WORLD DRAMA

Italy, Spain, France, Germany,
Denmark, Russia, and Norway

AN ANTHOLOGY EDITED BY
BARRETT H. CLARK

WITHDRAWN

DOVER PUBLICATIONS INC.

Copyright © 1933 by
Dover Publications, Inc.
All rights reserved under Pan American
and International Copyright Conventions.

International Standard Book Number: 0-486-20059-0
Library of Congress Catalog Card Number: 55-13854

Manufactured in the United States of America

Dover Publications, Inc.
180 Varick Street
New York 14, N. Y.

Dedicated To
BARRETT H. CLARK
in memory of his contribution
to the American drama and theater education

INTRODUCTION

The two volumes, *World Drama,* constitute a collection that is the first of its kind in English to offer a panoramic view of the dramatic achievement of the world from the earliest epoch of which any record exists to the beginning of the contemporary drama—which means the first of the modern plays of Ibsen. The modern period, from Ibsen to the present day, is well covered by fifty other collections. Aside from a very few dramatists who by universal consent could not be omitted from any such work as this, I have selected the plays of each country and epoch largely because they appeal to the mind of today, without attempting to exhibit in my table of contents a colorless reflection of the majority vote of the academic world. But in determining which nations and ages should be included I have been guided largely by historical considerations: in other words, ancient Greece could not possibly be left out, while the United States could not be admitted: our own country—until only a few years ago—had added nothing to the store of world drama. As for including a play of Shakespeare's, that would be a waste of good space: his presence may be taken for granted. I have included the living plays of the ages rather than their too glibly acknowledged masterpieces, preferring that students should read a few plays that may not take rank as supreme masterpieces to their praising the highest and being bored by them. I have tried my best not to include a single play in this book that has failed to move or delight me, in the hope that my pleasure may be shared by others; and in order to furnish historical data that has not before found its way into any anthology and to show that drama is not an exclusively literary affair, I have gone out of my way to print specimens of the informal folk drama that has undoubtedly exercised a far wider influence over the development of public taste (as well as the written drama) than we give it credit for. The Japanese farce *Abstraction,* the medieval French play of *The Wise Virgins and the Foolish Virgins,* the Italian Commedia dell'Arte *The Portrait,* and *The Play of St. George,* all belong in the picture I have tried to compose, because for every Euripides and every Shakespeare there existed a hundred humble playmakers whose very names are lost to us.

I hope therefore that the inclusion of such plays will give students the idea that drama at its best is a reflection of many phases of life; that the past as shown on the boards of the theater is not alone concerned with kings and great men, but with peasants and mechanics, saints and sinners; that it is not the exclusive province of fine writers but of inspired clowns, mountebanks and strolling mummers.

Of all the playwrights who have a place in this collection, Seneca alone is exceptional, in that it is not certain that his plays were actually written to be acted. But these have been so influential on the development of the drama of subsequent times that I have considered it wise to include one of the most brilliant examples of his extraordinary art.

To make my panorama as varied, as full and as colorful as the vast subject it aims to exhibit, I have gone to some trouble to have several plays translated that have never before been available to readers of English; others have been rescued from obscure or forgotten books or periodicals and restored to their proper places. With the assistance of generous and gifted scholars and able translators I am able to offer for the first time an authentic version of what is probably the greatest—certainly the most appealing—of Chinese plays, *The Chalk Circle*. The translator of that play has also provided me with a version of one of the most characteristic examples of the Italian improvised comedy, *The Portrait*. The Italian folk comedy *Bilora* and the French miracle play of *The Wise Virgins and the Foolish Virgins* are likewise for the first time made available in English translations. The *Adam* has not hitherto been accessible except in a back number of a scholarly university publication; *Abstraction* is reprinted from a collection that has for many years been out of print, and the same is true of several other items in the table of contents. The translations of *The Cave of Salamanca* and *Jeppe of the Hill* were made especially for these volumes; while the translations of *The King, the Greatest Alcalde, The Demi-Monde,* and *M. Poirier's Son-in-Law* were completely revised.

Taken as a whole, then, the plays in *World Drama* proclaim the never-ending stream of vital energy that underlies every form of artistic creation; they are a pageant of the life of man.

As such I am going to let them tell their own story, without comment. The student who wants to inquire into the background that produced these plays may refer to such books as Sheldon Cheney's *The Theater;* R. J. Taylor's *Story of the Drama;* and Thomas Wood Stevens' *The Theatre: From Athens to Broadway.*

B. H. C.

CONTENTS

BILORA

[The *Second Rustic Play*]

By ANGELO BEOLCO, called IL RUZZANTE

Written and produced probably, 1527

TRANSLATED ESPECIALLY FOR THIS WORK BY BABETTE AND GLENN HUGHES

CHARACTERS

BILORA
OLD PITTARO } *Peasants*
DINA, *wife of* BILORA
MESSIRE ANDRONICO, *a Venetian*
TONIN, *a Bergamese, his valet*

The scene represents a street in Venice, on which stands the house of Messire Andronico. At the back one sees a canal, with a small bridge. BILORA *discovered alone.*

BILORA. If there's any place a lover can't squeeze into, you couldn't shoot a cannon ball into it! Love—hell! Who would ever have thought that love would drag me wildly around like this, among people I never saw before, and such a long way from home? It's a fact I don't even know where I am! They say that love is a weak and helpless thing, but I know now that it can do absolutely anything it pleases. For example, if I—this once I must speak of myself—if I were moved only by the desire to recover my good wife, I certainly should not have trotted all day yesterday, all last night, and all this morning through woods, thickets, and across fields. And now I'm terribly gloomy, and sick of living. But never mind that. Love can outpull three pair oxen. And I am one who knows, too. It is a bad business, love. There are some who would have you believe that love seizes only striplings and disgraces only the young; but I can tell you it also pursues the old, and if a certain old fellow had not been shot in the rump with Cupid's arrow, he would never have stolen my wife. May love torture him and tear his heart to pieces—this old scoundrel! May canker-worms devour him—him and the other who brought him to my village —that money lender! May his money never bring him more pleasure and satisfaction than he allowed my wife and me! Meanwhile, curse the luck, I feel almost ill. I am not well at all. I preferred spending all my time, night and day,

1

hauling my shocks of grain, and while I was busy with that, the others were carrying off my wife. God knows if I will ever see her again. I'd have done better to stay near the house, where I was really needed. Damnation, I feel as if I were going out of my head! I'm almost starved, and I haven't so much as a crust of bread nor any money to buy some with. If I only knew where she was, and where they are taking her, I would beg of her at least to give me a piece of bread.

[*Enter* PITTARO.]

PITTARO. Well! By all that's holy! Is it you?

BILORA. Look here! The very person I was wishing for! Old Pittaro!

PITTARO. Is that so? Well, what's it all about?

BILORA. Haven't you heard what's happened the last few days? You must know.

PITTARO. I swear I don't. You'll have to tell me.

BILORA. Then you know nothing of this affair of . . . how shall I say it . . . of Messire Androtène, who has run off with my wife? You don't know this old man —this stranger?

PITTARO. Of course I do. And speak softly or he will hear you. He lives close by here, mind you. Who directed you here?

BILORA. I came by myself. No one directed me. Then he lives near here? Where? [*Indicating a house.*] Is that his door?

PITTARO. Yes, that's it. Well, then! What are you going to do? Do you want him to give her back? What do you want?

BILORA. I'll be honest with you. I never like to quarrel. You know that. I would always agree with a person rather than come to blows. What is done is done. Therefore I'll be satisfied if he gives me some money and returns my wife to me. You understand? It probably wouldn't do me any good to make a row here. Of course if we were somewhere else things could be handled differently, but you see, I don't know anyone around here, and he would probably have me drowned in one of these canals! Then he would come out on top.

PITTARO. You're absolutely right. He's a madman. Damn it all, you'd better go easy with him—come round him with "Fine Messire, dear Messire. . . ."

BILORA. What? Is his name Finemessire? I was told his name was Androtène, a very funny name.

PITTARO. No; you don't understand. His name is really what you say. I was only trying to tell you to be amiable, to approach him gently. Call him Your Excellency, Most Illustrious, and say, "I beg of you, dear Messire, to give her back to me." Understand? Be very humble.

BILORA. Ah! Very good! I understand. Damn it, I suppose he is illtempered. But does he just bark or does he bite?

PITTARO. He bites, worse luck. And in earnest, too, mind you.

BILORA. According to you, then, he's a dangerous fool who would hit a man hard enough to knock down a wall. The bastard! I've a mind to spit in his face. And then may the worms eat him! But meanwhile you show me how to come round him peaceably, so we shan't come to blows. Do you know whether he's at home? Has he come back from town?

PITTARO. No; he hasn't come back yet. Now listen and I'll tell you how to handle this in a good blood-and-thunder way.

BILORA. All right, then! Tell me and I'll do it.

PITTARO. Then listen! Go knock at that door. Dina is alone in the house. And don't be too rough with her, see? Tell her to come down, and then show her that you are not to be left out of this affair.

BILORA. Yes, yes; I'll do it.

PITTARO. First of all, say to her: "My dear, would you like to come home? Of course you have deserted me, but . . ." Hell, you know how to go about it.

BILORA. Yes, yes; I must speak kindly at first. But where do you think I should talk with her? On the doorstep or actually inside the house?

PITTARO. No! Outside the door. Right out here. Damn it, the old man might surprise you in the house and beat you up.

BILORA. Good! But what do you think? Will she go home with me?

PITTARO. I have no idea. Perhaps she will. Yes, she might. But of course she's leading a happy life here with him—no work, no worry; good food, good drink, good service.

BILORA. As for service, I'm damned if I'll believe that he serves her as well as I have. He isn't capable of it.

PITTARO. Not that, not that! They have a servant who waits on them both.

BILORA. But I ask you again—wouldn't it be better for me to go right into the house? I could settle matters before the other returned. You're sure there's no one in the house but Dina?

PITTARO. No one, I tell you. Damn you, do you think I'd lie about it? Go on! And as for me, I'm going down yonder, where I have some business. When I come back I'll stop and see what luck you've had. Don't stand around any longer. Get busy!

BILORA. Go ahead. In any case I'll be here when you come back.

[*Exit* PITTARO.]

Plague take it! God knows how all this will come out! Ah, yes, damn it all! However, I'll knock at the door no matter what happens—even if I am mashed like a turnip or boiled in the soup—even though it may be my own head that gets knocked, or my own frame that is jarred from its hinges. Bah! let happen what will! I am in the power of love, and I feel my liver, my heart, and my lungs jumping around inside me, making such a racket you would say a blacksmith was beating out a ploughshare. Yes, I must knock at that door, or I will go on feeling despondent. Hey, there! within! [*Knocking.*] Is no one home? I say, is no one home?

DINA [*from within*]. Who's knocking at the door? A beggar? Go in peace.

BILORA. I am a beggar all right, but you can't get rid of me that way. I'm a friend of yours. Open the door! It's me.

DINA. What friend? Who are you? Messire is not at home. Go in peace.

BILORA. Go on, Dina, open the door for me. It's me, confound it! You didn't recognize me, did you, you silly!

DINA [*appearing at the window*]. I tell you to get away from here. I don't know you. Messire is not at home. If you don't want to cause trouble, go on about your business.

BILORA. Damnation but you're mean! Listen! Come here; I want to have a little confidential talk with you. No use making a fuss; it is really me. Come now, Dina. You can see I am Bilora. I am your good husband.

DINA. All the worse for me! Just think of that! But what have you come here for?

BILORA. Eh? What's that you say? Come down a minute so I can see you.

DINA. I'm coming.

BILORA [*alone, speaking to himself*]. Now watch! I may be able to snatch some trinkets off her hands, or pinch some small change. I think my luck is turning. And a moment ago I was in despair!

DINA [*from behind the door*]. But . . . you won't hit me if I open the door?

BILORA. Why should you expect me to hit you? You didn't follow him here of your own free will. Come on outside. I give you my word that I'll gladly take you back as my helpmeet and my darling, as though nothing had happened.

DINA [*coming from the house*]. Hello. Now tell me, how did you find your way here, and how are you, anyway? Are you well?

BILORA. I'm all right. And how about yourself? You're looking well.

DINA. God help me, I don't feel any too well, to be honest with you. I'm about fed up, living with this old fellow.

BILORA. I believe it. Why, he can hardly get around. Besides, the young don't get on well with the old. You and I make a much better match.

DINA. By heaven, he's half sick. All night he tossed like a dying sheep. He never slept a wink, but spent every minute hugging and kissing me. And I suppose he thought I liked it. God knows I wish I never had to see him again!

BILORA. His breath stinks worse than a dungheap; you can smell his rotten carcass for a thousand miles; and he's as filthy in front as he is behind.

DINA. How excited you are! You're saying very nasty things.

BILORA. Come on now; tell me. Do you want to go home with me, or do you want me to go and leave you here with the old man?

DINA. For my own part I'd like to go back with you, but he doesn't want me to, and I'm sure he'd never allow it. If you could see the way he caresses me you would have a fit. Good heavens, how he loves me! And I certainly live well here.

BILORA. Just listen to you! "He doesn't want me to!" Damn it, you'd drive a person crazy. What if he doesn't want you to go? Can't you want to, yourself? You'll make me swear myself into hell! Come on, now; what do you say?

DINA. On my faith, I don't know. I'd like to, and yet . . . I wouldn't.

BILORA. Oh! If Fate isn't plaguing me to-night! Will it be long before he comes home? Do you think he'll come soon?

DINA. Pretty quick. He can never wait to get home. And I'd just as soon he didn't see us here talking together. Run along now, like a dear. Then after he gets here you can come back, and maybe you both can agree after all.

BILORA. We'll agree in the buttocks! And watch out for yourself if we don't agree. By the blood of Christ, if I get started I will do more damage than a soldier. I have a feeling that you're putting a trick over on me. But you oughtn't to go on living like this with another man. It's rotten. You're a filthy woman.

DINA. I wouldn't gain anything by going back to you! Now remember, he has a very quick temper. Listen! Honestly, I'm not joking. Go away for a while, and then, when he has got home, come and knock at the door and say you wish to talk with Messire. Tell him first thing that you want me to go back home with you. You can see what he says. If he consents, everything is all right; and if he refuses, I will go anyway.

BILORA. Honestly, will you go with me even if he objects?

DINA. I tell you, yes! I swear I will! Now go, so he won't find you here!

BILORA. Look here, couldn't you let me have a piece of bread? I give you my word I'm dying of hunger. I haven't eaten a bite since I left home last evening.

DINA. If you would just as soon, I'd rather give you some money. You only have to go down to the end of the street and you'll find an inn where you can eat and drink in comfort. I'm afraid he'll come back suddenly and see you leaving the house.

BILORA. Well, confound it, give me the money anyway. Where is this inn? Very far?

DINA. No, no; just there at the end of the street. When you get to the corner turn in at this side.

[DINA *reënters the house.*]

BILORA. Damn it, it'll be the very devil if I don't find it. But tell me . . . Hello, she's gone! I was so anxious to get something to eat that I forgot to ask her how long I should stay away. Never mind! Right now let's eat. And by the time I have satisfied my hunger he will have got home. Let's just see how much she has given me. Now what the hell is this! The very first piece I look at, I don't know what it is. Ah, yes! Damned if it isn't a two-lira piece. I didn't even recognize it, and it is the same as the first money I spent after I fell in love with her. This is a copper. And this other one? Lord, but it's big and heavy! It's the biggest of them all. Damned if it mustn't be worth a lot! But I can't remember what it's called. Oh, yes, it's a *cornacchion*. It's worth more than any of the others, I think. But I must go and eat. . . . [*Looking at the house.*] There's the door, all right, but will I be able to find it when I come back? I mustn't lose his trail. Meanwhile let's just count this money over again. Here's a two-lira piece, plus a copper, which makes four, plus a *cornacchion*, which makes five, plus one that I'll put away, which makes six, plus one which I'll spend, which makes seven—all of which means that I lack nineteen marks of having a ducat. [*He goes out.*]

[*Enter* ANDRONICO.]

ANDRONICO [*soliloquizing*]. Well, there's no doubt about it: if you don't do childish things when you are young, you're sure to want to do them when you're old. It reminds me of the time that Messires Nicolas d'Allegri and Panthasilus of the house of Bucentaure, heaven bless their memory, admonished me. Their Excellencies said to me: "What's the use, Andronico, of this melancholy mood in which you seem to take such delight? What the devil! Go and find yourself a girl and enjoy yourself with her. When do you expect to enjoy life—when you're no longer able to? You seem to us a most unnatural man, a strange man, a man bewitched. But take note and remember that in your old age you will commit some folly for the sake of love." And that is just what has happened. As a matter of fact I would almost rather be amorous now than to have been so in my youth were it not that a certain thing thwarts my desires: that is, knowing that *non respondent ultima primis*. Ah, the devil! but it is a miserable business, this growing old! *tamen* it is not that I lack courage. But enough! Let us say no more about it, for after all I am not really decrepit. Love works wonders. Look at the way I have stolen this girl

from her husband. I have risked my life in order to possess her—so deeply am I in love, and so fond of her. And then, *breviter concludendo*, she is a very angel of a girl, a cherubim, with a mouth that begs to be kissed. Altogether I fear only one thing, and that troubles me a good deal, the fear that someone will come to take her away from me. Ah, but such a one will be unwelcome, for I have decided to continue my pleasure, and never again be without it. If she does her duty by me, I will never be stingy with her, so she will always be happy. Already I have signed over securities to her, leaving her free to control my property as she likes, and to spend her leisure time in the house or outside of it, without consulting me or giving an account to anyone. It's a very fine thing for her, being a lady and a mistress. She rules everything, big and little. And all she has to do is give commands. Being satisfied, she will know how to treat me properly. But ah! what would I not give if she would only condescend to stir the very depths of my soul! But there—let us go up and pay her a little visit. She puts me in such a fine humor; she fondles me so! If I couldn't play with her I'd lose my head completely and neglect my business. I swear I feel so light on my feet I could dance the four figures of Badin, and after that the *Strapassao*, the *Rosina*, and in fact the whole bouquet of flower-figures. And that would be no small accomplishment. Ah yes, she will prove useful to me in a thousand ways, this girl: she will take care of me when I suffer from catarrh, and when I am bored; she will be a comfort to me when I want to talk over my business affairs. [*He knocks at the door.*] Hello! Quick! Open the door! God knows if my servant has come back yet with the boat.

TONIN [*within*]. Who is knocking?

ANDRONICO. Open, my dear! The devil! I thought it was she. Open, you numbskull! Can't you hear anything, eh?

TONIN [*opening the door*]. What is it you want?

ANDRONICO. Have you laid a fire upstairs?

[*He enters the house. Immediately* BILORA *and* PITTARO *appear from opposite directions.*]

BILORA. Well, I'm damned! How do we two happen to meet here?

PITTARO. Ah well! Have you had a good dinner? The wine isn't bad, is it?

BILORA. Damned if you're not right, Old Pittaro. I tell you I'm so full you could play a tune on my stomach as though it were a drum.

PITTARO. Well now, what do you want me to do? Shall we talk to the old man and find out at once what his intentions are, so we'll know what to count on? I tell you again that the girl will come back to you, whether he allows it or not.

BILORA. That's just what she told me herself. If only she hasn't changed her mind. By nature she's a bit fickle . . . you know what I mean.

PITTARO. I know. But one thing is sure: the quicker we straighten this matter out the better it will be for all of us. Now how do you want me to go about it? Shall I speak for you, or shall both of us speak?

BILORA. No; you do the talking. You know best what to say. But listen! if you notice that he is getting ill-tempered, you tell him that by heaven she has a husband who is a tough customer, and that if he doesn't send her back, her husband will kill him. Tell him I used to be a soldier. That may scare him.

PITTARO. Good. Leave it to me.

BILORA. And listen! Tell him I'm a regular cutthroat, a bad actor; and don't forget to tell him I used to be a soldier, eh?

PITTARO. Now get out of the way so he won't see you. I'm going to pound on the door. Leave it to me. I'll tell him something he'll understand!

BILORA. Do anything you like, so long as you make him give her back to me. And if he refuses, by the blood of the Virgin, I'll shoot him in the rump with an arrow. Yes, I'll knock his breakfast down to his shoe tops!

PITTARO. Just now be quiet! I don't need any more of your boasts. Get out of sight so I can knock at the door. What did you say his name is?

BILORA. Hell, I don't know how they pronounce that name. I think he's called Messire Ardochêne . . . but I'm not very sure . . . Messire Ardo . . . Messire Ardoché . . . that's it; yes, yes!

PITTARO [*knocking*]. Yes, yes, that's right. Hello! within there!

DINA [*at the window*]. Who's knocking?

PITTARO. A friend, young lady. Tell Messire I want a word with him.

DINA. Who are you?

PITTARO. Just say that it's me, and that I want to speak with him. He'll understand.

DINA. He'll be right down.

BILORA [*whispering to* PITTARO]. Listen! Tell him I have killed God knows how many men—that there's a price on my head. Will you?

PITTARO. All right, all right! Be quiet! Get back! You bother me.

[BILORA *hides again.*]

ANDRONICO [*appearing at the door*]. What is this anyway? What have you got to say?

PITTARO. Good evening to your Excellency.

ANDRONICO. Good evening, Pittaro. What do you want of me?

PITTARO. I'd like to have a few confidential words with you, Messire, if you don't mind. Just between you and me. If you will step this way a little.

ANDRONICO. What is it? Be quick about it.

PITTARO. I'm telling you now, Messire. There's no use beating around the bush. You know very well that the other day you stole this girl, the wife of that poor fellow, Bilora, who is now almost out of his head. Well then, I must tell you that I have come to beg your Excellency on his behalf to return her to him. Imagine, dear Messire, imagine for yourself how cruel and unnatural it must seem to one to have another steal his wife. And anyway, you should by now have gotten over your desire. You have had plenty of time in which to satisfy your passion for her. And finally, if I may give you a word of advice, this girl is not the skillet for your kitchen. You are old; she is young. Pardon me for speaking so frankly, Messire.

ANDRONICO. Do you want me to speak honestly? Then, I tell you I will do nothing about it, for it would be utterly impossible for me to get along without her. Is that clear? I have decided to spend the rest of my life with her. What the devil do you expect me to do—let that little girl go back to the farm and work for that big coward of a Bilora, who gives her beatings instead of bread. And you expect me to give her up? No, no! By God, no! I am going to protect my own happiness. And another reason why I refuse to give her up is that one of my principles is never to throw pearls to swine. You think I have gone to the trouble of bringing her here just to let her go again at once? I tell you I have girded on the sword and the shield like a veritable St. George, and I stand day and night under arms. I have spent my energy and risked my life in order to get her, and now, my good man, you may tell Bilora that he had best go home and tend to his own business.

PITTARO. But, Messire, this way his business will go to the dogs. I see you don't think much of my plan for helping him.

ANDRONICO. I would never agree to your plan, even if it cost me half my fortune and brought me to my grave.

PITTARO. Damnation! What do you want him to do? Do you want to drive him to despair?

ANDRONICO. I don't care a hang about his despair. So far as I'm concerned he can roast himself on a spit. Listen! What a devil of an idea! He is in despair! Well, what do you want me to do about it? You have already succeeded in boring me, and very quickly you will get my temper up. You can go to the deuce! Enough of this nonsense; I am getting hot under the collar.

PITTARO. No, no, Messire; you mustn't get excited. Listen! Do this much. Call the girl out here and see what she says. If she wants to go back home, let her go. If she doesn't want to, then keep her and get what pleasure you can from her. What do you say?

ANDRONICO. At last you're talking sensibly. But take care you don't regret your suggestion, for I know very well you'll be surprised. We will see who really counts. She has just got through telling me that she would not leave me for all the men in the world. And it's hardly possible that she has changed her mind since then. However, I am willing to oblige you, and besides, I would not have a clear conscience unless I brought the matter to a proof and made certain that she is not merely pretending when she responds so tenderly to my attentions. Hello! Do you hear me? Don't you hear me? Say there, my beautiful, do you hear me?

DINA [from within]. Is it me you are calling, Messire?

ANDRONICO. Yes, my child. Come down here a minute. [Aside.] I must admit that women have few brains . . . in fact most women haven't any . . . and if this one has suddenly changed her mind! . . .

[DINA appears.]

PITTARO. Here she is, Messire.

ANDRONICO. Ah there, my beautiful! What do you say?

DINA. About what, Messire? Not knowing, I can't say anything.

ANDRONICO. Listen! This good man has come on behalf of your husband to reclaim you, and we have agreed that if you want to go, I am to allow it, but if you want to stay, you are to do so. You know very well what your life is here with me, and whether or not I let you want for anything, but it is up to you to say what you'd like to do. As for me, I shall say nothing more.

DINA. Whether I should go with my husband? But why should you want me to do that? It would mean my being beaten every day. I should say I don't want to go! By heaven, I wish I had never known him! He's a miserable coward, as truly as bread is good to eat. Great God, no, Messire! I never want to go back to him. When I look at him I think of a wolf.

ANDRONICO. Enough, enough, enough! [To PITTARO.] Well, you have heard her. Are you satisfied? I told you she would refuse to go, and you wouldn't believe me!

PITTARO. Let me tell you, Messire, that I am very angry with this little jade, for it wasn't half an hour ago—in fact just before you came home—that she promised Bilora she would go with him, even if you objected.

DINA. What! I said that? I said . . . or rather, I was practically made to say—as the good woman said—I said . . . nothing at all. [To ANDRONICO.] Let him rave; he has imagined all this.

ANDRONICO. Then go back up to your room, and we'll stop this argument. [To PITTARO.] That will do. Go in peace. What do you think now? For my part I never doubted for an instant that she would stay with me. Do you need any further proof?

PITTARO. No . . . not for me, Messire. What could I demand? But I should warn you that Bilora is a bad man, who is not inclined at all toward decency, and that you will be safer if you return his wife to him.

ANDRONICO. Aha! What does all this mean? It's not very hard to guess. So! You are trying to threaten me! Don't irritate me further, or I swear some one will get his head broken. Without wasting words, I consider you an imbecile. Get out of here quickly, and don't forget that I refuse absolutely to return the girl. Do you understand? When I come

back out of the house in a few moments I don't want to find you here. If I do, then you will be . . . But enough! The matter is settled. [ANDRONICO reënters his house. BILORA appears.]

PITTARO. Go to the devil! And I hope I never see you again.

BILORA. By the blood of Dominustecum, you are a fine talker, you are! You didn't even swear at him, nor tell him I was an outlaw, nor blaspheme, nor anything! By the blessed blood of a sick bitch, what sort of a damned fool are you anyway? If you had blasphemed, if you had said I was an outlaw, I am sure he would have given me back my wife. What proves it is that when you told him I was a bad man and that I had no inclination toward decency, he began to tremble a little, and could think of nothing but getting himself safe inside the house.

PITTARO. So! Then why didn't you take a hand in the matter, if you're so brave? You'd like to have got me into an even worse mess, wouldn't you?

BILORA. I don't want to get you into any mess, but I owe you so little thanks it's hardly worth mentioning.

PITTARO. That's what I say. All right, all right. Are you coming?

BILORA. No; not me. Go on, then. I can say that you did your best by me. [PITTARO leaves.]

BILORA [alone]. By the blood of a limping bitch, but all my schemes have gone topsy-turvy, and I am flat on my back. Ah, yes! It's enough to make him split his breeches laughing. Never mind! The question is, what am I going to do about it? My life is ruined. It is best that I pick up my feet and get away from here. One thing is sure: I'll never be in danger of feeling bored so long as I'm so mad. Meanwhile I know exactly what I'm going to do. When I see him leave the house I'll jump on him all of a sudden and knock him off his legs. He will hit the ground at the first whack. Then I'll beat him up and down and across, and it will be a wonder if I don't scratch out his eyes and kill him. By God, yes, it will be too bad if I can't bully him into letting her go. Besides that, I'll talk to him in the language of a Spanish soldier; he will think there are at least eight men surrounding him. I had better practice a little the way I am going about it. First I will draw my knife. Let's see if it shines. Damned if it's very bright. He won't get much of a scare out of it. Now let's suppose, *verbo gratia*, that he is walking along over there, and that here am I, Bilora, who knows how to get what he wants. First I will commence to blaspheme and to swear by all the Christeleison of Padua, the Virgin Mary and the Dominustecum. A curse on you, son of a dog! Jew, go hang yourself. I know just how to kick the life out of your buttocks, and jerk you and maul you within an inch of death. Then I'll pull him out of his cloak, put it on my own back, undress him from head to foot, and then run away as fast as my legs will carry me, leaving him spread out on the ground like a big piece of filth. After that I will sell his cloak, buy myself a horse, and join the army. After all, I have no desire to go back home. Ah, yes! I know how to handle things! I wish he would show up, and not be so slow about leaving the house. Hush! Is that him coming now? Has he passed the door? Yes! May the worms eat you, old carcass! Suffering Christ, where is he then? No, he hasn't left the house yet. I'm lucky. Maybe he won't come out again at all. Hush! I swear I hear him coming. Yes, here he comes! I won't budge from this spot. Heaven keep me from jumping on him before he closes the door!

[ANDRONICO *appears in the door.*]

ANDRONICO. Who the devil is this idiot babbling around the streets at this hour? Some drunken sot. May the plague take him, and may he choke in the bargain! It makes my blood boil. I'd give a lot to be captain of the guard and lay hands on him. I'd give him something he'd remember. [*Calling off stage.*] Do you hear me? Hey, my man, don't you hear me?

TONIN [*in the house*]. Here I am!

ANDRONICO. Don't come. Stay in the house and keep Dina company. But come and get me at four o'clock. And bring along the lantern. Do you understand?

TONIN. I will come as soon as I can. Don't worry.

ANDRONICO [*coming forward*]. I had better go this way. If I cross the little bridge down there I will arrive in no time. Tonin, close the door.

BILORA. May the plague choke you, old villain! Take that! And that!

[*He strikes him.*]

ANDRONICO. Aha! my brave fellow! Alas! alas! Help! Fire! Fire! Fire! Ah, I am killed! Ha, traitor! Help! Fire! Murder! I am killed!

BILORA. Yes, fire! Fire! I'll set fire to your tail. And now give me back my wife. You should have left her with me in the first place. Hello! I believe he is actually dead. He doesn't so much as move his foot. Ah well, he has paid the piper! Good night, damn you! He has cashed in all right, that fellow. Didn't I give you warning enough?

THE PORTRAIT

By FLAMINIO SCALA

Written and produced probably about 1575

TRANSLATED ESPECIALLY FOR THIS WORK BY ETHEL VAN DER VEER

A troupe of actors were playing in Parma. As was the custom, the principal actress was visited by many callers. ORATIO, a cavalier of the city, while calling on her, took from his neck a locket in which was concealed the portrait of a very beautiful woman, who had herself given the locket to him.

Always catty, the actress, whose name was VITTORIA, slyly extracted the portrait from the locket before returning it to the cavalier at the end of his visit. A few days afterwards, the husband of the said lady, coming to see VITTORIA, who did not know him, was by chance shown the portrait of his wife.

The husband, whose name was PANTALONE, was greatly surprised. He made urgent entreaties to the actress to tell him the name of the man who had given her the portrait.

She answered him courteously. PANTALONE dissimulated the reason for his interest in the affair and returned home in a fury with the intention of inflicting an exemplary chastisement on his culpable better half. However, on his arrival, his wife exculpated herself with such good excuses that she succeeded in appeasing his wrath.

The persons are, besides the actress VITTORIA and her comrade PIOMBINO: the two old men, PANTALONE and GRATIANO; their wives ISABELLA and FLAMINIA, and the lovers of these last, ORATIO and

FLAVIO. PEDROLINO is valet to PANTALONE, HARLEQUIN is valet to CAPTAIN SPAVENTE. A young Milanese woman, SILVIA, disguised as a page, comes under the name of LESBINO to offer her services to the CAPTAIN, whom she loves.

ACT I

SCENE I

Following the quarrel which had occurred at their home between ISABELLA and her husband, upon the subject of the portrait which was last seen in the hands of the actress VITTORIA, ISABELLA becomes suspicious. She thereupon orders PEDROLINO to go to ORATIO and demand of him the portrait which she, ISABELLA, had given him some time before.

SCENE II

CAPTAIN SPAVENTE tells HARLEQUIN how, obliged to assist in the theater, he has fallen in love with the SIGNORA VITTORIA. HARLEQUIN tells him he is wasting his time.

SCENE III

Later, after asking a number of foolish questions as to LESBINO's bravery and military talents, the CAPTAIN consents to take him on as page.

10

Scene IV

FLAMINIA, at her window, calls HARLEQUIN and asks him to convey a letter to a cavalier named FLAVIO, whom he will encounter in the place where she gives rendezvous to gentlemen. HARLEQUIN takes the letter and promises to deliver it to him to whom it is addressed. FLAMINIA gives him some money and withdraws. HARLEQUIN attentively regards FLAMINIA's window.

Scene V

DOCTOR GRATIANO, husband of FLAMINIA, seeing HARLEQUIN gazing, letter in hand, at his wife's window, becomes suspicious. He demands what he wants and from whom the letter has come. HARLEQUIN replies that a certain FLAVIO gave it him to deliver to a lady. The doctor takes the letter and raps HARLEQUIN with his cane.

Scenes VI to X

PANTALONE interposes between the doctor and HARLEQUIN. FLAVIO presents himself. GRATIANO, exceedingly angry, returns the letter to him. FLAVIO receives it with deep humility. Alone, FLAVIO reads the letter, in which FLAMINIA begs him no longer to frequent the theater.

Scene XI

ORATIO, of whom PEDROLINO asks the return of the portrait to ISABELLA, explains that this is impossible at this time. He makes the excuse that the locket is being repaired at the jeweler's. PEDROLINO smiles and asks him how long it has been since he has visited the theater, questions him about all the actors and lastly about the SIGNORA VITTORIA.

Scene XII

ISABELLA comes in at this moment. She dissembles at first and requests the return of her portrait. ORATIO repeats what he had told PEDROLINO. She calls him a traitor and tells him that she is not ignorant of his love for the actress, to whom he has given her portrait. Vexed, and unwilling to listen to ORATIO, she goes back, ordering PEDROLINO to follow her. ORATIO complains of his ill-fortune and curses the presence of the players, whose coming brought all the trouble. He expresses himself in abusive terms regarding VITTORIA who had played him such a mischievous trick.

Scene XIII

The CAPTAIN, hearing what ORATIO says of the players and of VITTORIA in particular, takes up her defense. He maintains that the theater is a noble diversion and that the SIGNORA VITTORIA is an honorable lady. ORATIO, furious, replies that he is a liar. He puts his hand to his sword, whereupon the CAPTAIN asks ORATIO if he will fight a duel with him. ORATIO replies that he is ready. The CAPTAIN then says he goes to write a letter exculpating him from responsibility in the event that he is killed, and which he will give to him in case the police should misunderstand and seek his adversary. He suggests that ORATIO do the same for him, and leaves. HARLEQUIN comments that his master has all the appearances of wishing to sidestep the affair gracefully. Thus ends the first act.

ACT II

Scene I

VITTORIA, richly clad, with golden necklaces, pearl bracelets, diamonds and rubies on her fingers, rents herself, through PIOMBINO, to the DUKE and all his entourage, recalling the infinite courtesies she has received every day from the nobility of the city of Parma.

Scenes II to V

PEDROLINO boasts of his master PANTALONE to VITTORIA. PANTALONE unexpectedly appears, but seeing his wife at the window, dares not approach VITTORIA. PEDROLINO persuades PANTALONE that the actress is in love with him. PANTALONE, flattered, expresses the intention of making her a present.

SCENE VI

While ORATIO recounts the unhappy history of the portrait to his friend FLAVIO, HARLEQUIN offers the letter of release from the CAPTAIN. ORATIO receives him with a blow of the fist and dashes off to the theater.

SCENES VII TO XII

FLAVIO and PEDROLINO, and then FLAMINIA, attempt to reconcile ISABELLA with ORATIO. ISABELLA softens, but declares he will have nothing from her, so long as he does not return the portrait; and she forbids him, moreover, to go himself to negotiate for its restoration. PEDROLINO divulges to them the fact that the two old men, PANTALONE and GRATIANO, are attentive to the actress.

SCENE XIII

Now arrives the doctor. PEDROLINO pretends to be arguing with FLAMINIA and says: "How should I know whether your husband goes to the theater or not?" FLAMINIA, entering into the deception, pretends to be jealous of her husband.

SCENE XIV

PIOMBINO presents his compliments to the doctor on behalf of the SIGNORA VITTORIA. He requests him to provide the actress with a silver pitcher and basin of which she has need in a piece she is going to present. The doctor replies that he will send these by PEDROLINO. PIOMBINO assures him that the actress is smitten with him, and that on his account she scorns all the gentlemen who pay court to her at the theater. The doctor is vastly pleased, and promises a reward to PIOMBINO.

SCENE XV

The CAPTAIN converses with his page regarding the passion inspired in him by the actress. LESBINO endeavors to turn him away from this passion which he cannot make honorable. The page asks him if he has ever before been in love. The CAPTAIN says that, in Milan, he had been in love with a very beautiful young girl named SILVIA.

SCENE XVI

HARLEQUIN interrupts his master to inform him that VITTORIA is waiting near by, at the jeweler's. LESBINO, despairing, eeks to persuade HARLEQUIN that he must kill him, LESBINO, because he has conceived the intention of assassinating his master. HARLEQUIN abuses and maltreats the page. FLAMINIA and ISABELLA intervene.

SCENE XVII

Having divined a woman under the attire of LESBINO, they remove him to the residence of FLAMINIA. Thus ends the second act.

ACT III

SCENE I

VITTORIA and PIOMBINO go to dine at the house of a rich gentleman who gives them magnificent presents. They rejoice between themselves over the custom of making gifts to the players, a custom prevalent throughout the cities of Italy, and which is seldom neglected by persons of distinguished rank. VITTORIA confesses that she laughs at all the lovers who are not generous with her. PIOMBINO promises to provide well for her old age.

SCENES II AND III

PANTALONE comes to call. VITTORIA thanks him for the gifts he has brought and invites him to come to the theater at the première. PANTALONE promises to be present. Afterwards FLAVIO arrives, and the actress detains him with a diverting conversation.

SCENE IV

But FLAMINIA has observed them from her window. She goes out angrily and boxes FLAVIO'S ears, then returns into the house without uttering a word. VITTORIA bursts into laughter.

SCENE V

PANTALONE, who has witnessed this striking event, blames the effrontery of FLAMINIA. He felicitates himself upon the modesty and good breeding of his wife. After these reflections he exchanges compliments with the actress. But ISABELLA appears.

SCENE VI

She reproaches her husband for seeking other women and neglecting her. She recites all the facts, with embellishments, and adds that he does not deserve a wife like her. She flies into a mounting rage, exciting herself over him until he flees. Turning to VITTORIA she tells her that if his sense of honor does not keep him from compromising himself with an actress, she will teach him manners, and returns to her dwelling. VITTORIA laughs softly, remarking that wherever one finds a troupe of actors playing, there also one will find married women with a sour mouth.

SCENE VII

GRATIANO arrives in his turn. "Behold the other pigeon waiting to be plucked," says PIOMBINO. The actress does, in fact, coquette with the doctor. PIOMBINO reminds her of the silver pitcher and basin he has promised her. GRATIANO joyfully takes PEDROLINO with him in order to bring back the presents. The players jeer at his stupidity.

SCENE VIII

ORATIO, greeting VITTORIA, demands the portrait of ISABELLA. She laughingly replies that she doesn't know what he is talking about, and takes herself off with PIOMBINO.

SCENE IX

ISABELLA has seen ORATIO talking with the actress. She reproaches him for not keeping his promise. HARLEQUIN tells ORATIO that ISABELLA and FLAMINIA have taken away his master's page and are keeping him there with them. ISABELLA, seizing the occasion to spite ORATIO, calls FLAMINIA and tells her to bring her new lover to the window. LESBINO appears and says to ISABELLA: "What do you require of me, Signora?" ORATIO, at sight of this unknown person, becomes enraged and goes off cursing ISABELLA.

SCENE X

PANTALONE demands the cause of all this noise. ISABELLA says that ORATIO wished to take the page away from her. "And what do you want with this page?" inquires PANTALONE angrily. ISABELLA then recounts the adventure of SILVIA, the Milanese. She urges PANTALONE to go in search of the CAPTAIN and bring him there if possible. For PANTALONE, this is precisely the opportunity he himself needed to go to the theater.

SCENES XI TO XVII

The lovers start another quarrel. PEDROLINO suggests that as the husbands are at the play, which lasts just six hours in the evening, they might employ their time to better advantage. The lovers see the reasonableness of this and become reconciled. The valets take counsel as to the best means of restoring SILVIA to the CAPTAIN's favor. The latter appears.

SCENE XVIII

PEDROLINO tells the CAPTAIN that he will find VITTORIA at the residence of

PANTALONE. He enters by way of the basement and there discovers SILVIA divested of her masculine costume.

SCENE XIX

The two valets, PEDROLINO and HARLEQUIN, are alone in the theater. They seat themselves on the floor, agreeing between them what they would say if the two old men were suddenly to return. At this time some amusing pantomime takes place. A knave, bearing a lantern, sees the two valets. He weeps and laments because he has lost a great deal of money at cards, and has left not more than a dozen half-crowns. The valets invite him to play with them. They play. The swindler wins the money and finally the clothing of PEDROLINO and HARLEQUIN, and they suffer themselves to be left in their shirts. The valets are chagrined.

SCENE XX

There is great excitement in the theater. PANTALONE, GRATIANO and PIOMBINO rush in bringing VITTORIA, whom they beg to sustain herself amidst the dangers which threaten her, a brawl having taken place on her account. The gentlemen, the *bravi*, their swords bared, pour in and perceiving VITTORIA, seize her and hastily carry her off. PIOMBINO follows with a gesture of despair.

SCENE XXI

PANTALONE and GRATIANO, finding themselves face to face with their valets who are attired only in their shirts, demand of them what has happened. The valets cleverly explain that it is the men just going out of the theater who have robbed them. They add philosophically that while the theater brings pleasurable distraction,

it is also the source of a number of scandals. While they are giving themselves up to these sage reflections, ISABELLA and FLAMINIA descend upon them and demand of their husbands to know if the comedy is already ended.

SCENE XXII

PANTALONE replies that a brawl interrupted it and that he has not seen the CAPTAIN. ISABELLA recounts how they had told the CAPTAIN that he would find VITTORIA awaiting him in the basement where SILVIA, in lieu of the actress, is waiting. Fearing that the CAPTAIN, thus misled, might commit some kind of violence, they had urged the SIGNOR ORATIO and the SIGNOR FLAVIO to remain. PANTALONE and GRATIANO approve.

SCENE XXIII

The CAPTAIN goes out of the house swearing he has been betrayed. ORATIO and FLAVIO seek to calm him. PANTALONE and all the others intercede in SILVIA's behalf. He recognizes that SILVIA is of honorable lineage, that she is the daughter of a wealthy Milanese merchant and that he loves her. Bewitched by this diabolical actress, he had for a time forgotten poor SILVIA, but now returns to her and consents to marry her.

SCENE XXIV

They fetch SILVIA, who realizes that her lover reciprocates her tenderness.

ISABELLA and FLAMINIA exhort their husbands to keep away from the playhouse and watch over their households and the behavior of their wives. Everybody goes to PANTALONE's to celebrate the nuptials of SILVIA and the CAPTAIN, and it is thus that the comedy of *The Portrait* is ended.

THE FAN

By CARLO GOLDONI

Produced at Venice in 1764

TRANSLATED BY HENRY B. FULLER *

CHARACTERS

THE COUNT OF ROCCA MARINA
THE BARON DEL CEDRO
THE SIGNOR EVARISTO
CORONATO, *host of the inn*
CRESPINO, *shoemaker*
MORACCHIO, *peasant*
TIMOTEO, *apothecary*
THE SIGNORA GELTRUDE
THE SIGNORA CANDIDA, *her niece*
GIANNINA, *peasant girl*
SUSANNA, *shopkeeper*
LIMONCINO, *waiter at coffee-house*
TOGNINO, *Geltrude's servant*
SCAVEZZO, *servant at the inn*

The Square in a village near Milan

ACT I

SCENE I

All the characters on the stage. Grouping as follows: GELTRUDE *and* CANDIDA *seated on the terrace, engaged in fancywork.* EVARISTO *and the* BARON, *both in hunting-costume, seated on stools and drinking coffee, with their guns beside them. The* COUNT, *dressed for country walking (long coat, straw hat and stick), is seated near the apothecary-shop and is reading a book.* TIMOTEO, *at the front of his shop, is mixing drugs in a metal mortar, which rests on top of the enclosing railing.* GIANNINA, *in peasant dress, sits beside her door, spinning.* SUSANNA,

* Reprinted from the edition published by Samuel French, copyright 1925, by permission of the translator.

15

seated close to her shop, is engaged in some fine sewing. CORONATO *is seated on a bench close to his tavern, with a memorandum-book and a pencil.* CRESPINO, *on his cobbler's bench, is busy over a shoe on a last.* MORACCHIO, *between* GIANNINA *and the footlights, holds a hunting-dog in leash and gives him a piece of bread to eat.* SCAVEZZO, *between footlights and tavern, is plucking a fowl.* LIMONCINO, *near the two gentlemen at coffee, waits for the cups, saucers in hand.* TOGNINO *brushes the front and the threshold of the place.*

After the rise of the curtain, all remain several moments without speaking, and occupied as above described, so as to give audience time to take in the picture.

EVARISTO [*to* BARON]. How do you find this coffee?

BARON. Very good indeed.

EVARISTO. Just about perfect, isn't it? Bravo, Master Lemon-peel! [*To* LIMONCINO.] This morning you have done very well.

LIMONCINO. Thanks for your praise, sir; but I beg you not to call me by that name of Lemon-peel.

EVARISTO. Well, well, why not? Everybody knows you by that name. Under the name of Lemon-peel you are famous. Everybody says: "Come along; let's go and try a cup of Lemon-peel's coffee"; and now you are going to let that offend you?

LIMONCINO. That is not my name, sir.

EVARISTO. Oh, well, then, from now on we will call you Master Orange-peel, or Master Pumpkin-rind. [*Drinks coffee.*]

LIMONCINO. I tell you, I am not meant to serve as a butt for your jokes.

[CANDIDA *laughs, quite distinctly.*]

EVARISTO [*looking up*]. What does the Signorina Candida say to this?

CANDIDA [*moves her fan to and fro and then places it on the balustrade*]. What is there to say? You make me laugh.

GELTRUDE. Come, gentlemen, leave that poor young fellow alone. He serves very good coffee, and he is under my protection.

BARON. Ah, if he is under the protection of the Signora Geltrude, he shall be treated with all consideration. [*Aside to* EVARISTO.] You hear that?—the worthy widow protects him.

EVARISTO. Don't speak ill of Signora Geltrude. There is not a more sensible and respectable woman in all the world.

BARON. Just as you please; but this air of protection, of patronage. . . . Look at the Count sitting there and reading with the effect of a judge on the bench.

EVARISTO. You are not wrong, so far as he is concerned; he is a perfect caricature. But to compare him and Signora Geltrude is quite unjust.

BARON. A pair of them!—he's one, she's another. As for me, I find them equally ridiculous.

EVARISTO. And what do you find ridiculous in Signora Geltrude?

BARON. Too much prosing, too much deportment, too much self-sufficiency.

EVARISTO. Pardon me; you don't know her.

BARON. Candida, her niece, is worth a hundred of her?

[*The* BARON *and* EVARISTO *finish their coffee, rising and handing the cups to* LIMONCINO. *Each makes as if to pay; the* BARON *gets at his money first, and* EVARISTO *thanks him.* LIMONCINO *takes the cups and the money and goes into the café.* TIMOTEO *begins to pound harder with his pestle.*]

EVARISTO. Yes, you are quite right. . . . She *is* rather a nice girl. . . . [*Aside.*] I shouldn't want to find a rival in this fellow.

COUNT [*markedly, in tone of grave reproof*]. Eh—um,—you, Master Timoteo.

TIMOTEO. Yes, sir.

COUNT. This pounding of yours annoys me.

TIMOTEO [*pounding on*]. Excuse me . . .

COUNT. I can't read; you split my head.

TIMOTEO. Excuse me; I'm just finishing. [*He pounds, stops to sift, and begins to pound once more.*]

CRESPINO [*laughing, as he works at his bench*]. Hey, there, Coronato!

CORONATO. What's wanted, Master Crespino?

CRESPINO [*going it hard on his last*]. The Count doesn't want any pounding.

COUNT. What a deuced piece of impudence! [*To* CRESPINO.] Are you going to keep that up all the morning?

CRESPINO. Don't you see, illustrious sir, what I'm doing?

COUNT [*angry*]. Well, what *are* you doing?

CRESPINO. I'm mending your old shoes.

COUNT. Hush, there, you impudent rascal! [*He goes on with his reading.*]

CRESPINO [*pounding and laughing*]. Coronato!

[TIMOTEO *pounds.*]

COUNT [*fidgeting in his chair*]. I can't stand any more of *this!*

SCAVEZZO [*laughing*]. Moracchio!

MORACCHIO. What is it, Scavezzo?

SCAVEZZO [*laughing and poking fun*]. The Count!

MORACCHIO. Hush, hush! After all, he's a gentleman.

SCAVEZZO. On his uppers!

GIANNINA. Moracchio!

MORACCHIO. Well?

GIANNINA. What is that Scavezzo saying?

MORACCHIO. Nothing. Mind your own business, and go on with your spinning.

GIANNINA. Oh, he's civil, isn't he— that brother of mine! This is the way he always treats me. If I only saw my way to getting married! [*She jerks her seat round and goes on angrily with her spinning.*]

SUSANNA. What is it, Giannina? What's the matter with you?

GIANNINA. Oh, if you only knew, Susanna. I don't believe there's such another ugly, cross-grained fellow as my brother in all the world!

MORACCHIO. Well, you'll take me as I am. What are you driving at, anyway? As long as you are under my care——

GIANNINA. Under your care? That won't be for much longer, I hope.

[*Spins in anger.*]

EVARISTO [*To* MORACCHIO]. Come, now, why are you always tormenting that poor girl? [*Turning to* GIANNINA.] She doesn't deserve it, poor, dear child.

GIANNINA. He enrages me.

MORACCHIO. She wants to know everything.

EVARISTO. Come, come; have done.

BARON [*to* CANDIDA]. He's very tender-hearted,—Evaristo is.

CANDIDA [*with pique*]. So it seems to me.

GELTRUDE [*to* CANDIDA]. Well, now, don't let's criticise other people's actions so far as to have no eye for our own.

BARON [*aside*]. There, now—that's what I mean by her prosing: I can't stand it.

CRESPINO [*aside, working*]. Poor Giannina! When she's my wife we'll see if that big brute torments her any longer.

CORONATO [*aside*]. Poor Giannina! I should want to marry her if only to free her from her brother.

EVARISTO. Well, Baron, shall we go?

BARON. To tell you the truth, I don't feel very much inclined toward hunting this morning. I am still tired from yesterday. . . .

EVARISTO. Just as you like. But you won't mind if *I* go?

BARON. Please yourself. [*Aside.*] All the better for me. I shall be free to try my luck with Candida.

EVARISTO. Moracchio!

MORACCHIO. Sir?

EVARISTO. The dog has been fed?

MORACCHIO. Yes, sir.

EVARISTO. Go get your gun, then, and we'll be off.

MORACCHIO. At once, sir. [*To* GIANNINA]. Here, hold this.

GIANNINA. Hold what?

MORACCHIO. This dog, till I come back.

GIANNINA. Give it here, bother you.

[*She takes the dog, and pats it, as* MORAC-CHIO *goes into house.*]

CORONATO [*aside*]. She's a good-hearted girl, I'm sure. I wonder how soon I can make her mine.

CRESPINO [*aside*]. Ah, how prettily, how gracefully, she bestows her caresses. If she will do as much for a dog, how much more would she do for a husband!

BARON. Scavezzo!

SCAVEZZO [*coming forward*]. Yes, sir.

BARON. Take this gun and carry it up to my room.

SCAVEZZO Yes, sir. [*Aside.*] Well, anyhow, *this* one is rich and liberal—not a bit like that empty-pocketed old Count. [*Carries the gun into the inn.*]

EVARISTO [*to* BARON]. You are expecting to remain here for today?

BARON. Yes, I shall take a little rest at the inn.

EVARISTO. Arrange things so that I can come and dine with you.

BARON. Very happy, I'm sure. I shall look for you. [*To* GELTRUDE *and* CANDIDA.] Ladies, I take my leave. [*Aside.*] I must go, so as to give no occasion for suspicion. [*To* CORONATO.] I will go up to my room; and remember to have dinner for two. [*Enters inn.*]

CORONATO. Very well, sir.

SCENE II

MORACCHIO [*comes out of his house carrying the gun, and takes the dog from* GIANNINA. *To* EVARISTO]. Here I am, sir, all ready.

EVARISTO [*to* MORACCHIO]. Let's go, then. [*To* GELTRUDE *and* CANDIDA]. Ladies, if you will allow me, I'll amuse myself with a little shooting. [*Takes gun.*]

GELTRUDE. Use your own pleasure. Good luck to you.

CANDIDA. Good luck to you, and a big bagful of game.

EVARISTO [*to* CANDIDA, *as he fastens on his hunting equipment*]. I am sure to be lucky, if only I have your good wishes.

CANDIDA [*to* GELTRUDE]. Really, he's quite a nice young man.

GELTRUDE. And very well-mannered. But, my dear niece, don't trust yourself to anyone you don't know through and through.

CANDIDA. Why do you speak to me in that way, aunt?

GELTRUDE. The time has come when it's right that I should.

CANDIDA. I don't know that I've done anything to cause you to . . .

GELTRUDE. No; I'm not scolding you. You have conducted yourself very well, and all I mean is: Go on in the same way.

CANDIDA [*aside*]. A little too late—this advice. I'm as far gone in love as a girl may be!

EVARISTO [*to* MORACCHIO]. Well, everything is ready; come along. [*To the ladies.*] Once more, ladies, I salute you, and take my leave.

GELTRUDE [*rising and bowing*]. Adieu.

CANDIDA [*same action*]. Adieu. [*As she rises, she jostles against the fan on the balustrade. The fan falls into the street.*]

EVARISTO. Ah—h!

[*Picks the fan up.*]

CANDIDA. Never mind.

GELTRUDE. Don't trouble yourself.

EVARISTO. It's broken. I'm extremely sorry.

CANDIDA. No matter; it was only an old one.

EVARISTO. But I am to blame for this accident.

GELTRUDE. Don't feel troubled on account of that.

EVARISTO. Allow me to have the honor of . . . [*Makes as if to carry fan into house.*]

GELTRUDE. Don't inconvenience yourself. Just give it to the servant. [*Calls.*] Tognino!

TOGNINO. Yes, madam.

GELTRUDE. Just take the fan.

TOGNINO [*to* EVARISTO]. Allow me.

EVARISTO. If I am not to be permitted to . . . [*To* TOGNINO.] Take it. [*He gives the fan to* TOGNINO, *who takes it and goes in.*]

CANDIDA [*to* GELTRUDE]. See how disturbed he is—over the mere breaking of a fan!

GELTRUDE. A well-bred gentleman could scarcely be otherwise. [*Aside.*] The beginning of love—unless I am greatly mistaken.

SCENE III

[TOGNINO *appears on the terrace and gives the fan to the ladies, who look it over and try to adjust it.*]

EVARISTO [*aside*]. I'm extremely sorry to be the cause of breaking that fan. I must do what I can to set things right. [*He approaches* SUSANNA, *to whom he speaks softly.*] Madame Susanna.

SUSANNA. Yes, sir?

EVARISTO. I would like to speak with you. Suppose we go into your shop.

SUSANNA [*rising*]. Very well, sir, What can I do to serve you?

EVARISTO. Moracchio!

MORACCHIO. Yes, sir?

EVARISTO. You go on ahead. Wait for me at the edge of the wood—I'm coming along at once.

[*Enters shop with* SUSANNA.]

MORACCHIO. If we go on losing time like this, we shall bag more pumpkins than partridges. [*Exits with dog.*]

GIANNINA. My brother is finally off—good riddance! Now, how am I going to get a word with Crespino? Not while that bore of a Coronato is about, though. He is always tagging after me, and I can't endure him. [*To herself, while spinning.*]

COUNT [*reading*]. Oh! Ah! Beautiful, beautiful, beautiful indeed!—Signora Geltrude!

CRESPINO. What have you found that's so beautiful, Count?

COUNT. What business is it of yours, you great ignoramus?

CRESPINO [*aside, pounding hard on his last*]. I'll bet I know as much as you do!

GELTRUDE. What is it, Count?

COUNT. You are a clever woman, and you ought to hear what I have just this minute been reading—it's a real little masterpiece.

GELTRUDE. Something in history?

COUNT [*disdainfully*]. Ho!

GELTRUDE. Some treatise on philosophy?

COUNT [*as before*]. Ho!

GELTRUDE. Some fine bit of poetry?

COUNT [*as before*]. Ho!

GELTRUDE. What is it, then?

COUNT. It's a marvellous, magnificent thing, translated from the French. It is a little story—or, speaking in common parlance—a fable.

CRESPINO [*aside*]. Oh, lord! A fable! Marvellous! Magnificent!

[*Pounds noisily.*]

GELTRUDE. One of Æsop's?

COUNT. No.

GELTRUDE. One of Fontaine's?

COUNT. I don't know the author's name —that doesn't matter. Shall I read it to you?

GELTRUDE. Much pleased, I'm sure.

COUNT. Wait. Dear me, I've lost the place. I'll have it again in a moment. [*Looks for bookmark.*]

CANDIDA [*to* GELTRUDE]. You who are so fond of good books, do you care anything for these trashy fables?

GELTRUDE. Why not? If they are brightly and cleverly written, they may both please and instruct.

COUNT. Oh, here it is. Listen, now.

CRESPINO. Oh, Lord! He's going to read us fables! [*Pounds loudly.*]

COUNT [*to* CRESPINO]. You're going to start that up again, are you?

CRESPINO. Don't you want me to put on any heels? [*Pounds.*]

[TIMOTEO *returns to his mortar and pestle and pounds loudly.*]

COUNT. The deuce! Here's this other one starting up again! Ever going to come to an end, there?

TIMOTEO. Why, sir, I'm following my trade. [*Pounds.*]

COUNT. Listen. [*Reads to* GELTRUDE.]

"There was once a maiden of such amazing beauty . . ." [*To* TIMOTEO.] Here, you; be quiet there, or else go and do your pounding in some other place.

TIMOTEO. Excuse me, sir. I pay my rent, and have no better place than this. [*Pounds.*]

COUNT. The devil take you and your accursed mortar! I can't read here—I can't stand such a racket. Signora Geltrude, I will come up to you. And *then* you shall hear what a piece it is—such gaiety, such novelty . . . ! [*Raps on the book, and enters* GELTRUDE'S *house.*]

GELTRUDE. Well, truly, that apothecary *is* a little too enthusiastic. [*To* CANDIDA.] Let us go and receive the Count.

CANDIDA. Suppose you go. You know I don't care much for fables.

GELTRUDE. That isn't the point. Come. Civility requires it.

CANDIDA [*disdainfully*]. Oh, this Count!

GELTRUDE. My child, respect others, if you would have others respect you. Come, now; let us go.

CANDIDA. Ah, well, if you desire it. [*Rises to go. Exit* GELTRUDE.]

SCENE IV

[EVARISTO *and* SUSANNA *come out of shop.* CANDIDA *remains on terrace.*]

CANDIDA. How's this? Evaristo still here? Not gone hunting? I'm rather curious to know why. [*Steps back.*]

SUSANNA [*to* EVARISTO]. No, really, sir, you have nothing to complain of. I have let the fan go to you at a very low price.

EVARISTO [*aside*]. Candida no longer here? [*To* SUSANNA.] I only wish you had something better.

SUSANNA. I have nothing more, either better or worse. This is the last fan left in my shop.

EVARISTO. Very well; I will make it serve.

SUSANNA [*smiling*]. I imagine you are going to make a present of it.

EVARISTO. Certainly! Should I buy it for myself?

SUSANNA. You are going to give it to the Signorina Candida?

EVARISTO [*aside*]. This Susanna is a little too curious. [*Aloud.*] Why do you think I am going to give it to the Signorina Candida?

SUSANNA. Because I saw you break hers.

EVARISTO. No, no; I am meaning to put it to quite a different use.

SUSANNA. Oh, well, well, give it to whom you like. I never pry into other people's business. [*She seats herself and resumes her work.*]

EVARISTO [*aside*]. You didn't pry, still you'd like to know. But you won't know this time. [*He crosses over to* GIANNINA.]

CANDIDA. He has something very secret with that shop-keeper. I should like to know what it is. [*She comes forward a little.*]

EVARISTO [*softly*]. Giannina!

GIANNINA [*seated at her work*]. Well, sir?

EVARISTO. I would like to ask a favor of you.

GIANNINA. What's this you say, sir? Go on, if I can be of any use to you.

EVARISTO. The Signorina Candida, as I happen to know, has a great fondness for you.

GIANNINA. Yes, sir,—thanks to her good heart.

EVARISTO. She has even said something to me about using my influence with your brother.

GIANNINA. What an unfortunate girl I am! Left without father and mother, it is my fate to be under the thumb of a brother who is a brute—yes, sir, an out-and-out brute.

EVARISTO. Listen to me.

GIANNINA. Go on, sir. [*Spinning, with a lofty air.*] This spinning won't prevent my hearing you.

EVARISTO [*aside, ironically*]. Her brother carries things with a high hand, but she isn't so very far behind, herself!

SUSANNA [*aside*]. Could we have bought

the fan for Giannina? I don't believe so —not a bit.

[CORONATO *and* CRESPINO *show curiosity about the conversation between* EVARISTO *and* GIANNINA, *and stretch out their necks to overhear.*]

CANDIDA [*aside*]. Dealings with the shopwoman. Dealings with Giannini. I don't make this out.

[*Comes forward on the terrace.*]

EVARISTO [*to* GIANNINA]. May I ask a favor of you?

GIANNINA. Haven't I said yes? Haven't I said I would serve you if I could? If this distaff annoys you, I will throw it away.

[*Rises, and angrily casts distaff aside.*]

EVARISTO. This is a saucy piece to manage! But I need her.

CANDIDA [*aside*]. What is all that temper about?

CRESPINO [*aside*]. She throws away her distaff! [*He rises, shoe and hammer in hand, and comes forward a little.*]

CORONATO [*aside*]. Seems to me their talk is warming up. [*He too rises, book in hand, and comes forward a little.*]

SUSANNA [*looking on*]. If he were making her a present, she wouldn't lose her temper like that.

GIANNINA [*to* EVARISTO]. Well, here I am. What is it you wish?

EVARISTO. Come, be a good girl, Giannina.

GIANNINA. I don't know that I've ever been a bad one.

EVARISTO. You know that the Signorina Candida has broken her fan?

GIANNINA [*with set mouth*]. Yes, sir.

EVARISTO. And I have bought another at this shop?

GIANNINA [*as before*]. Very good, sir.

EVARISTO. But I shouldn't want Signora Geltrude to know it.

GIANNINA [*as before*]. Quite right, sir.

EVARISTO. And I should like to have you give it to Signorina Candida secretly.

GIANNINA [*as before*]. I cannot help you.

EVARISTO [*aside*]. What a rude reply!

CANDIDA [*aside*]. He gave me to understand that he was going hunting, and here he is yet.

CRESPINO [*coming forward, a boot in hand*]. I'd give a good deal to be able to hear.

CORONATO [*coming forward, and pretending to figure on his accounts*]. My curiosity grows greater every minute.

EVARISTO [*to* GIANNINA]. Why won't you do me this kindness?

GIANNINA. Because I've never learned the beautiful art of the go-between.

EVARISTO. Why do you put the thing in its worst light? Candida has a great fondness for you.

GIANNINA. I know she has; but in such a matter as this . . .

EVARISTO. They tell me you would like to marry Crespino. [*Turning, he sees the two men listening.*] What are you two fellows up to? What roguery is under way?

CRESPINO. I'm busy with my work, sir. [*Goes back and sits down.*]

CORONATO. Can't I write and walk at the same time? [*Also goes back and sits down.*]

CANDIDA [*aside*]. There's some great secret between them.

SUSANNA [*aside*]. What the dickens is there about that girl to make all the men run after her?

GIANNINA. If you have nothing more to say to me, I will go on with my spinning. [*Picks up distaff.*]

EVARISTO. Listen, Signorina Candida has asked me to interest myself in you, so that a dowry might be arranged for you and you might marry Crespino.

GIANNINA She has? [*Changes tone and throws away distaff.*]

EVARISTO. She has. And I am doing everything in my power to bring it about.

GIANNINA. Where is that fan?

EVARISTO. Here, in my pocket.

GIANNINA. Give it to me,—give it to me; but don't let anybody see.

EVARISTO. Take it.

[*Hands it over, secretly.*]

CRESPINO [*stretching his neck*]. He's giving her something.

CORONATO [*doing the same*]. What was it he handed her?

CANDIDA. Ah, yes! Evaristo is faithless. The Count but told the truth.

EVARISTO [*to* GIANNINA]. I must ask you to keep very quiet about this.

GIANNINA. Trust me for that. Don't have any fears.

EVARISTO. Adieu.

GIANNINA. Until we meet again.

EVARISTO. My best compliments.

GIANNINA. And mine to you. [*Takes up distaff, seats herself, and resumes spinning.*]

EVARISTO [*about to go, turns, and sees* CANDIDA, *above*]. Ah! there she is once more on the terrace. If I could only have a word with her! [*He looks about him, before speaking*]. Candida!

[CANDIDA *turns her back and walks away without answering.*]

EVARISTO. What is the meaning of this new turn? A little touch of disdain? Impossible; I know that she loves me, and she is certain that I adore her. Yet . . . Ah, I think I understand: she sees her aunt watching her and doesn't want to show her real feelings. That's it—it couldn't be anything different. But this silence must be broken; I must speak to Signora Geltrude and obtain from her the precious gift of her niece's hand.

[*Exit.*]

GIANNINA. Well, really, now, I'm very grateful to the Signorina Candida for keeping me in mind. Can I do less for her? With us girls, turn and turn about is fair play—we must lend each other a helping hand. [*Spins.*]

CORONATO [*rises and crosses over to* GIANNINA]. Great goings on with Signor Evaristo! Secret understandings and all that, eh?

GIANNINA. And what business is it of yours? And why must you come mixing yourself up in it?

CORONATO. If it was no business of mine, I shouldn't speak.

[CRESPINO, *rising, comes up behind* CORONATO *on tiptoe and listens.*]

GIANNINA. You have nothing to do with me. You have no control over me.

CORONATO. If I have nothing to do with you just now, I *shall* have, before long.

GIANNINA [*loud and quick*]. Who says so?

CORONATO. Who? I have the word of someone who has got the say of you, and who can dispose of you as he sees fit.

GIANNINA. You mean my brother, perhaps. [*Laughs.*]

CORONATO. Yes, I mean your brother. And I shall tell him about all these secrets, these private talks, these presents. . . .

CRESPINO. Hold on there, my good sir. [*Comes between the two.*] What claim have you got on this girl?

CORONATO. I am not to be held to account by you.

CRESPINO [*to* GIANNINA]. And you, what understanding have you got with Signor Evaristo?

GIANNINA. Leave me alone, both of you; you'll drive me out of my senses.

CRESPINO. I want you to tell me the whole truth about this.

CORONATO. You do, do you? You go with your wants to somebody that you've got a better right to order about. Giannina belongs to me—her brother has promised it.

CRESPINO. And I have her word to *me*. One word from the sister is worth a hundred from the brother.

CORONATO. We'll see about that.

CRESPINO [*to* GIANNINA]. What is it Evaristo said to you?

GIANNINA. Go to the deuce!

CORONATO. Aha! I saw him come out of the shop. The woman there will tell me. [*Runs toward* SUSANNA.]

CRESPINO. Could he have bought her some trinket? [*Runs also.*]

GIANNINA [*aside*]. Certainly *I* shall say nothing. And I shouldn't like to have Susanna . . .

CORONATO [*to* SUSANNA]. Tell me, if

you'll be so kind, what it was that Signor Evaristo bought of you.

SUSANNA [laughing]. A fan.

CRESPINO. Do you know what it was he gave to Giannina?

SUSANNA. Oh, do I? The fan.

GIANNINA [looking toward SUSANNA]. There's not a word of truth in that.

SUSANNA [rising, and approaching GIANNINA]. How's that?—not a word of truth in it?

CORONATO [violently to GIANNINA]. Let me see that fan.

CRESPINO [pushing CORONATO away]. This is none of your business. [To GIANNINA.] Let me see that fan.

[CORONATO raises his fist and threatens CRESPINO. CRESPINO does the same.]

GIANNINA [to SUSANNA]. You are to blame for this.

SUSANNA [to GIANNINA, angrily]. I am to blame for this?

GIANNINA. You are a gossip, a tattle-tale.

SUSANNA [advancing threateningly]. You call me a tattle-tale?

GIANNINA. Fall back, there, or I swear to heaven . . . [Raises her distaff.]

SUSANNA [drawing back]. I will go, before I risk my dignity.

GIANNINA. Before you risk your dignity?

SUSANNA. You are only a peasant wench, and you act according to your nature.

[GIANNINA tries to follow her. CRESPINO holds her back.]

GIANNINA. Leave me alone.

CRESPINO. Let me see that fan.

GIANNINA. I haven't got any fan.

CORONATO. What did Signor Evaristo give you?

GIANNINA. Your question is just so much impudence.

CORONATO [coming closer]. I've got to know, I tell you.

CRESPINO [pushing him back]. This is no affair of yours, I tell you.

GIANNINA [going toward her house]. This is no way to treat a respectable girl.

CRESPINO [following]. Tell me, Giannina.

GIANNINA [nearing her door]. No—never.

CORONATO [pushing back CRESPINO and approaching GIANNINA]. I'm the one who's got to know.

GIANNINA. The devil take you! [Enters house and slams door in his face.]

CORONATO. Such an insult to me! [To CRESPINO, threateningly.] You are to blame for this.

CRESPINO. What! you impudent rascal.

CORONATO. You don't want to get me too hot, now!

CRESPINO. I'm not afraid of you.

CORONATO [loud and emphatic]. Giannina must be mine!

CRESPINO. Never—never. And if it were so, I swear to heaven . . .

CORONATO. What do those threats amount to? Who is it you think you've got to deal with?

CRESPINO. I am a respectable man—everybody knows it.

CORONATO. And what am I?

CRESPINO. I don't know what you are.

CORONATO. I am an honest innkeeper.

CRESPINO. Honest?

CORONATO. What? You've got doubts about it?

CRESPINO. I'm not the one that has doubts about it.

CORONATO. Who, then?

CRESPINO. The whole village.

CORONATO. No, my friend; I'm not the one they talk about. I don't sell old leather for new.

CRESPINO. And I don't sell water for wine, nor mutton for lamb. And I don't go prowling round o' nights stealing cats, to sell them for rabbits . . .

CORONATO [holding up his hand]. I swear to heaven . . .

CRESPINO. Ha! [Does the same.]

CORONATO. By the great Lord . . . ! [Thrusts his hand into his pocket.]

CRESPINO. He's feeling for it! [Runs toward his bench for some weapon or other.]

CORONATO. Where is that knife? . . .

[*Runs and picks up his bench.* CRESPINO *leaves his search among his tools and picks up a stool belonging to the apothecary. The two men fight.*]

SCENE V

[*Enter* TIMOTEO, LIMONCINO, SCAVEZZO *and the* COUNT. TIMOTEO *from his shop, pestle in hand;* LIMONCINO *from café, with a stick of wood;* SCAVEZZO *from inn, with a spit.*]

COUNT [*from* GELTRUDE'S *house, trying to separate combatants*]. Stop, stop, stop, I tell you! It is I, you wretched brutes —I, the Count of Rocca Marina, who commands you. Stop, stop, I say.

[*He fears, however, to intervene.*]

CRESPINO. Yes, it is but right—[*to* CORONATO] that we show the proper respect to the Count.

CORONATO. Yes, thank the Count—for I should have broken every bone in your body.

COUNT. Come, come; this will do. Tell me, now, the cause of this quarrel. You others, there, go away. *I* am here, and nobody else is needed.

[*Exeunt* LIMONCINO *and* SCAVEZZO.]

TIMOTEO. Anybody hurt?

COUNT. You'd have liked them to crack their skulls and break their legs and dislocate their elbows, wouldn't you?—so as to show your skill and make an exhibition of your ability.

TIMOTEO. I'm not one to wish evil to anybody. But if there had been any need —if they'd been wounded, or crippled, or smashed all to pieces—I should have been glad enough to be of use. In such a case I would serve *you*, illustrious sir, with all my heart.

COUNT. You are too bold. I will have you run out of town.

TIMOTEO. Honest men can't be run out so easily as that.

COUNT. I've known towns to be rid of ignorant impostors, such as you are.

TIMOTEO. It astonishes me to hear you speak like that, sir. Without my pills you'd have been dead long ago.

COUNT. Insolent fellow!

TIMOTEO. And those same pills of mine you haven't paid me for, yet. [*Exit.*]

CORONATO [*aside*]. This is a case where the Count can help me.

COUNT. Well, now; what's been the trouble here? What is the reason for this quarrel?

CRESPINO. I will tell you, sir. I don't care who knows it; I love Giannina.

CORONATO. And she is promised to me.

COUNT. Aha! I understand. A battle for love. Two of Cupid's champions. Two valorous rivals. Two claimants for the hand of the beautiful Venus, the goddess of our village. [*Laughs.*]

CRESPINO [*going*]. If it's your idea to make a joke of me . . .

COUNT [*detains him*]. No; come here.

CORONATO. This is a serious matter, I assure you.

COUNT. So I see. Here we have two rival lovers. *Cospetto di Bacco*, what a combination! It seems, then, that the fable I read to Signora Geltrude . . . [*Opens book and reads.*] "There was once a maiden of such amazing beauty . . ."

CRESPINO [*aside*]. I understand. [*To* COUNT.] With your permission.

[*Going.*]

COUNT. Where are you off to? Come here.

CRESPINO. With your permission, I will go back and finish your shoes.

COUNT. Oh, yes; go along, so that I can have them by tomorrow morning.

CORONATO. And take care you don't mend them with old, worn-out leather.

CRESPINO. I will come to you to get new.

CORONATO. Thank heaven, I am neither a shoemaker nor a cobbler.

CRESPINO. Never mind; you can give me some horse-hide, or some cat-skin.

[*Exit.*]

CORONATO [*aside*]. I can see that this man is doomed to die by my hand.

COUNT. What does he say about cats? Have you been giving us cats to eat?

CORONATO. Sir, I am an honest man, and that fellow is an impudent scoundrel who is doing harm to my good name.

COUNT. That's an effect of passion, of rivalry. You are in love with Giannina, then?

CORONATO. Yes, sir; and I was hoping to put myself under your protection.

COUNT [with an air]. Under my protection? Very well; we will see about it. Are you sure that she returns your love?

CORONATO. To tell the truth, I think she inclines more to that fellow than she does to me.

COUNT. That's bad.

CORONATO. But I have her brother's promise.

COUNT. That isn't to be depended on very much.

CORONATO. Moracchio has pledged me his word, sure and certain.

COUNT [with emphasis]. That's very well, but you can't bring a woman round by main force.

CORONATO. It rests with her brother to dispose of her.

COUNT [sharply]. No, it doesn't; it rests with the girl herself.

CORONATO. But with your protection, your assistance . . .

COUNT. My protection is all well and good; my protection is valuable; my protection is powerful. But a gentleman, such as I am, cannot act as arbiter in the disposal of a woman's heart.

CORONATO. She's a peasant girl . . .

COUNT. What difference does that make? A woman's a woman, always. I distinguish degrees, conditions; but in the mass I respect the sex.

CORONATO [aside]. I understand. His protection is not worth a rap.

COUNT. How are you off for wine? Have you got something pretty good on hand?

CORONATO. Some of the very best—perfect, exquisite.

COUNT. I'll come and try it. My own, this year, hasn't done very well.

CORONATO [aside]. He sold his all out two years ago.

COUNT. If yours is good, I will let you supply me.

CORONATO [aside]. I don't insist on such a privilege.

COUNT. You understand?

CORONATO. I understand.

COUNT. Tell me, now. If I were to speak to this girl and bring her round to where she would be inclined to favor you . . . ?

CORONATO. Your words might serve to bring me some advantage.

COUNT. When we come down to it, you really deserve her preference.

CORONATO. It seems that between me and Crespino . . .

COUNT. There's no comparison at all. A man like you—solid, trustworthy, respectable . . .

CORONATO. You are too good, I'm sure.

COUNT. And then, I have a great respect for the women. And it's just this, I assure you—treating them as I do treat them—that makes them willing to do for me what they wouldn't do for anybody else.

CORONATO. That is what I was thinking myself; but you almost made me lose hope.

COUNT. My friend, you keep a good house here, and you could support a wife properly. Rely on me, and I will do what I can to advance your interests—like a good lawyer.

CORONATO. I depend on your protection.

COUNT. You shall have it, I promise you.

CORONATO. If you could put yourself out enough to come and try my wine . . .

COUNT. Very willingly. I am sure that everything will go all right for you.

CORONATO. Your humble servant.

COUNT. My worthy fellow! [Puts his hand on the other's shoulder.] Come. [Goes into tavern.]

CORONATO. Two or three barrels of wine couldn't be put to better use.

ACT II

Scene I

[Susanna *alone; she comes out from her shop and rearranges her display of wares.*]

Susanna. Little enough business going on in this village! So far I haven't sold a thing but one fan, and even that at such a price—just an out-and-out sacrifice! Everybody that's got money to spend goes to the city to buy; there's not much to be made out of these poor people here. It's foolish of me to waste my time in such a place. These wretched, mannerless rustics see no difference between a shopkeeper and anybody who sells milk, or eggs, or vegetables. I was well brought up in town; but that goes for nothing here in the country. All friends and equals: Susanna, Giannina, Mag and Betsy; the shopkeeper, the goat-girl, the peasant-wench—we're all bound together in one sheaf. With those two ladies there's some difference,—but little enough even with them. That saucy Giannina, who enjoys their favor a little, and thinks, on that account, she is something great! They have given her a fan! What is a mere peasant-girl to do with that fan? Oh, she will make a great figure, won't she?—like this—[*Business with imaginary fan.*] Oh, much good may it do her! The whole thing is enough to make you laugh—or to put you in a rage. I was well brought up and I can't stand clownishness and impudence. [*Seats herself and begins work.*]

Scene II

[Susanna *and* Candida, *who comes out from palace.*]

Candida. I can't enjoy a minute's peace until I get some light on these matters. I saw Evaristo leave the shop and go over to Giannina; and I'm perfectly certain he gave her something. I'm going to see if Susanna can't tell me something about it. My aunt is right when she advises me not to trust myself to anybody that I don't know through and through. Poor me!—if I were to find him unfaithful! He is my first love,—I have never cared for anyone else. [*Approaches* Susanna *little by little.*]

Susanna [*rising*]. Ah, Signorina, your humble servant.

Candida. Good day, Susanna. What pretty thing are you making now?

Susanna. I'm amusing myself by putting together a cap.

Candida. To sell?

Susanna. To sell, yes,—but heaven knows when.

Candida. I may have need of some such cap as this.

Susanna. I have a number already made. Would you like to see some?

Candida. Well, well; there is no hurry; another time will do.

Susanna [*offering chair*]. Wouldn't you like to sit down for a little?

Candida. And you?

Susanna. Oh, I will bring another chair. [*Goes into shop and brings out a straw-seated chair.*] Sit here,—this will be better.

Candida [*seating herself*]. Sit down too, and go on with your work.

Susanna [*seating herself*]. Thanks for your kindness in accepting my company. One well born and bred, like you, can condescend to anything. But these rude villagers are as proud as peacocks, and that Giannina——

Candida. Speaking of Giannina, did you notice when Signor Evaristo was speaking to her?

Susanna. Didn't I? How they went on!

Candida. He *did* have rather a long talk with her.

Susanna. And do you know what followed? Did you hear about the fight they had?

Candida. I heard some noise or other. They told me that Coronato and Crespino almost came to blows.

Susanna. Yes, indeed; and all on account of that lovely creature, that precious jewel!

CANDIDA. But why?

SUSANNA. Jealous of each other, and jealous of Signor Evaristo.

CANDIDA. Do you believe that Evaristo has come to have some—some attachment for Giannina?

SUSANNA. I'm sure I don't know anything about it. I attend to my own affairs and try not to think ill of anybody. But the innkeeper and the shoemaker are both jealous of him, and no doubt have their reasons.

CANDIDA [aside]. Ah, me—things are certainly not going in my favor!

SUSANNA. But excuse me. I shouldn't want to make any mistake——

CANDIDA. How do you mean?

SUSANNA. I shouldn't want to find that you yourself had some—some partiality for Signor Evaristo——

CANDIDA. What! I? Not in the least. I know him because he comes now and then to the house; he is a friend of my aunt's.

SUSANNA. Then I will tell you the truth. [Aside.] I don't believe that she will be offended by it. [Aloud.] I was inclined to think that between you and Evaristo there might be some good understanding—perfectly right and proper, of course; but after what has happened this morning, I find myself completely undeceived.

CANDIDA. Was he here with you this morning?

SUSANNA. He was. I will tell you: he came to buy a fan.

CANDIDA [with eager concern]. To buy a fan?

SUSANNA. Exactly. And since I knew that yours had been broken—by his fault, so to speak—I said to myself at once: He is buying this to give to the Signorina Candida——

CANDIDA. He did buy it for me, then?

SUSANNA. Oh, no, my dear young lady. I had the boldness to ask him if it was for you; and to tell the truth he answered me in such a way as to make me think

I had offended him. "That broken fan is no affair of mine," he said. "What have I to do with Signorina Candida? I'm buying this fan for someone else."

CANDIDA. For someone else? Who was it he gave it to?

SUSANNA. Who was it? It was Giannina.

CANDIDA [much moved]. Oh, me! I am in despair!

SUSANNA [observing CANDIDA'S emotion]. Signorina Candida——

CANDIDA [aside]. Unworthy fellow! Faithless wretch! Faithless!—and for whom? For a mere country wench.

SUSANNA [as before]. Signorina Candida——

CANDIDA [aside]. I will never forgive him—never!

SUSANNA [aside]. Oh, dear, I've done it now! [Aloud.] Calm yourself, do. It can't be so.

CANDIDA. Do you believe that he gave the fan to Giannina?

SUSANNA. Oh, as far as that goes, I saw it with my own eyes.

CANDIDA. Then why do you say to me —it can't be so?

SUSANNA. I—I don't know. I don't want to see you—I don't want to be to blame for——

SCENE III

[GELTRUDE at the door of the Palace.]

SUSANNA [to CANDIDA]. Oh, here comes your aunt.

CANDIDA [to SUSANNA]. For the love of heaven, don't say a word.

SUSANNA. Never fear. [Aside.] And she tried to make me think she didn't care for him! It's her own fault. Why didn't she tell me the truth?

GELTRUDE. What are you doing here, Candida? [CANDIDA and SUSANNA get up.]

SUSANNA. Your niece has been good enough to favor me with a little of her company.

CANDIDA. I just came down to look at a cap or two.

SUSANNA. Yes, quite true—she was inquiring after caps. Oh, don't be afraid —she is perfectly safe with me here. There's nothing too gay and frisky about me, and only the right kind of people come to my house.

GELTRUDE. Don't justify yourself beyond the needs of the case, Miss Susanna.

SUSANNA. Oh, I'm as particular as anybody, madam.

GELTRUDE [to CANDIDA]. Why didn't you tell *me* that you were in need of a cap?

CANDIDA. You were in your boudoir, writing, and I didn't want to disturb you.

SUSANNA. Would you like to see it? I will go and fetch it. Just take this seat, please. [*Gives seat to* GELTRUDE *and goes into shop.*]

GELTRUDE [*to* CANDIDA—*seating herself*]. Do you know anything about this quarrel between the inn-keeper and the shoemaker?

CANDIDA [*seating herself*]. It's some love trouble, they say; some jealousy, I understand, about Giannina.

GELTRUDE. I'm sorry, because she is a good girl.

CANDIDA. Oh, my dear aunt, excuse me; but I have heard such things about her that it would be well if we refused to let her come to the house any more.

GELTRUDE. *What* things? What do they say about her?

CANDIDA. I will tell you all about it presently. Do as *I* do, aunt. Don't see anything more of her, and you will be doing very well.

GELTRUDE. Since she came to see *you* rather than to see *me*, I leave you at liberty to treat her as you see fit.

CANDIDA [*aside*]. The insolent creature will never have the face to show herself before *me*, again!

SUSANNA [*coming back*]. Here are the caps, ladies. Look them over, make your selection, satisfy your own tastes. [*All three busy themselves over the caps and converse in low tones together.*]

SCENE IV

[*The* COUNT *and the* BARON *come out together from the inn.*]

COUNT. I am so glad that you have frankly told me all. Don't have any more doubts, but just put everything right into my hands.

BARON. I know you to be a friend of Signora Geltrude.

COUNT. Oh, I will tell you how it is, my friend. She is a woman of some cleverness; I love literature and am rather fonder of amusing myself with her than anybody else. As for the rest, she is a poor middle-class person. Her husband left her this little house and a few bits of land, and in order to be respected in the village, she has need of my protection.

BARON. Hurrah for the Count, who protects widows and all lovely damsels!

COUNT. How would you have it? In this world a man has got to be of some use one way or another.

BARON. So then, you will do me the kindness to——

COUNT. Never fear. I will speak to her; I will ask from her the hand of her niece for a gentleman who is a friend of mine. And when *I* ask, be very sure she won't have the boldness to say no.

BARON. Tell her who I am.

COUNT. What would be the good of that? When *I* ask——

BARON. But you're going to ask her for me?

COUNT. For you.

BARON. You know perfectly well who I am.

COUNT. Don't I?—your condition, your affairs, your circumstances. Ah, we men of title know all about each other.

BARON [*aside*]. How glad I should be if I didn't need his services.

COUNT [*with sudden eagerness*]. Ah! my dearest friend!

BARON. What is it?

COUNT. Look. Here is Signora Geltrude, with her niece.

BARON. They're busy; I don't believe they've seen us.

COUNT. Of course they haven't. If Geltrude had seen me she would have bestirred herself at once.

BARON. When are you going to speak to her?

COUNT. This very moment, if you like.

BARON. Better for me not to be here. Speak to her, and meanwhile I will go and wait in the apothecary's.

COUNT. Why the apothecary's?

BARON. I need a little rhubarb for my digestion. Adieu. I am in your hands.

COUNT [embracing him]. My dearest friend!

BARON. Adieu, my beloved associate. (He's the most gorgeous fool in all creation!) [BARON goes into apothecary's shop.]

COUNT. Signora Geltrude.

GELTRUDE. Oh, my dear Count, pardon me. I hadn't seen you. [Rises.]

COUNT. One word, if you please.

SUSANNA [to both]. Sit here, if you like; you are quite welcome.

COUNT. No, no. I have something— [To GELTRUDE.]—to say to you in private. Excuse my troubling you, but I must ask you to step this way.

GELTRUDE. In just a moment. Allow me to pay for a cap we have just bought, and then I am yours. [Takes out her purse to pay SUSANNA and to make delay.]

COUNT [aside]. She pays cash down! A bad trick that I have never learned!

SCENE V

[CORONATO comes out of the inn, with SCAVEZZO, who carries a barrel of wine on his back.]

CORONATO. Illustrious sir, here's a barrel of wine that's coming to you.

COUNT. Where's the other one?

CORONATO. That will follow this. Where do you want it carried?

COUNT. To my palace.

CORONATO. Whom shall we leave it with?

COUNT. With my steward, if he's there.

CORONATO. I'm afraid he won't be.

COUNT. Then leave it with anybody at all.

CORONATO. Very well. Off we go.

SCAVEZZO. Your excellency will give me a copper or two?

COUNT [to SCAVEZZO]. You take care not to drink any of this wine, and not to mix any water with it. [To CORONATO.] Don't let him go alone.

CORONATO. Never fear, never fear. I'm going along too. [Exit.]

SCAVEZZO [aside]. No, never fear— never fear but what between me and master, we've doctored it up by this time!

[GELTRUDE has paid by this time and goes toward COUNT. SUSANNA seats herself and resumes her work. CANDIDA remains seated and talks in low tone with SUSANNA.]

GELTRUDE. Here I am, Count. What can I do for you?

COUNT. In three words: Will you give me your niece?

GELTRUDE. Give? What do you mean by give?

COUNT. The deuce! Don't you understand? In marriage.

GELTRUDE. To you?

COUNT. Not to me, but to a person that I know and I propose for.

GELTRUDE. It is like this, Count. You know that my niece has lost her parents, and that as she is the daughter of my only brother, I have undertaken to fill the place of a mother to her.

COUNT. Pardon me, but all these words are quite unnecessary.

GELTRUDE. Pardon me. Let me come to the point of her present position.

COUNT. Very good. Well, then?

GELTRUDE. Candida has not inherited enough from her father to enable her to marry according to her rank in life.

COUNT. No matter; it's no question of that.

GELTRUDE. Let me go on. I was left very well off by my husband.

COUNT. I know.

GELTRUDE. And having no sons——
COUNT [*impatient*]. You will give her a dowry——
GELTRUDE [*with a bit of temper*]. Yes, sir, when I find a young man that pleases me.
COUNT. Oh, as far as *that* goes—I have one to propose, and when *I* propose him, he will please.
GELTRUDE. I feel sure, Count, that you would not propose an unsuitable person; but I hope you will do me the honor of telling me who he is.
COUNT. He is a friend of mine, a colleague.
GELTRUDE. How? A colleague?
COUNT. A man of title, as *I* am.
GELTRUDE. But let me say——
COUNT. Don't make difficulties.
GELTRUDE. Let me finish, if you please; and if not, I will go away, and relieve you of the burden of my company.
COUNT. Oh, come, come; be pleasant. I will listen to you. With the ladies I am always kindly, always indulgent; I will listen to you.
GELTRUDE. I will give you my idea in a few words. A title of nobility may add to the worth of a family but not to the worth of an individual. I do not believe my niece to be ambitious, nor have I any wish to sacrifice her on the altar of vanity.
COUNT [*jestingly*]. Oh, I see that you have been reading fables.
GELTRUDE. These sentiments do not come from fables, from story books. They are inspired by nature, and cultivated by good breeding.
COUNT. Nature — breeding — whatever you like. The man that I propose is the Baron Cedro.
GELTRUDE. The Baron is in love with my niece?
COUNT. Oui, Madame.
GELTRUDE. I know him, and have a great respect for him.
COUNT. You see what a good candidate I bring forward?
GELTRUDE. He is a gentleman of character, of merit.

COUNT. He is my colleague.
GELTRUDE. He is a little free of speech, but there's no harm in that.
COUNT. Come then. What do you say?
GELTRUDE. Slowly, slowly, if you please, Count. Such things are not decided on the spur of the moment. The Baron will be good enough to speak to me——
COUNT. Excuse me, but when *I* say a thing, one need have no doubts. I ask her hand of you on his behalf. He has put the affair in my charge, and has begged me, and implored me; and I speak to you, and implore you—no, I don't implore you; I ask you.
GELTRUDE. Well, let us suppose that the Baron has really said all this.
COUNT. *Cospetto!* What do you mean with your "supposing"? The thing is so, and when *I* say it——
GELTRUDE. Well, then, the thing is so. The Baron wants her, your lordship demands her for him. I must find out whether Candida herself consents.
COUNT. She won't know anything about it, if you don't speak to her.
GELTRUDE [*ironically*]. Be good enough to believe that I shall speak to her.
COUNT. There she is. Speak to her now.
GELTRUDE. I shall.
COUNT. Go on, then, I'll wait here.
GELTRUDE [*making reverence*]. With your permission. [*Aside, as she goes toward the shop.*] If this is true about the Baron it would be a piece of great good fortune for my niece. But I have an idea that there is somebody ahead of him.
COUNT. Oh, I've got such a taking way, that I can do just about anything with just about anybody! [*Pulls out his book, seats himself on bench and reads.*]
GELTRUDE. Candida, let us take a step or so to one side. I have something to say to you.
SUSANNA. If you would like to make use of my garden, it is quite at your disposal. [SUSANNA *and* CANDIDA *rise.*]
GELTRUDE. Yes, thanks, that will be

better, because I must come back here at once. [*Goes into shop.*]

CANDIDA. Whatever in the world has she got to say to me? I am far too wretched to hope for any consolation.

[*Goes into shop.*]

COUNT. She is quite capable of keeping me waiting here for an hour. Good thing that I've got this book to occupy myself with. First rate thing—literature. With a good book in his hand, a man is never alone. [*Reads to himself softly.*]

SCENE VI

[GIANNINA *comes out from house. The* COUNT *present.*]

GIANNINA. Well, the dinner is ready; so, when that brute of a Moracchio gets back there will be no scolding. Nobody to see me; good chance, now, to carry this fan to Signorina Candida. If I can give it to her without her aunt's seeing it, I will. If not, I'll wait until I happen to meet her again.

COUNT. Ha, there's Giannina! Hey, young woman! [*She goes toward palace.*]

GIANNINA [*turning where she stands*]. Yes, sir.

COUNT. A word. [*Calls her to him.*]

GIANNINA [*aside*]. Well, now; here's *this* hindrance. [*Moves forward very softly, slowly.*]

COUNT [*aside*]. I mustn't forget about Coronato. I have promised him my protection, and he deserves it. [*Rises, and lays aside his book.*]

GIANNINA. I am here. What do you wish?

COUNT. Where were you going?

GIANNINA [*brusquely*]. About my own business.

COUNT. Is *that* the way you answer? With such boldness? With such impertinence?

GIANNINA. How should I answer? I speak as I was taught to speak, and as I am accustomed to speak. I speak this way with everybody, and no one has ever called me impertinent.

COUNT. You must bear in mind whom you are speaking to.

GIANNINA. Oh, I don't know anything about bearing in mind. If you want anything, say so. If you are amusing yourself, I haven't got any time to waste on your highness.

COUNT. *Illustrious* highness.

GIANNINA. *Most* illustrious, if you like.

COUNT. Come here.

GIANNINA. I *am* here.

COUNT. Do you want to get married?

GIANNINA. Yes, sir, I do.

COUNT. Bravo! That's what I like.

GIANNINA. Oh, me—who has my heart in my mouth.

COUNT. Would you like to have *me* marry you?

GIANNINA. No, sir, I wouldn't.

COUNT. What do you mean by no?

GIANNINA. What do I mean by no? I mean no—no, because I wouldn't. Because, to get married I have no need of you.

COUNT. You have no need of my protection?

GIANNINA. No, I haven't—not the least bit.

COUNT. Do you know what I can do in this village?

GIANNINA. You can do everything in this village, but you can't do anything about my marriage.

COUNT. Nothing?

GIANNINA. Nothing,—not the least thing. [*Laughs softly.*]

COUNT. You are in love with Crespino.

GIANNINA. Well, he's plenty good enough for *me!*

COUNT. And you prefer him, do you, to that honest, well-to-do, steady-going Coronato?

GIANNINA. There are lots of others besides Coronato that I would prefer him to.

COUNT. Lots of others you would prefer him to?

GIANNINA. If you only know whom I preferred him to! [*Laughs.*]

COUNT. And whom do you prefer him to?

GIANNINA. What's the use of my saying? Don't make me talk.

COUNT. I won't, for you would be quite capable of getting off some insolence or other.

GIANNINA. Anything more you wish of me?

COUNT. Come now, I protect your brother, your brother has promised you to Coronato, and so Coronato you must marry.

GIANNINA. Your highness——

COUNT. *Illustrious* highness.

GIANNINA. Your illustrious highness protects [*affectedly*] my brother?

COUNT. I am pledged to that, yes.

GIANNINA. And my brother has promised Coronato?

COUNT. Certainly.

GIANNINA. Oh, if that's the case——

COUNT. Well?

GIANNINA. My brother shall marry Coronato.

COUNT. I swear to heaven, you shall never marry Crespino.

GIANNINA. No? Why not?

COUNT. I will have him run out of the village.

GIANNINA. I will follow him wherever he goes.

COUNT. I will have him soundly beaten.

GIANNINA. Oh, *he* will have something to say about that.

COUNT. I'll have him knocked down—felled like an ox.

GIANNINA. Truly, I shouldn't like that at all.

COUNT. What would you do if he were dead?

GIANNINA. Don't know.

COUNT. Would you take somebody else?

GIANNINA. Maybe so.

COUNT. Figure him as dead.

GIANNINA. Sir, I don't know how to read, nor how to write, nor how to figure.

COUNT. You saucy baggage!

GIANNINA. Anything more you wish of me?

COUNT. Go to the devil!

GIANNINA. Show me the way!

COUNT. By heavens, if you were not a woman——!

GIANNINA. What would you do to me?

COUNT. Go away from here, be off!

GIANNINA. I obey you at once;—and then you will tell me that I have no manners. [*Goes toward palace.*]

COUNT. Manners, manners! You are going off—[*Angrily, behind* GIANNINA.]—without making a curtsey.

GIANNINA. Oh, pardon me. Most humble servant of your highness.
[*Curtsies deeply.*]

COUNT. *Illustrious* highness.

GIANNINA. Of your illustrious highness. [*Runs laughing into palace.*]

COUNT [*Angrily, indignantly*]. This rustic rabble has no manners. I don't know what to do. If she doesn't want Coronato, I can't force her to take him—no failure of mine. Whatever put it into his head to want a girl who doesn't want *him?* I'll find him one yet—one better than this. He will see in full time the advantage of my protection.

SCENE VII

[GELTRUDE *and* CANDIDA *come out from* SUSANNA's *shop.*]

COUNT. Is it all right, Madam?

GELTRUDE. My niece, dear Count, is a wise and prudent young woman.

COUNT. Is it all right? Be brief.

GELTRUDE. But really, Count, you make me quite weary.

COUNT. Pardon me; if you only knew what I have just gone through, with a woman! [*Aside.*] Another woman, it is true; but these women—they're all alike! [*Aloud.*] Well, what does the wise and prudent Candida say?

GELTRUDE. Granted, now, that the Baron——

COUNT. "Granted!" Deuce take your "Granteds!"

GELTRUDE. Allowed, assumed, conceded —whatever may please your highness——

COUNT [*to himself, between his teeth*]. *Illustrious* highness.

GELTRUDE [*inquiringly*]. I beg pardon?
COUNT. Nothing, nothing; go ahead.
GELTRUDE. With all the conditions agreed upon, and all the usual forms observed, my niece is willing to marry the Baron.
COUNT. Brava, Bravissima! [*To* CANDIDA—*to himself.*] This time, at least, it goes through.
CANDIDA [*aside*]. Yes, to avenge myself upon that faithless Evaristo.
GELTRUDE [*aside*]. I did not think it at all likely that she would consent. I felt quite certain that she was occupied with some other affair;—but I was mistaken.

SCENE VIII

[GIANNINA *on terrace.*]
GIANNINA. She isn't here; I can't find her anywhere at all. Oh, there she is!
COUNT. So then, the Signorina Candida will marry the Baron del Cedro.
GIANNINA. What's this I hear? How will she answer?
GELTRUDE [*to the* COUNT]. She will, when the stipulations——
CANDIDA [*to* COUNT]. None at all, sir. I will marry him out of hand.
COUNT. Long live the Signorina Candida! This pleases me.
GELTRUDE [*to* CANDIDA]. Let us go and wait for them, then.
CANDIDA [*melancholy*]. Yes, let us go.
GELTRUDE. What's the matter with you? Don't you feel in good spirits?
CANDIDA. Yes, in good spirits. [*Aside.*] I have given my word;—there is no escape.
GELTRUDE. Poor girl! I feel for her. In such situations—in spite of love—there is always a certain amount of embarrassment. [*Goes toward palace.*]

SCENE IX

[GIANNINA *enters from the Palace.*]
GIANNINA. Oh, Signorina Candida.
CANDIDA [*angrily*]. What are you doing here?

GIANNINA. I have been looking for you——
CANDIDA. Go away, and never dare set foot in our house again.
GIANNINA. What! Why do you say such words to me?
CANDIDA. Such words to you? You are a wretched, worthless girl,—I can't endure you, I will not tolerate you! [*Goes into palace.*]
GELTRUDE. That's a little too strong, really.
GIANNINA [*aside*]. I'm turned to stone. [*Aloud.*] Signora Geltrude——
GELTRUDE. I'm sorry for the mortification you have been made to feel; but my niece is a young woman of good judgment, and if she has treated you so, she doubtless has her reasons for it.
GIANNINA. What reasons can she have? I wonder at her, I'm ashamed of her!
GELTRUDE. Come, come, don't raise your voice; don't forget the respect due me.
GIANNINA [*as if to leave*]. I've got to go and set myself right——
GELTRUDE. No, no; remain here. This isn't the time; you can do it later.
GIANNINA. I tell you, I'm going to do it now. [*Going toward palace door.*]
GELTRUDE [*in doorway*]. Don't you dare to pass this door.

SCENE X

[*The* COUNT *and the* BARON *come out from the apothecary shop to go into the palace.*]
COUNT. Come along; come along.
GIANNINA. I will, even if I have to force it!
GELTRUDE. Insolent creature! [*Goes inside and shuts the door in* GIANNINA'S *face just as the* COUNT *and the* BARON, *whom she has not seen, present themselves.*]

[GIANNINA *goes raging across the stage.* COUNT *remains speechless, looking at the door.*]
BARON. What! They shut the door in our faces?

COUNT. In our faces? Impossible.

BARON. Impossible? Is a thing that has just happened impossible?

GIANNINA [striding up and down in a rage.] Such an affront to me?

COUNT [to BARON]. Let us knock, and find out what this means.

GIANNINA. If they go in, I'll go in too.

BARON. No, stop—I don't want to know anything more. I don't care to expose myself to new insults. It is by reason of you that I am treated this way. They make a jest of you and turn me to ridicule on your account.

COUNT [hotly]. What way is that to talk?

BARON. I demand satisfaction.

COUNT. Of whom?

BARON. Of you.

COUNT. In what fashion?

BARON. Sword in hand.

COUNT. Sword? I've been living twenty years in this village, but I've never seen a sword here——

BARON. Pistols, then.

COUNT. Pistols? Very well, I will go and get mine. [Going.]

BARON. No, stay here, I've got two myself. [Takes them from pocket.] One for you, and one for me.

GIANNINA. Pistols, oh, help, help, everybody! Pistols, pistols! They're going to kill each other. [Runs into house.]

[COUNT is embarrassed.]

SCENE XI

[GELTRUDE on terrace. COUNT and BARON. Then, LIMONCINO and TOGNINO.]

GELTRUDE. Gentlemen, what does all this mean?

COUNT. Why did you shut the door in our faces?

GELTRUDE. I? Pardon me, I am not capable of treating anybody whomsoever with such discourtesy. Least of all you, and the Baron who has deigned to ask for the hand of my niece.

COUNT [to BARON]. Do you hear that?

BARON. But, madam, the door was shut in our faces just as we were on the point of entering your house.

GELTRUDE. I protest, gentlemen, I did not see you. I simply shut the door to keep out that little fool of a Giannina.

GIANNINA [thrusting her head out of her door]. Who's a little fool of a Giannina? [Draws it in again, bursting with vexation.]

COUNT [to GIANNINA]. Hush, there, saucebox.

GELTRUDE. If you wish to favor us, I will give orders to have you admitted. [Exit.]

COUNT [to BARON]. Do you hear that?

BARON. I have nothing more to say.

COUNT. What are you going to do with those pistols?

BARON. Excuse me if I have seemed over-sensitive about my honor—. [Puts pistols in pocket.]

COUNT. Do you want to present yourself to two ladies with a pair of pistols in your pocket?

BARON. I carry them about the country for my own protection.

COUNT. But if they know you've got those weapons—you understand what women are—they wouldn't want you to come anywhere near them.

BARON. You are right. I thank you for advising me on this point, and as a sign of friendship I make you a present of them. [Pulls them out again and offers them to COUNT.]

COUNT [afraid]. A present? To me?

BARON. Yes. I hope you won't decline them.

COUNT. I will accept them, because they come from you. Are they loaded?

BARON. What a question! Would you have me carrying them around empty?

COUNT. Wait. Hey, you there,—in the café.

LIMONCINO [entering from café]. What is it, sir?

COUNT. Take away those pistols, and keep good care of them until I send for them.

LIMONCINO. Very well, sir. [*Takes pistols from* BARON.]

COUNT. Look out, now; they're loaded.

LIMONCINO. Oh, well I know how to handle them. [*Handles pistols.*]

COUNT [*afraid*]. Come, come, now; don't act like a fool!

LIMONCINO [*aside*]. He's a brave man, the Count. [*Exit.*]

COUNT. I thank you. I shall not forget your kindness. [*Aside.*] I'll sell them to-morrow.

TOGNINO [*from palace*]. Gentlemen, my mistress is waiting for you.

COUNT. Come on, now.

BARON. Yes, let us go.

COUNT. Well, what do you say to all this? I'm a good deal of a man, eh, my dear colleague? We people with titles,— our protection is worth something. [*Going toward palace door.* GIANNINA *comes out of her house and follows behind softly, to go in with them. The* COUNT *and the* BARON *are admitted by* TOGNINO, *who remains standing in the doorway.* GIANNINA *tries to go in too, but is stopped by* TOGNINO.]

TOGNINO. You haven't got any business here.

GIANNINA. Yes, I have too got some business here.

TOGNINO. I have orders not to let you in! [*Goes inside and shuts the door.*]

GIANNINA. I'm boiling with a rage I can't choke down; I feel myself suffocating with indignation. [*Comes down.*] Such an affront to me! Such an insult to a girl of my sort! [*Goes raging up and down the stage.*]

SCENE XII

[EVARISTO *comes in, over the country road, with his gun on his shoulder;* MORACCHIO *gun in hand, with bag full of game, and dog in leash; and* GIANNINA, *then* TOGNINO.]

EVARISTO [*to* MORACCHIO]. Here, carry this gun into your house, and take charge of these pheasants until I can dispose of them; and look after the dog. [*Sits down before the cafe, takes out his tobacco, and lounges at ease.*]

MORACCHIO [*to* EVARISTO]. Never fear; everything will be looked after. [*To* GIANNINA.] Is dinner ready?

GIANNINA [*furious*]. It's ready.

MORACCHIO. What the deuce is the matter with you? You're always in a temper with everybody about everything, and then you scold about mine.

GIANNINA. Oh, quite true. We are brother and sister! There is nothing more to say.

MORACCHIO. Well, let us get to dinner; it's high time.

GIANNINA. Come, then, step along, and I'll follow you. [*Aside.*] I want to get a word with Evaristo.

MORACCHIO. If you're coming, come. If not, I'll eat alone. [*Goes into house.*]

GIANNINA. If I ate anything now, I should want it to be rank poison.

EVARISTO [*to himself*]. Nobody on the terrace. They're at dinner, probably. Better for me to go to the inn. The Baron is expecting me. [*Rises.*] Well, Giannina, have you nothing to say to me?

GIANNINA [*brusquely*]. Oh, yes, sir, I've got something to say to you.

EVARISTO. Have you given her the fan?

GIANNINA. Here's your accursed old fan!

EVARISTO. What do you mean? Haven't you been able to give it to her?

GIANNINA. I have received a thousand insults. I have endured a thousand insolences, and they have driven me out of the house just as they would any rogue or vagabond.

EVARISTO. Does Signora Geltrude know about this?

GIANNINA. She isn't the only one— nor the worst. The Signorina Candida has treated me the worst of all.

EVARISTO. Why? What did you do to her?

GIANNINA. I didn't do anything to her.

EVARISTO. Didn't you tell her that you had a fan for her?

GIANNINA. How could I tell her so when they didn't give me any time to? —when they ran me out of the house like a thief?

EVARISTO. But she must have had her reason.

GIANNINA. I haven't done a thing to her, and I'm perfectly certain that all the bad treatment I've received has been on your account.

EVARISTO. On my account? The Signorina Candida, who loves me so much?

GIANNINA. Oh, the Signorina Candida, who loves you so much!

EVARISTO. No doubt whatever. I'm absolutely certain of it.

GIANNINA. Oh, yes, and so am I. She loves you, she loves you well. Oh, how she loves you!

EVARISTO. Oh, what a terrible state of alarm you are throwing me into!

GIANNINA. Go, go and find her—your fair one, your sweet one, your dear one!

EVARISTO. And why not? Why can I not go and find her?

GIANNINA. Because your place is taken.

EVARISTO [agitated, distressed]. By whom?

GIANNINA. By the Baron Cedro.

EVARISTO [astounded]. The Baron is in their house?

GIANNINA. What difficulty would there be about that, if he were engaged to marry Candida?

EVARISTO. Giannina, you dream; you're in a delirium; what you say is nothing but so many wild words!

GIANNINA. You don't believe me? Go and see, and you will know whether I am telling the truth.

EVARISTO. In Signora Geltrude's house——?

GIANNINA. And Signorina Candida's.

EVARISTO. The Baron is there?

GIANNINA. The Baron del Cedro.

EVARISTO. Engaged to marry my Candida?

GIANNINA. I've seen it all with my own eyes; I've heard it all with my own ears.

EVARISTO. It cannot be. No, it can-

not! What you say is foolish, cruel, brutal——

GIANNINA. Go, see, and learn for yourself. You will find out whether I am foolish or not! [Singing.]

EVARISTO. I will, at once; this very instant. [Runs to the palace and knocks at the door.]

GIANNINA. Poor silly fool. He trusts in the love of one of those girls from town. They are not like us, no—those girls from town.

[EVARISTO, in a trembling rage, goes on knocking. TOGNINO opens door and shows his face.]

EVARISTO. Well, now?

TOGNINO. Excuse me, I cannot let anybody in just at present.

EVARISTO. Did you say who it was?

TOGNINO. I did.

EVARISTO. To Signorina Candida?

TOGNINO. To Signorina Candida.

EVARISTO. And Signora Geltrude does not wish me to come in?

TOGNINO. Quite the contrary. The Signora Geltrude said to let you in; it was the Signorina Candida who said No.

EVARISTO. Said No? By heavens, I will go in! [Tries to force his way past. TOGNINO shuts the door in his face.]

GIANNINA. Oh! What did I tell you?

EVARISTO. Where am I? What has happened to me? To shut the door in my face! To shut the door in my face!

GIANNINA. Don't be surprised. They treated me in the same fashion a few minutes ago.

EVARISTO. How is it possible that Candida could have so deceived me?

GIANNINA. An actual fact leaves no room for doubt.

EVARISTO. I won't believe it, yet; I can't believe; I never shall believe it.

GIANNINA. You don't believe it?

EVARISTO. No, there must be some mistake, some misunderstanding. I know Candida too well—she is not capable of such an action.

GIANNINA. Well, console yourself with that. Keep on hoping, if it gives you

any pleasure, and much good may you
get out of it.

EVARISTO. I must speak to Candida—
I must—I must!

GIANNINA. Even after she has refused
to receive you?

EVARISTO. No matter. There must be
some other reason. I will wait in the
café. I want only to see her,—only to
have a single word with her,—one little
sign to show which it is for me—life or
death.

GIANNINA. Here; take this.

SCENE XIII

[CORONATO and SCAVEZZO return from
the COUNT'S house. SCAVEZZO goes di-
rectly to the inn. CORONATO remains to
one side, listening; afterwards CRESPINO.]

EVARISTO [to GIANNINA]. What do
you want to give me?

GIANNINA. The fan.

EVARISTO. Keep it yourself; don't tor-
ment me.

GIANNINA. You give me the fan?

EVARISTO. Yes, keep it; I give it to
you. [Aside.] I am quite beside my-
self.

GIANNINA. If that's the case, why,
thank you.

CORONATO [aside]. Oho! Now I know
what his present to her is. It's a fan.
[Without being seen, goes into inn.]

EVARISTO. But if Candida will not let
me see her—if, by some chance she should
not come to the windows—if she should
see me, but refuse to listen to me—if her
aunt should forbid her to—I am on a
sea of doubt, agitation, confusion——

[CRESPINO with a bag over his
shoulder, full of bits of leather,
shoes, etc., comes on, going
toward his own shop; sees
EVARISTO and GIANNINA and
stops to listen.]

GIANNINA. My dear Signor Evaristo,
I pity you,—I really feel compassion for
you.

EVARISTO. Yes, my dear Giannina, I
have need of it, truly.

GIANNINA. A gentleman so kind, so
good, so courteous!

EVARISTO. You know my heart; you
are a witness to my affection.

CRESPINO [aside]. Good! I've got here
just in time. [Bag is still on his back.]

GIANNINA. Really, now, if I only knew
of some way to console you——

CRESPINO [aside]. Good—very good,
indeed!

EVARISTO. Yes, at any cost, I mean to
try my fate. I don't want to make it
possible to reproach myself with having
neglected to take every assurance. I will
go into the café. I go, Giannina, but I
go trembling. Do not let your love for
me fail, nor your kindness. [He presses
her hand, and goes into the coffee-house.]

GIANNINA. I hardly know whether to
laugh at him or to pity him.

[CRESPINO puts down his bag,
takes out the shoes, etc., and
sets them on the bench, then
goes into his shop without say-
ing a word.]

GIANNINA. Why, here's Crespino!
Welcome back! Where have you been all
this time?

CRESPINO. Don't you see? To buy
leather, and to get shoes to mend.

GIANNINA. All you do is just to mend
old shoes. I don't want to have people
say that—that . . . You know that there
are always plenty of evil tongues to
wag.

CRESPINO. Well, the evil tongues will
wag less about me than they will about
you. [Working.]

GIANNINA. About me? What is there
about me they can say?

CRESPINO. What difference to me if
folks do remark that I'm less a shoemaker
than a cobbler? For me it is enough to
be an honest man and to earn an honest
living. [Working.]

GIANNINA. But I wouldn't want to be
called a cobbler's wife.

CRESPINO. When?

GIANNINA. When we come to be mar-
ried.

CRESPINO. Ah!

GIANNINA. "Ah!" What do you mean by that "Ah"?

CRESPINO. I mean that the Signorina Giannina will be neither the cobbler's wife nor the shoemaker's wife,—she has ideas too grand, too high.

GIANNINA. Have you turned looney, or have you been drinking?

CRESPINO. I'm not looney, and I haven't been drinking. Neither am I blind—nor deaf.

GIANNINA. Now what the dickens do you mean? Explain yourself, if you want me to understand. [*Comes up to him.*]

CRESPINO. You want me to explain, do you? Well, I *will* explain. Do you think I didn't overhear that lovely talk of yours with Signor Evaristo?

GIANNINA. With Signor Evaristo?

CRESPINO. "Yes, my dear Giannina." [*Imitating* EVARISTO.] "You know my heart, you are a witness to my affection."

GIANNINA. Oh, you're crazy!

CRESPINO. "Really now," [*imitating* GIANNINA] "if I only knew of some way to console you."

GIANNINA [*as above*]. You're crazy.

CRESPINO. "Giannina." — [*Imitating* EVARISTO.] "Do not let your love for me fail, nor your kindness."

GIANNINA [*as above*]. You're crazy, crazy, crazy!

CRESPINO. I crazy?

GIANNINA. Yes, you, *you*. You're crazy, you're crazy as a loon; and, on top of that, you're—crazy!

CRESPINO. But, devil take it, didn't I see it all with my own eyes? Didn't I hear all that talk between you and Evaristo with my own ears?

GIANNINA. Crazy!

CRESPINO. Didn't I hear everything he said to you, and everything you replied to him?

GIANNINA. Crazy!

CRESPINO. Giannina, have done with that "crazy." In a minute or two— [*Threatening.*] you'll have me crazy in good earnest.

GIANNINA [*seriously*]. Oh! Oh! [*Changes tone.*] But do you really think that Evaristo cares anything in particular for me?

CRESPINO. I don't know anything about it.

GIANNINA. And that I could be so dreadful as to care anything for him?

CRESPINO. I don't know anything about it.

GIANNINA. Come here, and just listen. [*Very rapidly.*] Evaristo is in love with Candida; and Candida has played a joke on him, and is going to marry the Baron; and Evaristo is desperate, and came to talk to me to relieve himself; and I was pitying him to have *my* joke on him, and he was getting some consolation in my company. Do you understand?

CRESPINO. Not the least bit.

GIANNINA. But you are convinced of my innocence?

CRESPINO. Not too completely.

GIANNINA. If that's the way it is, go to the deuce! Coronato's always chasing after me, Coronato's simply wild over me—and my brother has promised me to him. And the Count has a high regard for me—he thinks everything of me. [*Suddenly.*] I shall marry Coronato.

CRESPINO. Come now, go slow. Don't fly into a rage. How can I be certain that you are telling me the truth—that there is nothing between you and Signor Evaristo?

GIANNINA. And yet you won't let me call you crazy! My dear Crespino— [*caressing him*] that I think so much of—the light of my soul, and my own dear little husband!—that is to be . . .

CRESPINO [*gently*]. And what was it that Evaristo gave you?

GIANNINA. Nothing.

CRESPINO. Nothing? Are you sure—nothing?

GIANNINA. When I say nothing, I mean nothing. [*Aside.*] He mustn't know about this fan—he would be suspicious in a second.

CRESPINO. You are perfectly sure about this?

GIANNINA. Go away, and stop tormenting me.

CRESPINO. Don't you love me?

GIANNINA. Yes, I love you.

CRESPINO. Come, then—[taking her hand] let us make up.

GIANNINA [laughing]. Crazy!

CRESPINO. Why crazy?

GIANNINA. You're crazy, because you are crazy.

SCENE XIV

[Enter CORONATO from the inn.]

CORONATO. Well, at last I know what Miss Giannina's present was.

GIANNINA. What business have you to meddle in my affairs?

CRESPINO [to CORONATO]. Who has been giving her a present?

CORONATO. Signor Evaristo.

GIANNINA. Not a word of truth in it.

CRESPINO. Not a word of truth in it?

CORONATO. There is, though. [To GIANNINA.] And I know what the present was.

GIANNINA. Well, whatever it was, it's none of your business anyway. I love Crespino; I shall be my dear little Crespino's wife.

CRESPINO [to CORONATO]. What was the present?

CORONATO. A fan.

CRESPINO [very angry, to GIANNINA]. A fan?

GIANNINA [aside]. Curse that fellow!

CRESPINO. Have you had a fan given you?   [To GIANNINA.]

GIANNINA. Not a word of truth in it!

CORONATO. There is, though. You've got it in your pocket now.

CRESPINO. Let me see that fan!

GIANNINA. I won't. I won't.

CORONATO. I'll find some way to bring it to view.

GIANNINA. You impudent creature!

SCENE XV

[Enter MORACCHIO from house, eating, with his napkin.]

MORACCHIO. What's all this racket about?

CORONATO. Your sister has had a fan given her, and she's got it in her pocket and she denies it.

MORACCHIO [to GIANNINA, in tone of command]. Give me that fan.

GIANNINA [to MORACCHIO]. You leave me alone.

MORACCHIO. Give me that fan, or I swear to heaven!   [Threatening.]

GIANNINA. Bother take you! Here it is!   [Produces it.]

CRESPINO. Give it to me. [Tries to seize it.]

CORONATO. Give it to me. [Angry, tries to seize it.]

GIANNINA. Leave me alone,—bother take all three of you!

MORACCHIO. Give it here—quick, quick.

GIANNINA. I won't either. I'd rather give it to Crespino.

MORACCHIO. Give it here, I say.

GIANNINA. Take it, Crespino. [She gives the fan to CRESPINO and runs into the house.]

CORONATO. Let me have that fan.

MORACCHIO. Let me have that fan.

CRESPINO. You shan't have it, either of you. [Both throw themselves upon him to get possession of the fan, but he evades them, and runs off, the two following him.]

SCENE XVI

[The COUNT on the terrace, TIMOTEO at his railing, then the BARON.]

COUNT [loudly, with concern]. Hey, there, Timoteo.

TIMOTEO. What do you want?

COUNT. Quick, quick! Bring spirits, bring cordials! Something is the matter with Signorina Candida.

TIMOTEO. I'll come at once.
                    [Disappears into shop.]

COUNT. Now what the deuce was it struck her there at that window? She stood looking down into the garden behind the café. Poisonous plants growing there, I wonder? [Retires into palace. CRESPINO comes running back across the stage, with CORONATO and MORACCHIO in hot pursuit of him.]

BARON [*entering from palace, to hurry up apothecary*]. Quick, quick, Timoteo! Make haste, make haste!

TIMOTEO [*entering from his shop with a tray full of bottles and phials*]. I'm coming, I'm coming!

BARON. Quick, quick; we need you. Hurry, hurry! [*He dashes back into the palace.*]

TIMOTEO. I'm right here! I'm right here!

[*As he is about to enter palace, CRESPINO runs across the stage once more, still pursued by CORONATO and MORACCHIO. They jostle against TIMOTEO, and make him drop his bottles, which all smash on the ground. CRESPINO stumbles and drops the fan. CORONATO picks it up, and starts off with it. TIMOTEO rises and returns to his shop.*]

CORONATO. Here it is, here it is! [*To MORACCHIO.*] I've got it! I've got it!

MORACCHIO. I'm glad you have. Keep good hold of it. And Miss Giannina will tell me now who it was that gave it to her. [*Goes into his house.*]

CORONATO. I've let him see it, but I've kept it in my own hands, all the same. [*Goes into inn.*]

CRESPINO. Curses on them both. I'm lamed for life. What's more, Coronato has got the fan. I'd give a dozen pairs of shoes if I could get it back and break it to bits. Yet why break it to bits? Just because it's a gift made to my sweetheart? How foolish that would be! Giannina is a good girl, and I love her, and I mustn't be too particular. [*Limps into his shop.*]

ACT III

SCENE I

DUMB SHOW: CRESPINO *comes out of his shop with a plate of bread and cheese and an empty wine bottle and settles himself on his bench for his meal.* TOGNINO *comes out of the palace with broom in hand and runs to the apothecary's.* CRESPINO *sets to work to cut up his bread, without speaking.* CORONATO *comes out of the inn, followed by* SCAVEZZO, *who carries a barrel on his shoulders, similar to the one carried to the* COUNT'S *in act two.* CORONATO *passes in front of* CRESPINO, *looks at him and laughs.* CRESPINO *looks back at him in a silent rage.* CORONATO *passes on laughing and goes off in the same direction as that in which he carried the first barrel.* CRESPINO *looks after the departing* CORONATO, *and when latter is out of sight goes on with his work.* TOGNINO *comes out from the apothecary-shop and sweeps up the broken bottles—* TIMOTEO *comes running out of the shop with tray and bottles, and goes into the palace.* TOGNINO *goes on sweeping.* CRESPINO *takes his wine bottle and enters the inn in slow and melancholy fashion.* SUSANNA *comes out of her shop, rearranges her display and then seats herself to work.* TOGNINO *goes into* GELTRUDE'S *house and shuts the door.* CRESPINO *comes out of the inn with his bottle full of wine, and laughs as he shows the fan under his work-apron (for his own consolation and for the instruction of the house), and goes back to his bench and sets the bottle on the ground.* GIANNINA *comes out of her house, seats herself and starts in spinning.* CRESPINO *seats himself, pulls out the fan, hides it laughing under his bits of leather, and falls to eating.* CORONATO *enters alone, passes before* CRESPINO *and laughs.* CORONATO *on the way to the inn turns toward* CRESPINO *and laughs again.* CRESPINO *eats and laughs.* CORONATO, *at the door of the inn, eats and laughs and then enters.* CRESPINO *pulls out the fan, looks at it, laughs, puts it back, then goes on with his eating and drinking. The* COUNT *and the* BARON *enter from palace.*

COUNT. No, my friend, pardon me, you have nothing to blame yourself for.

BARON. And nothing, I assure you, to congratulate myself for.

COUNT. If Candida has been taken ill,

that's just an accident. We must have patience. You know that women have a strong tendency to the splenetic, the historical——

BARON. Historical? Hysterical, do you mean?

COUNT. Well, perhaps I do mean hysterical,—arrange it to suit yourself. In fact, if she hasn't received you quite as she should have, it isn't her fault, but the fault of her illness.

BARON. But when we first went in she wasn't ill, yet within a moment or two after seeing me she withdrew to her own chamber.

COUNT. Perhaps she was just beginning to feel her illness coming on.

BARON. Did you notice Signora Geltrude when she came back from her niece's bedroom? Did you see with what eagerness, with what astonishment, she was reading some papers that looked like letters?

COUNT. She is a busy woman—she has a good many things to look after. They were probably some letters that had just arrived.

BARON. No, they were *old* letters. I'd be willing to bet you she found them on Candida's writing-desk or upon the girl's own person.

COUNT. Aren't you rather fussy, my friend? Aren't you a little over-particular? What are you imagining, anyway?

BARON. I am imagining what those letters might be. I have my suspicions. I believe there is some understanding between Candida and Evaristo.

COUNT. Oh, don't trouble yourself on *that* point. If it were so, I should know. I know everything. There's not a thing done in this village, but that I know all about it. Besides, if there was anything of the kind that you suspect, do you think that she would have accepted your proposal?—that she would have dared to put a slight upon the good offices of a man of my quality?

BARON. Truly she said yes without requiring to be persuaded; but her aunt, after reading those letters, was not quite

so civil as before;—on the contrary, she seemed to show pleasure at our coming away.

COUNT. I will tell you. All we can complain of about Signora Geltrude is just this: that she didn't invite us to stay to dinner.

BARON. That doesn't surprise me.

COUNT. I gave her a little jog, but she pretended not to understand.

BARON. She was very glad, I assure you, to escape the obligation.

COUNT. I'm sorry on your account. Where are you going to dine today?

BARON. I have ordered dinner for two at the inn.

COUNT. For two?

BARON. I am expecting Evaristo—he is off hunting.

COUNT. If you would like to come home to dinner with *me*——

BARON. With you?

COUNT. But my palace is a good half-mile away.

BARON. Thank you; but dinner is already ordered. [*Calls.*] Hey, you there; the inn! Coronato!

SCENE II

[CORONATO *enters from the inn.*]

CORONATO. What do you wish, sir?

BARON. Has Signor Evaristo come yet?

CORONATO. I haven't seen him yet, sir. I'm sorry, because dinner is all ready to serve, and it won't improve with waiting.

COUNT. Evaristo is quite capable of going on with his hunting from now till dark and of making you go without your dinner.

BARON. What would you have me do? I've promised to wait for him.

COUNT. Waiting is all right, up to a certain point. But, my dear friend, it isn't for you to wait upon a man of a rank inferior to your own. Do something for civility, something for humanity—well and good; but, my dearest colleague, let us maintain our own dignity.

BARON. Do you know I am half inclined to ask you to take Evaristo's place.

COUNT. If you don't want to wait any longer, and if you don't like to eat alone, come to my house and take pot-luck with me.

BARON. No, my dear Count, you shall do me the honor of dining with me. Let us sit down to table, and if Evaristo doesn't understand how to conduct himself, let the loss be his.

COUNT [*well content*]. Yes, let him learn good manners.

BARON [*to* CORONATO]. Have dinner put on the table.

CORONATO. You shall be served at once. [*Aside.*] There'll be little enough left for the kitchen, now!

BARON. Let's go and see what they have given us to eat. [*Enters inn.*]

COUNT [*to* CORONATO]. Have you had the other barrel of wine carried to my place.

CORONATO. Yes, sir—I've sent it.

COUNT. You've *sent* it? Without going along yourself? They'll be up to some trick or other.

CORONATO. I'll tell you. I went along with my young man as far as the fork in the road, where I met *your* man, who——

COUNT. My steward?

CORONATO. No, sir.

COUNT. My chamberlain?

CORONATO. No, sir.

COUNT. My footman?

CORONATO. No, sir.

COUNT. Who, then?

CORONATO. Oh, that man who stays with you, and goes about selling your fruits and vegetables for you——

COUNT. What! That fellow?

CORONATO. Yes, that—whatever you like. I met him, and showed him the barrel, and he went along with my boy here.

COUNT [*aside*]. The devil! Why, he never drinks wine from one year's end to another;—he'll drink up half the barrel!
[*About to enter inn.*]

CORONATO. One moment, please.

COUNT [*brusquely*]. Well, what is it?

CORONATO. Have you spoken for me to Giannina?

COUNT. Yes, I have.

CORONATO. What does she say?

COUNT [*embarrassed*]. Everything's going very well——

CORONATO. Very well?

COUNT [*about to enter inn*]. We will talk about this presently.

CORONATO. Tell me something—one way or another.

COUNT. Oh, come along, now; I don't want to keep the Baron waiting.
[*Passes in.*]

CORONATO. I have good hopes yet. When a man like that goes into a matter —something is sure to result. [*With sudden passion.*] Giannina! [GIANNINA *spins and does not answer.*] At least let me speak to you.

GIANNINA [*spinning, without looking up*]. It would be more to the purpose if you were to give me back my fan.

CORONATO. Yes—— [*Aside.*] H'm that reminds me that I left the fan in the taproom and forgot all about it. [*Aloud.*] Yes, yes, we will get to the fan in due course. [*Aside.*] I shouldn't care to have anybody make off with it. [*Enters inn.*]
[CRESPINO *laughs loudly.*]

SUSANNA. You must be feeling very good, Signor Crespino; you seem to laugh with a great deal of relish.

CRESPINO. I've got my own reason for laughing.

GIANNINA [*to* CRESPINO]. *You* laugh and *I* feel myself devoured by rage!

CRESPINO. Rage? What are you in a rage about?

GIANNINA. Coronato's got that fan of mine.

CRESPINO [*laughing*]. Yes, Coronato's got that fan of yours; so he has.

GIANNINA. What are you laughing at?

CRESPINO. I'm laughing because Coronato has got your fan.
[*Rises, takes up the remains of his dinner, and goes into his shop.*]

GIANNINA. He laughs like a perfect fool.

SUSANNA [*working*]. I should *never*

have thought that my fan would pass through so many hands.

GIANNINA [*turning angrily*]. Your fan?

SUSANNA. Yes, *my* fan; wasn't it sold out of my shop?

GIANNINA. I rather fancy they paid you for it.

SUSANNA. Of course they did. They wouldn't have got it if they hadn't.

GIANNINA. And they probably paid double what it was worth, at that.

SUSANNA. That isn't true; and even if it were true, what business would it be of yours? You can get it back by paying over again what it cost you.

GIANNINA. How do *you* know anything about what it cost me?

SUSANNA. Oh, if it *did* cost you something—but *I* don't know anything about that—— [*With cold satire.*] If whoever gave it to you was under any obligation to you——

GIANNINA. Obligation! What do you mean by obligation? I like your manners, I do! [*Bounds to her feet.*]

SUSANNA. Come, now, don't think you are going to frighten me.

CRESPINO [*from shop*]. What's the matter now? More racket, hey?—more yelling and squalling?

GIANNINA [*aside*]. I've got a good mind to break this distaff on—— [*Seats herself again, and goes on with her spinning.*]

SUSANNA. She doesn't do anything but stir people up, and then won't have them talk back.

CRESPINO [*seating himself at work*]. Lost your temper, Giannina?

GIANNINA [*spinning*]. Lost my temper? I *never* lose my temper.

SUSANNA [*ironical*]. Oh, she's as gentle as a lamb; she never gets on the rampage, oh, no!

GIANNINA. No, I don't—except when they pull me around by the hair of my head, and make a doormat of me. [*So that SUSANNA may hear. SUSANNA shakes her head and mutters to herself.*]

CRESPINO [*working*]. Am I the one that illtreats you? Am I the one that makes a doormat of you?

GIANNINA [*spinning angrily*]. I wasn't speaking of you.

SUSANNA [*making fun of GIANNINA*]. No, she wasn't speaking of you: she was speaking of me.

CRESPINO. Well, I vow! Here's a little neighborhood of only half a dozen houses, and yet we can't have a moment of peace in it.

GIANNINA. No, not when there are evil tongues wagging.

CRESPINO. Be quiet; this is shameful.

SUSANNA. She insults people, and then won't have them answer her.

GIANNINA. I've got good reason for any remark I make.

SUSANNA. Oh, I'd better be silent; I'd better not try to say anything.

GIANNINA. Of course you'd better be silent than to go on talking nonsense.

CRESPINO. Here, now; let that be an end.

[TIMOTEO *comes out of palace with tray and bottles.*]

GIANNINA. Whoever doesn't like me can lump me.

CRESPINO. 'Sh, 'sh; you don't want to be overheard.

TIMOTEO [*to himself*]. I'll never set foot in that house again. What fault is it of mine if these medicines are no good? I can't offer people except what I've got; but they expect to find out here in the country all the luxuries of the city. And when you come down to it, what are your spirits and your elixirs and your quintessences, after all? Mere humbugs. These are all three great things in medicine: water, quinine and mercury. [*Enters his shop.*]

CRESPINO [*turning toward GIANNINA*]. There must be some one ill in Signora Geltrude's house.

GIANNINA [*spitefully*]. Yes,—that dear, darling, precious Candida.

SUSANNA [*loudly*]. Poor Signorina Candida!

CRESPINO. What is the matter with her?

GIANNINA. How do I know what's the matter with her, you silly?

CRESPINO [to SUSANNA]. What is the trouble?

SUSANNA [hatefully]. Mistress Giannina ought to know.

GIANNINA. I? What have I got to do with it?

SUSANNA. A good deal. You're the one that's to blame for it.

GIANNINA [bounds to her feet]. I'm the one that's to blame for it?

SUSANNA. Oh, well, nobody can say anything to you.

CRESPINO. Now, I'd like to know what all this mix-up is about.

GIANNINA [to SUSANNA]. You, you! You can't open your mouth without putting your foot in it!

SUSANNA. Come, now, don't let her get too much warmed up.

CRESPINO [to GIANNINA]. Let her speak.

GIANNINA [to SUSANNA]. What reason have you got for saying what you do?

SUSANNA. Let's talk no more. Least said soonest mended.

GIANNINA. No, no; go on.

SUSANNA. No, Giannina; do not force me to speak.

GIANNINA. If you're one of the right sort, you won't stop there.

SUSANNA. Oh, if that's the way you put it, I'll go on.

CRESPINO. 'Sh, 'sh; here comes Signora Geltrude; don't let's have a scene before her. [Goes back to his work.]

GIANNINA [to herself as she goes toward her house]. Well, she's got to give me good reason for having spoken as she did.

SUSANNA [aside, as she seats herself at her work]. She wants me to speak, does she? Well, I will.

CRESPINO [aside]. I wish I could make either head or tail of this!
[Sits and goes on with work.]

SCENE III

[Enter GELTRUDE from palace.]

GELTRUDE [gravely to GIANNINA]. You, Giannina,—has your brother come back yet?

GIANNINA [ungraciously, as she goes on toward her house]. Yes, madam.

GELTRUDE [same manner]. Has Signor Evaristo come back too?

GIANNINA [as above]. Yes, madam.

GELTRUDE. Do you know where he is?

GIANNINA [pettishly]. I don't know anything about him. Your servant.
[Goes into house.]

GELTRUDE [aside]. Civil manners, there!—Crespino!

CRESPINO [rises]. Madam?

GELTRUDE. Do you know where Signor Evaristo is to be found?

CRESPINO. No, madam, I do not.

GELTRUDE. Please go and see for me if he isn't in the tavern.

CRESPINO. At once, madam.
[Goes into inn.]

SUSANNA [under her voice]. Madam.

GELTRUDE. What's wanted?

SUSANNA [rising]. A word with you.

GELTRUDE. Don't you know anything about Evaristo?

SUSANNA. Oh, my dear Madam, I know plenty of things. I've got ever so much to tell you.

GELTRUDE. Oh, heaven!—I've got plenty of things too, and they are disturbing me a good deal. I've,—I've seen some letters that—surprised me. Tell me what you know, I beg of you.

SUSANNA. But here, in public—— This dealing with people who haven't got any sense or reason in their heads—— If you would like me to go to your house——?

GELTRUDE. First of all, I want to see my dear Evaristo.

SUSANNA. Or if you would rather come to mine?

GELTRUDE. I should. But we must wait here for Crespino.

SUSANNA. Here he is now.
[Enter CRESPINO from inn.]

GELTRUDE. Is he there?

CRESPINO. No, Madam. They were expecting him for dinner, but he didn't come.

GELTRUDE. But he must surely have got back from hunting.

CRESPINO. Oh, yes, indeed, he's back. I've seen him myself.

GELTRUDE. But where in the world can he be?

SUSANNA [looking off]. He isn't in the café.

CRESPINO [looking off]. Nor in the apothecary's.

GELTRUDE. Look around a little. The village isn't so big but that he can be found.

CRESPINO. I'll go at once.

GELTRUDE. If you find him, tell him I'm very anxious to speak to him, and that I'm waiting for him here in this shop,—Susanna's.

CRESPINO. Glad to oblige you.
[Walking away.]

GELTRUDE [to SUSANNA]. Come; I want very much to hear what you have to say.
[Goes into SUSANNA'S shop.]

SUSANNA. Pass in, please. You shall hear some fine things, I promise you.
[Follows GELTRUDE into shop.]

CRESPINO. H'm; Evaristo is mixed up somehow or other in all these doings. That fan—I'm glad I've got it in my own hands—Coronato has found out that it has been carried off. All right; but he doesn't suspect me. Nobody likely to tell him that I have been into his place to buy wine. I was just in the nick of time! But who would have thought of my finding the fan lying there on top of a cask! Sometimes good things turn out of bad, and bad things turn out well. What a fool!—to leave the fan lying on top of a cask! While his man was busy at the spigot, I snatched it up and hid it away. [Indicates his apron.] And Coronato— imagine him feeble enough to ask me if I'd seen it, if I knew anything about it! And I was fool enough to tell him that I had taken it myself—oh, was I? The next thing will be that I went there on purpose and that I stole it. He is capable of saying that. He's the worst rascal going —he is quite capable of saying it. But where must I go to find Evaristo? To the Count's? No; for the Count is in there— [pointing to inn]—and working away with the best will in the world. [Motion of eating.] Well, I must search through our own neighborhood here;—not very many houses,—I'll be sure to find him. Sorry I'm still all in the dark as to what Susanna said. I'll talk to her about it, though. Oh, if I find Giannina to blame, if I find anything out of the way about her—what shall I do? Shall I give her up? Oh, well, it can't be anything great either way; and besides, after all, I love her. [About to go.]

SCENE IV

[Enter LIMONCINO from café. CRESPINO; then CORONATO.]

CRESPINO. Oh, you!—Could you tell me where Signor Evaristo is?

LIMONCINO. What do you take me for? —your servant?

CRESPINO. Don't fly off the handle for such a small thing as that. He might be in your place, there, mightn't he?

LIMONCINO. If he was, you would see him. [Advancing.]

CRESPINO. Lemon-peel is just the very deuce-and-all, isn't he?

LIMONCINO. What do you mean with your Lemon-peel?

CRESPINO. Come along; come along, my lad, and have your shoes mended. [Exit.]

LIMONCINO. You rogue! You idle rascal! I'm going to. tell, am I, that Signor Evaristo is in our back garden? He is; and he's feeling a good deal better, and he doesn't want to be disturbed. [Calls.] Hey, you there,—the inn!

CORONATO [at door]. What's wanted?

LIMONCINO. Signor Evaristo has sent me to tell you to say to the Baron to go on with his dinner and not wait for him any longer; he's busy, and he can't come.

CORONATO. You're rather late in the day. The Baron is at table now, and is almost done.

LIMONCINO. Very well, I'll tell him so when I see him. [About to leave.]

CORONATO. Just a minute, young fellow.

LIMONCINO. What is it?

CORONATO. Have you happened to hear of anybody's finding a fan?

LIMONCINO. I haven't; no.

CORONATO. If you do hear anything of the sort, I wish you'd let me know.

LIMONCINO. Why, yes—of course. Have you lost one?

CORONATO. I had one, and I don't know what the deuce has become of it. Some rogue has gone off with it, and these stupids of mine in here don't even know who has happened in to buy wine. But I'll find out—I'll find out yet. You'll remember, will you? [Goes back in.]

LIMONCINO. I'll do whatever I can for you. [Going.]

SCENE V

[COUNT at window of inn. LIMONCINO. Then GIANNINA.]

COUNT. Didn't I hear the voice of Lemon-peel? [Loudly.] Here, young man!

LIMONCINO [turning]. What is it, sir?

COUNT. Bring two good cups of coffee, will you?

LIMONCINO. For whom, most illustrious?

COUNT. For me.

LIMONCINO. Both of 'em?

COUNT. One for me, and one for the Baron Cedro.

LIMONCINO. Very good, sir.

COUNT. Be quick, now; and have it made fresh.

LIMONCINO [going]. Now that I know it's the Baron who pays, I'll bring them.

GIANNINA [from house, without distaff]. Hey, Lemon-peel!

LIMONCINO. And you want to annoy me with your Lemon-peel, too, do you?

GIANNINA. Oh, well, don't be vexed. I haven't called you banana-skin, or melon-rind, or potato-parings, have I?

LIMONCINO. Anything more?

GIANNINA [placidly]. Come, now; tell me; is Signor Evaristo still over there?

LIMONCINO. Over where?

GIANNINA. Over at your place.

LIMONCINO. Over at our place?

GIANNINA [warming up a little]. Yes, over at your place.

LIMONCINO. The place is there; and if he was in the place, you'd see him.

GIANNINA. Oh, pooh! In the garden, I mean.

LIMONCINO. Oh, pooh! I don't know anything about it. [Goes into café.]

GIANNINA. Hateful little fellow! If I had my distaff I'd break his head! They call me ill-tempered, but they all abuse and mistreat me: those ladies up there, that odious creature yonder [indicating SUSANNA'S shop], Moracchio, Coronato, Crespino . . . Oh, curse the lot of them!

SCENE VI

[EVARISTO comes running out of the café in great spirits. GIANNINA. Then, CORONATO.]

EVARISTO. Ah, here she is, here she is! [To GIANNINA.] I'm in luck, luck, luck!

GIANNINA. Ah! Ah! What does all this mean?

EVARISTO. Oh, Giannina, I'm the happiest, happiest man in the world!

GIANNINA. I'm glad. That's a great satisfaction. I hope you'll make it up to me for the way everybody has been treating me lately.

EVARISTO. Yes, yes; whatever you like. Let me just tell you, Giannina, how you have been under suspicion. Signorina Candida knew that I had given you the fan. She thought that I had bought it for you. She was jealous of me, and jealous of you!

GIANNINA. Jealous of me?

EVARISTO. Precisely.

GIANNINA [looking towards palace]. Ah! Rage as much as you please!

EVARISTO. She was so angry, so desperate, that she was going to marry somebody else, out of revenge. But she saw me in the garden there, and she fell down in a dead faint. For quite a time I lost sight of her. Then by good luck her aunt left the house, and Candida herself came down into the garden. I broke through a hedge, I jumped over a wall, I threw myself at her feet. I begged, I pleaded, I justified myself, and I won her. She is mine, mine, mine—there is nothing more to fear!

[*Jubilant and breathless.*]

GIANNINA [*somewhat piqued*]. I rejoice with you, I congratulate you; what a delight, what a consolation! She will be yours, yours always and forever. What a pleasure it gives me, what a satisfaction, what a content!

EVARISTO. She has placed but one condition between me and my certain and complete felicity.

GIANNINA. And what's that?

EVARISTO. For her own satisfaction and, at the same time, *your* justification, I must make her a present of the fan.

GIANNINA. Dear me! You don't say so!

EVARISTO. Yes, this is necessary for my dignity and for your good name. It would seem that I bought it for you—if her suspicions are to have their weight. Now, I know that you are a good, sensible girl; so please let me have the fan.

[*Always earnest and eager.*]

GIANNINA [*confused*]. But, sir—I haven't *got* the fan any more.

EVARISTO. Well, well, you are quite right. I gave it to you, of course, and I should never ask you for it if I didn't find myself driven to do so. I'll buy you another one, and a good deal better one. But, for heaven's sake, do give me *that* one, I beg of you.

GIANNINA. But I tell you, sir, I haven't got it any more.

EVARISTO. Giannina, this is a matter that concerns my very life and your good name. [*With vigorous emphasis.*]

GIANNINA. I tell you on my honor, I swear to you by anything you like, that I haven't got that fan.

EVARISTO [*hotly*]. Good heavens! What have you done with it, then?

GIANNINA. They knew I had it about me, and they went for me like three mad dogs.

EVARISTO [*furious*]. Who?

GIANNINA. My brother——

EVARISTO [*runs toward the house, and calls*]. Moracchio!

GIANNINA. Don't call him, he hasn't got it.

EVARISTO [*stamping*]. Who has, then?

GIANNINA. I gave it to Crespino——

EVARISTO [*runs to CRESPINO'S shop*]. Hey, you there; where are you, Crespino?

GIANNINA. Come back here, just listen——

EVARISTO. I'm beside myself——

GIANNINA. Crespino hasn't got it any longer.

EVARISTO. But who *has* got it? Tell me quick.

GIANNINA. That rascal of a Coronato has got it.

EVARISTO [*running toward inn*]. Coronato! Quick! Coronato!

CORONATO [*appearing*]. Yes, sir.

EVARISTO. Give me that fan.

CORONATO. What fan?

GIANNINA. The one that *I* had, and that you've got now.

EVARISTO. Come; be quick; don't lose time!

CORONATO. I'm very, very sorry, sir——

EVARISTO. What?

CORONATO. But the fan is not to be found.

EVARISTO. Not to be found?

CORONATO. I was careless enough to leave it lying on top of a cask. I went away, and when I came back it wasn't there any longer. Somebody had carried it off.

EVARISTO. Find it—find it!

CORONATO. Where? I've done everything I could.

EVARISTO. Would ten, twenty, thirty sequins help you to find it?

CORONATO. If it can't be found, it can't.

EVARISTO. I'm half-mad!

CORONATO. Sorry, sir; but I don't see what I can do for you. [*Exit.*]

EVARISTO [to GIANNINA]. It's you,
you, who have wrecked me, ruined me!
GIANNINA. I, sir? How am I to blame
for it?

SCENE VII

[CANDIDA on terrace.]
CANDIDA [calling]. Signor Evaristo!
EVARISTO [aside]. There she is, there
she is! I'm frantic!
GIANNINA. Oh, Lord! Oh, Lord! Has
the end of the world come for this poor
fellow?
CANDIDA. Signor Evaristo!
EVARISTO. Oh, Candida, my darling, I
am the most wretched, the most unfor-
tunate man in all the world.
CANDIDA. Do you mean that the fan is
not to be found?
GIANNINA [aside]. She has guessed it
the very first thing.
EVARISTO. How everything combines
against me! [To CANDIDA.] Yes, it is
only too true—the fan is lost, it is impos-
sible to lay hand on it yet awhile.
CANDIDA. Oh, I think I know where it is.
EVARISTO. Where? Where? If you
have any clue at all——
GIANNINA [to EVARISTO]. Who knows
but that somebody may have found it,
after all?
EVARISTO [to GIANNINA]. Let us hear.
CANDIDA. The fan is doubtless in the
hands of the person to whom you gave it;
and she won't return it; and right enough,
too.
GIANNINA [to CANDIDA]. Not a word
of truth in that.
CANDIDA. Hush!
EVARISTO. I swear to you on my
honor,——
CANDIDA. That's enough. I've made up
my mind. I am astonished at your pre-
ferring a mere peasant-girl to me!
GIANNINA [looking toward terrace].
Who's a mere peasant-girl?
EVARISTO [to GIANNINA]. By heaven,
it's you who have brought me to despair
and to death itself!
GIANNINA. Oh, come now—don't fly
into a foolish rage.

EVARISTO. Yes, she has made up her
mind, and I must make up mine. I will
await my rival and attack him sword in
hand. I will either kill the wretch or
sacrifice my own life to him. And it is
you, you, who have driven me to this
deadly hazard!
GIANNINA. I'd better get away from
here—I'm afraid he is going mad.
[Steals off softly toward her house.]
EVARISTO. But how can I confront it?
My passion racks my heart, my very
breath is leaving me. My feet fail me,
my head swims, my eyes are becoming
blinded! Poor wretched creature!—who
will help me? [Sinks upon a seat in front
of café, in a state of collapse.]
GIANNINA [turning, sees him fall].
What is it? What is the matter? He's
dying, poor fellow, he's dying! Help!
help! Come here, Moracchio! Ho, there,
Lemon-peel; come quick!

SCENE VIII

[LIMONCINO enters, carrying two cups of
coffee to inn. MORACCHIO comes running
out of house. CRESPINO. TIMOTEO.]
CRESPINO [arriving by way of street].
Oh, here is Signor Evaristo. Why, what's
the matter?
GIANNINA [to LIMONCINO]. Water,
water!
CRESPINO [running into shop]. Wine,
wine, wine!
LIMONCINO. Give him some wine. I've
got to carry this coffee to the inn. [Exit.]
MORACCHIO. Courage, courage, Signor
Evaristo. Was he hurt in hunting?
GIANNINA. I should say so! In heart-
hunting! He's in love—that's all the
matter with him.
TIMOTEO [entering from his shop].
What is the trouble?
MORACCHIO. Come here, Timoteo; come
here.
GIANNINA. Come and help save this
poor dear young man.
TIMOTEO. What ails him?
GIANNINA. He went down all in a
heap.

TIMOTEO. He must be bled.

MORACCHIO. Do you understand how to do it?

TIMOTEO. In case of need, I do all that is needed!

GIANNINA. Oh, poor Evaristo, they're going to butcher him now, sure enough!

CRESPINO [from shop with bottle of wine]. Here, this will bring him to. It's good strong wine, five years old.

GIANNINA. It seems as if he were coming around a little.

CRESPINO. Oh, this wine would bring back the dead.

MORACCHIO. Courage; courage, now!

TIMOTEO [from shop with tumbler, pieces of cloth, and razor]. Here I am. Get off his clothes as quick as you can.

MORACCHIO. And what are you going to do with that razor?

TIMOTEO. In a case like this, it's better than a lancet.

CRESPINO. A razor?

GIANNINA. A razor?

EVARISTO [feelingly, as he raises himself]. Who is it that wants to murder me with a razor?

GIANNINA. Timoteo.

TIMOTEO. I am an honest, respectable man;—I murder nobody. And when one does all that he can do, and all that he knows how to do, nobody has occasion to complain of him. [Aside.] They'll call me a long time before I come again!

[Goes into his shop.]

MORACCHIO [to EVARISTO]. Won't you come to my house, sir, and lie down awhile on my bed?

EVARISTO. Wherever you say.

MORACCHIO. Take my arm, then; lean on me.

EVARISTO. How much better for me if my wretched life would but come to an end!

[Walks across, supported by MORACCHIO.]

GIANNINA [aside]. If he wants to die, all he's got to do is to put himself in Timoteo's hands!

MORACCHIO. Here we are at the door. Come, now.

EVARISTO. Useless kindness, toward one who wishes only to die. [They go in.]

MORACCHIO [pausing at door]. Giannina, come along, and arrange the bed for Signor Evaristo. [Exit.]

[GIANNINA also starts to go in.]

CRESPINO [calls]. Giannina!

GIANNINA. Well?

CRESPINO. You've got a good deal of compassion for that young man!

GIANNINA. I shall do my duty, for you and I are the cause of all his trouble.

CRESPINO. That may be true as to you. But where do I come in?

GIANNINA. Oh, that accursed fan!

[Enters house.]

CRESPINO. Accursed fan say I, too. I've heard it referred to a million times, if I have once. But, anyway, while it's in my hands it's out of Coronato's. He is my enemy, and will be until I am married hard and fast to Giannina. I wonder if I couldn't set that fan down here somewhere;—but then somebody would come walking along and smash it. I've got to do something, though; I won't be bothered by it any longer. Still, I don't know; it was Giannina's, and so I feel as if I'd like to keep it, after all.

[Goes toward bench and takes up fan. LIMONCINO comes out of inn with coffee-cups, etc.]

COUNT [follows him out]. Here, you; wait a minute. [Takes a lump of sugar and puts it in his mouth.] That's for my cold.

LIMONCINO. For your sweet tooth.

COUNT. Eh?

LIMONCINO. I say it's for your sweet tooth. [Crosses over and enters café.]

[COUNT walks up and down in great content, showing himself to have dined well.]

CRESPINO. I'm just about ready to—— Yes, this will be the best way of all.

[Comes forward with fan.]

COUNT. Ah, good day, Crespino.

CRESPINO. Your illustrious highness' most humble servant.

COUNT [softly]. Are the shoes mended?

CRESPINO. They shall be ready for you tomorrow. [*Shows fan.*]

COUNT. What have you got nice in that paper?

CRESPINO. Something I just picked up a little way down the street.

COUNT. Let me see it.

CRESPINO. There it is, sir.
[*Gives it to him.*]

COUNT. Oh! a fan. Some lady passing by must have dropped it. What are you going to do with it?

CRESPINO. Well, to tell the truth, I don't know *what* to do with it.

COUNT. Do you want to sell it?

CRESPINO. Sell it? I shouldn't know what to ask for it. Do you think it is worth very much?

COUNT. I'm not so very well informed about such things. H'm; here are some figures painted—but a fan found lying in a country road couldn't have any great value, you know.

CRESPINO. I wish it *did* have.

COUNT. So as to sell it at a good figure?

CRESPINO. No, truly:—so as to have the pleasure of making a present of it to your illustrious highness.

COUNT [*well pleased*]. To me? You wish to give it to me?

CRESPINO. But since it isn't valuable enough to be suitable for you——

COUNT. Oh, well, well, it isn't at all bad; it is really very pretty. Thank you very much, my dear fellow. Whenever my protection can be of any use to you, don't fail to let me know. [*Aside.*] Now I'll just make a present of this to somebody, and get on that somebody's right side.

CRESPINO. Might I ask a favor of you!

COUNT [*aside*]. There! I knew it! These people never give anything without wanting to get something back. [*Aloud.*] What do you wish? Speak out.

CRESPINO. I would ask you not to say that I gave it to you.

COUNT. Is that all you want?

CRESPINO. That's all.

COUNT [*aside*]. Well, well, now, he's quite reasonable. [*Aloud.*] If that's all,

just tell me why it is you don't want anybody to know I got it from you. You didn't steal it?

CRESPINO. Pardon me, your highness, I am not capable of——

COUNT. But why don't you want anybody to know I got it from you? If you found it and the owner hasn't asked for it, I can't see any reason——

CRESPINO [*laughing*]. There *is* a reason, though.

COUNT. What reason?

CRESPINO. I'll tell you. I'm in love——

COUNT. I know that very well. With Giannina.

CRESPINO. And if Giannina knew that I had this fan and didn't give it to her, she would feel a good deal put out.

COUNT. You have done well in not giving it to her. It isn't the sort of fan for a peasant-girl. Don't be at all afraid of my saying I got it from you. And, by the way, how is your affair with Giannina coming on? You really want to marry her, do you?

CRESPINO. To tell the truth—— To confess my weakness—I really do.

COUNT. If that's the way it is, have no fears. I'll have her marry you this very evening, if you say.

CRESPINO. Truly?

COUNT. Truly? Don't you know who I am? Don't you know the value of my protection?

CRESPINO. But Coronato—*he's* got some claim on her.

COUNT. Coronato? Coronato is an ass. You really love Giannina?

CRESPINO. Well, rather.

COUNT. Very good, then. You're loved in return. She can't endure Coronato. Confide in my protection.

CRESPINO. But her brother.

COUNT. Brother, brother? What brother? If the sister is satisfied what has the brother got to do with it? You confide in my protection.

CRESPINO. I trust to your kindness.

COUNT. Yes, to my protection.

CRESPINO. I will go and finish mending your shoes.

COUNT. Just a minute. I need a pair of new ones.

CRESPINO. You shall have them.

COUNT. Yes, but you understand that I want to pay for them. You can't believe that I would *sell* my protection?!

CRESPINO. Oh, for a pair of shoes!

COUNT. Well, well, go about your business.

CRESPINO. At once, sir.

[*Goes toward Bench.* COUNT *takes out fan and makes leisurely examination of it.*]

CRESPINO [*to himself*]. Oh, cospetto di bacco!—I forgot all about it. Signora Geltrude sent me to look for Evaristo, and I found him and haven't said to a word *to* her. But that illness of his— And that fan—I forgot all about it. I would go and tell him, but I can't meet that Moracchio in his own house. I'll do this: I'll go and find Signora Geltrude again. I will tell her that Evaristo is in Giannina's house, and she may send anybody after him that she wants to.

[*Goes into* SUSANNA'S *shop.*]

COUNT [*vexedly*]. Ha! Well, a fan. What's it worth? How can *I* tell?—seven or eight pauls, perhaps. If it were a little better, I would give it to Candida—she broke hers this morning. Why not do so, anyway?—it isn't so very bad.

GIANNINA [*at window*]. I don't see Crespino anywhere. I wonder where he's gone to, this time of day.

COUNT. These figures are none too well painted, but they are not so badly drawn.

GIANNINA. Ah! What do I see! The fan!—the fan in the hands of the Count! Quick, Quick! Let me run and wake up Evaristo. [*Exit.*]

COUNT. Well, *something* can be done with it; *somebody* can be found to accept it.

SCENE IX

[*The* BARON *enters from inn. The* COUNT. *Then,* TOGNINO.]

BARON. My friend, you left me all to myself——

COUNT. I saw that you didn't seem to care about talking——

BARON. True. I don't feel quite right in my mind, even yet. Tell me, do you think we might try to visit those ladies once more?

COUNT. Why not?— Listen, I've got an idea. Would you like to have me make you a present?—something that you can give in turn to Candida?

BARON. What sort of a present is it?

COUNT. You know that she broke her fan this morning?

BARON. Yes, I heard something said about it.

COUNT. Now, *here's* a fan. Let's go and find her, and then you can give it to her with your own hands. [*Gives fan to* BARON.] Take a look at it; it isn't so bad.

BARON. You wish, then——

COUNT. Yes, give it to her—you'. I don't ask any of the credit for it. I leave the whole honor to you.

BARON. I shall be very glad to accept it from you; but you must allow me to ask how much it cost you.

COUNT. What difference does that make?

BARON. I should prefer to make the amount good to you.

COUNT. Oh, really, now; you quite surprise me. Why, didn't you give me that brace of pistols?

BARON. You quite deprive me of words. I thank you for your courtesy and accept your gift. [*Aside, looking at it.*] Now where the deuce could he have found this fan? He never bought and paid for it in the world!

COUNT. Well, how does it strike you? Rather a neat little trinket, eh? And arrives just in the nick of time. Oh, when it comes to occasions of this kind, I know about what is wanted. I know how to prepare beforehand;—I've got a whole roomful of these knick-knacks for the ladies—— Well, let's move along, and not lose any more time.

[*Runs and knocks at door of palace.*]

TOGNINO [*on terrace*]. What is it?

Count. We wish to pay our respects to the ladies.

Tognino. Signora Geltrude is away from home, and Signorina Candida is lying down in her room.

Count. As soon as she wakes up, let us know.

Tognino. I will do so, sir. [Exit.]

Count. You understand?

Baron. Yes, we must wait. I've got to send a letter in to town; I dare say the apothecary can let me have pen and ink. If you would like to come with me——

Count. No, no—I'm not very fond of the apothecary's. You go and write your letter, and I'll wait here for word from the servant.

Baron. Very well. The least sign will fetch me.

Count. Trust in me, make your mind completely easy.

Baron. Ah, I trust little in him, less in the aunt, and least of all in the niece. [Goes into apothecary shop.]

Count. I'll entertain myself with my book, with my precious collection of wonderful fables. [Draws out his book and seats himself.]

SCENE X

[Enter Evaristo from Giannina's house.]

Evaristo. Ah, he's still here, I see; I was afraid he had gone—I don't understand how sleep could have overcome me in the midst of so many afflictions. But I was so tired, so weak, so weary— Now I begin to feel more like myself again. The hope of getting back that fan—— Count, my best respects to you.

Count. Your servant, sir. [Reading and laughing.]

Evaristo. Will you allow me a word or two with you?

Count. Speak; I am all attention. [Reading and laughing.]

Evaristo [aside]. If he only had the fan in hand, I should know how to begin.

Count [rises, smiles, puts book in pocket and comes forward]. Well, I am all attention. What can I do for you?

Evaristo [looking for the fan]. Excuse me, if I am disturbing you.

Count. Not at all, not at all. I can finish my fable some other time.

Evaristo [still looking]. I shouldn't like to have you consider me too presumptuous——

Count. What are you looking at? Do you see some spot or other on me? [Looks himself over.]

Evaristo. Excuse me. I have been told that you have a fan in your possession.

Count [confused]. A fan? Yes, I had. It's you, perhaps, who lost it.

Evaristo. Yes, sir; I'm the one.

Count. But there are lots of fans in this world of ours. How do you know that the one I've got is the one you lost?

Evaristo. If you would be good enough to let me look at it——

Count. My dear friend, I'm sorry that you have come just a little too late.

Evaristo. Too late? How do you mean?

Count. The fan is no longer in my possession.

Evaristo [much moved]. No longer in your possession?

Count. No, I've given it to somebody.

Evaristo [warming up]. And who is that somebody?

Count. That's just what I don't want to tell you.

Evaristo. My dear Count, it's very important that I should know. I have got to have that fan, and you must tell me who has it.

Count. I shan't tell you one word.

Evaristo [enraged]. I swear by heaven that you shall!

Count. What, you treat me with disrespect?

Evaristo. I say you shall, and I'll back it up. No fair-minded man would do as you are doing now!

Count. Do you know that I've got a pair of loaded pistols?

Evaristo. What do I care about your pistols. Give me my fan, my fan!

COUNT. Oh, for shame! All this racket for a cheap ragged little fan that isn't worth sixpence.

EVARISTO. *You* don't know what it's worth—*you* don't know what it cost. Why, to get it back, I would give—yes, I would give fifty sequins.

COUNT. You would give fifty sequins?

EVARISTO. That's what I said, and that's what I stand by. If you can get it back for me, the fifty sequins are yours.

COUNT [aside]. Whew! That fan must have been painted by Titian, or by Raphael himself!

EVARISTO. I beg you, my dear Count, do me this kindness.

COUNT. I will see if I can get it back. That isn't likely to be easy.

EVARISTO. If whoever has got it would exchange it for fifty sequins, don't spare the money.

COUNT. If *I* had it, such a proposal would offend me.

EVARISTO. I have no doubt it would. But perhaps it won't offend the person who *has* got it.

COUNT. Oh, as far as that goes, the person would be no less offended than I should be. Yet perhaps, perhaps—— My friend, I assure you that this is a great embarrassment for me.

EVARISTO. I'll tell you what we'll do, Count. Here is a gold snuff-box that is worth fifty-four sequins by weight alone. The workmanship counts for as much more. But never mind, to get that fan back, I offer this in exchange, and do it willingly. Here, take it. [Gives it to him.]

COUNT. Were there any diamonds in that fan? I didn't notice——

EVARISTO. There are no diamonds. The fan is worth nothing save to me, but to me it is most precious.

COUNT. Well, I must try to satisfy you.

EVARISTO. Do your best, I beg you, I pray you. I shall be under the greatest obligations to you.

COUNT. Wait for me here. [Aside.] Now, how am I going to manage this? [Aloud.] I will do everything in my power—— And you wish me to offer this snuff-box in exchange?

EVARISTO. Yes, yes; offer it freely.

COUNT. Wait for me here [going], and if the person who has the fan should give it up, and yet not care for the snuff-box?

EVARISTO. Sir, the box that I have handed over to you is yours; put it to whatever use you like.

COUNT. Absolutely?

EVARISTO. Absolutely.

COUNT [aside]. When you come to it, the Baron is a good fellow, and my friend. [Aloud.] Wait for me here. [Aside.] If it was a matter of fifty sequins, he wouldn't accept them; but how about a gold snuff-box? Yes, that is a present fit for a man of title.

[He goes into apothecary shop.]

EVARISTO. Yes, to set myself right in my loved one's eyes, I would sacrifice my very heart's blood, if need be.

SCENE XI

[Enter CRESPINO from SUSANNA'S shop.]

CRESPINO [aside]. Ah, here he is. [Aloud.] Sir, I salute you. Signora Geltrude would like to speak with you. She is here in this shop, waiting for you, and hopes that you will give yourself the trouble of going to her.

EVARISTO. Say to her that I am quite at her disposal. But I must beg her to wait one moment, because *I* am waiting for a person that I must see. I will come to her as soon as possible.

CRESPINO. Very well, sir. How are you feeling now? Better?

EVARISTO. Yes, thanks; I feel a great deal better.

CRESPINO. I'm ever so glad of that. And Giannina?—is *she* pretty well?

EVARISTO. I believe so.

CRESPINO. She's a good girl—Giannina.

EVARISTO. So she is. And I know that she is very fond of you.

CRESPINO. So am I very fond of her. But——

EVARISTO. But what?

CRESPINO. But they have been telling me certain things——

EVARISTO. Certain things about me?

CRESPINO. Well, yes, sir—if you ask.

EVARISTO. My friend, I am a man of honor, and your Giannina is a good girl.

CRESPINO. Oh, yes, I believe that, all right enough. But there is always plenty of gossip going on.

[COUNT *coming on, pauses in door of apothecary's.*]

EVARISTO [*to* CRESPINO]. Just go to Signora Geltrude and tell her that I will be with her at once.

CRESPINO [*going*]. Very well, sir. Everything is coming out all right, I am sure. [*Passes close to* COUNT.] Say a good word for me to Giannina.

COUNT. Rely upon my protection.

CRESPINO. I'm all impatience—I can wait no longer. [*Goes into* SUSANNA'S *shop.*]

EVARISTO. Well, Count, how is it?

COUNT. Here's the fan. [*Shows it.*]

EVARISTO. Good! good! I'm ever so much obliged to you. [*Takes it eagerly.*]

COUNT. Just look and see if it is yours.

EVARISTO. Yes, it is; not a bit of doubt.

COUNT. And the snuff-box?

EVARISTO. Not a word about it. I'm immensely indebted to you. [*Runs into* SUSANNA'S *shop.*]

COUNT. That's what it is not to be well posted on things. I thought it was the most ordinary sort of fan, yet see what it turns out to be worth!—the value of a gold snuff-box of this quality! [*Takes out box.*] Evaristo didn't want it back. And the Baron,—well, perhaps he wouldn't have cared to accept it, anyway. He was a good deal put out when I asked to have the fan back, but when I told him that I would present it in his name he seemed a little better satisfied. I'll buy another for a shilling or so, and it will make just as much show.

CRESPINO [*coming out again from* SUSANNA'S *shop*]. Well, my little errand turned out as well as one could ask.

Signora Geltrude deserves to be well served—oh, there you are, Count. And do you give me good grounds for hope?

COUNT. The very best. This is one of my good days—everything is going my way.

CRESPINO. If this thing only went your way too!

COUNT. Oh, it will,—straight off. Just wait. Hey, Giannina!

GIANNINA [*from house, angry*]. Well, what is it? What do you want this time?

COUNT. Oh, oh, don't get angry; don't lose your temper. I want to do you a good turn—I want to marry you off.

GIANNINA. I don't need you.

CRESPINO [*to* COUNT]. Hear that?

COUNT [*to* CRESPINO]. Wait. [*To* GIANNINA.] I am going to marry you off in my own way.

GIANNINA. And I tell you you're not.

COUNT. And for a husband I'm going to give you Crespino.

GIANNINA [*pleased*]. Crespino?

COUNT [*to* GIANNINA]. Ha, what do you say to that?

GIANNINA. I say—yes, with all my heart, with all my soul.

COUNT [*to* CRESPINO]. Just see the benefits of my protection!

CRESPINO. Yes, sir, I do.

SCENE XII

[*Enter* MORACCHIO *from house. Others as above.*]

MORACCHIO. What's going on here?

GIANNINA. What business of yours?

COUNT. Giannina is to marry under the auspices of my protection,—of my distinguished patronage.

MORACCHIO. I'm glad to hear it. And you'll do it, too, Miss [*to* GIANNINA]— for love if you like, and by force if you don't.

GIANNINA [*seriously*]. Oh, I'll do it, willingly enough.

MORACCHIO. So much the better for you.

GIANNINA. And to show you *how* willingly, I give my hand, here and now, to —Crespino.

MORACCHIO [*badly taken back*]. Why, Count, how is this?

COUNT [*calmly*]. Let her do it.

MORACCHIO. But—but—wasn't she promised to Coronato?

SCENE XIII

[*Enter* CORONATO *from inn. Others as above.*]

CORONATO. Who's calling me?

MORACCHIO. You just come here! The Count is arranging a marriage for my sister.

CORONATO [*raging*]. Why, Count——

COUNT. I am a nobleman most just and honorable, a right-minded and humane protector of the lowly. Giannina doesn't want you, and I cannot, I should not, I will not, force her against her will.

GIANNINA. Yes, Count; I want Crespino, and I'll have him in the face of all the world.

CORONATO [*to* MORACCHIO]. What do you say to this?

MORACCHIO [*to* CORONATO]. What do you say to this?

CORONATO. I don't care a snap of my fingers. Anybody who doesn't want me doesn't deserve to get me.

GIANNINA. That settles it.

COUNT [*to* CRESPINO]. Just see the effects of my protection!

CORONATO. Count, I've just sent you another barrel of wine.

COUNT. Send in your bill; I'll pay it. [*Draws out the gold box and takes snuff.*]

CORONATO [*aside*]. Ha! he's got a gold snuff-box! He's good for the bill. [*Exit.*]

MORACCHIO [*to* GIANNINA]. So you've made up your mind to do things in your own way.

GIANNINA. It seems so, doesn't it?

MORACCHIO. You'll be sorry for it, though,—see if you're not.

COUNT. No such thing. She shall have my protection.

MORACCHIO. It'll be bread they'll want, not protection.   [*He goes into house.*]

COUNT. And now, then, when shall we have the wedding?

CRESPINO. Quick!

GIANNINA. Also—at once, right away, as soon as possible.

SCENE XIV

[*Enter* BARON *from apothecary's shop. The others.*]

BARON. Well, Count, have you seen the Signorina Candida? Have you given her the fan? Why wouldn't you let *me* have the satisfaction of giving it to her?

GIANNINA [*aside*]. What, didn't Evaristo have it?

COUNT. I haven't seen Candida yet. And as for the fan, I've got quite a number of them, and was arranging to put a better one at your service. Ah! here comes Signora Geltrude.

SCENE XV

[GELTRUDE, EVARISTO *and* SUSANNA *come out of* SUSANNA's *shop.*]

GELTRUDE [*to* SUSANNA]. Please go and ask my niece to come down. Tell her I am here, and would like to speak to her.

SUSANNA. Yes, Madam. [*Goes to door of palace, knocks, enters.*]

GELTRUDE [*in undertone to* EVARISTO]. I don't care about having the Count and the Baron in the house. At this time of day we can as well talk here.

COUNT [*to* GELTRUDE]. Madam, the Baron and I were just upon the point of making you a little visit.

GELTRUDE. Highly honored, I'm sure. But this is the time for promenading, so let us take the air for a while.

BARON [*serious*]. Welcome back, Evaristo.

EVARISTO [*grumpy*]. Thanks.

LAST SCENE

[*Enter* CANDIDA *and* SUSANNA *from palace.*]

CANDIDA. What is it you want of me, aunt?

GELTRUDE. Let us take a few steps up and down.

CANDIDA [*aside*]. Oh! here is that faithless Evaristo!

GELTRUDE [*to* CANDIDA]. But what does it mean that you haven't got your fan?

CANDIDA. Don't you remember that I broke it this morning?

GELTRUDE. Oh, so you did. If we could only find another one!

BARON [*softly to* COUNT, *whom he nudges eagerly*]. Now's the time!

COUNT [*softly to* BARON]. Oh no, not in public.

GELTRUDE. Evaristo, don't *you* happen to have one?

EVARISTO. I do. And here it is. [*Shows fan to* GELTRUDE *but does not give it to her.* CANDIDA *turns away in pique.*]

BARON [*sotto voce to* COUNT]. Bring out yours!

COUNT [*to* BARON]. Oh, the devil!

BARON [*to* COUNT]. Bring out yours, I say!

COUNT [*to* BARON]. No, not now.

GELTRUDE. Candida, won't you accept this little attention from Evaristo?

CANDIDA. No, Madam,—excuse me; I have no need of his attentions.

COUNT [*to* BARON]. You see? She won't take it.

BARON [*to* COUNT]. Give me yours—give me yours, quick!

COUNT [*to* BARON]. Do you want to arouse suspicion?

GELTRUDE. May I ask why you refuse to receive this fan?

CANDIDA. Because it isn't mine,—because it never was intended for me. [*With exaggerated emphasis.*] Neither my own dignity, nor yours, will permit me to accept it.

GELTRUDE. Signor Evaristo, it is for you to put yourself right.

EVARISTO. With your permission, I will do so.

CANDIDA [*going*]. Allow me to retire.

GELTRUDE. Stay where you are, I command you.

BARON [*to* COUNT]. What imbroglio is this?

COUNT [*to* BARON]. I don't know, I'm sure.

EVARISTO. Susanna, do you recognize this fan?

SUSANNA. Yes, sir; it's the one that you bought of me this morning, and that I imprudently thought you had purchased for Giannina.

GIANNINA. "Imprudently"—Oh, I like *that!*

SUSANNA. I acknowledge my error, and may *you* learn from me to do justice to the truth. For the rest, I had some show of reason, because Evaristo *did* give it to you.

EVARISTO [*to* GIANNINA]. Why did I give you this fan?

GIANNINA. That I might give it to the Signorina Candida. But when I wanted to give it to her, she scolded me and would not let me say a word. Then I tried to give it back to you, and you wouldn't take it, and so I gave it to Crespino.

CRESPINO. And I fell down, and Coronato took it away from *me*.

EVARISTO. But where is Coronato? And how did it get away from him?

CRESPINO. 'Sh! Don't call him. As long as he isn't here, I'll confess the truth. I went into the place to buy some wine, lit upon the fan by chance, and carried it away with me.

EVARISTO. And what did you do with it?

CRESPINO. I made a present of it to the Count.

COUNT. And *I* made a present of it to the Baron.

BARON [*to* COUNT *with angry scorn*]. You had it back again, did you?

COUNT. Yes, and I restored it to Signor Evaristo.

EVARISTO. And now I have the honor of placing it in the hands of the Signorina Candida.

[CANDIDA *makes a sweeping courtesy, receives the fan, with every sign of pleasure and content.*]

BARON [*to* COUNT]. What sort of doings are these, I'd like to know? Am I held up to ridicule by you?

COUNT. I swear to heaven, I swear to heaven, my dear——

EVARISTO. Come, come, Count,—calm yourself. Favor me with a pinch of tobacco.

COUNT. I am made so that when people take me the right way I never lose my temper.

BARON. Perhaps you can't lose yours, but I'll tell you I can lose mine!

GELTRUDE. My dear Baron——

BARON. And you, madam, you would make sport of me too?

GELTRUDE. Excuse me, sir—you do not know me. I have not failed in my duty in the slightest point. I listened to your proposals, my niece accepted them, and I gave her my consent with the greatest pleasure.

COUNT [to BARON]. Hear that? Because I spoke to her for you.

BARON [to CANDIDA]. And you, Signorina,—why delude me, why deceive me?

CANDIDA. I must beg your pardon, sir. I was driven to and fro by two contrary passions. Revenge would have made me yours, and love gave me back to Evaristo.

COUNT. Here's something that I'm not in.

EVARISTO [to BARON]. And if you had been less hasty as a lover and more trusty as a friend, you would not have found yourself in such a plight.

BARON. You are right. I confess my passion, and condemn my own weakness; but I detest the conduct and the friendship of the Count. [Exit.]

COUNT. Oh, never mind; we're friends; he's only joking—we persons of quality understand one another. And now for the wedding!

GELTRUDE. Let us go into the house, and I hope that everybody will share in the general joy.

[CANDIDA waves her fan to and fro.]

GELTRUDE [to CANDIDA]. Are you happy to have that much-wished-for fan at last in your hands?

CANDIDA. Happy? I cannot express the extent of my happiness!

GIANNINA. Great old fan!—it has turned everybody and everything topsy-turvy, from first to last, from highest to lowest!

CANDIDA [to SUSANNA]. This fan comes from Paris?

SUSANNA. From Paris, I assure you.

GELTRUDE. Come, I invite you one and all to supper. Let us drink to the health of him who devised it [to company], and let us humbly thank those [to house] who have done us the honor to listen to us so indulgently.

SAUL

By VITTORIO ALFIERI

1784

TRANSLATED BY E. A. BOWRING

CHARACTERS

SAUL
JONATHAN
MICHAL
DAVID
ABNER
AHIMELECH
SOLDIERS OF THE ISRAELITES
SOLDIERS OF THE PHILISTINES

SCENE—*The Camp of the Israelites in Gilboa.*

ACT I

SCENE I

[DAVID.]

DAVID. Here, God Omnipotent, wilt
Thou that I
Restrain that course to which Thou hast
impell'd me?
Here will I stand.—These are Gilboa's
mountains,
Now forming Israel's camp, exposed in
front
To the profane Philistines. Ah, that I
Might fall to-day beneath the foeman's
sword!
But, death awaits me from the hand of
Saul.

Ah, cruel and infatuated Saul!
Who, without giving him a moment's
respite,
Through caveins, and o'er cliffs, dost chase
thy champion.
And yet the self-same David formerly
Was thy defender; all thy confidence
In me hadst thou reposed; me didst thou
raise
To honor's pinnacle; and as a spouse
I was by thee selected for thy daugh-
ter . . .
But, as an inauspicious dowry, thou
Didst ask of me, dissever'd from thy foes,
A hundred heads: and I have brought of
them
To thee, full faithfully, a double har-
vest . . .

58

But Saul, I clearly see, in thought is
stricken;
Long hath he been so: to an evil spirit
His God abandons his perverted mind:
O Heav'ns! Distracted mortals! what are
we,
If God forsakes us?—Night, do thou soon
yield
Thy shades to the glad sun; for he to-
day
The witness of a gen'rous enterprise
Is destined to shine forth. Gilboa, thou
Shalt, to the latest ages, be renown'd;
They shall record of thee, that David
here
Himself surrender'd to ferocious Saul.—
March forth, O Israel, from thy peaceful
tents;
March forth from them, O king: I chal-
lenge you
To-day to witness, if I yet am versed
In military arts. And march thou forth,
Impious Philistia; march thou forth, and
see
Whether my sword have yet the pow'r to
smite.

SCENE II

[JONATHAN, DAVID.]
JONATHAN. What voice hath caught my
ears? I hear a voice
Skilful to penetrate my heart.
DAVID. Who comes? . . .
O that the dawn would rise! Fain would
not I
Like a base fugitive present myself . . .
JONATHAN. What! ho! Who art thou?
Near the royal tent,
What art thou doing? Speak.
DAVID. 'Tis Jonathan . . .
Courage.—A son of war, and Israel's stay,
Am I. And the Philistines know me
well.
JONATHAN. What do I hear? Ah!
David could alone
Thus answer.
DAVID. Jonathan . . .
JONATHAN. Heav'ns! David, . . .
brother . . .
DAVID. O joy! . . . To thee . . ,

JONATHAN. And can it, then, be true . . .
Thou in Gilboa? Fear'st thou not my
father?
I tremble for thee; ah! . . .
DAVID. Why speak'st thou thus?
Death present, in the fight, a thousand
times
Have I beheld and braved: for a long time
I have since fled thy father's rage unjust:
But to the valiant, fear alone is death.
No longer now I fear: with mighty dan-
ger
The monarch, and his people, are encom-
pass'd:
Shall David be the only one meanwhile
To skulk securely in untrodden forests?
While imminent o'er you the weapons
hang
Of the unfaithful, shall I take a thought
Of my own safety? I come here to die;
But, like a hero, in my country's cause,
Amid the clash of arms, and in the camp,
And also for ungrateful Saul himself,
Who now pursues me with the cry of
death.
JONATHAN. O virtue of a David! God's
elect
Thou art assuredly. That mighty God,
Who with such superhuman thoughts in-
spires
Thy lofty heart, gave thee a heav'nly
angel
To be thy guard.—Yet, to the monarch's
presence
How shall I bring thee? He believes, or
feigns,
That thou'rt enroll'd among the hostile
squadrons;
And taxes thee as a rebellious traitor.
DAVID. Alas! too forcibly he tempted
me
To seek a refuge 'mid his enemies.
But if those foes impugn him with their
arms,
I war with them, for him, till they're
subdued.
Then let him afterwards repeat to me
My ancient recompense; fresh hate, and
death.
JONATHAN. Unhappy father! There
are who deceive him.

Perfidious Abner, a dissembling friend,
Is ever at his side. The ghastly demon,
That hath possess'd, and subjugates his
    heart,
At least bestows on him a transient
    respite;
But Abner's unrelenting artifice
Never forsakes him. He alone is heard,
He only; he alone is loved: to Saul,
Like a malignant parasite, he paints
All that surpasses his frail excellence,
As dang'rous and uncertain. With my
    father,
In vain thy wife and I . . .
DAVID.   My wife! Loved name!
Where is my faithful Michal, where?
    Does she,
Spite of her cruel father, love me
    still? . . .
JONATHAN. Love thee, say'st thou?
. . . She, too, is in the camp . . .
DAVID. O Heav'ns! Shall I behold her,
    then? O joy!
How came she in the camp? . . .
JONATHAN.   Her father felt
Pity for her; alone he would not leave
    her,
A victim to her sorrow, in the palace:
And even she, though always sad, affords
To him some comfort. Ah! since thy de-
    parture,
Our house, indeed, has been the house of
    tears.
DAVID. Belovèd spouse! From me thy
    tender looks
Will banish ev'ry thought of past dis-
    tress;
Will banish ev'ry thought of coming woe.
JONATHAN. Ah, hadst thou seen her!
    . . . Scarcely had she lost thee,
When ev'ry ornament her grief disdain'd:
She strew'd with ashes her dishevell'd
    hair;
Pallor and tears sat on her sunken
    cheeks;
Profound mute grief was in her trem-
    bling heart.
A thousand times each day she prostrate
    fell
Before her father; and with sobs ex-
    claim'd:

"Restore my David; thou didst give him
    to me."
Her garments then she rent; and, weeping,
    bathed
Her father's hand, that even he shed tears.
Who did not shed them?—Only Abner; he
Insisted that, half dead e'en as she was,
She should be taken from her father's
    feet.
DAVID. O sight! O what dost thou
    recount to me?
JONATHAN. Would it were not the
    truth! . . . At thy departure,
Peace, glory, enterprise in arms, departed:
The hearts of Israel are benumb'd with
    dread;
Philistia's sons, who heretofore appear'd
Mere striplings when we fought beneath
    thy banners,
Now, since no more we have thee for our
    leader,
With port colossal stalk before our eyes:
Pent in this valley, mindless of ourselves,
Threats, insults, and derision, we endure.
Why should we wonder? Israel hath at
    once
In David lost her judgment and her sword.
I, who, pursuing thy heroic steps,
Elate with conscious glory trod the camp,
Now feel my right hand impotent to smite.
Now, that so often I behold thee, David,
Exposed to hardships, sever'd from my
    side,
Pursued by danger; now, no more I seem
To combat for my monarch, and my
    father,
My wife, my children: far more dear to
    me
Art thou than country, father, wife, and
    children . . .
DAVID. Thou lovest me, and more than
    I deserve:
May God reward thy love . . .
JONATHAN.   The God of justice,
The swift rewarder of true excellence,
He is with thee. By dying Samuel thou
In Rama wert received; the sacred lips
Of the anointed prophet, by whose means
My sire was crown'd, great marvels
    prophesied
Of thee in after-times: hence, in my sight

Thy life is no less sacred than beloved.
The cruel perils of the court alone
For thee alarm me; not those of the camp:
But death, and treachery, death's harbinger,
Round these pavilions hover evermore:
Death, Abner gives it; often Saul commands it.
Ah, David! hide thyself; until, at least,
The mountain echoes with the warlike trumpet.
To-day I deem that we shall be compell'd
To meet our foes.
    DAVID.   And shall a deed of valor
Be, like a scheme of guilt, by stealth transacted?
Saul shall behold me, ere I meet my foes.
I bring with me what must confound; what must
Reform the hardest of all harden'd hearts,
I bring; and first the fury of the king,
Then that of hostile swords, will I confront.—
What canst thou say, O king, if I to thee
Bend, as thy servant, my submissive brow?
I, who, the husband of thy daughter, ask
Pardon of thee for ne'er committed faults:
Thy ancient champion I, who in the jaws
Of mortal danger, as thy comrade, shield,
Or victim, offer now myself to thee.—
The sacred old man dying greeted me
In Rama; and address'd me like a father:
And in my arms expired. As his own son
He formerly loved Saul: but what reward
Had he for this?—The holy, dying man
Enjoin'd my love and homage to the king,
Not less than blind obedience to my God.
His latest words shall be, e'en till I die,
Indelibly engraven on my heart:
"Ah, wretched Saul! if thou art not more wise,
The wrath of the Most High will fall upon thee."
This Samuel said to me.—My Jonathan,
Fain would I see thee from the just revenge
Of Heav'n exempt: and thou, I trust, wilt be so;

And so we all shall be; and Saul, who yet
May pardon seek, and reconciliation.—
Ah, woe, if the Eternal sends His bolt
Of vengeance from the gaping firmament!
Thou know'st, that often in the fierce career
Of His retributory punishments,
He hath involved the guiltless with the guilty.
His irresistible, impetuous flash
Extirpates, crumbles, and beats down to earth,
And utterly destroys the flow'rs, fruits, leaves,
Equally with the foul and tainted plant.
    JONATHAN. —David can do, with God,
full much for Saul.
Oft in the visions of the night I've seen thee,
And so sublime in look, that at thy feet
Prostrate I've fallen.—More I shall not say;
Nor more shouldst thou to me. Long as I live,
I swear no sword of Saul shall e'er descend
To injure thee, no, never. But, O Heav'ns! . . .
How can I screen thee from vile stratagems? . . .
Here, 'mid the pleasures of the costly banquet,
Here, 'mid the harmony of festal song,
Is poison oft imbibed in faithless gold.
Ah! who from this can guard thee?
    DAVID.   Israel's God,
If I deserve deliv'rance; not a host,
If I deserve destruction.—But inform me:
Before my father, can I see my wife?
Till the dawn breaks, I would not enter there . . .
    JONATHAN. On downy couch doth she await the day?
Before the dawn she ever comes to me
To weep thy absence; and together here
We put up prayers to God for our sick father.—
Behold; a form in white not far from us
Gleams indistinctly: it is she, perchance:
A little step aside; and listen to her:

But, if it be another, do not now,
I pray thee, show thyself.
DAVID.   I will obey thee.

SCENE III

[MICHAL, JONATHAN.]
MICHAL. Abhorr'd, eternal night, wilt
   thou ne'er vanish? . . .
But, doth the sun, indeed, for me arise
The harbinger of joy? Unhappy I!
Who in an everlasting darkness live!—
Hast thou, my brother, left thy bed before
   me?
Yet, certainly, my frame, that never rests,
Was most exhausted. But, how can I rest
On easy pillows, while on the hard earth,
Banish'd, a fugitive, within the dens
Of cruel beasts, and watch'd by ambush'd
   foes,
My loved one lies? Ah, father, fiercer far
Than rav'ning monsters of the wilder-
   ness!
Hard-hearted Saul! Thou takest from thy
   child
Her husband, and thou takest not her
   life?—
Hear me, my brother; here no more I'll
   tarry:
'Twill be a noble deed, if thou go with
   me:
But, if thou go not, I alone will venture
His footsteps to trace out: I am resolved
To find my David, or to suffer death.
JONATHAN. Delay a little while; and
   dry thy tears:
P'rhaps to Gilboa will our David come . . .
MICHAL. What say'st thou? Can he
   e'er approach the place
Which Saul inhabits? . . .
JONATHAN.   David will be drawn,
Drawn irresistibly by his fond heart,
And his unswerving constancy, to seek
The place where Jonathan and Michal
   dwell.
Dost thou not think that his prevailing
   love
Can bid defiance to the pow'r of fear?
And wouldst thou wonder, if he dared
   come hither?

MICHAL. O, I should tremble for his
   life . . . But yet,
The seeing him would make me . . .
JONATHAN.   And if he
Fear'd nothing? . . . And should he with
   arguments
Defend his unexpected daring?—Saul,
Less terrible in his adversity
Than in prosperity, bewilder'd stands,
His strength mistrusting; this thou know-
   est well:
Since the invincible right hand of David
For him disperses not the hostile ranks,
Saul fears; but, arrogant, he speaks it
   not.
Each of us in his face can well discern
That hopes of triumph are not in his
   heart.
Perchance this moment he would see thy
   spouse.
MICHAL. Yes, it is maybe true: but he
   is far; . . .
Ah! where? . . . and in what state? . . .
   Alas! . . .
JONATHAN.   He's near thee,
More than thou thinkest.
MICHAL. Heav'ns! . . . why mock me
   thus? . . .

SCENE IV

[DAVID, MICHAL, JONATHAN.]
DAVID. Thy spouse is at thy side.
MICHAL.   O voice! . . . O sight!
O joy! . . . I cannot . . . speak.—Supreme
   amazement! . . .
And is it true . . . that I at last embrace
   thee? . . .
DAVID. Belovèd wife! . . . Hard has
   my absence been! . . .
Death, if I'm doom'd to meet with thee
   to-day,
By all who love me, and by all I love,
I am at least surrounded. Better die
At once, than languish on in solitude
A weary life, where thou by none art
   loved,
And where thou lovest none. Thou thirsty
   sword
Of Saul, I here expect thee; take my
   life:

Here will my eyes at least be closed in death
By my belovèd wife; my limbs composed;
And bathed by her with tears of genuine grief.

MICHAL. My David! ... Thou at once the source and end
Of all my hopes; ah, may thy coming here
To me be joyful! God, who rescued thee
From such prodigious oft-repeated dangers,
Restores thee not to us in vain to-day ...
O, with what strength thy sight alone inspires me!
So much I trembled for thee when remote;
Almost I cease to tremble for thee now ...
But, what do I behold? In what uncouth
And savage garment wrapt, the dawn of day
Displays thee to my eyes? My long'd-for champion;
How art thou stripp'd of ev'ry ornament?
No more thou wear'st that robe of gilded purple,
Which these hands wrought for thee! In all this squalor,
Who would deem thee the monarch's son-in-law?
Thou seem'st a vulgar warrior, and no more,
By thy accoutrements.

DAVID. We're in the camp:
Not in the centre of a timid court:
The common garment, and the sharpen'd sword,
Are most befitting here. I am resolved
To-day once more in the Philistines' blood
My garments to impurple. Thou, meanwhile,
Rely with me on Israel's mighty God,
Who from destruction can deliver me,
If I deserve not death.

JONATHAN. Behold, the day
Is fully now reveal'd: to linger here
Thou canst not with impunity persist.
Although, perchance, thou comest opportunely,
Still it behoves thee to advance with caution.—

Each morn we are accustom'd at this hour
To meet our father: we will scrutinize
How he to-day is govern'd and possess'd
By his distemper'd humor: by degrees
We will prepare him, if occasion smiles,
For thy reception; and will take good care
That no one first to him malignantly
Reports thy reappearance. Thou, meanwhile,
Keep thyself separate; lest any one
Should recognize thee here, and then betray thee;
And Abner even cause thee to be slain.
Lower the visor of thy helmet: mix
Among the undistinguish'd warriors here,
And, unobserved, await till I return
To thee, or send for thee ...

MICHAL. Among the warriors,
How can my David be conceal'd? What eye
Equal to his from 'neath the helmet darts?
Who wields a sword that may with his compare?
And whose arms clang with such a martial sound?
Ah, no! my love, 'twere better thou wert hid,
Till I return to thee. Unhappy I!
Scarce found, must I surrender thee already?
But only for an instant; after that,
Never, no never, will I leave thee more.
Yet first would I see thee conceal'd in safety.
Behold! dost thou not see a spacious cave
In the recesses of this gloomy wood?
There oft have I invoked thee, from the world
Retired, and sigh'd for thee, and thought on thee;
There with my bitter tears have I bedew'd
The rugged stones: in this conceal thyself,
Till the time come when thou shouldst show thyself.

DAVID. In all things, Michal, I would yield to thee.
Go in implicit trust: I am impell'd
By a sure instinct; I at random act not;

I love you both; for your sakes do I
live:
And in Jehovah only I confide.

ACT II

SCENE I

[SAUL, ABNER.]

SAUL. This dawn how beautiful! To-
day the sun
Arises not in bloody mantle wrapt;
He seems to promise a propitious day.—
O my past years! where are ye now all
fled?
Saul never from his martial bed, till now,
Rose in the camp, without the certain
trust
That, ere at eve his pillow he resumed,
He should be victor.
ABNER.   Wherefore now, O king,
Dost thou despair? Hast thou not here-
tofore
Discomfited Philistia's pride? The later
That thou beginn'st this fight—this Abner
tells thee—
The nobler, fuller, triumph thou shalt
win.
SAUL. O Abner, with what diff'rent
eyes do youth
And hoary age contemplate the events
Of human life! When with a well-knit
arm
I grasp'd this ponderous and gnarlèd
spear,
Which now I scarce can wield; I ill con-
ceived
The possibility of self-mistrust . . .
But, I have now not only lost my youth . . .
Ah! were but the invincible right hand
Of God still with me! . . . or with me at
least
David, my champion lost! . . .
ABNER.   What then are we?
Perchance without him we no longer con-
quer?
If I thought that, I never would un-
sheathe
My sword again, except to pierce my
heart.

David, who is the first, the only cause
Of all thy misadventures . . .
SAUL.   Ah! not so:
All my calamities may be referr'd
To a more dreadful cause . . . And what?
Wouldst thou
Conceal from me the horror of my state?
Ah! were I not a father, as I am,
Alas! too certainly, of much-loved chil-
dren, . . .
Should I desire life, victory, or throne?
I should already, and a long time since,
Headlong have cast myself 'mid hostile
swords:
I should already thus at least at once
Have closed the fearful life that I drag
on.
How many years have pass'd now, since a
smile
Was seen to play upon my lips? My
children,
Whom I so dearly love, if they caress me,
Most frequently inflame my heart to
rage . . .
Ever impatient, fierce, disturb'd, and
wrathful;
I am a burden to myself and others;
In peace I wish for war, in war for
peace:
Poison conceal'd I drink in ev'ry cup;
In ev'ry friend I see an enemy;
The softest carpets of Assyria seem
Planted with thorns to my unquiet limbs;
Anguish is my short sleep; my dreams
are terror.
What more? who would believe it? war's
loud trumpet
Speaks to my ears in an appalling voice;
The trumpet fills the heart of Saul with
fear.
Thou seest clearly that Saul's tott'ring
house
Is desolate, bereft of all its splendor;
Thou see'st that God hath cast me off for
ever.
And thou, thyself, (too well thou know'st
the truth,)
Dost sometimes, as thou art, appear to me
My kinsman, champion, and my real
friend,
The leader of my armies, the support

Of my renown; and sometimes dost appear
The interested minion of a court,
Hostile, invidious, crafty, and a traitor ...
ABNER. Now, Saul, that thou hast thus
regain'd thy reason,
Do thou, I pray thee, to thy mind recall
Each past transaction! Art thou not
aware
That all the wounds of thy afflicted heart
From Rama spring; yea, from the dwell-
ing spring
Of Rama's many prophets? Who to thee
First dared to say, that God had cast
thee off?
The daring, turbulent, ambitious Samuel,
The crafty, doting priest; whose palsying
words
His sycophantic worshippers repeat.
The royal wreath, which he thought his,
he saw
Glitt'ring upon thy brow with jealous
eyes.
Already he accounted it entwined
Around his hoary locks; when lo! the
voice,
At once unanimous, and loud spoken,
Of Israel's people, to the wind dispersed
His wishes, and a warrior king preferr'd.
This is thy crime, this only. Hence, when
thou
Ceasedst to be subordinate to him,
He ceased to call thee the elect of God.
This, this alone at first disturb'd thy rea-
son:
And then the eloquence inspired of David
The injury completed. He in arms
Was valiant, I deny it not; but still
He was implicitly the tool of Samuel;
And fitter for the altar than the camp:
In arm, a warrior; but in heart, a priest.
Of ev'ry adventitious ornament
Be truth divested; thou dost know the
truth.
I from thy blood am sprung; what con-
stitutes
Thy glory, constitutes my glory too:
But David, no, can never raise himself,
If first he tread not Saul beneath his
feet.
    SAUL. David? ... I hate him ... But
yet I to him

Have yielded as a consort my own daugh-
ter ...
Ah! thou canst never know.—That self-
same voice,
Imperative and visionary voice,
Which as a youth my nightly slumbers
broke,
When I in privacy obscurely lived
Far from the throne, and all aspiring
thoughts;
For many nights that self-same voice hath
been
Tremendous, and repell'd me, thund'ring
forth,
Like the deep roaring of the stormy
waves:
"Depart, depart, O Saul ..." The sacred
aspect,
The venerable aspect of the prophet,
Which I had seen in dreams, before he
had
Made manifest that God had chosen me
For Israel's king: that Samuel, in a
dream,
Now with far diff'rent aspect I behold.
I, from a hollow, deep, and dreadful
valley,
Behold him sitting on a radiant mount:
David is humbly prostrate at his feet:
The sacred prophet on his forehead pours
The holy oil; and with the other hand,
Extending to my head a hundred cubits,
He snatches from my brow the royal
crown;
And seeks to place it on the brow of
David:
But, wouldst thou think it? David pros-
trate falls,
With piteous gesture, at the prophet's
feet,
Refusing to receive it; and he weeps,
And cries, and intercedes so fervently,
That he refits it on my head at last ...
—O spectacle! O David, gen'rous
David!
Then thou art yet obedient to thy king?
My son? my faithful subject? and my
friend? ...
Distraction! Wouldst thou take from me
my crown
Thou, who daredst do it, insolent old man,

Tremble . . . Who art thou? . . . Let him
   die at once,
Who e'en conceived the thought . . .
   —Alas, alas!
I rave like one distracted! . . .
   ABNER.   Let him die;
Let David only die: and with him
   vanish
Dreams, terrors, omens, and distresses.

SCENE II

[JONATHAN, MICHAL, SAUL, ABNER.]
   JONATHAN.   Peace
Be with the king.
   MICHAL.   And God be with my father.
   SAUL. . . . Grief always is with me.—
I rose to-day,
Before my custom'd hour, in joyful
   hope . . .
But, like a vapor of the desert, hope
Hath disappear'd already.—O my son,
What boots it now the battle to defer?
To dread defeat is worse than to endure
   it;
And let us once endure it. Let us fight
To-day; I will it.
   JONATHAN.   We to-day shall conquer.
Father, resume thy hopes: hope never
   shone
With more authentic brightness on thy
   prospects.
Ah, calm thy looks again! my heart is
   big
With presages of victory. This plain
Shall with the bodies of our foes be
   cover'd;
And to the rav'nous vultures will we leave
A horrid banquet . . .
   MICHAL.   To a calmer spot
Within thy palace we will soon repair,
O father. There, amid thy palms en-
   throned,
Joyful thyself, thou, by restoring to her
Her much-loved husband, wilt restore to
   life
Thy mournful daughter . . .
   SAUL.   . . . Evermore in tears?
Are these, indeed, the pleasing objects
   destined

To renovate Saul's languid, wither'd
   mind?
Art thou a solace thus to my distress?
Daughter of tears, depart; go; leave me;
   hence!
   MICHAL. Alas! . . . Thou wouldst not,
   father, that I wept? . . .
Father, and who in everlasting tears
Now keeps me, if not thou? . . .
   JONATHAN.   Refrain; wouldst thou
Be irksome to thy father?—Saul, take
   comfort:
A minister of war and victory
Stands in the camp: a spirit of salvation,
With dawning light descended from the
   skies,
Which o'er all Israel's host will spread
   to-day
His brooding wings. A certainty of con-
   quest,
E'en on thy heart, will quickly be im-
   press'd.
   SAUL. Now, p'rhaps, thou wouldst that
   I should take a part
In thy weak transports? I?—What vic-
   tory?
What spirit comes . . . Let us all weep.
   To-day
That venerable oak, torn up, will show
Its squalid roots, where heretofore it
   spread
Its stately branches to the gales of
   Heaven.
All, all is weeping, tempest, blood, and
   death:
Rend, rend your garments; scatter on
   your hair
Polluting dust. Yes, this day is the last;
To us, the final day.
   ABNER.   Oft have I said it:
Your importuning presence evermore
Redoubles his fierce pangs.
   MICHAL.   And what? Must we
Leave our belovèd father? . . .
   JONATHAN.   At his side
Presumest thou alone to stand? Dost thou
Presume that in thy hands? . . .
   SAUL.   What, what is this?
Rage sits upon the faces of my children?
Who, who has wrong'd them? Abner,
   thou perchance?

These are my blood; dost know it not? . . .
Remember . . .
JONATHAN. Ah, yes! we are thy blood;
and for thy sake
Hold ourselves ready all our blood to
shed . . .
MICHAL. Father, when I of thee my
consort seek,
Am I by selfish love alone impell'd?
I ask of thee the champion of thy people,
The terror of Philistia, thy defender.
In thy disconsolate fantastic hours,
And in thy fatal presages of death,
Ah! did not David sometimes solace thee
With his celestial music? Was not he
A very beam of joy across thy darkness?
JONATHAN. And I; thou knowest, if
I wear a sword;
But, what boots that, if the resounding
steps
Of Israel's warrior to my steps give not
The law supreme? Should we of fighting
speak,
Were David here? We had already con-
quer'd.
SAUL. O times long past! . . . O my
illustrious days
Of joyful triumph! . . . Lo! they throng
before me,
Triumphant images of past success.
I from the camp return, with bloody
sweat
All cover'd, and with honorable dust:
In my extinguish'd pride, behold, I walk;
And praises to the Lord . . . I, praise the
Lord? . . . —
The ears of God are closed against my
voice;
Mute is my lip . . . Where is my glory?
where,
Where is the blood of my slain ene-
mies? . . .
JONATHAN. Thou wouldst have all in
David . . .
MICHAL. But, with thee
David is not, O no: to banishment
Thou drov'st him from thy presence,
sought'st his death . . .
David, thy son; thy noblest ornament;
Modest and docile; more than lightning
swift

To serve thee; and in loving thee more
warm,
Than thy own children. Father, ah!
desist . . .
SAUL. Tears from my eyes are gush-
ing? Who hath thus
Forced me to unaccustom'd tenderness?
Let me dry up my eyes.
ABNER. I counsel thee,
O king, to thy pavilion to withdraw.
Thy marshall'd forces, ready for the com-
bat,
Ere long I will display to thee. Now
come;
And be convinced that nothing is in
David . . .

SCENE III

[DAVID, SAUL, ABNER, JONATHAN,
MICHAL.]

DAVID. Except his innocence.
SAUL. What do I see?
MICHAL. O Heav'ns!
JONATHAN. What hast thou done?
ABNER. Audacious . . .
JONATHAN. Father . . .
MICHAL. Father, he is my spouse; to
me thou gav'st him.
SAUL. O what a sight is this!
DAVID. O Saul, my king!
Thou dost demand this head; for a long
time
Already hast thou sought it; here it is;
Sever it now, 'tis thine.
SAUL. What do I hear? . . .
O David, . . . David! In thee speaks a
God:
A God to-day doth usher thee to me . . .
DAVID. Yes, monarch; He who is the
only God;
He, who in Elah prompted me to meet,
Although a stripling, and yet inexpert,
The menacing colossal arrogance
Of fierce Goliath, clad in mail complete:
That God, who thence on thy wide-dreaded
arms
Heap'd victory on victory; and who,
Always in His designs inscrutable,
Chose, as an instrument, my hand obscure

For signal exploits: hither now that God
Doth usher me to thee, with victory.
Now, as thou likest best, a simple war-
    rior,
Or leader of thy bands, if I deserve
Such a distinction, take me. On the earth
First let thy foes be strewn: by the keen
    breath
Of northern blasts be all the clouds dis-
    persed,
That gather in dark masses round thy
    throne:
Thou afterwards, O Saul, with death shalt
    pay me.
Not one faint struggle, not a single
    thought,
Should my death cost thee. Thou, O king,
    shalt say:
"Be David slain:" and Abner instantly
Shall slay me.—I will grasp nor sword
    nor shield;
Within the palace of my sov'reign lord
All weapons misbecome me, saving pa-
    tience,
Humility, and prayers, and passive love,
And innocence. I ought, if God so will,
To perish as thy son, not as thy foe.
Thus was the son of the first ancestor
Of Israel's people ready to resign,
On the great mount, his sacrificial blood;
No disobedient word or sign escaped him:
Already had his father raised one hand
To slay him, while he fondly kiss'd the
    other.—
Saul gave my life; Saul takes that life
    away:
Through him I gain'd renown, through
    him I lose it:
He made me great, and now he makes me
    nothing.
    SAUL.   O, what a thick mist from my
        agèd eyes
Those words disperse! What voice sounds
    in my heart! . . .—
David, thou speakest as a man of valor,
And valiant were thy deeds; but, blind
    with pride,
Thou dar'dst despise me afterwards; dar'dst raise
Thyself above me; to my praise pretend,
And clothe thyself with my reflected light.

And, were I not thy king, does it become
A warrior young to scorn an agèd war-
    rior?
Thou, great in all things, wert not so in
    this.
Of thee the daughters of my people sang:
"David, the valiant, his ten thousands
    slew;
Saul slew his thousands." To my in-
    most heart,
David, thou woundedst me. Why saidst
    thou not:
"Saul, in his youth, not only slew a thou-
    sand,
But many thousands: he the warrior is;
Me he created"?
    DAVID.   I indeed said this;
But those, who to thy hearing gain'd ac-
    cess,
More loudly cried: "Too powerful is
    David:
In all men's mouths, and in the hearts
    of many;
If thou, Saul, slay him not, who will
    restrain him?"—
With less of art, and more of verity,
What said not Abner to the king?: "Ah,
    David
Too much surpasses me; hence I abhor
    him;
Hence envy, fear him; hence I wish him
    dead."
    ABNER.   Miscreant! the day that thou
        clandestinely
Didst with thy prophets trait'rously
    cabal;
When for thy monarch thou didst spread
    in secret
Infamous snares; when shelter thou didst
    seek
E'en in the bosom of Philistia's sons;
And spending days profane with foes im-
    pure,
Didst meanwhile with domestic traitors
    hold
A secret commerce: now, do I perchance
Only allege this? or didst thou not do it?
At first, who more install'd thee than my-
    self
Within thy monarch's heart?   Who
    prompted him

His son-in-law to make thee? Abner
    only . . .
MICHAL. 'Twas I: I at my father's
    hand obtain'd
David as consort; his I sought to be;
I, smitten by his virtues. He inspired
My earliest sighs; the idol of my heart,
My hope, my life was he, and he alone.
Although disguised in base obscurity,
Reduced to poverty, yet evermore
David had been more welcome to my heart,
Than any proud king whom the east
    adores.
SAUL. But thou, O David, canst thou
    controvert
The charges Abner brings? Didst thou
    not seek
A shelter in Philistia? Didst thou not
Sow in my people seeds of black revolt?
Hast thou not plotted many times to
    take
Thy monarch's life, thy second father's
    life?
DAVID. Behold; this border of thy royal
    garment
Answers for me. Dost recognize it, thou?
Take it; examine it.
SAUL.   Give it to me.
What do I see? 'Tis mine; assuredly . . .
Whence didst thou take it? . . .
DAVID.   From thyself I took it,
With this my sword, from off thy royal
    robe,
My own hands sever'd it.—Remember'st
    thou
En-gedi? There, where barbarously thou
Pursuedst me, a banish'd man, to death;
There was I, in the cave, that from the
    fount
Derives its name, a friendless fugitive;
There, thou alone, thy warriors having
    station'd
To guard the rugged entrance of the cave,
On downy pillows, in calm quietness,
Didst close thine eyes in sleep . . . Didst
    thou, O Heav'ns,
With rancorous and bloody thoughts in-
    flamed,
Yet slumber there? Thou see'st how
    mighty God
Defeats the schemes of human subtlety!

There with impunity I might have slain
    thee,
And by another issue have escaped:
This border of thy robe sufficiently
Proves this to thee. Behold thee, thou a
    king,
A haughty and a great one, in the midst
Of arm'd battalions, fallen in the hands
Of the proscribed calumniated youth . . .
Abner, the valiant Abner, where was he?
Thus does he guard thy life? Thus serve
    his king?
Thou see'st in whom thou hast reposed
    thy trust;
And against whom thou hast thine anger
    turn'd.—
Now, art thou satisfied? Now hast thou
    not,
Saul, of my heart proofs incontestable,
And of my fealty and innocence?
Not proofs persuasive of the little love,
Of the malignant and invidious rage,
And the precarious vigilance of Abner? . . .
SAUL. My son, thou hast prevail'd;
    . . . thou hast prevail'd.
Abner, do thou behold him; and be
    dumb.
MICHAL. Oh joy!
DAVID.   O father! . . .
JONATHAN.   O auspicious day!
MICHAL. O husband! . . .
SAUL.   Yes, this is a day of joy,
A day of restitution and of triumph.
I will that thou to-day command my
    armies:
Abner, oppose not; for I will it so.
Let no contention 'twixt you two arise,
Except an emulation which shall slay
Most of our enemies. Thou, Jonathan,
Beside the brother of thy heart shalt
    fight;
David to me is surety for thy life;
And thou art so for his.
JONATHAN.   When David leads
Our armies, God Himself becomes our
    surety.
MICHAL. God doth restore thee to me;
    He will save thee . . .
SAUL. Let this suffice. Before the
    fight begins,
Come to the tent, O son, a little while,

And rest thy wearied limbs. Thy spouse
beloved
Shall soothe the long affliction of thy ab-
sence:
With her own hands meanwhile shall she
provide
And minister thy food. My daughter,
now
Repair in part (for thou alone canst do
it)
The unintended errors of thy father.

ACT III

SCENE I

[DAVID, ABNER.]

ABNER. Behold me: at thy summons I
appear,
Ere scarce the king hath from the banquet
risen.
DAVID. I wish'd to speak to thee in
secret here.
ABNER. Thou wouldst perchance hear
of the coming fight? . . .
DAVID. And at the same time tell thee,
that thou'rt not
Subordinate to me; that both alike
Our people and our lawful king we serve,
And Israel's mighty God. Let not our
breasts
Harbor another thought.
ABNER. I, for our king,
From whose blood I descend, had in the
camp
Already brandish'd my ensanguined
sword,
Before the shrill twang of thy sling was
heard . . .
DAVID. The monarch's blood runs not
within my veins:
My deeds are known to all; I boast not
of them:
Abner well knows them.—In forgetfulness
Let them be buried; only recollect
Thine own: and, rivalling thy former
fame,
Seek only to surpass thyself to-day.
ABNER. I hitherto believed myself the
leader:

David was not here then: I ventured
hence
To order all things for the victory:
Hear what I should have done, had I
commanded.—
Full in our front, from north to south,
the camp
Of the Philistines fills the valley's length.
Behind it rise thick bushes; 'tis de-
fended
By lofty banks in front: eastward 'tis
flank'd
By a not lofty hill, of gentle slope
Towards the camp, but rough, precipitous,
Upon the other side; an ample outlet
Lies amid mountains to the west, through
which
By a vast plain the traveller may go,
Exempt from hindrance, to the murmur-
ing sea.
There, if we thither can decoy our foes,
Our triumph in the war will be assured.
But, to accomplish that, 'tis needful first
To feign retreat. In three battalions
form'd,
If we towards the valley's left side bend,
We shall in front encounter their right
flank.
The first battalion with forced march ad-
vances,
And seems to fly; the second, moving
slowly,
Remains behind, in thin, disorder'd ranks,
A sure temptation to the enemy.
Meanwhile, a band conspicuous for its
valor
The rugged hill towards the east has
gain'd,
And on the rear of the invading host
Re-issues. Thus in front is it enclosed,
Behind, transversely; and behold we make
A dreadful, universal carnage of it.
DAVID. Equally wise and valorous art
thou.
Nothing, O Abner, should be alter'd now
In thy arrangements. Valor I commend
Wherever found: a soldier I will be,
And not a leader: and my coming here
Shall, by addition of a sword alone,
Alter thy battle.
ABNER. David is the leader:

David is master of our armies. Who
Combats, compared with him?
DAVID. Who less indeed
Should stoop to jealousy than Abner, since
He is so highly gifted? Excellent,
However I behold it, is thy scheme.
Myself and Jonathan beside the tent
Of Saul shall combat; further, tow'rds the
    north,
Uz shall advance; with thousand chosen
    men
Zadok the eastern eminence shall gain;
And thou, with greatest numbers, shall
    command
The body of the army.
ABNER. This to thee
Belongs; it is the place of honor.
DAVID. Hence
I place thee there.—As yet the sun
    ascends:
Thou shalt keep all in steady preparation;
But till the fourth hour of the afternoon
Be not the trumpets heard. Thou seeest
    how
A furious west wind blows; the dazzling
    sun
And driven dust will, tow'rds the close of
    day,
Assist our enterprise.
ABNER. Thou speakest wisely.
DAVID. Now, go; command: and do not
    from thyself,
With base and courtly artifice, of which
Thou shouldst be ignorant, avert that
    praise,
Which, as a captain, thou so well de-
    servest.

SCENE II

[DAVID.]
DAVID. The order of the fight is wise
    and subtle.—
But, if he have not gain'd his soldiers'
    hearts,
What boots the foresight of a general?
Of this alone is Abner destitute;
And this to me God grants. To-day we
    conquer;
To-morrow once more will I leave the
    king;

For never by his side can there be peace
For me . . . What do I say? New vic-
    tory
Would be ascribed to me as a new crime.

SCENE III

[MICHAL, DAVID.]
MICHAL. My spouse, hast thou not
    heard? My father scarce
Rose from a joyous banquet, when towards
    him
Abner advanced, and spake to him an in-
    stant:
I enter'd, he retired; I found the king
No longer what he was.
DAVID. But yet, what said he?
What couldest thou infer? . . .
MICHAL. Just now was he
Devoted to our cause; with us he wept;
Alternately embraced us; and from us,
As if in his defence, he prophesied
A race of future heroes; he appear'd
To us, as he said this, more than a father:
More than a king he now appears to me.
DAVID. Ah! do not weep, O wife, be-
    fore the time:
Saul is the king; his will in us must be
Accomplish'd. So that he to-day may
    lose not
The battle; let him 'gainst myself to-
    morrow
Resume his cruel thoughts; I will resume
My abject state, my bitter banishment,
My fugitive and apprehensive life.
My true and only death will be to leave
    thee:
And yet I ought to do it . . . Ah, vain
    hopes!
Ah, nuptial ties for thee how inauspicious!
Another spouse a happy regal state
Had given thee; and I deprive thee of
    it.
Unhappy I! . . . Nor canst thou make me
    now,
Thy ever fugitive and homeless consort,
The father of a num'rous blooming off-
    spring . . .
MICHAL. Ah, no! we never shall again
    be parted:

No one shall dare to rend thee from my
    breast.
I never will return, no, never more.
To that unhappy life which I dragg'd on
Deprived of thee: the tomb shall sooner
    hold me.
I languish'd in that palace of despair,
Alone and weeping, through the tedious
    days;
The shades of night with dreadful dreams
    were fraught.
Now, I beheld my cruel father's sword
Suspended o'er thy head; thy voice I
    heard
Persuasive, weeping, supplicating, fit
To drive all cruel feelings from the
    breast;
And yet the barbarous Saul, in spite of
    this,
Plunged in thy heart the dagger: now, I
    saw thee
'Mid secret labyrinths of darksome caves,
Making thy couch of the unyielding flint;
While at the motion of each rustling leaf
Thy faint heart trembled; and thou
    sought'st another;
And thence another; yet without once
    finding
A place of rest, or quietness, or friends:
Sick, anxious, weary . . . worn with
    parching thirst . . .
O Heav'ns! . . . How tell my anguish,
    doubts, long trembling?—
No more, no, never will I leave thee;
    never . . .
    DAVID. Thou torturest my heart: ah,
    cease! . . . This day
To blood is consecrated, not to tears.
    MICHAL. Provided that an obstacle to-
    day
Arise not to thy fighting. I fear not
The fight on thy account; thou hast a
    shield
Proof against all assaults, Almighty
    God:
But I am fearful lest perfidious Abner
Frustrate on thy account, or intercept
The victory to-day.
    DAVID.   And what? did Saul
Appear to thee to hesitate to trust
The conduct of the enterprise to me?

MICHAL. I heard not that; but sternly
    did he frown,
And whisper'd to himself I know not
    what
Of trait'rous priests; of strangers in the
    camp;
Of simulated virtue . . . Broken, dark,
Mournful, tremendous words, to her who
    is
The wife of David and the child of Saul.
    DAVID. Behold him: let us hear.
    MICHAL.   Just God! I pray Thee,
Succor to-day Thy consecrated servant:
Confound blasphemers; give my father
    light;
Protect my husband; and defend Thy
    people.

SCENE IV

[SAUL, JONATHAN, MICHAL, DAVID.]
    JONATHAN. Ah come, belovèd father;
    to thy thoughts
Allow a little respite: the pure air
Will bring thee some refreshment; come:
    and sit
A little while among thy children now.
    SAUL. What are those words I hear?
    MICHAL.   Belovèd father! . . .
    SAUL. Who, who are ye? . . . Who
    speaks of pure air here? . . .
This? 'tis a thick impenetrable gloom;
A land of darkness; and the shades of
    death . . .
O see! Come nearer me; dost thou ob-
    serve it?
A fatal wreath of blood surrounds the
    sun . . .
Heard'st thou the singing of ill-omen'd
    birds?
The vocal air resounds with loud laments
That smite my ears, compelling me to
    weep . . .
But what? Ye, ye weep also? . . .
    JONATHAN.   Mighty God
Of Israel, dost Thou thus Thy face avert
From Saul the king? Is he, Thy servant
    once,
Abandon'd to the adversary thus?
    MICHAL. Father, thy much-loved daugh-
    ter is beside thee:

If thou art cheerful, she is also cheerful;
She, if thou weepest, weeps . . . But,
    wherefore now
Should we shed tears? For joy hath
    reappear'd.
SAUL. David, thou meanest. Ah! . . .
    Why doth not David
Also embrace me with my other children?
DAVID. O father! . . . I have been
    restrain'd by fear
Of importuning thee. Ah! why canst
    thou
Not read my heart? I evermore am
    thine.
SAUL. Thou lovest then . . . the house
    . . . of Saul?
DAVID.   I love it?
O Heav'ns! Dear as the apple of mine
    eye
To me is Jonathan; I neither know,
Nor heed a peril in the world, for thee;
Let my wife, if she can, say with what
    love,
And how much love, I love her . . .
SAUL.   Yet, thyself
Thou mightily dost prize . . .
DAVID.   I, prize myself? . . .
No despicable soldier in the camp,
In court thy son-in-law, I deem myself;
And nothing, nothing in the sight of God.
SAUL. Incessantly to me of God thou
    speakest;
Yet, thou well knowest that the crafty
    rage,
Cruel, tremendous, of perfidious priests
Has for a long time sever'd me from
    God.
Dost thou thus name Him to insult me?
DAVID.   I
Name Him, to give Him glory. Why dost
    thou
Believe that He no longer is with thee?
He doth not dwell with him who loves
    Him not:
But, doth He ever fail to succor him
Who doth invoke Him, and who hath re-
    posed
In Him implicit trust? He to the throne
Appointed thee; and on that throne He
    keeps thee:
And if in Him, in Him exclusively

Thou dost confide, He's thine, and thou
    art His.
SAUL. Who speaks of Heav'n? . . . Is
    he in snowy vest
Enrobed who thus his sacred lip unseals?
Let's see him . . . No: thou art a warrior:
    thou
Graspest the sword: approach; and let me
    see,
If David thus or Samuel doth accost
    me.—
What sword is this? 'Tis not the same,
    methinks,
Which I, with my own hands, on thee
    bestow'd . . .
DAVID. This is the sword that my poor
    sling acquired.
The sword that over me in Elah hung
Threat'ning my life; in fierce Goliath's
    hands
I saw it flash a horrid glare of death
Before my eyes: he grasp'd it: but it bears
Not mine, but his coagulated blood.
SAUL. Was not that sword, a conse-
    crated thing,
In Nob, within the tabernacle hung?
Was it not wrapp'd within the mystic
    Ephod,
And thus from all unhallow'd eyes con-
    ceal'd?
Devoted to the Lord of hosts for ever? . . .
DAVID. 'Tis true; but . . .
SAUL.   Whence didst thou obtain it,
    then?
Who dared to give it? who? . . .
DAVID.   I will explain.
Pow'rless and fugitive to Nob I came;
Wherefore I fled, thou knowest. Ev'ry
    path
Was crowded with unhappy wretches; I,
Defenceless, found myself at ev'ry step
Within the jaws of death. With humble
    brow
I kneel'd within the tabernacle, where
God's Spirit doth descend: and there,
    these arms
(Which if a living man might to his side
Refit them, David surely was that man)
Myself demanded of the priest.
SAUL.   And he? . . .
DAVID. Gave them to me.

SAUL.   He was?
DAVID.   Ahimelech.
SAUL.   Perfidious traitor! . . . Vile! . . .
     Where is the altar? . . .
O rage! . . . Ah, all are miscreants!
     traitors all! . . .
The foes of God; are ye his ministers? . . .
Black souls in vestments white . . . Where
     is the axe? . . .
Where is the altar? let him be
     destroy'd . . .
Where is the off'ring? I will slay him . . .
     MICHAL.   Father!
     JONATHAN. O Heav'ns! What mean
        these words? Where dost thou
        fly? . . .
Be pacified, I pray thee: there are not
Or altars here, or victims: in the priests
Respect that God who hears thee ever-
     more.
     SAUL. Who thus restrains me? . . .
        Who resists me thus? . . .
Who forces me to sit? . . .
     JONATHAN.   My father . . .
     DAVID.   Thou,
Great God of Israel, do Thou succor him!
Thy servant kneels to Thee, and this
     implores.
     SAUL. I am bereft of peace; the sun,
        my kingdom,
My children, and my pow'r of thought,
     all, all
Are taken from me! . . . Ah, unhappy
     Saul!
Who doth console thee? who is now the
     guide,
The prop of thy bewilder'd feebleness? . . .
Thy children all are mute; are harsh, and
     cruel . . .
And of the doting and infirm old man
They only wish the death: and nought
     attracts
My children, but the fatal diadem,
Which now is twined around thy hoary
     head.
Wrest it at once: and at the same time
     sever
From this now tremulous decaying form
Your father's palsied head . . .   Ah,
     wretched state!
Better were death. I wish for death . . .

     MICHAL.   O father! . . .
We all desire thy life: we each of us
Would die ourselves, to rescue thee from
     death . . .
     JONATHAN. —Now, since in tears his
        fury is dissolved,
Brother, do thou, to recompose his soul,
Exert thy voice. So many times already
Hast thou enthrall'd him with celestial
     songs
To calm oblivion.
     MICHAL.   Yes; thou seest row,
The breathing in his panting breast sub-
     sides;
His looks, just now so savage, swim in
     tears:
Now is the time to lend him thy as-
     sistance.
     DAVID. May God in mercy speak to
        him through me.—

Omnipotent, eternal, infinite,
     Thou, who dost govern each created
        thing;
Thou, who from nothing mad'st me by
        Thy might,
     Blest with a soul that dares to Thee
        take wing;
Thou, who canst pierce th' abyss of end-
        less night,
     And all its myst'ries into daylight
        bring;
The universe doth tremble at Thy nod,
And sinners prostrate own the out-
     stretch'd arm of God.

Oft on the gorgeous blazing wings ere
     now
     Of thousand cherubim wert Thou re-
        veal'd;
Oft did Thy pure divinity endow
     Thy people's shepherd in the martial
        field:
To him a stream of eloquence wert Thou;
     Thou wert his sword, his wisdom, and
        his shield:
From Thy bright throne, O God, bestow
     one ray
To cleave the gath'ring clouds that inter-
     cept the day.

In tears of darkness we . . .

SAUL. Hear I the voice
Of David? . . . From a mortal lethargy
It seems to wake me, and displays to me
The cheering radiance of my early years.

DAVID. Who comes, who comes, un-
seen, yet heard?
A sable cloud of dust appear'd,
Chased by the eastern blast.—
But it has burst; and from its womb
A thousand brandish'd swords illume
The track through which it pass'd . . .

Saul, as a tow'r, his forehead rears,
His head a flaming circlet wears.
The earth beneath his feet
Echoes with tramp of horse and men:
The sea, the sky, the hills, the plain,
The warlike sounds repeat.

In awful majesty doth Saul appear;
Horsemen and chariots from before him
fly:
Chill'd by his presence is each heart with
fear;
And god-like terrors lighten in his eye.

Ye sons of Ammon, late so proud,
Where now the scorn, the insults loud,
Ye raised against our host?
Your corpses more than fill the plain;
The ample harvest of your slain
Invalidates your boast.

See what it is thus to depend
On gods unable to defend.—
But wherefore from afar
Hear I another trumpet sound?
'Tis Saul's:—he levels with the ground
All Edom's sons of war.

Thus Moab, Zobah, by his arms laid low,
With impious Amalek, united fall:
Saul, like a stream fed by dissolving
snow,
Defeats, disperses, overwhelms them all.

SAUL. This is the voice of my departed
years,
That from the tomb to glory now recalls
me.

I live again in my victorious youth,
When I hear this . . . —What do I say?
. . . Alas!
Should cries of war be now address'd to
me? . . .
Oblivion, indolence, and peace, invite
The old man to themselves.
DAVID. Let peace be sung.—

Weary and thirsty, see he lies
Beside his native stream;
God's champion, whose past victories
Wake many a glorious dream.

The sigh'd-for laurel's evergreen
Doth screen his head from heat;
His children, all around him seen,
His sighs and smiles repeat.

They weep and smile, then smile and
weep,
With sympathy endued;
And still a strict accordance keep
To ev'ry varying mood.

One daughter's gentle hand unfits
His crested helm and sword;
His consort fond beside him sits,
Embracing her loved lord.

The other doth clear water bring
From the pure ambient flood,
To cleanse his stately brows, where cling
Commingled dust and blood.

A cloud of odorous flow'rs she spreads,
Which breathe their perfumes near;
And on his honor'd hand she sheds
The duteous filial tear.

But why sits one apart reclined,
In pensive mood alone?
Alas, she mourns that others find
A task, while she has none.

But diff'rent thoughts, with eager haste,
Attract the band of boys;
Till his turn comes to be embraced,
One son himself employs
To make the blood-encrusted blade
From spot and blemish clear:
With envy fired, another said:
"When shall I poise that spear?

"That pond'rous lance when shall I wield,
  That now defies my strength?"
Another grasps the blazon'd shield,
  And stalks behind its length.

Then tears of sweet surprise,
From forth the swimming eyes
Of Saul are seen to roll:
For of his blooming race,
So full of royal grace,
He knows that he's the soul.

The pleasure how entire,
How happy is the sire,
Whose waking thoughts inspire
Affections so sincere!
But now the day is o'er;
The zephyrs breathe no more;
And sleep's soft pow'rs restore
The monarch we revere.—

SAUL. Happy the father of a race like
    this!
O peace of mind, how precious are thy
    gifts! . . .
Through all my veins balsamic sweetness
    flows . . . —
But, what pretendest thou? To make Saul
    vile
Amid domestic ease? Does valiant Saul
Now lie an useless implement of war?

DAVID. The king reposes, but heroic
    dreams
  With fearful pomp before his eyes
      parade,
Pregnant with death and visionary themes.
  Behold, transfix'd with his victorious
      blade,
    The conquer'd tyrant of the haughty
        foes,
  All pow'r of harming gone, an awful
      shade.
    Behold a flash that instantaneous
        glows . . .
It is Saul's brandish'd sword, that no
    man spares,
    The weak and strong confounding
        with its blows.—

The dreaded lion thus sometimes forbears
  To make the forest with his cries re-
      sound,
For even he in sleep his strength repairs;
  But not the silence of his den profound,
Can courage to the trembling flocks re-
      store;
    Or make the swain with less fear look
        around,
For well he knows that he will prowl
    once more.

The monarch is roused from his slumbers:
  "Arms, arms," he imperiously cries.
They are vanish'd,—the enemy's numbers;
  What champion his valor defies?

I see, I see a track of fearful fire,
  To which perforce the hostile squadrons
      yield.
Before the arms of Israel they retire,
  Which, black with hostile gore, possess
      the field.

The wingèd thunderbolt huge stones doth
      shower,
  And far less promptly doth the foe re-
      treat,
Than our dread sov'reign in his mighty
      power
  Pursue him, and his overthrow com-
      plete.

Like a proud eagle, his audacious flight,
  Wing'd with immortal pinions, tow'rds
      the pole
He aims. His eyes are like the lightning
      bright;
  His talons God's own thunderbolts con-
      trol,

Annihilating those base sons of earth,
  Who in false temples have false gods
      adored;
Whose gods impure to rites impure gave
      birth,
  Who dare compare themselves with
      Israel's Lord.

Long, long have I pursued his ardent
      path;
  Now it behoves me once more to pursue

His foes on earth; with Heav'n-directed
wrath
To trample down and crush Philistia's
crew;

And with th' assistance of the God of
hosts,
Prove that, as he, so I maintain his
laws;
And prove that now the camp of Israel
boasts
Two swords resistless in a righteous
cause.

SAUL. Who, who thus boasts? Is there,
except my sword,
Which I unsheathe, another in the camp?
He's a blasphemer, let him perish, he
Who dares defy it.
MICHAL.   Ah forbear: O
Heav'ns! . . .
JONATHAN. Father, what wouldst thou
do? . . .
DAVID.   Unhappy king!
MICHAL. Ah fly! . . . Ah fly! . . .
With difficulty we
Can hold him back. Dear husband, fly!

SCENE V

[JONATHAN, SAUL, MICHAL.]
MICHAL.   O stop, . . .
Belovèd father! . . .
JONATHAN.   I beseech thee, stop . . .
SAUL. Who thus restrains me? who
presumes to do it? . . .
Where is my sword? Restore my sword at
once . . .
JONATHAN. Do thou retire with us,
belovèd father:
I will not let thee any farther go.
Behold, thy children now are all
alone:
Return with us to thy pavilion: now
Thou needest quietness. Ah, come! Re-
frain
From causeless rage; thy children stand
around thee . . .
MICHAL. And they shall never, never
quit thy presence . . .

ACT IV

SCENE I

[JONATHAN, MICHAL.]
MICHAL. Jonathan, tell me; to my
father's tent
May my dear spouse return?
JONATHAN.   Ah, no! with him
Saul is not reconciled; though he has
fully
Regain'd his reason: but his jealousy
Is too profound; and slow will be his
cure.
Return to David thou, and leave him not.
MICHAL. Alas! . . . Who is more
wretched than myself? . . .
I have so well conceal'd him, that no man
Will ever find him: to this hiding-place
I now return to him.
JONATHAN.   O Heav'ns! behold,
My poor distracted father once more
comes:
He never finds a resting-place.
MICHAL.   Alas!
What shall I say to him? . . . I will
retire . . .

SCENE II

[SAUL, MICHAL, JONATHAN.]
SAUL. Who flies at my approach?
Thou, woman, thou?
MICHAL. My lord . . .
SAUL.   Where, where is David?
MICHAL.   . . . I know not . . .
SAUL. Thou knowest not? . . .
JONATHAN.   My father . . .
SAUL.   Seek him then;
Go; bring him hither soon.
MICHAL.   I seek him out? . . .
But, . . . tell me, where? . . .
SAUL.   It was thy king that spake,
And hast thou not obey'd him?

SCENE III

[SAUL, JONATHAN.]
SAUL.   . . . Jonathan,
Lov'st thou thy father? . . .
JONATHAN. Father! . . . yes, I love thee:
But, loving thee, I also love thy glory:

Hence, sometimes I oppose, far as a son
Ought to oppose, thine impulses unjust.
 SAUL. Often thy father's arm dost thou
restrain:
But, thou dost turn against thyself that
sword
Which thou avertest from another's
breast.
Yes, yes, defend that David to the utmost;
Shortly will he . . . Dost thou not hear a
voice
That in thy heart cries: "David will be
king"?
—David? He shall be immolated first.
 JONATHAN. And doth not God, with a
more dreadful voice,
Cry in thy heart: "My favorite is David;
He is the chosen of the Lord of hosts"?
Doth not each act of his confirm this
truth?
Was not the frantic and invidious rage
Of Abner silenced by his mere approach?
And thou, when thou re-enter'st in thyself,
Dost thou not find that, only at his pres-
ence,
All thy suspicions vanish like a cloud
Before the sun? And dost thou fondly
dream,
When the malignant spirit visits thee,
That I restrain thy arm? 'Tis God re-
strains it.
Scarcely wilt thou have levell'd at his
breast
Thy evil-brandish'd sword, when thou wilt
be
Forced to withdraw it suddenly: in tears
Thou thyself prostrate at his feet wilt
fall;
Yes, father, thou, repentant: for thou art
Indeed not impious . . .
 SAUL. But too true thy words.
A strange inexplicable mystery
This David is to me. No sooner I
In Elah had beheld him, than he pleased
My eyes; but never, never won my heart.
When I might almost be disposed to love
him,
A fierce repulsion shoots athwart my
breast,
And weans me from him: scarcely do I
wish

For his destruction, than, if I behold him,
He straight disarms me, with such wonder
fills me,
That in his presence I become a noth-
ing . . .
Ah! this is surely, this the vengeance is
Of the inscrutable Almighty hand!
Tremendous hand, I now begin to know
thee . . .
But what? why should I seek for reasons
now? . . .
God have I ne'er offended: this is then
The vengeance of the priests. Yes, David
is
An instrument of sacerdotal malice.
Expiring Samuel he beheld in Ramah:
Th' implacable old man to him address'd
His dying words. Who knows, who
knows if he
Upon the head of this my enemy
Pour'd not the sacred oil with which be-
fore
My brows he had anointed? P'rhaps thou
knowest . . .
Speak . . . yes, thou knowest: I conjure
thee, speak.
 JONATHAN. Father, I know not: but if
it were so,
Should not I, equally with thee, esteem
Myself in this offended? Am not I
Thy eldest son? Dost thou not mean this
throne
For me, when thou art gather'd to thy
fathers?
If I then hold my peace, who else should
dare
To make complaints at this? In forti-
tude
David surpasses me; in virtue, sense,
In ev'ry quality: and as the more
His worth surpasses mine, the more I
love him.
Now, should that pow'r which gives and
takes away
Kingdoms at will, bestow this throne on
David,
What other greater proof can I require?
He is more worthy of that throne than
I:
And God hath summon'd him to lofty
deeds,

The shepherd of his children.—But mean-
while
I swear, that he has always been to thee
A faithful subject and a loyal son.
Now to that God to whom it doth belong,
The future yield: against that God, mean-
while,
Against the truth, ah, harden not thy
heart.
If a divinity in Samuel spake not,
How could an undesigning, weak old
man,
Half in the grave already, such effects
Produce by David's means? That mystery
Of love and hatred which thou feel'st for
David;
That apprehension at a battle's name,
(A terror hitherto to thee unknown,)
Whence, Saul, can it proceed? Is there a
power
On earth producing such effects as
these? . . .
SAUL. What language dost thou hold?
A son of Saul
Art thou?—Feel'st thou no int'rest for
the throne?—
Know'st not the cruel rights of him who'll
hold it?
My house will be abolish'd, from the
roots
Torn up, by him who seizes on my sceptre.
Thy sons, thy brothers, and thyself de-
stroy'd . . .
Not one of Saul's descendants will re-
main . . .
O guilty and insatiable thirst
Of pow'r, what horrors canst thou not
produce?
To reign, the brother immolates the
brother;
Mothers their children; wives their con-
sorts slay;
The son his father . . . Sacrilegious
throne!
Thou art the seat of blood and cruelty.
JONATHAN. Has man a shield against
the sword of Heaven?
Not menaces or prayers can turn aside
The wrath of God omnipotent, who oft
The proud abases, and exalts the hum-
ble.

SCENE IV

[SAUL, JONATHAN, ABNER, AHIMELECH,
SOLDIERS.]
ABNER. King, if thy presence I behold
once more,
Ere streams of hostile blood by my means
flow,
To this my mighty reasons am I urged.
David, the doughty champion, in whose
hands
Our victory was placed, has disappear'd.
Scarce is an hour now wanting to the
time
Appointed for attack: thou now dost hear
The warriors, chafing with impatient
ardor,
Filling with cries the air; the earth re-
sounds,
Beaten with iron hoof of fiery steeds:
Howlings and neighings, and the blaze of
helms,
And brandish'd swords, and loudly-echo-
ing shouts,
Enough to make the veriest coward vali-
ant; . . .
Yet who sees David?—Nowhere is he
found.—
Behold, (authentic succor of th' Al-
mighty!)
Behold, who in the camp stands in his
place.
This man, in soft, white, sacerdotal stole
Enveloped, having gain'd the camp by
stealth,
Tremblingly slunk beside the Benjamites.
Behold him; hear from him the lofty cause
Which to such peril guides him.
AHIMELECH. I will speak it,
If not forbidden by the king's displeas-
ure . . .
SAUL. The king's displeasure? Thou
dost then deserve it? . . .
Traitor, and who art thou? . . . It seems
to me
That I should know thee well. Art thou
not one
Of that fantastical and haughty flock
Of Ramah's seers?
AHIMELECH. The ephod I am wearing:
I, of the Levites chief, to holy Aaron,

In that high ministry, to which the Lord
Elected him, after a long descent
Of other consecrated priests, succeed.
Near to the sacred ark in Nob I'm sta-
tion'd:
The ark of covenant in former times
Stood in the centre of the camp: but now
'Tis deem'd too much, if e'en clandestinely
That camp is enter'd by God's minister:
Where Saul is monarch, a strange visitant
The priest is held: but he is not so,
no,
Where Israel fights; if still, as formerly,
Through God we triumph.—Dost thou
know me not?
What wonder? Dost thou better know
thyself?—
Thou hast withdrawn thy footsteps from
God's path;
And I within the tabernacle dwell,
Where dwells the great Jehovah; there,
where thou
For a long time, O Saul, hast not been
seen.
The name I go by is Ahimelech.

SAUL. That name proclaims thee, as
thou art, a traitor:
Now art thou recognized. Before my
sight
Thou comest opportunely. Now confess,
Art thou not he, who to the banish'd
David
Gav'st an asylum, nourishment, and
safety,
Deliverance and arms? And, then, what
arms!
Goliath's sacred sword, which, dedicated
To God, within the tabernacle hung,
Whence thou with hand profane removedst
it,
And girdedst it on the perfidious foe
Of thy sole lord and king?—Thou comest,
villain,
With treason to the camp: what doubt
is there? . . .

AHIMELECH. Assuredly, I to betray
thee come;
Since on thy arms I come to ask of God
For victory, which He to thee denies.
Yes, I am he, who, with benignant hand,
Assisted David. But, who is that David?

Of the king's daughter is not he the hus-
band?
Not the most valiant 'mid thy men of
valor?
Not the most graceful, most humane, most
just,
Of Israel's sons? Say, is he not in war
Thy shield, and thy defender? And in
peace,
Is he not in thy palace, with his songs,
The master of thy heart? The love of
maidens,
The people's joy, the terror of our foes;
Such, such was he whom I presumed to
rescue.
And thou thyself, didst thou not ere-
while choose him
For the first honors? Not select his arm
To guide thy battles? To bring back once
more
The shout of triumph to the camp? To
chase
That terror of defeat, which in thy heart
Thy God hath placed?—If thou con-
demnest me,
Thou, at the same time, dost condemn
thyself.

SAUL. Whence, whence in you springs
pity? whence in you,
O cruel priests, revengeful, thirsty ever
For human blood? To Samuel did it
seem
A crime unpardonable that I slew not
The king of Amalek, with arms in hand,
Taken in flight; a mighty king, a war-
rior,
Of ardent gen'rous temper, and profuse
Of his own life-blood in his people's ser-
vice.—
Unhappy king! dragg'd in my presence,
he
Came manacled: yet he preserved, though
vanquish'd,
A noble pride, as far from insolence,
As from all abjectness. Of courage guilty
To cruel Samuel he appear'd: three times
In his defenceless bosom did he plunge,
With sacerdotal hand, the reeking
sword.—
These are your battles, vile ones, these
alone.

But, he who dares to lift his haughty
    brow
Against his lawful monarch, he, in you,
Finds an asylum, a support, a shield.
All other objects occupy your hearts,
More than the altar. Who, yes, who are
    ye?
A selfish, cruel, and malignant tribe,
Who, yourselves shelter'd, at our dangers
    laugh;
And, in your easy mantles wrapp'd, pre-
    sume
To govern us who sweat in cumbrous
    mail:
Us, who, 'mid bloodshed, apprehension,
    death,
Lead, for our wives, our children, and
    yourselves,
Lives of distress and constant wretched-
    ness.
Cowards, less dignified than idle women,
Would ye with lithe wands, and fantastic
    hymns,
O'er us, and o'er our weapons, arbitrate?
    AHIMELECH. And thou, who art thou?
    of the earth a king:
But, in God's sight, what king?—Examine,
    Saul,
Thyself; thou art but a crown'd heap of
    dust.—
I, by myself, am nothing; but I am
A thunderbolt, a whirlwind, and a tem-
    pest,
If God descends in me: that mighty God
Who fashion'd thee; Who if He only look
Upon thee, where is Saul?—It ill befits
    thee
To plead the cause of Agag; foolishly
Dost thou pursue him in forbidden paths.
For a perverse king, save the hostile
    sword,
Is there a punishment? And does a sword
Smite unpermitted by Almighty God?
God writes His vengeances in adamant;
Nor to Philistines less than Israel's
    sons
Does He commit them.—Tremble, Saul: I
    see
Already in a sable cloud on high,
Death's dreadful angel poised on fiery
    wings:

Already, with one hand hath he un-
    sheathed
The pitiless, retributory sword;
And with the other, from thy guilty head
He plucks thy hoary tresses: tremble,
    Saul.—
There is who doth impel thee to destruc-
    tion:
'Tis he; this Abner, brother he of Satan;
He, who hath poison'd with suspicions vile
Thy agèd heart; he who hath dwindled
    thee
From a crown'd warrior to a less than
    child.
Thou, thou infatuate man, dost now re-
    move
The only true and steadfast prop of thee
And of thy house. Where is the house of
    Saul?
On quicksands it is built; it shakes al-
    ready;
It falls; it moulders into dust: 'tis
    gone.—
    SAUL. Prophet of my calamities art
    thou,
And not so of thy own. Thou has not
    seen,
Ere to the camp thou camest, that death
    here
Awaited thee: this I predict; and soon
Shall Abner's hand this prophecy fulfil.—
My faithful Abner, go thou; change at
    once
All the arrangements of the impious
    David;
For ev'ry one of them conceals a plot.
To-morrow fight we with the rising sun;
That beauteous day-star, of my hardi-
    hood
Shall be the witness. I am now aware,
That from malignity the thought arose
In David's breast, to choose the afternoon
For the attack, as most indicative
Of my declining arm: but, we shall see.—
I feel my martial spirits braced afresh
By thy rebukes; to-morrow I am leader;
The livelong day will be inadequate
To the great slaughter which I shall in-
    flict.—
Abner, now quickly from my presence drag
This miscreant, and dispatch him . . .

JONATHAN.　　　O my father! . . .
Great Heav'ns! . . . what art thou do-
ing? . . .
SAUL.　　　Hold thy peace.—
He shall be slain; and his unworthy blood
Shall fall on the Philistines.
ABNER.　　　Death is his
Already . . .
SAUL. But, to satisfy my vengeance
He only is too little. Let Nob feel
That vengeance also; let it smite, con-
sume,
Servants, and cattle, mothers, houses,
babes,
And to the desolating winds disperse
All the flagitious race. Thy priests may
now
Exclaim with truth: "There is a Saul."
My hand,
So oft by you provoked to homicide,
Never smote you: from hence, and hence
alone,
You scorn that hand.
AHIMELECH.　　No king can hinder me
From dying like a just man; whence my
death
Will be as welcome as it is illustrious.
Yours, for a long time, by Almighty God
Have been irrevocably seal'd: by swords,
Yet not in battle, not by hostile swords,
Abner and thou shall both be vilely
slain.—
Let me go hence.—I have at last ad-
dress'd
God's final sentence to the reprobate,
And he was deaf: my mission is accom-
plish'd:
I have lived faithful, faithful shall I die.
SAUL. Quick let him hence be dragg'd
to punishment;
To agonizing and protracted death.

SCENE V

[SAUL, JONATHAN.]
JONATHAN. Alas! rash king, what art
thou doing? pause . . .
SAUL. Must I once more command thee
to be silent?—
Art thou a warrior?—thou a son of mine?

Art thou a champion of the Israelites?—
Go, go; return to Nob; and there fill thou
His empty seat: thou worthy art alone
To live in indolence with drowsy priests,
Not 'mid the tumults of grim-visaged war,
Not 'mid the lofty cares of royalty . . .
JONATHAN. I also at thy side in combat
fierce
Have overcome, in multitudes, thy foes:
But this, which now thou dost presume
to shed,
Is sacerdotal, not Philistine, blood.
Alone thou standest in a fight so impious.
SAUL. I am alone sufficient for the con-
test,
Whate'er that contest be. Do thou to-
morrow,
Base one, reluctantly the battle join:
I only shall be Saul. What then avails
David? or Jonathan? Saul is the leader.
JONATHAN. Beside thee shall I fight.
Ah! may I fall
Lifeless beneath thine eyes, before I see
That which awaiteth thy unhappy blood!
SAUL. And what awaits it? death?
death in the field?
This is a monarch's death.

SCENE VI

[MICHAL, SAUL, JONATHAN.]
SAUL.　　　Thou, and no David? . . .
MICHAL. I cannot find him . . .
SAUL.　　　I will find him.
MICHAL.　　　He
P'rhaps is far distant; he avoids thy
anger . . .
SAUL. Though he had wings, my anger
should o'ertake him.
Woe, if in battle he presents himself:
Woe, if to-morrow, when my foes are con-
quer'd,
Thou bring'st him not to me.
MICHAL.　　　O Heav'ns!
JONATHAN.　　　Ah, father . . .
SAUL. I have no children.—Quickly,
Jonathan,
Resume thy place among the troops.—
And thou,
Seek, and find David.

MICHAL. Ah! . . . with thee . . .
SAUL. In vain.
JONATHAN. Father, shall I fight far
from thee?
SAUL. From me
Be all of you afar. Ye, all of you,
Vie with each other in betraying me.
Go, I command it: quickly fly from hence.

SCENE VII

[SAUL.]
SAUL. I to myself am left.—Myself
alone,
(Unhappy king!) myself alone I dread
not.

ACT V

SCENE I

[DAVID, MICHAL.]
MICHAL. Come forth, my consort;
come: the night already
Is far advanced . . . Dost hear what min-
gled sounds
Issue from yonder camp? The fierce en-
counter
To-morrow's dawn will witness.—Round
the tent
Where sleeps my father, ev'ry sound is
hush'd.
Behold; the heav'ns themselves assist thy
flight:
The moon is setting, and a black cloud
veils
Her latest rays. Let us depart: for no
one
Watches our footsteps now; let us depart;
We may descend the mountain by this
slope,
And God, where'er we go, will be our
guide.
DAVID. O spouse, the better portion of
my soul,
While Israel is preparing for attack,
Can it be true that I prepare for flight?
And what is death, that I should thus
avoid it?—
I will remain: Saul, if he will, may slay
me;

So that I first in numbers slay the foe.
MICHAL. Ah! thou know'st not: al-
ready hath the rage
Of Saul in blood his lifted arm embrued.
Ahimelech, discover'd here, hath fallen
The victim of his violence already.
DAVID. What do I hear? Hath he
indeed his sword
Turn'd on defenceless priests? Ill-fated
Saul! . . .
MICHAL. Thou must hear more. The
monarch gave himself
Cruel command to Abner, that, if thou
In battle shouldst be seen, our champions
should
Against thee turn their arms.
DAVID. And Jonathan,
My friend, bears this?
MICHAL. O Heav'ns! what can he do?
He too endured his father's rage; and ran
Distractedly 'mid combatants to die.
Now, thou see'st clearly, thou canst not
stay here:
Thou'rt forced to yield; to fly from hence;
and wait,
Or that my father change, or that he
bend
Beneath the weight of years . . . Ah, cruel
father!
'Tis thou thyself dost force thy wretched
daughter
To wish the fatal day . . . But yet, O no,
Thy death I do not wish for: live in
peace;
Live, if thou canst; 'twill be enough for
me
To dwell for ever in my consort's pres-
ence . . .
Ah, come then; let us go . . .
DAVID. How much I grieve
To leave the fight! I hear an unknown
voice
Cry in my heart: "For Israel and its
king
The dreadful day is come . . . Could I!
. . . But no:
The guiltless blood of sacred ministers
Was here pour'd out: the camp is now
impure,
Contaminate the soil; the face of God
Is hence averted: David now no more

Can combat here.—It is my duty, then,
To yield awhile to thy anxiety,
And careful love.—But, thou must yield
   to mine . . .
Ah! suffer me alone . . .
   MICHAL.   What! shall I leave thee?
Behold, I clasp thee by thy garment's
   hem;
No, never more I part from thee . . .
   DAVID.   Ah, hear me!
Ill could thy tardy steps keep pace with
   mine:
Paths rough with stocks and stones shall
   I be forced
To tread with indefatigable feet,
If I would seek, complying with thy wish,
A place of refuge. How can thy soft
   limbs
Bear up against the unaccustom'd tor-
   ment?
And shall I in the wilderness alone
Ever abandon thee? Thou seest clearly:
Owing to thee, I soon should be dis-
   cover'd:
Quickly would both of us be reconducted
To the fear'd vengeance of the king . . .
   O Heav'ns!
The mere thought makes me shudder . . .
   Further grant,
That we ensured our flight; can I remove
   thee
From thy sick sorrowing father? He is
   placed
Far from the dainty shelter of his palace,
Amid the hardships of a camp: his pangs,
His irritable age, some solace need.
Ah! soothe his grief, his fury, and his
   tears.
Thou only pleasest him; thou waitest on
   him,
And thou alone preservest him alive.
He wishes me destroy'd; but I would see
   him
Rescued from danger, happy, and tri-
   umphant: . . .
To-day I tremble for him—Ere thou wert
A wife, thou wert a daughter; 'tis not
   right
To love me overmuch. If I escape,
What further canst thou wish for me at
   present?

From thy already too-afflicted father
Do not depart. As soon as I'm in safety,
I'll cause the tidings to be sent to thee;
We shall, I hope, be reunited soon.
Think what it costs me to abandon
   thee . . .
Yet, . . . how? . . . alas! . . .
   MICHAL. Ah! must I once more lose
   thee? . . .
Once more permit thee to return alone
To former labors, to a wand'ring life,
To perils, and to solitary caves? . . .
Ah, if I only always were with thee! . . .
I might, perchanee, alleviate thy ills, . . .
By sharing them with thee . . .
   DAVID.   I do beseech thee,
By our affection; and, if there be need,
I also do command thee, as a lover;
Do not now follow me; thou canst not
   do it,
Without ensuring my effectual ruin.—
But, if God will my safety I ought not
To tarry longer here: the time advances:
Some spy from his pavilion might detect
   us,
And cruelly divulge our purposes.
I know each single corner of these hills;
And feel most certain that I can elude
All human vigilance.—Give, give me now
The last embrace. May God be thy sup-
   port!
And do thou never, never quit thy father,
Till Heav'n once more unite thee to thy
   consort . . .
   MICHAL. The last embrace? . . . And
   shall I then survive it? . . .
I feel, I feel my trembling heart-strings
   burst . . .
   DAVID. . . . And I? . . . But, . . . I be-
   seech thee . . . check thy tears.—
Wings to my feet now lend, Almighty
   God!

SCENE II

[MICHAL.]
   MICHAL. He flies? . . . O Heav'ns! . . .
   I will pursue him now . . .
But, with what iron fetters am I bound? . . .
I cannot follow him.—He flies from
   me! . . .

Scarce can I stand, much less o'ertake
  his steps . . .
Once more, then, have I lost him! . . .
  Who can tell,
When I shall see him? . . . And art thou
  a wife,
Thou wretched woman? . . . were thine
  nuptial rites? . . .
—No, no; no more beside my cruel father
Will I remain. I follow thee, O
  spouse . . . —
Yet, if I follow him, alas! I kill him;
Can I, to imitate his rapid steps,
Dissemble my slow pace? . . . —But, from
  yon camp
What murmur do I hear, like din of
  arms? . . .
I hear it plainly . . . and it waxes louder;
And with the trumpet's dissonance is
  mix'd . . .
The tramp of horses also . . . What is
  this? . . .
The fight before the rising of the sun,
Of this gave Saul no hint. Who knows?
  . . . Perchance
My brothers . . . Jonathan . . . Alas! . . .
  in danger . . .—
But, tears, and howlings, and deep groans
  I hear
From the pavilion of my father rise? . . .
Unhappy father! . . . I will run to meet
  him . . .
But . . . he himself approaches; O sad
  sight! . . .
How desolate he looks! . . . Alas, my
  father! . . .

SCENE III

[SAUL, MICHAL.]

SAUL. Incensed, tremendous shade, ah,
  go thy way!
Leave, leave me! . . . See: before thy feet
  I kneel . . .
Where can I fly? . . .—where can I hide
  myself?
O fierce, vindictive spectre, be appeased . . .
But to my supplications it is deaf;
And does it spurn me? . . . Burst asunder,
  earth,
Swallow me up alive . . . Ah! that at least

The fierce and threat'ning looks of that
  dire shade
May not quite pierce me through . . .
  MICHAL.   From whom dost fly?
No one pursues thee. Dost thou see me
  not,
Father? dost thou not know me?
  SAUL.   O most high,
Most holy priest, wilt thou that here I
  pause?
O Samuel, thou my real father once,
Dost thou command it? Prostrate, see,
  I fall
At thy supreme command. Thou, with thy
  hand,
Placedst the royal crown upon this head;
Thou didst adorn it; strip it, strip it
  now
Of all its honors; tread them under foot.
But O, . . . the flaming sword of God's
  revenge
Which glares eternally before my eyes, . . .
Thou, who canst do it, snatch it not from
  me,
O no, but from my children. Of my
  crime,
My children they are innocent . . .
  MICHAL.   O state
Of agony unparallel'd!—Thy sight
Bodies forth things that are not: father,
  turn
Thyself to me . . .
  SAUL.   O joy! . . . Is peace inscribed
Upon thy face? O fierce old man, hast
  thou
In part my prayers accepted? from thy
  feet
I will not rise, till thou hast first de-
  liver'd
My unoffending children from thy ven-
  geance.—
What voice exclaim'd: "And David was
  thy son;
"And thou didst persecute him, e'en to
  death"?
Of what dost thou accuse me? . . . Pause,
  O pause! . . .
David, where is he? find him: let him
  come;
And let him slay me at his will, and
  reign:

Provided only that he spare my children,
Be his the throne . . .—But, art thou
pitiless?
Thine eyes are orbs of blood; thy hand
is fire,
And fire thy sword; thy ample nostrils
breathe
Sulphureous flames, that glare and dart
at me . . .
They've caught me now; they burn my
heart to dust:
Where shall I fly? . . . I'll go in this
direction.
MICHAL. Cannot my hands restrain
thee, nor my voice
Convince thee of the truth? Ah, hear
me: thou . . .
SAUL. But no; on this side a prodi-
gious stream
Of blood restrains my steps. Atrocious
sight!
On both its shores in mountains are up-
piled
Great heaps of recent corpses: all is
death
On this side: thitherward I then will
fly . . .
But what do I behold? Who then are
ye?
"We are the children of Ahimelech.
I am Ahimelech. Die, Saul, then,
die."—
What cry is that? I recognize him
well:
With recent blood he reeks; let him drink
mine.
And who is this that drags me from be-
hind?
Thou, Samuel, thou?—What did he say?
that soon
We all should be with him? I only, I
Shall be with thee; but as for my poor
children . . .—
Where am I—In an instant from my
sight
Have all the spectres vanish'd. Where
am I?
What have I said? What am I doing?
Who
Art thou? What dissonance is this I
hear

It seems to me most like the din of
battle:
But the day dawns not yet: ah, yes, it is
The uproar of the battle. Quickly bring
My shield, my spear, my helmet: now with
speed
The weapons, the king's weapons. I will
die,
But in the camp.
MICHAL. What art thou doing, father?
Be tranquil . . . To thy daughter . . .
SAUL. I will have
My arms; what daughter? Now, thou
dost obey me.
My helm, my spear, my shield; behold
my children.
MICHAL. I will not leave thee, no . . .
SAUL. The trumpets sound
Louder and louder? Thither let me go:
For me my sword alone will be suffi-
cient.—
Thou, quit me, go; obey. I thither run:
There, where the death I seek for has its
home.

SCENE IV

[SAUL, MICHAL, ABNER, *with a few
fugitive Soldiers.*]
ABNER. O hapless king! . . . Now
whither dost thou fly?
This is a dreadful night.
SAUL. But, why this battle? . . .
ABNER. The foe assail'd us unawares:
we are
Wholly discomfited . . .
SAUL. Discomfited?
And liv'st thou, traitor?
ABNER. I? I live to save thee.
Hither perchance Philistia's hordes are
streaming:
We are compell'd to shun the first at-
tack:
Meanwhile the day will dawn. Thee will
I lead,
With my few followers, to yonder
slopes . . .
SAUL. Shall I then live, while all my
people fall?
ABNER. Ah, come! . . . Alas! the tumult
grows: approaches . . .

SAUL. My children, . . . Jonathan, . . .
do they too fly?
Do they abandon me?
ABNER. O Heav'ns! . . . Thy children, . . .
No, no; they fled not . . . Ill-starr'd
progeny! . . .
SAUL. I understand thee: they are all
destroy'd . . .
MICHAL. Alas! . . . My brothers? . . .
ABNER. Thou no more hast sons.
SAUL. —What now remains for me? . . .
Thou, thou alone,
But not for me, remainest.—In my heart
Have I been long time finally resolved:
And now the hour is come.—This, Abner,
is
The last of my commands. My daughter
now
Guide to some place of safety.
MICHAL. Father, no;
Around thee will I twine myself: the foe
Will never aim a sword against a woman.
SAUL. O daughter! . . . say no more:
compel me not
To weep. A conquer'd king should never
weep.
Save her, O Abner, go: but, if she fall
Within the foeman's hands, say not, O no,
That she's the child of Saul; but rather
tell them
That she is David's wife; they will respect
her.
Go; fly . . .
ABNER. She shall, I swear to thee, be
safe,

If I can aught avail; but thou mean-
time . . .
MICHAL. My father . . . ah! . . . I
will not, will not leave thee . . .
SAUL. I will it: and I yet am king.
But see,
The armèd bands approach. Fly, Abner,
fly:
Drag her by force with thee, if it be
needful.
MICHAL. O father! . . . and for
ever? . . .

SCENE V

[SAUL.]
SAUL. O my children! . . .
—I was a father.—See thyself alone,
O king; of thy so many friends and
servants,
Not one remains.—Inexorable God,
Is Thy retributory wrath appeased?—
But, thou remain'st to me, O sword: now
come,
My faithful servant in extremity.—
Hark, hark! the howlings of the haughty
victors:
The flashing of their burning torches
glares
Before my eyes already, and I see
Their swords by thousands . . .—O thou
vile Philistia,
Me thou shalt find, but like a king, here
. . . dead.—

THE CAVE OF SALAMANCA

By MIGUEL DE CERVANTES SAAVEDRA

Published in 1615, but probably produced before that time

TRANSLATED FOR THIS WORK BY M. JAGENDORF

CHARACTERS

PANCRACIO
LEONARDA, *his wife*
CRISTINA, *her maid*
CARRAOLANO, *a student*
REPONCE, *a sacristan*
THE VILLAGE BARBER
LEONISO, PANCRACIO'S *friend*

The stage shows PANCRACIO'S *house which is two stories high. A wall divides it from part of the stage which represents the street.*

[PANCRACIO'S *wife is discovered weeping while her maid* CRISTINA *and* PANCRACIO *stand by her side trying to console her.*]

PANCRACIO. Sweet wife and Madam, dry those tears; cease your sad weeping! Just remember it is but short four days that I'll be absent from you—not for eternity. On the fifth, at the very latest, I'll return, my pretty turtle dove—if the good Lord gives me life. Oh, oh, I'm so sorry to see you grieving. Perhaps . . . perhaps, just not to see those shimmering pearls in your eyes—I'd better break my word and give up this journey. My sister can enter solemn matrimony without me, I'm certain.

LEONARDA. Ah, no, my most agreeable Pancracio, most perfect of husbands, I'd not have you seem discourteous for my sake for anything in the world. Go, in God's name, my noble master, and fulfill your solemn, and serious, and worthy obligation. I shall control my uncontrollable grief and spend the lonely hours of your absence thinking of you. There is but one plea I have: do not stay a moment longer than you say, for if you do . . . I couldn't . . . Lord . . . Cristina . . . hold me . . . my heart is failing . . . from grief. . . .   [*She faints.*]

PANCRACIO. Lord! Water! A glass! Cristina, child . . . for her face. But hold! I know a few little words of magic . . . that cure fainting. [*He whispers into her ear and she recovers.*]

LEONARDA. Ah! Oh! Enough. That is a potent spell. What must be, must

88

be. I shall have patience, balm of my heart. Go quickly. The longer you tarry, the longer must my misery last. Leoniso, your friend, must surely be waiting for you at the coach. God be with you and may he direct your steps homeward as speedily and happily as I desire.

PANCRACIO. My adorable angel! Say but the word, and I shall be immovable as a statue riveted to this spot.

LEONARDA. No, my eternal love. Your wish is my command, and now I wish you to go, rather than stay. You gave your word of honor and your honor is mine as well.

CRISTINA. O model of perfect wifehood! On my word, were all wives as loving and as true to their husbands as my mistress Leonarda, this world would be a paradise.

LEONARDA. Come, Cristina, and get me my cloak. I would accompany my sweet husband to the coach.

PANCRACIO. No, not that. On my life that is thoughtfulness! All for my sake. Stay here, sweet—embrace me just once again. Cristina, dear, take care of your mistress. If you do, I shall bring you a pair of fine stockings when I return— just the kind you've been wishing for.

CRISTINA. Go along, good master, and don't worry about my mistress. I'll see to it that she doesn't grieve too much. I'll persuade her to have a little pleasure once in a while, so she won't think too often of your absence.

LEONARDA. I enjoy myself while my husband is away! Little do you understand my nature, child. Separated from the heart of my life's body no joy or pleasure can be mine, only pain and sorrow.

PANCRACIO. Lord! I can't stand this any longer. Farewell, happy light of my eyes, which henceforth shall see no light until they see you once again. [*He runs out overpowered by sorrow.*]

LEONARDA. Go! and may lightning strike you at the house of your sister, Anna Diaz! Go! and may you never return. By God! this time neither brag-ging nor avowals, neither cleverness nor watchfulness will help you.

CRISTINA. I was in terrible fear a thousand times that your protestings and weepings would prevent his going and our joys.

LEONARDA. Cristina, will they whose happy coming we long for be here this evening?

CRISTINA. Of course. I sent the good word long ago, and they were so overjoyed at the news they couldn't wait for evening to show it. This very afternoon, in full daylight, they sent by our washerwoman, whom you know we can trust, a load full of finest meats and wines and gifts, hidden in a basket of linen. It's a very treasure! It looks like the fruit baskets our good King gives to the poor on Holy Thursday, only it doesn't smack of Lent; rather of Easter: filled with meat pies, cold cuts, delicate fricassees and two capons which have not been even plucked. Besides there is every fruit you can think of. And best of all, there is a little skin of wine, pure, and clear, and with a rare bouquet.

LEONARDA. Just like Reponce. Always considerate and thoughtful—the sacristan of my soul.

CRISTINA. And what's wrong with my Nicolas, the barber of my heart and the shearer of my sorrows? No sooner am I in his presence than he clips and shears all unhappiness from me as if it had never existed.

LEONARDA. Did you hide the basket?

CRISTINA. I put it in the kitchen near the clothes hamper and covered it with old linen.

[*There is a knocking at the door.*]

LEONARDA. Cristina, look and see who is knocking.

[CARRAOLANO *the student enters without waiting to be invited.*]

CARRAOLANO. Charming ladies . . . only a poor student.

CRISTINA. That's not hard to guess. Your tattered clothes proclaim the student, your boldness the poverty. Queer, beggars never wait at the door for alms— no corner is safe from them. They never ask whether or not they disturb anyone.

CARRAOLANO. I expected a more generous and gracious reception from such lovely and sweet ladies; particularly since I ask no alms, only a corner in the stable or a bit of straw for protection against the threats of the darkened heavens, for the celestial sphere is threatening this sinful earth with the greatest severity.

LEONARDA. Where do you hail from, good friend?

CARRAOLANO. Salamancian am I, most gracious of mistresses—which means I come from the city of Salamanca. I was journeying with my uncle to Rome when the Lord, blessed be His name, took him from me on the way, while we were in the heart of sunny France. So when I found myself alone and forlorn, I decided to return to the land of my forefathers, but when I reached Catalonia, my servants, or the boon companions of Roque Guinarde, I don't know which, robbed me. I am certain the latter was not with the robbers, for he is kind and courteous and charitable and had he been there would never have permitted the robbery. I continued nevertheless until the threatening night overtook me at this hallowed door, for such it is to me at the moment. And that is why, good ladies, I am seeking shelter with you.

LEONARDA. In truth, Cristina, this student arouses my compassion.

CRISTINA. He has softened my heart as well. Let us keep him here for the night. He'll find plenty of consolation in the crumbs from the good basket. I mean your crying belly, poor student, will find silencing joys in the leftovers of a little treasure of food we have hereabouts right now. Besides, Mistress, he can help me pluck the fowls for supper.

LEONARDA. But hold, Cristina, are you willing to take into the house a witness to our coming lark?

CRISTINA. He looks as if he understood the wisdom of silent fishes. Come over here, good fellow, do you know anything about plucking?

CARRAOLANO. Eh, what! Plucking! I don't understand much about plucking unless you mean I look plucked. You need not rub it in, I confess myself the easiest fellow in the world for plucking.

CRISTINA. That's not what I mean; I swear, I only wanted to know if you could pluck a pair of capons.

CARRAOLANO. My sole reply to this, gracious Senorita, is that I am, by the grace of the good Lord, a graduate bachelor of the University of Salamanca. Which statement does not necessarily mean. . . .

LEONARDA. That is sufficient guarantee that you not only know how to pluck capons, but geese and humans as well. But how about the good virtue of silence? Does the fine scholar suffer from the temptation of telling all he sees—or hears—or imagines?

CARRAOLANO. You know the saying: Kill before my eyes a thousand more men than sheep in the slaughterhouse and I'll never open my lips to say a word.

CRISTINA. Well, if you'll close your mouth, sew your tongue at both ends and hold your teeth tight shut, you'll see marvels, feed like the king of Madrid, and get enough straw to stretch your limbs on to your heart's content.

CARRAOLANO. Seven feet of straw is all I seek, for I am far from greedy or pampered.

[*The sacristan,* REPONCE, *and the* BARBER *come in without knocking.*]

REPONCE. Greetings! How happy I am to see the driver and guide of my chariot of longing and joys! O burning star of my darkness! Fountain of tender caresses that are the foundation and pillars of my palace of desires!

LEONARDA. This talk always makes me angry. For Heaven's sake, Reponce, please speak in a more simple manner so I can understand you. Don't try to rise to where I cannot reach you.

BARBER. That's what I say. I speak straight as a shoe sole. What's on my lung, that's on my tongue, or something like that, as the saying goes.

REPONCE. Ah, quite true, quite true. Therein lies a difference between the learned sacristan and the ballad-whining barber.

CRISTINA. Well, for what I want him, my barber knows as much Latin as Antonio de Nebrija and a little more besides. But this is not the time to quarrel about highfalutin' talk or fine scholarship. Let us. all talk even as the tongue'll wag. And now to work, there's lots to be done.

CARRAOLANO. And plenty to pluck!

REPONCE. Who is the fellow there?

LEONARDA. A poor student from Salamanca who begged us for a night's shelter.

REPONCE. I'll give him a couple of coppers for supper and lodging and let him go in the Lord's name.

CARRAOLANO. Señor sacristan Reponce, I accept your generosity and alms with the deepest gratitude and wish to thank you eternally for it. But I am of the silent tribe and a perfect plucker, just as this charming young lady needs. She has invited me to stay and I swear by everything I'll not leave this house tonight even if the whole Universe tries to eject me. Don't you think you are a little hard on one with my accomplishments who is quite content to sleep on a bed of straw. And if you are so worried about the capons, my grand Turk, pluck them yourself. As far as I am concerned you may eat them bone, feathers and all, and may they rest easy in your stomach.

BARBER. Hm, this fellow seems more a rough knave than a poor beggar. I hope he doesn't turn things topsy-turvy.

CRISTINA. On my soul! he has courage, and his wit is to my liking. Let us go in and arrange the work. I'll see to it that he is busy with plucking and as silent as if he were at mass.

CARRAOLANO. Or at vespers.

REPONCE. Just the same, I'm a little bit afraid of your beggar student. I'll wager he knows more Latin than I do.

LEONARDA. I wish you had the courage he has. Don't worry so, my friend, charity is never wasted.

[*They go into the house. The stage is darkened a few seconds to indicate the lapse of some time.*]

[*Enter* PANCRACIO *and* LEONISO *his friend on the street.*]

LEONISO. I knew at once we'd lose a wheel. I knew it at once. There isn't a coachman who is not pigheaded when it comes to arguing. If he had gone but three paces the other way, we would have missed that rut and be now two leagues from here.

PANCRACIO. I mind it little. In truth I am happy to return so I can spend the night with my sweet wife Leonarda rather than at the inn. For when I left her she was almost dying with grief at my departure.

LEONISO. Ah, heaven blessed you with a treasure of a woman! a wonderful woman! Thank the Lord for that, good friend.

PANCRACIO. Aye, that I do indeed, very often—but I fear never enough to equal the blessing. No Lucretia is in her class, no Portia equals her. Honor and modesty have found their sanctuary in her.

LEONISO. If mine were not of a jealous disposition, I should have nothing to desire either. Which reminds me that I must go home too. Come with me and see me reach there. I feel safer than walking alone, just to this corner. [*They walk along to the opposite side of the stage.*] I'll see you to-morrow early, by then we'll surely have a coach for the journey. Good night, and may God be with you.

PANCRACIO. May God be with you as well. [*He walks out for a moment ostensibly to watch him.*]

[*Enter the* BARBER *and the* SACRISTAN *with guitars.* LEONARDA, CRISTINA *and the* STUDENT *follow and sit about. The* SACRISTAN'S *cassock is raised and girt around the waist. He is in high spirits and he shouts and sings while leaping about to the accompaniment of his guitar.*]

REPONCE. Perfect night! Glorious joys! Marvelous food, and oh, such wonderful love!

CRISTINA. Señor Sacristan Reponce, this is not a dancing hour, let us arrange the repast and the other little matters and leave dancing for later.

REPONCE [*keeping up his capers*]. Perfect night! Glorious joys! Marvelous food, and oh, such wonderful love!

LEONARDA. Oh, let him be, Cristina. I find a great deal of pleasure in watching his agility.

[PANCRACIO *comes back, goes over to door and knocks on it several times.*]

PANCRACIO [*without*]. Ho, there! Sleepyheads! Don't you hear me? How! The doors barred at this early hour. Ah, that shows the caution and virtue of my Leonarda.

LEONARDA. Oh, unfortunate me! The voice and knocking is that of my husband Pancracio. Something must have happened that caused him to return. Gentlemen, you must hide in the coal cellar. I mean the garret . . . where the coal is kept. Cristina, run, fly, lead 'm there while I stay Pancracio until you are safe.

CARRAOLANO. Frightful night! Terrible joy! Horrible food and miserable love!

CRISTINA. You are too slow. Come! Quick! everyone follow me.

[CARRAOLANO *lags behind.*]

PANCRACIO [*outside*]. What the fiends is this? Why don't you open the door, sleepysnails.

CARRAOLANO. Well . . . the truth is that I don't want to share the fate and accusation of these fellows. Hide them wherever you please, but put me in the straw loft so that if I am found I am taken for a beggar and not for a lover.

CRISTINA. Quick, quick, run; the door 'll crash in a minute from his beating. Quick, quick, run.

REPONCE. My heart's in my mouth.

BARBER. And mine is in my heels.

[*All except* LEONARDA *go out and the men follow her.* LEONARDA *goes to the little window near the door and peeps out.*]

LEONARDA. Who is this? Who is knocking?

PANCRACIO. It's your husband, my own loving Leonarda. Open the door; I've been banging at it for half an hour.

LEONARDA. From the voice I'd say you are my own sweet birdie, Pancracio, but then one cock's crowing is often the same as another's and therefore I am not yet quite convinced of your identity.

PANCRACIO. O unheard-of caution of a most virtuous and prudent wife! it's I, my sweetheart, your husband Pancracio. You may open the door in perfect safety.

LEONARDA. Step a bit the other way so I may see you the better. And now tell me what did I do when you left this afternoon?

PANCRACIO. You sighed and you cried and in the end you fell into a faint.

LEONARDA. Quite true. Quite right. Yet . . . tell me what kind of a mark have I on my left shoulder?

PANCRACIO. On your sweet left shoulder you have a birthmark—a delicate mole the size of half a royal, and three little hairs fine as three thousand threads of pure gold.

LEONARDA. Quite true, quite true . . . Yet . . . what is my maid's name?

PANCRACIO. Ei, ei, sweet silly, don't drag this on forever, Cristina is her name. Now, is there anything else?

LEONARDA. Oh, Cristina, Cristina dear, it really is your good master. It really is he. Open the door quickly, child.

CRISTINA [*within*]. Here I am, Señora, right here I am. One moment only. [*She comes in and walks slowly to the door and opens it.*] A thousand welcomes! But how is this, dear master? How is it that you returned so quickly from your journey?

LEONARDA. Ah, darling, tell us quickly. The fear that some misfortune caused your return leaves me almost lifeless.

PANCRACIO. Nothing happened; only a

wheel of the coach broke and so my good companion and I decided to return instead of spending the night in the open fields. To-morrow in the early morning we'll get once again under way, for there is still time. But what is this? Who is shouting?

CARRAOLANO [within]. Ho, there, open the door—kind people, I'm choking.

PANCRACIO. Ha! Was that voice in my house or in the street?

CRISTINA. May I die if it isn't the poor student whom I locked up in the straw loft so that he could sleep there for the night.

PANCRACIO. A student locked up in my house while I am away! Hm, that's not to my liking. Truly, good wife, if I weren't convinced of your great virtue, this locking up of a student would give me great cause for suspicion. But go Cristina, open the door, perhaps the bales of straw have fallen on his head.

CRISTINA. I'm going, I'm going at once. [Goes out.]

LEONARDA. He is a poor fellow from Salamanca who begged, in the name of the Lord, for a night's lodging, even if it were in the straw loft. And good sweet husband, you know my kind heart, I can't refuse anyone anything. But look, here he comes, that's him.

[CRISTINA and CARRAOLANO enter; the latter's hair and clothes are full of straw.]

CARRAOLANO. Ha, if I weren't so timid and less scrupulous and honorable I could have avoided the risk of choking in the straw, and besides, I would have dined better and slept on a softer and less dangerous bed.

PANCRACIO. And who pray, good fellow, would have given you better fare and bed.

CARRAOLANO. Who? why, my clever brain . . . but the fear of the law tied my hands.

PANCRACIO. Your clever brain, friend, must tread on dangerous paths to be afraid of the law.

CARRAOLANO. If I weren't in fear of the Inquisition, I'd use the rare knowledge I learned at home in the Cave of Salamanca—and dine—dine doubly well at my heir's expenses, as the saying goes. On second thought I may do it at that, for necessity not only compels, but excuses me as well. But am I certain that these lovely ladies would keep a secret even as I do.

PANCRACIO. Don't worry about them, good friend, but act as your impulse directs. I'll see to it that they are silent. I am burning with desire to see the marvelous miracles for which the famous Cave of Salamanca is renowned throughout the world.

CARRAOLANO. Señor, I wonder if you'd be satisfied with seeing me drag out here two devils in human form carrying on their shoulders a basket full of fine cold meats and other delicacies.

LEONARDA. Mother Mary! Devils in my house and before my very eyes! Lord help me, for I cannot help myself.

CRISTINA. That student has the devil in his heart. God grant that all ends well; I am shaking and quaking all over in fear.

PANCRACIO. Well then, I'd like to see this marvel—these Señores devils with their basket of delicacies—if it can be done without harm or danger to us. I must be certain that their appearance is not too frightful.

CARRAOLANO. I promise you they'll appear in the shape of the parish priest and the town barber his friend.

CRISTINA. Holy Lord! You don't mean to tell me in the guise of the good sacristan Reponce, and Master Roque, the town barber!!! Unfortunate men! to see themselves so changed to devils! But tell me, good brother, will they be baptized devils?

CARRAOLANO. An unusual new idea! Where the devil can you find baptized devils? Or why should devils be baptized at all? Though on the other hand, these may be baptized devils, for there is no rule that has not an exception.

Come on then, step aside. You are about to witness the great wonder.

LEONARDA [*low to* CRISTINA]. Oh, misfortune! Soon the cat'll be out of the bag. Our wickedness will be seen in full daylight. Lord, I am dead!

CRISTINA. Courage, Señora. A courageous heart can overcome any misfortune.

CARRAOLANO [*recitative*]. Come forth, ye avaricious knaves,
Who try to hide from misfortune in coal holes deep.
Come forth and bring out speedily and carefully,
The basket full of rare dainties for repast.
Quick, or I'll be forced to employ more forceful and harsh conjuring words—
Come forth and do not hesitate and procrastinate.
Come forth for if you wait,
There may be a tragic ending to the tale and I'll be forced to use more harsh and potent charm? [*He pauses here to see if they will come out while* PANCRACIO *watches him breathless and the women half scared to death from lack of knowledge as to what the student is driving at.*]
Ha! I know, I know how to treat these devils in human form who won't come out willingly. I shall go inside and cast on them so powerful an incantation, that not only will they come out, but fly out. That kind of fiend depends a great deal more on persuasion than on spells.
[*Exit.*]

PANCRACIO. If the fellow succeeds in his promise it will be the most marvelous and rare thing the world has ever seen.

LEONARDA. If he succeeds! Ah, I fear there is no doubt of that. Why should he make game of us?

CRISTINA. There is noise within. I swear he is bringing them out. See! Lord!!! He is coming back with the devils and the basket of food.

[*Enter the student followed by the* BARBER *and the sacristan with the basket.*]

LEONARDA. Lord Jesus! The two carrying the basket resemble the priest Reponce, and the barber of our square.

CRISTINA. Have a care, Lady, the good Lord's name should never be mentioned when devils are nigh.

REPONCE [*in a hollow voice*]. You may say what you please for we are like dogs in a smithy who sleep through all the hammering and the blowing. Nothing in this world can frighten or disturb us.

LEONARDA. Come a little nearer so I can taste what's in your basket—and you may all do likewise.

CARRAOLANO. I'll begin with the wine. [*He pours a glass from the skin that's in the basket, and drinks it.*] Fine! Excellent! Is it from Esquivias, Señor Sacri-Devil?

REPONCE. From Esquivias, I swear by . . .

CARRAOLANO. Stop! Control yourself. For the Lord's sake, say not another word. I'm no friend of cursing devils. Little Satan! Gentle little Satans, we are not here to commit mortal sins, but to spend a few happy hours and then in the Lord's name depart in peace.

CRISTINA. Will they eat with us?

PANCRACIO. Yes, can they? For devils don't eat.

BARBER. Some devils don't eat and some do. We are the eating kind.

CRISTINA. Good master, let these poor devils stay. It would be most discourteous to let them die of hunger, seeing it was they who brought the fine food for supper. Besides they seem honorable devils and very genteel people.

LEONARDA. As for me, I don't mind their staying one bit provided my good husband has no objections and they do nothing to frighten us.

PANCRACIO. They may remain for I would see with my own eyes what I've never seen before.

BARBER. May the good Lord repay you for your generous deed, kind Señores.

CRISTINA. Oh, how polite and well behaved! May I never meet good fortune if from now on I am not a good friend to all devils—provided they are like these.

REPONCE. If the wind blows this way then listen well so that henceforth you may truly love our kind. [*He plays on his guitar and sings; the* BARBER *joins him in the chorus.*]

REPONCE. Ye who know nothing, give ear and follow.

My tale of the marvels contained in that hollow.

BARBER. The Cave of Salamanca.

REPONCE. Tudanca, learned master, wrote wise words and fair

On the hintermost part of the hide from a mare,

Praising to heaven the wonders that were.

BARBER. The Cave of Salamanca.

REPONCE. Rich men and poor men from near and afar

Sit on long benches blackened with tar

Where teachers and students seek and devise;

And those who came simple, go away from here wise.

In one chosen spot only this great bounty lies:

BARBER. The Cave of Salamanca.

REPONCE. Dark Moors who work here come forth learned and whiter;

The dullest of scholars leave here much brighter.

Untold are the joys of those who study and live here;

So join us with zest, to eternity cheer.

BARBER. The Cave of Salamanca.

REPONCE. May each year our enchanter, if he be from Loranca,

Have ten hundred flasks of wine white and red;

And we pray that with stout hickory sticks will be whipped

The devil who touches a hair on his head,

And worse—may he never be served in good stead, by

BARBER. The Cave of Salamanca.

CRISTINA. Enough, enough. Now you can see that devils can be poets too.

BARBER. Aye, so they can. And all poets are devils.

PANCRACIO. But tell me, good Señores Devils, since devils are supposed to know everything, where were all the dances invented? The Sarabande, the Zambapalo, the Dello me Pesa, and the one I like least of all, the newfangled Escarramán?

BARBER. Where? Why, in hell. That is their birthplace and breeding place.

PANCRACIO. Aye, I believe that full well.

LEONARDA. Truly, were it not for my good name and honor, I think I'd try them myself. I honestly believe I have all the abilities of an Escarramán dancer.

REPONCE. If I were permitted to teach you four steps daily, dear lady, I am certain within a week you'd be the leader on the dance floor. For I know well you possess all qualifications for perfection.

CARRAOLANO. Well, everything in good time, but now let's to supper; that is the most important thing this moment.

PANCRACIO. Yes, let us go in for I am still anxious to find out whether devils eat or not, and the truth of a thousand other things I've heard about them. By God, they won't leave this house until they have taught me all the knowledge and all the arts of the Cave of Salamanca. [*They go out one behind the other while the curtain drops.*]

THE KING, THE GREATEST ALCALDE

By LOPE FELIX DE VEGA CARPIO

Published 1636

TRANSLATED BY JOHN GARRETT UNDERHILL *

CHARACTERS

SANCHO
DON TELLO
CELIO
JULIO
NUÑO
ELVIRA
FELICIANA
JUANA
LEONOR
DON ALFONSO VII *of León and Castile*
THE COUNT DON PEDRO
DON ENRIQUE
BRITO
PELAYO
FILENO
PEASANTS, SERVANTS, AND ATTENDANTS

The scene is laid at León and in a Galician town and its neighborhood.

ACT I

A field on the banks of the Sil.

SANCHO. You noble pastures of Galicia,

Under the shadow of these mountain sides,
Whose skirts the Sil amid his rushes green
Would kiss, sustenance to the marshalled host

---

* Revised by the translator for this work from an earlier version published in *Poet Lore*, 1918. Copyright, 1918, by the Poet Lore Company.

Of flowers, varied in a thousand hues,
you give.
You birds that sing of love, you beasts
that roam
Untrammeled of restraint, where have you
seen
More tender love in birds or beasts or
flowers?
But since it is impossible to see
Aught else of all the sun looks down upon
More beautiful than my Elvira is,
Nor aught else may be born, so, being
born,
Of her great beauty by necessity
My love is sprung, which from her favor
draws
Its brightest glory; no greater beauty is,
No greater beauty and no greater love.
Alas, sweet lady, may your beauty grow
That so in me may grow the love I
bear!
But ah! Most beautiful of them that
toil,
Since beauty cannot find in thee increase,
Nor loving in my heart betimes, then
know
I love you for the beauty that you show,
There is naught else to such endearment
binds.
The pallid sands of this swift rivulet
You turned but yesterday to gleaming
pearls,
Setting your feet therein, lilies of snow;
While I cried out, because I scarce could
see,
Unto the sun, your face, wherewith you
shed
Such radiance of light—who would not
stay—
That he should look upon the water there,
So all your beauty might be visible.
Linen, Elvira, you were washing linen,
Which all your labor never could make
white
For magic of the hands you laid thereon.
And I, behind these chestnuts, gazed on
you
With trembling, till suddenly I saw that
love
Had handed you the bandage from his
eyes,
In his rich favor given you to lave.

But heaven forbids that love should go
unblinded
I' the world! . . . Oh God! But when
shall come that day
(On which I too must die), when at the
last
I say to her: "Elvira, you are mine?"
What gifts and presents I shall shower on
you!
I am no fool not to esteem your worth,
Each year more priceless dear in my af-
fection.
Know in the realms of my heart's rich
possession,
There are no provinces of mean disdain.

[*Enter* ELVIRA.]

ELVIRA [*aside*]. Either Sancho came
down this way, or else my hopes deceive
me. In faith, there he is now! . . . I
knew my heart would find him out. He
was looking in the brook where he sur-
prised me yesterday. Does he think, I
wonder, my shadow stays behind? Ah!
But I was angry when I saw him looking
at me in the water! [*Aloud.*] What are
you looking for, Sancho—whom God bless!
—in the sands of these swift mountain
brooks, every time that you come out to
the pasture? Have you found the corals
which I lost here by the bank?

SANCHO. I was looking for myself—
I lost myself here yesterday, but now I
begin to find myself again, because I
find myself with you.

ELVIRA. I know you have come to help
me find them.

SANCHO. A pretty thing to do—to look
for what you are bringing with you in
your cheeks. I wonder is it modesty or
disdain? But I have found the jewels.

ELVIRA. Where?

SANCHO. There on your lips—and look
out! [*Kisses her.*] All bordered about
with silver!

ELVIRA. Let me go!

SANCHO. Always ungrateful for my
faith and loyalty!

ELVIRA. Sancho, you are too bold.
What more would you do, tell me that,
if by any chance it were the eve of your
wedding day?

SANCHO. But whose fault was it?

ELVIRA. Yours, by my faith!

SANCHO. Mine? No, because I warned you; my heart spoke but you said nothing.

ELVIRA. What better answer could you want than to have me say nothing?

SANCHO. We are both to blame.

ELVIRA. Since you are so cautious, Sancho, let me tell you that we women say most when we are silent. We give when we deny. Judge by this and by what you see and never believe us, whether we are cruel or kind. For everything we do is to be taken by opposites.

SANCHO. Then if that is so, you give me permission to ask Nuño to let us marry. You say nothing? You say yes then. Good! I have mastered the science.

ELVIRA. You have; but you must never tell him that I love you.

SANCHO. Here he comes.

ELVIRA. I will hide behind this elm and wait his answer.

SANCHO. Oh God! If it might be that we should marry! If not, I die.

[ELVIRA conceals herself.]

[Enter NUÑO and PELAYO.]

NUÑO [to PELAYO]. You serve me in such sort, Pelayo, it would be better for me to find some one who would keep a sharper watch over my flocks along the river bank. Are you discontented in my house?

PELAYO. God knows I am.

NUÑO. Then your employment ends today; service is not marriage.

PELAYO. It ought to come before it.

NUÑO. You have lost my hogs.

PELAYO. But with my mind where it was, what else was I to do? Listen; I want to become one of the family.

NUÑO. Why not? By all means do. But never blame then your hoggishness on me . . .

PELAYO. Wait; it's not easy to explain . . .

NUÑO. Wait, and it will be harder to do.

PELAYO. As she was coming out of the house yesterday, Elvira called to me: "Hello, Pelayo! Your pigs are fat."

NUÑO. Well, what did you answer?

PELAYO. Amen, like the sacristan.

NUÑO. You did? But what do you make of this?

PELAYO. Don't you see?

NUÑO. How should I?

PELAYO. She has lost all sense of shame.

SANCHO [apart]. Will the blockhead never go?

PELAYO. Don't you see she loves me, and this is the way she takes to let me know that she wants to marry?

NUÑO. God bless us!

PELAYO. I didn't tell you, though, so as to make you angry at our happiness.

NUÑO. Sancho! You here? . . .

SANCHO. Waiting to speak with you.

NUÑO. At once.—Pelayo, a moment . . . wait. [Leaving PELAYO.]

SANCHO. Nuño, my fathers ever as you know
Were humble laborers, who bore no stain;
Honest in station, in custom grave and slow.

PELAYO. Sancho, you know what tricks these lovers feign.
To have a rich and pretty woman say
To a poor fellow fresh as flowers of Spain,
"Your pigs are fat"—would she not mean, I pray,
She'd like to marry somehow with that man?

SANCHO. Her thoughts indeed might tend the marriage way.

NUÑO. Out, rascal, out! Begone!

SANCHO. You know how ran
Their fame and their integrity. My love
Will not offend your honor—no true love can.
I burn for my Elvira, consumed above, Below.

PELAYO. A friend of mine he had a herd
So thin—jerked beef hung up above the stove!
When I take my pigs out you'd cry absurd . . .

NUÑO. You here yet, booby? Now by all the blue! . . .

PELAYO. Shall we talk of Elvira or swop word
About the pigs?

SANCHO. Sir, since you know how true
My love . . .

PELAYO. Sir, since you know how far
she'd go . . .

NUÑO. What ruder savage ever Indies
grew?

SANCHO. Approve our marriage with
due rites and show.

PELAYO. I led a hog along the bank
here past her . . .

NUÑO. The wretched fool will split my
head I know.

PELAYO. Who would have made a per-
fect chapel master,
The voice he had it was so harsh and
rude.
While going in and out the grunts came
faster . . .

NUÑO. What does Elvira say?

SANCHO.   She has been wooed
And won, and gives consent I ask her
hand.

NUÑO. Happy her fortune with such
love endued!
Sancho, she knows what simple virtues
stand
Within your heart, well meriting in
meed
The noblest lady that e'er graced the
land.

PELAYO. With four or five hogs such as
now I feed—
Which would beget yet others in six
years—
I'd soon be having horses from the breed.

NUÑO. You serve Don Tello in his
flocks, who rears
His power over these lands, and is su-
preme
Through all Galicia, nor aught he fears
In foreign realms. His servant, Sancho,
I deem
It fit you lay perforce your full intent
Before him. Rich and bounteous in ex-
treme,
He might bestow a portion of his rent
On you, of these the flocks you tend. So
poor
Elvira's dowry is, that her consent
Is all its sum. See this rude house, whose
door

Is set amid these pastures; its rafters
bare
The thick smoke blackens, finding no
vent. Four
Far distant fields I have, waiting the
share—
Ten or a dozen chestnuts. All is naught,
Unless the master of these lands should
add
Some gift with clothing or employment
fraught.

SANCHO. To put my love in doubt
makes my heart sad!

PELAYO [aside]. Sunshine and heaven!
He marry Elvira? . . . Tiring!
Well, I abandon her; my love turns
bad.

SANCHO. What more could any lover
ask, expiring
For her great beauty than her beauty's
store?
Celestial wonder with the world admir-
ing!—
My mind is not so low, so crabbed, sore
But her great virtue moves me more than
dower.

NUÑO. It is no shame to speak with
your señor,
Nor need you fear to supplicate his power.
He and his sister else might easily
Withdraw their favor, Sancho, in ill hour.

SANCHO. I go against my judgment;
finally
I go since you command it.

NUÑO.   May God bless,
Sancho, both you and your posterity.—
Pelayo, come with me.

PELAYO.   What foolishness
To give him to Elvira and not me!

NUÑO. Sancho is young and honest;
noble no less.

PELAYO. And for a countryman you
shall not see
His equal. That's the truth, to put it
mild.
But in the house far better let me be,
And every month count on a fresh grand-
child.   [*Exeunt* NUÑO *and* PELAYO.]

SANCHO. Come forth, Elvira of my
eyes! Oh come
My priceless, beauteous treasure!

[ELVIRA *advances*.]

ELVIRA [*aside*]. O God! What doubts
Love harbors hiding, and trembles in dis-
    trust.
My anxious hopes hang only by a hair.

    SANCHO. Your father says that he has
    pledged your hand
To a youth in service of Don Tello here.
Alas! What strange extremity of fate!

    ELVIRA. Then not in vain did love hang
    all my hopes
Upon a hair. You say my father, Sancho,
Would give me to a squire in service?
    Then
To-day I end my life; I die to-day.
Ah, live, sweet sorrow, live! I take my
    life.

    SANCHO. An end, Elvira, this is jesting
    only.
See how my soul leaps up into my eyes
And yield you to their plain sincerity.
Because he answered *yes* a thousand times
Without delay.

    ELVIRA.   I do not weep for you.
No, Sancho, it is going to the Palace.
My bringing-up upon this humble farm
Will be a source of shame continually.
You know it is the truth.

    SANCHO.   Foolish love deceived me!
Ah, live, my foolish care! I end my life.
All was deception of Elvira only,
In whose pure snows I burn!

    ELVIRA. An end then, Sancho, this is
    jesting only;
See how my soul leaps up into my eyes,
For love and a too anxious expectation
Have taught this lesson by quick defini-
    tion:—
True love is but reprisal and disdain.

    SANCHO. But then I am your husband?
    ELVIRA.   Did you not say
It was arranged?

    SANCHO.   Elvira, without my asking
Your father yet has proffered his advice.
It is his wish I go and seek consent
Of Lord Don Tello, since he is my master
As of these lands, in peace and war su-
    preme.
Although, Elvira, I have gained in you
The summed and sovereign treasure of the
    world

(The sun beholds in you both Indian
    realms
Mirrored in beauty), yet Nuño wills it so,
Because he is my master. He, in sooth,
Is old in the world, experienced and wise;
So his opinion must command respect.
Besides he is your father. Light of my
    eyes,
I go to speak with him!

    ELVIRA.   I wait you here.

    SANCHO. May heaven grant a thousand
    happy gifts
From him and from his sister!

    ELVIRA.   It is enough
That he should know.

    SANCHO.   I leave my life and soul
Within these tender hands. But grant me
    one!

    ELVIRA. They both are yours. Take
    and look on it there.

    SANCHO. With this in mine, what can
    fate do against me?
Now you shall know the steadfast heart I
    bear
After such priceless favor. I learn of love
To see, to value and to understand!

                    [*Exeunt*.]

A Court or Enclosure before the House of
    DON TELLO *in Galicia*.

    [*Enter* DON TELLO, CELIO *and* JULIO
        from the chase.]

    DON TELLO. Take in the spear.

    JULIO.   It was a famous chase.

    CELIO. What sport we had to-day!

    DON TELLO.   Every field
Lies brilliant in the sun, so beautiful
To sense their hues is like a holiday.

    CELIO. How softly winding the rivulets
    creep up
To kiss the blossom's feet!

    DON TELLO.   Go feed the dogs,
Celio, as you love God.

    CELIO.   How well they rose
Over the crests and ridges of the moun-
    tains!

    JULIO. Two famous dogs.

    CELIO.   And Florisel's the flower
Of all the country.

    DON TELLO.   Galaor does well.

JULIO. He is a famous hound.
CELIO.   My lady, sir—
Your sister hears you come.

[*Enter* FELICIANA.]
DON TELLO.   What loving care!
And how repaid by me, Feliciana,
This watchfulness in you!
FELICIANA.   When you are gone,
I am in such disquiet for you, my lord,
As God knows. Nothing but vexes me;
I cannot sleep; I am deprived of rest,
Nor hare nor rabbit, puny howso'er,
But is as fearsome to me as wild beast.
DON TELLO. Among the mountains of
Galicia
There are no wild beasts, sister, though
blood of youth
Is avid of the wild. Sometimes, mayhap,
A boar runs out from the thick mountain
cover,
Whose marvellous exploits time and again
Myself have seen performed. They are
wild beasts
That with the tusk, e'en at the horse's
croup,
Will rive the armored collar from the
hound;
And yet therewith so ill appease their
rage,
To sum destruction at its savage full,
They barter their hot and fiercely foaming
breath
For the gushing blood which from his
flank is drawn.
There is beside, the roving bear, which
falls
Upon the huntsman as he roams along,
With such resistless, ungovernable rage
As ofttimes bears him lifeless to the
ground.
But day by day the ordinary chase
Is humble though various, not to tempt
heaven.
It is right worthy of the gentleman,
Of princes even, for in it are taught
The precepts of high war; it whets the
steel
And skills the body in the use of arms.
FELICIANA. I should not give myself
this anxious care
Were you but married, losing all my sleep.

DON TELLO. I know no equal, being so
powerful here.
FELICIANA. The daughter of some pros-
perous gentleman
Living near-by, would suit you well
enough.
DON TELLO. I believe you chide me for
my want of thought
About your marriage—a care that's ever
born
With women.
FELICIANA. On your life you are de-
ceived!
I only seek your good.

[*Enter* SANCHO *and* PELAYO, *behind the
bars of the enclosure.*]
PELAYO. Soft! Come in. They are alone.
No one is here who will prevent you.
SANCHO. You are right, for those who
are with them are all of the house.
PELAYO. Now you will see what they
give you.
SANCHO. I but comply with the de-
mands of duty. [*They pass the bars.*]
Most noble and illustrious Don Tello,
And you, O beautiful Feliciana,
Who are the lords and masters of these
lands
Whom I have oft-repeated cause to love,
Grant Sancho your most generous feet to
kiss—
Sancho who herds your flocks and tends
your pasture,
An office humble in so high a house.
But in Galicia, great lords and masters,
Each man is so high-born, only in this
That he is in the service of the rich,
The poor man yields to him. Know I am
poor,
And in the simple office of my speech,
Most plain you should not note me; for
your train
Passes a hundred thirty persons serving,
Who eat your food and wait upon your
bounty.
Yet sometimes in the chase I make so bold
To think you must have seen me.
DON TELLO.   I have indeed,
And with your bearing I have been well
pleased
And I esteem you well.

SANCHO.　　　　　　A thousand times
I kiss your feet in payment of such favor.
DON TELLO.　　　　　What would you?
SANCHO.　　Great my Lord, the years
　pass by
With such relentless pace, it seems post-
　haste
They rush with letters to the realms of
　death,
While life holds but brief lodging through
　the night,
Death coming in the morning. My days
　are lonely;
My father was a man of worth, who died
Ere he knew service. The line of our poor
　house
In me is ended. So I fain would wed
An honorable maid, who is the child
Of Nuño of Aibar, who tills your fields
But yet can point to the emblazoned
　shields
Upon the time-scarred scutcheon of his
　door,
And still retains with them from that
　proud day
Some lances. These—and the virtues of
　Elvira—
For so the bride is called—have won my
　heart.
She loves me and her father gives con-
　sent,
Though not without your license. Only
　to-day
He bade me learn it was the lord's to
　know
All that is done or happens in his house,
From deed of humblest vassal to his most
　proud
That fattens on his revenues; and kings
Are much at fault if they attend not this,
Which seldom they attend. I took his
　counsel
And here am come, my Lord, as he com-
　mands,
To tell you of my marriage.
DON TELLO.　　　　　Nuño is wise,
Nor may such excellent advice be paid
In moderation.—Celio!
CELIO.　　　　　　　Señor!
DON TELLO. Give Sancho twenty cows;
　a hundred sheep

Add you thereto. I and my sister both
Honor this wedding.
SANCHO.　　Such favor!
PELAYO.　　Favor such?
SANCHO.　　Such great bounty!
PELAYO.　　Such bounty? Great!
SANCHO.　　Oh, rare virtue!
PELAYO.　　Virtue—Oh, rare!
SANCHO.　　Lordly mien!
PELAYO.　　Mien? Lordly!
SANCHO.　　And pity, saintly lady!
PELAYO.　　Saintly lady? Pity!
DON TELLO.　　Who is this boor who
　mimics what you speak
And keeps you company?
PELAYO.　　　　　　　I am the one
Who puts hind-end first whatever he can
　say.
SANCHO.　　He is, my Lord, in Nuño's
　service.
PELAYO. My Lord,
I am indeed a prodigy of Nuño's.
DON TELLO.　　　　　　　What?
PELAYO. Why, the man who tends his
　pigs, of course!
I come to ask a favor of you too.
DON TELLO. Whom would you marry?
PELAYO.　　　Señor, no one just now;
But lest the devil get the best of me,
I'd like to ask you for a calf or two,
In case I need it. In Masalanca once
An old astrologer he told me this:
"Beware of bulls. There's always trouble
　with them."
He predicted water too was dangerous;
Since when I've never had the least desire
Either to marry or take a drink of water.
So as to avoid all trouble.
FELICIANA.　　　　　Simple fellow!
DON TELLO. No niggard of his wit.
FELICIANA.　　　　Sancho, begone
In happy hour.—And you look to it well
The cows and sheep be driven to his cot.
SANCHO.　　My poor rude tongue can
　never celebrate
Your towering glory.
DON TELLO.　　When do you marry?
SANCHO. This very night, for so my
　love commands.
DON TELLO. See where the sun shuts
　off his faltering light!

Amid his clouds of gold he sudden sinks
Into the West.   Go then, prepare the
    feast;
I and my sister grace it with our presence.
Ho there!   Make ready the coach!
    SANCHO.   My heart and tongue
Are bound, great Lord, in your eternal
    praise.   [*Exit.*]
    FELICIANA. But are you sure you will
not marry too?
    PELAYO. I was to marry, lady, too, the
    bride
Of this same fellow, who's a shapely lass
If ever one was in Galicia.
She knew, though, I kept pigs, and so she
    up
And turned me down for one.
    FELICIANA.   God keep you, friend,
For she was not deceived.
    PELAYO.   No more she was;
All of us are, Señora, what . . .
    FELICIANA.   Well, what?
    PELAYO. Well, what our parents passed
    along.   [*Exit.*]
    FELICIANA. The fellow pleases me.
    CELIO [*to* DON TELLO]. Now, by my
    troth,
The rustic is no fool in what he speaks;
Thereon Your Lordship may indeed rely.
The girl is first in all Galicia
In beauty—one who both by form and
    feature,
By rare discretion and by honesty,
With added virtues thereto infinite,
Might well shed lustre on the noblest scion
Of all the land of Spain.
    FELICIANA.   Is she so fair?
    CELIO. She is an angel.
    DON TELLO.   How easy 'tis to see
You speak, Celio, from the heart!
    CELIO.   I do.
I had some feeling once, and on my life
I could not be deceived.
    DON TELLO. Some country girls there
    are, devoid of paint
Or ornament, who draw all eyes to them,
And with the eyes the soul; but they are
    coy
And so uncommon disdainful of their
    favors,
The pretense wearies me.

    FELICIANA.   Rather, meseems,
Those who defend themselves are more
    esteemed.   [*Exeunt.*]

            A room in NUÑO'S *house.*

    NUÑO. Did Don Tello say that?
    SANCHO. He did, sir.
    NUÑO. Surely he answers in a manner
befitting his great worth.
    SANCHO. He commanded them to give
me the flock as I have told you.
    NUÑO. May he live a thousand years!
    SANCHO. And although it is too great
a gift, I value the honor he does me by
coming to be my sponsor more.
    NUÑO. But is his sister to be with him
too?
    SANCHO. She is.
    NUÑO. Such a generous disposition is
the direct gift of heaven.
    SANCHO. They are liberal masters.
    NUÑO. Oh, that this house might be a
splendid palace, since it is to entertain the
richest and the most powerful guests in all
the kingdom!
    SANCHO. Make no trouble about that.
It will be the same in their eyes as if it
covered infinite space. In short, they will
presently be here.
    NUÑO. What good advice I gave you!
    SANCHO. I have certainly found in Don
Tello a complete and perfect master. Take
generosity away from the master, in which
he is most like to God, and he is no more
a master; but that he is one is seen both
in his giving and his bestowing honor.
Since it is God's will to make his sov-
ereign virtue known by giving, without
giving and without bestowing honor, no
master can be master.
    NUÑO. A hundred sheep! Twenty cows!
It will be a goodly fortune as you lead
them out along the pastures of the Sil in
the springtime.   May God reward Don
Tello for so rich a gift and such priceless
favor!
    SANCHO. Where is Elvira, sir?
    NUÑO. Busy with her hair or some
frippery of her wedding dress.
    SANCHO. As long as she retains her

smile, she can dispense with curls and ornaments; for it is all sunshine.

NUÑO. You are no rustic lover.

SANCHO. I shall bring to her, sir, the steadfastness of the laborer and the devotion of the courtier.

NUÑO. No man can love worthily who is deficient in understanding; for the very essence of love is this—that we feel what we feel. I rejoice that it is so with you. Call in the men! I will have this gentleman to know I too am someone here—I am or I have been.

SANCHO. I think I hear my masters draw near; and they will follow them. Tell Elvira to leave her hair and make ready to receive their blessing.

[*Enter* DON TELLO *and* ATTENDANTS; *also* PELAYO, JUANA, LEONOR *and other* PEASANTS.]

DON TELLO. Where is my sister?

JUANA. She has gone in to the bride.

SANCHO. Señor . . .

DON TELLO. Sancho!

SANCHO. It would be madness, with my rude wit, to attempt to return thanks for this great honor.

DON TELLO. Where is the father of the bride?

NUÑO. Where his years have already been enriched by your unbounded favor!

DON TELLO. Come to my arms!

NUÑO. Would that my house were a world, and you lord of that world!

DON TELLO [*to* JUANA]. What is your name, little one?

PELAYO. Pelayo, sir.

DON TELLO. I did not speak to you.

PELAYO. You did not speak to me?

JUANA. Juana, at your service.

DON TELLO. Well said!

PELAYO. Even if he doesn't know it. But if a man gets after her in the kitchen, I tell you she hits him a blow with the ladle that's enough to curdle his wits. Once when I got as far as the *olla*, there was nothing left of me for two whole months together.

DON TELLO [*to* LEONOR]. And what is your name?

PELAYO. Pelayo, sir.

DON TELLO. I did not speak to you.

PELAYO. I thought you did speak to me.

DON TELLO. What is your name?

LEONOR. Mine? Leonor.

PELAYO [*aside*]. Why is he questioning the girls all the time, and never a word to us young fellows? [*Aloud.*] I am Pelayo, sir.

DON TELLO. Well? What have you to do with them?

PELAYO. I am the swineherd; yes, sir.

DON TELLO. I mean are you a husband, a brother?

NUÑO. What a blockhead you are!

SANCHO. What an ignorant clown!

PELAYO. As my mother made me.

SANCHO. Here come your sister and the bride.

[*Enter* FELICIANA *and* ELVIRA.]

FELICIANA. Brother, show them favor. Happy the masters who can count such vassals!

DON TELLO. You are right, in God's name! A beautiful girl!

FELICIANA. And spirited as well.

ELVIRA. Modesty overcomes me—it is the first time—I never looked upon your Lordship before.

NUÑO. My Lords, sit down; these chairs are all I have.

DON TELLO [*aside*]. I never saw such loveliness. What heavenly perfection! Their praise has been too small. Happy the hope that waits on such possession!

PELAYO. Give Sancho permission to sit down.

DON TELLO. Sit down.

SANCHO. No, my Lord.

DON TELLO. Sit down!

SANCHO. Such an honor to me in the presence of my Lady?

FELICIANA. Sit down by the bride; there is no one now to dispute the place with you.

DON TELLO [*aside*]. In all my life I never thought to see such strange, surpassing beauty.

PELAYO. And I—where shall I sit?

SANCHO. Out there in the stable; there you can solemnize the feast.

DON TELLO [aside]. In God's name, I am on fire! [Aloud.] What is your name?

PELAYO. Pelayo, sir.

NUÑO. Will you be silent? He was talking to the women; and you were counting yourself in with the girls. Elvira is her name, my Lord.

DON TELLO. By God then, but Elvira is beautiful and worthy, however great a miracle it seem, of a husband nobly born!

NUÑO. Girls, let the wedding be merry.

DON TELLO [aside]. What rare beauty!

NUÑO. Dance until the priest comes, as you are wont to do.

JUANA. The priest is already here.

DON TELLO. Then tell the priest that he shall not come in. [Aside.] Such heavenly beauty steals my heart away!

SANCHO. But why, Señor?

DON TELLO. Because it is my will, Knowing you further, to honor you the more.

SANCHO. I wish no other honor than to win Elvira, and I expect none other.

DON TELLO. To-morrow will do better.

SANCHO. Do not delay, my Lord, such priceless blessing;
But see my eager pain! An accident,
A trifle even betwixt this hour and morning
May snatch from me the good which now I hold,
Wherewith the present richly overflows.
For if philosophers speak any truth
Well spoke the sage who said it was the sun
Which brought all change and passing to the world.
How then can I tell
Subject to his spell,
What untoward thing
The dawn may bring
From other worlds to-morrow?

DON TELLO [aside].   Low in mind
And in condition low! *

_____

* A verse is missing here.—_Menéndez y Pelayo._

[Apart to FELICIANA.] I would do him honor
And make a holiday; but he, poor fool,
Before your face persists, dear sister mine,
In his dishonest purpose.—Nuño, I say!
Take her away! Rest all in peace to-night!

NUÑO. I do your bidding.
[Exeunt DON TELLO, FELICIANA and ATTENDANTS.]

NUÑO [apart]. This is unjust, meseems.
What is't should cause Don Tello such offense?

ELVIRA [apart]. I dare not answer, not to brand my thoughts
As evil.

NUÑO [to them both]. I do not understand his purpose.
Nor what he fain would do. He is my master,
But in my heart it irks me that he came.
[Exit.]

SANCHO. How much the more it must irk me,
Though I conceal my mind!

PELAYO. No wedding to-night?

JUANA. No.

PELAYO. Why not?

JUANA. Don Tello does not wish it.

PELAYO. Don Tello? What has he to do with it?

JUANA. He must have something; it was his command.

PELAYO. Upon my word, before the priest comes in
We shall be leaping over these obstructions!
[Exit, followed by the other PEASANTS.]

SANCHO. A word, Elvira.

ELVIRA.   Sancho, woe is me!
Alas, but I am little fortunate!

SANCHO. What would the master that he puts us off
Until to-morrow?

ELVIRA. I know not what he would.
[Aside.] But ah, it must be love!

SANCHO. Is it in reason that he bar from me,
O beautiful my eyes, this very night

The peace and solace which my burning
heart
Has craved so long?
ELVIRA.   You are my husband;
Sancho, come to my door to-night.
SANCHO.   My all! . . .
Will it stand open?
ELVIRA.   Will it not?
SANCHO.   Be thou
My remedy and cure! Hadst thou said
no,
Then I had slain myself.
ELVIRA. I too had slain myself.
SANCHO. The priest arrived but he
could not come in.
ELVIRA. He would not have the priest
come in.
SANCHO.   Relent
And open—our hearts a better way shall
prove;
No clumsy priest to heal desire is love!
[Exeunt.]

A Street before NUÑO'S *House.*

[*Enter* DON TELLO, CELIO *and*
ATTENDANTS.]

DON TELLO. You understand me well
enough.
CELIO. I hardly think a very subtle un-
derstanding is required to understand you,
great my Lord.
DON TELLO. Go in then; Elvira and
the old man are alone.
CELIO. The people went to their homes
in notable displeasure to see the wedding
so delayed.
DON TELLO. I acted, Celio, upon the
first counsel which love gave to me. It
would have been infamous in my passion
to have suffered a peasant to possess the
beauty which I crave. After I am tired
of her, this country fool can marry her,
and I will grant him a flock and a grange,
with money enough for him to live. It is
a compensation which comes to many, as
we have both of us seen in the world.
Finally, I have the power, and I will avail
me of it while I may, since the fellow is
not married.—Put on your masks.
CELIO. Shall we knock?

DON TELLO. Do.   [*They knock.*]
ATTENDANT. They open now.
[ELVIRA *appears at the door.*]
ELVIRA. Enter, Sancho, my soul!
CELIO. Elvira?
ELVIRA. Yes.
AN ATTENDANT [*aside*]. Fortunate en-
counter!
[*They overpower* ELVIRA.]
ELVIRA. It is not you, Sancho? Woe is
me! Father! Señor! Nuño! Help me,
heaven! They seize me! They carry me
away!
DON TELLO. Àway now!
[*They carry her off.*]
NUÑO [*within house*]. What is this?
ELVIRA [*in the distance*]. Father!
DON TELLO [*without*]. Cover her
mouth.
[*Enter* NUÑO.]
NUÑO. Daughter! Now I hear and see
you! But my feeble age and tottering
strength—what can they do against the
might of a young and powerful man? I
know now who it is.
[*Exit following the ravishers.*]

[*Enter* SANCHO *and* PELAYO, *muffled.*]
SANCHO. I thought I heard cries in the
valley in the direction of the Master's
house.
PELAYO. Speak low; don't let the serv-
ants hear.
SANCHO. While I am inside, remember,
you must not fall asleep.
PELAYO. I shall not; I understand. I
have had my opportunity already.
SANCHO. When the morning star rises
to beg alms of the dawn, I shall come out;
but the dawn need expect none from me,
for it will be driving me out of paradise.
PELAYO. While you are inside, do you
know what I shall be like? Like a doctor's
ass, chewing on his bit by the door.
SANCHO. Knock.
PELAYO. I'll lay you that Elvira is
peeping through the keyhole.
SANCHO. Here I stand, and knock.

[*Reënter* NUÑO.]
NUÑO. I shall lose my reason.

SANCHO. Who goes there?

NUÑO. A man!

SANCHO. Nuño?

NUÑO. Sancho?

SANCHO. But you in the street? What
is this?

NUÑO. What is this, you say?

SANCHO. Yes, but what is the matter?
I fear some harm.

NUÑO. The greatest that can befall;
some would be too little.

SANCHO. How?

NUÑO. A body of armed men broke
down these doors
And bore her off.

SANCHO. No more! My hope is ended!

NUÑO. I sought to track them by the
pale and fitful moon;
They would not stay nor have their faces
seen,
Covering their features sudden up with
masks,
Wherefore I could not know them.

SANCHO.   To what end, Nuño?
How should it profit us? What good were
served?
All, all are servants in Don Tello's train
To whom you bade me speak.
An evil counsel and I say amen!
There are ten houses standing in this
vale—
All ten of simple folk, who gather here
About this chapel. It could be none of
them.
It is the Master rather bore her off,
To his own town and close, whereof the
sign
Most sure and certain this:—he has re-
fused
To let us marry. What justice shall I
find
This side of heaven, he being a powerful
man
And richest in the kingdom? God knows
I . . .
I die! . . . It cannot be another thought
Lurks in his head—

NUÑO.   Hold, Sancho!

PELAYO.   By the river bank
If I can catch his pigs out on the
meadow—

Yes, though they have a guard along—I'll
stone them!

NUÑO. Now is the time to profit by
your wisdom,
My son . . .

SANCHO. How can I, father and señor?
You advised the hurt; advise the remedy.

NUÑO. To-morrow we shall speak with
the Señor;
For well I know, since what was done was
done
In heat of youth, repentance will have
come
With morning. I trust Elvira, Sancho;
Nor force nor prayers can overcome her.

SANCHO. I know and do believe it.
Alack! I die of love!
Ah me! I burn with jealousy!
On what unhappy human head till now
Has fallen ever such hideous mischance?
But how? To lead and welcome to my
house
The fierce and sanguinary lion, to seize
My white, my tender lamb? Say was I
blind?
Yes, yes, I was! Let never high-born
knight
Enter the humble dwellings of the poor
Wherein rich treasures lie!
I seem to see her face streaming with
tears,
Coursing like pearls adown her scarlet
cheeks,
While she defends her honor. I seem to
hear—
Unhappy thought!—her sad, protesting
moans,
While the cruel tyrant whispers in her ear
Outrageous profanation. I see her locks
Make of themselves close, friendly lattices,
Disheveled falling from her pallid brow,
To screen her from his hot and fierce de-
sires.
Unhand me, Nuño! I will take my life!
I lose the very sense and touch of reason!
Alack! I die of love!
Ah, me! I burn with jealousy!

NUÑO. Sancho, you are well born.
Where is your courage now?

SANCHO.   I fear such things
As once imagined, madden the very soul;

Yet have no hope nor power of remedy.
Show me Elvira's room.
PELAYO. Show me the kitchen;
Or hunger, sir, will be the death of me;
You know I had no supper. All of us
Were horribly put out.
NUÑO. Enter and rest;
So may we all take comfort till the morning.
Don Tello is no wild man.
SANCHO. Alack! I die of love!
Ah, me! I am consumed with jealousy!
[*Exeunt.*]

ACT II

A room in the Country Seat of
DON TELLO.

[DON TELLO *and* ELVIRA.]
ELVIRA. To what end, Tello, would you
torture me
With such dire cruelty? Do you not
know
I prize my honor? Further to persist
But wearies you and wearies me.
DON TELLO. Enough
Or you will slay me, being so rough and
hard.
ELVIRA. Return me to my husband,
Tello.
DON TELLO. No,
For he is not your husband, nor may a
clown
Though fortunate, deserve such passing
worth;
But were I Sancho, and he in turn were I,
How then, Elvira, could your cruel rage
Treat me thus foully? Cannot your rigor
see
That this is love?
ELVIRA. Never, my Lord; for love
That is deficient in a true respect
For honor is but vile desire, not love;
And being evil, love never can be called.
For love is born of loving what one loves
In mad desire;
And love that is not chaste
By no name of love is graced
Nor ever can to love's estate aspire.
DON TELLO. How so?

ELVIRA. But would you have me make
it plain?
Last night you saw me, Tello, for the
first;
Why, then, your love was such a sudden
thing
That you had scarce a moment to consider
What that thing was which you so much
desired;
Yet in that knowledge all true love resides.
For love is born of a great-grown desire,
And love goes mounting then the steps of
favor
Even to its own end and exercise.
So this you feel was never love we see
In simple truth—mad lust and longing
rather
To snatch from me my whole, my heart of
life
By heaven confided to me in pure honor;
But you would seek to load me with dishonor
And I defend my life.
DON TELLO. But my excuse
Is your intelligence, as in your arms.
Listen to reason.
ELVIRA. There is no argument
Can vanquish my assured intent.
DON TELLO. But how?
Do you maintain it is impossible
To see, desire and love, all at first sight?
ELVIRA. True.
DON TELLO. Then answer:
How can the basilisk, ungrateful girl,
Contrive to kill, and only with a glance?
ELVIRA. It is an animal.
DON TELLO. And so your beauty;
It is the basilisk.
ELVIRA. You argue falsely
As prompted by your wit.
DON TELLO. I argue falsely?
ELVIRA. The mortal basilisk kills with
a look,
Because his mind is wholly set to kill,
Which reason is so evident and plain
We could not say that he had power to kill
Did he but look upon us with affection.
Let us have no more arguments, my lord;
I am a woman and I am in love,
Nor have you aught to hope from me.

DON TELLO. How is it possible a country wench
Should answer in this wise? Confess to me
You are a fool, proving yourself discreet;
Because, when I behold your full perfection,
The more its sum, so much the more my love.
Oh, would to God you were my equal now!
But you know well the baseness of your state
Affronts my noble blood. Ill were it done
To join the brocade with the coarse homespun!
God knows what might of love now drives me on,
And turns to evil all my good intent!
The world made these vile laws in ages gone,
And I must yield to them, obedient.

[*Enter* FELICIANA.]

FELICIANA. Forgive me, brother, that my heart relents
And is more quick to pity than your wish.—
But hold! What angers you?
DON TELLO.   You are a fool!
FELICIANA. I am a fool, but yet a woman, Tello,
Amazed before this terrible desire.
Let some days pass. It was not said of love
"I came, I saw, I conquered," Cæsar of love
Above a subject world although you be.
DON TELLO. Can it be possible you are my sister?
FELICIANA. What? To use force against a poor peasant girl?
[*Knocking within.*]
ELVIRA. Have pity, Lady.
FELICIANA. Withholding "yes" to-day,
She may perhaps reserve it for the morrow.
Be patient, Tello; it is unnatural
That neither should have rest. Rest and return
Refreshed to the encounter.
DON TELLO.   Is this your pity,
Depriving me of life?   [*Knocking.*]

FELICIANA.   Be still, I say;
You are beside yourself. Did she tempt you?
Elvira has done naught. Blush and for shame!
Detain her here some days in company
With you and me; better we talk the while.
ELVIRA. Would that my tears might move you, noble lady,
To intercede in pity for my honor!
[*Knocking.*]
FELICIANA. Take note beside, my Lord, an hour has passed
Since her old father and the groom have stood
Knocking upon the gate. It is but meet
They find it open—whereto you are enforced,
Else they will say, entrance being denied,
You hold Elvira.
DON TELLO. All things augment my rage.
In, in, Elvira, and conceal yourself.—
Admit these hinds.
ELVIRA. Thank God you let me rest!
DON TELLO. Of what would you complain? You tie my hands.
[*Exit* ELVIRA.]
FELICIANA. Hello, without!
CELIO [*within*]. Señora! . . .
FELICIANA.   Summon these hinds.—
And look you treat them well, nor dare forget
The obligation of your quality.
[*To* DON TELLO.]

[*Enter* NUÑO *and* SANCHO.]
NUÑO. Kissing the pavement of this noble house
(All too unworthy we to kiss your feet),
Fain would we tell you what the time allows
Of ill-conditioned violence in your seat.
Sancho, Señor, Elvira's promised spouse,
To whom you both stand sponsors as is meet,
Comes to beg justice for the greatest wrong
That mortal tongue can speak through ages long.

SANCHO. Magnanimous Señor, whose
　　brow o'ertops
The summits of these mountains capped
　　with snow,
Which thence descending in clear foun-
　　tains drops
To kiss your feet amid green plains below,
Advised by Nuño and his friends, who
　　stops
Never to doubt the virtue that you show,
I sought your favor, begged your free
　　consent;
And with your presence you honored my
　　content.

Once having entered our poor house, alas,
To vengeance are you bound by dignity,
To right a wrong so bold, atrocious, crass,
As fouls your name and your nobility.
If ever love in you came to such pass
As paid in act desire's expectancy,
One moment had, that moment swept
　　away—
Think on the heart how sore the burden
　　lay!

I, a poor laborer within these fields,
But in the passion of the heart a lord—
One not so dulled to mountain use, but
　　wields
On fit occasion the bright shining sword—
Hearing foul rumor, no addled clown that
　　yields
Was I, nor might be—spineless, dull, un-
　　toward,
My honor trampled, by law she was not
　　mine,
But "yes" once said, that union is divine.

I rushed forth to the fields, and to the
　　light
Which dims the stars, I raised my eyes in
　　vain—
The swiftly gliding moon, drawn by whose
　　might
The tides recede and rise upon the main:
"Ah, happy thou!" I cried, "that night by
　　night
No human hand can bar the sun, thy wain,
Soft rising to thy throne within the sky
Though clouds may come like masks and
　　veil the eye!"

And then I turned me to the lonely earth,
Seeing Alcides' poplars lulled to sleep
With ivy twined, whose slim embracing
　　girth
Knotted them round, while close the
　　tendrils creep.
"Alas!" I cried, "What? Thrive you in my
　　dearth
Of joy, you vines? Nay, fool, will you
　　not sweep,
You base-born rustic, these rooted loves
　　asunder,
Slashing down boughs and trampling
　　blossoms under?"

All slept secure. But then I knew at last
They rapt, my Lord, my precious bride
　　away;
It sudden seemed the streamlets as they
　　passed
Wept too and murmured a more troubled
　　lay.
Within my hand I bore (how long outcast
From battle!) a sword in sheath of elder
　　day;
I flung me on the tallest tree—amain
With stroke and blow I leveled it like
　　grain.

Elvira had not suffered by the tree;
Ah, no! The tree was arrogant and
　　proud,
And looked upon the others pityingly;
With greatness such as this are giants
　　endowed.
But in the town they say—and lie to me,
Since you are what you are—that you
　　avowed
And open lover were of this my wife
And held her here—you author of this
　　strife.

"Base churls!" I cried, "What? Have you
　　not respect?
Don Tello is my lord, glory and honor
Of all the house of Neira. Stay! Reflect
He is my sponsor, and would my wedding
　　honor!"
Pity this truth, my lord, nor dare reject
My just complaint, to your and my dis-
　　honor.

Rather return with flashing eye and brand
Sancho his wife, Nuño his daughter's
  hand.
Don Tello. It grieves me sore, friend
  Sancho, to the heart,
To learn of such bold knavery, nor here
Shall any rustic dwell and scape the smart
Of vengeance, who takes or holds her, far
  or near.
Best you inquire and find what mad up-
  start,
Blinded with passion, by covert force, by
  fear,
Affronts us both with like contemptuous
  outrage.
Once he is known, I . . . I will assuage
Your hurt, and these base churls who
  flaunt my name
I will have whipped for their effrontery.
And go with God!
  Sancho [to Nuño, aside]. My jeal-
  ousy turns flame!
Nuño. Sancho, hold, in God's name!
Sancho. Death, come set me free!
Don Tello. Find out these knaves
  who boldly smirch my fame
With black dishonor.
  Sancho. But can such things be?
Don Tello. I know not where she lies.
            Show me your wife
And she is yours, upon Don Tello's life.

[Reënter Elvira.]
Elvira. He knows, my husband; Tello
  keeps me here
Hidden.
  Sancho. My wife, my life, my good,
  my all!
Don Tello. So this is what you would
  contrive against me?
Sancho. Alas! In what sad state I
  pined for you!
Nuño. Alas, my daughter! How you
  made me tremble!
My reason was clean gone!
  Don Tello. Hold rustics! Back!
Sancho. Let me but touch her hands;
  I am her husband.
Don Tello. Celio! Julio! What ho,
  my men!
Death to these peasants!

Feliciana. Brother, have pity; be less
  rough and hard.
Remember too that they are not to blame.
Don Tello. Had they been married,
  the impertinence were great.

[Enter Celio, Julio and Attendants.]
Kill them!
  Sancho. Yes, rather let me die than
  live,
However cruel death be!
  Elvira.   I lose the sense
Of life or death.
  Sancho. Elvira and my all,
But listen; better I let myself be slain.
Elvira. I too shall know how still to
  guard my honor,
Although they strike me with a thousand
  deaths.
Don Tello. But is it possible they
  flaunt their loves
Before my face? Can such hot passion be?
Celio! Julio! What ho!
  Julio.   My Lord . . .
Don Tello. Death! Beat them with
  clubs!
Celio. Death! Death! They die!
    [The Servants fall upon Nuño
    and Sancho and cudgel them
    from the room.]
Don Tello [to Elvira]. In vain your
  feeble plaints seek remedy
Against my rage. I had it well in mind
To send you back released, but such my
  fury
To see your brazen, base solicitations
All shameless shown, perforce you must
  be mine,
Or I not be the man I was in fine!
Feliciana. No, brother! I am here!
Don Tello. I'll force or kill her!
Feliciana. How is it possible to set
  her free
From one who has outrun self-mastery?
                        [Exeunt.]

Before the House of Don Tello.

Julio [without]. This is the way ras-
cals pay for effrontery.
Celio [without]. Out of the palace!
Servants [without]. Out!

[*Enter* SANCHO *and* NUÑO, *fleeing.*]

SANCHO. Yes, kill me, you squires! I have no sword myself.

NUÑO. My son, my fear is great lest this man will have your life, he is so turbulent and bold.

SANCHO. What is left for me in life?

NUÑO. Fortune perchance may relent; she is quick to change so long as life itself endures.

SANCHO. In God's name they shall not drive me from this threshold where I stand, although they strike me dead! Without Elvira I do not wish to live.

NUÑO. Live and you may yet find justice. These kingdoms have a king, and there is still a higher court of appeal, for you may petition heaven.

[*Enter* PELAYO.]

PELAYO. Oh, there you are!

SANCHO. Who is here?

PELAYO. Pelayo, and stuffed full with satisfaction. I come for a reward.

SANCHO. Reward? How? At a time like this?

PELAYO. I said a reward.

SANCHO. For what, Pelayo, when I am dead already and Nuño is at the last gasp?

PELAYO. I want a reward!

NUÑO. You know what this fool is.

PELAYO. Well, I have found Elvira out . . .

SANCHO. Ah, father! Then they have sent her back? Speak, my Pelayo! What is it you say?

PELAYO. The whole village is on tiptoe and everybody tells me that Don Tello has had her with him in his house since twelve o'clock last night.

SANCHO. Curses on you and amen!

PELAYO. They all think now that he will never want to give her up.

NUÑO. My son, we must find some remedy. Alfonso, King of Castile, by right and virtue of his mighty deeds, now holds his court at León. He is a just and an upright judge; wherefore go seek him out and lay your wrongs before him, for I verily believe that he will do us justice.

SANCHO. Alas! I very well know,

Nuño, that Alfonso, King of Castile, is a complete and perfect prince, but how think you shall it be that a rude peasant like myself may enter his presence? What gallery of the palace shall I dare desecrate with my presumption? What turnkey will be found who will suffer my presence, Nuño? The doors are flung wide open there to brocades and rich trappings, to grave and stately retinues; and this is as it should be, as we ourselves must confess. But the doorkeepers, Nuño, permit the poor people only to gaze from without upon the gates and the caparisons and the arms, and even this must be from far off. I will go to León and I will make my way into the palace, and then you will see what marks they will imprint with the flat sides of their swords upon my shoulders. What? Present myself with petitions before the King? I tell you they will drop from his hand into oblivion. I shall come back having had sight of the ladies and of the noble gentlemen, of the church, the palace, the park, the stately buildings; and I fear I shall bring back with me besides a distaste for this dwelling among yew trees and among oak trees and live oaks, where the birds sing and we hear the dogs bark. No, Nuño, you do not advise me well.

NUÑO. I know truly, Sancho, that I do advise you well. Go then and speak with King Alfonso, for if you remain here, I am certain that they will take your life.

SANCHO. I desire naught else, Nuño.

NUÑO. I have a chestnut horse which is so swift that he will wager his mane against the wings of the wind and lay his hoofs against the bridle. Take him and be gone, and let Pelayo take the little mottled horse which daily goes out with him into the fields.

SANCHO. To please you I obey. Pelayo, will you come with me to court?

PELAYO. And be so glad of the opportunity to see what I have never seen before, that I would stoop to kiss your feet, Sancho. They tell me that at court all the streets are laid with eggs and paved with rashers of bacon, and they greet strangers with a bounty so hearty

that for all the world it is the same as if
they had come out of Flanders or Italy or
else Morocco. They say the court is one
great bag wherein a man may draw naught
but prizes and all the counters unite to
spell fortune, whether they be black or
white. For God's sake, then, let us go to
court!

SANCHO. Father, farewell! I go. And
give me your blessing.

NUÑO. You have wisdom and discre-
tion, son; that we know. Speak out
boldly to the King.

SANCHO. You will learn presently how
bold I am. Come.

NUÑO. Good-bye, Sancho.

SANCHO. Good-bye, Elvira!

PELAYO. And good-bye, pigs. [*Exeunt.*]

A Room in the House of DON TELLO.

[DON TELLO *and* FELICIANA.]

DON TELLO. What? I shall not pos-
sess this woman's beauty?

FELICIANA. Tello, in vain this pas-
sion to persist;
For such her grief, she weeps continually.
While you confine her to this lonely tower
How is it possible you should not see
The part of greater wisdom? Though her
    love
Were all for you your lot were yet dis-
    dain.
If you will treat her with cold cruelty,
How shall she love you well? Pray be
    advised:
'Tis simple folly to be harsh with those
To whom we turn for pity at the close.

DON TELLO. Am I to suffer this most
    dire affront,
Seeing myself despised, when I am he
Who is most powerful in all the land,
Richest in goods and most magnificent?

FELICIANA. Give it less thought, nor
    be so much cast down
For a poor peasant.

DON TELLO.   Ah, Feliciana!
You do not know what love is, nor have
    felt
Its rigor.

FELICIANA. Patience, I say, until to-
    morrow;

And I will speak to her, and as I may
Soften this woman.

DON TELLO.   No, she is no woman;
A wild beast, rather, since she gives such
    pain.
Promise her silver, gold, and priceless
    gems,
Or what you will; tell her that I will
    give
A world of treasure. In presence of rich
    gifts
Women observe especial courtesy.
Say I will shower her with thank-offer-
    ings,
And say I will bestow on her a gown
That shall drain dry the gold from Milan
    town,
From her proud hair soft falling to her
    feet.
Tell her if she will remedy my pain
I will endow her with a farm and flocks,
For were she but my equal——

FELICIANA.   Is't possible
You talk like this? *

DON TELLO. Yes, sister, yes! My state,
My fortune ebbs; for either I must die
Or else enjoy her, once therewith for all
Ending my pain so grievous and so long.

FELICIANA. I go to plead with her,
though it be vain.

DON TELLO. How so?

FELICIANA. Because at least this much
    is plain—
There is no interest beneath the sun
By which an honest woman may be won.

DON TELLO. Go then and quickly bring
    my hope relief;
For if my steadfast faith shall not achieve
The goal desired, the love and troth I bear
Shall be transformed to vengeance by de-
    spair!   [*Exeunt.*]

A Hall in the Palace of the King in León.

[*The* KING DON ALFONSO VII, *the* COUNT
    DON PEDRO, DON ENRIQUE *and*
    ATTENDANTS.]

KING. While our decree is published
    and proclaimed

---

* A verse is missing here.—*Menéndez y
Pelayo.*

Unto Toledo, and due response returned
By our just judge and lord of Aragon
In Zaragoza resident, say, O Count,
Whether the soldiers and the suppliants
Be all despatched and learn if any stays
Who yet would speak with me?
 COUNT.   None, Sire, remains
To wait your pleasure.
 DON ENRIQUE. Propped up against the
  gate
I saw but now a poor Gallegan peasant,
And passing sad he seemed.
 KING.   Now by my hand
Who would resist the poor? Enrique of
  Lara,
In your own person go bring him to our
  presence. [*Exit* DON ENRIQUE.]
 COUNT. O virtue most heroical and
  rare!
Compassive pity and high clemency!
God-given model to the kings of air,
His law observing by thy Majesty!

[*Reënter* DON ENRIQUE *with* SANCHO *and*
  PELAYO.]
 DON ENRIQUE. Put down your spears.
 SANCHO. Pelayo, place them here
Against the wall.
 PELAYO. You put your best foot first.
 SANCHO. Which is the King, Señor?
 DON ENRIQUE.   He lifts his hand
To his breast there.
 SANCHO. Right well indeed he may,
Content with all his works. Fear not,
  Pelayo.
 PELAYO. These kings have in them a
  full strain of winter;
They make men shiver too all over.
 SANCHO.   Señor. . . .
 KING. Speak, and be calm.
 SANCHO. Who holds within his grasp
The government of Spain . . .
 KING.   Tell me your name
And whence you come.
 SANCHO. Grant me your hand to kiss,
For I would fain exalt this humble
  mouth,
O Prince and Sovereign! Once let my
  lips,
Unworthy howsoe'er, approach that hand,
And I am eloquent.

 KING. You bathe it in your tears!
But for what cause?
 SANCHO. My eyes did wrong to weep;
Yet since my lips give voice to their com-
  plaint
They would enforce it with a weight of
  woe
That should ensure, your hand set to the
  task,
The meting out of righteous chastisement
On one both mighty and my enemy.
 KING. Take courage, pray, and do not
  shed these tears;
Though holy pity most becomes my state
Yet you must know 'tis likewise mine to
  give
Its attribute to justice. Who does you
  wrong?
For he who wrongs the poor is never wise.
 SANCHO. Wrongs are like children,
  kings are fathers, Sire;
Then marvel not they pucker up their lips
In foolish grimaces, coming before them.
 KING [*apart*]. The man meseems is
  wise; before he speaks
He wins my sympathy.
 SANCHO.   Sire and Señor,
I am hidalgo born, though humbly poor,
Such is the mutability of fate,
Whose fickle changes sallied hand in hand
Forth with me from the warmth of my
  first cradle.
The which remembered, I sought an equal
  mate
In holy wedlock; but since that man errs
Who is forgetful of just obligation,
And ever errs, I made my 'purpose known
Unto the lord of all that country round,
By name and right Don Tello of Neira,
Less moved by art than frankness in the
  act,
Seeking his license. Freely he gave it me
And as my sponsor stands before the
  altar.
But love, which drives the wisest men to
  folly,
Blinded his sight and fired his heart to
  lust
Of my belovèd peasant girl, Señor.
He would not have us wed, and that same
  night

With armèd force he ravished her away,
Nor left thereafter life to me to live
Nor shadow of protection to invoke
This side of you and heaven, to whose
    bench
And sacred throne of justice I appeal;
For having begged her back with tears,
    Señor,
Her father and I, so fierce was his re-
    sponse
That to our breasts they bared their naked
    swords
And though hidalgos and high born, foul
    blows
With staves of oak they rained upon our
    shoulders.
KING.   Count—
COUNT.   Señor—
KING. Bring pen and paper on the
    moment.
A chair here where I stand.
               [*The* KING *sits and writes.*]
COUNT.   All is prepared.
SANCHO [*aside*]. His matchless worth
    amazes and strikes dumb.—
I spoke to the King, Pelayo.
                    [*Apart to him.*]
PELAYO.   By my jacket,
A good man!
SANCHO. Who would be so hard of
    heart
As to refuse the poor?
PELAYO.   The Kings of Spain
Must all be angels.
SANCHO. Do you not see them dressed
Like ordinary men?
PELAYO.   Another sort
Was one that Tello had in tapestry,
With blotchy face and hair all fallen
    down
About his knees; a staff he held in hand
And had a helmet like a lantern on
Atop there with his crown, which was
    all gold,
With a band around his chin like Turk
    or Moor.
I asked a page to tell me who he was——
He seemed to be a celebrated man——
Because I took a fancy to his clothes,
And he replied that he was called King
    Ball.

SANCHO. You fool! What he said was
    King Saul
PELAYO.   No, Ball,
Ball, trying to get rid of Badill.
SANCHO.   Nonsense!
Badill was David, fool, his son-in-law.
PELAYO. I know all that. The priest
    was preaching once
Down in the church, how he had hit him
    one
Flat on the crown, with one of Moses'
    tears,
Which was a hard stone, and killed the
    giant, the liar.
SANCHO. Goliath! You are a fool.
PELAYO.   The priest said so.
KING. Count, seal this letter. What
    is your name, good man?
SANCHO. My name is Sancho, Sire, who
    at your feet
Begs justice of your holy clemency
On one, vaunting in power, grown inso-
    lent,
Who rapt from me my true and lawful
    wife,
And would therewith deprive me of my
    life,
Did I not flee.
KING.   Can such a tyrant breathe
In all Galicia?
SANCHO.   So famed is he
That from the margin of those river
    glades
Unto the Roman Tower of Hercules,
He is obeyed. Once let his ire be roused
Against a man, then heaven succor him.
He makes and cancels laws; for such the
    state
Of haughty noblemen, who dwell in pride
And far removed from Kings.
COUNT. The letter's sealed.
KING. Which superscribe to Tello of
    Neira.
SANCHO. O Sire, you have cut down the
    sword which hung
Even above my neck!
KING.   Give him this letter;
He will return to you forthwith your
    wife.
SANCHO. Can greater favor be, even
    at your hand?

KING. You come afoot?

SANCHO. No, Sire, upon two horses,
Pelayo and myself.

PELAYO. We galloped like wind
Or even faster. The fact is, though, that
mine
Has some abominable, beastly tricks;
You scarcely mount him but he down and
rolls
Either in sand or else straight in the
river,
And runs besides like all profanity
And eats like a student. When he sees
an inn
He either goes in or stops still instanter.

KING. You are a likely knave.

PELAYO. I am one, Sire,
Who left his native land for sight of you.

KING. And what is your complaint?

PELAYO. Sire, of that horse.

KING. Have you, I say, a present
cause of trouble?

PELAYO. Yes, hunger; if the kitchen's
hereabouts . . .

KING. But is there nothing of the gar-
niture
Upon these walls, to which you would
incline,
Bearing it home?

PELAYO. I have no place to put it;
Better send it to Don Tello. He, belike,
Has three or four of the same kind al-
ready.

KING. A most amusing knave! What
may you be
In your own country when you are at
home?

PELAYO. I drive, Señor, all over the
mountain side;
I am my master's coachman.

KING. Are there coaches?
What? In that land?

PELAYO. Indeed not! So I drive
His pigs.

KING [aside]. How curious a pair that
land has joined,
One being so wise—the other such a fool!
[Aloud.] Accept this gift.

PELAYO. Oh, it is nothing, Sire!

KING. No, take them; they are dou-
bloons. [Then to SANCHO.]

You take the letter.
And go in happy hour.

SANCHO. May heaven guard you.
[Exeunt the KING, the COUNT,
DON ENRIQUE and ATTEND-
ANTS.]

PELAYO. Hello! I took them.

SANCHO. Money?

PELAYO. Plenty of it, too.

SANCHO. Ah, my Elvira! Fortune
here is writ
Upon these papers. In my hand I bear,
Prompted by hope, deliverance of thy
beauty! [Exeunt.]

A room in the Country Seat of DON TELLO.

[DON TELLO and CELIO.]

CELIO. In accordance with your com-
mands I have inquired about the churl,
and I had this information under threats,
although Nuño himself refused to answer.
He is not in the valley; he has been ab-
sent some days.

DON TELLO. Most strange behavior!

CELIO. They tell me that he has gone
to León.

DON TELLO. To León?

CELIO. And Pelayo keeps him company.

DON TELLO. To what end?

CELIO. To speak with the King.

DON TELLO. But for what purpose?
He is not Elvira's husband; and there-
fore I have not done him wrong. Had
Nuño made the complaint he might well
have been excused. But Sancho! . . .

CELIO. I had it from the shepherds
who tend your flocks. As the lad has wit
in his head, my Lord, and as he is in
love, in truth this daring does not sur-
prise me.

DON TELLO. Is it no more than dar-
ing for him to present himself to speak
with the King of Castile?

CELIO. Alfonso was reared in Galicia at
the hands of Count Don Pedro de An-
drada, and for that reason they say he will
never close his door to any Gallegan,
though never so humble his birth.
[Knocking within.]

DON TELLO. See who knocks, Celio.
What? Are there no pages in my hall?

CELIO. So help me God, my Lord, but it is Sancho, the very churl of whom we spoke but now!

DON TELLO. Can greater presumption be?

CELIO. May you live many years to learn how much I love you!

DON TELLO. Bid him come in; I will receive him here.

[*Enter* SANCHO *and* PELAYO.]

SANCHO. Great my Lord, I cast myself before your feet.

DON TELLO. Where have you been, Sancho? Some days have passed since last you came into my presence.

SANCHO. Rather they seemed years to me. My Lord, when I found how you persisted in the passion wherewith you were consumed—or call it love for my Elvira—I betook me to appeal to the King of Castile, who is the supreme and highest judge and who has the power to right all wrongs.

DON TELLO. So? And what, pray, did you tell him of me?

SANCHO. I told him that at the moment of my marriage you stole my wife away.

DON TELLO. Your wife? You lie, base knave! How? Did the priest come in, who was there that night?

SANCHO. No, my Lord, but he was advised that we both had given consent.

DON TELLO. If he never joined your hands, how then can it be marriage?

SANCHO. I have not come to discuss whether or not it be marriage. The King has granted me this letter which is writ in his own hand.

DON TELLO. I shake with rage. [*Reads.*] "Upon receipt of this you will deliver up to this poor peasant the woman whom you have taken from him, without word of reply; remember that the loyal vassal may be known, however distant he may be from his King, and that Kings are never distant when it is their duty to punish evil.

                                    "THE KING"

Man! What is this that you have done?

SANCHO. Señor, I bring this letter, given me by the King.

DON TELLO. By God, I am astonished at my own forbearance! Do you think, you hind, that by this insolence you shall teach me fear in my own despite? Do you know who I am?

SANCHO. I do, my Lord, and because I am assured of your nobility, I have brought this letter, not as you suppose to do you displeasure, but as a right friendly missive from my Lord of Castile, who is our King, that you may restore to me my wife.

DON TELLO. Then out of respect to this same letter, know that you and this miserable clown who comes with you . . .

PELAYO. Saint Blas! Saint Paul!

DON TELLO. I do not string you up here to the merlons of the battlements.

PELAYO. This not being my saint's day, by all the saints though altogether it has a devilish bad look for saints!

DON TELLO. Out of my palace on the instant, and look you linger not within my lands, or I will have you done to death with clubs! You knaves, you hinds, you low, earthly rascals of the clay! . . . What? To come to me! . . .

PELAYO. He is right too, and we were great fools to put him to this displeasure.

DON TELLO. If I have taken your wife, you knave, know I am who I am, and I reign here and here I do my will as the King does his in his Castile. My forebears never owed this land to him—they won it from the Moors.

PELAYO. Yes, they won it from the Moors and from the Christians too, and you don't owe a thing to the King.

DON TELLO. I am who I am . . .

PELAYO [*aside*]. Saint Macarius!

DON TELLO. That is the reason I do not take vengeance on you by my own hand. What? Give up Elvira! What is he to Elvira? Kill them, I say! But no —let them go! It is an unworthy thing in an hidalgo to stain his sword with peasants' blood!

PELAYO. No, don't you do it, on your life!

[*Exeunt* Don Tello *and* Celio.]

Sancho. Now what do you say?

Pelayo. I say out of Galicia.

Sancho. My brain whirls round when I consider that this fellow refuses to obey his King because he has three or four henchmen gathered here about him. For so help me God . . .

Pelayo. No, contain yourself, Sancho. It is good advice—and always was—never permit yourself a quarrel with a strong man and make no friendships among servants.

Sancho. Let us return to León.

Pelayo. Well, I have the doubloons yet which the King gave me. So come on then.

Sancho. I shall report to him what has happened. Ah, Elvira! Who now remains to bring you succor? Fly, fly to her, my sighs, and until I come again, tell her I die of love!

Pelayo. Better hurry, Sancho, for this fellow has not yet possessed Elvira.

Sancho. How do you know, Pelayo?

Pelayo. Because he would have given her back once he had done his will.

[*Exeunt.*]

ACT III

A Hall in the Palace of the King.

[*The* King, *the* Count *and* Don Enrique.]

King. Heaven be witness, Count, I hold supreme
The wishes of my mother.

Count.   And supreme
The duty that you show, great Lord and Sire,
Whose sovereign god-like thoughts in all transpire.

King. My mother gives me cause of great offense;
She is my mother—that my recompense.*

* This scene is fragmentary. Lope has scarcely employed a special measure for six verses only.—*Hartzenbusch.* The apparent purpose of the scene is the further characterization of the King.

[*Enter* Sancho *and* Pelayo.]

Pelayo [*apart to* Sancho]. I say you can come in.

Sancho.   I see him now
On whom, Pelayo, I would dower my soul,
The all of life I have to give. O sun
Of wide Castile, Trajan compassionate,
Thou true Alcides of our Christian faith
And Caesar of all Spain!

Pelayo.   Give me no kiddies
For pigs are what I chiefly understand.
Within his hands I read more victories
Than lines are graved therein. Draw near and bow,
Humbly abase yourself before his feet
And kiss that mighty hand.

Sancho. Most glorious Emperor and Sovereign,
O thou unconquered Sun and King of Spain,
Grant me the soles of these thy feet to kiss,
Which for their pillow Granada hold in fee,
Vouchsafed by Heaven in earnest of high favor,
And for their carpet Seville, rich in dyes
Of ships and myriad flowers, which deck the banks
Of its eternal river, mirrored in beauty!
Knowest thou me?

King.   Some farmer of Galicia
Meseems you are, who here besought my favor.

Sancho. I am, Señor.

King.   But do not be afraid.

Sancho. Señor, deeply it grieves me to return,
Making so bold to heap my cares upon you.
No other course was possible to me.
If in persistence I am peasant, Sire,
Then you are Emperor, a Roman Caesar
Quick to pardon him who humbly seeks
For justice of your royal clemency!

King. Say first what wrong you suffer.
Be advised
I bear you well. Ever with me the poor
Hold letters of high favor.

Sancho.   Unconquered Sire,
Then those you gave, Don Tello had and read,

By me delivered in Galicia,
Unto the end that he return forthwith
As meet and just, my bride so dearly
    loved.
But read and not respected, mortal rage
They stirred in him; he would not give
    me back
The prize I so had loved—not only this,
But a new chastisement bestowed on me
Because I bore them, and in such treacher-
    ous sort
They used us both, this countryman and I,
That right good fortune and a miracle
Was it to escape this side of death, Señor.
I took what steps I might to right the
    wrong,
Not to return with fresh importuning.
But naught availed to move his stubborn
    pride.
The priest then spoke for me, who in that
    land
Wields high authority, and to him spoke
A saint and holy abbot of our faith
In St. Pelayo of Samos resident,
Whose heart was stirred to pity. All was
    vain;
For none might move him, nor all together
    joined.
He would not let me see her—this had
    been salve
And brief assuagement to my burning
    pain.
Acting on this, again I sought your face,
Image of God, which shines therein re-
    splendent,
That justice might be done to me this
    day,
Since you reflect his glory!
KING.   In my own hand
Written and signed? He dared tear up
    that letter?
SANCHO. God would not have my grief
    insult with falsehood,
Although a crafty tongue had answered
    yes,
To feed your ire. He read but did not
    tear it;
Yet now I lie, to read and not comply
With what his King commanded—this was
    to tear it!
Upon two tables God set down His law.

Does he not break those tables who doth
    fail
To keep that law? Such is the law of
    Kings:
That faithlessness be clearly seen and
    known
Suffice it that respect be torn alone!
KING. Can it be possible that noble
    blood
Runs not within these veins, though daily
    toil
Oppresses and bears down? From noble
    lineage
Methinks you spring, as doth in truth
    appear
From your fair speech and mode of right
    procedure.
Enough! So shall I with a single stroke
Impose my remedy.—Count . . .
COUNT. Sire and Señor?
KING. Enrique!
DON ENRIQUE. Sire!
KING. We shall in person to Galicia,
For it behooves us justice should be
    done.—
And let no word of this be known.
COUNT. Señor . . .
KING. Who speaks? How now? Who
    dares reply to me?
Station our sentries at the Palace gates;
Command they close the Park.
COUNT.   Open they stand
To all the people.
KING. But how shall aught be known
When those of our own bedchamber do
    proclaim
That we are ill?
DON ENRIQUE. I am of other mind.
KING. It is my purpose. And make no
    further answer.
COUNT. Be gone two days and all Cas-
    tile shall see
What cure you make of your infirmity.
KING. Good swains——
SANCHO.   Great Lord and Sire——
KING.   Offended sore
At the cruelty, mad violence and rage
Of Tello, here we take upon ourselves
In our own person to do chastisement.
SANCHO. You, Sire? It will o'er much
    demean your crown,

Humbling it to the dust.

KING [*to* SANCHO].   Go on before
And look you the bride's father be prepared,
Holding his house against our coming. Breathe
No word of what impends to mortal living.
I charge you this on forfeit of your lives.

SANCHO.   Who should breathe word, Señor?

KING [*to* PELAYO].   Hark you, peasant;
Though all the world should question who I am,
You are to say a noble of Castile,
And lay your hand upon your mouth like this—
Take heed and mark me well—and never be
Without these first two fingers on your lips.

PELAYO.   Sire, I shall hold them there so firm and tight
That you shall never see me gape again;
But yet Your Majesty must pity me
While you admire the feat, and grant me leave
To eat from time to time.

KING.   I do not mean
To have you putting always hand to mouth.

SANCHO.   Consider, Sire, a peasant's humble honor
Touches you not so near. Despatch some judge,
Some just Alcalde to Galicia
To do your will.

KING.   The King the Greatest Alcalde!
[*Exeunt.*]

Before the House of DON TELLO.

[NUÑO *and* CELIO.]

NUÑO.   You say that I may see her?

CELIO.   To which intent
My master Lord Don Tello gives consent.

NUÑO.   What boots it now since the disgrace is mine?

CELIO.   There is no cause for fear; in her combine

Stout heart and courage of resistance, such
As are born to woman, who suffering much
Is much the greater grown.

NUÑO.   Shall I opine
That a fair woman may retain her honor
And man have power to wreak his will upon her?

CELIO.   So certain am I, should Elvira choose
Celio for her spouse, none should accuse
Him of suspicion; I would wed her sure
As had she in your house remained secure.

NUÑO.   Where do you say the grating is?

CELIO.   Here toward
The tower on this side a window will afford
Full view, whereat she takes her stand, as said.

NUÑO.   Methinks I see a form envelopèd
In white, which for my years I scarce descry.

CELIO.   Approach, I go . . . Should you be seen, why I
Must not be found.   Know I have done this thing
Upon your steadfast love's importuning.
[*Exit.*]

[ELVIRA *appears at a grating in the Tower.*]

NUÑO.   Is it you, unhappy child?

ELVIRA.   Who should it be but I?

NUÑO.   I never thought to see your face again,
Not that these bars confined you prisoner
In cruel duress, but rather in my sight
I held you for dishonored. So foul a thing
Dishonor is in honorable minds,
So vile, so loathsome ugly, even to me
Who brought you to the world, even to me
It must forbid that I should see you more.
Well you preserve your honor, that rich dower
Down handed from your sires, when you have struck
To instant pieces that crystal of great price!

Let her who renders count of her soul's
    treasure
In faithless wise, call me no more father.
Because a daughter of like infamy—
And all too weak are these the words I
    speak—
Upon a father has one single claim,
That he shall shed her blood!
ELVIRA.   My own dear father,
When those whose loving office is to
    salve
The dire misfortunes which close hedge
    me round,
This weary, wasteful siege of watchful-
    ness,
Do but augment my sufferings the more,
Then mine for the first time will mount
    in sum
To the heavy burden of my outward
    state;
For, sir, I am your daughter. If the life
Which stirs in me is wholly from you
    sprung,
From you perforce springs that nobility
Which proudly I repay. This is the
    truth:—
The tyrant had it in his mind to force
    me,
But I have known the practice of de-
    fense
With courage more than human. Hold
    up your head
In pride, for rather would I lose my life
Than that this murderer, this homicide
Should triumph o'er my honor, though
    with force
And cruel hand he holds me here con-
    cealed.
NUÑO. Already, daughter, I have freed
    my heart
From the extreme of jealousy.
ELVIRA.   Poor Sancho,
How fares he now, who was to be my
    spouse?
NUÑO. Perforce he seeks again that fa-
    mous king,
Alfonso of Castile.
ELVIRA. He is not in the village then?
NUÑO. I look for his return to-day.
ELVIRA.   And I
To see him slain!

NUÑO. Such cruelty passes belief.
ELVIRA. He swears by heaven to rend
    him limb from limb.
NUÑO. Sancho is wise and will protect
    himself.
ELVIRA. Oh, that I had it in my power
    to leap
Headlong from this high tower into your
    arms!
NUÑO. Here waiting with a thousand
    fold embrace!
ELVIRA. Father I go; 'tis best. They
    seek for me.
Farewell, father!
NUÑO.   Never to meet again!
I die! . . .   [ELVIRA disappears.]

          [Enter DON TELLO.]
DON TELLO. How now? With whom,
    churl, do you speak?
NUÑO. I speak my grief unto these
    stones, Señor,
Which mourn with me the usage I re-
    ceive;
For though you imitate the hardened
    stone
My anxious fears fly ever from relief
Hard following after on the trail of pain
How vainly! For though the stone be
    hardened stone
Yet heaven has lent it pity.
DON TELLO.   You peasant slaves,
Though you should voice laments and rain
    down tears
And heap thereon vast store of base in-
    vention,
The object of my passion shall not 'scape
From out my hands. You are the tyrants,
    churls,
Who will not whisper in her ear to yield
And lend occasion to my fixed intent;
For I adore and love her. How can it be,
Dying for her, Elvira dies by me?
What lady, think you, this Elvira is?
Or is she more than a poor farmer's daugh-
    ter?
You all live by the fields; yet well you
    say,
Seeing the base subjection of the heart,
There is no lordship like frail beauty's
    sway

With youth and spirit blended and wise
art.

NUÑO.   You speak the truth, Señor, so
help you God!

DON TELLO.   If she will do her part, I
shall in turn
Requite your just deserts.

NUÑO.   To hands like these
Must the long-suffering world confide its
laws?
The poor shall yield his honor to the rich
And then acclaim him just!   Only his
will
He holds for law, and he has power to
kill!   [*Exit*.]

DON TELLO.   Ho! Celio!

[*Enter* CELIO.]

CELIO.   Señor——

DON TELLO.   Lead out Elvira
To the place I have commanded.

CELIO.   Consider, my lord;
Look what you do . . .

DON TELLO.   He cannot see who's blind.

CELIO.   I pray you be advised; to force
her, sir,
Were cruelty.

DON TELLO.   Well, had she pitied me
I had not forced her, Celio.

CELIO.   Señor,
Such courage and such chastity are rare
And greatly to be prized.

DON TELLO.   Argue no more
Against my will!   An end to misery!
How base in me to suffer such disdain!
Did Tarquin stay to sate his royal lust?
No not an hour; and when the morning
came
His torment was assuaged.   And shall I
wait
Whole days upon a peasant?

CELIO.   Will you haste
And like him suffer equal punishment?
It is not well to ape the evil deed,
Only the good.

DON TELLO.   Or good or ill, today
She yields submission of her proud dis-
dain;
Obsession now, love once it may have been.
Elvira is not Tamar; she shall rue it
And I avenge me on her contumely!
                                    [*Exeunt*.]

A Room in NUÑO'S *House.*

[*Enter* SANCHO, PELAYO *and* JUANA.]

JUANA.   You are both welcome home.

SANCHO.   I cannot say how well we are
come, although some good may well come
out of it, Juana, so it be the will of
heaven.

PELAYO.   So it be the will of heaven,
Juana, at least it will come out . . .
well, that we have come.   Because a horse
is obliged to keep his thoughts to himself
is no reason, I say, why a man should
envy a horse.

JUANA.   Do you think they will murder
us all?

SANCHO.   Where is the master?

JUANA.   Gone, I think, to speak with
Elvira.

SANCHO.   What?   Will Don Tello per-
mit her to talk with him?

JUANA.   Through a window in a tower,
as Celio said.

SANCHO.   Does she still remain in the
tower?

PELAYO.   It makes no matter anyway,
because somebody is coming who will soon
make him . . .

SANCHO.   Take care, Pelayo . . .

PELAYO [*aside*].   I forgot both fingers.

JUANA.   Here comes Nuño.

[*Enter* NUÑO.]

SANCHO.   Señor!

NUÑO.   My son, what news?

SANCHO.   I return with a lighter heart
to your service.

NUÑO.   You return with a lighter heart?
In what way?

SANCHO.   I bring a just judge with me.

PELAYO.   We are bringing a judge with
us who will. . . .

SANCHO.   Take care, Pelayo . . .

PELAYO [*aside*].   I forgot both fingers.

NUÑO.   But has he a large force with
him?

SANCHO.   Two men.

NUÑO.   Then I must entreat you to at-
tempt nothing further, my son.   The ef-
fort will be useless, because a mighty
nobleman upon his own estates, where
he is provided with arms and vassals and

with money, will either twist justice to his liking, or else some night when we are all asleep he will have us murdered in our beds.

PELAYO. Murdered? Aha! But I like that! Didn't you ever play a trump, man? Why, I tell you Don Tello has led a two spot and—well we hold the ace of spades.

SANCHO. Pelayo, have you any sense?

PELAYO [aside]. I forgot both fingers.

SANCHO. You must have lodgings made ready for him, master, because he is a right worthy and an honorable man.

PELAYO. He is so honorable that I might almost say . . .

SANCHO. God help you, fool! . . .

PELAYO [aside]. I forgot both fingers . . . [Aloud.] I had better not say another word.

NUÑO. Rest yourself, my son. Before we are done, I fear this infatuation will have cost the forfeit of your life.

SANCHO. But first I must see the tower where my Elvira is confined. As surely as the sun casts a shadow some trace of her presence must be left behind her at the bars; but if the sun has set and there is none, then I know that my imagination will be able to conjure up an image of its own. [Exit.]

NUÑO. What rare devotion!

JUANA. I verily believe there was never anything like it in the world.

NUÑO. Come here, Pelayo.

PELAYO. I have to tell the cook something.

NUÑO. Come here, I say.

PELAYO. I'll be back in a moment.

NUÑO. Come here.

PELAYO. What do you want?

NUÑO. Who is this Sir Judge, this magistrate that Sancho brings home with him?

PELAYO. This judge, sir, this magistrate . . . Oh, we have hooked him! [Aside.] God help me with a good one! [Aloud.] He is a man of excellent fine judgment, pale yet fiery, and tall if somewhat dwarfed of person, with a mouth at the place where he eats and a red beard and a black one too; and if I make no mis-

take, he is a great doctor, or else he will shortly prove himself to be one, only when he orders people to be bled, it is always somehow at the neck . . .

NUÑO. Juana, was there ever such a stupid beast?

[Enter BRITO.]

BRITO. Hurry, Señor Nuño, three gentlemen are dismounting at the door of the house from three fine horses, all with new clothes on, and boots and spurs and plumes waving all over.

NUÑO. So help me God, but they are here! What? A judge who wears plumes?

PELAYO. Oh, there be such, sir, as do plume themselves, though frivolous mayhap, because a sober judge unless he is detained by some important bribery, goes back as impartial to the court again as he came out of it in the first place, which was a matter of course, and then he tells you what he makes out of it.

NUÑO. Who taught this animal this arrant nonsense?

PELAYO. Have I not just come from court? What is the matter with you?

[Enter the KING, the COUNT and DON ENRIQUE in traveling dress. With them SANCHO.]

SANCHO. I knew you as soon as I saw you a great way off.

KING [apart to SANCHO]. Remember, Sancho; no word that I am here.

NUÑO. You are welcome, sir.

KING. Who are you?

SANCHO. This is Nuño, my father-in-law.

KING. Well met, Nuño.

NUÑO. I kiss your feet a thousand times.

KING. Let all the laborers be warned, lest Don Tello be advised a judge has come.

NUÑO. Then it will be better, in my opinion, if we have them all locked up, so that none may wander from the house. [SANCHO speaks to BRITO and JUANA who go out.] Sir, my mind misgives me of this business. You have only brought two men. There is not a more powerful lord in all the kingdom, nor none richer nor more headstrong.

KING. Nuño, the King's staff is like the thunder—it gives warning where the lightning is about to strike. As you see, I came along to dispense justice for the King.

NUÑO. I behold such god-like worth in your presence as makes me tremble, although I am the wronged.

KING. I will take the depositions.

NUÑO. Rest yourself, first, sir; for you have more than time.

KING. I have never more than time. Did you arrive home well, Pelayo?

PELAYO. Yes, my Lord, I arrived home very well. Your Highness remembers . . .

KING. What I told you?

PELAYO. Yes, to put on the bridle. Your Grace had a pleasant journey?

KING. Thanks be to God, a very pleasant journey.

PELAYO. By my faith, if we ever get through with this business, I have made up my mind to present you with a pig as big as yourself.

SANCHO. Silence, you fool!

PELAYO. A little one then, like I am.

KING. Summon your people without further delay.

[PELAYO *goes to the door and calls.*]

[*Enter* BRITO, FILENO, JUANA *and* LEONOR.]

BRITO. What is your wish, master?

NUÑO. It will be necessary for you to wait a long while till the shepherds have come in from the valleys and the ridges.

KING. Those who are here will suffice. —Tell me, who are you?

BRITO. I am Brito, kind sir—a shepherd upon these pastures.

PELAYO. He is the son of some goatherds attached to the place hereabouts and something near a goat himself by the same token.

KING. What know you of Don Tello and this matter of Elvira?

BRITO. Some men carried her off on the night of her wedding day; and they broke down these gates.

KING. And you? . . . Who are you?

JUANA. Juana, sir, your servant who waits on Elvira; but now alas! I know she has lost her honor and her life!

KING. And who is this good man?

PELAYO. My Lord, this is Fileno the piper. At night he does nothing but pipe up and down after the witches, all over these ploughed fields; so one night they out and dragged him along behind after them, since when, like a salmon, he has had scales on the bottom.

KING. Declare what you know of this.

FILENO. I was coming in to pipe, sir, and I saw Don Tello give orders not to let the priest come in. And when the wedding was broken off he carried Elvira away with him to his house and her father and her kin have been there since to see her.

KING. Who is this country wench?

PELAYO. She is Leonora of Cueto, daughter of Pedro Miguel of Cueto, whose grandfather was Nuño of Cueto, while at the same time he had for uncle Martin Cueto, who was olive-presser for the entire neighborhood—all of them very noble people. He had two aunts, though, who were witches, but that was a long time ago, and he had a nephew who was squint-eyed, and he was the first man who planted turnips in Galicia.

KING. That will do for the present.— Gentlemen, to rest. We shall pay a visit to Don Tello—yes, this afternoon.

COUNT. Upon less testimony than this you might well be assured that Sancho has not deceived you. The guilelessness of these folk is the most convincing proof.

KING [*apart to* NUÑO]. Let a priest be sent for secretly, and a headsman.

[*Exeunt the* KING, *the* COUNT *and* DON ENRIQUE.]

NUÑO [*to* SANCHO, *apart*]. Sancho——

SANCHO. Master——

NUÑO. I cannot understand what sort of a judge this man is. Without entering a process, he sends for a priest and an executioner.

SANCHO. Nuño, I do not understand what he would do.

NUÑO. Even with an armed battalion he could not take him. How much less then with two men!

SANCHO. We had better make sure though that he has first food enough to eat. Afterwards we shall discover whether or not he is able to go through with the business.

NUÑO. Will they all eat at the same time?

SANCHO. I think that the judge will eat by himself and the others will eat afterwards together.

NUÑO. Belike his scribe and constable.

SANCHO. I think so too.   [*Exit.*]

NUÑO. Juana!

JUANA. Sir?

NUÑO. Spread a clean cloth and look you that four hens be killed without delay, and roast a good fat side of pork. And while it is being flayed put that young, tender turkey on; let it be roasted too, while Fileno goes down into the vault for wine.

PELAYO. Sunshine and heaven, Nuño, but I must break bread with that judge today!

NUÑO. You are the kind who never will learn judgment.   [*Exit.*]

PELAYO. It is a terrible thing that Kings must always eat alone. That is the reason, I suppose, they are willing to have dogs and fools around.   [*Exeunt.*]

Courtyard before the Country Seat of DON TELLO. *A wall or barred grating at the rear.*

[ELVIRA *fleeing from* DON TELLO, *and* FELICIANA *holding him back.*]

ELVIRA. Help, help, O heaven! I have no hope on earth
Nor succor . . .   [*Exit.*]

DON TELLO. I will kill her!

FELICIANA. Hold your hand!

DON TELLO. Have care! I shall forget that nice respect
I owe to you, Feliciana.

FELICIANA.   Yes,

Because I am your sister you accord
What you deny to woman.

DON TELLO.   Pest on the peasant!
She is mad. What? For a base, clownish love
Shall she be wanting in a due respect
Unto her master, out of vanity
And empty pride? She holds a steadfast belief
In her armor of resistance. I come to kill—
Either I slay her or bend her to my will!   [*Exit.*]
          [*Enter* CELIO.]

CELIO. I know not whether these be idle fears
Which vex me, lady. Nuño I saw but now
In entertainment of some guests of worth.
The shepherd Sancho has returned to town,
While all observe rare caution. With some complaint
Feigned cunningly, no doubt he was despatched
Into Castile. I never saw them act
With equal secrecy.

FELICIANA. You have not chosen wisely, Celio,
To rest in such suspicion. Ample occasion
To enter boldly and discern the truth
Were sure not wanting.

CELIO.   When he saw me enter
I feared lest Nuño might take quick offense,
For all there bear us ill.

FELICIANA.   Better at once
To warn my brother. The temper of this peasant
Is bold by nature, as being with him born.
You, Celio, remain and guard the gate
And watch if any come.   [*Exit.*]

CELIO.   A haunting dread
Pursues our conscience ever to its harm;
When cruelty exults beyond all bounds
It cries aloud to heaven for revenge.

[*Enter the* KING, *the* COUNT, DON ENRIQUE *and* SANCHO, *behind the grating.*]

KING. Enter and do as I command.

CELIO. Who are these people?

KING. Knock.

[*They knock. An* ATTENDANT *opens the gate and the* KING, *the* COUNT, DON ENRIQUE *and* SANCHO *enter the courtyard.*]

SANCHO. This fellow, sir, is a servant of Don Tello's.

KING. A word, hidalgo!

CELIO. Well, what do you want?

KING. Go and advise Don Tello I am here,
Making my journey from Castile posthaste
To speak with him.

CELIO. Whom shall I say?

KING. Say I.

CELIO. Have you no other name than I?

KING. Say no.

CELIO. No more than I, and yet of a good presence?
In faith you have me in a quandary;
I go to tell him I am at the gate. [*Exit.*]

DON ENRIQUE. He has gone in.

COUNT. I fear some hot reply;
'Twere better roundly to declare yourself.

KING. Indeed it were not, for his guilty fears
Will whisper quickly only I am I,
And only I say I with like import
In all these realms.

[*Reënter* CELIO.]

CELIO. I told Don Tello how you were called I,
He being my lord and master. He replies
In that case better turn you back again;
For only he is I by right of rule
And by just law of heaven as of earth
Where he is, and he alone, save him
Who is high God in heaven, and on earth
The King.

KING. Say then an Alcalde of his court
And of his house.

CELIO [*disturbed*]. I go to bear this name.

KING. Mark well what I have said.
[*Exit* CELIO.]

COUNT. The Squire's perturbed.

DON ENRIQUE. And the name the reason.

SANCHO. Nuño is here. Grant license,
Sire, I pray,
That he may enter, if so it be your will.

KING. Bid him come in, for he shall have a part
In all that passes as he may desire,
In the righting even as the bearing of the wrong.

[*Enter* NUÑO, PELAYO, JUANA *and* PEASANTS, *behind the grating.*]

SANCHO. Come, Nuño, approach; you may observe what passes from without.

NUÑO. The mere sight of this villain's house fills me with rage.—Be silent all!

JUANA. You talk, Pelayo, and keep our courage up; he is beside himself.

PELAYO. I'll show you now how little difference there is between me and a stone.

NUÑO. To come with only two men! Marvellous hardihood!

[*Enter* DON TELLO, FELICIANA *and* ATTENDANTS.]

FELICIANA. I pray you, sir, consider what you do . . .
Hold, brother! Whither would you go?

DON TELLO. Hidalgo,
Are you, perchance, that Alcalde of Castile
Who fain would speak with me?

KING. Do you wonder?

DON TELLO. And not a little, yea, I swear to God,
So you know who I am.

KING. In the King's name
How does he differ from our lord the King
Who comes for him?

DON TELLO. Wide worlds to me. But you—
Where is your wand of justice?

KING. In its sheathe,
From which it presently shall issue forth
And what will come will come.

DON TELLO. Only a wand in your sheathe? I like that well,

Indeed you do not know me! Unless the
King
Against me comes with iron bond and
brand,
No power throughout the world shall stay
my hand!
KING. I am the King, thou slave!
PELAYO. Saint Dominic of Silos!
DON TELLO. What, Sire? . . . What!
Can it be such state as this
Is the caparison of Spanish might?
You here yourself! In your own person,
you?
I humbly ask your pardon.
KING. Strip off his arms!—
[DON TELLO *is disarmed;* NUÑO
and the PEASANTS *come for-
ward through the gate.*]
Now by my crown, thou slave, thou shalt
respect
The letters of the King.
FELICIANA. Abate your rigor
I humbly pray, Señor!
KING. All prayer is vain.
Bring in the wife of this poor country-
man.
[*Exit an* ATTENDANT.]
DON TELLO. I pray you, Sire, but she
was not his wife.
KING. Enough for me that such was
her intent.
Is not her father here, who in our pres-
ence
Has uttered his complaint?
DON TELLO [*aside*]. My just death is
near;
I have offended God—God and the King!

[*Enter* ELVIRA, *her hair disheveled.*]
ELVIRA. The moment my sorrows
To thee might complain,
Castilian Alfonso
Who governs all Spain,
I broke from my prison,
The cell which confined,
To petition thy justice,
Royal mercy to find.
Daughter to Nuño
Of Aibar am I,
In honor and station
Well-known and high

Through all these lands.
Sancho of Roelas
Sought me in love;
My father consenting
His suit did approve.
Don Tello of Neira
By Sancho was served,
Who begged his lord's license
Ere the rite be observed.
He came with his sister,
Our sponsors they stood.
He saw me, he craved me
And foul plot he brewed.
He put off the wedding,
He came to my door
With men bearing weapons
And black masks before.
I was borne to his dwelling,
With treacherous art
He sought to destroy me,
My chaste firmness of heart.
And then from that dwelling
I was haled to a wood,
A farm house adjacent,
A fourth league removed.
There, where only
Was tangle of trees.
Which the sun could not peep through
To be witness with these—
The trees heard my mourning,
My sad, long lament.
My locks tell the story—
What struggles I bent
Against his offending,
And all the flowers know
How I left on their blooming
Fond tresses of woe;
My eyes tell the story—
What tears there I shed
That the hard rock might soften
Like down to the head.
I shall live now in weeping,
How shall she retain
Contentment or pleasure
Whose honor lies slain?
Yet in this I am happy—
That here I complain
To the Greatest Alcalde
That governs in Spain.
I plead for his justice,
I beg of his rule

Pity for wronging
So false and so cruel.
This be my petition,
Alfonso, whose feet
My poor lips with kisses
Humbly entreat.
And so may thy offspring
Rule conquered and free
The parts of thy kingdom
The Moor holds in fee,
Through happy war. Poor
My tongue in praise,
But endless song and story
Shall prolong thy days!

KING. It grieves my heart to have arrived too late;
I would have come in time to salve these wounds
And right the wrongs of Sancho and of Nuño.
But yet I may do justice, and strike off
The head from Tello.—Send for the headsman.

FELICIANA. Have pity, Sire, in royal clemency
Upon my brother.

KING.   Even without this cause,
Defiance and contempt of our own hand,
Our letter and our proper signature—
These had been crimes enough. Humbled today
Your pride lies, Tello, shattered at my feet.

DON TELLO. Although there were a direr penalty,
Unconquered Sire, than the death I now await,
I do confess of right it should be mine.

DON ENRIQUE. If humbly in your presence . . .

COUNT.   Mercy, Sire;

Be moved, for you were nurtured in this land.

FELICIANA. The Count Don Pedro, Sire, merits the life
Of Tello—a boon in payment of his service.

KING. The Count deserves of me a holy love
Such as one bears a father; but it is just
In equal wise the Count should know
What the allegiance he doth owe
Unto my justice, which admits no answer.

COUNT. Is mercy weakness, Sire?

KING. When justice fails and wanders from the mark
No mercy ever sets it right again.
In this divine and human writ agree
With copious example:—traitor that man
Who to his King is niggard of respect
Or absent speaks against his dignity.
Give, Tello, Elvira now that humbled hand,
So shall you expiate your full offense,
Becoming her husband; when they strike off your head
Then she shall marry Sancho, with a dower
Of half your lands and hoarded revenues.
And you, Feliciana, shall be dame
Of this our Court and Queen, until such time
As we shall find by grace a worthy spouse,
To match your noble blood.

NUÑO. I tremble . . .

PELAYO.   Good . . . King! . . .

SANCHO. Here ends the comedy "The Greatest Alcalde,"
A history the Chronicle of Spain
Records as true, the Fourth Part of the tale.

THE CONSTANT PRINCE

By PEDRO CALDERÓN DE LA BARCA

Produced at Madrid in 1635

TRANSLATED BY DENIS FLORENCE MAC CARTHY

CHARACTERS

DON FERNANDO, } *Princes of Portugal*
DON ENRIQUE,

DON JUAN COUTIÑO

ALPHONSO, *King of Portugal*

BRITO, *a Portuguese soldier*

THE KING OF FEZ

MULÉY, *his general*

TARUDANTE, *King of Morocco*

SELIM, *in the service of the* KING OF FEZ

THE PRINCESS PHENIX, *daughter of the* KING OF FEZ

ROSA,
ZARA,
ESTRELLA,   } *her attendants*
ZELIMA,

SOLDIERS, CHRISTIAN SLAVES, MUSICIANS, ATTENDANTS, etc.

ACT I

SCENE I—*The gardens of the* KING OF FEZ, *by the sea.*

[*Enter some* CHRISTIAN CAPTIVES *singing, and* ZARA.]

ZARA.   Sing, from out this thicket here.
While the beauteous Phenix dresses;—
Those sweet songs, whose air expresses
Fond regrets; which pleased her ear
Often in the baths,—those strains
Full of grief and sentiment.—

1ST CAPTIVE.   Can Music, whose strange instrument
Was our clanking gyves and chains—
Can it be, our wail could bring
Joy unto her heart? our woe
Be to her delight?—

129

ZARA.　　　　　'Tis so:—
She from this will hear you; sing.
2ND CAPTIVE. Ah! this anguish doth
　　exceed,
Beauteous Zara, all the rest—
Since from out a captive's breast
(Save a soulless bird's indeed)
Never has a willing strain
Of music burst.
ZARA.　　　　But have not you
Yourselves sung many a time?—
3RD CAPTIVE.　　　　　'Tis true;
But then it was no stranger's pain
To which we hoped some ease to bring,
It was our own too bitter grief
For which in song we sought relief.
ZARA. She is listening now—then sing.
CAPTIVES [sing]. Age doth not respect
The fair or the sublime;
Nothing stands erect
Before the face of time.

[Enter ROSA.]

ROSA. Captives, you can now retire,
And your pleasing concert end,
For fair Phenix doth descend
To this garden, to inspire
Joy, where'er her footsteps stray:—
Coming like a second morn,
Young Aurora newly born.—
　　　　[The CAPTIVES go out.]

[Enter PHENIX, attended by her Moorish
maidens, ESTRELLA and ZELIMA, etc.,
　　　　dressing her.]
ESTRELLA. Beauteous have you risen
　　today.
ZARA. Let the dawn, so purely bright,
Boast no more, this garden owes
To her its beauty—that the rose
Draws from her its purple light,
Or the jessamine its whiteness.
PHENIX. The glass.
ESTRELLA. Thou should'st not strive to
　　find
Specks the pencil ne'er designed
In its artificial brightness.
　　　[They present her with a mirror.]
PHENIX. What does loveliness avail
　　me,
(If, indeed, 'tis mine to vaunt it)—

If my joy of heart be wanted?—
If life's happiest feelings fail me?—
ZELIMA. How dost thou feel?
PHENIX.　　　　　If I but knew,
Ah! my Zelima, how I feel,
That certain knowledge soon would steal
Half of the grief that pains me through:—
I do not know its nature wholly,
Although it robs my heart of gladness;
For now it seemeth tearful sadness,—
And now 'tis pensive melancholy:—
I only know, I know I feel—
But what I feel I do not know,—
The sweet illusions mock me so.
ZARA. Since these gardens cannot steal
Away your oft-returning woes—
Though to beauteous spring, they build
Snow-white jasmine temples filled
With radiant statues of the rose,
Come unto the sea, and make
Thy bark the chariot of the sun.—
ROSA. And when the golden splendours
　　run
Athwart the waves, along thy wake—
The garden to the sea will say
(By melancholy fears deprest),
The sun already gilds the west,
How very short has been this day!—
PHENIX. Ah! no more can gladden me
Sunny shores, or dark projections,
Where in emulous reflections
Blend the rival land and sea;
When, alike in charms and powers,
Where the woods and waves are meet-
　　ing—
Flowers with foam are seen competing—
Sparkling foam with snow-white flowers;
For the garden, envious grown
Of the curling waves of ocean,
Loves to imitate their motion;
And the amorous zephyr, blown
Out to sea from fragrant bowers,
In the shining waters laving
Back returns, and makes the waving
Leaves an ocean of bright flowers:
When the sea too, sad to view
Its barren waste of waves forlorn,
Striveth swiftly to adorn
All its realm, and to subdue
The pride of its majestic mien,
To second laws it doth subject

Its nature, and with sweet effect
Blends fields of blue with waves of green.
Coloured now like heaven's blue dome,
Now plumed as if from verdant bowers,
The garden seems a sea of flowers,
The sea a garden of bright foam:
How deep my pain must be, is plain,
Since naught delights my heart or eye,
Nor earth, nor air, nor sea, nor sky.
  ZARA. Ah! deep, indeed, must be your
    pain!—

[*Enter the* KING *with a portrait in his
    hand.*]
  KING. If perchance the fever fit,
Quartan of thy beauty, let
Thee thy sadness to forget,—
This fair original (for it
Is too full of life, to be
But a picture) is the Infante
Of Morocco, Tarudante,
Who doth come to offer thee
His hand and crown; do not reprove
The ambassador who pleads his suit—
Do not doubt that he, though mute,
Bringeth messages of love:—
With favour I his wish behold,
For he hath sent to me, as liege,
Ten thousand horsemen, to besiege
Ceuta, which I long to hold:—
Let nor fears, nor vain alarms,
Nor coldness in your heart be found;
But let him soon in Fez be crowned
King of all thy beauteous charms.
  PHENIX [*aside*]. Protect me, Allah!
  KING.   What abhorred
Terror thus suspends thy breath?—
  PHENIX [*aside*]. It is the sentence of
    my death!
  KING. What is it you say?
  PHENIX [*aloud*].   My lord,
My master, and my king, to thee,
My father, what have I to say?—
[*Aside.*] What a happy chance, Muléy,
Hast thou lost! Ah! woe is me.
[*Aloud.*] Let my silence be a token
Of my dutiful reply.
[*Aside.*] In thinking it, my soul would
    lie,
My tongue would lie, if it had spoken.
  KING. Take the picture.

  PHENIX [*aside*].   Being desired,
My hand the hated gift hath got,
But my heart receives it not.
    [*The report of a cannon is heard.*]
  ZARA. This salute, my lord, is fired
For Muléy, arrived to-day
In the Sea of Fez.
  KING.   . . . 'Tis meet.

[*Enter* MULÉY *with the truncheon of a
    general.*]
  MULÉY. Give me, mighty lord, thy feet.
  KING. You are welcome home, Muléy.
  MULÉY. He who penetrates the light
Of so sovereign a sphere,
He who homeward drawing near
Finds a sun and dawn so sweet,
Well hath homeward come, indeed:—
Lady, let me kiss thy hand,
For *his* love and faith demand
Such reward, whose heart would bleed
To work his sovereign's least intent.
                    [*To the* KING.]
For newer triumphs still he burns
In thy service.—[*Aside to* PHENIX.] He
    returns
More thy lover than he went.
  PHENIX [*aside*]. Heaven protect me!
    [*To* MULÉY.] Thou, indeed,
Art most welcome. [*Aside.*] Life doth
    leave me!
  MULÉY [*aside*]. If my eyes do not de-
    ceive me,
Rather the reverse I read.
  KING. Well, Muléy, what news from
    sea?—
  MULÉY. Now thou'lt test thy suffering
Of misfortune: for I bring
Saddest news; [*Aside.*] as mine must be.
  KING. What thou knowest, let me hear,
For a firm and constant mind
Lets both good and evil find
Equal entrance: sit thou here,
Phenix.
  PHENIX. Yes.
  KING.   Let all be seated.
Now proceed thy news to tell,
Hiding nothing. [*The* KING *and ladies sit.*]
  MULÉY.   I, nor well
Can conceal it, or repeat it;—[*Aside.*]
With two galliasses only,

By command, my lord, of thee,
I departed to examine
All the coast of Barbary,
With the intention of approaching
That famed city of the South,
Known of old time as Eliza,
And which nearly at the mouth
Of the Herculean strait is founded;
Ceido is its latter name,—
For this Hebrew word and Ceuta
In the Arabic are the same,
Both expressive but of beauty,
Or the ever-beauteous town,—
That fair town, that, like a jewel,
Heaven has snatched from out thy crown.
Through, perhaps, Mahomet's anger,
Through the mighty prophet's wrath,
Which, opprobrium of our valour!
Now a foreign ruler hath.
Where we tamely gape and gaze at,
Where our slavish eye-sight sees,
Floating from its topmast turrets,
Banners of the Portuguese.
'Neath our very eyes prescribing
Limits that our arms deride—
'Tis a mockery of our praises,
'Tis a bridle to our pride,
'Tis a Caucasus, which, lying
Midway, doth the stream detain;
Back thy Nile of victory turning
From its onward course to Spain.
Hither, then, I went with orders
To examine, and to see
What the form and disposition
Of the place to-day might be;
How, with less expense and danger,
You might undertake its siege.
May heaven grant its restoration
Quickly unto you, my liege!
Though it be delayed a little
By a threatened new disgrace;
For this doubtful undertaking
To another must give place,
Far more pressing and important,
Since the thousand swords and spears
That for Ceuta you have marshall'd
Must be drawn around Tangiers
For that threatened city weepeth
Equal suffering, equal woe,
Equal ruin, equal trouble—
This, my gracious lord, I know.

For one morning on the ocean,
When the half-awaken'd sun,
Trampling down the lingering shadows
Of the western vapours dun,
Spread his ruby-tinted tresses
Over jessamine and rose,
Dried with cloths of gold, Aurora's
Tears of mingled fire and snows,
Which to pearls his glance converted.
It was then that, in the light
Of the horizon, a vast navy
Rose upon my startled sight:
First (so many a fair illusion
Oft the wandering seaman mocks),
I could not determine truly
Whether they were ships or rocks;
For, as on the coloured canvass
Subtle pencils softly blend!
Dark and bright, in such proportions
That the dim perspectives end—
Now, perhaps, like famous cities,
Now, like caves or misty capes,
For remoteness ever formeth
Monstrous and unreal shapes.
Thus, athwart the fields of azure,
Lights and shades alternate fly;
Clouds and waves in rich confusion,
Intermingling sea and sky,
Mock the sight with fair deceptions.
So it was, while I, alone,
Saw their bulk and vast proportions,
Though their form remained unknown.
First they seemed to us uplifting
High in heaven their pointed towers,
Clouds that to the sea descended,
To conceive in sapphire showers
What they would bring forth in crystal.
And this fancy seemed more true,
As from their untold abundance
They, methought, could drink the blue
Drop by drop. Again, sea-monsters,
Seemed to us the wandering droves,
Which, to form the train of Neptune,
Issued from their green alcoves.
For the sails, when lightly shaken,
Fanned by zephyrs as by slaves,
Seemed to us like outspread pinions,
Fluttering o'er the darkened waves;
Then the mass, approaching nearer,
Seemed a mighty Babylon,
With its hanging gardens pictured

By the streamers floating down.
But, although our certain vision
Undeceived, becoming true,
Showed it was a great armada,
For I saw the prows cut through
Foam, that, sparkling in the sunshine,
Like the fleece of snow-white flocks,
Rolled itself in silver mountains,
Curdled into crystal rocks.
I, so great a foe, beholding,
Turned my prow with utmost speed,
For a timely flight doth often
But to quicker victory lead—
And from being more experienced
In those seas, the entrance made,
Of a little creek, where, hidden
In the shelter and the shade,
I could best resist the powerful
Fury of a power so vast,
Which sea, sky and earth o'ershadowed;
Without seeing us, they passed:—
I, desiring to discover
(Who would not desire to know?)
Whither did this great armada
O'er the darkened ocean go—
Once again my anchor weighing,
Sought the blue sea's level plain,
And full knowledge, in this manner,
Heaven permitted me to gain:—
For I saw, of this armada
But one ship remained behind,
Which with difficulty struggled
With the warring wave and wind:
Since, as afterwards was told me,
From a tempest which had blown
Over all the fleet, it issued
Rent, disabled, and o'erthrown;
And so full of water was she,
That the men that worked thereat,
Scarcely baled her out, and reeling
Now on this side, now on that,
Seemed, with every fluctuation,
On the point of going down.
I approached, and though my Moorish
Garb and colours made them frown,
Still my company consoled them,
For companionship in woes
Ever gives alleviation,
Even though it be a foe's.
The desire of life arising
So provoked the hearts of some,

That by ladders made of twisted
Cords and cables, did they come
To our ship, although a prison;
But the rest, resisting, cried,
"Life is but to live with honour!"—
Proof of Portuguese vain pride!—
One of those who left the vessel
Thus informed me in detail:
Lately, thus he said, from Lisbon
Did the great armada sail
For Tangiers: and its heroic
Resolution seems to be,
To besiege it with such valour,
That upon its towers you'll see
The five shields, you see at Ceuta
Every time the sun doth rise.
Edward, Portugal's great monarch,
Whose renown of conquest flies
As on wings of Roman eagles,
Has sent thither to preside
Over them his own two brothers,
Fernando and Enrique,—pride
Of this age, which early sees them
Crowned with conquest: and each chief
Is Grand Master both of Avis
And of Christ: in white relief
On their breasts they bear two crosses,
One of green, the other red;
Fourteen thousand is the number
Of the paid troops, thither led—
Without mentioning the many
Volunteers, that with them serve,
At their own expense; a thousand
Are the steeds—whose fire and nerve,
Mixed with Spanish mettle, clothe them
With the tiger's glossy skin
And the swift foot of the panther:—
Now perhaps they enter in
Tangiers' waters,—at this moment,
If its shore they have not made,
They at least cleave through its waters:
Let us hasten to its aid:
You yourself, your arms assuming,
Mahomet's dread scourges bear—
And the brightest leaf it carries,
From death's mystic volume, tear:—
That this day may be accomplished
That brave prophecy of yore—
Of the Moors, which says, 'tis destined
That upon the sandy shore
Of our Africa, the glory

Of the crown of Portugal
There its hapless grave must meet with.
And these proud invaders shall
See thee, as thy curved sword waveth
O'er each prostrate foeman's head,
Turn the fields, both green and azure,
With their gushing hearts—blood red.

KING. Silence! do not speak the rest,
For my heart such wrath is feeling,
That each word is like the stealing
Of strong poison through my breast:
Graves amid the deserts yonder
I will ope, by sure disasters,
For the Infantes, those Grand Masters
Who have hither dared to wander:—
You, Muléy, along the coast
With a troop of horse depart,
And by every means that art
Can devise, engage the host
In such skirmishes of skill
That they cannot make the land
Until I can be at hand:—
And in doing so, you will
Show the blood that fills your veins.
I shall follow with all speed,
And the gallant rear-guard lead
Of the troops that fill these plains:
Thus, to-day, my many cares
And quarrels shall in one combine,
For great Ceuta shall be mine
And Tangiers shall not be theirs. [*Exit.*]

MULÉY. Though I must depart, yet I,
Lady, first would let thee hear,
Since my death approacheth near,
The malady with which I die.
And although my jealous fear
Disrespectful seem to thee,
Since my disease is jealousy,
Courtesy must disappear.
What picture—(ah! fair enemy!)
Is this thy beauteous fingers bear?
What is his happy name?—declare,
This favoured being, who is he?
But no; let not thy tongue eclipse
The pain thy touch hath made me bear;
Since in thy hand I see him there,
Thou needst not name him with thy lips!

PHENIX. Although, Muléy, thou hast
from me
Leave to love and to attend me,
Thou hast not any to offend me.

MULÉY. 'Tis true, fair Phenix, yes, I
see
That this is not the mode or style
Of speaking to thee; but the skies
Know, when jealous thoughts arise
Respect is overborne a while.
With utmost caution—secret pride—
I've hid the passion that I feel;
But, though my love I could conceal,
My jealousy I cannot hide—
In truth I cannot.

PHENIX. Though thy crime
Deserves not to be satisfied,
Still, will I, through wounded pride,
Satisfy thee this one time.
Friends their friendship ne'er should lose,
When a word might keep it still.

MULÉY. And wilt thou speak that
word?

PHENIX. I will.

MULÉY. God grant thee ever happy
news!

PHENIX. This picture has to me been
sent. . . .

MULÉY. By whom?

PHENIX. His Highness the Infante
Of Morocco, Tarudante.

MULÉY. And why?

PHENIX. It seems with this intent,—
My father, being ignorant
Of my feelings . . .

MULÉY. Well?—

PHENIX. Pretends
That their realms . . .

MULÉY. Is this the amends,
The satisfaction, thou dost grant?—
God grant thee evil news instead!—

PHENIX. Why for a fault must I atone
That was my father's act alone?

MULÉY. For taking, though he left
thee dead,
This picture as a willing bride?

PHENIX. Could I prevent it?

MULÉY. Yes, 'tis plain.

PHENIX. How?

MULÉY. Some excuse thou well
couldst feign.

PHENIX. What could I do?

MULÉY. Thou couldst have died,
As I would gladly do for thee.

PHENIX. 'Twas force prevailed.

MULÉY. A mere pretence—
'Twas fickleness.

PHENIX. 'Twas violence.

MULÉY. Nor violence.

PHENIX. What could it be?

MULÉY. Absence has been my hope's
dark tomb;
And since I cannot be secure,
Nor fix thy changing fancy sure,
I must return and meet my doom.
Thou wilt return, fair Phenix, too,
Once more to grieve me to the heart.

PHENIX. We now must separate: de-
part—

MULÉY. My soul first separates in two.

PHENIX. Thou to Tangiers, and I shall
wait
In Fez—to hear thee make an end
Of thy complaints.

MULÉY. And I'll attend,
If I am spared till then by fate.

PHENIX. Adieu! for it is heaven's de-
cree
We taste this bitter parting's woe.

MULÉY. But listen—wilt thou let me
go,
Nor give that portrait up to me?

PHENIX. 'Twere thine but for the
king's request.

MULÉY. Release it—justice doth de-
mand
That I should pluck from out thy hand
Him who has plucked me from thy breast.
[*Exeunt.*]

SCENE II—*The sea-coast near Tangiers.*

[*Amid the sound of trumpets and the
noise of disembarking, enter* DON FER-
NANDO, DON ENRIQUE, DON JUAN COUTIÑO,
*and Soldiers successively from their
ships.*]

FERNANDO. I must be first, fair Africa,
to tread
Upon the sandy margin of thy shore;
That as thou feelest on thy prostrate head
The weight of my proud footsteps tram-
pling o'er,
Thou may'st perceive to whom thy sway
is given.

ENRIQUE. I am the second whom the
swift waves bore
To tread this Africa! [*He stumbles and
falls.*]
Preserve me, Heaven!
Even here my evil auguries pursue.

FERNANDO. Let not, Enrique, thy stout
heart be riven
By fancied omens, as weak women do;
This fall should waken hopes and not
alarms.
The land a fitting welcome gives to you,
For, as its lord, it takes you to its arms.

ENRIQUE. The sight of us the Moorish
herd appalls,
And they have fled, deserting fields and
farms.

JUAN. Tangiers has closed the gates
around its walls.

FERNANDO. They all have fled for safer
shelter there.
On you, Don Juan, Count Miralva, falls
The duty of examining with care
All the approaches of the land, before
The sultry sun, o'ercoming with its glare
The temperate dawn, oppress and wound
us more.
Salute the city; call on it to yield;
Say 'tis in vain to squander human gore
In its defence; for though each conquered
field
Ran red with blood, and burning blew
the wind,
And 'neath our tread the tottering ram-
parts reeled,
We still would take it.

JUAN. You will quickly find
I'll reach its gates, although, volcano-
like,
With thickest clouds it strikes the bright
sun blind,
And lightnings flash and bolts around
me strike! [*Exit.*]

[*Enter* BRITO.]

BRITO. Thanks be to God! that April
and sweet May
Once more I walk on, and that, as I like,
Without unpleasant reelings and dismay
I go about upon the solid ground.
Not as just now at sea, when, yea or nay,

Within a wooden monster's caverns
    bound,
Though light of foot I could not get
    away
Even when in greatest fear of being
    drown'd.
So little weary of the world am I,
O dry land, mine! obtain for me, I pray,
That I may never in the water die,
Nor even on land till near to the last
    day.
    ENRIQUE [to FERNANDO]. Why dost
        thou listen to this fool?
    FERNANDO.   And why,
Against all reason, dost thou persevere,
In vague forebodings and unreal grief!
    ENRIQUE. My soul is full of some mys-
        terious fear;—
That Fate frowns darkly is my fixed be-
    lief;
For since I saw fair Lisbon disappear,
Its well-known heights fast fading one
    by one—
Of all the thoughts that haunt me Death
    is chief!
Scarcely had we our enterprise begun,
Scarce had our ships commenced their
    onward chase,
When, in a paroxysm, the great sun,
Shrouded in clouds, concealed his golden
    face,
And angry waves in foaming madness
    wreck'd
Some of our fleet. Where'er I look I
    trace
The same disaster;—O'er the sea project
A thousand shadows;—If I view the
    sky,
Its azure veil with bloody drops seems
    fleck'd;—
If to the once glad air I turn mine eye,
Dark birds of night their mournful
    plumage wave;—
If on the earth, my fall doth prophesy
And represent my miserable grave.
    FERNANDO. Let me decipher with affec-
        tionate care,
And so your breast from dark forebodings
    save,
These fancied omens from earth, sea, and
    air:

'Tis true we lost one ship amid the
    main;
That is to say, that we had troops to
    spare
From the great conquest we have come
    to gain.
The purple light that stains the radiant
    sky
Foretells a day of jubilee, not pain.
The monstrous shapes that round us float
    or fly,
Flew here, and floated ere we came; and
    thus
If they reveal a fatal augury,
It is to those who live here, not to us.
These idle fancies and unfounded fears
Came from the Moors, so darkly cred-
    ulous,
Not from the enlightened minds of Chris-
    tian seers.
Those who believe in them may feel
    alarms,
Not those who shut them from their
    doubting ears.
We two are Christians; we have taken
    arms,
Not through vainglory, nor the common
    prize
With which young Fame the soldier's
    bosom charms;
Nor that, perchance, in deathless books,
    men's eyes
Hereafter read of this great victory.
The faith of God we come to aggrandise;
Whether it be our fate to live or die,
Be His alone the glory and the praise.
'Tis true, we should not God's dread ven-
    geance try
Too rashly; but his anger knoweth ways
To curb the proud, and make the haughty
    bend.
You are a Christian; act a Christian's
    part:
We come to serve our God, and not offend.
But who is this?—

                [Enter DON JUAN.]
    JUAN.   My lord, obeying
Your commands, I sought the walls;
And when crossing o'er the mountain,
Where the sloping verdure falls,

I beheld a troop of horsemen
Riding by the road to Fez—
Riding with such wondrous fleetness
That the startled gazer says,
Are they birds, or are they horses?
Do they fly, or do they bound?
For the air doth not sustain them,
And they scarcely touch the ground.
Even the earth and air were doubtful
If they flew, or if they ran.
   FERNANDO. Let us hasten to receive
them,
Placing foremost in the van
Those who bear the arquebuses;
Let the horsemen next advance,
With the customary splendour
Of the harness and the lance.
On, Enrique! fortune offers
Now a noble opening fight.
Courage!
   ENRIQUE. Am I not thy brother?
Nothing can my soul affright,
Nor the accidents of fortune,
Nor the countenance of death! [*Exeunt.*]
   BRITO [*alone*]. I must somehow act the
soldier,
And *keep guard* upon—my breath!
What a very noble skirmish!
How they spill their blood and brains!
It is best, from under cover
To survey this "Game of Canes!"—
                   [*Exit.*]

SCENE III

[*A charge is sounded: enter* DON JUAN
and DON ENRIQUE, *fighting with the
Moors.*]
   ENRIQUE. After them! The Moors al-
ready,
Vanquished, from the fight have flown!—
   JUAN. Spoils of mingled men and
horses
Over all the fields are strown.
   ENRIQUE. Where has wandered Don
Fernando,
That he cannot be descried?—
   JUAN. Doubtless his impatient valour
Leads him onward far and wide.
   ENRIQUE. Let us seek him out, Cou-
tiño,

   JUAN. I am ever at thy side.
                   [*Exeunt.*]

[*Enter* DON FERNANDO *with the sword of
Muléy, and* MULÉY *with his shield alone.*]
   FERNANDO. In this desolate campagna,
Where, devoid of sense or breath,
Lie so many dead, or rather
In this theatre of death,
You alone, of all your people,
You alone, brave Moor, have stood:
All have fled, and even your war-horse,
After shedding seas of blood,
'Mid the dust and foam encircled,
Which it raised, and which it laid,
Leaves you here to be a trophy,
By my valorous right-hand made,
'Mid your late companions' horses,
Loosely flying o'er the ground.
I am prouder of this conquest,
Which to me doth more redound,
Than to see this broad campagna,
As with bright carnations crowned;
For so great has been the flowing
Of red blood on all around,
That my eyes, through deepest pity,
At beholding naught but dead—
Naught but ever new misfortunes—
Naught but ruins round me spread,—
O'er the desert plain went seeking
One green spot amid the red.
In effect, my arm subduing
Your courageous strength to mine,
'Mid the horses loosely flying,
One I seized, who was, in fine,
Such a prodigy, a wonder,
That, although he had for sire
Even the wind, his proud ambition
Claimed adoption of the fire;
Falsely thus, by both denying
His own hue, which being white,
Said the water, " 'Tis the offspring
Of my sphere so silver white.
I alone could thus have moulded
Such a form of curdled snow!"
Like the wind he went in fleetness,
Lightning-like flashed to and fro;
Like the swan his dazzling whiteness,
Speckled like the snake with blood,
Proud of his unrivall'd beauty,
Fearless in his haughtier mood;

Full of spirit in his neighing;
In his fetlocks firm and strong,
In the saddle, on his haunches,
You and I thus borne along—
On a sea of blood we entered,
Through whose cruel waves we steered,
Like an animated vessel,
For his head a prow appeared,
Breaking through the pearl-hued water.
And his mane and tail did float,
Blood and foam besprinkled over,
So that once again a boat,
Wounded by four spurs, he bounded,
As if heaven's four winds impelled;
He at length fell down exhausted
By the Atlas he upheld;—
For so great are some misfortunes,
That even brutes themselves must feel,
Or it may be, that some instinct
Through his softened soul did steal,
Saying, "Sad Arabia journeys,
And with joy departeth Spain;
Can I then betray my country,
Swelling the proud conqueror's train?
No, I do not wish to wander
One step farther from this spot."
And since thou thyself art coming
In such sorrow, though 'tis not
By the mouth or eyes acknowledged,
Still the smothered fire appears,
Of the bosom's hid volcanos,
By those flowing tender tears;
And the burning sighs thou heavest,
Wonderingly my valour views,
When I turn me round, how fortune
With one single blow subdues
Valour such as thine. Another
Cause, methinks, must sadden thee;
Since it is not just nor proper,
Even though for liberty,
That the man should weep so fondly,
Who so heavily can wound;
And, as in communicating
Evils, there is ever found
Something soothing to the feelings,
While we to my people go,
If I merit such a favour,
My desire is now to know,—
And with reason it entreats it,
Gently and with courtesy,—
What doth grieve thee? since 'tis certain

'Tis not thy captivity.
Sorrow, when communicated,
Is appeased, if not subdued,—
And since I have been the occasion
Partly of what hath ensued
From the accident of fortune,
I would wish to be likewise
Prompt in bringing consolation
To the cause of all thy sighs,
If the cause itself consenteth.
    MULÉY. Thou art truly valiant, Span-
    iard,
Victor both in act and word,
With the tongue às skilled to conquer,
As to conquer with the sword;
For my life was thine, when lately
With the sword my race among,
You subdued me, but this moment,
Since you take me with the tongue,
Even my soul is thine; with reason
Must my life and soul confess
They are thine, and thou their master.
For your arms and your address,
Cruel now, and now too clement,
Twice my soul have captive made.
Moved with pity to behold me,
Spaniard, you the cause have prayed
Of the burning sighs I'm breathing.
And although I own that woe,
When repeated, is accustomed
To grow lighter, still I know
That the person who repeats it
Wisheth that it should be so;
But *my* woe is such a master
Of my pleasures, that to keep
Them from any diminution,
Though itself be wide and deep,
It would rather not repeat it;
But 'tis needful I obey;
Grateful for the care you've shown me.
I am called the Cheik Muléy,
And the King of Fez's nephew.
Of an illustrious race and high,
Boasting many a Bey and Pasha.
But misfortune's son am I;
Being on life's early threshold
Folded in the arms of death,
On that plain, where many Spaniards
Found their graves, I first drew breath;
Hopeless boon to me that breathing!
For at Gelves, which you know,

I was born the year that witnessed
There, thy nation's overthrow.
To attend the King my uncle,
Came I young—but since increase
Day by day my pains and sorrows,
Cease enjoyments, wholly cease!
I to Fez came, and a beauty,
Whom since then my wondering eye
Worshipped, in the house adjoining
Lived, that I might, near her, die.
From the early years of childhood,
(For this love of mine became
Soon so constant, Time was powerless
To consume or quench its flame,)
We grew up beside each other.
Love within our childish hearts
Was not like the rapid lightning,
Which with greater fury darts
On the tender, weak, and humble,
Than upon the proud and strong;
So that he to show the varied
Powers that to love belong
Struck our hearts with different arrows;
But as water in its course
Dropping down on stone, doth mark it,
Not indeed through its own force,
No, but by continual falling,
So those tears of mine, for aye
On her heart's-stone downward dropping,
Finally did work their way
To it, though than diamond harder.
And by dint of constant love,
And through no excelling merits,
Finally did make it move.
In this state I lived a season,
Oh! how swift has been its flight!
Tasting, in their sweet aurora,
Many an amorous delight—
In an evil hour I left her,
Left her! more I need not say,
Since in my absence came another
Lover, all my peace to slay;
He is happy, I am wretched.
He is present, I away.
I a captive, he a freeman.
Ah! our fates how different,
Since your arm hath made me captive,
See how justly I lament.
    FERNANDO. Valiant-hearted Moor and
      gallant,
If thou adorest in this way,

If, as thou speakest, thou dost worship
If thou dost love as thou dost say;
If thou art jealous as thou sighest,
If thou dost fear with true dismay,
If thou dost love as thou dost suffer,
Thou sufferest in the happiest way,
And the acceptance of thy freedom
Is all the ransom thou must pay,
Return at once unto thy people,
And this unto thy lady say,
"That thou dost take me as thy servant,
A knight of Portugal doth pray;"
If she pretends her obligation
For this, to me, some price must pay,
I give to thee whate'er is owing,
So let her love the debt repay.
And thine be all the arrears of interest.
And see thy horse, which lately lay
Exhausted on the ground, hath risen
Refreshed and rested by our stay;
And since I know love's longing nature,—
How ill the absent brook delay,
I wish no longer to detain thee,
Mount on thy steed and go away.
    MULÉY. My voice to thee, doth answer
      nothing;
The flattery of a liberal heart
Is the acceptance of its offer:
Only tell me who thou art?
    FERNANDO. A man of noble birth, no
      further.
    MULÉY. Whoe'er thou art, thy conduct
      gave
This answer: I, through good and evil,
Am eternally thy slave.
    FERNANDO. Take the horse; it groweth
      late.
    MULÉY. If it appeareth so to thee,
How more to him who came a captive,
And to his lady goeth free?   [Exit.]
    FERNANDO. 'Tis generous to bestow a
      favour,
How much more, life?
    MULÉY [within]. Brave Portuguese.
    FERNANDO. 'Tis from the horse's back
      he speaketh;
What is it now that thou dost please?
    MULÉY [within]. To pay thee for so
      many favours,
Some day the duty shall be mine.
    FERNANDO. May thou enjoy them!

MULÉY [*within*].   A good action
Is never wholly lost; in fine,
Allah be thy protection, Spaniard!
FERNANDO.   If God be Allah, be he
     thine!
          [*Trumpets resound from within.*]
But what trumpet's this, whose sound
Thus disturbs the air, and echoeth o'er
     the ground?
          [*Drums from the opposite side.*]
And in this direction too
Drums are heard, the music of the two
Is that of Mars.

          [*Enter* DON ENRIQUE.]
ENRIQUE.   As swift as thought,
Have I, Fernando, for thy presence sought.
FERNANDO.   Brother, what hath hap-
     pened?
ENRIQUE.   These loud echoes
Rise from the troops of Fez, and from
     Morocco's,
For Tarudante hither flies
With succour to the king of Fez, who
     comes likewise,
Swollen with pride with all his troops
     around,
So that two mighty armies ours surround,
And their circling lines extend so far,
That we invaders and invaded are;
If upon one we turn our backs,
Badly we'll bear the other's fierce attacks,
For here and there around our leagured
     line
The dazzling lightnings of red Mars out-
     shine:
What shall we do in such disastrous
     plight?
FERNANDO.   What? Why in the fight,
With fearless minds, we'll die as brave
     men should.
Are we not Masters?—Princes of the
     blood?
Although it were enough that we had been
Two Portuguese, that never could be seen
Upon our faces any mark of fear:
Let Avis, then, and Christ our Saviour
     dear,
Be our resounding battle-cry,
Let us for the faith now die,
Since our death was here foreseen.

          [*Enter* DON JUAN.]
JUAN.   Our landing here has most un-
     lucky been.
FERNANDO.   This is no time to think of
     means gone by,
Upon our swords alone for help let us rely,
Since we betwixt two armies' loud alarms
Are placed—Avis and Christ!—
JUAN.   To arms! to arms!
          [*Exeunt with drawn swords.
          Sounds of a battle are heard.*]

          [*Enter* BRITO.]
BRITO.   Since betwixt two armies we
Are placed, there is no human remedy.
What a scurvy speech is this
Would that the key that locks the realms
     of bliss
In yonder sky, would open but a chink,
Through which securely a poor wretch
     might slink
Who hath wandered to this spot,
Nor knoweth wherefore or for what;
But I will pretend to die,
Hoping, hereafter, death will pass me by.
          [*He lies down on the ground.*]

          [*Enter a* MOOR *fighting with* DON
               ENRIQUE.]
MOOR.   Who is it that thus his breast
     defendeth
Against my arm, which like a bolt de-
     scendeth
From the fourth sphere of the skies?
ENRIQUE.   One who, though he stumbles,
     falls, and dies
Upon his fellow Christians' corses,—
Dreads no living foeman's forces,—
For who I am, let this be said.
          [*They walk over* BRITO *and
          exeunt.*]

[*Enter* MULÉY *and* DON JUAN COUTIÑO
          in conflict.]
MULÉY.   Valiant Portuguese, to see
Thy strength so great doth grieve not me,
For I would wish that thou shouldst gain
The victory to-day.
JUAN.   Oh! bitter pain,
Without consideration do I tread
Upon these corses of the Christian dead!—

BRITO [aside]. I would let him par-
doned be,
If my lord would lightlier tread on me.
[MULÉY and JUAN exeunt.]

[Enter DON FERNANDO retiring before the
KING and the Moors.]
KING. Yield thy sword, brave Portu-
guese,
If my hand alive can seize
And keep you captive, I do vow
To be thy friend: say, who art thou?
FERNANDO. A cavalier: no more reply
Expect to hear: now let me die!—

[Enter DON JUAN and places himself by
his side.]
JUAN. First, great lord, my breast will
be
A diamond wall to shelter thee,
Placed before thee in the strife
I still will guard thy princely life.
Now, my Fernando, by thy deeds declare
The race of which thou art the heir.
KING. If this I hear, what more do I
expect?
Suspend your arms!—no happier effect
From this day's glory any more can be,
This prize is victory enough for me:—
If you must die, or else a captive be,
Accept the sentence given by fate's decree:
Thy sword, Fernando,—give it up to me,
The King of Fez.

[Enter MULÉY.]
MULÉY [aside]. Ah! who is this I
see?—
FERNANDO. Only unto a king's hand
would I loose it:
Indeed, 'twere desperation to refuse it.

[Enter DON ENRIQUE.]
ENRIQUE. Is my brother taken?—
FERNANDO.   Do not thou,
Enrique, add to my misfortune now
By your lamenting. Fate high lessons
grants,
Even in the common accidents of chance.
KING. Enrique, in my power
Lies Don Fernando, and although this
hour,

Showing the vantage I have won
I could command your deaths; yet, as I've
done
Naught to-day, but in my own defence,
I can the easier with your blood dispense,
Since to me survives
A wider fame, by sparing of your lives;
And that you [to ENRIQUE] may bring
With greater speed his ransom from the
king,
Do you return: but in my power
Fernando stays, until doth shine the
hour
That you return to set him free:—
But say to Edward, that will never be,
That vain are all entreaties and demands,
Till Ceuta is surrendered to my hands;—
And now, your Highness, my illustrious
foe,
To whom that greatness I shall owe,
Come to Fez with me.
FERNANDO.   I go
To that sphere, whose rays I follow here
below.
MULÉY [aside]. Must I ever mourn,
By friendship's ties, and love's suspicions
torn!
FERNANDO. Enrique, though a prisoner
here,
Nor fate, nor fortune's malice do I fear:
Say to our brother, be thou of strong
heart,
And firmly act a Christian prince's part
In my misfortunes.
ENRIQUE.   Who is so unjust,
That would his magnanimity distrust?
FERNANDO. This again I charge you,
and I say,
Let him act the Christian.
ENRIQUE.   I obey,
And vow full early to return as such.
FERNANDO. Let me embrace thee.
ENRIQUE.   Is it not too much
That thou a captive still new bonds dost
take?   [Folds him in his arms.]
FERNANDO. Adieu, Don Juan.
JUAN.   I will not forsake
My gracious prince, so drive me not
away!
FERNANDO. O loyal friend!
ENRIQUE.   O most unhappy day!

FERNANDO.   Say to the king . . . but
  no, 'tis better say
Nothing; in silence, which my grief doth
  smother,
Bear thou these tears unto the king, my
  brother.   [*Exeunt.*]

[*Enter two* MOORS, *who see* BRITO *lying
  as dead.*]
  1ST MOOR.   Here is a Christian lying
  dead.
  2ND MOOR.   Let us, lest a plague should
  spread,
Throw these corses in the sea.
  BRITO [*starting up*].   First your skulls
  must opened be
By such cuts and thrusts as these;
For, even dead, we still are Portuguese.
        [*Exit, pursuing them with his
          sword.*]

ACT II

SCENE I—*A mountain district near Fez.*

[*Enter* PHENIX.]
  PHENIX.   Estrella! Zara! Rosa! no,
No one answers to my calling!
  MULÉY [*entering*].   One attends thee,
  like the falling
Shadow which the sun doth throw
Off its radiant disk.   For thou
Dost a sun to me appear—
Who am the shadow that it hath.
As I roamed this mountain path,
Thy sweet voice re-echoed near.
What hath happened lady?
  PHENIX.   Hear,
If I can its nature state:
Flattering, free, ungrateful, glides
Sweet and smooth, with peaceful tides,
A crystal fountain, all elate
With waves of molten silver plate.
Flattering, for it proffereth
Speech enough, yet doth not feel;
Smooth, for it can well conceal;
Free, for loud it uttereth;
Sweet, because it murmureth;
And ungrateful, for it flies!
To that fountain's shady place,
Wearied with a wild beast's chase,
Came I with a glad surprise,

For its fresh green canopies
Promised rest and relaxation;
Being upon one side bound
By a gentle hillock, crowned
With (as if for jubilation)
Wreaths of jasmine and carnation,
Which a shade of crimson light
Flung upon my emerald bed.
Scarcely had I render'd
Up my soul to the delight
Of solitude, when, 'mid the bright
Leaves, did me a sound alarm;
I attentive looked, and saw
An ancient dame of Africa—
A spirit in a human form,
Marked with all that can deform—
Wrinkles, scowling, haggard, dark—
A living skeleton, a shade;
But as if with features made
Of a tree's trunk, rude and stark,
Wrapt in rough, unpolished bark;
With mingled melancholy and
Sadness—doleful passions these.
That my heart's blood she might freeze,
She did take me by the hand,
I, to be like her, did stand
Tree-like, rooted to the ground;
Ice ran freezing through each vein
At her touch, and through my brain
Venomed horror flew its round.
She, with scarce articulate sound,
Thus appeared to speak to me—
"Hapless woman! fated woe!
Since, with all thy beauteous show,
All the graces crowning thee,
Thou a corse's prize must be!"
Thus she said, and thus I live
Sadly since, or rather die,
Waiting till the prophecy
Which that tree-like fugitive
Did with doubtful meaning give—
Which that prophet, through the force
Of fate fulfilled without remorse—
Is fulfilled by destiny.
Woe is me! for I must be
The worthless guerdon of a corse!   [*Exit.*]
  MULÉY.   It is easy to explain
This illusion, or this dream,
Since, indeed, it doth but seem
An image of my bosom's pain:
Tarudante is to gain

Thee; but though my heart doth burst
At the thought, my wrath and hate
Shall compel his joy to wait.
Never shall occur the worst,
Until he shall slay me first!
I may lose thee, that may be,
But I cannot lose and live:
Since my life I then must give,
Ere I come that hour to see,
The life that must abandon me
Is the price that buyeth thee;
Thou wilt then too surely be
The guerdon of a corse—for I
Shall be seen to pine and die
Through envy, love, and jealousy.

[*Enter* THREE CHRISTIAN CAPTIVES *with
the* INFANTE DON FERNANDO.]

1ST CAPTIVE. From the royal gardens
     near,
Where we work, we saw your Grace
Lately going to the chase,
And together we come here,
At your feet, in tears, to throw us.

2ND CAPTIVE. 'Tis the only consolation
Heaven doth grant our situation.

3RD CAPTIVE. It, in this, doth pity show
     us.

FERNANDO. Friends, come, let my arms
     enfold you;
And, God knows, if I, with these,
Could your necks a moment ease
Of the knots and bonds that hold you,
They would give you liberty,
Even before myself. But heaven
May this punishment have given
As a favour, it may be,
As a blessing, if we knew it.
Fate may better grow ere long;
No misfortune is so strong
But that patience may subdue it.
Bear with that whatever sorrow
Time or fortune makes you see;
For that fickle deity,
Now a flower, a corse to-morrow,
Ever changing o'er and o'er—
Yours may alter in a trice;
But, O God! to give advice
To the needy, and no more,
Is not wisdom. I would give
Gladly aught that would relieve you,

But, alas, I've naught to give you;
You the want, my friends, forgive.
I, from Portugal, expect
Succour—it will quickly come;
Yours will be whatever sum
May be sent for that effect.
I desire it but for ye,
If they come to lead away
Me from slavery, I say
That you all must come with me:—
Go, in God's name, to your tasks,
No offence, your masters giving.

1ST CAPTIVE. Lord, to know that thou
     art living,
Is the only joy that asks
Our enslavement.

2ND CAPTIVE. May the years
Of the Phenix be but few
To those granted unto you,
Gracious lord, to live.
          [*The* CAPTIVES *go out.*]

FERNANDO. With tears
Must the soul refuse relief,
Which their wretched state demands,
Bearing nothing from my hands;
Who will succour them? What grief!

MULÉY. I have stood with admiration,
Seeing the humane affection
With which you the deep dejection
Of these captives' situation
Have relieved.

FERNANDO. My grief was shown
Truly for the hapless state
Of these captives. By their fate
I may learn to bear my own;
It may be, perhaps, that some
Day the lesson I may need.

MULÉY. Says your Highness this in-
     deed?

FERNANDO. Born an Infante, I have
     come
To be a slave; and thus, I fear,
That from this, I yet may know
Even a lower depth of woe;
For the distance is less near
From an Infante, a king's brother,
And a captive, than can be
'Twixt degrees of slavery.
One day followeth another,
And thus sorrow follows sorrow,
Pains with pains thus intertwine.

MULÉY. Would no heavier pain were mine!
You, your Highness, may to-morrow
(Though to-day you here remain
In a brief captivity),
Your dear native country see;
But for me all hope is vain,
Fortune never will be seen
To grow kinder unto me,
Though the moon less fickle be.
FERNANDO. At the court of Fez I've been
Now some time, yet you have not,
Of the love you once confest,
Told me aught.
MULÉY. Within my breast
Lie the favours I have got;
Those I've sworn to conceal:
But to friendship's laws I bow,
Without breaking of my vow,
I a little may reveal:—
Without equal is her scorn,
So the grief my heart doth prove,
For the Phenix and my love
Were without their fellow born.
In seeing, hearing, and concealing
A Phenix, is my every thought;
A Phenix every love-distraught
Apprehension, fear, and feeling;
It is a Phenix that doth ope
The source of every pain and tear.
To feel I merit her yet fear,
A Phenix also is my hope.
The passion that I late revealed
Is now the Phenix I discover;
Thus, as a friend, and as a lover,
I both have spoken and concealed. [*Exit.*]
FERNANDO. With heart as skilful as discreet,
He thus his lady's name makes plain,
But if a Phenix be his pain,
I with it cannot compete:—
Mine is but a common pain,
And calmly should be borne as such,
Many have endured as much
Without boasts or wailings vain.

[*Enter the* KING.]
KING. By this mountain's brow, your Highness,
Have I to overtake you ridden,

That before the sun in coral
And in pearly clouds is hidden,
You the struggles of a tiger
In the meshes might admire,
For a circle now is closing
Round it by the huntsmen.
FERNANDO. Sire,
Every moment art thou planning
Means of pleasing me. If this
Is the way thy slaves thou fêtest,
They will not their country miss.
KING. Captives of such rare endowments,
That they to their owner pay
Highest honour, is the reason
They are treated in this way.

[*Enter* DON JUAN.]
DON JUAN. Come, my lord, unto the sea-shore,
And behold the fairest creature
That the hand of art e'er fashioned,
Or the mystic power of nature.
For, but now, a Christian galley
To our port has come; so fair,
That although her darkened bulwarks
Black and mournful colours wear,
Still, the wonder is how sorrow,
Thus, the eye, like gladness, charms.
From her topmasts gaily flutter
Portugal's emblazoned arms;
Since their Infante is a captive,
Thus they mourn his slavery—
Thus express the people's sorrow,
Though they come to set him free.
FERNANDO. No, my friend, Don Juan, no;
This is not their cause of mourning,
If they came to set me free,
On the faith of my returning,
Joyful would their signals be.

[*Enter* DON ENRIQUE *dressed in mourning, and holding an open paper in his hand.*]
ENRIQUE [*to the* KING]. Let me, mighty lord, embrace thee!
KING. May your Highness' years endure;
FERNANDO [*to* DON JUAN]. Ah! my death is sure, Don Juan.

KING [to MULÉY]. Ah! Muléy, my joy
  is sure!
ENRIQUE. Now that of your royal wel-
  fare
I, your presence may believe;
Thou wilt, to embrace my brother,
Mighty monarch, give me leave.
Ah! Fernando!   [They embrace.]
FERNANDO.   My Enrique,
Ah! what garb is this?—but stay,
Fully have your eyes informed me,
Nothing need your tongue now say;
Do not weep: if 'tis to tell me
Ever must my slavery be—
This is what my soul desireth:
Thanks you should have asked from
  me,
And in place of grief and mourning
Worn a gala festal suit.
How is my lord, the King? If well,
Nothing can I dread:—thou'rt mute!
  ENRIQUE. Since our sorrows, when re-
  peated,
Doubly touch affliction's chord,
I desire that you should feel them
Only once. Attend, great lord,
    [To the KING.]
For, although a rustic palace
This wild rugged mountain be,
Still, I ask you give me audience,
To this captive liberty,
And attention to my tidings.
Torn, and tempest-tossed, the fleet,
Which, with empty pride, so lately
Trod the waves beneath its feet,
Leaving here in Africa—
Thine and his own thoughts the prey—
The Infante's person taken,
Back to Lisbon took its way.
From the moment that King Edward
Heard the tragic news he pined,
For his heart was covered over
With a sadness, and his mind
Passing from the melancholy
Which oppressed it first, gave way
To a lethargy, and dying,
Gave the lie to those who say
Human sorrows are not mortal—
(Ah! how vainly this is said!)
For our brother, Don Fernando,
For the King himself is dead!

FERNANDO. Woe is me! how dear hath
  proved
My detention!
  KING.   This misfortune,
Allah knows, my heart hath moved.
Continue:—
  ENRIQUE. In his will when dying,
Thus, my lord, the King did say:—
That for the Infante's person
Ceuta should be given straightway;
Thus it is, that with full powers
From Alphonso I have run
(He the rising star of morning
That supplies the absent sun)
Hither, to yield up that city;
And since . . .
  FERNANDO. Ah! do not proceed;
Cease, Enrique, for such language
Is unworthy, not indeed
Of a Portuguese Infante,
Of a knight that doth profess
Christ's religion, but of even
The most vile, whose barbarousness
Never was illuminated
By Christ's everlasting laws.
If my brother, now in heaven,
In his will did leave this clause,
It was not that you should read it
Strictly, but he meant thereby,
That he so desired my freedom:
All proper methods you should try,
Whether peaceable or warlike,
To obtain my liberty;
For, to say, "Surrender, Ceuta,"
Is to say, to set him free
Prodigies should be effected.
Can it be? Oh! can it be,
That a just and Catholic monarch
Could surrender to a Moor
A fair city which did cost him
Even his own blood to secure;
When, with sword and buckler only,
On its ramparts he was first
To unfurl our country's standard?
And even this is not the worst:
But a city that confesses
The true Catholic faith in God,
Which has raised so many churches,
Consecrated to his laud,
With affection and devotion;—
Would it like a Catholic be?

Were it zeal for our religion?
Were it Christian piety,
Or a Portuguese achievement,
That these sovereign temples, which
Are the Atlases of Heaven,
All their golden glories rich,
Where the sun of grace is shining,
Should give place to Moorish shades,
And that their opposing crescents,
Through the churches' long arcades,
Thus should make these sad eclipses?
Is it right the sacred walls
Of their chapels become stables,
And their holy altars stalls?
Or if this should not so happen,
Turn to mosques! My cheek grows pale;
Here my tongue grows mute with horror,
Here my frightened breath doth fail,
Here the anguish overwhelms me;
For the thought doth through me send
Such a thrill, my heart is cloven,
And my hair doth stand on end,
And my body trembles over,
For it was not the first time
Stalls and stables gave a lodging
Unto God. But oh! the crime
Of becoming mosques! It seemeth
Like an epitaph—a wide
Mark of infamy undying—
Saying, Here did God abide,
And the Christians now deny it,
Giving it a gift instead
To the demon! Scarcely ever
(As is ordinarily said)
Does a man offend another
In his own house. Can it be,
Crime should enter thus God's mansion,
To offend him there; and we—
We ourselves become his escort—
We admit his impious rout—
And, to let the demon enter,
Driving the Almighty out?
And the Catholics, there dwelling
With their goods and families,
Must prevaricate henceforward
With the faith, or peril these.
Were it proper to occasion
This contingency of sin
By our conduct? And the tender
Little ones that dwell therein,—
Were it right, these helpless Christians,

From the Moors, through our neglect
Should adopt their rites and customs,
And grow up as of their sect
In a miserable thraldom?
Is it right, one life should cost
Many lives? and *that* one being
Of no import if 'twere lost?
Who am I? Am I then greater
Than a man? for if to be
An Infante makes distinction,
I'm a slave. Nobility
Cannot be a slave's adornment.
I am one; then wrong is he
Who doth call me an Infante.
And, if so, who gives advice,
That the poor life of a captive
Should be bought at such a price?
Death is but the loss of being,—
I lost mine amid the fight;
That being gone, my life departed,—
Being dead, it is not right
That so many lives should perish
For the ransom of a corse!
So, these vain and idle powers,
Thus I tear without remorse.
                    [*Tears the paper.*]
Let them be the sunbeam's atoms,
Or the sparkles of the fire,—
No, 'tis best that I devour them,
For my soul doth not desire
That there should survive a letter
Which would tell the world, the brave
Lusitanian spirit ever
Thought of this. I am thy slave,
And, O King, dispose and order
Of my freedom as you please,
For I would, nor could accept it
On unworthy terms like these:
Thou, Enrique, home returning
Say, in Africa I lie
Buried, for my life I'll fashion
As if I did truly die:—
Christians, dead is Don Fernando;
Moors, a slave to you remains;
Captives, you have a companion,
Who to-day doth share your pains:
Heaven, a man restores your churches
Back to holy calm and peace;
Sea, a wretch remains, with weeping
All your billows to increase;
Mountains, on ye dwells a mourner

Like the wild beasts soon to grow;
Wind, a poor man with his sighing
Doubleth all that thou canst blow;
Earth, a corse within they entrails
Comes to-day to lay his bones.
For King, Brother, Moors and Christians,
Sun, and moon, and starry zones,
Wind and sea, and earth and heaven,
Wild beasts, hills—let this convince
All of ye, in pains and sorrows,
How to-day a constant Prince
Loves the Catholic faith to honour,
And the law of God to hold.
If there were no other reason,
But that Ceuta doth enfold
A divine church consecrated
To the eternal reverence
Of the Conception of our Lady,
Queen of heaven and earth's events,
I would lose, so she be honoured,
Myriad lives in her defence.

KING. Thankless, thoughtless, both of us,
And of the great pride and glory
Of our kingdom; Is it thus
You deprive me, you deny me
What my heart desires so much?
But if in my realms you govern
More than in your own, can such
Servitude aught else conduct to?
But that I may now engrave
On your mind, you are my captive
I will treat you as my slave,—
That your friends here, that your brother,
To their eyes may give belief,
That you kiss my feet as vassal.

    [FERNANDO *kneels at the* KING'S
    feet.]

ENRIQUE. What misfortune!—
MULÉY [*aside*].   Oh! what grief!
ENRIQUE. What calamity!
JUAN.   What anguish!
KING. Now thou art my slave.
FERNANDO.   'Tis true,
Small in this, though, is your vengeance,
For as if all mankind do,
Man one day doth leave earth's bosom,
'Tis but to return to her
At the end of various journeys;
But to thank you, I prefer
To reproachings. Since you teach me,
Even in this way, how best

By the shortest road to reach to
My eternal wished-for rest.
KING. Being now a slave, you cannot
Titles hold, or rents possess;
Ceuta now is in thy power,
If, as slave, thou dost confess
That as master I am thine,
Why not, therefore, give me Ceuta?
FERNANDO. Because 'tis God's, and is
    not mine.
KING. Is it not a well-known precept,
That a slave in all things must
Be obedient to his master?
Be so now.
FERNANDO.   In all things just,
Heaven, no doubt, commands obedience,
And no slave should fail therein;
But, if it should chance, the master
Should command the slave to sin,
Then there is no obligation
To obey him: he who sins
When commanded, no less sinneth.
KING. Thou must die.
FERNANDO.   Then life begins.
KING. That this blessing may not
    happen,
Rather dying live: thou'lt see
I can be cruel.
FERNANDO.   And I patient.
KING. Thou'lt never gain thy liberty.
FERNANDO. Thou'lt never be the lord
    of Ceuta.
KING. Ho! there.

        [*Enter* SELIM.]
SELIM.   My lord?
KING.   Immediately
Let this captive here be treated
Like the others: let him be
Laden neck and feet with fetters;
Let him tend my horses' stall,
And the baths and gardens; so that
He be humbled as are all;
Let him wear no silken dresses,
But poor lowly serge instead;
Let him eat black bread, and swallow
Brackish water; let his bed
Be in dark and humid dungeons,
And to all who on him wait,
Let this sentence be extended:—
Hence remove them!

ENRIQUE. What a fate!

MULÉY [aside]. How unmerited!

JUAN. What sorrow!

KING. Now I'll see, 'twixt thee and me,
Barbarian, if thy patience lasteth
Like my wrath.

FERNANDO. Yes, thou shalt see,
For with me it is eternal. [He is led out.]

KING. Enrique, as my hand is given,
I permit thee to withdraw,
And to Lisbon, back returning,
Leave the sea of Africa;
Say at home, that their Infante,
Their Grand Master, dwells with me,
Occupied about my horses,
Let them come to set him free.

ENRIQUE. They will do so. If I leave
him
In this wretched misery,
And my heart bleeds, that I cannot
In it his companion be,
'Tis because I hope the sooner,
Coming in an army's van,
To return to give him freedom.

KING. Well, thou'lt do so, if you can.

MULÉY [aside]. Now has come a fit
occasion
All my gratitude to show,
Life I owe unto Fernando,
And I'll pay the debt I owe. [Exeunt.]

SCENE II—The KING's garden.

[Enter SELIM, and DON FERNANDO
dressed as a slave, and in chains.]

SELIM. The king commands that you
assist
In this garden; do thou not resist,
Disobeying what he hath decreed. [Exit.]

FERNANDO. My patience shall his
cruelty exceed.

[Enter some CHRISTIAN CAPTIVES; one
sings while the others dig in the garden.]

1ST CAPTIVE [sings]. To the conquest
of Tangiers,
'Gainst the tyrant king of Fez,
The Infante Don Fernando
Did the king, his brother, send.

FERNANDO. There's not a moment but
my story will

The sorrowing memory of mankind fill!
I am sad and troubled sore.

2ND CAPTIVE. Captive, why to sorrow
thus give o'er?
Do not weep—be cheerful—the Grand
Master
Said, he would bring from out of this
disaster
Back to his country every captive here.

FERNANDO [aside]. How soon this
cheering hope must disappear!

2ND CAPTIVE. Console yourself, and
trust to fortune's powers,
Assist me now to irrigate these flowers,
Take thou two pails, and water bring this
way
From yonder pond.

FERNANDO [aside]. I struggle to obey:
A fitting burden have you bid me bear,
Since it is water that you ask me, which
my care
Sowing sorrows, cultivating sighs,
Can fill from out the currents of mine
eyes! [Exit.]

2ND CAPTIVE. To the prison quarters
they are leading
Other captives.

[Enter DON JUAN and other CAPTIVES.]

JUAN. Let us look with careful heed-
ing,
If these shady gardens screen him,
Or, perchance, these captives may have
seen him,
For when in his company,
Less our sorrow and our grief will be,
And more our consolation:
Tell me, friend, and may heaven compensa-
tion
Grant you for it! Have you seen his
grace
Fernando, the Grand Master, working in
this place?

2ND CAPTIVE. No, friend, him I have
not seen.

JUAN. Scarcely can I, my tears and
sorrow screen.

3RD CAPTIVE. I repeat, they ope our
prison bounds,
And lead new captives to these garden
grounds.

[Enter DON FERNANDO *carrying two pails of water.]*

FERNANDO *[aside]*. Mortals, do not wonder at surveying
A grand master of Avis, an Infante, playing
Such an ignoble part; for Time
Oft acts these tragic scenes upon his stage
sublime.

JUAN. It is my lord!—but oh! 'tis past belief
I see your Highness in this state: with grief,
Within my breast, my heart doth burst in twain!

FERNANDO. May God forgive you, for the unconscious pain,
Don Juan, you have caused in thus revealing
Who I am. I hoped, my rank concealing,
Among my countrymen to live unknown,
And make their wretched poverty my own.

1ST CAPTIVE. My lord, for pardon I most humbly sue,
Being but now so rude and blind to you.

3RD CAPTIVE. Let me embrace your feet, my lord.

FERNANDO. My friend,
Arise: these ceremonies now must end.

JUAN. Your Highness . . .

FERNANDO. Highness! how can one be so,
Condemned to lead a life so meanly low?
See that an humbler name I crave,
For I will live among you as a slave,
Only as an equal and a friend
I must be treated.

JUAN. Why does Heaven not send
Its dreadful bolt to crush me with the slain?

FERNANDO. A man of noble soul should ne'er complain
Of fate, Don Juan: who distrusts in heaven?
Now an example should by us be given
Of prudence, valour, fortitude, my friend.

[Enter ZARA *with a basket.]*

ZARA. The lady Phenix hither doth descend,
And commands, with flowers of various shade,
A garland for this basket should be made.

FERNANDO. I hope to bring them to her, presently;
First in this pleasing service let me be.

1ST CAPTIVE. Let us, at least, assist you as you cull.

ZARA. Here I await you, while the flowers you pull.

FERNANDO. Pay me no idle courtesy,
Henceforth your pains and mine must equal be.
And if our sight to-day a difference strike,
Death comes to-morrow and makes all things like.
It were not wisdom, then, but cause of sorrow
Not to do now what must be done to-morrow.

[Exeunt the INFANTE *and the* CAPTIVES, *they following him respectfully.]*

[Enter PHENIX *and* ROSA.]*

PHENIX. Have you ordered they should choose me
Some fresh flowers?

ZARA. I so have ordered.

PHENIX. In my troubled and disordered
State, their colours may amuse me.

ROSA. Lady, I in wonder lose me,
Seeing fantasies continue
Thus to melancholy win you.

ZARA. What controls thee thus, what law?

PHENIX. Ah, it was no dream I saw
When I lay with frozen sinew,
But my own impending woe.
When a wretch doth dream with pleasure
That he owns some wished-for treasure,
Zara, I avow and know
That his bliss is only seeming;
But if he continues dreaming
That his fortune hath forsaken,
And that ruin hath o'ertaken,
Though both good and evil wind
Through his dreams, the wretch doth find
But the last when he doth waken!
Thus will be my fate; ah me!
Pitiless, without remorse.

ZARA. What remaineth for a corse,
If now you mourn thus piteously?
PHENIX. Ah! 'tis the fate reserved for
me.
The guerdon of a corse!—what eye
Ever saw such misery?
Naught remains to me but sighs;
Must I be a corse's prize?
Who will be that corse then?—

[*Enter* FERNANDO *with the flowers.*]
FERNANDO.   I!
PHENIX. Who is this, O heavens! I
view?
FERNANDO. What disturbs thee?
PHENIX.   Hearing, seeing
Such a wretched state of being?
FERNANDO. I can well believe that true:
Wishing, lady, upon you
To attend in humble duty,
I have brought thee flowers, whose beauty
Typifies my fate, Señora;
They are born with Aurora,
And they perish ere the dew.
PHENIX. When this *marvel* came to
light
It was given a fitting name.
FERNANDO. Is not every flower the same
That I bear thee in this plight?
PHENIX. It is true, but say whose spite
Caused this novelty?
FERNANDO.   My fate.
PHENIX. Is it then so strong?
FERNANDO.   So great.
PHENIX. You afflict me.
FERNANDO.   Do not grieve.
PHENIX. Why?
FERNANDO.   Because a man doth live
Death and fortune's abject mate.
PHENIX. Are you not Fernando?
FERNANDO.   Yes.
PHENIX. Changed by what?
FERNANDO.   The laws that wring
Captive souls.
PHENIX.   By whom?
FERNANDO.   The King.
PHENIX. Why?
FERNANDO. My life he doth possess.
PHENIX. To-day I saw him thee caress.
FERNANDO. And yet he doth abhor me
now.

PHENIX. How can it be that he and
thou
So late conjoined, twin stars of light,
But one short day could disunite?
FERNANDO. These flowers have come to
tell thee how.—
These flowers awoke in beauty and de-
light,
At early dawn, when stars began to set—
At eve they leave us but a fond regret,—
Locked in the cold embraces of the night.
These shades that shame the rainbow's
arch of light,
Where gold and snow in purple pomp are
met,
All give a warning, man should not forget,
When one brief day can darken things so
bright.
'Tis but to wither that the roses bloom—
'Tis to grow old they bear their beau-
teous flowers,
One crimson bud their cradle and their
tomb.
Such are man's fortunes in this world of
ours;
They live, they die, one day doth end
their doom.
For ages past but seem to us like hours!
PHENIX. Horror, terror, make me fear
thee;
I nor wish to see nor hear thee.
Be thou then the first of those
Whose woe hath scared another's woes.
FERNANDO. And the flowers?
PHENIX.   If they can bear thee
Emblems of mortality,
Let them broken, scattered be;—
They must know my wrath alone.
FERNANDO. For what fault must they
atone?
PHENIX. Like to stars they seem to me.
FERNANDO. Then you do not wish them?
PHENIX.   No;
All their rosy light I scorn.
FERNANDO. Why?
PHENIX.   A woman is, when born,
Subject to life's common foe,
And to fortune's overthrow,
Which methought this star did figure.
FERNANDO. Are the stars like flowers?
PHENIX.   'Tis so.

FERNANDO. This I do not see, although I myself have wept their rigour.

PHENIX. Listen.

FERNANDO. Speak, I wish to know.

PHENIX. These points of light, these sparkles of pure fire,
Their twinkling splendours boldly torn away
From the reluctant sun's departing ray,
Live when the beams in mournful gloom retire.
These are the flowers of night that glad Heaven's choir,
And o'er the vault their transient odours play.
For if the life of flowers is but one day,
In one short night the brightest stars expire.
But still we ask the fortunes of our lives,
Even from this flattering spring-tide of the skies,
'Tis good or ill, as sun or star survives.
Oh! what duration is there? who relies
Upon a star? or hope from it derives,
That every night is born again and dies?
[Exit.]

[Enter MULÉY.]

MULÉY. Until Phenix had departed,
Here I hid me from her sight,
For the most adoring eagle
Flieth sometimes from the light;
Are we now alone?

FERNANDO. Yes.

MULÉY. Hear me!

FERNANDO. Brave Muléy, what is thy will?

MULÉY. That you know—that faith and honour
Warm a Moorish bosom still.
I know not how first to speak of,
How to think of, such a crime!—
How to tell the pain I've suffered
For this fickle frown of Time!
For this ruin, this injustice!
This dark boon that Fortune grants,
This, the world's most sad example,—
This inconstancy of chance!
But I run some risk if people
See me speaking here to thee,

For, without respect to treat you
Is the king's proclaimed decree;
And thus, leaving to my sorrow
What my voice would fain repeat,
Let it tell, I come to throw me,
As thy slave, before thy feet.
I am thine, and thus, Infante,
I come here, but not to show
Favour to a fallen foeman,
But to pay the debt I owe!
The existence you have given me
I return thee, for indeed
A good action is a treasure
Guarded for the doer's need:
And since here I stand foot-fastened
By the unseen chains of fear—
And above my neck and bosom
Knife and cord hang threatening near—
I desire, in briefest language,
To inform you in one word,
That to-night I will have ready
By the shore, a vessel moored,
Full equipped; and in the loop-holes
Of the cells, I shall prepare
Instruments, which will unfasten
Those unworthy chains you wear.
On the outside of your dungeons
I myself the locks will break;
So that you and all the captives
Prisoned now in Fez, may take
Your departure for your country;
And be certain, that I stay
Here in Fez secure from danger;
Since I easily can say
That they overpowered their masters,
And escaped amid the strife.
Thus we two will put in safety
I my honour, you your life;
Though 'tis certain—if it reacheth
The King's ear, I let thee fly—
He will treat me as a traitor;
But I shall not grieve to die:
And as money may be needful
To conciliate the will
Of those near you, see these jewels,
Golden treasures amply fill
Their minute, but rich proportions;
This, Fernando, is the way
That I give to thee my ransom,
Thus my obligation pay.
For a true and noble captive

Ne'er should rest, until he bring
Payment back for such a favour.
FERNANDO. I would wish indeed to
    thank you
For my freedom; but the King
Cometh to the garden.
MULÉY.   Has he
Seen you with me?
FERNANDO.   No.
MULÉY.   If seen,
'Twere suspicious.
FERNANDO.   Of these branches
I will make a rustic screen,
Which will hide me while he passes.
              [*Conceals himself.*]

        [*Enter the* KING.]
KING [*aside*]. Ah! in secret stand
    Muléy
And Fernando! why in seeing
Me, does one thus go away,
And the other thus dissemble?
There is some concealment here,
Be it certain or not certain,
I must be secure from fear
Of all treason. [*Aloud.*] I am happy—
MULÉY. Lord, I greet thee on my knee.
KING. Here to find thee!
MULÉY.   Speak thy orders.
KING. Much it grieves me, not to see
    Ceuta mine.
MULÉY.   Then to its conquest,
Crowned with wreaths of laurel, wend;
For their swords against thy valour
Badly can its walls defend.
KING. By a more domestic warfare
I expect to gain my end.
MULÉY. In what manner?
KING.   In this manner,
I, Fernando's pride must bend,
Giving him such rigid treatment
That he must, or swiftly die,
Or to me surrender Ceuta;
Know then, friend Muléy, that I
Have some cause to fear the person
Of the Grand Master not secure,
Now in Fez. The captives, seeing
Him dishonoured thus, and poor,
Will, I do not doubt, soon murmur,
And break out in mutiny:
Were this not so, it is certain

Powerful interest has he;
And the strongest cells will open
Ever to a golden key.
MULÉY [*aside*]. I desire now to con-
    firm him
In the thought that this can be,
That he may have no suspicion
Of myself. [*Aloud.*] It seems to me
You are right—they mean to free him.
KING. There remains one remedy,
That my power may not be outraged.
MULÉY. And it is, my lord?
KING.   To thee—
To thy charge, Muléy, to trust him—
To thy care and custody—
Let not fear nor interest move thee,
Keep him safe in field and cell:—
Thou art the Infante's guardian,
Look to it, thou guard him well,
In what circumstance soever
You must be accountable.   [*Exit.*]
MULÉY. Without any doubt, our con-
    cert
By the king was overheard:
Bless me, Allah!

        [*Enter* FERNANDO.]
FERNANDO.   What afflicts thee?
MULÉY. Have you heard him?
FERNANDO.   Every word.
MULÉY. Then why is it that you ask
    me
What afflicts me? Suffering
In a blind and dark confusion,
And, between my friend and king,
Seeing friendship thus and honour
With each other combating;
If to thee I should be loyal,
I to him must traitor be;
If to him continue faithful,
Fail in gratitude to thee.
What then can I do? O heavens!
At the very time I came
To restore you to your freedom
He my confidence should claim,
Thus the better to secure thee.
What, I ask? And if the key
Of our secret is discovered
By the king himself! From thee
Do I ask advice and counsel,
Tell me what I ought to do?

FERNANDO. Brave Muléy, both love and
    friendship
Are inferior to those two—
Loyalty and upright honour.
No one equals to a king,
He alone himself doth equal;
This then is my counselling:
Heed not me, but serve *him* truly,
And that you may disregard
Any fears about your honour,
I myself will be its guard.
Should another come to offer
Freedom, I do promise thee
Not to take it—that your honour
Rest inviolate with me.
    MULÉY. Do not counsel me, Fernando,
As loyally, as courteously;
To you, I know, my life is owing,
And that to pay you is but right.
And so, the plan that I projected,
I will prepare against the night;
Be thou free, my life remaineth
Here to suffer in the stead
Of thy death: secure thy freedom,
After that I nothing dread.
    FERNANDO. Were it just that I should
    be
So tyrannic, and so cruel
With the man that pities me?
And destroy his stainless honour,
Who to me is giving life?
No: and thus I wish to make you
Umpire of my cause and life.
Do thou give me counsel also;
Ought I take my liberty
From a man who stays to suffer
In my place? and let him be
Cruel to his dearest honour?
What do you advise?
    MULÉY.   I know not
Which to say, or yea or nay;
If the latter, it will grieve me
That I e'er that word could say;
If the former—there is something
In my bosom that doth tell,
That in saying "yes" unto thee,
I do not advise thee well.
    FERNANDO. So advise; my God obeying,
And what his religion says,
I a constant Prince will show me
Here in servitude in Fez.

ACT III

SCENE I—*A hall in the country palace of*
    the KING OF FEZ.

[*Enter* MULÉY *and the* KING.]
    MULÉY [*aside*]. Since all aid is un-
    availing,
From the lines the king doth draw
Round Fernando: the detailing
Of his sufferings may:—the law
Of true friendships is unfailing. [*Aloud.*]
If, my lord, I thee have served,
On land or sea, in any way,—
If my heart hath never swerved
From the allegiance it should pay,
If a boon I have deserved,
Be it thy attention.
    KING.   Say.
    MULÉY. Don Fernando—
    KING.   Say no more.
    MULÉY. Wilt thou not hear me then,
    before
You thus refuse me?
    KING.   No, that word
Offends too much.
    MULÉY.   And why, my lord?
    KING. Because, now every chance is o'er
Of doing what thou wouldst require,
If 'tis for him that thou shouldst ask.
    MULÉY. My lord, and dost thou not
    desire
To know how I discharge the task
Thyself hath given?
    KING.   Well, speak; mine ire
Shall ne'er be seen in pity's mask.
    MULÉY. Fernando, whose unhappy fate
Survives his glory, once so great,
Still lives, but in such abject thrall,
That him the wondering world doth call
A miracle of adverse fate,
Feeling the wrath—a better word
Perhaps would be the boundless power—
Of thy imperial crown, my lord,
And victim of his pride—this hour
Doth feel a misery so abhorred,
That he in such a place doth lie
So lonely and so vile, that I
Will not offend your ears to name;
And there, infirm, and poor, and lame,
He asketh alms from passers by;

For as your orders were that he
Should sleep but in a dungeon's murk,
And on your steeds attendant be,
And in the prison quarters work;
And none should give him food, we see
Him so reduced from what he has been,
His pallid cheek so worn and wan;
His tottering limbs, that make him lean
Upon a staff; all changed or gone
His princely air, his royal mien;
Passing the chilly night away
In stony cells, as he begun,
Still firm in his resolve. When play,
At length, the pure beams of the sun,
Who is the father of the day,
His fellow-slaves (how grieved thereat!)
Upon a miserable mat,
Lifting him, place him, worn and weak,
Upon (since I the name must speak)
A dung-heap! for neglect begat
A state so loathsome, none will let
Him near their homes; and so he lies,
A sight no eye can e'er forget.
Shuddering, the gazer from him flies,
Nor feels compassion, nor regret.
Nor word nor aid to him doth send;
One servant, and one faithful friend,
A cavalier, alone remain
To solace him amid his pain,
And both divide, as they attend,
With him their scant supply of food,
Too small for one, to do one good,
For scarcely have the lips possess'd
The morsel, but it seeks the breast,
The mouth not tasting as it should;
And even your people punish these,
Because, by pity moved, they wait
To give their master some slight ease,
To them, no punishment so great,
As that your servants, should they please,
May rudely tear them each from each:
While one doth leave him, to beseech
Some food, the other doth remain
To give him solace in his pain
By kindly act, or soothing speech:
Conclude a suffering so severe,
And draw the Prince, so please your Grace,
From his sad state and dungeon drear,
Let horror move you in the place
Of pity's pang, or sorrow's tear.
KING.   'Tis well, Muléy.

[*Enter* PHENIX.]
PHENIX.   My lord, if ever
I have, by dutiful endeavour,
Deserved in aught to gain from thee
A boon, I come, your Majesty,
This day to ask of you a favour.
KING.   What could I then deny to thee?
PHENIX.   The Prince Fernando. . . .
KING.   Oh! 'tis well,—
Of this, no further speak to me!
PHENIX.   No human tongue has power
      to tell
The horror of his state. From thee
It was my only wish to pray. . . .
KING.   Oh! Phenix, cease, be silent, stay,
Who is it that Fernando then
Thus makes an outcast among men?
Thus slowly killeth day by day?
If he, for being madly brave,
And obstinate in a wild resolve,
Thus pines away, a lonely slave,
And sees the tardy days revolve—
'Twas he himself the sentence gave,
Not I who doomed him to this woe;
Is it not in his power to go
From out this misery and live?
A word can do it. Let him give
Up Ceuta to my hands, and so
Thus end those rigours and those pains.

[*Enter* SELIM.]
SELIM.   My lord, before the palace
      doors,
Crave audience, two ambassadors,
One from Morocco's neighbouring plains,
And one from Alphonso—he who reigns
O'er Portugal.
PHENIX [*aside*].   Still greater pains!
Doubtless he comes to lead the way
To Tarudante.
MULÉY [*aside*].   Heavens! from me
Now hope withdraws its cheering ray;
By friendship and by jealousy,
I have lost all things in one day!

[*Enter* ALPHONSO *and* TARUDANTE *from
      opposite sides.*]
TARUDANTE.   Most illustrious King of
      Fez. . . .
ALPHONSO.   King of Fez so proud and
      mighty. . . .

TARUDANTE. May thy glory. . . .
ALPHONSO.   Thy existence. . . .
TARUDANTE. Never die. . . .
ALPHONSO. Be ever gloriant. . . .
TARUDANTE [to PHENIX]. And thou,
this sun's serene Aurora. . . .
ALPHONSO. Thou its setting's hopeful
Orient. . . .
TARUDANTE. Spite of years, may you
continue. . . .
ALPHONSO. Spite of time, may you be
reigning. . . .
TARUDANTE. To be gladdened. . . .
ALPHONSO. To be honoured. . . .
TARUDANTE. Tasting pleasures. . . .
ALPHONSO. .   Laurels gaining. . . .
TARUDANTE. Great enjoyments. . . .
ALPHONSO.   Mighty triumphs. . . .
TARUDANTE. Little evil. . . .
ALPHONSO.   Good unsparing. . . .
TARUDANTE. While I speak, say, Chris-
tian, why
Thus to speak, art thou so daring?
ALPHONSO. Because whenever I am by,
I speak first, my wish declaring.
TARUDANTE. To me, as of the Moorish
nation,
The foremost place is surely own;
When kindred races meet, to strangers
A preference should ne'er be shown.
ALPHONSO. In lands where courtesy is
shown,
Quite a different rule prevaileth;
In every clime, in every zone,
A guest the foremost place receiveth.
TARUDANTE. However strong may be
this reason,
By it I am not overthrown;
Since as a guest I have come hither,
The foremost place is mine alone.
KING. Enough of this—let both of ye
With equal favour here be seated;
The Portuguese speak first, for he
Should, from his different faith, be treated
With greater honour.
TARUDANTE [aside].   I am wroth.
ALPHONSO. Brief will be my simple
story:—
Don Alphonso, Portugal's
Famous King, whose deathless glory
Will be told with tongues of bronze,

Spite of death's annihilation,
And of envy: unto thee
Greeting sends and salutation,
And doth ask you, since it seemeth
Don Fernando seeks not freedom,
Since the life that he redeemeth
Should the city of Ceuta cost;
That the fullest value of it
Should be rated at a price
More than avarice could covet
Or the most liberal despise:
Gold and silver he doth proffer
More than two such cities' worth,
For his ransom: and this offer
He doth make in friendly guise,
Which if you refuse, with bolder
Front he'll come to set him free;
For upon the smooth, white shoulder
Yonder of the labouring sea,
Towns arise amid the water
Of a thousand war-ships built,
And he swears with fire and slaughter
Him to free, and thee subdue—
Leaving all these bright plains covered
O'er with crimson blood, so that
What the rising sun discovered
Green-hued emeralds dewy wet,
He will leave behind him lying
Rubies red when he doth set.
TARUDANTE. Though, as an ambassador,
Mine should not be the replying,
Still in what concerns my King,
Christian, I will dare to venture,
For this insult is to him:
And my lord here will not censure
That his son at such a time
Could not patiently forget him:
So, on his part, you can say
To your King Alphonso, let him
Hither come, but in a space
Shorter than from night till morn,
He will see his veins' warm purple
Soon these verdant hills adorn;
So that even the heavens will think
They must have forgot to form
Any flower except the pink.
ALPHONSO. If thou wert my equal,
Moor,
This dispute were swiftly settled,
And the victory would lie
'Twixt two young men, manly-mettled.

Tell your King, that he come hither,
If renowned he wish to be,
Mine will not delay, believe me.

TARUDANTE. You almost said that thou
    wert he,
And if so, I, Tarudante,
Stand prepared to answer thee.

ALPHONSO. In the field I will await
    thee.

TARUDANTE. There, as thou wilt quickly
    find,
I shall not too long delay thee!
I am lightning!

ALPHONSO. I the wind!

TARUDANTE. I am fury!

ALPHONSO.   I am death!

TARUDANTE. Do you not tremble but to
    hear me?

ALPHONSO. Do you not die, but to come
    near me?

KING. My lords, will both your High-
    nesses—
Now that your wrath has torn asunder
The dark disguise of curtained shade,
Which hid each royal planet under—
Will you remember, 'neath this sky,
No battle-field can be selected
Without my leave: which I deny;
That time be mine, for my projected
Service. . . .

ALPHONSO.   I do not receive
Or hospitality or favour
From one who so has made me grieve;
I seek Fernando, the endeavour
To behold him is the cause
Why, disguised thus, I have ventured
Driven by duty here to Fez,
And before your court I entered
I was told that you did spend
At this pleasure-house a season,
And I hither came to end
My faint hope, or with more reason
To await a certain pain;
Be it known, my lord, I only
For your answer here remain.

KING. And that answer, King Alphonso,
Shall be very brief and plain;
If you do not give me Ceuta,
Him, for this, thou shalt not bear.

ALPHONSO. Since for him I have come
    hither,

And without him go, prepare
For the war I now declare;
And [to TARUDANTE] ambassador, whoe'er
Thou may'st be, amid the fray
We shall soon see one another;
Tremble Africa today.   [Exit.]

TARUDANTE. Since I cannot have the
    joy,
Beauteous Phenix, of thy seeing
Me as thy attendant slave,
Let me taste the bliss of being
At thy feet; thy hand present
To him, who his soul doth give thee.

PHENIX. Let your Highness not aug-
    ment,
Mighty lord, the suit and honour
You have shown me, which I prize,
Knowing what to me is owing.

MULÉY [aside]. What does he expect,
    whose eyes
See this sight and yet surviveth?

KING. Since your Highness thus in Fez
Unexpectedly arriveth,
You will pardon us the way
We receive you.

TARUDANTE. Pressing duty
Will not let me here delay
Longer than a passing moment;
And supposing that I came
As ambassador, with powers
My betrothed wife to claim—
You your full consent had given:
Not being so, yet still for this,
May I hope I shall not forfeit
That quick certainty of bliss?

KING. In everything, my lord, you con-
    quer,
And so, to set that doubt at rest,
And that all needful preparation
For such a war be made, 'tis best
Your mind be altogether freed from
Cares like these; and so return,
That you may be here the sooner
Joined with me the foe to spurn,
Should they dare to try the passage,—
These threatened hosts of Portugal.

TARUDANTE. That is but of small im-
    portance;
As I came here so I shall
Quick return, conducting with me
Such a host of armed men,

That these desert plains shall look like
Crowded murmuring cities then;
Soon shall I be here, thy soldier.
    KING. Then with speed let all things be
Ordered for the journey. Phenix,
It is right to Fez with me
Thou shouldst come, to glad that city.
Muléy!
    MULÉY. My gracious lord!
    KING.   Prepare
A chosen escort from the army,
As unto thy special care
Phenix I intrust, till safely
Thou dost leave her with her spouse.
                              [Exit.]
    MULÉY [aside]. This new ill was all I
        wanted,
Since stern fate no more allows
My poor succour to Fernando,
Let despair entwine his brows,
Now this glimmering hope hath vanished.
                              [Exeunt.]

SCENE II—-A street in Fez.

[DON JUAN COUTIÑO, BRITO, and other
CAPTIVES, enter, supporting DON FER-
NANDO: they place him on a mat upon
the ground.]
    FERNANDO. Place me here, where I can
        view,
With gladdened heart and will subdued,
The cloudless light of heaven's pure blue
O mighty Lord! so great and good,
To thee what boundless thanks are due!
When Job, as I, in anguish lay,
He curses on the day did pray,
But then it was because of sin
Which he had been engendered in;
But I, far different, bless the day
For all the graces God doth cheer
Our hearts through it—for it is clear
That every beauteous roseate hue,
And every beam that gilds the blue,
But living tongues of fire appear
To praise and bless him without end.
    BRITO. Does then your lordship feel so
        well?
    FERNANDO. Better than I deserve, my
        friend:

O Lord of Heaven! what tongue can tell
The mercies that to me you send?—
When from a dungeon's darksome gleam
Thou lead'st me forth, thou dost impart
To my chill blood the sun's warm beam.
O Lord! how liberal thou art!—
    1ST CAPTIVE. Heaven knows how great
        a boon we'd deem
The favour of being left with thee;
But the hour warns us, we must be
At work.
    FERNANDO. My sons, adieu!—
    2ND CAPTIVE. What bitter grief!
    3RD CAPTIVE. What sight to see!
                              [Exeunt.]
    FERNANDO. Will you remain with me,
        ye two?—
    JUAN. I too must also leave you now.
    FERNANDO. What can I do when thou
        art gone?—
    JUAN. My lord, I will return anon;
I only go to seek, somehow,
A little food; for since Muléy
From Fez was forced to go away,
On us has fallen a total dearth
Of human help upon the earth;
But I will go without delay
To try and gain it, even although
I make impossible demands;
For all who see me, fear to go
Against the edict, which commands
That even to a drop of water, no
Hand should give, or sell me aught,
Because they know it is for thee;—
To such a state has fortune brought
Our sad condition: but I see
People advancing hither.   [Exit.]
    FERNANDO.   Oh!
Would my voice could move to pity
Any heart in all this city!—
That the brief moments I may live
To greater suffering I may give!—

[Enter the KING, TARUDANTE, PHENIX,
        and SELIM.]
    SELIM. By a street, my lord, you've
        gone,
Where, perforce, you needs must be,
By the Infante, seen and known.
    KING [to TARUDANTE]. Thou hast come
        for this alone,

That my greatness thou mayst see.

TARUDANTE. Honours still thou showest me.

FERNANDO. Give a wretch in charity
Some relief, however scant;
Look, a fellow-man am I,
In affliction and in want,
And with very hunger die.
Men, take pity on a man;
Wild beasts pity one another;
Will not man a suffering brother?

BRITO. This I think is not the plan
Here of asking—try another.

FERNANDO. How?

BRITO. You should have thus began:—
Let your pity, Moors, be shown
Now unto this poor man's profit,
Let some food to him be thrown;
I ask it by the holiest bone
Of Mahomet, the great Prophet.

KING [aside]. That his constancy received
Naught of change, though thus bereaved,
Offends, insults me more than all.
[Aloud.] Infante! Prince!

BRITO. The king doth call.

FERNANDO. On me?—no, Brito, thou'rt deceived,
No Prince, no proud Infante, I,—
But the poor corse of what were they.—
And since almost in earth I lie,
Their names are not my names to-day,
Whate'er they've been in days gone by.

KING. Since you disown your rank and birth,
Then, as Fernando, answer me.

FERNANDO. Now must I raise me from the earth,
And slowly creeping unto thee,
Embrace thy feet.

KING. Thy constancy
Continues still to vex me so;
Is thy obedience humbleness
Or resolution?

FERNANDO. 'Tis to show
What great respect a slave doth owe
Unto his lord, nor more nor less;
And since I am thy slave at present,
And in thy presence now appear,
I will e'en venture to address thee,
My lord and King, and pray thee hear:

King I call thee, though thou beest
Of another law, for so august
Is the divinity of monarchs—
So strong and absolute—it must
Ever pitying minds engender,
And make all noble blood display
Pity and wisdom, as its nature.
For even 'mong brutes and beasts of prey
This name, authority so ample
Does in its wondrous way enforce,
That, by a certain law, obedience
Follows in Nature's usual course;
And thus, within his rude republics,
We read the lion-king doth reign,
Who, when his horrid front he wrinkleth,
And crowns him with his royal mane,
Feels pity, for he ne'er abuseth
Whatever prey his wrath hath slain.
So on the sea's salt foam the dolphin,
Who is the king of fish, we're told,
Worketh upon his azure shoulder,
In scales of silver and of gold,
The shape of crowns; and we behold him,
When the wild tempest shrieks with glee,
Bear on his back the sinking seaman,
Lest he should perish in the sea.
The eagle, too, so proud and noble,
He, with his tuft of plumes upcurled,
Diadem-like, by winds, is king
Of all the birds that from this world
Rise to salute the sun in heaven;
And he, through pity just and brave,
Downwards darts, lest man in drinking,
Should, amid the silver wave,
Drink his death; for o'er the crystal
Oft the snake his poison flings,
Which he scatters by the motion
Of his disturbing beak and wings.
So 'mong plants and precious stones
Is extended and deciphered
This imperial law of thrones.
The pomegranate which o'ershoots,
Crowned with flowers, the topmast branches,
Proof that it is queen of fruits,
Withers all its poisoned berries,
Which, like rubies, glisten through,
Turning them to yellow topaz,
Of a pale and sickly hue.
And the diamond, in whose presence
Even the loadstone turns away

From its beloved north, thus showing
How its true king it doth obey,
Is so noble, that the treason
Of its lord it cannot hide,
And its hardness, which the burin
Finds too flinty to divide,
Of its own accord dissolveth
Into small and shining dust.
If then, among beasts and fishes,
Plants, and stones, and birds, the august
Majesty of King, is pity—
It, my lord, were not unjust
That men's bosoms should possess it—
A different faith does not withdraw
You from this rule; since, to be cruel
Is condemned by every law.
Think not I desire to move thee
By my anguish and my pain,
To the end that life you give me:
This, my voice seeks not to gain;
For I know that I must perish
Of this malady which dims
All my senses, and which, frost-like,
Creepeth o'er my weary limbs;
I know well that I am wounded
By death's hand, for every word
That my feeble breath can utter
Cuts me like a keen-edged sword:
For I know that I am mortal,
Not secure of life one hour,
And 'tis doubtless to exhibit
Life and death's divided power,
That the cradle and the coffin
Are so like each other wrought;
For it is a natural action
When a man receiveth aught,
That his hands he raiseth upward,
Joined together in this way.
But should he express refusal,
By a similar action, may
His intent be known, by simply
Turning them averted down;
So, the world, to prove it seeks us
When we're born, without a frown
In a cradle doth receive us,
Leaving us securely lain
In its open arms: but should it,
Or through fury or disdain,
Wish to drive us forth, it turneth
Back her hands, with the intent,
That the coffin's mute material

Be of that same instrument,
For an upturned open cradle
When reversed, becomes a tomb.
Since we live in such assurance
Of our death—the common doom—
That when we are born, together
We our first and last bed see;
What expects he who this heareth?
Who that knows this, what waits he?
It is certain, that it cannot
Be to live; undoubtedly,
Then, 'tis death, and this I ask thee,
That the heavens may thus comply
With my earnest wish of dying
For the faith. But think not, I
Seek this boon through desperation,
Or from a dislike to live;
No, but from the strongest impulse
That I feel, my life to give
In the defence of my religion,
And to lay before God's feet
Life and soul breathed out together:
Thus, although I death entreat,
Will this impulse exculpate me.
If, through pity, thou dost slight
This request, let anger move thee.
Art thou a lion? then 'tis right,
That thou roar and tear in pieces
Him who in thy wrathful mood
Injures, wrongeth, and offends thee.
Art thou an eagle? then you should
Wound with vengeful beak and talons
Him who would dare despoil thy nest
Art thou a dolphin? then be herald
Of storms to move the seaman's breast,
How that the sea this huge world furrows.
Art thou a kingly tree? then show
Through all your bare and naked branches,
How wildly Time's dark tempests blow—
The ministers who work God's vengeance.
Art thou a diamond? then by
Thy own dust make deadliest poison,
Weary thyself out in wrath: but I,
Though I suffer greater torments,
Though I greater rigours see,
Though I weep still greater anguish,
Though I go through more misery,
Though I experience more misfortunes,
Though I more hunger must endure,
Though my poor body have no covering
But these few rags; and this impure

Dungeon be still my only dwelling,
All for the faith my soul derides;
For it is the sun that lights me,
For it is the star that guides!
It is the laurel that doth crown me;
No triumph o'er the Church thou'lt have;
O'er me, if you desire it, triumph:
God will my cause defend and save,
Since it is his for which I struggle.

KING. Can it be, in such a state,
Thou canst boast thus and console thee?
Being thine own, why idly rate
Me, for condoling not a fate,
When thou thyself wilt not condole thee?
Since then you your life resign
By your own deed, and not by mine,
No pity need'st thou hope from me,
Merciful thou to thyself must be
Ere I can feel those pains of thine.
                                        [*Exit.*]

FERNANDO [*to* TARUDANTE]. My lord,
    your gracious Majesty
Be my protector.

TARUDANTE.   What a sight!

FERNANDO [*to* PHENIX]. Since beauty
    owns no lovelier light,
Than when upon her face we see
Enthroned mild mercy's deity,—
Protect me with the king!

PHENIX.   What grief!

FERNANDO. What! not a look!

PHENIX.   'Tis past belief!

FERNANDO. 'Tis well: those beauteous
    eyes I know
Were never made to look at woe.

PHENIX. My very fear forbids relief!

FERNANDO. Since thou wilt not turn
    thine eye
Towards me, and desire to fly;
Lady, it is well to know,
Though thy beauty prides thee so,
That thou canst do less than I,
And perhaps I more than thou.

PHENIX. Horror comes, I know not how,
Wounding me, when thou dost speak.
Leave me, man; what dost thou seek?
More I cannot suffer now!   [*Exit.*]

[*Enter* DON JUAN *with some bread.*]

JUAN. This bread, I bring thee to
    assuage

Thy patient craving after food,
Have the cruel Moors pursued,—
Striking me with blows through rage.

FERNANDO. It is Adam's heritage.

JUAN. Take it.

FERNANDO.   Ah! my faithful friend,
'Tis too late; for now doth end
All my woes in death.

JUAN.   O heaven!
Now be thy consolation given.

FERNANDO. But since deathwards all
    men doth wend,
What is there that ends not so?
In the world's confused abyss,
Sickness ever leads to this,
When death strikes the fatal blow.
Man, be mindful, here below,
Of thy soul's sublimer part;
Think upon eternity,
Wait not till infirmity
Suddenly that truth impart—
For infirmity itself thou art.
On the hard earth, year by year,
Man is treading, hopeful, brave,
But each step is o'er his grave,
Daily drawing near and near.
Mournful sentence—law severe—
But which cannot be mistaken,
Every step (what fears awaken!)
Is to that dark goal commissioned,
So that God is not sufficient
To prevent that step being taken:
Friends, my end approaches nigher;
Bear me from this public place
In your arms.

JUAN.   Life's last embrace
For me, is this.

FERNANDO.   What I desire,
Noble friend, is, when I expire,
That these garments you unbind:
In my dungeon, you will find
My religious cloak, which I
Bore so oft in days gone by.
Uncovered thus and unconfined
Bury me—his wrath passed by—
If from the fierce King you procure
Leave to give me sepulture.
Mark the spot, for although I
Here to-day a captive die,
Ransomed yet, I hope to share
The blessed altar's sacred prayer,

For, my God! since I have given
So many churches unto Heaven,
One to me 'twill surely spare.
[*They bear him out in their arms.*]

SCENE III—*The sea-coast.*

[*Enter* DON ALPHONSO *and* SOLDIERS *with
arquebuses.*]

ALPHONSO. Leave to the fickle field of
green—
The azure wave—this arrogant machine
Of ships, whose vastness scaring heaven's
beholders,
The sea sustains upon its snow-white
shoulders,
And upon this sandy plain
Let the pregnant mountains of the main
Bring forth the troops, their fire-arms
brightly gleaming,
Each man-filled boat the Grecian structure
seeming.

[*Enter* DON ENRIQUE.]
ENRIQUE. My Lord, you did not wish
upon the strand
Of Fez, that we our armament should
land,
And this place, for debarkation,
You did choose—unhappy situation!—
For on one side, by the coast
Marching comes a numerous martial host
Whose speed the wind outvies;
Whose vastness makes the hills increase
in size;
And with a similar number, Tarudante
Leadeth his wife away (the fortunate
Infante)
From Fez unto Morocco,—
But learn the tidings better from the
echo.
ALPHONSO. Enrique, 'tis for this that
I advance
To meet them at this pass; 'tis not
through chance
That I, this spot have chosen, but re-
flection,
And this the reason is, of my selection:—
If I, at Fez had landed on the coast,
I must have fought with their united
host,

But being divided thus in two,
With smaller power I can each force sub-
due;
And so, before they can prepare,
Sound to arms.
ENRIQUE. My Lord, reflect—take care;
Unseasonable seems this movement.
ALPHONSO.   Oh! mine ire
No tardy-footed counsel doth desire,
Nor doth my vengeance know the way
Even to brook a moment's brief delay;
Let Africa beware,
In my strong hands the scourge of death
I bear.
ENRIQUE. Already hath the night be-
gun,
And see, the shining chariot of the sun
Has ceased the clouds of evening to
illume.
ALPHONSO. Well, let us combat in the
gloom;
The faith that animates my soul to-day,
Nor any power, nor time, can take away.
Fernando, if the martyrdom you suffer,
Since it is in his own cause, to God you
offer,
Certain is the sacred victory,
Mine will be the honour, thine the glory.
ENRIQUE. Thy daring pride doth lead
thee much too far.
[*The Ghost of* DON FERNANDO
speaks within.]
FERNANDO. Great Alphonso! to the
attack! war! war!
[*A trumpet sounds.*]
ALPHONSO. Hear you not these min-
gled voices breaking
The silence, and the swift, sad night-
winds waking?
ENRIQUE. Yes; and with them too do
I hear the rattle
Of arms, and trumpets charging to the
battle.
ALPHONSO. Forward, Enrique! doubts
had not delayed you
If you relied on Heaven.

[*Enter the Ghost of* DON FERNANDO,
*dressed in his capitulary cloak, and
with a torch in his hand.*]
FERNANDO. Yes! it will aid you;

For the Heavens regarding
Your faith and zeal, your piety rewarding,
Will this day defend you,
And to free me from my slavery doth
    send you;
For in return (a rare example)
Of many temples, God doth offer me one
    temple,
And with this flame-bespangled
Torch, from the streaming orient disen-
    tangled,
Before the army gliding,
Thus shall I go, the light your footsteps
    guiding,
That thy triumphs may be thus propi-
    tious,
And equal, great Alphonso, to thy wishes.
To Fez advance, not there new laurels get-
    ting,
But that thy morning rise upon my set-
    ting.   [*Exit.*]
ENRIQUE. Alphonso, I still doubt my
    eyes deceive.
ALPHONSO. And I do not. I bow and I
    believe,
And if it be for God's divinest glory,
No more cry "war!" the cry be "victory!"
                                    [*Exeunt.*]

SCENE IV—*Before the walls of Fez.*

[*Enter the* KING *and* SELIM; *on the
walls appear* DON JUAN *and a* CAPTIVE;
*before them is a coffin; in it appears to be
the body of* DON FERNANDO.]
JUAN. Now rejoice! rejoice! barbarian,
That thy tyranny hath ta'en
The noblest life of the world!
KING.   Who are you?
JUAN. A man, who though he should
    be slain
For it, shall not leave Fernando,
And though madness choke my breath,
Like the faithful dog, I shall not
Leave my master even in death.
KING. Christians, this is an example
Which, to future times may figure
What was due unto my justice,
For it cannot be called rigour—
That revenge which overtaketh

Wrongs to royal persons done.
Now let Alphonso come and free him,
With arrogant presumption,
From his chains; for though hath faded
The high hopes that once I had
Of Ceuta, *he* will lose the haughty
Hope of freeing him; I'm glad,
In this narrow cell to see him,
For though dead, he shall not be
Free of my renowned resentment:
Thus exposed, in mockery
Let him lie for all beholders.
JUAN. King, thy punishment is near,
For upon the fields and waters
I can plainly see, from here,
Coming swift my Christian standards.
KING. Let us mount upon the wall
To investigate these tidings. [*They go in.*]
JUAN. Down the drooping banners
    fall,
And the sullen drums are muffled,
Fires and lights are out, and all,
All things wear the signs of mourning.
        [*The drums beat a mournful
        march; enter the Ghost of* DON
        FERNANDO *bearing a lighted
        torch, and followed by* DON
        ALPHONSO *and* DON ENRIQUE
        *at the head of their troops,
        with whom as prisoners come*
        TARUDANTE, PHENIX, *and* MU-
        LÉY.]
FERNANDO. Through the darkness of
    the night,
By wild paths that no man knoweth,
Have I led you; now the sun
Faintly through the grey clouds gloweth.
Thus, victorious, great Alphonso,
I, to Fez have led thy feet.
This is Fez: behold the ramparts.
For my speedy ransom treat.   [*Disap-
                                    pears.*]
ALPHONSO. Ho, there! on the walls, to
    speak
To the King I crave an audience.

[*Enter the* KING *and* SELIM *on the walls.*]
KING. Valiant youth, what dost thou
    seek?
ALPHONSO. That you yield me the In-
    fante—

The Grand Master Don Fernando;
Phenix here and Tarudante,
Prisoners now, will be his ransom:
Thus we shall depart in peace.
Choose now which of these thou pleasest,
Thy daughter's death or his release.
 KING [*to* SELIM]. What can I now
  do, friend Selim,
In a perplexity so strange?
Fernando's dead, and see, my daughter
Is in their power—how great a change
In the condition of our fortunes,
Since I have fallen to such a state!
 PHENIX. How is this, my lord, that
  seeing
My person hemmed by ills so great,
My life in this extremest peril,
My honour, in this dangerous strait;
Can you hesitate to answer?
Can your anxiety delay
Even for a minute or an instant
The words of liberty to say?
In thy hand my life is lying,
And you consent (oh! bitter pain!)
That mine (oh! grief beyond expression!)
Should thus unjustly wear this chain!
On thy voice my life is hanging,
And (cruelty beyond compare!)
Thou permittest mine to trouble
Vainly thus the realms of air!
With thine eyes, you see my bosom
Thus the aim of pointed spears,
And you consent, that mine should sadly
Weep those useless tender tears!
Once my King—but now a wild beast,
Once my sire—an adder now—
Once my judge, but now my headsman,
Nor king, nor judge, nor father thou!
 KING. Phenix, if I have not given thee
Answer sooner—as 'tis known
Unto Heaven—'tis not to deny thee
Life, when thine would cost mine own,
And since now, both one and the other
Can no longer here delay,
Know, Alphonso, that when Phenix
Yester evening took her way
Out of Fez, two glorious planets
Down in two seas—one dark and dun—
The sea of death; one bright with sea-
  foam,—
Sank the Infante and the Sun.

Within this poor and narrow coffin
His lifeless body lieth lone;
Give death unto the beauteous Phenix,
And let my blood for his atone!
 PHENIX. Ah! woe is me! from this
  sad moment
For me, now every hope is o'er!
 KING. No remedy for me remaineth
By which to live one instant more!
 ENRIQUE. God of mercy! what sad tid-
  ings!
Ah! ye Heavens, we have delayed
Far too long to give him freedom!
 ALPHONSO. Do not say so, if the shade
Of Fernando said, thus darkly—
Free me from this slavery,—
It was for his corse he said it,
That, for many temples, he
Might obtain one for his body,
And for this be ransomèd;
King of Fez, do not imagine
That Fernando, even dead,
Is not worth this living beauty;
For him, though thus dead he lieth,
I exchange her: then, I pray,
Send us snow for these bright crystals—
January for this May,—
Roses dead for living diamonds,
And a hapless corse in fine
For a goddess-seeming image.
 KING. How! what mean these words of
  thine,
Brave, invincible Alphonso?
 ALPHONSO. Him, permit these slaves
  to lower.
 PHENIX. Thus I am a corse's ransom!
Now Heaven's prophecy is o'er.
 KING. Carefully let down the coffin
By the wall, with all things meet.
I myself, to make delivery,
Go to throw me at thy feet. [*Exit.*]
  [*The coffin is let down by cords
  from the walls.*]
 ALPHONSO. Let me in my arms receive
  thee,
Martyred prince—divinely grand.
 ENRIQUE. Accept my reverence—sainted
  brother.

[*Enter the* KING, DON JUAN, *and*
  CAPTIVES.]

JUAN. Let me kiss thy victor hand,
Brave Alphonso.
ALPHONSO.　　　　　Ah! Don Juan.
Ah! my friend, a piteous tale,
Have I learned of the Infante.
　JUAN. Till his death, I did not fail
In my attendance; till I saw him
Free beneath his native skies,
Dead or living, to be with him
I had vowed—see, there he lies.
　ALPHONSO. I must clasp thy hand, my
　　uncle,
For although, through luckless fate,
I, to draw thee from this danger,
Came, illustrious lord, too late,
Yet in death, which is the greatest,
Can true friendship be displayed;
In a sacred sovereign temple,
The grave deposit shall be made
Of thy consecrated body.
I deliver, king, to thee,

Tarudante and fair Phenix,
And I ask of you, that she
With Muléy be let to marry,—
For the friendship that I know
He did bear to the Infante.
Come, now, captives, let us go;
Look upon your prince, and bear him
On your shoulders to the fleet.
　KING. It is right they all go with
　　him.
　ALPHONSO. To the solemn sound and
　　sweet
Of trumpets, and the drum's low music
Let the army all attend,
Marching in the usual order
Of interment; and so end,
Humbly asking you to pardon
The great errors that it hath—
The Lusitanian Prince Fernando
Firm and Constant in the Faith.
　　　　　　　　　　　[Exeunt.]

THE CID

By PIERRE CORNEILLE

Produced at Paris, 1636

TRANSLATED BY FLORENCE KENDRICK COOPER *

CHARACTERS

FERNAND, *first King of Castile*
URRAQUE, *Infanta of Castile*
DIÈGUE, *father of Roderick*
GOMEZ, *Count of Gormaz, father of Chimène*
RODERICK, *lover of Chimène*
SANCHO, *enamored of Chimène*
ARIAS, }
ALONSO, } *Castilian gentlemen*
CHIMÈNE, *daughter of the Count of Gormaz*
LEONORA, *governess of the Infanta*
ELVIRE, *governess of Chimène*
A PAGE *of the Infanta*

SCENE—*Seville.*

ACT I

[*Enter* CHIMÈNE *and* ELVIRE.]

CHIMÈNE. Tell me, Elvire, is this a true report?
In naught dost thou disguise my father's words?
ELVIRE. My heart thrills with delight when I recall them.

Your love for Roderick vies with his esteem;
Unless I read amiss his inmost soul,
He will command that you return his love.
CHIMÈNE. Repeat, I pray, a second time the cause
Why thou dost think that he approves my choice;
What hope he gives me, let me learn anew;

---

* Reprinted from the edition published by D. Appleton, copyright, 1901, by permission of the publisher.

Such welcome news I could forever hear.
Thou canst not with too sure a promise
    pledge
The sunlight of his sanction to our love.
What utterance gave he on the secret plot
That Roderick and Sancho made with
    thee?
Hast thou not made too clear the differ-
    ences
Which draw me to my chosen Roderick's
    side?
    ELVIRE. No, an indifferent heart I pic-
    tured yours,
That kindles not, nor blights, the hope of
    either,
And, not too stern, nor yet too soft, but
    waits
Your father's wish in choosing you a hus-
    band.
This filial spirit charmed him, as his lips
And every feature quick assurance gave.
And since your heart demands his very
    words
Repeated o'er and o'er—why, here they
    are:
"Wisely she waits my choice; they both
    are worthy,
Of noble blood; of faithful, valiant soul.
Their youthful faces speak the unbroken
    line
Of shining virtues handed proudly down.
In Roderick's glance no slightest trace I
    see
Of aught but courage high and stainless
    honor.
Cradled amid war's trophies was this
    son,
So many warriors has his house pro-
    duced.
A marvelous tale of valor and emprise,
His father's glorious acts have long been
    told;
And the seamed brow that tells the flight
    of years
Speaks clearer still his mighty deeds in
    arms.
The son will prove fully worthy of the
    sire;
'T would please me should he win my
    daughter's love."
Then to the council-chamber did he haste,

Whose pressing hour an interruption
    made;
But from his hurried words I think 't is
    clear
He leans not strongly to the suit of either.
The king must choose a tutor for his
    son,
And this high service to your father
    gives;
The choice is certain, and his valor rare
Admits no fear of question or dispute;
His unmatched gifts ne'er meet a rival
    claim,
Whether in royal court or honor's field.
And since your Roderick has his father's
    word
To press the marriage, at the council's
    close,
Your heart may well assure you of his
    plea,
And in a tender hope will rest content.
    CHIMÈNE. My troubled heart in hope
    finds little ease,
But, burdened with sad doubt, asks cer-
    tainty:
Fate in a moment can reverse her will;
Even this happiness may mean a sorrow.
    ELVIRE. Nay, happily that fear shall
    be dispelled.
    CHIMÈNE. Away!—to wait the issue,
    what it be.
        [*Exeunt* CHIMÈNE *and* ELVIRE.]

[*Enter the* INFANTA, LEONORA, *and* PAGE.]
    INFANTA. Page, quickly tell Chimène
    she stays too long
Before her promised coming; my affection
Complains that she neglects the heart
    that loves her.   [*Exit* PAGE.]
    LEONORA. Madam, some longing burns
    within your soul,
For at each meeting anxiously you seek
The daily progress of her lover's suit.
    INFANTA. Have I not reason? Her
    young heart is pierced
By darts myself did level at her breast.
Her lover Roderick was my lover first,
And 't is to me she owes his passion deep;
Thus having forged these lovers' lasting
    chains,
I yearn to see the end of all their pains.

LEONORA. Madam, their dear delight in mutual love
Finds, as I read your heart, no echo there.
But sorrow weighs your spirit at their hopes.
Can your great soul feel grief at others' joy?
Why should your love for them react in pain,
And cause you suffering in their hour of rapture?
But, pardon, madam, I am overbold.
INFANTA. Concealment deepens sorrow, therefore hear
What struggles my too-loving heart has borne;
Listen what fierce assault my courage braves.
The tyrant Love spares neither high nor low;
This cavalier whose heart I've given away I love!
LEONORA. You love him!
INFANTA. Feel my bounding pulse!
Mark what its conqueror's name alone can do;
It knows its master.
LEONORA. Madam, pardon me,
I would not fail in gentle courtesy,
And rudely censure you for this affection.
But for a royal princess so to stoop
As to admit a simple cavalier
Within her heart—what would your father say?
What all Castile? Yours is the blood of kings!
Have you remembered that?
INFANTA. So well, alas!
That I would ope these veins ere I would prove
False to the sacred trust of rank and name.
In noble souls, 't is true, worth, worth alone
'Should kindle love's bright fires; and did I choose
To justify my passion, many a one
As high-born as myself could give me cause.
But honor heeds not Love's excuses fond,
And sense, surprised, makes not my courage less.
The daughter of a king must mate with kings;
No other hand than kingly sues for mine.
To save my heart from well-nigh fatal stroke,
With mine own hand I turned the steel away.
I drew the bond that binds him to Chimène,
And tuned their notes to love to still my own.
No longer wonder that my harassed soul,
With restless haste, will urge their nuptials on.
Love lives on hope, and dies when hope is dead—
A flame that needs perpetual renewal.
My heart has suffered much; but if this tie
Be consummated with no long delay,
My hope is dead, my wounded spirit healed.
But till that hour I'm rent with varying pangs;
I will to lose, yet suffer in my loss;
The love I would resign I still would keep;
And thus the court that to Chimène he pays
Excites the secret pain I cannot hide.
Love moves my sighs for one whose rank I scorn.
My mind divided feels a double pang;
My will is strong; my heart is all aflame.
I dare not hope from their united lives
More than a mingled sense of joy and pain.
Honor and Love war on this fatal field;
Neither can wholly conquer, neither yield.
LEONORA. Madam, I blame not, but I pity you,
And have no word to utter save that I
Sigh with your sighs and suffer in your grief.
But since your royal heart, unstained and strong,
Can front an ill so tempting and so sharp,
And bear it down, your noble spirit soon
Will know again its sweet serenity.

Time is the friend of Virtue; with its aid
You will forget; and Heaven, whose God
  is just,
Will not forsake you in this trying hour.
  INFANTA. My surest hope is hope's
  own swift defeat.

  [*Enter* PAGE.]

PAGE. Chimène awaits Your Highness
  at your wish.
INFANTA [*to* LEONORA]. Go, entertain
  her in the gallery.
LEONORA. Here, brooding o'er your sor-
  row, will you stay?
INFANTA. No, I but wish to hide my
  grief from her,
And to assume a joy I scarce can feel;
I follow soon.
INFANTA [*alone*]. Just Heaven, whence
  I must hope alone for aid,
Put to this bitter suffering an end;
Grant me repose; in honor's path be
  guide;
In others' bliss my own I fain would seek.
Three hearts are waiting for this mar-
  riage bond;
Oh, hasten it, or strengthen my weak
  soul!
The tie that makes these happy lovers one
Will break my fetters and my anguish
  end.
But I am lingering; I will seek Chimène;
Her gentle presence will assuage my pain.
  [*Exit.*]

  [*Enter the* COUNT *and* DIÈGUE.]

COUNT. At last you win the prize; the
  royal hand
Uplifts you to a place where I should
  stand.
You are to train the young prince of Cas-
  tile.
DIÈGUE. His justice and his gratitude
  the king
Has blended in this honor to my house.
COUNT. Kings, howsoever great they
  be, are men,
And, like us all, they ofttimes strangely
  err;
All courtiers may, in this, a warning see
That present service meets but poor re-
  ward.

DIÈGUE. No longer let us speak upon
  a theme
So chafing to your spirit; kindness may
Have turned the balance quite as much as
  merit.
But to a king whose power is absolute
'T is due to take, nor question, what he
  wills.
An added honor I would ask of you—
The union of our houses and our names.
You have a daughter, I an only son,
Their marriage would forever make us
  one
In more than friendship's bonds; this
  favor grant.
COUNT. To such alliance does this
  youth presume?
Will the new splendor of your office serve
To puff his mind with swelling vanity?
Use your new dignity, direct the prince,
Instruct him how a province should be
  ruled
So all his subjects tremble 'neath his laws,
And love and terror make his throne
  secure;
To civic duties add a soldier's life—
To laugh at hardship, ply the trade of
  Mars
Undaunted and unequaled; pass long days
And nights on horseback; to sleep fully
  armed;
To force a stronghold, and, the battle won,
To owe the glory to himself alone.
Instruct him by example; his young eyes
Must in yourself his perfect pattern see.
  DIÈGUE. Your envious soul speaks in
  your sneering words;
But, for example, he need only turn
The pages of my life; therein he'll read,
Through a long story of heroic acts,
How to subdue the nations, storm a fort,
Command an army, and to make a name
Whose wide renown shall rest on mighty
  deeds.
  COUNT. Living examples are the only
  guides;
Not from a book a prince his lesson
  learns.
Your boasted years a single day of mine
Equals not only, but surpasses oft.
Valiant you have been; I am valiant now!

On my strong arm this kingdom rests
  secure;
When my sword flashes, Aragon retreats,
Granada trembles; by my name of
  might
Castile is girdled round as by a wall.
Without me you would pass 'neath other
  laws,
And soon you'd have your enemies your
  kings.
Each day, each flying hour, exalts my
  fame,
Adds victory unto victory, praise to
  praise.
Under the guarding shadow of my arm
The prince should prove his mettle on the
  field,
Should learn by seeing conquest how to
  conquer.
In his young princehood he should early
  win
The loftiest heights of courage; he should
  see—
  DIÈGUE. I know! you serve the king,
  your master, well;
'Neath my command I've often watched
  you fight;
And since the stiffening currents of old
  age
Have chilled my powers, your prowess
  nobly shows—
No more; what I have been, you are to-
  day.
'T is true, however, that when choice is
  due,
Our monarch sees a difference 'twixt us
  still.
  COUNT. Nay! you have stolen what
  was mine by right!
  DIÈGUE. To win an honor is the proof
  of merit.
  COUNT. He is most worthy who can
  use it best.
  DIÈGUE. To be refused it is poor proof
  of worth.
  COUNT. You've used a courtier's wiles,
  and won by trick!
  DIÈGUE. My fame has been my only
  partisan.
  COUNT. Admit the king but honors
  your old age.

  DIÈGUE. My years the king but meas-
  ures by my deeds.
  COUNT. If deeds are years, I'm elder
  far than you!
  DIÈGUE. Who not obtained this honor
  not deserved it.
  COUNT. I not deserved it? I?
  DIÈGUE. Yes, you!
  COUNT. Old man,
Thine insolence shall have its due reward.
      [Gives him a blow.]
  DIÈGUE [drawing his sword]. Quick,
  run me through!—the first of all my
  race
To wear a flush of shame upon my brow.
  COUNT. What dost thou hope thine im-
  potence can do?
  DIÈGUE. O God! my worn-out strength
  at need forsakes me.
  COUNT. Thy sword is mine, but thou
  wouldst be too vain
If I should take this trophy of thy fall.
Adieu! Go read the prince, in spite of
  sneers,
For his instruction, thy life's history.
This chastisement of insolent discourse
Will prove, methinks, no slight embellish-
  ment.   [Exit COUNT.]
  DIÈGUE. Rage and despair! age, my
  worst enemy!
Must my great life end with a foul dis-
  grace?
Shall laurels gained with slowly whiten-
  ing locks,
In years of warlike toils, fade in a day?
And does the arm all Spain has wondered
  at,
Whose might has often saved the king his
  throne,
And kept the rod of empire in his grasp,
Betray me now, and leave me unavenged?
O sad remembrance of my vanished glory!
O years of life undone in one short hour!
This new-won height is fatal to my for-
  tune,
A precipice from which my honor falls.
Must the Count's triumph add the final
  pang
To death dishonorable, to life disgraced?
The office, Count, is thine; thine the high
  place

Of tutor to my prince, for thine own hand,
With envious insult, the king's choice re-
    versed,
And leaves me here with hope and honor
    gone.
And thou, brave instrument of my ex-
    ploits,
But useless ornament of feeble age,
Once terror of my enemies, but now
A bauble, not a man's defense at need—
My sword!—go, quit thy now dishonored
    master;
Pass, to avenge me, into worthier hands!

[*Enter* RODERICK.]
DIÈGUE. Hast thou a brave heart, Rod-
    erick?
RODERICK. Any man
Except my father soon would prove it so.
DIÈGUE. O pleasing choler! wrath that
    soothes my hurt!
My own blood speaks in this resentment
    swift,
And in thy heat my youth comes back to
    me.
My son, my scion, come, repair my wrong;
Avenge me instantly!
RODERICK. For what? for what?
DIÈGUE. For an affront so cruel, so
    unjust,
T is fatal to the honor of our house.
A blow! across my cheek! his life had
    paid,
Save that my nerveless arm betrayed my
    will.
This sword, which I again can never wield,
I pass to thee for vengeance to the death.
Against this arrogance thy courage set;
Only in blood such stains are cleansed, and
    thou
Must kill or die. This man, mine enemy,
Whom thou must meet, is worthy of thy
    steel;
Begrimed with blood and dust, I've seen
    him hold
An army terror-stricken at his will,
And break a hundred squadrons by his
    charge;
And, to say all, more than a leader
    brave,
More than a warrior great, he is—he is—

RODERICK. In mercy speak!
DIÈGUE. The father of Chimène!
RODERICK. Chimène!
DIÈGUE. Nay, answer not; I know thy
    love;
But who can live disgraced deserves not
    life.
Is the offender dear, worse the offense.
Thou know'st my wrong; its quittance lies
    with thee;
I say no more; avenge thyself and me!
Remember who thy father is—and was!
Weighed down with Fate's misfortunes
    heaped on me,
I go to mourn them. Do thou fly to
    vengeance! [*Exit* DIÈGUE.]
RODERICK. My heart's o'erwhelmed
    with woe.
A mortal stroke that mocks my tender
    trust
Makes me avenger of a quarrel just,
    And wretched victim of an unjust blow.
Though crushed in spirit, still my pride
    must cope
With that which slays my hope.
So near to love's fruition to be told—
    O God, the strange, strange pain!—
My father has received an insult bold,
    The offender is the father of Chimène.

'Mid conflicts wild I stand.
I lift my arm to strike my father's foe,
But Love with mighty impulse urges
    "No!"
    Pride fires my heart, affection stays my
    hand;
I must be deaf to Passion's calls, or face
    A life of deep disgrace.
Whate'er I do, fierce anguish follows me—
    O God, the strange, strange pain!
Can an affront so base unpunished be?
    But can I fight the father of Chimène?

To which allegiance give?—
To tender tyranny or noble bond?—
A tarnished name or loss of pleasures
    fond?
    Unworthy or unhappy must I live.
[*To his sword.*] Thou dear, stern hope of
    souls high-born and bold
And fired with love untold,

But enemy of my new dreams of bliss,
Sword, cause of all my pain,
Was't given me to use for this, for this?—
To save my honor, but to lose Chimène?

I must seek death's dread bourne.
To weigh my duty and my love is vain.
If I avenge his death, her hate I gain,
If I no vengeance take, I win her scorn;
Unfaithful must I prove to hope most
    sweet,
Or for that hope unmeet.
What heals my honor's wounds augments
    my grief,
And causes keener pain;
Be strong, my soul! Since death's my
    sole relief,
I'll die, nor lose the love of my Chimène.

What, die without redress?
Seek death—so fatal to my future fame?
Endure that Spain shall heap on me the
    shame
Of one who failed in honor's sorest
    stress?
All for a love whose hope my frenzied
    heart
Already sees depart?
I'll list no longer to the subtle plea
Which but renews my pain;
Come, arm of mine, my choice turns now
    to thee,
Since naught, alas! can give me back
    Chimène.

Yes, love my will misled.
My father—life and name to him I owe—
Whether of grief or from a mortal blow
I die, my blood all pure and true I'll
    shed.
Too long I've dallied with a purpose
    weak;
Now vengeance swift I seek.
The flush of shame mounts hotly to my
    brow,
That I can deem it pain
To save my father's house. I haste e'en
    now
To seek—woe's me!—the father of
    Chimène.   [Exit RODERICK.]

ACT II

[Enter ARIAS and the COUNT.]

COUNT. I grant you that my somewhat
    hasty blood
Took fire too soon, and carried me too far;
But—what is done, is done: the blow was
    struck.
ARIAS. To the king's will let your
    proud spirit yield.
This moves him deeply, and his anger
    roused
Will make you suffer penalty extreme.
No just defense can you before him plead;
The deed was gross, the aged victim great;
No common rule that serves 'twixt man
    and man
Will meet the high demand exacted here.
    COUNT. The king can use my life to
    suit his will.
    ARIAS. You add the fault of anger to
    your deed.
The king still loves you well; appease his
    wrath;
You know his wish; you will not disobey?
    COUNT. To disobey—a little—were no
    crime,
Should it preserve the fame I most do
    prize.
But were it such, forsooth, my valiant
    service
More than suffices for o'erlooking it.
    ARIAS. For deeds howe'er illustrious
    and high,
A king can ne'er become a subject's
    debtor.
Better than any other you should know
Who serves his king well does his simple
    duty;
This haughty confidence will cost you
    dear.
    COUNT. I will believe you when I pay
    the price.
    ARIAS. You should respect your mon-
    arch's sovereign will.
    COUNT. I can outlive a single day's
    displeasure.
Let the whole state be armed to hurl me
    down—
If I be made to suffer, Spain will fall!

ARIAS. What! you, forsooth, defy the power supreme!

COUNT. Why should I fear a sceptered hand whose grasp
Is weaker than my own? He knows my use;
My head, in falling, will shake off his crown.

ARIAS. Let reason rule your action; be advised.

COUNT. I wish no further counsel: all is said.

ARIAS. What message to your king shall I report?

COUNT. That I shall ne'er consent to my disgrace.

ARIAS. Remember that you brave a tyrant's power.

COUNT. The die is cast and longer speech is vain.

ARIAS. Adieu, then, since I cannot change your will.
E'en on your laureled head the bolt may strike!

COUNT. I wait it without fear.

ARIAS. 'T will cast you down.

COUNT. Then old Diègue will be well satisfied. [*Exit* ARIAS.]
Who fears not death need surely not fear threats.
My proud resolve yields not to weak disgrace;
Though I be stripped of fortune, rank, and name,
Myself alone can rob me of my honor.

[*Enter* RODERICK.]

RODERICK. Grant me a word, Count.

COUNT. Speak.

RODERICK. Dost know Diègue?

COUNT. Yes.

RODERICK. Listen, then, and let us softly speak.
Dost also know that his now feeble arm
Was once Spain's chiefest honor, valor, glory?

COUNT. Perhaps!

RODERICK. This fire enkindled in my eyes
Marks the same blood as his; dost thou know that?

COUNT. What matters that to me?

RODERICK. I'll teach you, Count,
At some four paces hence, what matters it.

COUNT. Presumptuous youth!

RODERICK. Speak quietly, I pray.
My years are few, but, Count, in high-born souls,
Valor and youth full oft united are.

COUNT. And thou wouldst stand 'gainst me! thou vain, untried,
Impudent upstart? Cease thy boyish brag!

RODERICK. The temper of my steel will not demand
A second proof; the first will be enough.

COUNT. Know'st thou to whom thou speakest?

RODERICK. I know well!
Another than I am would hear with dread
The mention of thy name: thy crowns of palm
Must mean to me, 't would seem, the stroke of doom.
But bold I meet thine all-victorious arm;
Where courage leads, there force will aye be found.
A father's honor is a triple shield;
Invincible thou art not, though unconquered.

COUNT. Thy fearless words a fearless heart reveal.
I've watched thy growing powers from day to day;
In thee the future glory of Castile
I have believed to see, and proud of heart,
Was laying in thine own my daughter's hand.
I know thy love, and charmed am I to learn
That duty is a dearer mistress still,
Nor soft emotions weaken warlike zeal.
Thy manly worth responds to my esteem;
And wishing for my son a noble knight,
I did not err when I made choice of thee.
But pity stirs within me at thy words;
Such boldness ill befits thy youthful form;
Let not thy maiden effort be thy last;
I cannot fight a combat so unequal;
A victory won without a peril braved
Is but inglorious triumph, and for me

Such contest is not fitting. None would
dream
Thou couldst withstand an instant, and
regret
At thy young, foolish death would e'er be
mine.
RODERICK. Thy pity more insults me
than thy scorn;
Thou fear'st my arm, but dar'st attack
my honor.
COUNT. Withdraw from here!
RODERICK. Let us to deeds, not words!
COUNT. Art tired of life?
RODERICK. Dost thou, then, fear to die?
COUNT. Come on! Thou'rt right. I'll
help thee do thy duty!
'T is a base son survives a father's fame!
[*Exeunt* COUNT *and* RODERICK.]

[*Enter the* INFANTA, CHIMÈNE, *and*
LEONORA.]
INFANTA. Nay, do not weep! allay thy
grief, Chimène!
This sorrow should disclose thy spirit's
strength.
After this transient storm a calm will fall,
And happiness, deferred and clouded now,
Will brighter seem in contrast. Do not
weep!
CHIMÈNE. My heart, worn out with
trouble, has no hope.
A storm so sudden and so terrible,
To my poor bark brings direful threat of
wreck.
Ere I set sail upon my smiling sea,
I perish in the harbor. I was loved
By him I fondly loved; our sires ap-
proved;
But even while I told my charming story
At that same moment was the quarrel on,
Whose sad recital changed my tale to woe.
O cursed ambition! wrath's insanity!
Pride, to my dearest wishes pitiless,
Whose tyranny the noblest nature rules!
In sighs and tears a heavy price I pay.
INFANTA. Thy fears o'ercome thee; 't
is a hasty word;
The quarrel of a moment dies as soon.
The king already seeks to make a peace;
And I, as well thou knowest, to dry thy
tears

And heal thy grief would try the impos-
sible.
CHIMÈNE. No reconciliation can avail.
Such wounds are mortal and defy all art
Of king or princess, of command or plead-
ing.
And though an outward show of peace be
gained,
The fires of hate, compressed within the
heart,
Burn fiercer, and will break at last in
flame.
INFANTA. When Love has bound Chi-
mène and Roderick
In sacred marriage, hatred will depart;
Their fathers will forget, and happiness
Will silence discord in sweet harmony.
CHIMÈNE. I wish for such an end, but
dare not hope.
'T is a matched combat between two
proud souls;
Neither will yield; I know them; I must
weep!
The past I mourn, the future frightens
me.
INFANTA. What fearest thou? an old
man's feebleness?
CHIMÈNE. Brave sires make braver
sons; Roderick is bold.
INFANTA. He is too young.
CHIMÈNE. Such men are born high-
hearted!
INFANTA. Thou shouldst not fear his
boldness overmuch;
He cannot wound thee, whom he loves so
well;
A word from thy sweet lips will check his
wrath.
CHIMÈNE. How shall I speak it? If
he do not yield,
'T is but an added burden to my heart;
And if he do, what will men say of him—
His father's son, to see his father's fall,
Nor lift an arm of vengeance? In this
strait
I stand confused, nor know what I would
choose—
His too weak love, or his too stern refusal.
INFANTA. In thy high soul, Chimène,
no thought can live
Unworthy of thee; love but more exalts.

But if, until this trouble be o'erpast,
I make a prisoner of this gallant youth,
Preventing thus the dread results you fear,
Would it offend thy proud and loving heart?
CHIMÈNE. Ah! madam, then my cares are quieted.

[*Enter the* PAGE.]

INFANTA. Page, summon Roderick hither; I would see him.
PAGE. He and the Count de Gormaz—
CHIMÈNE. Heaven, oh, help me!
INFANTA. What? Speak!
PAGE. Together they have left the palace.
CHIMÈNE. Alone?
PAGE. Yes, and they muttered angrily.
CHIMÈNE. They've come to blows! All words are useless now;
Madam, forgive this haste—my heart will break! [*Exeunt* CHIMÈNE *and* PAGE.]
INFANTA. Alas! that such inquietude is mine;
I weep her griefs, but Roderick still enthrals;
My peace is gone; my dying flame revives.
The fate that parts Chimène from him she loves
Renews alike my sorrow and my hope.
Their separation, cruel though it be,
Excites a secret ecstasy in me.
LEONORA. Surely, the noble virtue of your soul
Yields not so soon to passion's baser thrall.
INFANTA. Nay, do not name it thus, since in my heart,
Strong and triumphant, it controls my will,
Respect my love, for it is dear to me;
My nobler pride forbids it—yet I hope.
Ill-guarded 'gainst a madness so bewild'ring,
My heart flies to a love Chimène has lost.
LEONORA. And thus your high resolve all-powerless fails?
And Reason lays her wonted scepter down?

INFANTA. Ah! Reason has a harsh and rude effect,
When such sweet poison has inflamed the heart;
The patient loves his painful malady,
Nor willingly accepts a healing draught.
LEONORA. Be not beguiled by Love's seductions soft;
That Roderick is beneath you, all well know.
INFANTA. Too well myself must know it, but my heart
Hears subtle words which Love, the flaterer, speaks.
If from this combat Roderick victor comes,
And this great warrior falls beneath his blow,
What other plea need Love, the pleader, use?
Who could withstand that conqueror's conqueror!
My fancy sets no bounds to his exploits;
Whole kingdoms soon would fall beneath his laws;
I see him on Granada's ancient throne;
The subject Moors with trembling do his will;
Proud Aragon acknowledges him king,
And Portugal receives him, while the seas
Bear his high destiny to other lands.
In Afric's blood his laurels shall be dyed,
And all that e'er was said of greatest chief,
I hear of Roderick, this victory won;
Then in his love my highest glory lies.
LEONORA. Nay, madam, 't is your fancy makes you dream
Of conquests whose beginning may not chance.
INFANTA. The count has done the deed —Roderick enraged—
They have gone forth to combat—needs there more?
LEONORA. E'en should they fight—since you will have it so—
Will Roderick prove the knight you picture him?
INFANTA. Nay, I am weak; my foolish mind runs wild;

Love spreads its snares for victims such
  as I.
Come to my chamber; there console my
  grief,
Nor leave me till this troubled hour is
  o'er. [*Exeunt* INFANTA *and* LEONORA.]
[*Enter the* KING, ARIAS, *and* SANCHO.]
KING. Pray, is this haughty count
  bereft of sense?
Dares he believe his crime can be o'er-
  looked?
ARIAS. To him I have conveyed your
  strong desire;
Nothing I gained from long and earnest
  pleas.
KING. Just Heaven! A subject have
  I in my realm
So rash that he will disregard my wish?
My oldest, foremost courtier he affronts,
Then aims his boundless insolence at
  me!
The law, in my own court, he would de-
  cree:
Leader and warrior, great howe'er he be,
I'll school his haughty soul with lesson
  hard.
Were he the god of battles, valor's self,
Obedience to his sovereign he shall pay.
Although his act like chastisement de-
  served,
It was my will to show him leniency.
Since he abuses mercy, from this hour
He is a prisoner, all resistance vain.
SANCHO. Pray, sire, a brief delay may
  calm his mind.
Fresh from the quarrel he was first ap-
  proached,
Boiling with passion. Sire, a soul like
  his,
So hasty and so bold, belies itself
In its first impulse; soon he'll know his
  fault,
But cannot yet admit he was the offender.
KING. Be silent, Sancho, and be warned
  henceforth.
He who defends the guilty shares the
  guilt.
SANCHO. Yea, sire, I will obey, but
  grant me grace
To say one further word in his defense.

KING. What can you say for such a
  reckless man?
SANCHO. Concessions do not suit a
  lofty soul
Accustomed to great deeds; it can con-
  ceive
Of no submission without loss of honor.
He cannot bend his pride to make amends;
Too humble is the part you'd have him
  play;
He would obey you were he less a man.
Command his arm, nourished 'mid war's
  alarms,
To right this wrong upon the field of
  honor.
The boldest champion who his steel will
  face
He will accept and make atonement swift.
KING. You fail in due respect, but
  youth is rash,
And in your ardor I your fault excuse.
A king, whom prudence ever should in-
  form,
Is guardian of his subjects' life and death.
O'er mine I watch with care, and jeal-
  ously,
Like a great head, I guard my members
  well.
Your reason, then, no reason is for me;
You speak, a soldier; I must act, a king.
Moreover, let the count think what he
  will,
Obedience to his king ennobles him.
He has affronted me; he rudely stained
The honor of my son's appointed guide.
To strike a blow at him—'t is nothing less
Than to attack with blows the power su-
  preme.
I'll hear no more. Listen!—there have
  been seen
Ten hostile vessels, with their colors up;
They've dared approach clear to the
  river's mouth.
ARIAS. The Moors have learned, per-
  force, to know you well;
Conquered so oft, what courage can they
  feel
To risk themselves against their con-
  queror?
KING. They'll never see, without a
  jealous rage,

My scepter rule o'er Andalusia.
That lovely land, by them too long possessed,
Always with envious eye they closely watch.
That was the only cause why Castile's throne
In old Seville I placed, now years ago;
I would be near, and ready at demand,
To overthrow uprising or attack.

ARIAS. They know, at cost of many a mighty chief,
That triumph, sire, your presence only needs.
Naught ean you have to fear.

KING. Nor to neglect;
For confidence is danger's sure ally.
Well do you know with what an easy sweep
A rising tide may float them to our walls.
'T is but a rumor; let no panic rise,
Nor causeless fears be spread by false alarms.
Stir not the city in the hours of night;
But doubly fortify the walls and harbor.
Enough, till more is known.

[*Enter* ALONSO.]

ALONSO. The count is dead!
Diègue has taken vengeance by his son!

KING. Soon as the affront I learned, I feared revenge.
Would that I might have turned that fatal wrath!

ALONSO. Chimène approaches, bathed in bitter tears,
And at your feet would she for justice plead.

KING. Compassion moves my soul at her mishaps;
But the count's deed, methinks, has well deserved
This chastisement of his audacity.
And yet, however just may be his doom,
I lose with pain a warrior strong and true,
After long service rendered to our state,
His blood poured out for us a thousand times.
His pride excites my anger, but my throne
His loss enfeebles while his death bereaves.

[*Enter* DIÈGUE *and* CHIMÈNE.]

CHIMÈNE. Justice, sire, justice!

DIÈGUE. Ah, sire, let me speak!

CHIMÈNE. Behold me, at your feet!

DIÈGUE. I clasp your knees!

CHIMÈNE. 'T is justice I demand!

DIÈGUE. Hear my defense!

CHIMÈNE. Punish the insolence of this bold youth!
He has struck down your kingdom's chief support!
My father he has slain!

DIÈGUE. To avenge his own!

CHIMÈNE. A subject's blood demands his monarch's justice!

DIÈGUE. A vengeance just demands no punishment.

KING. Rise, and in calmness let us hear of this.
Chimène, my deepest sympathy is stirred;
A grief not less than yours affects my heart.
[*To* DIÈGUE.] You will speak after, nor disturb her plaint.

CHIMÈNE. My father, sire, is dead; mine eyes have seen
Great drops of blood roll from his noble side;
That blood that oft your walls has fortified;
That blood that many times your fights has won;
That blood which, shed, still holds an angry heat
To be outpoured for other lives than yours.
What in war's deadliest carnage ne'er was spilled,
The hand of Roderick sheds upon your soil.
Breathless and pale, I reached the fatal spot;
I found him lifeless, sire—forgive my tears;
In this sad tale words mock my trembling lips;
My sighs will utter what I cannot speak.

KING. Take courage, child; thy king henceforth shall be
Thy father, in the place of him that's lost.

CHIMÈNE. Such honor, sire, I ask not in my woe;
I said I found him lifeless: open wound
And blood outpoured, and mixed with horrid dust,
Showed me my duty, drove me here in haste;
That dreadful gaping mouth speaks with my voice,
And must be heard by the most just of kings.
O sire, let not such license reign unchecked
Beneath your sovereign sway, before your eyes;
So the most noble may, without restraint,
Suffer the blows of beardless insolence,
And a young braggart triumph o'er their glory,
Bathe in their blood and mock their memory.
This valiant warrior, slain, if unavenged,
Will surely cool the ardor of your knights.
O sire, grant vengeance for my father's death!
Your throne demands it more than my poor heart.
His rank was high, his death will cost you dear;
Pay death with death, and blood with blood avenge.
A victim, not for me, but for your crown,
Your person, and Your Majesty, I beg—
A victim that will show to all the state
The madness of a deed so arrogant.
KING. What say'st, Diègue?
DIÈGUE. Worthy of envy he
Who, losing life's best gift, can part with life!
For age's weakness brings to noble souls
A mournful fate before its closing scene.
I, whose proud 'scutcheon is graved o'er with deeds,
I, whom a victor laurels oft have crowned,
To-day, because too long with life I've stayed,
Affronted, prostrate lie and powerless.
What neither siege nor fight nor ambuscade,
Nor all your foes, nor all my envious friends,
Nor Aragon could do, nor proud Granada,

The count, your subject, jealous of your choice,
Bold in the power which youth has over age,
Has done within your court, beneath your eye.
Thus, sire, these locks, 'neath war's rough harness blanched,
This blood, so gladly lavished in your cause,
This arm, the lifelong terror of your foes,
To a dishonored grave would have descended,
Had not my son proved, worthy of his sire,
An honor to his country and his king.
He took his father's sword, he slew the count,
He gave me back my honor cleansed from stain.
If to show courage and resentment deep,
If to avenge a blow, claim punishment,
On me alone should fall your anger's stroke.
When the arm errs, the head must bear the blame.
Whether this be a crime of which we speak,
His was the hand, but mine, sire, was the will.
Chimène names him her father's murderer;
The deed was mine; I longed to take his place.
Spare for your throne the arm of youth and might,
But slay the chief whom Time o'ermasters soon.
If an old soldier's blood will expiate
And satisfy Chimène, 't is hers to shed;
Far from repining at such stern decree,
I'll glory in an honorable death.
KING. Of deep and serious import is this deed,
And in full council must be gravely met.
Lead the count's daughter home; and you, Diègue,
Shall be held prisoner by your word of honor.
Let Roderick be brought; I must do justice.

CHIMÈNE. 'T is justice, sire, a murderer should die.
KING. Allay your grief, my child, and take repose.
CHIMÈNE. When silence urges thought, then anguish grows. [*Exeunt omnes.*]

ACT III

[*Enter* RODERICK *and* ELVIRE.]

ELVIRE. Roderick, what hast thou done? why com'st thou here?
RODERICK. I follow my sad fate's unhappy course.
ELVIRE. Whence hast thou this audacity, to come
To places filled with mourning by thy deed?
Com'st here to brave the dead count's very shade?
Hast thou not killed him?
RODERICK. To my shame he lived;
My father's house demanded that he die.
ELVIRE. But why seek shelter 'neath thy victim's roof?
What murderer ever sought retreat so strange?
RODERICK. I come to yield myself up to my judge.
No more look on me with astonished eye;
I seek my death in penance for a death.
My love's my judge, my judge Chimène alone.
Sharper than death the knowledge of her hate;
That I deserve, and I have come to ask
The sentence of her lips, her hand's death blow.
ELVIRE. Nay, rather flee her sight, her passion's force,
Remove thy presence from her fresh despair.
Flee! shun the promptings of her anguish new
Which will but rouse to fury every feeling.
RODERICK. This dearest object of my heart's desire
Cannot too sorely chide me in her wrath;
That is a punishment I well deserve.

In seeking for a death from hand of hers
I shun a hundred others worse to face.
ELVIRE. Chimène is at the palace, drowned in tears,
And will return escorted from the king.
Flee, Roderick, flee! pray add not to my cares.
What would be said if here thou shouldst be seen?
Wouldst thou that slander, adding to her woe,
Charge that she hide her father's murderer?
She'll soon return! Hark! hark! she comes, she's here!
Hide thyself, then, for her sake; Roderick, hide! [*Exit* RODERICK.]

[*Enter* SANCHO *and* CHIMÈNE.]
SANCHO. True, madam, blood alone pays debts like this;
Your wrath is righteous, and your tears are just.
I would not try with weak and foolish words
To calm your anger or console your grief.
But if to serve you I am capable,
My sword is at your service to command;
My love is yours to avenge your father's death;
If you I serve, my arm will outmatch his.
CHIMÈNE. O wretched that I am!
SANCHO. Accept my sword!
CHIMÈNE. It would offend the king, who pledges justice.
SANCHO. The march of Justice often is so slow
That crime escapes the tardy loiterer.
Her oft uncertain course costs tears and pain!
Suffer a knight to avenge you with his sword;
The way is sure, the punishment is swift.
CHIMÈNE. It is the last resort. If come it must,
And still my sorrows move your soul to pity,
You shall be free to avenge my injury.
SANCHO. To that one happiness my soul aspires,

And hoping this, I leave you, well content.   [*Exit* SANCHO.]

CHIMÈNE. At last, in freedom from a forced restraint,
I can pour out to thee my poignant woe,
Can give an utterance to my mournful sighs,
And let my soul tell all its many griefs.
My father's dead, Elvire; the maiden thrust
Of Roderick's sword has cut his life-thread short.
Weep, weep, my eyes, dissolve yourselves in tears;
One half my heart the other half entombs;
And for this mortal stroke, my heart that loves
Must vengeance take for that which is no more.

ELVIRE. Rest, madam, rest.

CHIMÈNE. Nay, mock me not with words!
In misery like mine to speak of rest!
Whence-ever shall my agony be soothed
Unless I hate the hand that caused my grief?
What respite can I hope from torment aye,
When love and hate both seek the criminal?

ELVIRE. You still can love the one who killed your father?

CHIMÈNE. Love is a word too weak for what I feel;
I do adore him, spite of my resentment;
My lover and my enemy are one.
Still, notwithstanding all my hatred fierce,
Against my father Roderick contends;
My filial love resists his sweet assault,
And struggles, feeble now, and now triumphant.
In this rude war of anger and of love,
My heart is rent, but stronger grows my soul;
I feel Love's power, but duty's deeper claims
Forbid that I should change or hesitate;
I balance not, nor swerve, when honor leads.
To me is Roderick dear; I weep his fate;

My heart pleads in his favor, yet, alas!
I am my father's daughter; he is dead.

ELVIRE. Shall you pursue it further?

CHIMÈNE. Cruel thought!
And cruel path which I am forced to tread!
I seek his life, yet fear my end to gain;
My death will follow his, yet he must die.

ELVIRE. Nay, madam, quit so terrible a task,
Nor on yourself impose a law so stern.

CHIMÈNE. My father dead—nay, snatched from my embrace!
Shall his dear blood unheard for vengeance cry?
Shall my weak heart, snared by seducing spells,
With woman's tears alone pay honor's debt?
Shall guileful love betray my filial duty,
And in a shameful silence still its voice?

ELVIRE. Believe me, madam, there is much excuse.
For cooler counsels toward a loving heart,
Against a lover dear. You've made appeal
Unto the king himself; press not too far
Persistence in this purpose strange and sad.

CHIMÈNE. My word is pledged to vengeance; it must fall.
Love would beguile us with sweet subtleties;
To noble souls excuses shameful seem.

ELVIRE. If you love Roderick, he can not offend you.

CHIMÈNE. 'T is true!

ELVIRE. Then, after all, what will you do?

CHIMÈNE. I will avenge my father, end my woe;
I'll follow him, destroy him, then I'll—die!

[*Enter* RODERICK.]

RODERICK. Nay, madam, you shall find an easier way;
My life is in your hand; your honor's sure.

CHIMÈNE. Elvire, where are we? Who is this I see?

Is Roderick in my house?—before my eyes?

RODERICK. I offer you my life; taste, when you will,
The sweetness of my death and your revenge.

CHIMÈNE. Oh, woe!

RODERICK. Pray, hear me!

CHIMÈNE. Nay, I die!

RODERICK. A moment!

CHIMÈNE. Go; let me die!

RODERICK. I would but speak a word.
You shall reply with sword-thrust at my heart.

CHIMÈNE. What! with a blade stained with my father's blood?

RODERICK. Chimène!

CHIMÈNE. Remove that object from mine eyes!
Its sight recalls thy crime and sues for death!

RODERICK. Nay, gaze upon it; 't will excite still more
Thy hatred and thy wrath; 't will haste my doom.

CHIMÈNE. 'T is tinged with my own blood.

RODERICK. Plunge it in mine!
Wash in my veins what it has brought from thine.

CHIMÈNE. Oh, cruel steel, which in one awful day
A father's and a daughter's life can take.
I cannot live and see it! Take it hence!
Thou did'st me hear, and yet thou strik'st me dead!

RODERICK. I do thy will, but cherish still the wish
Of ending by thy hand my wretched life.
Not even love of thee works in my soul
Craven repentance for a righteous deed.
The fatal end of wrath too swift and hot
Brought shame upon my father's honored head.
The insult of a blow what heart can bear?
The affront was mine, I sought its author swift,
And swift avenged the honor of my sire.
Were it again to do, again 't were done!
But even 'gainst the inevitable deed,
My love long struggled for supremacy.

Judge how it ruled my heart, when I could pause,
In such an hour of rage, and hesitate
Between my house, my father, and—my love,
Compelled to wound thy heart or stand disgraced.
Myself I did accuse of haste undue,
Of passions too alive to feel affront.
Thy beauty might have turned the balance still,
But for the thought that pressed itself at last—
A man disgraced had naught to offer thee,
And vainly would thy heart's voice plead for me,
If nobleness were sunk in infamy.
To yield to love, to hearken to its cry,
Proved me unworthy of thy tenderness.
With sighs I tell thee o'er and o'er again,
And with my latest breath I still would say,
With cruel hand I've hurt thee, but naught else
Could blot my shame and leave me worthy thee.
Now, honor and my father satisfied,
To thee I come, to pay my final debt;
To offer thee my life, I seek thee here.
That duty done, this only rests to do.
Thou need'st not tell me that thy father slain
Arms thee against me—see, thy victim here!
Shrink not from offering up the blood of him
Who shed thy father's nor can mourn the deed.

CHIMÈNE. Ah! Roderick, strangely does my changeful heart
Defend thee who hast saved thy father's fame.
If my distracted mind has cruel seemed,
'T is not with blame for thee, but in despair.
The ardor of a high, unbroken spirit
That cannot brook an insult, well I know.
It was thy duty taught thee, but, alas!
In doing thine, thou teachest me mine own.

The very terror of thy deed compels;
For, as thy father's name thou hast restored,
Mine also calls upon his child for vengeance.
But, oh! my love for thee drives me to madness!
My father's loss by other hand had left
The solace of thy presence and thy love,
A consolation sweet in misery.
I still had felt in grief thy sympathy,
And loved the hand that wiped my tears away.
But now, in losing him thee too I lose;
This victory o'er my love his fame demands,
And duty, with the face of an assassin,
Drives me to work thy ruin and mine own.
For in my heart no more than in thine own
Must courage yield to luring dreams of love.
My strength must equal thine. In thine offense
Thou hast but proved thy worth. By thine own death
Alone can I be worthy of thy love.
    RODERICK. Defer no longer what thy cause demands.
It claims my head; I offer it to thee;
Make me the victim of thy just revenge.
I welcome the decree; I hail the stroke;
The tedious course of Justice to await
Retards thy glory, as my punishment.
'T is welcome fate to die by thy dear hand.
    CHIMÈNE. No, not thine executioner am I;
'T is not for me to take thine offered life;
'T is thine to make defense 'gainst my attack.
Some other hand than mine must work my will;
Challenge I must, but punish never, never!
    RODERICK. However love constrains thee for my sake,
Thy spirit must be equal to mine own,
Thyself hast said; then wouldst thou borrow arms
To avenge a father's death? Nay, my Chimène,

The soul of vengeance fails. No hand but mine
Could slay thy father; thine must punish me.
    CHIMÈNE. O cruelty, to stand upon this point!
Thou didst not need my aid, I need not thine!
I follow thine example, and my spirit
Will never share with thee my glory's task.
My father's fame and I shall nothing owe
To love of thine, or to thy late despair.
    RODERICK. 'T is thou that standest on a point of honor.
Shall I ne'er win this mercy at thy hand?
In thy dead father's name, for our love's sake,
In vengeance or in pity, slay me here!
Thy wretched lover keener pain will know
To live and feel thy hate than meet thy blow.
    CHIMÈNE. Leave me, I hate thee not.
    RODERICK. 'T is my desert.
    CHIMÈNE. I cannot.
    RODERICK. When my deed is fully known,
And men can say that still thy passion burns,
Dost thou not fear the cruel, stinging words
Of censure and of malice? Silence them;
Save thine own fame by sending me to death.
    CHIMÈNE. My fame will shine the brighter for thy life,
The voice of blackest slander will lift up
My honor to the heavens, and mourn my griefs,
Knowing I love thee and yet seek thy life.
Go, vex no longer my poor, troubled soul
By sight of what I love and what I lose.
Hide thy departure in the shade of night;
For calumny may touch me, art thou seen;
The sole occasion for a slanderous word
Is, that I suffer thee within my house.
See that thou guard my virtue, and withdraw.
    RODERICK. Oh, let me die!
    CHIMÈNE. Depart.
    RODERICK. What wilt thou do?

CHIMÈNE. The fires of wrath burn with
the flames of love.
My father's death demands my utmost
zeal;
'T is duty drives me with its cruel goad,
And my dear wish is—nothing to achieve.
RODERICK. O miracle of love!
CHIMÈNE. O weight of woe!
RODERICK. We pay our filial debt in
suffering!
CHIMÈNE. Roderick, who would have
thought—
RODERICK. Or could have dreamed—
CHIMÈNE. That joy so near so soon our
grasp would miss?
RODERICK. Or storm so swift, already
close to port,
Should shatter the dear bark of all our
hope?
CHIMÈNE. Oh, mortal griefs!
RODERICK. Regrets that count for
naught!
CHIMÈNE. Pray, leave me now; I can-
not longer hear.
RODERICK. Adieu! I go to drag a
dying life,
Till it is ended at thine own command.
CHIMÈNE. If my dire fate e'er bring
that hour to me,
Thy breath and mine together will de-
part.
Adieu! and let no eye have sight of thee.
[Exit RODERICK.]
ELVIRE. Madam, whatever ills kind
Heaven may send—
CHIMÈNE. Trouble me not; pray, leave
me with my grief.
I long for night's dark silence, and for
tears.
[Exeunt ELVIRE and CHIMÈNE.]

[Enter DIÈGUE.]
DIÈGUE. Never a perfect happiness is
ours;
Our best achievements have their bitter
drop;
In each event, whate'er its promise be,
Care troubles still the currents of our
peace.
In my rejoicing o'er my honor saved,
An anxious fear now seizes on my soul.

The count whose hand affronted me is
dead,
But now I seek in vain my avenger's face.
Hither and yon I strive, with labor vain,
To roam the city, broken as I am;
The remnant of my strength which age
has left
Consumes itself in fruitless hours of
search.
Each moment, in each place, I hear his
voice,
I see his form—a shadow of the night.
I would embrace him—lo, he is not
there!—
Till love, deceived, suspicious grows and
fearful.
No marks of hasty flight do I discern,
And that strong troop of friends who
served the count
Affrights me and suggests a thousand ills.
If Roderick lives, he breathes a dungeon's
air.—
Just Heaven! do I deceive myself again?
Or do I see at last my hope, my son?
'T is he! I doubt no more; my vows are
heard,
My fears dispelled, my anxious longings
o'er.

[Enter RODERICK.]
DIÈGUE. At last, my Roderick, Heaven
restores thee mine.
RODERICK. Alas!
DIÈGUE. Mar not my new delight with
sighs.
Let me find words to praise thee as I
would;
My valor sees in thee no cause to blush,
But marks a kindred spirit; live in thee
The heroes of thy race, bold and renowned.
Thine ancestors are they, my son thou
art.
Thine earliest sword-thrust equals all of
mine;
Thine untaught youth, inspired by ardor
great,
By this one effort, touches my renown.
Prop of my age, and crown of all my for-
tune,
On these white hairs lay thy redeeming
hand;

Come, kiss this check where still thou
  canst behold
The mark of that affront thou hast
  avenged.
RODERICK. The honor is your due; I
  could no less,
Your blood in mine, your care my school
  of arms.
Most happy am I that my maiden blow
Did not disgrace the author of my life.
But in your satisfaction do not shun
To grant me, also, what my soul demands.
Your words too long have silenced my de-
  spair,
Which bursts anew with every painful
  thought.
No mean regret for serving thee I feel;
But canst thou render back the price it
  cost?
My arm, for thee, I've raised against my
  love,
And with the stroke I cast away my
  all!
No more, no more; I owed you life itself;
That which I owed I've paid; your cause
  is won.
DIÈGUE. Nay, glory in the fruit of vic-
  tory;
I gave thee life, life's joy I owe to thee.
By all that honor means to men like me,
Far more than life I owe thee in return.
But spurn this weakness from thy warlike
  breast;
Love is a pleasure summoned when thou
  wilt;
Thy soul's one rightful master is thine
  honor.
RODERICK. What's this you teach me?
DIÈGUE. That which thou shouldst
  know.
RODERICK. My outraged honor turns
  upon myself,
And now thou dar'st to counsel treach-
  ery—
Treason to her I love! Baseness is one,
Whether in craven knight or lover false.
Wrong not with breath of doubt my faith-
  fulness;
To thee, to her, I would be wholly true.
Bonds such as mine cannot be broken
  thus;

A promise lives, though hope be dead for
  aye.
I cannot leave, nor can I win, Chimène;
In death I find my solace and my pain.
DIÈGUE. This is no time for thee to
  prate of death.
Thy country and thy prince demand thine
  arm.
The fleet, whose coming has aroused our
  fears,
Plots to surprise and pillage all our
  towns.
The Moors invade, the night's advancing
  tide
All silently may float them to our walls.
The court is shaken, and the people trem-
  ble;
Terror and tears are seen on every side;
'T is my good fortune, in this hour of
  need,
To find five hundred followers, ready
  armed
To avenge my quarrel, knowing my af-
  front.
Their zeal thou hast prevented; now their
  hands
They shall dip deep in blood of Moorish
  chiefs.
Go, lead their line; assume thy rightful
  place.
This valiant band calls thee to be their
  head;
Front the assault of these old enemies;
If die thou wilt, seek there a noble
  death
In service of thy king and war's emprise.
Let the king owe his safety to thy loss.
Nay, but return, far rather, crowned with
  bays,
Thy fame not narrowed to a vengeful
  deed,
But broadened to a kingdom's strong de-
  fense.
Win silence from Chimène, grace from the
  king.
And if thou still wouldst gain her maiden
  heart,
Know that to conquering hero it will
  yield.
I waste thy time in words. Come, fol-
  low me;

Forth to the fight, and let thy sovereign
see
What in the count he's lost he's gained
in thee.

[*Exeunt* DIÈGUE *and* RODERICK.]

ACT IV

[*Enter* CHIMÈNE *and* ELVIRE.]

CHIMÈNE. Is this no false report?—
art sure, Elvire?

ELVIRE. Should I repeat how all do
sound his praise,
And bear to heaven the fame of his ex-
ploits,
And wonder at his youth, you'd scarce
believe.
The Moors before him met a quick dis-
grace;
The attack was swift, but swifter still
the flight.
After three hours of combat we had won
Two captive kings and victory secure;
Naught could resist the young chief's on-
set fierce.

CHIMÈNE. And Roderick's arm this
miracle has wrought?

ELVIRE. Of his great prowess are two
kings the prize,
Conquered and captured by his hand alone.

CHIMÈNE. How knowest thou the truth
of this strange news?

ELVIRE. The people do extol him to the
skies—
Call him their liberator and their angel,
The author and the guardian of their
peace.

CHIMÈNE. The king, what thinks he of
these mighty deeds?

ELVIRE. Not yet has Roderick braved
the royal eye;
But the two captive kings, in fetters
bound,
Still wearing crowns, Diègue with joy
presents,
Entreating of the king, as recompense,
That he will see the conqueror and for-
give.

CHIMÈNE. Is Roderick wounded?

ELVIRE. I've heard naught of it.

You lose your color! pray take heart
again.

CHIMÈNE. I'll take again my weak
heart's failing wrath!
Must I forget myself in thought of him!
Shall my lips join in praises of his deeds!
While honor's mute, and duty, dull, con-
sents?
Be still, my love, and let my anger swell!
What are two conquered kings? My
father's slain!
This mourning garb, which speaks of my
distress,
Is the first token of his wondrous might!
Others may call his deeds magnanimous;
Here, every object testifies his crime.
May all this somber pomp which wraps
me round—
This sweeping veil, these heavy depths of
crape—
Add force to my resentment, fail it ever;
Nor let my love my honor overcome.
Should fond, alluring passion e'er prevail,
Recall my duty to my wavering mind,
And bid me fearless meet this hero proud.

ELVIRE. Calm yourself now; the In-
fanta is approaching.

[*Enter the* INFANTA *and* LEONORA.]

INFANTA. I come not vainly to console
thy grief;
Rather my tears to mingle with thine own.

CHIMÈNE. Ah, madam, thou canst share
the common joy;
'T is thine to taste this Heaven-sent hap-
piness;
The right to weep is mine, and mine alone.
The peril Roderick's wisdom could avert,
The public safety by his valor won,
Permit to me alone, to-day, a tear.
The city he has saved, the king has
served—
His valorous arm brings woe to me alone.

INFANTA. 'T is true, Chimène, he has
great marvels wrought.

CHIMÈNE. This grievous news already
reaches me;
On every side I hear him loud proclaimed
Noble in war, unfortunate in love.

INFANTA. Why shouldst thou suffer in
this generous praise?

But now this youthful Mars delighted
thee;
He dwelt within thy heart, he owned thy
sway;
To tell his praises is to sound thine own.
  CHIMÈNE. Others may boast his deeds;
    't is not for me;
His praises are but torture to my soul;
My anguish deepens with his rising fame;
My loss is greater as he greater grows.
Ah, cruel torture of a heart that loves!
My passion burns the brighter with his
    worth,
While duty, stern defender of my course,
Would follow him to death in love's de-
    spite.
  INFANTA. But yesterday thy duty's
    proud demands
Won from the court an admiration high,
So worthy of thy filial love it seemed;
Thy victory o'er thy passion was sublime;
But now—wilt have a faithful friend's
    advice?
  CHIMÈNE. Not to hear you would show
    me base indeed.
  INFANTA. To-day thy duty wears a dif-
    ferent face;
The chief support of a whole nation's life,
A people's love and hope, is Roderick now.
On him the Moors with hopeless terror
    gaze,
Securely leans on him our loved Castile.
The king himself can never now deny
Thy father's spirit moving in the youth;
Thou seek'st the public ruin in his death.
Thy country was thy father's country
    first,
And ne'er canst thou to hostile hands be-
    tray it.
Wilt thou pursue thy vengeance though
    its blow
Enwrap the kingdom in a fatal woe?
I plead not for thy lover; let thy heart
Cling to its filial ties; send him away,
And think no more of wedlock, but for
    us,
Thy country and thy king, preserve his
    life.
  CHIMÈNE. The gift of mercy is not
    mine to grant;
I cannot check the duty driving me;

Though in my heart the voice of love may
    plead,
Though prince and people praise him and
    adore,
Though all heroic souls encircle him—
My cypress-boughs his laurels shall o'er-
    spread.
  INFANTA. 'T is noble not to falter, my
    Chimène,
Though to avenge a father stabs our
    heart;
But 't is a higher nobleness to place
The public good above all private wrong.
Believe me, to exclude him from thy soul
Will be the bitterest pang thou canst be-
    stow.
Yield to the act thy country's weal de-
    mands,
Nor doubt thy king's most willing leni-
    ency.
  CHIMÈNE. Whether he hear, I still
    must plead for justice.
  INFANTA. Consider well what course
    you now will take.
Adieu! let solitude thy counsel aid.
  CHIMÈNE. My father dead!—what
    choice remains for me?
                        [*Exeunt omnes.*]

[*Enter the* KING, DIÈGUE, ARIAS, RODER-
        ICK, *and* SANCHO.]
  KING. Bold heir of an illustrious an-
    cestry,
Ever the hope and glory of Castile,
Son of a race of valor unexcelled,
Whose best exploits thine own already
    rank,
For due reward my power is all too
    weak—
What thou hast earned thy king can never
    pay.
Our land set free from barbarous enemy,
My scepter in my hand, by thine secured.
The Moors despatched before the call to
    arms
Had fully warned the people of attack—
Deeds such as these a king must ever find
Beyond the hope of suitable reward.
But thy two royal captives, they, in
    sooth,
In my own presence recognize thy might.

Their CID they name thee, sovereign, lord,
and head.
I well might envy thee this title proud,
The highest in their land; but, no, I call
On all to know that thou the CID shalt
be.
The CID henceforth art thou. To that
great name
May every foe succumb!—Granada yield.
Toledo tremble, but on hearing it.
To all my subjects ever shall it show
How great the debt to thee we proudly
owe.
RODERICK. Nay, sire, your words too
highly speak my praise,
And make me flush with shame before a
king
Whose generous honòr is so undeserved.
The blood within these veins, the air I
breathe—
All, all, to this great empire do I owe.
Had these been lost, and death alone been
won,
A subject's duty only had I done.
KING. E'en duty done is not the whole
of service;
Its glory is a courage quick and high,
Which, reckoning not with danger or de-
feat,
Pushes its way to triumph and renown.
Suffer thy praises from a grateful sover-
eign,
And now relate the story of thy deeds.
RODERICK. That in this sudden stress
of peril, sire,
A troop of followers of my father's house
Urged me to be their leader, well you
know.
My troubled soul was painfully per-
plexed—
I dared not lead the band without thy
word,
But to approach thee was a fatal step.
Pardon the rashness, sire, that dared to
act!
I chose to lose my head in serving thee,
Rather than while my followers stood in
arms.
KING. The state defended is thy full
defense,
And thy too heated vengeance I excuse.

Chimène, hereafter, has a cause forlorn;
I hear her but to comfort her; say on.
RODERICK. I take the lead, and, with
defiant front,
The little column slowly makes advance;
Five hundred at the starting, but ere
long
Three thousand was our number, strong
and bold.
The frightened gathered courage at the
sight.
A certain part I hurriedly conceal
In vessels lying at the river's mouth;
The rest, whose numbers every hour in-
creased,
Impatient for the fray, with me remain.
Close to the ground they crouched, and,
still as death,
They passed the night, nor slept, nor
scarcely breathed.
At my command, pretended, sire, from
you,
The guard itself conceals, and aids my
plot.
Just as the flow of tide comes rolling in,
By starlight pale, lo; thirty Moorish
sails,
Mounting the wave, sweep to the harbor's
mouth.
They enter; all seems tranquil; not a
guard,
No soldiers on the quay, none on the
walls.
Our ambush is complete, and fearlessly,
Not doubting their attack a full surprise,
They anchor, and debark; suspecting
naught,
They rush into the embraces of their foes.
We spring from every hiding-place, and
loud
A thousand cries of battle rise to heaven.
Then from the ships pour forth our armed
men;
But half have sprung to land when, terror-
struck,
They see the fight is lost ere 't is begun.
They came for pillage; they encounter
war.
We press them on the water, on the land;
Their blood, in rivers, flows upon our soil,
While dire disorder hinders all resistance.

But soon their leaders rally them with
  shouts,
Their panic is dispelled, their ranks are
  formed,
Their terrors are forgotten in their fury.
To die without a struggle were a shame,
And bravely with their sabers they oppose.
On sea, on land, on fleet, within the port,
All was a field of carnage, death its lord.
Their blood and ours in horrid mixture
  ran.
Brave deeds were wrought which never
  will be known;
The darkness was a veil, 'neath which
  each man
Fought as it were alone; nor any knew
How victory inclined. I praised my men,
Placed reënforcements here, changed or-
  ders there,
Nor knew till dawn which side was con-
  queror.
But day made clear our gain and their
  defeat.
Their courage fails them, with the fear of
  death;
And when they see approach a fresh com-
  mand,
They seek their ships, cut cables, and their
  cries
Of terror and of anguish fill the air.
They wait not to discover if their kings
Are dead or wounded: in a tumult wild,
On the ebb-tide which bore them in at
  flood,
They take their desperate flight and quit
  our shores.
The kings and others, left without re-
  treat
Or hope of succor, make a valiant stand;
They sell their lives at cost of life in turn,
And fight till nearly every man is dead.
I urge surrender, but they listen not,
Till the last follower falls, when yield
  they must.
Then the two kings demand to see the
  chief;
I tell them who I am, they seek my grace;
I send them straightway to Your Majesty.
So the fight ended, lacking combatants.
'T was in this manner, sire, that for your
  cause—

[*Enter* ALONSO.]

ALONSO. Chimène approaches, sire, to
  sue for justice.
KING. 'T is sorry news! a duty most
  untimely!
Go, for I would not force thee on her
  sight;
For sign of gratitude, I send thee hence;
But first receive thy monarch's kind em-
  brace.   [*Embraces him.*]
                    [*Exit* RODERICK.]
DIÈGUE. Chimène would save him from
  her own pursuit.
KING. 'T is said she loves him still;
  I'll test her heart;
Assume a mournful air—

[*Enter* CHIMÈNE *and* ELVIRE.]

KING. Chimène, your wishes with suc-
  cess are crowned;
Our foes have fallen beneath Roderick's
  hand.
Give thanks to Heaven, which hath
  avenged you thus.
[*Aside to* DIÈGUE.] Mark how her color
  changes at my words.
DIÈGUE. But see, she swoons, a token,
  sire, most sure,
Of perfect love; this grief the secret
  tells
Which rules her soul. No longer can you
  doubt
Her passion's flame still burns with glow
  unquenched.
CHIMÈNE. Tell me, is Roderick dead?
KING. Nay, nay, he lives,
And still his love unchanged for thee re-
  mains.
Forget the anxious grief that mourns for
  him.
CHIMÈNE. O sire, one swoons from joy
  as well as grief;
The soul surprised with happiness grows
  weak;
Too sudden gladness every sense o'er-
  whelms.
KING. Thou canst not so deceive my
  watchful eye;
Thy grief, Chimène, too manifest appeared.
CHIMÈNE. Add, then, this deeper pain
  to my distress;

My swoon but told my disappointment
sore;
My righteous wrath has brought me down
to this.
His death would snatch him from my just
revenge.
From wounds received in battle should he
die,
What place remains for my unyielding
will!
An end so honorable mocks my aim.
I wish him dead, but not with honor's
stroke,
Not in a blaze of glory should he pass,
But on a scaffold, shrouded in disgrace.
Grant him a murderer's, not a patriot's
death
To die for country is a noble fate;
Not that for him, but with a blemished
name,
A tarnished 'scutcheon, should his breath
depart.
His victory gives me pleasure unalloyed—
The state gains stableness, and I, I gain
A victim worthier still my father's house.
No longer a rash youth, whose violence
Condemns itself; but great, chief among
chiefs,
A warrior crowned with laurels, one whose
fall
Would vindicate my purpose. But, alas!
My hopes beyond my reason bear me on.
What force is in my tears, which men
despise?
The freedom of your empire is his own;
Under your power, he works his wicked
will.
He from my feebleness has naught to fear,
O'er me, as o'er his enemies, he triumphs.
To stifle Justice in his victory.
Makes a new trophy for this conqueror.
I serve his pomp when, trampling on the
law,
He, with his captives, hears me speak his
praise,
And from his car of triumph bids me fol-
low.
KING. My child, your words are all too
violent;
The scales of justice must not swerve a
hair.

Thy father was the aggressor; that thou
know'st.
Justice must see that mercy has a claim.
Nay, be not swift to oppose thy monarch's
plea;
Consult thy heart; there still thy Roder-
ick lives.
Thy love, though hidden, is a mighty
thing,
And will approve this favor from thy
king.
CHIMÈNE. Favor to him a cause of
thanks from me!
The author of my woes, my bitter foe!
Is anger o'er a father slain, and wrath
For the assassin, such a trifling thing
That I, forsooth, must grateful be to him
Who thinks to aid my cause by mocking
it?
Since tears call forth no justice from my
king,
Redress by arms I now, sire, will demand.
By arms alone my happiness was wrecked,
By arms alone my vengeance should be
wrought.
Of all you cavaliers I ask his head;
To him who brings it, I will give my hand.
Confirm the combat, sire, by your decree;
I wed the man who conquers Roderick.
KING. That ancient custom I would not
restore.
The state was oft enfeebled 'neath its rule.
Under the false pretence of righting
wrong,
The noblest oft would fall, the base es-
cape.
A life whose import deepens to our state
Shall not be left to Fate's capricious
whim;
From that ordeal of arms is Roderick free.
Whatever crime his hasty wrath has
wrought
The flying Moors have borne with them
afar.
DIÈGUE. What, sire, for him alone re-
verse the laws
Your court so oft has honored by observ-
ance?
What will your people think, or envy say,
If 'neath your arm, a coward, he retreat,
Nor make redress upon the field of honor,

Where men of spirit seek a worthy death?
Such favors would but tarnish his renown.
Nay, let him drain unto the sweetest drops
The draught of triumph. Bravely did he front
The bragging count; he will be brave again.

KING. Since you demand it, let it be; but know
A thousand warriors will replace the slain
By Roderick conquered; for the offered prize
Will make an eager foe of every knight.
To oppose them all would be a grievous wrong;
Once only shall he enter in the lists.
Choose whom thou wilt, Chimène, but choose with care;
No more reproaches will thy sovereign bear.

DIÈGUE. Let none be overlooked—not those who most
Do tremble at the prowess of his arm.
The deeds of valor wrought by him to-day
Will fright the boldest. Who would dare confront
A warrior so audacious and so keen?

SANCHO. Declare an open field! I enter it.
Rash though I be, I dare confront this knight.
Madam, this favor grant to my devotion;
Your word's fulfillment shall I surely claim.

KING. Chimène, do you accept this champion?

CHIMÈNE. It is a promise, sire.

KING. To-morrow, then.

DIÈGUE. Nay, sire, why should there longer be delay?
The brave are ever ready. Now's the time.

KING. He scarce has quit his battle with the Moors.

DIÈGUE. While in your presence he took breathing space.

KING. An hour or two of respite I impose.
And lest this combat seem to speak my will—
To show the deep reluctance that I feel

In suffering this bloody pass at arms—
I and my court will straight withdraw us hence.
[To ARIAS.] You shall be judge between these combatants;
See that the laws of honor govern them.
The combat ended, lead to me the victor.
Whoe'er he be, the prize is still the same.
With mine own hand Chimène I would present,
And for his guerdon she her faith shall plight.

CHIMÈNE. What, sire, impose on me a law so stern?

KING. Thou murmurest, but thy changeful, loving heart,
If Roderick wins, will gladly take his part.
Cease to complain of such a mild decree;
The victor shall thy husband surely be.
[Exeunt omnes.]

ACT V

[Enter RODERICK and CHIMÈNE.]

CHIMÈNE. What, Roderick! whence this boldness—to my face?
Go!—this will cost my honor. Leave me, pray.

RODERICK. Madam, to death I go, but ere I die,
To offer you a last farewell I come.
The love that keeps me vassal to your laws
Even in death demands my homage still.

CHIMÈNE. And wilt thou die?

RODERICK. I count the moment blest
That satisfies your hatred with my life.

CHIMÈNE. But wilt thou die? Sancho is not the one
To terrify that dauntless soul of thine!
What renders thee so weak, or him so strong?
Before the combat, Roderick talks of death!
He who nor feared my father nor the Moors,
Is going to fight one Sancho, and despairs!
Does courage thus desert thee, valorous knight?

RODERICK. I haste to punishment, and not to combat.
Since you desire my death, what wish have I
To keep my life? My courage fails me not;
But my indifferent arm will not preserve
What thou dost find displeàsing. Not a blow
Could I have struck against the fiery Moors
For wrong of mine alone; 't was tor my king,
His people, and his kingdom, that I fought.
To poorly guard myself were treachery.
Life is not yet so hateful to my heart
That basely I can sacrifice its claims.
The question now is different. I alone
Am in the balance. You demand my death;
Your sentence I accept, although the hand
You let inflict it should have been your own.
He who shall wield your weapon in your stead
Shall meet no sword-thrust answering to his steel.
I cannot strike the man that fights for you;
I joy to think his blow is from your hand.
Since 't is your honor that his arms maintain,
Unguarded shall I offer every point,
Seeing in his your hand which slays me thus.
    CHIMÈNE. Let no blind folly lead thee to forget
That glory ends with life. Though my just wrath
Impels me to a course which I abhor,
And forces me to follow thee to death—
E'en though a sense of honor would demand
A nerveless arm, an undefended blow—
Remember, all the splendor of thy deeds
Will change to shame when death has conquered thee.
Who will believe thou didst not raise thy hand?
Though I am dear, honor is dearer still,
Else I had still my father, and the hope
That fatal blow has cost thee would remain—
The hope of calling me thine own Chimène.
Thou canst not hold so cheap thy high renown
To weakly, unresisting yield it up.
What strange inconstancy can valor show!
Thou shouldst have more or else thou shouldst have less!
Is it to grieve me only thou art bold,
And courage fails when courage I demand?
Wilt thou my father's might so disallow
That, conquering him, thou'lt to a weaker yield?
Go, do not will to die, o'ercome my will;
If life no longer charms thee, honor pleads.
    RODERICK. The count is dead, the Moors defeated fly—
Still, other claims to glory need I prove?
Henceforth, my fame can scorn all self-defense.
None would believe this heart of mine could quail.
What can I not accomplish? Who will doubt
That, honor gone, naught dear to me remains?
No, doubt it if you will, this fatal fight
Increases not nor lessens my renown.
None e'er will dare my courage to impugn,
Nor deem that I did meet my conqueror.
"He loved Chimène"—'t is thus the court will say—
"He would not live and her resentment face.
To the stern hand of Fate that followed him—
Her vengeful hand—he yielded up his breath.
She sought his life; to his great soul it seemed
'T would be ignoble did he care to live.
He lost his love to save his father's name;
He loses life for his dear mistress' sake.
Whate'er of hope his heart had cherished still,

Honor for love, and love for life, he
chose."
'T will not obscure my glory thus to die,
But brighter will its growing splendor
shine.
My willing death this honor high will
win,
No life but mine for thee redress could
make.

CHIMÈNE. Since life and honor feebly
plead my cause,
Nor stay thee from a death unwished by
me,
Let mine old love speak for me, Roderick,
And, in return, shield me from Sancho's
power.
Save me from such a fate as will be mine
If I, the prize, am won by him I hate.
Need I say more? Go, plan a sure de-
fense,
Silence my wrath, my filial duty done.
Then, if thy heart still beats for .thy
Chimène,
As conqueror, thou lovest not in vain.
Adieu! my cheek is hot at this avowal.
                                      [Exit CHIMÈNE.]
RODERICK. What foe can daunt my
valiant spirit now?
Come on, Navarre, Morocco, and Castile!
Come, all the valor of our kingdom's
might!
In one great host unite to hurl me down!
My arm alone will equal all your force.
Against a hope so sweet, the flower of
Spain
Were all too weak! I fight for my
Chimène!   [Exit RODERICK.]

                [Enter INFANTA.]
INFANTA. Thou pride of birth, which
turns my love to crime,
Thy warning shall I list, or thy sweet
voice
My heart, whose soft constraint compels
revolt
Against that tyrant stern? In worth
alone
Thou, Roderick, art mine equal; but thy
blood,
Though brave and pure, flows not from
royal veins.

Unhappy lot, which rudely separates
My duty and my love. Must loyalty
To valor rare condemn to misery
A loving soul? What anguish must I bear
If ne'er I learn, despite my high resolve,
Nor lover to embrace, nor love to quell!
'Twixt love and pride my reason bids me
choose
Though birth's high destiny demand a
throne,
Thou, Roderick, art of kings the con-
queror,
And 'neath thy sway with honor shall I
dwell.
The glorious name of Cid that now is
thine
Points clearly to the realm where thou
shalt reign.

Worthy is he, but 't is Chimène he loves.
Her father's death so slightly breaks their
bonds,
That, though her duty slays him, she
adores.
No hope to my long grief his crime can
bring.
Alas for me! ordains a wretched fate
That love outlast the bitterness of hate.

                [Enter LEONORA.]
INFANTA. Why com'st thou, Leonora?
LEONORA. 'T is to praise thee,
That thou at last hast conquered all thy
pain,
And hast repose.
INFANTA. Repose? whence shall that
come
To a heart burdened with a hopeless woe?
LEONORA. Love lives·on hope; without
it, surely dies.
No more can Roderick's image charm your
heart;
For whether in this combat he prevail,
Or whether fall, he is her victim still.
Your hope is dead, your wounded heart is
healed.
INFANTA. That time—how distant still!
LEONORA. Why mock yourself?
INFANTA. Say, rather, why forbid me
still to hope?
I can invent a thousand happy shifts

This combat's hard conditions to evade.
Love tortures me, but 't is from love I
learn
To use a lover's skillful artifice.
LEONORA. The flame of love, enkindled
in their hearts,
Survives a father slain. What, then, can
you?
No deadly hate inspires Chimène's pur-
suit.
She claims a combat, but she straight ac-
cepts
The combatant who offers first his sword.
None does she choose among the valiant
knights
Whose bold exploits match Roderick's own
renown.
A youth whose steel has never yet been
tried
Suits her cause well—young Sancho is
her choice.
His highest merit is his unskilled blade.
Without a name, no fame has he to save;
And this too easy choice full plainly shows
This combat is but duty's weak pretence.
To Roderick she gives a victim sure,
Whose harmless death her honor seems to
crown.
INFANTA. I read her plan, and still this
restless heart
Rivals Chimène, and loves this conqueror.
Unhappy that I am! what shall I do?
LEONORA. Recall the high conditions of
your birth.
Shall a king's daughter love her father's
subject?
INFANTA. My love has changed its ob-
ject; listen, pray!
It is no longer Roderick I love,
A simple gentleman; not so, not so!
I love the author of most noble deeds,
The valorous Cid, the conqueror of two
kings.
But still my love I'll conquer; not in
fear,
But lest their sweet devotion I betray.
If for my sake a crown he should re-
ceive,
I would not take again the gift I gave.
Since to no doubtful combat he is gone,
Another happy scheme must I employ.

Do thou, the confidant of all my woes,
Help me to finish what I have begun.
[*Exeunt* INFANTA *and* LEONORA.]

[*Enter* CHIMÈNE *and* ELVIRE.]
CHIMÈNE. Elvire, I suffer—pity, pity
me!
I can but hope, yet everything I fear.
A vow escapes me I would fain withdraw;
A swift repentance follows every wish.
Two rivals for my sake are now at arms;
Of dear success my tears the price will
pay.
Though Fate may seem to grant my great
desire,
I still must carry in my heart the pain
Of father unavenged or lover dead.
ELVIRE. Nay, 't is of consolation you
must dream.
Your lover or your vengeance is assured.
Whatever issue destiny decrees,
Your honor and a husband are your
own.
CHIMÈNE. What! him I hate, or him
I've wished to slay!
The murderer of my father, or of Roder-
ick?
The victory of either gives to me
A husband stained with blood that I
adore.
From this most wretched choice my soul
revolts.
Far more than death I dread this quar-
rel's end.
Hence, vengeance, love, disturbers of my
peace!
I can no longer pay your cruel price.
Almighty author of my direful fate,
Bring thou this combat to no certain
close—
Let there be neither conqueror nor con-
quered.
ELVIRE. Nay, wish not a result so
profitless.
If still you cherish Justice' stern de-
mands,
And still your deep resentment you would
nurse,
Unsatisfied, because your lover lives,
This combat will but torture you anew.
Far rather hope his valor may secure

New bays for him, and silence for your
plaints;
That by the law of combat, still revered,
Your sighs be stifled and your heart con-
soled.
    CHIMÈNE. To him, though conqueror,
think'st thou I will yield?
Too strong my duty, and my loss too
dear.
No law of combat, nor the king's decree,
Can force a daughter's conscience to be
quiet.
An easy victory he may win in fight,
Chimène will prove an adversary still.
    ELVIRE. 'T were well if Heaven prevent
your vengeance just,
To punish pride so strange and impious!
What! will you now the happiness re-
ject
Of silence with your honor reconciled?
What means such duty? Pray, what hope
you for?
Your lover slain, will't give your father
back?
Does one such sorrow not suffice for
you,—
Must you heap loss on loss, and grief on
grief?
'T is a caprice of temper you indulge,
Which of your promised lord makes you
unfit.
The wrath of Heaven will snatch him
from your arms,
And leave you as young Sancho's right-
ful bride.
    CHIMÈNE. Elvire, the conflicts which
my soul endures
Pray deepen not by prophecy malign.
Would Heaven ordain I might escape
them both;
If not, for Roderick all my vows ascend.
Not that my foolish love inclines me
thus,
But Sancho's prize I cannot, cannot be!
That fear o'ermasters every wish besides.
What is 't I see? Undone!—I am un-
done!

            [*Enter* SANCHO.]
    SANCHO. 'T is mine this sword to offer
at your feet.

    CHIMÈNE. What! dripping still with
Roderick's life-blood pure?
Perfidious wretch! how dar'st thou show
thyself
To me, of my dear love by thee bereft?
Burst forth, my love! no longer need'st
thou fear!
My father's death restrains thee never-
more;
By one fell blow my honor is assured,
My love set free, my soul plunged in de-
spair.
    SANCHO. With calmer mind—
    CHIMÈNE. Thou speak'st to me again!
Assassin of a hero I adore!
Away! thou wast a traitor! Well I know
That valiant knight by thee was never
slain
In open combat. Nothing hope from me.
My champion thou!—my death thou'lt
surely be!
    SANCHO. What strange illusion! Hear
me, I entreat!
    CHIMÈNE. Think'st thou I'll listen to
thy bragging tale—
With patience bear thine insolence which
paints
His fall, my crime, and, chiefest still, thy
valor?

    [*Enter the* KING, DIÈGUE, ARIAS, *and*
            ALONSO.]
    CHIMÈNE. Ah, sire, no more need I
dissimulate
What vainly I have struggled to conceal.
I loved; 't was known to you; but for
my father
I could devote to death so dear a head.
Love, sire, to duty's desperate cause I
gave;
Now Roderick is dead, my heart is
changed
From foe relentless to afflicted lover.
To him who gave me life was vengeance
due;
But now my tears can fall for him I love.
Young Sancho in defending me destroys,
And of his murderous arm I am the prize.
In pity, sire, if pity move a king,
Revoke a law so terrible to me!
As recompense for victory, whose end

To me is loss of all on earth I love,
All that I have is his; myself, I pray,
May to a holy cloister now retire,
Where death shall find me weeping life
  away.
DIÈGUE. No longer, sire, it seems to
  her a shame
To openly avow her heart's desire.
KING. Be undeceived, Chimène: thy
  Roderick lives!
The champion has, though vanquished,
  told thee false.
SANCHO. 'T was her too hasty thought
  deceived herself.
To tell the issue of the fight I came—
How the brave warrior who her heart en-
  chains,
After disarming me, thus nobly spoke:
"Fear naught! I'd leave the combat all
  in doubt,
Rather than pierce a heart that loves
  Chimène.
My duty summons me at once to court.
Do thou convey to her the final chance,
And lay thy sword, her trophy, at her
  feet."
This had I done, but seeing me return,
Bearing my sword, she deemed me con-
  queror.
Then love and anger, mingled suddenly,
Betrayed her into transports uncontrolled,
Nor could I gain a hearing for my tale.
Vanquished in combat, still I am content,
And gratefully accept my own defeat;
For though I love and lose my love, 't is
  sweet
This perfect love of theirs to consummate.
KING. My child, no flush of shame
  should mount thy cheek.
No longer seek to disavow thy flame.
Thy faithful love unmeasured praise shall
  win,
Thy honor's safe, thy filial duty done.
Thy father is avenged; to do thy will
Thy Roderick's life thou hast in peril set.
'T was Heaven ordained to save him for
  thine own;
Thou hast not shunned thy part; take thy
  reward;
Be not rebellious toward my wise decree,
Thy lover in thy loving arms enfold.

[*Enter* RODERICK, INFANTA, *and* LEONORA.]
INFANTA. No longer weep, Chimène.
  With joy receive
This noble conqueror from thy princess'
  hand.
RODERICK. I crave indulgence, sire,
  that love's high claim
Impels me, in thy presence, to her feet.—
To ask no promised prize, Chimène, I
  come,
But once again my life to offer thee.
My love cannot for thee obey alone
The code of honor or a sovereign's will.
If still your father's death seem un-
  avenged,
But speak your wish; you shall be satis-
  fied.
A thousand rivals I will yet o'ercome,
To utmost bounds of earth I'll fight my
  way.
Alone I'll force a camp, an army rout,
The fame of demigods I'll cast in shade;
Whate'er the deeds my crime to expiate,
All things will I attempt and all achieve.
But if the voice of honor unappeased
Still clamors for the guilty slayer's death,
Arm not against me warrior such as I.
My head is at your feet: strike now the
  blow!
You only can o'ercome the invincible;
No other hand than yours can vengeance
  take.
One thing I pray: let death end punish-
  ment;
From your dear memory ne'er banish me.
Your honor is exalted in my death;
As recompense let my remembrance live.
Say sometimes, thinking of my love for
  you,
"He died, because he ne'er could be un-
  true."
CHIMÈNE. Nay, Roderick, rise.—Ah,
  sire, no more I hide
The feelings which have burst their long
  control.
His virtues high compel my heart to love.
A king commands; obedience is his due;
Yet, though my fate is sealed by sentence
  stern,
Can you with eye approving give consent?
If duty drive me on to do your will,

Can justice the unnatural act confirm?
For Roderick's service to his monarch's
    cause
Must I, the guerdon, though reluctant,
    be?
A prey forever to remorseful shame
That in paternal blood my hands I've
    stained.
    KING. Time changes all; a deed to-day
    unmeet,
May seem hereafter lawful and benign.
Thou has been won by Roderick; thou art
    his.
This day his valor rightly gained the
    prize.
But since so freshly from the field he
    comes,
And still thy heart unreconciled remains,
I well might seem thy fair fame's enemy,
If I so soon reward his victory.
My law decreed no hour for nuptial vows,
Nor does delay show change in royal will.
Let a round year bring solace to thy
    heart,
And dry the fountain of a daughter's
    tears.
For thee, brave knight, wait mighty deeds
    of arms:
The Moors on our own borders thou hast
    slain,

Their plots confounded, their assaults re-
    pelled;
Now into their own country push the
    war,
Command my army, plunder all their
    land.
Thy name of Cid their terrors will in-
    flame;
Themselves have given it—king they'll
    choose thee now.
Fidelity is valor's noblest crown;
Return yet worthier of this lovely maid.
Let thy great deeds so loudly plead for
    thee,
That pride and love will join to make her
    thine.
    RODERICK. To win Chimène and serve
    my glorious king,
My arm is iron and my heart is flame.
Though absence from her eyes I must en-
    dure,
I thank you, sire, for hope's unfailing
    bliss.
    KING. Thy valor and my word assure
    thy hopes;
Her heart already is confessed thine
    own.
The filial honor that resists thee now,
To time, thy king, and thy high deeds
    will bow.

BERENICE

By JEAN RACINE

Produced at Paris, 1670

TRANSLATED BY R. B. BOSWELL

CHARACTERS

TITUS, *emperor of Rome*
BERENICE, *queen of Palestine*
ANTIOCHUS, *king of Commagene*
PAULINUS, *friend of Titus*
ARSACES, *friend of Antiochus*
PHŒNICE, *friend of Berenice*
RUTILUS, *a Roman*
ATTENDANTS *of* TITUS

The scene is laid at Rome, in a chamber between the apartments of TITUS *and those of* BERENICE.

ACT I

SCENE I

[ANTIOCHUS, ARSACES.]
ANTIOCHUS. Let us stay here a moment! All this pomp
Is a new sight to you, my Arsaces.
This chamber so superb, and so secluded
Is ofttimes privy to the Emperor's secrets:
Hither he sometimes from the Court retires,
To pour his passion forth into the ears
Of Berenice. Thro' this door he passes
From his apartments; that one leads to hers.

Go, tell her I regret to trouble her,
But must entreat a secret interview.
   ARSACES. To trouble her, my lord!
And you her friend,
So true and generous in your care for her!
Her lover once, Antiochus, whom all
The East holds great among her greatest monarchs!
What! Tho' in hope she shares the throne with Titus,
Is she so far removed in rank from you?
   ANTIOCHUS. Go, nor concern yourself with other matters,
See if I soon may speak with her in private.

196

Scene II

[Antiochus.]

Antiochus. Antiochus, art thou the same as ever?
Canst say to her, "I love thee," without trembling?
I quake already, and my throbbing heart
Dreads now as much as it desired this moment.
Has not fair Berenice slain my hopes,
And did she not enjoin eternal silence?
Five years have they been dead; and, till this day,
My passion has assumed the mask of friendship.
Can I expect the destined bride of Titus
To hear me better than in Palestine?
He weds her. Have I then until this hour
Delay'd to come and own me still her lover?
What fruit will follow from a rash confession?
Since part we must, let's part without displeasure.
I will withdraw unseen, and from her sight
Go, to forget her, or perchance to die.
What! suffer torments that she knows not of
For ever, and for ever feed on tears!
Fear to offend her now when losing her!
And why, fair queen, should I incur thine anger?
Come I to ask you to resign the throne
Of empire, and to love me? Nay, I come
Only to say that, flatter'd for so long
By hope that obstacles might cross my rival,
To-day I find he can do all, and Hymen
Has lit his torch. Vain all my constancy!
After five years of love and wasted hopes,
I leave thee, faithful still, tho' hope be dead,
Can that displease her? Nay she needs must pity;
In any case I can hold out no longer.
And wherefore should a hopeless lover fear,
Who is resolved to see her nevermore?

Scene III

[Antiochus, Arsaces.]

Antiochus. Have we admittance?
Arsaces. I have seen the Queen;
But hard it was to struggle thro' the crowd
That surged around of ever fresh adorers,
Attracted by the news of coming greatness.
Titus, eight days in strict seclusion spent,
Ceases at length to mourn his father's loss,
And gives himself once more to amorous cares;
And, may I trust the rumours of the Court,
Perhaps ere nightfall happy Berenice
Shall change the name of Queen for that of Empress.
Antiochus. Alas!
Arsaces. Can this report disturb my lord?
Antiochus. So then I cannot speak with her alone?
Arsaces. Sire, you shall see her: I have told the Queen
You wish to have a secret interview,
And with a look she deign'd to grant assent,
Willing to lend herself to your entreaty:
Doubtless she waits a favourable moment
T' escape from troublesome congratulations.
Antiochus. 'Tis well. But has my Arsaces neglected
None of the weighty matters he was charged with?
Arsaces. You know, my lord, my prompt obedience.
Ships have been fitted out at Ostia,
Ready to quit the port at any moment,
And stay but for your orders. But I know not
Whom you are sending back to Commagene.
Antiochus. When I have seen her, then departure follows.
Arsaces. Who must depart?
Antiochus. Myself.
Arsaces. You?

ANTIOCHUS. When I leave
This palace, I leave Rome; and that for
ever.

ARSACES. Your words surprise me, and
with justice, Sire.
After Queen Berenice for so long
Has forced you to forsake your throne
and country,
Detaining you for three whole years at
Rome;
And when this queen, her victory achieved,
Expects your presence at her royal nup-
tials,
When amorous Titus, giving her his hand,
Surrounds her with a glory which reflects
Its light on you—

ANTIOCHUS. Let her enjoy her fortune!
We've talk'd enough. Pray, leave me,
Arsaces.

ARSACES. I understand you, Sire.
These dignities
Have made the Queen ungrateful for your
kindness;
Friendship betray'd brings hatred in its
train.

ANTIOCHUS. No, Arsaces, I never held
her dearer.

ARSACES. Has then the Emperor, daz-
zled with new splendour,
Ventur'd to slight you? Does his waning
favour
Warn you to take your flight from him
and Rome?

ANTIOCHUS. Titus is constant as a
friend can be;
I should do wrong to blame him.

ARSACES. Why depart, then?
Some fancy makes you your own enemy.
Heav'n places on the throne a prince who
loves you,
Who erst was witness of your valiant
prowess,
When in his steps you follow'd death
and glory;
Who, aided by your valour, in the end
Reduced beneath his yoke the rebel
Jews.
With mingled pride and pain he well re-
members
The day that closed the long and doubtful
siege.

The enemy upon their triple rampart
Watch'd at their ease our ineffectual
efforts,
And all in vain we plied the battering
ram.
You, you alone, bearing a ladder, brought
Death and destruction, as you scaled their
walls.
That day had well nigh proved your last,
and Titus
Embraced you, lying wounded in my
arms,
While Rome's victorious legions wept your
fall.
And now the time is come for you to
reap
The fruit of all the blood they saw you
shed.
If, eager to behold your realm again,
You weary of a life without a sceptre,
Can you not wait at least till, honour
laden
From Cæsar's triumph, glad Euphrates
greet you
With such additions to your royal title
As Rome bestows in token of her friend-
ship?
Can nought prevail to change your pur-
pose, Sire?
You answer nothing!

ANTIOCHUS. What wouldst have me
say?
I wait to have a word with Berenice.

ARSACES. And then, my lord?

ANTIOCHUS. Hers will decide my fate.

ARSACES. How, Sire?

ANTIOCHUS. I wait to learn from her
own lips
The truth or falsehood of the voice of
rumour
That seats her on th' imperial throne
with Titus.
If she is pledged to wed him, I go hence.

ARSACES. And why so fatal in your
eyes, this marriage?

ANTIOCHUS. The rest I'll tell you after
we are gone.

ARSACES. In what perplexity your
words involve me!

ANTIOCHUS. She comes. Farewell. Do
all that I have said.

SCENE IV

[BERENICE, ANTIOCHUS, PHŒNICE.]

BERENICE. At last from these oppressive gratulations
I steal away, from friends made mine by fortune;
Escaping from their vain and tedious homage,
To find a friend whose words come from his heart.
I'll not deny it, that my just impatience
Blamed you for some degree of negligence.
"Why does Antiochus," said I, "whose care
For me has had for witness Rome and Asia,
Constant and true, whatever cross'd my path,
In close attendance on my varied fortunes;
Why, when to-day Heav'n seems to promise me
An honour that I fain would share with him,
Hides he himself, and leaves me to the mercy
Of stranger crowds?"
ANTIOCHUS. 'Tis true then, Madam, is it?
Am I to understand from what you say
That your long wooing is to end in marriage?
BERENICE. I will confide to you my late alarms.
The last few days not without tears I've spent;
The mourning Titus on his Court imposed
Had held his love suspended e'en in secret;
No more for me that ardour he display'd
When by my eyes entranced the livelong day
He sat, and sigh'd, and could not speak for tears;
He bade me for a while a sad farewell.
Think how I must have grieved, whose fervent passion
Adores him for himself alone, as ofttimes
To you I've own'd; who, were his state as mean

As 'tis exalted, would have chosen him
But for his virtues.
ANTIOCHUS. Has he now resumed
His amorous suit?
BERENICE. You witness'd how last night
The senate, seconding his pious cares,
Enroll'd his father as a deity.
His filial duty, satisfied thereby,
Has given place to love and care for me.
E'en at this moment, tho' he told me not
Of his intention, his command has gather'd
The senate, that the bounds of Palestine
May beyond Syria and Arabia reach;
And if I may believe his friends' report
And his own promise sworn a thousand times,
He will crown Berenice queen of all,
Adding to other titles that of empress.
Hither he comes himself for my assurance.
ANTIOCHUS. And I am come to bid farewell for ever.
BERENICE. Farewell for ever! What is this you say?
Prince, you look pale, and trouble dims your eye!
ANTIOCHUS. Yes, I must leave you.
BERENICE. What! may I not know
The reason—
ANTIOCHUS [aside]. Without seeing her again
'Twere better to have gone.
BERENICE. What fear you? speak: too long
You keep me in suspense. What mystery
Surrounds this parting?
ANTIOCHUS. 'Tis to your command
I bow, remember, as you hear me now
For the last time. If from your present greatness
Your memory recalls your birthplace, Madam,
You cannot have forgotten that my heart
There felt love's arrows first from your sweet eyes:
Agrippa gave his sanction to my passion,
And, as your brother, spoke on my behalf;
Nor seem'd you angry at the suit so urged.
But to my loss came Titus, saw, and won

Your admiration dazzled by a hero
Who carried in his hands the wrath of
  Rome.
Judæa quail'd before him, and I fell
The earliest victim of his vanquish'd foes.
Soon did your lips, making my fate more
  bitter,
Bid mine be silent. Long did I dispute
That cruel sentence, with my eyes I spoke,
Follow'd you everywhere with sighs and
  tears.
At last your rigour turn'd the trembling
  scale,
I must conceal my passion, or be ban-
  ish'd.
You made me swear obedience to that
  compact:
But I confess, e'en at that very moment,
When you extorted promise so unfair,
I swore that I would never cease to love
  you.
  BERENICE. Alas, what words are these?
  ANTIOCHUS. Five years have I
Quell'd mine own heart, and will be silent
  still.
I follow'd my victorious rival's arms,
And hoped, since tears were vain, that I
  might shed
My blood; or that my name, by many a
  feat
Renown'd, might reach your ears, deaf to
  my voice.
Heav'n seem'd disposed to end my misery,
You mourn'd my death, but a worse fate
  was mine,
And, disappointed, I survived the danger.
The Emperor's valour more than match'd
  my rage;
His merit I must own with true esteem.
Tho' near in prospect gleam'd th' imperial
  sceptre,
The darling of the universe, and loved
By you, he seem'd the mark for every
  blow;
Whilst hopeless, scorn'd, and weary of his
  life,
His hapless rival follow'd where he led.
I see your heart echoes my praise of him
In secret, and, attentive to my tale
Of woe, you hear me now with less regret,
For Titus' sake forgiving all the rest.

At last the long and cruel siege was
  o'er,
He tamed the rebels left by feuds in-
  testine,
By fire and famine, bleeding, sick, and
  pale,
And laid their ramparts low 'neath heaps
  of ruins.
Rome saw you with the conqueror arrive.
How in my desert home I pined and lan-
  guish'd!
Long stay'd I roaming about Cæsarea,
Those charming gardens where I learn'd
  to love you,
And made my quest for you thro' your
  dominions
Sad at your absence, sought to trace your
  steps,
And wept my failure; till in mere de-
  spair,
Master'd by grief, I turn'd tow'rds Italy;
Where Fate reserved for me her latest
  stroke.
Titus, embracing me, brought me to you;
A veil of friendship so deceived you both
That you reveal'd your love to me who
  loved you.
But still some lingering hope soothed my
  displeasure,
Rome and Vespasian frown'd upon your
  sighs,
For all his conquests Titus might be
  foil'd.
  The sire is dead, and now the son is
  master.
Why fled I not at once? Some days I
  wish'd
Wherein to watch the progress of affairs.
My cup is full of sorrow, yours of joy.
You, without me, will have enough to
  witness
Your happiness with glad congratulations.
I, who could only add ill-omen'd tears,
Too constant victim of a fruitless love,
Relieved to tell this story of my woes,
Stain'd by no wild revenge, to her who
  caused them.
Depart, altho' I love you more than ever.
  BERENICE. I would not have believed
  that on this day
Which is to join my destiny with Cæsar's,

I could have suffer'd mortal, unrebuked,
To tell me to my face he is my lover.
But friendship kept me silent; for its
sake
I pardon language that might well offend
me,
Nor check'd the torrent of unjust upbraid-
ing;
Yet more, I grieve to hear that we must
part.
Heav'n knows that in the midst of all my
honours
I yearn'd for one thing more, that you
might witness
My joy; like all the world I held your
virtues
Esteem'd; my Titus met your admiration
With warm regard. And many a time
I joy'd
As if with Titus when I talk'd with you.
ANTIOCHUS. 'Tis this that wings my
flight. I shun, too late,
Converse wherein you give no thought to
me.
I fly from Titus, from a name that tor-
tures
Each moment that your cruel lips repeat
it.
Shall I say more? I cannot bear those
eyes
Whose absent gaze seems fix'd upon an-
other.
Farewell. Your image in my heart
abides;
I go to wait for death, still loving you.
But fear not that my passion so deluded
Will make the world resound with my
misfortunes:
The tidings of a death that I desire
Alone will tell you that I lived so long.
Farewell.

SCENE V

[BERENICE, PHŒNICE.]
PHŒNICE. Ah, how I pity him! Such
faith
Deserved a happier lot. Madam, do you
Not pity him?
BERENICE. This sudden parting leaves
me

(I own it, my Phœnice) secret sorrow.
PHŒNICE. I would have kept him
back.
BERENICE. I keep him back!
Nay, I should rather force me to forget
him.
Would'st have me, then, encourage a mad
passion?
PHŒNICE. Not yet has Titus all his
heart unbosomed.
With eyes of jealousy Rome sees you,
Madam:
I dread for you the rigour of her laws,
They count a foreign marriage a dis-
grace:
All monarchs Rome detests, and Berenice
Is one.
BERENICE. The time is gone when I
could tremble.
The Emperor loves me, and his word
has pow'r
Unlimited. He'll see the senate bring me
Their homage, and the people crown his
statues
With garlands.
         Have you seen this
night's rare splendour?
Are not your eyes fill'd with its dazzling
glory?
That funeral pyre, the darkness lost in
light
Of blazing torches, armies with their
eagles,
Long lines of lictors, consuls, senators,
A crowd of Kings, and all with glory
borrow'd
From Titus; gold and purple which en-
hanced
His majesty, and bays that crown'd the
victor;
All eyes of visitors from every land
Turning their eager gaze on him alone;
That noble carriage, and that air be-
nign,—
Good gods! with what affection and re-
spect
All hearts assured him of their loyalty!
Could any then behold him and not think,
As I did, that, however lowly born,
The world would still have own'd him as
its master?

But whither does my fond remembrance
wander?
All Rome, Phœnice, at this very moment
Offers her vows for Titus, and with smoke
Of sacrifice inaugurates his reign.
Why should we linger? Let us add our
pray'rs
For his success to Heav'n that watches
o'er him.
Then straightway, without waiting to be
summon'd,
I'll seek him, and in loving colloquy
Say all that warm affection, long re-
press'd,
Inspires in hearts contented with each
other.

ACT II

Scene I

[TITUS, PAULINUS, ATTENDANTS.]
TITUS. Has Commagene's monarch
been inform'd
That I desire to see him?
PAULINUS.   To the Queen
I went, and found the Prince had been
with her,
But he was gone or ever I arrived.
I have left word to let him know your
wishes.
TITUS. 'Tis well. And what does she,
Queen Berenice?
PAULINUS. The Queen this moment,
grateful for your goodness,
Loads Heav'n with pray'rs for your pros-
perity.
She is gone forth, my lord.
TITUS.   Too kind a Princess!
Alas!
PAULINUS. Why breathe for her that
sigh of sorrow?
When well nigh all the East will bow
before her,
Needs she your pity?
TITUS.   Let us talk in private.

Scene II

[TITUS, PAULINUS.]
TITUS. Rome, still uncertain of my
purpose, waits

To learn the future fortune of the Queen;
The secrets of her heart and mine,
Paulinus,
Are now become the theme of every
tongue.
'Tis time that I should make my mean-
ing plain.
What says the public voice of her and
me?
Tell me, what hear you?
PAULINUS.   By all lips, my liege,
I hear your virtues and her beauty
praised.
TITUS. What say they of the sighs I
breathe for her?
What end expect they of a love so faith-
ful?
PAULINUS. Nought balks your pow'r;
love on, or quench this passion,
The Court will be subservient to your
wishes.
TITUS. Ah yes, I know the Court is
insincere,
Too ready always to content its masters,
Approving e'en a Nero's horrid crimes;
I've seen them on their knees adore his
madness.
I will not take for judge a servile Court,
I'll play my part upon a nobler stage;
And, without giving ear to Flattery's
voice,
I wish to hear the heart of Rome thro'
you,
As you have promised. Fear and rever-
ence
Close me the door to murmurs and com-
plaint:
For better eyes and ears, my dear Paul-
inus,
To you I make appeal, and borrow yours:
'Tis this return I ask for private friend-
ship,
That what my people feel you should
express,
That thro' the mists of flattery the truth
Should reach me, thanks to your sin-
cerity.
Speak, then. For what must Berenice
look?
Will Rome to her show harshness or in-
dulgence?

Am I to think that she would be offended
Were Queen so fair to grace th' imperial throne?
PAULINUS. Doubt not, my lord, be't reason or caprice,
Rome will be loath to have her for an Empress.
They know her charms, and own that hand so fair
May seem to you worthy to wield your sceptre;
No Roman dame, say they, has heart more noble;
She has a thousand virtues, but, my lord,
She is a Queen. Rome, by a changeless law
Admits no foreign blood with hers to mingle,
Nor will she recognize the lawless issue
Of unions which our customs have forbidden.
Rome, too, you know, when banishing her Kings,
Condemn'd that name, so sacred hitherto,
To the black stigma of eternal hatred;
And, tho' she stoops submissive to her Cæsars,
That hatred, the last relic of her pride,
Survives in hearts whence freedom has departed.
Julius, whose martial glory first subdued her,
And drown'd the voice of law 'mid din of arms,
Smitten with Cleopatra's beauty, fear'd
To wed her, and in Egypt left her lonely
To mourn his absence. Antony, whose love
Made her his idol, in her lap forgot
Country and fame, yet dared not call her wife:
Rome track'd the traitor to his charmer's knees,
Nor let her vengeful fury be disarm'd
Till she had overwhelm'd the amorous pair.
Since then, my lord, Caligula and Nero,
Monsters whose very name I blush to mention,

Whose outward aspect only show'd them human,
Who trampled under foot all other laws,
Fear'd this one only, and refrain'd from lighting
Before our eyes a hymeneal torch
Hateful to Rome. You bade me speak with frankness.
We've seen the brother of the freedman Pallas,
Felix, whose back still bears the brand of Claudius,
Become the husband of two foreign Queens,
And, if I needs must tell unvarnish'd truth,
Both Queens were of the blood of Berenice.
Think you that Rome without offence could see
Partner of Cæsar's bed this Eastern princess,
Whose countrymen beheld one of our slaves
Leave chains and fetters for their Queens' caresses!
Thus public feeling views your present passion;
Nor am I sure that, ere this sun has set,
The senate will not, in the name of Rome,
Repeat to you what I have dared to say,
And the whole city, falling at your feet,
Add their entreaties for a choice more worthy
Of you and them. Weigh well what you will answer.
TITUS. Ah! What a love they wish me to renounce!
PAULINUS. That love is ardent, I must e'en confess it.
TITUS. Stronger a thousand times than you can think.
It has become to me a needful pleasure
To see her every day, and win her favour.
Yet more, (no secrets have I with Paulinus,)
How oft has Heav'n received my warmest thanks
For her, that she embraced my father's side
In Edom, and beneath his banners ranged

The armies of the East, and, all mankind
Rousing, entrusted to his peaceful sway
Rome, drunk with blood! I wish'd my
father's throne,
E'en I, Paulinus, who to save his life
Would willingly have died, had Fate
consented
To lengthen out the thread of his ex-
istence:
And all in hopes, (how ill a lover knows
What he desires!) to share that throne
with her,
Her love and loyalty to recognize,
And lay my heart with all the world be-
fore her.
In spite of all my love and all her beauty,
After so many oaths, so many tears,
Now when I have the pow'r to crown
such charms,
Now when my heart adores her more than
ever,
And can, united to her own in marriage,
Pay in one day the vows of five long
years,
I am about—Ye gods, how shall I say it?
　　PAULINUS. What, Sire?
　　TITUS. To part from her for evermore.
This moment only seals my heart's sur-
render:
If I desired to hear your frank avowal,
'Twas only that your zeal might aid in
secret
Th' extinction of a love with anguish
silenced.
Long has fair Berenice held the balance
Suspended, and if glory outweighs pas-
sion,
Believe me it has been a desp'rate con-
flict,
From which my heart will bleed for many
a day.
Calm was life's ocean when love's bark
I launch'd,
The sceptre of the world by other hands
Was sway'd. Consulting no one but my-
self,
Free felt I to indulge each amorous sigh;
But scarce had Heav'n recall'd my father's
spirit,
And I, with sad farewell, had closed his
eyes,

When I awoke from that fools' paradise.
I felt the burden that was laid upon me,
I knew that soon, instead of soft in-
dulgence,
I should be call'd on to renounce my-
self,
And that Heav'n's choice, thwarting the
course of love,
Would make the world henceforth engross
my care.
To-day Rome watches my new line of
conduct;
What shame for me, for her what evil
omen,
If at my first step all her claims I
spurn'd,
And based my happiness upon the ruin
Of ancient laws! Bent on this sacri-
fice,
I wish'd to break the blow to Berenice:
But where can I begin? These last eight
days,
How oft have I been minded to disclose
My purpose! And each time my tongue
refused
To speak a single word, as if 'twere frozen
Within my mouth. I hoped the pain I
felt
Might give her warning of our common
woe:
But touch'd by my alarm, all unsuspect-
ing,
She sought to dry the tears whose source
she knew not,
And nought foreboded less than that a
love,
So well deserved, was drawing to an
end.
At length this morning I have steel'd my
heart
To tell the truth: Paulinus, I must see
her.
I wait to ask Antiochus to take
This precious charge, no longer mine to
guard,
Back to the Eastern clime from which
she came.
To-morrow Rome shall see the Queen de-
part
With him. Soon she shall learn her fate
from me,

When for the last time we converse to-
gether.
PAULINUS. I thought no less from that
heroic soul
Which Victory has follow'd everywhere.
Captive Judæa, and her smoking ram-
parts,
Eternal monuments of noble courage,
Assured me well enough you would not
mar
The fame that you have won by feats of
arms,
And that the victor of so many nations
Sooner or later would subdue his pas-
sions.
TITUS. Under what specious names
does Glory mask
Her cruel will! How would her charms
seem fairer,
Were it but death she call'd on me to
face!
Till now, 'twas Berenice who inspired
The ardour that I felt for her attractions.
You know that once Renown no lustre
shed
Around my name; brought up at Nero's
Court,
My youth, by ill example led astray,
Too prone to heed the voice of self-in-
dulgence,
Scorn'd nobler aims, Paulinus. Berenice
Enthrall'd my heart. What cannot Love
achieve
To please the loved one, and to win tho'
vanquish'd?
I spent my blood; all to my sword gave
way;
Triumphant I return'd. But tears and
blood
Sufficed not to deserve my lady's favour:
A thousand wretches bless'd the aid I
brought them.
On every side they saw my bounty spread,
And I was happy, more than you can
guess,
When in her eyes I read warm approba-
tion
Of countless hearts won by my benefits.
I owe her all. And what reward is hers?
That debt about to be flung back upon
her!

As recompense for virtues so unrivall'd
My tongue will say: "Depart, see me no
more."
PAULINUS. What, Sire, is all that new-
born grandeur nothing,
Which to Euphrates will extend her
pow'r?
Honours so great as to surprise the sen-
ate,
A hundred tribes added to her dominion,
Are novel tokens of ingratitude.
TITUS. Weak trifles to engage so great
a sorrow!
I know too well how Berenice's heart
Craves nothing but mine own. I loved
her fondly,
And was beloved as well. Since that glad
day,
(Should I not rather call it most disas-
trous),
Loving me only for myself, in Rome
A stranger, unfamiliar with my Court,
She lives without a wish but for the
hour
When she may see my face, meanwhile
content
To wait. And if at times my footstep
lingers,
And I appear not at th' expected mo-
ment,
I find her when I come all bathed in
tears,
Which long refuse my efforts to dispel
them.
All the most binding ties of love, re-
proaches
That sweetly merge in transports of de-
light
Dash'd with fresh fears, charms uncon-
strain'd by art,
Beauty and virtue, all I find in her.
For five whole years have I beheld her
daily,
And every day her face wears new at-
tractions.
No more I'll think of it. Let's go, Paul-
inus,
My resolution wavers while we linger.
Great Heav'ns, that I should greet her
with such tidings!
Once more, let's go, I must not hesitate.

I know my duty, 'tis for me to follow:
Without concern whether I live or die.

SCENE III

[TITUS, PAULINUS, RUTILUS.]
RUTILUS.   The Queen, your Majesty,
would speak with you.
TITUS.   Alas, Paulinus!
PAULINUS.   Drawing back already!
Remember, Sire, your noble resolution;
Now is the time.
TITUS.   We'll see her. Let her come.

SCENE IV

[TITUS, BERENICE, PAULINUS, PHŒNICE.]
BERENICE.   Be not offended, if my zeal
outruns
Discretion, and disturbs your privacy.
While your Court, gathering around, re-
peat
The favours show'r'd so freely on my
head,
Sir, is it right that I at such a moment
Should stay alone, and gratitude be
silent?
I know your friend sincere, nor need I
shun
His presence, well acquainted as he is
With our hearts' secret; you have done
with mourning,
Nought hinders you, and yet you seek me
not.
I hear you offer me another sceptre,
But from yourself I hear no word of it.
Let us have more repose and less dis-
play;
Is your love dumb except before the
senate?
Ah, Titus (for my heart disowns those
titles
Of majesty which fear and reverence
prompt),
Why should your love be burden'd with
such cares?
Are crowns the only prize that it can
offer?
How long have you supposed I covet
grandeur?

A sigh, a look, a word that falls from
you,
Are all th' ambition of a heart like mine.
See me more often, and come empty
handed.
Is all your time devoted to your empire?
Eight days have pass'd, and have you
nought to tell me?
One word would reassure this timid heart!
But was your speech of me, when I sur-
prised you?
Were my concerns the subject of dis-
course?
Was I at least, Sir, present to your
thought?
TITUS.   Of that you may be sure: for
Heav'n is witness
That Berenice is before me always.
Nor time, nor absence, once again I swear
it,
Can banish you from my adoring soul.
BERENICE.   Why, what is this? You
swear eternal ardour,
But, even while you swear, are cold as
ice!
Why make appeal to Heav'n's omnipo-
tence?
What need have I of oaths to strengthen
trust?
I have no wish to think you false, my
lord,
And will believe the witness of a sigh.
TITUS.   Madam—
BERENICE.   I listen. But, without re-
ply,
You turn away your eyes and seem per-
plex'd!
Why is your countenance so full of
woe?
Will you for ever mourn your father's
death?
Can nothing charm away this gnawing
sorrow?
TITUS.   Ah! would to Heav'n my father
yet were living,
How happy should I be!
BERENICE.   Sir, this regret
Does honour to your filial piety,
But to his memory your tears have paid
Due tribute. Other cares you owe to
Rome;

I dare not say how much your glory
  moves
My own concern. Once I could soothe
  your troubles,
And Berenice's voice you heard with pleas-
  ure;
For your sake vex'd with manifold mis-
  fortunes,
A word from you has made me check my
  tears.
You mourn a father: 'tis a common sor-
  row,
While I (the bare remembrance makes
  me shudder,)
So nearly torn from him whom more than
  life
I loved, the anguish of whose heart you
  know
When parted from my Titus for a mo-
  ment,
I, who would die if banish'd from your
  sight,
Never to see you more—
  TITUS.   Alas! What say you?
Why choose this time? Pray cease, for
  pity's sake:
Your kindness crushes an ungrateful
  wretch.
  BERENICE. Ungrateful! can it be that
  you are that?
Are you so weary of my tender-
  ness?
  TITUS. No, never; since I must the
  truth confess,
My heart burns now with fiercer flames
  than ever.
But—
  BERENICE. Speak.
  TITUS.   Alas!
  BERENICE.   Go on.
  TITUS.   Rome and the empire—
  BERENICE. Well, Sir?
  TITUS.   Let's go, Paulinus; I am
  dumb.

SCENE V

[BERENICE, PHŒNICE.]
BERENICE. So soon to leave me! and
  without a word!
A doleful meeting truly, dear Phœnice!

What have I done? What means he by
  this silence?
  PHŒNICE. Like you I'm puzzled to
  account for it.
Does nothing to your memory occur
Which may have raised a prejudice
  against you?
Consider well.
  BERENICE. Alas! you may believe me,
The more I wish to bring to mind the
  past,
From the first day I saw him till this
  hour,
The only fault I find is too much fond-
  ness.
You heard us. Tell me frankly, my
  Phœnice,
Did I say anything that could displease
  him?
I know not if, perchance, with too much
  heat
I scorn'd his gifts, or blamed the grief
  that vex'd him—
Is it his people's hatred that he dreads?
He fears, it may be, to espouse a Queen.
Alas, if that were true.—It cannot be,
A hundred times at least he has assured
  me
He slights their cruel laws. Why does
  he not
Explain so harsh a silence? This sus-
  pense
Will kill me. How could I endure to live
Neglected, feeling I had him offended?
Let us go after him. But thro' my brain
Flashes a thought that may the source
  reveal
Of this disorder. Has he learn'd where
  loves
Antiochus? Can that have moved his
  anger?
I heard the King was summon'd to his
  presence.
Why further seek for cause of my dis-
  tress?
Doubtless this trouble that has so alarm'd
  me
Is but a light suspicion, which with ease
May be disarm'd. This feeble victory
Brings me no pride, my Titus. Would
  to Heav'n

A rival worthier of your jealous fears
Might try my faith, and offer empire
  wider
Than Rome can boast, to pay me for my
  love;
While you had nought to give me but
  yourself!
Then would you see, victorious and be-
  loved,
How much I prize your heart, my dearest
  Titus.
Come, let us go.   One word will clear
  his doubts.
Let me take courage, I can please him
  still.
Too soon have I counted myself unhappy;
Titus must love me if his heart is jealous.

ACT III

Scene I

[Titus, Antiochus, Arsaces.]
Titus.   So you would leave us, Prince!
  What sudden reason
Speeds your departure, shall I say your
  flight?
Would you have gone in secret, without
  taking
Our farewell wishes?   Is it as a foe
You quit us?   What will Rome then say
  to this?
I, as your friend, my Court, and all the
  empire?
Wherein have I offended?   Did I treat
  you
Without distinction just like other kings?
While yet my father lived my heart was
  yours,
That was the only present I could make
  you;
Now, when my hand can open with my
  heart,
You shun the favours I would fain be-
  stow.
Think you, the hazards of the past for-
  gotten,
My present grandeur every thought en-
  grosses,
And all my friends, fast fading in the
  distance,

Wanted no longer, are accounted stran-
  gers?
Of you, dear Prince, who thus would steal
  away,
My need is greater than it ever was.
  Antiochus.   Of me?
  Titus.   Of you.
  Antiochus.   Alas! what can you look
  for
From one so luckless, Sire, but useless
  wishes?
  Titus.   Can I forget, Prince, that my
  victory
Owed half its glory to your valiant deeds,
That in the train of captives Rome be-
  held
More than one vanquish'd by Antiochus?
And laid up in the Capitol she saw
Spoils that your hands had taken from
  the Jews?
These brave achievements are enough for
  me,
No further claim I make but on your
  counsel.
I know that Berenice, to your care
A debtor, has in you a faithful friend;
Her eyes and ears are giv'n to you alone
In Rome, you share with us one heart
  and soul.
For friendship's sake, so constant and
  devoted,
Exert the influence that you have with
  her;
See her for me.
  Antiochus.   I? Nay, I cannot face her.
She has received my last farewell for
  ever.
  Titus.   Prince, speak to her again on
  my behalf.
  Antiochus.   Plead your own cause, my
  lord.   The Queen adores you;
Why should you at this hour deny your-
  self
The pleasure of so charming an avowal?
She waits you with impatience.   I will
  answer
For her obedience with my parting breath;
Ready to yield consent, herself has told
  me
That when you see her next, 'twill be to
  woo her.

TITUS. Ah; would that I could thus confess my passion!
To do so would be happiness indeed!
My love was ready to burst forth to-day,
This very day when I, dear Prince, must leave her.

ANTIOCHUS. Leave her, my lord?

TITUS. Such my sad destiny:
For her and Titus is no longer hope
Of wedlock, vainly that sweet thought has lured me:
To-morrow, Prince, she must depart with you.

ANTIOCHUS. Heav'ns! What is this?

TITUS. Pity the pow'r that galls me:
Lord of the universe, I rule its fortunes;
I set up Kings, and cast them down at will;
Yet can I not of mine own heart dispose.
Rome, the eternal foe of royal titles,
Disdains a beauty born to wear the purple:
The glitter of a crown and long descent
From kingly sires are in her eyes a scandal
To smirch my flame. This heart of mine is free
To rove elsewhere, and choose the meanest bride
Of Roman blood, nor need I dread a murmur
To mar the shouts of welcome and delight.
The mighty Julius could not stem that tide
Which sweeps me on. If Rome to-morrow sees not
The Queen's departure, she will hear the people
Demand of me her instant banishment.
Let us then spare ourselves that base affront,
And yield, since yield we must, without disgrace.
My eight days' silence and averted eyes
Will have prepared her for this sad announcement;
E'en at this moment, restless and excited,
She longs to learn my purpose from myself.

Soothe the keen anguish of a tortured lover,
And spare me the sore task of explanation.
Go, make her understand my troubled silence,
And why it is I must avoid her presence;
Be you sole witness of her tears and mine,
Take her my last farewell, and bring me hers.
I shrink from parting words and looks of sadness,
Which might o'erthrow my tottering resolution.
If it can ease her misery to know
That in my soul her image lives and reigns,
Assure her, Prince, that, faithful to the end,
My broken heart, banish'd from happiness
No less than she, and bearing to the tomb
Her name beloved, will, like a captive bird,
Pine for release, as long as Heav'n that tears
Her from me, may protect my weary life.
You, Prince, whom friendship's ties alone have bound
To her, forsake her not in her affliction;
By you escorted to her Eastern realms,
Let her appear in triumph, not in flight.
And to confirm a friendship so devoted,
And keep my name fresh in your memories,
Let your dominions reach each other's borders;
Euphrates only shall divide your kingdoms.
I know the senate holds your name so honour'd,
They with one voice will ratify this gift,
I join Cilicia to your Commagene.
Farewell. Desert her not, my Berenice,
Queen of my heart, sole object of desire,
Whom only I can love till I expire.

SCENE II

[ANTIOCHUS, ARSACES.]

ARSACES. Thus is kind Heav'n prepared to do you justice:

You will leave Rome, Sire, but with
    Berenice.
You force her not away, they to your
    hands
Consign her.
    ANTIOCHUS. Give me time, good Ar-
        saces.
The change is great, and my surprise
    extreme;
Titus to me resigns his dearest treasure!
Gods! can I credit what mine ears have
    heard?
And should my heart be glad, could I
    believe it?
    ARSACES. And what am I, my lord, to
        think of you?
With what fresh hindrance is your joy
    confronted?
Did you deceive me when just now, at
    parting,
Still moved with anguish at a last fare-
    well,
You told me all your heart had dared to
    tell her,
And trembled at your own audacity?
'Twas her impending marriage urged your
    flight,
That fear removed, what care can trou-
    ble you?
Follow where love invites your willing
    footsteps.
    ANTIOCHUS. With her safe conduct I
        am charged, my friend,
And sweetest intercourse shall long en-
    joy;
Her eyes will grow accustom'd to the
    sight
Of mine, and learn, perchance, how much
    my ardour,
So persevering, makes the suit of Titus
Seem weak and cold. Here all his gran-
    deur daunts me;
In Rome nought else is seen beside his
    splendour;
But, tho' his name is in the East re-
    nown'd,
The traces of my glory too are there
For her to see.
    ARSACES.   Ay, Fortune favours you.
    ANTIOCHUS. Ah! How we mock our-
        selves with self-deception!

ARSACES. Why, what deception?
ANTIOCHUS.   Could I ever please her?
Or Berenice cease to thwart my love?
Would she let fall a word to ease my
    pain?
Think you that she, in her unhappiness,
Tho' all the world besides should slight
    her charms,
Would thank me for my tears, or con-
    descend
So far as to accept the zealous service
Which she should feel she owed to my
    affection?
    ARSACES. And who can better solace
        her disgrace?
Her prospect now is changed from what
    it was:
Titus forsakes her.
    ANTIOCHUS. Ah! this turn of fortune
Will bring me nothing but an added tor-
    ture,
To learn how much she loves him from
    her tears;
I shall behold her grief, and pity her
Myself. The fruit of all my love will be
To see her weep, but not, alas, for me.
    ARSACES. Why thus continue to tor-
        ment yourself?
Was ever known a noble heart more
    feeble?
Open your eyes, and see how many rea-
    sons
Must move fair Berenice to be yours.
Now that no longer Titus courts her fa-
    vour,
She will perforce accept your hand, my
    master.
    ANTIOCHUS. And why perforce?
    ARSACES. Give her some days to
        weep,—
Let the first sobs of grief be unrestrain'd;
Then all will work for you, vexation, ven-
    geance,
His absence and your presence, time it-
    self,
Her single hand too weak to wield three
    sceptres,
Your realms so ready to be join'd with
    hers,
Interest, reason, friendship, all unites
    you.

ANTIOCHUS. I breathe once more, you
give me back my life,
With joy I hail a presage so agreeable.
Why tarry? Let my mission be dis-
charged.
I'll see the Queen, and since the task is
mine,
Tell her that Titus has deserted her—
But stay, what would I do? Is it for
me
To take upon myself such cruel errand?
My heart revolts, whether from love or
pity.
Shall my dear Berenice hear from me
She is forsaken? Who would e'er have
guess'd it,
That such a word should strike upon her
ear?
ARSACES. Her indignation will all fall
on Titus;
And if you speak, 'twill be at her de-
sire.
ANTIOCHUS. No, let us not intrude
upon her sorrow;
Let others come to tell of her misfortune.
Do you not think it will be hard enough
For her to hear how Titus spurns her
from him,
Without the further bitterness of learn-
ing
His scornful treatment from a rival's
lips?
Once more, let's fly; nor by such evil
tidings
Incur the weight of her undying hatred.
ARSACES. Ah! Here she comes. Now
to your part, my lord.
ANTIOCHUS. Good Heav'ns!

SCENE III

[BERENICE, ANTIOCHUS, ARSACES,
PHŒNICE.]

BERENICE. Why, how is this? I
thought you gone.
ANTIOCHUS. I see that you are disap-
pointed, Madam,
And it was Cæsar that you here expected.
Him must you blame if, spite of my fare-
well,

My presence still offends unwilling eyes.
I should, perhaps, have been ere now at
Ostia,
Had not his orders kept me at his Court.
BERENICE. Your presence then he wel-
comes, mine he shuns.
ANTIOCHUS. He has detain'd me but
to speak of you.
BERENICE. Of me, Prince?
ANTIOCHUS. Yes, of you.
BERENICE. What could he say?
ANTIOCHUS. A thousand others are
more fit to tell you.
BERENICE. What, Sir!—
ANTIOCHUS. Suspend, dear Madam,
your resentment.
Another, far from seeking to be silent,
Perhaps would triumph, and with ready
boldness
Might gladly yield to your impatient
wish;
But I, whose heart shrinks ever, as you
know,
From wounding feelings dearer than mine
own,
Would rather risk displeasure than dis-
tress you,
Dreading your sorrow even more than
anger.
Ere sunset you will justify my silence.
Madam, farewell.
BERENICE. What words are these?
Stay, Prince,
I cannot hide my trouble from your eye.
You see before you a distracted Queen;
Speak but two words, for I am sick at
heart.
You fear, say you, to trouble my repose;
This cruel reticence spares me no pain,
It pierces deep, it stirs my wrath, my
hatred.
Sir, if you hold my peace of mind so
precious,
If ever I myself to you was dear,
Lighten this darkness that you see o'er-
whelms me.
Tell me what Titus said.
ANTIOCHUS. For Heav'n's sake,
Madam—
BERENICE. Do you so little fear to
disobey me?

ANTIOCHUS. To tell the truth would
  be to make you hate me.
BERENICE. Speak, I command you.
ANTIOCHUS. Gods! What vehemence!
Once more, believe me, you will praise my
  silence.
BERENICE. This moment, Prince, com-
  ply with what I ask,
Or be assured that I shall always hate
  you.
ANTIOCHUS. That sentence, Madam,
  shall release my tongue.
Since you will have it so, I must content
  you.
But do not be deceived: I have to tell
Of troubles peradventure little dream'd
  of.
I know your heart; you must expect a
  blow
To strike it where your feeling is most
  tender.
Titus commands me—
BERENICE. What?
ANTIOCHUS. To let you know
That you must part for ever from each
  other.
BERENICE. Part! He and I? Titus
  from Berenice?
ANTIOCHUS. Yet at the same time I
  must do him justice;
All the repugnance that a generous heart
Can feel when love is vanquish'd by
  despair,
I've seen in him. He worships while he
  weeps.
But he's convinced 'tis vain to love you
  longer.
Rome holds the very name of Queen
  suspected;
Yes, you and he must part. You leave
  to-morrow.
BERENICE. Part! Oh, Phœnice!
PHŒNICE. You must show, dear Madam,
The greatness of your soul. This sudden
  blow
Is doubtless hard to bear, and well may
  stun you.
BERENICE. Titus forsake me! All his
  vows forgotten!
Titus, who swore to me—I'll not believe
  it;

Honour forbids him so to cast me off.
It is a slander on his innocence,
A trap to tear two loving hearts asunder.
Too dear he holds me to desire my death.
Come, I will see him, speak with him
  forthwith.
Come, let us go.
ANTIOCHUS. Is falsehood in my face?—
BERENICE. Too much you wish it true,
  Sir, to persuade me.
No, I believe you not. Be't as it may,
Take heed you never see my face again.
                        [To PHŒNICE.]
Do not desert me in this dire distress.
I struggle hard to keep myself deluded.

SCENE IV

[ANTIOCHUS, ARSACES.]
ANTIOCHUS. Heard I aright? or did my
  ears deceive me?
Me did she bid, me, ne'er to see her more?
I'll take good care of that. Was I not
  leaving,
Had Titus not detain'd me 'gainst my
  will?
Yes, I must go. Get ready, Arsaces.
Her hatred, wherewithal she thinks to
  blast me,
Strikes off my chains. Just now you saw
  a lover
Departing, jealous with a wild despair;
Now, with this warning ringing in mine
  ears,
I'll go, methinks, in proud indifference.
ARSACES. There is less need to leave
  her now than ever.
ANTIOCHUS. Shall I then stay to see
  myself disdain'd,
And bear the blame of Cæsar's cruelty?
See myself punish'd because he offends?
With what injustice and unworthy scorn
She tells me to my face that I'm dis-
  honest!
For thanks she taxes me with perfidy,
Saying that I'm a traitor, he is true!
And when forsooth? Just at the bitter
  moment
When I was setting forth my rival's
  tears;

When to console her I presented Titus
More tenderly attach'd than truth may
warrant.
ARSACES. Why vex yourself, my lord,
with thoughts like these?
Give to this angry torrent time to flow;
A week, or at the most a month, will
dry it.
Only remain.
ANTIOCHUS. No, Arsaces, I leave her.
Her sorrow might excite my sympathy;
My peace, my honour urge me to be gone.
Let us fly far enough from Berenice
To hear her very name no longer men-
tion'd.
Still there is time, the day is not yet
spent.
I'll seek my palace, there to wait for
you;
Haste, see how she supports this crush-
ing blow,
Until I know she lives, I cannot go.

ACT IV

SCENE I

BERENICE. Phœnice comes not! Tan-
talizing moments,
How slow ye seem to my impatient
wishes!
Restless I pace this floor, faint, sick at
heart;
Strength fails me, yet it kills me to be
quiet.
Phœnice comes not! Ah, how this delay
Appals my heart with a too fatal
presage!
Phœnice has no answer to bring back;
Titus, ungrateful Titus will not hear her;
He seeks in flight a refuge from my fury.

SCENE II

[BERENICE, PHŒNICE.]
BERENICE. Well, dear Phœnice, have
you seen the Emperor?
What says he? Will he come?

PHŒNICE. Yes, I have seen him,
And painted your distress in darkest
tints;
Tears he would fain have check'd flow'd
from his eyes.
BERENICE. And comes he?
PHŒNICE. He will come; doubt it not,
Madam.
But will you show yourself in this dis-
order?
Calm yourself, dearest lady, be com-
posed.
Let me replace the veil that from its
place
Has slipt, and smooth this too dishevell'd
hair:
No trace of weeping must your charms
disfigure.
BERENICE. Nay, let them be, Phœnice;
he shall see
His handiwork. What boots this vain
apparel?
If my true love, my tears and sighs, nor
they
Alone, but certain death whose near ap-
proach
I feel, avail not to recall him to me,
Will your superfluous cares be more suc-
cessful,
Aiding attractions that have ceased to
move him?
PHŒNICE. Why will you load him with
unjust reproaches?
I hear a step, dear Madam; it is Cæsar's.
This place is public, haste to your apart-
ments.
There you in private may converse to-
gether.

SCENE III

[TITUS, PAULINUS, ATTENDANTS.]
TITUS. Do what you can to soothe the
Queen, Paulinus;
Tell her I'm coming.
                    I would be alone
A moment. Let them leave me.
PAULINUS [aside].   How I fear
This conflict! May the gods protect his
glory,
And Rome's! I'll see the Queen.

Scene IV

Titus. What dost thou, Titus?
How rash art thou, thus to seek Berenice!
Art thou prepared to take a last farewell?
And is thine heart steel'd to such cruelty?
For in the conflict that awaits thee now
Firmness is not enough, thou must be
  ruthless.
How shall I bear those eyes whose tender
  glance
Knows but too well the way to reach
  my heart?
When I encounter that soul-piercing gaze
Fix'd upon mine, can I resist her tears,
Or bear in mind the stern behest of duty?
How shall I say: "See me no more for
  ever?"
  I am about to stab a heart that loves
  me,
Beloved by me. And why? At whose
  command?
Mine own, for Rome has not declared her
  wishes.
I hear no cries surging around this
  palace,
Nor see the State hanging o'er ruin's
  brink.
Needs it a sacrifice like this to save it?
Its voice is silent: I, my own tormentor,
Rush to meet troubles I may keep at bay.
Who knows but Rome, owning the Queen's
  rare virtues,
Will count her one of her own citizens?
Rome by her choice may justify my own;
I will not court destruction, no, not I.
Let Rome against her laws weigh in the
  balance
Such love as hers, such tears, such con-
  stancy,
And she will side with me—
              Open thine eyes;
What air is this that thou dost breathe?
  Can love
Or fear eradicate the hate of Kings
That Romans with their mothers' milk
  imbibe?
Their sentence against Kings condemns
  thy Queen.
Hast thou not heard it from thine earliest
  years?

And even in the camp the voice of Fame
Proclaim'd thy duty in thine ears once
  more.
When Berenice hither follow'd thee,
Rome did not fail to let thee know her
  judgment.
How often must that judgment be re-
  peated?
Coward, let love prevail, renounce the
  throne,
Seek Earth's remotest bounds, and, there
  confined,
Resign to worthier hands the reins of
  empire.
Is this the end then of those glorious
  projects
Which were t' enshrine my memory in all
  hearts?
Eight days have I been reigning, and till
  now
Nought have I done for honour, all for
  love.
What record can I give of time so
  precious?
Where are the boons I led men to expect?
The tears that I have dried? The happy
  eyes
Wherein I read the fruit of kindly
  service?
How have the burdens of the world been
  lighten'd?
What span of life to me has been allotted
I know not; and how much of these few
  days,
So long expected, have I lost already!
Delay no longer: do what honour bids,
And break the only tie—

Scene V

[Berenice, Titus.]
Berenice [coming from her apart-
  ment]. Nay, let me go.
Your counsel all is vain to keep me back;
And I must see him—
              Ah, my lord, you here!
Then it is true Titus abandons me!
And we must part! 'Tis he will have it
  so!
Titus. Spare, Madam, to o'erwhelm a
  hapless prince.

We must not melt each other's hearts
with woe.
I am consumed with cruel griefs enough
Without the added torture of those tears.
Recall that noble spirit which so oft
Has made me recognize the voice of duty.
Yet there is time. Reduce your love to
silence;
And, with an eye clear'd from the mists
of passion,
Regard that duty with unflinching
courage.
Strengthen this heart of mine against
yourself,
Help me to nerve its weakness, if I can;
To keep back tears that will not cease to
rise;
Or, if we cannot stanch those tender
springs,
Let dignity at least support our woes.
So that the whole world without blame
may mark
When weeps an Emperor and when weeps
a Queen.
For, after all, my Princess, we must part.
BERENICE. Ah, cruel Titus, you repent
too late.
What have you done? You made me
think you loved me,
Accustom'd me to see you with delight,
Till but for that I lived. You knew your
laws
When first you brought me to such fond
confession,
Why did you let my love grow to this
height?
Why said you not: "Poor Princess, fix
your heart
Elsewhere, nor let deceitful hopes ensnare
it;
Give it to one free to accept the gift?"
You took it gladly, will you now reject
it
With cruel scorn, when to your own it
clings?
How oft did all the world conspire
against us!
Still there was time, you should have
left me then.
A thousand reasons might have soothed
my woe;

I might have blamed your father for my
death,
The senate, and the people, all the empire,
The whole world, rather than a hand so
dear.
Their enmity, so long declared against
me,
Had long prepared me to expect misfor-
tune.
I did not look, Sir, for this cruel blow
To fall when hope seem'd crown'd with
happiness,
Now, when your love can do whate'er it
wishes,
When Rome is silent, and your father
dead,
When all the world bends humbly at your
knees,
When there is nothing left to fear but
you.
TITUS. Yes, it is I who wreak my own
destruction!
Till now I lived the victim of delusion,
My heart refused to look into the future,
To think that we might one day have to
part.
To eager wishes nothing seems too hard,
And blinded hope grasps the impossible.
Haply I thought to die before your eyes,
And so forestall more cruel separation.
All opposition made my flame burn
brighter;
Rome and the empire spoke, but glory's
voice
Not yet had to my heart appeal'd in
tones
Like those with which it strikes an Em-
peror's ears.
I know what torments wait on this re-
solve,
I feel my heart ready to take its flight,
I cannot any longer live without you.
Come life or death, my duty is to reign.
BERENICE. Be cruel, then, and reign, a
slave to glory!
I'm ready to submit. Yes, I expected,
For trusting you, to hear those lips, that
swore
A thousand vows of everlasting love,
Confess before mine eyes that they were
faithless.

And banish me for ever from your presence.
I wish'd to hear that sentence from yourself!
But I will hear no more. Farewell for ever—
For ever! Ah, my lord, think how those words,
Those cruel words, dismay a heart that loves!
A year, a month will be to us an age
Of suff'ring, when the wide sea rolls between us,
And each fresh sun that dawns shall sink in darkness
Without presenting to the eyes of Titus
His Berenice, he unseen by her
The livelong day. But how am I deceived!
No sorrow feels he at the thought of absence,
He will not count the days when I am gone,
So long to me, they'll seem too short for him!

TITUS.   They'll not be many I shall have to count:
I hope ere long the tidings of my death
Will bring assurance that I loved you truly.
Then you will own that Titus could not live—

BERENICE. Ah, my dear lord, why part if that be so?
I speak not now to you of happy marriage.
Has Rome condemn'd me never more to see you?
Why grudge to me the selfsame air you breathe?

TITUS.   I can't resist you, Madam. Stay, I yield;
But not without a sense of mine own weakness;
Ceaseless must be the conflict and the fears,
Ceaseless the watch to keep my steps from you,
Whose charms will ever like a magnet draw me.
Ay, at this very instant, love distracts me
From memory of all things but itself.

BERENICE. Well, well, my lord, what ill can come of it?
Where see you any sign of Rome's displeasure?

TITUS. Who knows how they will look on this offence?
If they complain, if cries succeed to murmurs,
Must I shed blood to justify my choice?
If they in silence let me break their laws,
To what do you expose me? I must purchase
Their patience at the price of base compliance
With whatsoever else they dare to ask me;
Too weak t' inforce the laws I cannot keep.

BERENICE. You count as nothing Berenice's tears!

TITUS. I count them nothing! Heavens! What injustice!

BERENICE. Why then, for unjust laws that you can change,
O'erwhelm yourself in ceaseless miseries?
Have you no rights, my lord, as well as Rome?
Why should you hold her interests more sacred
Than ours? Come, tell me.

TITUS.   How you rend my heart!

BERENICE. You are the Emperor, and yet you weep!

TITUS. Yes, Madam, it is true, with sighs and tears
I am unnerved. But when the throne I mounted
Rome made me swear to vindicate her laws,
And I must keep them. More than once already
Her rulers have been call'd on to display
Their constancy in trial. From her birth
Those whom she honour'd readily obey'd her:
See Regulus who, faithful unto death,
Return'd to Carthage to be slain with tortures,
Torquatus dooming his victorious offspring,
Brutus with tearless eyes seeing his sons

Slain by his orders 'neath the lictor's axe.
Hard lot was theirs! But patriotic duty
Has ever won the victory with Romans.
I know in leaving you unhappy Titus
Attempts what throws their virtues in
the shade,
A sacrifice surpassing any other's:
But think you, after all, I am unworthy
To leave posterity a high example
Which those who follow will be task'd to
equal?
BERENICE. No! To your cruel heart I
deem it easy;
Worthy are you to rob me of my life.
The veil is torn aside, I read your heart.
I will not ask you more to let me stay,—
Me, who had willingly endured the shame
Of ridicule and scorn from those who
hate me.
I wish'd to drive you to this harsh re-
fusal.
'Tis done, and soon you'll have no more
to fear me.
Think not that I shall vent my wrongs
in fury,
Or call on Heav'n to punish perjury:
No, if a wretch's tears still move the gods,
I pray them to forget the pangs I suffer.
If, ere I die, victim of your injustice,
I cherish any wish to leave behind me
Avengers of poor Berenice's death,
I need but seek them in your cruel heart;
Remorse will dwell there, all my love re-
calling,
Paint my past kindness, and my present
anguish,
Show you my blood staining your royal
palace,
And haunt you with abiding memories:
I have made every effort to dissuade you,
'Tis vain: to your own heart I trust for
vengeance.
Farewell.

SCENE VI

[TITUS, PAULINUS.]
PAULINUS. What seem'd her purpose
when she left you?
Is she disposed, my lord, to go away?

TITUS. I am undone, Paulinus. She is
bent
On self-destruction. How should I sur-
vive it?
Haste, let us follow her!
PAULINUS. Did you not order,
Just now, that all her movements should
be watch'd?
Her women are not backward in their
duty,
And they will turn her from these gloomy
thoughts.
Fear nothing. This is her last throw, my
lord;
With perseverance victory is yours.
I know you could not hear her without
pity,
I was myself affected at the sight.
But take a wider and more distant
view,
Think how a moment's pain will lead to
glory,
With what applause the universe will
ring,
Rank'd in the future—
TITUS. No, I am a monster.
I hate myself. Nero, by all detested,
Ne'er reach'd a depth of cruelty like
this.
I will not let poor Berenice die.
Come, let us go, and Rome say what she
will.
PAULINUS. My lord!
TITUS. I know not what I say,
Paulinus;
Excess of sorrow overpow'rs my senses.
PAULINUS. Soil not the current of your
pure renown:
The news, already spread, of your fare-
well
Makes Rome exchange her sighs for shouts
of triumph;
In all her temples fumes of incense rise
For you, your virtues to the skies are
lauded,
And everywhere your statues crown'd
with bays.
TITUS. Ah, Rome! Ah, Berenice! Woe
is me,
That I should be an Emperor, and a
lover!

SCENE VII

[TITUS, ANTIOCHUS, PAULINUS, ARSACES.]
  ANTIOCHUS. What have you done, my
    lord? The lovely Queen
Lies in Phœnice's arms, death hovering
  o'er her:
Deaf to our tears, to counsel, and to
  reason,
She cries aloud for daggers or for poison.
You, you alone can tear that longing from
  her—
For when they breathe your name her
  life comes back;
Her eyes are ever turn'd to your apart-
  ments,
As tho' they look'd to see you every mo-
  ment.
The sight is more than I can bear, it
  kills me.
Go, show yourself to her. Why tarry
  longer?
Save to the world such virtue and such
  beauty,
Or waive all title to humanity.
Speak but one word.
    TITUS.   Alas! What can I say?
I scarcely know if I'm alive or dead.

SCENE VIII

[TITUS, ANTIOCHUS, PAULINUS, ARSACES,
        RUTILUS.]
  RUTILUS. My lord, the senate, consuls,
    all the tribunes
Seek audience of you in the name of
  Rome:
With them a multitude, full of impatience,
Throng your apartments, and await your
  presence.
  TITUS. Great gods, ye thus would re-
    assure my heart,
Distracted as ye see till like to break!
  PAULINUS. Come, Sire, and let us pass
    to the next chamber.
There see the senate.
  ANTIOCHUS. Haste, Sir, to the Queen!
  PAULINUS. Nay, treat them not with
    such indignity,
Nor trample on the majesty of Rome,
Whose envoys—

  TITUS. 'Tis enough. Yes, I will see
    them.   [To ANTIOCHUS.]
Prince, 'tis a duty that I cannot shun.
Go to the Queen. I hope, on my return,
She will no longer need to doubt my love.

ACT V

SCENE I

  ARSACES. Where shall I find this Prince
    of peerless faith?
May Heav'n conduct my steps, and aid
  my zeal:
Grant me this moment to announce to
  him
A happiness which he has ceased to hope
  for!

SCENE II

    [ANTIOCHUS, ARSACES.]
  ARSACES. Ah! What good fortune
    sends you hither, Sire?
  ANTIOCHUS. If my return can bring
    you any joy,
It is to my despair your thanks are due.
  ARSACES. My lord, the Queen goes
    hence.
  ANTIOCHUS. She goes!
  ARSACES.   To-night.
Her orders have been giv'n. She is of-
  fended
That Titus leaves her to her tears so
  long.
Her passion has cool'd down to proud
  displeasure;
Rome and the Emp'ror she alike re-
  nounces,
And wishes to be gone ere Rome can learn
Her trouble, and rejoice to see her flight.
She writes to Cæsar.
  ANTIOCHUS. Heavens! Who'd have
    thought it?
And Titus?
  ARSACES. Has not met her eyes again.
The multitude in transport press around
  him,
Shouting his praises and the names of
  honour

The senate have conferr'd, and these loud
  plaudits,
These titles, and these tokens of respect
To Titus seem so many binding pledges,
Links in a chain to fix his wavering will,
Despite his sighs and Berenice's tears.
I think he will not see her more. All's
  over.
ANTIOCHUS. I feel fresh hope; I own
  it, Arsaces.
But cruel Fate has ofttimes play'd me
  false,
And mock'd me with such bitter disap-
  pointments,
That 'tis with fear and trembling that I
  hear you:
Evil forebodings mingle with my joy,
And make me dread the turn of Fortune's
  wheel.
But who is this? Titus is coming hither!
With what intent?

SCENE III

[TITUS, ANTIOCHUS, ARSACES.]
TITUS [to his Attendants]. Stay, let
  none follow me. [To ANTIOCHUS.]
I come at last, Prince, to redeem my
  promise.
The Queen's distress engrosses all my
  thoughts,
Her tears and yours have pierced me to
  the heart;
I come to calm sorrows than mine less
  cruel.
Come, Prince; I would that you yourself
  should see
For the last time if I love Berenice.

SCENE IV

[ANTIOCHUS, ARSACES.]
ANTIOCHUS. Thus ends the hope, then,
  that you came to offer!
You see the triumph that awaited me!
Justly incensed was Berenice leaving,
For Titus had refused to see her more!
Great gods! What have I done, that thus
  misfortune

Is destined to pursue me all my life?
My days are pass'd in constant quick
  transition
From fear to hope, from hope to wild
  despair,
Yet still I breathe! O Berenice! Titus!
Ah, cruel gods! ye shall no longer mock
  me.

SCENE V

[TITUS, BERENICE, PHŒNICE.]
BERENICE. Nay, I'll hear nothing. I am
  quite resolved:
I mean to go. Why show yourself be-
  fore me?
Why come you to embitter hopeless sor-
  row?
Are you not yet content? No more I'll
  see you.
TITUS. Pray hear me.
BERENICE.   No, the time is past.
TITUS.   Dear Madam,
One word.
BERENICE. Not one.
TITUS.   Into what grief she casts
  me!
Whence comes, my Princess, this so sud-
  den change?
BERENICE. You said you wish'd me to
  depart to-morrow;
I am determined to depart this moment;
The die is cast; I go.
TITUS.   Stay.
BERENICE.   Why, forsooth?
To hear myself insulted everywhere,
My trouble made the theme of every
  tongue?
Can you not hear their cries of cruel joy,
While I am drown'd in tears of lonely
  sorrow?
What have I done to make myself so
  hated?
No crime I know save loving you too
  much.
TITUS.   Why heed the malice of a
  senseless mob?
BERENICE. Nought see I here but sights
  that wound mine eyes.
This chamber furnish'd by your thought-
  ful care,

These walls so long the witness of my
  love,
All seem'd to pledge that yours would last
  for ever;
These garlands, where our names close
  link'd together
Meet my sad gaze whene'er I look around,
Are more than I can bear, smiling im-
  postors!
Phœnice, let us go.
  TITUS.   Heav'ns! How unjust!
  BERENICE. Return, return to that au-
  gust assembly
Which welcomes with applause your
  cruelty.
Say, did their praises gratify your ear?
Was your fierce thirst for glory fully
  slaked?
Confess that you have promised to forget
  me.
But that would not suffice to seal re-
  pentance:
Have you not sworn an everlasting
  hatred?
  TITUS. Nay, I have promised nothing.
  Hatred, say you?
How can I e'er forget my Berenice?
Gods! What a bitter moment thus to feel
Crush'd 'neath the weight of her unjust
  suspicion!
Ah, you should know me better. Count
  the hours,
The days I spent, these five years past, in
  telling
My heart's desires with passion that out-
  ran
Your own, and fervent sighs when words
  were dumb.
This day surpasses all. Ne'er, I protest,
Were you beloved with so much tender-
  ness,
Ay, and for ever—
  BERENICE. You maintain you love me;
Yet I'm departing, and by your command!
Find you such charms, my lord, in my
  despair?
Fear you that these mine eyes shed tears
  too few?
What boots it that your heart returns so
  late?
For pity's sake, at least show me less love,

Recall not an idea too fondly cherish'd;
Let me go hence, persuaded that, already
Banish'd in secret from your soul, I leave
A wretch who loses me without regret.
              [TITUS *reads a letter.*]
The letter you have seized I had just
  written.
There you may read all that of you I ask,
And of your love: read it, and let me go.
  TITUS. Nay, that you never shall with
  my consent.
What! this departure then was but a
  scheme
Veiling more cruel purpose! You would
  die!
So should there but remain sad memories
Of all I love.
          Go, call Antiochus.
      [BERENICE *sinks upon a seat.*]

SCENE VI

          [TITUS, BERENICE.]
  TITUS. Madam, a true confession I
  must make.
Whilst my mind brooded on that dreaded
  moment
When, in obedience to stern laws of duty,
I should be forced to see your face no
  longer;
When I foresaw that sad farewell ap-
  proaching,
Contending fears in me, from your rebuke
Of tearful eyes, I arm'd my soul to suffer
All that affliction most intense could bring
  me:
But I must own that e'en my worst fore-
  bodings
Fell short, far short of the reality;
I thought my courage was less prone to
  yield,
And feel with shame how feeble was its
  strength.
Before mine eyes I saw all Rome as-
  sembled;
The senate spoke, but my distracted soul
Heard without comprehending, and in
  silence,
As cold as ice, I met their warmest
  greetings.

Rome knows not yet what destiny awaits you;
I scarcely know myself if at this moment
I am an Emperor, or e'en a Roman.
Uncertain of my purpose, I am come,
Drawn hither by my love, where, peradventure,
Self-consciousness may to my soul return.
What have I found? Death pictured in your eyes.
In search of death I see you mean to leave me.
At this sad prospect I'm o'erwhelm'd with anguish,
The devastating flood has reach'd its height,
The worst that man can feel 'tis mine to suffer.
Nay, not the worst; I see a way of rescue.
Yet hope not for a refuge from these terrors
In happy wedlock that may dry these tears:
Tho' sore the straits to which I am reduced,
Glory asserts inexorable claims,
And evermore reminds me that our marriage
Is incompatible with sovereignty,
That, after all the fame I sought and won,
'Tis less than ever meet that I should wed you,
That I, dear Madam, should declare me ready
For you the throne of empire to resign,
To follow you and, going, hug my chains,
To breathe forth amorous sighs in realms remote.
You would yourself blush at such feeble conduct,
And see with shame an Emperor so unworthy
As humbly to attach himself to you,
Forfeit his crown, and make himself a mark
For all men's scorn. To 'scape my present torments
There is, you know it well, a nobler way;
Many a hero, many a son of Rome
Has shown me, Madam, how to tread that path;

When constant woes have wearied out their patience,
Fate's ceaseless persecution has to them
Seem'd like a se ret order from on high
No longer to resist. If still your tears
Reproach me when I look on Berenice,
If I behold you still resolved to die,
If I must ever tremble for your life,
Unless your solemn oath this fear removes,
You will have other tears to shed ere long.
My present strait prompts me to desperate deeds,
Nor can I answer for it that my hand
May not with blood seal our last sad farewell.

BERENICE. Alas!
TITUS. What is there that I dare not do!
See how my fate rests wholly in your hands;
Ponder it well, and if I still am dear—

SCENE VII

[TITUS, BERENICE, ANTIOCHUS.]
TITUS. You're welcome, Prince, I sent to bid you come.
Be witness of the weakness of my heart;
Judge whether with too little tenderness
It loves.
ANTIOCHUS. I doubt it not; I know you both;
Know in your turn what misery is mine.
You, Sire, have honour'd me with your regard,
And I can here assure you without falsehood,
I have competed with your dearest friends,
And shed my blood, to hold the foremos t place.
The Queen and you, my lord, have both confided
Your mutual love to me, against my will:
She hears me and can say if I speak truth,
She never saw me eager in your praises,
Well I responded to your confidence.
You owe me thanks, ay, more than you suppose,

For little you imagine at this moment
That such a faithful friend was yet your
    rival.
TITUS. My rival!
ANTIOCHUS. Listen to my explanation.
This heart has ever worshipp'd Berenice;
A hundred times I struggled to forget
    her,
In vain, but not in vain to make my love
Seem dead. When I was flatter'd with
    the signs
Of change in you, new hopes within me
    rose.
But Berenice's tears those hopes have
    quench'd:
With weeping eyes she begg'd that she
    might see you,
And, as you know, I summon'd you my-
    self.
You have return'd to her beloved and
    loving,
The breach between you heal'd, I cannot
    doubt it.
In final consultation with my heart,
I have resolved to test its utmost courage,
And Reason has resumed her sovereign
    sway.
I never loved her more than at this mo-
    ment,
But one strong effort may effect my free-
    dom;
To death I fly for succour, which alone
Can burst my bonds. This is what I de-
    sired
To tell you. I recall'd him to you,
    Madam,
Nor do I now repent what I have done.
May Heav'n pour forth its blessings in
    rich store
On all your future years, link'd each to
    other
By happiness! Or, if its wrath still
    threatens
A life so precious, I implore the gods
To turn it all on this devoted head,
And consummate my sacrifice for you.
    BERENICE [rising]. Cease, Prince,
    cease. This generosity
Is more than I can bear and drives me
    mad!
Where'er I look, whether on you or him,

I meet the very image of despair,
Eyes full of tears, and lips that utter
    nought
But words of horror and impending blood-
    shed.   [To TITUS.]
My lord, you know my heart, and I am
    bold
To say I never sigh'd to be an Empress.
Rome's grandeur and the purple of her
    Cæsars
Could not attract the gaze of Berenice.
My love was all for you, your love alone
My heart's desire; and, when I thought
    to-day
That I had lost it, 'twas with wild alarm.
I know my error now, you never ceased
To love me. I have seen your deep emo-
    tion,
Your heart is troubled more than I de-
    serve.
Let not your love eclipse "the World's
    Delight,"
Nor rob her of yourself just at the time
When the first taste of your transcendent
    virtues
Allures her hopes. For five years I have
    wish'd
To prove to you how faithful is my love;
Now must a crowning effort seal devotion,
Your will shall be obey'd and I will live.
Reign, noble Cæsar! Berenice bids
Adieu to you for ever. [To ANTIOCHUS.]
                    Prince, this parting
May well convince you that no other
    passion
(Tho' far I go from Rome) can e'er sup-
    plant
My love for Titus. Do as we have done,
In generous self-conquest vie with us
Who tear asunder our united hearts.
Live, and, if sigh you must, let it be far
From Berenice. Fare you well.
                    We three
Shall offer to the world the saddest in-
    stance
In History's page of fond affections
    blighted.
My bark is ready. Do not follow me.
                    [To TITUS.]
For the last time, farewell, my lord.
    ANTIOCHUS. Alas!

THE CIT TURNED GENTLEMAN

By JEAN BAPTISTE POQUELIN, CALLED MOLIÈRE*

Produced at Paris, 1670.

CHARACTERS

MR. JORDAN, *the Cit*
MRS. JORDAN
LUCILIA, *daughter to* MR. JORDAN
CLEONTES, *in love with* LUCILIA
DORIMÈNE, *a marchioness*
DORANTES, *a count,* DORIMÈNE'S *lover*
NICOLA, *a maid-servant to* MR. JORDAN
COVIEL, *servant to* CLEONTES
MUSIC-MASTER
MUSIC-MASTER'S SCHOLAR
DANCING-MASTER
FENCING-MASTER
PHILOSOPHY-MASTER
MASTER-TAILOR
JOURNEYMAN-TAILOR
TWO LACKEYS

ACT I

SCENE I

[MUSIC-MASTER, a SCHOLAR to the MUSIC-MASTER *(composing at a table in the middle of the stage)*, a WOMAN SINGER, and TWO MEN SINGERS, a DANCING-MASTER *and* DANCERS.]

MUSIC-MASTER [*to the musicians*]. Here, step into this hall, and sit there till he comes.

DANCING-MASTER [*to the dancers*]. And you too, on this side.

MUSIC-MASTER [*to his scholar*]. Is it done?

SCHOLAR. Yes.

MUSIC-MASTER. Let's see. . . . 'Tis mighty well.

DANCING-MASTER. Is it anything new?

MUSIC-MASTER. Yes, 'tis an air for a serenade, which I set him to compose here, while we wait till our gentleman's awake.

* Translation reprinted from the first complete English translation of Molière's works, carried out in 1739, by the two playwrights, H. Baker and J. Miller.

DANCING-MASTER. May one see what it is?

MUSIC-MASTER. You will hear it, with the dialogue, when he comes. He won't be long.

DANCING-MASTER. We have no want of business, either of us, at present.

MUSIC-MASTER. 'Tis true. We have found a man here, just such a one as we both of us want. This same Mr. Jordan is a sweet income, with his visions of nobility and gallantry, which he has got into his noddle; and it would be well for your capers and my crotchets, were all the world like him.

DANCING-MASTER. Not altogether so well; I wish, for his sake, that he were better skilled than he is in the things we give him.

MUSIC-MASTER. It is true he understands 'em ill, but he pays for 'em well. And that's what our art has more need of at present than of anything else.

DANCING-MASTER. For my part, I own it to you, I regale a little upon glory. I am sensible of applause, and think it a very grievous punishment in the liberal arts, to display one's self to fools, and to expose our compositions to the barbarous judgment of the stupid. Talk no more of it, there is a pleasure in working for persons, who are capable of relishing the delicacies of an art; who know how to give a kind reception to the beauties of a work, and, by titillating approbation, regale you for your labour. Yes, the most agreeable recompense one can receive for the things one does, is to see them understood; to see 'em caressed with an applause that does you honour. There's nothing, in my opinion, which pays us better than this, for all our fatigues. And the praises of connoisseurs give an exquisite delight.

MUSIC-MASTER. I grant it, and I relish them as well as you. There is nothing certainly that tickles more than the applause you speak of; but one cannot live upon this incense. Sheer praises won't make a man easy. There must be something solid mixed withal, and the best method of praising is to praise with the open hand. This indeed is one whose understanding is very shallow, who speaks of everything awry, and cross of the grain, and never applauds but in contradiction to sense. But his money sets his judgment right. He has discernment in his purse. His praises are current coin; and this ignorant cit is more worth to us, as you see, than that grand witty lord who introduced us here.

DANCING-MASTER. There's something of truth in what you say; but I find you lean a little too much towards the pelf. And mere interest is something so base, that an honest man should never discover an attachment to it.

MUSIC-MASTER. For all that, you decently receive the money our spark gives you.

DANCING-MASTER. Certainly; but I don't place all my happiness in that: and I wish that, with his fortune, he had also some good taste of things.

MUSIC-MASTER. I wish the same; 'tis what we both labour at as much as we can. But however he gives us the opportunity of making ourselves known in the world; and he'll pay for others, what others praise for him.

DANCING-MASTER. Here he comes.

SCENE II

[MR. JORDAN (in a nightgown and cap), MUSIC-MASTER, DANCING-MASTER, SCHOLAR to the MUSIC-MASTER, VIOLINS, MUSICIANS, DANCERS, two LACKEYS.]

MR. JORDAN. Well, gentlemen? What have you there? will you let me see your little drollery?

DANCING-MASTER. How? what little drollery?

MR. JORDAN. Why the—how do you call that thing? your prologue, or dialogue of songs and dancing.

DANCING-MASTER. Ha, ha!

MUSIC-MASTER. You see we are ready.

MR. JORDAN. I have made you wait a little; but 'tis because I am to be dressed out to-day like your people of quality; and my hosier has sent me a pair of silk-stockings, which I thought I should never have got on.

MUSIC-MASTER. We are here only to wait your leisure.

MR. JORDAN. I desire you'll both stay till they have brought me my clothes, that you may see me.

DANCING-MASTER. As you please.

MR. JORDAN. You shall see me most exactly equipped from head to foot.

MUSIC-MASTER. We don't doubt it.

MR. JORDAN. I have had this Indian thing made up for me.

DANCING-MASTER. 'Tis very handsome.

MR. JORDAN. My tailor tells me that people of quality go thus in a morning.

MUSIC-MASTER. It fits you to a miracle.

MR. JORDAN. Why, hoh! Fellow there! both my fellows!

FIRST LACKEY. Your pleasure, sir?

MR. JORDAN. Nothing: 'Tis only to try whether you hear me readily. [*To the* TWO MASTERS.] What say you of my liveries?

DANCING-MASTER. They are magnificent.

MR. JORDAN [*half-opens his gown and discovers a strait pair of breeches of scarlet velvet, and a green velvet jacket which he has on*]. Here again is a kind of dishabille to perform my exercises in a morning.

MUSIC-MASTER. 'Tis gallant.

MR. JORDAN. Lackey!

FIRST LACKEY. Sir?

MR. JORDAN. T'other lackey!

SECOND LACKEY. Sir?

MR. JORDAN [*taking off his gown*]. Hold my gown. [*To the* MUSIC *and* DANCING-MASTERS.] Do you like me so?

DANCING-MASTER. Mighty well; nothing can be better.

MR. JORDAN. Now for your affair a little.

MUSIC-MASTER. I should be glad first to let you hear an air [*Pointing to his* SCHOLAR.] he has just composed for the serenade, which you gave me orders about. He is one of my scholars, who has an ad-

mirable talent for these sort of things.

MR. JORDAN. Yes; but that should not have been put to a scholar to do; you were not too good for that business yourself.

MUSIC-MASTER. You must not let the name of scholar impose upon you, sir. These sort of scholars know as much as the greatest masters, and the air is as good as can be made. Hear it only.

MR. JORDAN [*to his* SERVANTS]. Give me my gown that I may hear the better. —Stay, I believe I shall be better without the gown.—No, give it me again, it will do better.

MUSICIAN. I languish night and day, nor sleeps my pain,
Since those fair eyes imposed the rigorous chain;
But tell me, Iris, what dire fate attends
Your enemies, if thus you treat your friends?

MR. JORDAN. This song seems to me a little upon the dismal; it inclines one to sleep; I should be glad you could enliven it a little here and there.

MUSIC-MASTER. 'Tis necessary, sir, that the air should be suited to the words.

MR. JORDAN. I was taught one perfectly pretty some time ago. Stay—um—how is it?

DANCING-MASTER. In good troth, I don't know.

MR. JORDAN. There's lamb in it.

DANCING-MASTER. Lamb?

MR. JORDAN. Yes—Hoh. [*He sings.*]

I thought my dear Namby
As gentle as fair-o;
I thought my dear Namby
As mild as a lamb-y.
Oh dear, oh dear, oh dear-o!
For now the sad scold, is a thousand times told,
More fierce than a tiger or bear-o.

Isn't it pretty?

MUSIC-MASTER. The prettiest in the world.

DANCING-MASTER. And you sing it well.

MR. JORDAN. Yet I never learnt music.

MUSIC-MASTER. You ought to learn it, sir, as you do dancing. They are two arts which have a strict connection one with the other.

DANCING-MASTER. And which open the human mind to see the beauty of things.

MR. JORDAN. What, do people of quality learn music too?

MUSIC-MASTER. Yes, sir.

MR. JORDAN. I'll learn it then. But I don't know how I shall find time. For, besides the fencing-master who teaches me, I have also got me a philosophy-master, who is to begin this morning.

MUSIC-MASTER. Philosophy is something; but music, sir, music—

DANCING-MASTER. Music and dancing —Music and dancing, that is all that's necessary.

MUSIC-MASTER. There's nothing so profitable in a state, as music.

DANCING-MASTER. There's nothing so necessary for men, as dancing.

MUSIC-MASTER. A state cannot subsist without music.

DANCING-MASTER. Without dancing, a man can do nothing.

MUSIC-MASTER. All the disorders, all the wars one sees in the world, happen only from not learning music.

DANCING-MASTER. All the disasters of mankind, all the fatal misfortunes that histories are replete with, the blunders of politicians, the miscarriages of great commanders, all this comes from want of skill in dancing.

MR. JORDAN. How so?

MUSIC-MASTER. Does not war proceed from want of concord amongst men?

MR. JORDAN. That's true.

MUSIC-MASTER. And if all men learnt music, would not that be a means of keeping them better in tune, and of seeing universal peace in the world?

MR. JORDAN. You're in the right.

DANCING-MASTER. When a man has been guilty of a defect in his conduct, be it in the affairs of his family, or in the government of the state, or in the command of an army; don't we always say,

such a one has made a false step in such an affair?

MR. JORDAN. Yes, we say so.

DANCING-MASTER. And can making a false step proceed from anything but not knowing how to dance?

MR. JORDAN. 'Tis true, and you are both in the right.

DANCING-MASTER. This is to let you see the excellence and advantage of dancing and music.

MR. JORDAN. I now comprehend it.

MUSIC-MASTER. Will you see each of our compositions.

MR. JORDAN. Yes.

MUSIC-MASTER. I have told you already that this is a slight essay which I formerly made upon the different passions that may be expressed by music.

MR. JORDAN. Very well.

MUSIC-MASTER [to the MUSICIANS]. Here, come forward. [To MR. JORDAN.] You are to imagine with yourself that they are dressed like shepherds.

MR. JORDAN. Why always shepherds? One sees nothing but such stuff everywhere.

MUSIC-MASTER. When we are to introduce persons, as speaking in music, 'tis necessary to probability that we give into the pastoral way. Singing has always been appropriated to shepherds; and it is by no means natural in dialogue, that princes or citizens should sing their passions.

MR. JORDAN. Be it so, be it so. Let's see.

[Dialogue in music between a WOMAN and two MEN.]

WOMAN. The heart that must tyrannic love obey,
A thousand fears and cares oppress.
Sweet are those sighs and languishments they say;
Say what they will for me,
Nought is so sweet as liberty.

FIRST MAN. Nothing so sweet as love's soft fire,
Which can two glowing hearts inspire,
With the same life, the same desire.

The loveless swain no happiness can prove.
From life take soothing love,
All pleasure you remove.
SECOND MAN. Sweet were the wanton archer's sway,
Would all with constancy obey:
But, cruel fate!
No nymph is true:
The faithless sex more worthy of our hate,
To love should bid eternally adieu.
FIRST MAN. Pleasing heat!
WOMAN. Freedom blest!
SECOND MAN. Fair deceit!
FIRST MAN. O how I love thee!
WOMAN. How I approve thee!
SECOND MAN. I detest!
FIRST MAN. Against love's ardour quit this mortal hate.
WOMAN. Shepherd, myself I bind here, To show a faithful mate.
SECOND MAN. Alas! but where to find her?
WOMAN. Our glory to retrieve, My heart I here bestow.
SECOND MAN. But, nymph, can I believe
That heart no change will know?
WOMAN. Let experience decide, Who loves best of the two.
SECOND MAN. And the perjured side May vengeance pursue.
ALL THREE. Then let us kindle soft desire,
Let us fan the amorous fire.
Ah! how sweet it is to love,
When hearts united constant prove!
MR. JORDAN. Is this all?
MUSIC-MASTER. Yes.
MR. JORDAN. I find 'tis very concise, and there are some little sayings in it pretty enough.
DANCING-MASTER. You have here, for my composition, a little essay of the finest movements, and the most beautiful attitudes with which a dance can possibly be varied.
MR. JORDAN. Are they shepherds too?
DANCING-MASTER. They're what you please. [To the DANCERS.] Hola!

ACT II

SCENE I

[MR. JORDAN, MUSIC-MASTER, DANCING-MASTER.]
MR. JORDAN. This is none of your stupid things, and these same fellows flutter it away bravely.
MUSIC-MASTER. When the dance is mixed with the music, it will have a greater effect still, and you will see something gallant in the little entertainment we have prepared for you.
MR. JORDAN. That's however for by and by; and the person for whom I have ordered all this, is to do me the honour of dining with me here.
DANCING-MASTER. Everything's ready.
MUSIC-MASTER. But in short, sir, this is not enough, 'tis necessary such a person as you, who live great, and have an inclination to things that are handsome, should have a concert of music at your house every Wednesday, or every Thursday.
MR. JORDAN. Why so? have people of quality?
MUSIC-MASTER. Yes, sir.
MR. JORDAN. I'll have one then. Will it be fine?
MUSIC-MASTER. Certainly. You must have three voices, a treble, a counter-tenor, and bass, which must be accompanied with a bass-viol, a theorbo-lute, and a harpsicord for the thorough-bass, with two violins to play the symphonies.
MR. JORDAN. You must add also a trumpet-marine. The trumpet-marine is an instrument that pleases me, and is very harmonious.
MUSIC-MASTER. Leave us to manage matters.
MR. JORDAN. However don't forget by and by to send the musicians to sing at table.
MUSIC-MASTER. You shall have everything you should have.
MR. JORDAN. But above all, let the entertainment be fine.
MUSIC-MASTER. You will be pleased

with it. and amongst other things, with certain minutes, you will find in it.

MR. JORDAN. Ay, the minutes are my dance; and I have a mind you should see me dance 'em. Come, master.

DANCING-MASTER. Your hat, sir, if you please. [MR. JORDAN *takes off his foot-boy's hat, and puts it on over his own nightcap; upon which his master takes him by the hand, and makes him dance to a minuet-air which he sings.*] Tol, lol, lol, lol, lol, lol, Tol, lol, lol, twice; Tol, lol, lol; tol, lol. In time, if you please, Tol, lol, the right leg. Tol, lol, lol. Don't shake your shoulders so much. Tol, lol, lol, lol, lol. Why, your arms are out of joint. Tol, lol, lol, lol, lol. Hold up your head. Turn out your toes. Tol, lol, lol. Your body erect.

MR. JORDAN. Heh?

MUSIC-MASTER. Admirably well performed.

MR. JORDAN. Now I think of it, teach me how I must bow to salute a marchioness; I shall have occasion for it by and by.

DANCING-MASTER. How you must bow to salute a marchioness?

MR. JORDAN. Yes, a marchioness whose name is Dorimène.

DANCING-MASTER. Give me your hand.

MR. JORDAN. No. You need only to do it, I shall remember it easily.

DANCING-MASTER. If you would salute her with a great deal of respect, you must first of all make a bow and fall back, then advancing towards her, bow thrice, and at the last bow down to her very knees.

MR. JORDAN. Do it a little. [*After the* DANCING-MASTER *has made three bows.*] Right.

SCENE II

[MR. JORDAN, MUSIC-MASTER, DANCING-MASTER, LACKEY.]

LACKEY. Sir, your fencing-master is here.

MR. JORDAN. Bid him come in that he may give me a lesson. [*To the* MUSIC- *and* DANCING-MASTERS.] I'd have you stay and see me perform.

SCENE III

[MR. JORDAN, A FENCING-MASTER, MUSIC-MASTER, DANCING-MASTER, LACKEY (*holding two foils*).]

FENCING-MASTER [*taking the two foils out of the* LACKEY'S *hand, and giving one to* MR. JORDAN]. Come, sir, your salute. Your body straight. A little bearing upon the left thigh. Your legs not so much a straddle. Your feet both on a line. Your wrist opposite to your hip. The point of your sword over-against your shoulder. Your arm not quite so much extended. Your left hand on a level with your eye. Your left shoulder more square. Hold up your head. Your look bold. Advance. Your body steady. Beat carte, and push carte. One, two. Recover. Again with it, your foot firm. One, two. Leap back. When you make a pass, sir, 'tis necessary your sword should disengage first, and your body make as small a mark as possible. One, two. Come, beat tierce, and push the same. Advance. Your body firm. Advance. Quit after that manner. One, two. Recover. Repeat the same. One, two. Leap back. Parry, sir, parry. [*The* FENCING-MASTER *gives him two or three home-thrusts, crying, Parry.*]

MR. JORDAN. Ugh!

MUSIC-MASTER. You do wonders.

FENCING-MASTER. I have told you already; the whole secret of arms consists but in two things, in giving and not receiving. And as I showed you t'other day by demonstrative reason, it is impossible you should receive, if you know how to turn your adversary's sword from the line of your body; which depends only upon a small motion of your wrist, either inward, or outward.

MR. JORDAN. At that rate therefore, a man without any courage, is sure to kill his man, and not to be killed.

FENCING-MASTER. Certainly. Don't you see the demonstration of it?

MR. JORDAN. Yes.

FENCING-MASTER. By this one may see of what consideration such persons as we should be esteemed in a state, and how highly the science of arms excels all the other useless sciences, such as dancing, music, and——

DANCING-MASTER. Soft and fair, Mr. Sa, sa. Don't speak of dancing but with respect.

MUSIC-MASTER. Pray learn to treat the excellence of music in a handsomer manner.

FENCING-MASTER. You're merry fellows, to pretend to compare your sciences with mine.

MUSIC-MASTER. Do but see the importance of the creature!

DANCING-MASTER. The droll animal there, with his leathern stomacher!

FENCING-MASTER. My little master skipper, I shall make you skip as you should do. And you my little master scraper, I shall make you sing to some tune.

DANCING-MASTER. Mr. Tick-tack, I shall teach you your trade.

MR. JORDAN [to the DANCING-MASTER]. Are you bewitched to quarrel with him, who understands tierce and carte, who knows how to kill a man by demonstrative reason?

DANCING-MASTER. I laugh at his demonstrative reason, and his tierce and his carte.

MR. JORDAN [to the DANCING-MASTER]. Softly, I say.

FENCING-MASTER [to the DANCING-MASTER]. How? Master Impertinence!

MR. JORDAN. Nay, my dear fencing-master!

DANCING-MASTER [to the FENCING-MASTER]. How? You great dray-horse!

MR. JORDAN. Nay, my dancing-master.

FENCING-MASTER. If I lay my——

MR. JORDAN [to the FENCING-MASTER]. Gently.

DANCING-MASTER. If I lay my clutches on you——

MR. JORDAN. Easily.

FENCING-MASTER. I shall curry you with such an air——

MR. JORDAN [to the FENCING-MASTER]. For goodness' sake.

DANCING-MASTER. I shall drub you after such a manner——

MR. JORDAN [to the DANCING-MASTER]. I beseech you.

MUSIC-MASTER Let us teach him a little how to speak.

MR. JORDAN [to the MUSIC-MASTER]. Lack-a-day, be quiet.

SCENE IV

[PHILOSOPHY-MASTER, MR. JORDAN, MUSIC-MASTER, DANCING-MASTER, FENCING-MASTER, LACKEY.]

MR. JORDAN. Hola, Mr. Philosopher, you are come in the nick of time with your philosophy. Come, and make peace a little amongst these people here.

PHILOSOPHY-MASTER. What's to do? What's the matter, gentlemen?

MR. JORDAN. They have put themselves into such a passion about the preference of their professions, as to call names, and would come to blows.

PHILOSOPHY-MASTER. O fie, gentlemen, what need was there of all this fury? Have you not read the learned treatise upon anger, composed by Seneca. Is there anything more base and shameful than this passion, which makes a savage beast of a man? And should not reason be master of all our commotions?

DANCING-MASTER. How, sir? Why he has just now been abusing us both, in despising dancing which is my employment, and music which is his profession.

PHILOSOPHY-MASTER. A wise man is above all foul language that can be given him; and the grand answer one should make to all affronts, is moderation and patience.

FENCING-MASTER. They had both the assurance to compare their professions to mine.

PHILOSOPHY-MASTER. Should this disturb you? Men should not dispute about vainglory and rank; that which perfectly distinguishes one from another, is wisdom and virtue.

DANCING-MASTER. I maintained to him

that dancing was a science, to which one cannot do sufficient honour.

MUSIC-MASTER. And I, that music is one of those that all ages have revered.

FENCING-MASTER. And I maintained against 'em both, that the science of defence is the finest and most necessary of all sciences.

PHILOSOPHY-MASTER. And what becomes of philosophy then? You are all three very impertinent fellows, methinks, to speak with this arrogance before me; and impudently to give the name of science to things that one ought not to honour even with the name of art, that can't be comprised but under the name of a pitiful trade of gladiator, ballad-singer, and morris-dancer.

FENCING-MASTER. Out, ye dog of a philosopher.

MUSIC-MASTER. Hence, ye scoundrel of a pedant.

DANCING-MASTER. Begone, ye arrant pedagogue.

PHILOSOPHY-MASTER. How? Varlets as you are——
[*The* PHILOSOPHER *falls upon them, they all three lay him on.*]

MR. JORDAN. Mr. Philosopher!

PHILOSOPHY-MASTER. Infamous dogs! Rogues! Insolent curs!

MR. JORDAN. Mr. Philosopher!

FENCING-MASTER. Plague on the animal!

MR. JORDAN. Gentlemen!

PHILOSOPHY-MASTER. Impudent villains!

MR. JORDAN. Mr. Philosopher!

DANCING-MASTER. Deuce take the pack-saddled ass!

MR. JORDAN. Gentlemen!

PHILOSOPHY-MASTER. Profligate vermin!

MR. JORDAN. Mr. Philosopher!

MUSIC-MASTER. De'il take the impertinent puppy!

MR. JORDAN. Gentlemen!

PHILOSOPHY-MASTER. Knaves! Ragamuffins! Traitors! Impostors!

MR. JORDAN. Mr. Philosopher! Gen-tlemen! Mr. Philosopher! Gentlemen! Mr. Philosopher! [*They beat each other out.*]

SCENE V

[MR. JORDAN, LACKEY.]

MR. JORDAN. Nay, beat your hearts out if you will, I shall neither meddle nor make with you, I shan't spoil my gown to part you. I should be a great fool to thrust myself among them, and receive some blow that might do me a mischief.

SCENE VI

[PHILOSOPHY-MASTER, MR. JORDAN, LACKEYS.]

PHILOSOPHY-MASTER [*setting his band right*]. Now to our lesson.

MR. JORDAN. Ah! Sir, I'm sorry for the blows they have given you.

PHILOSOPHY-MASTER. 'Tis nothing at all. A philosopher knows how to receive things in a proper manner; and I'll compose a satire against 'em, in the manner of Juvenal, that shall cut 'em most gloriously. Let that pass. What have you a mind to learn?

MR. JORDAN. Everything I can, for I have all the desire in the world to be a scholar, and it vexes me that my father and mother had not made me study all the sciences, when I was young.

PHILOSOPHY-MASTER. 'Tis a very reasonable sentiment. *Nam, sine doctrinâ vita est quasi mortis imago.* You understand that, and are acquainted with Latin, without doubt?

MR. JORDAN. Yes; but act as if I were not acquainted with it. Explain me the meaning of that.

PHILOSOPHY-MASTER. The meaning of it is, that without learning, life is as it were an image of death.

MR. JORDAN. That same Latin's in the right.

PHILOSOPHY-MASTER. Have you not some principles, some rudiments of science?

MR. JORDAN. Oh! yes, I can read and write.

PHILOSOPHY-MASTER. Where would you please to have us begin? Would you have me teach you logic?

MR. JORDAN. What may that same logic be?

PHILOSOPHY-MASTER. It's that which teaches us the three operations of the mind.

MR. JORDAN. What are those three operations of the mind?

PHILOSOPHY-MASTER. The first, the second, and the third. The first is to conceive well. by means of universals. The second, to judge well, by means of categories. The third, to draw the conclusion right, by means of figures: Barbara, Celarent, Darii, Ferio, Baralipton, etc.

MR. JORDAN. These words are too crabbed. This logic does not suit me by any means. Let's learn something else that's prettier.

PHILOSOPHY-MASTER. Will you learn morality?

MR. JORDAN. Morality?

PHILOSOPHY-MASTER. Yes.

MR. JORDAN. What means morality?

PHILOSOPHY-MASTER. It treats of happiness; teaches men to moderate their passions, and——

MR. JORDAN. No, no more of that. I'm as choleric as the devil, and there's no morality holds me; I will have my belly full of passion, whenever I have a mind to it.

PHILOSOPHY-MASTER. Would you learn physics?

MR. JORDAN. What is it that physics treat of?

PHILOSOPHY-MASTER. Physics are what explain the principles of things natural, and the properties of bodies; which discourse of the nature of elements, of metals, of minerals, of stones, of plants, and animals, and teach us the cause of all the meteors; the rainbow, *ignes fatui*, comets, lightnings, thunder, thunderbolts, rain, snow, hail, winds, and whirlwinds.

MR. JORDAN. There's too much hurly-burly in this, too much confusion.

PHILOSOPHY-MASTER. What would you have me teach you then?

MR. JORDAN. Teach me orthography.

PHILOSOPHY-MASTER. With all my heart.

MR. JORDAN. Afterwards you may teach me the almanack, to know when there's a moon, and when not.

PHILOSOPHY-MASTER. Be it so. To pursue this thought of yours right, and treat this matter like a philosopher, we must begin, according to the order of things, with an exact knowledge of the nature of letters, and the different manner of pronouncing them. And on this head I am to tell you, that letters are divided into vowels, called vowels because they express the voice: and into consonants, so called because they sound with the vowels, and only mark the different articulations of the voice. There are five vowels or voices, A, E, I, O, U.

MR. JORDAN. I understand all that.

PHILOSOPHY-MASTER. The vowel A is formed by opening the mouth very wide, A.

MR. JORDAN. A, A. Yes.

PHILOSOPHY-MASTER. The vowel E is formed by drawing the under-jaw a little nearer to the upper, A, E.

MR. JORDAN. A, E. A, E. In troth it is. How pretty that is!

PHILOSOPHY-MASTER. And the vowel I, by bringing the jaws still nearer one to the other, and stretching the two corners of the mouth towards the ears, A, E, I.

MR. JORDAN. A, E, I, I, I, I. 'Tis true. Long live learning!

PHILOSOPHY-MASTER. The vowel O is formed by re-opening the jaws, and drawing the lips near at the two corners, the upper and the under, O.

MR. JORDAN. O, O. There's nothing more just, A, E, I, O, I, O. 'Tis admirable! I, O, I, O.

PHILOSOPHY-MASTER. The opening of the mouth makes exactly a little ring, which resembles an O.

MR. JORDAN. O, O, O. You're right, O.

How fine a thing it is but to know something!

PHILOSOPHY-MASTER. The vowel U is formed by bringing the teeth near together without entirely joining them, and pouting out both your lips, bringing them also near together without absolutely joining 'em, U.

MR. JORDAN. U, U. There's nothing more true, U.

PHILOSOPHY-MASTER. Your two lips pout out, as if you were making faces. Whence it comes that if you would do that to anybody, and make a jest of him, you need say nothing to him but U.

MR. JORDAN. U, U. It's true. Ah! why did not I study sooner, that I might have known all this!

PHILOSOPHY-MASTER. To-morrow we shall take a view of the other letters, which are the consonants.

MR. JORDAN. Is there anything as curious in them, as in these?

PHILOSOPHY-MASTER. Doubtless. The consonant D, for example, is pronounced by clapping the tip of your tongue above the upper teeth, DE.

MR. JORDAN. DE, DE. 'Tis so. Oh! charming things! charming things!

PHILOSOPHY-MASTER. The F, in leaning the upper teeth upon the lower lip, EF.

MR. JORDAN. EF, EF. 'Tis truth. Ah! father and mother o'mine, how do I owe you a grudge!

PHILOSOPHY-MASTER. And the R, in carrying the tip of the tongue up to the roof of your mouth; so that being grazed upon by the air which bursts out with a force, it yields to it, and returns always to the same part, making a kind of trill R, ra.

MR. JORDAN. R, r, ra. R, r, r, r, r, ra. That's true. What a clever man are you! And how have I lost time! R, r, r, ra.

PHILOSOPHY-MASTER. I will explain to you all these curiosities to the bottom.

MR. JORDAN. Pray do. But now, I must commit a secret to you. I'm in love with a person of great quality, and I should be glad you would help me to write something to her in a short *billet-doux*, which I'll drop at her feet.

PHILOSOPHY-MASTER. Very well.

MR. JORDAN. That will be very gallant, won't it?

PHILOSOPHY-MASTER. Without doubt. Is it verse that you would write to her?

MR. JORDAN. No, no, none of your verse.

PHILOSOPHY-MASTER. You would only have prose?

MR. JORDAN. No, I would neither have verse nor prose.

PHILOSOPHY-MASTER. It must be one or t'other.

MR. JORDAN. Why so?

PHILOSOPHY-MASTER. Because, sir, there's nothing to express one's self by, but prose, or verse.

MR. JORDAN. Is there nothing then but prose, or verse?

PHILOSOPHY-MASTER. No, sir, whatever is not prose, is verse! and whatever is not verse, is prose.

MR. JORDAN. And when one talks, what may that be then?

PHILOSOPHY-MASTER. Prose.

MR. JORDAN. How? When I say, Nicola, bring me my slippers, and give me my nightcap, is that prose?

PHILOSOPHY-MASTER. Yes, sir.

MR. JORDAN. On my conscience, I have spoken prose above these forty years, without knowing anything of the matter; and I have all the obligations in the world to you, for informing me of this. I would therefore put into a letter to her: Beautiful marchioness, your fair eyes make me die with love; but I would have this placed in a gallant manner; and have a gentle turn.

PHILOSOPHY-MASTER. Why, add that the fire of her eyes has reduced your heart to ashes: that you suffer for her night and day all the torments——

MR. JORDAN. No, no, no, I won't have all that—I'll have nothing but what I told you. Beautiful marchioness, your fair eyes make me die with love.

PHILOSOPHY-MASTER. You must by all means lengthen the thing out a little.

MR. JORDAN. No, I tell you, I'll have

none but those very words in the letter:
but turned in a modish way, ranged hand-
somely as they should be. I desire you'd
show me a little, that I may see the
different manners, in which one may place
them.

PHILOSOPHY-MASTER. One may place
them first of all as you said: Beautiful
marchioness, your fair eyes make me die
for love. Or suppose: For love die me
make, beautiful marchioness, your fair
eyes. Or perhaps: Your eyes fair, for
love me make, beautiful marchioness, die.
Or suppose: Die your fair eyes, beautiful
marchioness, for love me make. Or, how-
ever: Me make your eyes fair die, beau-
tiful marchioness, for love.

MR. JORDAN. But of all these ways,
which is the best?

PHILOSOPHY-MASTER. That which you
said: Beautiful marchioness, your fair
eyes make me die for love.

MR. JORDAN. Yet at the same time, I
never studied it, and I made the whole
of it at the first touch. I thank you
with all my heart, and desire you would
come in good time to-morrow.

PHILOSOPHY-MASTER. I shall not fail.

SCENE VII

[MR. JORDAN, LACKEY.]

MR. JORDAN [to his LACKEY]. What?
Are my clothes not come yet?

LACKEY. No, sir.

MR. JORDAN. This cursed tailor makes
me wait unreasonably, considering it's a
day I have so much business in. I shall
go mad. A quartan ague wring this
villain of a tailor. D——l take the
tailor. A plague choke the tailor. If I
had him but here now, this detestable
tailor, this dog of a tailor, this traitor
of a tailor: I——

SCENE VIII

[MR. JORDAN, MASTER-TAILOR, JOURNEY-
MAN-TAILOR (bringing a suit of clothes
for MR. JORDAN), LACKEY.]

MR. JORDAN. Oh! You're there. I was
going to be in a passion with you.

MASTER-TAILOR. I could not possibly
come sooner; and I set twenty fellows to
work at your clothes.

MR. JORDAN. You have sent me a pair
of silk-hose so strait, that I had all the
difficulty in the world to get 'em on,
and there are two stitches broke in 'em.

MASTER-TAILOR. They'll grow rather
too large.

MR. JORDAN. Yes, if I break every day
a loop or two. You have made me a pair
of shoes too, that pinch me execrably.

MASTER-TAILOR. Not at all, sir.

MR. JORDAN. How, not at all?

MASTER-TAILOR. No, they don't pinch
you at all.

MR. JORDAN. I tell you they do hurt
me.

MASTER-TAILOR. You fancy so.

MR. JORDAN. I fancy so, because I feel
it. There's a fine reason indeed.

MASTER-TAILOR. Hold, stay, here's one
of the handsomest suits at court, and the
best-matched. 'Tis a masterly work to
invent a grave suit of clothes, that should
not be black; and I'll give the cleverest
tailor in town six trials to equal it.

MR. JORDAN. What a deuce have we
here? You have put the flowers down-
wards.

MASTER-TAILOR. Why, you did not tell
me you would have 'em upwards.

MR. JORDAN. Was there any need to
tell you of that?

MASTER-TAILOR. Yes certainly. All
the people of quality wear 'em in that
way.

MR. JORDAN. Do people of quality wear
the flowers downwards?

MASTER-TAILOR. Yes, sir.

MR. JORDAN. Oh, 'tis very well then.

MASTER-TAILOR. If you please I'll put
'em upwards.

MR. JORDAN. No, no.

MASTER-TAILOR. You need only say the
word.

MR. JORDAN. No, I tell you, you have
done right. Do you think my clothes
will fit me?

MASTER-TAILOR. A pretty question! I
defy a painter with his pencil to draw

you anything that shall fit more exact. I have a fellow at home, who, for mounting a rhingrave, is the greatest genius in the world; another, who for the cut of a doublet, is the hero of the age.

MR. JORDAN. Are the peruke and feather as they should be?

MASTER-TAILOR. Everything's well.

MR. JORDAN [looking earnestly at the tailor's clothes]. Ah, hah! Mr. Tailor, here's my stuff of the last suit you made for me. I know it very well.

MASTER-TAILOR. The stuff appeared to me so handsome, that I had a mind to cut a coat out of it for myself.

MR. JORDAN. Yes, but you should not have cabbaged it out of mine.

MASTER-TAILOR. Will you put on your clothes?

MR. JORDAN. Yes, give 'em me.

MASTER-TAILOR. Stay; the matter must not go so. I have brought men along with me, to dress you to music; these sort of suits are put on with ceremony. Soho! come in there, you.

SCENE IX

[MR. JORDAN, MASTER-TAILOR, JOURNEY-MAN-TAILOR, JOURNEYMEN-TAILORS (dancing), LACKEY.]

MASTER-TAILOR [to his journeymen]. Put on this suit of the gentleman's, in the manner you do to people of quality. [Enter four JOURNEYMEN-TAILORS, two of which pull off his straight breeches made for his exercises, and two others his waistcoat; then they put him on his new suit to music; and MR. JORDAN walks amongst them to show them his clothes to see whether they fit or no.]

JOURNEYMAN-TAILOR. My dear gentleman, please to give the tailor's men something to drink.

MR. JORDAN. How do you call me?

JOURNEYMAN-TAILOR. My dear gentleman.

MR. JORDAN. My dear gentleman! See what it is to dress like people of quality. You may go clothed like a cit all your days, and they'll never call you, my dear gentleman. [Gives them something.] Stay, there's for my dear gentleman.

JOURNEYMAN-TAILOR. My lord, we are infinitely obliged to you.

MR. JORDAN. My lord! Oh, hoh! My lord! Stay, friend; my lord deserves something. My lord is none o' your petty words. Hold, there my lord gives you that.

JOURNEYMAN-TAILOR. My lord, we shall go drink your grace's health.

MR. JORDAN. Your grace! oh, oh, oh! stay, don't go. Your grace, to me! [Aside.] I'faith if he goes as far as highness, he'll empty my purse. [Aloud.] Hold, there's for my grace.

JOURNEYMAN-TAILOR. My lord, we most humbly thank your grace for your liberality.

MR. JORDAN. He did very well, I was going to give him all.

ACT III

SCENE I

[MR. JORDAN and his TWO LACKEYS.]

MR. JORDAN. Follow me, that I may go and show my clothes a little through the town; and especially take care, both of you, to walk immediately at my heels, that people may plainly see you belong to me.

LACKEYS. Yes, sir.

MR. JORDAN. Call me Nicola, that I may give her some directions. You need not go, here she comes.

SCENE II

[MR. JORDAN, NICOLA, TWO LACKEYS.]

MR. JORDAN. Nicola?

NICOLA. Your pleasure, sir?

MR. JORDAN. Harkee.

NICOLA [laughing]. Ha, ha, ha, ha, ha.

MR. JORDAN. Who do ye laugh at?

NICOLA. Ha, ha, ha, ha, ha, ha.

MR. JORDAN. What does this slut mean?

NICOLA. Ha, ha, ha. How you are bedizened! Ha, ha, ha.

MR. JORDAN. How's that?

NICOLA. Oh! oh! my stars! ha, ha, ha, ha, ha.

MR. JORDAN. What a jade is here! What! do ye make a jest of me?

NICOLA. No, no, sir, I should be very sorry to do so. Ha, ha, ha, ha, ha, ha.

MR. JORDAN. I shall give ye a slap o' the chops, if you laugh any more.

NICOLA. Sir, I cannot help it. Ha, ha, ha, ha, ha, ha.

MR. JORDAN. Won't ye have done?

NICOLA. Sir, I ask your pardon; but you are so comical, that I cannot hold from laughing. Ha, ha, ha.

MR. JORDAN. Do but see the insolence!

NICOLA. You are so thoroughly droll there! Ha, ha.

MR. JORDAN. I shall——

NICOLA. I beg you would excuse me. Ha, ha, ha, ha.

MR. JORDAN. Hold, if you laugh again the least in the world, I protest and swear, I'll give ye such a box o' the ear, as ye never had in your life.

NICOLA. Well, sir, I have done; I won't laugh any more.

MR. JORDAN. Take care you don't. You must clean out against by and by——

NICOLA. Ha, ha.

MR. JORDAN. You must clean out as it should be——

NICOLA. Ha, ha.

MR. JORDAN. I say, you must go clean out the hall, and——

NICOLA. Ha, ha.

MR. JORDAN. Again?

NICOLA [tumbles down with laughing]. Hold, sir, beat me rather, and let me laugh my belly-full, that will do me more good. Ha, ha, ha, ha.

MR. JORDAN. I shall run mad!

NICOLA. For goodness' sake, sir, I beseech you let me laugh. Ha, ha, ha.

MR. JORDAN. If I take you in hand——

NICOLA. Si—ir, I shall bu—urst, if I do—not laugh. Ha, ha, ha.

MR. JORDAN. But did ever anybody see such a jade as that, who insolently laughs in my face, instead of receiving my orders!

NICOLA. What would you have me do, sir?

MR. JORDAN. Why, take care to get ready my house, for the company that's to come by and by.

NICOLA [getting up]. Ay, i'fakins, I've no more inclination to laugh; all your company makes such a litter here, that the very word's enough to put one in an ill humour.

MR. JORDAN. What! I ought to shut my doors against all the world for your sake?

NICOLA. You ought at least to shut it against certain people.

SCENE III

[MRS. JORDAN, MR. JORDAN, NICOLA, TWO LACKEYS.]

MRS. JORDAN. Ah, hah! Here's some new story. What means this, husband, this same equipage? D'ye despise the world, that you harness yourself out in this manner? Have you a mind to make yourself a laughing-stock wherever ye go?

MR. JORDAN. None but fools, wife, will laugh at me.

MRS. JORDAN. In truth, people have not stayed thus long to laugh, 'tis a good while ago that your ways have furnished all the world with a laugh.

MR. JORDAN. Who is that all the world, pray?

MRS. JORDAN. That all the world, is a world perfectly in the right, and much wiser than yourself. For my part, I am shocked at the life you lead. I don't know what to call our house. One would swear 'twere carnival here all the year round; and from break o' day, for fear there should be any respite, there's nothing to be heard here, but an uproar of fiddles and songsters, which disturb the whole neighbourhood.

NICOLA. Madam says right. I shall never see my things set to rights again for that gang of folks that you bring to the house. They ransack every quarter of the town with their feet for dirt to bring here; and poor Frances is e'en almost slaved off her legs with scrubbing of the floors, which your pretty masters come to daub as regularly as the day comes.

MR. JORDAN. Hey-day! our maid Nicola! you have a pretty nimble tongue of your own, for a country-wench.

MRS. JORDAN. Nicola's in the right, and she has more sense than you have. I should be glad to know what you think to do with a dancing-master, at your age?

NICOLA. And with a lubberly fencing-master, that comes here with his stamping to shake the whole house, and tear up all the pavement of the hall.

MR. JORDAN. Peace, our maid, and our wife.

MRS. JORDAN. What! will you learn to dance against the time you'll have no legs?

NICOLA. What! have you a mind to murder somebody?

MR. JORDAN. Hold your prate, I tell you you are ignorant creatures, both of you, and don't know the advantage of all this.

MRS. JORDAN. You ought much rather to think of marrying your daughter, who is of age to be provided for.

MR. JORDAN. I shall think of marrying my daughter, when a suitable match presents itself; but I shall think too of learning the *belles sciences*.

NICOLA. I've heard say further, madam, that to pin the basket, he has got him a philosophy-master to-day.

MR. JORDAN. Very well. I've a mind to have wit, and to know how to reason upon things with your genteel people.

MRS. JORDAN. Won't you go to school one of these days, and be whipped at your age?

MR. JORDAN. Why not? Would I were whipped this very instant before all the world, so I did but know what they learn at school!

NICOLA. Yes, forsooth, that would be a mighty advantage t'ye.

MR. JORDAN. Without doubt.

MRS. JORDAN. This is all very necessary to the management of your house.

MR. JORDAN. Certainly. You talk, both of you, like asses, and I'm ashamed of your ignorance. [*To* MRS. JORDAN.] For example, do you know, you, what it is you now speak?

MRS. JORDAN. Yes, I know that what I speak is very right, and that you ought to think of living in another manner.

MR. JORDAN. I don't talk of that. I ask you what the words are that you now speak?

MRS. JORDAN. They are words that have a good deal of sense in them, and your conduct is by no means such.

MR. JORDAN. I don't talk of that, I tell you. I ask you, what is that I now speak to you, which I say this very moment?

MRS. JORDAN. Mere stuff.

MR. JORDAN. Pshaw, no, 'tis not that. That which we both of us say, the language we speak this instant?

MRS. JORDAN. Well?

MR. JORDAN. How is it called?

MRS. JORDAN. 'Tis called just what you please to call it.

MR. JORDAN. 'Tis prose, you ignorant creature.

MRS. JORDAN. Prose?

MR. JORDAN. Yes, prose. Whatever is prose, is not verse; and whatever is not verse, is prose. Now, see what it is to study. And you, [*To* NICOLA.] do you know very well how you must do to say U?

NICOLA. How?

MR. JORDAN. Yes. What is it you do when you say U?

NICOLA. What?

MR. JORDAN. Say U a little, to try.

NICOLA. Well, U.

MR. JORDAN. What is it you do?

NICOLA. I say U.

MR. JORDAN. Yes, but when you say U, what is it you do?

NICOLA. I do as you bid me.

MR. JORDAN. O! what a strange thing it is to have to do with brutes! You pout out your lips, and bring your under-jaw to your upper, U, d'ye see? I make a mouth, U.

NICOLA. Yes, that's fine.

MRS. JORDAN. 'Tis admirable!

MR. JORDAN. 'Tis quite another thing, had but you seen O, and DE, DE, and EF, EF.

MRS. JORDAN. What is all this ridiculous stuff?

NICOLA. What are we the better for all this?

MR. JORDAN. It makes one mad, to see these ignorant women.

MRS. JORDAN. Go, go, you should send all these folks apacking with their silly stuff.

NICOLA. And especially that great lubberly fencing-master, who fills all my house with dust.

MR. JORDAN. Hey-day! This fencing-master sticks strangely in thy stomach. I'll let thee see thy impertinence presently. [*He orders the foils to be brought, and gives one to* NICOLA.] Stay, reason demonstrative, the line of the body. When they push in carte one need only do so; and when they push in tierce one need only do so. This is the way never to be killed; and is not that clever to be upon sure grounds, when one has an encounter with anybody? There, push at me a little, to try.

NICOLA. Well, how? [NICOLA *gives him several thrusts.*]

MR. JORDAN. Gently! hold! Oh! Softly; deuce take the hussy.

NICOLA. You bid me push.

MR. JORDAN. Yes, but you push me in tierce, before you push in carte; and you have not patience while I parry.

MRS. JORDAN. You are a fool, husband, with all these whims, and this is come to you since you have taken upon you to keep company with quality.

MR. JORDAN. When I keep company with quality, I show my judgment; and that's much better than herding with your cits.

MRS. JORDAN. Yes, truly, there's a great deal to be got by frequenting your nobility; and you have made fine work with that count you are so bewitched with.

MR. JORDAN. Peace, take care what you say. Do you well know, wife, that you don't know whom you speak of, when you speak of him? He's a man of more importance than you think of; a nobleman of consideration at court, who speaks to the king just for all the world as I speak to you. Is it not a thing that does me great honour, that you see a person of that quality come so often to my house, who calls me his dear friend, and treats me as if I were his equal? He has more kindness for me than one would ever imagine; and he caresses me in such a manner before all the world, that I myself am perfectly confounded at it.

MRS. JORDAN. Yes, he has a great kindness for you, and caresses you; but he borrows your money of you.

MR. JORDAN. Well, and is it not a great honour to me to lend money to a man of that condition? And can I do less for a lord who calls me his dear friend?

MRS. JORDAN. And what is it this lord does for you?

MR. JORDAN. Things that would astonish you, if you did but know 'em.

MRS. JORDAN. And what may they be?

MR. JORDAN. Peace, I can't explain myself. 'Tis sufficient that if I have lent him money, he'll pay it me honestly, and that before 'tis long.

MRS. JORDAN. Yes, stay you for that.

MR. JORDAN. Certainly. Did he not tell me so?

MRS. JORDAN. Yes, yes, and he won't fail to disappoint you.

MR. JORDAN. He swore to me on the faith of a gentleman.

MRS. JORDAN. A mere song.

MR. JORDAN. Hey! You are mighty obstinate, wife of mine; I tell you he will keep his word with me, I am sure of it.

MRS. JORDAN. And I am sure that he will not; and all the court he makes to you, is only to cajole you.

MR. JORDAN. Hold your tongue. Here he comes.

Mrs. Jordan. That's all we shall have of him. He comes perhaps to borrow something more of you; the very sight of him gives me my dinner.

Mr. Jordan. Hold your tongue, I say.

Scene IV

[Dorantes, Mr. Jordan, Mrs. Jordan, Nicola.]

Dorantes. My dear friend, Mr. Jordan, how do you do?

Mr. Jordan. Very well, sir, to do you what little service I can.

Dorantes. And Madam Jordan there, how does she do?

Mrs. Jordan. Madam Jordan does as well as she can.

Dorantes. Hah! Mr. Jordan, you're dressed the most genteely in the world!

Mr. Jordan. As you see.

Dorantes. You have a very fine air with that dress, and we have ne'er a young fellow at court, that's better made than you.

Mr. Jordan. He, he.

Mrs. Jordan [aside]. He scratches him where it itches.

Dorantes. Turn about. 'Tis most gallant.

Mrs. Jordan [aside]. Yes, as much of the fool behind as before.

Dorantes. 'Faith, Mr. Jordan, I was strangely impatient to see you. You're the man in the world I most esteem, and I was talking of you again this morning at the king's levee.

Mr. Jordan. You do me a great deal of honour, sir. [To Mrs. Jordan.] At the king's levee!

Dorantes. Come, be covered.

Mr. Jordan. Sir, I know the respect I owe you.

Dorantes. Lack-a-day, be covered; no ceremony pray between us two.

Mr. Jordan. Sir——

Dorantes. Put on your hat, I tell you, Mr. Jordan, you are my friend.

Mr. Jordan. Sir, I am your humble servant.

Dorantes. I won't be covered, if you won't.

Mr. Jordan. [Puts on his hat.] I choose rather to be unmannerly than troublesome.

Dorantes. I am your debtor, you know.

Mrs. Jordan [aside]. Yes, we know it but too well.

Dorantes. You have generously lent me money upon several occasions; and have obliged me, most certainly, with the best grace in the world.

Mr. Jordan. You jest, sir.

Dorantes. But I know how to repay what is lent me, and to be grateful for the favours done me.

Mr. Jordan. I don't doubt it, sir.

Dorantes. I'm willing to get out of your books, and came hither to make up our accounts together.

Mr. Jordan [aside to Mrs. Jordan]. Well, you see your impertinence, wife.

Dorantes. I'm one who love to be out of debt as soon as I can.

Mr. Jordan [aside to Mrs. Jordan]. I told you so.

Dorantes. Let's see a little what 'tis I owe you.

Mr. Jordan [aside to Mrs. Jordan]. You there, with your ridiculous suspicions.

Dorantes. Do you remember right all the money you have lent me?

Mr. Jordan. I believe so. I made a little memorandum of it. Here it is. Let you have at one time two hundred louis d'or.

Dorantes. 'Tis true.

Mr. Jordan. Another time, six-score.

Dorantes. Yes.

Mr. Jordan. And another time a hundred and forty.

Dorantes. You are right.

Mr. Jordan. These three articles make four hundred and sixty louis d'or, which come to five thousand and sixty livres.

Dorantes. The account is very right. Five thousand and sixty livres.

Mr. Jordan. One thousand eight hundred and thirty-two livres to your plume-maker.

DORANTES. Just.

MR. JORDAN. Two thousand seven hundred and four-score livres to your tailor.

DORANTES. 'Tis true.

MR. JORDAN. Four thousand three hundred and seventy-nine livres, twelve sols and eight deniers to your tradesman.

DORANTES. Very well. Twelve sols, eight deniers. The account is just.

MR. JORDAN. And a thousand seven hundred and forty-eight livres seven sols four deniers to your saddler.

DORANTES. 'Tis all true. What does that come to?

MR. JORDAN. Sum total, fifteen thousand eight hundred livres.

DORANTES. The sum total, and just. Fifteen thousand and eight hundred livres. To which add two hundred pistoles, which you are going to lend me, that will make exactly eighteen thousand francs, which I shall pay you the first opportunity.

MRS. JORDAN [aside to MR. JORDAN]. Well, did I not guess how 'twould be!

MR. JORDAN [aside to MRS. JORDAN]. Peace.

DORANTES. Will it incommode you to lend me what I tell you?

MR. JORDAN. Oh! no.

MRS. JORDAN [aside to MR. JORDAN]. This man makes a mere milch cow of you.

MR. JORDAN [aside to MRS. JORDAN]. Hold your tongue.

DORANTES. If this will incommode you, I'll seek it elsewhere.

MR. JORDAN. No, sir.

MRS. JORDAN [aside to MR. JORDAN]. He'll ne'er be satisfied till he has ruined you.

MR. JORDAN [aside to MRS. JORDAN]. Hold your tongue, I tell you.

DORANTES. You need only tell me if this puts you to any straits.

MR. JORDAN. Not at all, sir.

MRS. JORDAN [aside to MR. JORDAN]. 'Tis a true wheedler.

MR. JORDAN [aside to MRS. JORDAN]. Hold your tongue then.

MRS. JORDAN [aside to MR. JORDAN]. He'll drain you to the last farthing.

MR. JORDAN [aside to MRS. JORDAN]. Will you hold your tongue?

DORANTES. I've a good many people would be glad to lend it me, but as you are my very good friend, I thought I should wrong you if I asked it of anybody else.

MR. JORDAN. 'Tis too much honour, sir, you do me. I'll go fetch what you want.

MRS. JORDAN [aside to MR. JORDAN]. What! going to lend him still more?

MR. JORDAN [aside to MRS. JORDAN]. What can I do? Would you have me refuse a man of that rank, who spoke to me this morning at the king's levee.

MRS. JORDAN [aside to MR. JORDAN]. Go, you're a downright dupe.

SCENE V

[DORANTES, MRS. JORDAN, NICOLA.]

DORANTES. You seem to me very melancholy. What ails you, Mrs. Jordan?

MRS. JORDAN. My head's bigger than my fist, even if it is not swelled.

DORANTES. Where is Miss your daughter that I don't see her?

MRS. JORDAN. Miss my daughter is pretty well where she is.

DORANTES. How does she go on?

MRS. JORDAN. She goes on her two legs.

DORANTES. Won't you come with her, one of these days, and see the ball, and the play that's acted at court.

MRS. JORDAN. Yes truly, we've a great inclination to laugh, a great inclination to laugh have we.

DORANTES. I fancy, Madam Jordan, you had a great many sparks in your younger years, being so handsome and good-humoured as you were.

MRS. JORDAN. Tredame, sir! what, is Madam Jordan grown decrepit, and does her head totter already with a palsy?

DORANTES. Odso, Madam Jordan, I ask your pardon. I was not thinking that you are young. I'm very often absent. Pray excuse my impertinence.

SCENE VI

[MR. JORDAN, MRS. JORDAN, DORANTES, NICOLA.]

MR. JORDAN [to DORANTES]. Here's two hundred pieces for you, hard money.

DORANTES. I do assure you, Mr. Jordan, I am absolutely yours; and I long to do you service at court.

MR. JORDAN. I'm infinitely obliged to you.

DORANTES. If Madam Jordan inclines to see the royal diversion, I'll get her the best places in the ballroom.

MRS. JORDAN. Madam Jordan kisses your hand.

DORANTES [aside to MR. JORDAN]. Our pretty marchioness, as I informed you in my letter, will be here by and by to partake of your ball and collation; I brought her, at last, to consent to the entertainment you design to give her.

MR. JORDAN. Let us draw to a distance a little, for a certain reason.

DORANTES. 'Tis eight days since I saw you, and I gave you no tidings of the diamond you put into my hands to make her a present of, as from you; but the reason was, I had all the difficulty in the world to conquer her scruples, and 'twas no longer ago than to-day, that she resolved to accept of it.

MR. JORDAN. How did she like it?

DORANTES. Marvellously; and I am much deceived if the beauty of this diamond has not an admirable effect upon her.

MR. JORDAN. Grant it, kind Heaven!

MRS. JORDAN [to NICOLA]. When he's once with him, he can never get rid of him.

DORANTES. I made her sensible in a proper manner, of the richness of the present, and the strength of your passion.

MR. JORDAN. These kindnesses perfectly overwhelm me; I am in the greatest confusion in the world to see a person of your quality demean himself on my account as you do.

DORANTES. You jest sure. Does one ever stop at such sort of scruples among friends? And would not you do the same thing for me, if occasion offered?

MR. JORDAN. Oh! certainly, and with all my soul.

MRS. JORDAN [aside to NICOLA]. How the sight of him torments me!

DORANTES. For my part, I never mind anything when a friend is to be served; and when you imparted to me the ardent passion you had entertained for the agreeable marchioness, with whom I was acquainted, you see that I made an immediate offer of my service.

MR. JORDAN. 'Tis true, these favours are what confound me.

MRS. JORDAN [to NICOLA]. What, will he never be gone?

NICOLA. They are mighty great together.

DORANTES. You've taken the right way to smite her. Women, above all things, love the expense we are at on their account; and your frequent serenades, your continual entertainments; that sumptuous firework she saw on the water, the diamond she received by way of present from you, and the regale you are now preparing; all this speaks much better in favour of your passion than all the things you yourself could possibly have said to her.

MR. JORDAN. There's no expense I would not be at, if I could by that means find the way to her heart. A woman of quality has powerful charms for me, and 'tis an honour I would purchase at any rate.

MRS. JORDAN [aside to NICOLA]. What can they have to talk of so long together? Go softly, and listen a little.

DORANTES. By and by you will enjoy the pleasure of seeing her at your ease, your eyes will have full time to be satisfied.

MR. JORDAN. To be at full liberty, I have ordered matters so, that my wife shall dine with my sister, where she'll pass the whole afternoon.

DORANTES. You have done wisely, for your wife might have perplexed us a little. I have given the proper orders for yon to the cook, and for everything necessary for the ball. 'Tis of my own invention; and provided the execution answers the plan, I am sure 'twill be——

MR. JORDAN [*perceives that* NICOLA *listens, and gives her a box on the ear*]. Hey, you're very impertinent. [*To* DORANTES.] Let us go if you please.

SCENE VII

[MRS. JORDAN, NICOLA.]

NICOLA. I'faith, curiosity has cost me something; but I believe there's a snake in the grass; for they were talking of some affair, which they were not willing you should be present at.

MRS. JORDAN. This is not the first time, Nicola, that I have had suspicions of my husband. I am the most deceived person in the world, or there is some amour in agitation, and I am labouring to discover what it should be. But let's think of my daughter. You know the love Cleontes has for her. He is a man who hits my fancy, and I have a mind to favour his addresses, and help him to Lucilia, if I can.

NICOLA. In truth, madam, I am the most ravished creature in the world, to find you in these sentiments; for if the master hits your taste, the man hits mine no less; and I could wish our marriage might be concluded under favour of theirs.

MRS. JORDAN. Go, and talk with him about it, as from me, and tell him to come to me presently, that we may join in demanding my daughter of my husband.

NICOLA. I fly, madam, with joy, and I could not have received a more agreeable commission. [*Alone.*] I believe I shall very much rejoice their hearts.

SCENE VIII

[CLEONTES, COVIEL, NICOLA.]

NICOLA [*to* CLEONTES]. Hah, most luckily met. I'm an ambassadress of joy, and I come——

CLEONTES. Be gone, ye perfidious slut, and don't come to amuse me with thy traitorous speeches.

NICOLA. Is it thus you receive——

CLEONTES. Be gone, I tell thee, and go directly and inform thy false mistress, that she never more, while she lives, shall impose upon the too simple Cleontes.

NICOLA. What whim is this? My dear Coviel, tell me a little what does this mean.

COVIEL. Thy dear Coviel, wicked minx? Away quickly out of my sight, hussy, and leave me at quiet.

NICOLA. What dost thou·too——

COVIEL. Out o' my sight, I tell thee, and talk not to me, for thy life.

NICOLA [*aside*]. Hey-day! What gadfly has stung 'em both? Well, I must march and inform my mistress of this pretty piece of history.

SCENE IX

[CLEONTES, COVIEL.]

CLEONTES. What! treat a lover in this manner; and a lover the most constant, the most passionate of all lovers?

COVIEL. 'Tis a horrible trick they have served us both.

CLEONTES. I discover all the ardour for her, all the tenderness one can imagine. I love nothing in the world but her, have nothing in my thoughts besides her. She is all my care, all my desire, all my joy. I speak of nought but her, think of nought but her, dream of nought but her, I breathe only for her, my heart lives wholly in her; and this is the worthy recompense of such a love! I am two days without seeing her, which are to me two horrible ages; I meet her accidentally, my heart feels all transported at the sight; joy sparkles in my face; I fly to her with ecstasy, and the faithless creature turns away her eyes, and brushes hastily by me, as if she had never seen me in her life!

COVIEL. I say the same as you do.

CLEONTES. Is it possible to see anything, Coviel, equal to this perfidy of the ungrateful Lucilia?

COVIEL. Or to that, sir, of the villainous jade Nicola?

CLEONTES. After so many ardent sacrifices of sighs and vows that I have made to her charms!

COVIEL. After so much assiduous sneaking, cares, and services that I have paid her in the kitchen!

CLEONTES. So many tears that I have shed at her feet!

COVIEL. So many buckets of water that I have drawn for her!

CLEONTES. Such ardour as I have shown, in loving her more than myself!

COVIEL. So much heat as I have endured, in turning the spit in her place!

CLEONTES. She flies me with disdain!

COVIEL. She turns her back upon me with impudence!

CLEONTES. This is a perfidy worthy the greatest punishment.

COVIEL. This is a treachery that deserves a thousand boxes o' the ear.

CLEONTES. Prithee, never think to speak once more to me in her favour.

COVIEL. I, sir? marry Heaven forbid.

CLEONTES. Never come to excuse the action of this perfidious woman.

COVIEL. Fear it not.

CLEONTES. No, d'ye see, all discourses in her defence will signify nothing.

COVIEL. Who dreams of such a thing?

CLEONTES. I'm determined to continue my resentment against her, and break off all correspondence.

COVIEL. I give my consent.

CLEONTES. This same count that visits her, pleases perhaps her eye; and her fancy, I see plainly, is dazzled with quality. But I must, for my own honour, prevent the triumph of her inconstancy. I'll make as much haste as she can do towards the change, which I see she's running into, and won't leave her all the glory of quitting me.

COVIEL. 'Tis very well said, and for my share, I enter into all your sentiments.

CLEONTES. Second my resentments, and support my resolutions against all the remains of love, that may yet plead for her. I conjure thee, say all the ill things of her thou canst. Paint me her person so as to make her despicable; and, in order to disgust me, mark me out well all the faults thou canst find in her.

COVIEL. She, sir? A pretty mawkin, a fine piece to be so much enamoured with. I see nothing in her, but what's very indifferent, and you might find a hundred persons more deserving of you. First of all she has little eyes.

CLEONTES. That's true, she has little eyes; but they are full of fire, the most sparkling, the most piercing in the world, the most striking that one shall see.

COVIEL. She has a wide mouth.

CLEONTES. Yes; but one sees such graces in it, as one does not see in other mouths, and the sight of that mouth inspires desire; 'tis the most attractive, the most amorous in the world.

COVIEL. As to her height, she's not tall.

CLEONTES. No; but she's easy, and well-shaped.

COVIEL. She affects a negligence in speaking and acting.

CLEONTES. 'Tis true; but all this has a gracefulness in her, and her ways are engaging; they have I don't know what charms. that insinuate into our hearts.

COVIEL. As to her wit——

CLEONTES. Ah! Coviel, she has the most refined, the most delicate turn of wit.

COVIEL. Her conversation——

CLEONTES. Her conversation is charming.

COVIEL. She's always grave.

CLEONTES. Would you have flaunting pleasantry, a perpetual profuse mirth? And d'ye see anything more impertinent than those women who are always upon the giggle?

COVIEL. But in short, she is the most capricious creature in the world:

CLEONTES. Yes, she is capricious I grant ye; but everything sits well upon fine women; we bear with everything from the fair.

COVIEL. Since that's the case, I see plainly you desire always to love her.

CLEONTES. I! I should love death sooner; and I am now going to hate her as much as ever I loved her.

COVIEL But how, if you think her so perfect?

CLEONTES. Therein shall my vengeance be more glaring; therein shall I better display the force of my resolution in hating her, quitting her, most beautiful as she is; most charming, most amiable, as I think her. Here she is.

SCENE X

[LUCILIA, CLEONTES, COVIEL, NICOLA.]

NICOLA [to LUCILIA]. For my part, I was perfectly shocked at it.

LUCILIA. It can be nothing else, Nicola, but what I said. But there he comes.

CLEONTES [to COVIEL]. I won't so much as speak to her.

COVIEL. I'll follow your example.

LUCILIA. What means this, Cleontes, what's the matter with you?

NICOLA. What ails thee, Coviel?

LUCILIA. What trouble has seized you?

NICOLA. What cross humour possesses thee?

LUCILIA. Are you dumb, Cleontes?

NICOLA. Hast thou lost thy speech, Coviel?

CLEONTES. The abandoned creature!

COVIEL. Oh! the Judas!

LUCILIA. I see very well that the late meeting has disordered your mind.

CLEONTES [to COVIEL]. O, hoh! She sees what she has done.

NICOLA. The reception of this morning has made thee take snuff.

COVIEL [to CLEONTES]. She has guessed where the shoe pinches.

LUCILIA. Is it not true, Cleontes, that this is the reason of your being out of humour?

CLEONTES. Yes, perfidious maid, that is it, since I must speak; and I can tell you, that you shall not triumph, as you imagine, by your unfaithfulness, that I shall be beforehand in breaking with you, and you won't have the credit of discarding me. I shall, doubtless, have some difficulty in conquering the passion I have for you: 'twill cause me uneasiness; I shall suffer for a while; but I shall compass my point, and I would sooner stab myself to the heart than have the weakness of returning to you.

COVIEL [to NICOLA]. As says the master, so says the man.

LUCILIA. Here's a noise indeed about nothing. I'll tell you, Cleontes, the reason that made me avoid joining you this morning.

CLEONTES [endeavouring to go to avoid LUCILIA]. No, I'll hear nothing.

NICOLA [to COVIEL]. I'll let thee into the cause that made us pass you so quick.

COVIEL [endeavouring to go to avoid NICOLA]. I will hear nothing.

LUCILIA [following CLEONTES]. Know that this morning——

CLEONTES [walks about without regarding LUCILIA]. No, I tell you.

NICOLA [following COVIEL]. Learn that——

COVIEL [walks about likewise without regarding NICOLA]. No, traitress.

LUCILIA. Hear me.

CLEONTES. Not a bit.

NICOLA. Let me speak.

COVIEL. I'm deaf.

LUCILIA. Cleontes!

CLEONTES. No.

NICOLA. Coviel!

COVIEL. No.

LUCILIA. Stay.

CLEONTES. Idle stuff.

NICOLA. Hear me.

COVIEL. No such thing.

LUCILIA. One moment.

CLEONTES. Not at all.

NICOLA. A little patience.

COVIEL. A fiddle-stick.

LUCILIA. Two words.

CLEONTES. No, 'tis over.

NICOLA. One word.

COVIEL. No more dealings.

LUCILIA [stopping]. Well, since you won't hear me, keep your opinion, and do what you please.

NICOLA [stopping likewise]. Since that's thy way, e'en take it all just as it pleases thee.

CLEONTES. Let's know the subject then of this fine reception.

LUCILIA [going in her turn to avoid CLEONTES]. I've no longer an inclination to tell it.

COVIEL. Let us a little into this history.

NICOLA [going likewise in her turn to avoid COVIEL]. I won't inform thee now, not I.

CLEONTES [following LUCILIA]. Tell me——

LUCILIA. No, I'll tell you nothing.

COVIEL [following NICOLA]. Say——

NICOLA. No, I say nothing.

CLEONTES. For goodness' sake.

LUCILIA. No, I tell you.

COVIEL. Of all charity.

NICOLA. Not a bit.

CLEONTES. I beseech you.

LUCILIA. Let me alone.

COVIEL. I conjure thee.

NICOLA. Away with thee.

CLEONTES. Lucilia!

LUCILIA. No.

COVIEL. Nicola!

NICOLA. Not at all.

CLEONTES. For Heaven's sake.

LUCILIA. I will not.

COVIEL. Speak to me.

NICOLA. Not a word.

CLEONTES. Clear up my doubts.

LUCILIA. No, I'll do nothing towards it.

COVIEL. Cure my mind.

NICOLA. No, 'tis not my pleasure.

CLEONTES. Well, since you are so little concerned to ease me of my pain, and to justify yourself as to the unworthy treatment my passion has received from you, ungrateful creature, 'tis the last time you shall see me, and I am going far from you to die of grief and love.

COVIEL [to NICOLA]. And I'll follow his steps.

LUCILIA [to CLEONTES, who is going]. Cleontes!

NICOLA [to COVIEL, who follows his master]. Coviel!

CLEONTES [stopping]. Hey?

COVIEL [likewise stopping]. Your pleasure?

LUCILIA. Whither do you go?

CLEONTES. Where I told you.

COVIEL. We go to die.

LUCILIA. Do you go to die, Cleontes?

CLEONTES. Yes, cruel, since you will have it so.

LUCILIA. I? I have you die?

CLEONTES. Yes, you would.

LUCILIA. Who told you so?

CLEONTES [going up to LUCILIA]. Would you not have it so, since you would not clear up my suspicions?

LUCILIA. Is that my fault? Would you but have given me the hearing, should I not have told you that the adventure you make such complaints about, was occasioned this morning by the presence of an old aunt who will absolutely have it, that the mere approach of a man is a dishonour to a girl; who is perpetually lecturing us upon this head, and represents to us all mankind as so many devils, whom one ought to avoid.

NICOLA [to COVIEL]. There's the whole secret of the affair.

CLEONTES. Don't you deceive me, Lucilia?

COVIEL [to NICOLA]. Dost thou not put a trick upon me?

LUCILIA [to CLEONTES]. There's nothing more true.

NICOLA [to COVIEL]. 'Tis the very thing, as it is.

COVIEL [to CLEONTES]. Shall we surrender upon this?

CLEONTES. Ah, Lucilia, what art have you to calm my passions with a single word! How easily do we suffer ourselves to be persuaded by those we love!

COVIEL. How easily is one wheedled by these plaguy animals!

SCENE XI

[MRS. JORDAN, CLEONTES, LUCILIA, CO-
VIEL, NICOLA.]

MRS. JORDAN. I am very glad to see
you, Cleontes, and you are here apropos.
My husband's acoming, catch your op-
portunity quick, and demand Lucilia in
marriage.

CLEONTES. Ah, madam, how sweet is
that word, how it flatters my wishes!
Could I receive an order more charming?
A favour more precious?

SCENE XII

[MR. JORDAN, MRS. JORDAN, CLEONTES,
LUCILIA, COVIEL, NICOLA.]

CLEONTES. Sir, I was not willing to
employ any other person to make a cer-
tain demand of you, which I have long
intended. It concerns me sufficiently to
undertake it in my own person; and,
without farther circumlocution, I shall
inform you that the honour of being your
son-in-law is an illustrious favour which
I beseech you to grant me.

MR. JORDAN. Before I give you an an-
swer, sir, I desire you would tell me
whether you are a gentleman.

CLEONTES. Sir, the generality of peo-
ple don't hesitate much on this question.
People speak out bluff, and with ease.
They make no scruple of taking this title
upon 'em, and custom nowadays seems
to authorise the theft. For my part, I
confess to you, my sentiments in this
matter are somewhat more delicate. I
look upon all imposture as unworthy an
honest man; and that there is cowardice
in denying what Heaven has made us;
in tricking ourselves out, to the eyes of
the world, in a stolen title; in desiring
to put ourselves off for what we are not.
I am undoubtedly born of parents who
have held honourable employments. I
have had the honour of six years' service
in the army; and I find myself of conse-
quence enough to hold a tolerable rank
in the world; but for all this I won't
give myself a name, which others in my
place would think they might pretend to,
and I'll tell you frankly that I am no
gentleman.

MR. JORDAN. Your hand, sir, my daugh-
ter is no wife for you.

CLEONTES. How?

MR. JORDAN. You are no gentleman,
you shan't have my daughter.

MRS. JORDAN. What would you be at
then with your gentlemen? D'ye think
we sort of people are of the line of St.
Louis?

MR. JORDAN. Hold your tongue, wife,
I see you're acoming.

MRS. JORDAN. Are we either of us
otherwise descended than of plain citi-
zens?

MR. JORDAN. There's a scandalous re-
flection for you!

MRS. JORDAN. And was not your father
a tradesman as well as mine?

MR. JORDAN. Plague take the woman.
She never has done with this. If your
father was a tradesman, so much was the
worse for him; but as for mine, they are
numskulls that say he was. All that I
have to say to you is, that I will have a
gentleman for my son-in-law.

MRS. JORDAN. Your daughter should
have a husband that's proper for her;
and an honest man who is rich and well
made, would be much better for her than
a gentleman who is deformed and a
beggar.

NICOLA. That's very true. We have
a young squire in our town who is the
most awkward looby, the veriest driveller
that I ever set eyes on.

MR. JORDAN. Hold your prate, Mrs.
Impertinence. You are always thrusting
yourself into conversation. I've means
sufficient for my daughter, and want noth-
ing but honour, and I will have her a
marchioness.

MRS. JORDAN. A marchioness!

MR. JORDAN. Yes, a marchioness.

MRS. JORDAN. Marry, Heavens preserve
me from it.

MR. JORDAN. 'Tis a determined thing.

MRS. JORDAN. 'Tis what I shall never
consent to. Matches with people above

one, are always subject to grievous inconveniences. I don't like that a son-in-law should have it in his power to reproach my daughter with her parents, or that she should have children who should be ashamed to call me grandmother. Should she come and visit me with the equipage of a grand lady, and through inadvertency, miss curtsying to some of the neighbourhood, they would not fail, presently, saying a hundred idle things. Do but see, would they say, this lady marchioness, what haughty airs she gives herself! She's the daughter of Mr. Jordan, who was over and above happy, when she was a little one, to play children's play with us. She was not always so lofty as she is now; and her two grandfathers sold cloth near St. Innocent's Gate. They amassed great means for their children, which they are paying for now, perhaps very dear, in the other world. People don't generally grow so rich by being honest. I won't have all these tittle-tattle stories; in one word, I'll have a man who shall be beholden to me for my daughter, and to whom I can say, Sit you down there, son-in-law, and dine with me.

MR. JORDAN. See there the sentiments of a little soul, to desire always to continue in a mean condition. Let me have no more replies; my daughter shall be a marchioness in spite of the world; and if you put me in a passion, I'll make her a duchess.

SCENE XIII

[MRS. JORDAN, LUCILIA, CLEONTES, NICOLA, COVIEL.]

MRS. JORDAN. Cleontes, don't be discouraged for all this. [To LUCILIA.] Follow me, daughter, and come tell your father resolutely, that if you have not him, you won't marry anybody at all.

SCENE XIV

[CLEONTES, COVIEL.]

COVIEL. You have made a pretty piece of work of it with your fine sentiments.

CLEONTES. What wouldst thou have me do? I have a scrupulousness in this case that no precedents can conquer.

COVIEL. You're in the wrong to be serious with such a man as that. Don't you see that he's a fool? And would it cost you anything to accommodate yourself to his chimeras?

CLEONTES. You're in the right; but I did not dream it was necessary to bring your proofs of nobility, to be son-in-law to Mr. Jordan.

COVIEL [laughing]. Ha, ha, ha.

CLEONTES. What d'ye laugh at?

COVIEL. At a thought that's come into my head to play our spark off, and help you to obtain what you desire.

CLEONTES. How?

COVIEL. The thought is absolutely droll.

CLEONTES. What is it?

COVIEL. There was a certain masquerade performed a little while ago, which comes in here the best in the world; and which I intend to insert into a piece of roguery I design to make for our coxcomb. This whole affair looks a little like making a joke of him; but with him we may hazard everything, there's no need here to study finesse so much, he's a man who will play his part to a wonder; and will easily give in to all the sham tales we shall take in our heads to tell him. I have actors, I have habits all ready, only let me alone.

CLEONTES. But inform me of it.

COVIEL. I am going to let you into the whole of it. Let's retire; there he comes.

SCENE XV

[MR. JORDAN.]

MR. JORDAN [alone]. What a deuce can this mean? They have nothing but great lords to reproach me with; and I for my part see nothing so fine as keeping company with your great lords; there's nothing but honour and civility among 'em; and I would it had cost me two fingers of a hand to have been born a count, or a marquis.

SCENE XVI

[MR. JORDAN, LACKEY.]
LACKEY. Sir, here's the count, and a lady, whom he's handing in.
MR. JORDAN. Good lack-a-day, I have some orders to give. Tell 'em that I'm acoming in a minute.

SCENE XVII

[DORIMÈNE, DORANTES, LACKEY.]
LACKEY. My master says that he's acoming in a minute.
DORANTES. 'Tis very well.

SCENE XVIII

[DORIMÈNE, DORANTES.]
DORIMÈNE. I don't know, Dorantes; I take a strange step here in suffering you to bring me to a house where I know nobody.
DORANTES. What place then, madam, would you have a lover choose to entertain you in, since, to avoid clamour, you neither allow of your own house nor mine?
DORIMÈNE. But you don't mention that I am every day insensibly engaged to receive too great proofs of your passion. In vain do I refuse things, you weary me out of resistance, and you have a civil kind of obstinacy, which makes me come gently into whatsoever you please. Frequent visits commenced, declarations came next, which drew after them serenades and entertainments, which were followed by presents. I opposed all these things, but you are not disheartened, and you become master of my resolutions step by step. For my part, I can answer for nothing hereafter, and I believe in the end you will bring me to matrimony, from which I stood so far aloof.
DORANTES. Faith, madam, you ought to have been there already. You are a widow, and depend upon nobody but yourself. I am my own master, and love you

more than my life. What does it stick at then, that you should not, from this day forward, complete my happiness?
DORIMÈNE. Lack-a-day, Dorantes, there must go a great many qualities on both sides, to make people live happily together; and two of the most reasonable persons in the world have often much ado to compose a union to both their satisfactions.
DORANTES. You're in the wrong, madam, to represent to yourself so many difficulties in this affair; and the experience you have had concludes nothing for the rest of the world.
DORIMÈNE. In short, I always abide by this. The expenses you put yourself to for me, disturb me for two reasons; one is, they engage me more than I could wish; and the other is, I'm sure, no offence to you, that you can't do this, but you must incommode yourself, and I would not have you do that.
DORANTES. Fie, madam, these are trifles, and 'tis not by that——
DORIMÈNE. I know what I say; and, amongst other things, is the diamond you forced me to take, is of value——
DORANTES. Nay, madam, pray don't enhance the value of a thing my love thinks unworthy of you: and permit—— Here's the master of the house.

SCENE XIX

[MR. JORDAN, DORIMÈNE, DORANTES.]
MR. JORDAN [after having made two bows, finding himself too near DORIMÈNE]. A little farther, madam.
DORIMÈNE. How?
MR. JORDAN. One step, if you please.
DORIMÈNE. What then?
MR. JORDAN. Fall back a little for the third.
DORANTES. Mr. Jordan, madam, knows the world.
MR. JORDAN. Madam, 'tis a very great honour that I am fortunate enough to be so happy, but to have the felicity, that you should have the goodness, to grant

me the favour, to do me the honour, to honour me with the favour of your presence; and had I also the merit to merit a merit like yours, and that Heaven—envious of my good—had granted me—the advantage of being worthy—of——

DORANTES. Mr. Jordan, enough of this; my lady does not love great compliments, and she knows you are a man of wit. [*Aside to* DORIMÈNE.] 'Tis a downright cit, ridiculous enough, as you see, in his whole behaviour.

DORIMÈNE [*aside to* DORANTES]. It is not very difficult to perceive it.

DORANTES. Madam, this is a very good friend of mine.

MR. JORDAN. 'Tis too much honour you do me.

DORANTES. A very polite man.

DORIMÈNE. I have a great esteem for him.

MR. JORDAN. I have done nothing yet, madam, to merit this favour.

DORANTES [*aside to* MR. JORDAN]. Take good care however not to speak to her of the diamond you gave her.

MR. JORDAN [*aside to* DORANTES]. Mayn't I ask her only how she likes it?

DORANTES [*aside to* MR. JORDAN]. How! Take special care you don't. 'Twould be villainous of you; and to act like a man of gallantry, you should make as if it were not you who made the present. [*Aloud.*] Mr. Jordan, madam, says that he's in raptures to see you at his house.

DORIMÈNE. He does me a great deal of honour.

MR. JORDAN [*aside to* DORANTES]. How am I obliged to you, sir, for speaking to her in that manner on my account!

DORANTES [*aside to* MR. JORDAN]. I have had a most terrible difficulty to get her to come hither.

MR. JORDAN [*aside to* DORANTES]. I don't know how to thank you enough for it.

DORANTES. He says, madam, that he thinks you the most charming person in the world.

DORIMÈNE. 'Tis a great favour he does me.

MR. JORDAN. Madam, it's you who do the favours, and——

DORANTES. Let's think of eating.

SCENE XX

[MR. JORDAN, DORIMÈNE, DORANTES, LACKEY.]

LACKEY [*to* MR. JORDAN]. Everything is ready, sir.

DORANTES. Come then, let us sit down to table; and fetch the musicians.

ACT IV

SCENE I

[DORIMÈNE, MR. JORDAN, DORANTES, *three* MUSICIANS, LACKEYS.]

DORIMÈNE. How, Dorantes? why here's a most magnificent repast!

MR. JORDAN. You are pleased to banter, madam, I would it were more worthy of your acceptance.

[DORIMÈNE, MR. JORDAN, DORANTES, *and three* MUSICIANS *sit down at the table.*]

DORANTES. Mr. Jordan, madam, is in the right in what he says, and he obliges me in paying you, after so handsome a manner, the honours of his house. I agree with him that the repast is not worthy of you. As it was myself who ordered it, and I am not so clearly sighted in these affairs, as certain of our friends, you have here no very learned feast; and you will find incongruities of good cheer in it, some barbarisms of good taste. Had our friend Damis had a hand here, everything had been done by rule; elegance and erudition would have run through the whole, and he would not have failed exaggerating all the regular pieces of the repast he gave you, and force you to own his great capacity in the science of good eating; he would have told you of bread *de rive*, with the golden kissing-crust, raised too all round with a crust that crumbles tenderly in your teeth; of wine with a velvet sap, heightened with a smartness not too overpowering; of a breast of mutton stuffed with parsley; of a loin of veal de rivière, thus long, white, delicate, and which is a true almond paste between the teeth; of your partridges heightened with a surprising goût; and then by way of farce or entertainment, of a soup with jelly broth, fortified with a young plump turkey-pout, cantoned with pigeons, and garnished with white onions married to succory. But, for my part, I confess to you my ignorance; and, as Mr. Jordan has very well said, I wish the repast were more worthy of your acceptance.

DORIMÈNE. I make no other answer to this compliment than eating as I do.

MR. JORDAN. Ah! what pretty hands are there!

DORIMÈNE. The hands are so so, Mr. Jordan; but you mean to speak of the diamond which is very pretty.

MR. JORDAN. I, madam? Marry Heaven forbid I should speak of it; I should not act like a gentleman of gallantry, and the diamond is a very trifle.

DORIMÈNE. You are wondrous nice.

MR. JORDAN. You have too much goodness——

DORANTES [having made signs to MR. JORDAN]. Come, give some wine to Mr. Jordan, and to those gentlemen who will do us the favour to sing us a catch.

DORIMÈNE. You give a wondrous relish to the good cheer by mixing music with it; I am admirably well regaled here.

MR. JORDAN. Madam, it is not——

DORANTES. Mr. Jordan, let us listen to these gentlemen, they'll entertain us with something better than all we can possibly say.

[FIRST and SECOND MUSICIANS together with a glass in their hands.]
Put it round, my dear Phyllis, invert the bright glass;
Oh what charms to the crystal those fingers impart!
You and Bacchus combined, all resistance surpass,

And with passion redoubled have ravished my heart.
'Twixt him, you and me, my charmer, my fair,
Eternal affection let's swear.

At the touch of those lips how he sparkles more bright!
And his touch, in return, those lips does embellish:
I could quaff 'em all day, and drink bumpers all night.
What longing each gives me, what gusto, what relish!
'Twixt him, you and me, my charmer, my fair,
Eternal affection let's swear.

[SECOND and THIRD MUSICIANS together.]
Since time flies so nimbly away,
Come drink, my dear boys, drink about;
Let's husband him well while we may,
For life may be gone before the mug's out.
When Charon has got us aboard,
Our drinking and wooing are past;
We ne'er to lose time can afford,
For drinking's a trade not always to last.

Let your puzzling rogues in the schools,
Dispute of the bonum of man;
Philosophers dry are but fools,
The secret is this, drink, drink off your can.
When Charon has got us aboard,
Our drinking and wooing are past,
We ne'er to lose time can afford,
For drinking's a trade not always to last.

[All three together.]
Why bob there! some wine, boys! come fill the glass, fill,
Round and round let it go, till we bid it stand still.

DORIMÈNE. I don't think anything can be better sung; and 'tis extremely fine.

MR. JORDAN. I see something here though, madam, much finer.

Dorimène. Hey! Mr. Jordan is more gallant than I thought he was.

Dorantes. How, madam! who do you take Mr. Jordan for?

Mr. Jordan. I wish she would take me for what I could name.

Dorimène. Again?

Dorantes [to Dorimène]. You don't know him.

Mr. Jordan. She shall know me whenever she pleases.

Dorimène. Oh! Too much.

Dorantes. He's one who has a repartee always at hand. But you don't see, madam, that Mr. Jordan eats all the pieces you have touched.

Dorimène. Mr. Jordan is a man that I am charmed with.

Mr. Jordan. If I could charm your heart, I should be——

SCENE II

[Mrs. Jordan, Mr. Jordan, Dorimène, Dorantes, Musicians, Lackeys.]

Mrs. Jordan. Hey-day! why here's a jolly company of you, and I see very well you did not expect me. It was for this pretty affair then, Mr. Husband o' mine, that you were in such a violent hurry to pack me off to dine with my sister; I just now found a play-house below, and here I find a dinner fit for a wedding. Thus it is you spend your money, and thus it is you feast the ladies in my absence, and present 'em with music and a play, whilst I'm sent abroad in the meantime.

Dorantes. What do you mean, Madam Jordan? And what's your fancy to take it into your head, that your husband spends his money, and that 'tis he who entertains my lady? Know, pray, that 'tis I do it, that he only lends me his house, and that you ought to consider a little better what you say.

Mr. Jordan. Yes, Mrs. Impertinence, 'tis the count that presents the lady with all this, who is a person of quality. He does me the honour to borrow my house, and is pleased to let me be with him.

Mrs. Jordan. 'Tis all stuff this. I know what I know.

Dorantes. Mrs. Jordan, take your best spectacles, take 'em.

Mrs. Jordan. I've no need of spectacles, sir, I see clear enough; I've smelt things out a great while ago, I am no ass. 'Tis base in you, who are a great lord, to lend a helping hand, as you do, to the follies of my husband. And you, madam, who are a great lady, 'tis neither handsome, nor honest in you, to sow dissension in a family, and to suffer my husband to be in love with you.

Dorimène. What can be the meaning of all this? Go, Dorantes, 'tis wrong in you to expose me to the silly visions of this raving woman.

Dorantes [following Dorimène who goes out]. Madam, why madam, where are you running?

Mr. Jordan. Madam—My lord, make my excuses to her and endeavour to bring her back.

SCENE III

[Mrs. Jordan, and Mr. Jordan, Lackeys.]

Mr. Jordan. Ah! impertinent creature as you are, these are your fine doings; you come and affront me in the face of all the world, and drive people of quality away from my house.

Mrs. Jordan. I value not their quality.

Mr. Jordan. I don't know what hinders me, you plaguy hussy, from splitting your skull with the fragments of the feast you came here to disturb. [Lackeys take away the table.]

Mrs. Jordan [going]. I despise all this. I defend my own rights, and I shall have all the wives on my side.

Mr. Jordan. You do well to get out of the way of my fury.

SCENE IV

Mr. Jordan [alone]. She came here at a most unlucky time. I was in the humour of saying fine things, and never did I find myself so witty. What have we got here?

SCENE V

[MR. JORDAN, COVIEL, *disguised.*]

COVIEL. Sir, I don't know whether I have the honour to be known to you.

MR. JORDAN. No, sir.

COVIEL. I have seen you when you were not above thus tall.

MR. JORDAN. Me?

COVIEL. You were one of the prettiest children in the world; and all the ladies used to take you in their arms to kiss you.

MR. JORDAN. To kiss me?

COVIEL. Yes, I was an intimate friend of the late gentleman your father.

MR. JORDAN. Of the late gentleman my father!

COVIEL. Yes. He was a very honest gentleman.

MR. JORDAN. What is't you say?

COVIEL. I say that he was a very honest gentleman.

MR. JORDAN. My father?

COVIEL. Yes.

MR. JORDAN. Did you know him very well?

COVIEL. Certainly.

MR. JORDAN. And did you know him for a gentleman?

COVIEL. Without doubt.

MR. JORDAN. I don't know then what the world means.

COVIEL. How?

MR. JORDAN. There is a stupid sort of people, who would face me down that he was a tradesman.

COVIEL. He a tradesman? 'Tis mere scandal, he never was one. All that he did was, that he was very obliging, very officious, and as he was a great connoisseur in stuffs, he used to pick them up everywhere, have 'em carried to his house, and gave 'em to his friends for money.

MR. JORDAN. I'm very glad of your acquaintance, that you may bear witness that my father was a gentleman.

COVIEL. I'll maintain it in the face of all the world.

MR. JORDAN. You will oblige me. What business brings you here?

COVIEL. Since my acquaintance with the late gentleman your father, honest gentleman, as I was telling you, I have travelled round the world.

MR. JORDAN. Round the world?

COVIEL. Yes.

MR. JORDAN. I fancy 'tis a huge way off, that same country.

COVIEL. Most certainly. I have not been returned from these tedious travels of mine but four days. And because I have an interest in everything that concerns you, I come to tell you the best news in the world.

MR. JORDAN. What?

COVIEL. You know that the son of the Great Turk is here.

MR. JORDAN. I? No.

COVIEL. How? He has a most magnificent train. All the world goes to see him, and he has been received in this country as a person of importance.

MR. JORDAN. In troth, I did not know that.

COVIEL. What is of advantage to you in this affair is, that he is in love with your daughter.

MR. JORDAN. The son of the Great Turk?

COVIEL. Yes, and wants to be your son-in-law.

MR. JORDAN. My son-in-law, the son of the Great Turk?

COVIEL. The son of the Great Turk your son-in-law. As I have been to see him, and perfectly understand his language, he held a conversation with me; and after some other discourse, says he to me: Acciam croc soler, onch alla moustaph gidelum amanahem varahini oussere carbulath. That is to say, Have you not seen a young handsome person, who is the daughter of Mr. Jordan, a gentleman of Paris?

MR. JORDAN. The son of the Great Turk said that of me?

COVIEL. Yes, as I made answer to him,

that I knew you particularly well, and that I had seen your daughter. Ah, says he to me, Marababa sahem; that is to say, Ah! how am I enamoured with her!

Mr. Jordan. Marababa sahem means: Ah! how am I enamoured with her?

Coviel. Yes.

Mr. Jordan. Marry, you did well to tell me so, for as for my part, I should never have believed that Marababa sahem had meant, Ah! how am I enamoured with her! 'Tis an admirable language, this same Turkish!

Coviel. More admirable than one can believe. Do you know very well what is the meaning of Cacaramouchen?

Mr. Jordan. Cacaramouchen? No.

Coviel. 'Tis as if you should say, My dear soul.

Mr. Jordan. Cacaramouchen means, My dear soul?

Coviel. Yes.

Mr. Jordan. Why, 'tis very wonderful! Cacaramouchen, my dear soul. Would one ever have thought it? I am perfectly confounded at it.

Coviel. In short, to finish my embassy, he comes to demand your daughter in marriage; and to have a father-in-law who should be suitable to him, he designs to make you a Mamamouchi, which is a certain grand dignity of his country.

Mr. Jordan. Mamamouchi?

Coviel. Yes, Mamamouchi: that is to say, in our language, a Paladin. Paladin, is your ancient—Paladin in short: there's nothing in the world more noble than this; and you will rank with the grandest lord upon earth.

Mr. Jordan. The son of the Great Turk does me a great deal of honour, and I desire you would carry me to him, to return him my thanks.

Coviel. How? Why he's just acoming hither.

Mr. Jordan. Is he acoming hither?

Coviel. Yes. And he brings all things along with him for the ceremony of your dignity.

Mr. Jordan. He's main hasty.

Coviel. His love will suffer no delay.

Mr. Jordan. All that perplexes me, in this case, is, that my daughter is an obstinate hussy, who has took into her head one Cleontes, and vows she'll marry no person besides him.

Coviel. She'll change her opinion, when she sees the son of the Grand Turk; and then there happens here a very marvellous adventure, that is, that the son of the Grand Turk resembles this Cleontes, with a trifling difference. I just now came from him, they showed him me; and the love she bears for one, may easily pass to the other, and—I hear him coming; there he is.

SCENE VI

[Cleontes (like a Turk), three Pages carrying the vest of Cleontes, Mr. Jordan, Coviel.]

Cleontes. Ambousahim oqui boraf, Iordina, salamalequi.

Coviel [to Mr. Jordan]. That is to say, Mr. Jordan, may your heart be all the year like a rose-tree in flower. These are obliging ways of speaking in that country.

Mr. Jordan. I am His Turkish Highness's most humble servant.

Coviel. Carigar camboto oustin moraf.

Cleontes. Oustin yoc catamalequi basum base alla moran.

Coviel. He says that Heaven has given you the strength of lions, and the prudence of serpents.

Mr. Jordan. His Turkish Highness does me too much honour; and I wish him all manner of prosperity.

Coviel. Ossa binamin sadoc babally oracaf ouram.

Cleontes. Bel-men.

Coviel. He says that you should go quickly with him, to prepare yourself for the ceremony, in order afterwards to see your daughter, and to conclude the marriage.

Mr. Jordan. So many things in two words?

COVIEL. Yes, the Turkish language is much in that way; it says a great deal in a few words. Go quickly where he desires you.

SCENE VII

COVIEL [alone]. Ha, ha, ha. I'faith, this is all absolutely droll. What a dupe! Had he had his part by heart, he could not have played it better. O, hoh!

SCENE VIII

[DORANTES, COVIEL.]

COVIEL. I beseech you, sir, lend us a helping hand here, in a certain affair which is in agitation.

DORANTES. Ah! ah! Coviel, who could have known thee? How art thou trimmed out there!

COVIEL. You see, ha, ha.

DORANTES. What do ye laugh at?

COVIEL. At a thing, sir, that well deserves it.

DORANTES. What?

COVIEL. I could give you a good many times, sir, to guess the stratagem we are making use of with Mr. Jordan, to bring him over to give his daughter to my master.

DORANTES. I don't at all guess the stratagem, but I guess it will not fail of its effect, since you undertake it.

COVIEL. I know, sir, you are not unacquainted with the animal.

DORANTES. Tell me what it is.

COVIEL. Be at the trouble of withdrawing a little farther off, to make room for what I see acoming. You will see one part of the story, whilst I give you a narration of the rest.

SCENE IX

THE TURKISH CEREMONY

[THE MUFTI, DERVISHES, TURKS (assisting to the MUFTI), SINGERS and DANCERS.]

Six TURKS *enter gravely, two and two, to the sound of instruments. They bear three carpets, with which they dance in several figures, and then lift them up very high. The* TURKS *singing, pass under the carpets, and range themselves on each side of the stage. The* MUFTI *accompanied by* DERVISHES, *close the march.*

Then the TURKS *spread the carpets on the ground, and kneel down upon them; the* MUFTI *and the* DERVISHES *standing in the middle of them; while the* MUFTI *invokes Mahomet in dumb contortions and grimaces, the* TURKS *prostrate themselves to the ground, singing Allah, raising their hands to heaven, singing Allah, and so continuing alternately to the end of the invocation. When they all rise up, singing Allahekber; then two* DERVISHES *bring* MR. JORDAN.]

SCENE X

[*The* MUFTI, DERVISHES, TURKISH SINGERS *and* DANCERS, MR. JORDAN (*clothed like a Turk, his head shaved, without a turban or sabre*).]

THE MUFTI [*to* MR. JORDAN]. If thou understandest,
　　Answer;
If thou dost not understand,
Hold thy peace, hold thy peace.

I am Mufti,
Thou! who thou art
I don't know:
Hold thy peace, hold thy peace.
　　　　[*Two* DERVISHES *retire with* MR. JORDAN.]

SCENE XI

[THE MUFTI, DERVISHES, TURKS (*singing and dancing*).]

MUFTI. Say, Turk, who is this,
An Anabaptist, an anabaptist?

THE TURKS. No.

MUFTI. A Zuinglian?
THE TURKS. No.
MUFTI. A Coffite?
THE TURKS. No.
MUFTI. A Hussite? A Morist? A Fronest?
THE TURKS. No, no, no.
MUFTI. No, no, no. Is he a Pagan?
THE TURKS. No.
MUFTI. A Lutheran?
THE TURKS. No.
MUFTI. A Puritan?
THE TURKS. No.
MUFTI. A Brahmin? A Moffian? A Zurian?
THE TURKS. No, no, no.
MUFTI. No, no, no. A Mahometan, a Mahometan?
THE TURKS. There you have it, there you have it.
MUFTI. How is he called? How is he called?
THE TURKS. Jordan, Jordan.
MUFTI [*dancing*]. Jordan! Jordan!
THE TURKS. Jordan, Jordan.
MUFTI. To Mahomet for Jordan:
I pray night and day,
That he would make a Paladin
Of Jordan, of Jordan.
Give him a turban, and give a sabre,
With a galley and a brigantine,
To defend Palestine.
To Mahomet for Jordan,
I pray night and day. [*To the* TURKS.]
Is Jordan a good Turk?
THE TURKS. That he is, that he is.
MUFTI [*singing and dancing*]. Ha, la ba, ba la chou, ba la ba, ba la da.
THE TURKS. Ha la ba, ba la chou, ba la ba, ba la da.

SCENE XII

[MUFTI, DERVISHES, MR. JORDAN, TURKS (*singing and dancing*).]
[*The* MUFTI *returns with the State Turban, which is of an immeasurable largeness, garnished with lighted wax candles, four or five rows deep,* accompanied by two DERVISHES bearing the Alcoran with conic caps, garnished also with lighted candles.
The two other DERVISHES *lead up* MR. JORDAN, *and place him on his knees with his hands to the ground, so that his back on which the Alcoran is placed, may serve for a desk to the* MUFTI, *who makes a second burlesque invocation, knitting his eyebrows, striking his hands sometimes upon the Alcoran, and tossing over the leaves with precipitation; after which, lifting up his hands, and crying with a loud voice,* Hou.
During this second invocation, the assistant TURKS *bowing down and raising themselves alternately, sing likewise,* Hou, hou, hou.]
MR. JORDAN [*after they have taken the Alcoran off his back*]. Ouf.
MUFTI [*to* MR. JORDAN]. Thou wilt not be a knave?
THE TURKS. No, no, no.
MUFTI. Not be a thief?
THE TURKS. No, no, no.
MUFTI [*to the* TURKS]. Give the turban.
THE TURKS. Thou wilt not be a knave?
No, no, no.
Not be a thief?
No, no, no.
Give the turban.
[*The* TURKS *dancing put the turban on* MR. JORDAN'S *head at the sound of the instruments.*]
MUFTI [*giving the sabre to* MR. JORDAN]. Be brave, be no scoundrel,
Take the sabre.
THE TURKS [*drawing their sabres*]. Be brave, be no scoundrel,
Take the sabre.
[*The* TURKS *dancing strike* MR. JORDAN *several times with their sabres, to music.*]

MUFTI. Give, give
The bastonade.
THE TURKS. Give, give
The bastonade.

[*The* TURKS *dancing give* MR.
JORDAN *several strokes with a
cudgel to music.*]

MUFTI. Don't think it a shame,
This is the last affront.
THE TURKS. Don't think it a shame,
This is the last affront.

[*The* MUFTI *begins a third in-
vocation. The* DERVISHES *sup-
port him with great respect,
after which the* TURKS *singing
and dancing round the* MUFTI,
retire with him, and lead off
MR. JORDAN.]

ACT V

SCENE I

[MRS. JORDAN, MR. JORDAN.]

MRS. JORDAN. Bless us all! Mercy
upon us! What have we got here? What
a figure! What! dressed to go a mum-
ming, and is this a time to go masked?
Speak therefore, what does this mean?
Who has trussed you up in this manner?

MR. JORDAN. Do but see the imper-
tinent slut, to speak after this manner to
a Mamamouchi.

MRS. JORDAN. How's that?

MR. JORDAN. Yes, you must show me
respect now I am just made a Mama-
mouchi.

MRS. JORDAN. What d'ye mean with
your Mamamouchi?

MR. JORDAN. Mamamouchi, I tell you.
I am a Mamamouchi.

MRS. JORDAN. What beast is that?

MR. JORDAN. Mamamouchi, that is to
say, in our language, a Paladin.

MRS. JORDAN. A Paladin? Are you of
an age to be a morris-dancer?

MR. JORDAN. What an ignoramus! I
say, Paladin. 'Tis a dignity, of which
I have now gone through the cere-
mony.

MRS. JORDAN. What ceremony then?

MR. JORDAN. Mahameta per Jordina.

MRS. JORDAN. What does that mean?

MR. JORDAN. Jordina, that is to say,
Jordan.

MRS. JORDAN. Well, how Jordan?

MR. JORDAN. Voler far un Paladina
de Jordina.

MRS. JORDAN. What?

MR. JORDAN. Dar turbanta con galera.

MRS. JORDAN. What's the meaning of
that?

MR. JORDAN. Per deffender Palestina.

MRS. JORDAN. What is it you would
say?

MR. JORDAN. Dara, dara, bastonnara.

MRS. JORDAN. What is this same jar-
gon?

MR. JORDAN. Non tener honta, questa
star l'ultima affronta.

MRS. JORDAN. What in the name of
wonder, can all this be?

MR. JORDAN [*singing and dancing*].
Hou la ba, ba la chou, ba la ba, ba la da.
[*Falls down to the ground.*]

MRS. JORDAN. Alas and well-a-day!
My husband is turned fool.

MR. JORDAN [*getting up and walking
off*]. Peace, insolence, show respect to
Mr. Mamamouchi.

MRS. JORDAN [*alone*]. How could he
lose his senses? I must run and prevent
his going out. [*Seeing* DORIMÈNE *and*
DORANTES.] So, here come the rest
of our gang. I see nothing but vexation
on all sides.

SCENE II

[DORANTES, DORIMÈNE.]

DORANTES. Yes, madam, you'll see the
merriest thing that can be seen; and I
don't believe it's possible, in the whole
world, to find another man so much a
fool as this here. And besides, madam,
we must endeavour to promote Cleontes's
amour, and to countenance his masquer-
ade. He's a very pretty gentleman and
deserves that one should interest one's
self in his favour.

DORIMÈNE. I've a very great value for him, and he deserves good fortune.

DORANTES. Besides, we have here, madam, an entertainment that will suit us, and which we ought not to suffer to be lost; and I must by all means see whether my fancy will succeed.

DORIMÈNE. I saw there magnificent preparations, and these are things, Dorantes, I can no longer suffer. Yes, I'm resolved to put a stop, at last, to your profusions; and to break off all the expenses you are at on my account, I have determined to marry you out of hand. This is the real secret of the affair, and all these things end, as you know, with marriage.

DORANTES. Ah! madam, is it possible you should form so kind a resolution in my favour?

DORIMÈNE. I only do it to prevent you from ruining yourself; and without this, I see plainly, that before 'tis long you won't be worth a groat.

DORANTES. How am I obliged to you, madam, for the care you take to preserve my estate! 'Tis entirely at your service, as well as my heart, and you may use both of 'em just in the manner you please.

DORIMÈNE. I shall make a proper use of them both. But here comes your man; an admirable figure.

SCENE III

[MR. JORDAN, DORIMÈNE, DORANTES.]

DORANTES. Sir, my lady and I are come to pay our homage to your new dignity, and to rejoice with you at the marriage you are concluding betwixt your daughter and the son of the Grand Turk.

MR. JORDAN [bowing first in the Turkish manner]. Sir, I wish you the force of serpents, and the wisdom of lions.

DORIMÈNE. I was exceeding glad to be one of the first, sir, who should come and congratulate you upon the high degree of glory to which you are raised.

MR. JORDAN. Madam, I wish your rose-tree may flower all the year round; I am infinitely obliged to you for interesting yourselves in the honour that's paid me; and I am greatly rejoiced to see you returned hither, that I may make my most humble excuses for the impertinence of my wife.

DORIMÈNE. That's nothing at all, I can excuse a commotion of this kind in her; your heart ought to be precious to her, and 'tis not at all strange the possession of such a man as you are, should give her some alarms.

MR. JORDAN. The possession of my heart is a thing you have entirely gained.

DORANTES. You see, madam, that Mr. Jordan is none of those people whom prosperity blinds, and that he knows, in all his grandeur, how to own his friends.

DORIMÈNE. 'Tis the mark of a truly generous soul.

DORANTES. Where is His Turkish Highness? We should be glad, as your friends, to pay our devoirs to him.

MR. JORDAN. There he comes, and I have sent to bring my daughter to join hands with him.

SCENE IV

[MR. JORDAN, DORIMÈNE, DORANTES, CLEONTES (in a Turkish habit).]

DORANTES [to CLEONTES]. Sir, we come to compliment Your Highness, as friends of the gentleman your father-in-law, and to assure you, with respect, of our most humble services.

MR. JORDAN. Where's the dragoman, to tell him who you are, and make him understand what you say; you shall see that he'll answer you, and he speaks Turkish marvellously. Hola! there; where the deuce is he gone? [To CLEONTES.] Stref, strif, strof, straf. The gentleman is a grande segnore, grande segnore, grande segnore; and madam is a granda dama, granda dama. [Seeing he cannot make himself be understood.] Lack-a-day! [To CLEONTES.] Sir, he be a French Mamamouchi, and madam a

French Mamamouchess. I can't speak plainer. Good, here's the dragoman.

SCENE V

[MR. JORDAN, DORIMÈNE, DORANTES, CLEONTES (*in a Turkish habit*), COVIEL (*disguised*).]

MR. JORDAN. Where do you run? We can say nothing without you. [*Pointing to* CLEONTES.] Inform him a little that the gentleman and lady are persons of great quality, who come to pay their compliments to him, as friends of mine, and to assure him of their services. [*To* DORIMÈNE *and* DORANTES.] You shall see how he will answer.

COVIEL. Alabala crociam, acci boram alabamen.

CLEONTES. Catalequi tubal ourin soter amalouchan.

MR. JORDAN [*to* DORIMÈNE *and* DORANTES]. Do ye see?

COVIEL. He says that the rain of prosperity waters, at all seasons, the gardens of your family.

MR. JORDAN. I told you that he speaks Turkish.

DORANTES. This is admirable.

SCENE VI

[CLEONTES, MR. JORDAN, LUCILIA, DORIMÈNE, DORANTES, COVIEL.]

MR. JORDAN. Come, daughter, come nearer, and give the gentleman your hand, who does you the honour of demanding you in marriage.

LUCILIA. What's the matter, father, how are you dressed here? what! are you playing a comedy?

MR. JORDAN. No, no, 'tis no comedy, 'tis a very serious affair; and the most honourable for you that possibly can be wished. [*Pointing to* CLEONTES.] This is the husband I bestow upon you.

LUCILIA. Upon me, father?

MR. JORDAN. Yes upon you, come take him by the hand, and thank Heaven for your good fortune.

LUCILIA. I won't marry.

MR. JORDAN. I'll make you, am I not your father?

LUCILIA. I won't do it.

MR. JORDAN. Here's a noise indeed! Come, I tell you. Your hand here.

LUCILIA. No, father, I've told you before that there's no power can oblige me to take any other husband than Cleontes; and I am determined upon all extremities rather than—[*Discovering* CLEONTES.] 'Tis true that you are my father; I owe you absolute obedience; and you may dispose of me according to your pleasure.

MR. JORDAN. Hah, I am charmed to see you return so readily to your duty; and it is a pleasure to me to have my daughter obedient.

SCENE VII

[CLEONTES, MRS. JORDAN, MR. JORDAN, LUCILIA, DORIMÈNE, DORANTES, COVIEL.]

MRS. JORDAN. How, how, what does this mean? They tell me you design to marry your daughter to a mummer.

MR. JORDAN. Will you hold your tongue, impertinence? You're always coming to mix your extravagances with everything; there's no possibility of teaching you common sense.

MRS. JORDAN. 'Tis you whom there's no teaching to be wise, and you go from folly to folly. What's your design, what would you do with this flock of people?

MR. JORDAN. I design to marry my daughter to the son of the Grand Turk.

MRS. JORDAN. To the son of the Grand Turk?

MR. JORDAN. Yes. [*Pointing to* COVIEL.] Make your compliments to him by the dragoman there.

MRS. JORDAN. I have nothing to do with the dragoman, and I shall tell him plainly to his face that he shall have none of my daughter.

MR. JORDAN. Will you hold your tongue once more?

DORANTES. What, Mrs. Jordan, do you oppose such an honour as this? Do you refuse His Turkish Highness for a son-in-law?

MRS. JORDAN. Lack-a-day, sir, meddle you with your own affairs.

DORIMÈNE. 'Tis a great honour, 'tis by no means to be rejected.

MRS. JORDAN. Madam, I desire you too not to give yourself any trouble about what no ways concerns you.

DORANTES. 'Tis the friendship we have for you, that makes us interest ourselves in what is of advantage to you.

MRS. JORDAN. I shall easily excuse your friendship.

DORANTES. There's your daughter consents to her father's pleasure.

MRS. JORDAN. My daughter consent to marry a Turk?

DORANTES. Certainly.

MRS. JORDAN. Can she forget Cleontes?

DORANTES. What would one not do to be a great lady?

MRS. JORDAN. I would strangle her with my own hands, had she done such a thing as this.

MR. JORDAN. Here's tittle-tattle in abundance. I tell you this marriage shall be consummated.

MRS. JORDAN. And I tell you that it shall not be consummated.

MR. JORDAN. What a noise is here?

LUCILIA. Mother!

MRS. JORDAN. Go, you are a pitiful hussy.

MR. JORDAN [to MRS. JORDAN]. What! do you scold her for being obedient to me?

MRS. JORDAN. Yes, she belongs to me as well as you.

COVIEL [to MRS. JORDAN]. Madam.

MRS. JORDAN. What would you say to me, you?

COVIEL. One word.

MRS. JORDAN. I've nothing to do with your word.

COVIEL [to MR. JORDAN]. Sir, would she hear me but one word in private, I'll promise you to make her consent to what you have a mind.

MRS. JORDAN. I won't consent to it.

COVIEL. Only hear me.

MRS. JORDAN. No.

MR. JORDAN [to MRS. JORDAN]. Give him the hearing.

MRS. JORDAN. No, I won't hear him.

MR. JORDAN. He'll tell you——

MRS. JORDAN. He shall tell me nothing.

MR. JORDAN. Do but see the great obstinacy of the woman! Will it do you any harm to hear him?

COVIEL. Only hear me; you may do what you please afterwards.

MRS. JORDAN. Well, what?

COVIEL [aside to MRS. JORDAN]. We have made signs to you, madam, this hour. Don't you see plainly that all is done purely to accommodate ourselves to the visions of your husband; that we are imposing upon him under this disguise, and that it is Cleontes himself who is the son of the Great Turk?

MRS. JORDAN [aside to COVIEL]. Oh, oh!

COVIEL [aside to MRS. JORDAN]. And that 'tis me, Coviel, who am the dragoman?

MRS. JORDAN [aside to COVIEL]. Oh! in that case, I give up.

COVIEL [aside to MRS. JORDAN]. Don't seem to know anything of the matter.

MRS. JORDAN [aloud]. Yes, 'tis all done, I consent to the marriage.

MR. JORDAN. Ay, all the world submits to reason. [To MRS. JORDAN.] You would not hear him. I knew he would explain to you what the son of the Great Turk is.

MRS. JORDAN. He has explained it to me sufficiently, and I'm satisfied with it. Let us send to see for a notary.

DORANTES. 'Tis well said. And, Mrs. Jordan, that you may set your mind perfectly at rest, and that you should this day quit all jealousy which you may have entertained of the gentleman your husband, my lady and I shall make use of the same notary to marry us.

MRS. JORDAN. I consent to that too.

MR. JORDAN [aside to DORANTES]. 'Tis to make her believe.

DORANTES [aside to MR. JORDAN]. We

must by all means amuse her a little with this pretence.

MR. JORDAN. Good, good. [*Aloud.*] Let somebody go see for the notary.

DORANTES. In the meantime, till he comes and has drawn up the contracts, let us see our entertainment, and give His Turkish Highness the diversion of it.

MR. JORDAN. Well advised; come let us take our places.

MRS. JORDAN. And Nicola?

MR. JORDAN. I give het to the drago-man; and my wife, to whosoever pleases to take her.

COVIEL. Sir, I thank you. [*Aside.*] If it's possible to find a greater fool than this, I'll go and publish it at Rome.

THE BARBER OF SEVILLE

By PIERRE AUGUSTIN CARON DE BEAUMARCHAIS

Produced at Paris, 1775

TRANSLATED BY W. R. TAYLOR *

CHARACTERS

COUNT ALMAVIVA, *Spanish Grandee, incognito lover of* ROSINE
BARTHOLO, *physician and guardian of* ROSINE
ROSINE, *young lady of noble birth, ward of* BARTHOLO
FIGARO, *the barber of Seville*
DON BAZILE, *organist and* ROSINE'S *music teacher*
YOUNGMAN, *an old servant of* BARTHOLO
WIDEAWAKE, *another servant of* BARTHOLO, *a dolt and a sluggard*
A NOTARY PUBLIC
A JUSTICE OF THE PEACE
SEVERAL POLICEMEN *and* SERVANTS, *with torches*

ACT I.   Street in Seville; outside Bartholo's house in the morning.
ACT II.   Reception-room in Bartholo's house; the same morning.
ACT III.   The same in the afternoon.
ACT IV.   The same in the evening.

ACT I

SCENE—*The morning in a street in Seville where all the windows are barred and fitted with shutters.*

[*As the curtain rises* THE COUNT *is walking to and fro alone, in a voluminous brown cape and hat with a turned-down brim.*]

THE COUNT [*looking at his watch*]. It is earlier than I thought: still quite a

while till the time when she usually appears in her window. Well, never mind; it is better to get here too soon than to miss seeing her even one minute. If some court dandy should nose me out a hundred leagues from Madrid, loitering every morning under the window of a girl to whom I have never spoken, he would take me for some gallant of the time of Isabella of Castile. Why not? Every one seeks happiness. Happiness for me exists

---

* Reprinted from the edition published by Walter H. Baker & Co., copyright 1922, by permission of the publisher.

in the heart of Rosine. But then! to follow a girl to Seville when Madrid and the court offer everywhere such easy pleasures! That's just it. That's just what I am fleeing. I am tired of love conquests which self-interest, fitness, or vanity present to us without end. It is so sweet to be loved for oneself! And if I could make sure that in this disguise——Oh! The devil take this intruder!

[FIGARO enters with a guitar slung over his shoulder, a wide ribbon serving as a strap. He hums gaily, a piece of paper in his hand. He also has a pencil. THE COUNT hides.]

FIGARO.   Away with the corrosion of sorrow!
The fire of good wine let us borrow.
For without its inspiration
Man enters a declination,
And dieth on the morrow.

Pretty good up to that point, isn't it?

And dieth on the morrow.
Glowing wine and restful ease
In my heart madly struggle——

Oh, no, no, no, no! They do not struggle; they live in it together peacefully enough.

Divide between them my heart.

Is it good English to say divide between them or divide among them? Eh? Oh, dear me, we makers of musical comedies must not be too particular. To-day things not worth being said are sung.

Glowing wine and restful ease
Share my heart between them.

Now I would like to finish with something pretty, sparkling, brilliant which may have the trace of a thought.

[He kneels on one knee and writes, singing at the same time.]

Share my heart between them.
If the one has my love,
The other gives me happiness.

Oh, come now; that falls flat. That isn't the thing. What I need is an antithesis.

If the one is my mistress,
The other——

Ah, to be sure. I have it.

The other is my slave.

Very good for you, Figaro, old man.
[He writes, at the same time singing.]

Glowing wine and restful ease
Share my heart between them;
If the one is my mistress,
The other is my slave;
The other is my slave;
The other is my slave!

What do you say to that? With the accompaniment added we will see yet, my friends of the conspiracy against me, if I do not know what I am talking about. [He catches sight of THE COUNT.] I have seen that priest there somewhere.
[He arises.]

THE COUNT [aside]. This man is no stranger to me.

FIGARO. Oh, no; he isn't a priest. That proud and noble bearing——

THE COUNT. That grotesque figure.

FIGARO. I am not at all mistaken; it is the Count Almaviva.

THE COUNT. I believe it is that rascal of a Figaro.

FIGARO. It is he indeed. My Lord——

THE COUNT. Rascal, if you say a word——

FIGARO. Yes, I recognize you. These are the kind of familiarities with which you have always honored me.

THE COUNT. For my part, I do not recognize you. You are so fat and sleek——

FIGARO. No wonder, my lord; I've seen such hard times.

THE COUNT. Poor little fellow! But what are you doing in Seville? It hasn't been so long since I recommended you to the government civil service for a position.

FIGARO. I secured it, my lord, and my gratitude——

THE COUNT. Call me Lindor. Don't you see by my disguise that I wish to be unknown?

FIGARO [*with dignity*]. I'll withdraw, my lord.

THE COUNT. Not at all. I am waiting something here, and two men who chat are less suspected than one who loiters around. Let's have the appearance of chatting amiably about—let's see—this position.

FIGARO. The Minister, complying with your request, had me appointed right away as assistant druggist.

THE COUNT. In the Army Medical Corps?

FIGARO. No, in the horse-breeding farms of Andalusia.

THE COUNT [*laughing*]. Fine beginning.

FIGARO. Oh, the position wasn't so bad; because, having charge of the dressings for the wounds and of the drugs, I often sold good horse medicine to the enlisted men.

THE COUNT. Which killed the loyal subjects of the king?

FIGARO [*laughs*]. Oh, well, there isn't any universal remedy but what sometimes has failed to cure even Galicians, Catalonians, and Auvergnians.

THE COUNT. Why then did you quit?

FIGARO. Quit? They quit me. Some one spoke ill of me to the authorities.

"Envy with clutching fingers, with pale and livid face——"

THE COUNT. Oh, for pity's sake! Are you a maker of verses too? I have just seen you scribbling on your knee and humming.

FIGARO. That is just the cause of my misfortune, your Excellency. When it was reported to the Minister that I was making, prettily enough I dare say, occasional verses to the ladies; that I was sending articles to the newspapers; that there were in circulation some madrigals written according to my style; when he

knew, in short, that I was head and ears in print, he took it tragically and made me give up my position under the pretext that love of letters does not sit well with strict attention to business.

THE COUNT. Well reasoned. And you did not present to him your side of——

FIGARO. I believed myself only too fortunate in having been forgotten by him, being persuaded that you of the upper class do us positive good when you are doing us no ill.

THE COUNT. You are not telling the whole story. I remember that in my service you were a bad enough fellow.

FIGARO. Oh, but dear me, my lord, would you have a poor fellow without any faults?

THE COUNT. Lazy, unsteady——

FIGARO. How many masters does your Excellency know who measure up to the standard of perfection you are demanding in a servant?

THE COUNT [*laughing*]. Not bad. And you have retired in this city?

FIGARO. No, not just yet——

THE. COUNT [*silencing him*]. One moment—— I thought it was she—— Go ahead; I hear you well enough.

FIGARO. On returning to Madrid, I wished to try anew my literary talents, and the theatre seemed to me a field of honor.

THE COUNT. Oh, mercy on us!

FIGARO [*during* FIGARO'S *reply* THE COUNT *anxiously watches* ROSINE'S *window*]. In truth I do not know why I have not had the greatest success; for I filled the pit of the theatre with excellent workmen, their hands like—butter paddles; I banned the use of canes, gloves, everything that produces only dull-sounding applause; and, on my honor, before the first night of my play, the critics and the club gossipers had the best good will in the world toward me. But the effort of my enemies in the conspiracy——

THE COUNT. Ah, a conspiracy against you. And Monsieur the author failed.

FIGARO. Just as has many another. Why not? They hissed me off the stage.

But if I can ever get them together again——

THE COUNT. You will get revenge by boring them to death?

FIGARO. Ah, what a treat I have in store for them, by Jove!

THE COUNT. You swear! Do you not know that at the Palace of Justice one has only twenty-four hours in which to curse his judges?

FIGARO. One has twenty-four years in the theatre; life is too short to wear out such a grudge.

THE COUNT. Your merry anger delights me. But you are not telling me what made you leave Madrid.

FIGARO [with the air of making a fine speech]. It was my Good Angel, your Excellency, since I have been fortunate enough to find again in you my former master. [In a serious vein.] Seeing at Madrid that the republic of letters is a republic of wolves, each snarling at the other; and that the contempt caused by this ridiculous bitterness made it easy for all the insects, the mosquitoes, the gnats, the crawling things, the envious, the hack writers, the publishers, the censors,—the whole pack of wolves which fastens itself to the skins of the unfortunate men of letters, to bite to pieces and suck dry the little substance left them; tired of writing, bored with myself, disgusted with others, buried under debts, light of purse, at last convinced that the tangible revenue of the razor is preferable to the empty honors of the pen, I left Madrid; and my pack on my back, philosophically travelling about through the two Castilles, Manca, Estramadura, Sierra-Morena, Andalusia, welcomed in one town, emprisoned in another, and everywhere rising above events; praised by some, harshly criticized by others; making the best of good and of bad weather, putting up with misfortune, making fun of fools, defying the wicked, laughing at my misery, and shaving everybody, you see me finally established in Seville, and ready again to serve your lordship in anything that you may be pleased to order.

THE COUNT. What has given you so cheerful a philosophy of life?

FIGARO. Long experience with misfortune. I hasten to laugh at everything for fear that otherwise I might be forced to weep over it.

THE COUNT. Let's be off, quick!

FIGARO. Why?

THE COUNT. Come now, you wretch. You will be the undoing of me.

[They conceal themselves just as the shutters of the window in the first story are opened. BARTHOLO and ROSINE appear at the window.]

ROSINE. How sweet to get a breath of fresh air! This window is so rarely opened.

BARTHOLO. What is that paper you have there?

ROSINE. Some couplets from the "Useless Precaution" which my music teacher gave me yesterday.

BARTHOLO. What is this "Useless Precaution"?

ROSINE. It is a new musical comedy.

BARTHOLO. Another one of those prose plays! More of that new bosh!

ROSINE. I know nothing at all about it.

BARTHOLO. Anyway, creditable critics call it that. The world is going to the dogs. These barbarous times now—— This century——

ROSINE. You are always maligning our century.

BARTHOLO. Pardon the liberty that I take. What has our century produced worth praising? Follies of all sorts: liberty of thought, electricity, religious tolerance, vaccination, quinine, the encyclopedia, these prose plays——

ROSINE [the paper drops from her hand and falls into the street]. Oh! My song! My song dropped while I was listening to you—Run! Run now, please! My song will be lost!

BARTHOLO. The devil! Why didn't you hold to it while you had it?

[BARTHOLO leaves the balcony. ROSINE, as soon as he has dis-

*appeared into the house, sig-
nals to* THE COUNT.]

ROSINE. *St! St!* [THE COUNT *ap-
pears.*] Pick it up quickly, and go!

[THE COUNT *makes just one
bound, grasps the paper, and
hides again.*]

BARTHOLO [*comes out of the house and
looks around*]. Where is it then? I do
not see anything.

ROSINE. Under the balcony at the foot
of the wall.

BARTHOLO. Fine errand you have sent
me on. Has any one passed?

ROSINE. I haven't seen a soul.

BARTHOLO [*to himself*]. And I had the
simplicity to look for it! Bartholo, you're
only a fool, my friend; this ought to
teach you never to open a window look-
ing on the street.

[*He goes back into the house.*]

ROSINE [*still on the balcony*]. My un-
happiness is the excuse for this decep-
tion: lonely, shut-in, the victim of a hate-
ful old man's persecution; is it a crime
to attempt to escape slavery?

BARTHOLO [*appearing on the balcony*].
Come back in, my lady; it is my fault
that you have lost your song; but that
misfortune will not happen again,—I can
assure you of that.

[*He closes the shutters and locks
them.* THE COUNT *and* FIGARO
enter, making sure that BAR-
THOLO *doesn't see them.*]

THE COUNT. Now that they have gone
in, let's take a look at this song, in which
some mystery is surely bottled up. It is
a note!

FIGARO. Ha! He asked what the "Use-
less Precaution" was.

THE COUNT [*reads rapidly*]. "Your ar-
dent attentions excite my curiosity; as
soon as my guardian goes out, sing care-
lessly to the air of this song a few verses
that will teach me the name, the rank,
and the intentions of one who appears to
interest himself so obstinately in the af-
fairs of unfortunate Rosine."

FIGARO [*imitating* ROSINE'S *voice*]. My
song! My song has fallen! Run, run

now! [*He laughs.*] Ha! Ha! Ha! Ha!
Oh, these women! If you want to teach
cunning to the most unsophisticated, just
lock her up.

THE COUNT. My darling Rosine!

FIGARO. My lord, I am no longer in
doubt as to the motives of your disguise;
you are making love here for future use.

THE COUNT. Well, you have caught on,
but if you blab——

FIGARO. What! I blab! Give away se-
crets! In allaying your fear, I shall not
use any of the fine phrases of honor and
devotion, phrases that are abused all day
long; I have only a word: it is to my
interest to keep silent; weigh that in the
balance——

THE COUNT. Very well then, know that
six months ago on the Prado I met by
chance a young girl of marvellous beauty.
You have just seen her. I have had her
sought for all over Madrid—in vain. Just
a few days ago I discovered that her
name is Rosine, that she is of noble ex-
traction, an orphan, and married to an
old doctor of this city, Bartholo by name.

FIGARO. 'Pon my honor, a pretty bird,
and hard to get from the nest. But who
told you that she was the wife of the
doctor?

THE COUNT. Everybody.

FIGARO. It is a story he patched up
upon arriving from Madrid, in order to
get rid of her admirers and to put her
pursuers on a false trail. So far she is
only his ward, but soon——

THE COUNT [*quickly*]. Never! Oh!
What a relief! I had determined to dare
all, in order to tell her how sorry I was
that she was married, and I find her
free! There's not a moment to lose; I
must make her love me and snatch her
from this unholy .engagement that is in
store for her. You say you know this
guardian?

FIGARO. As I know my mother.

THE COUNT. What kind of a fellow is
he?

FIGARO [*quickly*]. He's a slim, fat,
short, young, doddering old fool, dappled-
gray, clean shaven, cynic, who spies and

peeps, and scolds and whines at the same time.

THE COUNT. Oh, come! I've seen him. His disposition?

FIGARO. Brutal, avaricious, excessively amorous and jealous of his ward who hates him like poison.

THE COUNT. His good points are——?

FIGARO. None.

THE COUNT. So much the better. His honesty?

FIGARO. Just enough for him to escape hanging.

THE COUNT. So much the better. To punish a scoundrel, at the same time gaining my own happiness would——

FIGARO. Be both a personal and a public blessing, which is, in truth, my lord, the essence of morality.

THE COUNT. You say that fear of her lovers made him close his gates?

FIGARO. To everybody. If he could daub the chinks——

THE COUNT. Oh, the devil! So much the worse. You do not happen to have access to his house, do you?

FIGARO. Oh, yes I do! In the first place, the house in which I live belongs to the doctor, who puts me up there for nothing.

THE COUNT. Ha! Ha!

FIGARO. Yes, and I, in gratitude, promise him one hundred dollars a year for nothing also.

THE COUNT [impatiently]. You are his tenant?

FIGARO. More, his barber, his surgeon, his druggist. There isn't a razor, a lancette, or a hypodermic syringe used in his house except by the hand of your humble servant.

THE COUNT [kisses him on both cheeks]. Ah, Figaro, my friend, you shall be my Good Angel, my savior, my tutelary god.

FIGARO. Plague on't! How my usefulness to you has lessened the distance between us! Talk about your impassioned people!

THE COUNT. Lucky Figaro! You are going to see my Rosine; you are going to see her. Do you realize your good fortune?

FIGARO. Now that's the speech of a lover for you. Am I the one who adores her? I wish you could take my place!

THE COUNT. If we could only get rid of all prying eyes.

FIGARO. That is what I am thinking about.

THE COUNT. To get rid of them for twelve hours only.

FIGARO [meditating]. By keeping people busy about their own affairs you keep them from meddling with others, don't you?

THE COUNT. Doubtless. Why?

FIGARO [meditating]. I am just trying to think whether the pharmacopœia can furnish me with some little innocent means——

THE COUNT [in a laughing tone]. You rascal!

FIGARO. Oh, I don't mean to harm them. They have need of my services, and now to treat them all together.

THE COUNT. But this physician might smell a rat.

FIGARO. We must act so quickly that the rat will not have time to die. I have an idea. The regiment of the heir-apparent is just being quartered in this city.

THE COUNT. The Colonel is one of my friends.

FIGARO. Good. Present yourself at the doctor's house dressed like a trooper and with a quartermaster's billet. He will have to take you in, and I will take care of the rest.

THE COUNT. Excellent!

FIGARO. It would not be a bad idea for you to appear to be half drunk.

THE COUNT. What good will that do?

FIGARO. And treat him a bit cavalierly; your apparent drunkenness will be excuse enough for being unreasonable.

THE COUNT. Again I ask you why?

FIGARO [patiently]. So that he will take no offense, and so that he will believe you more in need of sleep than of love affairs in his house.

THE COUNT. Masterly conception! But why do you have no part in this plan?

FIGARO. Oh, yes, why not? We shall be lucky enough if he doesn't recognize you, you whom he has never seen. And how should I get you into the house afterwards?

THE COUNT. You are right——

FIGARO. Perhaps you will not be able to play this difficult part. A trooper—— Half drunk——

THE COUNT. You are mocking me. [*Assuming the speech of a drunken person.*] Isn't the house of Doctor Bartholo around here nowhere at all, m' friend?

FIGARO. Not so bad after all; your legs ought to be a trifle more wobbly. [*With a still more drunken tone.*] Izhn't thish th' housh——?

THE COUNT. Come now. You are imitating the drunkenness of a low fellow.

FIGARO. That is the best way to be drunk; it is the drunkenness of pleasure.

THE COUNT. Some one is opening the door.

FIGARO. It is our man. Let's move away till he leaves.

[THE COUNT *and* FIGARO *conceal themselves;* BARTHOLO *comes out of the house.*]

BARTHOLO [*speaks to some one inside the house*]. I am coming back directly; do not let any one in. What a fool I was to search for that song. When she began teasing, I should have suspected—— And this Bazile doesn't come either. He was to arrange things so that my marriage may secretly take place to-morrow; and no news from him. Well, I'll see what is keeping him.   [*Exit L.*]

[THE COUNT *and* FIGARO *come forward.*]

THE COUNT. What have I heard? To-morrow he marries Rosine secretly!

FIGARO. My lord, the difficulty of succeeding only adds to the necessity of trying.

THE COUNT. What then is this Bazile who is meddling with the marriage?

FIGARO. A poor beggar who teaches music to Bartholo's ward, wrapped up in his art, petty rascal, needy, on his knees in the presence of a dollar, and whom it will be easy to checkmate, noble sir——[*Glancing at the window.*] Look! Look! There she is.

THE COUNT. Who?

FIGARO. Behind the shutter; there she is. Do not look that way now!

THE COUNT. Why?

FIGARO. Didn't she write you: "Sing carelessly"? That is to say sing—as if you were singing—only sing—— Oh, there she is! There she is!

THE COUNT. Since I have succeeded in attracting her without being known to her, I shall not give up the name of Lindor which I have assumed; my triumph will have more charm that way. [*He unfolds the note of* ROSINE.] But how shall I sing to this air? I am neither verse-maker nor musician.

FIGARO. Excellent things, my lord, will come into your mind; in love the heart assists the productions of the mind. And take my guitar.

THE COUNT. And what am I to do with that? I am a miserable player.

FIGARO. Is it possible that there is one thing that a man like you cannot do? With the back of your hand like this: tum—tum—tum——Sing without the accompaniment of a guitar in Seville? You would be recognized right away, I swear, and run down immediately.

[FIGARO *flattens himself against the wall under the balcony.*]

THE COUNT [*sings, walking to and fro and accompanying himself on the guitar to the tune of "The Spanish Cavalier"*]. No longer unknown, I dare love you. You have ordained it, my dear! What can I gain by breathing my name? My mistress so desires and I obey, dear.

FIGARO [*whispers*]. Good, by Jove. Courage, my lord.

THE COUNT. I am Lindor; my birth is ordinary.
My love is that of a simple student.
Alas, that I have not to offer you
The rank and fortune of a noble chevalier!

FIGARO. Deuce take it! I who pride myself couldn't do better.

THE COUNT. Every morning here with a tender voice,
I shall sing of my hopeless love;
I shall limit my pleasures to seeing you;
And, oh, that you might find it a pleasure to listen to me!

FIGARO. Oh! My word! As for that refrain——

[*Words fail him. He comes closer and kisses the hem of* THE COUNT'S *cape.*]

THE COUNT. Figaro!

FIGARO. My lord?

THE COUNT. Do you think she heard me?

ROSINE [*sings from within*]. All things with delight in telling unite
That Lindor is charming
My heart as his right possessing——
[*The noise of a banging window is heard.*]

FIGARO. Now do you think that you have been heard?

THE COUNT. She closed her window. Some one apparently entered her room.

FIGARO. Oh, the poor little thing! How she trembled while she was singing! You have won her, my lord.

THE COUNT. She is making use of the means that she herself has pointed out:

"All things with delight in telling unite
That Lindor is charming."

How graceful! What love!

FIGARO. What cunning! What love!

THE COUNT. Do you think she will be mine, Figaro?

FIGARO. She would crawl through that shutter rather than miss being yours.

THE COUNT. I am done for. I am my Rosine's forever!

FIGARO. You are forgetting, my lord, that she cannot hear you now.

THE COUNT. Master Figaro, I have but one word to say to you: she shall be my wife; and if you help me out in this affair, all the while keeping my name hid —you hear, you understand?

FIGARO. I agree. Come, Figaro, my boy, your fortune is made.

THE COUNT. Let's withdraw for fear of exciting suspicion.

FIGARO [*quickly*]. I shall enter this house where by means of my art, with a single wave of the wand, I shall put vigilance to sleep, awaken love, lead jealousy astray, checkmate intrigue, and overturn all obstacles. You, my lord, at my house, trooper's uniform, quartermaster's billet, and your pockets lined with gold——

THE COUNT. Why gold?

FIGARO. Gold! Mercy me, gold! It is the backbone of intrigue!

THE COUNT. Calm yourself, Figaro, I shall bring plenty of it.

FIGARO [*making off*]. I shall rejoin you after a while.

THE COUNT. Figaro!

FIGARO. Well?

THE COUNT. What about your guitar?

FIGARO [*coming back*]. Forgetting my guitar! Surely I am losing my wits.
[*He goes off.*]

THE COUNT [*as* FIGARO *goes*]. You haven't told me where you live, addlepate.

FIGARO [*coming back*]. Ah, really I am daffy! My shop is just a little way from here, painted blue, lead window cases, sign over the door: three surgical instruments, an eye in a hand, with a motto, "Consilio Manuque."
[*He flees as if the devil were after him.*]

ACT II

SCENE—*The apartment of* ROSINE. *The window up stage is closed, and the shutters locked from the inside.*

[*As the curtain rises* ROSINE *enters alone, a candlestick in her hand. She places paper on the table and begins writing.*]

ROSINE. Marceline is sick; every one else is busy; and no one sees fit to write to me. I know not whether these walls have eyes and ears, or whether my hundred-eyed Argus has some evil genius who tells him things just at the wrong time; but I cannot take a step nor speak a word the significance of which he doesn't at once guess.—Oh, Lindor! [*She sighs, looks pensive for a moment, and then seals the letter.*] Anyway I'll seal my letter though I know not when nor how I can get it to him. From behind my closed shutters I have seen him talk a long time to the barber Figaro. That good fellow has now and then shown the pity he felt for me; if I could only speak to him for a moment——[FIGARO *enters.* ROSINE *surprised.*] Ah, Figaro, how glad I am to see you!

FIGARO. I trust that your health is good, my lady

ROSINE. Not too good, Figaro, I am bored to death.

FIGARO. I can well believe it. Ennui fattens only fools.

ROSINE. With whom were you holding such lively conversation down there just now? I did not hear, but——

FIGARO. With a young student, a relative of mine, of the greatest promise; a man of brains, of feelings, of abilities, and of very pleasing appearance.

ROSINE. Oh, that is all very nice, certainly. His name?

FIGARO. Lindor. He has nothing; but if he had not left Madrid so abruptly, he could have found a good position there.

ROSINE [*unthinkingly*]. He shall find one. Figaro, he shall find one. A young man such as you have described is not made to remain unknown.

FIGARO [*aside*]. Good! [*Aloud.*] But he has one great fault which will always hinder his advancement.

ROSINE. A fault, Figaro? A fault? Are you sure?

FIGARO. He is in love.

ROSINE. He is in love! And you call that a fault!

FIGARO. In truth, it is a fault only when we consider his poverty.

ROSINE. Oh, how unjust fate is! And did he tell you whom he loves? I have such a curiosity——

FIGARO. You are the last person, my lady, to whom I should like to entrust a secret of this kind.

ROSINE [*beseechingly*]. Why, Master Figaro? I am discreet. This young man is related to you. He interests me—oh, so much. Please tell me.

FIGARO [*observing her slyly*]. Imagine the prettiest little darling, sweet, gentle, engaging and full of life, temptingly attractive, dainty foot, neat figure, slender and willowy, plump arms, rosy lips, and hands! Oh! Cheeks! Oh! Teeth! Oh! Eyes! Oh!

ROSINE [*excitedly*]. She lives in this city?

FIGARO. In this part of this city.

ROSINE. In this street, perhaps?

FIGARO. Not far from my house.

ROSINE. Ah! How nice!—for your kinsman. And this girl is?

FIGARO. I haven't told you yet?

ROSINE [*all aquiver with excitement.*] It is the only thing that you have forgotten, Master Figaro. Tell me now. Oh, please tell me quickly! If some one should interrupt us, I might never know——

FIGARO. You really wish to know, my lady? [ROSINE *indicates vigorously that she does.*] Oh, well, this young person is —the ward of your guardian.

ROSINE. The ward?

FIGARO. Of Doctor Bartholo. Yes, my lady.

ROSINE [*with emotion.*] Ah, Figaro, I cannot believe you.

FIGARO. Well, at any rate, he is dying to convince you that it is true.

ROSINE. You make me tremble, Master Figaro.

FIGARO. Tremble? Oh, no. Bad plan, my lady; when one fears to suffer, one suffers from fear. Besides I have just gotten rid of all prying eyes till tomorrow.

ROSINE. If he loves me, he ought to prove it by remaining absolutely quiet.

FIGARO. Eh? What's that, my lady? Can love and repose dwell in the same heart? Young people are so unfortunate to-day. They have this terrible choice: love without repose, or repose without love.

Rosine [*dropping her eyes*]. Repose without love—seems——

Figaro. Oh, very tiresome! It seems that love without repose is more attractive, and as for me, if I were a woman——

Rosine [*embarrassed*]. It is certain that a girl cannot keep a gentleman from esteeming her.

Figaro. That is just what my kinsman does, esteems you—passionately!

Rosine. But if he should do something foolish or careless, Figaro, he would ruin our chances.

Figaro [*aside*]. Ruin *our* chances! [*Aloud.*] If you would caution him expressly in a little note—a little note can do much.

Rosine [*gives him the letter that she has just written*]. I haven't time to rewrite this; but when you give it to him, tell him—be sure to tell him——
[*She listens.*]

Figaro. No one, my lady.

Rosine. That all I am doing is through pure friendship.

Figaro. That is understood. That is a fact, by Jove; love does have another way with it.

Rosine. Only from pure friendship. [Figaro *looks knowing.* Rosine *petulantly stamps her foot.*] Do you understand? I fear only that, disheartened by difficulties——

Figaro. Aye, if his were some flitting flame. You must remember, my lady, that the wind which blows out a candle makes a hotter blaze in a furnace, and that we are that furnace. Just in speaking of his love he breathes such ardor that he has almost given the fever of his passion to me, *me* who am totally unconcerned in the matter.

Rosine. Merciful Heavens! I hear the doctor. He must not find you here.—Go out through the music-room and be as quiet as a cat.

Figaro. Don't worry. [*Aside, holding up the letter.*] This is worth more than all my observations.
[*Exit* Figaro *to music-room.*]

Rosine [*aloud*]. I am worried to death till he has left the house.—How I like Figaro! He is a good fellow, an excellent relation! Ah! There is my tyrant. I must take up my work.
[*She blows out the candle, sits down, and takes up some embroidery.* Bartholo *enters in a rage.*]

Bartholo. Ah! Curses! That maniac, that rascally pirate of a Figaro! There you see that one cannot leave his house for a single moment without being sure that on his return——

Rosine. What has made you so extremely angry, sir?

Bartholo. That damned barber who has just in the time it takes to turn your hand put my entire household out of commission. He has given a sleeping powder to Wideawake, a sneezing powder to Youngman. He has bled Marceline in the foot—no one not maimed—not even my mule.—He put a poultice on the eyes of the poor blind beast. Because he owes me a hundred dollars he takes pains to run up his bills! Ah! Let him bring them in! One could get in this room as easily as get in—in—in a drill ground.

Rosine. And who would wish to get in but yourself, sir?

Bartholo. I'd rather have a groundless fear than take the risk. There are scheming people everywhere. Didn't one of them only this morning pick up your music sheet while I was going down to look for it? Oh, I——

Rosine. Oh, you take pleasure in giving importance to trifles. The wind could easily have blown this paper away; the first passer-by, or anything——

Bartholo. The wind! A passer-by! There wasn't any wind, and not a passer-by in the world. And it is always some one there posted on purpose who picks up papers that a woman pretends to drop accidentally.

Rosine. Pretends, sir?

BARTHOLO. Yes, my lady! Pretends!

ROSINE [aside]. The old wretch!

BARTHOLO. But that will happen no more. I am going to have that window sealed up.

ROSINE. Better still; while you are at it, wall up the windows all around; make a dungeon cell out of a prison; the difference is so little.

BARTHOLO. To wall up those looking on the street wouldn't be a bad idea. That barber hasn't been in here surely——?

ROSINE. Are you jealous of him too?

BARTHOLO. As I am of all others!

ROSINE. How civil your replies are!

BARTHOLO. Ah! You trust everybody, and you will soon have in your house a fine woman to deceive you, good friends to spirit her away from you, and good servants to aid them in doing it.

ROSINE. What! You do not even allow that I might have principles against coquetting with a servant, with Figaro?

BARTHOLO. Who the devil knows what a woman might take the notion to do! [Sneeringly.] And how often I have seen these high and mighty virtues——

ROSINE [angrily]. Well, sir, since I am so easily captivated by anything in breeches, why is it that just to look at you gives me a nervous headache?

BARTHOLO [stupefied]. Why?—Why?—but you are not answering my question about this barber.

ROSINE [beside herself]. Oh well! Yes! This man did come into my apartment; I saw him; I spoke to him. I do not hesitate to tell you that I found him quite pleasing, and now I hope that what I have told you gives you a stroke of apoplexy.   [Exit ROSINE, angrily.]

BARTHOLO. Ah! These rascals! These dogs of servants! [He calls.] Youngman. Wideawake! Wideawake, curse you!

[WIDEAWAKE comes in yawning and half asleep.]

WIDEAWAKE [yawning]. Aaaah, aah, ah, ah——

BARTHOLO. Where were you, pest of a giddy pate, when that barber got in?

WIDEAWAKE. Why, sir, I was—aah, ah, aah——

BARTHOLO. Up to some deviltry, no doubt. And you didn't see him?

WIDEAWAKE. Certainly I saw him. According to what he said, he found me pretty sick too; and it musta been so, too, becuz I commenced to have the misery in my legs and arms just from hearing him talk—ah, aah, ah——

BARTHOLO [mocking him]. Just from hearing him talk! Where, then, is that good-for-nothing Youngman? Drugging this poor little fellow without my prescription. There is some rascality under all that.

[YOUNGMAN enters. He is an old man, leaning on a crutch stick. He sneezes several times.]

WIDEAWAKE [still yawning]. Youngman!

BARTHOLO. Oh, sneeze some other day.

YOUNGMAN. That's more than fifty—a-chew—fifty times—a-chew—enduring of a moment—a-chew—; I'm all broken up.

BARTHOLO. How does it happen that when I asked you both if any one had been in Miss Rosine's rooms you didn't say that this barber——?

WIDEAWAKE [still yawning]. He ain't nobody, that Figaro. Aaah, aah, ah——

BARTHOLO. I'll wager that that sneak had an understanding with you.

WIDEAWAKE [crying like a fool]. Me! —Me have an understanding!

YOUNGMAN. But, sir, you are unjust to us.

BARTHOLO. Justice! That's a fine word for you boobs. Justice! Ha! I am your master, I, and I am right always.

YOUNGMAN [sneezing]. But you know when a thing is so——

BARTHOLO. When a thing is so! Umph! I do not wish that it be so; I mean to see that it isn't so. Just permit all you flunkies to be right about anything, and right away you will see what becomes of authority.

YOUNGMAN [sneezing]. I'd much rather

be turned off. An awful job I've got. There's always the devil to pay.

WIDEAWAKE [*crying*]. A poor respectable fellow treated like a rascal!

BARTHOLO. Get out then, poor respectable fellow. [*He mocks them.*] And a-chew—and a-cha. One sneezes in my nose and the other yawns at me.

YOUNGMAN. Oh, sir, I swear that if it wasn't for Miss Rosine I couldn't stand to stay in this house.

[*Exit* YOUNGMAN, *sneezing.*]

BARTHOLO. In what a plight Figaro has left us all! I see what he is up to. The villain wants to pay me my hundred dollars without taking out his purse. [BAZILE *enters*. FIGARO *is hidden in the music-room and appears from time to time to listen to them*. BARTHOLO *continues.*] Ah, Bazile! You are come then to give Rosine her music lesson?

BAZILE. That is the least pressing thing.

BARTHOLO. I have been to your house but couldn't find you.

BAZILE. I was out attending to your affairs. I have bad enough news.

BARTHOLO. For you?

BAZILE. No, for you. Count Almaviva is in the city.

BARTHOLO. Speak in a whisper. The fellow who had Rosine searched for all over Madrid?

BAZILE. He is rooming on the main square, and he comes out every day disguised.

BARTHOLO. He is surely after us! What is to be done?

BAZILE. If he were not a nobleman, he could be made to disappear——

BARTHOLO [*eagerly*]. Yes, we will lay a trap for him, ambush him, with sword and buckler——

BAZILE. Good God! Get ourselves in trouble! No! Stir up some underhand piece of business? That is more like it; and during the excitement slander right and left. Yes!

BARTHOLO. Singular means of getting rid of a man.

BAZILE. You belittle slander, sir? You scarcely know what you are making light of. I have seen the most respectable people very near to being overwhelmed by it. There is no silly piece of malice, no abomination, no absurd story that we could not get taken up and repeated by the idlers of a big city, provided we go about it in the right way. And we have in Seville such skilled people in affairs of that kind—— To start with a low sound, skimming the ground like the swallow before the storm, *pianissimo*, very softly it murmurs, spreads swiftly, and hurls while running the poisoned dart. Here such and such a mouth takes it up, and *piano, piano* it slips easily into your ear. The evil is done; it trails; it winds; and *rinforzando*, from mouth to mouth it goes the deuce of a pace; then suddenly, no one knows how, you see slander rear itself, hiss, swell, and grow before your eyes. It hurls itself forward, enlarges its flight, whirls, envelops, uproots, explodes, thunders, and becomes, thanks to heavens, a universal cry, a public *crescendo*, a general chorus of hatred and condemnation. What the devil could resist it?

BARTHOLO. What is all this poppycock you are giving me, Bazile? What has all this *piano-crescendo* talk to do with my situation?

BAZILE. Hey? What connection! That which is done everywhere to get rid of an enemy, you must in your case do to keep your enemy from appearing on the scene.

BARTHOLO. From appearing? I mean to marry Rosine before she learns of the existence of this count.

BAZILE. In that case you have not a minute to lose.

BARTHOLO. And who is responsible for my delay, Bazile, you or I? I have entrusted the management of the whole affair to you.

BAZILE. Yes, but you have been stingy with expense money; and in the music of order, a disparity between parties to a marriage, an iniquitous judgment, an evident violation of right, are discords that must be introduced and smoothed over by the perfect agreement of golden tinklings.

BARTHOLO [*giving him money*]. I must submit to your wishes. But let's use dispatch.

BAZILE. That goes without saying. To-morrow all will be over; to-day you must see that no one sees your ward.

BARTHOLO. Trust me for that. Are you coming this evening, Bazile?

BAZILE. Don't count on it. This business will take all my time to-day; so don't count on it.

BARTHOLO [*accompanying him*]. Goodbye.

BAZILE. Stay where you are, Doctor, you need not show me out.

BARTHOLO. Not at all. I want to close the street door after you.

[*Exit* BARTHOLO *and* BAZILE.]

[ROSINE *enters running.* FIGARO *comes from the music-room.*]

ROSINE. What! You still here, Figaro?

FIGARO. Very fortunately for you, Miss, I am. Your guardian and your music master, believing themselves alone here, have just unbosomed themselves——

ROSINE. And you listened to them, Figaro? But do you not know that that is naughty?

FIGARO. To listen? That is the best way to learn things. Know then that your guardian is arranging to marry you to-morrow.

ROSINE. Oh, merciful heavens!

FIGARO. Don't let that worry you; we will give him so much to do that he will not have time to think of getting married.

ROSINE. Here he comes; go out by the back stairs. You frighten me to death with your boldness. [FIGARO *flees.* BARTHOLO *enters.*] Some one has been here with you, sir?

BARTHOLO. Bazile. I have just shown him out—and for a good reason. You would much prefer to hear that it was this Master Figaro, eh?

ROSINE. It makes no difference to me, I am sure.

BARTHOLO. Now look here, I must know what it was so important that this barber had to say to you.

ROSINE. Do you really want me to tell you? He informed me of Marceline's condition, which from what he says, is not so good.

BARTHOLO. Informed you! I am willing to wager that he was commissioned to deliver to you some letter.

ROSINE. From whom, please?

BARTHOLO. Oh, from whom? From some one that you women never name. How do I know? Perhaps the reply to the letter that you dropped out of the window.

ROSINE [*aside*]. He hasn't missed guessing a single thing right. [*Aloud.*] You deserve that it be that.

BARTHOLO [*examines* ROSINE'S *hands*]. That's it. You have been writing.

ROSINE [*embarrassed*]. It would be a good joke for you to undertake to make me agree with you.

BARTHOLO [*taking her right hand*]. I! Oh, I shan't try to make you admit it. For you see now that your ink-stained finger does that for you. Eh? Tricky lady!

ROSINE [*aside*]. You wretch!

BARTHOLO [*still holds her hand*]. A woman believes herself safe because she is alone.

ROSINE. Ah, without doubt! Wonderful reasoning! Unhand me, sir; you are twisting my arm. I burned myself snuffing this candle, and I have been told that steeping a burn wound in ink was a good remedy. That is what I did.

BARTHOLO. That is what you did? Let's see then if the second witness confirms the deposition of the first. This is the box of writing-paper in which I am certain there were six sheets only this morning. I know because I count them every morning.

ROSINE [*aside*]. Oh, fool that I am!

BARTHOLO [*counting*]. Three, four, five——

ROSINE [*hastily*]. Six!

BARTHOLO. I can see well enough that the sixth isn't there.

Rosine [*lowering her eyes*]. The sixth?
Oh, yes! I used it in making a sack for
some bonbons that I sent Figaro's little
sister.

Bartholo. To little sister? And this
pen that was new, how comes it black-
ened? Perhaps you used it in writing
the address of little sister.

Rosine [*aside*]. Jealousy is an instinct
with this man. [*Aloud.*] I used it to
trace a flower on the vest I am embroid-
ering for you.

Bartholo. How edifying that is! To
have all that believed, my child, you
should not blush so at piling up false-
hoods. [*Commiseratingly.*] But you do
not know that yet; you are a novice at
deceit.

Rosine. Who would not blush to see
such evil interpretations placed on things
most innocently done?

Bartholo. Certainly. I am wrong:
burn a finger, steep it in ink, make sacks
for candy, embroider my vest, nothing
more innocent. How many lies it takes
to conceal a single deed!—I am alone;
no one sees me; when the time comes I
shall be able to tell lies at my ease; but
the end of the finger remains soiled, the
pen is black, the paper is missing. Poor
little thing! She couldn't think up in
advance answers to everything. [*Shaking
his finger at her.*] Rest assured though,
young lady, that from now on a double
lock will make me certain that you are
up to no mischief while I am out.

[THE COUNT *in a trooper's uni-
form enters, feigning partial
drunkenness and singing.*]

The Count. "Let's wake her up," etc.

Bartholo. But what does this man
want of us? A soldier! Go to your room,
Miss!

The Count [*sings*]. "Let's wake her
up——" [*He proceeds toward* Rosine.]
Which of you two, my ladies, is named
Doctor Balordo? [*Aside to* Rosine.] I
am Lindor.

Bartholo [*with emphasis*]. Bartholo!

Rosine. He speaks of Lindor!

The Count. Balordo, Barbe-a-l'eau, I
don't care a snap of my finger which. It
is a question only of knowing which of
you two is Doctor—— [*To* Rosine, *show-
ing her a note.*] Take this letter.

Bartholo. Which one? You know well
enough that I am the one. Which one?
Go to your room, Rosine; this man ap-
pears to be drunk.

Rosine. That is just why I do not wish
to go; you are alone; a woman sometimes
inspires respect.

Bartholo. Go to your room! Go to
your room! I am not afraid.

[*Exit* Rosine.]

The Count. Oh, I recognized you at
first from your card of description.

Bartholo [*to* The Count, *who puts
away the letter*]. What is that you are
hiding in your pocket?

The Count. I am hiding it in my
pocket just so that you may not know
what it is.

Bartholo. My card of description!
You soldiers always talk in military
terms.

The Count. Do you think it would be
so hard to describe you on a rating card?

Wagging pate, skin-shaved head;
Lop-sided figure, heavy as lead;
Beastlike stare of a wall-eyed loon,
Bed-canopy nose. steeped in maroon;
Right shoulder high, left shoulder low;
Legs both gnarled and twisted in a bow;
Tone is gruff, voice is thick;
Dangerous apparition to the seriously
    sick;
Fierce appearance of an Algonquin chief,
Ugly and destructive beyond all belief.
In short, of doctors
    The paragon;
In all this world, of his like
    There's nary a one.

[THE COUNT *clogs a few steps to
the staccato movement of his
description.*]

Bartholo. What does all that mean?
Are you here to insult me? Get out right
now.

The Count. Get out? Oh fie! How

naughty you are talking. Can you read, Dr. Barbe-a-l'eau?

BARTHOLO. Another one of your foolish questions!

THE COUNT. Oh, do not let that worry you, for I am at least as much physician as you.

BARTHOLO. What do you mean?

THE COUNT. Am I not horse doctor for the regiment? That is why they billeted me in the home of a colleague.

BARTHOLO. To dare compare me with a veterinarian!——

THE COUNT [chanting, but not singing.] No, Doctor, I do not claim:

That our art takes precedence
Over Hippocrates and·his crew. [Singing.]
Your knowledge, my comrade,
Has a more general success.
If it doesn't get rid of the ill,
At least it gets rid of the patient.

Now isn't all this that I am singing to you civil?

BARTHOLO. It is worthy of you, ignorant manipulator, to abuse thus the first, the greatest, and the most useful of all arts.

THE COUNT. Quite useful to those who practise it.

BARTHOLO. An art the success of which the sun honors itself in shining upon.

THE COUNT. And the blunders of which the earth makes haste to cover up.

BARTHOLO. I can well see, boor, that you are accustomed to talk only to horses.

THE COUNT. Talk to horses! Ah, Doctor! That you, such a clever doctor, should make a mistake of that kind! Isn't it notorious that the veterinarian always cures his patients without talking to them, while the doctor on the other hand talks a lot to his——

BARTHOLO. Without curing them, eh?

THE COUNT [solemnly]. You have said it.

BARTHOLO. Who the devil sent this drunken fellow here?

THE COUNT. I believe that you are firing off naughty words at me, my love. [He lightly slaps BARTHOLO'S wrist.]

BARTHOLO. In short, what do you wish? What do you demand?

THE COUNT [feigning great anger]. Oh, well then! [He flies into a passion.] What do I wish? Cannot you see?

[ROSINE enters. THE COUNT is looking directly at her as he asks the last question above.]

ROSINE [hastily and with much feigned concern]. Oh, good Master Soldier, do not lose your temper, please! [To BARTHOLO.] Speak gently to him, sir. A man who hasn't full use of his reason——

THE COUNT [pretending to understand that she is speaking to him.] You are right; he hasn't full use of his reason, he! But we, you and I, we are sensible people. I good-natured, and you pretty—in short that suffices. The truth is, I do not wish to have anything to do with any one in this house except you.

ROSINE. How can I be of service to you, Master Soldier?

THE COUNT. Just a mere trifle, my child. But if my words explaining what I want are somewhat ambiguous——

ROSINE [eagerly]. I'll get the spirit of them.

THE COUNT [showing her the letter and saying with double meaning]. No, get the letter; stick to the letter. It is a question only—that you give me somewhere to sleep.

BARTHOLO. Nothing but that?

THE COUNT. Nothing else. Read the love letter that our quartermaster sends you.

BARTHOLO. Let's see it. [THE COUNT hides the letter intended for ROSINE and gives BARTHOLO another paper. BARTHOLO reads.] "Doctor Bartholo will receive, feed, lodge, and give a bed to——"

THE COUNT [emphasizing]. "Give a bed to!"

BARTHOLO. "—for one night only, one Lindor, called the scholar, trooper in the Xth regiment——"

ROSINE [in a low tone]. It is he! It is he himself!

BARTHOLO [quickly to ROSINE]. What is that?

THE COUNT. Eh? Now, Doctor Barbaro, am I wrong?

BARTHOLO. One would say that this man takes a devilish delight in murdering my name in all possible manners. Go to the devil with your Balordos, your Barbaros, your Barbe-a-l'eaus! And tell your impertinent quartermaster that since my trip to Madrid I have been exempt from lodging military people.

THE COUNT [aside]. Oh, the deuce! This is an awkward hitch!

BARTHOLO. Ah, ha! My friend! That jars you, and sobers you up a little? But don't go just yet.

THE COUNT [aside]. I almost gave myself away. [Aloud.] Go? If you are exempt from having soldiers billeted in your house, you are not lacking in courtesy, perhaps. Go? Show me your papers of exemption. Although I do not know how to read, I shall see soon——

BARTHOLO. Never mind about that letter of exemption; I have it here in my desk.

THE COUNT [while BARTHOLO goes to the desk, says without leaving his place]. Ah! My beautiful Rosine!

ROSINE. Why, Lindor, is it you?

THE COUNT. Yes. I must get this letter to you.

ROSINE. Take care. He is watching us.

THE COUNT. Take out your handkerchief. I will drop this. [He draws closer to her.]

BARTHOLO. Gently there, gently, my noble soldier; I do not at all like any one to observe my wife so closely.

THE COUNT. She is your wife?

BARTHOLO. And why not?

THE COUNT. I took you for her paternal, maternal, sempiternal great-grandfather. There are at least three generations between you and her.

BARTHOLO [reads a paper]. "In consideration of good and faithful testimony proffered us."

THE COUNT [with a quick movement knocks the paper out of BARTHOLO'S hands]. I don't want all that pack of words!

BARTHOLO. Do you know, sir, that if I have to call my people, I will have you thrashed?

THE COUNT. A fight? Ah, I fight willingly; that is my trade. [He lovingly fondles the handle of his pistol.] And here is what I throw powder in people's eyes with. You have never seen a battle, my lady?

ROSINE. No, nor ever wish to see one.

THE COUNT. And yet there is nothing more cheerful than a battle. Just imagine—[Giving BARTHOLO a violent push.] in the first place that the enemy is on one side of a ravine, and our friends on the other. [Low to ROSINE, showing her the letter.] Now take out your handkerchief. [He spits on the floor.] Now that is the ravine, you understand.

[ROSINE takes out her handkerchief; THE COUNT lets the letter fall between them, trying to make it appear as if ROSINE had pulled the letter out herself with her handkerchief.]

BARTHOLO [stooping]. Ah! Ah!

THE COUNT [quickly takes the letter up and says]. Wait! I was going to teach you the secrets of my trade. You are a very discreet girl in truth. Now isn't this a billet-doux that she has dropped from her pocket?

BARTHOLO [with frantic greediness]. Give me! Give me!

THE COUNT [calmly holding him off]. Gently, dad, old dear! Every one to his calling. This is just as natural coming from her pocket as for a rhubarb prescription to fall out of yours.

ROSINE [holds out her hand]. Ah, I know what it is, Master Soldier.

[She takes the note and conceals it in one of her pockets.]

BARTHOLO. Are you ever going?

THE COUNT. Oh yes, I am going. Good-bye, Doctor, no hard feelings! One little pretty speech, my heart: pray that death may overlook me for some few campaigns yet; life before has never been so dear to me.

BARTHOLO. Never you mind; if I had any influence over death——

THE COUNT. Influence death? Aren't you a doctor? You do so many good things for death that it couldn't refuse you anything. [*Exit.*]

BARTHOLO [*watches him leave*]. He has finally gone. [*Aside.*] Now to hide my little game.

ROSINE [*still gazing in the direction of* THE COUNT'S *departure*]. You must admit, sir, that he is really nice, this young soldier. Despite his drunkenness, I can see that he does not lack wit, nor a certain amount of education.

BARTHOLO. Fortunate we are, my life, to be rid of him. But aren't you extremely anxious to read with me the paper that he handed you?

ROSINE. What paper?

BARTHOLO. The one he pretended to pick up to hand you.

ROSINE. Oh, that was the letter from my cousin, the officer; it fell from my pocket.

BARTHOLO. I had the idea that he took it from his.

ROSINE. But I know that it was mine.

BARTHOLO. But we can settle the question easily by looking at it.

ROSINE. I don't know what I did with it.

BARTHOLO [*pointing to her pocket*]. You put it there.

ROSINE. Oh yes. Absent-mindedly.

BARTHOLO. You are going to see that it will be some piece of foolishness.

ROSINE [*aside*]. If I do not make him angry, there will be no way of refusing him.

BARTHOLO. Give it to me then, my love.

ROSINE. But what is your reason for insisting, sir? Do you distrust me?

BARTHOLO. But what reason have you for not showing it to me?

ROSINE. I tell you again, sir, that this letter is no other than the one you gave me unsealed this morning, from my cousin; and in regard to its being unsealed, I tell you frankly that this liberty displeases me excessively.

BARTHOLO. I do not know what you mean.

ROSINE. Do I read your letters? Why do you assume the right to read those addressed to me? If jealousy is the reason, that is insulting; if it is abuse of an usurped authority, I am still more angry.

BARTHOLO. What! Angry! You have never before spoken to me like this.

ROSINE. If I have controlled myself thus far, it was not to give you the right to insult me with impunity.

BARTHOLO. Of what insult are you speaking?

ROSINE. It is an unheard of offense to open other people's letters.

BARTHOLO. The letters of one's wife?

ROSINE. I am not that yet. But why should a wife be singled out for an indignity that one offers no one else?

BARTHOLO. You are trying to put me on a false trail and make me forget the letter which without doubt is a missive from some lover! But I shall see it, I tell you!

ROSINE. You shall not see it! If you come a step nearer me, I will flee from this house and ask shelter of the first person I meet.

BARTHOLO. Who will have none of you.

ROSINE. We shall see.

BARTHOLO. We are not in France, where they always give in to women; but to take false hopes out of your head, I will lock the door.

ROSINE [*while he goes to lock the door*]. Oh! Heavens! What shall I do? I'll replace this quickly with the one from my cousin and let him take that as much as he likes.

[*She makes the exchange and places the letter from her cousin in her pocket in such a way that a little of it shows.*]

BARTHOLO. Now I intend to see it.

ROSINE. By what right, please?

BARTHOLO. By the most universally recognized right, that of might.

ROSINE. I'll die before I let you see it!

BARTHOLO [*stamping his foot*]. My lady! My lady!

ROSINE [*falls into an armchair and feigns illness*]. Oh! What an outrage!

BARTHOLO. Give me that letter, or fear my anger!

ROSINE [*falling backward*]. Unhappy Rosine!

BARTHOLO. What is the matter now?

ROSINE. What a frightful future!

BARTHOLO. Rosine!

ROSINE. I'm stifling with fury!

BARTHOLO. She is ill.

ROSINE. I'm fainting! I'm dying!

BARTHOLO [*feels her pulse and says aside*]. Ye gods! The letter! I'll read it without her knowedge.

[*He continues to feel her pulse and tries to turn the letter in her pocket so that he can read a little of it.*]

ROSINE [*still reclining*]. Unhappy me! Ah! [*She sighs.*]

BARTHOLO [*drops her arm and says aside*]. What an insane desire I have to learn what I am always afraid to know.

ROSINE [*sighs*]. Ah! Poor Rosine!

BARTHOLO. The use of perfumes produces spasmodic affections. [*He reads from behind the armchair while feeling her pulse. ROSINE raises herself a little, watches him slyly, nods her head, and resumes her original position without speaking. BARTHOLO aside.*] Oh, heavens! It is the letter from her cousin. Cursed suspicion! Now how can I appease her? At least, I'll not let her know that I have read it. [*He pretends to lift her and replaces the letter.*]

ROSINE [*sighs*]. Ah!

BARTHOLO. You are all right now. It is nothing, my child; a little rush of blood to the head, that's all. Your pulse hasn't varied a beat. [*He goes to get a flask from the table.*]

ROSINE [*aside*]. He has replaced the letter. Good!

BARTHOLO. My dear Rosine, a little sip of this wine.

ROSINE. I wish nothing from you; leave me alone.

BARTHOLO. I admit that I have been unreasonable in this matter of the letter.

ROSINE. Oh, I do not care anything about the letter; it is your revolting manner of demanding things.

BARTHOLO [*on his knees*]. Pardon. I realized right away my fault; you see me at your feet and ready to make reparation.

ROSINE. Yes, pardon you! When you believe that this letter did not come from my cousin.

BARTHOLO. Let it come from where it will, I wish no explanation.

ROSINE [*offering the letter to him*]. You see that with kindness one can get anything from me. Read it.

BARTHOLO. This frankness would dispel my suspicions even if I were unhappy enough to retain any of them.

ROSINE. But read it, sir.

BARTHOLO. God forbid that I should so insult you!

ROSINE. You are displeasing me by refusing.

BARTHOLO. Take in recompense this mark of my perfect confidence. I am going up to see poor Marceline, whom this Figaro, I know not why, has bled in the foot; do you not want to go too?

ROSINE. I'll come up in a moment.

BARTHOLO. Since we have made peace, darling, give me your hand. If you were only able to love me, how happy you might be!

ROSINE [*lowering her eyes*]. If you were only able to please me, ah! how I would love you!

BARTHOLO. I will please you; I will please you; I repeat: I will please you. [*Exit BARTHOLO wagging his head.*]

ROSINE [*alone; she watches him go*]. Ah, Lindor! He says that he will please me. Let's read this letter which came near causing me so much trouble. [*She reads and cries out.*] Ha! I am too late reading it; he advises me to have an open quarrel with my guardian. I had such a good opportunity, and I let it slip. On receiving the letter, I felt myself blushing even behind my ears. My guardian is right: I am far from having the worldly experience which, he often tells me, assures the composure of women on all occasions. But an unjust man succeeds in making a crafty thing of innocence itself.

ACT III

SCENE—*The apartments of* ROSINE *in* BARTHOLO'S *house as in* ACT II.

[*Curtain rises, disclosing* BARTHOLO *alone and downcast.*]

BARTHOLO. What caprice! What caprice! She seemed in a good humor. Then can any one tell me what the devil put the notion into her head not to take any more music lessons from Bazile? She knows that he has something to do with my marriage—— [*Some one knocks at the door.*] Do everything in the world for a woman, and if you forget a single thing—I say, a single thing—— [*Another knock on the door.*] Well, let's see who it is. [*Goes to the door.*]

[*The* COUNT *enters, dressed as a student.*]

THE COUNT. May joy and peace dwell herewithin forever!

BARTHOLO [*shortly*]. Never was wish more opportune. What do you want?

THE COUNT. Sir, I am Alonzo, Master of Arts, licensed to teach——

BARTHOLO. I have no need of an instructor.

THE COUNT [*continuing what he had begun to say*].—Student under Bazile, organist of the Grand Convent, who has the honor of teaching music to your——

BARTHOLO. Bazile! Organist! Who has the honor! I know it. Come to the point.

THE COUNT [*aside*]. Phew! What a man! [*Aloud.*] A sudden illness has forced him to stay in bed——

BARTHOLO. Bazile? Stay in bed? He

has done well to send; I will go to see him immediately.

THE COUNT [*aside*]. Oh, the devil! [*Aloud.*] When I say the bed, sir, it is —it is—it is—the room I mean.

BARTHOLO [*making ready to go out*]. Even if he be only slightly indisposed— go ahead; I'll be with you in a moment.

THE COUNT [*embarrassed*]. Sir, I was commissioned—no one can hear us?

BARTHOLO [*aside*]. It is some trickery. [*Aloud.*] Oh no, my mysterious friend! Speak without fear if you can.

THE COUNT [*aside*]. Damned old fool! [*Aloud.*] Bazile entrusted me with telling you——

BARTHOLO. Speak louder; I am deaf in one ear.

THE COUNT [*raising his voice*]. Oh, certainly—that Count Almaviva, who is lodging on the main square——

BARTHOLO. Not so loud; don't speak so loud, I beg.

THE COUNT [*still louder*]. —gave up his rooms this morning. Since it was through me that he knew Count Almaviva——

BARTHOLO. Not so loud; not so loud, please.

THE COUNT [*in the same tone*]. —was in this city, and since I learned that Miss Rosine has written to him——

BARTHOLO [*shrieks*]. Rosine written to him? My dear fellow, please speak in a whisper, I beseech you. Come, let's sit down and chat amiably. You have discovered, you say, that Rosine——

THE COUNT [*proudly*]. Assuredly. Bazile, disturbed on your account about this correspondence, asked me to show you her letter; but the manner in which you take things——

BARTHOLO. Oh, my God! I take them well enough. But isn't it possible for you to whisper?

THE COUNT. You told me that you were deaf in one ear.

BARTHOLO. Pardon me, Professor Alonzo, if you have found me suspicious and hard; but I am surrounded by intriguers, snares—— And then your

make-up, your age, your manners——
Pardon me, pardon me! Oh well, you
have the letter.

THE COUNT. Now you are talking! In
that tone of voice.—But I am afraid that
some one is eavesdropping.

BARTHOLO. Who do you think? All
my servants laid up; Rosine in a rage
shut up in her room. The devil has
gotten into my house. But I'll go to be
certain——

[BARTHOLO *opens* ROSINE's *door
gently, peeps in, and listens.*]

THE COUNT [*aside*]. I have gotten my-
self into this fix through sheer irritation.
Shall I refuse to show him the letter
now? I would have to flee and might
just as well not come—— Shall I show it
to him? If I can forewarn Rosine, to
show it would be a trick of genius.

BARTHOLO [*returning on tiptoes*]. She
is sitting near the window, her back
turned to the door, reading a letter from
her cousin,—a letter that I unsealed.
Now let's see hers.

THE COUNT [*hands him* ROSINE's *let-
ter*]. Here it is. [*Aside.*] It is my let-
ter that she is reading.

BARTHOLO [*reads*]. "Since you have
told me your position and name." Ah!
The little vixen! It is surely her hand-
writing.

THE COUNT [*frightened*]. Sh! Now it
is your turn not to speak so loud.

BARTHOLO. How can I ever repay you
for this, my dear sir?

THE COUNT. When all is over, if you
still think there is any obligation on your
part, I relieve you of it now in advance.
After Bazile finishes his business with a
lawyer to whom he is just now talk-
ing——

BARTHOLO [*interrupting*]. With a law-
yer, about my marriage?

THE COUNT. That is just what I was
going to say. He charged me with tell-
ing you that all will be ready for to-
morrow. Then if she resists——

BARTHOLO. She will resist, all right.

THE COUNT [*attempts to take the let-
ter*, BARTHOLO *holding it all the tighter*].

Here is the way that I can serve you:
we will show her this letter, and if it
is necessary [*More mysteriously.*] I shall
go as far as to tell her that I secured it
from a woman to whom the Count sur-
rendered it. You see that confusion,
shame, spite may induce her to yield to
you on the spot.

BARTHOLO [*laughing*]. Slander the
Count! My dear friend, I see well enough
now that you come from Bazile. But in
order that this may not look like a put-up
job, would it not be good for her to
know you beforehand?

THE COUNT [*overcomes an irrepressible
movement of joy*]. That was just the
opinion of Bazile. But how manage it?
It is so late—— In the little remaining
time——

BARTHOLO. I shall say that you come
in his place. Can't you give her a music
lesson?

THE COUNT. There is nothing that I
would not do to please you. But bear
in mind that all these fabrications of sub-
stitute teachers are old dodges, worn-out
comedy tricks; if she suspects——

BARTHOLO [*breaks in*]. What likeli-
hood, since you will be introduced by
me? You look more like a disguised
lover than an officious friend.

THE COUNT. Yes? You believe then
that my appearance may aid in the de-
ception?

BARTHOLO. Yes. No one would take
you for what you are. She is in a ter-
rible humor this evening. If she would
only see you. Her harpsichord is in this
music-room; I am going to do the im-
possible by presenting you to her.

THE COUNT. Do not say a word about
the letter.

BARTHOLO. Not before the psychologi-
cal moment? It would lose all its effect.
You do not have to tell me things twice;
I'm not so dense.

[*He goes out grotesquely chuck-
ling and wagging his head.*]

THE COUNT [*alone*]. Saved! Phew!
How hard this devilish fellow is to han-
dle! Figaro knew what he was talking

about. I could just see myself telling lies; I was stupid and awkward, and he has cat's eyes. My faith, without the sudden inspiration of that letter, I'll admit that I would have been in a pretty pickle! [*He goes over toward door and listens.*] They are quarreling in there. Suppose she holds out in not coming. I'll listen. She is refusing to come from her room, and I have lost the fruits of my trick. [*He goes back to listen.*] There she is; I'll not show myself at first.

[*Exit* COUNT *into the music-room.*]

[BARTHOLO *and* ROSINE *enter.* ROSINE *feigns great anger.*]

ROSINE. All that you are going to say isn't worth while, sir. I have made up my mind; I do not wish to hear the word music.

BARTHOLO [*wheedling tone*]. Listen now, my child, it is Professor Alonzo, the pupil and friend of Don Bazile, chosen by him to be one of our witnesses. Music will make you feel better, I warrant you.

ROSINE. Oh! As for that, you might as well give up hope. If I sing this evening—— Where is this Professor Alonzo that you are afraid to send in? In two words I will send him about his business, and that of Bazile. [*She sees her lover and utters a cry.*] Ah!

BARTHOLO. What is the matter?

ROSINE [*both hands over her heart in great confusion*]. Ah, sir, merciful heavens!

BARTHOLO. She is ill again, Professor Alonzo.

ROSINE. No, I am not ill, but just in turning—— Ah!

THE COUNT [*suggesting a way out of her confusion*]. You twisted your ankle, Miss?

ROSINE [*looking her thanks*]. Oh, yes! Yes! That's it. I twisted my ankle. I hurt myself horribly.

THE COUNT. Yes, certainly. I saw it myself.

ROSINE [*looking significantly toward* THE COUNT]. The shock of it has gone even to my heart.

BARTHOLO. A chair! A chair! And not an armchair here! [*He goes to look for a chair.*]

THE COUNT. Ah, Rosine!

ROSINE. What imprudence!

THE COUNT. I have a thousand important things to say to you.

ROSINE. He will not leave us alone.

THE COUNT. Figaro is coming to help us.

BARTHOLO [*bringing up an armchair*]. Wait, little one, come sit down. No hopes now, Professor, of her taking a music lesson. Some other day, perhaps. Goodbye.

ROSINE [*to* THE COUNT]. No, wait. I feel much better. [*To* BARTHOLO.] I shall believe, sir, that you do not wish to oblige me, if you keep me from proving my sincerity by taking the lesson.

THE COUNT [*aside*]. Take my advice, and do not cross her.

BARTHOLO. I yield, my love. I am so far from seeking to displease you that I wish to be with you all the time that you are taking your lesson.

ROSINE. No, sir. I know that music has no charms for you.

BARTHOLO. I assure you that this evening it will enchant me.

ROSINE [*aside to* THE COUNT]. I am being put to torture.

THE COUNT [*taking a sheet of music from the music-stand*]. Will you sing this, my lady?

ROSINE. Yes, it is a charming number from the "Useless Precaution."

BARTHOLO. Still talking about that "Useless Precaution."

THE COUNT. It is the newest thing out; it is a springtime picture of a lively enough class. Now will my lady please try it?

ROSINE [*looking at* THE COUNT]. With great pleasure; a springtime selection delights me. Spring is the youth of Nature. The heart after a long winter acquires a higher degree of sensibility, as a slave chained for a long time tastes with the greatest of pleasure the charm of liberty that has just been offered him.

BARTHOLO [*whispers to* THE COUNT]. Her head is filled with those romantic ideas.

THE COUNT [*in a whisper*]. Do you sense the application of it?

BARTHOLO. Yes, damn it! [*He sits in the armchair that* ROSINE *had occupied.*]

ROSINE [*sings*]. When hand in hand
Through Springtime's wonderland
Come love and flowers,
Then all things new life do take,
Tender and adoring young hearts awake;
Then speed the hours
In green twined bowers
Where swain and shepherdess their tasks
forsake.

Far rove the flocks
O'er hills and mossy rocks,
The hamlet spurning.
Sweetly the cries of young lambs re-
sound
As gaily they gambol and sprightly they
bound.
The blossoms are blowing,
All things else growing
And rejoicing in sweet pleasures new
found.

Faithful dogs keep
Watch o'er the sheep
That nearby graze.
While Lindor passion-shaken,
His gentle charge quite forsaken,
Of his shepherdess dreams
Nor ever deems
Life possible without love's thrilling
maze.

Far from her mother
To the green recess
Where waits her anxious lover,
Singing and tripping goes the sweet shep-
herdess.
By this device does love entice
And snare the pretty rover.
But will singing save her?

The melodious reeds
She lists and heeds;
Filled with alarms
From her budding charms

From the birds as they sweetly sing,
The poor little thing,
The timorous maid,
As she trips along,
Trembles afraid.

From his hidden retreat
Her advance to meet
Lindor springs forward.
With rapture he has kissed her;
She, well content, and with amorous joy
pent,
In feigned anger rails,
And loudly wails,
So that he will appease her.

Now come the sighs, the moving fears,
The promises, the joyful tears,
Tender dalliance, amorous treasures,
Gentle repartee, and lover's pleasures.
The shepherdess her anger has forgot-
ten quite:
In love's name all kisses are right.

If some wretched intruding swain
Awkwardly surprises their lover's re-
treat,
With one accord the height of indifference
they feign,
And his early departure they greet:
Restraint can naught but heighten
The pleasures of love we feel.

[BARTHOLO *goes to sleep as he listens.* THE COUNT *during the last verse risks taking one of* ROSINE'S *hands which he covers with kisses. Emotion causes* ROSINE'S *song to become slower in movement, softens it, and ends even by stopping her voice in the middle of the cadence on the last word. Absence of the sounds which put* BARTHOLO *to sleep now awakes him.* THE COUNT *straightens up,* ROSINE *and the orchestra take up suddenly the air of the song where they left off. In this manner the third verse is repeated, and the byplay commences again.*]

THE COUNT. Truly this is a charming selection, and my lady renders it with intelligence——

ROSINE. You flatter me, sir; the credit is due my teacher.

BARTHOLO [yawning]. Why, I believe that I have slept a little during this charming selection. I have my failings: I come; I go; I traipse around; and as soon as I sit down, my poor tired legs—— [He gets up slowly and pushes back the armchair.]

ROSINE [in a whisper to THE COUNT]. Figaro doesn't seem to be coming at all.

THE COUNT [whispers]. Let's kill time.

BARTHOLO. But, Professor, I have already spoken to Bazile about it; isn't there some way of having her study some more lively things than these grand arias which go up, down, roll around: hi, ho, a,a,a,a,a, and which seem to me to be just so many funeral dirges? Now some of these little tunes that were sung in my day, and which any one can easily hold in mind. I used to know some of them. For example—[During the prelude, he tries to remember, scratching his head; and finally begins to sing, snapping his fingers and dancing with his knees bent in the old-fashioned way.]

Do you, my Rosinette,
Desire to get
The very prince of husbands?

[To THE COUNT, laughing.] It was Fanchonette in the song, but I substituted Rosinette to make it more pleasing to her and to make it fit our particular case. He! He! He! He! Very neat, eh? [He gives THE COUNT a nudge in the ribs.]

THE COUNT [laughing]. Ha! Ha! Ha! Yes, deuced clever, by Jove!

[FIGARO appears in the background.]

BARTHOLO [sings]. Do you, my Rosinette,
Desire to get
The very prince of husbands?
No young gallant am I;

But in the shadows of night
You'll find me gay and spry.
Those cats most gaily bedight
Lose color when darkness is nigh.

[He repeats the refrain, at the same time dancing. FIGARO, behind him, imitates his movements.]

No young gallant——

[Seeing FIGARO.] Ah! Ha! Come in, my friend the barber; come forward; you are charming!

FIGARO [salutes]. Sir, my mother used to pay me the same compliment; but I am become a little deformed since those days. [Aside to THE COUNT.] Bravo! My lord!

[During all this passage, THE COUNT does all he can to speak to ROSINE, but the vigilant and suspicious eye of BARTHOLO prevents him, which makes a dumb show of all the actors not in the passages between BARTHOLO and FIGARO.]

BARTHOLO. Do you come to bleed, to drug, and to cripple all my household again?

FIGARO. Why, sir, Christmas comes but once a year; but without taking into consideration daily cares, you have seen that when there was need for it, my zeal has awaited only your command.

BARTHOLO. Your zeal has only awaited! What have you to say, my friend the zealot, to that poor fellow who yawns and sleeps even when he is awake? and to the other one who has been sneezing for three hours fit to shake his head off and blow out his brains? What do you say to them?

FIGARO. What do I say to them?

BARTHOLO. Yes.

FIGARO. I shall say to them—oh, to be sure, I shall say to the one who sneezes, "May God bless you"; and, "Go to bed" to the one who yawns. I do not charge you anything for that advice.

BARTHOLO. No, it is the bleeding and

the powders that you charge for, if I stand for it. Was it through zeal too that you plastered up the eyes of my blind mule? And will your poultice give him his sight?

FIGARO. If it doesn't do him any good, it certainly can't do him any harm.

BARTHOLO. Just you let me find it charged on my bill! I am not extravagant enough to buy medicine to restore the sight of a blind mule.

FIGARO. My word, sir! Since men have little to choose between stupidity and folly, where I see no profit, I try at least to get pleasure; so long live joy! Who knows that the world will last three weeks more?

BARTHOLO. You would do much better, my friend the reasoner, to pay me my hundred dollars and interest without beating around the bush. I warn you.

FIGARO. Do you doubt my honesty, sir? Why, before I would beat you out of them, I'd owe them to you all my life.

BARTHOLO. And pray tell me how little Miss Figaro found the bonbons that you carried her?

FIGARO. What bonbons? What are you talking about?

BARTHOLO. Yes, the bonbons, in the sack made out of the sheet of note paper —this morning.

FIGARO. Devil take me if I——

ROSINE. Why surely you gave them to her for me, Figaro. I asked you to.

FIGARO. Oh! Ah! The bonbons of this morning. How stupid I am! I had completely lost sight—— Oh, they were excellent, my lady, delicious!

BARTHOLO. Excellent! Delicious! Yes, without doubt, Mister Barber. Take back all you said: fine business that, sir!

FIGARO. What fault do you find with it, sir?

BARTHOLO. Lie as easily as that? What about your reputation, sir?

FIGARO. I'll live up to my reputation, sir.

BARTHOLO. Say, rather, that you will live it down, sir.

FIGARO. As you will, sir.

BARTHOLO. You are on a high horse, sir. Know that when I dispute with a coxcomb, I never yield to him.

FIGARO. We differ in that, sir. [Turns his back to BARTHOLO.] I always give in to him.

BARTHOLO. Hey? What does he mean by that, Professor?

FIGARO. You think that you are dealing with some village barber who knows how to wield nothing but a razor. Know, sir, that I made my living at Madrid by the pen, and if it had not been for the envious——

BARTHOLO. Eh? Then why didn't you stay there without coming here to change your profession?

FIGARO. One does as one can; put yourself in my place.

BARTHOLO. Put myself in your place! Ah, to be sure! Then I'd bray like a jackass.

FIGARO. You do that anyway, sir! I appeal to your colleague who is there dreaming.

THE COUNT [who has been too openly courting ROSINE, comes to himself]. I— I am not the colleague of this gentleman.

FIGARO [with double meaning]. No? Seeing you here in consultation, I thought that you were both pursuing the same object.

BARTHOLO [in anger]. To come to an end, what brings you here? Some other letter to my lady? Speak up! Is it necessary for me to retire?

FIGARO. How rough you are with the poor world! To be sure, sir, I came to shave you. That's all. Isn't to-day your time?

BARTHOLO. Come back a little later.

FIGARO. Oh yes, come back later! The whole garrison is to take a course of medicine to-morrow morning; I obtained the contract for the drugs through my influential friends. Imagine then how much time I have to lose. Will you please to walk into your room, sir?

BARTHOLO. No, I do not please to step into my room at all. Er—why—what is to hinder my being shaved here?

ROSINE [*with sarcasm*]. Well now you are respectful.—Shaving in my rooms!

BARTHOLO. You are offended? Pardon me, my child; you are going to finish having your music lesson; I am staying so as not to miss one instant's pleasure of hearing you.

FIGARO [*whispers to* THE COUNT]. We can't budge him from here. [*Aloud.*] Come here, Youngman! Hey, Wideawake! the basin, the water, all that the doctor needs.

BARTHOLO. That's right, call them. Tired out, done up, crippled at your hands, didn't they have to go to bed?

FIGARO. Oh, well, I'll go find the things; are they in your room? [*Whispers to* THE COUNT.] I'll pull him out now.

BARTHOLO [*detaches his key-ring and says after reflecting*]. No, no, I am going myself. [*Whispers to* THE COUNT.] Keep your eyes on them, please. [*Exit.*]

FIGARO. We have missed a grand opportunity! He was on the point of giving me his key-ring. Isn't the key to that window on it?

ROSINE. Yes, it is the newest one.

BARTHOLO [*returns and says aside*]. Well, I do not know what I am doing leaving that cursed barber in here. [*To* FIGARO.] Here. [*He gives the key-ring to him.*] In my dressing-room under the bureau; but don't you touch anything else!

FIGARO. Plague on't! You deserve it, distrustful as you are. [*He goes out and says aside.*] See how heaven takes care of the innocent.

BARTHOLO [*whispers to* THE COUNT]. That's the rascal who carried her letter to Count Almaviva.

THE COUNT [*whispers*]. He looks like a tricky fellow to me.

BARTHOLO [*whispers*]. He'll not catch me napping any more.

THE COUNT [*whispers*]. I believe that the worst of that matter is over.

BARTHOLO [*whispers*]. Taking everything into consideration, I thought it wiser to send him to my room than to leave him here with her.

THE COUNT [*whispers*]. I would have overheard every word they said.

ROSINE. It is surely polite, gentlemen, to keep on whispering! And what about my lesson?

[*They hear a noise as of crashing dishes.*]

BARTHOLO [*shrieking*]. What do I hear now? The heartless barber must have dropped on the stairs my dressing-case with the most beautiful pieces in it. [*He rushes out.*]

THE COUNT. Let's profit by this moment that Figaro's intelligence has gained for us. Grant me, I beseech, this evening one word of conversation absolutely necessary if you are to be saved from the slavery into which you are about to fall.

ROSINE. Ah, Lindor!

THE COUNT. I can climb up to your window; and as for the letter that I received from you this morning, I was forced——

BARTHOLO [*enters wringing his hands and saying*]. I wasn't mistaken; everything is broken into a thousand pieces.

FIGARO. Where there was so much noise there must have been a grand calamity. It is pitch dark on the stairs. [*He shows a key to* THE COUNT, *and says with double meaning.*] I—— Why, I stumbled upon a key, as I came up-stairs.

BARTHOLO. Why didn't you watch your step? Stumble upon a key! The clever man!

FIGARO. My word, sir, you may search far for a cleverer.

[DON BAZILE *enters.*]

ROSINE [*frightened, aside*]. Don Bazile!

THE COUNT [*aside*]. Good heavens!

FIGARO [*aside*]. The deuce is to pay now!

BARTHOLO [*going to meet him*]. Ah, Bazile, my friend, I am glad that you are well again. Your illness hasn't had any bad consequences then? To-day Professor Alonzo frightened me considerably about your condition. Just ask him: I was going out to see you, and if he hadn't restrained me——

BAZILE. Professor Alonzo?

FIGARO [*stamps his foot.*] My heavens! Still more delay? Two hours just for one shave! Such customers would lead me a dog's life.

BAZILE. Will you do me the favor, gentlemen, of telling me——

FIGARO. You shall talk your fill when I am gone.

BAZILE. But then I must——

THE COUNT. You must hush, Bazile.— Do you think you are telling the doctor something he doesn't know? I have told him that you sent me in your place to give the music lesson.

BAZILE [*more astonished*]. Music lesson! Alonzo!

ROSINE [*aside to* BAZILE]. Oh, please do not say any more.

BAZILE. She, too?

THE COUNT [*whispers to* BARTHOLO]. Just whisper to him that we are all together in this.

BARTHOLO [*to* BAZILE, *aside*]. Do not give us the lie, Bazile, by saying that he is not your pupil. That would spoil everything.

BAZILE. Ha! Ha!

BARTHOLO [*aloud*]. Truly, Bazile, your pupil is a most talented fellow.

BAZILE [*stupefied*]. That my pupil? [*Whispers.*] I came to tell you that the Count has moved——

BARTHOLO [*whispers*]. I know it; be silent.

BAZILE [*whispers*]. Who told you?

BARTHOLO. He, of course.

THE COUNT [*whispers*]. I, of course; you just listen and do not talk.

ROSINE [*whispers to* BAZILE]. Is it so hard to silence you?

FIGARO [*whispers*]. Humph! Fat hipponoceros! He is deaf!

BAZILE [*aside*]. Some one is being fooled here; but I'm hanged if I know who. Everybody is in the secret but me.

BARTHOLO [*aloud*]. Oh, well, Bazile, what about the lawyer?

FIGARO. You have all the evening to talk about lawyers.

BARTHOLO [*to* BAZILE]. In a word, just tell me if you are satisfied with the lawyer.

BAZILE [*bewildered*]. With the lawyer?

THE COUNT [*smiling*]. You haven't seen the lawyer?

BAZILE [*impatiently*]. No, I haven't seen any lawyer.

THE COUNT [*aside to* BARTHOLO]. Do you want him to explain before her? Send him away.

BARTHOLO [*whispers to* THE COUNT]. You are right. [*To* BAZILE.] But what made you sick so suddenly?

BAZILE. I do not understand you.

THE COUNT [*unobserved slips a purse into* BAZILE'S *hand*]. He is asking you what you are doing out of your house as sick as you are.

FIGARO. He is as pale as death.

BAZILE. Ah, I understand.

THE COUNT. Go to bed, my dear Bazile; you are not well, and you are frightening us terribly. Go to bed.

FIGARO. He looks all upset. Go to bed!

BARTHOLO. On my honor, you could tell a block away that he is feverish. Go to bed!

ROSINE. Why on earth did you come out? You can see that your illness is infectious. Go to bed!

BAZILE [*woefully bewildered*]. I go to bed?

ALL. Yes, certainly!

BAZILE [*looking at them all*]. Well really, gentlemen, I believe that it wouldn't be a bad idea for me to go to bed; I do feel a little out of sorts.

BARTHOLO. See you to-morrow if you are better.

THE COUNT. Bazile, I will come to your house early.

FIGARO. Better keep yourself warm in bed.

ROSINE. Good day, Don Bazile.

BAZILE [*aside*]. Devil take me if I understand anything, and if it were not for this purse——

ALL. Good day, Bazile, good day!

BAZILE [*going out*]. Oh, well then, good day, good day!

[*They accompany him, all laughing unrestrainedly.*]

BARTHOLO [*in a pompous tone*]. That man isn't at all well.

ROSINE. He has a wild look in his eyes.

THE COUNT. He must have had a chill.

FIGARO. Did you notice how he talked to himself? What frail beings we humans are! [*To* BARTHOLO.] Now make up your mind to be shaved forthwith.

[FIGARO *pushes an armchair to some distance from* THE COUNT *and hands him the towel.*]

THE COUNT. Before finishing, my lady, I should tell you one thing essential to progress in the art which I have the honor of teaching.

[*He draws closer to her and whispers in her ear.*]

BARTHOLO [*to* FIGARO]. But it seems that you have placed yourself right in front of me to keep me from seeing——

THE COUNT [*whispers to* ROSINE]. We have the key to the window, and we shall be here at midnight.

FIGARO [*places the towel around* BARTHOLO'S *neck*]. What is there to see? If it were a dancing lesson, I shouldn't blame you for looking; but singing! Aie! Aie!

BARTHOLO. What is it?

FIGARO. Something, I don't know what, has gotten into my eye. [*He bends his head forward.*]

BARTHOLO. Do not rub it.

FIGARO. It is the left. Will you please blow into it a little stronger?

[BARTHOLO *seizes* FIGARO'S *head, looks over it, pushes him away violently, and creeps behind the lovers to listen to their conversation.*]

THE COUNT [*whispers to* ROSINE]. And as for your letter, I found myself hard put to it for an excuse to stay here——

FIGARO [*at a distance to warn them*]. Ahem! Ahem!

THE COUNT. Disheartened at seeing my disguise useless——

BARTHOLO [*coming between them*]. Your disguise useless!

ROSINE [*terrified*]. Ah!

BARTHOLO. Very good, my lady, do not be alarmed! What now, under my very eyes, in my presence you dare outrage me in this fashion!

THE COUNT. What is the matter, Doctor?

BARTHOLO. Perfidious Alonzo!

THE COUNT. Doctor Bartholo, if you often have such whims as this of which chance has made me a witness, I am no longer astonished at the aversion which my lady here has to becoming your wife.

ROSINE. His wife! I! Pass my days with a jealous old fool, who offers me as the only happiness an abominable slavery.

BARTHOLO. Ah! What do I hear?

ROSINE. Yes, I say it to you, you: I shall give my heart and hand to that one who will be able to save me from this horrible prison where my person and my property are retained against all justice. [*Exit.*]

BARTHOLO. Anger is choking me!

THE COUNT. Truly, Doctor, it is hard for a young girl——

FIGARO. Yes, youth and old age; that is what troubles the heads of old men.

BARTHOLO. What, when I caught them in the act! Cursed barber! I have a great mind to——

FIGARO. I am leaving. He is crazy.

THE COUNT. And I also; on my honor, he is crazy.

FIGARO. He is crazy; he is crazy—— [*Exeunt.*]

BARTHOLO [*follows them leering and muttering*]. I am crazy, am I? Infamous barber! Agents of the devil, whose work you are doing here, and who, I hope, will fly away with you all. I am crazy! I saw them as plainly as I see this music stand.—And to face it out so brazenly.—Only Bazile can explain and set things aright. I'll send some one after him. Holloa there!—Oh, I forgot; I have no one to send.—A neighbor, the first-comer, —it doesn't matter who.—I am crazy, am

I? I have enough to make me lose my wits!

[NOTE—*During the interval between acts the theatre is darkened, and the noise of a terrific storm is heard.*]

ACT IV

SCENE—*Same as in* ACT III.

[*As the curtain rises the theatre is dark.* BARTHOLO *and* DON BAZILE *with a paper lantern in his hand enter.*]

BARTHOLO. What, Bazile, you do not know him? Is it possible that what you say is true?

BAZILE. You might ask me a hundred times, and my answer would still be no. If he has given you Rosine's letter, he is without doubt one of the Count's retainers. Yet judging by the magnificence of his present to me, it might be that he is the Count himself.

BARTHOLO. More than likely. But about this present—er—why did you take it?

BAZILE. You all seemed to be in accord; I couldn't make heads nor tails of your actions; and in delicate and fine points of judgment, a purse of gold throws the balances its way.—Besides, you know the proverb, One good turn de——

BARTHOLO. Yes, I know. Deserves——

BAZILE [*quickly*].—that I make good use of it.

BARTHOLO [*surprised*]. Ha!

BAZILE. Yes, I have arranged some little variations like that for several proverbs. But to get back to business: what have you decided upon?

BARTHOLO. If you were in my place, Bazile, wouldn't you make use of every means to possess her?

BAZILE. My word, no, Doctor! In all kinds of property, possession is the smallest part; it is the enjoyment of them that makes one happy. My opinion is that to marry a woman by whom one isn't loved at all, is to expose oneself——

BARTHOLO. You would fear unfaithfulness?

BAZILE [*snickers*]. He! He! I have seen enough of that this year. I shouldn't do any outrage to her heart.

BARTHOLO. That will do, Bazile. I'd much rather that she weeps from having me than that I die from not having her.

BAZILE. Oh, if it is a question of life and death, why marry her, Doctor, marry her.

BARTHOLO. I shall do that and this very night.

BAZILE. Good-bye then.—Remember in talking to Rosine about him paint him blacker than hell.

BARTHOLO. You are right.

BAZILE. Slander, Doctor, slander! You must come to that finally.

BARTHOLO. Here is Rosine's letter that this Alonzo gave me; he taught me, without meaning to, to what good advantage I may use it with her.

BAZILE. Good-bye. We will be here at four o'clock.

BARTHOLO. Why not sooner?

BAZILE. Impossible; the notary is engaged.

BARTHOLO. For a marriage?

BAZILE. Yes, at the home of the barber Figaro; his niece is getting married.

BARTHOLO. His niece? He hasn't any niece.

BAZILE. That is what they told the notary.

BARTHOLO. That rascal is in with them. What the deuce——

BAZILE. Do you think——?

BARTHOLO. My word, they are so alert. Wait, my friend, I am uneasy. You go see the notary. Let him come here immediately with you.

BAZILE. It is raining cats and dogs—devilish weather outside; but nothing keeps me from serving you. Where are you going now?

BARTHOLO. I am going with you to the door. Hasn't this Figaro crippled all my servants? I am alone here.

BAZILE. I have my lantern.

BARTHOLO. Here, Bazile, take my pass-key. I await you, I stay up; and come who will, with the exception of you and the notary, no one shall enter here this night.

BAZILE. With such precautions, you are sure of your step. [*Exeunt.*]

[*In a moment* ROSINE *comes from her bedroom.*]

ROSINE. I thought I heard talking. It is midnight; Lindor isn't come at all! This weather, and all, favors his coming. He is sure not to meet any one. Ah, Lindor! If you have deceived me—— What noise is that? Heavens, it is my guardian! I must get back to my room.

[BARTHOLO *enters, holding a light.*]

BARTHOLO. Ah, Rosine, since you have not yet gone to bed——

ROSINE. I was just going——

BARTHOLO. In such a frightful storm as this, you would not sleep. Besides, I have some very pressing things to say to you.

ROSINE. What do you wish of me, sir? Isn't it enough to be tormented all day?

BARTHOLO. Rosine, listen to me.

ROSINE. To-morrow, please!

BARTHOLO. Be good enough to spare me one moment.

ROSINE [*aside*]. Suppose Lindor comes now!

BARTHOLO [*shows her the letter*]. Do you recognize this letter?

ROSINE [*recognizing it*]. Oh, merciful heavens!

BARTHOLO. It is not at all my intention, Rosine, to reproach you; at your age, one may err; but I am your friend: please listen to me.

ROSINE. I am helpless.

BARTHOLO. This letter that you wrote to Count Almaviva——

ROSINE [*astonished*]. To Count Almaviva?

BARTHOLO. You see what an unprincipled man this Count is. As soon as he received it, he made a trophy of it. I secured it from a woman to whom he gave it.

ROSINE. Count Almaviva!

BARTHOLO. You can hardly persuade yourself that he is so vile. Inexperience, Rosine, makes your sex confiding and credulous; but just see what a snare you have been drawn into. This woman had me fully informed, apparently to get rid of such a dangerous rival as you. I tremble at it! The most abominable conspiracy hatched up by Almaviva, Figaro, and this Alonzo, the supposed pupil of Bazile, who bears an alias and is only the low panderer of the Count, was about to sweep you down into a chasm from which nothing could have drawn you.

ROSINE [*overwhelmed*]. How terrible! What? Lindor? What, this young man do that?

BARTHOLO. So *he* is Lindor.

ROSINE. He is acting for Count Almaviva.—He is making love for another!

BARTHOLO. That is what they told me when they brought the letter.

ROSINE [*beside herself*]. Oh, what an insult! He shall be punished for it. You were anxious to marry me, sir?

BARTHOLO. You know the sincerity of my affections.

ROSINE. If you still have any left, I am yours.

BARTHOLO. Fine! The notary will come to marry us this very night.

ROSINE. That is not all. Oh, heavens! I am sufficiently humiliated. Know that in a little while the wretch will dare come in through that window, the key of which they have artfully stolen from you.

BARTHOLO [*fingering his key-ring*]. The scoundrels! My child, I shall not leave you.

ROSINE [*frightened*]. Oh, but, sir, suppose—suppose they are armed.

BARTHOLO. You are right. I would lose my vengeance. Go up to Marceline's room; double lock the door. I am going to get the police and await Bazile outside the house. By arresting this Lindor for burglary, we shall have the pleasure of being both avenged and freed of him. And remember that my love will repay you——

ROSINE [*in despair*]. Only forget my mistake. [*Aside*]. Oh, I am punishing myself enough for it!

BARTHOLO [*going out, and aside*]. Now to fix my trap. At last, I have got her.

ROSINE [*alone*]. His love will repay me.—Unhappy me! [*She takes out her handkerchief and gives away to tears*]. What must I do? He is certain to come. I want to stay and dissemble in order to observe him in all his blackness. The lowness of his conduct will be my safeguard. Ah! I have great need of protection! Noble face! Gentle manners! A voice,—oh, so tender!—And he is only the vile agent of a libertine. Oh, miserable me! Unhappy me! Heavens! Some one is opening the shutters.

[*She flees.* THE COUNT *and* FIGARO *both wearing long capes appear at the window.*]

FIGARO [*speaks off stage*]. Some one is fleeing. Shall I go in?

THE COUNT [*off stage*]. A man?

FIGARO. No.

THE COUNT. It is Rosine. Your hideous appearance must have frightened her.

[FIGARO *jumps into the room.*]

FIGARO. I can well believe that. Well, here we are in spite of rain, thunder, and lightning.

THE COUNT. Give me your hand. [*He in turn jumps into the room.*] Ah, victory!

FIGARO [*throws cape aside*]. We are wet to the skin. Wonderful weather to go philandering. My lord, how does this night suit you?

THE COUNT. Superb for a lover.

FIGARO. Yes, but for a confidant? And suppose some one should catch us here.

THE COUNT. Aren't you with me? I have quite another concern: it is to persuade her to leave this night the home of her guardian.

FIGARO. You have in your favor three very powerful arguments: love, hate, and fear.

THE COUNT. How shall I abruptly announce that the notary is waiting at your home to marry us? She will find my project too bold. She will call me audacious.

FIGARO. If she calls you that, you call her cruel. Women adore being called cruel. Moreover, if her love is as sincere as you wish, and if you tell her who you are, she will no longer be doubtful about your feelings and your intentions.

[FIGARO *lights all the candles on the table.* ROSINE *enters just as he finishes.*]

THE COUNT. There she is! My beautiful Rosine!

ROSINE [*in a very cool tone*]. I was beginning to fear, sir, that you were not coming.

THE COUNT. Charming anxiety! My lady, it is not at all my nature to take an unfair advantage of circumstances in proposing that you share the lot of a poor fellow. But whatever refuge you may choose, I swear on my honor——

ROSINE. If the gift of my hand, sir, did not go with that of my heart, you would not be here. Let the plea of necessity justify you in whatever of irregularity there is in this interview.

THE COUNT. You, Rosine! The wife of an unlucky fellow without fortune, without birth——!

ROSINE. Birth! Fortune! Stop talking of things that come by chance, and if you assure me that your intentions are honorable——

THE COUNT [*at her feet*]. Ah, Rosine! I love you!

ROSINE [*in great indignation*]. Stop, wretch! You dare profane! You love me!—Go! You are no longer hard for me to understand; I was awaiting this word to detest you. But before abandoning you to the remorse in store for you—[*Weeping.*] know that I loved you; know that I was going to make it my happiness to share with you your low estate. Miserable Lindor! I intended to give up everything to follow you, but the cowardly abuse you have made of my gifts and the insult of this Count Almaviva to whom you have sold me, have served to return to me this evidence of my weakness. Do you recognize this letter?

THE COUNT [*realizing the trick that*

Bartholo *has played, says quickly*]. That your guardian gave you?

Rosine [*proudly*]. Yes, I am indebted to him for it.

The Count. Ye gods! How happy I am! He secured it from me. In my embarrassment yesterday, I made use of it to force his confidence, and I have not been able to find a moment to tell you about it. Ah, Rosine! It is true that you really love me?

Figaro. Your Excellency was seeking a woman who would love you for yourself.

Rosine. Your Excellency? What is he saying?

The Count [*throwing aside his cape, appears dressed magnificently*]. O most beloved of women! It is no longer necessary to abuse your confidence: the happy man you see at your feet is not Lindor at all; I am Count Almaviva, who is dying of love, and has sought six months in vain for you.

Rosine [*falls into the arms of* The Count]. Ah!

The Count [*alarmed*]. Figaro?

Figaro. Do not be alarmed, my lord; the sweet emotion of joy has never had ill consequences. There, she is coming to herself. Jove! How beautiful she is!

Rosine. Oh, Lindor! How guilty I am! I was going to give myself to my guardian this very night.

The Count. You, Rosine?

Rosine. Only see my punishment: I would have passed my life in detesting you. Ah, Lindor! isn't *hating* the most frightful torture when one feels herself made for loving?

Figaro [*looks out the window*]. My lord, our way of retreat is cut off; the ladder has been removed.

The Count. Removed?

Rosine [*confused*]. Yes, it is I—it is the doctor. That is the fruit of my credulity. He deceived me. I told all, betrayed all; he knows that you were here, and he has gone for the police.

Figaro [*still looking out*]. My lord, some one is opening the street door.

Rosine [*in fright throws herself into* the arms of The Count]. Oh, Lindor!

The Count [*with firmness and an air of protectiveness*]. Rosine, you love me! That is enough; I fear no one; you shall be my wife. I shall then have the pleasure of punishing that old man to my taste!

Rosine. No, no, have pity on him, dear Lindor! My heart is so full that vengeance has no place in it.

[Don Bazile *and the* Notary *enter.*]

Figaro. My lord, this is our notary.

The Count. And friend Bazile with him.

Bazile [*rubbing his eyes*]. What do I see?

Figaro. Eh? By what chance, friend——?

Bazile. By what accident, gentlemen——?

The Notary. Is this the bride, and is that the groom?

The Count. Yes. You were to marry the Señora Rosine and me to-night at the home of Figaro, but we have selected this house instead for reasons that you shall know. Have you the license?

The Notary. I have the honor then of speaking to His Excellency, the Count Almaviva?

Figaro. You have.

Bazile [*aside*]. If this is the reason he gave me the pass-key——

The Notary. But then I have two marriage licenses, my lord: let's not get them mixed. Here is yours, and this is the one of Doctor Bartholo with Miss— Miss——[*He fits his glasses and peers at the paper.*] Rosine too? The ladies are apparently two sisters who bear the same name.

The Count. At any rate sign the certificate. Bazile will be just the man for a second witness.

[*They all sign.*]

Bazile [*hesitating to sign*]. But your Excellency, I do not understand.

The Count. My good Bazile, a trifle embarrasses you, and everything astonishes you.

BAZILE. But your Excellency—if the doctor——

THE COUNT [*tossing him a purse*]. Come now, you are acting childishly. Sign now and quickly!

BAZILE [*astonished*]. Ah! Ah!

FIGARO. Where then is your trouble in signing?

BAZILE [*weighing the purse*]. There isn't any more; but I am the kind of fellow that when I have once given my word must have motives of great weight before breaking it——

[*He signs just as* BARTHOLO, *a* JUSTICE OF THE PEACE, POLICE-MEN, *and* SERVANTS *with torches burst into the room.* BARTHOLO *sees* THE COUNT *kissing* ROSINE'S *hand and* FIGARO *grotesquely hugging and dancing with* DON BAZILE. BARTHOLO *takes the* NOTARY *by the neck and shouts.*]

BARTHOLO. Rosine with these scoundrels! Arrest them all; I have one of them by the collar.

THE NOTARY. I am your notary.

BAZILE. He is your notary; are you trying to play a joke?

BARTHOLO. Ah, Don Bazile, why are you here?

BAZILE. Better ask why are you *not* here.

JUSTICE [*pointing to* FIGARO]. Just a minute: I know this one. What are you doing in this house in the dead hours of night?

FIGARO. Middle of the night? You well see, sir, that it is as near to morning as it is to evening. Besides, I am a retainer of His Excellency, the Count Almaviva.   [*He bows to* THE COUNT.]

BARTHOLO. Almaviva!

JUSTICE. Then there aren't any burglars here?

BARTHOLO. Oh, let that go. At any other time, my lord, I am the humble servant of your Excellency; but you understand that here superiority of rank counts for nothing. Will you, therefore,

if it please you, have the goodness to withdraw.

THE COUNT. You are right: rank ought not to count here; but that which should and does count far more is that my lady here has just shown her preference for me by giving herself willing to me.

BARTHOLO. What is he saying, Rosine?

ROSINE. The truth. Whence comes your surprise? Was I not due this very night to be revenged upon a deceiver? Well, I am.

BAZILE. Didn't I tell you that it was the Count himself, Doctor?

BARTHOLO. What difference does it make what you told me? Preposterous marriage! Where are your witnesses?

NOTARY. Oh, the marriage is in good form all right. I was assisted by these two gentlemen.

BARTHOLO. What? You too, Bazile? You served as a witness?

BAZILE. What else could you expect? This devil of a man always has his pockets full of unanswerable arguments.

BARTHOLO. I don't give a snap of my fingers for his arguments. I shall make use of my authority.

THE COUNT. You have lost it by abusing it.

BARTHOLO. The girl is not of age.

FIGARO. This marriage has just made her of age.

BARTHOLO. Who is talking to you, arch-knave?

THE COUNT. The lady is noble and beautiful. I am of good birth, young, and rich; she is my wife; does any one wish to dispute me this title which honors us both?

BARTHOLO. You shall never take her from me.

THE COUNT. She is no longer in your power. I place her under the authority of the law; and this gentleman, whom you yourself brought here, will protect her against the violence that you wish to do her. True magistrates are defenders of the oppressed.

JUSTICE. Certainly, and this useless resistance to a most honorable marriage indicates well enough his fright over the fraudulent administration of his ward's property; but he must render an account.

THE COUNT. Oh, let him consent to this marriage, and I ask nothing else of him.

FIGARO. Wait a minute! Wait a minute! Do not be too hasty! nothing except a receipt for my hundred dollars.

BARTHOLO [in irritation]. They were all against me.—I have thrust my head into a hornet's nest.

BAZILE. What hornet's nest? Failing to get a wife, Doctor, just consider that you get the money. Oh, yes.—You get the money.

BARTHOLO. Oh, let me be, Bazile. You think only of money. Much I care about money now! To be sure, I will keep it; but do not think that that is the motive that determines my signing. [He signs the certificate.]

FIGARO [laughing]. Ha! Ha! My lord, they are of the same family.

NOTARY. But, gentlemen, I do not quite understand yet. Are there not two ladies who have the same name?

FIGARO. No, sir, the two are only one.

BARTHOLO [in great distress]. And I carried the ladder away in order that my marriage be made more sure! Oh, I am ruined in spite of my pains!

FIGARO. Ruined from lack of sense. But let's be serious, Doctor; when youth and love work together to deceive an old fellow, everything he does to prevent it may well be called the "Useless Precaution."

HERNANI

By VICTOR HUGO

Produced at Paris, 1830

TRANSLATED BY MRS. NEWTON CROSLAND*.

CHARACTERS

HERNANI
DON CARLOS
DON RUY GOMEZ DE SILVA
DOÑA SOL DE SILVA
THE KING OF BOHEMIA
THE DUKE OF BAVARIA
THE DUKE OF GOTHA
THE BARON OF HOHENBOURG
THE DUKE OF LUTZELBOURG
DON SANCHO
DON MATIAS
DON RICARDO
DON GARCIA SUAREZ
DON FRANCISCO
DON JUAN DE HARO
DON PEDRO GUZMAN DE LARA
DON GIL TELLEZ GIRON
DOÑA JOSEFA DUARTE
JAQUEZ
A MOUNTAINEER
A LADY
FIRST, SECOND, AND THIRD CONSPIRATORS

*Conspirators of the Holy League, Germans and Spaniards,
Mountaineers, Nobles, Soldiers, Pages, Attendants, etc.*

* Reprinted from the *Dramatic Works of Victor Hugo*, published by Little, Brown & Co., copyright, 1909, by permission of the publisher.

ACT I

Saragossa. A Chamber. Night: a lamp on the table.

[*Enter* DOÑA JOSEFA DUARTE, *an old woman dressed in black, with body of her dress worked in jet in the fashion of Isabella the Catholic. She draws the crimson curtains of the window, and puts some armchairs in order. A knock at a little secret door on the right. She listens. A second knock.*]

DOÑA JOSEFA. Can it be he already?
[*Another knock.*] 'T is, indeed,
At th' hidden stairway. [*A fourth knock.*]
I must open quick.
[*She opens the concealed door.*]

[*Enter* DON CARLOS, *his face muffled in his cloak, and his hat drawn over his brows.*]
Good-evening to you, sir!
[*She ushers him in. He drops his cloak and reveals a rich dress of silk and velvet in the Castilian style of 1519. She looks at him closely, and recoils astonished.*]
What now?—not you,
Signor Hernani! Fire! fire! Help, oh, help!

DON CARLOS [*seizing her by the arm*].
But two words more, duenna, and you die! [*He looks at her intently. She is frightened into silence.*]
Is this the room of Doña Sol, betrothed
To her old uncle, Duke de Pastrana?
A very worthy lord he is—senile,
White-hair'd and jealous. Tell me, is it true
The beauteous Doña loves a smooth-faced youth,
All whiskerless as yet, and sees him here
Each night, in spite of envious care? Tell me,
Am I informed aright?
[*She is silent. He shakes her by the arm.*]
Will you not speak?

DOÑA JOSEFA. You did forbid me, sir, to speak two words.

DON CARLOS. One will suffice. I want a yes, or no.
Say, is thy mistress Doña Sol de Silva?

DOÑA JOSEFA. Yes, why?

DON CARLOS. No matter why. Just at this hour
The venerable lover is away?

DOÑA JOSEFA. He is.

DON CARLOS. And she expects the young one now?

DOÑA JOSEFA. Yes.

DON CARLOS. Oh, that I could die!

DOÑA JOSEFA. Yes.

DON CARLOS. Say, duenna,
Is this the place where they will surely meet?

DOÑA JOSEFA. Yes.

DON CARLOS. Hide me somewhere here.

DOÑA JOSEFA. You?

DON CARLOS. Yes, me.

DOÑA JOSEFA. Why?

DON CARLOS. No matter why.

DOÑA JOSEFA. I hide you here!

DON CARLOS. Yes, here.

DOÑA JOSEFA. No, never!

DON CARLOS [*drawing from his girdle a purse and a dagger*]. Madam, condescend to choose
Between a purse and dagger.

DOÑA JOSEFA [*taking the purse*]. Are you, then,
The devil?

DON CARLOS. Yes, duenna.

DOÑA JOSEFA [*opening a narrow cupboard in the wall*]. Go—go in.

DON CARLOS [*examining the cupboard*]. This box!

DOÑA JOSEFA [*shutting up the cupboard*]. If you don't like it, go away.

DON CARLOS [*reopening cupboard*].
And yet! [*Again examining it.*] Is this the stable where you keep
The broom-stick that you ride on?
[*He crouches down in the cupboard with difficulty.*]
Oh! Oh! Oh!

DOÑA JOSEFA [*joining her hands and looking ashamed*]. A man here!

DON CARLOS [*from the cupboard, still open*]. And was it a woman, then, Your mistress here expected?

DOÑA JOSEFA. Heavens! I hear The step of Doña Sol! Sir, shut the door! Quick—quick!

[*She pushes the cupboard door, which closes.*]

DON CARLOS [*from the closed cupboard*]. Remember, if you breathe a word You die!

DOÑA JOSEFA [*alone*]. Who is this man? If I cry out, Gracious! there's none to hear. All are asleep Within the palace walls—madam and I Excepted. Pshaw! The other'll come. He wears A sword; 't his affair. And Heav'n keep us From powers of hell. [*Weighing the purse in her hand.*] At least no thief he is.

[*Enter DOÑA SOL in white. DOÑA JOSEFA hides the purse.*]

DOÑA SOL. Josefa!

DOÑA JOSEFA. Madam?

DOÑA SOL. I some mischief dread, For 't is full time Hernani should be here.

[*Noises of steps at the secret door.*] He's coming up; go—quick; at once, undo Ere he has time to knock.

[*JOSEFA opens the little door.*]

[*Enter HERNANI in large cloak and large hat; underneath, costume of mountaineer of Aragon—gray, with a cuirass of leather; a sword, a dagger, and a horn at his girdle.*]

DOÑA SOL [*going to him*]. Hernani! Oh!

HERNANI. Ah, Doña Sol! It is yourself at last I see—your voice it is I hear. Oh, why Does cruel fate keep you so far from me? I have such need of you to help my heart Forget all else!

DOÑA SOL [*touching his clothes*]. Oh! Heav'ns! Your cloak is drench'd! The rain must pour!

HERNANI. I know not.

DOÑA SOL. And the cold— You must be cold!

HERNANI. I feel it not.

DOÑA SOL. Take off This cloak, then, pray.

HERNANI. Doña, beloved, tell me, When night brings happy sleep to you, so pure And innocent—sleep that half opes your mouth, Closing your eyes with its light finger-touch— Does not some angel show how dear you are To an unhappy man, by all the world Abandoned and repulsed?

DOÑA SOL. Sir, you are late; But tell me, are you cold?

HERNANI. Not near to you. Ah! when the raging fire of jealous love Burns in the veins, and the true heart is riven By its own tempest, we feel not the clouds O'erhead, though storm and lightning they fling forth!

DOÑA SOL. Come, give me now the cloak, and your sword too.

HERNANI [*his hand on his sword*]. No. 'T is my other love, faithful and pure, The old Duke, Doña Sol,—your promised spouse, Your uncle,—is he absent now?

DOÑA SOL. Oh, yes; This hour to us belongs.

HERNANI. And that is all! Only this hour! And then comes afterwards!— What matter! For I must forget or die! Angel! One hour with thee—with whom I would Spend life, and afterwards eternity!

DOÑA SOL. Hernani!

HERNANI. It is happiness to know The Duke is absent. I am like a thief Who forces doors. I enter—see you—rob An old man of an hour of your sweet voice And looks. And I am happy, though, no doubt

He would deny me e'en one hour, although
He steals my very life.
    DOÑA SOL. Be calm. [*Giving the cloak
to the duenna.*] Josefa!
This wet cloak take and dry it.
                [*Exit* JOSEFA.]
    [*She seats herself, and makes a
    sign for* HERNANI *to draw near.*]
Now, come here.
    HERNANI [*without appearing to hear
her*]. The Duke, then, is not in the mansion now?
    DOÑA SOL. How grand you look!
    HERNANI. He is away?
    DOÑA SOL. Dear one,
Let us not think about the Duke.
    HERNANI. Madam,
But let us think of him, the grave old
    man
Who loves you—who will marry you!
    How now?
He took a kiss from you the other day.
Not think of him!
    DOÑA SOL. Is 't that which grieves you
    thus?
A kiss upon my brow—an uncle's kiss—
Almost a father's.
    HERNANI. No, not so; it was
A lover's, husband's, jealous kiss. To
    him—
To him it is that you will soon belong.
Think'st thou not of it! Oh, the foolish
    dotard,
With head drooped down to finish out his
    days!
Wanting a wife, he takes a girl; himself
Most like a frozen specter. Sees he not,
The senseless one! that while with one
    hand he
Espouses you, the other mates with
    Death!
Yet without shudder comes he 'twixt our
    hearts!
Seek out the grave-digger, old man, and
    give
Thy measure.
Who is it that makes for you
This marriage? You are forced to it, I
    hope?
    DOÑA SOL. They say the King desires
    it.

    HERNANI. King! This king!
My father on the scaffold died condemned
By his; and, though one may have aged
    since then,—
For e'en the shadow of that king, his son,
His widow, and for all to him allied,
My hate continues fresh. Him dead, no
    more
We count with; but while still a child I
    swore
That I'd avenge my father on his son.
I sought him in all places—Charles the
    King
Of the Castiles. For hate is rife between
Our families. The fathers wrestled long
And without pity, and without remorse,
For thirty years! Oh, 't is in vain that
    they
Are dead; their hatred lives. For them
    no peace
Has come; their sons keep up the duel
    still.
Ah! then I find 't is thou who hast made
    up
This execrable marriage! Thee I sought—
Thou comest in my way!
    DOÑA SOL. You frighten me!
    HERNANI. Charged with the mandate
    of anathema,
I frighten e'en myself; but listen now:
This old, old man, for whom they destine
    you,
This Ruy de Silva, Duke de Pastrana,
Count and grandee, rich man of Aragon,
In place of youth can give thee, oh! young
    girl,
Such store of gold and jewels that your
    brow
Will shine 'mong royalty's own diadems;
And for your rank and wealth, and pride
    and state,
Queens many will perhaps envy you. See,
    then,
Just what he is. And now consider me.
My poverty is absolute, I say.
Only the forest, where I ran barefoot
In childhood, did I know. Although perchance
I too can claim illustrious blazonry,
That's dimm'd just now by rusting stain
    of blood.

Perchance I've rights, though they are shrouded still,
And hid 'neath ebon folds of scaffold cloth,
Yet which, if my attempt one day succeeds,
May, with my sword from out their sheath leap forth.
Meanwhile, from jealous Heaven I've received
But air, and light, and water—gifts bestowed
On all. Now, wish you from the Duke, or me,
To be delivered? You must choose 'twixt us,
Whether you marry him, or follow me.
DOÑA SOL. You, I will follow!
HERNANI. 'Mong companions rude,
Men all proscribed, of whom the headsman knows
The names already. Men whom neither steel
Nor touch of pity softens; each one urged
By some blood feud that's personal. Wilt thou
Then come? They'd call thee mistress of my band,
For know you not that I a bandit am?
When I was hunted throughout Spain, alone
In thickest forests, and on mountains steep,
'Mong rocks which but the soaring eagle spied,
Old Catalonia like a mother proved.
Among her hills—free, poor, and stern—I grew;
And now, to-morrow if this horn should sound,
Three thousand men would rally at the call.
You shudder, and should pause to ponder well.
Think what 't will prove to follow me through woods
And over mountain paths, with comrades like
The fiends that come in dreams! To live in fear,
Suspicious of a sound, of voices, eyes:

To sleep upon the earth, drink at the stream,
And hear at night, while nourishing perchance
Some wakeful babe, the whistling musket balls.
To be a wanderer with me proscribed,
And when my father I shall follow—then,
E'en to the scaffold, you to follow me!
DOÑA SOL. I'll follow you.
HERNANI. The Duke is wealthy, great
And prosperous, without a stain upon
His ancient name. He offers you his hand,
And can give all things—treasures, dignities,
And pleasure—
DOÑA SOL. We'll set out to-morrow. Oh!
Hernani, censure not th' audacity
Of this decision. Are you angel mine
Or demon? Only one thing do I know,
That I'm your slave. Now, listen: wheresoe'er
You go, I go—pause you or move I'm yours.
Why act I thus? Ah! that I cannot tell;
Only I want to see you evermore.
When sound of your receding footstep dies
I feel my heart stops beating; without you
Myself seems absent, but when I detect
Again the step I love, my soul comes back,
I breathe—I live once more.
HERNANI [embracing her]. Oh! angel mine!
DOÑA SOL. At midnight, then, to-morrow, clap your hands
Three times beneath my window, bringing there
Your escort. Go! I shall be strong and brave.
HERNANI. Now know you who I am?
DOÑA SOL. Only my lord.
Enough—what matters else?—I follow you.
HERNANI. Not so. Since you, a woman weak, decide

To come with me, 't is right that you
should know
What name, what rank, what soul, per-
chance what fate
There hides beneath the low Hernani here.
Yes, you have willed to link yourself for
aye
With brigand—would you still with out-
law mate?
DON CARLOS [*opening the cupboard*].
When will finish all this history?
Think you 't is pleasant in this cupboard
hole?

[HERNANI *recoils, astonished.*
DOÑA SOL *screams and takes
refuge in* HERNANI'S *arms,
looking at* DON CARLOS *with
frightened gaze.*]

HERNANI [*his hand on the hilt of his
sword*]. Who is this man?
DOÑA SOL. Oh, Heavens, help!
HERNANI. Be still,
My Doña Sol! you'll wake up dangerous
eyes.
Never—whatever be—while I am near,
Seek other help than mine.
[*To* DON CARLOS.] What do you here?
DON CARLOS. I?—Well, I am not rid-
ing through the wood,
That you should ask.
HERNANI. He who affronts, then jeers,
May cause his heir to laugh.
DON CARLOS. Each, sir, in turn.
Let us speak frankly. You the lady love,
And come each night to mirror in her eyes
Your own. I love her, too, and want to
know
Who 't is I have so often seen come in
The window way, while I stand at the
door.
HERNANI. Upon my word, I'll send you
out the way
I enter.
DON CARLOS. As to that we'll see. My
love
I offer unto madam. Shall we, then,
Agree to share it? In her beauteous soul
I've seen so much of tenderness, and
love,
And sentiment, that she, I'm very sure,
Has quite enough for ardent lovers twain.

Therefore, to-night, wishing to end sus-
pense
On your account, I forced an entrance,
hid,
And—to confess it all—I listened too.
But I heard badly, and was nearly
choked;
And then I crumpled my French vest—
and so,
By Jove! come out I must!
HERNANI. Likewise my blade
Is not at ease, and hurries to leap out.
DON CARLOS [*bowing*]. Sir, as you
please.
HERNANI [*drawing his sword*]. Defend
yourself!
[DON CARLOS *draws his sword.*]
DOÑA SOL. Oh, Heaven!
DON CARLOS. Be calm, señora.
HERNANI [*to* DON CARLOS]. Tell me,
sir, your name.
DON CARLOS. Tell me yours!
HERNANI. It is a fatal secret,
Kept for my breathing in another's ear,
Some day when I am conqueror, with my
knee
Upon his breast, and dagger in his
heart.
DON CARLOS. Then tell to me this
other's name.
HERNANI. To thee
What matters it? On guard! Defend
thyself!
[*They cross swords.* DOÑA SOL
*falls trembling into a chair.
They hear knocks at the door.*]
DOÑA SOL [*rising in alarm*]. Oh, Heav-
ens! There's some one knocking at the
door!
[*The champions pause.*]
[*Enter* JOSEFA, *at the little door, in a
frightened state.*]
HERNANI [*to* JOSEFA]. Who knocks in
this way?
DOÑA JOSEFA [*to* DOÑA SOL]. Madam,
a surprise!
An unexpected blow. It is the Duke
Come home.
DOÑA SOL [*clasping her hands*]. The
Duke. Then every hope is lost!
DOÑA JOSEFA [*looking round*]. Gra-

cious!—the stranger out!—and swords, and fighting
Here's a fine business!

[*The two combatants sheath their swords.* DON CARLOS *draws his cloak round him, and pulls his hat down on his forehead. More knocking.*]

HERNANI. What is to be done?
[*More knocking.*]

A VOICE [*without*]. Doña Sol, open to me.

[DOÑA JOSEFA *is going to the door, when* HERNANI *stops her.*]

HERNANI. Do not open.

DOÑA JOSEFA [*pulling out her rosary*]. Holy St. James! Now draw us through this broil! [*More knocking.*]

HERNANI [*pointing to the cupboard*]. Let's hide!

DON CARLOS. What! in the cupboard?

HERNANI. Yes, go in; I will take care that it shall hold us both.

DON CARLOS. Thanks. No; it is too good a joke.

HERNANI [*pointing to secret door*]. Let's fly That way.

DON CARLOS. Good-night! But as for me I stay Here.

HERNANI. Fire and fury, sir, we will be quits For this.
[*To* DOÑA SOL.] What if I firmly barr'd the door?

DON CARLOS [*to* JOSEFA]. Open the door.

HERNANI. What is it that he says?

DON CARLOS [*to* JOSEFA, *who hesitates bewildered*]. Open the door, I say.

[*More knocking.* JOSEFA *opens the door, trembling.*]

DOÑA SOL. Oh, I shall die!

[*Enter* DON RUY GOMEZ DE SILVA, *in black; white hair and beard. Servants with lights.*]

DON RUY GOMEZ. My niece with two men at this hour of night!

Come all! The thing is worth exposing here.
[*To* DOÑA SOL.] Now, by St. John of Avila, I vow
That we three with you, madam, are by two Too many.
[*To the two young men.*] My young sirs, what do you here?
When we'd the Cid and Bernard—giants both
Of Spain and of the world—they traveled through
Castile protecting women, honoring
Old men. For them steel armor had less weight
Than your fine velvets have for you. These men
Respected whitened beards, and when they loved,
Their love was consecrated by the Church.
Never did such men cozen or betray,
For reason that they had to keep unflawed
The honor of their house. Wished they to wed,
They took a stainless wife in open day,
Before the world, with sword, or axe, or lance
In hand. But as for villains such as you,
Who come at eve, peeping behind them oft,
To steal away the honor of men's wives
In absence of their husbands, I declare,
The Cid, our ancestor, had he but known
Such men, he would have plucked away from them
Nobility usurped, have made them kneel,
While he with flat of sword their blazon dashed.
Behold what were the men of former times
Whom I, with anguish, now compare with these
I see to-day! What do you here? Is it
To say, a white-haired man's but fit for youth
To point at when he passes in the street,
And jeer at there? Shall they so laugh at me,
Tried soldier of Zamora? At the least
Not yours will be that laugh.

HERNANI. But, Duke—
DON RUY GOMEZ. Be still!
What! You have sword and lance, falcons, the chase,
And songs to sing 'neath balconies at night,
Festivals, pleasures, feathers in your hats,
Raiment of silk—balls, youth, and joy of life;
But wearied of them all, at any price
You want a toy, and take an old man for it.
Ah, though you've broke the toy, God wills that it
In bursting should be flung back in your face!
Now follow me!
HERNANI. Most noble Duke—
DON RUY GOMEZ. Follow—
Follow me, sirs. Is this alone a jest?
What! I've a treasure, mine to guard with care,
A young girl's character, a family's fame.
This girl I love—by kinship to me bound,
Pledged soon to change her ring for one from me.
I know her spotless, chaste, and pure. Yet when
I leave my home one hour, I—Ruy Gomez
De Silva—find a thief who steals from me
My honor, glides unto my house. Back, back,
Make clean your hands, oh, base and soulless men,
Whose presence, brushing by, must serve to taint
Our women's fame! But no, 't is well. Proceed.
Have I not something more?
[*Snatches off his collar.*] Take, tread it now
Beneath your feet. Degrade my Golden Fleece.
[*Throws off his hat.*] Pluck at my hair, insult me every way,
And then, to-morrow through the town make boast
That lowest scoundrels in their vilest sport

Have never shamed a nobler brow, nor soiled
More whitened hair.
DOÑA SOL. My lord—
DON RUY GOMEZ [*to his servants*]. A rescue! grooms!
Bring me my dagger of Toledo, axe,
And dirk.
[*To the young men.*] Now, follow—follow me—ye two.
DON CARLOS [*stepping forward a little*].
Duke, this is not the pressing thing just now;
First we've to think of Maximilian dead,
The Emperor of Germany.
[*Opens his cloak, and shows his face, previously hidden by his hat.*]
DON RUY GOMEZ. Jest you!
Heavens, the King!
DOÑA SOL. The King!
HERNANI. The King of Spain!
DON CARLOS [*gravely*]. Yes, Charles, my noble Duke, are thy wits gone?
The Emperor, my grandsire, is no more.
I knew it not until this eve, and came
At once to tell it you and counsel ask,
Incognito, at night, knowing you well
A loyal subject that I much regard.
The thing is very simple that has caused
This hubbub.
[*DON RUY GOMEZ sends away servants by a sign, and approaches DON CARLOS. DOÑA SOL looks at the King with fear and surprise. HERNANI from a corner regards him with flashing eyes.*]
DON RUY GOMEZ. But oh, why was it the door
Was not more quickly opened?
DON CARLOS. Reason good.
Remember all your escort. When it is
A weighty secret of the state I bear
That brings me to your palace, it is not
To tell it to thy servants.
DON RUY GOMEZ. Highness, oh!
Forgive me, some appearances—
DON CARLOS. Good father,
Thee Governor of the Castle of Figuère

I've made. But whom thy governor shall
I make?

DON RUY GOMEZ. Oh, pardon—

DON CARLOS. 'T is enough. We'll say
no more
Of this. The Emperor is dead.

DON RUY GOMEZ. Your Highness's
Grandfather dead!

DON CARLOS. Aye! Duke, you see me
here
In deep affliction.

DON RUY GOMEZ. Who'll succeed to
him?

DON CARLOS. A Duke of Saxony is
named. The throne
Francis the First of France aspires to
mount.

DON RUY GOMEZ. Where do the Elec-
tors of the Empire meet?

DON CARLOS. They say at Aix-la-Cha-
pelle, or at Spire,
Or Frankfort.

DON RUY GOMEZ. But our King, whom
God preserve!
Has he not thought of Empire?

DON CARLOS. Constantly.

DON RUY GOMEZ. To you it should re-
vert.

DON CARLOS. I know it, Duke.

DON RUY GOMEZ. Your father was
Archduke of Austria.
I hope 't will be remembered that you
are
Grandson to him, who but just now has
changed
Th' imperial purple for a winding-sheet.

DON CARLOS. I am, besides, a citizen
of Ghent.

DON RUY GOMEZ. In my own youth
your grandfather I saw.
Alas! I am the sole survivor now
Of all that generation past. All dead!
He was an Emperor magnificent
And mighty.

DON CARLOS. Rome is for me.

DON RUY GOMEZ. Valiant, firm,
And not tyrannical, this head might well
Become th' old German body.
[*He bends over the King's hands
and kisses them.*]
Yet so young.

I pity you, indeed, thus plunged in such
A sorrow.

DON CARLOS. Ah! the Pope is anxious
now
To get back Sicily—the isle that's mine;
'T is ruled that Sicily cannot belong
Unto an Emperor; therefore it is
That he desires me Emperor to be made;
And then, to follow that, as docile son
I give up Naples too. Let us but have
The Eagle, and we'll see if I allow
Its wings to be thus clipp'd!

DON RUY GOMEZ. What joy 't would
be
For this great veteran of the throne to
see
Your brow, so fit, encircled by his crown!
Ah, Highness, we together weep for him,
The Christian Emperor, so good, so great!

DON CARLOS. The Holy Father's clever.
He will say—
This isle unto my States should come;
't is but
A tatter'd rag that scarce belongs to
Spain.
What will you do with this ill-shapen
isle
That's sewn upon the Empire by a thread?
Your Empire is ill-made; but quick, come
here,
The scissors bring, and let us cut away!—
Thanks, Holy Father, but if I have luck
I think that many pieces such as this
Upon the Holy Empire will be sewn!
And if some rags from me are ta'en, I
mean
With isles and duchies to replace them
all.

DON RUY GOMEZ. Console yourself, for
we shall see again
The dead more holy and more great.
There is
An Empire of the Just.

DON CARLOS. Francis the First
Is all ambition. The old Emperor dead,
Quick he'll turn wooing. Has he not fair
France
Most Christian? 'T is a place worth hold-
ing fast.
Once to King Louis did my grandsire
say—

If I were God, and had two sons, I'd make
The elder God, the second, King of
France.
[*To* DON RUY GOMEZ.] Think you that
Francis has a chance to win?
DON RUY GOMEZ. He is a victor.
DON CARLOS. There'd be all to change—
The golden bull doth foreigners exclude.
DON RUY GOMEZ. In a like manner,
Highness, you would be
Accounted King of Spain.
DON CARLOS. But I was born
A citizen of Ghent.
DON RUY GOMEZ. His last campaign
Exalted Francis mightily.
DON CARLOS. The Eagle
That soon perchance upon my helm will
gleam
Knows also how to open out its wings.
DON RUY GOMEZ. And knows Your
Highness Latin?
DON CARLOS. Ah, not much.
DON RUY GOMEZ. A pity that. The
German nobles like
The best those who in Latin speak to
them.
DON CARLOS. With haughty Spanish
they will be content,
For trust King Charles, 't will be of
small account,
When masterful the voice, what tongue it
speaks.
To Flanders I must go. Your King, dear
Duke,
Must Emperor return. The King of
France
Will stir all means. I must be quick to
win.
I shall set out at once.
DON RUY GOMEZ. Do you, then, go,
Oh, Highness, without clearing Aragon
Of those fresh bandits who, among the
hills,
Their daring insolence show everywhere?
DON CARLOS. To the Duke D'Arcos I
have orders given
That he should quite exterminate the
band.
DON RUY GOMEZ. But is the order
given to its chief
To let the thing be done?

DON CARLOS. Who is this chief—
His name?
DON RUY GOMEZ. I know not. But
the people say
That he's an awkward customer.
DON CARLOS. Pshaw! I know
That now he somewhere in Galicia hides;
With a few soldiers, soon we'll capture
him.
DON RUY GOMEZ. Then it was false,
the rumor which declared
That he was hereabouts?
DON CARLOS. Quite false. Thou canst
Accommodate me here to-night?
DON RUY GOMEZ [*bowing to the
ground*]. Thanks! Thanks!
Highness! [*He calls his servants.*]
You'll do all honor to the King,
My guest.
      [*The servants reënter with lights.
      The Duke arranges them in
      two rows to the door at the
      back. Meanwhile* DOÑA SOL
      approaches HERNANI *softly.
      The King observes them.*]
DOÑA SOL [*to* HERNANI]. To-morrow,
midnight, without fail
Beneath my window clap your hands three
times.
HERNANI [*softly*]. To-morrow night.
DON CARLOS [*aside*]. To-morrow!
[*Aloud to* DOÑA SOL, *whom he approaches
with politeness.*] Let me now
Escort you hence, I pray. [*He leads her
to the door. She goes out.*]
HERNANI [*his hand in his breast on
dagger hilt*]. My dagger true!
DON CARLOS [*coming back, aside*]. Our
man here has the look of being
trapped. [*He takes* HERNANI *aside.*]
I've crossed my sword with yours; that
honor, sir,
I've granted you. For many reasons I
Suspect you much, but to betray you
now
Would shame the King; go therefore
freely. E'en
I deign to aid your flight.
DON RUY GOMEZ [*coming back, and
pointing to* HERNANI]. This lord—who's
he?

DON CARLOS. One of my followers, who'll soon depart.
[*They go out with servants and lights, the Duke preceding with waxlight in his hand.*]
HERNANI. One of thy followers! I am, O King!
Well said. For night and day and step by step
I follow thee, with eye upon thy path
And dagger in my hand. My race in me
Pursues thy race in thee. And now, behold
Thou art my rival! For an instant I
'Twixt love and hate was balanced in the scale.
Not large enough my heart for her and thee;
In loving her oblivious I became
Of all my hate of thee. But since 't is thou
That comes to will I should remember it,
I recollect. My love it is that tilts
Th' uncertain balance, while it falls entire
Upon the side of hate. Thy follower!
'Tis thou hast said it. Never courtier yet
Of thy accursed court, or noble, fain
To kiss thy shadow—not a seneschal
With human heart abjured in serving thee;
No dog within the palace, trained the King
To follow, will thy steps more closely haunt
And certainly than I. What they would have,
These famed grandees, is hollow title, or
Some toy that shines—some golden sheep to hang
About the neck. Not such a fool am I.
What I would have is not some favor vain,
But 't is thy blood, won by my conquering steel—
Thy soul from out thy body forced—with all
That at the bottom of thy heart was reached
After deep delving. Go—you are in front—

I follow thee. My watchful vengeance walks
With me, and whispers in mine ear. Go where
Thou wilt I'm there to listen and to spy,
And noiselessly my step will press on thine.
No day, should'st thou but turn thy head, O King,
But thou wilt find me, motionless and grave,
At festivals; at night, should'st thou look back,
Still wilt thou see my flaming eyes behind.   [*Exit by the little door.*]

ACT II

Saragossa. A square before the palace of SILVA. *On the left the high walls of the palace, with a window and a balcony. Below the window a little door. To the right, at the back, houses of the street. Night. Here and there are a few windows still lit up, shining in the front of the houses.*

[*Enter* DON CARLOS, DON SANCHO SANCHEZ DE ZUÑIGA, COUNT DE MONTEREY, DON MATIAS CENTURION, MARQUIS D'ALMUÑAN, DON RICARDO DE ROXAS, LORD OF CASAPALMA, DON CARLOS *at the head, hats pulled down, and wrapped in long cloaks, which their swords inside raise up.*]
DON CARLOS [*looking up at the balcony*]. Behold! 'We're at the balcony—the door.
My heart is bounding.
[*Pointing to the window, which is dark.*]
Ah, no light as yet. [*He looks at the windows where light shines.*]
Although it shines just where I'd have it not,
While where I wish for light is dark.
DON SANCHO. Your Highness,
Now let us of this traitor speak again.
And you permitted him to go!
DON CARLOS. 'T is true.

DON MATIAS. And he, perchance, was major of the band.

DON CARLOS. Were he the major or the captain e'en,
No crown'd king ever had a haughtier air.

DON SANCHO. Highness, his name?

DON CARLOS [*his eyes fixed on the window*]. Muñoz—Fernan—
[*With gesture of a man suddenly recollecting.*] A name
In *i*.

DON SANCHO. Perchance Hernani?

DON CARLOS. Yes.

DON SANCHO. 'T was he.

DON MATIAS. The chief, Hernani!

DON SANCHO. Cannot you recall
His speech?

DON CARLOS. Oh, I heard nothing in the vile
And wretched cupboard.

DON SANCHO. Wherefore let him slip
When there you had him?

DON CARLOS [*turning round gravely and looking him in the face*]. Count de Monterey,
You question me!
        [*The two nobles step back, and are silent.*]
Besides, it was not he
Was in my mind. It was his mistress, not
His head, I wanted. Madly I'm in love
With two dark eyes, the loveliest in the world,
My friends! Two mirrors, and two rays! two flames!
I heard but of their history these words:
"To-morrow come at midnight." 'T was enough.
The joke is excellent! For while that he,
The bandit lover, by some murd'rous deed
Some grave to dig, is hindered and delayed,
I softly take his dove from out its nest.

DON RICARDO. Highness, 't would make the thing far more complete
If we, the dove in gaining, killed the kite.

DON CARLOS. Count, 't is most capital advice. Your hand
Is prompt.

DON RICARDO [*bowing low*]. And by what title will it please
The King that I be count?

DON SANCHO. 'T was a mistake.

DON RICARDO [*to* DON SANCHO]. The King has called me count.

DON CARLOS. Enough—enough!
[*To* DON RICARDO.] I let the title fall;
but pick it up.

DON RICARDO [*bowing again*]. Thanks, Highness.

DON SANCHO. A fine count—count by mistake!
        [*The King walks to the back of the stage, watching eagerly the lighted windows. The two lords talk together at the front.*]

DON MATIAS [*to* DON SANCHO]. What think you that the King will do, when once
The beauty's taken?

DON SANCHO [*looking sideways at* DON RICARDO]. Countess she'll be made;
Lady of honor afterwards, and then,
If there's a son, he will be King.

DON MATIAS. How so?—
My lord! a bastard! Let him be a count.
Were one His Highness, would one choose as king
A countess' son?

DON SANCHO. He'd make her marchioness
Ere then, dear marquis.

DON MATIAS. Bastards—they are kept
For conquer'd countries. They for viceroys serve.
        [DON CARLOS *comes forward.*]

DON CARLOS [*looking with vexation at the lighted windows*]. Might one not say they're jealous eyes that watch?
Ah! there are two which darken; we shall do.
Weary the time of expectation seems—
Sirs, who can make it go more quickly?

DON SANCHO. That
Is what we often ask ourselves within
The palace.

DON CARLOS. 'T is the thing my people say
Again with you.
[*The last window light is extinguished.*]
The last light now is gone. [*Turning toward the balcony of* DOÑA SOL, *still dark.*]
Oh, hateful window! When wilt thou light up?
The night is dark; come, Doña Sol, and shine
Like to a star!
[*To* DON RICARDO.] Is't midnight yet?
DON RICARDO. Almost.
DON CARLOS. Ah! we must finish, for the other one
At any moment may appear.
[*A light appears in* DOÑA SOL'S *chamber. Her shadow is seen through the glass.*]
My friends!
A lamp! and she herself seen through the pane!
Never did daybreak charm me as this sight.
Let's hasten with the signal she expects.
We must clap hands three times. An instant more
And you will see her. But our number, perhaps,
Will frighten her. Go, all three out of sight
Beyond there, watching for the man we want.
'Twixt us, my friends, we'll share the loving pair,
For me the girl—the brigand is for you.
DON RICARDO. Best thanks.
DON CARLOS. If he appear from ambuscade,
Rush quickly, knock him down, and, while the dupe
Recovers from the blow, it is for me
To carry safely off the darling prize.
We'll laugh anon. But kill him not outright,
He's brave, I own;—killing's a grave affair.
[*The lords bow and go.* DON CARLOS *waits till they are*

quite gone, then claps his hands twice. At the second time the window opens, and DOÑA SOL appears on the balcony.]
DOÑA SOL [*from the balcony*]. Hernani, is that you?
DON CARLOS [*aside*]. The devil! We must
Not parley! [*He claps his hands again.*]
DOÑA SOL. I am coming down.
[*She closes the window, and the light disappears. The next minute the little door opens, and she comes out, the lamp in her hand, and a mantle over her shoulders.*]
DOÑA SOL. Hernani!
[DON CARLOS *pulls his hat down on his face, and hurries toward her.*]
DOÑA SOL [*letting her lamp fall*].
Heavens! 'T is not his footstep!
[*She attempts to go back, but DON CARLOS runs to her and seizes her by the arm.*]
DON CARLOS. Doña Sol!
DOÑA SOL. 'T is not his voice! Oh, misery!
DON CARLOS. What voice
Is there that thou could'st hear that would be more
A lover's? It is still a lover here,
And King for one.
DOÑA SOL. The King!
DON CARLOS. Ah! wish, command,
A kingdom waits thy will; for he whom thou
Hast vanquish'd is the King, thy lord—
't is Charles,
Thy slave!
DOÑA SOL [*trying to escape from him*].
To the rescue! Help, Hernani! Help!
DON CARLOS. Thy fear is maidenly, and worthy thee.
'T is not thy bandit—'t is thy King that holds
Thee now!
DOÑA SOL. Ah, no. The bandit's you. Are you

Not 'shamed? The blush unto my own
    cheek mounts
For you. Are these the exploits to be
    noised
Abroad? A woman thus at night to seize!
My bandit's worth a hundred of such
    kings!
I do declare, if man were born at level
Of his soul, and God made rank propor-
    tional
To his heart, he would be king and prince,
    and you
The robber be!
    Don Carlos [*trying to entice her*].
    Madam!—
    Doña Sol. Do you forget
My father was a count?
    Don Carlos. And you I'll make
A duchess.
    Doña Sol [*repulsing him*]. Cease! All
    this is shameful;—go! [*She retreats
                    a few steps.*]
Nothing, Don Carlos, can there 'twixt us
    be.
My father for you freely shed his blood.
I am of noble birth, and heedful ever
Of my name's purity. I am too high
To be your concubine—too low to be
Your wife.
    Don Carlos. Princess!
    Doña Sol. Carry to worthless girls,
King Charles, your vile addresses. Or, if
    me
You treat insultingly, I'll show you well
That I'm a woman, and a noble dame.
    Don Carlos. Well, then but come, and
    you shall share my throne,
My name—you shall be Queen and Em-
    press—
    Doña Sol. No.
It is a snare. Besides, I frankly speak,
Since, Highness, it concerns you. I avow
I'd rather with my king, Hernani, roam,
An outcast from the world and from the
    law—
Know thirst and hunger, wandering all
    the year,
Sharing the hardships of his destiny—
Exile and warfare, mourning hours of
    terror,
Than be an Empress with an Emperor!

    Don Carlos. Oh, happy man is he!
    Doña Sol. What! poor, proscribed!
    Don Carlos. 'T is well with him,
    though poor, proscribed he be,
For he's beloved!—an angel watches him!
I'm desolate. You hate me, then?
    Doña Sol. I love
You not.
    Don Carlos [*seizing her violently*].
    Well, then, it matters not to me
Whether you love me, or you love me not!
You shall come with me—yes, for that
    my hand's
The stronger, and I will it! And we'll
    see
If I 'for nothing am the King of Spain
And of the Indies!
    Doña Sol [*struggling*]. Highness!
    Pity me!
You're King, you only have to choose
    among
The countesses, the duchesses, the great
Court ladies, all have love prepared to
    meet
And answer yours; but what has my pro-
    scribed
Received from niggard fortune? You
    possess
Castile and Aragon—Murcia and Léon,
Navarre, and still ten kingdoms more,
    Flanders,
And India with the mines of gold you
    own,
An empire without peer, and all so
    vast
That ne'er the sun sets on it. And when
    you,
The King, have all, would you take me,
    poor girl,
From him who has but me alone.
        [*She throws herself on her knees.
            He tries to draw her up.*]
    Don Carlos. Come—come!
I cannot listen. Come with me. I'll give
Of Spain a fourth part unto thee. Say,
    now,
What wilt thou? Choose.
    Doña Sol [*struggling in his arms*].
    For mine own honor's sake
I'll only from Your Highness take this
    dirk.

[*She snatches the poniard from his girdle.*]
Approach me now but by a step!
DON CARLOS. The beauty!
I wonder not she loves a rebel now.
[*He makes a step towards her. She raises the dirk.*]
DOÑA SOL. Another step, I kill you—and myself.
[*He retreats again. She turns and cries loudly.*]
Hernani! Oh, Hernani!
DON CARLOS. Peace!
DOÑA SOL. One step,
And all is finished.
DON CARLOS. Madam, to extremes
I'm driven. Yonder there I have three men
To force you—followers of mine.
HERNANI [*coming suddenly behind him*].
But one
You have forgotten.
[*The King turns, and sees HER-NANI motionless behind him in the shade, his arms crossed under the long cloak which is wrapped round him, and the brim of his hat raised up. DOÑA SOL makes an exclamation and runs to him.*]
HERNANI [*motionless, his arms still crossed, and his fiery eyes fixed on the King*]. Heaven my witness is,
That far from here it was I wished to seek him.
DOÑA SOL. Hernani! Save me from him.
HERNANI. My dear love,
Fear not.
DON CARLOS. Now, what could all my friends in town
Be doing, thus to let pass by the chief
Of the Bohemians? Ho! Monterey!
HERNANI. Your friends are in the hands of mine just now,
So call not on their powerless swords; for three
That you might claim, sixty to me would come
Each one worth four of yours. So let us now

Our quarrel terminate. What! You have dared
To lay a hand upon this girl! It was
An act of folly, great Castilian King,
And one of cowardice!
DON CARLOS. Sir Bandit, hold!
There must be no reproach from you to me!
HERNANI. He jeers! Oh, I am not a king; but when
A king insults me, and above all jeers,
My anger swells and surges up, and lifts
Me to his height. Take care! When I'm offended,
Men fear far more the reddening of my brow
Than helm of king. Foolhardy, therefore, you
If still you're lured by hope. [*Seizes his arm.*] Know you what hand
Now grasps you? Listen. 'T was your father who
Was death of mine. I hate you for it. You
My title and my wealth have taken. You
I hate. And the same woman now we love.
I hate—hate—from my soul's depths you I hate.
DON CARLOS. That's well.
HERNANI. And yet this night my hate was lull'd.
Only one thought, one wish, one want I had—
'T was Doña Sol! And I, absorbed in love,
Came here to find you daring against her
To strive, with infamous design! You—you,
The man forgot—thus in my pathway placed!
I tell you, King, you are demented! Ah!
King Charles, now see you're taken in the snare
Laid by yourself: and neither flight nor help
For thee is possible. I hold thee fast,
Besieged, alone, surrounded by thy foes,
Bloodthirsty ones,—what wilt thou do?
DON CARLOS [*proudly*]. Dare you
To question me!

HERNANI. Pish! pish! I would not wish
An arm obscure should strike thee. 'T is not so
My vengeance should have play. 'T is I alone
Must deal with thee. Therefore defend thyself. [*He draws his sword.*]
DON CARLOS. I am your lord, the King. Strike! but no duel.
HERNANI. Highness, thou may'st remember yesterday
Thy sword encountered mine.
DON CARLOS. I yesterday
Could do it. I your name knew not, and you
Were ignorant of my rank. Not so to-day.
You know who I am, I who you are now.
HERNANI. Perchance.
DON CARLOS. No duel. You can murder. Do.
HERNANI. Think you that kings to me are sacred? Come,
Defend thyself.
DON CARLOS. You will assassinate Me, then?
[HERNANI *falls back. The King looks at him with eagle eyes.*]
Ah, bandits, so you dare to think
That your most vile brigades may safely spread
Through towns—ye blood-stained, murderous, miscreant crew—
But that you'll play at magnanimity!
As if we'd deign th' ennobling of your dirks
By touch of our own swords—we victims duped.
No, crime enthralls you—after you it trails.
Duels with you! Away! and murder me.
[HERNANI, *morose and thoughtful, plays for some instants with the hilt of his sword, then turns sharply toward the King and snaps the blade on the pavement.*]
HERNANI. Go, then.
[*The King half turns toward him and looks at him haughtily.*]
We shall have fitter meetings. Go.
Get thee away.
DON CARLOS. 'T is well. I go, sir, soon
Unto the ducal palace. I, your King,
Will then employ the magistrate. Is there
Yet put a price upon your head?
HERNANI. Oh, yes.
DON CARLOS. My master, from this day
I reckon you
A rebel, trait'rous subject; you I warn.
I will pursue you everywhere, and make
You outlaw from my kingdom.
HERNANI. That I am
Already.
DON CARLOS. That is well.
HERNANI. But France is near
To Spain. There's refuge there.
DON CARLOS. But I shall be
The Emperor of Germany, and you
Under the Empire's ban shall be.
HERNANI. Ah, well!
I still shall have the remnant of the world,
From which to brave you—and with havens safe
O'er which you'll have no power.
DON CARLOS. But when I've gain'd
The world?
HERNANI. Then I shall have the grave.
DON CARLOS. Your plots
So insolent I shall know how to thwart.
HERNANI. Vengeance is lame, and comes with lagging steps,
But still it comes.
DON CARLOS [*with a half laugh of disdain*]. For touch of lady whom
The bandit loves!
HERNANI [*with flashing eyes*]. Dost thou remember, King,
I hold thee still? Make me not recollect
O future Roman Cæsar, that despised
I have thee in my all too loyal hand,
And that I only need to close it now
To crush the egg of thy Imperial Eagle!
DON CARLOS. Then do it.
HERNANI. Get away.
[*He takes off his cloak, and throws it on the shoulders of the King.*]
Go, fly, and take

This cloak to shield thee from some knife
I fear
Among our ranks.
[*The King wraps himself in the cloak.*]
At present safely go,
My thwarted vengeance for myself I keep.
It makes 'gainst every other hand thy life
Secure.
DON CARLOS. And you who've spoken
thus to me
Ask not for mercy on some future day.
[*Exit* DON CARLOS.]
DOÑA SOL [*seizing* HERNANI'S *hand*].
Now, let us fly—be quick.
HERNANI. It well becomes
You, loved one, in the trial hour to prove
Thus strong, unchangeable, and willing
e'er
To th' end and depth of all to cling to me;
A noble wish, worthy a faithful soul!
But thou, O God, dost see that to accept
The joy that to my cavern she would
bring
The treasure of a beauty that a king
Now covets—and that Doña Sol to me
Should all belong—that she with me
should 'bide,
And all our lives be joined—that this
should be
Without regret, remorse—it is too late.
The scaffold is too near,
DOÑA SOL. What is 't you say?
HERNANI. This king, whom to his face
just now I braved,
Will punish me for having dared to show
Him mercy. He already, perhaps, has
reached
His palace, and is calling round his guards
And servants, his great lords, his heads-
men—
DOÑA SOL. Heavens!
Hernani! Oh, I shudder. Never mind,
Let us be quick and fly together, then.
HERNANI. Together! No; the hour
has passed for that.
Alas! When to my eyes thou didst reveal
Thyself, so good and generous, deigning
e'en
To love me with a helpful love, I could
But offer you—I, wretched one!—the
hills,

The woods, the torrents, bread of the pro-
scribed,
The bed of turf, all that the forest gives;
Thy pity then emboldened me—but now
To ask of thee to share the scaffold! No,
No, Doña Sol. That is for me alone.
DOÑA SOL. And yet you promised even
that!
HERNANI [*falling on his knees*]. Angel!
At this same moment, when perchance
from out
The shadow Death approaches, to wind
up
All mournfully a life of mournfulness,
I do declare that here a man proscribed,
Enduring trouble great, profound,—and
rock'd
In blood-stained cradle,—black as is the
gloom
Which spreads o'er all my life, I still de-
clare
I am a happy, to-be-envied man,
For you have loved me, and your love
have owned!
For you have whispered blessings on my
brow
Accursed!
DOÑA SOL [*leaning over his head*]. Her-
nani!
HERNANI. Praisèd be the fate
Sweet and propitious that for me now sets
This flower upon the precipice's brink!
[*Raising himself.*] 'T is not to you that I
am speaking thus;
It is to Heaven that hears, and unto God.
DOÑA SOL. Let me go with you.
HERNANI. Ah, t' would be a crime
To pluck the flower while falling in the
abyss.
Go: I have breathed the perfume—'t is
enough.
Remould your life, by me so sadly marred.
This old man wed; 't is I release you
now.
To darkness I return. Be happy thou—
Be happy and forget.
DOÑA SOL. No, I will have
My portion of thy shroud. I follow thee.
I hang upon thy steps.
HERNANI [*pressing her in his arms*].
Oh, let me go

Alone!   Exiled—proscribed—a   fearful
man
Am I.
> [*He quits her with a convulsive
> movement, and is going.*]

Doña Sol [*mournfully, and clasping
her hands*].   Hernani, do you fly from
me!

Hernani [*returning*].   Well, then, no,
no.   You will it, and I stay.
Behold me!   Come into my arms.   I'll
wait
As long as thou wilt have me.   Let us
rest,
Forgetting them.   [*He seats her on a
bench.*]
Be seated on this stone.
> [*He places himself at her feet.*]

The liquid light of your eyes inundates
Mine own.   Sing me some song, such as
sometimes
You used at eve to warble, with the tears
In those dark orbs.   Let us be happy
now,
And drink; the cup is full.   This hour is
ours,
The rest is only folly.   Speak and say,
Enrapture me.   Is it not sweet to love,
And know that he who kneels before you
loves?
To be but two alone?   Is it not sweet
To speak of love in stillness of the night
When Nature rests?   Oh, let me slumber
now,
And on thy bosom dream.   Oh, Doña
Sol,
My love, my darling!
> [*Noise of bells in the distance.*]

Doña Sol [*starting up frightened*].
Tocsin?—dost thou hear?
The tocsin!

Hernani [*still kneeling at her feet*].
Eh!   No, 't is our bridal bell
They're ringing.
> [*The noise increases.   Confused
> cries.   Lights at all the win-
> dows, on the roofs, and in the
> streets.*]

Doña Sol.   Rise—oh, fly,—great God!
the town
Lights up!

Hernani [*half rising*].   A torchlight
wedding for us 't is!

Doña Sol.   The nuptials these of
Death, and of the tombs!
> [*Noise of swords and cries.*]

Hernani [*lying down on the stone
bench*].   Let us to sleep again.

A Mountaineer [*rushing in, sword in
hand*].   The runners, sir.
The alcaldes rush out in cavalcades
With mighty force.   Be quick—my Cap-
tain,—quick.   [*Hernani rises.*]

Doña Sol [*pale*].   Ah, thou wert right!

The Mountaineer.   Oh, help us!

Hernani [*to Mountaineer*].   It is
well—
I'm ready.
[*Confused cries outside.*]   Death to the
bandit!

Hernani [*to Mountaineer*].   Quick,
thy sword—
[*To Doña Sol*].   Farewell!

Doña Sol.   'T is I have been thy ruin!
Oh,
Where canst thou go?
[*Pointing to the little door.*]   The door is
free.   Let us
Escape that way.

Hernani.   Heavens!   Desert my friends!
What dost thou say?

Doña Sol.   These clamors terrify.
Remember, if thou diest I must die.

Hernani [*holding her in his arms*].   A
kiss!

Doña Sol.   Hernani!   Husband!   Mas-
ter mine!

Hernani [*kissing her forehead*].   Alas!
it is the first!

Doña Sol.   Perchance the last!
> [*Exit Hernani.   She falls on the
> bench.*]

ACT III

*The Castle of Silva in the midst of the
mountains of Aragon.   The gallery of
family portraits of Silva; a great hall of
which these portraits—surrounded with
rich frames, and surmounted by ducal
coronets and gilt escutcheons—form the*

decoration. At the back a lofty Gothic door. Between the portraits complete panoplies of armour of different centuries. DOÑA SOL, *pale, and standing near a table.* DON RUY GOMEZ DE SILVA, *seated in his great carved oak chair.*

DON RUY GOMEZ. At last the day has come!—and in an hour
Thou'lt be my duchess, and embrace me! Not
Thine uncle then! But hast thou pardoned me?
That I was wrong I own. I raised thy blush,
I made thy cheek turn pale. I was too quick
With my suspicions—should have stayed to hear
Before condemning; but appearances
Should take the blame. Unjust we were. Certes
The two young handsome men were there. But then—
No matter—well I know that I should not
Have credited my eyes. But, my poor child,
What would'st thou with the old?
DOÑA SOL [*seriously, and without moving*]. You ever talk
Of this. Who is there blames you?
DON RUY GOMEZ. I myself.
I should have known that such a soul as yours
Never has gallants; when 't is Doña Sol,
And when good Spanish blood is in her veins.
DOÑA SOL. Truly, my Lord, 't is good and pure; perchance
'T will soon be seen.
DON RUY GOMEZ [*rising, and going toward her*]. Now list. One cannot be
The master of himself, so much in love
As I am now with thee. And I am old
And jealous, and am cross—and why? Because
I'm old; because the beauty, grace, or youth

Of others frightens, threatens me. Because,
While jealous thus of others, of myself
I am ashamed. What mockery! that this love
Which to the heart brings back such joy and warmth,
Should halt, and but rejuvenate the soul,
Forgetful of the body. When I see
A youthful peasant, singing blithe and gay,
In the green meadows, often then I muse—
I, in my dismal paths, and murmur low:
Oh, I would give my battlemented towers,
And ancient ducal donjon, and my fields
Of corn, and all my forest lands, and flocks
So vast which feed upon my hills, my name
And all my ancient titles—ruins mine,
And ancestors who must expect me soon,
All—all I'd give for his new cot, and brow
Unwrinkled. For his hair is raven black,
And his eyes shine like yours. Beholding him
You might exclaim: A young man this! And then
Would think of me so old. I know it well.
I am named Silva. Ah, but that is not
Enough; I say it, see it. Now behold
To what excess I love thee. All I'd give
Could I be like thee—young and handsome now!
Vain dream! that I were young again, who must
By long, long years precede thee to the tomb.
DOÑA SOL. Who knows?
DON RUY GOMEZ. And yet, I pray you, me believe,
The frivolous swains have not so much of love
Within their hearts as on their tongues. A girl
May love and trust one; if she dies for him,
He laughs. The strong-winged and gay-painted birds
That warble sweet, and in the thicket trill,

Will change their loves as they their
plumage moult.
They are the old, with voice and color
gone,
And beauty fled, who have the resting
wings
We love the best.   Our steps are slow,
and dim
Our eyes.   Our brows are furrowed,—but
the heart
Is never wrinkled.   When an old man
loves
He should be spared.   The heart is ever
young,
And always it can bleed.   This love of
mine
Is not a plaything made of glass to shake
And break.   It is a love severe and sure,
Solid, profound, paternal,—strong as is
The oak which forms my ducal chair.   See,
then,
How well I love thee—and in other ways
I love thee—hundred other ways, e'en as
We love the dawn, and flowers, and
heaven's blue!
To see thee, mark thy graceful step each
day,
Thy forehead pure, thy brightly beaming
eye,
I'm joyous—feeling that my soul will
have
Perpetual festival!
DoÑA Sol.   Alas!
DON RUY GOMEZ.   And then,
Know you how much the world admires,
applauds,
A woman, angel pure, and like a love,
When she an old man comforts and con-
soles
As he is tott'ring to the marble tomb,
Passing away by slow degrees as she
Watches and shelters him, and conde-
scends
To bear with him, the useless one, that
seems
But fit to die?   It is a sacred work
And worthy of all praise—effort supreme
Of a devoted heart to comfort him
Unto the end, and without loving, per-
haps,
To act as if she loved.   Ah, thou to me

Wilt be this angel with a woman's heart
Who will rejoice the old man's soul again
And share his latter years, and by respect
A daughter be, and by your pity like
A sister prove.
DoÑA Sol.   Far from preceding me,
'T is likely me you'll follow to the grave.
My lord, because that we are young is not
A reason we should live.   Alas! I know
And tell you, often old men tarry long,
And see the young go first, their eyes shut
fast
By sudden stroke, as on a sepulcher
That still was open falls the closing stone.
DON RUY GOMEZ.   Oh, cease, my child,
such saddening discourse,
Or I shall scold you.   Such a day as this
Sacred and joyous is.   And, by-the-bye,
Time summons us.   Are you not ready
yet
For chapel when we're called?   Be quick
to don
The bridal dress.   Each moment do I
count.
DoÑA Sol.   There is abundant time.
DON RUY GOMEZ.   Oh, no, there's not.

[*Enter a* PAGE.]
What want you?
THE PAGE.   At the door, my lord, a
man—
A pilgrim—beggar—or I know not what,
Is craving here a shelter.
DON RUY GOMEZ.   Let him in
Whoever he may be.   Good enters with
The stranger that we welcome.   What's
the news
From th' outside world?   What of the
bandit chief
That filled our forests with his rebel
band?
THE PAGE.   Hernani, Lion of the moun-
tains, now
Is done for.
DoÑA Sol [*aside*].   God!
DON RUY GOMEZ [*to the* PAGE].   How
so?
THE PAGE.   The troops destroyed.
The King himself has led the soldiers on.
Hernani's head a thousand crowns is
worth

Upon the spot; but now he's dead, they
say.
DOÑA SOL [*aside*]. What! Without
me, Hernani!
DON RUY GOMEZ. And thank Heaven!
So he is dead, the rebel! Now, dear love,
We can rejoice; go then and deck thyself,
My pride, my darling. Day of double joy.
DOÑA SOL. Oh, mourning robes! [*Exit.*]
DON RUY GOMEZ [*to the* PAGE]. The
casket quickly send
That I'm to give her. [*He seats himself
in his chair.*]
'T is my longing now
To see her all adorned Madonna like.
With her bright eyes, and aid of my rich
gems,
She will be beautiful enough to make
A pilgrim kneel before her. As for him
Who asks asylum, bid him enter here,
Excuses from us offer; run, be quick.
[*The* PAGE *bows and exit.*]
'T is ill to keep a guest long waiting thus.
[*The door at the back opens.*]

[HERNANI *appears disguised as a Pilgrim.
The Duke rises.* HERNANI *pauses at the
threshold of the door.*]
HERNANI. My lord, peace and all hap-
piness be yours!
DON RUY GOMEZ [*saluting up with his
hand*]. To thee be peace and happi-
ness, my guest!

[HERNANI *enters. The Duke reseats him-
self.*]
Art thou a pilgrim?
HERNANI [*bowing*]. Yes.
DON RUY GOMEZ. No doubt you come
From Armillas?
HERNANI. Not so. I hither came
By other road, there was some fighting
there.
DON RUY GOMEZ. Among the troop of
bandits, was it not?
HERNANI. I know not.
DON RUY GOMEZ. What's become of
him—the chief
They call Hernani? Dost thou know?
HERNANI. My lord,
Who is this man?

DON RUY GOMEZ. Dost thou not know
him, then?
For thee so much the worse! Thou wilt
not gain
The good round sum. See you a rebel he
That has been long unpunished. To Ma-
drid
Should you be going, perhaps you'll see
him hanged.
HERNANI. I go not there.
DON RUY GOMEZ. A price is on his head
For any man who takes him.
HERNANI [*aside*]. Let one come!
DON RUY GOMEZ. Whither, good pil-
grim, goest thou?
HERNANI. My lord.
I'm bound for Saragossa.
DON RUY GOMEZ. A vow made
In honor of a saint, or of Our Lady?
HERNANI. Yes, of Our Lady, Duke.
DON RUY GOMEZ. Of the Pillar?
HERNANI. Of the Pillar.
DON RUY GOMEZ. We must be soulless
quite
Not to acquit us of the vows we make
Unto the saints. But thine accomplished,
then
Hast thou not other purposes in view?
Or is to see the Pillar all you wish?
HERNANI. Yes. I would see the lights
and candles burn,
And at the end of the dim corridor
Our Lady in her glowing shrine, with cope
All golden—then would satisfied return.
DON RUY GOMEZ. Indeed, that's well.
Brother, what is thy name?
Mine, Ruy de Silva is.
HERNANI [*hesitating*]. My name—
DON RUY GOMEZ. You can
Conceal it if you will. None here has
right
To know it. Cam'st thou to asylum ask?
HERNANI. Yes, Duke.
DON RUY GOMEZ. Remain, and know
thou'rt welcome here.
For nothing want; and as for what
thou'rt named,
But call thyself my guest. It is enough
Whoever thou may'st be. Without demur
I'd take in Satan if God sent him me.
[*The folding doors at the back open.*]

[*Enter* DOÑA SOL *in nuptial attire. Behind her* PAGES *and* LACKEYS, *and two women carrying on a velvet cushion a casket of engraved silver, which they place upon a table, and which contains a jewel case, with duchess' coronet, necklaces, bracelets, pearls, and diamonds in profusion.* HERNANI, *breathless and scared, looks at* DOÑA SOL *with flaming eyes without listening to the Duke.*]

DON RUY GOMEZ [*continuing*]. Behold my blessed Lady—to have prayed
To her will bring thee happiness.

[*He offers his hand to* DOÑA SOL, *still pale and grave.*]

Come, then,
My bride. What! not thy coronet, nor ring!

HERNANI [*in a voice of thunder*]. Who wishes now a thousand golden crowns
To win?

[*All turn to him astonished. He tears off his pilgrim's robe, and crushes it under his feet, revealing himself in the dress of a mountaineer.*]

I am Hernani.

DOÑA SOL [*joyfully*]. Heavens! Oh, He lives!

HERNANI [*to the* LACKEYS]. See! I'm the man they seek.
[*To the Duke.*] You wished
To know my name—Diego or Perez?
No, no! I have a grander name—Hernani.
Name of the banished, the proscribed. See you
This head? 'T is worth enough of gold to pay
For festival.
[*To the* LACKEYS.] I give it to you all.
Take; tie my hands, my feet. But there's no need,
The chain that binds me's one I shall not break

DOÑA SOL [*aside*]. Oh, misery!

DON RUY GOMEZ. Folly! This my guest is mad—
A lunatic!

HERNANI. Your guest a bandit is.

DOÑA SOL. Oh, do not heed him.

HERNANI. What I say is truth.

DON RUY GOMEZ. A thousand golden crowns—the sum is large.
And, sir, I will not answer now for all My people.

HERNANI. And so much the better, should
A willing one be found.
[*To the* LACKEYS.] Now seize, and sell me!

DON RUY GOMEZ [*trying to silence him*]. Be quiet, or they'll take you at your word.

HERNANI. Friends, this your opportunity is good.
I tell you, I'm the rebel—the proscribed Hernani!

DON RUY GOMEZ. Silence!

HERNANI. I am he!

DOÑA SOL [*in a low voice to him*]. Be still!

HERNANI [*half turning to* DOÑA SOL]. There's marrying here! My spouse awaits me too.
[*To the Duke.*] She is less beautiful, my lord, than yours,
But not less faithful. She is Death.
[*To the* LACKEYS.] Not one
Of you has yet come forth!

DOÑA SOL [*in a low voice*]. For pity's sake!

HERNANI [*to the* LACKEYS]. A thousand golden crowns. Hernani here!

DON RUY GOMEZ. This is the demon!

HERNANI [*to a young* LACKEY]. Come! thou'lt earn this sum,
Then rich, thou wilt from lackey change again
To man.
[*To the other* LACKEYS, *who do not stir.*] And also you—you waver. Ah,
Have I not misery enough?

DON RUY GOMEZ. My friend,
To touch thy life they'd peril each his own.
Wert thou Hernani, or a hundred times
As bad, I must protect my guest,—were e'en
An Empire offered for his life—against
The King himself; for thee I hold from God.

If hair of thine be injured, may I die.
[*To* DoÑA SoL.]
My niece, who in an hour will be my wife,
Go to your room. I am about to arm
The Castle—shut the gates.
[*Exit, followed by servants.*]
HERNANI [*looking with despair at his empty girdle*]. Not e'en a knife!
[DoÑA SoL, *after the departure of the Duke, takes a few steps, as if to follow her women, then pauses, and when they are gone, comes back to* HERNANI *with anxiety.* HERNANI *looks at the nuptial jewel-case with a cold and apparently indifferent gaze; then he tosses back his head, and his eyes light up.*]
Accept my 'gratulations! Words tell not
How I'm enchanted by these ornaments.
[*He approaches the casket.*]
This ring is in fine taste,—the coronet
I like,—the necklace shows surpassing skill.
The bracelet's rare—but oh, a hundred times
Less so than she, who 'neath a forehead pure
Conceals a faithless heart.
[*Examining the casket again.*]
What for all this
Have you now given? Of your love some share?
But that for nothing goes! Great God! to thus
Deceive, and still to live and have no shame!
[*Looking at the jewels.*]
But after all, perchance, this pearl is false,
And copper stands for gold, and glass and lead
Make out sham diamonds—pretended gems!
Are these false sapphires and false jewels all?
If so, thy heart is like them, Duchess false,

Thyself but only gilded. [*He returns to the casket.*] Yet no, no!
They are all real, beautiful, and good,
He dares not cheat, who stands so near the tomb.
Nothing is wanting. [*He takes up one thing after another.*]
Necklaces are here,
And brilliant earrings, and the Duchess' crown
And golden ring. Oh, marvel! Many thanks
For love so certain, faithful and profound.
The precious box!
DoÑA SoL [*going to the casket, feeling in it, and drawing forth a dagger.*]
You have not reached its depths.
This is the dagger which, by kindly aid
Of patron saint, I snatched from Charles the King
When he made offer to me of a throne,
Which I refused for you, who now insult me.
HERNANI [*falling at her feet*]. Oh, let me on my knees arrest those tears,
The tears that beautify thy sorrowing eyes.
Then after thou canst freely take my life.
DoÑA SoL. I pardon you, Hernani. In my heart
There is but love for you.
HERNANI. And she forgives—
And loves me still! But who can also teach
Me to forgive myself, that I have used
Such words? Angel, for heaven reserved, say where
You trod, that I may kiss the ground.
DoÑA SoL. My love!
HERNANI. Oh, no, I should to thee be odious.
But listen. Say again—I love thee still!
Say it, and reassure a heart that doubts.
Say it, for often with such little words
A woman's tongue hath cured a world of woes.
DoÑA SoL [*absorbed, and without hearing him*]. To think my love had such short memory!
That all these so ignoble men could shrink

A heart, where his name was enthroned,
to love
By them thought worthier.
HERNANI. Alas! I have
Blasphemed! If I were in thy place I
should
Be weary of the furious madman, who
Can only pity after he has struck.
I'd bid him go. Drive me away, I say,
And I will bless thee, for thou hast been
good
And sweet. Too long thou hast myself
endured,
For I am evil; I should blacken still
Thy days with my dark nights. At last
it is
Too much; thy soul is lofty, beautiful,
And pure; if I am evil, is't thy fault?
Marry the old Duke, then, for he is good
And noble. By the mother's side he has
Olmédo, by his father's Alcala.
With him be rich and happy by one act.
Know you not what this generous hand of
mine
Can offer thee of splendor? Ah, alone
A dowry of misfortune, and the choice
Of blood or tears. Exile, captivity
And death, and terrors that environ me.
These are thy necklaces and jeweled
crown.
Never elated bridegroom to his bride
Offered a casket filled more lavishly,
But 't is with misery and mournfulness.
Marry the old man—he deserves thee
well!
Ah, who could ever think my head pro-
scribed
Fit mate for forehead pure? What looker-
on
That saw thee calm and beautiful, me
rash
And violent—thee peaceful, like a flower
Growing in shelter, me by tempests dash'd
On rocks unnumber'd—who could dare
to say
That the same law should guide our des-
tinies?
No, God, who ruleth all things well, did
not
Make thee for me. No right from Heav'n
above

Have I to thee; and I'm resigned to fate.
I have thy heart; it is a theft! I now
Unto a worthier yield it. Never yet
Upon our love has Heaven smiled; 't is
false
If I have said thy destiny it was.
To vengeance and to love I bid adieu!
My life is ending; useless I will go,
And take away with me my double dream,
Ashamed I could not punish, nor could
charm.
I have been made for hate, who only
wished
To love. Forgive and fly me, these my
prayers
Reject them not, since they will be my
last.
Thou livest—I am dead. I see not why
Thou should'st immure thee in my tomb.
DOÑA SOL. Ingrate!
HERNANI. Mountains of old Aragon!
Galicia!
Estremadura! Unto all who come
Around me I bring misery!
The best, without remorse I've ta'en to
fight,
And now behold them dead! The bravest
brave
Of all Spain's sons, lie, soldier-like, upon
The hills, their backs to earth, the living
God
Before; and if their eyes could ope they'd
look
On heaven's blue. See what I do to all
Who join me! Is it fortune any one
Should covet? Doña Sol, oh! take the
Duke,
Take hell, or take the King—all would be
well,
All must be better than myself, I say.
No longer have I friend to think of me.
And it is fully time that thy turn comes,
For I must be alone. Fly from me, then,
From my contagion. Make not faithful
love
A duty of religion! Fly from me,
For pity's sake. Thou think'st me, per-
haps, a man
Like others, one with sense, who knows
the end
At which he aims, and acts accordingly.

Oh, undeceive thyself. I am a force
That cannot be resisted—agent blind
And deaf of mournful mysteries! A soul
Of misery made of gloom. Where shall I
go?
I cannot tell. But I am urged, compelled
By an impetuous breath and wild decree;
I fall, and fall, and fall, and cannot stop descent.
If sometimes breathless I dare turn my
head,
A voice cries out, "Go on!" and the abyss
Is deep, and to the depths I see it red
With flame or blood! Around my fearful
course
All things break up—all die. Woe be to
them
Who touch me. Fly, I say! Turn thee
away
From my so fatal path. Alas! without
Intending I should do thee ill.
DOÑA SOL. Great God!
HERNANI. My demon is a formidable
one.
But there's a thing impossible to it—
My happiness. For thee is happiness.
Therefore, go seek another lord, for thou
Art not for me. If Heaven, that my
fate
Abjures, should smile on me, believe it
not:
It would be irony. Marry the Duke!
DOÑA SOL. 'T was not enough to tear
my heart, but you
Must break it now! Ah me! no longer,
then
You love me!
HERNANI. Oh! my heart—its very life
Thou art! The glowing hearth whence all
warmth comes
Art thou! Wilt thou, then, blame me
that I fly
From thee, adored one?
DOÑA SOL. No, I blame thee not,
Only I know that I shall die of it.
HERNANI. Die! And for what? For
me? Can it then be
That thou should'st die for cause so
small?
DOÑA SOL [bursting into tears]. Enough.
        [She falls into a chair.]
HERNANI [seating himself near her].

And thou art weeping; and 't is still
my fault!
And who will punish me? for thou I know
Wilt pardon still! Who, who can tell thee
half
The anguish that I suffer when a tear
Of thine obscures and drowns those radi-
ant eyes
Whose luster is my joy. My friends are
dead!
Oh, I am crazed—forgive me—I would
love
I know not how. Alas! I love with love
Profound. Weep not—the rather let us
die!
Oh that I had a world to give to thee!
Oh, wretched, miserable man I am!
DOÑA SOL [throwing herself on his
neck]. You are my lion, generous and
superb!
I love you.
HERNANI. Ah, this love would be a good
Supreme, if we could die of too much love!
DOÑA SOL. Thou art my lord! I love
thee and belong
To thee!
HERNANI [letting his head fall on her
shoulder]. How sweet would be a
poniard stroke
From thee!
DOÑA SOL [entreatingly]. Fear you not
God will punish you
For words like these?
HERNANI [still leaning on her shoul-
der]. Well, then, let Him unite us!
I have resisted; thou would'st have it
thus.
        [While they are in each other's
        arms, absorbed and gazing with
        ecstasy at each other, DON RUY
        GOMEZ enters by the door at
        the back of the stage. He sees
        them, and stops on the thresh-
        old as if petrified.]
DON RUY GOMEZ [motionless on the
threshold, with arms crossed]. And
this is the requital that I find
Of hospitality!
DOÑA SOL. Oh, Heavens—the Duke!
        [Both turn as if awakening with
        a start.]

DON RUY GOMEZ [*still motionless*].
This then's the recompense from thee,
my guest?
Good Duke, go see if all thy walls be high,
And if the door is closed, and archer
placed
Within his tower, and go the castle round
Thyself for us; seek in thine arsenal
For armor that will fit—at sixty years
Resume thy battle-harness—and then see
The loyalty with which we will repay
Such service! Thou for us do thus, and we
Do this for thee! Oh, blessed saints of
Heaven!
Past sixty years I've lived, and met some-
times
Unbridled souls; and oft my dirk have
drawn
From out its scabbard, raising on my path
The hangman's game birds: murd'rers I
have seen
And coiners, traitorous varlets poisoning
Their masters; and I've seen men die
without
A prayer, or sight of crucifix. I've seen
Sforza and Borgia; Luther still I see,
But never have I known perversity
So great that feared not thunderbolt, its
host
Betraying! 'T was not of my age—such
foul
Black treason, that at once could petrify
An old man on the threshold of his door,
And make the master, waiting for his
grave,
Look like his statue ready for his tomb.
Moors and Castilians! Tell me, who's this
man? [*He raises his eyes and looks
round on the portraits on the wall.*]
Oh, you, the Silvas who can hear me
now,
Forgive if, in your presence by my wrath
Thus stirr'd, I say that hospitality
Was ill advised.
HERNANI [*rising*]. Duke—
DON RUY GOMEZ. Silence!
[*He makes three steps into the
hall looking at the portraits of
the* SILVAS.]
Sacred dead!
My ancestors! Ye men of steel, who know

What springs from heav'n or hell, reveal,
I say,
Who is this man? No, not Hernani he,
But Judas is his name—oh, try to speak
And tell me who he is!
[*Crossing his arms.*] In all your days
Saw you aught like him? No.
HERNANI. My lord—
DON RUY GOMEZ [*still addressing the
portraits*]. See you
The shameless miscreant? He would speak
to me,
But better far than I you read his soul.
Oh, heed him not! he is a knave—he'd
say
That he foresaw that in the tempest wild
Of my great wrath I brooded o'er some
deed
Of gory vengeance shameful to my roof.
A sister deed to that they call the feast
Of Seven Heads. He'll tell you he's pro-
scribed,
He'll tell you that of Silva they will talk
E'en as of Lara. Afterwards he'll say
He is my guest and yours. My lords, my
sires,
Is the fault mine? Judge you between
us now.
HERNANI. Ruy Gomez de Silva, if ever
'neath
The heavens clear a noble brow was raised,
If ever heart was great and soul was high,
Yours are, my lord; and oh, my noble
host,
I, who now speak to you, alone have
sinn'd.
Guilty most damnably am I, without
Extenuating word to say. I would
Have carried off thy bride—dishonor'd
thee.
'T was infamous. I live; but now my life
I offer unto thee. Take it. Thy sword
Then wipe, and think no more about the
deed.
DOÑA SOL. My lord, 't was not his
fault—strike only me.
HERNANI. Be silent, Doña Sol. This
hour supreme
Belongs alone to me; nothing I have
But it. Let me explain things to the
Duke.

Oh, Duke, believe the last words from my
mouth,
I swear that I alone am guilty. But
Be calm and rest assured that she is pure,
That's all. I guilty and she pure. Have
faith
In her. A sword or dagger thrust for me.
Then throw my body out of doors, and
have
The flooring washed, if you should will
it so.
What matter?
DOÑA SOL. Ah! I only am the cause
Of all; because I love him.
[DON RUY *turns round trembling
at these words, and fixes on*
DOÑA SOL *a terrible look. She
throws herself at his feet.*]
Pardon! Yes.
My lord, I love him!
DON RUY GOMEZ. Love him—you love
him.
[*To* HERNANI.] Tremble! [*Noise of trum-
pet outside.*]
[*Enter a* PAGE.]
What is this noise?
THE PAGE. It is the King,
My lord, in person, with a band complete
Of archers, and his herald, who now
sounds.
DOÑA SOL. Oh, God! This last fatality
—the King!
THE PAGE [*to the Duke*]. He asks the
reason why the door is closed,
And order gives to open it.
DON RUY GOMEZ. Admit.
The King. [*The* PAGE *bows and exit.*]
DOÑA SOL. He's lost!
[DON RUY GOMEZ *goes to one of
the portraits—that of himself
and the last on the left; he
presses a spring, and the por-
trait opens out like a door, and
reveals a hiding-place in the
wall. He turns to* HERNANI.]
DON RUY GOMEZ. Come hither, sir.
HERNANI. My life
To thee is forfeit; and to yield it up
I'm ready. I thy prisoner am.
[*He enters the recess.* DON RUY
again presses the spring, and

*the portrait springs back to its
place looking as before.*]
DOÑA SOL. My lord,
Have pity on him!
THE PAGE [*entering*]. His Highness the
King! [DOÑA SOL *hurriedly lowers
her veil. The folding-doors open.*]

[*Enter* DON CARLOS *in military attire, fol-
lowed by a crowd of gentlemen equally
armed with halberds, arquebuses, and
cross-bows.* DON CARLOS *advances slowly,
his left hand on the hilt of his sword, his
right hand in his bosom, and looking at
the Duke with anger and defiance. The
Duke goes before the King and bows low.
Silence. Expectation and terror on all.
At last the King, coming opposite the
Duke, throws back his head haughtily.*]
DON CARLOS. How comes it, then, my
cousin, that to-day
Thy door is strongly barr'd? By all the
saints
I thought your dagger had more rusty
grown,
And know not why, when I'm your visitor,
It should so haste to brightly shine again
All ready to your hand.
[DON RUY GOMEZ *attempts to
speak, but the King continues
with an imperious gesture.*]
Late in the day
It is for you to play the young man's
part!
Do we come turban'd? Tell me, are we
named
Boabdil or Mahomet, and not Charles,
That the portcullis 'gainst us you should
lower
And raise the drawbridge?
DON RUY GOMEZ [*bowing*]. Highness—
DON CARLOS [*to his gentlemen*]. Take
the keys
And guard the doors.
[*Two officers exeunt. Several
others arrange the soldiers in a
triple line in the hall from the
King to the principal door.*
DON CARLOS *turns again to the
Duke.*]
Ah! you would wake to life

Again these crushed rebellions. By my faith,
If you, ye dukes, assume such airs as these
The King himself will play his kingly part,
Traverse the mountains in a warlike mode,
And in their battlemented nests will slay
The lordlings!
　DON RUY GOMEZ [*drawing himself up*].
Ever have the Silvas been,
Your Highness, loyal.
　DON CARLOS [*interrupting him*]. Without subterfuge
Reply, or to the ground I'll raze thy towers
Eleven! Of extinguished fire remains
One spark—of brigands dead the chief survives,
And who conceals him? It is thou, I say!
Hernani, rebel ringleader, is here,
And in thy castle thou dost hide him now.
　DON RUY GOMEZ. Highness, it is quite true.
　DON CARLOS. Well, then, his head
I want—or if not, thine. Dost understand,
My cousin?
　DON RUY GOMEZ. Well, then, be it so.
You shall
Be satisfied.
　　　[DOÑA SOL *hides her face in her hands and sinks into the armchair.*]
　DON CARLOS [*a little softened*]. Ah! you repent. Go seek
Your prisoner.
　　　[*The Duke crosses his arms, lowers his head, and remains some moments pondering. The King and* DOÑA SOL, *agitated by contrary emotions, observe him in silence. At last the Duke looks up, goes to the King, takes his hand, and leads him with slow steps toward the oldest of the portraits, which is where the gallery commences to the right of the spectator.*]

　DON RUY GOMEZ [*pointing out the old portrait to the King*]. This is the eldest one,
The great forefather of the Silva race,
Don Silvius our ancestor, three times
Was he made Roman consul.
[*Passing to the next portrait.*] This is he—
Don Galceran de Silva—other Cid!
They keep his body still at Toro, near
Valladolid; a thousand candles burn
Before his gilded shrine. 'T was he who freed
Leon from tribute o' the hundred virgins.
[*Passing to another.*] Don Blas—who, in contrition for the fault
Of having ill-advised the king, exiled
Himself of his own will.
[*To another.*] This Christoval!
At fight of Escalon, when fled on foot
The King Don Sancho, whose white plume was mark
For general deadly aim, he cried aloud,
Oh, Christoval! And Christoval assumed
The plume, and gave his horse.
[*To another.*] This is Don Jorge,
Who paid the ransom of Ramire, the King
Of Aragon.
　DON CARLOS [*crossing his arms and looking at him from head to foot*].
By Heavens, now, Don Ruy,
I marvel at you! But go on.
　DON RUY GOMEZ. Next comes
Don Ruy Gomez Silva; he was made
Grand Master of St. James, and Calatrava.
His giant armor would not suit our heights.
He took three hundred flags from foes, and won
In thirty battles. For the King Motril
He conquer'd Antequera, Suez,
Nijar; and died in poverty. Highness,
Salute him.
　　　[*He bows, uncovers, and passes to another portrait. The King listens impatiently, and with increasing anger.*]
Next him is his son, named Gil,
Dear to all noble souls. His promise worth

The oath of royal hands.
[*To another.*] Don Gaspard this,
The pride alike of Mendocé and Silva.
Your Highness, every noble family
Has some alliance with the Silva race.
Sandoval has both trembled at, and wed
With us. Manrique is envious of us: Lara
Is jealous. Alencastre hates us. We
All dukes surpass, and mount to kings.
DON CARLOS.   Tut! tut!
You're jesting.
     DON RUY GOMEZ.   Here behold Don
     Vasquez, called
The Wise. Don Jayme surnamed the
     Strong. One day
Alone he stopped Zamet and five score
     Moors.
I pass them by, and some the greatest.
          [*At an angry gesture of the
          King, he passes by a great
          number of portraits, and
          speedily comes to the three
          last at the left of the audi-
          ence.*]
This,
My grandfather, who lived to sixty years,
Keeping his promised word even to Jews.
[*To the last portrait but one.*] This ven-
     erable form my father is,
A sacred head. Great was he, though he
     comes
The last. The Moors had taken prisoner
His friend Count Alvar Giron. But my
     sire
Set out to seek him with six hundred men
To war inured. A figure of the count
Cut out of stone by his decree was made
And dragged along behind the soldiers, he,
By patron saint, declaring that until
The count of stone itself turned back and
     fled,
He would not falter; on he went and
     saved
His friend.
     DON CARLOS. I want my prisoner.
     DON RUY GOMEZ. This was
A Gomez de Silva. Image—judge
What in this dwelling one must say who
     sees
These heroes—
     DON CARLOS.   Instantly—my prisoner!

          [*DON RUY GOMEZ bows low be-
          fore the King, takes his hand,
          and leads him to the last por-
          trait, which serves for the door
          of HERNANI'S hiding-place.
          DOÑA SOL watches him with
          anxious eyes. Silence and ex-
          pectation in all.*]
DON RUY GOMEZ. This portrait is my
     own. Mercy! King Charles!
For you require that those who see it
     here
Should say, "This last, the worthy son of
     race
Heroic, was a traitor found, that sold
The life of one he sheltered as a guest!"
          [*Joy of DOÑA SOL. Movement
          of bewilderment in the crowd.
          The King, disconcerted, moves
          away in anger, and remains
          some moments with lips trem-
          bling and eyes flashing.*]
DON CARLOS. Your castle, Duke, an-
     noys me, I shall lay
It low.
     DON RUY GOMEZ.   Thus, Highness,
     you'd retaliate,
Is it not so?
     DON CARLOS.   For such audacity
Your towers I'll level with the ground,
     and have
Upon the spot the hemp-seed sown.
     DON RUY GOMEZ. I'd see
The hemp spring freely up where once
     my towers
Stood high, rather than stain should eat
     into
The ancient name of Silva.
[*To the portraits.*] Is't not true?
I ask it of you all.
     DON CARLOS. Now, Duke, this head,
'T is ours, and thou hast promised it to
     me.
     DON RUY GOMEZ. I promised one or
     other.
[*To the portraits.*] Was't not so?
I ask you all?
[*Pointing to his head.*] This one I give.
          [*To the King.*] Take it.
     DON CARLOS. Duke, many thanks; but
     't would not do. The head

I want is young; when dead the heads-
man must
Uplift it by the hair. But as for thine,
In vain he'd seek, for thou hast not
enough
For him to clutch.
  Don Ruy Gomez. Highness, insult me
  not.
My head is noble still, and worth far
more
Than any rebel's poll. The head of Silva
You thus despise!
  Don Carlos. Give up Hernani!
  Don Ruy Gomez. I
Have spoken, Highness.
  Don Carlos [to his followers]. Search
  you everywhere
From roof to cellar, that he takes not
wing—
  Don Ruy Gomez. My keep is faithful
  as myself; alone
It shares the secret which we both shall
guard
Right well.
  Don Carlos. I am the King!
  Don Ruy Gomez. Out of my house
Demolished stone by stone, they'll only
make
My tomb,—and nothing gain.
  Don Carlos. Menace I find
And prayer alike are vain. Deliver up
The bandit, Duke, or head and castle
both
Will I beat down.
  Don Ruy Gomez. I've said my word.
  Don Carlos. Well, then,
Instead of one head I'll have two.
[To the Duke d'Alcala.] You, Jorge,
Arrest the Duke.
  Doña Sol [plucking off her veil and
  throwing herself between the King,
  the Duke, and the Guards]. King
  Charles, an evil king
Are you!
  Don Carlos. Good Heavens! Is it
Doña Sol I see?
  Doña Sol. Highness! Thou hast no
  Spaniard's heart!
  Don Carlos [confused]. Madam, you
  are severe upon the King.
  [He approaches her, and speaks low.]

'T is you have caused the wrath that's in
my heart.
A man approaching you perforce becomes
An angel or a monster. Ah, when we
Are hated, swiftly we malignant grow!
Perchance, if you had willed it so, young
girl,
I'd noble been—the lion of Castile;
A tiger I am made by your disdain.
You hear it roaring now. Madam, be
still! [Doña Sol looks at him. He
bows.]
However, I'll obey. [Turning to the
Duke.] Cousin, may be
Thy scruples are excusable, and I
Esteem thee. To thy guest be faithful still,
And faithless to thy King. I pardon thee.
'T is better that I only take thy niece
Away as hostage.
  Don Ruy Gomez. Only!
  Doña Sol. Highness! Me!
  Don Carlos. Yes, you.
  Don Ruy Gomez. Alone! Oh, won-
  drous clemency!
Oh, generous conqueror, that spares the
head
To torture thus the heart! What mercy
this!
  Don Carlos. Choose 'twixt the traitor
  and the Doña Sol,
I must have one of them.
  Don Ruy Gomez. The master you!
    [Don Carlos approaches Doña
    Sol to lead her away. She flies
    toward the Duke.]
  Doña Sol. Save me, my lord!
[She pauses.—Aside.] Oh, misery! and
yet
It must be so. My uncle's life, or else
The other's!—rather mine!
[To the King.] I follow you.
  Don Carlos [aside]. By all the saints!
  the thought triumphant is!
Ah, in the end you'll soften, princess
mine!
    [Doña Sol goes with a grave and
    steady step to the casket, opens
    it, and takes from it the dag-
    ger, which she hides in her
    bosom. Don Carlos comes to
    her and offers his hand.]

DON CARLOS. What is 't you're taking thence?

DOÑA SOL. Oh, nothing!

DON CARLOS. Is 't Some precious jewel?

DOÑA SOL. Yes.

DON CARLOS [*smiling*]. Show it to me.

DOÑA SOL. Anon you'll see it.

[*She gives him her hand and prepares to follow him.* DON RUY GOMEZ, *who has remained motionless and absorbed in thought, advances a few steps crying out.*]

DON RUY GOMEZ. Heavens, Doña Sol! Oh, Doña Sol! Since he is merciless, Help! Walls and armor come down on us now!

[*He runs to the King.*] Leave me my child! I have but her, O King!

DON CARLOS [*dropping* DOÑA SOL'S *hand*]. Then yield me up my prisoner.

[*The Duke drops his head, and seems the prey of horrible indecision. Then he looks up at the portraits with supplicating hands before them.*]

DON RUY GOMEZ. Oh, now Have pity on me all of you!

[*He makes a step toward the hiding-place,* DOÑA SOL *watching him anxiously. He turns again to the portraits.*]

Oh, hide Your faces! They deter me.

[*He advances with trembling steps toward his own portrait, then turns again to the King.*]

Is't your will?

DON CARLOS. Yes. [*The Duke raises a trembling hand toward the spring.*]

DOÑA SOL. O God!

DON RUY GOMEZ. No! [*He throws himself on his knees before the King.*]

In pity take my life!

DON CARLOS. Thy niece!

DON RUY GOMEZ [*rising*]. Take her, and leave me honor, then.

DON CARLOS [*seizing the hand of the trembling* DOÑA SOL.] Adieu, Duke.

DON RUY GOMEZ. Till we meet again!

[*He watches the King, who retires slowly with* DOÑA SOL. *Afterwards he puts his hand on his dagger.*]

May God Shield you!

[*He comes back to the front of the stage panting, and stands motionless, with vacant stare, seeming neither to see nor hear anything, his arms crossed on his heaving chest. Meanwhile the King goes out with* DOÑA SOL, *the suite following two by two according to their rank. They speak in a low voice among themselves.*]

[*Aside.*] Whilst thou go'st joyous from my house, O King, my ancient loyalty goes forth From out my bleeding heart.

[*He raises his head, looks all round, and sees that he is alone. Then he takes two swords from a panoply by the wall, measures them, and places them on a table. This done, he goes to the portrait, touches the spring, and the hidden door opens.*]

Come out.

[HERNANI *appears at the door of the hiding-place.* DON RUY GOMEZ *points to the two swords on the table.*]

Now, choose. Choose, for Don Carlos has departed now, And it remains to give me satisfaction. Choose, and be quick. What, then! trembles thy hand?

HERNANI. A duel! Oh, it cannot be, old man, 'Twixt us.

DON RUY GOMEZ. Why not? Is it thou art afraid? Or that thou art not noble? So or not, All men who injure me, by Hell, I count Noble enough to cross their swords with mine.

HERNANI. Old man—
DON RUY GOMEZ. Come forth, young
man, to slay me, else
To be the slain.
HERNANI. To die, ah, yes! Against
My will thyself hast saved me, and my
life
Is yours. I bid you take it.
DON RUY GOMEZ. This you wish?
[*To the portraits.*] You see he wills it.
[*To* HERNANI.] This is well. Thy prayer
Now make.
HERNANI. It is to thee, my lord, the
last
I make.
DON RUY GOMEZ. Pray to the other
Lord.
HERNANI. No, no,
To thee. Strike me, old man,—dagger
or sword,—
Each one for me is good,—but grant me
first
One joy supreme. Duke, let me see her ere
I die.
DON RUY GOMEZ. See her!
HERNANI. Or at the least I beg
That you will let me hear her voice once
more—
Only this one last time!
DON RUY GOMEZ. Hear her!
HERNANI. Ah, well,
My lord, I understand thy jealousy,
But death already seizes on my youth.
Forgive me. Grant me—tell me that
without
Beholding her, if it must be, I yet
May hear her speak, and I will die to-
night.
I'll grateful be to hear her. But in peace
I'd calmly die, if thou would'st deign that
ere
My soul is freed, it sees once more the
soul
That shines so clearly in her eyes. To
her
I will not speak. Thou shalt be there to
see,
My father, and canst slay me afterwards.
DON RUY GOMEZ [*pointing to the recess
still open*]. Oh, saints of Heaven!
Can this recess, then, be

So deep and strong that he has nothing
heard?
HERNANI. No, I have nothing heard.
DON RUY GOMEZ. I was compelled
To yield up Doña Sol or thee.
HERNANI. To whom?
DON RUY GOMEZ. The King.
HERNANI. Madman! He loves her.
DON RUY GOMEZ. Loves her! He!
HERNANI. He takes her from us! He
our rival is!
DON RUY GOMEZ. Curses be on him!
Vassals! all to horse—
To horse! Let us pursue the ravisher!
HERNANI. Listen! The vengeance that
is sure of foot
Makes on its way less noise than this
would do.
To thee I do belong. Thou hast the right
To slay me. Wilt thou not employ me
first
As the avenger of thy niece's wrongs?
Let me take part in this thy vengeance
due;
Grant me this boon, and I will kiss thy
feet,
If so must be. Let us together speed
The King to follow. I will be thine arm.
I will avenge thee, Duke, and afterwards
The life that's forfeit thou shalt take.
DON RUY GOMEZ. And then,
As now, thou'lt ready be to die?
HERNANI. Yes, Duke.
DON RUY GOMEZ. By what wilt thou
swear this?
HERNANI. My father's head.
DON RUY GOMEZ. Of thine own self
wilt thou remember it?
HERNANI [*giving him the horn which he
takes from his girdle*]. Listen! Take
you this horn, and whatso'er
May happen—what the place, or what the
hour—
Whenever to thy mind it seems the same
Has come for me to die, blow on this horn
And take no other care; all will be
done.
DON RUY GOMEZ [*offering his hand*].
Your hand! [*They press hands.*]
[*To the portraits.*] And all of you are
witnesses.

ACT IV

The Tomb, Aix-la-Chapelle. The vaults which enclose the Tomb of Charlemagne at Aix-la-Chapelle. Great arches of Lombard architecture, with semicircular columns, having capitals of birds and flowers. At the right a small bronze door, low and curved. A single lamp suspended from the crown of the vault shows the inscription: CAROLVS MAGNVS. *It is night. One cannot see to the end of the vaults, the eye loses itself in the intricacy of arches, steps, and columns which mingle in the shade.*

[*Enter* DON CARLOS, DON RICARDO DE ROXAS, COUNT DE CASAPALMA, *lanterns in hand, and wearing large cloaks and slouched hats.*]

DON RICARDO [*hat in hand*]. This is the place.

DON CARLOS. Yes, here it is the League
Will meet; they that together in my power
So soon shall be. Oh, it was well, my Lord
Of Trèves th' Elector—it was well of you
To lend this place; dark plots should prosper best
In the dank air of catacombs, and good
It is to sharpen daggers upon tombs.
Yet the stake's heavy—heads are on the game,
Ye bold assassins, and the end we'll see.
By Heaven, 't was well a sepulcher to choose
For such a business, since the road will be
Shorter for them to traverse.
[*To* DON RICARDO.] Tell me now
How far the subterranean way extends?

DON RICARDO. To the strong fortress.

DON CARLOS. Farther than we need.

DON RICARDO. And on the other side it reaches quite
The Monastery of Altenheim.

DON CARLOS. Ah, where
Lothaire was overcome by Rodolf. Once
Again, Count, tell me o'er their names and wrongs.

DON RICARDO. Gotha.

DON CARLOS. Ah, very well I know why 't is

The brave Duke is conspirator: he wills
For Germany, a German Emperor.

DON RICARDO. Hohenbourg.

DON CARLOS. Hohenbourg would better like
With Francis hell, than heaven itself with me.

DON RICARDO. Gil Tellez Giron.

DON CARLOS. Castile and our Lady!
The scoundrel!—to be traitor to his king!

DON RICARDO. One evening it is said that you were found
With Madam Giron. You had just before
Made him a baron; he revenges now
The honor of his dear companion.

DON CARLOS. This, then, the reason he revolts 'gainst Spain?
What name comes next?

DON RICARDO. The Reverend Vasquez, Avila's Bishop.

DON CARLOS. Pray does he resent
Dishonor of his wife!

DON RICARDO. Then there is named
Guzman de Lara, who is discontent,
Claiming the collar of your order.

DON CARLOS. Ah!
Guzman de Lara! If he only wants
A collar he shall have one.

DON RICARDO. Next the Duke
Of Lutzelbourg. As for his plans, they say—

DON CARLOS. Ah! Lutzelbourg is by the head too tall.

DON RICARDO. Juan de Haro—who Astorga wants.

DON CARLOS. These Haros! Always they the headsman's pay
Have doubled.

DON RICARDO. That is all.

DON CARLOS. Not by my count.
These make but seven.

DON RICARDO. Oh, I did not name
Some bandits, probably engaged by Trèves
Or France.

DON CARLOS. Men without prejudice of course,
Whose ready daggers turn to heaviest pay,
As truly as the needle to the pole.

DON RICARDO. However, I observed two sturdy ones

Among them, both new comers—one was
young,
The other old.
  Don Carlos. Their names?
      [Don Ricardo *shrugs his shoul-
          ders in sign of ignorance.*]
Their age, then, say?
  Don Ricardo. The younger may be
    twenty.
  Don Carlos. Pity, then.
  Don Ricardo. The elder must be sixty,
    quite.
  Don Carlos. One seems
Too young—the other, over-old; so much
For them the worse 't will be. I will take
    care—
Myself will help the headsman, be there
    need.
My sword is sharpened for a traitor's
    block,
I'll lend it him if blunt his ax should
    grow,
And join my own imperial purple on
To piece the scaffold cloth, if it must
    be
Enlarged that way. But shall I Emperor
    prove?
  Don Ricardo. The College at this hour
    deliberates.
  Don Carlos. Who knows? Francis the
    first, perchance, they'll name,
Or else their Saxon Frederick the Wise.
Ah, Luther, thou art right to blame the
    times
And scorn such makers-up of royalty,
That own no other rights than gilded
    ones.
A Saxon heretic! Primate of Trèves,
A libertine! Count Palatine, a fool!
As for Bohemia's king, for me he is.
Princes of Hesse, all smaller than their
    states!
The young are idiots, and the old de-
    bauched,
Of crowns a plenty—but for heads we
    search
In vain! Council of dwarfs ridiculous,
That I in lion's skin could carry off
Like Hercules; and who of violet robes
Bereft, would show but heads more shal-
    low far

Than Triboulet's. See'st thou I want
    three votes
Or all is lost, Ricardo? Oh! I'd give
Toledo, Ghent, and Salamanca too,
Three towns, my friends, I'd offer to their
    choice
For their three voices—cities of Castile
And Flanders. Safe I know to take them
    back
A little later on [Don Ricardo *bows low
    to the King, and puts on his hat.*]
You cover, sir!
  Don Ricardo. Sire, you have called me
    thou [*bowing again*]. And thus I'm
    made
Grandee of Spain.
  Don Carlos [*aside*]. Ah, how to pit-
    eous scorn
You rouse me! Interested brood devour'd
By mean ambition. Thus across my plans
Yours struggle. Base the court where
    without shame
The King is plied for honors, and he
    yields,
Bestowing grandeur on the hungry crew.
[*Musing.*] God only, and the Emperor
    are great,
Also the Holy Father! For the rest,
The kings and dukes, of what account are
    they?
  Don Ricardo. I trust that they Your
    Highness will elect.
  Don Carlos. Highness—still Highness!
    Oh, unlucky chance!
If only King I must remain.
  Don Ricardo [*aside*]. By jove,
Emperor or King, Grandee of Spain I am.
  Don Carlos. When they've decided
    who shall be the one
They choose for Emperor of Germany,
What sign is to announce his name?
  Don Ricardo. The guns.
A single firing will proclaim the Duke
Of Saxony is chosen Emperor;
Two if 't is Francis; for Your Highness
    three.
  Don Carlos. And Doña Sol! I'm
    crossed on every side.
If, Count, by turn of luck, I'm Emperor
    made,
Go seek her; she by Cæsar might be won.

DON RICARDO [*smiling*]. Your Highness pleases.

DON CARLOS [*haughtily*]. On that subject peace!
I have not yet inquired what's thought of me.
But tell me when will it be truly known
Who is elected?

DON RICARDO. In an hour or so,
At latest.

DON CARLOS. Ah, three votes; and only three!
But first this trait'rous rabble we must crush,
And then we'll see to whom the Empire falls,

[*He counts on his fingers and stamps his foot.*]

Always by three too few! Ah, they hold power.
Yet did Cornelius know all long ago:
In Heaven's ocean thirteen stars he saw
Coming full sail toward mine, all from the north.
Empire for me—let's on! But it is said,
On other hand, that Jean Trithème Francis
Predicted! Clearer should I see my fate
Had I some armament the prophecy
To help. The sorcerer's predictions come
Most true when a good army—with its guns
And lances, horse and foot, and martial strains,
Ready to lead the way where Fate alone
Might stumble—plays the midwife's part to bring
Fulfillment of prediction. That's worth more
Than our Cornelius Agrippa or
Trithème. He, who by force of arms expounds
His system, and with sharpen'd point of lance
Can edge his words, and uses soldiers' swords
To level rugged fortune—shapes events
At his own will to match the prophecy.
Poor fools! who with proud eyes and haughty mien
Only look straight to Empire, and declare

"It is my right!"—They need great guns in files
Whose burning breath melts towns; and soldiers, ships,
And horsemen. These they need their ends to gain
O'er trampled peoples. Pshaw! At the crossroads
Of human life, where one leads to a throne,
Another to perdition, they will pause
In indecision,—scarce three steps will take
Uncertain of themselves, and in their doubt
Fly to the necromancer for advice
Which road to take.

[*To* DON RICARDO.] Go now, 't is near the time
The trait'rous crew will meet. Give me the key.

DON RICARDO [*giving key of tomb*].
Sire, 't was the guardian of the tomb, the Count
De Limbourg, who to me confided it,
And has done everything to pleasure you.

DON CARLOS. Do all, quite all that I commanded you.

DON RICARDO [*bowing*]. Highness, I go at once.

DON CARLOS. The signal, then,
That I await is cannon firing thrice?

[DON RICARDO *bows and exit.*
DON CARLOS *falls into a deep reverie, his arms crossed, his head drooping; afterwards he raises it, and turns to the tomb.*]

Forgive me, Charlemagne! Oh, this lonely vault
Should echo only unto solemn words.
Thou must be angry at the babble vain
Of our ambition at your monument.
Here Charlemagne rests! How can the somber tomb
Without a rifting spasm hold such dust!
And art thou truly here, colossal power,
Creator of the world? And canst thou now
Crouch down from all thy majesty and might?
Ah, 't is a spectacle to stir the soul

What Europe was, and what by thee 't was
made,
Mighty construction with two men su-
preme
Elected chiefs to whom born kings submit.
States, duchies, kingdoms, marquisates
and fiefs—
By right hereditary most are ruled,
But nations find a friend sometimes in
Pope
Or Cæsar; and one chance another chance
Corrects; thus even balance is maintained
And order opens out. The cloth-of-gold
Electors, and the scarlet cardinals.
The double, sacred senate, unto which
Earth bends, are but paraded outward
show,
God's fiat rules it all. One day He wills
A thought, a want, should burst upon the
world,
Then grow and spread, and mix with
everything,
Possess some man, win hearts, and delve
a groove
Though kings may trample on it, and
may seek
To gag;—only that they some morn may
see
At diet, conclave, this the scorned
idea,
That they had spurned, all suddenly ex-
pand
And soar above their heads, bearing the
globe
In hand, or on the brow tiara. Pope
And Emperor, they on earth are all in
all,
A mystery supreme dwells in them both,
And Heaven's might, which they still
represent,
Feasts them with kings and nations, hold-
ing them
Beneath its thunder-cloud, the while they
sit
At table with the world served out for
food.
Alone they regulate all things on earth,
Just as the mower manages his field.
All rule and power are theirs. Kings at
the door
Inhale the odor of their savory meats.

Look through the window, watchful on
tiptoe,
But weary of the scene. The common
world
Below them groups itself on ladder-rungs.
They make and all unmake. One can re-
lease,
The other surely strike. The one is Truth,
The other Might. Each to himself is
law,
And is, because he is. When—equals they
The one in purple, and the other swathed
In white like winding-sheet—when they
come out
From sanctuary, the dazzled multitude
Look with wild terror on these halves of
God,
The Pope and Emperor. Emperor! oh, to
be
Thus great! Oh, anguish, not to be this
Power
When beats the heart with dauntless
courage fill'd!
Oh, happy he who sleeps within this
tomb!
How great, and oh! how fitted for his
time!
The Pope and Emperor were more than
men,
In them two Romes in mystic Hymen
joined
Prolific were, giving new form and soul
Unto the human race, refounding realms
And nations, shaping thus a Europe new,
And both remoulding with their hands the
bronze
Remaining of the great old Roman world.
What destiny! And yet 't is here he
lies?
Is all so little that we come to this!
What then? To have been Prince and
Emperor,
And King—to have been sword, and also
law;
Giant, with Germany for pedestal—
For title Cæsar—Charlemagne for name:
A greater to have been than Hannibal
Or Attila—as great as was the world.
Yet all rests here! For Empire strive
and strain
And see the dust that makes an Emperor!

Cover the earth with tumult, and with noise
Know you that one day only will remain—
Oh, madd'ning thought—a stone! For sounding name
Triumphant, but some letters 'graved to serve
For little children to learn spelling by.
How high soe'er ambition made thee soar,
Behold the end of all! Oh, Empire, power,
What matters all to me! I near it now
And like it well. Some voice declares to me
Thine—thine—it will be thine. Heavens, were it so!
To mount at once the spiral height supreme
And be alone—the keystone of the arch,
With states beneath, one o'er the other ranged,
And kings for mats to wipe one's sandal'd feet!
To see 'neath kings the feudal families,
Margraves and cardinals, and doges—dukes,
Then bishops, abbés—chiefs of ancient clans,
Great barons—then the soldier class and clerks,
And know yet farther off—in the deep shade
At bottom of th'abyss there is Mankind—
That is to say a crowd, a sea of men,
A tumult—cries, with tears, and bitter laugh
Sometimes. The wail wakes up and scares the earth
And reaches us with leaping echoes, and
With trumpet tone. Oh, citizens, oh, men!
The swarm that from the high church towers seems now
To sound the tocsin!
[*Musing.*] Wondrous human base
Of nations, bearing on your shoulders broad
The mighty pyramid that has two poles,
The living waves that ever straining hard

Balance and shake it as they heave and roll,
Make all change place, and on the highest heights
Make stagger thrones, as if they were but stools.
So sure is this, that ceasing vain debates
Kings look to Heaven! Kings look down below,
Look at the people!—Restless ocean, there
Where nothing's cast that does not shake the whole;
The sea that rends a throne, and rocks a tomb—
A glass in which kings rarely look but ill.
Ah, if upon this gloomy sea they gazed
Sometimes, what Empires in its depths they'd find!
Great vessels wrecked that by its ebb and flow
Are stirr'd—that wearied it—known now no more!
To govern this—to mount so high if called,
Yet know myself to be but mortal man!
To see the abyss—if not that moment struck
With dizziness bewildering every sense.
Oh, moving pyramid of states and kings
With apex narrow,—woe to timid step!
What shall restrain me? If I fail when there
Feeling my feet upon the trembling world,
Feeling alive the palpitating earth,
Then when I have between my hands the globe
Have I the strength alone to hold it fast,
To be an Emperor? O God, 't was hard
And difficult to play the kingly part.
Certes, no man is rarer than the one
Who can enlarge his soul to duly meet
Great Fortune's smiles, and still increasing gifts.
But I! Who is it that shall be my guide,
My counselor, and make me great?
[*Falls on his knees before the tomb.*] 'T is thou,
Oh, Charlemagne! And since 't is God for whom
All obstacles dissolve, who takes us now

And puts us face to face—from this
    tomb's depths
Endow me with sublimity and strength.
Let me be great enough to see the truth
On every side. Show me how small the
    world
I dare not measure—me this Babel show
Where, from the hind to Cæsar mounting
    up,
Each one, complaisant with himself, re-
    gards
The next with scorn that is but half re-
    strained.
Teach me the secret of thy conquests
    all.
And how to rule. And show me certainly
Whether to punish, or to pardon, be
The worthier thing to do.
Is it not fact
That in his solitary bed sometimes
A mighty shade is wakened from his sleep,
Aroused by noise and turbulence on earth;
That suddenly his tomb expands itself,
And bursts its doors—and in the night
    flings forth
A flood of light? If this be true, indeed,
Say, Emperor! what can after Charle-
    magne
Another do! Speak, though thy sovereign
    breath
Should cleave this brazen door. Or rather
    now
Let me thy sanctuary enter lone!
Let me behold thy veritable face,
And not repulse me with a freezing breath.
Upon thy stony pillow elbows lean,
And let us talk. Yes, with prophetic
    voice
Tell me of things which make the fore-
    head pale,
And clear eyes mournful. Speak, and do
    not blind
Thine awe-struck son, for doubtlessly thy
    tomb
Is full of light. Or if thou wilt not speak,
Let me make study in the solemn peace
Of thee, as of a world, thy measure take,
O giant, for there's nothing here below
So great as thy poor ashes. Let them
    teach,
Failing thy spirit.

[*He puts the key in the lock.*] Let us
    enter now.
[*He recoils.*] O God, if he should really
    whisper me!
If he be there and walks with noiseless
    tread,
And I come back with hair in moments
    bleached!
I'll do it still.   [*Sound of footsteps.*]
Who comes? who dares disturb
Besides myself the dwelling of such dead!
        [*The sound comes nearer.*]
My murderers! I forgot! Now, enter
    we. [*He opèns the door of the tomb,
    which shuts upon him.*]

[*Enter several men walking softly, dis-
guised by large cloaks and hats. They
take each other's hands, going from one
to another and speaking in a low tone.*]
    FIRST CONSPIRATOR [*who alone carries
    a lighted torch*]. Ad augusta.
    SECOND CONSPIRATOR. Per angusta.
    FIRST CONSPIRATOR. The saints
Shield us.
    THIRD CONSPIRATOR. The dead assist
us.
    FIRST CONSPIRATOR. Guard us, God!
        [*Noise in the shade.*]
    FIRST CONSPIRATOR. Who's there?
    A VOICE. Ad augusta.
    SECOND CONSPIRATOR. Per angusta.

[*Enter fresh Conspirators—noise of
footsteps.*]
    FIRST CONSPIRATOR [*to* THIRD]. See!
    there is some one still to come.
    THIRD CONSPIRATOR. Who's there?
    VOICE [*in the darkness*]. Ad augusta.
    THIRD CONSPIRATOR. Per angusta.

[*Enter more Conspirators, who exchange
signs with their hands with the others.*]
    FIRST CONSPIRATOR. 'T is well.
All now are here. Gotha, to you it falls
To state the case. Friends, darkness
    waits for light.
        [*The Conspirators sit in a half-
        circle on the tombs. The* FIRST
        CONSPIRATOR *passes before
        them, and from his torch each*

one lights a wax taper which he holds in his hand. Then the FIRST CONSPIRATOR *seats himself in silence on a tomb a little higher than the others in the center of the circle.*]

DUKE OF GOTHA [*rising*]. My friends!
This Charles of Spain, by mother's side
A foreigner, aspires to mount the throne
Of Holy Empire.

FIRST CONSPIRATOR. But for him the grave.

DUKE OF GOTHA [*throwing down his light and crushing it with his foot*].
Let it be with his head as with this flame.

ALL. So be it.

FIRST CONSPIRATOR. Death unto him.

DUKE OF GOTHA. Let him die.

ALL. Let him be slain.

DON JUAN DE HARO. German his father was.

DUKE DE LUTZELBOURG. His mother Spanish.

DUKE OF GOTHA. Thus you see that he
Is no more one than other. Let him die.

A CONSPIRATOR. Suppose th' Electors at this very hour
Declare him Emperor!

FIRST CONSPIRATOR. Him! oh, never him!

DON GIL TELLEZ GIRON. What signifies? Let us strike off the head,
The Crown will fall.

FIRST CONSPIRATOR. But if to him belongs
The Holy Empire, he becomes so great
And so august, that only God's own hand
Can reach him.

DUKE OF GOTHA. All the better reason why
He dies before such power august he gains.

FIRST CONSPIRATOR. He shall not be elected.

ALL. Not for him
The Empire.

FIRST CONSPIRATOR. Now, how many hands will't take
To put him in his shroud?

ALL. One is enough.

FIRST CONSPIRATOR. How many strokes to reach his heart?

ALL. But one.

FIRST CONSPIRATOR. Who, then, will strike?

ALL. All! All!

FIRST CONSPIRATOR. The victim is
A traitor proved. They would an Emperor choose,
We've a high-priest to make. Let us draw lots.
[*All the Conspirators write their names on their tablets, tear out the leaf, roll it up, and one after another throw them into the urn on one of the tombs.*]
Now, let us pray. [*All kneel.*]
Oh, may the chosen one
Believe in God, and like a Roman strike,
Die as a Hebrew would, and brave alike
The wheel and burning pincers, laugh at rack,
And fire, and wooden horse, and be resigned
To kill and die. He might have all to do. [*He draws a parchment from the urn.*]

ALL. What name?

FIRST CONSPIRATOR [*in low voice*]. Hernani!

HERNANI [*coming out from the crowd of Conspirators*]. I have won, yes, won!
I hold thee fast! Thee I've so long pursued
With vengeance.

DON RUY GOMEZ [*piercing through the crowd and taking* HERNANI *aside*].
Yield—oh, yield this right to me.

HERNANI. Not for my life! Oh, signor, grudge me not
This stroke of fortune—'t is the first I've known.

DON RUY GOMEZ. You nothing have!
I'll give you houses, lands,
A hundred thousand vassals shall be yours
In my three hundred villages, if you
But yield the right to strike to me.

HERNANI. No—no.

DUKE OF GOTHA. Old man, thy arm would strike less sure a blow.

DON RUY GOMEZ. Back! I have strength of soul, if not of arm.

Judge not the sword by the mere scabbard's rust.

[*To* HERNANI.] You do belong to me.

HERNANI. My life is yours,

As his belongs to me.

DON RUY GOMEZ [*drawing the horn from his girdle*]. I yield her up.

And will return the horn.

HERNANI [*trembling*]. What life! My life

And Doña Sol! No, I my vengeance choose.

I have my father to revenge—yet more,

Perchance I am inspired by God in this.

DON RUY GOMEZ. I yield thee Her—and give thee back the horn!

HERNANI. No!

DON RUY GOMEZ. Boy, reflect.

HERNANI. Oh, Duke, leave me my prey.

DON RUY GOMEZ. My curses on you for depriving me

Of this my joy.

FIRST CONSPIRATOR [*to* HERNANI]. Oh, brother, ere they can

Elect him—'t would be well this very night

To watch for Charles.

HERNANI. Fear nought, I know the way

To kill a man.

FIRST CONSPIRATOR. May every treason fall

On traitor, and may God be with you now.

We Counts and Barons, let us take the oath

That if he fall, yet slay not, we go on

And strike by turn unflinching till Charles dies.

ALL [*drawing their swords*]. Let us all swear.

DUKE OF GOTA [*to* FIRST CONSPIRATOR]. My brother, let's decide.

On what we swear.

DON RUY GOMEZ [*taking his sword by the point and raising it above his head*]. By this same cross,

ALL [*raising their swords*]. And this That he must quickly die impenitent.

[*They hear a cannon fired afar off. All pause and are silent. The door of the tomb half opens, and* DON CARLOS *appears at the threshold. A second gun is fired, then a third. He opens wide the door and stands erect and motionless without advancing.*]

DON CARLOS. Fall back, ye gentlemen —the Emperor hears.

[*All the lights are simultaneously extinguished. A profound silence.* DON CARLOS *advances a step in the darkness, so dense, that the silent, motionless Conspirators can scarcely be distinguished.*]

Silence and night! From darkness sprung, the swarm

Into the darkness plunges back again!

Think ye this scene is like a passing dream,

And that I take you, now your lights are quenched,

For men's stone figures seated on their tombs?

Just now, my statues, you had voices loud,

Raise, then, your drooping heads, for Charles the Fifth

Is here. Strike. Move a pace or two and show

You dare. But no, 't is not in you to dare.

Your flaming torches, blood-red 'neath these vaults,

My breath extinguished; but now turn your eyes

Irresolute, and see that, if I thus

Put out the many, I can light still more.

[*He strikes the iron key on the bronze door of the tomb. At the sound all the depths of the cavern are filled with soldiers bearing torches and halberts. At their head the* DUKE D'ALCALA, *the* MARQUIS D'ALMUÑAN, *etc.*]

Come on, my falcons! I've the nest—the prey.

[*To Conspirators.*] I can make blaze of light, 't is my turn now,

Behold!

[*To the Soldiers.*] Advance—for flagrant is the crime.

HERNANI [*looking at the Soldiers*]. Ah, well! At first I thought 't was Charlemagne,

Alone he seemed so great—but after all 'T is only Charles the Fifth.

DON CARLOS [*to the* DUKE D'ALCALA]. Come, Constable

Of Spain.

[*To* MARQUIS D'ALMUÑAN.] And you Castilian Admiral,

Disarm them all.

> [*The Conspirators are surrounded and disarmed.*]

DON RICARDO [*hurrying in and bowing almost to the ground*]. Your Majesty!

DON CARLOS. Alcalde

I make you of the palace.

DON RICARDO [*again bowing*]. Two Electors,

To represent the Golden Chamber, come To offer to Your Sacred Majesty Congratulations now.

DON CARLOS. Let them come forth.

[*Aside to* DON RICARDO.] The Doña Sol.

[RICARDO *bows and exit.*]

[*Enter with flambeaux and flourish of trumpets the* KING OF BOHEMIA *and the* DUKE OF BAVARIA, *both wearing cloth of gold, and with crowns on their heads. Numerous followers. German nobles carrying the banner of the Empire, the double-headed Eagle, with the escutcheon of Spain in the middle of it. The Soldiers divide, forming lines between which the Electors pass to the Emperor, to whom they bow low. He returns the salutation by raising his hat.*]

DUKE OF BAVARIA. Most Sacred Majesty

Charles, of the Romans King, and Emperor,

The Empire of the world is in your hands—

Yours is the throne to which each king aspires!

The Saxon Frederick was elected first, But he judged you more worthy, and declined.

Now, then, receive the crown and globe, O King—

The Holy Empire doth invest you now, Arms with the sword, and you indeed are great.

DON CARLOS. The College I will thank on my return.

But go, my brother of Bohemia, And you,, Bavarian cousin.—Thanks; but now

I do dismiss you—I shall go myself.

KING OF BOHEMIA. Oh! Charles, our ancestors were friends. My sire

Loved yours, and their two fathers were two friends—

So young! exposed to varied fortunes! say,

Oh, Charles, may I be ranked a very chief

Among thy brothers? I cannot forget I knew you as a little child.

DON CARLOS. Ah, well—

King of Bohemia, you presume too much.

[*He gives him his hand to kiss, also the* DUKE OF BAVARIA, *both bow low.*] Depart.

> [*Exeunt the two* ELECTORS *with their followers.*]

THE CROWD. *Long live the Emperor!*

DON CARLOS [*aside*]. So 't is mine.

All things have helped, and I am Emperor—

By the refusal, though, of Frederick Surnamed the Wise!

[*Enter* DOÑA SOL *led by* RICARDO.]

DOÑA SOL. What, soldiers!—Emperor!

Hernani! Heaven, what an unlooked-for chance!

HERNANI. Ah! Doña Sol!

DON RUY GOMEZ [*aside to* HERNANI]. She has not seen me.

[DOÑA SOL *runs to* HERNANI,

*who makes her recoil by a look
of disdain.*]
HERNANI. Madam!
DOÑA SOL [*drawing the dagger from
her bosom*]. I still his poniard have!
HERNANI [*taking her in his arms*]. My
dearest one!
DON CARLOS. Be silent all.
[*To the Conspirators.*] Is 't you re-
morseless are?
I need to give the world a lesson now,
The Lara of Castile, and Gotha, you
Of Saxony—all—all—what were your
plans
Just now? I bid you speak.
HERNANI. Quite simple, Sire,
The thing, and we can briefly tell it you.
We 'graved the sentence on Belshazzar's
wall. [*He takes out a poniard and
brandishes it.*]
We render unto Cæsar Cæsar's due.
DON CARLOS. Silence!
[*To DON RUY GOMEZ.*] And you! You
too are traitor, Silva!
DON RUY GOMEZ. Which of us two is
traitor, Sire?
HERNANI [*turning toward the Con-
spirators*]. Our heads
And Empire—all that he desires he has.
[*To the EMPEROR.*] The mantle blue of
kings encumbered you;
The purple better suits—it shows not
blood.
DON CARLOS [*to DON RUY GOMEZ*].
Cousin of Silva, this is felony,
Attaining your baronial rank. Think
well,
Don Ruy—high treason!
DON RUY GOMEZ. Kings like Roderick
Count Julians make.
DON CARLOS [*to the DUKE D'ALCALA*].
Seize only those who seem
The nobles,—for the rest!—
[DON RUY GOMEZ, *the* DUKE DE
LUTZELBOURG, *the* DUKE OF
GOTHA, DON JUAN DE HARO,
DON GUZMAN DE LARA, DON
TELLEZ GIRON, *the* BARON OF
HOHENBOURG *separate them-
selves from the group of Con-
spirators, among whom is*

HERNANI. *The* DUKE D'ALCALA
surrounds them with guards.]
DOÑA SOL [*aside*]. Ah, he is saved!
HERNANI [*coming from among the Con-
spirators*]. I claim to be included!
[*To DON CARLOS.*] Since to this
It comes, the question of the axe—that
now
Hernani, humble churl, beneath thy feet
Unpunished goes, because his brow is not
At level with thy sword—because one
must
Be great to die, I rise. God, who gives
power,
And gives to thee the scepter, made me
Duke
Of Segorbe and Cardona, Marquis too
Of Monroy, Albaterra's Count, of Gor
Viscount, and Lord of many places, more
Than I can name. Juan of Aragon
Am I, Grand Master of Avis—the son
In exile born, of murder'd father slain
By king's decree, King Charles, which
me proscribed,
Thus death 'twixt us is family affair;
You have the scaffold—we the poniard
hold.
Since Heaven a duke has made me, and
exile
A mountaineer,—since all in vain I've
sharpen'd
Upon the hills my sword, and in the tor-
rents
Have tempered it. [*He puts on his hat.*]
[*To the Conspirators.*] Let us be cov-
ered now,
Us the Grandees of Spain. [*They cover.*]
[*To DON CARLOS.*] Our heads, O King,
Have right to fall before thee covered
thus.
[*To the Prisoners.*] Silva, and Haro—
Lara—men of rank
And race make room for Juan of Ara-
gon.
Give me my place, ye dukes and counts—
my place.
[*To the Courtiers and Guards.*] King,
headsmen, varlets—Juan of Aragon
Am I. If all your scaffolds are too small
Make new ones. [*He joins the group of
nobles.*]

DoñA Sol. Heavens!

Don Carlos. I had forgotten quite
This history.

Hernani. But they who bleed remember
Far better. Th' evil that wrong-doer thus
So senselessly forgets, forever stirs
Within the outraged heart.

Don Carlos. Therefore, enough
For me to bear this title, that I'm son
Of sires, whose power dealt death to ancestors
Of yours!

DoñA Sol [falling on her knees before
the Emperor]. Oh, pardon—pardon!
Mercy, Sire.

Be pitiful, or strike us both, I pray,
For he my lover is, my promised spouse,
In him it is alone I live—I breathe;
Oh, Sire, in mercy us together slay.
Trembling—oh, Majesty!—I trail myself
Before your sacred knees. I love him,
Sire,
And he is mine—as Empire is your own.
Have pity.
[Don Carlos looks at her without moving.]
Oh, what thought absorbs you?

Don Carlos. Cease.
Rise—Duchess of Segorbe—Marchioness
Of Monroy—Countess Albaterra—and—
[To Hernani.] Thine other names, Don
Juan?

Hernani. Who speaks thus,
The King?

Don Carlos. No, 't is the Emperor.

DoñA Sol. Just Heav'n!

Don Carlos [pointing to her]. Duke
Juan, take your wife.

Hernani [his eyes raised to heaven,
DoñA Sol in his arms]. Just God!

Don Carlos [to Don Ruy Gomez]. My
cousin,
I know the pride of your nobility,
But Aragon with Silva well may mate.

Don Ruy Gomez [bitterly]. 'T is not
a question of nobility.

Hernani [looking with love on DoñA
Sol and still holding her in his arms].
My deadly hate is vanishing away.
[Throws away his dagger.]

Don Ruy Gomez [aside, and looking at
them]. Shall I betray myself? Oh,
no,—my grief,
My foolish love would make them pity
cast
Upon my venerable head. Old man
And Spaniard! Let the hidden fire consume,
And suffer still in secret. Let heart
break
But cry not;—they would laugh at thee.

DoñA Sol [still in Hernani's arms].
My Duke!

Hernani. Nothing my soul holds now
but love!

DoñA Sol. Oh, joy!

Don Carlos [aside, his hand in his
bosom]. Stifle thyself, young heart
so full of flame,
Let reign again the better thoughts which
thou
So long hast troubled. Henceforth let
thy loves,
Thy mistresses, alas!—be Germany
And Flanders—[Looking at the banner.]
Spain.
The Emperor is like
The Eagle his companion, in the place
Of heart, there's but a 'scutcheon.

Hernani. Cæsar you!

Don Carlos. Don Juan, of your ancient name and race
Your soul is worthy [Pointing to DoñA
Sol.]—worthy e'en of her.
Kneel, Duke.
[Hernani kneels. Don Carlos
unfastens his own Golden
Fleece and puts it on Hernani's neck.]
Receive this collar.
[Don Carlos draws his sword
and strikes him three times on
the shoulder.]
Faithful be,
For by St. Stephen now I make thee
Knight. [He raises and embraces
him.]
Thou hast a collar softer and more
choice;
That which is wanting to my rank supreme,—

The arms of loving woman, loved by
thee.
Thou wilt be happy—I am Emperor.
[*To Conspirators.*] Sirs, I forget your
names. Anger and hate
I will forget. Go—go—I pardon you.
This is the lesson that the world much
needs.
THE CONSPIRATORS. Glory to Charles!
DON RUY GOMEZ [*to* DON CARLOS]. I
only suffer, then!
DON CARLOS. And I!
DON RUY GOMEZ. But I have not like
Majesty
Forgiven!
HERNANI. Who is't has worked this
wondrous change?
ALL, NOBLES, SOLDIERS, CONSPIRATORS.
Honor to Charles the Fifth, and Ger-
many!
DON CARLOS [*turning to the tomb*].
Honor to Charlemagne! Leave us
now together.
    [*Exeunt all.* DON CARLOS, *alone,
    bends toward the tomb.*]
Art thou content with me, O Charle-
magne!
Have I the kingship's littleness stripped
off?
Become as Emperor another man?
Can I Rome's miter add unto my helm?
Have I the right the fortunes of the world
To sway? Have I a steady foot that safe
Can tread the path, by Vandal ruins
strewed,
Which thou has beaten by thine armies
vast?
Have I my candle lighted at thy flame?
Did I interpret right the voice that spake
Within this tomb? Ah, I was lost—alone
Before an Empire—a wide howling world
That threatened and conspired! There
were the Danes
To punish, and the Holy Father's self
To compensate—with Venice—Soliman,
Francis, and Luther—and a thousand
dirks
Gleaming already in the shade—snares—
rocks;
And countless foes; a score of nations
each

Of which might serve to awe a score of
kings.
Things ripe, all pressing to be done at
once.
I cried to thee—with what shall I begin?
And thou didst answer—Son, by clem-
ency!

ACT V

*Saragossa. A terrace of the palace of
Aragon. At the back a flight of steps
leading to the garden. At the right and
left, doors on to a terrace which shows
at the back of the stage a balustrade sur-
mounted by a double row of Moorish
arches, above and through which are seen
the palace gardens, fountains in the shade,
shrubberies and moving lights, and the
Gothic and Arabic arches of the palace
illuminated. It is night. Trumpets afar
off are heard. Masks and dominoes, either
singly or in groups, cross the terrace here
and there. At the front of the stage a
group of young lords, their masks in their
hands, laugh and chat noisily.*

[*Enter* DON SANCHO SANCHEZ DE ZUÑIGA,
COUNT DE MONTEREY, DON MATIAS CEN-
TURION, MARQUIS D'ALMUÑAN, DON RI-
CARDO DE ROXAS, COUNT DE CASAPALMA,
DON FRANCISCO DE SOTOMAYOR, COUNT DE
VALALCAZAR, DON GARCIA SUAREZ DE
CARBAJAL, COUNT DE PENALVER.]
DON GARCIA. Now to the bride long
life—and joy—I say!
DON MATIAS [*looking to the balcony*].
All Saragossa at its windows shows.
DON GARCIA. And they do well. A
torchlight wedding ne'er
Was seen more gay than this, nor love-
lier night,
Nor handsomer married pair.
DON MATIAS. Kind Emp'ror!
DON SANCHO. When we went with him
in the dark that night
Seeking adventure, Marquis, who'd have
thought
How it would end?
DON RICARDO [*interrupting*]. I, too

was there. [*To the others.*] Now,
list.
Three gallants, one a bandit, his head due
Unto the scaffold; then a duke, a king,
Adoring the same woman, all laid siege
At the same time. The onset made—who
won?
It was the bandit.
Don Francisco. Nothing strange in
that,
For love and fortune, in all other lands
As well as Spain, are sport of the cogg'd
dice.
It is the rogue who wins.
Don Ricardo. My fortune grew
In seeing the love-making. First a count
And then grandee, and next an alcalde
At court. My time was well spent, though
without
One knowing it.
Don Sancho. Your secret, sir, appears
To be the keeping close upon the heels
O' the King.
Don Ricardo. And showing that my
conduct's worth
Reward.
Don Garcia. And by a chance you
profited.
Don Matias. What has become of the
old Duke? Has he
His coffin ordered?
Don Sancho. Marquis, jest not thus
At him! For he a haughty spirit
has;
And this old man loved well the Doña
Sol.
His sixty years had turned his hair to
gray,
One day has bleached it.
Don Garcia. Not again, they say,
Has he been seen in Saragossa.
Don Sancho. Well?
Wouldst thou that to the bridal he should
bring
His coffin?
Don Francisco. What's the Emperor
doing now?
Don Sancho. The Emperor is out of
sorts just now,
Luther annoys him.
Don Ricardo. Luther!—subject fine

For care and fear! Soon would I finish
him
With but four men-at-arms!
Don Matias. And Soliman
Makes him dejected.
Don Garcia. Luther—Soliman—
Neptune—the devil—Jupiter! What are
They all to me? The women are most
fair,
The masquerade is splendid, and I've said
A hundred foolish things!
Don Sancho. Behold you now
The chief thing.
Don Ricardo. Garcia's not far wrong,
I say.
Not the same man am I on festal days.
When I put on the mask in truth I
think
Another head it gives me.
Don Sancho [*apart to* Don Matias].
Pity 't is
That all days are not festivals!
Don Francisco. Are those
Their rooms?
Don Garcia [*with a nod of his head*].
Arrive they will, no doubt, full soon.
Don Francisco. Dost think so?
Don Garcia. Most undoubtedly!
Don Francisco. 'T is well.
The bride is lovely!
Don Ricardo. What an Emperor!
The rebel chief, Hernani, to be pardoned—
Wearing the Golden Fleece! and married
too!
Ah, if the Emperor had been by me
Advised, the gallant should have had a bed
Of stone, the lady one of down.
Don Sancho [*aside to* Don Matias].
How well
I'd like with my good sword this lord to
smash,
A lord made up of tinsel coarsely joined;
Pourpoint of count filled out with bailiff's
soul!
Don Ricardo [*drawing near*]. What
are you saying?
Don Matias [*aside to* Don Sancho].
Count, no quarrel here!
[*To* Don Ricardo.] He was reciting one
of Petrarch's sonnets
Unto his lady love.

DON GARCIA. Have you not seen
Among the flowers and women, and dresses
gay
Of many hues, a figure specter-like,
Whose domino all black, upright against
A balustrade, seems like a spot upon
The festival?
DON RICARDO. Yes, by my faith!
DON GARCIA. Who is 't?
DON RICARDO. By height and mien I
judge that it must be—
The Admiral—the Don Prancasio.
DON FRANCISCO. Oh, no.
DON GARCIA. He has not taken off his
mask.
DON FRANCISCO. There is no need; it
is the Duke de Soma,
Who likes to be observed. 'T is nothing
more.
DON RICARDO. No; the Duke spoke to
me.
DON GARCIA. Who, then, can be
This Mask! But see—he's here.

[*Enter a* BLACK DOMINO, *who slowly
crosses the back of the stage. All turn
and watch him without his appearing to
notice them.*]
DON SANCHO. If the dead walk,
That is their step.
DON GARCIA [*approaching the* BLACK
DOMINO]. Most noble Mask——
    [*The* BLACK DOMINO *stops and
    turns.* GARCIA *recoils.*]
I swear,
Good sirs, that I saw flame shine in his
eyes.
DON SANCHO. If he's the devil, he'll
find one he can
Address. [*He goes to the* BLACK DOMINO,
who is still motionless.]
Ho, Demon! Comest thou from hell?
THE MASK. I come not thence—'t is
thither that I go.
    [*He continues his walk and dis-
    appears at the balustrade of
    the staircase. All watch him
    with a look of horrified dis-
    may.*]
DON MATIAS. Sepulchral is his voice,
as can be heard.

DON GARCIA. Pshaw! What would
frighten elsewhere, at a ball
We laugh at.
DON SANCHO. Silly jesting 't is!
DON GARCIA. Indeed,
If Lucifer is come to see us dance,
Waiting for lower regions, let us dance!
DON SANCHO. Of course it's some buf-
foonery.
DON MATIAS. We'll know
To-morrow.
DON SANCHO [*to* DON MATIAS]. Look
now what becomes of him,
I pray you!
DON MATIAS [*at the balustrade of the
terrace*]. Down the steps he's gone.
That's all.
DON SANCHO. A pleasant jester he!
[*Musing.*] 'T is strange.
DON GARCIA [*to lady passing*]. Mar-
quise,
Let us pray dance this time. [*He bows
and offers his hand.*]
THE LADY. You know, dear sir,
My husband will my dances with you all
Count up.
DON GARCIA. All the more reason.
Pleased is he
To count, it seems, and it amuses him.
He calculates—we dance.
    [*The lady gives her hand. Ex-
    eunt.*]
DON SANCHO [*thoughtfully*]. In truth,
't is strange!
DON MATIAS. Behold the married pair!
Now, silence all!

[*Enter* HERNANI *and* DOÑA SOL *hand in
hand.* DOÑA SOL *in magnificent bridal
dress.* HERNANI *in black velvet and with
the Golden Fleece hanging from his neck.
Behind them a crowd of Masks and of
ladies and gentlemen who form their
retinue. Two halberdiers in rich liveries
follow them, and four pages precede them.
Every one makes way for them and bows
as they approach. Flourish of trumpets.*]
HERNANI [*saluting*]. Dear friends!
DON RICARDO [*advancing and bowing*].
    Your Excellency's happiness
Makes ours.

DON FRANCISCO [looking at DOÑA SOL). Now, by St. James, 't is Venus' self That he is leading.

DON MATIAS. Happiness is his!

DON SANCHO [to DON MATIUS]. 'T is late now, let us leave.

[All salute the married pair and retire—some by the door, others by the stairway at the back.]

HERNANI [escorting them]. Adieu!

DON SANCHO [who has remained to the last, and pressing his handle]. Be happy!

[Exit DON SANCHO. HERNANI and DOÑA SOL remain alone. The sound of voices grows fainter and fainter till it ceases altogether. During the early part of the following scene the sound of trumpets grows fainter, and the lights by degrees are extinguished— till night and silence prevail.]

DOÑA SOL. At last they all are gone.

HERNANI [seeking to draw her to his arms]. Dear love!

DOÑA SOL [drawing back a little]. Is't late?—

At least to me it seems so.

HERNANI. Angel, dear, Time ever drags till we together are.

DOÑA SOL. This noise has wearied me. Is it not true, Dear lord, that all this mirth but stifling is To happiness?

HERNANI. Thou sayest truly, love, For happiness is serious, and asks For hearts of bronze on which to 'grave itself. Pleasure alarms it, flinging to it flowers; Its smile is nearer tears than mirth.

DOÑA SOL. Thy smile's Like daylight in thine eyes.

[HERNANI seeks to lead her to the door.]

Oh, presently.

HERNANI. I am thy slave; yes, linger if thou wilt, Whate'er thou dost is well. I'll laugh and sing

If thou desirest that it should be so. Bid the volcano stifle flame, and 't will Close up its gulfs, and on its sides grow flowers, And grasses green.

DOÑA SOL. How good you are to me, My heart's Hernani!

HERNANI. Madam, what name's that? I pray in pity speak it not again! Thou call'st to mind forgotten things. I know That he existed formerly in dreams, Hernani, he whose eyes flashed like a sword, A man of night and of the hills, a man Proscribed, on whom was seen writ everywhere The one word vengeance. An unhappy man That drew down malediction! I know not The man they called Hernani. As for me, I love the birds and flowers, and woods— and song Of nightingale. I'm Juan of Aragon, The spouse of Doña Sol—a happy man!

DOÑA SOL. Happy am I!

HERNANI. What does it matter now, The rags I left behind me at the door! Behold, I to my palace desolate Come back. Upon the threshold-sill there waits For me an angel; I come in and lift Upright the broken columns, kindle fire, And ope again the windows; and the grass Upon the courtyard I have all pluck'd up; For me there is but joy, enchantment, love, Let them give back my towers, and donjon-keep, My plume, and seat at the Castilian board Of council, comes my blushing Doña Sol, Let them leave us—the rest forgotten is. Nothing I've seen, nor said, nor have I done. Anew my life begins, the past effacing. Wisdom or madness, you I have and love, And you are all my joy!

DOÑA SOL. How well upon The velvet black the golden collar shows!

HERNANI. You saw it on the King ere
now on me.

DOÑA SOL. I did not notice. Others,
what are they

To me? Besides, the velvet is it, or
The satin? No, my Duke, it is thy neck
Which suits the golden collar. Thou art
proud

And noble, my own lord.
[*He seeks to lead her indoors.*] Oh, pres-
ently,

A moment! See you not, I weep with
joy?

Come look upon the lovely night. [*She
goes to the balustrade.*] My Duke,

Only a moment—but the time to breathe
And gaze. All now is o'er, the torches
out,

The music done. Night only is with us.
Felicity most perfect! Think you not
That now while all is still and slumber-
ing,

Nature, half waking, watches us with
love?

No cloud is in the sky. All things like
us

Are now at rest. Come, breathe with me
the air

Perfumed by roses. Look, there is no
light,

Nor hear we any noise. Silence prevails.
The moon just now from the horizon
rose

E'en while you spoke to me; her trem-
bling light

And thy dear voice together reached my
heart.

Joyous and softly calm I felt, oh, thou
My lover! And it seemed that I would
then

Most willingly have died.

HERNANI. Ah, who is there

Would not all things forget when listen-
ing thus

Unto this voice celestial! Thy speech
But seems a chant with nothing human
mixed,

And as with one, who gliding down a
stream

On summer eve, sees pass before his
eyes

A thousand flowery plains, my thoughts
are drawn

Into thy reveries!

DOÑA SOL. This silence is

Too deep, and too profound the calm.
Say, now,

Wouldst thou not like to see a star shine
forth

From out the depths—or hear a voice of
night,

Tender and sweet, raise suddenly its
song?

HERNANI [*smiling*]. Capricious one!
Just now you fled away

From all the songs and lights.

DOÑA SOL. Ah, yes, the ball!
But yet a bird that in the meadow sings,
A nightingale in moss or shadow lost,
Or flute far off. For music sweet can
pour

Into the soul a harmony divine,
That like a heavenly choir wakes in the
heart

A thousand voices! Charming would it
be!

[*They hear the sound of a horn
from the shade.*]

My prayer is heard.

HERNANI [*aside, trembling*]. Oh, miser-
able man!

DOÑA SOL. An angel read my thought
—'t was thy good angel

Doubtless?

HERNANI [*bitterly*]. Yes, my good
angel! [*Aside.*] There, again!

DOÑA SOL [*smiling*]. Don Juan, I rec-
ognize your horn.

HERNANI. Is't so?

DOÑA SOL. The half this serenade to
you belongs?

HERNANI. The half, thou hast declared
it.

DOÑA SOL. Ah, the ball

Detestable! Far better do I love
The horn that sounds from out the woods!
And since

It is your horn 't is like your voice to
me.

[*The horn sounds again.*]

HERNANI [*aside*]. It is the tiger howl-
ing for his prey!

DOÑA SOL. Don Juan, this music fills my heart with joy.

HERNANI [drawing himself up and looking terrible]. Call me Hernani! call me it again! For with that fatal name I have not done.

DOÑA SOL [trembling]. What ails you?

HERNANI. The old man!

DOÑA SOL. O God, what looks! What is it ails you?

HERNANI. That old man who in The darkness laughs. Can you not see him there?

DOÑA SOL. Oh, you are wand'ring! Who is this old man?

HERNANI. The old man!

DOÑA SOL. On my knees I do entreat Thee, say what is the secret that afflicts Thee thus?

HERNANI. I swore it!

DOÑA SOL. Swore! [She watches his movements with anxiety. He stops suddenly and passes his hand across his brow.]

HERNANI [aside]. What have I said? Oh, let me spare her. [Aloud.] I— nought. What was it I said?

DOÑA SOL. You said—

HERNANI. No, no, I was disturbed— And somewhat suffering I am. Do not Be frightened.

DOÑA SOL. You need something? Order me, Thy servant. [The horn sounds again.]

HERNANI [aside]. Ah, he claims! He claims the pledge! [Feeling for his dagger.] Not there. It must be done! Ah!—

DOÑA SOL. Suff'rest thou so much?

HERNANI. 'T is an old wound That I thought healed—it has reopened now. [Aside]. She must be got away. [Aloud.] My best beloved, Now, listen; there's a little box that in Less happy days I carried with me—

DOÑA SOL. Ah,

I know what 't is you mean. Tell me your wish.

HERNANI. It holds a flask of an elixir which Will end my sufferings.—Go!

DOÑA SOL. I go, my lord. [Exit by the door to their apartments.]

HERNANI [alone]. This, then, is how my happiness must end! Behold the fatal finger that doth shine Upon the wall! My bitter destiny Still jests at me. [He falls into a profound yet convulsive reverie. Afterwards he turns abruptly.] Ah, well! I hear no sound. Am I myself deceiving?—

[THE MASK in black domino appears at balustrade of steps. HERNANI stops petrified.]

THE MASK. "Whatsoe'er May happen, what the place, or what the hour, Whenever to thy mind it seems the time Has come for me to die—blow on this horn And take no other care. All will be done." This compact had the dead for witnesses. Is it all done?

HERNANI [in a low voice]. 'T is he!

THE MASK. Unto thy home I come, I tell thee that it is the time. It is my hour. I find thee hesitate.

HERNANI. Well, then, thy pleasure say. What wouldest thou Of me?

THE MASK. I give thee choice 'twixt poison draught And blade. I bear about me both. We shall Depart together.

HERNANI. Be it so.

THE MASK. Shall we First pray?

HERNANI. What matter?

THE MASK. Which of them wilt thou?

HERNANI. The poison.

THE MASK. Then hold out your hand.

[*He gives a vial to* HERNANI, *who pales at receiving it.*]
Now drink,
That I may finish.
[HERNANI *lifts the vial to his lips, but recoils.*]
HERNANI. Oh, for pity's sake,
Until to-morrow wait! If thou hast heart
Or soul, if thou art not a specter just
Escaped from flame, if thou art not a soul
Accursed, forever lost; if on thy brow
Not yet has God inscribed his "never."
Oh,
If thou hast ever known the bliss supreme
Of loving, and at twenty years of age
Of wedding the beloved; if ever thou
Hast clasped the one thou lovedst in thine arms,
Wait till to-morrow. Then thou canst come back!
THE MASK. Childish it is for you to jest this way!
To-morrow! Why, the bell this morning toll'd
Thy funeral! And I should die this night,
And who would come and take thee after me!
I will not to the tomb descend alone,
Young man, 't is thou must go with me!
HERNANI. Well, then,
I say thee nay; and, demon, I from thee
Myself deliver. I will not obey.
THE MASK. As I expected. Very well.
On what,
Then, didst thou swear? Ah, on a trifling thing,
The mem'ry of thy father's head. With ease
Such oath may be forgotten. Youthful oaths
Are light affairs.
HERNANI. My father!—father! Oh
My senses I shall lose!
THE MASK. Oh, no,—'t is but
A perjury and treason.
HERNANI. Duke!
THE MASK. Since now
The heirs of Spanish houses make a jest

Of breaking promises, I'll say Adieu!
[*He moves as if to leave.*]
HERNANI. Stay!
THE MASK. Then—
HERNANI. Oh, cruel man. [*He raises the vial.*] Thus to return
Upon my path at heaven's door!

[*Reënter* DOÑA SOL *without seeing* THE MASK, *who is standing erect near the balustrade of the stairway at the back of the stage.*]
DOÑA SOL. I've failed
To find that little box.
HERNANI [*aside*]. O God! 't is she!
At such a moment here!
DOÑA SOL. What is't, that thus
I frighten him,—e'en at my voice he shakes!
What hold'st thou in thy hand? What fearful thought!
What hold'st thou in thy hand? Reply to me.
[*The* DOMINO *unmasks; she utters a cry in recognizing* DON RUY.]
'T is poison!
HERNANI. Oh, great Heaven!
DOÑA SOL [*to* HERNANI]. What is it
That I have done to thee? What mystery
Of horror? I'm deceived by thee, Don Juan!
HERNANI. Ah, I had thought to hide it all from thee.
My life I promised to the Duke that time
He saved it. Aragon must pay this debt
To Silva.
DOÑA SOL. Unto me you do belong,
Not him. What signify your other oaths?
[*To* DON RUY GOMEZ.] My love it is
which gives me strength, and, Duke,
I will defend him against you and all
The world.
DON RUY GOMEZ [*unmoved*]. Defend
him if you can against
An oath that's sworn.
DOÑA SOL. What oath?
HERNANI. Yes, I have sworn.
DOÑA SOL. No, no; naught binds thee;
it would be a crime,

A madness, an atrocity—no, no,
It cannot be.
Don Ruy Gomez. Come, Duke.
    [Hernani *makes a gesture to*
    obey. Doña Sol *tries to stop*
    him.]
Hernani. It must be done.
Allow it, Doña Sol. My word was pledged
To the Duke, and to my father now in
    heaven!
Doña Sol [*to* Don Ruy Gomez]. Better that to a tigress you should go
And snatch away her young, than take
    from me
Him whom I love. Know you at all what
    is
This Doña Sol? Long time I pitied
    you,
And, in compassion for your age, I seemed
The gentle girl, timid and innocent,
But now see eyes made moist by tears of
    rage.
    [*She draws a dagger from her bosom.*]
See you this dagger? Old man imbecile!
Do you not fear the steel when eyes flash
    threat?
Take care, Don Ruy! I'm of thy family.
Listen, mine uncle! Had I been your
    child
It had been ill for you, if you had laid
A hand upon my husband!
    [*She throws away the dagger,*
    and falls on her knees before
    him.]
At thy feet
I fall! Mercy! Have pity on us both.
Alas! my lord, I am but woman weak,
My strength dies out within my soul, I
    fail
So easily; 't is at your knees I plead,
I supplicate—have mercy on us both!
Don Ruy Gomez. Doña Sol!
Doña Sol. Oh, pardon! With us
    Spaniards
Grief bursts forth in stormy words, you
    know it.
Alas! you used not to be harsh! My
    uncle,
Have pity, you are killing me indeed
In touching him! Mercy, have pity now,
So well I love him!

Don Ruy Gomez [*gloomily*]. You love
    him too much!
Hernani. Thou weepest!
Doña Sol. No, my love, no, no, it must
Not be. I will not have you die.
[*To* Don Ruy.] To-day
Be merciful, and I will love you well,
You also.
Don Ruy Gomez. After him; the dregs
    you'd give,
The remnants of your love, and friendliness.
Still less and less.—Oh, think you thus to
    quench
The thirst that now devours me?
[*Pointing to* Hernani.] He alone
Is everything. For me kind pityings!
With such affection, what, pray, could I
    do?
Fury! 't is he would have your heart,
    your love,
And be enthroned, and grant a look from
    you
As alms; and if vouchsafed a kindly word
'T is he would tell you,—say so much,
    it is
Enough,—cursing in heart the greedy one
The beggar, unto whom he's forced to
    fling
The drops remaining in the emptied glass.
Oh, shame! derision! No, we'll finish.
    Drink!
Hernani. He has my promise, and it
    must be kept.
Don Ruy Gomez. Proceed.
    [Hernani *raises the vial to his*
    lips; Doña Sol *throws herself*
    on his arm.]
Doña Sol. Not yet. Deign both of
    you to hear me.
Don Ruy Gomez. The grave is open
    and I cannot wait.
Doña Sol. A moment only,—Duke,
    and my Don Juan,—
Ah! both are cruel! What is it I ask?
An instant! That is all I beg from you.
Let a poor woman speak what's in her
    heart,
Oh, let me speak—
Don Ruy Gomez. I cannot wait.
Doña Sol. My lord,

You make me tremble! What, then, have I done?

HERNANI. His crime is rending him.

DOÑA SOL [*still holding his arm*]. You see full well
I have a thousand things to say.

DON RUY GOMEZ [*to* HERNANI]. Die—die
You must.

DOÑA SOL [*still hanging on his arm*]. Don Juan, when all's said, indeed,
Thou shalt do what thou wilt.
[*She snatches the vial.*] I have it now!
[*She lifts the vial for* HERNANI *and the old man to see.*]

DON RUY GOMEZ. Since with two women I have here to deal,
It needs, Don Juan, that I elsewhere go
In search of souls. Grave oaths you took to me,
And by the race from which you sprang. I go
Unto your father, and to speak among
The dead. Adieu.
[*He moves as if to depart.* HERNANI *holds him back.*]

HERNANI. Stay, Duke.
[*To* DOÑA SOL.] Alas! I do
Implore thee. Wouldst thou wish to see in me
A perjured felon only, and e'erwhere
I go "a traitor" written on my brow?
In pity give the poison back to me.
'T is by our love I ask it, and our souls
Immortal—

DOÑA SOL [*sadly*]. And thou wilt?
[*She drinks.*] Now, take the rest.

DON RUY GOMEZ [*aside*]. 'T was, then, for her!

DOÑA SOL [*returning the half-emptied vial to* HERNANI]. I tell thee, take.

HERNANI [*to* DON RUY]. See'st thou,
Oh, miserable man!

DOÑA SOL. Grieve not for me,
I've left thy share.

HERNANI [*taking the vial*]. O God!

DOÑA SOL. Not thus would'st thou
Have left me mine. But thou! Not thine the heart
Of Christian wife! Thou knowest not to love

As Silvas do—but I've drunk first—made sure.
Now, drink it, if thou wilt!

HERNANI. What hast thou done,
Unhappy one?

DOÑA SOL. 'T was thou who willed it so.

HERNANI. It is a frightful death!

DOÑA SOL. No—no—why so?

HERNANI. This philter leads unto the grave.

DOÑA SOL. And ought
We not this night to rest together? Does
It matter in what bed?

HERNANI. My father, thou
Thyself avengest upon me, who did
Forget thee!
[*He lifts the vial to his mouth.*]

DOÑA SOL [*throwing herself on him*].
Heavens, what strange agony!
Ah, throw this philter far from thee! My reason
Is wand'ring. Stop! Alas! oh, my Don Juan,
This drug is potent, in the heart it wakes
A hydra with a thousand tearing teeth
Devouring it. I knew not that such pangs
Could be! What is the thing? 'T is liquid fire.
Drink not! For much thou'dst suffer!

HERNANI [*to* DON RUY]. Ah, thy soul
Is cruel! Could'st thou not have found for her
Another drug?
[*He drinks and throws the vial away.*]

DOÑA SOL. What dost thou?

HERNANI. What thyself
Hast done.

DOÑA SOL. Come to my arms, young lover, now.
[*They sit down close to each other.*]
Does not one suffer horribly?

HERNANI. No, no.

DOÑA SOL. These are our marriage rites! But for a bride
I'm very pale, say am I not?

HERNANI. Ah me!

DON RUY GOMEZ. Fulfilled is now the fatal destiny!

HERNANI. Oh, misery and despair to know her pangs!

DoÑa Sol. Be calm. I'm better.
Toward new brighter light
We now together open out our wings
Let us with even flight set out to reach
A fairer world. Only a kiss—a kiss!
[*They embrace.*]
Don Ruy Gomez. Oh, agony supreme!
Hernani [*in a feeble voice*]. Oh,
bless'd be Heav'n
That will'd for me a life by specters followed,
And by abysses yawning circled still,
Yet grants, that weary of a road so rough,
I fall asleep my lips upon thy hand.
Don Ruy Gomez. How happy are they!
Hernani [*in voice growing weaker and weaker*]. Come—come, Doña Sol,
All's dark. Dost thou not suffer?
DoÑa Sol [*in a voice equally faint*].
Nothing now.
Oh, nothing.

Hernani. Seest thou not fires in the gloom?
DoÑa Sol. Not yet.
Hernani [*with a sigh*]. Behold—
[*He falls.*]
Don Ruy Gomez [*raising the head, which falls again*]. He's dead!
DoÑa Sol [*disheveled and half raising herself on the seat*]. Oh, no, we sleep.
He sleeps. It is my spouse that here you see.
We love each other—we are sleeping thus.
It is our bridal. [*In a failing voice.*]
I entreat you not
To wake him, my Lord Duke of Meudocé,
For he is weary.
[*She turns round the face of* Hernani.]
Turn to me, my love.
More near—still closer— [*She falls back.*]
Don Ruy Gomez. Dead! Oh, I am
damn'd! [*He kills himself.*]

M. POIRIER'S SON-IN-LAW

By EMILE AUGIER AND JULES SANDEAU

Produced at Paris, 1855

TRANSLATED BY BARRETT H. CLARK *

CHARACTERS

POIRIER
GASTON, *Marquis de Presles*
HECTOR, *Duke de Montmeyran*
VERDELET
ANTOINETTE
SALOMON, ⎫
CHEVASSUS, ⎬ *creditors*
COGNE,   ⎭
VATEL
THE PORTER
A SERVANT

The home of M. POIRIER, *at Paris.*

ACT I

A richly-furnished drawing-room. Doors on either side, and windows at the back, looking out on the garden. A fireplace with a fire burning.

[A SERVANT *and the* DUKE *are present.*]

SERVANT. I repeat, Corporal, Monsieur le Marquis cannot possibly receive. He is not up yet.

DUKE. At nine! The sun rises slowly during the honeymoon. What time is breakfast served here?

SERVANT. At eleven; but what business is that of yours?

DUKE. You will lay another place.

SERVANT. For your colonel?

DUKE. For my colonel. Is this to-day's paper?

SERVANT. Yes: February 15, 1846.

DUKE. Give it to me.

SERVANT. I haven't read it yet.

DUKE. You refuse to let me have it?

You see, don't you, that I can't wait?
Announce me.

SERVANT. Who are you?

DUKE. The Duke de Montmeyran.

SERVANT. You're joking!

[*Enter* GASTON.]

GASTON. Why, it's. you! [*They embrace.*]

SERVANT. The devil! I've put my foot in it!

DUKE. My dear Gaston!

GASTON. My dear Hector! I'm so glad to see you!

DUKE. And I you!

GASTON. You couldn't possibly have arrived at a better time.

DUKE. How do you mean?

GASTON. Let me tell you—but, my poor fellow, the way you're dressed up! Who would recognize under that tunic one of the princes of youth, the perfect model of prodigal sons?

DUKE. Next to you, old man. We've both settled down: you have married, I have become a soldier. Whatever you may think of my uniform, I prefer my regiment to yours.

GASTON [*looking at the* DUKE'S *uniform*]. Thank you!

DUKE. Look at the tunic. It's the only costume that can keep me from boring myself to death. And this little decoration you pretend not to notice—

[*He shows his corporal's stripes.*]

GASTON. Stripes!

DUKE. Which I picked up on the field of Isly.

GASTON. And when will you get the star for bravery?

DUKE. My dear fellow, please don't joke about those things. It was all very well in the past, but to-day the Cross is my one ambition. I would willingly shed a pint of my blood for it.

GASTON. A real soldier, I see!

DUKE. Yes, I love my profession. It's the only one for a ruined gentleman. I have but one regret: that I did not enter it long ago. This active and adventurous life is infinitely attractive. Even disci-pline has its peculiar charm: it's healthy, it calms the mind—this having one's life arranged in advance, without any possible discussion, and consequently without hesitation and without regret. That's why I can feel so carefree and happy. I know my duty, I do it, and I am content.

GASTON. Without great cost on your part.

DUKE. And then, old man, those patriotic ideas we used to make fun of at the *Café de Paris* and call chauvinism, make our hearts swell when we face the enemy. The first cannon-shot knocks forever the last vestige of that nonsénse out of our minds; the flag then is no longer a bit of cloth at the end of a stick: it is the very incarnation of the *patrie*.

GASTON. That's all very well, but this enthusiasm for a flag which is not your own—

DUKE. Nonsense, you can't see its color in the midst of the powder smoke.

GASTON. The important point is that you are satisfied. Are you in Paris for some time?

DUKE. Just a month. You know how I've arranged my manner of living?

GASTON. Tell me.

DUKE. It's very clever: before leaving I place the remains of my fortune with a certain banker: about a hundred thousand francs, the income from which allows me during one month in the year to live as I used to. So that I live for one month at a six thousand francs' rate, and for the rest of the year on six sous a day. Naturally, I have chosen carnival season for my prodigalities. It began yesterday, but my first visit was to you.

GASTON. Thanks! But I shan't hear of your staying anywhere but here.

DUKE. I don't want to be in the way.

GASTON. You shan't be: there's a small pavilion here, at the end of the garden.

DUKE. To be perfectly frank; I'm not afraid of you, but of myself. You see, you lead a family life here: there's your wife, your father-in-law—

GASTON. You imagine that, simply because I have married the daughter of a retired dry-goods merchant, my home is a temple of boredom, that my wife brought with her a heap of bourgeois virtues, that all that remains for me is write an inscription over my door: "Here lies Gaston Marquis de Presles." Make no mistake, I live like a prince, race my horses, gamble like the devil, buy pictures, have the finest chef in Paris,—the fellow pretends he's a direct descendant of Vatel, and takes his art ever so seriously,—I invite whom I like to meals (by the way, you'll dine with all my friends to-morrow, and you'll see how I treat them). In short, marriage has not changed me in the least, except to rid me of my creditors.

DUKE. So your wife and father-in-law leave you free?

GASTON. Absolutely. My wife is a nice little boarding-school miss, rather pretty, somewhat awkward, timid, still wide-eyed with wonder at the sudden change in her station in life, passing the greater part of her time, I'll warrant, looking at the Marquise de Presles in her mirror. As for Monsieur Poirier, my father-in-law, he is worthy of his name. Modest and nutritious like all fruit-trees, he was born to the part. His highest ambition is to serve as a gentleman's dessert: that ambition is now satisfied.

DUKE. Do such bourgeois still exist?

GASTON. In a word, he is Georges Dandin become a father-in-law. Really, I've made a magnificent match.

DUKE. I can well believe you had good reasons for contracting this misalliance.

GASTON. Judge for yourself. You know the desperate straits I was in? An orphan at fifteen, and master of a fortune at twenty. I quickly spent my patrimony and was rapidly running up a capital of debts, worthy the nephew of my uncle. Now, at the very moment when that capital reached the figure of five hundred thousand francs, thanks to my activities, what did my seventy-year-old uncle do but marry a young girl who had fallen in love with him? Corvisart said that at seventy one always has children. I didn't count on cousins, but it soon became necessary.

DUKE. And you then occupied the position of honorary nephew.

GASTON. I thought of taking a position in the rank of active sons-in-law. At that time heaven sent Monsieur Poirier across my path.

DUKE. How did you happen to meet him?

GASTON. He had some money he wanted to invest—it was the merest chance. I lacked sufficient guarantee as a debtor, but I offered him enough as a son-in-law. I made inquiries about his person, assured myself that his fortune had been honorably acquired, and then, by Jove, I married his daughter.

DUKE. And he gave you—?

GASTON. The old fellow had four millions; now he has only three.

DUKE. A dowry of a million?

GASTON. Better still: he agreed to pay my debts. By the way, to-day a visible proof of the phenomenon can be seen, I believe. It was a matter of five hundred thousand francs. The day we signed the contract he gave me stock which will net me an income of twenty-five thousand; five hundred thousand francs more!

DUKE. There's your million. And then?

GASTON. He insisted on not being separated from his daughter and agreed to defray all household expenses so long as we lived with him. So, after receiving lodging, heat, carriages and board, I still have an income of twenty-five thousand for my wife and myself.

DUKE. Very neat.

GASTON. Wait a moment.

DUKE. Something else?

GASTON. He bought back the Château de Presles, and I expect any day to find the deeds under my plate at breakfast.

DUKE. A delightful father-in-law!

GASTON. Wait a moment!

DUKE. More?

GASTON. As soon as the contract was signed, he came to me, took my hands in his, and made profuse excuses for being no more than sixty years old; but he assured me that he would hurry on to the age of eighty. But I'm in no great haste

—he's not in the way, poor man. He knows his place, goes to bed with the chickens, rises at cock-crow, keeps his accounts and is ready to satisfy my every whim. He is a steward who does not rob me; I should have to look long to find a better.

DUKE. Really, you are the most fortunate of men.

GASTON. And wait—you might imagine that my marriage has lessened me in the eyes of the world, that it has "taken the shine out of me," as Monsieur Poirier says. Never worry, I still hold my place in the social world. I still lead in matters of fashion. The women have forgiven me. As I was saying, you have arrived in the nick of time.

DUKE. Why?

GASTON. Don't you understand, you, my born second?

DUKE. A duel?

GASTON. Yes, a nice little duel, as in the days of our youth. Well, what do you say? Is the old Marquis de Presles dead? Are you thinking of burying him yet?

DUKE. Whom are you fighting with, and why?

GASTON. The Viscount de Pontgrimaud —a gambling quarrel.

DUKE. Gambling quarrel? Can't it be decided otherwise?

GASTON. Is that the way you are taught to regulate affairs of honor in the regiment?

DUKE. Yes, in the regiment. There we are taught what use to make of our blood. But you can't persuade me that you must shed it over a gambling quarrel?

GASTON. But what if this particular quarrel were only a pretext? What if there be something else behind it?

DUKE. A woman!

GASTON. That's it.

DUKE. An intrigue—so soon? That's bad!

GASTON. How could I help it? A last year's passion I had imagined dead of the cold, and which, a month after my marriage had its Indian Summer. There's nothing serious in it, and no cause for worry.

DUKE. And might I know?

GASTON. I can have no secrets from you: the Countess de Montjay.

DUKE. My compliments, but the matter *is* serious. I once thought of making love to her, but I retired before the dangers of such an intrigue—that sort of danger has little enough chivalry in it. You know, of course, that the Countess has no money of her own?

GASTON. That she is waiting for the fortune of her aged husband; that he would have the bad taste to disinherit her in case he discovered her guilt? I know all that.

DUKE. And out of sheer lightness of heart you have imposed that bond on yourself?

GASTON. Habit, a certain residue of my former love, the temptation of forbidden fruit, the pleasure of cutting out that little fool Pontgrimaud, whom I detest—

DUKE. You're doing him an honor!

GASTON. What else can I do? He gets on my nerves, the little imp; he imagines he is a noble by reason of his knightly achievements, simply because his grandfather Monsieur Grimaud supplied arms to the Government. He's a Viscount, Heaven knows how or why, and imagines that he belongs to a nobility older than our own. He never loses an opportunity to pose as champion of the nobility, and tries to make people believe for that very reason that he represents it. If a Montmorency is scratched, he howls as if he himself had been hit. I tell you there was a quarrel brewing between us and last night it came to a head over a game of cards. I'll let him off with a scratch— the first in the history of his family.

DUKE. Has he sent his seconds to you?

GASTON. I expect them at any moment. You and Grandlieu will help me.

DUKE. Very well.

GASTON. Of course, you will stay with me?

DUKE. Delighted.

GASTON. Though this is carnival season, you don't intend to parade about as a hero, do you?

DUKE. No, I've written to my tailor—

GASTON. Wait! I hear some one talking. It's my father-in-law. You'll now have an opportunity of seeing him, with his old friend Verdelet, a former partner. You're in luck!

[*Enter* POIRIER *and* VERDELET.]

GASTON. How are you, Monsieur Verdelet?

VERDELET. Your servant, messieurs.

GASTON. A dear friend of mine, my dear Monsieur Poirier: the Duke de Montmeyran.

DUKE. Corporal of the African Cavalry.

VERDELET [*aside*]. Indeed!

POIRIER. Most honored, Monsieur le Duc!

GASTON. More honored than you think, dear Monsieur Poirier: for Monsieur le Duc has been good enough to accept the hospitality I have offered him.

VERDELET [*aside*]. Another rat in the cheese!

DUKE. I beg your pardon, monsieur, for having accepted an invitation which my friend Gaston has possibly been a trifle too hasty in offering.

POIRIER. Monsieur le Marquis, my son-in-law, need never feel obliged to consult me before inviting his friends to stay with him here. The friends of our friends—

GASTON. Very well, Monsieur Poirier. Hector will stay in the garden pavilion. Is it ready?

POIRIER. I shall attend to it at once.

DUKE. I am very sorry, monsieur, to cause you any annoyance.

GASTON. None at all; Monsieur Poirier will be only too happy—

POIRIER. Too happy!

GASTON. And you will of course give orders that the little blue coupé be placed at his disposal?

POIRIER. The one I usually use?

DUKE. Oh, I positively refuse—

POIRIER. But I can easily hire one; there is a stand at the end of the street.

VERDELET [*aside*]. Fool! Idiot!

GASTON [*to the* DUKE]. Now, let us take a look at the stables. Yesterday I got a superb Arabian—tell me what you think of him. Come.

DUKE [*to* POIRIER]. With your permission, monsieur. Gaston is impatient to show me his luxurious surroundings. I don't blame him. He can then tell me more about you.

POIRIER. Monsieur le Duc is well acquainted with my son-law's delicate nature and tastes.

GASTON [*aside to the* DUKE]. You'll spoil my father-in-law! [*Going toward the door, and stopping.*] By the way, Monsieur Poirier, you know I am giving an elaborate dinner party to-morrow night. Will you give us the pleasure of your company?

POIRIER. No, thank you, I am dining with Verdelet.

GASTON. Ah, Monsieur Verdelet, I am angry with you for carrying off my father-in-law every time I have company.

VERDELET [*aside*]. Impertinent!

POIRIER. A man of my age would only be in the way!

VERDELET [*aside*]. You old Géronte!

GASTON. As you please, Monsieur Poirier. [*He goes out with the* DUKE.]

VERDELET. That son-in-law of yours is mighty obsequious with you. You told me beforehand you'd know how to make him respect you.

POIRIER. I'm doing what pleases me. I prefer to be loved than feared.

VERDELET. You've not always thought that way. Well, you've succeeded: your son-in-law is on a more familiar footing with you than with the other servants.

POIRIER. I can do without your clever remarks, and I advise you to mind your own business.

VERDELET. This is my own business, I tell you! Aren't we partners? Why, we're a bit like the Siamese twins. When you grovel before that marquis, I have a hard time keeping my temper.

POIRIER. Grovel? That marquis! Do you think I am dazzled by his title? I've always been more of a Liberal than you, and I still am. I don't care a snap of my finger for the nobility! Ability and virtue are the only social distinctions I recognize and before which I bow down.

VERDELET. Is your son-in-law virtuous?

POIRIER. You make me tired. Do you want me to make him feel he owes everything to me?

VERDELET. Oh, oh; you have become very considerate in your old age, doubtless the result of your economical habits. Look here, Poirier, I never did approve of this marriage; you know I always wanted my dear goddaughter to marry a man of our own class. But you refused to listen to reason.

POIRIER. Listen to monsieur! That's the last straw!

VERDELET. Well, why not?

POIRIER. Monsieur Verdelet, you are most clever and you have the noblest ideals; you have read amusing books, you have your own ideas on every subject, but in the matter of commonsense I can give you enormous odds.

VERDELET. Oh, as to commonsense— you mean business sense. I don't deny that: you've piled up four millions, while I've barely made forty thousand a year.

POIRIER. And that you owe to me.

VERDELET. I don't deny it. What I have I owe to you. But it is all going eventually to your daughter, after your son-in-law has ruined you.

POIRIER. Ruined me?

VERDELET. Yes—in ten years' time.

POIRIER. You're crazy.

VERDELET. At the rate he's going now, you know only too well how long it will take him to run through his money.

POIRIER. That's my business.

VERDELET. If you were the only one concerned I'd never open my lips.

POIRIER. Why not? Don't you take any interest in my welfare? You don't care if I am ruined? I, who have made your fortune?

VERDELET. What is the matter with you?

POIRIER. I don't like ungrateful people.

VERDELET. The devil! You're taking out your son-in-law's familiarities on me.

I was going to say, if you were the only one concerned, I could at least be patient about it: you aren't my godson, but it happens that your daughter is my goddaughter.

POIRIER. I was a fool to give you that right over her.

VERDELET. You might easily have found someone who loved her less.

POIRIER. Yes, I know—you love her more than I do. I know, you claim that, and you've even persuaded her—

VERDELET. Are we going to quarrel about that again? For Heaven's sake, then, go ahead!

POIRIER. I will! Do you think I like to see myself left out and pushed aside by a stranger? Have I no place in my own daughter's heart?

VERDELET. She has the tenderest affection for you.

POIRIER. That's not so: you've taken my place. All her secrets, all her nice pleasing little ways are for you.

VERDELET. Because I don't frighten her. How can you expect the little one to be confidential with an old bear like you? She can never find an opening, you're always so crabbed.

POIRIER. You are the one who has made me play the part of a kill-joy, while you usurp that of a sugar-plum father. It's not right to make up to children by giving in to all their wishes, and forgetting what's good for them. That's loving them for your sake instead of for theirs.

VERDELET. Now, Poirier, you know very well that when the real interests of your daughter were at stake, her whims were opposed by me, and by me alone. Heaven knows, I went against poor Toinon's wishes in this marriage, while you were ass enough to urge her on.

POIRIER. She was in love with the Marquis.—Let me read my paper.

[He sits down and runs his eyes over the "Constitutionnel."]

VERDELET. It's all very well for you to say the child was in love: you forced her into it. You brought the Marquis de Presles here.

POIRIER [*rising*]. Another one has arrived at the top! Monsieur Michaud, the ironmaster, has just been appointed a peer of France.

VERDELET. What do I care?

POIRIER. What do you care! Does it make no difference to you to see a man of our class arrive at the top? To see the Government honor industry by calling one of her representatives into its midst? Don't you think it admirable that we live in a country and age in which labor opens every door? You have a right to look forward to becoming a peer some day, and you ask, "What do I care?"

VERDELET. Heaven preserve me from aspiring to the peerage! And Heaven preserve my country should I become a peer!

POIRIER. But why? Can't Monsieur Michaud fill his position?

VERDELET. Monsieur Michaud is not only a business man, but a man of great personal merit. Molière's father was an upholsterer, but that is no reason why every upholsterer's son should believe himself a writer.

POIRIER. I tell you, commerce is the true school for statesmen. Who shall lay his hand on the wheel unless it is those who have first learned to steer their own barks?

VERDELET. A bark is not a ship, a little captain is not necessarily a true pilot, and France is no commercial house. I can hardly restrain myself when I see this mania taking root in people's minds. I declare, you might imagine that statesmanship in this country was nothing more than a pastime for people who have nothing else to do! A business man like you or me attends to his own little concerns for thirty years; he makes his fortune and one fine day closes his shop and sets up as a statesman. With no more effort than that! How simple! Good Lord, messieurs, you might just as well say, "I have measured so many yards of cloth, and I therefore know how to play the violin!"

POIRIER. I don't exactly see what connection—?

VERDELET. Instead of thinking about governing France, learn to govern your own home. Don't marry off your daughters to ruined marquesses who imagine they are doing you an honor in allowing you to pay off their debts with your own hard cash.

POIRIER. Are you saying that for my benefit?

VERDELET. No; for my own!

[*Enter* ANTOINETTE.]

ANTOINETTE. How are you, father? How is everything? Hello, godfather. Are you going to lunch with us? How nice you are!

POIRIER. He is nice. But what am I, I who invited him?

ANTOINETTE. You are charming.

POIRIER. But only when I invite Verdelet. Agreeable for me!

ANTOINETTE. Where is my husband?

POIRIER. In the stable. Where else would he be?

ANTOINETTE. Do you blame him for liking horses? Isn't it natural for a gentleman to like horses and arms?

POIRIER. I wish he cared for something else.

ANTOINETTE. He is very fond of the arts: poetry, painting, music.

POIRIER. Huh, the agreeable arts! Pleasures!

VERDELET. Would you expect him to care for the unpleasant arts? Would you want him to play the piano?

POIRIER. There you are again, taking his part before Toinon. You're trying to get into her good graces. [*To* ANTOINETTE.] He was just saying that your husband was ruining me. Didn't you?

VERDELET. Yes, but all you have to do is to pull tight your purse-strings.

POIRIER. It would be much simpler if the young man had some occupation.

VERDELET. It seems to me that he is very much occupied as it is.

POIRIER. Yes: spending money from morning till night. I'd prefer a more lucrative occupation.

ANTOINETTE. What, for instance? He can't sell cloth.

POIRIER. He wouldn't be able to. I don't ask for so very much, after all. Let him take a position that befits his rank: an embassy, for instance.

VERDELET. An embassy? You don't take an embassy the way you take cold.

POIRIER. When a man is called the Marquis de Presles, he can aspire to anything.

ANTOINETTE. On the other hand, father, he need not aspire to anything.

VERDELET. True. Your son-in-law has his own ideas.

POIRIER. Only one: to be lazy.

ANTOINETTE. That's not fair, father: my husband has very fine ideals.

VERDELET. At least, if he hasn't, he possesses that chivalrous obstinacy of his rank. Do you think for one moment that your son-in-law is going to give up the traditions of his family, just for the sake of changing his lazy life?

POIRIER. You don't know my son-in-law, Verdelet; I have studied him thoroughly—I did that before giving my daughter to him. He's hare-brained, and the lightness of his character prevents his being obstinate. As to his family traditions, well, if he had thought very much of them he would never have married Mademoiselle Poirier.

VERDELET. That makes no difference. It would have been much wiser to have sounded him on this subject before the marriage.

POIRIER. What a fool you are! It would have looked as if I were making a bargain with him, and he would have refused point-blank. You can't get things of that sort unless you go about it in the right way, slowly, tenaciously, perseveringly. He has been living here this past three months on the fat of the land.

VERDELET. I see: you wanted to make it pleasant for him before you came down to business.

POIRIER. Exactly. [*To* ANTOINETTE.] A man is always indulgent toward his wife during the honeymoon. Now, if you ask him in a nice way—in the evening—when you're taking down your hair—?

ANTOINETTE. Oh, father!

POIRIER. That's the way Madame Poirier used to get me to promise to take her to the Opéra. I always took her the next day. See?

ANTOINETTE. But I'd never dare speak to my husband on so serious a subject.

POIRIER. Your dowry will surely give you a good enough right to speak.

ANTOINETTE. He would only shrug his shoulders, and not answer.

VERDELET. Does he do that when you talk with him?

ANTOINETTE. No, but—

VERDELET. Ah, you look away! So your husband treats you a little—? I've been afraid of that.

POIRIER. Have you any reason to complain of him?

ANTOINETTE. No, father.

POIRIER. Doesn't he love you?

ANTOINETTE. I don't say that.

POIRIER. Then what do you say?

ANTOINETTE. Nothing.

VERDELET. Come, dear, you should speak frankly with your old friends. Our whole object in life is to provide for your happiness. Whom have you left to confide in unless it's your father and your godfather? Are you unhappy?

ANTOINETTE. I haven't the right to be: my husband is very kind and good.

POIRIER. Well?

VERDELET. Is that enough? He's kind and good, but he pays no more attention to you than to some pretty doll, is that it?

ANTOINETTE. It's my fault. I'm so timid with him; I've never dared open my heart. I'm sure he thinks me a little boarding-school miss who wanted to become a marquise.

POIRIER. The fool!

VERDELET. Why don't you explain to him?

ANTOINETTE. I tried to more than once, but the tone of his first answer was so different from what I thought it should be, I couldn't go on. There are certain kinds of intimacy that must be encouraged; the heart has a reticence of its own.

You ought to be able to understand that, dear Tony?

POIRIER. Well, what about me? Don't I understand, too?

ANTOINETTE. You, too, father. How can I tell Gaston that it wasn't his title that pleased me, but his manners, his mind, his knightly bearing, his contempt for the pettinesses of life? How can I tell him that he is the man of my dreams? how can I do that if he stops me at once with some joke?

POIRIER. That shows the boy is in a good humor.

VERDELET. No: it's because his wife bores him.

POIRIER [to ANTOINETTE]. Do you bore your husband?

ANTOINETTE. I'm afraid I do!

POIRIER. I tell you it isn't you, it's his own confounded laziness that bores him. A husband doesn't love his wife very long when he has nothing else to do.

ANTOINETTE. Is that true, Tony?

POIRIER. I'm telling you! You needn't ask Verdelet.

VERDELET. Yes, I do believe that passion is soon exhausted unless it is managed like a fortune: economically.

POIRIER. Every man wants to be actively engaged in some pursuit. When his way is barred, that desire is wasted, lost.

VERDELET. A wife should be the preoccupation, not the occupation, of her husband.

POIRIER. Why did I always adore your mother? Because I never had time to think about her.

VERDELET. Your husband has twenty-four hours a day to love you.

POIRIER. That's twelve too many.

ANTOINETTE. You're opening my eyes.

POIRIER. Let him take a position and everything will turn out satisfactorily.

ANTOINETTE. What do you say, Tony?

VERDELET. Possibly! The difficulty is in making him take the position.

POIRIER. Leave the matter in my hands.

VERDELET. Are you going to attack the question at once?

POIRIER. No, after lunch. I have noticed that the Marquis is in splendid humor after his meals.

[Enter GASTON and the DUKE.]

GASTON [introducing the DUKE to his wife]. My dear Antoinette, Monsieur de Montmeyran, who is not entirely unknown to you.

ANTOINETTE. Gaston has told me so much about you, monsieur, that I seem to be shaking hands with an old friend.

DUKE. You are not mistaken, madame; you have made me feel that only a moment was necessary to resume, as it were, a former friendship. [Aside to the MARQUIS.] Your wife is charming.

GASTON [aside to the DUKE]. Yes, she is nice. [To ANTOINETTE.] I have some good news for you: Hector is going to stay with us during his leave.

ANTOINETTE. How good of you, monsieur! I trust your leave is a long one?

DUKE. One month, after which I return to Africa.

VERDELET. You afford us a noble example, Monsieur le Duc: you do not consider laziness a family inheritance.

GASTON [aside]. Aha! Monsieur Verdelet.

[Enter a SERVANT, carrying a picture.]

SERVANT. This picture has just come for Monsieur le Marquis.

GASTON. Lay it on that chair, by the window. There—good. [The SERVANT goes out.] Take a look at it, Montmeyran.

DUKE. Charming—beautiful evening effect! Don't you think so, madame?

ANTOINETTE. Yes—charming—and how real it is! How calm and quiet. You feel as if you would like to walk about in that silent landscape.

POIRIER [aside to VERDELET]. Peer of France!

GASTON. Look at that strip of greenish light, running between the orange tones of the horizon, and that cold blue of the rest of the sky. Splendid technique!

DUKE. Then the foreground! And the coloring, the handling of the whole thing!

GASTON. Then the almost imperceptible reflection of that little spot of water behind the foliage—charming!

POIRIER. Let's take a look at it, Verdelet. [POIRIER *and* VERDELET *go to look at the picture.*] Well? What does it represent?

VERDELET. It represents some fields at nine o'clock at night.

POIRIER. The subject isn't interesting; it doesn't *tell* anything. In my room I have an engraving showing a dog on the seashore barking at a sailor's hat. There now, you can understand that: it's clever, and simple, and touching.

GASTON. My dear Monsieur Poirier, if you like touching pictures let me have one made for you; the subject I take from nature: on the table is a little onion, cut into quarters, a poor little white onion. The knife lies beside it. Nothing at all, yet it brings tears to the eyes!

VERDELET [*aside to* POIRIER]. He's making fun of you.

POIRIER. Let him!

DUKE. Who painted this?

GASTON. Poor devil—lots of talent, but without a sou.

POIRIER. What did you pay for the picture?

GASTON. Fifty louis.

POIRIER. Fifty louis? For the picture of an unknown painter who is dying of hunger! If you'd gone around at mealtime you could have got it for twenty-five francs.

ANTOINETTE. Oh, father!

POIRIER. A fine example of misplaced generosity!

GASTON. Then you don't think that the arts should be protected?

POIRIER. Protect the arts as much as you like, but not the artists—they're all rascals or debauchees. Why, the stories they tell about them are enough to raise the hair on your head, things I couldn't repeat to my own daughter.

VERDELET [*aside to* POIRIER]. What?

POIRIER. They say that—
[*He takes* VERDELET *to one side and whispers.*]

VERDELET. And do you believe things of that kind?

POIRIER. The people who told me knew what they were talking about.

[*Enter a* SERVANT.]

SERVANT. Dinner is served.

POIRIER [*to the* SERVANT]. Bring up a bottle of 1811 Pomard. [*To the* DUKE.] The year of the comet, Monsieur le Duc—fifteen francs a bottle! The king drinks no better. [*Aside to* VERDELET.] You mustn't drink any—neither will I!

GASTON [*to the* DUKE]. Fifteen francs, the bottle to be returned when empty!

VERDELET [*aside to* POIRIER]. Are you going to allow him to make fun of you like that?

POIRIER [*aside to* VERDELET]. In matters of this sort, you must take your time.
[*They all go out.*]

ACT II

The scene is the same. VERDELET, POIRIER, GASTON, *the* DUKE, *and* ANTOINETTE *enter from the dining-room.*

GASTON. Well, Hector, what do you say? This is the house, and this is what we do every mortal day. Can you imagine a happier man than myself?

DUKE. I must confess you make me very envious; you almost reconcile me to the idea of marriage.

ANTOINETTE [*aside to* VERDELET]. Charming young man, that Duke de Montmeyran, isn't he?

VERDELET [*aside to* ANTOINETTE]. Yes, I like him.

GASTON. Monsieur Poirier, I must say you are an excellent soul. Believe me, I'm not ungrateful to you.

POIRIER. Oh, Monsieur le Marquis!

GASTON. Come, now, call me Gaston. Monsieur Verdelet, delighted to see you.

ANTOINETTE. He is a member of the family, dear.

GASTON. Shake hands, uncle!

VERDELET [*shaking hands with* GASTON —*aside*]. He's not so bad, after all!

GASTON. You can't deny, Hector, that I'm downright lucky. Monsieur Poirier, something has been weighing on my conscience. You know, you think of nothing but how to make my existence one long series of good times. Will you never give me a chance to repay you? Try, now, I beg you, to think of something I might do for you in return—anything in my power.

POIRIER. Well, since you're in so good a humor, let me have a quarter of an hour's conversation with you—a serious conversation.

DUKE. I shall be glad to retire.

POIRIER. Please don't, monsieur; be good enough to stay with us. This is to be a kind of family council. You are not in the way, any more than is Monsieur Verdelet.

GASTON. What the devil, father-in-law! A family council! Are you going to give me a legal adviser?

POIRIER. Far from it, my dear Gaston. Let us sit down.

[*They all seat themselves.*]

GASTON. Monsieur Poirier has the floor.

POIRIER. You say you are happy, my dear Gaston. That is the finest recompense I could have.

GASTON. I ask nothing better than to increase my gratitude twofold.

POIRIER. You have spent three months of your honeymoon in the lap of idleness and luxury, and I think that that part of the romance is enough. It's now time to give your attention to hard facts.

GASTON. You talk like a book, I do declare! Very well, let us give our attention to history.

POIRIER. What do you intend to do?

GASTON. To-day?

POIRIER. And to-morrow—in the future. You surely have some idea?

GASTON. Of course: to-day I intend to do what I did yesterday; to-morrow what I did to-day. I'm not capricious, even though I may appear light-hearted. So long as the future promises to be as bright as the present, I am content.

POIRIER. Yet you are far too reason-able a man to believe that the honeymoon can last forever.

GASTON. Exactly; too reasonable, and too well posted on astronomy—of course, you have read Heinrich Heine?

POIRIER. You have, haven't you, Verdelet?

VERDELET. I admit I have.

POIRIER. He passed his school-days playing truant.

GASTON. Well, when Heinrich Heine was asked what became of all the full moons, he replied that they were broken in pieces and made into stars.

POIRIER. I don't quite see.

GASTON. When our honeymoon grows old, we shall break it up and there will remain enough fragments to make a whole Milky Way.

POIRIER. Very pretty idea, I suppose.

DUKE. The sole merit of which is its extreme simplicity.

POIRIER. But, seriously, son-in-law, doesn't this lazy life you are leading seem to threaten the happiness of a young household?

GASTON. Not in the least.

VERDELET. A man of your ability shouldn't be always condemned to a life of inactivity.

GASTON. Ah, but one can resign one's self.

ANTOINETTE. Aren't you afraid that in time you may be bored, dear?

GASTON. You fail to do yourself justice, my dear.

ANTOINETTE. I am not vain enough to believe I can be everything in your life, and I must confess I should be very happy to see you follow Monsieur de Montmeyran's example.

GASTON. Do you mean that I should enlist?

ANTOINETTE. Oh, no.

GASTON. Then, what?

POIRIER. We want you to take a position worthy of your name.

GASTON. There are but three: in the army, the church, and agriculture. Choose.

POIRIER. We all owe our services to France: she is our mother.

VERDELET. I can readily understand the sorrow of a son who sees his mother remarry; I can sympathize with his not joining in the wedding festivities; but if he is honest and sincere he will not blame the mother. And if the second husband makes the mother happy the son cannot with a good conscience help offering the second husband his hand.

POIRIER. The nobility won't always keep away as it does now; it's even beginning to recognize the fact already. More than one great noble has given a good example: Monsieur de Valchevrière, Monsieur de Chazerolles, Monsieur de Mont-Louis.

GASTON. Those gentlemen did what they thought best. I am not judging them, but I cannot emulate them.

ANTOINETTE. Why not, dear?

GASTON. Ask Montmeyran.

VERDELET. Monsieur le Duc's uniform answers for him.

DUKE. Allow me, monsieur: the soldier has but one idea, to obey; but one adversary, the enemy.

POIRIER. Still, monsieur, I might answer that—

GASTON. Let us drop the subject, Monsieur Poirier; this is not a question of politics. We may discuss opinions, never sentiments. I am bound by gratitude: my fidelity is that of a servant and of a friend. Let us say no more about this. [*To the* DUKE.] I beg your pardon, my dear fellow, but this is the first time we have talked politics here and I promise it shall be the last.

DUKE [*aside to* ANTOINETTE]. You have been led into an indiscretion, madame!

ANTOINETTE [*aside to the* DUKE]. I realize it—only too late!

GASTON. I bear you no malice, Monsieur Poirier. I have been a trifle direct, but I am dreadfully thin-skinned on that subject, and, doubtless without intending it you have scratched me. I don't blame you, however. Shake hands.

POIRIER. You're only too good!

VERDELET [*aside to* POIRIER]. A pretty mess!

POIRIER [*aside to* VERDELET]. First attack repulsed, but I'm not lifting the siege.

[*Enter a* SERVANT.]

SERVANT. There are some persons in the small waiting-room who say they have an appointment with Monsieur Poirier.

POIRIER. Ask them to wait a moment. I'll be there directly. [*The* SERVANT *goes out.*] Your creditors, son-in-law.

GASTON. Yours, my dear father-in-law. I have given them to you.

DUKE. A wedding present.

VERDELET. Good-bye, Monsieur le Marquis.

GASTON. Are you leaving us so soon.

VERDELET. Very good of you. Antoinette has asked me to do something for her.

POIRIER. What?

VERDELET. It's a secret between us.

GASTON. You know, if I were inclined to be jealous—

ANTOINETTE. But you are not.

GASTON. Is that a reproach? Very well, Monsieur Verdelet. I have made up my mind to be jealous, and I ask you in the name of the law to unveil the mystery!

VERDELET. You are the last person in the world whom I should think of telling!

GASTON. And why, please?

VERDELET. You are Antoinette's right hand, and the right hand should not know what—

GASTON. The left gives. You are right; I am indiscreet. Allow me to pay my indemnity. [*He gives his purse to* ANTOINETTE.] Put this with your own, my dear child.

ANTOINETTE. Thank you on behalf of my poor.

POIRIER [*aside*]. He *is* mighty generous!

DUKE. Will you allow me, too, madame, to steal a few blessings from you? [*He also gives her his purse.*] It is not heavy, but it is the corporal's mite.

ANTOINETTE. Offered from the heart of a true duke.

POIRIER [*aside*]. Hasn't a sou to his name, and he gives to charity!

VERDELET. Aren't you going to add something, Poirier?

POIRIER. I've already given a thousand to the charity organization.

VERDELET. I see. Good-day, messieurs. Your names won't appear on the lists, but your charity won't be less welcome.

[*He goes out with* ANTOINETTE.]

POIRIER. See you later, Monsieur le Marquis; I'm going to pay your creditors.

GASTON. Now, Monsieur Poirier, simply because those fellows have lent me money is no reason why you should think you must be polite with them. They're unconscionable rascals. You must have had something to do with them. Hector, —old Père Salomon, Monsieur Chevassus, Monsieur Cogne?

DUKE. Did I! They're the first Arabs I ever had anything to do with. Lent me money at fifty per cent.

POIRIER. Highway robbery! And you were fool enough—I beg your pardon, Monsieur le Duc, I beg your pardon!

DUKE. What else could I do? Ten thousand francs at two per cent is better than nothing at all at five per cent.

POIRIER. But, monsieur, there is a law against usury.

DUKE. Which the usurers respect and obey; they take only legal interest, but you get only one half the face value of the note in cash, you see.

POIRIER. And the other half?

DUKE. Stuffed lizards, as in Molière's day. Usurers do not progress: they were born perfect.

GASTON. Like the Chinese.

POIRIER. I hope, son-in-law, that you haven't borrowed at any such outrageous rate?

GASTON. I hope so too, father-in-law.

POIRIER. At fifty per cent!

GASTON. No more, no less.

POIRIER. And did you get stuffed lizards?

GASTON. Any number.

POIRIER. Why didn't you tell me sooner? I could have come to an agreement with them before the marriage.

GASTON. That is precisely what I did

not want. Would it not be fine to see the Marquis de Presles buying back his pledged word, insulting his noble name!

POIRIER. But if you owe only half the amount?

GASTON. I received only half, but I owe the whole. I don't owe the money to those thieves, but to my own signature.

POIRIER. Allow me, Monsieur le Marquis, I believe I may say that I am an honest man; I have never cheated anyone out of a single sou and I am incapable of advising you to do something underhand, but it appears to me that in paying back those scoundrels their principal at six per cent, you will have acted in an honorable and scrupulous way.

GASTON. This is not a question of honesty, but of honor.

POIRIER. What difference do you see between the two?

GASTON. Honor is a gentleman's honesty.

POIRIER. So, virtues change names when you want to put them into practice? You polish up their vulgarity in order to use them for yourself? I'm surprised at only one thing: that the nose of a nobleman deigns to be called by the same name when it happens to be on a tradesman's face!

GASTON. That is because all noses are similar.

DUKE. Within six inches!

POIRIER. Then don't you think that men are?

GASTON. It's a question.

POIRIER. Which was decided long ago, Monsieur le Marquis.

DUKE. Our rights and privileges have been abolished, but not our duties. Of all that remains to us there are only two words, but they are words which nothing can snatch from us: *Noblesse oblige!* No matter what happens we shall abide by a code more severe than the law, that mysterious code which we call honor.

POIRIER. Well, Monsieur le Marquis, it is very fortunate for your honor that my honesty pays your debts. Only, as I am not a gentleman, I warn you I shall do my best to get out of this fix as cheaply as I can.

GASTON. You must be very clever indeed to make any sort of compromise with those highway robbers: they are masters of the situation.

[*Reënter* ANTOINETTE.]

POIRIER. We'll see. [*Aside.*] I have an idea: I'm going to play my own little game. [*Aloud.*] I'll go at once, so that they shan't get impatient.

DUKE. Don't wait; they will devour you if you do. [*POIRIER goes out.*]

GASTON. Poor Monsieur Poirier, I feel sorry for him. This latest revelation takes away all his pleasure in paying my debts.

DUKE. Listen to me: there are very few people who know how to be robbed. It is an art worthy a great lord.

[*Enter a* SERVANT.]

SERVANT. Messieurs de Ligny and de Chazerolles would like to speak to Monsieur le Marquis on behalf of Monsieur de Pontgrimaud.

GASTON. Very well. [*The* SERVANT *goes out.*] You receive the gentlemen, Hector. You don't need me to help you arrange the party.

ANTOINETTE. A party?

GASTON. Yes, I won a good deal of money from Pontgrimaud and promised him a chance to take revenge. [*To* HECTOR.] To-morrow, some time in the morning, will be satisfactory for me.

DUKE [*aside to* GASTON]. When shall I see you again?

GASTON [*aside to* HECTOR]. Madame de Montjay is expecting me. At three, then, here. [*The* DUKE *goes out.*]

GASTON [*sitting on a sofa, opens a magazine and yawns*]. Would you like to go to the *Italiens* to-night?

ANTOINETTE. If you are going.

GASTON. I am. What gown are you going to wear?

ANTOINETTE. Any one you like.

GASTON. It makes no difference to me

—I mean, you look very pretty in any of them.

ANTOINETTE. But you have such excellent taste, dear; you ought to advise me.

GASTON. I am not a fashion magazine, my dear child; all you have to do is to watch the great ladies and make them your models: Madame de Nohan, Madame de Villepreux—

ANTOINETTE. Madame de Montjay.

GASTON. Why Madame de Montjay, rather than anyone else?

ANTOINETTE. Because she pleases you more.

GASTON. Where did you get that idea?

ANTOINETTE. The other evening at the Opéra you paid her a rather long visit in her box. She is pretty. Is she clever too?

GASTON. Very. [*A pause.*]

ANTOINETTE. Why don't you tell me when I do something that doesn't please you?

GASTON. I have never failed to do so.

ANTOINETTE. You never said you were displeased.

GASTON. Because you never gave me an occasion.

ANTOINETTE. Why, just a few moments ago, when I insisted that you take some position, I know I displeased you.

GASTON. I'd forgotten about that—it doesn't matter.

ANTOINETTE. If I had had any notion what your ideas on that subject were, do you think for an instant that I should have—?

GASTON. Truly, my dear, it almost seems as if you were making excuses.

ANTOINETTE. That is because I am afraid you will think me childish and vain.

GASTON. What if you were a little proud? Is that a crime?

ANTOINETTE. I swear I haven't an ounce of pride.

GASTON [*rising*]. My dear, you haven't a single fault. And do you know you have quite won the admiration of Montmeyran? You ought to be proud of that. Hector is difficult to please.

ANTOINETTE. Less so than you.

GASTON. Do you think me difficult? You see, you have some vanity—I've caught you in the act!

ANTOINETTE. I have no illusions about myself: I know very well what I need in order to be worthy of you. But if you will only take the trouble to guide me, tell me something about the ideas of the world you know, I love you so much I would completely change myself.

GASTON [kissing her hand]. I could not but lose by the change, madame, and furthermore, I am only a middling teacher. There is but one school in which to learn what you think you lack: society. Study it.

ANTOINETTE. Very well, then, I shall study Madame de Montjay.

GASTON. Again! Are you doing me the honor to be jealous? Take care, my dear, that failing is distinctly bourgeois. You must learn, since you allow me to be your guide, that in our circle marriage does not necessarily mean a home and a household; only the noble and elegant things in life do we have in common among ourselves. When I am not with you, pray do not worry about what I am doing; merely say to yourself, "He is dissipating his imperfections in order that he may bring to me one hour of perfection, or nearly so."

ANTOINETTE. I think that your greatest imperfection is your absence.

GASTON. Neatly turned. Thank you. Who's this? My creditors!

[Enter the Creditors.]

GASTON. You here, messieurs! You have mistaken the door; the servants' entrance is on the other side.

SALOMON. We didn't want to leave without seeing you, Monsieur le Marquis.

GASTON. I can dispense with your thanks.

COGNE. We have come to ask for yours.

CHEVASSUS. You've treated us long enough as usurers.

COGNE. Leeches.

SALOMON. Blood-suckers.

CHEVASSUS. We're delighted to have this occasion to tell you that we are honest men.

GASTON. I fail to see the joke.

COGNE. This is not a joke, monsieur. We have loaned you money at six per cent.

GASTON. Have my notes not been paid in full?

SALOMON. There's a trifle lacking: some two hundred and eighteen thousand francs.

GASTON. What's that?

CHEVASSUS. We were obliged to submit to that!

SALOMON. And your father-in-law insisted on your being sent to the debtors' prison.

GASTON. My father-in-law?

COGNE. It seems you have been playing some underhanded trick with him, poor fellow!

SALOMON. It'll teach him better next time!

COGNE. But meantime, we must bear the burden.

GASTON [to ANTOINETTE]. Your father, madame, has behaved in a very undignified way. [To the Creditors.] I confess myself in your debt, messieurs, but I have an income of only twenty-five thousand francs.

SALOMON. You know very well you can't touch the principal without your wife's consent. We have seen your marriage contract.

COGNE. You're not making your wife very happy.

GASTON. Leave the house!

SALOMON. You can't kick honest people out of the house like dogs—people who've helped you [ANTOINETTE has meantime sat down and is now writing.]—people who believed that the signature of the Marquis de Presles was worth something.

COGNE. Who were mistaken!

CREDITORS. Yes, mistaken!

ANTOINETTE [handing SALOMON a check]. You are not mistaken, messieurs: you are paid in full.

GASTON [taking the check, glances at it, and hands it back to SALOMON]. Now that you really are thieves—leave the house! Hurry up, or we'll have you swept out!

CREDITORS. Too good of you, Monsieur le Marquis! A thousand thanks!

[*They go out.*]

GASTON. You dear! I adore you!

[*He takes her in his arms and kisses her.*]

ANTOINETTE. Dear Gaston!

GASTON. Where in the world did your father find the heart he gave you?

ANTOINETTE. Don't judge my father too severely, dear. He is good and generous, but his ideas are narrow. He can't see beyond his own individual rights. It's the fault of his mind, not his heart. Now, if you consider I have done my duty, forgive my father for that one moment of agony.

GASTON. I should be very ungrateful to refuse you anything.

ANTOINETTE. You won't blame him, will you?

GASTON. No, since you wish it, Marquise. Marquise, you hear?

ANTOINETTE. Call me your wife—the only title of which I am proud!

GASTON. You do love me a little?

ANTOINETTE. Haven't you noticed it, ungrateful man?

GASTON. Oh, yes, but I like to hear you say it—especially at this moment. [*The clock strikes three.*] Three o'clock! [*Aside.*] The devil! Madame de Montjay!

ANTOINETTE. You smile—what are you thinking about?

GASTON. Would you like to take a ride with me in the Bois?

ANTOINETTE. I'm not dressed.

GASTON. Throw a shawl over your shoulders and ring for your maid. [*ANTOINETTE rings.*]

[*Enter POIRIER.*]

POIRIER. Well, son-in-law, have you seen your creditors?

GASTON [*with evident ill-humor*]. Yes, monsieur.

ANTOINETTE [*aside to GASTON, as she takes his arm*]. Remember your promise.

GASTON. Yes, my dear father-in-law, I have seen them.

[*Enter the Maid.*]

ANTOINETTE [*to the Maid*]. Bring me my shawl and hat and have the horses hitched. [*The Maid goes out.*]

GASTON [*to POIRIER*]. Allow me to congratulate you on your good stroke of business; you did play them a very clever trick. [*Aside to ANTOINETTE.*] Am I not nice?

POIRIER. You take it better than I thought you would; I was prepared for any number of objections on the score of your "honor."

GASTON. I am reasonable, father-in-law. You have acted according to your own ideas. I have little objection to that: we have acted according to *our* ideas.

POIRIER. What's that?

GASTON. You gave those rascals only the actual sum of money borrowed from them: we have paid the rest.

POIRIER [*to ANTOINETTE*]. What! Did you sign away—? [*ANTOINETTE nods.*] Good God, what have you done!

ANTOINETTE. I beg your pardon, father.

POIRIER. I've moved heaven and earth to give you a good round sum and you throw it out of the window! Two hundred and eighteen thousand francs!

GASTON. Don't worry about that, Monsieur Poirier; we are the ones who lose: the benefit is yours.

[*Reënter the Maid, with a hat and shawl.*]

ANTOINETTE. Good-bye, father, we are going to the Bois.

GASTON. Your arm, wife! [*They go.*]

POIRIER. He gets on my nerves, that son-in-law of mine. I see I can never get any satisfaction out of him. He's an incurable gentleman! He refuses to do anything—he's good for nothing—he's a frightful expense—he is master of my own house. This has got to end.

[*He rings. A moment later—*]

[*Enter a SERVANT.*]

Have the porter and cook come here. [*The SERVANT goes out.*] We'll see, son-in-law. I've been too soft and kind and generous. So you won't give in, my fine friend? Very well, do as you please? Neither will I: you remain a marquis, and I shall remain a bourgeois. I'll at least have the consolation of living as I want to live.

[*Enter the* PORTER.]

PORTER. Monsieur?

POIRIER. François, monsieur asked for you. Put up a sign on the house at once.

PORTER. A sign?

POIRIER. "To let, a magnificent apartment on the first floor, with stables and appurtenances."

PORTER. Monsieur le Marquis' apartment?

POIRIER. Exactly.

PORTER. But Monsieur le Marquis gave me no orders about this.

POIRIER. Idiot, who is master here? Who owns this house?

PORTER. You, monsieur.

POIRIER. Then do as I tell you. I can dispense with your opinions.

PORTER. Very well, monsieur.

[*The* PORTER *goes out.*]

[*Enter* VATEL.]

POIRIER. Hurry, François.—Come here, Monsieur Vatel. You are preparing a grand dinner for to-morrow?

VATEL. Yes, monsieur, and I may even say that the menu would be no disgrace to my illustrious ancestor. It will be a veritable work of art. Monsieur Poirier will be astonished.

POIRIER. Have you the menu with you?

VATEL. No, monsieur, it is being copied, but I know it by heart.

POIRIER. Be good enough to recite it to me.

VATEL. *Potage aux ravioles à l'Italienne* and *potage à l'orge à la Marie Stuart.*

POIRIER. Instead of those two unknown soups you will have ordinary vegetable soup.

VATEL. What, monsieur?

POIRIER. No arguments. Continue.

VATEL. After the soup: *Carpe du Rhin à la Lithuanienne, poulardes à la Godard,* *filet de bœuf braisé aux raisins à la Napolitaine,* Westphalian ham, Madeira sauce.

POIRIER. Here's an easier and much healthier after-soup course for you: Brill with caper sauce; Bayonne ham with spinach; larded veal with gooseberries; and rabbit.

VATEL. But, Monsieur Poirier, I shall never consent to—

POIRIER. I am master here, do you understand? Continue.

VATEL. Entrées: *Filets de volaille à la concordat—croustades de truffes garnies de foie à la royale;* stuffed pheasants *à la Montpensier,* red partridges *farcis à la bohémienne.*

POIRIER. Instead of these entrées we'll have nothing at all. Proceed at once to the roasts. That's the important part.

VATEL. But this is against all the precepts of my art.

POIRIER. I'll take the responsibility for that. Now, what are your roasts?

VATEL. There is no use going any further, monsieur; my ancestor thrust a sword through his heart for a lesser insult. I resign.

POIRIER. I was just going to ask you to do that. Of course, you still have a week here, while I can look for another servant.

VATEL. A servant! Monsieur, I am a chef!

POIRIER. I am going to replace you by a woman-cook. Meantime, during the week you are in my service, you will be good enough to execute my orders.

VATEL. I would rather blow my brains out than be false to my name!

POIRIER [*aside*]. Another stickler for his name! [*Aloud.*] Blow your brains out, Monsieur Vatel, but be careful not to burn my sauces. Good-day to you. [VATEL *goes out.*] And now I'm going to invite some of my old friends from the Rue des Bourdonnais. Monsieur le Marquis de Presles, we are going to make you come down a few pegs!

[*He goes out humming the first verse of "Monsieur et Madame Denis."*]

ACT III

The scene is the same. GASTON *and* ANTOINETTE *are present.*

GASTON. What a delightful ride! Charming spring weather. You might almost think it was April!

ANTOINETTE. Really, weren't you too bored?

GASTON. With you, my dear? As a matter of fact, you are the most charming woman I know.

ANTOINETTE. Compliments, Monsieur?

GASTON. Oh, no: the truth in its most brutal form. And what a delightful journey I made into your mind and heart. How many undiscovered points I have found. Why, I have been living near you without knowing you, like a Parisian in Paris.

ANTOINETTE. And I don't displease you too much?

GASTON. It is my place to ask you that question. I feel like a peasant who has been entertaining a queen in disguise: all at once the queen puts on her crown and the peasant feels embarrassed and makes excuses for not having been more attentive and hospitable.

ANTOINETTE. Be assured, good peasant, that your queen blamed nothing except her own incognito.

GASTON. For having kept it so long, cruel queen? Was it out of sheer coquetry, and to have another honeymoon? You have succeeded. Hitherto I have been only your husband; now I want to become your lover.

ANTOINETTE. No, my dear Gaston, remain my husband. I think that a woman can cease to love her lover, never her husband.

GASTON. Ah, so you are not romantic?

ANTOINETTE. I am, but in my own way. My ideas on the subject are perhaps not fashionable, but they are deeply rooted in me, like childhood impressions. When I was a little girl I could never understand how it was that my father and mother weren't related, and ever since then marriage has seemed to me the tenderest and closest of all relationships. To love a man who is not my husband seems contrary to nature.

GASTON. The ideas rather of a Roman matron, my dear Antoinette, but keep them, for the sake of my honor and my happiness.

ANTOINETTE. Take care! There is another side: I am jealous, I warn you. If there is only one man in the world I can love, I must have all his love. The day I discover that this is not so, I shall make no complaint or reproach, but the link will be broken. At once my husband will become a stranger to me: I should consider myself a widow.

GASTON [*aside*]. The devil! [*Aloud.*] Fear nothing, dear Antoinette, we shall live like two lovers, like Philemon and Baucis—with the exception of the hut— you don't insist on the hut, do you?

ANTOINETTE. Not in the least.

GASTON. I am going to hold a brilliant celebration of our wedding, and I want you to eclipse all the other women and make all the men envious of me.

ANTOINETTE. Must we proclaim our happiness so loud?

GASTON. Don't you like entertainments?

ANTOINETTE. I like everything that you like. Are we going to have company at dinner to-day?

GASTON. No—to-morrow. To-day we have only Montmeyran. Why did you ask?

ANTOINETTE. Should I dress?

GASTON. Yes, because I want you to make married life attractive to Hector. Go now, my dear child. I shan't forget this happy day!

ANTOINETTE. How happy I am!
[*She goes out.*]

GASTON. There is no denying the fact: she is prettier than Madame de Montjay. Devil take me if I am not falling in love with my wife! Love is like good fortune: while we seek it afar, it is waiting for us at home.

[*Enter* POIRIER.]

Well, my dear father-in-law, how are you taking your little disappointment? Are you still angry on account of the money? Have you decided to do something?

POIRIER. I have.

GASTON. Violent?

POIRIER. Something necessary.

GASTON. Might I be so indiscreet as to inquire what?

POIRIER. On the contrary, monsieur, I even owe you an explanation. When I gave you my daughter together with a million francs dowry, I never for a moment thought you would refuse to take a position.

GASTON. Please let's drop that subject.

POIRIER. I wanted to remind you. I confess I was wrong in thinking that a gentleman would ever consent to work like a man; I own my mistake. As a result of that error, however, I have allowed you to run my house on a scale which I don't myself keep up with; and since it is understood that my fortune alone is our only source of income, it seems to me just, reasonable and necessary to cut down, because I see I have no hope of any further increase in revenue. I have therefore thought of making a few reforms, which you will undoubtedly approve.

GASTON. Proceed, Sully! Go on, Turgot! Cut, slash. You find me in splendid humor! Take advantage of the fact.

POIRIER. I am most delighted at your condescension. I have, I say, decided, resolved, commanded—

GASTON. I beg your pardon, father-in-law, but if you have decided, resolved, commanded, it seems quite superfluous for you to consult me.

POIRIER. I am not consulting you; I am merely telling you the facts.

GASTON. You are not consulting me?

POIRIER. Are you surprised?

GASTON. A little but, as I told you, I am in splendid humor.

POIRIER. Well, the first reform, my dear boy—

GASTON. You mean, your dear Gaston, I think? A slip of the tongue!

POIRIER. Dear Gaston, dear boy—it's the same. Some familiarity between father-in-law and son-in-law is allowed, doubtless?

GASTON. And on your part, Monsieur Poirier, it flatters and honors me. You were about to say that your first reform—?

POIRIER. That you, monsieur, do me the favor to stop making fun of me. I'm tired of being the butt of all your jokes.

GASTON. Now, now, Monsieur Poirier, don't be angry.

POIRIER. I know very well that you think I'm of little account, that I'm not very intelligent, but—

GASTON. Where did you get that idea?

POIRIER. But let me tell you, there is more brains in my little finger than there is in your whole body.

GASTON. This is ridiculous.

POIRIER. *I'm* no marquis!

GASTON. Hush! Not so loud! Someone might hear you.

POIRIER. It makes no difference to me whether they do or not. I don't pretend to be a gentleman, thank God! It's not worth troubling my mind about.

GASTON. Not worth troubling about?

POIRIER. No, monsieur, I'm an old dyed-in-the-wool Liberal, that's what I am, and I judge men on their merits, and not according to their titles. I laugh at the mere accident of birth. The nobility don't dazzle me: I think no more of them than I do of the Judgment Day. I'm delighted to have this occasion of telling you so.

GASTON. Do you think I have merits?

POIRIER. No, monsieur, I do not.

GASTON. Then, why did you give me your daughter?

POIRIER. Why did I—?

GASTON. Possibly you had some afterthought?

POIRIER [*embarrassed*]. Afterthought?

GASTON. Allow me: your daughter did not love me when you brought me to your home; and certainly it was not my debts which appealed to you, and which caused the honor of your choice to fall upon me. Now, since it was not my title either, I am forced to assume that you must have had some afterthought.

POIRIER. And what of it, monsieur? What if I did try to combine my own interest with my daughter's happiness? Where would be the harm? Who could blame me, I who gave a million right out of my pocket, for choosing a son-in-law who could in some way pay me back for my sacrifice? My daughter loved you, didn't she? I thought of her first: that was my duty, in fact my right.

GASTON. I don't contest that, Monsieur Poirier; I only say that you were wrong in one respect: not to have had confidence is me.

POIRIER. Well, you are not a very encouraging sort of man.

GASTON. Are you blaming me for my occasional jokes at your expense? Possibly I am not the most respectful son-in-law in the world; I admit it; only allow me to state that in serious matters I know how to be serious.

POIRIER [aside]. Can he really have understood the situation?

GASTON. Look here, my dear father-in-law, can I help you in any way? That is, if I am good for anything?

POIRIER. Well, I once dreamed of being introduced at court.

GASTON. Ah, so you still have that desire to dance at court?

POIRIER. It's not a matter of dancing. Do me the honor of thinking me not quite so frivolous as that. I am not vain or trivial.

GASTON. Then, in the name of Heaven, what are you? Explain yourself.

POIRIER [piteously]. I am ambitious.

GASTON. Why, you're not blushing, are you? Why? With all the experience you have acquired in the realm of business, you might well aspire to any heights. Commerce is the true school for statesmanship.

POIRIER. That's what Verdelet was telling me only this morning.

GASTON. That is where one can obtain a high and grand view of things, and stand detached from the petty interests which—that is the sort of condition from which your Richelieus and Colberts sprang.

POIRIER. Oh, I don't pretend—!

GASTON. Now, my good Monsieur Poirier, what would suit you? A prefecture? Nonsense! Council of State? No! Diplomatic service? Let me see, the Turkish Embassy is vacant at present.

POIRIER. I'm a stay-at-home—and besides I don't understand Turkish.

GASTON. Wait! [Striking POIRIER on the shoulder.] The peerage—it would fit you to a T.

POIRIER. Do you really think so?

GASTON. That's the trouble: you don't fall into any category, you see. The Institute? No. You're not a member of the Institute?

POIRIER. Oh, don't worry about that. I'll pay—three thousand francs, if necessary—direct contributions. I have three millions now at the bank; they await only a word from you to be put to good use.

GASTON. Ah, Machiavelli! Sixtus V! You'll outstrip them all!

POIRIER. Yes, I think I will!

GASTON. But I sincerely hope your ambition will not stop there? You must have a title.

POIRIER. I don't insist on such vain baubles. I'm an old Liberal, as I told you.

GASTON. All the more reason. A Liberal must despise only the nobility of the old régime; now, the new nobility, which has no ancestors—

POIRIER. The nobility that owes everything to itself!

GASTON. You might be a count.

POIRIER. No, I'll be reasonable: a baronetcy would suffice.

GASTON. Baron Poirier! Sounds well!

POIRIER. Yes, Baron Poirier!

GASTON [looks at POIRIER and then bursts out laughing]. I beg your pardon! But—really—this is too funny! Baron!

Monsieur Poirier! Baron de Catillard!

POIRIER [aside]. He's been making fun of me!

GASTON [calling]. Come here, Hector!

[Enter the DUKE.]

Come here! Do you know why Jean Gaston de Presles received three wounds from an arquebuse at the battle of Ivry? Do you know why François Gaston de Presles led the attack on La Rochelle? Why Louis Gaston de Presles was blown to pieces at La Hogue? Why Philippe Gaston de Presles captured two flags at Fontenoy? Why my grandfather gave up his life at Quiberon? It was all in order that some day Monsieur Poirier might be peer of France and a baron!

DUKE. What do you mean?

GASTON. This is the secret of that little attack on me this morning.

DUKE [aside]. I see!

POIRIER. And do you know, Monsieur le Duc, why I have worked fourteen hours a day for thirty years? Why I heaped up, sou by sou, four millions of cash, while I deprived myself of everything but the bare necessities? It was all in order that some day Monsieur le Marquis Gaston de Presles, who died neither at Quiberon nor at Fontenoy nor at La Hogue nor anywhere else, might die of old age on a feather bed, after having spent his life doing nothing at all.

DUKE. Well said, monsieur!

GASTON. You are a born orator!

[Enter a SERVANT.]

SERVANT. There are some gentlemen here who would like to see the apartment.

GASTON. What apartment?

SERVANT. Monsieur le Marquis'.

GASTON. Do they think this is a natural history museum?

POIRIER [to the SERVANT]. Tell the gentlemen to call again. [The SERVANT goes out.] Pardon me, son-in-law, I was so carried away by your gaiety, I forgot to mention that I am renting the first floor of my house.

GASTON. What's that?

POIRIER. That is one of the little reforms I was speaking about.

GASTON. And where do you intend to lodge me?

POIRIER. On the floor above: the apartment is large enough for us all.

GASTON. A Noah's Ark!

POIRIER. Of course, it goes without saying that I am renting the stables and carriages, too.

GASTON. And my horses—are you going to lodge them on the second floor?

POIRIER. You will sell them.

GASTON. And go on foot?

DUKE. It will do you good; you don't do half enough walking.

POIRIER. I shall, however, keep my own blue coupé. I'll lend it to you when you need it.

DUKE. When the weather is nice!

GASTON. Now, see here, Monsieur Poirier, this is—!

[Enter a SERVANT.]

SERVANT. Monsieur Vatel would like a word with Monsieur le Marquis.

GASTON. Tell him to come in.

[Enter VATEL, dressed in black.]

What does this mean, Monsieur Vatel? Are you going to a funeral? And on the eve of battle!

VATEL. The position in which I have been placed is such that I am forced to desert in order to escape dishonor. Will Monsieur le Marquis kindly cast his eyes over the menu Monsieur Poirier has imposed upon me!

GASTON. Monsieur Poirier imposed on you? Let us see. [Reading.] "Lapin sauté!"

POIRIER. My old friend Ducaillou's favorite dish.

GASTON. "Stuffed turkey and chestnuts!"

POIRIER. My old comrade Groschenet is very fond of it.

GASTON. Are you entertaining the whole Rue des Bourdonnais?

POIRIER. Together with the Faubourg Saint-Germain.

GASTON. I accept your resignation, Monsieur Vatel. [VATEL *goes out*.] So, to-morrow my friends are to have the honor of meeting yours?

POIRIER. Exactly; they will have that honor. Monsieur le Duc will not, I hope, feel humiliated at having to eat soup— my soup—as he sits between Monsieur and Madame Pincebourde?

DUKE. Not at all. This little debauch is not in the least displeasing. Undoubtedly Madame Pincebourde will sing during the dessert?

GASTON. And after dinner we shall have a game of piquet, too?

DUKE. Or lotto.

POIRIER. And Pope Joan.

GASTON. And I trust we shall repeat the debauch from time to time?

POIRIER. My home will be open every evening, and your friends will always be welcome.

GASTON. Really, Monsieur Poirier, your home will soon become a center of marvellous pleasures, a miniature Capua. But I am afraid I should become a slave of luxury and I shall, therefore, leave no later than to-morrow.

POIRIER. I am sorry to hear it, but my home is not a prison. What career do you intend to follow? Medicine or Law?

GASTON. Who said anything about a career?

POIRIER. Or will you enter the Department of Roads and Bridges? For you will certainly be unable to keep up your rank on nine thousand francs income?

GASTON. Nine thousand francs?

POIRIER. Well, the account is easy to make out: you received five hundred thousand francs as my daughter's dowry. The wedding and installation took about a hundred thousand. You have just given two hundred and eighteen thousand to your creditors; you have, therefore, one hundred and eighty-two thousand left, which, at the usual interest, will yield you nine thousand francs income. You see? On that can you supply your friends with *Carpe à la Lithuanienne* and *Volailles à la concordat?* Take my word for it, my dear Gaston, stay with me; you will be more comfortable than in a home of your own. Think of your children, who will not be sorry some day to find in the pockets of the Marquis de Presles the savings of old man Poirier. Goodbye, son-in-law, I'm going to settle accounts with Monsieur Vatel.

[POIRIER *goes out.*]

GASTON [*as he and the* DUKE *exchange glances and the* DUKE *bursts into laughter*]. You think it funny?

DUKE. Indeed I do! So this is the modest and generous fruit-tree of a father-in-law! This Georges Dandin! At last you've found your master. In the name of Heaven, don't look so miserable! See there, you look like a prince starting on a crusade, turning back because of the rain! Smile a little; this isn't so tragic after all!

GASTON. You are right. Monsieur Poirier, you are rendering me a great service that you little dream of!

DUKE. A service?

GASTON. Yes, my dear fellow. I was about to make a fool of myself: fall in love with my wife. Fortunately, Monsieur Poirier has put a stop to that.

DUKE. Your wife is not to blame for the stupidity of her father. She is charming!

GASTON. Nonsense! She's just like her father!

DUKE. Not the least bit.

GASTON. There is a family resemblance, I insist! I couldn't kiss her without thinking of the old fool. Now I *did* want to sit at home with my wife by the fireside, but the moment it is to be a kitchen fireside— [*He takes out his watch.*] Good-evening!

DUKE. Where are you going?

GASTON. To Madame de Montjay's; she's been waiting two hours already.

DUKE. Gaston, don't go.

GASTON. They want to make my life a hardship for me here, make me feel penitent!

DUKE. Listen to me!

GASTON. You can't persuade me.

DUKE. What about your duel?

GASTON. That's so—I'd forgotten.

DUKE. You are going to fight to-morrow at two in the Bois de Vincennes.

GASTON. Very well. With this humor on me, Pontgrimaud is going to have a pleasant quarter-hour to-morrow!

[*Enter* VERDELET *and* ANTOINETTE.]

ANTOINETTE. Are you going out, dear?

GASTON. Yes, madame. [*He goes out.*]

VERDELET. Well, Toinon, his humor isn't quite so charming as you described it?

ANTOINETTE. I don't understand?

DUKE. Very serious things are happening, madame.

ANTOINETTE. What?

DUKE. Your father is ambitious.

VERDELET. Poirier ambitious?

DUKE. He was counting on his son-in-law's title to—

VERDELET. Get into the peerage—like Monsieur Michaud! [*Aside.*] Old fool!

DUKE. He's adopted childish measures in retaliation after Gaston refused to help him. I'm afraid it is you, however, who will bear the expenses of war.

ANTOINETTE. How do you mean?

VERDELET. It's only too simple: if your father is making the house disagreeable to your husband, he will seek distraction elsewhere.

ANTOINETTE. Distraction elsewhere?

DUKE. Monsieur Verdelet has put his finger on the spot. You, madame, are the only person who can prevent disaster. If your father loves you, you must stand between him and Gaston. Make a truce between them at once. There is no harm done yet, and everything can be as it was.

ANTOINETTE. No harm done yet? Everything can be as it was? You make me very much afraid. Against whom am I to defend myself?

DUKE. Against your father.

ANTOINETTE. No: you are not telling me everything. What my father has done is not enough to take my husband from me in the space of a single day. He's making love to some woman, is he not?

DUKE. No, madame, but—

ANTOINETTE. Please, Monsieur le Duc, don't try to hide the truth. I have a rival!

DUKE. Do calm yourself!

ANTOINETTE. I feel it. I know it. He is with her now!

DUKE. No, madame: he loves you.

ANTOINETTE. But he has just come to know me since an hour ago. Ha, it wasn't to me that he felt he must tell of his anger—he went elsewhere with his troubles!

VERDELET. Now, now, Toinon, don't get so excited. He went out for a walk, that's all. That was what I always did when Poirier made me angry.

[*Enter a* SERVANT *carrying a letter on a silver plate.*]

SERVANT. A letter for Monsieur le Marquis.

ANTOINETTE. He has gone out. Lay it there. [*The* SERVANT *lays the letter on a table.* ANTOINETTE *looks at it, and says, aside:*] A woman's hand! [*Aloud.*] From whom does this come?

SERVANT. Madame de Montjay's footman brought it. [*He goes out.*]

ANTOINETTE [*aside*]. Madame de Montjay!

DUKE. I shall see Gaston before you, madame. Would you like me to give him the letter?

ANTOINETTE. Are you afraid I might open it?

DUKE. Oh, madame!

ANTOINETTE. It must have crossed Gaston.

VERDELET. The idea! Your husband's mistress would never dare write him here!

ANTOINETTE. She must despise me, if she would dare to write him here. But I don't say she is his mistress. I only say he is making love to her. I say that because I am positive.

DUKE. But I swear, madame—

ANTOINETTE. Would you dare swear,— seriously swear—Monsieur le Duc?

DUKE. My oath would prove nothing, for a gentleman has the right to lie in a case of this sort. No matter what the truth is, I have warned you of the danger and suggested a means of escape. I have done my duty as a friend and an honorable man. Do not ask anything else of me. [*He goes out.*]

ANTOINETTE. I have just lost everything I had won in Gaston's affection. An hour ago he called me Marquise, and my father has just brutally reminded him that I was Mademoiselle Poirier.

VERDELET. Well, is it impossible to love Mademoiselle Poirier?

ANTOINETTE. Possibly my own devotion might have touched him, my own love have awakened his. That was beginning, but my father has just stopped it. His mistress! She can't be that yet, can she? You don't really believe she is, do you?

VERDELET. Certainly not!

ANTOINETTE. I understand how he might have been making love to her for the last few days. But if he is really her lover, then he must have begun the day after our marriage. That would be vile!

VERDELET. Yes, my dear child.

ANTOINETTE. Of course, he didn't marry me with the idea that he would never love me, but he shouldn't have condemned me so soon.

VERDELET. No, of course he shouldn't.

ANTOINETTE. You don't seem very sure. You must be mad to suspect a thing of that sort! You know very well my husband wouldn't be capable of it! Tell me, there's no doubt, is there? You don't think him so low?

VERDELET. No!

ANTOINETTE. Then you can swear he is innocent. Swear it, dear Tony, swear it!

VERDELET. I swear it.

ANTOINETTE. Why is she writing a letter to him?

VERDELET. It's an invitation, probably, to a party of some sort.

ANTOINETTE. It must be very important, if she sends it by a footman. To think that the secret of my whole fu-

ture life is in that envelope. Let's go—that letter tempts me.

[*She lays the letter, which she has meanwhile picked up, on the table and stands looking at it.*]

VERDELET. Come, then, you are right.

[*Enter* POIRIER.]

POIRIER. Why, Antoinette. [*To* VERDELET.] What is she looking at? A letter? [*He picks it up.*]

ANTOINETTE. Leave it, father, it is addressed to Monsieur de Presles.

POIRIER [*looking at the address.*] Pretty handwriting! [*He sniffs the letter.*] Doesn't smell of tobacco! It's from a woman!

ANTOINETTE. Yes, from Madame de Montjay.

POIRIER. How excited you are! You're feverish, aren't you? [*He takes her hand.*] You are.

ANTOINETTE. No, father.

POIRIER. You are. What's the matter? Tell me.

ANTOINETTE. Nothing.

VERDELET [*aside to* POIRIER]. Don't worry her. She's jealous.

POIRIER. Jealous? Is the Marquis unfaithful to you? By God, if that's so—

ANTOINETTE. Father, dear, if you love me, don't.

POIRIER. If I love you!

ANTOINETTE. Don't torment Gaston.

POIRIER. Who's tormenting him? I'm just economizing.

VERDELET. You irritate the Marquis, and your daughter suffers for it.

POIRIER. You mind your own business. [*To* ANTOINETTE.] What has that man done to you? I must know.

ANTOINETTE [*frightened*]. Nothing—nothing. Don't quarrel with him, for Heaven's sake!

POIRIER. Then, why are you jealous? Why are you looking at that letter, eh? [*He takes the letter.*] Do you think that Madame de Montjay—?

ANTOINETTE. No, no!

POIRIER. She does, doesn't she, Verdelet?

VERDELET. Well, she thinks—

POIRIER. It's very easy to find out. [*He breaks the seal.*]

ANTOINETTE. Father! A letter is sacred.

POIRIER. There is nothing so sacred to me as your happiness.

VERDELET. Take care, Poirier. What will your son-in-law say?

POIRIER. I don't care a hang about my son-in-law. [*He opens the letter.*]

ANTOINETTE. Please, don't read that letter.

POIRIER. I will read it. If it isn't my right, it is my duty. [*Reading:*] "Dear Gaston." The blackguard!
[*He drops the letter.*]

ANTOINETTE. She is his mistress! Oh, God! [*She falls into a chair.*]

POIRIER [*taking* VERDELET *by the collar*]. You allowed me to arrange this marriage!

VERDELET. This is too much!

POIRIER. When I asked for your advice, why didn't you oppose me? Why didn't you warn me what was going to happen?

VERDELET. I told you twenty times—but, no, monsieur was ambitious!

POIRIER. Much good it did me!

VERDELET. She's fainting!

POIRIER. Good God!

VERDELET [*kneeling before* ANTOINETTE]. Toinon, my child, come to yourself!

POIRIER. Get out! You don't know what to say to her. [*Kneeling before* ANTOINETTE.*] Toinon, my child, come to yourself!

ANTOINETTE. It was nothing—I'm all right, father.

POIRIER. Don't worry, I'll get rid of the monster for you.

ANTOINETTE. What have I done to deserve this! And after three months of marriage! Why—the day after, the day after! He wasn't faithful to me for a single day. He ran to her from my arms. Didn't he feel my heart beating? He didn't understand that I was giving myself and my love completely up to him. The wretch! I can't live—after this!

POIRIER. You must! What would become of me? The scoundrel! Where are you going?

ANTOINETTE. To my room.

POIRIER. Do you want me to come with you?

ANTOINETTE. Thank you, father,—no.

VERDELET [*to* POIRIER]. Leave her to cry alone. Tears will make her feel better. [*ANTOINETTE goes out.*]

POIRIER. What a marriage! What a marriage! [*He strides back and forth.*]

VERDELET. Calm yourself, Poirier, everything can be arranged again. At present our duty is to bring these two hearts together again.

POIRIER. I know my duty and I am going to do it. [*He picks up the letter.*]

VERDELET. Please, now, don't do anything foolish!

[*Enter* GASTON.]

POIRIER. Are you looking for something, monsieur?

GASTON. A letter.

POIRIER. From Madame de Montjay. You needn't look for it, it is in my pocket.

GASTON. Have you by any chance opened it?

POIRIER. Yes, monsieur, I have.

GASTON. Do you realize, monsieur, that that is an infamous trick? The act of a dishonest and dishonorable man?

VERDELET. Monsieur le Marquis! Poirier!

POIRIER. There is only one dishonorable man here, and that is you!

GASTON. Let us drop that! In stealing from me the secret of my fault, you have forfeited the right to judge it. There is but one thing more sacred than the lock of a safe, monsieur, and that is the seal of a letter—because *it* cannot defend itself.

VERDELET [*to* POIRIER]. What did I tell you?

POIRIER. Ridiculous! Do you mean

to tell me that a father hasn't the right—? Why, I'm doing you a great favor even to answer you! You'll explain in court, Monsieur le Marquis.

VERDELET. In court!

POIRIER. Do you think a man can bring despair and sin into our family and not be punished? I'll have a divorce, monsieur!

GASTON. Will you drag all this into court? Where that letter will be read?

POIRIER. In public. Yes, monsieur, in public.

VERDELET. You're crazy, Poirier. Think of the scandal!

GASTON. Of course, you're forgetting: a woman will lose her reputation!

POIRIER. Now, say something about her honor! I expected that.

GASTON. Yes, her honor, and if that isn't enough to dissuade you, her ruin—

POIRIER. So much the better! I'm delighted! She will get all she deserves, the—!

GASTON. Monsieur!

POIRIER. She'll get no sympathy! To take a husband from his poor young wife, after three months of marriage!

GASTON. She is less to blame than I. I am the only one you should accuse.

POIRIER. You needn't worry: I despise you as the lowest of the low! Aren't you ashamed of yourself? To sacrifice a charming woman like Antoinette! Has she ever given you cause for complaint? Find a single fault, a single one, in order to excuse yourself! She has a heart of gold—and what eyes! And her education! You know what it cost me, Verdelet.

VERDELET. Do keep calm, Poirier!

POIRIER. I am, am I not? If I only— No, there is justice—I'm going to see my lawyer at once.

GASTON. Please wait until to-morrow, monsieur, I beg you. Just take time to think it over.

POIRIER. I have thought it over.

GASTON [to VERDELET]. Please help me to prevent him from committing an irreparable blunder, monsieur.

VERDELET. Ah, you don't know him.

GASTON [to POIRIER]. Take care, monsieur. It is my duty to save that woman, save her at any price. Let me tell you that I am responsible for everything.

POIRIER. I know that very well.

GASTON. You have no idea how desperate I can be.

POIRIER. So you're threatening?

GASTON. Yes, I am threatening. Give me that letter. You are not going to leave this room until I have it.

POIRIER. Violence, eh? Must I ring for the servants?

GASTON. That's so—I'm losing my head. At least, listen to me. You are not naturally mean; you are just angry. And now your sorrow makes you so excited that you have no idea what you are doing.

POIRIER. I have a right to be angry, and my sorrow is decent and fitting.

GASTON. I have told you, monsieur, I confess I am to blame; I am sorry. But if I promised you never to see Madame de Montjay again, if I swore that I would spend my life in trying to make your daughter happy—?

POIRIER. It would merely be the second time you have sworn! Let's stop this nonsense!

GASTON. Very well. You were right this morning: it is lack of an occupation that has been my ruin.

POIRIER. Ah, now, you admit it!

GASTON. Well, what if I took a position?

POIRIER. You—? A position?

GASTON. You have the right to doubt my word, that is true, but I ask you to keep that letter, and if I fail to keep my promise, you can always—

VERDELET. That's a good guarantee, Poirier.

POIRIER. Of what?

VERDELET. That he will stand by his promise: that he will never see that lady again, that he will take a position, that he will make your daughter happy. What more can you ask?

POIRIER. I see; but what assurance can I have?

VERDELET. The letter. What the devil, the letter!

POIRIER. That's so, yes, that's so.

VERDELET. Well, do you accept? Anything is better than a divorce.

POIRIER. I don't quite agree with that, but if you insist— [*To the* MARQUIS.] For my part, monsieur, I am willing to accept your offer. Now we have only to consult my daughter.

VERDELET. She will surely not want any scandal.

POIRIER. Let's go and find her. [*To* GASTON.] Believe me, monsieur, my only object in all this is to assure my daughter's happiness. And the proof of my own sincerity is that I expect nothing from you, that I will receive no favor from your hands, that I am firmly decided to remain the same plain business man I have always been.

VERDELET. Good, Poirier!

POIRIER [*to* VERDELET]. So long, at least, as he doesn't make my daughter so happy that— [*They go out.*]

GASTON. Blame it on yourself, Marquis de Presles. What humiliations! Ah, Madame de Montjay! This is the hour of my fate. What are they going to do with me? Condemn me, or that unfortunate woman? Shame or remorse? And it has all been because of one caprice—a single day! Blame it on yourself, Marquis de Presles—you have no one else to blame. [*He stands plunged in thought.*]

[*Enter the* DUKE, *who comes up to* GASTON *and slaps him on the shoulder.*]

DUKE. What's the matter?

GASTON. You know what my father-in-law asked me this morning?

DUKE. Yes.

GASTON. What if I told you I was going to accede to his wishes?

DUKE. I should say, Impossible!

GASTON. And yet it's a fact: I am.

DUKE. Are you crazy? You said yourself that if there was one man who had not the right—

GASTON. It must be. My father-in-law has opened a letter to me from Madame de Montjay. He was so angry that he declared he would take it to a lawyer. In order to stop that, I had to offer to accept his conditions.

DUKE. Poor fellow! You are in a difficult situation!

GASTON. Pontgrimaud would be rendering me a great service if he were to kill me to-morrow.

DUKE. Come, come, put that idea out of your head.

GASTON. That would be a solution.

DUKE. You are only twenty-five—you still have a happy life before you.

GASTON. Life? Look at my situation: I am ruined, I am the slave of a father-in-law whose despotism makes capital of my faults, husband of a wife whom I have cruelly wounded, and who will never forget. You say that I may have a happy life before me, but I tell you I am disgusted with life and with myself! My cursed foolishness, my caprices, have brought me to a point where I have lost everything: liberty, domestic happiness, the esteem of the world, self-respect. How horrible!

DUKE. Courage, my friend. Don't lose hope!

GASTON [*rising*]. Yes, I am a coward. A gentleman may lose everything except his honor.

DUKE. What are you going to do?

GASTON. What you would do in my place.

DUKE. I should not kill myself! No!

GASTON. You see, then, you have guessed!—Sh-h! I have only my name now, and I want to keep that intact. Someone's coming!

[*Enter* POIRIER, ANTOINETTE, *and* VERDELET.]

ANTOINETTE. No, father, no. It's impossible. All is over between Monsieur de Presles and me!

VERDELET. I can't believe it's you speaking, my dear child.

POIRIER. But I tell you, he is going to

take a position! He has promised never to see that woman again. He's going to make you happy!

ANTOINETTE. Happiness is no longer possible for me. If Monsieur de Presles has not been able to love me of his own accord, do you think he can ever love me when he is forced to?

POIRIER [to the MARQUIS]. Speak, monsieur.

ANTOINETTE. Monsieur de Presles says nothing, because he knows I will not believe him. He is well aware, too, that every bond which held us together has been broken, and that he can never be anything but a stranger to me. Let us each, therefore, take what liberty the law allows us. I want a separation, father. Give me that letter: it is mine and mine alone, to make what use of I please. Give it to me.

POIRIER. Please, my child, think of the scandal. It will affect us all.

ANTOINETTE. It will harm only those who are guilty.

VERDELET. Think of that woman whom you will ruin—

ANTOINETTE. Did she have pity on me? Father, give me the letter. It is not as your daughter that I ask for it, but as the outraged Marquise de Presles.

POIRIER. There.—But I tell you he is willing to take a position—

ANTOINETTE. Give it to me. [To the MARQUIS.] Here is my revenge, monsieur; I have you absolutely in my power. You placed your own honor at stake in order to save your mistress; I absolve you in this way.

[She tears up the letter and throws it into the fireplace.]

POIRIER. Well—! What's she done?

ANTOINETTE. My duty.

VERDELET. Dear child! [He kisses her.]

DUKE. Noble heart!

GASTON. Ah, madame, how can I hope to express to you—? I was so haughty and proud—I thought I had made a misalliance, but I see that you bear my name better than I! My whole life will not

suffice to make up for the evil I have done you.

ANTOINETTE. I am a widow, monsieur— [She takes VERDELET'S arm, and starts to leave, as the curtain falls.]

ACT IV

The scene is the same. ANTOINETTE is seated between VERDELET and POIRIER.

VERDELET. I tell you you still love him.

POIRIER. I tell you you hate him.

VERDELET. No, no, Poirier—

POIRIER. Yes, I say! Evidently what happened yesterday is not enough for you! I suppose you'd like to see that good-for-nothing carry her off now?

VERDELET. I don't want Antoinette's whole life ruined, but from the way you go about things I—

POIRIER. I go about things the way I want to, Verdelet. It's all very well and easy to play the part of mediator, but you're not at swords' points with the Marquis. Once let him carry her off and you'd be always with her, while I'd be sitting alone in my hole like an old screech-owl —that's what you'd like! I know you! You're selfish, like all old bachelors!

VERDELET. Take care, Poirier! Are you positive that while you're pushing things to extremes, you yourself are not acting selfishly—?

POIRIER. Ha, so I'm the selfish one, am I? Because I'm trying to safeguard my girl's happiness? Because I have no intention of allowing that blackguardly son-in-law of mine to take my child from me and make her life a torture! [To ANTOINETTE.] Say something, can't you? It concerns you more than it does us!

ANTOINETTE. I don't love him any more, Tony. He crushed out of my heart everything that made me love him.

POIRIER. You see!

ANTOINETTE. I don't hate him, father; I am simply indifferent to him. I don't know him any more.

POIRIER. That's enough for me.

VERDELET. But, my poor Toinon, you are just beginning life. Have you ever thought what would become of a divorced woman? Did you ever consider—?

POIRIER. Verdelet, never mind your sermons! She won't have a very hard time of it with her good old father, who is going to spend all his time loving her and taking care of her. You'll see, dearie, what a lovely life we'll lead, we two [*Indicating* VERDELET]—we three! And I'm worth more than you, you selfish brute! You'll see how we'll love you, and do everything in the world for you. We won't leave you alone here and run after countesses! Now, smile at your father, and say that you're happy with him.

ANTOINETTE. Yes, father, very happy.

POIRIER. Hear that, Verdelet?

VERDELET. Yes, yes.

POIRIER. Now, as for your rascal of a husband—why, you've been much too good to him. We have him in our power at last. I'll allow him a thousand crowns a year, and he can go hang himself.

ANTOINETTE. Let him take everything that I have.

POIRIER. Oh, no!

ANTOINETTE. I ask only one thing: never to see him again.

POIRIER. He'll hear from me before long. I've just delivered a last blow.

ANTOINETTE. What have you done?

POIRIER. Offered the Château de Presles for sale, the château of his worthy ancestors.

ANTOINETTE. Have you done that? And would you allow him, Tony?

VERDELET [*aside to* ANTOINETTE]. Don't worry.

POIRIER. Yes, I have. The land speculators know their business, and I hope in a month's time that that vestige of feudalism will have disappeared and no longer soil the land of a free people. They'll plant beets over the site. From the old materials they will build huts for workingmen, useful farmers, and vine-growers. The park of his fathers will be cut down and the wood sawed into little pieces,

which will be burned in the fireplaces of good bourgeois, who have earned the money to buy firewood for themselves. And I myself will buy a cord or two for my own use.

ANTOINETTE. But he will think this is all revenge.

POIRIER. He will be perfectly right.

ANTOINETTE. He will think it is I who—

VERDELET [*aside to* ANTOINETTE]. Don't worry, my dear.

POIRIER. I'm going to see if the signs are ready. They're going to be huge, huge enough to cover the great walls all over Paris. "For sale, the Château de Presles!"

VERDELET. Perhaps it's already sold!

POIRIER. Since last evening? Nonsense! I'm going to the printer's.

[*He goes out.*]

VERDELET. Your father is absurd. If we let him have his way, he'd make reconciliation impossible between you and your husband.

ANTOINETTE. But what can you possibly hope for, poor Tony? My love has fallen from too great a height to be able ever to rise again. You have no idea how much Monsieur de Presles meant to me—

VERDELET. Oh, indeed I do.

ANTOINETTE. He was not only a husband, but a master whose slave I was proud to be. I not only loved him, I admired him as a great representative of a former age. Oh, Tony, what a horrible awakening I've had!

[*Enter a* SERVANT.]

SERVANT. Monsieur le Marquis asks whether madame will see him?

ANTOINETTE. No.

VERDELET. See him, dear. [*To the* SERVANT.] Monsieur le Marquis may come in. [*The* SERVANT *goes out.*]

ANTOINETTE. What good can come of it?

[*Enter* GASTON.]

GASTON. You need have no apprehension, madame; I shall not trouble you long with my company. You said yesterday that you considered yourself a widow, and I am far too guilty not to feel that your decision is irrevocable. I have come to say good-bye to you.

VERDELET. What's this, monsieur?

GASTON. Yes; I am going to do the only honorable thing that remains. You should be able to understand that.

VERDELET. But, monsieur—?

GASTON. I understand. Fear nothing for the future, and reassure Monsieur Poirier. There is one position I can take, that of my father: in the army. I am leaving to-morrow for Africa with Monsieur de Montmeyran, who has been good enough to sacrifice his leave of absence for my sake.

VERDELET [aside to ANTOINETTE]. What a splendid fellow!

ANTOINETTE [aside to VERDELET]. I never said he was a coward!

VERDELET. Now, my dear children, don't do anything extreme. Monsieur le Marquis, you are very much at fault, but I am sure that you ask nothing better than to make amends.

GASTON. If there were anything I could do—! [A pause.] There is nothing—I know! [To ANTOINETTE.] I leave you my name, madame; I am sure you will keep it spotless. I carry away with me the remorse of having troubled your existence, but you are still young and beautiful. And war carries with it happy chances—

[Enter the DUKE.]

DUKE. I have come to get him.

GASTON. Come. [Offering his hand to VERDELET.] Good-bye, Monsieur Verdelet. [They embrace.] Good-bye, madame, —for always.

DUKE. For always! He loves you, madame.

GASTON. Hush!

VERDELET. He loves you desperately. The moment he emerged from the black abyss from which you have helped him, his eyes were opened. He has seen you as you really are.

ANTOINETTE. Mademoiselle Poirier has triumphed over Madame de Montjay. How admirable!

VERDELET. You are cruel!

GASTON. She is only doing justice, monsieur. She deserved the purest sort of love, and I married her for her money. I made a bargain, a bargain which I was not honest enough to abide by. [To ANTOINETTE.] Yes, the very day after our marriage I sacrificed you, out of pure viciousness, for a woman who is far beneath you. Your youth, your charm, your purity, were not enough; no, in order to bring light to this darkened heart it was necessary for you to save my honor twice on the same day! How low I was to resist such devotion, and what does my love now prove? Can it possibly reinstate me in your eyes? When I loved you, I did what any man in my place would have done; in blinding myself to your virtues and your splendid qualities, I did what no one else would have done. You are right, madame, to despise a man who is utterly unworthy of you. I have lost all, even the right to pity myself —I don't pity myself.—Come, Hector.

DUKE. Wait. Do you know where he is going, madame? To fight a duel.

VERDELET and ANTOINETTE. To fight a duel?

GASTON. What are you saying?

DUKE. Well, if your wife doesn't love you any longer, there is no reason for hiding the truth.—Yes, madame, he is going to fight a duel.

ANTOINETTE. Oh, Tony, his life is in danger—!

DUKE. What difference does that make to you, madame? Is it possible that everything is not over between you, then?

ANTOINETTE. Oh, no: everything is over. Monsieur de Presles may dispose of his life as he thinks best—he owes me nothing—

DUKE [to GASTON]. Come, then—

[They go as far as the door.]

ANTOINETTE. Gaston!

DUKE. You see, she still loves you!

GASTON [throwing himself at her feet].

Oh, madame, if that is true, if I still have a place in your affection, say some word —give me the wish to live.

[*Enter* POIRIER.]

POIRIER. What are you doing there, Monsieur le Marquis?

ANTOINETTE. He is going to fight a duel!

POIRIER. A duel! And are you the least bit surprised? Mistresses, duels— that's to be expected. He who has land has war.

ANTOINETTE. What do you mean, father? Do you imagine—?

POIRIER. I'd wager my head on it.

ANTOINETTE. That's not true, is it, monsieur? You don't answer?

POIRIER. Do you think he would be honest enough to admit it?

GASTON. I cannot lie, madame. This duel is the last remnant of an odious past.

POIRIER. He's a fool to confess it! The impudence!

ANTOINETTE. And I was led to understand that you still loved me! I was even ready to forgive you—while you were on the point of fighting a duel for your mistress! Why, this was a trap for my weakness. Ah, Monsieur le Duc!

DUKE. He has already told you, madame, that this duel was the remnant of a past which he detests and wants to lay at rest and obliterate.

VERDELET [*to the* MARQUIS]. Very well, monsieur, then I have a simple plan: If you don't love Madame de Montjay any longer, then don't fight for her.

GASTON. What, monsieur, make excuses?

VERDELET. You must give Antoinette a proof of your sincerity, and this is the only one which you can give. Then didn't you just now ask for something to do as an expiation? Time was the only proof she could impose. Aren't you happy that you now have a chance, and that you can give that proof at once? I know it's a great sacrifice, but if it were any less, could it be a real expiation?

POIRIER [*aside*]. The fool! He's going to patch up matters!

GASTON. I would gladly sacrifice my life, but my honor—the Marquise de Presles would never accept that sort of sacrifice.

ANTOINETTE. What if you were mistaken, monsieur? What if I would accept it?

GASTON. What, madame, would you ask me—?

ANTOINETTE. To do for me almost as much as you would for Madame de Montjay? Yes, monsieur. For her sake you consented to forget the past of your family, and now would you refuse to forget a duel, a duel which is most offensive to me? How can I believe in your love, if it is less strong than your pride?

POIRIER. Then what good would a sword-scratch do you? Take my word for it, prudence is the mother of safety.

VERDELET [*aside*]. Old fool!

GASTON. See? That is what people will say.

ANTOINETTE. Who would doubt your courage? Haven't you given ample proofs of it?

POIRIER. And then what do you care for the opinion of a lot of know-nothings? You will have the respect of my friends, and that ought to be enough—

GASTON. You see, madame, people would laugh at me, and you could not love a ridiculous man very long.

DUKE. No one would laugh at you. Let me take your excuses to the ground, and I promise you that there will be no levity.

GASTON. What! Do you, too, think that—?

DUKE. Yes, my friend. Your affair is not one of those that can't possibly be arranged. The sacrifice your wife is asking affects only your own personal pride.

GASTON. But to make excuses on the ground—?

POIRIER. I would!

VERDELET. Really, Poirier, one might think you were trying to make him fight!

POIRIER. I'm doing all in my power to prevent him.

DUKE. Come, Gaston, you have no right to refuse this proof to your wife.

GASTON. Well—no! It's out of the question!

ANTOINETTE. That is the price of my forgiveness.

GASTON. Then I refuse it, madame. I shan't carry my sorrow very long.

POIRIER. Nonsense. Don't listen to him, dearie. Wait till he has his sword in his hand: he'll defend himself, I tell you. It would be like an expert swimmer trying to drown himself: once in the water, the devil himself couldn't keep him from saving himself.

ANTOINETTE. If Madame de Montjay objected to your fighting, you would give in to her. Good-bye.

GASTON. Antoinette, for God's sake—!

DUKE. She is exactly right.

GASTON. Excuses! I offer excuses!

ANTOINETTE. I see, you are thinking only of your own pride!

DUKE. Gaston! Give in! I swear I would do the same thing in your place.

GASTON. Very well—but to Pontgrimaud!—Go without me, then.

DUKE [to ANTOINETTE]. Madame, are you now satisfied with him?

ANTOINETTE. Yes, Gaston, you have now made up for everything. I have nothing else to forgive you; I believe in you, I am happy, and I love you. [The MARQUIS stands still, his head bowed. ANTOINETTE goes to him, takes his head in her hands, and kisses his forehead.] Now, go and fight! Go!

GASTON. My dearest wife, you have my mother's heart!

ANTOINETTE. No, my mother's, monsieur—

POIRIER [aside]. What idiots women are!

GASTON [to the DUKE]. Quick, or we shall be late.

ANTOINETTE. You are a good swordsman, are you not?

DUKE. He's as good as St. George, madame, and he has a wrist of steel.

Monsieur Poirier, pray for Pontgrimaud!

ANTOINETTE [to GASTON]. Please don't kill the young man.

GASTON. I'll let him off with a scratch—because you love me. Come, Hector.

[Enter a SERVANT with a letter on a silver plate.]

ANTOINETTE. Another letter?

GASTON. Open it yourself.

ANTOINETTE. It will be the first of yours that I have opened.

GASTON. I am sure of that.

ANTOINETTE [opening the letter]. It is from Monsieur de Pontgrimaud.

GASTON. Bah!

ANTOINETTE [reading:]. "My dear Marquis—"

GASTON. Snob!

ANTOINETTE. "We have both proved our valor—"

GASTON. In different ways, however!

ANTOINETTE. "I therefore have no hesitation in telling you that I regret having for a moment lost my head—"

GASTON. I was the one who lost mine!

ANTOINETTE. "You are the only man in the world to whom I should think of making excuses—"

GASTON. You flatter me, monsieur.

ANTOINETTE. "And I have no doubt that you will accept them as gallantly as they are offered—"

GASTON. Exactly!

ANTOINETTE. "With all my heart, Viscount de Pontgrimaud."

DUKE. He is not a viscount, and he has no heart. Otherwise his letter is most appropriate.

VERDELET [to GASTON]. Everything has turned out splendidly, my dear boy. I hope you have learned your lesson?

GASTON. For the rest of my life, dear Monsieur Verdelet. From this day on I begin a serious and calm existence. In order to break definitely with the follies of my past, I ask you for a place in your office.

VERDELET. In my office! You! A gentleman!

GASTON. Have I not my wife to support?

DUKE. You will do as the Breton nobles did, when they laid down their swords in Parliament in order to enter the field of commerce, and took them up again after having set their houses in order.

VERDELET. Very good, Monsieur le Marquis.

POIRIER [aside]. It's now my turn to give in. [Aloud.] My dear son-in-law, that is a most liberal sentiment; you really deserve to be a bourgeois. Now that we can understand each other, let us make peace. Stay with me.

GASTON. I ask for nothing better than to make my peace with you, monsieur. But as to staying with you, that is another matter. You have made me understand the happiness which the woodchopper feels when he is master of his own home. I do not blame you, but I cannot help remembering.

POIRIER. Are you going to take away my daughter? Are you going to leave me alone?

ANTOINETTE. I'll come to see you often, father.

GASTON. And you will always be welcome.

POIRIER. So my daughter is going to be the wife of a tradesman!

VERDELET. No, Poirier, your wife will be mistress of the Château de Presles. The château was sold this morning, and, with the permission of your husband, Toinon, it will be my wedding present.

ANTOINETTE. Dear Tony! May I accept it, Gaston?

GASTON. Monsieur Verdelet is one of those to whom it is a pleasure to be grateful.

VERDELET. I am retiring from business, and, if you will allow me, I shall come and live with you, Monsieur le Marquis. We shall cultivate your land together. That is a gentleman's profession.

POIRIER. Well, what about me, then? Aren't you going to invite me? All children are ungrateful—yes, my poor father was right.

VERDELET. Buy some neighboring land, and live near us.

POIRIER. That's an idea!

VERDELET. That's all you have to do; and besides—you're cured of your ambition, aren't you? I think you are.

POIRIER. Yes, yes. [Aside.] Let me see: this is 1846. I'll be deputy of the arrondissement of Presles in forty-seven, and peer of France in forty-eight¹

THE DEMI-MONDE

By ALEXANDRE DUMAS FILS

Produced at Paris, 1855

TRANSLATED BY HAROLD HARPER *

CHARACTERS

OLIVIER DE JALIN

RAYMOND DE NANJAC

HIPPOLYTE RICHOND

DE THONNERINS

FIRST SERVANT

SECOND SERVANT

THIRD SERVANT

BARONESS SUZANNE D'ANGE

VISCOUNTESS DE VERNIÈRES

VALENTINE DE SANTIS

MARCELLE

A CHAMBERMAID

*The action takes place at Paris; the first and fifth
acts in the home of Olivier, the second in that of the
Viscountess, the third and fourth, in that of Suzanne.*

ACT I

A drawing-room in the home of OLIVIER
DE JALIN.

[*As the curtain rises, the* VISCOUNTESS
and OLIVIER *are discovered.*]

VISCOUNTESS. Then you promise that
the affair will go no further?

OLIVIER. It cannot.

VISCOUNTESS. I wanted to come my-
self and ask you, even at the risk of being
found in your home with Heaven knows
whom!

OLIVIER. Do I keep evil company?

VISCOUNTESS. People say so.

OLIVIER. People are mistaken. No
women except those who are your inti-
mate friends come here.

VISCOUNTESS. That's flattering to my friends!

OLIVIER. But your presence here is quite explicable. Two friends of yours, Monsieur de Maucroix and Monsieur de Latour, were playing cards at your home and had a little misunderstanding. An explanation became necessary; that explanation should be made in this place. I am Monsieur de Maucroix's second; you have come to ask me to arrange the affair. What more natural?

VISCOUNTESS. I see that clearly enough, but I shouldn't like it known that I came, because I prefer all Paris not to know that I gamble at home. If anything serious happens there will be a trial, and no respectable woman should appear in court, even as witness, and have her name in the papers. Please do your best to come to an amicable arrangement or, if that is impossible, for the sake of my friendship, make the cause of the duel something with which I am not connected, even indirectly. I open my house to gambling in order that people may amuse themselves, not quarrel.

OLIVIER. I understand.

VISCOUNTESS. Well, as Madame de Santis hasn't come yet, I must go.

OLIVIER. Is Madame de Santis to do me the honor?

VISCOUNTESS. When she heard I was coming to see you she said to me: "I'll call for you. I shan't be sorry to see him either, the naughty man!" But she's so careless she may have forgotten all about it. I can't wait an instant longer. Good-bye. Let me remind you that you haven't asked after my niece, who was nice enough to ask me to convey to you all sorts of things.

OLIVIER. Pleasant things?

VISCOUNTESS. Of course.

OLIVIER. Very kind of her.

VISCOUNTESS. Certainly it is kind; she didn't have to do it: she knows very well you are not going to marry her.

OLIVIER. Oh, no!

VISCOUNTESS. My dear friend, you might find someone much worse.

OLIVIER. One never *happens* on anyone worth while.

VISCOUNTESS. But we're better off than you.

OLIVIER. Are you sure?

VISCOUNTESS. You are of the petty nobility—and, you're not rich?

OLIVIER. I have thirty thousand.

VISCOUNTESS. Dividends?

OLIVIER. Land.

VISCOUNTESS. Not bad. You have a family?

OLIVIER. One always has a family. But my family consists only of a mother —remarried; as I had to sue her husband when I came of age in order to get my father's fortune, we see each other very rarely. I don't think she cares very much for me. A widowed mother ought never to remarry. When she casts aside her husband's name she becomes practically a stranger to her family. That is how, my dear Viscountess, I was thrown so much on my own resources at an early age; that is why I have sown my wild oats, and contracted debts which I have since paid, and why to-day I am far too reasonable a man to marry your niece, in spite of the fact that I think her charming, that as an orphan she appeals to me, and that at one time I was afraid I might marry her.

VISCOUNTESS. Indeed!

OLIVIER. Yes! I actually fell deeply in love with her, and if I had continued to visit your home, as I am an honest and upright man, I should have ended by asking you for her hand, which would have been absurd.

VISCOUNTESS. Because she has no money?

OLIVIER. That made no difference to me; I am not the man to marry for money. There is another reason.

VISCOUNTESS. What is that?

OLIVIER. We men of the world are not such fools as we may appear to be. When we marry, we choose in our wives what we have been unable to find in the wives of others, and the longer we live the more insistent we are that our wives should know nothing of life. Those little ladies who have ready-made reputations for wit and independence before marriage, make a very sorry showing as wives. Look at Madame de Santis!

VISCOUNTESS. But Marcelle hasn't Valentine's character.

OLIVIER. Which does not prevent Madame de Santis, who is separated from an unknown husband,—a woman who is compromised and who compromises,—from having as her bosom friend Mademoiselle de Sancenaux, your niece. Tell me, now, is Madame de Santis a fit companion for a girl of twenty?

VISCOUNTESS. Why not? Marcelle has few amusements, and I have no fortune. Madame de Santis likes the theater and owns a carriage. Marcelle is merely taking advantage of all that. The poor girl must have some distractions. She is keeping out of mischief, after all.

OLIVIER. She does keep out of mischief, but she gives people the idea that she doesn't, and she will end by getting into it.

VISCOUNTESS. My dear Olivier!

OLIVIER. You are wrong! Do you know what you ought to have done? Sent your niece to the Marquis de Thonnerins three years ago, when she left boarding-school. He wanted to have her with him for his own daughter's sake. To-day Marcelle would be living in respectable society, and would have married or been able to marry as she should. Now, I doubt whether she will ever be able to do that.

VISCOUNTESS. I loved her so much I couldn't think of being separated from her.

OLIVIER. That was selfishness, which you will later regret, and for which she will some day blame you.

VISCOUNTESS. No; because if she wishes, she may marry in two months' time. She'll make a charming wife: women are what their husbands make them.

OLIVIER. But husbands are also what

their wives make them—and the compensation is not sufficient. Whom are you going to marry her to this time?

VISCOUNTESS. A young man.

OLIVIER. Who is in love with Mademoiselle de Sancenaux and who is loved by her?

VISCOUNTESS. No, but that makes little difference. In marriage if there is love it is killed by familiarity, and when it does not exist it gives birth to it.

OLIVIER. You talk like La Rochefoucauld. Where did you find the young man?

VISCOUNTESS. Monsieur de Latour introduced him to her.

OLIVIER. Introduced by Monsieur de Latour, specialist in shoddy: half string, half cotton!

VISCOUNTESS. Listen to me: I know good respectable men when I see them, and I tell you this man is one. He's exactly the husband for Marcelle: young, he looks imposing, he's not over thirty-two at the outside, in the army, decorated, no family with the exception of a young sister who is a widow and lives a retired life in the depths of her Faubourg Saint-Germain; he has twenty thousand francs' income, is free to do as he likes and may marry to-morrow. The only people he knows in Paris are Monsieur de Latour, Marcelle, and me. This is a splendid chance, I couldn't hope for a finer. You'll be the first to admit it when you've seen the man.

OLIVIER. Oh, I am to meet him?

VISCOUNTESS. To-day: he is Monsieur de Latour's second.

OLIVIER. Then he's that Monsieur de Nanjac who left his card here yesterday, and who is going to call to-day at three?

VISCOUNTESS. Yes. Now, be nice; you can when you want to be. If Monsieur de Nanjac takes to you, there's nothing out of the way in that, and if he speaks to you about Marcelle, try not to say too many of those stupid things you referred to a few moments ago.

[Enter a SERVANT.]
SERVANT. Madame de Santis.
[He goes out.]

[Enter VALENTINE.]
VISCOUNTESS. Come here, my dear child! Where have you been?
VALENTINE. Don't speak about it—I thought I'd never get away! [*To* OLIVIER.] How are you?
OLIVIER. Splendid, thanks.
VALENTINE. Just think! My dressmaker came and I had to try on some dresses. You'll see the one I'm having made for the races to-morrow. Then I went to hire a coach with two horses. I made them show me the coachman first—he's English—very nice. Then I went to see my landlord—you know I'm moving. What rent do you pay here?
OLIVIER. Three thousand francs.
VALENTINE. You're in a new neighborhood, a real desert. You might be murdered here and no one would ever know. I'd die of boredom. I found the dearest little apartment on the third floor—it's in the Rue de la Paix—seven thousand five hundred a year—landlord will re-paper. The drawing-room is to be decorated in red and gold, the bedroom in yellow, the boudoir in blue satin. I'm getting new furniture for it—it'll be lovely!
OLIVIER. How can you afford all that?
VALENTINE. Haven't I my dowry?
OLIVIER. You can't have very much of it left, at the pace you are living?
VALENTINE. I have about thirty thousand. [*To the* VISCOUNTESS.] My dear, if you ever need money, don't forget my agent: Monsieur Michel. I didn't have time to wait for the sale of some property of mine in Touraine, so I let him have the deeds, and he advanced me five thousand cash at once—interest at eight per cent—that isn't too high. From here I'm going straight to him and get the rest of the money.
OLIVIER. Isn't that Michel a thin little fellow with a mustache, who wears em-broidered shirts, and enameled buttons on his waistcoat?
VALENTINE. He's very nice-looking.
OLIVIER. That depends on where you see him. You know, he is a thief. I know him: he loaned me money before I became of age. If you're in the hands of that man, your thirty thousand francs won't last long. When they are gone, what are you going to do?
VALENTINE. There's still my husband. He must give me an allowance. Or if he doesn't, I can always return to him.
OLIVIER. What luck for him! And to think that at this moment he hasn't the slightest inkling of the happiness that awaits him! But what if he were to re-fuse?
VALENTINE. He can't—our separation isn't a judicial one. I have the right to return to my home whenever I like; he's forced to receive me. But I know, he'd ask for nothing better than to take me back: he's still in love with me.
OLIVIER. I'd be very curious to know how that comes out.
VALENTINE. You'll see—I've got to decide soon. Now, where else have I been? That's all! I came back by way of the Champs-Élysées—what crowds of people there were! I met heaps of my men friends: little de Bonchamp, the Count de Bryade, Monsieur de Casavaux. I invited them to tea to-morrow. Will you come, too?
OLIVIER. Thank you, no.
VALENTINE. I reserved a box at the theater for to-night, a stage-box down-stairs. I paid my bill at the modiste's. I'm leaving her: she works now only for actresses. That's what I've done to-day. [*To the* VISCOUNTESS.] Oh, by the way, we dine Tuesday at Monsieur de Calvillot's—a house-warming. What a charming apartment he has! He asked me to invite the ladies. You'll come with Marcelle, won't you? We'll have a gay time.
OLIVIER [*looking at her*]. Poor woman!
VALENTINE. What's the matter?
OLIVIER. Nothing: I pity you.
VALENTINE. Why?

OLIVIER. You deserve to be pitied. If you can't understand, I shan't waste time trying to explain.

VALENTINE. By the way, I knew I wanted to ask you something!

OLIVIER. She didn't even hear what I said! Can she have anything at all in her brain? And what did you want to know?

VALENTINE. Have you heard anything of Madame d'Ange?

OLIVIER. Why do you ask?

VALENTINE. Didn't she write you from Baden?

OLIVIER. No.

VALENTINE. And you tell that to *me*, to me who—   [*She laughs.*]

OLIVIER. To you who?

VALENTINE. Who mailed her letters for her. I can keep a secret, though I may look a fool. She wrote you charming letters.   [*She laughs again.*]

OLIVIER. Why do you laugh?

VALENTINE. Because you tried to appear discreet with me, and because I know more about it all than you do.

OLIVIER. I haven't heard from her for two weeks.

VALENTINE. Exactly: not since I left.

OLIVIER. Didn't she write to you, either?

VALENTINE. She never writes.
[*She laughs in his face.*]

OLIVIER [*looking into the whites of her eyes*]. What have you—there?

VALENTINE. Where do you mean?

VISCOUNTESS. He wants to make you angry.

OLIVIER. It's all black around your eyes.

VALENTINE. You're just like all the others: you're going to tell me I paint my eyebrows and lashes. When I think that fully half my friends believe I paint!

OLIVIER. And the other half are sure!

VALENTINE. The idea!

OLIVIER. Don't you use powder?

VALENTINE. As every woman does.

OLIVIER. And rouge?

VALENTINE. Never.

OLIVIER. Never?

VALENTINE. Just a touch, in the evenings—sometimes.

OLIVIER. And don't you touch up a little around the eyes?

VALENTINE. It's the fashion.

OLIVIER. Not among *decent* women.

VALENTINE. If it's becoming, what's the difference? So long as people know I'm decent, too.

OLIVIER. It is evident.

VISCOUNTESS. What a gossip you are, dear! We must go now!

VALENTINE [*to the* VISCOUNTESS]. Would you like to come with me to my apartment?

VISCOUNTESS. Delighted—I haven't anything to do.

VALENTINE [*to* OLIVIER]. Come with us: you can advise me about shades.

OLIVIER. I can't go: I am waiting for someone.

VALENTINE. For whom?

OLIVIER. A friend.

VALENTINE. What's his name?

OLIVIER. How can that interest you?

VALENTINE [*feigning indifference*]. I just asked.

OLIVIER. His name is Hippolyte Richond. He's been traveling a good deal during the past ten years. He returned to Paris about a week ago. He's the son of a rich merchant of Marseille, now deceased; he was in the oil business. Are you satisfied? Do you know him?

VALENTINE [*troubled*]. No.

VISCOUNTESS. Is he married?

OLIVIER. Yes, so you needn't trouble—

VALENTINE. Do you know his wife?

OLIVIER. And his son, too.

VALENTINE [*astonished*]. He has a son?

OLIVIER. Five or six years old. Why are you surprised? You say you don't know him?

VALENTINE. And this Monsieur Richond lives at—?

OLIVIER. Number seven, Rue de Lille. Would you care to see him? Wait a moment, I'll introduce you.

VALENTINE. No, no, I don't want to see him.

OLIVIER. What's the matter?

VALENTINE. Nothing! Good-bye!

[*Enter a* SERVANT.]

SERVANT. Monsieur Hippolyte Richond. [*He goes out.*]

OLIVIER [*to* VALENTINE]. Won't you—?

VALENTINE. Don't try to persuade me. [*She lets down her veil, and, as* HIPPOLYTE *enters, turns her head to one side. She goes out with the* VISCOUNTESS.]

OLIVIER. How are you?

HIPPOLYTE. Very well. And you?

OLIVIER. Splendid. How's your wife?

HIPPOLYTE. Everybody is very well.— Who is that woman?

OLIVIER. Madame de Santis.

HIPPOLYTE. Valentine!

OLIVIER. You know her?

HIPPOLYTE. Not personally, but I knew her husband intimately.

OLIVIER. Is she really married?

HIPPOLYTE. As much married as a person can possibly be.

OLIVIER. Really? She claims that her husband has greatly wronged her.

HIPPOLYTE. True: first he did wrong to marry her, for it seems she'd lost all sense of modesty.

OLIVIER. Not quite.

HIPPOLYTE. Do you know her very well?

OLIVIER. Yes. She has just been here for that old lady whom you saw with her. When I mentioned your name, her expression changed. Yet she denied knowing you.

HIPPOLYTE. We have never exchanged a word; but she must know that I am well acquainted with every detail of her life.

OLIVIER. And where is Monsieur de Santis?

HIPPOLYTE. Her husband's name is not de Santis; she got that name from her mother, and used it just after she was separated. Her husband refused to allow her to use his.

OLIVIER. What cause for complaint did he have against her?

HIPPOLYTE. She deceived him—vilely.

He was madly in love with her. I must say, she was charming: everyone called her the beautiful Mademoiselle de Santis. She didn't have a sou to her name. Her suitor was rich, very much in love, young, timid, he didn't dare ask for her hand. A friend of his, who first introduced him to the family, offered to make the proposal on his behalf, and the man accepted. The girl took the offer, and the friend was one of the two witnesses at the ceremony.

OLIVIER. And you were the other?

HIPPOLYTE. Yes. Six months after the wedding the husband came to me: he had incontrovertible proof that his wife was the mistress of the scoundrel who had brought about their marriage. He fought a duel with the fellow, killed him, and went away, leaving his wife the stipulated dowry of two hundred thousand francs, but forbidding her to use his name, or even to say that she had ever known him. Since that time they have not seen each other. That was ten years ago.

OLIVIER. And where is the husband now?

HIPPOLYTE. He lives abroad. I met him in Germany two months ago.

OLIVIER. Does he still love his wife?

HIPPOLYTE. I don't think so.

OLIVIER. Yet she maintains that he loves her as much as ever, and that it rests with her whether or not she shall return to him.

HIPPOLYTE. She is mistaken. Who is that old lady she went out with?

OLIVIER. The remains of a woman of quality whom the need for luxury and pleasure has gradually dragged into a rather free-and-easy social circle. She ruined her husband, who took it into his head to die ten or twelve years ago. She has a few old friends, some few shares which are given her at par and which she sells at a premium, a few scattered fragments of her fortune which the wind casts up from time to time—those are her sole resources. She has a pretty niece, upon whose marriage she counts to regild her 'scutcheon; the only trouble is that the husband is not yet forthcoming. Meantime, she struggles on as best she is able; gives parties at which you instinctively feel that the coffers are empty, and that the day after she will have to pawn a jewel or sell something in order to pay for the pink candles, the punch and the ices. The young people she invites drink the punch, send bonbons on New Year's, marry girls in real society, and just tip their hats to the Viscountess and her niece when they meet them, in order not to have to invite them to meet their mothers and wives.

HIPPOLYTE. And is Madame de Santis a friend of that woman?

OLIVIER. In what other social circle would she move?

HIPPOLYTE. That's true! Well, you wrote that you had a favor to ask me. What is it?

OLIVIER. What time is it?

HIPPOLYTE. Two o'clock.

OLIVIER [*ringing*]. Let me finish something I have to do, then we can talk at our ease.

HIPPOLYTE. Please! I have plenty of time.

[*Enter a* SERVANT.]

OLIVIER [*to the* SERVANT, *as he hands him a letter*]. Take this letter to Monsieur le Comte de Lornan. You know him, of course. In case he is not at home, give the letter to Madame la Comtesse. That will do. [*The* SERVANT *goes out.*]

HIPPOLYTE. So you write letters that can be opened by both—?

OLIVIER. No! I wrote a letter that can be read only by the wife, but in order not to compromise her, I address it to the husband.

HIPPOLYTE. But what if it is handed to the husband?

OLIVIER. Stupid! The husband is in the country.

HIPPOLYTE. Very ingenious, I declare!

OLIVIER. I recommend it to you in case you should ever need to make use of it. This is the first and the last time that I employ the means—it is only for the sake of the lady.

HIPPOLYTE. Are you sure?

OLIVIER. Here's the story—it's very simple, you see. I'll mention the people, in order to show you that the husband has nothing to fear from the wife, and the wife nothing to fear from me. Last autumn—that's a dangerous season, especially in the country, where the solitude gives rein to the imagination, where each leaf that falls is a ready-made elegy, where one feels the need of becoming a consumptive in order to be in closer harmony with melancholy and fading nature—

HIPPOLYTE. See Millevoye, *The Falling of the Leaves,* volume one, page twentyone. I know that! I've suffered from consumption myself.

OLIVIER. Who hasn't? Consumption and the mounted National Guard of 1830 —everyone has been in both. Well, last autumn I was introduced to the Countess de Lornan, who was spending the month of October in the country with the mother of one of my friends—why, de Maucroix's mother, it was! We were just speaking of him. She's a blonde, very distinguished-looking, poetic, sentimental, always in the clouds,—her husband was away,—you know, the usual situation! I made love to her, and now I believe I am still in love with her. On our return to Paris she introduces me to her husband.

HIPPOLYTE. Who is a fool?

OLIVIER. Charming fellow of forty, who took to me, and for whom I feel a deep affection. At the end of two weeks I became his intimate friend and forgot all about the woman—absolutely. Now, there was a woman who gave me no hopes whatsoever, and who, between you and me, was no more intended for love affairs and intrigues than—

[*He tries to find the word.*]

HIPPOLYTE. Never mind: you'll find the comparison some other time.

OLIVIER. Her pride was hurt; she believed I had been trifling with her. Yesterday she wrote me that her husband had gone away for a few days; that she wanted an explanation from me, and that she was waiting for me to-day at two o'clock. I burned her letter, and instead of having an altogether unnecessary explanation with her, I have just written the truth: that I want to become her friend, that I don't love her enough, or rather that I care too much for her to do the other thing. She will blame me a little, but, good Heavens! it will be something to be proud of to have saved the good name of a woman.

HIPPOLYTE. Splendid, I say!

OLIVIER. And I decided that without any afterthought, I swear! Granted that I have had a great deal of experience, I am an honest man, and I have decided not to commit any more of those petty infamies for which love is only too often the excuse. To go to a man's home, accept his friendship and hospitality, call him friend, and then take his wife,—well, so much the worse for those who don't agree with me,—but I think that it is shameful, repugnant, disgusting.

HIPPOLYTE. You're really magnificent!

OLIVIER. Well—yes!

HIPPOLYTE. You must be in love with someone else.

OLIVIER. Sceptic!

HIPPOLYTE. Confess it!

OLIVIER. Well, it's a fact that—

HIPPOLYTE. I was saying to myself: "There's a gay fellow who's playing the Joseph—he must have good reasons—" Do I know the fair lady?

OLIVIER. No. She went to take the waters before you arrived at Paris. But I should never have mentioned her name to you: I don't want to compromise her. She is a woman of the world.

HIPPOLYTE. Nonsense!

OLIVIER. She says so. Meantime, she is free, she pretends to be a widow, she is no more than twenty. She's wonderful, clever, and knows how to keep up appearances. There's no danger at present, no possibility of remorse in the future; she is the sort of woman who can foresee every eventuality of a *liaison* and who

lead their love with ready-made phrases and a smile on the lips, along past every relay, up to the point where it is necessary to change horses. I entered this *liaison* as a traveler would who is in no particular hurry, and who prefers to take the post-chaise instead of the railroad. It's much more amusing, and I can get out whenever I like.

HIPPOLYTE. And this has been going on for how long?

OLIVIER. For six months.

HIPPOLYTE. And it will last?

OLIVIER. As long as she wishes it.

HIPPOLYTE. Until you marry!

OLIVIER. I shall never marry.

HIPPOLYTE. You say so, but some fine day—

[*Enter a* SERVANT.]

SERVANT. Monsieur.

OLIVIER. What is it?

SERVANT [*in an undertone*]. The lady who was away.

OLIVIER [*pointing to a door*]. Tell her to go in there; I shall be with her in a moment. [*The* SERVANT *goes out*.]

HIPPOLYTE. Is it she?

OLIVIER. Yes.

HIPPOLYTE. I'm going.

OLIVIER. When shall I see you again?

HIPPOLYTE. Whenever you say.

OLIVIER. Well?

HIPPOLYTE. Well, what?

OLIVIER. Are you running off like this?

HIPPOLYTE. How else should I?

OLIVIER. But what about Maucroix? We've been talking about everything else except his affair.

HIPPOLYTE. That's so. We forgot. What fools we are!

OLIVIER. Use the singular, please!

HIPPOLYTE. Very well. What a fool you are!

OLIVIER. Is monsieur pleased to be clever?

HIPPOLYTE. Sometimes.

OLIVIER. This is the case, then: Monsieur de Maucroix had a quarrel at cards with Monsieur de Latour; it took place at the home of the Madame de Vernières, whom you saw here. De Latour is going to send his second here at three o'clock. Now, the moment he sends me a second, I know that the matter can be arranged. But, if this is out of the question, we must have another meeting, with two seconds for each side. That meeting will doubtless take place this evening. We might as well have it over with as soon as possible. Where can I find you in case I need you?

HIPPOLYTE. At my home, up to six, and from six to eight at the Café Anglais. Will you have dinner with me there?

OLIVIER. Good! Come for me at six; this is not out of your way.

[HIPPOLYTE *goes out. As soon as the door at the back has closed,* OLIVIER *goes to the side door, which has opened meantime.*]

[*Enter* SUZANNE.]

OLIVIER. What! It's you!

[*He offers his hand to her.*]

SUZANNE [*shaking hands and smiling*]. Yes it's I.

OLIVIER. I thought you were dead.

SUZANNE. I'm very well, you see.

OLIVIER. When did you come from Baden?

SUZANNE. A week ago.

OLIVIER. A week ago!

SUZANNE. Yes.

OLIVIER. And to-day I see you for the first time! There must be some news?

SUZANNE. Possibly. [*A pause*]. Are you as clever as ever?

OLIVIER. More so.

SUZANNE. Since when?

OLIVIER. Since your return.

SUZANNE. That's almost a compliment.

OLIVIER. Almost.

SUZANNE. So much the better.

OLIVIER. Why?

SUZANNE. Because on my return from Baden, I'm not at all sorry to talk over a number of things.

OLIVIER. Don't people talk at Baden?

SUZANNE. No—they just speak!

OLIVIER. Well, it seems that you weren't any too anxious to talk this last week. Otherwise you would have come to see me sooner.

SUZANNE. I've been in the country. I've come to Paris to-day for the first time, and no one knows I'm here. You were saying that you were as clever as ever?

OLIVIER. Yes.

SUZANNE. We'll see.

OLIVIER. What are you driving at?

SUZANNE. One point: a question. Will you marry me?

OLIVIER. You?

SUZANNE. Don't be too surprised; that would be most impolite.

OLIVIER. What an idea!

SUZANNE. Then you won't? Don't say any more about it. Well, my dear Olivier, I must now let you know that we shall never see each other again. I'm going away.

OLIVIER. For long?

SUZANNE. Yes.

OLIVIER. Where are you going?

SUZANNE. Far away.

OLIVIER. I'm puzzled.

SUZANNE. It's very simple. People talk; you find them everywhere. It was for such people that carriages and steamboats were invented.

OLIVIER. True. Well, what about me?

SUZANNE. You?

OLIVIER. Yes.

SUZANNE. You stay here at Paris, I imagine.

OLIVIER. Ah!

SUZANNE. At least—unless you want to go away, too?

OLIVIER. With you?

SUZANNE. Oh, no.

OLIVIER. Then—it's all over?

SUZANNE. What?

OLIVIER. We don't love each other any more?

SUZANNE. Have we ever done so?

OLIVIER. I once thought it.

SUZANNE. I did all in my power to believe it.

OLIVIER. Really?

SUZANNE. I have spent my life wanting to love. Up to now, it has been impossible.

OLIVIER. Thank you!

SUZANNE. I'm not referring to you alone.

OLIVIER. Thank you on *our* behalf, then!

SUZANNE. You must know that when I left for Baden, I went there less as a woman who wanted to be lazy than as one who wanted time to reflect—like a sensible woman. At a distance, one can better realize what one truly feels and thinks. Possibly you were of more importance to me than I had wanted to believe. I went away in order to see whether I could do without you.

OLIVIER. Well?

SUZANNE. I can. You did not follow me; and the most that can be said of your letters is that they were clever. Two weeks after I left, you were completely indifferent to me.

OLIVIER. Your words possess the inestimable advantage of being absolutely clear.

SUZANNE. My first idea on returning was not even to see you and have that explanation, but to wait until chance should bring us together. But then I knew we were both sensible people, and that in place of trying to escape that situation, it was a much more dignified proceeding to try to have it over with at once. And here I am, asking you whether you wish to make out of our false love a true friendship? [OLIVIER *smiles*.] Why do you smile?

OLIVIER. Because, except for the form, I said or rather wrote the same thing not two hours ago.

SUZANNE. To a woman?

OLIVIER. Yes.

SUZANNE. To the beautiful Charlotte de Lornan?

OLIVIER. I don't know the lady.

SUZANNE. Toward the end of my last stay in Paris you did not come to see me so regularly as you used to. I soon saw that the excuses you gave for not coming, or rather the pretexts you made before

not coming, were hiding some mystery. That mystery could be nothing other than a woman. One day when you were leaving my home, after saying that you were to meet some man friend, I followed you to the house where you were going; I gave the porter twenty francs, and learned that Madame de Lornan lived there, and that you went to see her every day. That's how simple it was. Then I understood that I didn't love you: I did my best to be jealous, and failed.

OLIVIER. And how does it happen that you have not spoken to me before about Madame de Lornan?

SUZANNE. If I had, I should have had to ask you to choose between that woman and me. As she was more recent than I, I should have been sacrificed for her, and my pride would have suffered cruelly. I didn't want to speak to you.

OLIVIER. But you were mistaken. I did go to see Madame de Lornan, but I declare she has never been, is not, and never will be, other than a good friend of mine.

SUZANNE. That is nothing to me. You are free to love whom you like. All I ask is your friendship; may I have it?

OLIVIER. What is the use, since you are going away?

SUZANNE. Exactly. Friends are rare and more precious at a distance than near at hand.

OLIVIER. Tell me the whole truth.

SUZANNE. What truth?

OLIVIER. Why are you going away?

SUZANNE. Merely in order to—get away.

OLIVIER. Is there no other reason?

SUZANNE. No other.

OLIVIER. Then stay.

SUZANNE. There are reasons to prevent that.

OLIVIER. Don't you want to tell me?

SUZANNE. To ask for a secret in exchange for one's friendship is not friendship, but a venal transaction.

OLIVIER. You are logic incarnate. And what are you going to do before you leave?

SUZANNE. Stay in the country. I know you are bored to death with the country, that is why I am not asking you to come.

OLIVIER. Very well. Then this is a dismissal in good form. Well, my task as friend will not be difficult.

SUZANNE. It will be more difficult than you imagine. I don't mean by that word friendship one of those banal traditional affairs that every lover offers to every other when the two separate; that is nothing more than the mite of a reciprocal indifference. What I want is an intelligent friendship, a useful attachment, a form of devotion and protection, if need be, and above all, of discretion. You will doubtless have but one occasion, and that lasting five minutes, to prove your friendship. But that will be a sufficient proof. Do you accept?

OLIVIER. I do.

[*Enter a* SERVANT.]

SERVANT. Monsieur Raymond de Nanjac asks whether monsieur can see him. Here is his card. He has come on behalf of Monsieur le Comte de Latour, and says monsieur is awaiting him.

OLIVIER. That's so. I shall see him in a moment.

SUZANNE [*to the* SERVANT]. Wait! Let me see that card.

OLIVIER [*handing her the card*]. Here.

SUZANNE. Good. Monsieur de Nanjac is a friend of yours?

OLIVIER. I have never set eyes on him.

SUZANNE. How is it that he is here to see you?

OLIVIER. He is acting as second to Monsieur de Latour, who had a quarrel with a friend of mine.

SUZANNE. What strange coincidences there are!

OLIVIER. What is it?

SUZANNE. Where can I escape without being seen?

OLIVIER. You know very well. How agitated you are! Do you know Monsieur de Nanjac?

SUZANNE. I was introduced to him at Baden—I spoke to him two or three times.

OLIVIER. Oh! I'm getting warm, I think, as little children say when they are playing games. Is Monsieur de Nanjac—?

SUZANNE. You're dreaming!

OLIVIER. Hm!

SUZANNE. Well, if you insist that Monsieur de Nanjac see me in your apartment, ask him in.

OLIVIER. I shouldn't think of it.

SUZANNE [*regaining control over herself*]. No, better ask him in.

OLIVIER [*motioning to the* SERVANT]. I don't understand, now?

SERVANT [*announcing*]. Monsieur Raymond de Nanjac.

[*Enter* RAYMOND.]

OLIVIER [*going to greet him at the door*]. Pardon my having made you wait, monsieur.

[RAYMOND *bows, then looks at* SUZANNE *in astonishment. He is deeply moved.*]

SUZANNE. Don't you recognize me, Monsieur de Nanjac?

RAYMOND. I thought I did, madame, but I was not quite sure.

SUZANNE. When did you come from Baden?

RAYMOND. The day before yesterday I thought I should have the honor of paying you a visit to-day, but it is likely I shall be prevented from doing so by certain things which have happened, contrary to all expectation.

SUZANNE. Whenever you would like to call, I shall be delighted to see you. Good-bye, my dear Olivier, and don't forget our agreement.

OLIVIER. I am less inclined to do so now than ever before.

SUZANNE [*to* RAYMOND]. Good-bye, monsieur. I hope to see you again.

[*She goes out.*]

OLIVIER. Now, monsieur, I am at your service. [*He motions* RAYMOND *to a seat.*]

RAYMOND [*sitting down—dryly*]. Monsieur, the matter is most simple. Monsieur de Latour, a friend of mine—

OLIVIER. Pardon me, monsieur, for interrupting: is Monsieur de Latour a friend of yours?

RAYMOND. Yes, monsieur. Why do you ask?

OLIVIER. Because sometimes—Are you a soldier, monsieur?

RAYMOND. Yes, monsieur.

OLIVIER. Sometimes a soldier believes himself in honor bound not to refuse to act as second to a person whom he scarcely knows, or even whom he does not know at all.

RAYMOND. True, we rarely refuse. But as a matter of fact, I do know Monsieur de Latour; I like him and consider him a friend. Does he not deserve the title? Is that what you mean to convey?

OLIVIER. Not in the least, monsieur. Continue, please.

RAYMOND. Well, Monsieur de Latour was the day before yesterday at the home of the Viscountess de Vernières. I was there with him; they were playing *lansquenet*. A young man, Monsieur Georges de Maucroix—

OLIVIER. A friend of mine.

RAYMOND. Monsieur de Maucroix "had the hand." I believe that is the term— I am not acquainted with the technical expressions used in cards. I have never played.

OLIVIER. That is the expression which has been consecrated by time.

RAYMOND. Monsieur de Maucroix had "passed" three or four times, and there were twenty-five louis on the table. Monsieur de Latour's turn came next, but as he had lost a great deal during the evening, he found that he hadn't any money left, and told Monsieur de Maucroix that he would take the hand and owe the money: give his *word* for it. At that, Monsieur de Maucroix, who was about to lay down his cards, handed them to his right-hand neighbor, and said: "I pass." Monsieur de Latour was pleased to see in this simple occurrence a refusal to accept his word about the money. He be-

lieved that he had been offended, and demanded an explanation from Monsieur de Maucroix, who replied that the place where they were was not suitable for that sort of discussion. He mentioned your name and address. Monsieur de Latour has asked me to come and receive the explanation from you which your friend thought he could not make in person.

OLIVIER. The explanation is very simple, monsieur, and in this affair there will result, I hope, one advantage for me: the pleasure of making your acquaintance. Georges had no intention of offending Monsieur de Latour: he "passed," as anyone may when he does not wish to risk losing on one hand all that he had won.

RAYMOND. But it was Monsieur de Maucroix's place to decide that before beginning the hand with Monsieur de Latour.

OLIVIER. He merely reconsidered.

RAYMOND. He would have played the hand with anyone else; of that I am firmly convinced. He would have played it if Monsieur de Latour's money had been on the table.

OLIVIER. Allow me to say that we cannot know that, monsieur. We can discuss only the visible and known fact. I have the honor of repeating what Monsieur de Maucroix himself said to me: that he did nothing but what he had often done, a thing everyone does. For my part, I can say that if I had been in Monsieur de Latour's place, I should never have noticed that detail.

RAYMOND. It is possible, monsieur, that in ordinary society it might be as you say, but in military circles—

OLIVIER. I beg your pardon, monsieur, but I was not aware that Monsieur de Latour was in the army.

RAYMOND. But I am.

OLIVIER. Allow me to remark, monsieur, that in this matter neither of *us* is concerned; this is between Monsieur de Latour and Monsieur de Maucroix, neither of whom is in the army.

RAYMOND. But the moment Monsieur

de Latour chooses me to represent him, I treat the matter as if it were my own.

OLIVIER. Let me tell you, monsieur, that you are making a mistake. I grant that the seconds should be as careful of the honor of the principals as they would be of their own, but they ought in their discussions to adopt a conciliatory manner or at least a certain impartiality, which will, in case of a tragic outcome, relieve them of responsibility. It is surely sufficient to discuss facts, without making suppositions—*those* should be made only by the principals. Monsieur, believe me, there are not two kinds of honor—one for the uniform you wear, one for the clothes I wear: the same heart beats under each. You see, a man's life appears so serious a matter to me that it deserves serious discussion, and only when no other course is open should one cold-bloodedly bring two men face to face on the dueling-ground. If you like, monsieur, let us have another meeting, for, if you will allow me to speak frankly, you seem in a rather irritable humor, and your friend and mine cannot come to a satisfactory agreement unless for some reason which I cannot guess (this is the first time I have had the honor of meeting you) we are ourselves two adversaries needing seconds, and not seconds trying to conciliate two adversaries.

RAYMOND [*with a change of tone and manner*]. You are right, monsieur; it was personal feeling that led me to speak as I did. Pardon me, and allow me at the same time to speak freely.

OLIVIER. Speak, monsieur.

RAYMOND. I am very frank—as soldiers usually are—and I ask you to be frank with me.

OLIVIER. Very well.

RAYMOND. We are both men of honor; about the same age; we move in similar circles; and if I had not been living like a bear in Africa for the past ten years, we should undoubtedly have met and become friends long ago. You agree with me, do you not?

OLIVIER. I am beginning to.

RAYMOND. I ought to have begun in this tone, instead of allowing myself to go on in that ill-humored manner, and receiving the little lesson you so cleverly and delightfully administered to me. If I had happened upon a man of my own disposition, instead of a man of sense like yourself, we should now have been at each other's throats—which would have been ridiculous. Now, let me ask you a few delicate questions which only an old friend would ordinarily have the right to ask. I give you my word that not a syllable will go beyond this room.

OLIVIER. Proceed.

RAYMOND. Thank you. This conversation may have the greatest influence over my life.

OLIVIER. I am listening.

RAYMOND. What is the name of the woman who was here when I came in?

OLIVIER. Baroness d'Ange.

RAYMOND. In society?

OLIVIER. Yes.

RAYMOND. Widow?

OLIVIER. Yes.

RAYMOND. What are the relations—answer me, monsieur, on your honor, as I should answer you if you asked me—what are the relations between her and you?

OLIVIER [*after a pause*]. Simple friendship.

RAYMOND. You are just her friend?

OLIVIER [*emphasizing the word "am"*]. I *am* simply her friend.

RAYMOND. Thank you, monsieur. One word more: how did it happen that Madame d'Ange was here? Surely a friend—?

OLIVIER. May not a respectable woman visit a respectable man? Why not? The proof that Madame d'Ange's business here was nothing that she need be ashamed of is that, although she might have left here by that door unseen, she waited, talked with you, and went quite openly.

RAYMOND. That's so. I needed this explanation. Now, as I wish to fulfill my obligations to you for your frankness, let me tell you everything. I am an officer in an African regiment; three months ago I was rather severely wounded, and I obtained a leave of absence during my convalescence. Two weeks ago I arrived at Baden. I saw Madame d'Ange and obtained an introduction; she produced an instantaneous and profound impression on me. I followed her to Paris, and I am desperately in love with her. She has never in any way encouraged my passion. She is young and beautiful, and I wondered whether she were in love with someone, because her behavior at Baden was irreproachable. Now you can easily understand how excited I was when I found her here. You will understand my very natural fears, all my suppositions, my ill-humor which was dissipated by your own good commonsense, and finally this explanation I so frankly asked for and which you so courteously gave me. I hope, monsieur, that we shall have occasion to see each other again. Please consider me among your friends; if ever I can help you, remember that I am at your service.

OLIVIER. I have already told you what I had to tell you, monsieur. Good luck to you!

RAYMOND. I believe that this duel affair can be satisfactorily settled.

OLIVIER. I believe so, too.

RAYMOND. We'll outline our conference, give copies to our friends, and nothing more need be done about it.

OLIVIER. Exactly. Shall I see you to-morrow? I shall come to you. I have your address on this card. At the same hour?

RAYMOND. Very well. Until to-morrow, monsieur.

[*They shake hands, then* RAYMOND *goes out.* HIPPOLYTE *opens the door and looks through.*]

HIPPOLYTE. May I come in?

OLIVIER [*bowing to* RAYMOND, *who is in the hallway—aside*]. Poor fellow!

HIPPOLYTE. What's happening?

OLIVIER. A great deal, my dear man.

HIPPOLYTE. What about Monsieur de Maucroix's affair?

OLIVIER. Settled.

HIPPOLYTE. Good. And the lady who came from Baden?

OLIVIER. All my plans for the future have crumbled. Harlequin proposed beautifully, but Columbine disposed in her own way.

HIPPOLYTE. That makes two ruptures in a single day.

OLIVIER. One before, one after. If Titus were in my place, he would be able to retire early, and he would not have misspent his day.

HIPPOLYTE. Something has happened to me, too.

OLIVIER. What?

HIPPOLYTE. I have just received the following invitation from Madame de Vernières: "Madame la Vicomtesse de Vernières has the honor to ask Monsieur Hippolyte Richond to spend the evening with her next Wednesday—" the address follows. But guess what was written at the bottom of the page? "On behalf of Madame de Santis, who sends her compliments." Madame de Santis wants to talk to me about her husband, no doubt.

OLIVIER. What did you answer?

HIPPOLYTE. Nothing as yet, but I am going to accept.

OLIVIER. I'll go with you.

HIPPOLYTE. Were you invited, too?

OLIVIER. An invitation is not necessary at Madame de Vernières'. I am sure there is some intrigue afoot with those people, and I prefer to be present while it is in process of incubation rather than after it is hatched. Are you hungry?

HIPPOLYTE. Oh, yes!

OLIVIER. Then let's go to dinner.

ACT II

The drawing-room at MADAME DE VER-NIÈRES'. *The* VISCOUNTESS *is speaking to a* SERVANT.

VISCOUNTESS. Light up the boudoir and my bedroom.

SERVANT [*just as he is leaving, announces*]. Madame la Baronne d'Ange.
[*He goes out.*]

[*Enter* SUZANNE.]

SUZANNE. I'm not as prompt as I wanted to be, my dear Viscountess, but you know when one lives in the country one cannot always be punctual. I dressed at home, at Paris, but everything was upside down there, as if I'd been away. But to-morrow everything will be in order again.

VISCOUNTESS. You are not late.

SUZANNE. One is always late when one comes to do a favor.

VISCOUNTESS. How good of you! You received my letter? You don't blame me too much for my indiscretion, do you?

SUZANNE. But we're friends! Here is what you asked me for. [*She gives the* VISCOUNTESS *a bank-note.*] If that is not enough—

VISCOUNTESS. Thank you, that will be plenty—and I needed it to-day!

SUZANNE. Why didn't you ask for it yesterday?

VISCOUNTESS. Because up to the last moment I thought I could get it from Madame de Santis' broker; he promised me. But at noon he said it would be impossible. Valentine is hard-pressed, too, and I couldn't ask her. Now I can tell you: I'm being sued. I had good reason to believe that my goods would have been seized to-morrow, and I wanted to avoid that scandal.

SUZANNE. You are quite right. You must pay the bailiff to-night.

VISCOUNTESS. There are two.

SUZANNE. Then, the bailiffs.

VISCOUNTESS. I'm going to send my maid with the money.

SUZANNE. Don't take servants into your confidence in matters of that sort.

VISCOUNTESS. But I can't wait until to-morrow. Those men might come the first thing in the morning.

SUZANNE. Then go yourself.

VISCOUNTESS. What about my guests?

SUZANNE. I'll receive them for you.

You can be back before the first arrives. Who are coming?

VISCOUNTESS. Valentine; a Monsieur Richond whom she wanted me to ask— a friend of her husband; Monsieur de Nanjac (oh, if that were only a match! I'm counting on you for that—if it materializes, we'll be saved!); Marcelle: you; I; and the Marquis de Thonnerins. I'm counting on these. I don't know whether Monsieur de Maucroix and Monsieur de Latour are coming, even though their quarrel has been settled.

SUZANNE. Didn't you invite Monsieur de Jalin?

VISCOUNTESS. He never comes.

SUZANNE. Will the Marquis de Thonnerins?

VISCOUNTESS. He sent no reply, which means he is coming.

SUZANNE. Quick now, attend to your affairs—I'll wait for you.

VISCOUNTESS. I'll take a cab and be back in twenty minutes. You're going to be bored—or shall I leave Marcelle with you? I don't think she need go with me.

SUZANNE. What has she to do with it?

VISCOUNTESS. I'll tell you: my affairs are in such confusion that the only way I can hope to save a few odds and ends is by putting them under someone else's name. I have made Marcelle legally independent; you know her mother left her a little money, of which I was made a trustee. You see, she can claim what I still have: it's her only guarantee. That will protect me from further persecution. Still, I think possibly she may have to sign something.

SUZANNE. Then take her with you.

[*Enter a* SERVANT.]

SERVANT. Monsieur le Marquis de Thonnerins. [*He goes out.*]

SUZANNE. I'll talk with the Marquis while I'm waiting for you.

VISCOUNTESS. Good. I'll go before he comes; otherwise I couldn't get away. Tell him about Marcelle and Monsieur de Nanjac, he might be of use to us.
[*She goes out.*]

[*Enter the* MARQUIS.]

MARQUIS. Who just left?

SUZANNE. The mistress of the house, who has an errand to do. She will be back soon.

MARQUIS. Oh, never mind! I probably shan't see her.

SUZANNE. Aren't you going to spend the evening with us?

MARQUIS. No: I have only a short time to spare. My daughter just returned from the country, and I am going to take her to my brother's to-day. I came only because you wrote.

SUZANNE. I wished to speak with you, but I did not want to make you come out to the country—that would be taking advantage of you. Is Mademoiselle de Thonnerins well?

MARQUIS. Very well.

SUZANNE. Aren't you ever going to let me see her? You know, I'd so like to, even at a distance, because you might never bring her.

MARQUIS. My dear Suzanne, I think I've made that clear once for all. Why open the discussion again? You have something to tell me; I am listening.

SUZANNE. You once told me that no matter what might happen, I should always find you ready to help me.

MARQUIS. I repeat it.

SUZANNE. Yes, but so distantly that I am not sure whether it would be discreet of me to count on your promise.

MARQUIS. I don't remember ever having made you a promise I did not keep. The way in which I spoke is because of my age. The time has come when I should remember that I am no longer a young man of twenty, or even of forty. I should be ridiculous if I pretended to be anything but what I am: an old man who is happy if he can be of service to those whom he has occasionally bored, and who have been generous enough not to make him aware of the fact.

SUZANNE. Then let me answer in the same spirit. I owe everything to you, Monsieur le Marquis. Perhaps you have forgotten that, because you are the bene-factor; I have not, because I am the recipient of your favors. You might have had for me only a passing fancy; you honored me with a little love.

MARQUIS. Suzanne!

SUZANNE. I was nothing, and you made something of me. Thanks to you, I have attained a position on the social ladder which might be considered a descent for women who started at the top, but which is for me, who started at the bottom, the apex. Now you can readily understand that since I have risen through you—to this position which I should never otherwise have dared aspire to, I cannot help having certain ambitions; they are inevitable under the circumstances. Now, I must either fall lower than where I began, or rise to the very top. Marriage is my only salvation.

MARQUIS. Marriage?

SUZANNE. Yes.

MARQUIS. You are ambitious.

SUZANNE. Do not discourage me. I said to myself, as you seem to say now, that it was out of the question, because I had to find a man who had enough confidence to believe in me, was strong and fine enough to force society to accept me, brave enough to defend me, sufficiently in love to devote his whole life to me; young enough, handsome enough to believe that he is loved and that I *shall* love him.

MARQUIS. Have you found this confident, noble, and loving husband?

SUZANNE. Yes.

MARQUIS. Is he young enough to believe he is loved?

SUZANNE. He is young enough for me to love him.

MARQUIS. *Do* you love him?

SUZANNE. Yes. What of it? No one is perfect!

MARQUIS. Is he going to marry you?

SUZANNE. I have only a word to say, and he will ask me.

MARQUIS. Why haven't you said it?

SUZANNE. Because I wanted to speak to you first. It was the least I could do.

MARQUIS. There is this to fear, you know: that this man, who appears so splendid to you, may be merely speculating. He may know your past and, believing you to be rich, offering to sell you a name as a final resource for saving yourself. That is often the case.

SUZANNE. He left France ten years ago, and knows nothing of my life. If he were to find out the slightest detail, he would leave me at once. He has an income of twenty or twenty-five thousand francs, and he need not sell, because he is able to buy. When you hear his name—

MARQUIS. I don't want, I have no right, to know it. My interest in your welfare may lead me so far as to wish to see your desires fulfilled, but I really cannot help you in an affair of this sort, no matter how honorable your motives. If by chance you should mention the name of a man I know, you would be placing me in a situation where I should have either to deceive a man of honor, or betray you.

SUZANNE. Of course, people of honor must stand by one another.

MARQUIS. What have you decided to do?

SUZANNE. I am going away, that's the wisest course, but I must be able to be absolute mistress of my life: I must be able to leave France, Europe even, if need be, and never return. My marriage must not for an instant seem to my husband in any way the result of calculation. To do this I must have a fortune of about the same size as his—I must have it in two hours' time. You are my guardian, and you know how much I have; tell me.

MARQUIS. Just at present your income is fifteen thousand francs.

SUZANNE. Yes?

MARQUIS. Which means a capital of three hundred thousand, figured at five per cent.

SUZANNE. And this capital—?

MARQUIS. A word to my solicitor,—he has charge of your affairs, too—and he will hand you over all your papers.

SUZANNE. You are a wonderful man!

MARQUIS. I am merely rendering you your account.

SUZANNE. I owe everything to you, even the happiness I am about to find in another.

MARQUIS. A clever woman never owes anything to anyone.

SUZANNE. That is an indirect reproach.

MARQUIS. No: merely a receipt of "paid in full." [*He kisses her hand.*] Please offer my excuses to the Viscountess.

[*He goes out.*]
[*Enter a* SERVANT.]

SERVANT. Monsieur Raymond de Nanjac. [*He goes out.*]

[*Enter* RAYMOND.]

RAYMOND. I have just côme from your apartment. I had hoped we might spend a few moments together before coming to the Viscountess's, and I was looking forward to the pleasure of accompanying you.

SUZANNE. I received a note from Madame de Vernières, who asked me to come a little earlier. There is a favor to do.

RAYMOND. That would be an excuse if you needed her. Were you speaking to the Viscountess when I came?

SUZANNE. No: with the Marquis de Thonnerins.

RAYMOND. Has he not a sister?

SUZANNE. The Duchess d'Haubeney.

RAYMOND. My sister knows her intimately, and ever since I arrived she has been tormenting me to have her introduced at this house. But I always refused—what was the use?

SUZANNE. The Marquis has a charming daughter.

RAYMOND. What is that to me?

SUZANNE. Whose dowry will amount to four or five millions.

RAYMOND. What difference can that make to me? I don't want to marry her.

SUZANNE. Why not?

RAYMOND. How can I think of Mademoiselle de Thonnerins, or anyone else, when I love you?

SUZANNE. How ridiculous! You scarcely know me.

RAYMOND. The day a man sees for the first time the woman he is going to love, he already loves her. Perhaps he even loved her the day before he meets her. Love comes; it is not reasoned about. It is sure and instantaneous, or else it never comes. It seems I have known you for ten years.

SUZANNE. That may be, but if love takes no time to be born, it must take time to live, and while we women do not believe in the permanence of these sudden passions we inspire, we still want to believe in the durability of true love. Now, you say you love me and yet you are going to leave in six weeks and will probably never return. Do I seem to you like one of those women whose amorous caprices hardly outlast a month? If you have imagined that, you have done me a grave injustice.

RAYMOND. What did I tell you yesterday?

SUZANNE. Nonsense—that you did not want to leave—that you wanted to marry me. A night has passed since then, and night brings counsel.

RAYMOND. I am not going away. I sent in my resignation to-day.

SUZANNE. Madness! You will surely regret the sacrifice you are making for me —in a year's time, in a month, perhaps. I'm talking to you as a true friend. Think, I'm an old woman compared with you: I am twenty-eight. At twenty-eight a woman is older than a man of thirty. I must be reasonable for both of us.

RAYMOND. But is it necessary to have lived, as you say, to have worn out one's heart in the banal and vulgar intrigues of what masquerades under the name of love, in order to have the right to give one's self up to a true passion at thirty? I thank God for having granted me since my early youth an active life, for keeping intact all my feelings and energies until I should be old enough to respond to the call of a true passion! You treat me like a child! I was only ten, Suzanne, when I lost a mother whom I worshiped. No matter how soon one loses his mother, that event makes him old all at once. Can't you see that the camp-life I have led, the long days spent in the silent soli-tudes by the sea, the memory of my dearest friends who fell at my side—can't you see that all this has matured me and made me live two years in one? I have gray hair, Suzanne; I am an old man; love me.

SUZANNE. But if I love you and if you continue to be suspicious of me, as you were when you saw me at Monsieur de Jalin's (I went there to speak about you); if I must continually struggle against your doubts, your jealousy, what will become of me?

RAYMOND. What I told Olivier proved my love. Is there a man who really loves and can harbor a single suspicion about the woman he loves? There can be no true love without respect and esteem.

SUZANNE. True. I can understand this jealousy of yours; I might even feel it myself; perhaps I do. What I like in you is that you have never loved. If I were to become your wife I should want to hide my love and happiness from everyone. I want to forget this society in which I live, to forget that it ever existed, because it is full of women who are younger and more beautiful than I, whom you might some day come to love. Marriage, in my opinion, is being always alone with one's husband.

RAYMOND. Suzanne, that is the way I love you, the way I want to be loved. We shall go away as soon as you like— to-morrow, if you say—and never come back.

SUZANNE. But what will your sister say?

RAYMOND. She will say: "If you love her, and if she loves you and is worthy of you, marry her."

SUZANNE. She does not know me, dear. She thinks I am young and beautiful; she imagines I belong to a family to which she might belong. She does not know I am alone in the world, and that my marriage will separate her from you—because we must leave. If she knew all that she would give you the same advice I gave you not long ago. You love her, and you will end by believing her.

RAYMOND. My sister will live near us; she has no attachments anywhere.

SUZANNE. Let me know her first. I want her to like me; I want to win her respect and affection; I want her to wish to have me for a sister, to want our marriage instead of merely accepting it.

RAYMOND. I shall do as you wish.

SUZANNE. How about the friends whose advice you are going to ask?

RAYMOND. I have no friends.

SUZANNE. Monsieur de Jalin?

RAYMOND. He is the only one. You must admit that he is worthy. He has a loyal heart.

SUZANNE. He has. Just think by how slender a thread our reputation hangs! You speak of marriage, yet, if for some reason it should not take place, just see in what a false and ridiculous a position I should be! If I should ever cause you pain you may tell Olivier; otherwise, keep our secret to yourself. True happiness is that of which no one else knows.

RAYMOND. You are always right. Though Olivier practically deserves this confidence, though we have scarcely been apart during the past four days, he never questioned me, nor was your name once mentioned. Well, I promise to say nothing either to my sister or to Olivier. Is that satisfactory?

SUZANNE. Yes.

RAYMOND. How I love you!

SUZANNE. Here comes someone.

[*Enter a* SERVANT.]

SERVANT. Monsieur Olivier de Jalin. Monsieur Hippolyte Richond.

[*He goes out.*]

SUZANNE [*aside*]. Olivier! What can he want here?

[*Enter* HIPPOLYTE *and* OLIVIER.]

OLIVIER. The Viscountess not here? And she calls this "receiving"!

SUZANNE. The Viscountess will soon return.

OLIVIER. In any event, she could not have chosen a better representative. Since you are doing the honors, Baroness, al-low me to present my friend Monsieur Hippolyte Richond.

HIPPOLYTE [*bowing*]. Madame.

SUZANNE [*likewise bowing*]. Monsieur.

OLIVIER. And how are you to-day, my dear Raymond?

RAYMOND. Very well, thank you.

SUZANNE. How pleasant it is to see two men who haven't been acquainted over a week on terms of such intimacy!

OLIVIER. Between upright and honorable people, my dear Baroness, there exists a mysterious bond which unites them even before they become acquainted, and which very shortly after their meeting develops into true friendship. My dear Raymond, let me introduce you to one of my best friends—I have two now—to Monsieur Hippólyte Richond, who has traveled widely and who has likewise been in Africa. You may chat about it together.

RAYMOND. Ah, monsieur, so you know that beautiful country about which so much evil is spoken! [*They draw aside and converse.*]

OLIVIER [*to* SUZANNE]. I thought you were in the country?

SUZANNE. I returned this evening.

OLIVIER. Have you anything new of interest to tell me?

SUZANNE. Absolutely nothing.

OLIVIER. Then let me give you some news.

SUZANNE. What?

OLIVIER. Monsieur de Nanjac is in love with you.

SUZANNE. You're joking!

OLIVIER. Hasn't he spoken to you?

SUZANNE. No.

OLIVIER. Strange. He spoke to me.

SUZANNE. He went about it indirectly.

OLIVIER. You may expect a proposal.

SUZANNE. Thank you for preparing me.

OLIVIER. Why?

SUZANNE. Because I'm going to let him know as soon as possible that he would be wasting his time.

OLIVIER. Don't you love Monsieur de Nanjac?

SUZANNE. The idea!

OLIVIER. Not even a little?

SUZANNE. Not even a great deal!

OLIVIER. Nor passionately. Then, not at all?

SUZANNE. Not at all, as you say.

OLIVIER. Then I've been much mistaken, but I am very glad to hear what you tell me.

SUZANNE. Why?

OLIVIER. I'll tell you when we're alone together.

SUZANNE. Tell me soon, you know I'm going away.

OLIVIER. You haven't gone yet.

SUZANNE. Who can prevent my going?

OLIVIER. I—I hope.

SUZANNE. Take care, or I shall ask Madame de Lornan to protect me.

OLIVIER. Madame de Lornan has nothing to do with me. I've called there daily for the past three days, and each time she has refused to see me.

SUZANNE. Do you want me to see her and make it up between you?

OLIVIER. You?

SUZANNE. Yes.

OLIVIER. Do you think she would receive you and not me?

SUZANNE. Perhaps. People receive me when I *want* them to.—At your service! [*She turns and goes away.*]

OLIVIER [*to himself*]. That looks like a threat. We'll see.

[*Enter the* VISCOUNTESS *and* MARCELLE.]

VISCOUNTESS. I hope you will excuse me, gentlemen?

SUZANNE [*to the* VISCOUNTESS]. Well?

VISCOUNTESS. Everything is arranged. Thanks.

MARCELLE [*to* SUZANNE]. I trust you are well, madame?

SUZANNE. And you, my dear?

MARCELLE. Well, I'm sorry to say. When a woman is always well, no one is interested in her.

SUZANNE. I have occasionally heard you cough when we passed the night together.

MARCELLE. That doesn't count: I've had colds as long as I can remember. I must have been born with a cold.

VISCOUNTESS [*to* HIPPOLYTE, *to whom* OLIVIER *has meantime introduced her*]. Very good of you, monsieur, to accept my invitation, though it was sent in a rather irregular fashion. Madame de Santis, whose husband you know—

HIPPOLYTE. Yes, madame.

VISCOUNTESS. Madame de Santis was anxious to consult you on a matter of some importance, and she is not yet settled in her own home. She complimented me by believing and saying that you would come here. I think the world of Valentine, and my dearest wish is that she may realize her dreams.

HIPPOLYTE. If that depends on me, madame, she shall.

MARCELLE. Didn't Monsieur de Thonnerins come?

SUZANNE. Yes, but he asked me to offer you his excuses. He called to say that he could not be present: his sister is receiving this evening.

MARCELLE. I wish I might have seen him!

VISCOUNTESS. By the way, Monsieur de Nanjac, didn't you promise me you would bring your sister?

RAYMOND. Yes, madame, but you know she is still in mourning, and is ailing a little at present. As soon as she is better, I shall be delighted to introduce her.

OLIVIER [*to* RAYMOND]. Tell me—?

RAYMOND. Yes?

MARCELLE. Monsieur de Nanjac?

OLIVIER [*to* RAYMOND]. I'll ask you later.

RAYMOND. Mademoiselle?

MARCELLE [*to* OLIVIER]. Monsieur Olivier, lend me Monsieur de Nanjac a moment; I'll give him back. [*To* RAYMOND.] I have something to talk to you about, but beforehand please take this pin out of my hat.

HIPPOLYTE [*to* OLIVIER]. That young lady seems very clever.

OLIVIER. She's only a girl. How could you think she was anything more?

MARCELLE. Tell me, Monsieur de Nanjac, do you know there is a conspiracy hatching against us?

RAYMOND. Really, mademoiselle?

MARCELLE. Yes: they are trying to get you to marry me.

RAYMOND. But—

MARCELLE. Don't try to be gallant, now! You don't any more want to be my husband than I ought to be your wife. You are in love with a woman who is much better than I; I have guessed that, but I shan't say any more about it. Now that you have nothing to fear, come with me and my aunt will believe you are making love to me. She'll be so pleased. One must do something for one's relatives. But I'm a good girl, and I thought it best to warn unfortunate people what is in store for them. Now, take care not to spoil my hat; it's the only one I have, and I don't think it's paid for yet.

[*She goes out laughing, with* RAYMOND.]

VISCOUNTESS [*to* SUZANNE]. What did I tell you? Everything is going splendidly.

HIPPOLYTE. Monsieur de Nanjac seems a fine fellow.

OLIVIER. He is charming. I am going to try to save him, too, even at the risk of repenting later.

[*Enter a* SERVANT.]

SERVANT. Madame de Santis.

[*He goes out.*]

OLIVIER. This is your affair.

[*Enter* VALENTINE.]

VISCOUNTESS. You are the last to arrive.

VALENTINE [*aside to the* VISCOUNTESS]. Monsieur de Latour didn't want to let me go; I had an awful time getting away; he doesn't know I am here. Is Monsieur Richond here?

VISCOUNTESS. He's talking with Olivier over there.

VALENTINE. Oh, how my heart's beating!

SUZANNE. Courage!

OLIVIER [*going to* VALENTINE]. How are you?

VALENTINE. Very well, thank you.

OLIVIER. You're dressed like a little middle-class housekeeper. Suits you beautifully! Let me introduce you to my friend Richond. You had him asked, so I imagine you would like to meet him?

VALENTINE. Introduce me.

OLIVIER [*introducing her to* HIPPOLYTE]. Monsieur Hippolyte Richond—Madame de Santis.

HIPPOLYTE. Madame.

VALENTINE [*bowing*]. I have been wanting to meet you for ever so long, monsieur.

HIPPOLYTE. Very good of you, madame, to say so. I have been away from France for ten years.

VALENTINE [*after making sure that she will not be overheard—to* HIPPOLYTE]. Tell me, Hippolyte, what are you going to do with me?

HIPPOLYTE. With you, madame?

VALENTINE. Yes!

HIPPOLYTE. Why—what I have been doing so far!

VALENTINE. But I tell you my situation is impossible.

HIPPOLYTE. Why?

VALENTINE. You ask that! We haven't spoken to each other for ten years. I am still your wife.

HIPPOLYTE. Legally.

VALENTINE. You once loved me.

HIPPOLYTE. Deeply. I nearly died—luckily, I escaped death.

VALENTINE. And now?

HIPPOLYTE. Now I don't even think of you; you are as indifferent to me as if you had never lived.

VALENTINE. Yet you came here, knowing you would see me. If I were indifferent to you, you would not have come.

HIPPOLYTE. You are mistaken: I came precisely because I had nothing to fear in seeing you again.

VALENTINE. Then will you never forgive me?

HIPPOLYTE. Never!

VALENTINE. Your home will never be open to me?

HIPPOLYTE. I hope it never will.

VALENTINE. Is it true what people have told me?

HIPPOLYTE. What have you been told?

VALENTINE. That your home is—occupied?

HIPPOLYTE. Yes: by people for whom I care a great deal.

VALENTINE. But whom I might drive out.

HIPPOLYTE. You know very well that only one of us two has the right to threaten, and that is I. Don't forget that. Even after three years of sorrow, despair, loneliness, during which, if your heart had found a single word of regret, if you had shed a single tear of repentence, I would have forgiven you,—because I loved you. But now I have earned the right to feel and live as I think best. It is in the bosom of a family happened upon by chance, at a borrowed hearth, as it were, that I found the happiness you did not think fit to give me. Just see the strange situation into which a wife's sin can bring an honest man. I know everything you have done since our separation, and I know that to-day is the first time you have thought of returning to me. You have wasted your fortune in idleness and luxury, and now that you are at the end of your resources, you say to yourself: "Let's see whether my husband will take me back!" Never has a single word come straight from your heart. No, madame, everything is over between us: you are dead to me.

VALENTINE. So, you don't care what becomes of me?

HIPPOLYTE. You may do what you like; I have no more love for you. You cannot make me suffer any more. I am an upright man, and you cannot render me ridiculous.

VALENTINE. That is all I wanted to know. You can blame yourself now for whatever happens to me.

HIPPOLYTE. Good-bye, then. We shall never see each other again.

MARCELLE [who has entered meanwhile and is anxious to speak with HIPPOLYTE]. Are you going, monsieur?

HIPPOLYTE. Yes, mademoiselle. [To VALENTINE.] Madame. [He bows to her.]

VALENTINE [bowing]. Monsieur.

VISCOUNTESS. Are you leaving us so soon, monsieur? That's not at all nice!

HIPPOLYTE. I promised to return early.

VISCOUNTESS. Why didn't you bring Madame Richond?

HIPPOLYTE. Madame de Santis did not ask her.

VISCOUNTESS. I am at home every Wednesday, monsieur, and whenever you and Madame Richond wish to give me the pleasure of your company at tea, I shall be glad to receive you.

HIPPOLYTE [to OLIVIER]. I shall see you to-morrow; I want to talk to you.
[He bows and goes out.]

MARCELLE. You can never count on these married men!

RAYMOND [to OLIVIER]. You had something to say to me awhile ago?

OLIVIER. Yes. Tell me, my dear Raymond, you have never, since that once, referred to Madame d'Ange. What has become of your consuming passion?

RAYMOND. I have given it up.

OLIVIER. So soon?

RAYMOND. I was only wasting my time.

OLIVIER. You came to that conclusion at once?

RAYMOND. What else could I do?

OLIVIER. That's so. Do you know, you are becoming quite Parisian; you are more reasonable that I had thought. I congratulate you. You have also encouraged me to give you some advice.

RAYMOND. What?

OLIVIER. You promised the Viscountess, did you not, that you would introduce her to your sister?

RAYMOND. Yes.

OLIVIER. Don't bring her here.

RAYMOND. Why not? Is the Viscountess' home not quite respectable?

OLIVIER. I don't say that, only the best homes are not necessarily those which present the best appearance. If you scratch the surface you will see what lies just beneath.—Listen! [Aloud.] Are we not to have the pleasure of seeing Monsieur de Latour?

VISCOUNTESS. He wrote asking to be excused—urgent business—

MARCELLE. If the person who invented those two words, "urgent business," had taken out a patent, he would have made a mint of money.

OLIVIER. Perhaps Monsieur de Latour is not lying: once, by chance, he might be telling the truth.

MARCELLE. What has he done to you? You invariably speak ill of him, and he never speaks anything but good of you.

OLIVIER. He is only doing his duty.

VALENTINE. He is most charming, respectable, distinguished-looking, and well-bred; you can't make the same reproach to everyone.

OLIVIER. Very well, then, everything is in his favor; he squanders his money—

VALENTINE. True enough.

OLIVIER. True for what it costs him to make: he gambles every night and invariably wins.

VISCOUNTESS. I suppose you will say he cheats?

OLIVIER. No, only that he is lucky at play, and one does not always have luck as one has a paunch—without having it purposely.

RAYMOND. My dear Olivier, don't forget that I was once a second for Monsieur de Latour.

OLIVIER. Whose acquaintance you made at the hotel in Baden. You are a man of honor, my dear Raymond, and you imagine that everyone else is like yourself. That is very dangerous. I tell you, I should never have consented to the duel which Monsieur de Latour appears to have provoked.

SUZANNE. Do you deny his courage? He fought his first duel when he was eighteen, and killed his adversary.

VISCOUNTESS. A good beginning in life!

OLIVIER. The life of other people! I don't question Monsieur de Latour's courage; I only say that a man of honor like Monsieur de Maucroix ought no more to fight with Monsieur de Latour than a man of honor like Monsieur de Nanjac to serve as his second.

SUZANNE. But, my dear Olivier, surely Monsieur de Latour is as fine a man as Monsieur de Maucroix?

OLIVIER. No, because Monsieur de Latour, who calls himself Count, is the son of a little Marais money-lender who left him fifty thousand francs, with the aid of which his son, thanks to cards, nets an income of forty thousand.

VALENTINE. Nonsense!. He comes of an excellent family.

OLIVIER. What family?

VALENTINE. The Latour of Auvergne.

OLIVIER. Hm! . . . I am astonished that women who claim to belong to society——

VISCOUNTESS. Who do, my dear friend.

OLIVIER. Who do, if you like, should receive so readily a man whom no one else receives, and who will end by forcing every decent man to stay away. I am positive that if Monsieur de Briade or Monsieur de Bonchamp, or any of those gentlemen, as Madame de Santis calls them, have not come here to-day, it was for fear of meeting Monsieur de Latour.

VISCOUNTESS. Let us not discuss the matter further. [A pause.]

OLIVIER. Madame de Santis! Madame de Santis!

VALENTINE. Well?

OLIVIER. Has the lease of your apartment in the Rue de la Paix expired yet?

VALENTINE. What is that to you? I don't think you came very often.

OLIVIER. Thank you—and your husband?

VALENTINE. My husband?

OLIVIER. He has expired, I know. My friend Richond has just given me news of him. Has he swallowed the reconciliation bait? Is he going to pay for the blue-and-yellow rooms?

VALENTINE. My husband? He'll hear from me!

OLIVIER. That will please him.

VALENTINE. I'm going to sue him.

OLIVIER. An idea. But is it a good one? Why sue?

VALENTINE. You'll see why. I know some very interesting facts about him; I leave the rest with my lawyer. I am his wife, after all.

OLIVIER. The lawyer's.

VALENTINE. My dear, you are witty once a week, and yesterday was your day. Keep still now!

OLIVIER. Rather good, you know.

MARCELLE. Let him talk, Valentine, dear. You have the right on your side, and you'll win your case, take my word for it. You don't say anything more, Monsieur Olivier?

OLIVIER. No, mademoiselle: *you* have begun. I speak only of things I know about, and since I know nothing of dolls or lunches, I never converse with little girls.

MARCELLE. Is that for my benefit?

OLIVIER. Yes, mademoiselle.

MARCELLE. But I speak of the same things you do. When grand people speak of certain things before little girls, the little girls have a right to join the conversation. And then—well, I'm no longer a little girl.

OLIVIER. Then what are you, mademoiselle?

MARCELLE. A woman, and I speak like a woman!

OLIVIER. You might even say, "like a man!"

MARCELLE. Monsieur!

VALENTINE. I thought you would end up with some impertinence!

VISCOUNTESS [*taking* MARCELLE *aside*]. You are going a little too far, Monsieur de Jalin; that child never harmed you. If, in the future, you feel the need of saying disagreeable things to someone, you may do so to me, when you are in my home, and to me alone.—Come, Marcelle. Are you coming with us, Monsieur de Nanjac?

RAYMOND. One moment, please.

[*The women go out.*]

OLIVIER. You heard that, my dear Ray-mond? Are you going to bring your sister to Madame de Vernières'?

RAYMOND. Then everything you said is true?

OLIVIER. Absolutely.

RAYMOND. And this Monsieur de La-tour?

OLIVIER. An unprincipled rascal.

RAYMOND. And Madame de Santis?

OLIVIER. A creature without heart and brain, who would be dishonoring her husband's name if he had not forbidden her the use of it.

RAYMOND. And Mademoiselle de Sance-naux?

OLIVIER. A little girl looking for a husband; a new product of our present-day society.

RAYMOND. But what *is* this society? I must confess, I can't understand a thing about it.

OLIVIER. My dear fellow, you must live for a long time, as I have, in the intimate circles of Parisian society in order to understand the various shades of this particular stratum. It is not easy to explain.—Do you like peaches?

RAYMOND [*surprised*]. Peaches? Yes.

OLIVIER. Well, go to a large fruit dealer, Chevet's, say, or Potel's, and ask for his best peaches. He will show you a basket of magnificent ones, each one separated from the other by leaves, in order to keep them from touching, from decaying by the contact. Ask him the price, and he will tell you: "Thirty sous each," I imagine. Look about you then and you will not fail to see another basket filled with peaches looking at first sight exactly like the others, but they are packed closer together; only one side is visible. The dealer will not offer you these. Ask him their price, and he will reply: "Fifteen sous." You will naturally ask why these peaches, as large, as beautiful and ripe as the others, are cheaper. Then he will pick one up with the tips of his fingers as delicately as he can, turn it around, and show you on the bottom a tiny black speck. That is the explanation of the lower price. My dear fellow, you are now in the fifteen-sous peach basket. Each woman here has some blot in her past life; they are crowded close to one another in order that these blots may be noticed as little as possible. Although they have the same origin, the same appearance and the same prejudices as women of society, they do not belong to it: they constitute the "Demi-monde" or "Half-world," a veritable floating island on the ocean of Paris, which calls to itself, welcomes, accepts everything that falls, emigrates, everything that escapes from *terra firma*—not to mention those who have been shipwrecked or who come from God knows where.

RAYMOND. And has this social stratum any particular visible characteristics?

OLIVIER. You see it everywhere, but rather indistinctly; a Parisian can recognize it at a glance.

RAYMOND. How?

OLIVIER. By the absence of husbands. It is full of married women whose husbands are never seen.

RAYMOND. But what is the origin of this strange social world?

OLIVIER. It is a modern creation. In former times adultery, as we now think of it, did not exist: morals were much more lax; there was a word much more trivial to denote what is now thought of as adultery. Molière made frequent use of it, and made rather the husband ridiculous than the wife at fault. But since the husband, aided by the law, has acquired the right to expel the erring wife from his home, a modification of the manner of looking at such things has come, and this modification has created a new society. What was to become of all these compromised and repudiated wives? The first who saw herself sent from the conjugal roof went into distant retirement somewhere to hide her grief and shame; but—the second? The second followed the first, and the two gave the name of misfortune to what was really a fault; an error to what was actually a crime. They began to console and excuse each other. With the advent of a third, they invited one another to lunch; with the fourth, they had a dance. Then about this nucleus came in turn young girls who have "made a false step," questionable widows, women who bear the name of the man they are living with, some truly-married couples who made their *début* in a *liaison* of many years' standing; finally, the women who think they have done something of importance and who do not want to appear as they really are. To-day this irregular society functions regularly; this bastard society holds charms for the younger generation. "Love" is more easily obtained than higher up, and cheaper than at the bottom.

RAYMOND. Where do these people go?

OLIVIER. It's impossible to say. Only, beneath the brilliant surface, gilded by youth, beauty, money, under this social fabric of laces, smiles, fêtes, and passion, dark and tragic dramas are played, dramas of expiation, scandal, ruin, of the dishonor of whole families, law-suits, children separated from their mothers, children who are forced to forget them at an early age in order not to curse them later on. Then youth passes away, lovers disappear, and out of the past come regrets, remorse, abandonment, and solitude. Among these women are some who attach themselves to men who have been fools enough to take them seriously; they ruin the lives of these men as they have ruined their own; others disappear and no one ever troubles to find out where they have gone. Some cling to this society—like the Viscountess de Vernières— and die not knowing whether they prefer to rise or fear to fall; others, either because they sincerely repent or because they fear the desert about them, pray, in the name of their children or on behalf of the good of the family, to be taken back by their husbands. Then friends intervene and a few good reasons are set forth: the wife is old, people will not gossip about her. The ruined marriage is patched up again, the façade is given a new coat of paint, the couple go to the country for a year or two; they return, society closes its eyes, and allows from time to time those who publicly went out by the front door to creep in through the small door at the back.

RAYMOND. Is all that true? How delighted the Baroness would be if she heard!

OLIVIER. Why so?

RAYMOND. Because she has already told me the same thing.

OLIVIER. She did? *She!*

RAYMOND. But not so cleverly, I must admit.

OLIVIER. Ah! [*Aside.*] Very clever of her to do it. [*Aloud.*] But since the Baroness knows this section of society so well, why does she frequent it?

RAYMOND. I asked her and she replied that the early friends she made brought her here from time to time: Madame de Santis, for instance, is a childhood friend. Then she is interested in Mademoiselle de Sancenaux, whom she wants to extricate from her unpleasant situation. But she is not going to remain here long.

OLIVIER. What?

RAYMOND. It's a secret, but in a week you will hear great news.

[*Enter* MARCELLE.]

MARCELLE. Monsieur de Nanjac, Madame d'Ange would like to see you; she has something she wants to say to you. [RAYMOND *goes out.*] Don't go, Monsieur de Jalin, I have something to say to you.

OLIVIER. At your service, mademoiselle.

MARCELLE. You were very hard on me a little while ago: you made me cry. What have I done to you?

OLIVIER. Nothing at all.

MARCELLE. This isn't the first time you've not treated me nicely. I know you have a bad opinion of me—I've been told so.

OLIVIER. You have not been told the truth.

MARCELLE. You used not to be that way with me: you used to say pleasant things occasionally. I even thought you considered me a friend. You weren't happy in your home-life; you told me that; I, too,

had my own troubles: there should have been a bond of sympathy between us. Why aren't you nice to me now? What have I done?

OLIVIER. I feel that bond of sympathy, mademoiselle, as I used to, only—

MARCELLE. Oh, tell me!

OLIVIER. Well, a young girl must be a young girl, and she should only have to do with those things which are befitting her age. There are times when your conversation actually makes me blush, me, a man! And I can't think what answer to make. I sometimes regret that you have been brought up in this evil society, and that you can speak as you did not long ago.

MARCELLE. Then you were purposely severe? Thank you. But what can I do? I can't leave this society in which I live: I have no parents; the conversation I indulge in is the kind I have heard for many years. After all, perhaps it's not so great a misfortune that I have lived in this atmosphere? When I see every day of my life what is happening to women who have erred for the first time, I have learned not to err myself.

OLIVIER. That's true.

MARCELLE. But that's not enough, it seems, especially in view of the future. Since you have been kind enough to take an interest in me, Monsieur Olivier, I'm going to ask your advice.

OLIVIER. What is it, mademoiselle?

MARCELLE. If a young girl like me, without money, without a family, with no other protector than a relative like Madame Vernières, a girl who has been brought up in a society like this, wants to escape the evil influences, the possible scandal, the nasty advice, the discouragement, how is she to go about it? [*A pause.*] You don't answer? I see: you blame me, you even pity me, but you cannot advise me. Can I say now that I am no longer a young girl?

OLIVIER [*touched*]. Forgive me!

MARCELLE. I do more than forgive you, I thank you for having opened my eyes before it was too late. But I am going to beg you, no matter what happens, to defend me a little, and in return I promise to find a way of remaining a decent woman. Perhaps I shall some day meet an honorable man who will be grateful to me for that. Good-bye, Monsieur Olivier, and thank you.

[*She shakes hands with* OLIVIER.]

[*Enter* SUZANNE.]

SUZANNE. I am delighted to see that peace is once more established.

MARCELLE. Yes, and I am very happy.

[*She goes out.*]

OLIVIER. Strange girl!

SUZANNE. She is in love with you.

OLIVIER. With me!

SUZANNE. She has been for ever so long.

OLIVIER. Well, one learns strange things every day!

SUZANNE. Yes: for instance, I have just learned that your pledged word is not to be taken seriously.

OLIVIER. And why?

SUZANNE. Because you have not been a friend to me as you promised.

OLIVIER. What have I done?

SUZANNE. Monsieur de Nanjac has just repeated your conversation to me.

OLIVIER. I did not speak of you.

SUZANNE. That's too subtle for me. In saying what you said to Monsieur de Nanjac, you spoke evil of me and harmed me —or would have if I had not taken the reins in my hands.

OLIVIER. What difference can it possibly make to you, if you don't love Monsieur de Nanjac?

SUZANNE. What do you know about that?

OLIVIER. Do you love him?

SUZANNE. I'm not forced to tell you.

OLIVIER. Perhaps you are!

SUZANNE. Then, it's—war?

OLIVIER. Very well: war!

SUZANNE. You have letters of mine; please return them.

OLIVIER. To-morrow I shall do so in person.

SUZANNE. Until to-morrow, then.

OLIVIER. Until to-morrow!

[*He goes out.*]

ACT III

[*The drawing-room in the home of* SUZANNE. SUZANNE *and* SOPHIE *are present.*]

SUZANNE. Has my solicitor called yet?

SOPHIE. No, madame.

SUZANNE. I am going out. If any one comes, ask him to wait.

SOPHIE [*opening the door, ready to leave*]. Mademoiselle de Sancenaux.

SUZANNE. Tell her to come in.

[SOPHIE *goes out.*]

[*Enter* MARCELLE.]

SUZANNE. My dear child, to what do I owe this lovely visit?

MARCELLE. Am I keeping you from something?

SUZANNE. You never do that. You know how much I think of you; I'm always ready to do anything I can for you. What is it, now?

MARCELLE. You can do a great deal for my future.

SUZANNE. What is it?

MARCELLE. You have great influence with Monsieur de Thonnerins, haven't you?

SUZANNE. He is good enough to count me among his friends.

MARCELLE. Four or five years ago he offered my aunt to take me to live in his home and bring me up with his daughter; he wanted a companion of her own age for her.

SUZANNE. He told me about it at the time. But your aunt refused.

MARCELLE. Unfortunately. If she had consented, I shouldn't have been in the situation I now am.

SUZANNE. What's the trouble?

MARCELLE. I don't want to blame my aunt: it isn't her fault if the meager fortune my parents left me was soon eaten up in household expenses. If we balanced accounts I should be in her debt, because there are cares and affection which cannot be repaid. However, the continual fight for money often hardens the kindest hearts. After you went yesterday we had a rather sharp discussion, when I told her I didn't love Monsieur de Nanjac, and that I refused to make any effort to become his wife.

SUZANNE. Especially as you love someone else!

MARCELLE. Possibly! At last my aunt gave me to understand that if I was not ready to do as she directed, I could no longer count on her help. I didn't sleep a wink, I was trying to think of some plan whereby I should not have to trouble her any further. Then I happened to remember Monsieur de Thonnerins' offer, and I decided to come to you, who have always been so kind to me, and ask you to ask the Marquis to do for me to-day what he was willing to do four years ago. Mademoiselle de Thonnerins won't marry for another year or two; she lives a lonely life, and I'm sure I'll like her extremely well. I'm positive, too, that she will like me. Even after she marries, I don't doubt that she'll have me with her then. And I'm certain that if you stand sponsor for me, my little scheme will succeed, and I'll owe to you, if not a brilliant career, at least one that's all I could desire: independent, obscure, and quiet.

SUZANNE. I shall see the Marquis to-day.

MARCELLE. Really?

SUZANNE. I must go out now, and I'll call on my way.

MARCELLE. How good you are!

SUZANNE. Write me a letter to give him.

MARCELLE. I'll go home and send it to you.

SUZANNE. No, write it here; it's much easier—while I'm putting on my hat and cloak. Bring it to me in my bedroom, and then wait for the answer; I shall return in an hour. [*She rings the bell.*]

MARCELLE. I'll go back to see my aunt while you are gone. I went out with the maid without telling her where I was going. She might worry.

[*Enter a* SERVANT.]

SUZANNE [*to the* SERVANT]. If Monsieur de Jalin comes, ask him to wait.

Also Monsieur de Nanjac. [*The* SERVANT *goes out.—To* MARCELLE.] I'll go to my room and wait: we might be delayed by visitors. [*She goes out.*]

MARCELLE [*as she is writing the letter*]. That was a splendid inspiration! He will protect me. [*Meanwhile,* OLIVIER *has come in. He stands watching* MARCELLE *for a few moments. She rises, seals the letter and, turning round, catches sight of* OLIVIER.] Oh!

OLIVIER. Did I frighten you, mademoiselle?

MARCELLE. I didn't expect to see you.

OLIVIER. You seem happy this morning.

MARCELLE. I'm so hopeful, and now I'm glad to see you. You know, I owe this great feeling of hope to you. Since yesterday the future has taken on an entirely different aspect.

OLIVIER. What has happened?

MARCELLE. I'll tell you later. Could I hold secrets from you, my best friend? See you later.

OLIVIER. Going so soon?

MARCELLE. I'm coming back in an hour. You'll still be here: I'll tell the Baroness, whom I'm going to see now, to keep you. [*Taking his hand.*] Please always be as frank as you were yesterday.

[*She goes out.*]

OLIVIER. Possibly some day some one will explain a woman' heart, but the man who can decipher that of a young girl! God knows what I thought about that child yesterday, and God knows what she will make me think to-day! [*Taking a packet of letters from his pocket.*] Meantime, let us put an epitaph on this dead past; may the earth lie light over it! [*Writing.*] "To Madame la Baronne d'Ange—"

[*Enter* RAYMOND.]

Raymond! the devil! [*He puts the letters back into his pocket.*] It's you! My dear Raymond! I felt sure I was going to see you: I was speaking of you only a short while ago.

RAYMOND. Where?

OLIVIER. With de Maucroix, Senior, with whom I lunched. When I say, "I was speaking of you," I mean, "He was speaking of you."

RAYMOND. Does Monsieur de Maucroix, Senior, know me?

OLIVIER. Not personally, but he knows the Minister of War, and as de Maucroix knows that I know you, and as he is an old soldier, he takes an interest in those who wear the uniform and honor it. He asked if I knew why you resigned from the service. I said that, so far was I from knowing the reason, I was ignorant of the very fact. I added that I doubted it, but he said the Minister himself had vouchsafed the information.

RAYMOND. Well, it is a fact, and if I have not yet spoken to you—

OLIVIER. Your secrets are your own, my dear Raymond. I consider that my friendship can go as far as interest in you, not indiscretion. If you have resigned, though it is a serious step, you must have had compelling reasons, reasons which a friend could not have combatted. You are well?

RAYMOND. Perfectly well. Are you going?

OLIVIER. Yes, the Baroness does not seem to come.

RAYMOND. Then let us wait for her together.

OLIVIER. I haven't time; I have a call to make.

RAYMOND. Shall I deliver some message to her from you?

OLIVIER [after a pause]. If you will, please tell her I brought what she asked for.

RAYMOND. What a mysterious message! Are you annoyed with me?

OLIVIER. Why should I be? Good Lord!

RAYMOND. It's only natural. You are a friend, you have the right to be surprised and even to blame me for concealing something from you. Forgive me! I have promised silence, promised it to someone whom I could not refuse. Not only have I not told you the truth, but yesterday I confess I told you a little lie. Now I am going to tell you everything, because, since then, I have been very much worried. I am ashamed to have deceived you.

OLIVIER. I had just as soon you told me nothing. I even beg you not to say a word.

RAYMOND. That's childish spite, my dear Olivier; men of our age should be above such things, especially as I was going to call on you to-day and ask a favor.

OLIVIER. A favor?

RAYMOND. I am going to be married.

OLIVIER. You!

RAYMOND. Yes, I.

OLIVIER. And you are marrying?

RAYMOND. Guess.

OLIVIER. How can I?

RAYMOND. When we met for the first time I told you that the information I asked for might have the greatest possible influence over my life. I am going to marry Madame d'Ange.

OLIVIER. Suzanne! [Quickly.] The Baroness?

RAYMOND. Yes.

OLIVIER. You're joking!

RAYMOND. I am not joking.

OLIVIER. You mean it?

RAYMOND. Seriously.

OLIVIER. Was the marriage her idea?

RAYMOND. It was mine.

OLIVIER. Oh!—my compliments, Raymond!

RAYMOND. The news seems to surprise you?

OLIVIER. I don't deny that it's unexpected. I rather imagined, though you tried to throw me off the scent yesterday, that you were still in love with Madame d'Ange; I thought, too, that you gave up your commission in order to be with her as long as possible, but I never thought for a second, I must say, that it might be a question of marriage.

RAYMOND. Why not?

OLIVIER. Because, according to my notion, marriage is a serious matter, and when one is going to pledge one's life with a single word, one ought to reflect much longer than you have.

RAYMOND. But I think, for my part,

my dear friend, that when one believes he has found true happiness, he should lose no time in seizing it. I am free, I have no family, and I have never loved before. Madame d'Ange is free—a widow—a woman of the world (you told me that yourself); I love her, she loves me, and we are going to marry. That's all very natural, isn't it?

OLIVIER. Perfectly. And when is the wedding to take place?

RAYMOND. As soon as the law allows. But don't breathe a word to anyone; the Baroness doesn't want it even suspected. We are going to live alone some place; she even wanted the ceremony performed away from Paris. But I insisted on its taking place here, on your account.

OLIVIER. My account?

RAYMOND. Yes; I must have witnesses and I felt sure you would do me the favor.

OLIVIER. I a witness to your marriage with the Baroness? Impossible.

RAYMOND. You refuse?

OLIVIER. I am going away to-morrow.

RAYMOND. But you never said a word! My dear Olivier, what's the matter? You seem so embarrassed—you have for the past few moments.

OLIVIER. It *is* very embarrassing.

RAYMOND. What is? Tell me.

OLIVIER. Raymond, are you willing to believe that if I were to advise you in a serious situation, the advice could not but be for your good?

RAYMOND. Yes.

OLIVIER. Then, take my advice, delay this wedding—there is still time.

RAYMOND. What do you mean?

OLIVIER. I mean that no matter how deeply in love you are, there is no need of your marrying—when you can do otherwise.

RAYMOND. When I told you that I was in love with Madame d'Ange, my dear Olivier, I doubtless neglected to say that I respected and esteemed her.

OLIVIER. Very well, then, let us say no more about it. Good-day!

RAYMOND. Aren't you going to wait for the Baroness?

OLIVIER. I'll return later.

RAYMOND. Olivier!

OLIVIER. Raymond?

RAYMOND. You have something on your mind?

OLIVIER. Nothing.

RAYMOND. You have.

OLIVIER. My dear fellow, you are not like other men.

RAYMOND. What is there unusual about me?

OLIVIER. I don't seem able to talk with you; you always turn the good to evil. At the slightest word, you ignite like powder, you reason like a cannon-ball of '48, which shatters one's arms and legs. I tell you, it's discouraging. I advise you as a friend; I think it my duty, and you stop the words on my lips with one of those marble answers that no one else but you can make. We Parisians are not familiar with those characters which lack subtlety and cannot understand half-uttered phrases. You make me afraid.

RAYMOND. My dear fellow, the profession of soldier has not altogether crushed out of me all commonsense and intelligence. I am still aware that a situation—that is doubtless what you mean? —can have two sides, a serious and a comic. Up to now, I have taken my situation seriously; if it is comic, and I can't see that side, it is because I am inexperienced, and it is the right and duty of a friend to tell me. Take my word for it, the moment I see the point, I promise I shall be the first to laugh.

OLIVIER. So you say, but you won't laugh.

RAYMOND. You don't know me—a man can be mistaken every day of his life. I tell you, the day a man is shown his mistake, the best he can do is to see the humor of it and laugh. Everything or nothing! That is my motto!

OLIVIER. Word of honor?

RAYMOND. Word of honor!

OLIVIER. Then, my dear fellow, let us laugh.

RAYMOND. Have I been on the wrong track?

OLIVIER. Exactly.

RAYMOND. Doesn't she love me?

OLIVIER. On the contrary, I think she loves you deeply, but, between you and me, that is no good reason for your marrying. She has another reason in mind. Husbands like you are not found every day, and when you are, you must be played for.

RAYMOND. You mean the Baroness—? Tell me.

OLIVIER. It would take too long, and then other people's affairs do not concern me. All that I have a right to tell you is, do not marry Madame d'Ange.

RAYMOND. Truly?

OLIVIER. Only your recent arrival from Africa could allow such an idea to creep into your head.

RAYMOND. You are opening my eyes! Now I understand why she wanted me to say nothing about the marriage, why she wanted to be married far from Paris, and why she told me to be on my guard against you.

OLIVIER. She knew I thought too much of you to allow you to do a thing of this sort, without giving you a little information.

RAYMOND. You know, the woman is very clever! She had me bound hand and foot, body and heart.

OLIVIER. She is most seductive, I admit; she has a charming personality, and she is far above the women about her, because the mere fact of her being introduced into their society and holding the place she does is a proof of her superiority. Don't marry Suzanne, but love her: she is well worth your while.

RAYMOND. You know something about this?

OLIVIER. No.

RAYMOND. Why be so discreet at this point? This isn't the same sort of situation as when we first met. That day you were discreet, which was most natural, because you didn't know me.

OLIVIER. I have told you the truth.

RAYMOND. Come, now!

OLIVIER. Word of honor! You said to me: "You are only a friend of Madame d'Ange?" and I replied: "Yes"; that was true, I was only her friend. I did not know you, as you say; you came ready to kill and I had no good reasons for being interested in your welfare. I said to myself: "There's a young man who is in love with the Baroness; he is or will soon be her lover; he will leave here two months hence with the firm conviction that he has been loved by a woman of the world, and he will then blow his brains out. *Bon voyage!*" But, now that I have come to know and value your open heart, your frankness, to appreciate your character—now you tell me that you are on the point of giving this woman your name! The devil! That's another matter, and silence on my part would be treason, for which you would later have good right to call me to account. I shan't hide anything now. Things have followed their natural course. You're not blaming me, are you?

RAYMOND. Blame you, my dear friend? Are you mad? Believe me, on the contrary, I shall never forget what you are doing for me.

OLIVIER. You never know just how people in love will behave.

RAYMOND. I don't love that woman now.

OLIVIER. You understand, of course, that everything I say is in strict confidence?

RAYMOND. Of course. Now, what do you advise me to do?

OLIVIER. This concerns *you.*

RAYMOND. It's not easy, and it's going to be embarrassing. Things have gone so far—I must have a good reason.

OLIVIER. In a case of this sort, all reasons are good reasons. At the psychological moment, you are sure to have an inspiration. But, you see, at that moment, she will be forced to confess her situation to you. That will give you a reason.

RAYMOND. What situation?

OLIVIER. In order to become a widow, there must have been a husband—and that husband must be dead; now, a dead husband is harder to get than a living one.

RAYMOND. Then she is not a widow?

OLIVIER. She was never married.

RAYMOND. Are you sure?

OLIVIER. I am. No one has ever seen the Baron d'Ange! If you want authentic information about her, see the Marquis de Thonnerins: his sister knows her. There's a man who must know a great deal about her. But don't mention me. This is the sort of favor a friend does for another friend, but it is useless to speak of the matter to a third party. And now, good-bye; I prefer not to be found here: she would suspect something, and she must not know of this conversation.

RAYMOND. I understand. Then there is no use my giving her the message you spoke of?

OLIVIER. What message?

RAYMOND. Didn't you ask me to tell her that you were going to bring later what you brought her this morning?

OLIVIER. Say nothing about it.

RAYMOND. What did you bring?

OLIVIER. Some papers.

RAYMOND. Business papers?

OLIVIER. Yes.

RAYMOND. About her income?

OLIVIER. Yes. Good-bye.

RAYMOND. My dear Olivier, to-day is not the first day we have met, and I think it's wrong of you not to be quite frank with me. Those "papers" are letters—don't deny it. [A pause.] Come, while we're on the point: the more you tell me, the better it will be.

OLIVIER. Well, yes, they are letters.

RAYMOND. Which she wrote you, and which she, intending to marry, wants back. Now, do your duty.

OLIVIER. How?

RAYMOND. Prove you are really a friend.

OLIVIER. What must I do?

RAYMOND. Give me the letters.

OLIVIER. You?

RAYMOND. Yes.

OLIVIER. Impossible.

RAYMOND. Why?

OLIVIER. Because one doesn't give away a woman's letters.

RAYMOND. That depends.

OLIVIER. On what?

RAYMOND. On the situation in which the person who asks happens to be placed.

OLIVIER. A woman's letters are sacred, no matter who the woman is.

RAYMOND [very seriously]. I think it's a little late to come forth with maxims of that sort, my dear Olivier.

OLIVIER. You think so?

RAYMOND. Yes, because when you begin a confidential conversation of this sort, you ought to carry it through to the bitter end.

OLIVIER. My dear Raymond, I see I have made a grave blunder; I ought to say nothing more.

RAYMOND. Why?

OLIVIER. Because you are not in a laughing mood; because you love Madame d'Ange more than you admitted; because that mask of gayety you assumed just now was only in order to make me speak. You are more clever than I thought you. Good-morning.

RAYMOND. Olivier, in the name of our friendship, give me those letters!

OLIVIER. That's out of the question. I tell you it would be unworthy of both of us. I am surprised at your asking.

RAYMOND. I merely ask for a proof of what you have told me.

OLIVIER. You may doubt it all, if you like.

RAYMOND. I would willingly do it for your sake.

OLIVIER. Swear to me on your honor.

RAYMOND. I— [He stops.]

OLIVIER. You see?

RAYMOND. You are right. Well, I swear on my honor not to read the letters. Give them to me, and I promise to hand them to Madame d'Ange to-day.

OLIVIER. No!

RAYMOND. Do you doubt my word?

OLIVIER. Good Heavens, no!

RAYMOND. Well, then?

OLIVIER. Listen to me, Raymond: you will never forgive me for having told you the truth. I cannot repent, because I have acted as I believe I ought to have acted. I could not hesitate between a silent complicity for Madame d'Ange's sake, and giving you the information I have given. Between men like you and me an explanation of this sort ought to be sufficient. I see it is not; let us therefore say no more about the matter. I came here to-day to give to Madame d'Ange, or leave for her in case she was not in, some papers which belonged to her the moment she asked for them. Here they are, in this sealed envelope. Madame d'Ange is out; I leave the papers on the table, where she will find them on her return. I shall be back in half an hour to see whether she has them. And now, my dear Raymond, do as you think best! I was your friend; I will continue to be such so long as you wish me to be. Good-bye—or—au revoir. [He goes out.]

RAYMOND. Olivier! [He makes for the letters, which OLIVIER has left on the table.] After all, that woman's past belongs to me, because I am giving her my name. I shall read the letters. [He picks up, then lays down the envelope.] He is right: it is impossible!

[Enter SUZANNE.]

SUZANNE. I've been out long, my dear, haven't I?

RAYMOND. No. I wasn't alone.

SUZANNE. Who was here?

RAYMOND. Monsieur de Jalin.

SUZANNE. Why didn't he wait?

RAYMOND. He seemed in a hurry.

SUZANNE. Is he coming back?

RAYMOND. In half an hour. Where have you been, dear Suzanne?

SUZANNE. Some tiresome errands. I don't complain, because they were for you.

RAYMOND. For me?

SUZANNE. For you, monsieur. When a person marries, he must put all his affairs in order, mustn't he? I shouldn't complain at all—unless you happened to change your mind.

RAYMOND. Not yet.

SUZANNE. Any chance of it?

RAYMOND. That will depend on you.

SUZANNE. Then I have nothing to fear. Do you still love me?

RAYMOND. Always, more than you can know. Now, Suzanne, you have been—?

SUZANNE. To see my solicitor. My husband ought to know the state of my finances.

RAYMOND. Never mind that.

SUZANNE. I have just got my birth-certificate. See, I didn't lie: I'm an old woman of twenty-eight. There's no denying facts. [She reads:] "Infant; sex, feminine; born February 4, 1818, at 11 o'clock in the evening; daughter of Jean-Hyacinthe, Count de Berwach, and of Joséphine-Henriette de Crousserolles, his wife." You see, I come of a good family! This is all that remains of the first two love affairs of my life: an almost illegible scrap of paper, an official document, cold and dry as the epitaph on a tombstone. Here is my marriage-contract. I wasn't in a happy mood that day, Raymond dear, because I didn't love my husband; I was simply giving in to the wishes of my parents. But I can't reproach the Baron, he was as good to me as he could be; he came of an old family, and was the last of the line. And here is my husband's death-certificate: that is to say, my right to love you before all the world. You see, I have been a widow for eight years. The past is over and laid at rest; we have only the future to think of. What's the matter?

RAYMOND. Will you let me have those documents?

SUZANNE. Don't lose them.

RAYMOND. You may be sure I shan't; I'll put them with my own, as soon as I get them. Is that all you've done this morning?

SUZANNE. No, I went to see my guardian, the Marquis de Thonnerins; Mademoiselle de Sancenaux, you know, begged me to ask him for something. I was not

successful, and I'm very much put out
about it. The poor child is coming here
for her answer, and I don't know how to
tell her.

RAYMOND. There is a way.

SUZANNE. How?

RAYMOND. Write her before she comes.
Isn't that the best way to break bad
news?

SUZANNE. But it's such a bother to
write!

RAYMOND. It depends: to those we
love, for instance.

SUZANNE. That's different.

RAYMOND. You never wrote to me.

SUZANNE. I have seen you every day;
what did I have to write? But you've
lost nothing: I write a fearful hand.

RAYMOND. Let me see a sample?

SUZANNE. Do you really wish to?

RAYMOND. Yes.

SUZANNE. Very well. [*She writes:*]
"My dear child—" Horrid pen! "I have
been to see Monsieur de Thonnerins, as
I promised, but I did not find our old
friend in the frame of mind I had ex-
pected—" [*To* RAYMOND, *who is watching
closely what she writes.*] Can hardly
read it, can you?

RAYMOND. Hardly. Let me have the
beginning of the letter, please.

SUZANNE. Why?

RAYMOND. Give it to me.

SUZANNE. There.

RAYMOND [*after having examined the
letter*]. My dear Suzanne, I forgot to
tell you that Monsieur de Jalin left a
little package for you.

SUZANNE. What is it?

RAYMOND. Letters.

SUZANNE. What letters?

RAYMOND. Which you asked him for.

SUZANNE. I?

RAYMOND. Yes.

SUZANNE. From whom are they?

RAYMOND. From you!

SUZANNE. I don't understand. Where
are they?

RAYMOND. Here.

SUZANNE. Give them to me.

RAYMOND. I beg your pardon, Suzanne,

dear, but I'm going to ask your permis-
sion to open the package.

SUZANNE. Did Monsieur de Jalin bring
these for me?

RAYMOND. As I told you.

SUZANNE. Very well, then, open it and
read the letters if you wish. If you
wanted to see anything in them, you
needn't have waited until I came home.
Only, after you have seen what you wanted
to see, I am going to ask you the mean-
ing of all this, for I don't understand in
the least.

RAYMOND. I shall explain everything,
I promise; or, rather, *we* shall explain.

[*He opens the package, takes one
of the letters and compares it
with the one which* SUZANNE
has just written to MARCELLE.]

SUZANNE. Well?

RAYMOND. Suzanne, someone is being
deceived somewhere.

SUZANNE. I, I think, for I hope to die
if I can guess a word of the riddle!

RAYMOND. Look at those letters.

SUZANNE. They are from a woman.

RAYMOND. Read them.

SUZANNE [*glancing through a few*].
Love-letters, or practically—the expres-
sions are not particularly tender. But
they might pass for love-letters. Well?

RAYMOND. Don't you know who wrote
these?

SUZANNE. How should I? They're not
signed.

RAYMOND. Are they not in your hand-
writing?

SUZANNE. My handwriting? Are you
mad? Is my handwriting like that? I
wish it were! That woman writes very
nicely.

RAYMOND. Then why Olivier's lie? He
seemed so sure!

SUZANNE. What lie? What does this
mean? Did Monsieur de Jalin say that
these letters were from me?

RAYMOND. Yes.

SUZANNE [*indignantly*]. Then, Mon-
sieur de Jalin must have been my lover!

RAYMOND. So it appears.

SUZANNE. Did he tell you that?

RAYMOND. He gave me to understand—

SUZANNE. Please—where is the joke?

RAYMOND. Monsieur de Jalin was not joking.

SUZANNE. He was making fun of you. You lied to him yesterday, and to-day he takes his revenge. I have known Monsieur de Jalin longer than you have; I know he is incapable of anything cowardly. You now accuse him of it. He made love to me once, and wrote letters to me, which I can show you. I think he is rather hurt that I am marrying, because it takes his last hope from him. But there's a vast difference between trying to prevent the marriage and inventing a calumny of that kind. I have no idea what has actually occurred, but I am positive that Monsieur de Jalin is incapable of committing an act like that.

RAYMOND. We shall see.

SUZANNE. Have *you* any doubts?

RAYMOND. This matter is between him and me. Will you swear that what Monsieur de Jalin told me was false?

SUZANNE. Do you want me to swear? So, it's something more than a joke, or even a libel on Monsieur de Jalin's part: it is treason on yours, monsieur.

RAYMOND. Treason!

SUZANNE. Yes, you are already beginning to regret the promises you made me. Why didn't you tell me frankly rather than resort to such means, which really do more honor to your cleverness than to your delicacy.

RAYMOND. Suzanne, you are accusing me of something infamous.

SUZANNE. What am I accusing you of?

RAYMOND. Monsieur de Jalin is coming here shortly; let us clear matters up in his presence.

SUZANNE. Must you await Monsieur de Jalin's permission to believe I am telling the truth? I am going to have Monsieur de Jalin himself tell you that he was never my lover; you will believe me then. Whom do you take me for? I loved you, Raymond, but I must say, this suspicion and jealousy terrify me. That is why I hesitated to become your wife.

I at least thought that you respected and honored me. I have no intention of looking into the causes for this sudden outbreak, but I declare you have put me to a humiliating test, me and my love for you and my dignity. You have doubted me. Everything is over between us.

RAYMOND. My jealousy is only a proof of my love. I love you so deeply, Suzanne!

SUZANNE. I don't want to be loved that way!

RAYMOND. I swear—

SUZANNE. Please!

RAYMOND. Suzanne!

[*Enter* SOPHIE.]

SOPHIE. Mademoiselle de Sancenaux wishes to know if madame will see her?

SUZANNE. Ask her to come in.

[SOPHIE *goes out.*]

RAYMOND. I shall stay with you.

[*Enter* MARCELLE.]

MARCELLE. It's I, madame.

SUZANNE. I'm so glad to see you, dear child. [*To* RAYMOND.] Please excuse us, Monsieur de Nanjac, mademoiselle and I wish to be alone.

RAYMOND. When shall I have the pleasure of seeing you again, madame?

SUZANNE. On my return: I'm leaving to-night, and I shan't see anyone in the meantime.

[RAYMOND *bows and goes out, as* SUZANNE *rings.*]

[*Enter a* SERVANT.]

[*To the* SERVANT.] If Monsieur de Nanjac calls again to-day, tell him I am not at home; if he insists, add that I refuse to see him. Go! [*The* SERVANT *goes out.*] I have seen the Marquis, and I have bad news to report, my poor dear: Monsieur de Thonnerins is interested in you, but—

MARCELLE. He refuses.

SUZANNE. He would like to do what you ask.

MARCELLE. Only—worldly considerations prevent him. I have thought a good deal since I saw you, and I came to the conclusion that perhaps it would not be right of him to have as a companion for his daughter a person in so exceptional a position as I am. Mademoiselle de Thonnerins is fortunate in having a father to protect and care for her. Thank you, dear madame, and forgive me for having troubled you.

SUZANNE. I do wish I had been successful. The Marquis is very fond of you, and he told me he would do what he could to help you, and that if you found some fine young man whom you could love, and if there were no other obstacle except the matter of fortune, he would see to it that that obstacle was removed.

MARCELLE. I asked for help, not alms.

SUZANNE. That isn't kind. Why do you get so discouraged, dear? How do you know that the man you love may not some day return your love? Perhaps he loves you even now. If he does, what is there to prevent your becoming his wife?

MARCELLE. I don't love anyone.

SUZANNE. Very well, Marcelle, I'm not asking for secrets.

MARCELLE. Didn't I hear you say you were going away to-night?

SUZANNE. Yes.

MARCELLE. Perhaps we shan't see each other again, but I shall never forget how good you have been to me.

SUZANNE. I'll let you know where I am. Write me, and no matter where I am, I shall do everything in my power to help you.

MARCELLE. Thank you. [*She kisses* SUZANNE.] Good-bye.

SUZANNE. Good-bye—and courage!

[*Enter a* SERVANT.]

SERVANT. Monsieur Olivier de Jalin.
[MARCELLE *makes ready to go, as the* SERVANT *leaves.*]

[*Enter* OLIVIER.]

OLIVIER. Am I sending you away, mademoiselle?

MARCELLE. No, monsieur, I was going anyway.

OLIVIER. How sad you look. What's the matter?

MARCELLE. One hour follows another, and not one resembles another. I was too quick to hope: life is more difficult than I had imagined, when one is alone to struggle.

OLIVIER. But—when there are two? Am I not your friend? I don't want you to be sad any longer. Will you let me come to see you? Then you'll tell me all your troubles!

MARCELLE. I will do everything you tell me.

OLIVIER. I shall see you soon, possibly very soon. [*He shakes hands with her, and she goes out.*]

SUZANNE. Touching, isn't it? I should very much like to see you marry Mademoiselle de Sancenaux, after what you have said about her.

OLIVIER. I did not know her then, now I do.

SUZANNE. All of which goes to show that it is never wise to speak evil of people before you know! By the way, you and I have an account to balance.

OLIVIER. What?

SUZANNE. Now pretend not to understand! You told Monsieur de Nanjac that it would be wrong of him to marry me.

OLIVIER. True.

SUZANNE. Did you tell him why?

OLIVIER. Yes.

SUZANNE. You are at least frank. However, that is no excuse for your having committed a—What is it? There is a word for such things.

OLIVIER [*appearing to be searching for the word*]. A blunder?

SUZANNE. No.

OLIVIER. Something tactless?

SUZANNE. Not altogether. Something —er—

OLIVIER. Cowardly? Say it; it burns your lips.

SUZANNE. Exactly: something cowardly!

OLIVIER. And why did I do it?

SUZANNE. Because a man of honor keeps such things to himself.

OLIVIER. Which proves that you and I do not agree on the question of honor, fortunately!

SUZANNE. You have nothing more to add?

OLIVIER. Nothing.

SUZANNE. And did you imagine that Monsieur de Nanjac would fail to repeat your conversation to me?

OLIVIER. I did, because he gave me his word of honor.

SUZANNE. But you gave me your word of honor, my friend!

OLIVIER. To be your friend, yes, but not your accomplice.

SUZANNE. "Accomplice" is rather brutal. [*She laughs.*] Olivier.

OLIVIER. Yes?

SUZANNE. What you have done has turned out to my advantage.

OLIVIER. So much the better! Well, I have done my duty on the one hand, and you a favor on the other.

SUZANNE. He loves me more than ever.

OLIVIER. Indeed?

SUZANNE. I really can't be angry with you. And you pretend to be a clever man! Can't you see that you've been caught in a trap?

OLIVIER. Caught in a trap?

SUZANNE. You poor dear! You are trying to deal with a woman! Haven't you learned that the stupidest of women —and I am not that by a long way—is a hundred times more resourceful than the cleverest man? I rather suspected yesterday, after your conversation with Monsieur de Nanjac, that your great friendship for me would end, and that the moment there was any question of my marriage, your loyal self would declare war on me. You had to strike a final blow and lay low the truth so emphatically, that any lies or calumnies could not afterward have the slightest chance. Then I asked you to bring me those letters. That should have opened your eyes? Do you think I am the sort of woman who asks for her letters? Of course you didn't sus-

pect a thing, and you were so nice as to come this morning, with your little letters in your pocket! A short while before you were due here, I went out in order to leave you alone with Monsieur de Nanjac and you did your duty as an honest man. You told him what you had been to me, and found means of giving him my letters. I returned, he did not know my handwriting, so he asked me to give him a sample of it before his very eyes; then he compared the two hands.

OLIVIER. And?

SUZANNE. And as they bear no resemblance to each other, he is convinced that I am the victim of a libelous story. He loves me more than ever, and has only one thought: to cut your throat. The idea! To think that, at your age, you don't yet know that the very best way to fall out with a friend is to speak evil of the woman he loves, even when it can be proved. And can you prove it? I sent him away because he dared entertain such suspicions. I told him I didn't want to see him any more, that I was going away to-day—and any number of other things: everything an intelligent woman says under similar circumstances. I told him I could never think of becoming his wife. He will be here in ten minutes, and in a week's time we shall be married. I owe all this to you, my dear. You have lost, you see, and you owe me a forfeit.

OLIVIER. Have you two samples of the handwriting?

SUZANNE. I have only one, but that is enough.

OLIVIER. Then how does it happen that—?

SUZANNE. I'll tell you everything, because at bottom I am obliging, and I have nothing against you. My dear friend, when a woman like me has spent ten years in building up her life, piece by piece, her first care must be to get out of her way every possible chance of danger. Now, among these chances, in the first place, is the desire to write. Out of a hundred compromised women, two-thirds have met their ruin through their letters. Women's letters seem destined to be lost by those to whom they are sent, returned to those who wrote them, intercepted by the one person who ought never to see them, stolen by servants, and shown to the whole world. In matters of love, it is dangerous to write, not to say useless. Consequently, I have made it a rule never to write a compromising letter, and for the last ten years I have adhered to that rule.

OLIVIER. Then the letters you wrote me—?

SUZANNE. Were dictated to Madame de Santis, the greatest known letter-writer. She has a pen in her hand from morning to night; that is her great passion. She was with me all the time at Baden, and I made use of her mania occasionally, asking her to answer letters from you, which I never read. She writes a lovely English hand, long, delicate, aristocratic, like a lady of rank taking a walk. And she was so well brought up! So you see, my dear, you were corresponding with Valentine. But you needn't worry; I shan't breathe a word to your friend Monsieur Richond; you might fall out with him!

OLIVIER [bowing]. I have nothing more to say. You are a most powerful—

SUZANNE. Now, let us talk seriously. By what right have you behaved this way? In what way can you reproach me? If Monsieur de Nanjac were an old friend of yours, a childhood comrade, or a brother, I might see, but you have known him scarcely a week or ten days. If you were disinterested, too, I might understand, but are you quite sure you haven't been prompted by wounded pride? I know you don't love me, but a man always rather resents being told by a woman who once loved him that she no longer does so. Simply because you happened to make love to me and because I was confiding enough to believe you, because I thought you an honorable man, because I loved you, perhaps, are you going to be an obstacle to the happiness of my whole life? Did I compromise you? ruin you? Did I even deceive you? I will admit,—I must admit, because it's true—that I am not worthy on moral grounds, of the name and position I aspire to; but is it your place—you helped make me unworthy!—to close to me the honorable path I have chosen to tread? No, my dear Olivier, it's not right; when a person has himself succumbed to certain weaknesses, he ought not to forge weapons and use them against those with whom he has sinned. A man who has been loved, no matter how little, provided the love was based neither on interest nor calculation, is under an eternal obligation to the woman, and he should remember that no matter how much he does for her, he can never hope to repay her.

OLIVIER. You are right: perhaps I did give in to an evil impulse, to jealousy, thinking I was prompted by honor. Still, there is no honest man who would not have acted likewise in my place. For Raymond's sake I was right in speaking; for yours, I should have said nothing. The Arabian proverb is right: "Speech is silver, but silence is golden."

SUZANNE. That is all I wanted to hear from you. Now—

OLIVIER. Now?

SUZANNE [seeing SOPHIE enter]. Nothing. [To SOPHIE.] What is it?

SOPHIE. Monsieur de Nanjac has called.

SUZANNE. I have already given my orders.

SOPHIE. He insisted on seeing Madame la Baronne. I told him that Madame la Baronne was not receiving. He asked whether Monsieur de Jalin was with madame, and told me if he was, to ask him to step out and see him.

SUZANNE. Tell Monsieur de Nanjac to come in.

OLIVIER. Are you going to see him?

SUZANNE. No, but you will, and you will please tell him what you think you ought to tell him. Only remember that he loves me, that I love him, and that what I want, I want. Au revoir, my dear Olivier. [She goes out.]

OLIVIER. I'll get this over with at once.

[Enter RAYMOND.]

You wished to see me, my dear Raymond? The Baroness is not present—we are alone. I am listening.

RAYMOND. I don't wish to forget that I once called you friend, but—

OLIVIER. But?

RAYMOND. You have deceived me.

OLIVIER [staccato]. I have not.

RAYMOND. Listen to me: I have decided not to consider proofs; furthermore, Madame d'Ange convinced me that what you told me was not so. You said she was never married; I have seen the marriage contract with my own eyes. Are you going to tell me the document is a forgery?

OLIVIER. No.

RAYMOND. You told me she was not a widow; I have seen her husband's death-certificate. Are you going to tell me that document is an invention?

OLIVIER. No.

RAYMOND. I have just come from the Marquis de Thonnerins, whom I have questioned, and who said he knew nothing about the Baroness. And, finally, these letters you told me were written by Madame d'Ange—

OLIVIER. Are not from her, I now know: one of her friends wrote them for her, and I was led to believe they were her own. Both of them were making game of me. But it was not I who deceived you, I myself have been deceived. I believed I had the right to warn you, but I did not have it. I felt positive I had incontrovertible proofs against the Baroness, but even my own stupidity didn't furnish one. When I tried to prove I was truly your friend I succeeded only in proving that I was a fool. I have been beautifully deceived, take my word for it.

RAYMOND. So you take back everything you said?

OLIVIER. Everything. She comes of a good family, she was married, she is a baroness, a widow, she loves you, she was never any more than a stranger to me; she is worthy of you. Whoever denies this is a defamer, who speaks evil he cannot prove. Good-bye, Raymond; after what has happened, I can't show my face to the Baroness again. I shan't see her again until she asks for me, and I hardly think she will do that soon. Please don't think of me as being anything but clumsy. Good-bye.

RAYMOND Good-bye. [OLIVIER goes out.] I must hear the final word from that man!

[Enter a SERVANT.]

SERVANT. Monsieur knows, of course, that Madame la Baronne has gone out, and will not return until late?

RAYMOND [sitting down]. Very well, I shall wait.

ACT IV

The scene is the same. SUZANNE is present.

[Enter a SERVANT.]

SERVANT. Monsieur le Marquis de Thonnerins. [He goes out.]

[Enter the MARQUIS.]

MARQUIS. How do you do, Baroness!

SUZANNE. To what do I owe the pleasure of your visit, my dear Marquis?

MARQUIS. I have come to learn, my dear Suzanne, if my solicitor has given you what he was to give you?

SUZANNE. He gave me everything, thank you.

MARQUIS. And I wanted to learn how you are getting on?

SUZANNE. Very well.

MARQUIS. And your marriage?

SUZANNE. My marriage?

MARQUIS. Is it going to take place?

SUZANNE. That's so—I haven't seen you for a long time. Haven't you heard?

MARQUIS. Nothing.

SUZANNE [with a sigh.] You are right, Monsieur le Marquis, I was too ambitious: some things are impossible.

MARQUIS. You admit it?

SUZANNE. I must.

MARQUIS. Tell me.

SUZANNE. Someone told!

MARQUIS. Who?

SUZANNE. Someone in whom I had too great confidence: Monsieur de Jalin.

MARQUIS. And did he tell Monsieur de Nanjac?

SUZANNE. You know his name?

MARQUIS. Yes. And what did Monsieur de Nanjac do?

SUZANNE. He believed Monsieur de Jalin; then, because he loved me, he believed *me*.

MARQUIS. And now?

SUZANNE. Now he still loves me—only jealously, and without confidence. There's no end of questions, suspicion, spying; I declare I haven't the strength to endure such a life. And it used to be my ambition! To be incessantly trembling for fear the past should tumble down on our heads, start each morning of my life with some new lie I have to confess every night, and at the same time love sincerely and loyally—it's out of the question. I have already used up my strength in the struggle, and my love as well. I don't love Monsieur de Nanjac any longer.

MARQUIS. Is that true?

SUZANNE. You are the only person I never lie to.

MARQUIS. You don't love Monsieur de Nanjac?

SUZANNE. I love no one.

MARQUIS. Then the marriage will not take place?

SUZANNE. No; I shall remain free. I'm going to Italy; they rarely ask where a woman comes from, and so long as she has money and is not too homely, they believe everything she says. I am going to buy a house on the shores of Lake Como; I'll powder and rouge like Madame de Santis, and wander about the lake in the light of the stars, write poetry *à la* Byron, pose as a misunderstood woman, receive and protect artists, and some day, if I like, marry a ruined Italian prince of questionable title, who will squander my fortune, keep a dancing-girl, and beat me besides. Don't you think I'd be doing what I ought, and that a woman like me hasn't anything better to look forward to?

MARQUIS. So you're going away?

SUZANNE. In three or four days.

MARQUIS. Alone?

SUZANNE. With my maid.

MARQUIS. Does Monsieur de Nanjac know?

SUZANNE. He has no suspicion of it.

MARQUIS. Are you not going to let him know where you will be?

SUZANNE. If I wanted to continue to see him, I might better remain in Paris. No; I am leaving in order to escape from an unbearable situation, which cannot but become worse as time goes on.

MARQUIS. I congratulate you. Your commonsense is leading you to do what necessity would have forced on you later.

SUZANNE [*distractedly*]. How is that?

MARQUIS. Chance is a clumsy bungler in what does not concern it. Now, chance had it that Monsieur de Nanjac's sister is a friend of my own sister. Monsieur de Nanjac did not hide his plans from his sister, who came to see mine. That was how I heard the name I had no wish to learn from you. But that is not all: Monsieur de Nanjac himself came to ask me questions about you. I told him nothing, because, as a man of honor, I preferred to allow you to extricate yourself from this delicate situation with all the honors of war. To-day I have come to tell you what I have told you once before: namely, that the day I should meet (by chance, of course) the man you wish to marry, I should tell him the whole truth. I have waited a little, and I am glad, because I see you have decided not to marry. It's all for the best, if you mean what you say—

SUZANNE. I do. To-morrow Monsieur de Nanjac will be freed from all obligations, and you will be at perfect liberty, if you like, to give him to Mademoiselle de Thonnerins as a husband.

MARQUIS. My daughter has nothing to do in all this, my dear Suzanne; remember that. Everything I have said is in sober earnest.

SUZANNE. Sober earnest, yes.

MARQUIS. Be happy; that is my last wish. Good-bye, Baroness, and remember!

SUZANNE. I shall never forget.

[The MARQUIS goes out as VALENTINE enters. They bow to each other.]

VALENTINE [who wears a traveling dress, looks at the door through which the MARQUIS has gone]. Was that the Marquis de Thonnerins?

SUZANNE. Yes.

VALENTINE. He's always a little brusque, isn't he?

SUZANNE. Where are you going? You're dressed for traveling?

VALENTINE. I'm going away.

SUZANNE. When?

VALENTINE. In an hour.

SUZANNE. Where?

VALENTINE. To London, and from there to Belgium, and then Germany.

SUZANNE. With—?

VALENTINE. Yes, someone is going with me.

SUZANNE. But your law-suit?

VALENTINE. I'm not going to sue. I applied, but I lost. When I told the judge of my troubles he said: "Believe me, madame, you had better not bother your husband. That's the best you can do." So, I'm going.

SUZANNE. I haven't seen you for a long time.

VALENTINE. Oh, the things I have to buy for the trip! It seems one can't get anything in England. And I must do something about my apartment. I paid a year's rent to the landlord, who let me go; I gave an indemnity to the upholsterer, who took back his furniture, and now I'm free as the winds of heaven.

SUZANNE. But you didn't find time to bring me the answer I asked you for.

VALENTINE. I've written it. Didn't you get my note?

SUZANNE. Yes, only—

VALENTINE. I'll tell you everything; it's much simpler.

SUZANNE. Very well.

VALENTINE. I sent Madame de Lornan an anonymous letter.

SUZANNE. Good.

VALENTINE. I was careful to disguise my hand. I told her that a woman who takes the greatest interest in her welfare but who must remain unnamed, insists upon speaking with her. I gave her to understand that the matter concerned Monsieur de Jalin. I advised her to be very discreet, and suggested that we meet: it was the day before yesterday, in the evening.

SUZANNE. Did she come?

VALENTINE. Yes. We met in the Tuileries; it was dusk, and I was heavily veiled. She couldn't possibly have seen my face, but I saw hers: she is beautiful.

SUZANNE. What did you say to her?

VALENTINE. Exactly what we agreed I should say: that Olivier was deceiving her, that he was in love with Mademoiselle de Sancenaux whom he wants to marry; I told her how foolish it was of him, how tragic it would be, because the girl is not worthy of him. I pretended to think Madame de Lornan was no more than a friend of Olivier's. As a matter of fact, she is only a friend, but she loves him and is fearfully jealous.

SUZANNE. Did you mention me?

VALENTINE. She was the first to speak of you. I told her I knew you, that you knew all about the matter, and that she and you together might prevent the marriage; it would be doing a service to Monsieur de Jalin. All she would have to do would be to see you and come to an understanding. She hesitated a long time, and made me promise that you would be alone when she came. I promised and, as I wrote you, she will be here at two. The poor woman doesn't know where she is. Who would ever believe that Monsieur de Jalin could inspire such passion? Have you heard from him?

SUZANNE. Yes.

VALENTINE. On what sort of terms is he with Monsieur de Nanjac?

SUZANNE. Bad; but Olivier wrote me—

VALENTINE. What does he say?

SUZANNE. That he loves me, that if he wished to prevent my marriage, it was for that reason.

VALENTINE. That may be true.

SUZANNE. Who knows? Perhaps; but the chances are it is not, because he asks me to call on him. He wants to explain something which, it seems, he cannot explain here.

VALENTINE. There is some trick in this.

SUZANNE. I am certain that he and Monsieur de Nanjac are not on speaking terms.

VALENTINE. If Monsieur de Nanjac could only give him one good sword-thrust and teach him not to meddle in what doesn't concern him! I can't bear this Monsieur de Jalin; he's the one who set Hippolyte against me. Now, my dear, if you want to play him a turn, go ahead, I'll be only too glad to help.

SUZANNE. Never worry, I shan't forget. What is the use of offending, so long as the offenses are forgiven? Among other things, Monsieur de Jalin remarked that it was wrong to introduce a respectable woman into our society; well, to-day he will be found at my home in the company of Madame de Lornan; that will possibly force him to modify his ideas a little.

VALENTINE. Is he coming?

SUZANNE. Yes.

VALENTINE. He'll be furious. What if he were to get angry with you?

SUZANNE. The idea! The first angry word would mean a duel with Monsieur de Nanjac, and he doesn't want that. He will learn his lesson and hold his tongue in the future.

VALENTINE. Isn't it too bad I have to go? Good-bye. Write me to London, general delivery, care of Mademoiselle Rose—that's my maid's name. Until I'm quite safe, I don't want my husband to know where I am. It's funny to see me leaving Paris: this is the only place where one can enjoy one's self, but I must go. Good-bye.

SUZANNE. You'll let me hear from you?

VALENTINE. I shan't fail to. Good-bye. Remember, in Mademoiselle Rose's name.

[*Enter* RAYMOND *through one door, as* VALENTINE *disappears through another.*]

SUZANNE. Another woman I shan't receive after I marry! [*To* RAYMOND.] I've been so anxious to see you!

RAYMOND. Everything is ready.

SUZANNE. The contract?

RAYMOND. We shall sign it to-morrow.

SUZANNE. And we leave?

RAYMOND. Whenever you like.

SUZANNE. Will you always love me?

RAYMOND. And you, Suzanne?

SUZANNE. Can you doubt it now? Haven't I given you every proof? Oh, yes, I love you!

RAYMOND. Have you seen Monsieur de Jalin again?

SUZANNE. No. Why?

RAYMOND. I saw him not long ago, coming in this direction with his friend Monsieur Richond.

SUZANNE. Yes; he is coming here.

RAYMOND. I thought you weren't to see him any more. I asked you not to and you promised.

SUZANNE. He wrote that he had to speak to me, and I am going to receive him as if nothing had happened. I shall even pretend that nothing has, and I advise you to forget, too.

RAYMOND. Please give your final orders about the signing of the contract to-morrow. I want our marriage officially announced to all our friends, including Monsieur de Jalin, whom I shall receive; I wish to be the first person he sees here. I want him to understand how he is to behave in your home. I shall be with you shortly. [SUZANNE *goes out.*]

[*Enter a* SERVANT.]
SERVANT. Monsieur Olivier de Jalin.
Monsieur Hippolyte Richond.
[*He goes out.*]

[*Enter* OLIVIER *and* HIPPOLYTE.]
RAYMOND [*bowing formally*]. Messieurs!
OLIVIER. How are you, Raymond?
RAYMOND. In the best of health, thank you.
OLIVIER. Is the Baroness in?
RAYMOND. She asked me to beg you to wait for her; she will be here in a few moments. Messieurs—
[*He bows and goes out.*]
OLIVIER. What a face!
HIPPOLYTE. You might have expected it when you decided to come. Why did you? You were clear of all this intriguing. You have done your duty. Monsieur de Nanjac is determined to marry the woman; if he insists on seeing no obstacle, like Guzman, leave him alone. After all, it doesn't concern you.
OLIVIER. Perfectly right, and, as a matter of fact I did make up my mind to have nothing further to do with it all, in spite of the fact that I believe there are certain people who are worth saving from themselves; but women are extremists, and Suzanne has just dealt me a blow and provoked me to continue. It's not my fault.
HIPPOLYTE. You have been waiting only for a pretext to return to her.
OLIVIER. Possibly; but that is only another reason why you ought not to furnish me with this pretext.
HIPPOLYTE. Tell me what she did.
OLIVIER. Your wife wrote an anonymous letter to Madame de Lornan.
HIPPOLYTE. My wife?
OLIVIER. Yes; the writing was disguised but I recognized it. The letter asked Madame de Lornan for a meeting; her housekeeper showed it to me (she knows the interest I have in her mistress, though Charlotte still refuses to receive me). I know Suzanne is at the bottom of this, but I warn her to take care! If what

I believe is true, if she makes the slightest move against Madame de Lornan, I don't know just how I shall go about it but I declare I will so ruin her prospects of marriage that I'm hanged if she even finds the tiniest fragment!
HIPPOLYTE. What if I tried to stop her? So long as she confined herself to wronging me it wasn't so bad, but the moment she touches others—
OLIVIER. I'll attend to it myself. The moment I heard of these new goings-on I wrote Suzanne asking her to come to see me, but she took good care not to accept. She replied that she would see me if I called to-day. Just allow me to cast my line where I want, and don't make any noise; in an hour, the fish will bite.
[*Enter the* VISCOUNTESS, *very agitated.*]
VISCOUNTESS. Where is the Baroness?
OLIVIER. What is the trouble, my dear Viscountess? You come in like a tempest.
VISCOUNTESS. I'm furious!
OLIVIER. I'm not sorry to see you that way. It changes one.
VISCOUNTESS. I am in no mood for joking.
OLIVIER. Then let me answer your question: the Baroness is with Monsieur de Nanjac; we are now waiting for her.
VISCOUNTESS [*taking* OLIVIER *to one side, as she says to* HIPPOLYTE]. Pardon me, monsieur. [*To* OLIVIER.] Do you know what Marcelle has done?
OLIVIER. She told Monsieur de Nanjac to his face that she wouldn't marry him.
VISCOUNTESS. Yes.
OLIVIER. Because she does not love him.
VISCOUNTESS. A fine reason! But that isn't all: when I went to Marcelle's room this morning, she wasn't there.
OLIVIER. She must have left a letter?
VISCOUNTESS. Yes; she said she had found means of not being a burden to me any more, that I should fear nothing, and that I should never have reason to be ashamed of her.
OLIVIER. And added that she was going back to the school where she was educated, eh?

VISCOUNTESS. Have you seen her?
OLIVIER. Not long ago.
VISCOUNTESS. Where?
OLIVIER. At her school.
VISCOUNTESS. How did that happen?
OLIVIER. She wrote.
VISCOUNTESS. To you?
OLIVIER. To me.
VISCOUNTESS. Why?
OLIVIER. I advised her.
VISCOUNTESS. What business is it of yours?
OLIVIER. It *is* my business.
VISCOUNTESS. You, too, advised her to leave Paris?
OLIVIER. Yes; she is going to-morrow. The head of the school has found her a position.
VISCOUNTESS. A position?
OLIVIER. With an excellent family at Besançon. Mademoiselle de Sancenaux will give lessons in English and music to a little girl. She will receive eight hundred francs a year, with board and lodging. It will hardly be amusing, but she considers it more honorable than to stay in Paris, fail to get married, play cards, and compromise herself. I agree with her.
VISCOUNTESS. Well, you have done a splendid thing! Do you know what I am going to do? Write and tell her at least to change her name. To think of having a Sancenaux, my own brother's daughter, compromise her family like that! A Sancenaux teaching! Why not make her a chambermaid?
OLIVIER. Is that what you call compromising her family? My dear Viscountess, the person who sold you your logic, cheated you shamelessly! It must have been Monsieur de Latour.
VISCOUNTESS. What hope has she of marriage after a scandal like that?
OLIVIER. She will doubtless marry sooner than if she stayed with you.
VISCOUNTESS. She's not taking the right road.
OLIVIER. All roads lead to Rome, and the longest is frequently the surest.

VISCOUNTESS. We'll see. I've done all I could for her. She is only my niece, after all.
[*Enter* SUZANNE.]
SUZANNE. How are you, Viscountess?
VISCOUNTESS. And you, dear?
SUZANNE. What's the matter?
VISCOUNTESS. I'll tell you later. I've returned what you were good enough to lend me.
SUZANNE. There's no hurry.
VISCOUNTESS. Thank you, but I have fallen heir to a little money.
SUZANNE [*to* HIPPOLYTE]. Very good of you, monsieur, to pay me this visit with Monsieur de Jalin.
HIPPOLYTE. I hesitated for fear of being indiscreet, but Olivier—
SUZANNE. The friends of Monsieur de Jalin are my friends.
HIPPOLYTE. Thank you, madame.
SUZANNE [*to* OLIVIER]. So you are here?
OLIVIER. You wrote me to come.
SUZANNE. In order to find out what you had to say to me.
OLIVIER. I wrote you that.
SUZANNE. Do you love me?
OLIVIER. I love you.
SUZANNE. So that was why you wanted me to come to you? Yes, in order that Monsieur de Nanjac might know, and see me go into your home! Really, you're waging a child's war, using wooden cannons and bread-crumb bullets. Do you intend to disarm me?
OLIVIER. Don't you believe me?
SUZANNE. No.
OLIVIER. Very well. Good-bye.
SUZANNE. Don't go; I want to show you something.
OLIVIER. What?
SUZANNE. It's a surprise.
[*During this,* RAYMOND *has entered and begun speaking with the* VISCOUNTESS *and* HIPPOLYTE.]
RAYMOND. My dear Viscountess, you surely know Madame de Lornan?
VISCOUNTESS. I used to, but we have since drifted apart.

SUZANNE. She is said to be very virtuous.

VISCOUNTESS. True.

SUZANNE. She is most particular as to what homes she visits.

VISCOUNTESS. She sees very few people.

SUZANNE. She is coming here. I'll introduce her to you, my dear Monsieur de Nanjac; you'll see, she's most charming.

OLIVIER. If she comes!

SUZANNE. That's so; you know Madame de Lornan very well, don't you, dear Monsieur de Jalin?

OLIVIER. That is why I am willing to wager that she is not coming, or at least if she does, that she will not enter the house.

SUZANNE. How much will you wager?

OLIVIER. Whatever you like, whatever a respectable woman can wager: a box of candy or a bouquet.

SUZANNE. I accept [*seeing a* SERVANT *enter*], and I think I am going to win immediately. [*To the* SERVANT.] What is it?

SERVANT. A lady who would like to speak with Madame la Baronne.

SUZANNE. Her name?

SERVANT. She would not tell me.

SUZANNE. Tell the lady that I do not receive people who refuse to give their names. [*The* SERVANT *goes out.*]

OLIVIER [*aside to* RAYMOND]. Raymond, for the sake of our former friendship, prevent Madame de Lornan's entering this room.

RAYMOND. Why?

OLIVIER. Because it may have dire results.

RAYMOND. For whom?

OLIVIER. For several people.

RAYMOND. I have no rights in the home of Madame d'Ange.

OLIVIER. Very well.

SERVANT [*opening the door*]. Madame de Lornan asks whether Madame la Baronne will receive her?

SUZANNE. Ask her to come in.

OLIVIER. Poor woman!

[*He hastens out.*]

HIPPOLYTE. God grant that you may never regret what you are doing, madame!

SUZANNE. I have never regretted anything. [*To* RAYMOND, *who is about to leave.*] Don't go! Monsieur de Jalin will offer his arm to Madame de Lornan. He has lost his wager, and is doing the best thing he can do.

[RAYMOND *goes toward the door. The moment he gets there, it opens, and* OLIVIER *appears.*]

RAYMOND. Where have you been, monsieur?

OLIVIER. I have just told Madame de Lornan that I object to her coming in here.

RAYMOND. By what right?

OLIVIER. By the right of an honest man who wishes to prevent an honest woman's losing her good name.

SUZANNE. Especially when that honest woman is the mistress of that honest man.

OLIVIER. You lie, madame!

RAYMOND. Monsieur, you are insulting a woman.

OLIVIER. During the past week, monsieur, you have been trying to pick a quarrel with me, but allow me to tell you I did not come here to give you an opportunity to do so. You believe that a sword-thrust can extricate you from the situation you are now in; very well, I am at your service.

RAYMOND. In an hour's time, monsieur, my seconds will pay you a call.

OLIVIER. I shall await them.

RAYMOND. They have only the conditions to fix; the cause should remain unknown. [*The men prepare to go.*]

SUZANNE. Raymond!

RAYMOND. Wait for me, Suzanne; I shall return at once. [*He goes out.*]

OLIVIER. Come, Hippolyte.

[*They bow, and go out, opposite.*]

VISCOUNTESS. My dear, a provocation to a duel in your home, between two men who were such good friends a few days ago? How could it happen?

SUZANNE. I know nothing about it.

VISCOUNTESS. But you surely won't allow it?

SUZANNE. Oh, no; I've done more difficult things than that.

VISCOUNTESS. Can't I help you?

SUZANNE. No, thank you.

VISCOUNTESS. Then I'll go; you haven't too much time. Keep me posted on developments.

SUZANNE. I shan't fail. Come back later in the day, or I'll drop in to see you.

VISCOUNTESS. I'll see you soon again. [*As she goes.*] What does it all mean?
[*She leaves.*]

SUZANNE. Really, Olivier is braver than I had thought him. He's a splendid, upright man. Olivier is not in love with Madame de Lornan—but what if he were?

[*Enter a* SERVANT.]

SERVANT. A letter for Madame la Baronne.

[*He gives her the letter and goes out.*]

SUZANNE. That will do. [*She opens the letter.*] From the Marquis! [*Reading:*] "You have deceived me: you have seen Monsieur de Nanjac again and you insist on marrying, in spite of the fact that I forbade it. I give you one hour in which to break it off. If by the end of that time you have not found the means, I shall tell everything to Monsieur de Nanjac." Oh, this past of mine, that keeps crumbling before me, fragment by fragment! Shall I never be able to bury it? Confess everything? No; I am going to fight it out to the bitter end. [*She rings.*] I must gain time, that's the principal thing. [*She writes a note, and gives it to* SOPHIE, *who enters.*] Take this letter to Monsieur de Thonnerins, and deliver it to him yourself. Close this door.

[SOPHIE *goes to the door, and as she is about to close it, announces.*]

SOPHIE. Monsieur de Nanjac.

SUZANNE [*closing her writing-portfolio, as she says in a loud voice to* SOPHIE]. Very well. Never mind, Sophie, you may do that errand later. [SOPHIE *goes out as* RAYMOND *enters.—To* RAYMOND.] Well, dear?

RAYMOND. I have just been to see two officers, old comrades of mine, and asked them to act as seconds for me. They were not in, but I left word for them.

SUZANNE. Raymond, this duel cannot take place.

RAYMOND. You must be mad, Suzanne. I may allow compromises between Monsieur de Latour and Monsieur de Maucroix, but not for my own duels. Monsieur de Jalin is right: I hate him.

SUZANNE. Give me up, Raymond: I have done you nothing but harm so far.

RAYMOND. I have sworn that you are to be my wife, and you will be! I may be killed: in a duel one man is as good as another, and Monsieur de Jalin is no coward; he will do his best to defend himself. I do not want to die without having kept my promise.

[*He sits by the table and starts to open the writing-portfolio.*]

SUZANNE [*with an involuntary start*]. What are you going to do?

RAYMOND. Ask my solicitor to come here. Please have this letter taken to him.

SUZANNE. Never mind.

RAYMOND. What's the matter. Didn't we agree?

SUZANNE. Yes, but you have plenty of time.

RAYMOND. I have very little.

SUZANNE. I'll give you pen and paper.

RAYMOND. Here is everything I need.

SUZANNE. No.

RAYMOND. You're mistaken—why, you were writing when I came in.

SUZANNE. Raymond, I ask you not to open that.

RAYMOND. I shan't, then, if you have been writing things I have no business seeing.

SUZANNE. Do you suspect something else?

RAYMOND. No, dear Suzanne: if you have secrets, I shall respect them.

SUZANNE. Then open it and read.

RAYMOND. Will you allow me?

SUZANNE. Yes. [RAYMOND *is on the point of opening the portfolio, when she stops him.*] So you defy me?

RAYMOND. You should not accuse me of that! This is not defiance, but curiosity. You have given me permission, and I am going to look.

SUZANNE. Do you promise not to make fun of me?

RAYMOND. I promise.

SUZANNE. If you only knew what it's about!

RAYMOND. We shall soon see.

SUZANNE. You will know so much more when you see the list of things I have ordered for our trip.

RAYMOND. What have you ordered?

SUZANNE. Dresses, skirts, silk gowns with figured corsages, and—How interesting those details must be to a man!

RAYMOND. Is that the whole secret?

SUZANNE. Yes.

RAYMOND. So you were writing to your dressmaker?

SUZANNE. Yes.

RAYMOND. While I was seeing the seconds for my duel, you were ordering dresses. Really, Suzanne, do you think I am a fool?

SUZANNE. Raymond!

RAYMOND. I want to know whom you were writing to!

SUZANNE. Oh ho, well, I won't tell you!

[*She opens the writing-portfolio and takes out a letter.*]

RAYMOND. Take care!

SUZANNE. Threats! And by what right? Thank God, I am not your wife yet. I am here in my own home, free, mistress of my own actions, as I leave you free to do as you like. Do I ask you questions? Do I search through your private papers?

RAYMOND [*seizing her wrist*]. Let me see that letter!

SUZANNE. You shall not! I have never given in to violence. I have told you the truth; you may now believe what you like.

RAYMOND. I believe that you are deceiving me.

SUZANNE. Very well!

RAYMOND. Suzanne!

SUZANNE. That will do, monsieur! I release you of all your obligations, and I take back my promise. You and I are now nothing to each other.

RAYMOND. You have once before made use of that trick, madame, but this time I shall remain.

SUZANNE. What sort of man are you?

RAYMOND. A man who asked nothing of you in exchange for an honorable name, except one moment's sincerity; a man who has sworn you had nothing with which to reproach yourself; a man who to-morrow is going to fight a duel with a man of honor who had cast a slur on your good name; a man who, for the past two weeks, has had to deal with lies and deceptions, with no other help than loyalty, frankness, and confidence; a man who is determined to know the whole truth at any cost. If that letter does not contain all of it, I imagine from your excitement that it contains a part. I must see that letter; give it to me or I will take it!

SUZANNE [*crumpling the letter and trying to tear it*]. You are not going to have it.

RAYMOND [*shaking her by the arm*]. The letter!

SUZANNE. You dare use violence with a woman!

RAYMOND [*more and more excited*]. That letter!

SUZANNE. I don't love you! I never loved you! I did deceive you. Now, go!

RAYMOND. That letter! [*He tries to force her hand.*]

SUZANNE. Raymond, I'll tell you everything—you're hurting me—I'm not to blame. Please, for God's sake! [*He snatches the letter from her.*] Oh, you—! [*She falls exhausted into a chair.*] All right—read it—I'll have my revenge, I swear!

RAYMOND [*reading, with emotion*]. "I beg you, don't ruin me. I must see you; I shall explain everything. I will do as you say. It is not my fault if Monsieur de Nanjac loves me: I love him, that is my excuse. I depend on you. Please be generous and forgive me. If he knew the truth I should die of shame. I promise you I shall never marry him, but you must never let him know. Wait till I am free, I—" And I still doubted! [*He hides his face in his hands.*] What did I ever do to you, Suzanne? Why did you deceive me? Here is your letter. Good-bye. [*He starts to go out, but falls into a chair and bursts out crying.*]

SUZANNE [*seeing that he is overcome, says, timidly*]. Raymond?

RAYMOND. You have made a man cry who has not cried since his mother's death. I thank you—it has done me good.

SUZANNE [*reproachfully*]. You hurt my arms and hands cruelly, Raymond.

RAYMOND. I am sorry; forgive me; it was cowardly. But I did so love you!

SUZANNE [*going toward him*]. I loved you, too.

RAYMOND. If you had loved me, you would not have lied to me.

SUZANNE. There is not a woman who would have confessed what you asked me to confess. I loved you; I respected you; I wanted to be loved and respected. Let me tell you about my life. There is one thing I should keep from you, but only one. If you only knew: I am not so much to blame as I may seem to be; I had no one to advise or help me. I ought to have told you everything; you are generous and would have forgiven me. Now, you can't believe me any longer. But, if I am not pure enough to become the wife of a man like you, I love you enough to deserve your love in return. There is nothing now to force me to tell you. [*She falls to her knees and takes his hand.*] Raymond, believe in me: I love you!

RAYMOND. To whom were you sending that letter?

SUZANNE. You would want to challenge him if you knew.

RAYMOND. I shan't say a word about it to him, but tell me his name!

SUZANNE. That man has no rights over me; you see, I wrote that I loved you.

RAYMOND. Then why does he forbid you to become my wife?

SUZANNE. I will tell you all, if you promise to be calm.

RAYMOND [*rising*]. Good-bye.

SUZANNE [*retaining him*]. I'll tell you everything.

RAYMOND. Well?

SUZANNE. I was going to send that letter to—

RAYMOND. Olivier?

SUZANNE [*forcefully*]. No, I swear! But promise me you won't challenge him.

RAYMOND. I promise.

SUZANNE. To the Marquis de Thonnerins. [RAYMOND *makes a gesture of surprise and anger.*] Raymond, put yourself in the place of a woman who has been cast off by everyone, who had at last found an unhoped-for though secret protector. I owe everything to the Marquis! If you only realized—I never had any family!

RAYMOND. Then your marriage—?

SUZANNE. A lie!

RAYMOND. But the documents you showed me?

SUZANNE. Belonged to a young woman who died abroad—she had no friends or relatives.

RAYMOND. Your fortune?

SUZANNE. Comes from Monsieur de Thonnerins.

RAYMOND. And you were prepared to exchange that shame for my confidence and love? Instead of confessing everything to me, frankly, nobly, you were about to bring me a stolen name and a fortune acquired at the price of your honor! You did not see that, after I had become your husband, had I found out about this infamous bargain, the only thing I could do would have been to kill you, and then myself. You not only did not love me, Suzanne, you did not respect me.

SUZANNE. I am the lowest of creatures, I know; I don't deserve your love, not even that you should remember me. Leave me, Raymond, and forget me.

RAYMOND. This is not all, doubtless? Please continue; what else have you to confess?

SUZANNE. Nothing.

RAYMOND. What about Olivier? Neither misery nor loneliness could ha ve led you to go to him. If that man was ever your lover, it means that you have loved him, and that love is what I cannot forgive!

SUZANNE. Olivier has never been anything to me. He told you that himself, and you know it.

RAYMOND. Will you swear to that?

SUZANNE [calmly]. I swear.

RAYMOND. Do you love me?

SUZANNE. Do you think I would have confessed unless I did?

RAYMOND. Well, Suzanne, I ask for only one proof of that love.

SUZANNE. What?

RAYMOND. Return to Monsieur de Thonnerins everything you have from him.

SUZANNE [ringing]. At once! [She takes papers from a drawer, wraps and seals them. To the SERVANT, who enters.] Take these at once to Monsieur de Thonnerins; there is no answer.

SERVANT. Monsieur le Marquis de Thonnerins is just this moment coming up the stairs.

SUZANNE. He is!

RAYMOND [to the SERVANT]. Ask Monsieur le Marquis to wait! [The SERVANT goes out.—To SUZANNE.] Let me have those papers; I shall give them to him myself.

SUZANNE. You frighten me!

RAYMOND. Don't be afraid. There is still time, Suzanne. Choose. Keep these papers; I shall go away, for always; or, if you decide to make those promises again, and in case I am not killed tomorrow, I shall hold you to account only from this moment on. We may then go away together

SUZANNE. I have told you the truth.

RAYMOND. Oh, Suzanne, I had no idea myself how much I loved you!

[He goes out.]

SUZANNE. I am staking my whole life, past and future! Olivier is the only one now who can ruin or save me! If he loves me as he says he does—it would be strange. [She puts on her cloak and hat.] We shall see!   [She goes out.]

ACT V

The scene is the same as in the First Act. OLIVIER *is writing. A moment later, enter* HIPPOLYTE.

HIPPOLYTE [touching OLIVIER on the shoulder]. It's I.

OLIVIER [as he seals the letter]. Well?

HIPPOLYTE. I have done everything.

OLIVIER. Have you seen Madame de Lornan?

HIPPOLYTE. Yes, but through the agency of her housekeeper, because her husband has returned. That is why Madame de Lornan wrote you asking for news. She can't leave her house now. I told her the duel was not going to take place.

OLIVIER. And that in no event would her name be mentioned? Undoubtedly, she cares more about that than about anything else?

HIPPOLYTE. She cares something about it, but she is anxious that nothing should happen to you. You wanted to save her, and you succeeded; you should be the last one to blame her for refusing to compromise herself even for your sake. She received a good lesson, and she will profit by it. I reassured her. It was not difficult, because I felt very sure myself.

OLIVIER. How do you mean?

HIPPOLYTE. The duel will not take place, I tell you.

OLIVIER. Why?

HIPPOLYTE. Because I have seen the Marquis; there is something new.

OLIVIER. There can't be anything new to prevent us, Monsieur de Nanjac and I, from fighting this duel: we have gone too far—unless he makes excuses to me, which is not likely.

HIPPOLYTE. That depends on you alone.

OLIVIER. Tell me what you mean.

HIPPOLYTE. I have seen the Marquis.

OLIVIER. Does he refuse to act as my second?

HIPPOLYTE. Yes.

OLIVIER. I rather thought he would. He is afraid of compromising himself—he, too.

HIPPOLYTE. He is right. Things of this sort do not go with his years or position. For his daughter's sake, his name ought not to be dragged into the affair. But he has seen Monsieur de Nanjac, who knows the whole truth.

OLIVIER. The whole truth?

HIPPOLYTE. So far as the Marquis is concerned. He found a letter that Suzanne had written to Monsieur de Thonnerins. There was a violent quarrel between Raymond and Madame d'Ange. Suzanne was forced to tell about her relations with the Marquis. Raymond forgave her, on condition that she restore to the Marquis everything he had given her.

OLIVIER. Did she do it?

HIPPOLYTE. So it seems.

OLIVIER. I am surprised; but, tell me, how can this prevent the duel?

HIPPOLYTE. Monsieur de Nanjac gave back everything himself, and Monsieur de Thonnerins, who was told of the provocation, informed Monsieur de Nanjac that the marriage, like the duel, was out of the question; that Madame d'Ange was not worthy of him, and that your conduct throughout was that of a gallant man and a good friend. You know what a man in love is like when he finds himself in a false position: the more violently the woman is attacked, the more he believes it due his dignity to defend her. Monsieur de Nanjac took it all in a high-handed way and replied: "The moment I restore what Madame d'Ange has received from you, monsieur, it means that I wish to forget everything in Madame d'Ange's life in which you have played a part. As to Monsieur de Jalin, who began by telling me he was no more than a friend to Madame d'Ange, and ended by relating the exact opposite; as to Monsieur de Jalin, who I once thought was my friend and who was not enough of a friend either to affirm or to deny anything outright, let him say to me, 'I give you my word of honor that I have been that woman's lover,'—that is what he ought to do if he ever cared anything for me,—I give him my word of honor to make excuses to him, to offer him my hand as I used to, and never see Madame d'Ange again." You see now how senseless a duel would be?

OLIVIER. Are you through?

HIPPOLYTE. Yes.

OLIVIER. Well, my poor Hippolyte, I thank you for your splendid intentions; but we have been wasting good time.

HIPPOLYTE. Why?

OLIVIER. Because Madame d'Ange has nothing to do with the question. I do not know and I cannot know anything but one fact: that there is cause for a duel between Monsieur de Nanjac and me, and that any effort to prevent a duel, the basis of which is an insult to a woman (even if it is true), would be undignified and unworthy of a man of honor. Monsieur de Nanjac is a soldier, I belong to what is called the middle-class. What would be said if the duel were stopped? Let us allow things to follow their course. Monsieur de Nanjac is more to be pitied than I, but I can understand his conduct. I want to grasp his hand, but I am perhaps on the point of killing him. Such is the false logic of our code of honor. I did not make it, but I must submit to it.

HIPPOLYTE. It's not very amusing to kill a man. When I look at my wife and remember that I killed a man for her sake—well, you know what my wife did?

OLIVIER. No.

HIPPOLYTE. I have just found out, myself. She ran away with Monsieur de Latour, who leaves a deficit of 400,000 francs at the Bourse. She was bound to do that some day, though she has not yet reached the end. She is one of those women whom nothing can stop; once they start going down, they must continue straight to the bottom, without having, as those who are at the bottom of the ladder have, the excuse of evil example, misery, and ignorance.

OLIVIER. I'm sorry, but it is now half-past two.

HIPPOLYTE. That's true. After Monsieur de Thonnerins refused to be your second, I went to see Monsieur de Maucroix, and he and I went to see Monsieur de Nanjac. We meet at three. We still have three quarters of an hour.

OLIVIER. Where is it to take place?

HIPPOLYTE. In the fields behind your home; they are large and always deserted. No one will disturb us—and then we shall be only a step from where you live. In case of accident, we shall have a safe place to carry the wounded.

OLIVIER. What weapons?

HIPPOLYTE. The seconds left the choice to us.

OLIVIER. Did you refuse?

HIPPOLYTE. Yes, because you told us that you wanted no concessions; we drew lots, and the choice fell to us.

OLIVIER. What did you decide on?

HIPPOLYTE. Swords.

OLIVIER. If anything should happen to me, you will find a letter in this drawer; please have it sent to Mademoiselle de Sancenaux at once; she is going away to-night. This letter will prevent her leaving.

HIPPOLYTE. Is that all?

OLIVIER. Yes.

HIPPOLYTE. Nothing for Madame d'Ange?

OLIVIER. No, nothing—she is coming.

HIPPOLYTE. Did she send word?

OLIVIER. No; but she is brave and proud only when she is victorious; if she knows that I have to say only a word in order to break off her marriage, she will stop at nothing to obtain my silence. She will come.

HIPPOLYTE. Do you know what I am thinking of?

OLIVIER. Tell me.

HIPPOLYTE. That you were more in love with Suzanne than you let anyone

see, and that perhaps you still are, more than you will admit.

OLIVIER [smiling]. Who knows? The heart of a man is so strange.

[Enter a SERVANT.]

SERVANT. There is a young lady below in a carriage who would like to speak with monsieur.

OLIVIER. Who is it?

SERVANT. She wrote this note.

[He hands OLIVIER a note.]

OLIVIER [reading]. "Marcelle"! Ask the lady to come in. [The SERVANT goes out.—To HIPPOLYTE.] Go into my room. I am to see someone who does not want to be seen. When the time comes for us to leave, rap on the door, and I shall join you.

HIPPOLYTE. You have only half an hour.

OLIVIER. Don't worry; we shall be on time. [HIPPOLYTE goes out; OLIVIER goes toward the door. Enter MARCELLE.] You here, Marcelle? How imprudent!

MARCELLE. No one saw me come in, though I don't care what anyone may think. I am going away to-night; perhaps I shall never come back. I didn't want to go without seeing you.

OLIVIER. I should have called on you before you went.

MARCELLE. That might not have been possible, perhaps? Or didn't you think of that?

OLIVIER. Is that a reproach?

MARCELLE. What right have I to reproach you? Am I a friend of yours? Am I worthy of your confidence? If you are in trouble, do you come to me? If you are in danger would you even think of saying good-bye to me before exposing yourself? How miserable I am!

OLIVIER. What is the trouble, Marcelle?

MARCELLE. You are going to fight; perhaps you will be killed! Do you expect me to be calm? And you ask what's the trouble?

OLIVIER. Who told you I was going to fight?

MARCELLE. My aunt, who came to see me after she had been to see Madame d'Ange; she told me everything and gave me the name of the woman for whose sake you are fighting: Madame de Lornan.

OLIVIER. She was mistaken.

MARCELLE. No. If something had happened to you I should have heard about it the way everyone else did—that you were killed! Not to have a single memory or souvenir of you in the moment of danger! How ungrateful of you! I declare, if I were in danger, you would be the only person I would ask to help me! You might at least do for me what I would do for you. But, never mind: I am going to stop the duel.

OLIVIER. How?

MARCELLE. You don't deny it! I'm going to report you to the first police officer I can find.

OLIVIER. By what right?

MARCELLE. By the right of a woman who wants to save the life of the man she loves.

OLIVIER. Do you love me?

MARCELLE. You know I do.

OLIVIER. Marcelle!

MARCELLE. Who else could have induced me, by a word, to change my whole life? Who made me leave the society where I was living? For whose sake would I have been willing to bury myself in the provinces to make a living in sadness and obscurity? For whose sake am I going away, with no other consolation but the thought that I was respected and perhaps would soon be forgotten by you? And, at last, for whose sake does a woman change herself in this way, unless for the sake of the man she loves? Deep down in my heart I was taking one hope with me; I said to myself: "Perhaps he is trying to test me? When he sees I am making an honest effort to live a respectable life, and after he has made of me the woman he wants me to be, who knows but that some day he may come to love me?" I dreamed that—and now I suddenly hear you are fighting a duel for another woman. Do you think I'm going to allow that? Let her allow it, the woman you love; very well; but I, I who love you? No.

OLIVIER. Listen to me, Marcelle; I swear if you attempt in any way to stop this duel—and dishonor me, as it surely will, because it will be said that I made a woman my excuse to avoid fighting—I swear, Marcelle, I will not survive the dishonor.

MARCELLE. I shan't say a word; I shall only pray.

OLIVIER. Now, Marcelle, you must go home. I shall see you soon.

MARCELLE. You're sending me away because the duel is going to take place to-day.

OLIVIER. No—perhaps it will not even take place at all. Now that I know you love me, I want to live. There is a way out of it all.

MARCELLE. Will you promise you are not going to fight to-day?

OLIVIER. I promise. [HIPPOLYTE'S *knock is heard.*] Very well—one moment.

MARCELLE. What's that?

OLIVIER. A friend who wants me.

MARCELLE. One of your seconds?

OLIVIER. Yes.

MARCELLE. To take you to the dueling-ground. Olivier, I'm not going to leave you.

OLIVIER. My seconds are already here: they are conferring with Monsieur de Nanjac's seconds. They must see me. That is why Hippolyte wants to speak to me.

MARCELLE. I'm so afraid!

OLIVIER. Listen, Marcelle: I, too, perhaps, have dreamed your dream. I was happy and proud to have had something to do with developing those good qualities I felt sure were within you. Some mysterious instinct for happiness has urged me toward you. I was unable to say why I wanted you to be worthy of everyone's respect. I see now, it was a basic need in my own heart. That is all I can tell you, because a man whose life is in imminent danger has no right to speak of hope and the future.

MARCELLE. Olivier!

OLIVIER. Everything will have been decided in one hour; then I can explain. Meantime you must not be seen here. Go back to the Viscountess and wait for me. We shall meet again, I promise. I shall be there, and when I leave it will be only to see you. Courage! [He goes out.]

MARCELLE. O God, protect me! [She makes ready to leave, as SUZANNE enters.]

SUZANNE. Marcelle!

MARCELLE [turning round]. You, madame!

SUZANNE. How does it happen that you are here?

MARCELLE. I came the moment I heard of the duel.

SUZANNE. Have you seen Olivier?

MARCELLE. Yes.

SUZANNE. When does it take place?

MARCELLE. I hope it won't take place.

SUZANNE. How is that?

MARCELLE. There is one means of stopping it.

SUZANNE. What?

MARCELLE. I don't know, but Olivier told me he would make use of it.

SUZANNE. That is infamous!

MARCELLE. Do you know what it is?

SUZANNE. Yes; and I tell you Olivier would not compromise any woman in order to avoid fighting. He deceived you.

MARCELLE. He did!

SUZANNE. What did you tell him when you came?

MARCELLE. That I didn't want the duel to take place.

SUZANNE. And that you loved him?

MARCELLE. Yes.

SUZANNE. That if he persisted you would not leave him?

MARCELLE. How do you know that?

SUZANNE. I know what a woman would say. Then did he promise to come to an understanding with his opponent?

MARCELLE. Yes.

SUZANNE. He said, too, that he loved you?

MARCELLE. I could see that.

SUZANNE. He deceived you. He wanted to gain time. He went out to fight.

MARCELLE. No: he is in there.

SUZANNE. Are you sure?

MARCELLE. If I call he will come.

SUZANNE. Call him.

MARCELLE [calling]. Olivier! Olivier!

SUZANNE [opening the door]. No one! Now are you convinced?

MARCELLE. It's—impossible!

SUZANNE [ringing]. Do you still doubt? [To the SERVANT, who enters.] Has your master gone out?

SERVANT. Yes, madame.

SUZANNE. Alone?

SERVANT. With Monsieur Richond and Monsieur de Maucroix, who came to get him.

SUZANNE. Did he leave word either for mademoiselle or for me?

SERVANT. No, madame.

SUZANNE. That will do. [The SERVANT goes out.—To MARCELLE.] Where are you going?

MARCELLE. I must find him and save him!

SUZANNE. Do you know where he is? How can you save him? Wait! That is all we can do—everything rests on chance. Olivier and Raymond are now fighting. They are both brave men, they hate each other, and one of them is sure to be killed.

MARCELLE. My God!

SUZANNE. Now, listen to me: Olivier has lied both to you and to me—he told me, too, that he loved me.

MARCELLE. You? When?

SUZANNE. Two hours ago. I may lose love, fortune, future, in one second. If Raymond survives, I am saved; if he dies, Olivier's love is my last resource. He must love me, otherwise I should die of shame. You ought to know the truth: the same man has told us both that he loved us. It is our right to know whether he does love us. If he is the one who survives, he must find only one of us here—you understand that, of course? He would never explain before us both.

One of us will meet him, the other will remain hidden behind this door, and hear everything: I'll dɔ that, if you like. If he persists in telling you that he loves you, I will sacrifice myself, and go away without saying a word. Tell me—?

MARCELLE. I don't understand, madame; I don't know what you are saying. How calm you are—it's frightful!

SUZANNE. Listen!

MARCELLE. What?

SUZANNE. A carriage!

MARCELLE. It's he!

SUZANNE. Something has happened! Go in there!

MARCELLE. I must see him.

SUZANNE. Go in there, I tell you! It's he—Olivier!

MARCELLE. He is saved! He is living! Now, O God, let me suffer!

SUZANNE [*pushing her toward the door*]. Go in! [MARCELLE *goes out.*]

[*Enter* OLIVIER.]

OLIVIER [*feebly*]. Is that you, Suzanne?

SUZANNE. You didn't expect to see me?

OLIVIER. No.

SUZANNE. Are you wounded?

OLIVIER. It's nothing!

SUZANNE. But Raymond?

OLIVIER [*whose voice grows stronger*]. Suzanne, was I in the right? Did I deceive him?

SUZANNE. No. Well?

OLIVIER. Did I do my duty as an honest man? Answer me.

SUZANNE. Yes. Well?

OLIVIER. When you forced us to fight, whom did you consider was right?

SUZANNE. You.

OLIVIER. Then his death is only a misfortune, and not a crime?

SUZANNE. His death!

OLIVIER. Yes, his death. Listen, Suzanne. The day you came to tell me that you did not love me any longer, a great jealousy was born in me. I wanted to behave generously, and I wore a smile, but my love for you was the strange, fatal sort you inspire in all who love you: in Monsieur de Thonnerins, that old man

who for a moment forgot his daughter for your sake; in Raymond, whom nothing could convince, who believed no one but you, who *would* believe no one but you, who preferred trying to kill me to being convinced by me. If I wanted to prevent this marriage, if I told Raymond all I did tell him, if on the dueling-ground I forgot that he was a friend, if I—I—killed the man who was dear to me only a week ago —it was not because of any offense, it was because I didn't want you to belong to him, because I loved you—because I love you! In a single moment I have made you lose everything; but in a moment I can restore everything to you. I can't think of anyone but you; you must be mine. Don't leave me! Let us go away together!

SUZANNE [*looking him straight in the eyes*]. Yes, let us go!

OLIVIER [*clasping her to him*]. At last!—[*He bursts out laughing.*] Oh! It *was* such trouble!

SUZANNE. What!

OLIVIER. You have lost, my dear. You owe me a forfeit! Look!

SUZANNE [*seeing* RAYMOND *appear, followed by* HIPPOLYTE]. Raymond!

[*Enter* MARCELLE, *who throws herself into* OLIVIER'S *arms.*]

MARCELLE. Oh!

OLIVIER. Forgive me, dear child; I had to save a friend.

RAYMOND [*to* OLIVIER]. Thank you, Olivier. I must have been mad. You have taken my honor into your hands; nothing stopped your attempts to convince me—not even my own blindness, my unjust hatred, even this wound, which is luckily only a slight one. Everything is over between madame and me, except a few practical matters, which I shall ask you to regulate. [*He gives him a slip of paper.*] I don't wish to have to speak with her.

[MARCELLE *goes to* RAYMOND, *who takes her hands in his.* OLIVIER *goes to* SUZANNE.]

SUZANNE. You are a blackguard!

OLIVIER. Careful, please! When one implicates the life and honor of two men, and loses, one should bow to Fate with a good grace. It seems I had to receive a sword-thrust in order to prove the truth of my assertions. I am not preventing your marriage; reason, commonsense and justice are, and the social law which requires that an honest man marry none but an honest woman. You have lost, but you have a consolation prize.

SUZANNE. What?

OLIVIER. In this document, Raymond gives you back the fortune he made you abdicate.

SUZANNE [*playing her last card*]. Give it to me! [*She destroys the document as she looks at* RAYMOND.] What I wanted from him was his name, not his fortune.

I shall leave Paris in an hour, on my way to a foreign country.

[RAYMOND *pretends not to hear.*]

OLIVIER. But you have nothing to live on! You returned everything to the Marquis.

SUZANNE. I don't know what it was, but I was so agitated when I gave those documents to Monsieur de Nanjac that I found most of the deeds and other things on my table after he left. Good-bye, Olivier. [*She goes out.*]

OLIVIER. And to think that all that woman needed to turn her bad into good was a small proportion of the intelligence she used in doing evil!

RAYMOND [*to* MARCELLE]. You are going to be happy, mademoiselle: you are marrying the finest man I know!

MISS SARA SAMPSON

BY GOTTHOLD EPHRAIM LESSING

Produced at Frankfort-on-the-Oder, 1755

TRANSLATED BY ERNEST BELL

CHARACTERS

SIR WILLIAM SAMPSON
MISS SARA SAMPSON, *his daughter*
MELLEFONT
MARWOOD, *formerly* MELLEFONT'S *mistress*
ARABELLA, *a child, daughter of* MARWOOD
WAITWELL, *an old servant of* SIR WILLIAM
NORTON, *servant of* MELLEFONT
BETTY, SARA'S *maid*
HANNAH, MARWOOD'S *maid*
The INNKEEPER *and others*

ACT I

SCENE I—*A room in an inn.*

[SIR WILLIAM SAMPSON, WAITWELL.]

SIR WILLIAM. My daughter, here? Here in this wretched inn?

WAITWELL. No doubt, Mellefont has purposely selected the most wretched one in the town. The wicked always seek the darkness, because they are wicked. But what would it help them, could they even hide themselves from the whole world? Conscience after all is more powerful than the accusations of a world. Ah, you are weeping again, again, Sir!—Sir!

SIR WILLIAM. Let me weep, my honest old servant! Or does she not, do you think, deserve my tears?

WAITWELL. Alas! She deserves them, were they tears of blood.

SIR WILLIAM. Well, let me weep!

WAITWELL. The best, the loveliest, the most innocent child that ever lived beneath the sun, must thus be led astray! Oh, my Sara, my little Sara! I have watched thee grow; a hundred times have I carried thee as a child in these arms, have I admired thy smiles, thy lispings. From every childish look beamed forth the dawn of an intelligence, a kindliness, a——

SIR WILLIAM. Oh, be silent! Does not the present rend my heart enough? Will

434

you make my tortures more infernal still by recalling past happiness? Change your tone, if you will do me a service. Reproach me, make of my tenderness a crime, magnify my daughter's fault; fill me with abhorrence of her, if you can; stir up anew my revenge against her cursed seducer; say, that Sara never was virtuous, since she so lightly ceased to be so; say that she never loved me, since she clandestinely forsook me!

WAITWELL. If I said that, I should utter a lie, a shameless, wicked lie. It might come to me again on my deathbed, and I, old wretch, would die in despair. No, little Sara has loved her father; and doubtless, doubtless she loves him yet. If you will only be convinced of this, I shall see her again in your arms this very day.

SIR WILLIAM. Yes, Waitwell, of this alone I ask to be convinced. I cannot any longer live without her; she is the support of my age, and if she does not help to sweeten the sad remaining days of my life, who shall do it? If she loves me still, her error is forgotten. It was the error of a tender-hearted maiden, and her flight was the result of her remorse. Such errors are better than forced virtues. Yet I feel, Waitwell, I feel it, even were these errors real crimes, premeditated vices—even then I should forgive her. I would rather be loved by a wicked daughter, than by none at all.

WAITWELL. Dry your tears, dear sir! I hear some one. It will be the landlord coming to welcome us.

SCENE II

[*The* LANDLORD, SIR WILLIAM SAMPSON, WAITWELL.]

LANDLORD. So early, gentlemen, so early? You are welcome; welcome, Waitwell! You have doubtless been travelling all night! Is that the gentleman, of whom you spoke to me yesterday?

WAITWELL. Yes, it is he, and I hope that in accordance with what we settled——

LANDLORD. I am entirely at your service, my lord. What is it to me, whether I know or not, what cause has brought you hither, and why you wish to live in seclusion in my house? A landlord takes his money and lets his guests do as they think best. Waitwell, it is true, has told me that you wish to observe the stranger a little, who has been staying here for a few weeks with his young wife, but I hope that you will not cause him any annoyance. You would bring my house into ill repute and certain people would fear to stop here. Men like us must live on people of all kinds.

SIR WILLIAM. Do not fear; only conduct me to the room which Waitwell has ordered for me; I come here for an honourable purpose.

LANDLORD. I have no wish to know your secrets, my lord! Curiosity is by no means a fault of mine. I might for instance have known long ago, who the stranger is, on whom you want to keep a watch, but I have no wish to know. This much however I have discovered, that he must have eloped with the young lady. The poor little wife—or whatever she may be!—remains the whole day long locked up in her room, and cries.

SIR WILLIAM. And cries?

LANDLORD. Yes, and cries; but, my lord, why do your tears fall? The young lady must interest you deeply. Surely you are not——

WAITWELL. Do not detain him any longer!

LANDLORD. Come, come! One wall only will separate you from the lady in whom you are so much interested, and who may be——

WAITWELL. You mean then at any cost to know, who——

LANDLORD. No, Waitwell! I have no wish to know anything.

WAITWELL. Make haste, then, and take us to our rooms, before the whole house begins to stir.

LANDLORD. Will you please follow me, then, my lord? [*Exeunt.*]

SCENE III—MELLEFONT'S *room*.

[MELLEFONT, NORTON.]

MELLEFONT [*in dressing-room, sitting in an easy chair*]. Another night, which I could not have spent more cruelly on the rack!—[*calls*] Norton!—I must make haste to get sight of a face or two. If I remained alone with my thoughts any longer, they might carry me too far. Hey, Norton! He is still asleep. But is not it cruel of me, not to let the poor devil sleep? How happy he is! However, I do not wish any one about me to be happy! Norton!

NORTON [*coming*]. Sir!

MELLEFONT. Dress me!—Oh, no sour looks please! When I shall be able to sleep longer myself I will let you do the same. If you wish to do your duty, at least have pity on me.

NORTON. Pity, sir! Pity on you? I know better where pity is due.

MELLEFONT. And where then?

NORTON. Ah, let me dress you and don't ask.

MELLEFONT. Confound it! Are *your* reproofs then to awaken together with my conscience? I understand you; I know on whom you expend your pity. But I will do justice to her and to myself. Quite right, do not have any pity on me! Curse me in your heart; but—curse yourself also!

NORTON. Myself also?

MELLEFONT. Yes, because you serve a miserable wretch, whom earth ought not to bear, and because you have made yourself a partaker in his crimes.

NORTON. I made myself a partaker in your crimes? In what way?

MELLEFONT. By keeping silent about them.

NORTON. Well, that is good! A word would have cost me my neck in the heat of your passions. And, besides, did I not find you already so bad, when I made your acquaintance, that all hope of amendment was vain? What a life I have seen you leading from the first moment! In the lowest society of gamblers and va-grants—I call them what they were without regard to their knightly titles and such like—in this society you squandered a fortune which might have made a way for you to an honourable position. And your culpable intercourse with all sorts of women, especially with the wicked Mar-wood——

MELLEFONT. Restore me—restore me to that life. It was virtue compared with the present one. I spent my fortune; well! The punishment follows, and I shall soon enough feel all the severity and humiliation of want. I associated with vicious women; that may be. I was myself seduced more often than I seduced others; and those whom I did seduce wished it. But—I still had no ruined virtue upon my conscience. I had carried off no Sara from the house of a beloved father and forced her to follow a scoundrel, who was no longer free. I had . . . who comes so early to me?

SCENE IV

[BETTY, MELLEFONT, NORTON.]

NORTON. It is Betty.

MELLEFONT. Up already, Betty? How is your mistress?

BETTY. How is she? [*Sobbing.*] It was long after midnight before I could persuade her to go to bed. She slept a few moments; but God, what a sleep that must have been! She started suddenly, sprang up and fell into my arms, like one pursued by a murderer. She trembled, and a cold perspiration started on her pale face. I did all I could to calm her, but up to this morning she has only answered me with silent tears. At length she sent me several times to your door to listen whether you were up. She wishes to speak to you. You alone can comfort her. O do so, dearest sir, do so! My heart will break, if she continues to fret like this.

MELLEFONT. Go, Betty! Tell her, I shall be with her in a moment.

BETTY. No, she wishes to come to you herself.

MELLEFONT. Well, tell her, then, that I am awaiting her—— [*Exit* BETTY.]

SCENE V

[MELLEFONT, NORTON.]

NORTON. O God, the poor young lady!

MELLEFONT. Whose feelings is this exclamation of yours meant to rouse? See, the first tear which I have shed since my childhood is running down my cheek. A bad preparation for receiving one who seeks comfort. But why does she seek it from me? Yet where else shall she seek it? I must collect myself [*Drying his eyes.*] Where is the old firmness with which I could see a beautiful eye in tears? Where is the gift of dissimulation gone by which I could be and could say whatsoever I wished? She will come now and weep tears that brook no resistance. Confused and ashamed I shall stand before her; like a convicted criminal I shall stand before her. Counsel me, what shall I do? What shall I say?

NORTON. You shall do what she asks of you!

MELLEFONT. I shall then perpetrate a fresh act of cruelty against her. She is wrong to blame me for delaying a ceremony which cannot be performed in this country without the greatest injury to us.

NORTON. Well, leave it, then. Why do we delay? Why do you let one day after the other pass, and one week after the other? Just give me the order, and you will be safe on board to-morrow! Perhaps her grief will not follow her over the ocean; she may leave part of it behind, and in another land may——

MELLEFONT. I hope that myself. Silence! She is coming! How my heart throbs!

SCENE VI

[SARA, MELLEFONT, NORTON.]

MELLEFONT [*advancing towards her*]. You have had a restless night, dearest Sara.

SARA. Alas, Mellefont, if it were nothing but a restless night.

MELLEFONT [*to his servant*]. Leave us!

NORTON [*aside, in going*]. I would not stay if I was paid in gold for every moment.

SCENE VII

[SARA, MELLEFONT.]

MELLEFONT. You are faint, dearest Sara! You must sit down!

SARA [*sits down*]. I trouble you very early! Will you forgive me that with the morning I again begin my complaints?

MELLEFONT. Dearest Sara, you mean to say that you cannot forgive me, because another morning has dawned, and I have not yet put an end to your complaints?

SARA. What is there that I would not forgive you? You know what I have already forgiven you. But the ninth week, Mellefont! the ninth week begins to-day, and this miserable house still sees me in just the same position as on the first day.

MELLEFONT. You doubt my love?

SARA. I doubt your love? No, I feel my misery too much, too much to wish to deprive myself of this last and only solace.

MELLEFONT. How, then, can you be uneasy about the delay of a ceremony?

SARA. Ah, Mellefont! Why is it that we think so differently about this ceremony! Yield a little to the woman's way of thinking! I imagine in it a more direct consent from Heaven. In vain did I try again, only yesterday, in the long tedious evening, to adopt your ideas, and to banish from my breast the doubt which just now—not for the first time, you have deemed the result of my distrust. I struggled with myself; I was clever enough to deafen my understanding; but my heart and my feeling quickly overthrew this toilsome structure of reason. Reproachful voices roused me from my sleep, and my imagination united with them to torment me. What pictures, what dreadful pictures hovered about me! I would willingly believe them to be dreams——

MELLEFONT. What? Could my sensible Sara believe them to be anything else? Dreams, my dearest, dreams!—How unhappy is man!—Did not his Creator find tortures enough for him in the realm of reality? Had he also to create in him the still more spacious realm of imagination in order to increase them?

SARA. Do not accuse Heaven! It has left the imagination in our power. She is guided by our acts; and when these are in accordance with our duties and with virtue the imagination serves only to increase our peace and happiness. A single act, Mellefont, a single blessing bestowed upon us by a messenger of peace, in the name of the Eternal One, can restore my shattered imagination again. Do you still hesitate to do a few days sooner for love of me, what in any case you mean to do at some future time? Have pity on me, and consider that, although by this you may be freeing me only from torments of the imagination, yet these imagined torments are torments, and are real torments for her who feels them. Ah! could I but tell you the terrors of the last night half as vividly as I have felt them. Wearied with crying and grieving—my only occupations—I sank down on my bed with half-closed eyes. My nature wished to recover itself a moment, to collect new tears. But hardly asleep yet, I suddenly saw myself on the steepest peak of a terrible rock. You went on before, and I followed with tottering, anxious steps, strengthened now and then by a glance which you threw back upon me. Suddenly I heard behind me a gentle call, which bade me stop. It was my father's voice—I unhappy one, can I forget nothing which is his? Alas if his memory renders him equally cruel service; if he too cannot forget me!— But he has forgotten me. Comfort! cruel comfort for his Sara!—But, listen, Melle-

font! In turning round to this well-known voice, my foot slipped; I reeled, and was on the point of falling down the precipice, when just in time, I felt myself held back by one who resembled myself. I was just returning her my passionate thanks, when she drew a dagger from her bosom. "I saved you," she cried, "to ruin you!" She lifted her armed hand—and—! I awoke with the blow. Awake, I still felt all the pain which a mortal stab must give, without the pleasure which it brings—the hope for the end of grief in the end of life.

MELLEFONT. Ah! dearest Sara, I promise you the end of your grief, without the end of your life, which would certainly be the end of mine also. Forget the terrible tissue of a meaningless dream!

SARA. I look to you for the strength to be able to forget it. Be it love or seduction, happiness or unhappiness which threw me into your arms, I am yours in my heart and will remain so for ever. But I am not yet yours in the eyes of that Judge, who has threatened to punish the smallest transgressions of His law——

MELLEFONT. Then may all the punishment fall upon me alone!

SARA. What can fall upon you, without touching me too? But do not misinterpret my urgent request! Another woman, after having forfeited her honour by an error like mine, might perhaps only seek to regain a part of it by a legal union. I do not think of that, Mellefont, because I do not wish to know of any other honour in this world than that of loving you. I do not wish to be united to you for the world's sake but for my own. And I will willingly bear the shame of not appearing to be so, when I am united to you. You need not then, if you do not wish, acknowledge me to be your wife, you may call me what you will! I will not bear your name; you shall keep our union as secret as you think good, and may I always be unworthy of it, if I ever harbour the thought of drawing any other advantage from it than the appeasing of my conscience.

MELLEFONT. Stop, Sara, or I shall die before your eyes. How wretched I am, that I have not the courage to make you more wretched still! Consider that you have given yourself up to my guidance; consider that it is my duty to look to our future, and that I must at present be deaf to your complaints, if I will not hear you utter more grievous complaints throughout the rest of your life. Have you then forgotten what I have so often represented to you in justification of my conduct?

SARA. I have not forgotten it, Mellefont! You wish first to secure a certain bequest. You wish first to secure temporal goods, and you let me forfeit eternal ones, perhaps, through it.

MELLEFONT. Ah, Sara! If you were as certain of all temporal goods as your virtue is of the eternal ones——

SARA. My virtue? Do not say that word! Once it sounded sweet to me, but now a terrible thunder rolls in it!

MELLEFONT. What? Must he who is to be virtuous, never have committed a trespass? Has a single error such fatal effect that it can annihilate a whole course of blameless years? If so, no one is virtuous; virtue is then a chimera, which disperses in the air, when one thinks that one grasps it most firmly; if so, there is no Wise Being who suits our duties to our strength; if so, there is. . . . I am frightened at the terrible conclusions in which your despondency must involve you. No, Sara, you are still the virtuous Sara that you were before your unfortunate acquaintance with me. If you look upon yourself with such cruel eyes, with what eyes must you regard me!

SARA. With the eyes of love, Mellefont!

MELLEFONT. I implore you, then, on my knees I implore you for the sake of this love, this generous love which overlooks all my unworthiness, to calm yourself! Have patience for a few days longer!

SARA. A few days! How long even a single day is!

MELLEFONT. Cursed bequest! Cursed nonsense of a dying cousin, who would only leave me his fortune on the condition that I should give my hand to a relation who hates me as much as I hate her! To you, inhuman tyrants of our freedom, be imputed all the misfortune, all the sin, into which your compulsion forces us! Could I but dispense with this degrading inheritance! As long as my father's fortune sufficed for my maintenance, I always scorned it, and did not even think it worthy of mentioning. But now, now, when I should like to possess all the treasures of the world only to lay them at the feet of my Sara, now, when I must contrive at least to let her appear in the world as befits her station, now I must have recourse to it.

SARA. Which probably will not be successful after all.

MELLEFONT. You always forbode the worst. No, the lady whom this also concerns is not disinclined to enter into a sort of agreement with me. The fortune is to be divided, and as she cannot enjoy the whole with me, she is willing to let me buy my liberty with half of it. I am every hour expecting the final intelligence, the delay of which alone has so prolonged our sojourn here. As long as I receive it, we shall not remain here one moment longer. We will immediately cross to France, dearest Sara, where you shall find new friends, who already look forward to the pleasure of seeing and loving you. And these new friends shall be the witnesses of our union——

SARA. They shall be the witnesses of our union? Cruel man, our union, then, is not to be in my native land? I shall leave my country as a criminal? And as such, you think, I should have the courage to trust myself to the ocean. The heart of him must be calmer or more impious than mine, who, only for a moment, can see with indifference between himself and destruction, nothing but a quivering plank. Death would roar at me in every wave that struck against the vessel, every wind would howl its curses after me from my native shore, and the slightest storm would seem a sentence of death pronounced upon me. No, Mellefont, you cannot be so cruel to me! If I live to see the completion of this agreement, you must not grudge another day, to be spent here. This must be the day, on which you shall teach me to forget the tortures of all these tearful days. This must be the sacred day—alas! which day will it be?

MELLEFONT. But do you consider, Sara, that our marriage here would lack those ceremonies which are due to it?

SARA. A sacred act does not acquire more force through ceremonies.

MELLEFONT. But——

SARA. I am astonished. You surely will not insist on such a trivial pretext? O Mellefont, Mellefont! had I not made for myself an inviolable law, never to doubt the sincerity of your love, this circumstance might. . . . But too much of this already, it might seem as if I had been doubting it even now.

MELLEFONT. The first moment of your doubt would be the last moment of my life! Alas, Sara, what have I done, that you should remind me even of the possibility of it? It is true the confessions, which I have made to you without fear, of my early excesses cannot do me honour, but they should at least awaken confidence. A coquettish Marwood held me in her meshes, because I felt for her that which is so often taken for love which it so rarely is. I should still bear her shameful fetters, had not Heaven, which perhaps did not think my heart quite unworthy to burn with better flames, taken pity on me. To see you, dearest Sara, was to forget all Marwoods! But how dearly have you paid for taking me out of such hands! I had grown too familiar with vice, and you know it too little——

SARA. Let us think no more of it.

SCENE VIII

[NORTON, MELLEFONT, SARA.]

MELLEFONT. What do you want?

NORTON. While I was standing before the house, a servant gave me this letter. It is directed to you, sir!

MELLEFONT. To me? Who knows my name here? [Looking at the letter.] Good heavens!

SARA. You are startled.

MELLEFONT. But without cause, Sara, as I now perceive. I was mistaken in the handwriting.

SARA. May the contents be as agreeable to you as you can wish.

MELLEFONT. I suspect that they will be of very little importance.

SARA. One is less constrained when one is alone, so allow me to retire to my room again.

MELLEFONT. You entertain suspicions, then, about it?

SARA. Not at all, Mellefont.

MELLEFONT [going with her to the back of the stage]. I shall be with you in a moment, dearest Sara.

SCENE IX

[MELLEFONT, NORTON.]

MELLEFONT [still looking at the letter]. Just Heaven!

NORTON. Woe to you, if it is only just!

MELLEFONT. Is it possible? I see this cursed handwriting again and am not chilled with terror? Is it she? Is it not she? Why do I still doubt? It is she! Alas, friend, a letter from Marwood! What fury, what demon has betrayed my abode to her? What does she still want from me? Go, make preparations immediately that we may get away from here. Yet stop! Perhaps it is unnecessary; perhaps the contempt of my farewell letters has only caused Marwood to reply with equal contempt. There, open the letter; read it! I am afraid to do it myself.

NORTON [*reads*]. "If you will deign, Mellefont, to glance at the name which you will find at the bottom of the page, it will be to me as though I had written you the longest of letters."

MELLEFONT. Curse the name! Would I had never heard it! Would it could be erased from the book of the living!

NORTON [*reads on*]. "The labour of finding you out has been sweetened by the love which helped me in my search."

MELLEFONT. Love? Wanton creature! You profane the words which belong to virtue alone.

NORTON [*continues*]. "Love has done more still"——

MELLEFONT. I tremble——

NORTON. "It has brought me to you"——

MELLEFONT. Traitor, what are you reading? [*Snatches the letter from his hand and reads himself.*] "I am here; and it rests with you, whether you will await a visit from me, or whether you will anticipate mine by one from you. Marwood." What a thunderbolt! She is here! Where is she? She shall atone for this audacity with her life!

NORTON. With her life? One glance from her and you will be again at her feet. Take care what you do! You must not speak with her, or the misfortunes of your poor young lady will be complete.

MELLEFONT. O, wretched man that I am! No, I must speak with her! She would go even into Sara's room in search of me, and would vent all her rage on the innocent girl.

NORTON. But, sir——

MELLEFONT. Not a word! Let me see [*Looking at the letter.*] whether she has given the address. Here it is! Come, show me the way! [*Exeunt.*]

ACT II

SCENE I—MARWOOD'S *room in another inn.*

[MARWOOD (*in negligée*), HANNAH.]

MARWOOD. I hope Belfort has delivered the letter at the right address, Hannah?

HANNAH. He has.

MARWOOD. To him himself?

HANNAH. To his servant.

MARWOOD. I am all impatience to see what effect it will have. Do I not seem a little uneasy to you, Hannah? And I am so. The traitor! But gently! I must not on any account give way to anger. Forbearance, love, entreaty are the only weapons which I can use against him, if I rightly understand his weak side.

HANNAH. But if he should harden himself against them?

MARWOOD. If he should harden himself against them? Then I shall not be angry. I shall rave! I feel it, Hannah, and I would rather do so to begin with.

HANNAH. Calm yourself! He may come at any moment.

MARWOOD. I only hope he may come; I only hope he has not decided to await me on his own ground. But do you know, Hannah, on what I chiefly found my hopes of drawing away the faithless man from this new object of his love? On our Bella!

HANNAH. It is true, she is a little idol to him; and there could not have been a happier idea than that of bringing her with you.

MARWOOD. Even if his heart should be deaf to an old love, the language of blood will at least be audible to him. He tore the child from my arms a short time ago under the pretext of wishing to give her an education such as she could not have with me. It is only by an artifice that I have been able to get her again from the lady who had charge of her. He had paid more than a year in advance, and had given strict orders the very day before his flight that they should by no means give admission to a certain Marwood, who would perhaps come and give herself out as mother of the child. From this order I see the distinction which he draws between us. He regards Arabella as a precious portion of himself, and me as an unfortunate creature, of whose charms he has grown weary.

HANNAH. What ingratitude!

MARWOOD. Ah, Hannah! Nothing more infallibly draws down ingratitude, than favours for which no gratitude would be too great. Why have I shown him these fatal favours? Ought I not to have foreseen that they could not always retain their value with him; that their value rested on the difficulty in the way of their enjoyment, and that the latter must disappear with the charm of our looks which the hand of time imperceptibly but surely effaces?

HANNAH. You, Madam, have not anything to fear for a long time from this dangerous hand! To my mind your beauty is so far from having passed the point of its brightest bloom, that it is rather advancing towards it, and would enchain fresh hearts for you every day if you only would give it the permission.

MARWOOD. Be silent, Hannah! You flatter me on an occasion which makes me suspicious of any flattery. It is nonsense to speak of new conquests, if one has not even sufficient power to retain possession of those which one has already made.

SCENE II

[A SERVANT, MARWOOD, HANNAH.]
SERVANT. Some one wishes to have the honour of speaking with you.
MARWOOD. Who is it?
SERVANT. I suppose it is the gentleman to whom the letter was addressed. At least the servant to whom I delivered it is with him.
MARWOOD. Mellefont!—Quick, bring him up! [Exit SERVANT.] Ah, Hannah! He is here now! How shall I receive him? What shall I say? What look shall I put on? Is this calm enough? Just see!
HANNAH. Anything but calm.
MARWOOD. This, then?
HANNAH. Throw a little sweetness into it.
MARWOOD. So, perhaps?
HANNAH. Too sad.
MARWOOD. Would this smile do?

HANNAH. Perfectly—only less constrained—He is coming.

SCENE III

[MELLEFONT, MARWOOD, HANNAH.]
MELLEFONT [entering with wild gestures]. Ha! Marwood——
MARWOOD [running to meet him smiling, and with open arms]. Ah, Mellefont!
MELLEFONT [aside]. The murderess! What a look!
MARWOOD. I must embrace you, faithless, dear fugitive! Share my joy with me! Why do you tear yourself from my caresses?
MELLEFONT. I expected, Marwood, that you would receive me differently.
MARWOOD. Why differently? With more love, perhaps? With more delight? Alas, how unhappy I am, that I cannot express all that I feel! Do you not see, Mellefont, do you not see that joy, too, has its tears? Here they fall, the offspring of sweetest delight! But alas, vain tears! His hand does not dry you!
MELLEFONT. Marwood, the time is gone, when such words would have charmed me. You must speak now with me in another tone. I come to hear your last reproaches and to answer them.
MARWOOD. Reproaches? What reproaches should I have for you, Mellefont? None!
MELLEFONT. Then you might have spared yourself the journey, I should think.
MARWOOD. Dearest, capricious heart. Why will you forcibly compel me to recall a trifle which I forgave you the same moment I heard of it? Does a passing infidelity which your gallantry, but not your heart, has caused, deserve these reproaches? Come, let us laugh at it!
MELLEFONT. You are mistaken; my heart is more concerned in it, than it ever was in all our love affairs, upon which I cannot now look back but with disgust.
MARWOOD. Your heart, Mellefont, is a good little fool. It lets your imagination

persuade it to whatever it will. Believe me, I know it better than you do yourself! Were it not the best, the most faithful of hearts, should I take such pains to keep it?

MELLEFONT. To keep it? You have never possessed it, I tell you.

MARWOOD. And I tell you, that in reality I possess it still!

MELLEFONT. Marwood! if I knew that you still possessed one single fibre of it, I would tear it out of my breast here before your eyes.

MARWOOD. You would see that you were tearing mine out at the same time. And then, then these hearts would at last attain that union which they have sought so often upon our lips.

MELLEFONT [aside]. What a serpent! Flight will be the best thing here.—Just tell me briefly, Marwood, why you have followed me, and what you still desire of me! But tell it me without this smile, without this look, in which a whole hell of seduction lurks and terrifies me.

MARWOOD [insinuatingly]. Just listen, my dear Mellefont! I see your position now. Your desires and your taste are at present your tyrants. Never mind, one must let them wear themselves out. It is folly to resist them. They are most safely lulled to sleep, and at last even conquered, by giving them free scope. They wear themselves away. Can you accuse me, my fickle friend, of ever having been jealous, when more powerful charms than mine estranged you from me for a time? I never grudged you the change, by which I always won more than I lost. You returned with new ardour, with new passion to my arms, in which with light bonds, and never with heavy fetters I encompassed you. Have I not often even been your confidante though you had nothing to confide but the favours which you stole from me, in order to lavish them on others. Why should you believe then, that I would now begin to display a capriciousness just when I am ceasing, or, perhaps have already ceased, to be justified in it. If your ardour for the pretty

country girl has not yet cooled down, if you are still in the first fever of your love for her; if you cannot yet do without the enjoyment she gives you; who hinders you from devoting yourself to her, as long as you think good? But must you on that account make such rash projects, and purpose to fly from the country with her?

MELLEFONT. Marwood! You speak in perfect keeping with your character, the wickedness of which I never understood so well as I do now, since, in the society of a virtuous woman, I have learned to distinguish love from licentiousness.

MARWOOD. Indeed! Your new mistress is then a girl of fine moral sentiments, I suppose? You men surely cannot know yourselves what you want. At one time you are pleased with the most wanton talk and the most unchaste jests from us, at another time we charm you when we talk nothing but virtue, and seem to have all the seven sages on our lips. But the worst is, that you get tired of one as much as the other. We may be foolish or reasonable, worldly or spiritual; our efforts to make you constant are lost either way. The turn will come to your beautiful saint soon enough. Shall I give you a little sketch? Just at present you are in the most passionate paroxysm over her. I allow this two or at the most three days more. To this will succeed a tolerably calm love; for this I allow a week. The next week you will only think occasionally of this love. In the third week, you will have to be reminded of it; and when you have got tired of being thus reminded, you will so quickly see yourself reduced to the most utter indifference, that I can hardly allow the fourth week for this final change. This would be about a month altogether. And this month, Mellefont, I will overlook with the greatest pleasure; but you will allow that I must not lose sight of you.

MELLEFONT. You try all the weapons in vain which you remember to have used successfully with me in bygone days. A virtuous resolution secures me against both your tenderness and your wit. However, I will not expose myself longer to either. I go, and have nothing more to tell you but that in a few days you shall know that I am bound in such a manner as will utterly destroy all your hope of my ever returning into your sinful slavery. You will have learned my justification sufficiently from the letter which I sent to you before my departure.

MARWOOD. It is well that you mention this letter. Tell me, who did you get to write it?

MELLEFONT. Did not I write it myself?

MARWOOD. Impossible! The beginning of it, in which you reckoned up—I do not know what sums—which you say you have wasted with me, must have been written by an innkeeper, and the theological part at the end by a Quaker. I will now give you a serious reply to it. As to the principal point, you well know that all the presents which you have made are still in existence. I have never considered your cheques or your jewels as my property, and I have brought them all with me to return them into the hands which entrusted them to me.

MELLEFONT. Keep them all, Marwood!

MARWOOD. I will not keep any of them. What right have I to them without you yourself? Although you do not love me any more, you must at least do me justice and not take me for one of those venal females, to whom it is a matter of indifference by whose booty they enrich themselves. Come, Mellefont, you shall this moment be as rich again as you perhaps might still be if you had not known me; and perhaps, too, might *not* be.

MELLEFONT. What demon intent upon my destruction speaks through you now! Voluptuous Marwood does not think so nobly.

MARWOOD. Do you call that noble? I call it only just. No, Sir, no, I do not ask that you shall account the return of your gifts as anything remarkable. It costs me nothing, and I should even consider the slightest expression of thanks on your part as an insult, which could have no other meaning than this: "Mar-

wood, I thought you a base deceiver; I am thankful that you have not wished to be so towards me at least."

MELLEFONT. Enough, Madam, enough! I fly, since my unlucky destiny threatens to involve me in a contest of generosity, in which I should be most unwilling to succumb.

MARWOOD. Fly, then! But take everything with you that could remind me of you. Poor, despised, without honour, and without friends, I will then venture again to awaken your pity. I will show you in the unfortunate Marwood only a miserable woman, who has sacrificed to you her person, her honour, her virtue, and her conscience. I will remind you of the first day, when you saw and loved me; of the first, stammering, bashful confession of your love, which you made me at my feet; of the first assurance of my return of your love, which you forced from me; of the tender looks, of the passionate embraces, which followed, of the eloquent silence, when each with busy mind divined the other's most secret feelings, and read the most hidden thoughts of the soul in the languishing eye; of the trembling expectation of approaching gratification; of the intoxication of its joys; of the sweet relaxation after the fulness of enjoyment, in which the exhausted spirits regained strength for fresh delights. I shall remind you of all this, and then embrace your knees, and entreat without ceasing for the only gift, which you cannot deny me, and which I can accept without blushing—for death from your hand.

MELLEFONT. Cruel one! I would still give even my life for you. Ask it, ask it, only do not any longer claim my love. I must leave you, Marwood, or make myself an object of loathing to the whole world. I am culpable already in that I only stand here and listen to you. Farewell, farewell!

MARWOOD [*holding him back*]. You must leave me? And what, then, do you wish, shall become of me? As I am now, I am your creature; do, then, what becomes a creator; he may not withdraw his hand from the work until he wishes to destroy it utterly. Alas, Hannah, I see now, my entreaties alone are too feeble. Go, bring my intercessor, who will now, perhaps, return to me more than she ever received from me. [*Exit* HANNAH.]

MELLEFONT. What intercessor, Marwood?

MARWOOD. Ah, an intercessor of whom you would only too willingly have deprived me. Nature will take a shorter road to your heart with her grievances.

MELLEFONT. You alarm me. Surely you have not——

SCENE IV

[ARABELLA, HANNAH, MELLEFONT, MARWOOD.]

MELLEFONT. What do I see? It is she! Marwood, how could you dare to——

MARWOOD. Am I not her mother? Come, my Bella, see, here is your protector again, your friend, your. . . . Ah! his heart may tell him what more he can be to you than a protector and a friend.

MELLEFONT [*turning away his face*]. God, what shall I have to suffer here?

ARABELLA [*advancing timidly towards him*]. Ah, Sir! Is it you? Are you our Mellefont? No, Madam, surely, surely it is not he! Would he not look at me, if it were? Would he not hold me in his arms? He used to do so. What an unhappy child I am! How have I grieved him, this dear, dear man, who let me call him my father?

MARWOOD. You are silent, Mellefont? You grudge the innocent child a single look?

MELLEFONT. Ah!

ARABELLA. Why, he sighs, Madam! What is the matter with him? Cannot we help him? Cannot I? Nor you? Then let us sigh with him! Ah, now he looks at me! No, he looks away again! He looks up to Heaven! What does he want? What does he ask from Heaven? Would that Heaven would grant him everything, even if it refused me everything for it!

MARWOOD. Go, my child, go, fall at his feet! He wants to leave us, to leave us for ever.

ARABELLA [*falling on her knees before him*]. Here I am already. You will leave us? You will leave us for ever? Have not we already been without you for a little "for ever." Shall we have to lose you again? You have said so often that you loved us. Does one leave the people whom one loves? I cannot love you then, I suppose, for I should wish never to leave you. Never, and I never will leave you either.

MARWOOD. I will help you in your entreaties, my child! And you must help me too! Now, Mellefont, you see me too at your feet. . . .

MELLEFONT [*stopping her, as she throws herself at his feet*]. Marwood, dangerous Marwood! And you, too, my dearest Bella [*Raising her up.*], you too are the enemy of your Mellefont?

ARABELLA. I your enemy?

MARWOOD. What is your resolve?

MELLEFONT. What it ought not to be, Marwood; what it ought not to be.

MARWOOD [*embracing him*]. Ah, I know that the honesty of your heart has always overcome the obstinacy of your desires.

MELLEFONT. Do not importune me any longer! I am already what you wish to make me; a perjurer, a seducer, a robber, a murderer!

MARWOOD. You will be so in imagination for a few days, and after that you will see that I have prevented you from becoming so in reality. You will return with us, won't you?

ARABELLA [*insinuatingly*]. Oh yes, do!

MELLEFONT. Return with you! How can I?

MARWOOD. Nothing is easier, if you only wish it.

MELLEFONT. And my Sara——

MARWOOD. And your Sara may look to herself.

MELLEFONT. Ha! cruel Marwood, these words reveal the very bottom of your heart to me. And yet I, wretch, do not repent?

MARWOOD. If you had seen the bottom of my heart, you would have discovered that it has more true pity for your Sara than you yourself have. I say true pity; for your pity is egotistic and weak. You have carried this love-affair much too far. We might let it pass, that you as a man, who by long intercourse with our sex has become master in the art of seducing, used your superiority in dissimulation and experience against such a young maiden, and did not rest until you had gained your end. You can plead the impetuosity of your passion as your excuse. But, Mellefont, you cannot justify yourself for having robbed an old father of his only child, for having rendered to an honourable old man his few remaining steps to the grave harder and more bitter, for having broken the strongest ties of nature for the sake of your desires. Repair your error, then, as far as it is possible to repair it. Give the old man his support again, and send a credulous daughter back to her home, which you need not render desolate also, because you have dishonored it.

MELLEFONT. This only was still wanting—that you should call in my conscience against me also. But even supposing what you say were just, must I not be brazenfaced if I should propose it myself to the unhappy girl?

MARWOOD. Well, I will confess to you, that I have anticipated this difficulty, and considered how to spare you it. As soon as I learned your address, I informed her old father privately of it. He was beside himself with joy, and wanted to start directly. I wonder he has not yet arrived.

MELLEFONT. What do you say?

MARWOOD. Just await his arrival quietly, and do not let the girl notice anything. I myself will not detain you any longer. Go to her again; she might grow suspicious. But I trust that I shall see you again to-day.

MELLEFONT. Oh, Marwood! With what feelings did I come to you, and with what must I leave you! A kiss, my dear Bella.

ARABELLA. That was for you, now one for me! But come back again soon, do!
[*Exit* MELLEFONT.]

SCENE V

[MARWOOD, ARABELLA, HANNAH.]

MARWOOD [*drawing a deep breath*]. Victory, Hannah! but a hard victory! Give me a chair, I feel quite exhausted. [*Sitting down.*] He surrendered only just in time, if he had hesitated another moment, I should have shown him quite a different Marwood.

HANNAH. Ah, Madam, what a woman you are! I should like to see the man who could resist you.

MARWOOD. He has resisted me already too long. And assuredly, assuredly, I will not forgive him that he almost let me go down on my knees to him.

ARABELLA. No, no! You must forgive him everything. He is so good, so good——

MARWOOD. Be silent, little silly!

HANNAH. I do not know on what side you did not attack him! But nothing, I think, touched him more, than the disinterestedness with which you offered to return all his presents to him.

MARWOOD. I believe so too. Ha! ha! ha! [*Contemptuously.*]

HANNAH. Why do you laugh, Madam? You really risked a great deal, if you were not in earnest about it. Suppose he had taken you at your word?

MARWOOD. Oh, nonsense, one knows with whom one has to deal.

HANNAH. I quite admit that! But you too, my pretty Bella, did your part excellently, excellently!

ARABELLA. How so? Could I do it, then, any other way? I had not seen him for such a long time. I hope you are not angry, Madam, that I love him so? I love you as much as him, just as much.

MARWOOD. Very well, I will pardon you this time that you do not love me better than him.

ARABELLA [*sobbing*]. This time?

MARWOOD. Why, you are crying actually? What is it about?

ARABELLA. Ah, no! I am not crying. Do not get angry! I will love you both so much, so much, that it will be impossible to love either of you more.

MARWOOD. Very well.

ARABELLA. I am so unhappy.

MARWOOD. Now be quiet—but what is that?

SCENE VI

[MELLEFONT, MARWOOD, ARABELLA, HANNAH.]

MARWOOD. Why do you come back again so soon, Mellefont? [Rising.]

MELLEFONT [passionately]. Because I needed but a few moments to recover my senses.

MARWOOD. Well?

MELLEFONT. I was stunned, Marwood, but not moved! You have had all your trouble in vain. Another atmosphere than this infectious one of your room has given me back my courage and my strength, to withdraw my foot in time from this dangerous snare. Were the tricks of a Marwood not sufficiently familiar to me, unworthy wretch that I am?

MARWOOD [impatiently]. What language is that?

MELLEFONT. The language of truth and anger.

MARWOOD. Gently, Mellefont! or I too shall speak in the same language.

MELLEFONT. I return only in order not to leave you one moment longer under a delusion with regard to me, which must make me despicable even in your eyes.

ARABELLA [timidly]. Oh, Hannah!

MELLEFONT. Look at me as madly as you like. The more madly the better! Was it possible that I could hesitate only for one moment between a Marwood and a Sara, and that I had well nigh decided for the former?

ARABELLA. Oh, Mellefont!

MELLEFONT. Do not tremble, Bella! For your sake too I came back. Give me your hand, and follow me without fear!

MARWOOD [stopping them]. Whom shall she follow, traitor?

MELLEFONT. Her father!

MARWOOD. Go, pitiable wretch, and learn first to know her mother.

MELLEFONT. I know her. She is a disgrace to her sex.

MARWOOD. Take her away, Hannah!

MELLEFONT. Remain here, Bella.

[Attempting to stop her.]

MARWOOD. No force, Mellefont, or——

[Exeunt HANNAH and ARABELLA.]

SCENE VII

[MELLEFONT, MARWOOD.]

MARWOOD. Now we are alone! Say now once more, whether you are determined to sacrifice me for a foolish girl?

MELLEFONT [bitterly]. Sacrifice you? You recall to my mind that impure animals were also sacrificed to the ancient gods.

MARWOOD [mockingly]. Express yourself without these learned allusions.

MELLEFONT. I tell you, then, that I am firmly resolved never to think of you again but with the most fearful of curses. Who are you? And who is Sara? You are a voluptuous, egoistic, shameful strumpet, who certainly can scarcely remember any longer that she ever was innocent. I have nothing to reproach myself with but that I have enjoyed with you that which otherwise you would perhaps have let the whole world enjoy. You have sought me, not I you, and if I now know who Marwood is, I have paid for this knowledge dearly enough. It has cost me my fortune, my honour, my happiness——

MARWOOD. And I would that it might also cost you your eternal happiness. Monster! Is the devil worse than you, when he lures feeble mortals into crimes and himself accuses them afterwards for these crimes which are his own work! What is my innocence to you? What does it matter to you when and how I lost it. If I could not sacrifice my virtue, I have at least staked my good name for you.

The former is no more valuable than the latter. What do I say? More valuable? Without it the former is a silly fancy, which brings one neither happiness nor guilt. The good name alone gives it some value, and can exist quite well without it. What did it matter what I was before I knew you, you wretch! It is enough that in the eyes of the world I was a woman without reproach. Through you only it has learned that I am not so; solely through my readiness to accept your heart, as I then thought, without your hand.

MELLEFONT. This very readiness condemns you, vile woman!

MARWOOD. But do you remember to what base tricks you owed it? Was I not persuaded by you, that you could not be publicly united to me without forfeiting an inheritance which you wished to share with me only? Is it time now to renounce it? And to renounce it, not for me but for another!

MELLEFONT. It is a real delight to me to be able to tell you that this difficulty will soon be removed. Content yourself therefore with having deprived me of my father's inheritance, and let me enjoy a far smaller one with a more worthy wife.

MARWOOD. Ha! Now I see what it is that makes you so perverse. Well, I will lose no more words. Be it so! Be assured I shall do everything to forget you. And the first thing that I will do to this end, shall be this. You will understand me! Tremble for your Bella! Her life shall not carry the memory of my despised love down to posterity; my cruelty shall do it. Behold in me a new Medea!

MELLEFONT [frightened]. Marwood!——

MARWOOD. Or, if you know a more cruel mother still, behold her cruelty doubled in me! Poison and dagger shall avenge me. But no, poison and dagger are tools too merciful for me! They would kill your child and mine too soon. I will not see it dead. I will see it dying! I will see each feature of the face which she has from you disfigured, distorted, and obliterated by slow torture. With eager hand will I part limb from limb, vein from vein, nerve from nerve, and will not cease to cut and burn the very smallest of them, even when there is nothing remaining but a senseless carcass! I—I shall at least feel in it—how sweet is revenge!

MELLEFONT. You are raving, Marwood——

MARWOOD. You remind me that my ravings are not directed against the right person. The father must go first! He must already be in yonder world, when, through a thousand woes the spirit of his daughter follows him. [She advances towards him with a dagger which she draws from her bosom.] So die, traitor!

MELLEFONT [seizing her arm, and snatching the dagger from her]. Insane woman! What hinders me now from turning the steel against you? But live, and your punishment shall be left for a hand void of honour.

MARWOOD [wringing her hands]. Heaven, what have I done? Mellefont——

MELLEFONT. Your grief shall not deceive me. I know well why you are sorry —not that you wished to stab me, but that you failed to do so.

MARWOOD. Give me back the erring steel! Give it me back, and you shall see for whom it was sharpened! For this breast alone, which for long has been too narrow for a heart which will rather renounce life than your love.

MELLEFONT. Hannah!

MARWOOD. What are you doing, Mellefont?

SCENE VIII

[HANNAH (in terror), MARWOOD, MELLEFONT.]

MELLEFONT. Did you hear, Hannah, how madly your mistress was behaving? Remember that I shall hold you responsible for Arabella!

HANNAH. Madam, how agitated you are!

MELLEFONT. I will place the innocent child in safety immediately. Justice will doubtless be able to bind the murderous hands of her cruel mother. [*Going.*]

MARWOOD. Whither, Mellefont? Is it astonishing that the violence of my grief deprived me of my reason? Who forces me to such unnatural excess? Is it not you yourself? Where can Bella be safer than with me? My lips may rave, but my heart still remains the heart of a mother. Oh, Mellefont, forget my madness, and to excuse it think only of its cause.

MELLEFONT. There is only one thing which can induce me to forget it.

MARWOOD. And that is?

MELLEFONT. That you return immediately to London! I will send Arabella there under another escort. You must by no means have anything further to do with her.

MARWOOD. Very well! I submit to everything; but grant me one single request more. Let me see your Sara once.

MELLEFONT. And what for?

MARWOOD. To read in her eyes my future fate. I will judge for myself whether she is worthy of such a breach of faith as you commit against me; and whether I may cherish the hope of receiving again, some day at any rate, a portion of your love.

MELLEFONT. Vain hope!

MARWOOD. Who is so cruel as to grudge even hope to the unhappy? I will not show myself to her as Marwood, but as a relation of yours. Announce me to her as such; you shall be present when I call upon her, and I promise you, by all that is sacred, to say nothing that is in any way displeasing to her. Do not refuse my request, for otherwise I might perhaps do all that is in my power to show myself to her in my true character.

MELLEFONT. Marwood! This request ——[*After a moment's reflection.*] might be granted.—But will you then be sure to quit this spot?

MARWOOD. Certainly; yes, I promise you. Even more, I will spare you the visit from her father, if that is still possible.

MELLEFONT. There is no need of that! I hope that he will include me too in the pardon which he grants to his daughter. But if he will not pardon her, I too shall know how to deal with him. I will go and announce you to my Sara. Only keep your promise, Marwood. [*Exit.*]

MARWOOD. Alas, Hannah, that our powers are not as great as our courage. Come, help me to dress. I do not despair of my scheme. If I could only make sure of him first. Come!

ACT III

SCENE I—*A room in the first inn.*

[SIR WILLIAM SAMPSON, WAITWELL.]

SIR WILLIAM SAMPSON. There, Waitwell, take this letter to her! It is the letter of an affectionate father, who complains of nothing but her absence. Tell her that I have sent you on before with it, and that I only await her answer, to come myself and fold her again in my arms.

WAITWELL. I think you do well to prepare them for your arrival in this way.

SIR WILLIAM SAMPSON. I make sure of her intentions by this means, and give her the opportunity of freeing herself from any shame or sorrow which repentance might cause her, before she speaks verbally with me. In a letter it will cost her less embarrassment, and me, perhaps, fewer tears.

WAITWELL. But may I ask, Sir, what you have resolved upon with regard to Mellefont?

SIR WILLIAM SAMPSON. Ah, Waitwell, if I could separate him from my daughter's lover, I should make some very harsh resolve. But as this cannot be, you see, he is saved from my anger. I myself am most to blame in this misfortune. But for me Sara would never have made the acquaintance of this dangerous man. I admitted him freely into my house on account of an obligation under which I believed myself to be to him. It was natural that the attention which in gratitude I paid him, should win for him the esteem of my daughter. And it was just as natural, that a man of his disposition should suffer himself to be tempted by this esteem to something more. He had been clever enough to transform it into love before I noticed anything at all, and before I had time to inquire into his former life. The evil was done, and I should have done well, if I had forgiven them everything immediately. I wished to be inexorable towards him, and did not consider that I could not be so towards him alone. If I had spared my severity, which came too late, I would at least have prevented their flight. But here I am now, Waitwell! I must fetch them back myself and consider myself happy if only I can make a son of a seducer. For who knows whether he will give up his Marwoods and his other creatures for the sake of a girl who has left nothing for his desires to wish for and who understands so little the bewitching arts of a coquette?

WAITWELL.   Well, Sir, it cannot be possible, that a man could be so wicked——

SIR WILLIAM SAMPSON.   This doubt, good Waitwell, does honour to your virtue. But why, at the same time, is it true that the limits of human wickedness extend much further still? Go now, and do as I told you! Notice every look as she reads my letter. In this short deviation from virtue she cannot yet have learned the art of dissimulation, to the masks of which only deep-rooted vice can have recourse. You will read her whole soul in her face. Do not let a look escape you which might perhaps indicate indifference to me—disregard of her father. For if you should unhappily discover this, and if she loves me no more, I hope that I shall be able to conquer myself and abandon her to her fate. I hope so, Waitwell. Alas! would that there were no heart here, to contradict this hope.

[*Exeunt on different sides.*]

SCENE II

[MISS SARA, MELLEFONT.]

[*Sara's room.*]

MELLEFONT.   I have done wrong, dearest Sara, to leave you in uneasiness about the letter which came just now.

SARA.   Oh dear, no, Mellefont! I have not been in the least uneasy about it. Could you not love me even though you still had secrets from me?

MELLEFONT.   You think, then, that it was a secret?

SARA.   But not one which concerns me. And that must suffice for me.

MELLEFONT.   You are only too good. Let me nevertheless reveal my secret to you. The letter contained a few lines from a relative of mine, who has heard of my being here. She passes through here on her way to London, and would like to see me. She has begged at the same time to be allowed the honour of paying you a visit.

SARA.   It will always be a pleasure to me to make the acquaintance of the respected members of your family. But consider for yourself, whether I can yet appear before one of them without blushing.

MELLEFONT.   Without blushing? And for what? For your love to me? It is true, Sara, you could have given your love to a nobler or a richer man. You must be ashamed that you were content to give your heart for another heart only, and that in this exchange you lost sight of your happiness.

SARA.   You must know yourself how wrongly you interpret my words.

MELLEFONT.   Pardon me, Sara; if my interpretation is wrong, they can have no meaning at all.

SARA.   What is the name of your relation?

MELLEFONT.   She is—Lady Solmes. You will have heard me mention the name before.

SARA.   I don't remember.

MELLEFONT.   May I beg you to see her?

SARA. Beg me? You can command me to do so.

MELLEFONT. What a word! No, Sara, she shall not have the happiness of seeing you. She will regret it, but she must submit to it. Sara has her reasons, which I respect without knowing them.

SARA. How hasty you are, Mellefont! I shall expect Lady Solmes, and do my best to show myself worthy of the honour of her visit. Are you content?

MELLEFONT. Ah, Sara! let me confess my ambition. I should like to show you to the whole world! And were I not proud of the possession of such a being, I should reproach myself with not being able to appreciate her value. I will go and bring her to you at once. [Exit.]

SARA [alone]. I hope she will not be one of those proud women, who are so full of their own virtue that they believe themselves above all failings. With one single look of contempt they condemn us, and an equivocal shrug of the shoulders is all the pity we seem to deserve in their eyes.

SCENE III

[WAITWELL, SARA.]

BETTY [behind the scenes]. Just come in here, if you must speak to her yourself!

SARA [looking round]. Who must speak to me? Whom do I see? Is it possible? You, Waitwell?

WAITWELL. How happy I am to see our young lady again!

SARA. Good God, what do you bring me? I hear already, I hear already; you bring me the news of my father's death! He is gone, the excellent man, the best of fathers! He is gone, and I—I am the miserable creature who has hastened his death.

WAITWELL. Ah, Miss——

SARA. Tell me, quick; tell me, that his last moments were not embittered by the thought of me; that he had forgotten me; that he died as peacefully as he used to hope to die in my arms; that he did not remember me even in his last prayer——

WAITWELL. Pray do not torment yourself with such false notions! Your father is still alive! He is still alive, honest Sir William!

SARA. Is he still alive? Is it true? Is he still alive? May he live a long while yet, and live happily! Oh, would that God would add the half of my years to his life! Half! How ungrateful should I be, if I were not willing to buy even a few moments for him with all the years that may yet be mine! But tell me at least, Waitwell, that it is not hard for him to live without me; that it was easy for him to renounce a daughter who could so easily renounce her virtue, that he is angry with me for my flight, but not grieved; that he curses me, but does not mourn for me.

WAITWELL. Ah! Sir William is still the same fond father, as his Sara is still the same fond daughter that she was.

SARA. What do you say? You are a messenger of evil, of the most dreadful of all the evils which my imagination has ever pictured to me! He is still the same fond father? Then he loves me still! And he must mourn for me, then! No no, he does not do so; he cannot do so? Do you not see how infinitely each sigh which he wasted on me would magnify my crime? Would not the justice of heaven have to charge me with every tear which I forced from him, as if with each one I repeated my vice and my ingratitude? I grow chill at the thought. I cause him tears? Tears? And they are other tears than tears of joy? Contradict me, Waitwell! At most he has felt some slight stirring of the blood on my account; some transitory emotion, calmed by a slight effort of reason. He did not go so far as to shed tears, surely not to shed tears, Waitwell?

WAITWELL [wiping his eyes]. No, Miss, he did not go so far as that.

SARA. Alas! your lips say no, and your eyes say yes.

WAITWELL. Take this letter, Miss, it is from him himself——

SARA. From whom? From my father? To me?

WAITWELL. Yes, take it! You can learn more from it, than I am able to say. He ought to have given this to another to do, not to me. I promised myself pleasure from it; but you turn my joy into sadness.

SARA. Give it me, honest Waitwell! But no! I will not take it before you tell me what it contains.

WAITWELL. What can it contain? Love and forgiveness.

SARA. Love? Forgiveness?

WAITWELL. And perhaps a real regret, that he used the rights of a father's power against a child, who should only have the privileges of a father's kindness.

SARA. Then keep your cruel letter.

WAITWELL. Cruel? Have no fear. Full liberty is granted you over your heart and hand.

SARA. And it is just this which I fear. To grieve a father such as he, this I have had the courage to do. But to see him forced by this very grief—by his love which I have forfeited, to look with leniency on all the wrong into which an unfortunate passion has led me; this, Waitwell, I could not bear. If his letter contained all the hard and angry words which an exasperated father can utter in such a case, I should read it—with a shudder it is true—but still I should be able to read it. I should be able to produce a shadow of defence against his wrath, to make him by this defence if possible more angry still. My consolation then would be this—that melancholy grief could have no place with violent wrath and that the latter would transform itself finally into bitter contempt. And we grieve no more for one whom we despise. My father would have grown calm again, and I would not have to reproach myself with having made him unhappy for ever.

WAITWELL. Alas, Miss! You will have to reproach yourself still less for this if you now accept his love again, which wishes only to forget everything.

SARA. You are mistaken, Waitwell! His yearning for me misleads him, perhaps, to give his consent to everything. But no sooner would this desire be appeased a little, than he would feel ashamed before himself of his weakness. Sullen anger would take possession of him, and he would never be able to look at me without silently accusing me of all that I had dared to exact from him. Yes, if it were in my power to spare him his bitterest grief, when on my account he is laying the greatest restraint upon himself: if at a moment when he would grant me everything I could sacrifice all to him; then it would be quite a different matter. I would take the letter from your hands with pleasure, would admire in it the strength of the fatherly love, and, not to abuse this love, I would throw myself at his feet a repentant and obedient daughter. But can I do that? I shall be obliged to make use of his permission, regardless of the price this permission has cost him. And then, when I feel most happy, it will suddenly occur to me that he only outwardly appears to share my happiness and that inwardly he is sighing —in short, that he has made me happy by the renunciation of his own happiness. And to wish to be happy in this way,— do you expect that of me, Waitwell?

WAITWELL. I truly do not know what answer to give to that.

SARA. There is no answer to it. So take your letter back! If my father must be unhappy through me, I will myself remain unhappy also. To be quite alone in unhappiness is that for which I now pray Heaven every hour, but to be quite alone in my happiness—of that I will not hear.

WAITWELL [aside]. I really think I shall have to employ deception with this good child to get her to read the letter.

SARA. What are you saying to yourself?

WAITWELL. I was saying to myself that the idea I had hit on to get you to read this letter all the quicker was a very clumsy one.

SARA. How so?

WAITWELL. I could not look far enough. Of course you see more deeply into things than such as I. I did not wish to frighten you; the letter is perhaps only too hard; and when I said that it contained nothing but love and forgiveness, I ought to have said that I wished it might not contain anything else.

SARA. Is that true? Give it me then! I will read it. If one has been unfortunate enough to deserve the anger of one's father, one should at least have enough respect for it to submit to the expression of it on his part. To try to frustrate it means to heap contempt on insult. I shall feel his anger in all its strength. You see I tremble already. But I must tremble; and I will rather tremble than weep. [*Opens the letter.*] Now it is opened! I sink! But what do I see? [*She reads.*] "My only, dearest daughter" —ah, you old deceiver, is that the language of an angry father? Go, I shall read no more——

WAITWELL. Ah, Miss! You will pardon an old servant! Yes, truly, I believe it is the first time in my life that I have intentionally deceived any one. He who deceives once, Miss, and deceives for so good a purpose, is surely no old deceiver on that account. That touches me deeply, Miss! I know well that the good intention does not always excuse one; but what else could I do? To return his letter unread to such a good father? That certainly I cannot do! Sooner will I walk as far as my old legs will carry me, and never again come into his presence.

SARA. What? You too will leave him?

WAITWELL. Shall I not be obliged to do so if you do not read the letter? Read it, pray! Do not grudge a good result to the first deceit with which I have to reproach myself. You will forget it the sooner, and I shall the sooner be able to forgive myself. I am a common, simple man, who must not question the reasons why you cannot and will not read the letter. Whether they are true, I know not, but at any rate they do not appear to me to be natural. I should think thus, Miss: a father, I should think, is after all a father; and a child may err for once, and remain a good child in spite of it. If the father pardons the error, the child may behave again in such a manner that the father may not even think of it any more. For who likes to remember what he would rather had never happened? It seems, Miss, as if you thought only of your error, and believed you atoned sufficiently in exaggerating it in your imagination and tormenting yourself with these exaggerated ideas. But, I should think, you ought also to consider how you could make up for what has happened. And how will you make up for it, if you deprive yourself of every opportunity of doing so. Can it be hard for you to take the second step, when such a good father has already taken the first?

SARA. What daggers pierce my heart in your simple words! That he has to take the first step is just what I cannot bear. And, besides, is it only the first step which he takes? He must do all! I cannot take a single one to meet him. As far as I have gone from him, so far must he descend to me. If he pardons me, he must pardon the whole crime, and in addition must bear the consequences of it continually before his eyes. Can one demand that from a father?

WAITWELL. I do not know, Miss, whether I understand this quite right. But it seems to me, you mean to say that he would have to forgive you too much, and as this could not but be very difficult to him, you make a scruple of accepting his forgiveness. If you mean that, tell me, pray, is not forgiving a great happiness to a kind heart? I have not been so fortunate in my life as to have felt this happiness often. But I still remember with pleasure the few instances when I have felt it. I felt something so sweet, something so tranquillising, something so divine, that I could not help thinking of the great insurpassable blessedness of God, whose preservation of miserable mankind is a perpetual forgiveness. I wished that I could be forgiving continually, and was ashamed that I had only such trifles to pardon. To forgive real painful insults, deadly offences, I said to myself, must be a bliss in which the whole soul melts. And now, Miss, will you grudge your father such bliss?

SARA. Ah! Go on, Waitwell, go on!

WAITWELL. I know well there are people who accept nothing less willingly than forgiveness, and that because they have never learned to grant it. They are proud, unbending people, who will on no account confess that they have done wrong. But you do not belong to this kind, Miss! You have the most loving and tender of hearts that the best of your sex can have. You confess your fault too. Where then is the difficulty? But pardon me, Miss! I am an old chatterer, and ought to have seen at once that your refusal is only a praiseworthy solicitude, only a virtuous timidity. People who can accept a great benefit immediately without any hesitation are seldom worthy of it. Those who deserve it most have always the greatest mistrust of themselves. Yet mistrust must not be pushed beyond limits!

SARA. Dear old father! I believe you have persuaded me.

WAITWELL. If I have been so fortunate as that it must have been a good spirit that has helped me to plead. But no, Miss, my words have done no more than given you time to reflect and to recover from the bewilderment of joy. You will read the letter now, will you not? Oh, read it at once!

SARA. I will do so, Waitwell! What regrets, what pain shall I feel!

WAITWELL. Pain, Miss! but pleasant pain.

SARA. Be silent! [*Begins reading to herself.*]

WAITWELL [*aside*]. Oh! If he could see her himself!

SARA [*after reading a few moments*]. Ah, Waitwell, what a father! He calls my flight "an absence." How much more culpable it becomes through this gentle word! [*Continues reading and interrupts*

herself again.] Listen! he flatters himself I shall love him still. He flatters himself! He begs me—he begs me? A father begs his daughter? his culpable daughter? And what does he beg then? He begs me to forget his over-hasty severity, and not to punish him any longer with my absence. Over-hasty severity! To punish! More still! Now he thanks me even, and thanks me that I have given him an opportunity of learning the whole extent of paternal love. Unhappy opportunity! Would that he also said it had shown him at the same time the extent of filial disobedience. No, he does not say it! He does not mention my crime with one single word. [*Continues reading.*] He will come himself and fetch his children. His children, Waitwell! that surpasses everything! Have I read it rightly? [*Reads again to herself.*] I am overcome! He says, that he without whom he could not possess a daughter deserves but too well to be his son. Oh that he had never had this unfortunate daughter! Go, Waitwell, leave me alone! He wants an answer, and I will write it at once. Come again in an hour! I thank you meanwhile for your trouble. You are an honest man. Few servants are the friends of their masters!

WAITWELL. Do not make me blush, Miss! If all masters were like Sir William, servants would be monsters, if they would not give their lives for them. [*Exit.*]

SCENE IV

SARA [*sits down to write*]. If they had told me a year ago that I should have to answer such a letter! And under such circumstances! Yes, I have the pen in my hand. But do I know yet what I shall write? What I think; what I feel. And what then does one think when a thousand thoughts cross each other in one moment? And what does one feel, when the heart is in a stupor from a thousand feelings. But I must write! I do not guide the pen for the first time. After assist-

ing me in so many a little act of politeness
and friendship, should its help fail me at
the most important office? [*She pauses,
and then writes a few lines.*] It shall
commence so? A very cold beginning!
And shall I then begin with his love? I
must begin with my crime. [*She scratches
it out and writes again.*] I must be on
my guard not to express myself too leni-
ently. Shame may be in its place any-
where else, but not in the confession of
our faults. I need not fear falling into
exaggeration, even though I employ the
most dreadful terms. Ah, am I to be in-
terrupted now?

SCENE V

[MARWOOD, MELLEFONT, SARA.]

MELLEFONT. Dearest Sara, I have the
honour of introducing Lady Solmes to
you; she is one of the members of my
family to whom I feel myself most in-
debted.

MARWOOD. I must beg your pardon,
Madam, for taking the liberty of convinc-
ing myself with my own eyes of the hap-
piness of a cousin, for whom I should
wish the most perfect of women if the
first moment had not at once convinced
me, that he has found her already in you.

SARA. Your ladyship does me too much
honour! Such a compliment would have
made me blush at any time, but now I
would almost take it as concealed re-
proach, if I did not think that Lady
Solmes is much too generous to let her
superiority in virtue and wisdom be felt
by an unhappy girl.

MARWOOD [*coldly*]. I should be incon-
solable if you attributed to me any but
the most friendly feelings towards you.
[*Aside.*] She is good-looking.

MELLEFONT. Would it be possible Ma-
dam, to remain indifferent to such beauty,
such modesty? People say, it is true, that
one charming woman rarely does another
one justice, but this is to be taken only
of those who are over-vain of their su-
periority, and on the other hand of those
who are not conscious of possessing any

superiority. How far are you both re-
moved from this. [*To* MARWOOD, *who
stands in deep thought.*] Is it not true,
Madam, that my love has been anything
but partial? Is it not true, that though I
have said much to you in praise of my
Sara, I have not said nearly so much as
you yourself see? But why so thoughtful.
[*Aside to her.*] You forget whom you
represent.

MARWOOD. May I say it? The admira-
tion of your dear young lady led me to
the contemplation of her fate. It touched
me, that she should not enjoy the fruits of
her love in her native land. I recollected
that she had to leave a father, and a very
affectionate father as I have been told, in
order to become yours; and I could not
but wish for her reconciliation with him.

SARA. Ah, Madam! how much am I
indebted to you for this wish. It en-
courages me to tell you the whole of my
happiness. You cannot yet know, Melle-
font, that this wish was granted before
Lady Solmes had the kindness to wish it.

MELLEFONT. How do you mean, Sara.

MARWOOD [*aside*]. How am I to in-
terpret it?

SARA. I have just received a letter from
my father. Waitwell brought it to me.
Ah, Mellefont, such a letter!

MELLEFONT. Quick, relieve me from my
uncertainty. What have I to fear? What
have I to hope? Is he still the father
from whom we fled? And if he is, will
Sara be the daughter who loves me so
tenderly as to fly again? Alas, had I but
done as you wished, dearest Sara, we
should now be united by a bond which no
caprice could dissolve. I feel now all the
misfortune which the discovery of our
abode may bring upon me.—He will come
and tear you out of my arms. How I hate
the contemptible being who has betrayed
us to him! [*With an angry glance at
MARWOOD.*]

SARA. Dearest Mellefont, how flatter-
ing to me is this uneasiness! And how
happy are we both in that it is unneces-
sary. Read his letter! [*To* MARWOOD,
whilst MELLEFONT *reads the letter.*] He

will be astonished at the love of my father. Of *my* father? Ah, he is *his* now too.

MARWOOD [*perplexed*]. Is it possible?

SARA. Yes, Madam, you have good cause to be surprised at this change. He forgives us everything; we shall now love each other before his eyes; he allows it, he commands it. How has this kindness gone to my very soul! Well, Mellefont? [*Who returns the letter to her.*] You are silent? Oh no, this tear which steals from your eye says far more than your lips could say.

MARWOOD [*aside*]. How I have injured my own cause. Imprudent woman that I was!

SARA. Oh, let me kiss this tear from your cheek.

MELLEFONT. Ah, Sara, why was it our fate to grieve such a godlike man? Yes, a godlike man, for what is more godlike than to forgive? Could we only have imagined such a happy issue possible, we should not now owe it to such violent means, we should owe it to our entreaties alone. What happiness is in store for me! But how painful also will be the conviction, that I am so unworthy of this happiness!

MARWOOD [*aside*]. And I must be present to hear this.

SARA. How perfectly you justify my love by such thoughts.

MARWOOD [*aside*]. What restraint must I put on myself!

SARA. You too, Madam, must read my father's letter. You seem to take too great an interest in our fate to be indifferent to its contents.

MARWOOD. Indifference? [*Takes letter.*]

SARA. But, Madam, you still seem very thoughtful, very sad——

MARWOOD. Thoughtful, but not sad!

MELLEFONT [*aside*]. Heavens! If she should betray herself!

SARA. And why then thoughtful?

MARWOOD. I tremble for you both. Could not this unforeseen kindness of your father be a dissimulation? An artifice?

SARA. Assuredly not, Madam, assur-edly not. Only read and you will admit it yourself. Dissimulation is always cold, it is not capable of such tender words. [MARWOOD *reads.*] Do not grow suspicious, Mellefont, I beg. I pledge myself that my father cannot condescend to an artifice. He says nothing which he does not think, falseness is a vice unknown to him.

MELLEFONT. Oh, of that I am thoroughly convinced, dearest Sara! You must pardon Lady Solmes for this suspicion, since she does not know the man whom it concerns.

SARA [*whilst* MARWOOD *returns the letter to her*]. What do I see, my lady? You are pale! You tremble! What is the matter with you?

MELLEFONT [*aside*]. What anxiety I suffer! Why did I bring her here?

MARWOOD. It is nothing but a slight dizziness, which will pass over. The night air on my journey must have disagreed with me.

MELLEFONT. You frighten me! Would you not like to go into the air? You will recover sooner than in a close room.

MARWOOD. If you think so, give me your arm!

SARA. I will accompany your ladyship!

MARWOOD. I beg you will not trouble to do so! My faintness will pass over immediately.

SARA. I hope then, to see you again soon.

MARWOOD. If you permit me. [MELLE-FONT *conducts her out.*]

SARA [*alone*]. Poor thing! She does not seem exactly the most friendly of people; but yet she does not appear to be either proud or ill-tempered. I am alone again. Can I employ the few moments, while I remain so, better than by finishing my answer? [*Is about to sit down to write.*]

SCENE VI

[BETTY, SARA.]

BETTY. That was indeed a very short visit.

SARA. Yes, Betty! It was Lady Solmes, a relation of my Mellefont. She was suddenly taken faint. Where is she now?

BETTY. Mellefont has accompanied her to the door.

SARA. She is gone again, then?

BETTY. I suppose so. But the more I look at you—you must forgive my freedom, Miss—the more you seem to me to be altered. There is something calm, something contented in your looks. Either Lady Solmes must have been a very pleasant visitor, or the old man a very pleasant messenger.

SARA. The latter, Betty, the latter! He came from my father. What a tender letter I have for you to read! Your kind heart has often wept with me, now it shall rejoice with me, too. I shall be happy again, and be able to reward you for your good services.

BETTY. What services could I render you in nine short weeks?

SARA. You could not have done more for me in all the rest of my life, than in these nine weeks. They are over! But come now with me, Betty. As Mellefont is probably alone again, I must speak to him. It just occurs to me that it would be well if he wrote at the same time to my father, to whom an expression of gratitude from him could hardly come unexpectedly. Come! [Exeunt.]

SCENE VII—The drawing-room.

[SIR WILLIAM SAMPSON, WAITWELL.]

SIR WILLIAM. What balm you have poured on my wounded heart with your words, Waitwell! I live again, and the prospect of her return seems to carry me as far back to my youth as her flight had brought me nearer to my grave. She loves me still? What more do I wish! Go back to her soon, Waitwell? I am impatient for the moment when I shall fold her again in these arms, which I had stretched out so longingly to death! How welcome would it have been to me in the moments of my grief! And how terrible will it be to me in my new happiness! An old man, no doubt, is to be blamed for drawing the bonds so tight again which still unite him to the world. The final separation becomes the more painful. But God who shows Himself so merciful to me now, will also help me to go through this. Would He, I ask, grant me a mercy in order to let it become my ruin in the end? Would He give me back a daughter, that I should have to murmur when He calls me from life? No, no! He gives her back to me that in my last hour I may be anxious about myself alone. Thanks to Thee, Eternal Father! How feeble is the gratitude of mortal lips! But soon, soon I shall be able to thank Him more worthily in an eternity devoted to Him alone!

WAITWELL. How it delights me, Sir, to know you happy again before my death! Believe me, I have suffered almost as much in your grief as you yourself. Almost as much, for the grief of a father in such a case must be inexpressible.

SIR WILLIAM. Do not regard yourself as my servant any longer, my good Waitwell. You have long deserved to enjoy a more seemly old age. I will give it you, and you shall not be worse off than I am while I am still in this world. I will abolish all difference between us; in yonder world, you well know, it will be done. For this once be the old servant still, on whom I never relied in vain. Go, and be sure to bring me her answer, as soon as it is ready.

WAITWELL. I go, Sir! But such an errand is not a service. It is a reward which you grant me for my services. Yes, truly it is so! [Exeunt on different sides of the stage.]

ACT IV

SCENE I—MELLEFONT'S room.

[MELLEFONT, SARA.]

MELLEFONT. Yes, dearest Sara, yes! That I will do! That I must do.

SARA. How happy you make me!

MELLEFONT. It is I who must take the whole crime upon myself. I alone am guilty; I alone must ask for forgiveness.

SARA. No, Mellefont, do not take from me the greater share which I have in our error! It is dear to me, however wrong it is, for it must have convinced you that I love my Mellefont above everything in this world. But is it, then, really true, that I may henceforth combine this love with the love of my father? Or am I in a pleasant dream? How I fear it will pass and I shall awaken in my old misery! But no! I am not merely dreaming, I am really happier than I ever dared hope to become; happier than this short life may perhaps allow. But perhaps this beam of happiness appears in the distance, and delusively seems to approach only in order to melt away again into thick darkness, and to leave me suddenly in a night whose whole terror has only become perceptible to me through this short illumination. What forebodings torment me! Are they really forebodings, Mellefont, or are they common feelings, which are inseparable from the expectation of an undeserved happiness, and the fear of losing it? How fast my heart beats, and how wildly it beats. How loud now, how quick! And now how weak, how anxious, how quivering! Now it hurries again, as if these were its last throbbings, which it would fain beat out rapidly. Poor heart!

MELLEFONT. The tumult of your blood, which a sudden surprise cannot fail to cause, will abate, Sara, and your heart will continue its work more calmly. None of its throbs point to aught that is in the future, and we are to blame—forgive me, dearest Sara!—if we make the mechanic pressure of our blood into a prophet of evil. But I will not leave anything undone which you yourself think good to appease this little storm within your breast. I will write at once, and I hope that Sir William will be satisfied with the assurances of my repentance, with the expressions of my stricken heart, and my vows of affectionate obedience.

SARA. Sir William? Ah, Mellefont, you must begin now to accustom yourself to a far more tender name. My father, your father, Mellefont——

MELLEFONT. Very well, Sara, our kind, our dear father! I was very young when I last used this sweet name; very young, when I had to unlearn the equally sweet name of mother.

SARA. You had to unlearn it, and I— I was never so happy, as to be able to pronounce it at all. My life was her death! O God, I was a guiltless matricide! And how much was wanting—how little, how almost nothing was wanting to my becoming a parricide too! Not a guiltless, but a voluntary parricide. And who knows, whether I am not so already? The years, the days, the moments by which he is nearer to his end than he would have been without the grief I have caused him—of those I have robbed him. However old and weary he may be when Fate shall permit him to depart, my conscience will yet be unable to escape the reproach that but for me he might have lived yet longer. A sad reproach with which I doubtless should not need to charge myself, if a loving mother had guided me in my youth. Through her teaching and her example my heart would —you look tenderly on me, Mellefont? You are right; a mother would perhaps have been a tyrant for very love, and I should not now belong to Mellefont. Why do I wish then for that, which a wiser Fate denied me out of kindness? Its dispensations are always best. Let us only make proper use of that which it gives us; a father who never yet let me sigh for a mother; a father who will also teach you to forget the parents you lost so soon. What a flattering thought. I fall in love with it, and forget almost, that in my innermost heart there is still something which refuses to put faith in it. What is this rebellious something?

MELLEFONT. This something, dearest Sara, as you have already said yourself, is the natural, timid incapability to realize a great happiness. Ah, your heart hesitated less to believe itself unhappy than now, to its own torment, it hesitates to believe in its own happiness! But as to one who has become dizzy with quick movement, the external objects still appear to move round when again he is sitting still, so the heart which has been violently agitated cannot suddenly become calm again; there remains often for a long time, a quivering palpitation which we must suffer to exhaust itself.

SARA. I believe it, Mellefont, I believe it, because you say it, because I wish it. But do not let us detain each other any longer! I will go and finish my letter. And you will let me read yours, will you not, after I have shown you mine?

MELLEFONT. Each word shall be submitted to your judgment; except what I must say in your defence, for I know you do not think yourself so innocent as you are. [*Accompanies* SARA *to the back of the stage*.]

SCENE II

MELLEFONT [*after walking up and down several times in thought*]. What a riddle I am to myself! What shall I think myself? A fool? Or a knave? Heart, what a villain thou art! I love the angel, however much of a devil I may be. I love her! Yes, certainly! certainly I love her. I feel I would sacrifice a thousand lives for her, for her who sacrificed her virtue for me; I would do so,—this very moment without hesitation would I do so. And yet, yet—I am afraid to say it to myself —and yet—how shall I explain it? And yet I fear the moment which will make her mine for ever before the world. It cannot be avoided now, for her father is reconciled. Nor shall I be able to put it off for long. The delay has already drawn down painful reproaches enough upon me. But painful as they were, they were still more supportable to me than the melancholy thought of being fettered for life. But am I not so already? Certainly,— and with pleasure! Certainly I am al-

ready her prisoner. What is it I want, then? At present I am a prisoner, who is allowed to go about on parole; that is flattering! Why cannot the matter rest there? Why must I be put in chains and thus lack even the pitiable shadow of freedom? In chains? Quite so! Sara Sampson, my beloved! What bliss lies in these words! Sara Sampson, my wife! The half of the bliss is gone! and the other half—will go! Monster that I am! And with such thoughts shall I write to her father? Yet these are not my real thoughts, they are fancies! Cursed fancies, which have become natural to me through my dissolute life! I will free myself from them, or live no more.

SCENE III

[NORTON, MELLEFONT.]
MELLEFONT. You disturb me, Norton!
NORTON. I beg your pardon, Sir.
[*Withdrawing again.*]
MELLEFONT. No, no! Stay! It is just as well that you should disturb me. What do you want?
NORTON. I have heard some very good news from Betty, and have come to wish you happiness.
MELLEFONT. On the reconciliation with her father, I suppose you mean? I thank you.
NORTON. So Heaven still means to make you happy.
MELLEFONT. If it means to do so,— you see, Norton, I am just towards myself—it certainly does not mean it for my sake.
NORTON. No, no; if you feel that, then it will be for your sake also.
MELLEFONT. For my Sara's sake alone. If its vengeance, already armed, could spare the whole of a sinful city for the sake of a few just men, surely it can also bear with a sinner, when a soul in which it finds delight, is the sharer of his fate.
NORTON. You speak with earnestness and feeling. But does not joy express itself differently from this?

MELLEFONT. Joy, Norton? [*Looking sharply at him.*] For me it is gone now for ever.

NORTON. May I speak candidly?

MELLEFONT. You may.

NORTON. The reproach which I had to hear this morning of having made myself a participator in your crimes, because I had been silent about them, may excuse me, if I am less silent henceforth.

MELLEFONT. Only do not forget who you are!

NORTON. I will not forget that I am a servant, and a servant, alas, who might be something better, if he had lived for it. I am your servant, it is true, but not so far as to wish to be damned along with you.

MELLEFONT. With me? And why do you say that now?

NORTON. Because I am not a little astonished to find you different from what I expected.

MELLEFONT. Will you not inform me what you expected?

NORTON. To find you all delight.

MELLEFONT. It is only the common herd who are beside themselves immediately when luck smiles on them for once.

NORTON. Perhaps, because the common herd still have the feelings which among greater people are corrupted and weakened by a thousand unnatural notions. But there is something besides moderation to be read in your face—coldness, irresolution, disinclination.

MELLEFONT. And if so? Have you forgotten who is here besides Sara? The presence of Marwood——

NORTON. Could make you anxious, I daresay, but not despondent. Something else troubles you. And I shall be glad to be mistaken in thinking you would rather that the father were not yet reconciled. The prospect of a position which so little suits your way of thinking——

MELLEFONT. Norton, Norton! Either you must have been, or still must be, a dreadful villain, that you can thus guess my thoughts. Since you have hit the nail upon the head, I will not deny it. It is true—so certain as it is that I shall love my Sara for ever so little does it please me, that I *must*—*must* love her for ever! But do not fear; I shall conquer this foolish fancy. Or do you think that it is no fancy? Who bids me look at marriage as compulsion? I certainly do not wish to be freer than she will permit me to be.

NORTON. These reflections are all very well. But Marwood will come to the aid of your old prejudices, and I fear, I fear——

MELLEFONT. That which will never happen! You shall see her go back this very evening to London. And as I have confessed my most secret—folly we will call it for the present—I must not conceal from you either, that I have put Marwood into such a fright that she will obey the slightest hint from me.

NORTON. That sounds incredible to me.

MELLEFONT. Look! I snatched this murderous steel from her hand [*Showing the dagger which he has taken from* MARWOOD.] when in a fearful rage she was on the point of stabbing me to the heart with it. Will you believe now, that I offered her a stout resistance? At first she well nigh succeeded in throwing her noose around my neck again. The traitoress!—She has Arabella with her.

NORTON. Arabella?

MELLEFONT. I have not yet been able to fathom by what cunning she got the child back into her hands again. Enough, the result did not fall out as she no doubt had expected.

NORTON. Allow me to rejoice at your firmness, and to consider your reformation half assured. Yet,—as you wish me to know all—what business had she here under the name of Lady Solmes?

MELLEFONT. She wanted of all things to see her rival. I granted her wish partly from kindness, partly from rashness, partly from the desire to humiliate her by the sight of the best of her sex. You shake your head, Norton?

NORTON. I should not have risked that.

MELLEFONT. Risked? I did not risk

anything more, after all, than what I should have had to risk if I had refused her. She would have tried to obtain admittance as Marwood; and the worst that can be expected from her incognito visit is not worse than that.

NORTON. Thank Heaven that it went off so quietly.

MELLEFONT. It is not quite over yet, Norton. A slight indisposition came over her and compelled her to go away without taking leave. She wants to come again. Let her do so! The wasp which has lost its sting [*Pointing to the dagger.*] can do nothing worse than buzz. But buzzing too shall cost her dear, if she grows too troublesome with it. Do I not hear somebody coming? Leave me if it should be she. It is she. Go!

[*Exit* NORTON.]

SCENE IV

[MELLEFONT, MARWOOD.]

MARWOOD. No doubt you are little pleased to see me again.

MELLEFONT. I am very pleased, Marwood, to see that your indisposition has had no further consequences. You are better, I hope?

MARWOOD. So, so.

MELLEFONT. You have not done well, then, to trouble to come here again.

MARWOOD. I thank you, Mellefont, if you say this out of kindness to me; and I do not take it amiss, if you have another meaning in it.

MELLEFONT. I am pleased to see you so calm.

MARWOOD. The storm is over. Forget it, I beg you once more.

MELLEFONT. Only remember your promise, Marwood, and I will forget everything with pleasure. But if I knew that you would not consider it an offence, I should like to ask——

MARWOOD. Ask on, Mellefont! You cannot offend me any more. What were you going to ask?

MELLEFONT. How you liked my Sara?

MARWOOD. The question is natural. My answer will not seem so natural, but it is none the less true for that. I liked her very much.

MELLEFONT. Such impartiality delights me. But would it be possible for him who knew how to appreciate the charms of a Marwood to make a bad choice?

MARWOOD. You ought to have spared me this flattery, Mellefont, if it is flattery. It is not in accordance with our intention to forget each other.

MELLEFONT. You surely do not wish me to facilitate this intention by rudeness? Do not let our separation be of an ordinary nature. Let us break with each other as people of reason who yield to necessity; without bitterness, without anger, and with the preservation of a certain degree of respect, as behoves our former intimacy.

MARWOOD. Former intimacy! I do not wish to be reminded of it. No more of it. What must be, must, and it matters little how. But one word more about Arabella. You will not let me have her?

MELLEFONT. No, Marwood!

MARWOOD. It is cruel, since you can no longer be her father, to take her mother also from her.

MELLEFONT. I can still be her father, and will be so.

MARWOOD. Prove it, then, now!

MELLEFONT. How?

MARWOOD. Permit Arabella to have the riches which I have in keeping for you, as her father's inheritance. As to her mother's inheritance I wish I could leave her a better one than the shame of having been borne by me.

MELLEFONT. Do not speak so! I shall provide for Arabella without embarrassing her mother's property. If she wishes to forget me, she must begin by forgetting that she possesses anything from me. I have obligations towards her, and I shall never forget that really—though against her will—she has promoted my happiness. Yes, Marwood, in all seriousness I thank you for betraying our retreat to a father whose ignorance of it alone prevented him from receiving us again.

MARWOOD. Do not torture me with gratitude which I never wished to deserve. Sir William is too good an old fool; he must think differently from what I should have thought in his place. I should have forgiven my daughter, but as to her seducer I should have——

MELLEFONT. Marwood!

MARWOOD. True; you yourself are the seducer! I am silent. Shall I be presently allowed to pay my farewell visit to Miss Sampson?

MELLEFONT. Sara could not be offended, even if you left without seeing her again.

MARWOOD. Mellefont, I do not like playing my part by halves, and I have no wish to be taken, even under an assumed name, for a woman without breeding.

MELLEFONT. If you care for your own peace of mind you ought to avoid seeing a person again who must awaken certain thoughts in you which——

MARWOOD [smiling disdainfully]. You have a better opinion of yourself than of me. But even if you believed that I should be inconsolable on your account, you ought at least to believe it in silence. —Miss Sampson would awaken certain thoughts in me? Certain thoughts! Oh, yes; but none more certain than this— that the best girl can often love the most worthless man.

MELLEFONT. Charming, Marwood, perfectly charming. Now you are as I have long wished to see you; although I could almost have wished, as I told you before, that we could have retained some respect for each other. But this may perhaps come still when once your fermenting heart has cooled down. Excuse me for a moment. I will fetch Miss Sampson to see you.

SCENE V

MARWOOD [looking round]. Am I alone? Can I take breath again unobserved, and let the muscles of my face relax into their natural position? I must just for a moment be the true Marwood in all my features to be able again to bear the restraint of dissimulation! How I hate thee, base dissimulation! Not because I love sincerity, but because thou art the most pitiable refuge of powerless revenge. I certainly would not condescend to thee, if a tyrant would lend me his power or Heaven its thunderbolt.—Yet, if thou only servest my end! The beginning is promising, and Mellefont seems disposed to grow more confident. If my device succeeds and I can speak alone with his Sara; then —yes, then, it is still very uncertain whether it will be of any use to me. The truths about Mellefont will perhaps be no novelty to her; the calumnies she will perhaps not believe, and the threats, perhaps, despise. But yet she shall hear truths, calumnies and threats. It would be bad, if they did not leave any sting at all in her mind. Silence; they are coming. I am no longer Marwood, I am a worthless outcast, who tries by little artful tricks to turn aside her shame,— a bruised worm, which turns and fain would wound at least the heel of him who trod upon it.

SCENE VI

[SARA, MELLEFONT, MARWOOD.]

SARA. I am happy, Madam, that my uneasiness on your account has been unnecessary.

MARWOOD. I thank you! The attack was so insignificant that it need not have made you uneasy.

MELLEFONT. Lady Solmes wishes to take leave of you, dearest Sara!

SARA. So soon, Madam?

MARWOOD. I cannot go soon enough for those who desire my presence in London.

MELLEFONT. You surely are not going to leave to-day?

MARWOOD. To-morrow morning, first thing.

MELLEFONT. To-morrow morning, first thing? I thought to-day.

SARA. Our acquaintance, Madam, commences hurriedly. I hope to be honoured with a more intimate intercourse with you at some future time.

MARWOOD. I solicit your friendship, Miss Sampson.

MELLEFONT. I pledge myself, dearest Sara, that this desire of Lady Solmes is sincere, although I must tell you beforehand that you will certainly not see each other again for a long time. Lady Solmes will very rarely be able to live where we are.

MARWOOD [aside]. How subtle!

SARA. That is to deprive me of a very pleasant anticipation, Mellefont!

MARWOOD. I shall be the greatest loser!

MELLEFONT. But in reality, Madam, do you not start before to-morrow morning?

MARWOOD. It may be sooner! [Aside.] No one comes.

MELLEFONT. We do not wish to remain much longer here either. It will be well, will it not, Sara, to follow our answer without delay? Sir William cannot be displeased with our haste.

SCENE VII

[BETTY, MELLEFONT, SARA, MARWOOD.]

MELLEFONT. What is it, Betty?

BETTY. Somebody wishes to speak with you immediately.

MARWOOD [aside]. Ha! now all depends on whether——

MELLEFONT. Me? Immediately? I will come at once. Madam, is it agreeable to you to shorten your visit?

SARA. Why so, Mellefont? Lady Solmes will be so kind as to wait for your return.

MARWOOD. Pardon me; I know my cousin Mellefont, and prefer to depart with him.

BETTY. The stranger, sir—he wishes only to say a word to you. He says, that he has not a moment to lose.

MELLEFONT. Go, please! I will be with him directly. I expect it will be some news at last about the agreement which I mentioned to you. [Exit BETTY.]

MARWOOD [aside]. A good conjecture!

MELLEFONT. But still, Madam——

MARWOOD. If you order it, then, I must bid you——

SARA. Oh, no, Mellefont; I am sure you will not grudge me the pleasure of entertaining Lady Solmes during your absence?

MELLEFONT. You wish it, Sara?

SARA. Do not stay now, dearest Mellefont, but come back again soon! And come with a more joyful face, I will wish! You doubtless expect an unpleasant answer. Don't let this disturb you. I am more desirous to see whether after all you can gracefully prefer me to an inheritance, than I am to know that you are in the possession of one.

MELLEFONT. I obey. [In a warning tone.] I shall be sure to come back in a moment, Madam.

MARWOOD [aside]. Lucky so far.

[Exit MELLEFONT.]

SCENE VIII

[SARA, MARWOOD.]

SARA. My good Mellefont sometimes gives his polite phrases quite a wrong accent. Do not you think so too, Madam?

MARWOOD. I am no doubt too much accustomed to his way already to notice anything of that sort.

SARA. Will you not take a seat, Madam?

MARWOOD. If you desire it. [Aside, whilst they are seating themselves.] I must not let this moment slip by unused.

SARA. Tell me! Shall I not be the most enviable of women with my Mellefont?

MARWOOD. If Mellefont knows how to appreciate his happiness, Miss Sampson will make him the most enviable of men. But——

SARA. A "but," and then a pause, Madam——

MARWOOD. I am frank, Miss Sampson.

SARA. And for this reason infinitely more to be esteemed.

MARWOOD. Frank—not seldom imprudently so. My "but" is a proof of it. A very imprudent "but."

SARA. I do not think that my Lady Solmes can wish through this evasion to make me more uneasy. It must be a cruel mercy that only rouses suspicions of an evil which it might disclose.

MARWOOD. Not at all, Miss Sampson! You attach far too much importance to my "but." Mellefont is a relation of mine——

SARA. Then all the more important is the slightest charge which you have to make against him.

MARWOOD. But even were Mellefont my brother, I must tell you, that I should unhesitatingly side with one of my own sex against him, if I perceived that he did not act quite honestly towards her. We women ought properly to consider every insult shown to one of us as an insult to the whole sex, and to make it a common affair, in which even the sister and mother of the guilty one ought not to hesitate to share.

SARA. This remark——

MARWOOD. Has already been my guide now and then in doubtful cases.

SARA. And promises me—I tremble.

MARWOOD. No, Miss Sampson, if you mean to tremble, let us speak of something else——

SARA. Cruel woman!

MARWOOD. I am sorry to be misunderstood. I at least, if I place myself in imagination in Miss Sampson's position, would regard as a favour any more exact information which one might give me about the man with whose fate I was about to unite my own for ever.

SARA. What do you wish, Madam? Do I not know my Mellefont already? Believe me I know him, as I do my own soul. I know that he loves me——

MARWOOD. And others——

SARA. *Has* loved others. That I know also. Was he to love me, before he knew anything about me? Can I ask to be the only one who has had charm enough to attract him? Must I not confess it to myself, that I have striven to please him? Is he not so lovable, that he must have awakened this endeavour in many a breast? And isn't it but natural, if several have been successful in their endeavour?

MARWOOD. You defend him with just the same ardour and almost the same words with which I have often defended him already. It is no crime to have loved; much less still is it a crime to have been loved. But fickleness is a crime.

SARA. Not always; for often, I believe, it is rendered excusable by the objects of one's love, which seldom deserve to be loved for ever.

MARWOOD. Miss Sampson's doctrine of morals does not seem to be of the strictest.

SARA. It is true; the one by which I judge those who themselves confess that they have taken to bad ways is not of the strictest. Nor should it be so. For here it is not a question of fixing the limits which virtue marks out for love, but merely of excusing the human weakness that has not remained within those limits and of judging the consequences arising therefrom by the rules of wisdom. If, for example, a Mellefont loves a Marwood and eventually abandons her; this abandonment is very praiseworthy in comparison with the love itself. It would be a misfortune if he had to love a vicious person for ever because he once had loved her.

MARWOOD. But do you know this Marwood, whom you so confidently call a vicious person?

SARA. I know her from Mellefont's description.

MARWOOD. Mellefont's? Has it never occurred to you then that Mellefont must be a very invalid witness in his own affairs?

SARA. I see now, Madam, that you wish to put me to the test. Mellefont will smile, when you repeat to him how earnestly I have defended him.

MARWOOD. I beg your pardon, Miss Sampson, Mellefont must not hear anything about this conversation. You are of too noble a mind to wish out of gratitude for a well-meant warning to estrange from him a relation, who speaks against him only because she looks upon his unworthy behaviour towards more than one of the most amiable of her sex as if she herself had suffered from it.

SARA. I do not wish to estrange anyone, and would that others wished it as little as I do.

MARWOOD. Shall I tell you the story of Marwood in a few words?

SARA. I do not know. But still—yes, Madam! but under the condition that you stop as soon as Mellefont returns. He might think that I had inquired about it myself; and I should not like him to think me capable of a curiosity so prejudicial to him.

MARWOOD. I should have asked the same caution of Miss Sampson, if she had not anticipated me. He must not even be able to suspect that Marwood has been our topic; and you will be so cautious as to act in accordance with this. Hear now! Marwood is of good family. She was a young widow when Mellefont made her acquaintance at the house of one of her friends. They say, that she lacked neither beauty, nor the grace without which beauty would be useless. Her good name was spotless. One single thing was wanting. Money. Everything that she had possessed,—and she is said to have had considerable wealth,—she had sacrificed for the deliverance of a husband from whom she thought it right to withhold nothing, after she had willed to give him heart and hand.

SARA. Truly a noble trait of character, which I wish could sparkle in a better setting!

MARWOOD. In spite of her want of fortune she was sought by persons who wished nothing more than to make her happy. Mellefont appeared amongst her rich and distinguished admirers. His offer was serious, and the abundance in which he promised to place Marwood was the least on which he relied. He knew, in their earliest intimacy, that he had not to deal with an egoist, but with a woman of refined feelings, who would have preferred to live in a hut with one she loved, than in a palace with one for whom she did not care.

SARA. Another trait which I grudge Miss Marwood. Do not flatter her any more, pray, Madam, or I might be led to pity her at last.

MARWOOD. Mellefont was just about to unite himself with her with due solemnity, when he received the news of the death of a cousin who left him his entire fortune on the condition that he should marry a distant relation. As Marwood had refused richer unions for his sake, he would not now yield to her in generosity. He intended to tell her nothing of this inheritance, until he had forfeited it through her. That was generously planned, was it not?

SARA. Oh, Madam, who knows better than I, that Mellefont possesses the most generous of hearts?

MARWOOD. But what did Marwood do? She heard late one evening, through some friends, of Mellefont's resolution. Mellefont came in the morning to see her, and Marwood was gone.

SARA. Where to? Why?

MARWOOD. He found nothing but a letter from her, in which she told him that he must not expect ever to see her again. She did not deny, though, that she loved him; but for this very reason she could not bring herself to be the cause of an act, of which he must necessarily repent some day. She released him from his promise, and begged him by the consummation of the union, demanded by the will, to enter without further delay into the possession of a fortune, which an honourable man could employ for a better purpose than the thoughtless flattery of a woman.

SARA. But, Madam, why do you attribute such noble sentiments to Marwood? Lady Solmes may be capable of such, I daresay, but not Marwood. Certainly not Marwood.

MARWOOD. It is not surprising, that you are prejudiced against her. Mellefont was almost distracted at Marwood's resolution. He sent people in all directions to search for her, and at last found her.

SARA. No doubt, because she wished to be found!

MARWOOD. No bitter jests! They do not become a woman of such gentle disposition. I say, he found her; and found her inexorable. She would not accept his hand on any account; and the promise to return to London was all that he could get from her. They agreed to postpone their marriage until his relative, tired of the long delay, should be compelled to propose an arrangement. In the meantime Marwood could not well renounce the daily visits from Mellefont, which for a long time were nothing but the respectful visits of a suitor who has been ordered back within the bounds of friendship. But how impossible is it for a passionate temper not to transgress these bounds. Mellefont possesses everything which can make a man dangerous to us. Nobody can be more convinced of this than you yourself, Miss Sampson.

SARA. Alas!

MARWOOD. You sigh! Marwood too has sighed more than once over her weakness, and sighs yet.

SARA. Enough, Madam, enough! These words I should think, are worse than the bitter jest which you were pleased to forbid me.

MARWOOD. Its intention was not to offend you, but only to show you the unhappy Marwood in a light in which you could most correctly judge her. To be brief—love gave Mellefont the rights of a husband; and Mellefont did not any longer consider it necessary to have them made valid by the law. How happy would Marwood be, if she, Mellefont, and Heaven alone knew of her shame! How happy if a pitiable daughter did not reveal to the whole world that which she would fain be able to hide from herself.

SARA. What do you say? A daughter——

MARWOOD. Yes, through the intervention of Sara Sampson, an unhappy daughter loses all hope of ever being able to name her parents without abhorrence.

SARA. Terrible words! And Mellefont has concealed this from me? Am I to believe it, Madam?

MARWOOD. You may assuredly believe that Mellefont has perhaps concealed still more from you.

SARA. Still more? What more could he have concealed from me?

MARWOOD. This,—that he still loves Marwood.

SARA. You will kill me!

MARWOOD. It is incredible that a love which has lasted more than ten years can die away so quickly. It may certainly suffer a short eclipse, but nothing but a short one, from which it breaks forth again with renewed brightness. I could name to you a Miss Oclaff, a Miss Dorcas, a Miss Moore, and several others, who one after another threatened to alienate from Marwood the man by whom they eventually saw themselves most cruelly deceived. There is a certain point beyond which he cannot go, and as soon as he gets face to face with it he draws suddenly back. But suppose, Miss Sampson, you were the one fortunate woman in whose case all circumstances declared themselves against him; suppose you succeeded in compelling him to conquer the disgust of a formal yoke which has now become innate to him; do you then expect to make sure of his heart in this way?

SARA. Miserable girl that I am! What must I hear?

MARWOOD. Nothing less than that! He would then hurry back all the more into the arms of her who had not been so jealous of his liberty. You would be called his wife and she would be it.

SARA. Do not torment me longer with such dreadful pictures! Advise me rather, Madam, I pray you, advise me what to do. You must know him! You must know by what means it may still be possible to reconcile him with a bond without which even the most sincere love remains an unholy passion.

MARWOOD. That one can catch a bird, I well know; but that one can render its cage more pleasant than the open field, I do not know. My advice, therefore, would be that one should rather not catch it, and should spare oneself the vexation of the profitless trouble. Content yourself, young lady, with the pleasure of having seen him very near your net; and as you can foresee, that he would certainly tear it if you tempted him in altogether, spare your net and do not tempt him in.

SARA. I do not know whether I rightly understand your playful parable——

MARWOOD. If you are vexed with it, you have understood it. In one word. Your own interest as well as that of another—wisdom as well as justice, can, and must induce Miss Sampson to renounce her claims to a man to whom Marwood has the first and strongest claim. You are still in such a position with regard to him that you can withdraw, I will not say with much honour, but still without public disgrace. A short disappearance with a lover is a stain, it is true; but still a stain which time effaces. In some years all will be forgotten, and for a rich heiress there are always men to be found, who are not so scrupulous. If Marwood were in such a position, and she needed no husband for her fading charms nor father for her helpless daughter, I am sure she would act more generously towards Miss Sampson than Miss Sampson acts towards her when raising these dishonourable difficulties.

SARA [rising angrily]. This is too much! Is that the language of a relative of Mellefont's? How shamefully you are betrayed, Mellefont! Now I perceive, Madam, why he was so unwilling to leave you alone with me. He knows already, I daresay, how much one has to fear from your tongue. A poisoned tongue! I speak boldly—for your unseemly talk has continued long enough. How has Marwood been able to enlist such a mediator; a mediator who summons all her ingenuity to force upon me a dazzling romance

about her; and employs every art to rouse my suspicion against the loyalty of a man, who is a man but not a monster? Was it only for this that I was told that Marwood boasted of a daughter from him; only for this that I was told of this and that forsaken girl—in order that you might be enabled to hint to me in cruel fashion that I should do well if I gave place to a hardened strumpet.

MARWOOD. Not so passionate, if you please, young lady! A hardened strumpet? You are surely using words whose full meaning you have not considered.

SARA. Does she not appear such, even from Lady Solmes's description? Well, Madam, you are her friend, perhaps her intimate friend. I do not say this as a reproach, for it may well be that it is hardly possible in this world to have virtuous friends only. Yet why should I be so humiliated for the sake of this friendship of yours? If I had had Marwood's experience, I should certainly not have committed the error which places me on such a humiliating level with her. But if I had committed it, I should certainly not have continued in it .for ten years. It is one thing to fall into vice from ignorance; and another to grow intimate with it when you know it. Alas, Madam, if you knew what regret, what remorse, what anxiety my error has cost me! My error, I say, for why shall I be so cruel to myself any longer, and look upon it as a crime? Heaven itself ceases to consider it such; it withdraws my punishment, and gives me back my father.—But I am frightened, Madam; how your features are suddenly transformed! They glow—rage speaks from the fixed eye, and the quivering movement of the mouth. Ah, if I have vexed you, Madam, I beg for pardon! I am a foolish, sensitive creature; what you have said was doubtless not meant so badly. Forget my rashness! How can I pacify you? How can I also gain a friend in you as Marwood has done? Let me, let me entreat you on my knees [Falling down upon her knees.] for your friendship, and if I cannot have this, at least for the justice not to place me and Marwood in one and the same rank.

MARWOOD [*proudly stepping back and leaving* SARA *on her knees*]. This 'position of Sara Sampson is too charming for Marwood to triumph in it unrecognized. In me, Miss Sampson, behold the Marwood with whom on your knees you beg—Marwood herself—not to compare you.

SARA [*springing up and drawing back in terror*]. You Marwood? Ha! Now I recognize her—now I recognize the murderous deliverer, to whose dagger a warning dream exposed me. It is she! Away, unhappy Sara! Save me, Mellefont; save your beloved! And thou, sweet voice of my beloved father, call! Where does it call? Whither shall I hasten to it?—here?—there?—Help, Mellefont! Help, Betty! Now she approaches me with murderous hand! Help! [*Exit.*]

SCENE IX

MARWOOD. What does the excitable girl mean? Would that she spake the truth, and that I approached her with murderous hand! I ought to have spared the dagger until now, fool that I was! What delight to be able to stab a rival at one's feet in her voluntary humiliation! What now? I am detected. Mellefont may be here this minute. Shall I fly from him? Shall I await him? I will wait, but not in idleness. Perhaps the cunning of my servant will detain him long enough? I see I am feared. Why do I not follow her then? Why do I not try the last expedient which I can use against her? Threats are pitiable weapons; but despair despises no weapons, however pitiable they may be. A timid girl, who flies stupid and terror-stricken from my mere name, can easily take dreadful words for dreadful deeds. But Mellefont! Mellefont will give her fresh courage, and teach her to scorn my threats. He will! Perhaps he will not! Few things would have been undertaken

in this world, if men had always looked to the end. And am I not prepared for the most fatal end? The dagger was for others, the drug is for me! The drug for me! Long carried by me near my heart, it here awaits its sad service; here, where in better times I hid the written flatteries of my lovers,—poison for us equally sure if slower. Would it were not destined to rage in my veins only! Would that a faithless one—why do I waste my time in wishing? Away! I must not recover my reason nor she hers. He will dare nothing, who wishes to dare in cold blood!

ACT V

SCENE I—SARA'S *room.*

[SARA (*reclining in an armchair*), BETTY.]

BETTY. Do you feel a little better, Miss?

SARA. Better—I wish only that Mellefont would return! You have sent for him, have you not?

BETTY. Norton and the landlord have gone for him.

SARA. Norton is a good fellow, but he is rash. I do not want him by any means to be rude to his master on my account. According to his story, Mellefont is innocent of all this. She follows him; what can he do? She storms, she raves, she tries to murder him. Do you see, Betty, I have exposed him to this danger? Who else but me? And the wicked Marwood at last insisted on seeing me or she would not return to London. Could he refuse her this trifling request? Have not I too often been curious to see Marwood. Mellefont knows well that we are curious creatures. And if I had not insisted myself that she should remain with me until his return, he would have taken her away with him. I should have seen her under a false name, without knowing that I had seen her. And I should perhaps have been pleased with this little deception at some future time. In short, it is all my fault. Well, well, I was frightened; nothing more! The swoon was nothing. You know, Betty, I am subject to such fits.

BETTY. But I had never seen you in so deep a swoon before.

SARA. Do not tell me so, please! I must have caused you a great deal of trouble, my good girl.

BETTY. Marwood herself seemed moved by your danger. In spite of all I could do she would not leave the room, until you had opened your eyes a little and I could give you the medicine.

SARA. After all I must consider it fortunate that I swooned. For who knows what more I should have had to hear from her! She certainly can hardly have followed me into my room without a purpose! You cannot imagine how terrified I was. The dreadful dream I had last night recurred to me suddenly, and I fled, like an insane woman who does not know why and whither she flies. But Mellefont does not come. Ah!

BETTY. What a sigh, Miss! What convulsions!

SARA. God! what sensation was this——

BETTY. What was that?

SARA. Nothing, Betty! A pain! Not one pain, a thousand burning pains in one! But do not be uneasy; it is over now!

SCENE II

[NORTON, SARA, BETTY.]

NORTON. Mellefont will be here in a moment.

SARA. That is well, Norton! But where did you find him?

NORTON. A stranger had enticed him beyond the town gate, where he said a gentleman waited for him, to speak with him about matters of the greatest importance. After taking him from place to place for a long time, the swindler slunk away from him. It will be bad for him if he lets himself be caught. Mellefont is furious.

SARA. Did you tell him what has happened?

NORTON. All.

SARA. But in such a way!——

NORTON. I could not think about the way. Enough! He knows what anxiety his imprudence has again caused you.

SARA. Not so, Norton; I have caused it myself.

NORTON. Why may Mellefont never be in the wrong? Come in, sir; love has already excused you.

SCENE III

[MELLEFONT, NORTON, SARA, BETTY.]

MELLEFONT. Ah, Sara! If this love of yours were not——

SARA. Then I should certainly be the unhappier of the two. If nothing more vexatious has happened to you in your absence than to me, I am happy.

MELLEFONT. I have not deserved to be so kindly received.

SARA. Let my weakness be my excuse, that I do not receive you more tenderly. If only for your sake, I would that I was well again.

MELLEFONT. Ha! Marwood! this treachery too! The scoundrel who led me with a mysterious air from one street to another can assuredly have been a messenger of her only! See, dearest Sara, she employed this artifice to get me away from you. A clumsy artifice certainly, but just from its very clumsiness, I was far from taking it for one. She shall have her reward for this treachery! Quick, Norton, go to her lodging; do not lose sight of her, and detain her until I come!

SARA. What for, Mellefont? I intercede for Marwood.

MELLEFONT. Go! [*Exit* NORTON.]

SCENE IV

[SARA, MELLEFONT, BETTY.]

SARA. Pray let the wearied enemy who has ventured the last fruitless assault retire in peace! Without Marwood I should be ignorant of much——

MELLEFONT. Much? What is the "much"?

SARA. What you would not have told me, Mellefont! You start! Well, I will forget it again, since you do not wish me to know it.

MELLEFONT. I hope that you will not believe any ill of me which has no better foundation than the jealousy of an angry slanderer.

SARA. More of this another time! But why do you not tell me first of all about the danger in which your precious life was placed? I, Mellefont, I should have been the one who had sharpened the sword, with which Marwood had stabbed you.

MELLEFONT. The danger was not so great. Marwood was driven by blind passion, and I was cool, so her attack could not but fail. I only wish that she may not have been more successful with another attack—upon Sara's good opinion of her Mellefont! I must almost fear it. No, dearest Sara, do not conceal from me any longer what you have learned from her.

SARA. Well! If I had still had the least doubt of your love, Mellefont, Marwood in her anger would have removed it. She surely must feel that through me she has lost that which is of the greatest value to her; for an uncertain loss would have let her act more cautiously.

MELLEFONT. I shall soon learn to set some store by her bloodthirsty jealousy, her impetuous insolence, her treacherous cunning! But Sara! You wish again to evade my question and not to reveal to me——

SARA. I will; and what I said was indeed a step towards it. That Mellefont loves me, then, is undeniably certain. If only I had not discovered that his love lacked a certain confidence, which would be as flattering to me as his love itself. In short, dearest Mellefont—Why does a sudden anxiety make it so difficult for me to speak?—Well, I suppose I shall have to tell it without seeking for the most prudent form in which to say it. Marwood mentioned a pledge of love; and the talkative Norton—forgive him, pray—told me a name—a name, Mellefont, which must rouse in you another tenderness than that which you feel for me.

MELLEFONT. Is it possible? Has the shameless woman confessed her own disgrace? Alas, Sara, have pity on my confusion! Since you already know all, why do you wish to hear it again from my lips? She shall never come into your sight,—the unhappy child, who has no other fault than that of having such a mother.

SARA. You love her, then, in spite of all?

MELLEFONT. Too much, Sara, too much for me to deny it.

SARA. Ah, Mellefont! How I too love you, for this very love's sake! You would have offended me deeply, if you had denied the sympathy of your blood for any scruples on my account. You have hurt me already in that you have threatened me never to let her come into my sight. No, Mellefont! That you will never forsake Arabella must be one of the promises which you vow to me in the presence of the Almighty! In the hands of her mother she is in danger of becoming unworthy of her father. Use your authority over both, and let me take the place of Marwood. Do not refuse me the happiness of bringing up for myself a friend who owes her life to you—a Mellefont of my own sex. Happy days, when my father, when you, when Arabella will vie in your calls on my filial respect, my confiding love, my watchful friendship. Happy days! But, alas! They are still far distant in the future. And perhaps even the future knows nothing of them, perhaps they exist only in my own desire for happiness! Sensations, Mellefont, sensations which I never before experienced, turn my eyes to another prospect. A dark prospect, with awful shadows! What sensations are these? [*Puts her hand before her face.*]

MELLEFONT. What sudden change from exultation to terror! Hasten, Betty! Bring help! What ails you, generous Sara! Divine soul! Why does this jealous hand [*Moving it away.*] hide these sweet looks from me? Ah, they are looks which unwillingly betray cruel pain. And yet this hand is jealous to hide these looks from me. Shall I not share your pain with you? Unhappy man, that I can only share it—that I may not feel it alone! Hasten, Betty!

BETTY. Whither shall I hasten?

MELLEFONT. You see, and yet ask? For help!

SARA. Stay. It passes over. I will not frighten you again, Mellefont.

MELLEFONT. What has happened to her, Betty? These are not merely the results of a swoon.

SCENE V

[NORTON, MELLEFONT, SARA, BETTY.]

MELLEFONT. You are back again already, Norton? That is well! You will be of more use here.

NORTON. Marwood is gone——

MELLEFONT. And my curses follow her! She is gone? Whither? May misfortune and death, and, were it possible, a whole hell lie in her path! May Heaven thunder a consuming fire upon her, may the earth burst open under her, and swallow the greatest of female monsters!

NORTON. As soon as she returned to her lodgings, she threw herself into her carriage, together with Arabella and her maid, and hurried away, at full gallop. This sealed note was left behind for you.

MELLEFONT [*taking the note*]. It is addressed to me. Shall I read it, Sara?

SARA. When you are calmer, Mellefont.

MELLEFONT. Calmer? Can I be calmer, before I have revenged myself on her, and before I know that you are out of danger, dearest Sara?

SARA. Let me not hear of revenge! Revenge is not ours.—But you open the letter. Alas, Mellefont! Why are we less prone to certain virtues with a healthy body, which feels its strength, than with a sick and wearied one? How hard are gentleness and moderation to you, and how unnatural to me appears the impatient heat of passion! Keep the contents for yourself alone.

MELLEFONT. What spirit is it that seems to compel me to disobey you? I opened it against my will, and against my will I must read it!

SARA [*whilst* MELLEFONT *reads to himself*]. How cunningly man can disunite his nature, and make of his passions another being than himself, on whom he can lay the blame for that which in cold blood he disapproves.—The water, Betty! I fear another shock, and shall need it. Do you see what effect the unlucky note has on him? Mellefont! You lose your senses, Mellefont! God! he is stunned! Here, Betty. Hand him the water! He needs it more than I.

MELLEFONT [*pushing* BETTY *back*]. Back, unhappy girl! Your medicines are poison!

SARA. What do you say? Recover yourself! You do not recognise her.

BETTY. I am Betty,—take it!

MELLEFONT. Wish rather, unhappy girl, that you were not she! Quick! Fly, before in default of the guiltier one you become the guilty victim of my rage.

SARA. What words! Mellefont, dearest Mellefont——

MELLEFONT. The last "dearest Mellefont" from these divine lips, and then no more for ever! At your feet, Sara. . . . [*Throwing himself down.*] But why at your feet? [*Springing up again.*] Disclose it? I disclose it to you? Yes! I will tell you, that you will hate me, that you must hate me! You shall not hear the contents, no, not from me. But you will hear them. You will. . . . Why do you all stand here, stock still, doing nothing? Run, Norton, bring all the doctors! Seek help, Betty! Let your help be as effective as your error! No, stop here! I will go myself——

SARA. Whither, Mellefont? Help for what? Of what error do you speak?

MELLEFONT. Divine help, Sara! or inhuman revenge! You are lost, dearest Sara! I too am lost! Would the world were lost with us!

SCENE VI

[SARA, NORTON, BETTY.]

SARA. He is gone! I am lost? What does he mean? Do you understand him, Norton? I am ill, very ill; but suppose the worst, that I must die, am I therefore lost? And why does he blame you, poor Betty? You wring your hands? Do not grieve: you cannot have offended him; he will bethink himself. Had he only done as I wished, and not read the note! He could have known that it must contain the last poisoned words from Marwood.

BETTY. What terrible suspicion! No, it cannot be. I do not believe it!

NORTON [who has gone towards the back of the stage]. Your father's old servant, Miss.

SARA. Let him come in, Norton.

SCENE VII

[WAITWELL, SARA, BETTY, NORTON.]

SARA. I suppose you are anxious for my answer, dear Waitwell. It is ready except a few lines. But why so alarmed? They must have told you that I am ill.

WAITWELL. And more still.

SARA. Dangerously ill? I conclude so from Mellefont's passionate anxiety more than from my own feelings. Suppose, Waitwell, you should have to go with an unfinished letter from your unhappy Sara to her still more unhappy father! Let us hope for the best! Will you wait until to-morrow? Perhaps I shall find a few good moments to finish off the letter to your satisfaction. At present, I cannot do so. This hand hangs as if dead by my benumbed side. If the whole body dies away as easily as these limbs . . . you are an old man, Waitwell, and cannot be far from the last scene. Believe me, if that which I feel is the approach of death, then the approach of death is not so bitter. Ah! Do not mind this sigh! Wholly without unpleasant sensation it cannot be. Man could not be void of feeling; he must not be impatient. But, Betty, why are you so inconsolable?

BETTY. Permit me, Miss, permit me to leave you.

SARA. Go; I well know it is not every one who can bear to be with the dying. Waitwell shall remain with me! And you, Norton, will do me a favour, if you go and look for your master. I long for his presence.

BETTY [going]. Alas, Norton, I took the medicine from Marwood's hands!

SCENE VIII

[WAITWELL, SARA.]

SARA. Waitwell, if you will do me the kindness to remain with me, you must not let me see such a melancholy face. You are mute! Speak, I pray! And if I may ask it, speak of my father! Repeat all the comforting words which you said to me a few hours ago. Repeat them to me, and tell me too, that the Eternal Heavenly Father cannot be less merciful. I can die with that assurance, can I not? Had this befallen me before your arrival, how would I have fared? I should have despaired, Waitwell. To leave this world burdened with the hatred of him, who belies his nature when he is forced to hate —what a thought! Tell him that I died with the feelings of the deepest remorse, gratitude and love. Tell him—alas, that I shall not tell him myself—how full my heart is of all the benefits I owe to him. My life was the smallest amongst them. Would that I could yield up at his feet the ebbing portion yet remaining!

WAITWELL. Do you really wish to see him, Miss?

SARA. At length you speak—to doubt my deepest, my last desire!

WAITWELL. Where shall I find the

words which I have so long been vainly seeking? A sudden joy is as dangerous as a sudden terror. I fear only that the effect of his unexpected appearance might be too violent for so tender a heart!

SARA. What do you mean? The unexpected appearance of whom?

WAITWELL. Of the wished-for one! Compose yourself!

SCENE IX

[SIR WILLIAM SAMPSON, SARA, WAITWELL.]

SIR WILLIAM. You stay too long, Waitwell! I must see her!

SARA. Whose voice——

SIR WILLIAM. Oh, my daughter!

SARA. Oh, my father! Help me to rise, Waitwell, help me to rise that I may throw myself at his feet. [*She endeavors to rise and falls back again into the arm-chair.*] Is it he, or is it an apparition sent from Heaven like the angel who came to strengthen the Strong One? Bless me, whoever thou art, whether a messenger from the Highest in my father's form or my father himself!

SIR WILLIAM. God bless thee, my daughter! Keep quiet. [*She tries again to throw herself at his feet.*] Another time, when you have regained your strength, I shall not be displeased to see you clasp my faltering knees.

SARA. Now, my father, or never! Soon I shall be no more! I shall be only too happy if I still have a few moments to reveal my heart to you. But not moments —whole days—another life, would be necessary to tell all that a guilty, chastened and repentant daughter can say to an injured but generous and loving father. My offence, and your forgiveness——

SIR WILLIAM. Do not reproach yourself for your weakness, nor give me credit for that which is only my duty. When you remind me of my pardon, you remind me also of my hesitation in granting it. Why did I not forgive you at once? Why did I reduce you to the necessity of flying from me? And this very day, when I had already forgiven you, what was it that forced me to wait first for an answer from you? I could already have enjoyed a whole day with you if I had hastened at once to your arms. Some latent spleen must still have lain in the innermost recesses of my disappointed heart, that I wished first to be assured of the continuance of your love before I gave you mine again. Ought a father to act so selfishly? Ought we only to love those who love us? Chide me, dearest Sara! Chide me! I thought more of my own joy in you than of you yourself. And if I were now to lose this joy? But who, then, says that I must lose it? You will live; you will still live long. Banish all these black thoughts! Mellefont magnifies the danger. He put the whole house in an uproar, and hurried away himself to fetch the doctors, whom he probably will not find in this miserable place. I saw his passionate anxiety, his hopeless sorrow, without being seen by him. Now I know that he loves you sincerely; now I do not grudge him you any longer. I will wait here for him and lay your hand in his. What I would otherwise have done only by compulsion, I now do willingly, since I see how dear you are to him. Is it true that it was Marwood herself who caused you this terror? I could understand this much from your Betty's lamentations, but nothing more. But why do I inquire into the causes of your illness, when I ought only to be thinking how to remedy it. I see you growing fainter every moment, I see it and stand helplessly here. What shall I do, Waitwell? Whither shall I run? What shall I give her? My fortune? My life? Speak!

SARA. Dearest father! all help would be in vain! The dearest help, purchased with your life, would be of no avail.

SCENE X

[MELLEFONT, SARA, SIR WILLIAM, WAITWELL.]

MELLEFONT. Do I dare to set my foot again in this room? Is she still alive?

SARA. Step nearer, Mellefont!

MELLEFONT. Am I to see your face again? No, Sara; I return without consolation, without help. Despair alone brings me back. But whom do I see? You, Sir? Unhappy father! You have come to a dreadful scene! Why did you not come sooner? You are too late to save your daughter! But, be comforted! You shall not have come too late to see yourself revenged.

SIR WILLIAM. Do not remember in this moment, Mellefont, that we have ever been at enmity! We are so no more, and we shall never be so again. Only keep my daughter for me, and you shall keep a wife for yourself.

MELLEFONT. Make me a god, and then repeat your prayer! I have brought so many misfortunes to you already, Sara, that I need not hesitate to announce the last one. You must die! And do you know by whose hand you die?

SARA. I do not wish to know it—that I can suspect it is already too much——

MELLEFONT. You must know it, for who could be assured that you did not suspect wrongly? Marwood writes thus: [He reads.] "When you read this letter, Mellefont, your infidelity will already be punished in its cause. I had made myself known to her and she had swooned with terror. Betty did her utmost to restore her to consciousness. I saw her taking out a soothing-powder, and the happy idea occurred to me of exchanging it for a poisonous one. I feigned to be moved, and anxious to help her, and prepared the draught myself. I saw it given to her, and went away triumphant. Revenge and rage have made me a murderess; but I will not be like a common murderess who does not venture to boast of her deed. I am on my way to Dover; you can pursue me, and let my own handwriting bear witness against me. If I reach the harbour unpursued I will leave Arabella behind unhurt. Till then I shall look upon her as a hostage. Marwood." Now you know all, Sara! Here, Sir, preserve this paper! You must bring the murderess to punishment, and for this it is indispensable.—How motionless he stands!

SARA. Give me this paper, Mellefont! I will convince myself with my own eyes. [He hands it to her and she looks at it for a moment.] Shall I still have sufficient strength? [Tears it.]

MELLEFONT. What are you doing, Sara!

SARA. Marwood will not escape her fate; but neither you nor my father shall be her accusers. I die, and forgive the hand through which God chastens me. Alas, my father, what gloomy grief has taken hold of you? I love you still, Mellefont, and if loving you is a crime, how guilty shall I enter yonder world! Would I might hope, dearest father, that you would receive a son in place of a daughter! And with him you will have a daughter, too, if you will acknowledge Arabella as such. You must fetch her back, Mellefont; her mother may escape. Since my father loves me, why should I not be allowed to deal with this love as with a legacy? I bequeath this fatherly love to you and Arabella. Speak now and then to her of a friend from whose example she may learn to be on her guard against love. A last blessing, my father! —Who would venture to judge the ways of the Highest?—Console your master, Waitwell! But you too stand there in grief and despair, you who lose in me neither a lover nor a daughter?

SIR WILLIAM. We ought to be giving you courage, and your dying eyes are giving it to us. No more, my earthly daughter—half angel already; of what avail can the blessing of a mourning father be to a spirit upon whom all the blessings of heaven flow? Leave me a ray of the light which raises you so far above everything human. Or pray to God, who hears no prayer so surely as that of a pious and departing soul—pray to Him that this day may be the last of my life also!

SARA. God must let the virtue which has been tested remain long in this world as an example; only the weak virtue which would perhaps succumb to too many temptations is quickly raised above the dangerous confines of the earth. For whom do these tears flow, my father? They fall like fiery drops upon my heart; and yet—yet they are less terrible to me than mute despair. Conquer it, Mellefont!—My eyes grow dim.—That sigh was the last! But where is Betty?—Now I understand the wringing of her hands.— Poor girl!—Let no one reproach her with carelessness, it is excused by a heart without falsehood, and without suspicion of it. —The moment is come! Mellefont—my father— [*Dies.*]

MELLEFONT. She dies! Ah, let me kiss this cold hand once more. [*Throwing himself at her feet.*] No! I will not venture to touch her. The old saying that the body of the slain bleeds at the touch of the murderer, frightens me. And who is her murderer? Am I not he, more than MARWOOD? [*Rises.*] She is dead now, Sir; she does not hear us any more. Curse me now. Vent your grief in well-deserved curses. May none of them miss their mark, and may the most terrible be fulfilled twofold! Why do you remain silent? She is dead! She is certainly dead. Now, again, I am nothing but Mellefont! I am no more the lover of a tender daughter, whom you would have reason to spare in him. What is that? I do not want your compassionate looks! This is your daughter! I am her seducer. Bethink yourself, Sir! In what way can I rouse your anger? This budding beauty, who was yours alone, became my prey! For my sake her innocent virtue was abandoned! For my sake she tore herself from the arms of a beloved father! For my sake she had to die! You make me impatient with your forbearance, Sir! Let me see that you are a father!

SIR WILLIAM. I am a father, Mellefont, and am too much a father not to respect the last wish of my daughter. Let me

embrace you, my son, for whom I could not have paid a higher price!

MELLEFONT. Not so, Sir! This angel enjoined more than human nature is capable of! You cannot be my father. Behold, Sir [*Drawing the dagger from his bosom.*], this is the dagger which Marwood drew upon me to-day. To my misfortune, I disarmed her. Had I fallen a guilty victim of her jealousy, Sara would still be living. You would have your daughter still, and have her without Mellefont. It is not for me to undo what is done—but to punish myself for it is still in my power! [*He stabs himself and sinks down at SARA's side.*]

SIR WILLIAM. Hold him, Waitwell! What new blow upon my stricken head! Oh, would that my own might make the third dying heart here.

MELLEFONT [*dying*]. I feel it. I have not struck false. If now you will call me your son and press my hand as such, I shall die in peace. [*SIR WILLIAM embraces him.*] You have heard of an Arabella, for whom Sara pleaded; I should also plead for her; but she is Marwood's child as well as mine. What strange feeling seizes me? Mercy—O Creator, mercy!

SIR WILLIAM. If the prayers of others are now of any avail, Waitwell, let us help him to pray for this mercy! He dies! Alas! He was more to pity than to blame.

SCENE XI

[NORTON, THE OTHERS.]

NORTON. Doctors, Sir!——

SIR WILLIAM. If they can work miracles, they may come in! Let me no longer remain at this deadly spectacle! One grave shall enclose both. Come and make immediate preparations, and then let us think of Arabella. Be she who she may, she is a legacy of my daughter!
[*Exeunt.*]

EGMONT

By JOHANN WOLFGANG GOETHE

Published 1786; produced at Weimar in revised form several years later

TRANSLATED BY ANNA SWANWICK

CHARACTERS

MARGARET OF PARMA, *daughter of Charles V, and Regent of the Netherlands*

COUNT EGMONT, *Prince of Gaure*

WILLIAM OF ORANGE

THE DUKE OF ALVA

FERDINAND, *his natural son*

MECHIAVEL, *in the service of the Regent*

RICHARD, EGMONT'S *private secretary*

SILVA,
GOMEZ, } *in the service of* ALVA

CLARA, *the beloved of* EGMONT

HER MOTHER

BRACKENBURG, *a citizen's son*

SOEST, *a Shopkeeper,*
JETTER, *a Tailor,*
A CARPENTER,
A SOAPBOILER, } *citizens of Brussels*

BUYCK, *a Hollander, a soldier under* EGMONT

RUYSUM, *a Frieslander, an invalid soldier, and deaf*

VANSEN, *a Clerk*

PEOPLE, ATTENDANTS, GUARDS, *etc.*

The scene is laid in Brussels.

ACT I

[SOEST, BUYCK, RUYSUM, SOLDIERS *and* CITIZENS *with cross-bows.* JETTER *steps forward, and bends his cross-bow.*]

SOEST. Come, shoot away, and have done with it! You won't beat me! Three black rings, you never made such a shot in all your life. And so I'm master for this year.

JETTER. Master and king to boot; who envies you? You'll have to pay double reckoning; 'tis only fair you should pay for your dexterity.

BUYCK. Jetter, I'll buy your shot, share the prize, and treat the company. I have already been here so long, and am a debtor for so many civilities. If I miss, then it shall be as if you had shot.

SOEST. I ought to have a voice, for in fact I am the loser. No matter! Come, Buyck, shoot away.

BUYCK [*shoots*]. Now, corporal, look out!—One! Two! Three! Four!

SOEST. Four rings! So be it!

ALL. Hurrah! Hurrah! Long live the king! Hurrah! Hurrah!

BUYCK. Thanks, sirs, master even were too much! Thanks for the honor.

JETTER. You have no one to thank but yourself.

RUYSUM. Let me tell you!——

SOEST. How now, gray beard?

RUYSUM. Let me tell you!—He shoots like his master, he shoots like Egmont.

BUYCK. Compared with him, I am only a bungler. He aims with the rifle as no one else does. Not only when he's lucky or in the vein; no! he levels, and the bull's eye is pierced. I have learned from him. He were indeed a blockhead, who could serve under him and learn nothing! —But, sirs, let us not forget! A king maintains his followers; and so, wine here, at the king's charge!

JETTER. We have agreed among ourselves that each——

BUYCK. I am a foreigner and a king, and care not a jot for your laws and customs.

JETTER. Why you are worse than the Spaniard, who has not yet ventured to meddle with them.

RUYSUM. What does he say?

SOEST [*loud to* RUYSUM]. He wants to treat us; he will not hear of our clubbing together, the king paying only a double share.

RUYSUM. Let him! under protest, however! 'Tis his master's fashion, too, to be munificent, and to let the money flow in a good cause.

[*Wine is brought.*]

ALL. Here's to his majesty! Hurrah!

JETTER [*to* BUYCK]. That means your majesty, of course.

BUYCK. My hearty thanks, if it be so.

SOEST. Assuredly! A Netherlander does not find it easy to drink the health of his Spanish majesty from his heart.

RUYSUM. Who?

SOEST [*aloud*]. Philip the Second, King of Spain.

RUYSUM. Our most gracious king and master! Long life to him!

SOEST. Did you not like his father, Charles the Fifth, better?

RUYSUM. God bless him! He was a king indeed! His hand reached over the whole earth, and he was all in all. Yet, when he met you, he'd greet you just as one neighbour greets another,—and if you were frightened, he knew so well how to put you at your ease,—ay, you understand me,—he walked out, rode out, just as it came into his head, with very few followers. We all wept when he resigned the government here to his son. You understand me,—he is another sort of man, he's more majestic.

JETTER. When he was here, he never appeared in public, except in pomp and royal state. He speaks little, they say.

SOEST. He is no king for us Netherlanders. Our princes must be joyous and free like ourselves, must live, and let live. We will neither be despised nor oppressed, good-natured fools though we be.

JETTER. The king, methinks, were a gracious sovereign enough, if he had only better counsellors.

SOEST. No, no! He has no affection for us Netherlanders; he has no heart for the people; he loves us not; how then can we love him? Why is everybody so fond of Count Egmont? Why are we all so devoted to him? Why, because one can read in his face that he loves us; because joyousness, open-heartedness, and good-nature, speak in his eyes; because he possesses nothing that he does not share with him who needs it, ay, and with him who needs it not. Long live Count Egmont! Buyck, it is for you to give the first toast! give us your master's health.

BUYCK. With all my heart; here's to Count Egmont! Hurrah!

RUYSUM. Conqueror of St. Quintin.

BUYCK. The hero of Gravelines.

ALL. Hurrah!

RUYSUM. St. Quintin was my last battle. I was hardly able to crawl along, and could with difficulty carry my heavy rifle. I managed, notwithstanding, to singe the skin of the French once more, and, as a parting gift, received a grazing shot in my right leg.

BUYCK. Gravelines! Ha, my friends, we had sharp work of it there! The victory was all our own. Did not those French dogs carry fire and desolation into the very heart of Flanders? We gave it them, however! The old hard-fisted veterans held out bravely for awhile, but we pushed on, fired away, and laid about us, till they made wry faces, and their lines gave way. Then Egmont's horse was shot under him; and for a long time we fought pell-mell, man to man, horse to horse, troop to troop, on the broad, flat, sea-sand. Suddenly, as if from heaven, down came the cannon shot from the mouth of the river, bang, bang, right into the midst of the French. These were English, who, under Admiral Malin, happened to be sailing past from Dunkirk. They did not help us much, 'tis true; they could only approach with their smallest vessels, and that not near enough;—besides, their shot fell sometimes among our troops. It did some good, however! It broke the French lines, and raised our courage. Away it went. Helter, skelter! topsy, turvy! all struck dead, or forced into the river; the fellows were drowned the moment they tasted the water, while we Hollanders dashed in after them. Being amphibious, we were as much in our element as frogs, and hacked away at the enemy, and shot them down as if they had been ducks. The few who struggled through, were struck dead in their flight by the peasant women, armed with hoes and pitchforks. His Gallic majesty was compelled at once to humble himself, and make peace; and that peace you owe to us, to the great Egmont.

ALL. Hurrah, for the great Egmont! Hurrah! Hurrah!

JETTER. Had they but appointed him Regent, instead of Margaret of Parma!

SOEST. Not so! Truth is truth! I'll not hear Margaret abused. Now it is my turn. Long live our gracious lady!

ALL. Long life to her!

SOEST. Truly, there are excellent women in that family. Long live the Regent!

JETTER. She is prudent and moderate in all she does; if she would only not hold so fast to the priests. It is partly her fault, too, that we have the fourteen new mitres in the land. Of what use are they, I should like to know? Why, that foreigners may be shoved into the good benefices, where formerly abbots were chosen out of the chapters! And we're to believe it's for the sake of religion. We know better. Three bishops were enough for us; things went on decently and reputably. Now each must busy himself as if he were needed; and this gives rise every moment to dissensions and ill-will. And the more you agitate the matter, the worse it grows. [They drink.]

SOEST. But it was the will of the king; she cannot alter it, one way or another.

JETTER. Then we may not even sing the new psalms; but ribald songs, as many as we please. And why? There is heresy in them, they say, and heaven knows what. I have sung some of them, however; they are new to be sure, but I see no harm in them.

BUYCK. Ask their leave, forsooth! In our province we sing just what we please. That's because Count Egmont is our stadtholder, who does not trouble himself about such matters. In Ghent, Yyprès, and throughout the whole of Flanders, any body sings them that chooses. [*Aloud to* RUYSUM.] There is nothing more harmless than a spiritual song. Is there, father?

RUYSUM. What, indeed! It is a godly work, and truly edifying.

JETTER. They say, however, that they are not of the right sort, not of their sort, and, since it is dangerous, we had better leave them alone. The officers of the Inquisition are always lurking and spying about, and many an honest fellow has already fallen into their clutches. They had not gone so far as to meddle with conscience, that was yet wanting. If they will not allow me to do what I like, they might at least let me think and sing as I please.

SOEST. The Inquisition won't do here. We are not made like the Spaniards, to let our consciences be tyrannized over. The nobles must look to it, and clip its wings betimes.

JETTER. It is a great bore. Whenever it comes into their worships' heads to break into my house, and I am sitting there at my work, humming a French psalm, thinking nothing about it, neither good nor bad; singing it just because it is in my throat; forthwith I'm a heretic, and am clapped into prison. Or if I am passing through the country, and stand near a crowd listening to a new preacher, one of those who have come from Germany; instantly I'm called a rebel, and am in danger of losing my head! Have you ever heard one of these preachers?

SOEST. Brave fellows! Not long ago, I heard one of them preach in a field, before thousands and thousands of people. A different sort of dish he gave us from that of our humdrum preachers, who, from the pulpit, choke their hearers with scraps of Latin. He spoke from his heart; told us how we had, till now, been led by the nose, how we had been kept in darkness, and how we might procure more light;—ay, and he proved it all out of the Bible.

JETTER. There may be something in it. I always said as much, and have often pondered the matter over. It has long been running in my head.

BUYCK. All the people run after them.

SOEST. No wonder, since they hear both what is good and what is new.

JETTER. And what is it all about? Surely they might let every one preach after his own fashion.

BUYCK. Come, sirs! While you are talking, you forget the wine and the prince of Orange.

JETTER. We must not forget him. He's a very wall of defence. In thinking of him, one fancies, that if one could only hide behind him, the devil himself could not get at one. Here's to William of Orange! Hurrah!

ALL. Hurrah! Hurrah!

SOEST. Now, gray beard, let's have your toast.

RUYSUM. Here's to old soldiers! To all soldiers! War for ever!

BUYCK. Bravo, old fellow! Here's to all soldiers! War for ever!

JETTER. War! War! Do ye know what ye are shouting about? That it should slip glibly from your tongue is natural enough; but what wretched work it is for us, I have not words to tell you. To be stunned the whole year round by the beating of the drum; to hear of nothing except how one troop marched here, and another there; how they came over this height, and halted near that mill; how many were left dead on this field, and how many on that; how they press forward, and how one wins, and another loses, without being able to comprehend what they are fighting about; how a town is taken, how the citizens are put to the sword, and how it fares with the poor women and innocent children. This is grievous work, and then one thinks every moment: "Here they come! It will be our turn next."

SOEST. Therefore every citizen must be practised in the use of arms.

JETTER. Fine talking, indeed, for him who has a wife and children. And yet I would rather hear of soldiers than see them.

BUYCK. I might take offence at that.

JETTER. It was not intended for you, countryman. When we got rid of the Spanish garrison, we breathed freely again.

SOEST. Faith! They pressed on you heavy enough.

JETTER. Mind your own business.

SOEST. They came to sharp quarters with you.

JETTER. Hold your tongue.

SOEST. They drove him out of kitchen, cellar, chamber—and bed. [*They laugh.*]

JETTER. You are a blockhead.

BUYCK. Peace, sirs! Must the soldier cry peace? Since you will not hear anything about us, let us have a toast of your own—a citizen's toast.

JETTER. We're all ready for that! Safety and peace!

SOEST. Freedom and order!

BUYCK. Bravo! That will content us all.

> [*They ring their glasses together, and joyously repeat the words, but in such a manner that each utters a different sound, and it becomes a kind of chaunt. The old man listens, and at length joins in.*]

ALL. Safety and peace! Freedom and order!

Palace of the REGENT.

[MARGARET OF PARMA, *in a hunting dress.* COURTIERS, PAGES, SERVANTS.]

REGENT. Put off the hunt, I shall not ride to-day. Bid Mechiavel attend me.

> [*Exeunt all but the* REGENT.]

The thought of these terrible events leaves me no repose! Nothing can amuse, nothing divert my mind. These images, these cares, are always before me. The king will now say that these are the natural fruits of my kindness, of my clemency; yet my conscience assures me that I have adopted the wisest, the most prudent course. Ought I sooner to have kindled, and spread abroad these flames with the breath of wrath? My hope was to keep them in, to let them smoulder in their own ashes. Yes, my inward conviction, and my knowledge of the circumstances, justify my conduct in my own eyes, but in what light will it appear to my brother! For, can it be denied that the insolence of these foreign teachers waxes daily more audacious? They have desecrated our sanctuaries, unsettled the dull minds of the people, and conjured up amongst them a spirit of delusion. Impure spirits have mingled among the insurgents, deeds horrible to think of have been perpetrated, and of these a circumstantial account must be transmitted instantly to court. Prompt and minute must be my communication, lest rumour outrun my messenger, and the king suspect that some particulars have been purposely withheld. I can see no means, severe or mild, by which to stem the evil. Oh, what are we great ones on the billows of life? We think to control them, and are ourselves driven to and fro, hither and thither.

> [*Enter* MECHIAVEL.]

REGENT. Are the despatches to the king prepared?

MECHIAVEL. In an hour they will be ready for your signature.

REGENT. Have you made the report sufficiently circumstantial?

MECHIAVEL. Full and circumstantial, as the king loves to have it. I relate how the rage of the iconoclasts first broke out at St. Omer. How a furious multitude, with stones, hatchets, hammers, ladders, and cords, accompanied by a few armed men, first assailed the chapels, churches, and convents, drove out the worshippers, forced the barred gates, threw everything into confusion, tore down the altars, destroyed the statues of the saints, defaced the pictures, and dashed to atoms, and trampled under foot, whatever came in their way that was consecrated and holy. How the crowd increased as it advanced, and how the inhabitants of Yprès opened their gates at its approach. How, with incredible rapidity, they demolished the cathedral, and burned the library of the bishop. How a vast multitude, possessed by the like frenzy, dispersed themselves through Menin, Comines, Verviers, Lille, nowhere encountered opposition; and how, through almost the whole of Flanders, in a single moment, the monstrous conspiracy broke forth, and accomplished its object.

REGENT. Alas! Your recital rends my heart anew; and the fear that the evil will increase, adds to my grief. Tell me your thoughts, Mechiavel!

MECHIAVEL. Pardon me, your Highness, my thoughts will appear to you but as idle fancies; and though you always seem well satisfied with my services, you have seldom felt inclined to follow my advice. How often have you said in jest: "You see too far, Mechiavel! You should be an historian; he who acts, must provide for the exigence of the hour." And yet, have I not predicted this terrible history? Have I not foreseen it all?

REGENT. I too can foresee many things, without being able to avert them.

MECHIAVEL. In one word, then:—you will not be able to suppress the new faith. Let it be recognized, separate its votaries from the true believers, give them churches of their own, include them within the pale of social order, subject them to the restraints of law,—do this, and you will at once tranquillize the insurgents. All other measures will prove abortive, and you will depopulate the country.

REGENT. Have you forgotten with what aversion the mere suggestion of toleration was rejected by my brother? Know you not, how in every letter he urgently recommends to me the maintenance of the true faith? That he will not hear of tranquillity and order being restored at the expense of religion? Even in the provinces, does he not maintain spies, unknown to us, in order to ascertain who inclines to the new doctrines? Has he

not, to our astonishment, named to us this or that individual residing in our very neighbourhood, who, without its being known, was obnoxious to the charge of heresy? Does he not enjoin harshness and severity? and am I to be lenient? Am I to recommend for his adoption measures of indulgence and toleration? Should I not thus lose all credit with him, and at once forfeit his confidence?

MECHIAVEL. I know it. The king commands and puts you in full possession of his intentions. You are to restore tranquillity and peace by measures which cannot fail still more to embitter men's minds, and which must inevitably kindle the flames of war from one extremity of the country to the other. Consider well what you are doing. The principal merchants are infected—nobles, citizens, soldiers. What avails persisting in our opinion, when everything is changing around us? Oh, that some good genius would suggest to Philip that it better becomes a monarch to govern subjects of two different creeds, than to excite them to mutual destruction!

REGENT. Never let me hear such words again. Full well I know that the policy of statesmen rarely maintains truth and fidelity; that it excludes from the heart candour, charity, toleration. In secular affairs, this is, alas! only too true; but shall we trifle with God as we do with each other? Shall we be indifferent to our established faith, for the sake of which so many have sacrificed their lives? Shall we abandon it to these far-fetched, uncertain, and self-contradicting heresies?

MECHIAVEL. Think not the worse of me for what I have uttered.

REGENT. I know you and your fidelity. I know too that a man may be both honest and sagacious, and yet miss the best and nearest way to the salvation of his soul. There are others, Mechiavel, men whom I esteem, yet whom I needs must blame.

MECHIAVEL. To whom do you refer?

REGENT. I must confess that Egmont caused me to-day deep and heart-felt annoyance.

MECHIAVEL. How so?

REGENT. By his accustomed demeanour, his usual indifference and levity. I received the fatal tidings as I was leaving church, attended by him and several others. I did not restrain my anguish, I broke forth into lamentations, loud and deep, and turning to him, exclaimed, "See what is going on in your province! Do you suffer it, count, you, in whom the king confided so implicitly?"

MECHIAVEL. And what was his reply?

REGENT. As if it were a mere trifle, an affair of no moment, he answered: "Were the Netherlanders but satisfied as to their constitution, the rest would soon follow."

MECHIAVEL. There was, perhaps, more truth than discretion or piety in his words. How can we hope to acquire and to maintain the confidence of the Netherlander, when he sees that we are more interested in appropriating his possessions, than in promoting his welfare, temporal or spiritual? Does the number of souls saved by the new bishops exceed that of the fat benefices they have swallowed? And are they not for the most part foreigners? As yet, the office of stadtholder has been held by Netherlanders; but do not the Spaniards betray their great and irresistible desire to possess themselves of these places? Will not people prefer being governed by their own countrymen, and according to their ancient customs, rather than by foreigners, who, from their first entrance into the land, endeavour to enrich themselves at the general expense, who measure everything by a foreign standard, and who exercise their authority without cordiality or sympathy?

REGENT. You take part with our opponents?

MECHIAVEL. Assuredly not in my heart. Would that with my understanding I could be wholly on our side!

REGENT. If such your disposition, it were better I should resign the regency to them; for both Egmont and Orange entertained great hopes of occupying this position. Then they were adversaries, now they are leagued against me, and have become friends,—inseparable friends.

MECHIAVEL. A dangerous pair.

REGENT. To speak candidly, I fear Orange,—I fear for Egmont.—Orange meditates some dangerous scheme, his thoughts are far-reaching, he is reserved, appears to accede to everything, never contradicts, and while maintaining the show of reverence, with clear foresight accomplishes his own designs.

MECHIAVEL. Egmont, on the contrary, advances with a bold step, as if the world were all his own.

REGENT. He bears his head as proudly, as if the hand of majesty were not suspended over him.

MECHIAVEL. The eyes of all the people are fixed upon him, and he is the idol of their hearts.

REGENT. He has never assumed the least disguise, and carries himself as if no one had a right to call him to account. He still bears the name of Egmont. Count Egmont is the title by which he loves to hear himself addressed, as though he would fain be reminded that his ancestors were masters of Guelderland. Why does he not assume his proper title,—Prince of Gaure? What object has he in view? Would he again revive extinguished claims?

MECHIAVEL. I hold him for a faithful servant of the king.

REGENT. Were he so inclined, what important service could he not render to the government; whereas now, without benefiting himself, he has caused us unspeakable vexation. His banquets and entertainments have done more to unite the nobles and to knit them together, than the most dangerous secret associations. With his toasts, his guests have drunk in a permanent intoxication, a giddy frenzy, that never subsides. How often have his facetious jests stirred up the minds of the populace? and what an excitement was produced among the mob, by the new liveries, and the extravagant devices of his followers!

MECHIAVEL. I am convinced he had no design.

REGENT. Be that as it may, it is bad enough. As I said before, he injures us without benefiting himself. He treats as a jest matters of serious import; and not to appear negligent and remiss, we are forced to treat seriously what he intended as a jest. Thus one urges on the other; and what we are endeavouring to avert is actually brought to pass. He is more dangerous than the acknowledged head of a conspiracy; and I am much mistaken if it is not all remembered against him at court. I cannot deny that scarcely a day passes in which he does not wound me, deeply wound me.

MECHIAVEL. He appears to me to act on all occasions according to the dictates of his conscience.

REGENT. His conscience has a convenient mirror. His demeanour is often offensive. He carries himself as if he felt he were the master here, and were withheld by courtesy alone from making us feel his supremacy; as if he would not exactly drive us out of the country; there'll be no need for that.

MECHIAVEL. I entreat you, put not too harsh a construction upon his frank and joyous temper, which treats lightly matters of serious moment. You but injure yourself and him.

REGENT. I interpret nothing. I speak only of inevitable consequences, and I know him. His patent of nobility, and the Golden Fleece upon his breast, strengthen his confidence, his audacity. Both can protect him against any sudden outbreak of royal displeasure. Consider the matter closely, and he is alone responsible for the disorders that have broken out in Flanders. From the first, he connived at the proceedings of the foreign teachers, avoided stringent measures, and perhaps rejoiced in secret, that they gave us so much to do. Let me alone; on this occasion, I will give utterance to that which weighs upon my heart; I will not shoot my arrow in vain. I know where he is vulnerable. For he is vulnerable.

MECHIAVEL. Have you summoned the council? Will Orange attend?

REGENT. I have sent for him to Antwerp. I will lay upon their shoulders the burden of responsibility; they shall either strenuously co-operate with me in quelling the evil, or at once declare themselves rebels. Let the letters be completed without delay, and bring them for my signature. Then hasten to dispatch the trusty Vasca to Madrid; he is faithful and indefatigable; let him use all diligence, that he may not be anticipated by common report, that my brother may receive the intelligence first through him. I will myself speak with him ere he departs.

MECHIAVEL. Your orders shall be promptly and punctually obeyed.

Citizen's house.

[CLARA, HER MOTHER, BRACKENBURG.]

CLARA. Will you not hold the yarn for me, Brackenburg?

BRACKENBURG. I entreat you, excuse me, Clara.

CLARA. What ails you? Why refuse me this trifling service?

BRACKENBURG. When I hold the yarn, I stand as it were spell-bound before you, and cannot escape your eyes.

CLARA. Nonsense! Come and hold!

MOTHER [*knitting in her arm-chair*]. Give us a song! Brackenburg sings so good a second. You used to be merry once, and I had always something to laugh at.

BRACKENBURG. Once!

CLARA. Well, let us sing.

BRACKENBURG. As you please.

CLARA. Merrily, then, and sing away! 'Tis a soldier's song, my favourite.

[*She winds yarn, and sings with* BRACKENBURG.]

The drum is resounding,
And shrill the fife plays,
My love for the battle,
His brave troop arrays,

He lifts his lance high
And the people he sways.
My blood it is boiling!
My heart throbs pit-pat!
Oh, had I a jacket
With hose and with hat!

How boldly I'd follow,
And march through the gate;
Through all the wide province
I'd follow him straight.
The foe yield, we capture
Or shoot them! Ah, me!
What heart-thrilling rapture
A soldier to be!

> [*During the song,* BRACKENBURG
> *has frequently looked at* CLARA,
> *at length his voice falters, his
> eyes fill with tears, he lets the
> skein fall, and goes to the
> window.* CLARA *finishes the
> song alone, her mother motions
> to her, half displeased, she
> rises, advances a few steps to-
> wards him, turns back, as if ir-
> resolute, and again sits down.*]

MOTHER. What is going on in the street, Brackenburg? I hear soldiers marching.

BRACKENBURG. It is the Regent's body-guard.

CLARA. At this hour? What can it mean? [*She rises and joins* BRACKEN-BURG *at the window.*] That is not the daily guard; it is more numerous! almost all the troops! Oh, Brackenburg, do go! Learn what it means. It must be something unusual. Go, good Bracken-burg, do me this favour.

BRACKENBURG. I am going! I will return immediately.

> [*He offers his hand to* CLARA,
> *and she gives him hers. Exit*
> BRACKENBURG.]

MOTHER. Do you send him away so soon!

CLARA. I long to know what is going on; and, besides,—do not be angry, mother,—his presence pains me. I never know how I ought to behave towards him. I have done him a wrong, and it goes to my very heart, to see how deeply he feels it. Well,—it can't be helped now!

MOTHER. He is such a true-hearted fellow!

CLARA. I cannot help it, I must treat him kindly. Often, without a thought, I return the gentle loving pressure of his hand. I reproach myself that I am de-ceiving him, that I am nourishing in his heart a vain hope. I am in a sad plight. God knows, I do not willingly deceive him. I do not wish him to hope, yet I cannot let him despair!

MOTHER. That is not as it should be.

CLARA. I liked him once, and in my soul I like him still. I could have mar-ried him; yet I believe I was never really in love with him.

MOTHER. You would have been always happy with him.

CLARA. I should have been provided for, and have led a quiet life.

MOTHER. And it has all been trifled away through your own folly.

CLARA. I am in a strange position. When I think how it has come to pass, I know it, indeed, and I know it not. But I have only to look upon Egmont, and I understand it all; ay, and stranger things would seem natural then. Oh, what a man he is. All the provinces worship him. And in his arms, shall I not be the happiest creature in the world?

MOTHER. And how will it be in the future?

CLARA. I only ask, does he love me?—does he love me?—as if there were any doubt about it.

MOTHER. One has nothing but anxiety of heart with one's children. Always care and sorrow, whatever may be the end of it! It cannot come to good! Alas, you have made yourself wretched! You have made your mother wretched too.

CLARA [*quietly*]. Yet, you allowed it in the beginning.

MOTHER. Alas, I was too indulgent, I am always too indulgent.

CLARA. When Egmont rode by, and I ran to the window, did you chide me then? Did you not come to the window yourself? When he looked up, smiled, nodded, and greeted me; was it displeasing to you? Did you not feel honoured in your daughter?

MOTHER. Go on with your reproaches.

CLARA [*with emotion*]. Then, when he passed more frequently, and we felt sure that it was on my account that he came this way, did you not remark it, yourself, with secret joy? Did you call me away, when I stood at the closed window waiting for him?

MOTHER. Could I imagine that it would go so far?

CLARA [*with faltering voice, and repressed tears*]. And then, one evening, when, enveloped in his mantle, he surprised us as we sat at our lamp, who busied herself in receiving him, while I remained, lost in astonishment, as if fastened to my chair?

MOTHER. Could I imagine that the prudent Clara would so soon be carried away by this unhappy love? I must now endure that my daughter——

CLARA [*bursting into tears*]. Mother! How can you? You take pleasure in tormenting me.

MOTHER [*weeping*]. Ay, weep away! Make me yet more wretched by your grief. Is it not misery enough that my only daughter is a cast-away?

CLARA [*rising, and speaking coldly*]. A cast-away! The beloved of Egmont, a cast-away?—What princess but would envy the poor Clara her place in his heart? Oh, mother,—my own mother, you were not wont to speak thus! Dear mother, be kind!—Let the people think, let the neighbours whisper what they like,—this chamber, this lowly house is a paradise, since Egmont's love dwelt here.

MOTHER. One cannot help liking him! that is true. He is always so kind, frank, and open-hearted.

CLARA. There is not a drop of false blood in his veins. And then, mother, he is indeed the great Egmont; yet, when he comes to me, how tender he is, how kind! How he tries to conceal from me his rank, his bravery! How anxious he is about

me! so entirely the man, the friend, the lover.

MOTHER. Do you expect him to-day?

CLARA. Have you not noticed how often I go to the window? How I listen to every noise at the door? Though I know that he will not come before night, yet, from the time when I rise in the morning, I keep expecting him every moment. Were I but a boy, to follow him always, to the court and everywhere! Could I but carry his colours in the field!

MOTHER. You were always such a lively, restless creature; even as a little child, now wild, now thoughtful. Will you not dress yourself a little better?

CLARA. Perhaps I may, if I want something to do.—Yesterday, some of his people went by, singing songs in his honour. At least his name was in the songs! I could not understand the rest. My heart leaped up into my throat,—I would fain have called them back if I had not felt ashamed.

MOTHER. Take care! Your impetuous nature will ruin all. You will betray yourself before the people; as, not long ago, at your cousin's, when you found the wood-cut with the description, and exclaimed, with a cry: "Count Egmont!"— I grew as red as fire.

CLARA. Could I help crying out? It was the battle of Gravelines, and I found in the picture, the letter C, and then looked for it in the description below. There it stood, "Count Egmont, with his horse shot under him." I shuddered, and afterwards I could not help laughing at the wood-cut figure of Egmont, as tall as the neighbouring tower of Gravelines, and the English ships at the side.—When I remember how I used to conceive of a battle, and what an idea I had, as a girl, of Count Egmont, when I listened to descriptions of him, and of all the other earls and princes;—and think how it is with me now!

[*Enter* BRACKENBURG.]

CLARA. Well, what is going on?

BRACKENBURG. Nothing certain is

known. It is rumoured that an insurrection has lately broken out in Flanders; the Regent is afraid of its spreading here. The castle is strongly garrisoned, the citizens are crowding to the gates, and the streets are thronged with people. I will hasten at once to my old father.

[*As if about to go.*]

CLARA. Shall we see you to-morrow? I must change my dress a little. I am expecting my cousin, and I look too untidy. Come, mother, help me a moment. Take the book, Brackenburg, and bring me such another story.

MOTHER. Farewell.

BRACKENBURG [*extending his hand*]. Your hand!

CLARA [*refusing hers*]. When you come next. [*Exeunt* MOTHER *and* DAUGHTER.]

BRACKENBURG [*alone*]. I had resolved to go away again at once, and yet, when she takes me at my word, and lets me leave her, I feel as if I could go mad.— Wretched man! Does the fate of thy fatherland, does the growing disturbance fail to move thee?—Are countryman and Spaniard the same to thee? and carest thou not who rules, and who is in the right?—I was a different sort of fellow as a schoolboy!—Then, when an exercise in oratory was given; "Brutus' speech for liberty," for instance, Fritz was ever the first, and the rector would say: "If it were only spoken more deliberately, the words not all huddled together."—Then my blood boiled, and I longed for action; —Now I drag along, bound by the eyes of a maiden. I cannot leave her! yet she, alas, cannot love me!—ah—no—she—she cannot have entirely rejected me—not entirely—yet half love is no love!—I will endure it no longer!—Can it be true, what a friend lately whispered in my ear, that she secretly admits a man into the house by night, when she always sends me away modestly before evening? No, it cannot be true! It is a lie! A base, slanderous, lie! Clara is as innocent as I am wretched.—She has rejected me, has thrust me from her heart—and shall I live on thus? I cannot, I will not endure

it. Already my native land is convulsed by internal strife, and do I perish abjectly amid the tumult? I will not endure it! When the trumpet sounds, when a shot falls, it thrills through my bone and marrow! But, alas, it does not rouse me! It does not summon me to join the onslaught, to rescue, to dare.—Wretched, degrading position! Better end it at once! Not long ago, I threw myself into the water; I sank—but nature in her agony was too strong for me; I felt that I could swim, and saved myself against my will. Could I but forget the time when she loved me, seemed to love me!— Why has this happiness penetrated my very bone and marrow? Why have these hopes, while disclosing to me a distant paradise, consumed all the enjoyment of life?—and that first, that only kiss!— Here [*Laying his hand upon the table.*], here we were alone,—she had always been kind and friendly towards me,—then she seemed to soften,—she looked at me,—my brain reeled,—I felt her lips on mine,— and—and now?—Die, wretch! Why dost thou hesitate? [*He draws a phial from his pocket.*] Thou healing poison, it shall not have been in vain that I stole thee from my brother's medicine chest! From this anxious fear, this dizziness, this death-agony, thou shalt deliver me at once.

ACT II

Square in Brussels.

[JETTER *and a* MASTER CARPENTER *meeting.*]

CARPENTER. Did I not tell you beforehand? Eight days ago, at the guild, I said there would be serious disturbances.

JETTER. Is it then true that they have plundered the churches in Flanders?

CARPENTER. They have utterly destroyed both churches and chapels. They have left nothing standing but the four bare walls. The lowest rabble! And this it is that damages our good cause. We ought rather to have laid our claims before the Regent, formally and decidedly, and then have stood by them. If we now speak, if we now assemble, it will be said that we are joining the rebels.

JETTER. Ay, so every one thinks at first. Why should you thrust your nose into the mess? The neck is closely connected with it.

CARPENTER. I am always uneasy when tumults arise among the mob, among people who have nothing to lose. They use as a pretext that to which we also must appeal, and plunge the country in misery.

[*Enter* SOEST.]

SOEST. Good day, sirs! What news? Is it true that the insurgents are coming straight in this direction?

CARPENTER. Here they shall touch nothing, at any rate.

SOEST. A soldier came into my shop just now to buy tobacco; I questioned him about the matter The Regent, though so brave and prudent a lady, has for once lost her presence of mind. Things must be bad indeed when she thus takes refuge behind her guards. The castle is strongly garrisoned. It is even rumoured that she means to fly from the town.

CARPENTER. Forth she shall not go! Her presence protects us, and we will ensure her safety better than her mustachioed gentry. If she only maintains our rights and privileges, we will stand faithfully by her.

[*Enter a* SOAPBOILER.]

SOAPBOILER. An ugly business this! a bad business! Troubles are beginning; all things are going wrong! Mind you keep quiet, or they'll take you also for rioters.

SOEST. Here come the seven wise men of Greece.

SOAPBOILER. I know there are many who in secret hold with the Calvinists, abuse the bishops, and care not for the king. But a loyal subject, a sincere Catholic!——

[*By degrees others join the speakers and listen.*]

[*Enter* VANSEN.]

VANSEN. God save you, sirs! What news?

CARPENTER. Have nothing to do with him, he's a dangerous fellow.

JETTER. Is he not secretary to Dr. Wiets?

CARPENTER. He has already had several masters. First he was a clerk, and as one patron after another turned him off, on account of his roguish tricks, he now dabbles in the business of notary and advocate, and is a brandy-drinker to boot.

[*More people gather round and stand in groups.*]

VANSEN. So here you are, putting your heads together. Well, it is worth talking about.

SOEST. I think so too.

VANSEN. Now if only one of you had heart and another head enough for the work, we might break the Spanish fetters at once.

SOEST. Sirs! you must not talk thus. We have taken our oath to the king.

VANSEN. And the king to us. Mark that!

JETTER. There's sense in that! Tell us your opinion.

OTHERS. Hearken to him; he's a clever fellow. He's sharp enough.

VANSEN. I had an old master once, who possessed a collection of parchments, among which were charters of ancient constitutions, contracts, and privileges. He set great store, too, by the rarest books. One of these contained our whole constitution; how, at first, we Netherlanders had princes of our own, who governed according to hereditary laws, rights, and usages; how our ancestors paid due honour to their sovereign so long as he governed them equitably; and how they were immediately on their guard the moment he was for overstepping his bounds. The states were down upon him at once; for every province, however small, had its own chamber and representatives.

CARPENTER. Hold your tongue! We knew that long ago! Every honest citizen learns as much about the constitution as he needs.

JETTER. Let him speak; one may always learn something.

SOEST. He is quite right.

SEVERAL CITIZENS. Go on! Go on! One does not hear this every day.

VANSEN. You citizens, forsooth! You live only in the present; and as you tamely follow the trade inherited from your fathers, so you let the government do with you just as it pleases. You make no inquiry into the origin, the history, or the rights of a Regent; and in consequence of this negligence, the Spaniard has drawn the net over your ears.

SOEST. Who cares for that, if one has only daily bread? ♦

JETTER. The devil! Why did not some one come forward and tell us this in time?

VANSEN. I tell it you now. The King of Spain, whose good fortune it is to bear sway over these provinces, has no right to govern them otherwise than the petty princes who formerly possessed them separately. Do you understand that?

JETTER. Explain it to us.

VANSEN. Why, it is as clear as the sun. Must you not be governed according to your provincial laws? How comes that?

A CITIZEN. Certainly!

VANSEN. Are not the laws of Brussels different from those of Antwerp? The laws of Antwerp different from those of Ghent? How comes that?

ANOTHER CITIZEN. By heaven!

VANSEN. But if you let matters run on thus, they will soon tell you a different story. Fye on you! Philip, through a woman, now ventures to do what neither Charles the Bold, Frederick the Warrior, nor Charles the Fifth could accomplish.

SOEST. Yes, yes! The old princes tried it also.

VANSEN. Ay! But our ancestors kept a sharp look-out. If they thought themselves aggrieved by their sovereign, they would perhaps get his son and heir into their hands, detain him as a hostage, and surrender him only on the most favourable conditions. Our fathers were men! They knew their own interests! They knew how to lay hold on what they wanted, and to get it established! They were men of the right sort; and hence it is that our privileges are so clearly defined, our liberties so well secured.

SOEST. What are you saying about our liberties?

ALL. Our liberties! our privileges! Tell us about our privileges.

VANSEN. All the provinces have their peculiar advantages, but we of Brabant are the most splendidly provided for. I have read it all.

SOEST. Say on.

JETTER. Let us hear.

A CITIZEN. Pray do.

VANSEN. First, it stands written:— The Duke of Brabant shall be to us a good and faithful sovereign.

SOEST. Good! Stands it so?

JETTER. Faithful? Is that true?

VANSEN. As I tell you. He is bound to us as we are to him. Secondly;—in the exercise of his authority he shall neither exert arbitrary power, nor exhibit caprice, himself, nor shall he, either directly or indirectly, sanction them in others.

JETTER. Bravo! Bravo! Not exert arbitrary power.

SOEST. Not exhibit caprice.

ANOTHER. And not sanction them in others! That is the main point. Not sanction them, either directly or indirectly.

VANSEN. In express words.

JETTER. Get us the book.

A CITIZEN. Yes, we must have it.

OTHERS. The book! The book!

ANOTHER. We will to the Regent with the book.

ANOTHER. Sir doctor, you shall be spokesman.

SOAPBOILER. Oh, the dolts!

OTHERS. Something more out of the book!

SOAPBOILER. I'll knock his teeth down his throat if he says another word.

PEOPLE. We'll see who dares to lay hands upon him. Tell us about our privileges! Have we any more privileges?

VANSEN. Many, very good and very wholesome ones too. Thus it stands: The sovereign shall neither benefit the clergy, nor increase their number, without the consent of the nobles and of the states. Mark that! Nor shall he alter the constitution of the country.

SOEST. Stands it so?

VANSEN. I'll show it you, as it was written down two or three centuries ago.

A CITIZEN. And we tolerate the new bishops? The nobles must protect us, we will make a row else!

OTHERS. And we suffer ourselves to be intimidated by the Inquisition?

VANSEN. It is your own fault.

PEOPLE. We have Egmont! We have Orange! They will protect our interests.

VANSEN. Your brothers in Flanders are beginning the good work.

SOAPBOILER. Dog! [*Strikes him.*]

OTHERS [*oppose the* SOAPBOILER *and exclaim*]. Are you also a Spaniard?

ANOTHER. What! This honourable man?

ANOTHER. This learned man?

[*They attack the* SOAPBOILER.]

CARPENTER. For heaven's sake, peace!

[*Others mingle in the fray.*]

CARPENTER. Citizens, what means this?

[*Boys whistle, throw stones, set on dogs; citizens stand and and gape, people come running up, others walk quietly to and fro, others play all sorts of pranks, shout and huzza.*]

OTHERS. Freedom and privilege! Privilege and freedom!

[*Enter* EGMONT, *with followers.*]

EGMONT. Peace! Peace! good people. What is the matter? Peace, I say! Separate them.

CARPENTER. My good lord, you come like an angel from heaven. Hush! See you nothing? Count Egmont! Greet Count Egmont.

EGMONT. Here, too! What are you about? Citizen against citizen! Does not even the neighbourhood of our royal mistress oppose a barrier to this frenzy? Disperse yourselves, and go about your business. 'Tis a bad sign when you thus keep holiday on working days. How did the disturbance begin.

[*The tumult gradually subsides, and the people gather around* EGMONT.]

CARPENTER. They are fighting about their privileges.

EGMONT. Which they will forfeit through their own folly—and who are you? You seem honest people.

CARPENTER. 'Tis our wish to be so.

EGMONT. Your calling?

CARPENTER. A carpenter, and master of the guild.

EGMONT. And you?

SOEST. A shopkeeper.

EGMONT. And you?

JETTER. A tailor.

EGMONT. I remember, you were employed upon the liveries of my people. Your name is Jetter.

JETTER. To think of your grace remembering it!

EGMONT. I do not easily forget any one whom I have seen or conversed with. Do what you can, good people, to keep the peace; you stand in bad repute enough already. Provoke not the king still farther. The power, after all, is in his hands. An honest citizen, who maintains himself industriously, has everywhere as much freedom as he wants.

CARPENTER. That now is just our misfortune! With all due deference, your grace, 'tis the idle portion of the community, your drunkards and vagabonds, who quarrel for want of something to do, and clamour about privilege because they are hungry; they impose upon the curious and the credulous, and in order to obtain a pot of beer, excite disturbances that will bring misery upon thousands. That is just what they want. We keep our houses and chests too well guarded; they would fain drive us away from them with firebrands.

EGMONT. You shall have all needful assistance; measures have been taken to stem the evil by force. Make a firm stand against the new doctrines, and do not imagine that privileges are secured by sedition. Remain at home, suffer no crowds to assemble in the streets. Sensible people can accomplish much.

[*In the meantime the crowd has for the most part dispersed.*]

CARPENTER. Thanks, your excellency—thanks for your good opinion. We will do what in us lies. [*Exit* EGMONT.] A gracious lord! A true Netherlander! Nothing of the Spaniard about him.

JETTER. If we had only him for a regent! 'Tis a pleasure to follow him.

SOEST. The king won't hear of that. He takes care to appoint his own people to the place.

JETTER. Did you notice his dress? It was of the newest fashion—after the Spanish cut.

CARPENTER. A handsome gentleman.

JETTER. His head now were a dainty morsel for a headsman.

SOEST. Are you mad? What are you thinking about?

JETTER. It is stupid enough that such an idea should come into one's head! But so it is. Whenever I see a fine long neck, I cannot help thinking how well it would suit the block. These cursed executions! One cannot get them out of one's head. When the lads are swimming, and I chance to see a naked back, I think forthwith of the dozens I have seen beaten with rods. If I meet a portly gentleman, I fancy I already see him roasting at the stake. At night, in my dreams, I am tortured in every limb; one cannot have a single hour's enjoyment; all merriment and fun have long been forgotten. These terrible images seem burnt in upon my brain.

EGMONT'S *residence.*
[*His* SECRETARY *at a desk with papers. He rises impatiently.*]

SECRETARY. Still he comes not! And I have been waiting already full two hours, pen in hand, the papers before me; and just to-day I was anxious to be out so early. The floor burns under my feet. I can with difficulty restrain my impatience. "Be punctual to the hour." Such was his parting injunction; now he comes not. There is so much business to get through, I shall not have finished before midnight. He overlooks one's faults, it is true; methinks it would be better though, were he more strict, so he dismissed one at the appointed time. One could then arrange one's plans. It is now full two hours since he left the Regent; who knows whom he may have chanced to meet by the way?

[*Enter* EGMONT.]

EGMONT. Well, how do matters look?

SECRETARY. I am ready, and three couriers are waiting.

EGMONT. I have detained you too long; you look somewhat out of humour.

SECRETARY. In obedience to your command I have already been in attendance for some time. Here are the papers!

EGMONT. Donna Elvira will be angry with me, when she learns that I have detained you.

SECRETARY. You are pleased to jest.

EGMONT. Nay, be not ashamed. I admire your taste. She is pretty, and I have no objection that you should have a friend at court. What say the letters?

SECRETARY. Much, my lord, but withal little that is satisfactory.

EGMONT. 'Tis well that we have pleasures at home, we have the less occasion to seek them from abroad. Is there much that requires attention?

SECRETARY. Enough, my lord; three couriers are in attendance.

EGMONT. Proceed! The most important.

SECRETARY. All is important.

EGMONT. One after the other; only be prompt.

SECRETARY. Captain Breda sends an account of the occurrences that have further taken place in Ghent and the surrounding districts. The tumult is for the most part allayed.

EGMONT. He doubtless reports individual acts of folly and temerity?

SECRETARY. He does, my lord.

EGMONT. Spare me the recital.

SECRETARY. Six of the mob who tore down the image of the Virgin at Verviers, have been arrested. He inquires whether they are to be hanged like the others?

EGMONT. I am weary of hanging; let them be flogged and discharged.

SECRETARY. There are two women among them; are they to be flogged also?

EGMONT. He may admonish them and let them go.

SECRETARY. Brink, of Breda's company, wants to marry; the captain hopes you will not allow it. There are so many women among the troops, he writes, that when on the march, they resemble a gang of gipsies rather than regular soldiers.

EGMONT. We must overlook it in his case. He is a fine young fellow, and moreover entreated me so earnestly before I came away. This must be the last time, however; though it grieves me to refuse the poor fellows their best pastime; they have enough without that to torment them.

SECRETARY. Two of your people, Seter and Hart, have ill-treated a damsel, the daughter of an inn-keeper. They got her alone and she could not escape from them.

EGMONT. If she be an honest maiden and they used violence, let them be flogged three days in succession; and if they have any property, let him retain as much of it as will portion the girl.

SECRETARY. One of the foreign preachers has been discovered passing secretly through Comines. He swore that he was on the point of leaving for France. According to law, he ought to be beheaded.

EGMONT. Let him be conducted quietly to the frontier, and there admonished, that, the next time, he will not escape so easily.

SECRETARY. A letter from your steward. He writes that money comes in slowly, he can with difficulty send you the required sum within the week; the late disturbances have thrown everything into the greatest confusion.

EGMONT. Money must be had! It is for him to look to the means.

SECRETARY. He says he will do his utmost, and at length proposes to sue and imprison Raymond, who has been so long in your debt.

EGMONT. But he has promised to pay!

SECRETARY. The last time he fixed a fortnight himself.

EGMONT. Well, grant him another fortnight; after that he may proceed against him.

SECRETARY. You do well. His non-payment of the money proceeds not from inability, but from want of inclination. He will trifle no longer when he sees that you are in earnest. The steward further proposes to withhold, for half a month, the pensions which you allow to the old soldiers, widows, and others. In the meantime some expedient may be devised; they must make their arrangements accordingly.

EGMONT. But what arrangements can be made here? These poor people want the money more than I do. He must not think of it.

SECRETARY. How then, my lord, is he to raise the required sum?

EGMONT. It is his business to think of that. He was told so in a former letter.

SECRETARY. And therefore he makes these proposals.

EGMONT. They will never do;—he must think of something else. Let him suggest expedients that are admissible, and, before all, let him procure the money.

SECRETARY. I have again before me the letter from Count Oliva. Pardon my recalling it to your remembrance. Before all others, the aged count deserves a detailed reply. You proposed writing to him with your own hand. Doubtless, he loves you as a father.

EGMONT. I cannot command the time; —and of all detestable things, writing is to me the most detestable. You imitate my hand so admirably, do you write in my name. I am expecting Orange. I cannot do it;—I wish, however, that something soothing should be written, to allay his fears.

SECRETARY. Just give me a notion of what you wish to communicate; I will at once draw up the answer, and lay it before you. It shall be so written that it might pass for your hand in a court of justice.

EGMONT. Give me the letter. [*After glancing over it.*] Dear, excellent, old man! Wert thou then so cautious in thy youth? Did'st thou never mount a breach? Did'st thou remain in the rear of battle at the suggestion of prudence?— What affectionate solicitude! He has indeed my safety and happiness at heart, but considers not, that he who lives but to save his life, is already dead.—Charge him not to be anxious on my account; I act as circumstances require, and shall be upon my guard. Let him use his influence at court in my favour, and be assured of my warmest thanks.

SECRETARY. Is that all? He expects still more.

EGMONT. What more can I say? If you choose to write more fully, do so. The matter turns upon a single point; he would have me live as I cannot live. That I am joyous, live fast, take matters easily, is my good fortune; nor would I exchange it for his tomb-like safety. My blood rebels against the Spanish mode of life, nor have I the least inclination to regulate my movements by the new and cautious measures of the court. Do I live only to think of life? Am I to forego the enjoyment of the present moment in order to secure the next? And must that in its turn be consumed in anxieties and idle fears?

SECRETARY. I entreat you, my lord, be not so harsh towards the venerable man. You are wont to be friendly towards every one. Say a kindly word to allay the anxiety of your noble friend. See how considerate he is, with what delicacy he warns you.

EGMONT. Yet he harps continually on the same string. He knows of old how I detest these admonitions. They serve only to perplex and are of no avail. What if I were a somnambulist, and trod the giddy summit of a lofty house,—were it the part of friendship to call me by my name, to warn me of my danger, to waken, to kill me? Let each choose his own path, and provide for his own safety.

SECRETARY. It may become you, my lord, to be without a fear, but those who know and love you——

EGMONT [*looking over the letter*]. Then he recalls the old story of our sayings and doings, one evening, in the wantonness of conviviality and wine; and what conclusions and inferences were thence drawn and circulated throughout the whole kingdom! Well, we had a cap and bells embroidered on the sleeves of our servants' liveries, and afterwards exchanged this senseless device for a bundle of arrows;— a still more dangerous symbol for those who are bent upon discovering a meaning where nothing is meant. These and similar follies were conceived and brought forth in a moment of merriment. It was at our suggestion, that a noble troop, with beggars' wallets, and a self-chosen nickname, with mock humility recalled the king's duty to his remembrance. It was at our suggestion too—well what does it signify? Is a carnival jest to be construed into high treason? Are we to be grudged the scanty, variegated rags, wherewith a youthful spirit and heated imagination would adorn the poor nakedness of life? Take life too seriously, and what is it worth? If the morning wake us to no new joys, if in the evening we have no pleasures to hope for, is it worth the trouble of dressing and undressing? Does the sun shine on me to-day, that I may reflect on what happened yesterday? That I may endeavour to foresee and control, what can neither be foreseen nor controlled,—the destiny of the morrow? Spare me these reflections; we will leave them to scholars and courtiers. Let them ponder and contrive, creep hither and thither, and surreptitiously achieve their ends.—If you can make use of these suggestions, without swelling your letter into a volume, it is well. Everything appears of exaggerated importance to the good old man. 'Tis thus the friend, who has long held our hand, grasps it more warmly ere he quits his hold.

SECRETARY. Pardon me, the pedestrian grows dizzy when he beholds the charioteer drive past with whirling speed.

EGMONT. Child! Child! Forbear! As if goaded by invisible spirits, the sun-steeds of time bear onward the light car of our destiny; and nothing remains for us but, with calm self-possession, firmly to grasp the reins, and now right, now left, to steer the wheels, here from the precipice and there from the rock. Whither he is hasting, who knows? Does any one consider whence he came?

SECRETARY. My lord! my lord!

EGMONT. I stand high, but I can and must rise yet higher. Courage, strength, and hope possess my soul. Not yet have I attained the height of my ambition; that once achieved, I will stand firmly and without fear. Should I fall, should a thunder-clap, a storm-blast, ay, a false step of my own, precipitate me into the abyss, so be it! I shall lie there with thousands of others. I have never disdained, even for a trifling stake, to throw the bloody die with my gallant comrades; and shall I hesitate now, when all that is most precious in life is set upon the cast?

SECRETARY. Oh, my lord! you know not what you say! May heaven protect you!

EGMONT. Collect your papers. Orange is coming. Dispatch what is most urgent, that the couriers may set forth before the gates are closed. The rest may wait. Leave the Count's letter till to-morrow. Fail not to visit Elvira, and greet her from me. Inform yourself concerning the Regent's health. She cannot be well, though she would fain conceal it.

[*Exit* SECRETARY.]

[*Enter* ORANGE.]

EGMONT. Welcome, Orange; you appear somewhat disturbed.

ORANGE. What say you to our conference with the Regent?

EGMONT. I found nothing extraordinary in her manner of receiving us. I have often seen her thus before. She appeared to me to be somewhat indisposed.

ORANGE. Marked you not that she was more reserved than usual? She began by cautiously approving our conduct during the late insurrection; glanced at the false light in which, nevertheless, it might be viewed; and finally turned the discourse to her favourite topic—that her gracious demeanour, her friendship for us Netherlanders, had never been sufficiently recognized, never appreciated as it deserved; that nothing came to a prosperous issue; that for her part she was beginning to grow weary of it; that the king must at last resolve upon other measures. Did you hear that?

EGMONT. Not all; I was thinking at the time of something else. She is a woman, good Orange, and all women expect that every one shall submit passively to their gentle yoke; that every Hercules shall lay aside his lion's skin, assume the distaff, and swell their train; and, because they are themselves peaceably inclined, imagine, forsooth, that the ferment which seizes a nation, the storm which powerful rivals excite against one another, may be allayed by one soothing word, and the most discordant elements be brought to unite in tranquil harmony at their feet. 'Tis thus with her; and since she cannot accomplish her object, why she has no resource left but to lose her temper, to menace us with direful prospects for the future, and to threaten to take her departure.

ORANGE. Think you not that this time she will fulfil her threat?

EGMONT. Never! How often have I seen her actually prepared for the journey! Whither should she go? Being here a stadtholder, a queen, think you that she could endure to spend her days in insignificance at her brother's court? Or to repair to Italy, and there drag on her existence among her old family connexions.

ORANGE. She is held incapable of this determination, because you have already seen her hesitate and draw back; nevertheless, it is in her to take this step; new circumstances may impel her to the long delayed resolve. What if she were to depart, and the king to send another?

EGMONT. Why he would come, and he also would have business enough upon his hands. He would arrive with vast projects and schemes, to reduce all things to order, to subjugate, and combine; and to-day he would be occupied with this trifle, to-morrow with that, and the day following have to deal with some unexpected hindrance. He would spend one month in forming plans, another in mortification at their failure, and half a year would be consumed in cares for a single province. With him also time would pass, his head grow dizzy, and things hold on their ordinary course, till instead of sailing into the open sea, according to the plan which he had previously marked out, he might thank God, if, amid the tempest, he were able to keep his vessel off the rocks.

ORANGE. What if the king were advised to try an experiment?

EGMONT. Which should be——?

ORANGE. To try how the body would get on without the head.

EGMONT. How?

ORANGE. Egmont, our interests have for years weighed upon my heart; I ever stand as over a chess-board, and regard no move of my adversary as insignificant; and as men of science carefully investigate the secrets of nature, so I hold it to be the duty, ay, the very vocation of a prince, to acquaint himself with the dispositions and intentions of all parties. I have reason to fear an outbreak. The king has long acted according to certain principles; he finds that they do not lead to a prosperous issue; what more probable than that he should seek it some other way?

EGMONT. I do not believe it. When a man grows old, has attempted much, and finds that the world cannot be made to move according to his will, he must needs grow weary of it at last.

ORANGE. One thing he has not yet attempted.

EGMONT. What?

ORANGE. To spare the people, and put an end to the princes.

EGMONT. How many have long been haunted by this dread! There is no cause for such anxiety.

ORANGE. Once I felt anxious; gradually I became suspicious; suspicion has at length grown into certainty.

EGMONT. Has the king more faithful servants than ourselves?

ORANGE. We serve him after our own fashion; and between ourselves, it must be confessed, that we understand pretty well how to make the interests of the king square with our own.

EGMONT. And who does not? He has our duty and submission, in so far as they are his due.

ORANGE. But what if he should arrogate still more, and regard as disloyalty what we esteem the maintenance of our just rights?

EGMONT. We shall know in that case how to defend ourselves. Let him assemble the knights of the Golden Fleece; we will submit ourselves to their decision.

ORANGE. What if the sentence were to precede the trial? punishment, the sentence?

EGMONT. It were an injustice of which Philip is incapable; a folly, which I cannot impute either to him or his counsellors.

ORANGE. And how if they were both foolish and unjust?

EGMONT. No, Orange, it is impossible. Who would venture to lay hands on us? The attempt to capture us were a fruitless enterprise. No, they dare not raise the standard of tyranny so high. The breeze that should waft these tidings over the land would kindle a mighty conflagration. And what object would they have in view? The king alone has no power either to judge or to condemn us; and would they attempt our lives by assassination? They cannot intend it. A terrible league would unite the entire people. Direful hate, and eternal separation from the crown of Spain would, on the instant, be forcibly declared.

ORANGE. The flames would then rage over our grave, and the blood of our enemies flow, a vain oblation. Let us consider, Egmont.

EGMONT. But how could they effect this purpose?

ORANGE. Alva is on the way.

EGMONT. I do not believe it.

ORANGE. I know it.

EGMONT. The Regent appeared to know nothing of it.

ORANGE. And, therefore, the stronger is my conviction. The Regent will give place to him. I know his blood-thirsty disposition, and he brings an army with him.

EGMONT. To harass the provinces anew? The people will be exasperated to the last degree.

ORANGE. Their leaders will be secured.

EGMONT. No! No!

ORANGE. Let us retire, each to his province. There we can strengthen ourselves; the duke will not begin with open violence.

EGMONT. Must we not greet him when he comes?

ORANGE. We will delay.

EGMONT. What if, on his arrival, he should summon us in the king's name?

ORANGE. We will answer evasively.

EGMONT. And if he is urgent?

ORANGE. We will excuse ourselves.

EGMONT. And if he insist?

ORANGE. We shall be the less disposed to come.

EGMONT. Then war is declared; and we are rebels. Do not suffer prudence to mislead you, Orange. I know it is not fear that makes you yield. Consider this step.

ORANGE. I have considered it.

EGMONT. Consider for what you are answerable if you are wrong. For the most fatal war that ever yet desolated a country. Your refusal is the signal that at once summons the provinces to arms, that justifies every cruelty for which Spain has hitherto so anxiously sought a pretext. With a single nod, you will excite to the direst confusion what, with patient effort, we have so long kept in abeyance. Think of the towns, the nobles, the people; think of commerce, agriculture, trade! Realize the murder, the desolation! Calmly the soldier beholds his comrade fall beside him in the battlefield. But towards you, carried downwards by the stream, shall float the corpses of citizens, of children, of maidens, till, aghast with horror, you shall no longer know whose cause you are defending, since you shall see those, for whose liberty you drew the sword, perishing around you. And what will be your emotions when conscience whispers, "It was for my own safety that I drew it."

ORANGE. We are not ordinary men, Egmont. If it becomes us to sacrifice ourselves for thousands, it becomes us no less to spare ourselves for thousands.

EGMONT. He who spares himself becomes an object of suspicion even to himself.

ORANGE. He who is sure of his own motives can, with confidence, advance or retreat.

EGMONT. Your own act will render certain the evil that you dread.

ORANGE. Wisdom and courage alike prompt us to meet an inevitable evil.

EGMONT. When the danger is imminent the faintest hope should be taken into account.

ORANGE. We have not the smallest footing left; we are on the very brink of the precipice.

EGMONT. Is the king's favour ground so narrow?

ORANGE. Not narrow, perhaps, but slippery.

EGMONT. By heavens! he is belied. I cannot endure that he should be so meanly thought of! He is Charles's son and incapable of meanness.

ORANGE. Kings of course do nothing mean.

EGMONT. He should be better known.

ORANGE. Our knowledge counsels us not to await the result of a dangerous experiment.

EGMONT. No experiment is dangerous, the result of which we have the courage to meet.

ORANGE. You are irritated, Egmont.

EGMONT. I must see with my own eyes.

ORANGE. Oh that for once you saw with mine! My friend, because your eyes are open, you imagine that you see. I go! Await Alva's arrival, and God be with you! My refusal to do so may perhaps save you. The dragon may deem the prey not worth seizing, if he cannot swallow us both. Perhaps he may delay, in order more surely to execute his purpose; in the meantime you may see matters in their true light. But then, be prompt! Lose not a moment! Save,—oh, save yourself! Farewell!—Let nothing escape your vigilance:—how many troops he brings with him; how he garrisons the town; what force the Regent retains; how your friends are prepared. Send me tidings— Egmont.

EGMONT. What would you?

ORANGE [grasping his hand]. Be persuaded! Go with me!

EGMONT. How! Tears, Orange!

ORANGE. To weep for a lost friend is not unmanly.

EGMONT. You deem me lost?

ORANGE. You are lost. Consider! Only a brief respite is left you. Farewell.
[Exit.]

EGMONT [alone]. Strange that the thoughts of other men should exert such an influence over us. These fears would never have entered my mind; and this man infects me with his solicitude. Away! 'Tis a foreign drop in my blood! Kind nature, cast it forth! And to erase the furrowed lines from my brow there yet remains indeed a friendly means.

ACT III

Palace of the REGENT.

[MARGARET OF PARMA.]

REGENT. I might have expected it. Ha! when we live immersed in anxiety and toil, we imagine that we achieve the utmost that is possible; while he, who, from a distance, looks on and commands, believes that he requires only the possible. O ye kings! I had not thought it could have galled me thus. It is so sweet to reign!—and to abdicate? I know not how my father could do so; but I will also.

[MECHIAVEL *appears in the back-ground.*]

REGENT. Approach, Mechiavel. I am thinking over this letter from my brother.

MECHIAVEL. May I know what it contains?

REGENT. As much tender consideration for me, as anxiety for his states. He extols the firmness, the industry, the fidelity, with which I have hitherto watched over the interests of his majesty in these provinces. He condoles with me that the unbridled people occasion me so much trouble. He is so thoroughly convinced of the depth of my views, so extraordinarily satisfied with the prudence of my conduct, that I must almost say the letter is too politely written for a king—certainly for a brother.

MECHIAVEL. It is not the first time that he has testified to you his just satisfaction.

REGENT. But the first time that it is a mere rhetorical figure.

MECHIAVEL. I do not understand you.

REGENT. You soon will.—For after this preamble, he is of opinion, that without soldiers, without a small army indeed,— I shall always cut a sorry figure here! He intimates that we did wrong to withdraw our troops from the provinces at the remonstrance of the inhabitants; and thinks that a garrison which shall press upon the neck of the citizen, will prevent him, by its weight, from making any lofty spring.

MECHIAVEL. It would irritate the public mind to the last degree.

REGENT. The king thinks, however,—attend to this,—he thinks that a clever general, one who never listens to reason, will be able to deal promptly with all parties;—people and nobles, citizens and peasants; he therefore sends, with a powerful army, the duke of Alva.

MECHIAVEL. Alva?

REGENT. You are surprised.

MECHIAVEL. You say, he sends, he asks doubtless whether he should send.

REGENT. The king asks not, he sends.

MECHIAVEL. You will then have an experienced warrior in your service.

REGENT. In my service? Speak out, Mechiavel.

MECHIAVEL. I would not anticipate you.

REGENT. And I would I could dissimulate. It wounds me—wounds me to the quick. I had rather my brother would speak his mind, than attach his signature to formal epistles, drawn up by a secretary of State.

MECHIAVEL. Can they not comprehend——

REGENT. I know them thoroughly. They would fain make a clean sweep; and since they cannot set about it themselves, they give their confidence to any one who comes with a besom in his hand. Oh, it seems to me as if I saw the king and his council worked upon this tapestry.

MECHIAVEL. So distinctly!

REGENT. No feature is wanting. There are good men among them. The honest Roderigo, so experienced and so moderate, who does not aim too high, yet lets nothing sink too low; the upright Alonzo, the diligent Freneda, the steadfast Las Vargas, and others who join them when the good party are in power. But there sits the hollow-eyed Toledan, with brazen front and deep fire-glance, muttering between his teeth about womanish softness, ill-timed concession, and that women can ride trained steeds well enough, but are them-selves bad horse-breakers, and the like pleasantries, which, in former times, I have been compelled to hear from political gentlemen.

MECHIAVEL. You have chosen good colours for your picture.

REGENT. Confess, Mechiavel, among the tints from which I might select, there is no hue so livid, so jaundice-like, as Alva's complexion, and the colour he is wont to paint with. He regards every one as a blasphemer or traitor; for under this head they can be racked, impaled, quartered, and burnt at pleasure. The good I have accomplished here, appears as nothing seen from a distance, just because it is good. Then he dwells on every outbreak that is past, recalls every disturbance that is quieted, and brings before the king such a picture of mutiny, sedition, and audacity, that we appear to him to be actually devouring one another, when with us the transient explosion of a rude people has long been forgotten. Thus he conceives a cordial hatred for the poor people; he views them with horror, as beasts and monsters; looks around for fire and sword, and imagines that by such means human beings are subdued.

MECHIAVEL. You appear to me too vehement; you take the matter too seriously. Do you not remain regent?

REGENT. I am aware of that. He will bring his instructions. I am old enough in state affairs to understand how people can be supplanted, without being actually deprived of office. First, he will produce a commission, couched in terms somewhat obscure and equivocal; he will stretch his authority, for the power is in his hands; if I complain, he will hint at secret instructions; if I desire to see them, he will answer evasively; if I insist, he will produce a paper of totally different import; and if this fail to satisfy me, he will go on precisely as if I had never interfered. Meanwhile he will have accomplished what I dread, and have frustrated my most cherished schemes.

MECHIAVEL. I wish I could contradict you.

REGENT. His harshness and cruelty will again arouse the turbulent spirit, which, with unspeakable patience, I have succeeded in quelling; I shall see my work destroyed before my eyes, and have besides to bear the blame of his wrongdoing.

MECHIAVEL. Await it, your highness.

REGENT. I have sufficient self-command to remain quiet. Let him come; I will make way for him with the best grace ere he pushes me aside.

MECHIAVEL. So important a step thus suddenly?

REGENT. 'Tis harder than you imagine. He who is accustomed to rule, to hold daily in his hand the destiny of thousands, descends from the throne as into the grave. Better thus, however, than linger a spectre among the living, and with hollow aspect endeavour to maintain a place which another has inherited, and already possesses and enjoys.

CLARA'S *dwelling.*
[CLARA *and her* MOTHER.]

MOTHER. Such a love as Brackenburg's I have never seen; I thought it was to be found only in romance books.

CLARA [*walking up and down the room, humming a song*]. With love's thrilling rapture
What joy can compare!

MOTHER. He suspects your attachment to Egmont; and yet, if you would but treat him a little kindly, I do believe he would marry you still, if you would have him.

CLARA [*sings*]. Blissful
And tearful,
With thought-teeming brain;
Hoping
And fearing
In passionate pain;
Now shouting in triumph,
Now sunk in despair;—
With love's thrilling rapture
What joy can compare!

MOTHER. Have done with your baby-nonsense.

CLARA. Nay, do not abuse it; 'tis a song of marvellous virtue. Many a time I have lulled a grown child to sleep with it.

MOTHER. Ay! You can think of nothing but your love. If it only did not put everything else out of your head. You should have more regard for Brackenburg, I tell you. He may make you happy yet some day.

CLARA. He?

MOTHER. Oh, yes! A time will come! You children live only in the present, and give no ear to our experience. Youth and happy love, all has an end; and there comes a time when one thanks God if one has any corner to creep into.

CLARA [*shudders, and after a pause stands up*]. Mother, let that time come—like death. To think of it beforehand is horrible! And if it come! If we must—then—we will bear ourselves as we may. Live without thee, Egmont! [*Weeping.*] No! It is impossible.

[*Enter* EGMONT, *enveloped in a horseman's cloak, his hat drawn over his face.*]

EGMONT. Clara!

CLARA [*utters a cry and starts back*]. Egmont! [*She hastens towards him.*] Egmont! [*She embraces and leans upon him.*] O you good, kind, sweet Egmont! Are you come? Is it you indeed?

EGMONT. Good evening, mother!

MOTHER. God save you, noble sir! My daughter has well nigh pined to death, because you have stayed away so long; she talks and sings about you the live-long day.

EGMONT. You will give me some supper?

MOTHER. You do us too much honour. If we only had anything——

CLARA. Certainly! Be quiet, mother; I have provided everything; there is something prepared. Do not betray me, mother.

MOTHER. There's little enough.

CLARA. Never mind! When he is with me I am never hungry; so he cannot, I should think, have any great appetite when I am with him.

EGMONT. Do you think so?

[CLARA *stamps with her foot and turns pettishly away.*]

EGMONT. What ails you?

CLARA. How cold you are to-day! You have not yet offered me a kiss. Why do you keep your arms enveloped in your mantle, like a new-born babe. It becomes neither a soldier nor a lover to keep his arms muffled up.

EGMONT. Sometimes, dearest, sometimes. When the soldier stands in ambush and would delude the foe, he collects his thoughts, gathers his mantle around him, and matures his plan; and a lover——

MOTHER. Will you not take a seat, and make yourself comfortable? I must to the kitchen, Clara thinks of nothing when you are here. You must put up with what we have.

EGMONT. Your good-will is the best seasoning. [*Exit* MOTHER.]

CLARA. And what then is my love?

EGMONT. Just what you please.

CLARA. Liken it to anything, if you have the heart.

EGMONT. But first. [*He flings aside his mantle, and appears arrayed in a magnificent dress.*]

CLARA. Oh heavens!

EGMONT. Now my arms are free!

[*Embraces her.*]

CLARA. Don't! You will spoil your dress. [*She steps back.*] How magnificent! I dare not touch you.

EGMONT. Are you satisfied? I promised to come once arrayed in Spanish fashion.

CLARA. I had ceased to remind you of it; I thought you did not like it—ah, and the Golden Fleece!

EGMONT. You see it now.

CLARA. And did the emperor really hang it round your neck?

EGMONT. He did, my child! And this chain and Order invest the wearer with the noblest privileges. On earth I acknowledge no judge over my actions, except the grand master of the Order, with the assembled chapter of knights.

CLARA. Oh, you might let the whole world sit in judgment over you. The velvet is too splendid! and the braiding! and the embroidery! One knows not where to begin.

EGMONT. There, look your fill.

CLARA. And the Golden Fleece! You told me its history, how it is the symbol of everything great and precious, of everything that can be merited and won by diligence and toil. It is very precious—I may liken it to your love;—even so I wear it next my heart;—and then——

EGMONT. Well—what then?

CLARA. And then again it is not like.

EGMONT. How so?

CLARA. I have not won it by diligence and toil, I have not deserved it.

EGMONT. It is otherwise in love. You deserve it because you have not sought it—and, for the most part, those only obtain love who seek it not.

CLARA. Is it from your own experience that you have learned this? Did you make that proud remark in reference to yourself? you, whom all the people love?

EGMONT. Would that I had done something for them! That I could do anything for them! It is their own good pleasure to love me.

CLARA. You have doubtless been with the Regent to-day?

EGMONT. I have.

CLARA. Are you upon good terms with her?

EGMONT. So it would appear. We are kind and serviceable to each other.

CLARA. And in your heart?

EGMONT. I like her. True, we have each our own views; but that is nothing to the purpose. She is an excellent woman, knows with whom she has to deal, and would be penetrating enough were she not quite so suspicious. I give her plenty of employment, because she is always suspecting some secret motive in my conduct when, in fact, I have none.

CLARA. Really none?

EGMONT. Well, with one little exception, perhaps. All wine deposits lees in the cask in the course of time. Orange furnishes her still better entertainment, and is a perpetual riddle. He has got the credit of harbouring some secret design; and she studies his brow to discover his thoughts, and his steps, to learn in what direction they are bent.

CLARA. Does she dissemble?

EGMONT. She is regent—and do you ask?

CLARA. Pardon me; I meant to say, is she false?

EGMONT. Neither more nor less than every one who has his own objects to attain.

CLARA. I should never feel at home in the world. But she has a masculine spirit, and is another sort of woman from us housewives and sempstresses. She is great, steadfast, resolute.

EGMONT. Yes, when matters are not too much involved. For once, however, she is a little disconcerted.

CLARA. How so?

EGMONT. She has a moustache, too, on her upper lip, and occasionally an attack of the gout. A regular Amazon.

CLARA. A majestic woman! I should dread to appear before her.

EGMONT. Yet you are not wont to be timid! It would not be fear, only maidenly bashfulness.

[CLARA casts down her eyes, takes his hand, and leans upon him.]

EGMONT. I understand you, dearest! You may raise your eyes.

[He kisses her eyes.]

CLARA. Let me be silent! Let me embrace thee! Let me look into thine eyes, and find there everything—hope and comfort, joy and sorrow! [She embraces and gazes on him.] Tell me! Oh, tell me! It seems so strange—art thou indeed Egmont! Count Egmont! The great Egmont, who makes so much noise in the world, who figures in the newspapers, who is the support and stay of the provinces?

EGMONT. No, Clara, I am not he.

CLARA. How?

EGMONT. Seest thou, Clara? Let me sit down! [He seats himself, she kneels on a footstool before him, rests her arms on his knees, and looks up in his face.] That Egmont is a morose, cold, unbending Egmont, obliged to be upon his guard, to assume now this appearance and now that; harassed, misapprehended and perplexed, when the crowd esteem him light-hearted and gay; beloved by a people who do not know their own minds; honoured and extolled by the intractable multitude; surrounded by friends in whom he dares not confide; observed by men who are on the watch to supplant him; toiling and striving, often without an object, generally without a reward. O let me conceal how it fares with him, let me not speak of his feelings! But this Egmont, Clara, is calm, unreserved, happy, beloved and known by the best of hearts, which is also thoroughly known to him, and which he presses to his own with unbounded confidence and love. [He embraces her.] This is thy Egmont.

CLARA. So let me die! The world has no joy after this!

ACT IV

A street.

[JETTER. CARPENTER.]

JETTER. Hist! neighbour,—a word!

CARPENTER. Go your way and be quiet.

JETTER. Only one word. Is there nothing new?

CARPENTER. Nothing, except that we are anew forbidden to speak.

JETTER. How?

CARPENTER. Step here, close to this house. Take heed! Immediately on his arrival, the Duke of Alva published a decree, by which two or three, found conversing together in the streets, are, without trial, declared guilty of high treason.

JETTER. Alas!

CARPENTER. To speak of state affairs is prohibited on pain of perpetual imprisonment.

JETTER. Alas for our liberty!

CARPENTER. And no one, on pain of death, shall censure the measures of government.

JETTER. Alas, for our heads!

CARPENTER. And fathers, mothers, children, kindred, friends, and servants, are invited, by the promise of large rewards, to disclose what passes in the privacy of our homes, before an expressly appointed tribunal.

JETTER. Let us go home.

CARPENTER. And the obedient are promised that they shall suffer no injury, either in person or estate.

JETTER. How gracious!—I felt ill at ease the moment the duke entered the town. Since then, it has seemed to me, as though the heavens were covered with black crape, which hangs so low, that one must stoop down to avoid knocking one's head against it.

CARPENTER. And how do you like his soldiers? They are a different sort of crabs from those we have been used to.

JETTER. Faugh! It gives one the cramp at one's heart to see such a troop march down the street, as straight as tapers, with fixed look, only one step, however many there may be; and when they stand sentinel, and you pass one of them, it seems as though he would look you through and through; and he looks so stiff and morose, that you fancy you see a task-master at every corner. They offend my sight. Our militia were merry fellows; they took liberties, stood their legs astride, their hats over their ears, they lived and let live; these fellows are like machines with a devil inside them.

CARPENTER. Were such an one to cry, "Halt!" and to level his musket, think you, one would stand?

JETTER. I should fall dead upon the spot.

CARPENTER. Let us go home!

JETTER. No good can come of it. Farewell.

[Enter SOEST.]

SOEST. Friends! Neighbours!

CARPENTER. Hush! Let us go.

SOEST. Have you heard?

JETTER. Only too much!

SOEST. The Regent is gone.

JETTER. Then heaven help us.

CARPENTER. She was some stay to us.

SOEST. Her departure was sudden and secret. She could not agree with the duke; she has sent word to the nobles that she intends to return. No one believes it, however.

CARPENTER. God pardon the nobles for letting this new yoke be laid upon our necks. They might have prevented it. Our privileges are gone.

JETTER. For heaven's sake not a word about privileges. I already scent an execution; the sun will not come forth; the fogs are rank.

SOEST. Orange, too, is gone.

CARPENTER. Then are we quite deserted!

SOEST. Count Egmont is still here.

JETTER. God be thanked! Strengthen him all ye saints to do his utmost; he is the only one who can help us.

[Enter VANSEN.]

VANSEN. Have I at length found a few brave citizens who have not crept out of sight?

JETTER. Do us the favour to pass on.

VANSEN. You are not civil.

JETTER. This is no time for compliments. Does your back itch again? are your wounds already healed?

VANSEN. Ask a soldier about his wounds! Had I cared for blows, nothing good would have come of me.

JETTER. Matters may grow more serious.

VANSEN. You feel from the gathering storm, a pitiful weakness in your limbs, it seems.

CARPENTER. Your limbs will soon be in motion elsewhere, if you do not keep quiet.

VANSEN. Poor mice! The master of the house procures a new cat, and ye are straight in despair! The difference is very trifling; we shall get on as we did before, only be quiet.

CARPENTER. You are an insolent knave.

VANSEN. Gossip! Let the duke alone.

The old cat looks as though he had swallowed devils, instead of mice, and could not now digest them. Let him alone I say; he must eat, drink, and sleep, like other men. I am not afraid if we only watch our opportunity. At first he makes quick work of it; by and by, however, he too will find that it is pleasanter to live in the larder, among flitches of bacon, and to rest by night, than to entrap a few solitary mice in the granary. Go to! I know the stadtholders.

CARPENTER. What such a fellow can say with impunity! Had I said such a thing, I should not hold myself safe a moment.

VANSEN. Do not make yourselves uneasy! God in heaven does not trouble himself about you, poor worms, much less the Regent.

JETTER. Slanderer!

VANSEN. I know some for whom it would be better, if instead of their own high spirits, they had a little tailor's blood in their veins.

CARPENTER. What mean you by that?

VANSEN. Hum! I mean the count.

JETTER. Egmont! What has he to fear?

VANSEN. I'm a poor devil, and could live a whole year round on what he loses in a single night; yet he would do well to give me his revenue for a twelvemonth, to have my head upon his shoulders for one quarter of an hour.

JETTER. You think yourself very clever; yet there is more sense in the hairs of Egmont's head, than in your brains.

VANSEN. Perhaps so! Not more shrewdness, however. These gentry are the most apt to deceive themselves. He should be more chary of his confidence.

JETTER. How his tongue wags! Such a gentleman!

VANSEN. Just because he is not a tailor.

JETTER. You audacious scoundrel!

VANSEN. I only wish he had your courage in his limbs for an hour to make him uneasy, and plague and torment him, till he were compelled to leave the town.

JETTER. What nonsense you talk; why he's as safe as a star in heaven.

VANSEN. Have you ever seen one snuff itself out? Off it went!

CARPENTER. Who would dare to meddle with him, I should like to know?

VANSEN. Will you interfere to prevent it? Will you stir up an insurrection if he is arrested?

JETTER. Ah!

VANSEN. Will you risk your ribs for his sake?

SOEST. Eh!

VANSEN [mimicking him]. Eh! Oh! Ah! Run through the alphabet in your wonderment. So it is, and so it will remain. Heaven help him!

JETTER. Confound your impudence. Can such a noble, upright man, have anything to fear?

VANSEN. In this world the rogue has everywhere the advantage. At the bar, he makes a fool of the judge; on the bench, he takes pleasure in convicting the accused. I have had to copy out a protocol, where the commissary was handsomely rewarded by the court, both with praise and money, because through his cross-examination, an honest devil, against whom they had a grudge, was made out to be a rogue.

CARPENTER. Why that again is a downright lie. What can they want to get out of a man if he is innocent?

VANSEN. Oh you blockhead! When nothing can be worked out of a man by cross-examination, they work it into him. Honesty is rash and withal somewhat presumptuous; at first they question quietly enough, and the prisoner, proud of his innocence, as they call it, comes out with much that a sensible man would keep back; then, from these answers the inquisitor proceeds to put new questions, and is on the watch for the slightest contradiction; there he fastens his line; and let the poor devil lose his self-possession, say too much here, or too little there, or, heaven knows from what whim or other, let him withhold some trifling circumstance, or at any moment give way to fear,—then we're on the right track, and, I assure you, no beggar-woman seeks for rags among the rubbish with more care, than such a fabricator of rogues, from trifling, crooked, disjointed, misplaced, misprinted, and concealed facts and information, acknowledged or denied, endeavours at length to patch up a scarecrow, by means of which he may at least hang his victim in effigy; and the poor devil may thank heaven, if he is in a condition to see himself hanged.

JETTER. He has a ready tongue of his own.

CARPENTER. This may serve well enough with flies. Wasps laugh at your cunning well.

VANSEN. According to the kind of spider. The tall duke now, has just the look of your garden spider; not the large-bellied kind, they are less dangerous; but your long-footed, meagre-bodied gentleman, that does not fatten on his diet, and whose threads are slender indeed, but not the less tenacious.

JETTER. Egmont is knight of the Golden Fleece, who dare lay hands on him? He can be tried only by his peers, by the assembled knights of his order. Your own foul tongue and evil conscience betray you into this nonsense.

VANSEN. Think you that I wish him ill? I would you were in the right. He is an excellent gentleman. He once let off, with a sound drubbing, some good friends of mine, who would else have been hanged. Now take yourselves off! be gone, I advise you! yonder I see the patrol again commencing their round. They do not look as if they would be willing to fraternize with us over a glass. We must wait, and bide our time. I have a couple of nieces and a gossip of a tapster; if after enjoying themselves in their company, they are not tamed, they are regular wolves.

The Palace of Eulenberg. Residence of the DUKE OF ALVA.

SILVA. Have you executed the duke's commands?

GOMEZ. Punctually. All the day patrols have received orders to assemble at the appointed time, at the various points that I have indicated. Meanwhile, they march as usual through the town to maintain order. Each is ignorant respecting the movements of the rest, and imagines the command to have reference to himself alone; thus in a moment the cordon can be formed, and all the avenues to the palace occupied. Know you the reason of this command?

SILVA. I am accustomed blindly to obey; and to whom can one more easily render obedience than to the duke, since the event always proves the wisdom of his commands.

GOMEZ. Well! Well! I am not surprised that you are become as reserved and monosyllabic as the duke, since you are obliged to be always about his person; to me, however, who am accustomed to the lighter service of Italy, it seems strange enough. In loyalty and obedience I am the same old soldier as ever; but I am wont to indulge in gossip and discussion; here, you are all silent, and seem as though you knew not how to enjoy yourselves. The duke, methinks, is like a brazen tower without gates, the garrison of which must be furnished with wings. Not long ago I heard him say at the table of a gay, jovial fellow, that he was like a bad spirit-shop, with a brandy sign displayed to allure idlers, vagabonds, and thieves.

SILVA. And has he not brought us hither in silence?

GOMEZ. Nothing can be said against that. Of a truth, we, who witnessed the address with which he led the troops hither out of Italy, have seen something. How he advanced warily through friends and foes; through the French, both royalists and heretics; through the Swiss and their confederates; maintained the strictest discipline, and accomplished with ease, and without the slightest hindrance, a march that was esteemed so perilous!—We have seen and learned something.

SILVA. Here too! Is not everything as still and quiet as though there had been no disturbance?

GOMEZ. Why, as for that, it was tolerably quiet when we arrived.

SILVA. The provinces have become much more tranquil; if there is any movement now, it is only among those who wish to escape; and to them, methinks, the duke will speedily close every outlet.

GOMEZ. This service cannot fail to win for him the favour of the king.

SILVA. And nothing is more expedient for us than to retain his. Should the king come hither, the duke doubtless and all whom he recommends will not go without their reward.

GOMEZ. Do you really believe then that the king will come?

SILVA. So many preparations are being made, that the report appears highly probable.

GOMEZ. I am not convinced, however.

SILVA. Keep your thoughts to yourself, then. For if it should not be the king's intention to come, it is at least certain that he wishes the rumour to be believed.

[*Enter* FERDINAND.]

FERDINAND. Is my father not yet abroad?

SILVA. We are waiting to receive his commands.

FERDINAND. The princes will soon be here.

GOMEZ. Are they expected to-day?

FERDINAND. Orange and Egmont.

GOMEZ [*aside to* SILVA]. A light breaks in upon me.

SILVA. Well, then, say nothing about it.

[*Enter the* DUKE OF ALVA. *As he advances the rest draw back.*]

ALVA. Gomez.

GOMEZ [*steps forward*]. My lord.

ALVA. You have distributed the guards and given them their instructions?

GOMEZ. Most accurately. The day patrols——

ALVA. Enough. Attend in the gallery. Silva will announce to you the moment when you are to draw them together, and to occupy the avenues leading to the palace. The rest you know.

GOMEZ. I do, my lord. [*Exit.*]

ALVA. Silva.

SILVA. Here, my lord.

ALVA. I shall require you to manifest to-day all the qualities which I have hitherto prized in you: courage, resolve, unswerving execution.

SILVA. I thank you for affording me an opportunity of showing that your old servant is unchanged.

ALVA. The moment the princes enter my cabinet, hasten to arrest Egmont's private secretary. You have made all needful preparations for securing the others who are specified?

SILVA. Rely upon us. Their doom, like a well-calculated eclipse, will overtake them with terrible certainty.

ALVA. Have you had them all narrowly watched?

SILVA. All. Egmont especially. He is the only one whose demeanour, since your arrival, remains unchanged. The livelong day he is now on one horse and now on another; he invites guests as usual, is merry and entertaining at table, plays at dice, shoots, and at night steals to his mistress. The others, on the contrary, have made a manifest pause in their mode of life; they remain at home, and, from the outward aspect of their houses, you would imagine that there was a sick man within.

ALVA. To work then, ere they recover in spite of us.

SILVA. I shall bring them without fail. In obedience to your commands we load them with officious honours; they are alarmed; cautiously, yet anxiously, they tender us their thanks, feel that flight would be the most prudent course, yet none venture to adopt it; they hesitate, are unable to work together, while the bond which unites them prevents their acting boldly as individuals. They are anxious to withdraw themselves from suspicion, and thus only render themselves more obnoxious to it. I already contemplate with joy the successful realization of your scheme.

ALVA. I rejoice only over what is accomplished, and not lightly over that; for there ever remains ground for serious and anxious thought. Fortune is capricious; the common, the worthless, she oft-times ennobles, while she dishonours with a contemptible issue the most maturely-considered schemes. Await the arrival of the princes, then order Gomez to occupy the streets, and hasten yourself to arrest Egmont's secretary, and the others who are specified. This done, return, and announce to my son that he may bring me the tidings in the council.

SILVA. I trust this evening I shall dare to appear in your presence. [ALVA *approaches his son, who has hitherto been standing in the gallery.*] I dare not whisper it even to myself; but my mind misgives me. The event will, I fear, be different from what he anticipates. I see before me spirits, who, still and thoughtful, weigh in ebon scales the doom of princes and of many thousands. Slowly the beam moves up and down; deeply the judges appear to ponder; at length one scale sinks, the other rises, breathed on by the caprice of destiny, and all is decided. [*Exit.*]

ALVA [*advancing with his son*]. How did you find the town?

FERDINAND. All is again quiet. I rode as for pastime, from street to street. Your well-distributed patrols hold fear so tightly yoked, that she does not venture even to whisper. The town resembles a plain when the lightning's glare announces the impending storm: no bird, no beast is to be seen, that is not stealing to a place of shelter.

ALVA. Has nothing further occurred?

FERDINAND. Egmont, with a few companions, rode into the market-place; we exchanged greetings; he was mounted on an unbroken charger, which excited my admiration. "Let us hasten to break in our steeds," he exclaimed; "we shall need them ere long!" He said that he should see me again to-day; he is coming here, at your desire, to deliberate with you.

ALVA. He will see you again.

FERDINAND. Among all the knights whom I know here, he pleases me the best. I think we shall be friends.

ALVA. You are always rash and inconsiderate. I recognize in you the levity of your mother, which threw her unconditionally into my arms. Appearances have already allured you precipitately into many dangerous connexions.

FERDINAND. You will find me ever submissive.

ALVA. I pardon this inconsiderate kindness, this heedless gaiety, in consideration of your youthful blood. Only forget not on what mission I am sent, and what part in it I would assign to you.

FERDINAND. Admonish me, and spare me not, when you deem it needful.

ALVA [*after a pause*]. My son!

FERDINAND. My father!

ALVA. The princes will be here anon; Orange and Egmont. It is not mistrust that has withheld me till now, from disclosing to you what is about to take place. They will not depart hence.

FERDINAND. What do you purpose?

ALVA. It has been resolved to arrest them.—You are astonished! Learn what you have to do; the reasons you shall know when all is accomplished. Time fails now to unfold them. With you alone I wish to deliberate on the weightiest, the most secret matters; a powerful bond holds us linked together; you are dear and precious to me; on you I would bestow everything. Not the habit of obedience alone would I impress upon you; I desire also to implant within your mind the power to realize, to execute, to command; to you I would bequeath a vast inheritance, to the king a most useful servant; I would endow you with the noblest of my possessions, that you may not be ashamed to appear among your brethren.

FERDINAND. How deeply am I indebted to you for this love, which you manifest for me alone, while a whole kingdom trembles before you.

ALVA. Now hear what is to be done.

As soon as the princes have entered, every avenue to the palace will be guarded. This duty is confided to Gomez. Silva will hasten to arrest Egmont's secretary, together with those whom we hold most in suspicion. You, meanwhile, will take the command of the guards stationed at the gates and in the courts. Before all, take care to occupy the adjoining apartment with the trustiest soldiers. Wait in the gallery till Silva returns, then bring me any unimportant paper, as a signal that his commission is executed. Remain in the ante-chamber till Orange retires, follow him; I will detain Egmont here as though I had some further communication to make to him. At the end of the gallery demand Orange's sword, summon the guards, secure promptly the most dangerous man; I meanwhile will seize Egmont here.

FERDINAND. I obey, my father—for the first time with a heavy and an anxious heart.

ALVA. I pardon you; this is the first great day of your life.

[*Enter* SILVA.]

SILVA. A courier from Antwerp. Here is Orange's letter. He does not come.

ALVA. Says the messenger so?

SILVA. No, my own heart tells me.

ALVA. In thee speaks my evil genius. [*After reading the letter, he makes a sign to the two, and they retire to the gallery.* ALVA *remains alone in front of the stage.*] He comes not! Till the last moment he delays declaring himself. He ventures not to come! So then, the cautious man, contrary to all expectation, is for once sagacious enough to lay aside his wonted caution. The hour moves on! Let the finger travel but a short space over the dial, and a great work is done or lost— irrevocably lost; for the opportunity can never be retrieved, nor can our intention remain concealed. Long had I maturely weighed everything, foreseen even this contingency, and firmly resolved in my own mind what, in that case, was to be done; and now, when I am called upon to act, I

can with difficulty guard my mind from being again distracted by conflicting doubts. Is it expedient to seize the others if he escape me? Shall I delay, and suffer Egmont to elude my grasp, together with his friends, and so many others who now, and perhaps for to-day only, are in my hands? How! Does destiny control even thee—the uncontrollable? How long matured! How well prepared! How great, how admirable the plan! How nearly had hope attained the goal! And now, at the decisive moment, thou art placed between two evils; as in a lottery, thou dost grasp in the dark future; what thou hast drawn remains still unrolled, to thee unknown whether it is a prize or a blank! [*He becomes attentive, like one who hears a noise, and steps to the window.*] 'Tis he! Egmont! Did thy steed bear thee hither so lightly, and started not at the scent of blood, at the spirit with the naked sword who received thee at the gate? Dismount! Lo, now thou hast one foot in the grave! And now both! Ay, caress him, and for the last time stroke his neck for the gallant service he has rendered thee. And for me no choice is left. The delusion, in which Egmont ventures here to-day, cannot a second time deliver him into my hands! Hark! [FERDINAND *and* SILVA *enter hastily.*] Obey my orders! I swerve not from my purpose. I shall detain Egmont here as best I may, till you bring me tidings from Silva. Then remain at hand. Thee, too, fate has robbed of the proud honour of arresting with thine own hand the king's greatest enemy. [*To* SILVA.] Be prompt! [*To* FERDINAND.] Advance to meet him.

[ALVA *remains some moments alone, pacing the chamber in silence.*]

[*Enter* EGMONT.]

EGMONT. I come to learn the king's commands; to hear what service he demands from our loyalty, which remains eternally devoted to him.

ALVA. He desires, before all, to hear your counsel.

EGMONT. Upon what subject? Does Orange come also? I thought to find him here.

ALVA. I regret that he fails us at this important crisis. The king desires your counsel, your opinion as to the best means of tranquillizing these states. He trusts indeed that you will zealously co-operate with him in quelling these disturbances, and in securing to these provinces the benefit of complete and permanent order.

EGMONT. You, my lord, should know better than I, that tranquillity is already sufficiently restored, and was still more so, till the appearance of fresh troops again agitated the public mind, and filled it anew with anxiety and alarm.

ALVA. You seem to intimate that it would have been more advisable if the king had not placed me in a position to interrogate you.

EGMONT. Pardon me! It is not for me to determine whether the king acted advisedly in sending the army hither, whether the might of his royal presence alone would not have operated more powerfully. The army is here, the king is not. But we should be most ungrateful were we to forget what we owe to the Regent. Let it be acknowledged! By her prudence and valour, by her judicious use of authority and force, of persuasion and finesse, she pacified the insurgents, and, to the astonishment of the world, succeeded, in the course of a few months, in bringing a rebellious people back to their duty.

ALVA. I deny it not. The insurrection is quelled; and the people appear to be already forced back within the bounds of obedience. But does it not depend upon their caprice alone to overstep these bounds? Who shall prevent them from again breaking loose? Where is the power capable of restraining them? Who will be answerable to us for their future loyalty and submission? Their own good will is the sole pledge we have.

EGMONT. And is not the good-will of a people the surest, the noblest pledge? By heaven! when can a monarch hold himself more secure, ay, both against foreign and domestic foes, than when all can stand for one, and one for all?

ALVA. You would not have us believe, however, that such is the case here at present?

EGMONT. Let the king proclaim a general pardon; he will thus tranquillize the public mind; and it will be seen how speedily loyalty and affection will return, when confidence is restored.

ALVA. How! And suffer those who have insulted the majesty of the king, who have violated the sanctuaries of our religion, to go abroad unchallenged! living witnesses that enormous crimes may be perpetrated with impunity!

EGMONT. And ought not a crime of frenzy, of intoxication, to be excused, rather than horribly chastised? Especially when there is the sure hope, nay, more, where there is positive certainty, that the evil will never again recur? Would not sovereigns thus be more secure? Are not those monarchs most extolled by the world and by posterity, who can pardon, pity, despise an offense against their dignity? Are they not on that account likened to God himself, who is far too exalted to be assailed by every idle blasphemy?

ALVA. And therefore, should the king maintain the honour of God and of religion, we the authority of the king. What the supreme power disdains to avert, it is our duty to avenge. Were I to counsel, no guilty person should live to rejoice in his impunity.

EGMONT. Think you that you will be able to reach them all? Do we not daily hear that fear is driving them to and fro, and forcing them out of the land. The more wealthy will escape to other countries, with their property, their children, and their friends; while the poor will carry their industrious hands to our neighbours.

ALVA. They will, if they cannot be prevented. It is on this account that the king desires counsel and aid from every prince, zealous co-operation from every stadtholder; not merely a description of the present posture of affairs, or conjectures as to what might take place were events suffered to hold on their course without interruption. To contemplate a mighty evil, to flatter oneself with hope, to trust to time, to strike a blow, like the clown in a play, so as to make a noise, and appear to do something, when in fact one would fain do nothing; is not such conduct calculated to awaken a suspicion that those who act thus contemplate with satisfaction a rebellion, which they would not indeed excite, but which they are by no means unwilling to encourage?

EGMONT [*about to break forth, restrains himself, and after a brief pause, speaks with composure*]. Every design is not immediately obvious, and a man's intentions are often misconstrued. It is widely rumoured, however, that the object which the king has in view is not so much to govern the provinces according to uniform and clearly defined laws, to maintain the majesty of religion, and to give his people universal peace, as unconditionally to subjugate them, to rob them of their ancient rights, to appropriate their possessions, to curtail the fair privileges of the nobles, for whose sake alone they are ready to serve him with life and limb. Religion, it is said, is merely a splendid device, behind which every dangerous design may be contrived with the greater ease; the prostrate crowds adore the sacred symbols pictured there, while behind lurks the fowler ready to ensnare them.

ALVA. Must I hear this from you?

EGMONT. I speak not my own sentiments! I but repeat what is loudly rumoured, and uttered here and there by rich and poor, by wise men and fools. The Netherlanders fear a double yoke, and who will be surety to them for their liberty?

ALVA. Liberty! A fair word when rightly understood. What liberty would they have? What is the freedom of the most free? To do right! And in that the monarch will not hinder them. No! No! They imagine themselves enslaved, when they have not the power to injure themselves and others. Would it not be better to abdicate at once, rather than rule such a people? When the country is threatened by foreign invaders, the citizens, occupied only with their immediate interests, bestow no thought upon the advancing foe, and when the king requires their aid, they quarrel among themselves, and thus, as it were, conspire with the enemy. Far better is it to circumscribe their power, to control and guide them for their good, as children are controlled and guided. Trust me, a people grows neither old nor wise, a people remains always in its infancy.

EGMONT. How rarely does a king attain wisdom! And is it not fit that the many should confide their interests to the many rather than to the one? And not even to the one, but to the few servants of the one, men who have grown old under the eyes of their master. To grow wise, it seems, is the exclusive privilege of these favoured individuals.

ALVA. Perhaps for the very reason that they are not left to themselves.

EGMONT. And therefore they would fain leave no one else to his own guidance. Let them do what they like, however; I have replied to your questions, and I repeat, the measures you propose will never do! They cannot succeed! I know my countrymen. They are men worthy to tread God's earth; each complete in himself, a little king, steadfast, active, capable, loyal, attached to ancient customs. It may be difficult to win their confidence, but it is easy to retain it. Firm and unbending! They may be crushed, but not subdued.

ALVA [*who during this speech has looked round several times*]. Would you venture to repeat what you have uttered, in the king's presence?

EGMONT. It were the worse, if in his presence I were restrained by fear! The better for him, and for his people, if he inspired me with confidence, if he encouraged me to give yet freer utterance to my thoughts.

ALVA. What is profitable, I can listen to as well as he.

EGMONT. I would say to him—'Tis easy for the shepherd to drive before him a flock of sheep; the ox draws the plough without opposition; but if you would ride the noble steed, you must study his thoughts, you must require nothing unreasonable, nor unreasonably, from him. The citizen desires to retain his ancient constitution; to be governed by his own countrymen; and why? Because he knows in that case how he shall be ruled, because he can rely upon their disinterestedness, upon their sympathy with his fate.

ALVA. And ought not the Regent to be empowered to alter these ancient usages? Should not this constitute his fairest privilege? What is permanent in this world? And shall the constitution of a state alone remain unchanged? Must not every relation alter in the course of time? And an ancient constitution become the source of a thousand evils, because not adapted to the present condition of the people? These ancient rights afford, doubtless, convenient loopholes, through which the crafty and the powerful may creep, and wherein they may lie concealed, to the injury of the people and of the entire community; and it is on this account, I fear, that they are held in such high esteem.

EGMONT. And these arbitrary changes, these unlimited encroachments of the supreme power, are they not indications that one will permit himself to do what is forbidden to thousands? The monarch would alone be free, that he may have it in his power to gratify his every wish, to realize his every thought. And though we should confide in him as a good and virtuous sovereign, will he be answerable to us for his successors? That none who come after him shall rule without consideration, without forbearance! And who would deliver us from absolute caprice, should he send hither his servants, his minions, who, without knowledge of the country and its requirements, should govern according to their own good pleas-

ure, meet with no opposition, and know themselves exempt from all responsibility?

ALVA [who has meanwhile again looked round]. There is nothing more natural than that a king should choose to retain the power in his own hands, and that he should select as the instruments of his authority, those who best understand him, who desire to understand him, and who will unconditionally execute his will.

EGMONT. And just as natural is it, that the citizen should prefer being governed by one born and reared in the same land, whose notions of right and wrong are in harmony with his own, and whom he can regard as his brother.

ALVA. And yet the noble, methinks, has shared rather unequally with these brethren of his.

EGMONT. That took place centuries ago, and is now submitted to without envy. But should new men, whose presence is not needed in the country, be sent, to enrich themselves a second time, at the cost of the nation; should the people see themselves exposed to their bold unscrupulous rapacity, it would excite a ferment that would not soon be quelled.

ALVA. You utter words to which I ought not to listen;—I too am a foreigner.

EGMONT. That they are spoken in your presence is a sufficient proof that they have no reference to you.

ALVA. Be that as it may, I would rather not hear them from you. The king sent me here in the hope that I should obtain the support of the nobles. The king wills, and will have his will obeyed. After profound deliberation, he at length discerns what course will best promote the welfare of the people; matters cannot be permitted to go on as heretofore; it is his intention to limit their power for their own good; if necessary, to force upon them their salvation; to sacrifice the more dangerous citizens, that the rest may find repose, and enjoy in peace the blessing of a wise government. This is his resolve; this I am commissioned to announce to the nobles; and in his name I require from them advice, not as to the course to be pursued,—on that he is resolved,—but as to the best means of carrying his purpose into effect.

EGMONT. Your words, alas, justify the fears of the people, the fears of all! The king has then resolved as no sovereign ought to resolve. In order to govern his subjects more easily, he would crush, subvert, nay, ruthlessly destroy, their strength, their spirit, and their self-respect! He would violate the core of their individuality, doubtless with the view of promoting their happiness. He would annihilate them, that they may assume a new, a different shape. Oh! if his purpose be good, he is fatally misguided! It is not the king whom we resist;—we but place ourselves in the way of the monarch, who, unhappily, is about to take the first rash step in a wrong direction.

ALVA. Such being your sentiments, it were a vain attempt for us to endeavour to agree. You must indeed think poorly of the king, and contemptibly of his counsellors, if you imagine that everything has not already been thought of and maturely weighed. I have no commission a second time to balance conflicting arguments. From the people I demand submission;—and from you, their leaders and princes, I demand counsel and support, as pledges of this unconditional duty.

EGMONT. Demand our heads and your object is attained; to a noble soul it must be indifferent whether he stoop his neck to such a yoke, or lay it upon the block. I have spoken much to little purpose. I have agitated the air, but accomplished nothing.

[*Enter* FERDINAND.]

FERDINAND. Pardon my intrusion. Here is a letter, the bearer of which urgently demands an answer.

ALVA. Allow me to peruse its contents.
[*Steps aside.*]

FERDINAND [*to* EGMONT]. 'Tis a noble steed that your people have brought for you.

EGMONT. I have seen worse. I have had him some time; I think of parting with him. If he pleases you we shall probably soon agree as to the price.

FERDINAND. We will think about it.

ALVA [*motions to his son, who retires to the back-ground*].

EGMONT. Farewell! Allow me to retire; for by heaven I know not what more I can say.

ALVA. Fortunately for you, chance prevents you from making a fuller disclosure of your sentiments. You incautiously lay bare the recesses of your heart, and your own lips furnish evidence against you, more fatal than could be produced by your bitterest adversary.

EGMONT. This reproach disturbs me not. I know my own heart; I know with what honest zeal I am devoted to the king; I know that my allegiance is more true than that of many who, in his service, seek only to serve themselves. I regret that our discussion should terminate so unsatisfactorily, and trust that in spite of our opposing views, the service of the king, our master, and the welfare of our country, may speedily unite us; another conference, the presence of the princes who to-day are absent, may, perchance, in a more propitious moment, accomplish what at present appears impossible. In this hope I take my leave.

ALVA [*who at the same time makes a sign to* FERDINAND]. Hold, Egmont!—Your sword!—

[*The centre door opens and discloses the gallery, which is occupied with guards, who remain motionless.*]

EGMONT [*after a pause of astonishment*]. Was this then your intention? Was it for this purpose that I was summoned here? [*Grasping his sword as if to defend himself.*] Am I then weaponless?

ALVA. The king commands. You are my prisoner.

[*At the same time guards enter from both sides.*]

EGMONT [*after a pause*]. The king?—
Orange! Orange! [*After a pause, resign-
ing his sword.*] Take it! It has been
employed far oftener in defending the
cause of my king, than in protecting this
breast.

[*He retires by the centre door,
followed by the guard and
ALVA's son. ALVA remains
standing while the curtain
falls.*]

ACT V

A street. Twilight.

[CLARA, BRACKENBURG, CITIZENS.]
BRACKENBURG. Dearest, for heaven's
sake, what would'st thou do?
CLARA. Come with me, Brackenburg!
You cannot know the people, we are cer-
tain to rescue him; for what can equal
their love for him? I could swear it, the
breast of every citizen burns with the de-
sire to deliver him, to avert danger from
a life so precious, and to restore freedom
to the most free. Come, a voice only is
wanting to call them together. In their
souls the memory is still fresh of all they
owe him, and well they know that his
mighty arm alone shields them from de-
struction. For his sake, for their own
sake, they must peril everything. And
what do we peril? At most, our lives,
which, if he perish, are not worth pre-
serving.
BRACKENBURG. Unhappy girl! Thou
seest not the power that holds us fettered
as with bands of iron.
CLARA. To me it does not appear in-
vincible. Let us not lose time in idle
words. Here come some of our old, hon-
est, valiant citizens! Hark ye, friends!
Neighbours! Hark—Say, how fares it
with Egmont?
CARPENTER. What does the girl want?
Tell her to hold her peace.
CLARA. Step nearer, that we may
speak low, till we are united and more
strong. Not a moment is to be lost! Au-

dacious tyranny, that dared to fetter him,
already lifts the dagger against his life.
Oh, my friends! With the advancing
twilight my anxiety grows more intense.
I dread this night. Come! Let us dis-
perse; let us hasten from quarter to
quarter, and call out the citizens. Let
every one grasp his ancient weapons. In
the market-place we meet again, and
every one will be carried onward by our
gathering stream. The enemy will see
themselves surrounded, overwhelmed, and
be compelled to yield. How can a hand-
ful of slaves resist us? And he will re-
turn among us, he will see himself res-
cued, and can for once thank us, us, who
are already so deeply in his debt. He will
behold, perchance, ay doubtless, he will
again behold the morn's red dawn in the
free heavens.
CARPENTER. What ails thee, maiden?
CLARA. Can ye misunderstand me? I
speak of the Count! I speak of Eg-
mont.
JETTER. Speak not the name, 'tis
deadly.
CLARA. Not speak his name? Not Eg-
mont's name? Is it not on every tongue?
Does it not appear everywhere legibly in-
scribed? I read it emblazoned in golden
letters among the stars. Not utter it?
What mean ye? Friends! Good, kind
neighbours; ye are dreaming; collect
yourselves. Gaze not upon me with those
fixed and anxious looks! Cast not such
timid glances on every side! I but give
utterance to the wish of all. Is not my
voice the voice of your own hearts? Who,
in this fearful night, ere he seeks his rest-
less couch, but on bended knee, will in
earnest prayer seek to wrest his life as a
cherished boon from heaven? Ask each
other! Let each ask his own heart! And
who but exclaims with me,—"Egmont's
liberty, or death!"
JETTER. God help us! This is a sad
business.
CLARA. Stay! Stay! Shrink not away
at the sound of his name, to meet whom
ye were wont to press forward so joy-
ously!—When rumour announced his ap-

proach, when the cry arose, "Egmont comes! He comes from Ghent!"—then happy indeed were those citizens who dwelt in the streets through which he was to pass. And when the neighing of his steed was heard, did not every one throw aside his work, while a ray of hope and joy, like a sunbeam from his countenance, stole over the toilworn faces that peered from every window. Then, as ye stood in the doorways, ye would lift up your children in your arms, and pointing to him, exclaim: "See, that is Egmont, he who towers above the rest! 'Tis from him that ye must look for better times than those your poor fathers have known." Let not your children inquire at some future day, "Where is he? Where are the better times ye promised us?"— Thus we waste the time in idle words! do nothing,—betray him.

SOEST. Shame on thee, Brackenburg! Let her not run on thus; prevent the mischief.

BRACKENBURG. Dear Clara! Let us go! What will your mother say? Perchance——

CLARA. Think you I am a child, a lunatic? What avails perchance?—With no vain hope can you hide from me this dreadful certainty.

Ye shall hear me and ye will: for I see it, ye are overwhelmed, ye cannot hearken to the voice of your own hearts. Through the present peril cast but one glance into the past,—the recent past. Send your thoughts forward into the future. Could ye live, would ye live, were he to perish? With him expires the last breath of freedom. What was he not to you? For whose sake did he expose himself to the direst perils? His blood flowed, his wounds were healed for you alone. A dungeon now confines that mighty spirit that upheld you all, while around him hover the terrors of secret assassination. Perhaps, he thinks of you,—perhaps he hopes in you,—he who has been accustomed only to grant favours to others and to fulfil their prayers.

CARPENTER. Come, gossip.

CLARA. I have neither the arms, nor the strength of a man; but I have that which ye all lack—courage and contempt of danger. Oh that my breath could kindle your souls! That, pressing you to this bosom, I could arouse and animate you! Come! I will march in your midst! —As a waving banner, though weaponless, leads on a gallant army of warriors, so shall my spirit hover, like a flame, over your ranks, while love and courage shall unite the dispersed and wavering multitude into a terrible host.

JETTER. Take her away, I pity her, poor thing. [Exeunt CITIZENS.]

BRACKENBURG. Clara! See you not where we are?

CLARA. Where? Under the dome of heaven, which has so often seemed to arch itself more gloriously as the noble Egmont passed beneath it. From these windows I have seen them look forth, four or five heads one above the other; at these doors the cowards have stood, bowing and scraping, if the hero but chanced to look down upon them! Oh how dear they were to me, when they honoured him. Had he been a tyrant they might have turned with indifference from his fall; but they loved him! O ye hands, so prompt to wave caps in his honour, can ye not grasp a sword? And yet, Brackenburg, is it for us to chide them? These arms that have so often embraced him, what do they for him now? Stratagem has accomplished so much in the world. You know the ancient castle, every passage, every secret way.—Nothing is impossible,—suggest some plan——

BRACKENBURG. If you would but come home.

CLARA. Well.

BRACKENBURG. There at the corner I see Alva's guard; let the voice of reason penetrate to your heart! Do you deem me a coward? Do you doubt that for your sake I would peril my life? Here we are both mad, I as well as you. Do you not perceive that your scheme is impracticable? Oh be calm! You are beside yourself.

CLARA. Beside myself! Horrible. You Brackenburg are beside yourself. When you hailed the hero with loud acclaim, called him your friend, your hope, your refuge, shouted vivats as he passed;— then I stood in my corner, half opened the window, concealed myself while I listened, and my heart beat higher than yours who greeted him so loudly. Now it again beats higher! In the hour of peril you conceal yourselves, deny him, and feel not, that if he perish, you are lost.

BRACKENBURG. Come home.

CLARA. Home?

BRACKENBURG. Recollect yourself! Look around! These are the streets in which you were wont to appear only on the sabbath day, when you walked modestly to church; where, over-decorous perhaps, you were displeased if I but joined you with a kindly greeting. And now you stand, speak, and act before the eyes of the whole world. Recollect yourself, love! How can this avail us?

CLARA. Home! Yes, I remember. Come, Brackenburg, let us go home! Know you where my home lies?

[*Exeunt.*]

A prison.

Lighted by a lamp, a couch in the background.

[EGMONT *alone.*]

EGMONT. Old friend! Ever faithful sleep, dost thou too forsake me, like my other friends? How wert thou wont of yore to descend unsought upon my free brow, cooling my temples as with a myrtle wreath of love! Amidst the din of battle, on the waves of life, I rested in thine arms, breathing lightly as a growing boy. When tempests whistled through the leaves and boughs, when the summits of the lofty trees swung creaking in the blast, the inmost core of my heart remained unmoved. What agitates thee now? What shakes thy firm and steadfast mind? I feel it, 'tis the sound of the murderous axe, gnawing at thy root. Yet I stand erect, but an inward shudder runs through my frame. Yes, it prevails, this treacherous power; it undermines the firm, the lofty stem, and ere the bark withers, thy verdant crown falls crashing to the earth.

Yet wherefore now, thou who hast so often chased the weightiest cares like bubbles from thy brow, wherefore can'st thou not dissipate this dire foreboding which incessantly haunts thee in a thousand different shapes. Since when hast thou trembled at the approach of death, amid whose varying forms, thou wert wont calmly to dwell, as with the other shapes of this familiar earth. But 'tis not he, the sudden foe, to encounter whom the sound bosom emulously pants;—'tis the dungeon, dread emblem of the grave, revolting alike to the hero, and the coward. How intolerable I used to feel it, in the stately hall, girt round by gloomy walls, when, seated on my cushioned chair, in the solemn assembly of the princes, questions, which scarcely required deliberation, were overlaid with endless discussions, while the rafters of the ceiling seemed to stifle and oppress me. Then I would hurry forth as soon as possible, fling myself upon my horse with deepdrawn breath, and away to the wide champaigne, man's natural element, where, exhaling from the earth, nature's richest treasures are poured forth around us, while, from the wide heavens, the stars shed down their blessings through the still air; where, like earthborn giants, we spring aloft, invigorated by our mother's touch; where the energies of our being throb in every vein; where the soul of the young hunter glows with the desire to overtake, to conquer, to capture, to possess; where the warrior, with rapid stride, assumes his inborn right to dominion over the world; and, with terrible liberty, sweeps like a desolating hailstorm over field and grove, knowing no boundaries, traced by the hand of man.

Thou art but a shadow, a dream of the happiness I so long possessed; where has treacherous fate conducted thee? Did she deny thee, to meet the rapid stroke of never-shunned death, in the open face of day, only to prepare for thee a foretaste of the grave, in the midst of their loathsome corruption? How revoltingly its rank odour exhales from these damp stones! Life stagnates, and my foot shrinks from the couch as from the grave.

Oh care, care! Thou who dost begin prematurely the work of murder,—forbear!—Since when has Egmont been alone, so utterly alone in the world? 'Tis doubt renders thee insensible, not happiness. The justice of the king, in which, through life thou hast confided, the friendship of the Regent, which, thou may'st confess it, was akin to love,—have these suddenly vanished, like a meteor of the night, and left thee alone upon thy gloomy path? Will not Orange, at the head of thy friends, contrive some daring scheme? Will not the people assemble, and with gathering might, attempt the rescue of their faithful friend?

Ye walls, which thus gird me round, separate me not from the well intentioned zeal of so many kindly souls. And may the courage with which my glance was wont to inspire them, now return again from their hearts to mine. Yes! they assemble in thousands! they come! they stand beside me! their prayers rise to heaven, and implore a miracle; and if no angel stoops for my deliverance, I see them grasp eagerly their lance and sword. The gates are forced, the bolts are riven, the walls fall beneath their conquering hands, and Egmont advances joyously, to hail the freedom of the rising morn! How many well known faces receive me with loud acclaim! Oh Clara! wert thou a man, I should see thee here the very first, and thank thee for that which it is galling to owe even to a king—liberty.

CLARA'S *house.*

[CLARA.]

CLARA [*enters from her chamber with a lamp and a glass of water; she places*
the glass upon the table and steps to the window]. Brackenburg, is it you? What noise was that? No one yet? No one! I will set the lamp in the window, that he may see that I am still awake, that I still watch for him. He promised me tidings. Tidings? horrible certainty!—Egmont condemned!—What tribunal has the right to summon him?—And they dare to condemn him!—Is it the king who condemns him, or the duke? And the Regent withdraws herself! Orange hesitates, as do all his friends!—Is this the world, of whose fickleness and treachery I have heard so much, and as yet experienced nothing? Is this the world?—Who could be so base as to bear malice against one so dear? Could villainy itself be audacious enough to overwhelm with sudden destruction the object of a nation's homage? Yet so it is—it is—Oh Egmont, I held thee safe before God and man, safe as in my arms! What was I to thee? Thou hast called me thine, my whole being was devoted to thee. What am I now? In vain I stretch out my hand to the toils that environ thee. Thou helpless, and I free!—Here is the key that unlocks my chamber door. My going out and my coming in, depend upon my own caprice; yet, alas, to aid thee I am powerless!—Oh bind me that I may not go mad; hurl me into the deepest dungeon, that I may dash my head against the damp walls, groan for freedom, and dream how I would rescue him if fetters did not hold me bound.—Now I am free, and in freedom lies the anguish of impotence.—Conscious of my own existence, yet unable to stir a limb in his behalf, alas! even this insignificant portion of thy being, thy Clara, is, like thee, a captive, and separated from thee, consumes her expiring energies in the agonies of death.—I hear a stealthy step,—a cough—Brackenburg, —'tis he!—Kind, unhappy man, thy destiny remains ever the same; thy love opens to thee the door at night,—alas! to what a doleful meeting.

[*Enter* BRACKENBURG.]

CLARA. You look so pale, so terrified! Speak, Brackenburg! What is the matter?

BRACKENBURG. I have sought you through perils and circuitous paths. The principal streets are occupied with troops; —through lanes and by-ways I have stolen to you!

CLARA. Tell me what is going on.

BRACKENBURG [*seating himself*]. Oh Clara, let me weep, I loved him not. He was the rich man who lured to better pasture the poor man's solitary lamb. Yet I cursed him not, God has created me with a true and tender heart. My life was consumed in anguish, and each day I hoped would end my misery.

CLARA. Let that be forgotten, Brackenburg! Forget thyself. Speak to me of him! Is it true? Is he condemned?

BRACKENBURG. He is! I know it.

CLARA. And still lives?

BRACKENBURG. Yes, he still lives.

CLARA. How can you be sure of that? Tyranny murders its victim in the night! His blood flows concealed from every eye. The people, stunned and bewildered, lie buried in sleep, dream of deliverance, dream of the fulfilment of their impotent wishes, while, indignant at our supineness, his spirit abandons the world. He is no more! Deceive me not; deceive not thyself!

BRACKENBURG. No,—he lives! and the Spaniards, alas, are preparing for the people, on whom they are about to trample, a terrible spectacle, in order to crush, by a violent blow, each heart that yet pants for freedom.

CLARA. Proceed! Calmly pronounce my death-warrant also! Near and more near I approach that blessed land, and already from those realms of peace, I feel the breath of consolation. Say on.

BRACKENBURG. From casual words, dropped here and there by the guards, I learned that secretly in the market-place they were preparing some terrible spectacle. Through by-ways and familiar lanes I stole to my cousin's house, and

from a back window, looked out upon the market-place. Torches waved to and fro, in the hands of a wide circle of Spanish soldiers. I strained my unaccustomed sight, and out of the darkness there arose before me a scaffold, dark, spacious, and lofty! The sight filled me with horror. Several persons were employed in covering with black cloth such portions of the wood-work as yet remain exposed. The steps were covered last, also with black; —I saw it all. They seemed preparing for the celebration of some horrible sacrifice. A white crucifix, that shone like silver through the night, was raised on one side. As I gazed, the terrible conviction strengthened in my mind. Scattered torches still gleamed here and there; gradually they flickered and went out. Suddenly the hideous birth of night returned into its mother's womb.

CLARA. Hush, Brackenburg! Be still! Let this veil rest upon my soul. The spectres are vanished; and thou, gentle night, lend thy mantle to the inwardly fermenting earth, she will no longer endure the loathsome burden, shuddering, she rends open her yawning chasms, and with a crash swallows the murderous scaffold. And that God, whom in their rage they have insulted, sends down his angel from on high; at the hallowed touch of the messenger bolts and bars fly back; he pours around our friend a flood of splendour, and leads him gently through the night to liberty. My path leads also through the darkness to meet him.

BRACKENBURG [*detaining her*]. My child, whither would'st thou go? What would'st thou do?

CLARA. Softly, my friend, lest some one should awake! Lest we should awake ourselves! Know'st thou this phial, Brackenburg? I took it from thee once in jest, when thou, as was thy wont, didst threaten, in thy impatience, to end thy days.—And now my friend—

BRACKENBURG. In the name of all the saints!

CLARA. Thou can'st not hinder me. Death is my portion! Grudge me not the quiet and easy death which thou had'st prepared for thyself. Give me thine hand! At the moment when I unclose that dismal portal through which there is no return, I may tell thee, with this pressure of the hand, how sincerely I have loved, how deeply I have pitied thee. My brother died young; I chose thee to fill his place; thy heart rebelled, thou didst torment thyself and me, demanding with still increasing fervour, that which fate had not destined for thee. Forgive me and farewell! Let me call thee brother! 'Tis a name that embraces many names. Receive, with a true heart, the last fair token of the departing spirit —take this kiss. Death unites all, Brackenburg—us too it will unite!

BRACKENBURG. Let me then die with thee! Share it! oh share it! There is enough to extinguish two lives.

CLARA. Hold! Thou must live, thou can'st live.—Support my mother, who, without thee, would be a prey to want. Be to her what I can no longer be, live together, and weep for me. Weep for our fatherland, and for him who could alone have upheld it. The present generation must still endure this bitter woe; vengeance itself could not obliterate it. Poor souls, live on, through this gap in time. To-day the world suddenly stands still, its course is arrested, and my pulse will beat but for a few minutes longer. Farewell!

BRACKENBURG. Oh, live with us, as we live only for thy sake! In taking thine own life thou wilt take ours also; still live and suffer. We will stand by thee, nothing shall sever us from thy side, and love, with ever-watchful solicitude, shall prepare for thee the sweetest consolation in its loving arms. Be ours! Ours! I dare not say, mine.

CLARA. Hush, Brackenburg! You know not what chord you touch. Where you see hope, I see only despair.

BRACKENBURG. Share hope with the living! Pause on the brink of the precipice, cast one glance into the gulf below, and then look back on us.

CLARA. I have conquered; call me not back to the struggle.

BRACKENBURG. Thou art stunned; enveloped in night thou seekest the abyss. Every light is not yet extinguished, yet many days!——

CLARA. Alas! Alas! Cruelly thou dost rend the veil from before mine eyes. Yes, the day will dawn! Despite its misty shroud it needs must dawn. The citizen gazes timidly from his window, night leaves behind an ebon speck; he looks, and the scaffold looms fearfully in the morning light. With re-awakened anguish the desecrated image of the Saviour lifts to the Father its imploring eyes. The sun veils his beams, he will not mark the hero's death-hour. Slowly the fingers go their round—one hour strikes after another—hold! Now is the time! The thought of the morning scares me into the grave. [*She goes to the window as if to look out, and drinks secretly.*]

BRACKENBURG. Clara! Clara!

CLARA [*goes to the table, and drinks water*]. Here is the remainder. I invite thee not to follow me. Do as thou wilt; farewell. Extinguish this lamp silently and without delay; I am going to rest. Steal quietly away, close the door after thee. Be still! Wake not my mother! Go, save thyself, if thou wouldst not be taken for my murderer. [*Exit.*]

BRACKENBURG. She leaves me for the last time as she has ever done. What human soul could conceive how cruelly she lacerates the heart that loves her. She leaves me to myself, leaves me to choose between life and death, and both are alike hateful to me. To die alone! Weep ye tender souls! Fate has no sadder doom than mine. She shares with me the death-potion, yet sends me from her side! She draws me after her, yet thrusts me back into life! Oh, Egmont, how glorious is thy lot! She goes before thee! From her hand thou wilt receive the victor's crown. She will bring heaven itself to meet thy departing spirit. And shall I follow? Again to stand aloof? To carry this inextinguishable jealousy even to yon distant realms? Earth is no longer a tarrying place for me, and hell and heaven offer equal torture. How welcome to the wretched the dread hand of annihilation! [*Exit.*]

[*The scene remains some time unchanged. Music sounds, indicating* CLARA'S *death; the lamp which* BRACKENBURG *had forgotten to extinguish, flares up once or twice, and then suddenly expires. The scene changes.*]

A prison.

[EGMONT *is discovered sleeping on a couch. A rustling of keys is heard; the door opens; servants enter with torches;* FERDINAND *and* SILVA *follow, accompanied by soldiers.* EGMONT *starts from his sleep.*]

EGMONT. Who are ye that thus rudely banish slumber from my eyes? What mean these vague and insolent glances? Why this fearful procession? With what dream of horror come ye to delude my half awakened soul?

SILVA. The duke sends us to announce your sentence.

EGMONT. Do ye also bring the headsman who is to execute it?

SILVA. Listen, and you will know the doom that awaits you.

EGMONT. It is in keeping with the rest of your infamous proceedings. Alike conceived and executed in the night, so would this audacious act of injustice shroud itself from observation! Step boldly forth, thou who dost bear the sword concealed beneath thy mantle; here is my head, the freest ever doomed by tyranny to the block.

SILVA. You err! The righteous judges who have condemned you, will not conceal their sentence from the light of day.

EGMONT. Then does their audacity exceed all imagination and belief.

SILVA [*takes the sentence from an attendant, unfolds it, and reads*]. "In the king's name, and invested by his majesty with authority to judge all his subjects, of whatever rank, not excepting the knights of the Golden Fleece, we declare——"

EGMONT. Can the king transfer that authority?

SILVA. "We declare, after a strict and legal investigation, you, Henry, Count Egmont, Prince of Gaure, guilty of high treason, and pronounce your sentence:—That at early dawn you be led from this prison to the market-place, and that there, in sight of the people, and as a warning to traitors, your head be severed from your body. Given at Brussels. [*Date and year so indistinctly read as to be imperfectly heard by the audience.*] Ferdinand, Duke of Alva, president of the tribunal of twelve."

You know your doom. Brief time remains for you to prepare for the impending stroke, to arrange your affairs, and to take leave of your friends.

[*Exit* SILVA, *with followers.* FERDINAND *remains with two torch-bearers. The stage is dimly lighted.*]

EGMONT [*stands for a time, as if buried in thought, and allows* SILVA *to retire without looking round. He imagines himself alone, and, on raising his eyes, beholds* ALVA'S *son*]. Thou tarriest here? Wouldst thou, by thy presence, augment my amazement, my horror? Wouldst thou carry to thy father the welcome tidings that thou hast seen me overpowered by womanish despair? Go, tell him that he deceives neither the world nor me. At first it will be whispered cautiously behind his back, then spoken more and more loudly, and when, at some future day, the ambitious man descends from his proud eminence, a thousand voices will proclaim —that 'twas not the welfare of the state, nor the honour of the king, nor the tranquillity of the provinces, that brought him hither. For his own selfish ends he, the warrior, has counselled war, that the value of his services might be enhanced. He has excited this monstrous insurrection that his presence might be deemed necessary in order to quell it. And I fall a victim to his mean hatred, his contemptible envy. Yes, I know it, dying and mortally wounded I may utter it; long has the proud man envied me, long has he meditated and planned my ruin.

Even then, when still young, we played at dice together, and the heaps of gold passed rapidly from his side to mine, he would look on with affected composure, while inwardly consumed with rage, more at my success than at his own loss. Well do I remember the fiery glance, the treacherous pallor that overspread his features, when, at a public festival, we shot for a wager before assembled thousands. He challenged me, and both nations stood by; Spaniards and Netherlanders wagered on either side; I was the victor; his ball missed, mine hit the mark, and the air was rent by acclamations from my friends. His shot now hits me. Tell him that I know this, that I know him, that the world despises every trophy that a paltry spirit erects for itself by base and surreptitious arts. And thou! If it be possible for a son to swerve from the manners of his father, practise shame betimes, while thou art compelled to feel shame for him whom thou wouldst fain revere with thy whole heart.

FERDINAND. I listen without interrupting thee! Thy reproaches fall like blows upon a helm of steel. I feel the shock, but I am armed. They strike, but do not wound me; I am sensible only to the anguish that lacerates my heart. Alas! Alas! Have I lived to witness such a scene? Am I sent hither to behold a spectacle like this?

EGMONT. Dost thou break out into lamentations! What moves, what agitates thee thus? Is it a late remorse at having lent thyself to this infamous conspiracy? Thou art so young, thy exterior is so prepossessing. Thy demeanour towards me was so friendly, so unreserved! So long as I beheld thee, I was reconciled with thy father; and crafty, ay, more crafty than he, thou hast lured me into the toils. Thou art the wretch! The monster! Whoso confides in him, does so at his own peril; but who could apprehend danger in trusting thee? Go! Go! Rob me not of the few moments that are left to me! Go, that I may collect my thoughts, forget the world, and thee, first of all!

FERDINAND. What can I say! I stand, and gaze on thee, yet see thee not; I am scarcely conscious of my own existence. Shall I seek to excuse myself? Shall I aver that it was not till the last moment that I was made aware of my father's intentions? That I acted as the constrained, the passive instrument of his will? What signifies now the opinion thou mayst entertain of me? Thou art lost; and I, miserable wretch, stand here but to assure thee of it, and to lament thy doom.

EGMONT. What strange voice, what unexpected consolation comes thus to cheer my passage to the tomb? Thou, the son of my first, of almost my only enemy, thou dost pity me, thou art not associated with my murderers? Speak! In what light must I regard thee?

FERDINAND. Cruel father! Yes, I recognize thy nature in this command. Thou didst know my heart, my disposition, which thou hast so often censured as the inheritance of a tender-hearted mother. To mould me into thine own likeness thou hast sent me hither. Thou dost compel me to behold this man on the verge of the yawning grave, in the grasp of an arbitrary doom, that I may experience the profoundest anguish; that thus, rendered callous to every fate, I may henceforth meet every event with a heart unmoved.

EGMONT. I am amazed! Be calm! Act and speak like a man.

FERDINAND. Oh, that I were a woman! That they might say—what moves, what agitates thee? Tell me of a greater, a more monstrous crime, make me the spectator of a more direful deed; I will thank thee, I will say this was nothing.

EGMONT. Thou dost forget thyself. Consider where thou art?

FERDINAND. Let this passion rage, let me give vent to my anguish. I will not seem composed when my whole inner being is convulsed. Must I behold thee here? Thee? It is horrible? Thou understandest me not! How shouldst thou understand me? Egmont! Egmont!

[*Falling on his neck.*]

EGMONT. Explain this mystery.

FERDINAND. It is no mystery.

EGMONT. How can the fate of a mere stranger thus deeply move thee?

FERDINAND. Not a stranger! Thou art no stranger to me. Thy name it was that, even from my boyhood, shone before me like a star in heaven! How often have I made inquiries concerning thee, and listened to the story of thy deeds. The youth is the hope of the boy, the man of the youth. Thus didst thou walk before me, ever before me; I saw thee without envy, and followed after, step by step; at length I hoped to see thee—I saw, and my heart embraced thee. I had destined thee for myself, and when I beheld thee, I made choice of thee anew. I hoped now to know thee, to associate with thee, to be thy friend—'tis over, and I meet thee here!

EGMONT. My friend, if it can be any comfort to thee, be assured that the very moment we met, my heart was drawn towards thee. Now listen! Let us exchange a few quiet words; is it the stern, the settled purpose of thy father to take my life?

FERDINAND. It is.

EGMONT. This sentence is not a mere scarecrow, designed to terrify me, to punish me through fear and intimidation, to humiliate me, that he may then raise me again by the royal favour?

FERDINAND. Alas, no! At first I flattered myself with this delusive hope, and even then my heart was filled with anguish to behold thee thus. Thy doom is real! Is certain! I cannot command myself. Who will counsel, who will aid me to meet the inevitable?

EGMONT. Listen! If thy heart is impelled so powerfully in my favour, if thou dost abhor the tyranny that holds me fettered, then deliver me! The moments are precious. Thou art the son of the all-powerful, and thou hast power thyself. Let us fly! I know the roads; the means of effecting our escape cannot be unknown to thee. These walls, a few short miles, alone separate us from my friends. Loose these fetters, conduct me to them; be ours. The king, on some future day, will doubtless thank my deliverer. Now he is taken by surprise, or perchance he is ignorant of the whole proceeding. Thy father ventures on this daring step, and majesty, though horror-struck at the deed, must needs sanction the irrevocable. Thou dost deliberate? Oh, contrive for me the way to freedom! Speak; nourish hope in a living soul.

FERDINAND. Cease! Oh cease! Every word deepens my despair. There is here no outlet, no counsel, no escape.—'Tis this thought that tortures me, that lays hold of my heart, and rends it as with talons. I have myself spread the net; I know its firm, inextricable knots; I know that every avenue is barred alike to courage and to stratagem. I feel that I too am fettered, like thyself, like all the rest. Think'st thou that I should give way to lamentation if any means of safety remained untried? I have thrown myself at his feet, I have remonstrated, I have implored. He has sent me hither, in order to blast in this fatal moment, every remnant of joy and happiness that yet survived within my heart.

EGMONT. And is there no deliverance?

FERDINAND. None!

EGMONT [*stamping his foot*]. No deliverance!—Sweet life! Sweet, pleasant habitude of being and of activity! Must I part from thee! So calmly part! Not amid the tumult of battle, the din of arms, the excitement of the fray, dost thou send me a hasty farewell; thine is no hurried leave; thou dost not abridge the moment of separation. Once more let me clasp thy hand, gaze once more into thine eyes, feel with keen emotion, thy beauty and thy worth, then resolutely tear myself away, and say;—depart!

FERDINAND. Must I stand by, and look passively on; unable to save thee, or to give thee aid! What voice avails for lamentation! What heart but must break under the pressure of such anguish?

EGMONT. Be calm!

FERDINAND. Thou can'st be calm, thou can'st renounce life: led on by necessity, thou can'st advance to the direful struggle, with the courage of a hero. What can I do? What ought I to do? Thou dost conquer thyself and us; thou art the victor; I survive both myself and thee. I have lost my light at the banquet, my banner on the field. The future lies before me, dark, desolate, perplexed.

EGMONT. Young friend, whom by a strange fatality, at the same moment, I both win and lose, who dost feel for me, who dost suffer for me the agonies of death,—look on me;—thou wilt not lose me. If my life was a mirror in which thou didst love to contemplate thyself, so be also my death. Men are not together only when in each other's presence;—the distant, the departed, still live for us. I shall live for thee, and for myself I have lived long enough. I have enjoyed each day; each day, I have performed, with prompt activity, the duties enjoined by my conscience. Now my life ends, as it might have ended, long, long, ago, on the sands of Gravelines. I shall cease to live; but I have lived. My friend, follow in my steps, lead a cheerful and a joyous life, and dread not the approach of death.

FERDINAND. Thou should'st have saved thyself for us, thou could'st have saved thyself. Thou art the cause of thine own destruction. Often have I listened when able men discoursed concerning thee; foes and friends, they would dispute long as to thy worth; but on one point they were agreed, none ventured to deny that thou wert treading a dangerous path. How often have I longed to warn thee! Hadst thou no friends?

EGMONT. I was warned.

FERDINAND. And I found all these allegations, point for point, in the indictment, together with thy answers, containing much that might serve to palliate thy conduct, but no evidence weighty enough fully to exculpate thee.

EGMONT. No more of this. Man imagines that he directs his life, that he governs his actions, when in fact his existence is irrisistibly controlled by his destiny. Let us not dwell upon this subject; these reflections I can dismiss with ease—not so my apprehensions for these provinces; yet they too will be cared for. Could my blood bring peace to my people, how freely should it flow. Alas! This may not be. Yet it ill becomes a man idly to speculate, when the power to act is no longer his. If thou canst restrain or guide the fatal power of thy father; do so. Alas, who can?—Farewell!

FERDINAND. I cannot leave thee.

EGMONT. Let me urgently recommend my followers to thy care! I have worthy men in my service; let them not be dispersed, let them not become destitute! How fares it with Richard, my Secretary?

FERDINAND. He is gone before thee. They have beheaded him, as thy accomplice in high treason.

EGMONT. Poor soul!—Yet one word, and then farewell, I can no more. However powerfully the spirit may be stirred, nature at length irresistibly asserts her rights; and like a child who enjoys refreshing slumber though enveloped in a serpent's folds, so the weary one lays himself down to rest before the gates of death, and sleeps soundly, as though a toilsome journey yet lay before him.—One word more,—I know a maiden; thou wilt not despise her because she was mine. Since I can commend her to thy care, I shall die in peace. Thy soul is noble; in such a man, a woman is sure to find a protector. Lives my old Adolphus? Is he free?

FERDINAND. The active old man, who always attended thee on horseback?

EGMONT. The same.

FERDINAND. He lives, he is free.

EGMONT. He knows her dwelling; let him guide thy steps thither, and reward him to his dying day, for having shown thee the way to this jewel.—Farewell!

FERDINAND. I cannot leave thee.

EGMONT [*urging him towards the door*]. Farewell!

FERDINAND. Oh let me linger yet a moment!

EGMONT. No leave-taking, my friend.

[*He accompanies* FERDINAND *to the door, and then tears himself away;* FERDINAND *overwhelmed with grief, hastily retires.*]

EGMONT [*alone*]. Cruel man! Thou didst not think to render me this service through thy son. He has been the means of relieving my mind from the pressure of care and sorrow, from fear and every anxious thought. Gently, yet urgently, nature claims her final tribute. 'Tis past! —'Tis resolved! And the reflections which, in the suspense of last night, kept me wakeful on my couch, now with resistless certainty, lull my senses to repose. [*He seats himself upon the couch; music.*] Sweet sleep! Like the purest happiness, thou comest most willingly, uninvited, unsought. Thou dost loosen the knots of earnest thoughts, dost mingle all images of joy and of sorrow, unimpeded the circle of inner harmony flows on, and wrapped in fond delusion, we sink into oblivion, and cease to be.

[*He sleeps; music accompanies his slumber. The wall behind his couch appears to open and discovers a brilliant apparition. Freedom, in a celestial garb, surrounded by a glory, reposes in a cloud. Her features are those of* CLARA *and she inclines towards the sleeping hero. Her countenance betokens compassion, she seems to lament his fate. Quickly she recovers herself and with an encouraging gesture exhibits the symbols of freedom, the bundle of arrows, with the*

staff and cap. She encourages him to be of good cheer, and while she signifies to him, that his death will secure the freedom of the provinces, she hails him as a conqueror, and extends to him a laurel crown. As the wreath approaches his head, EGMONT *moves like one asleep, and reclines with his face towards her. She holds the wreath suspended over his head;—martial music is heard in the distance, at the first sound the vision disappears. The music grows louder and louder.* EGMONT *awakes. The prison is dimly illumined by the dawn.—His first impulse is to lift his hand to his head, he stands up, and gazes round, his hand still upraised.*]

The crown is vanished! Beautiful vision, the light of day has frighted thee! Yes, they revealed themselves to my sight, uniting in one radiant form the two sweetest joys of my heart. Divine Liberty borrowed the mien of my beloved one; the lovely maiden arrayed herself in the celestial garb of her friend. In a solemn moment they appeared united with aspect more earnest than tender. With bloodstained feet the vision approached, the waving folds of her robe also were tinged with blood. It was my blood, and the blood of many brave hearts. No! It shall not be shed in vain! Forward! Brave people! The goddess of liberty leads you on! And as the sea breaks through and destroys the barriers that would oppose its fury, so do ye overwhelm the bulwark of tyranny, and with your impetuous flood sweep it away from the land which it usurps. [*Drums.*] Hark! Hark! How often has this sound summoned my joyous steps to the field of battle and of victory! How bravely did I tread, with my gallant comrades, the dangerous path of fame! And now, from this dungeon I shall go forth, to meet a glorious death; I die for freedom, for whose cause I have lived and fought, and for whom I now offer myself up a sorrowing sacrifice.

[The back-ground is occupied by Spanish soldiers with halberts.]

Yes, lead them on! Close your ranks, ye terrify me not. I am accustomed to stand amid the serried ranks of war, and environed by the threatening forms of death, to feel, with double zest, the energy of life. *[Drums.]*

The foe closes round on every side! Swords are flashing; courage, friends!

Behind are your parents, your wives, your children! *[Pointing to the guard.]* And these are impelled by the word of their leader, not by their own free will. Protect your homes! And to save those who are most dear to you, be ready to follow my example, and to fall with joy.

[Drums. As he advances through the guards towards the door in the back-ground, the curtain falls. The music joins in, and the scene closes with a symphony of victory.]

WILLIAM TELL

By JOHANN CHRISTOPH FRIEDRICH VON SCHILLER

Produced at Weimar, 1804

TRANSLATED BY SIR THEODORE MARTIN

CHARACTERS

HERMANN GESSLER, *governor of Schwyz and Uri*
WERNER, *baron of Attinghausen, free noble of Switzerland*
ULRICH VON RUDENZ, *his nephew*

WERNER STAUFFACHER,	
KONRAD HUNN,	
HANS AUF DER MAUER,	
JÖRG IM HOFE,	*People of Schwyz*
ULRICH DER SCHMIDT,	
JOST VON WEILER,	
ITEL REDING,	
WALTER FÜRST,	
WILHELM TELL,	
RÖSSELMANN, *the priest,*	
PETERMANN, *sacristan,*	*of Uri*
KUONI, *herdsman,*	
WERNI, *huntsman,*	
RUODI, *fisherman,*	
ARNOLD OF MELCHTHAL,	
KONRAD BAUMGARTEN,	
MEYER VON SARNEN,	
STRUTH VON WINKELRIED,	*of Unterwald*
KLAUS VON DER FLÜE,	
BURKHART AM BÜHEL,	
ARNOLD VON SEWA,	

PFEIFFER OF LUCERNE
KUNZ OF GERSAU
JENNI, *fisherman's son*
SEPPI, *herdsman's son*
GERTRUDE, *Stauffacher's wife*
HEDWIG, *wife of Tell, daughter of Fürst*
BERTHA OF BRUNECK, *a rich heiress*
ARMGART,
MECHTHILD,
ELSBETH,
HILDEGARD, } *peasant women*
WALTER,
WILHELM, } *Tell's sons*
FRIESSHARDT,
LEUTHOLD, } *soldiers*
RUDOLPH DER HARRAS, *Gessler's master of the horse*
JOHANNES PARRICIDA, *Duke of Suabia*
STÜSSI, *overseer, ranger*
THE MAYOR OF URI
A COURIER
MASTER STONEMASON, COMPANIONS AND WORKMEN
TASKMASTER
A CRIER, *the Stier of Uri (the horn-blower of Uri)*
MONKS OF THE ORDER OF CHARITY
HORSEMEN OF GESSLER AND LANDENBERG
MANY PEASANTS; MEN AND WOMEN FROM THE WALD-
STETTEN

ACT I

SCENE I

A high rocky shore of the lake of Lucerne opposite Schwyz. The lake makes a bend into the land; a hut stands at a short distance from the shore; the fisher boy is rowing about in his boat. Beyond the lake are seen the green meadows, the hamlets and farms of Schwyz, lying in the clear sunshine. On the left are observed the peaks of the Hacken, surrounded with clouds; to the right, and in the remote distance, appear the Glaciers. The Ranz des Vaches and the tinkling of cattle bells, continue for some time after the rising of the curtain.

FISHER BOY [*sings in his boat*].
Melody of the Ranz des Vaches
The clear smiling lake woo'd to bathe in its deep
A boy on its green shore had laid him to sleep;
  Then heard he a melody
    Flowing and soft,
  And sweet, as when angels
    Are singing aloft.

And as thrilling with pleasure he wakes from his rest,
The waters are murmuring over his breast;
 And a voice from the deep cries,
 "With me thou must go,
 I charm the young shepherd,
 I lure him below."

HERDSMAN [on the mountains].

Air—Variation of the Ranz des Vaches
 Farewell, ye green meadows,
 Farewell, sunny shore,
 The herdsman must leave you,
 The summer is o'er.
We go to the hills, but you'll see us again,
When the cuckoo is calling, and wood-notes are gay,
When flow'rets are blooming in dingle and plain,
And the brooks sparkle up in the sunshine of May.
 Farewell, ye green meadows,
 Farewell, sunny shore,
 The herdsman must leave you,
 The summer is o'er.

CHAMOIS HUNTER [appearing on the top of a cliff].

Second Variation of the Ranz des Vaches
On the heights peals the thunder, and trembles the bridge.
The huntsman bounds on by the dizzying ridge.
 Undaunted he hies him
 O'er ice-covered wild,
 Where leaf never budded,
 Nor Spring ever smiled;
And beneath him an ocean of mist, where his eye
No longer the dwellings of man can espy;
 Through the parting clouds only
 The earth can be seen,
 Far down 'neath the vapor
 The meadows of green.
 [A change comes over the land-
  scape. A rumbling, cracking
  noise is heard among the
  mountains. Shadows of clouds
  sweep across the scene.]

[RUODI, the fisherman, comes out of his cottage. WERNI, the huntsman, descends from the rocks. KUONI, the shepherd, enters, with a milkpail on his shoulders, followed by SEPPI, his assistant.]

RUODI. Bestir thee, Jenni, haul the boat on shore.
The grizzly Vale-King comes, the Glaciers moan,
The lofty Mytenstein draws on his hood,
And from the Stormcleft chilly blows the wind;
The storm will burst before we are prepared.

KUONI. 'Twill rain ere long; my sheep browse eagerly,
And Watcher there is scraping up the earth.

WERNI. The fish are leaping, and the water-hen
Dives up and down. A storm is coming on.

KUONI [to his boy]. Look, Seppi, if the cattle are not straying.

SEPPI. There goes brown Liesel, I can hear her bells.

KUONI. Then all are safe; she ever ranges farthest.

RUODI. You've a fine yoke of bells there, master herdsman.

WERNI. And likely cattle, too. Are they your own?

KUONI. I'm not so rich. They are the noble lord's
Of Attinghaus, and trusted to my care.

RUODI. How gracefully yon heifer bears her ribbon!

KUONI. Ay, well she knows she's leader of the herd,
And, take it from her, she'd refuse to feed.

RUODI. You're joking now. A beast devoid of reason—

WERNI. That's easy said. But beasts have reason, too,—
And that we know, we men that hunt the chamois:
They never turn to feed—sagacious creatures!—
Till they have placed a sentinel ahead,
Who pricks his ears whenever we approach,

And gives alarm with clear and piercing
pipe.

RUODI [to the shepherd]. Are you for
home?

KUONI. The Alp is grazed quite
bare.

WERNI. A safe return, my friend!

KUONI. The same to you!
Men come not always back from tracks
like yours.

RUODI. But who comes here, running
at topmost speed?

WERNI. I know the man; 'tis Baum-
gart of Alzellen.

KONRAD BAUMGARTEN [rushing in
breathless]. For God's sake, ferry-
man, your boat!

RUODI. How now?
Why all this haste?

BAUMGARTEN. Cast off! My life's
at stake!
Set me across!

KUONI. Why, what's the matter,
friend?

WERNI. Who are pursuing you? First
tell us that.

BAUMGARTEN [to the fisherman].
Quick, quick, e'en now they're close
upon my heels!
The Viceroy's horsemen are in hot pur-
suit!
I'm a lost man, should they lay hands
upon me.

RUODI. Why are the troopers in pur-
suit of you?

BAUMGARTEN. First save my life, and
then I'll tell you all.

WERNI. There's blood upon your gar-
ments—how is this?

BAUMGARTEN. The imperial Seneschal,
who dwelt at Rossberg—

KUONI. How! What! The Wolfshot?
Is it he pursues you?

BAUMGARTEN. He'll ne'er hurt man
again; I've settled him.

ALL [starting back]. Now, God forgive
you, what is this you've done?

BAUMGARTEN. What every free man in
my place had done.
I have but used mine own good house-
hold right

'Gainst him that would have wrong'd
my wife—my honor.

KUONI. And has he wrong'd you in
your honor, then?

BAUMGARTEN. That he did not fulfil
his foul desire
Is due to God and to my trusty axe.

WERNI. You've cleft his skull then,
have you, with your axe?

KUONI. O, tell us all! You've time
enough, before
The boat can be unfastened from its
moorings.

BAUMGARTEN. When I was in the for-
est felling timber,
My wife came running out in mortal fear.
The Seneschal, she said, was in my house,
Had order'd her to get a bath prepared,
And thereupon had ta'en unseemly free-
doms,
From which she rid herself, and flew to
me.
Arm'd as I was, I sought him, and my
axe
Has given his bath a bloody benediction.

WERNI. And you did well; no man can
blame the deed.

KUONI. The tyrant! Now he has his
just reward!
We men of Unterwald have owed it
long.

BAUMGARTEN. The deed got wind, and
now they're in pursuit.
Heavens! whilst we speak, the time is
flying fast.
                    [It begins to thunder.]

KUONI. Quick, ferryman, and set the
good man over.

RUODI. Impossible! a storm is close
at hand,
Wait till it pass! You must.

BAUMGARTEN. Almighty heavens!
I cannot wait; the least delay is death.

KUONI [to the fisherman]. Push out—
God with you! We should help our
neighbors;
The like misfortune may betide us all.
            [Thunder and the roaring of the
            wind.]

RUODI. The South-wind's up! See how
the lake is rising!

I cannot steer against both storm and
    wave.
BAUMGARTEN [clasping him by the
    knees]. God so help you, as now you
    pity me!
WERNI. His life's at stake. Have pity
    on him, man!
KUONI. He is a father: has a wife and
    children.
            [Repeated peals of thunder.]
RUODI. What! and have I not, then,
    a life to lose,
A wife and child at home as well as he?
See, how the breakers foam, and toss,
    and whirl,
And the lake eddies up from all its
    depths!
Right gladly would I save the worthy
    man,
But 'tis impossible, as you must see.
BAUMGARTEN [still kneeling]. Then
    must I fall into the tyrant's hands,
And with the port of safety close in sight!
Yonder it lies! My eyes can measure
    it,
My very voice can echo to its shores.
There is the boat to carry me across,
Yet must I lie here helpless and forlorn.
KUONI. Look! who comes here?
RUODI. 'Tis Tell, brave Tell, of Bürglen.

    [Enter TELL with a cross-bow.]
TELL. Who is the man that here im-
    plores for aid?
KUONI. He is from Alzellen, and to
    guard his honor
From touch of foulest shame, has slain
    the Wolfshot,
The Imperial Seneschal, who dwelt at
    Rossberg.
The Viceroy's troopers are upon his
    heels;
He begs the boatman here to take him
    over,
But he, in terror of the storm, refuses.
RUODI. Well, there is Tell can steer as
    well as I,
He'll be my judge, if it be possible.
    [Violent peals of thunder—the
    lake becomes more tempestu-
    ous.]

Am I to plunge into the jaws of hell?
I should be mad to dare the desperate
    act.
TELL. The brave man thinks upon him-
    self the last.
Put trust in God, and help him in his
    need!
RUODI. Safe in the port, 'tis easy to
    advise.
There is the boat, and there the lake!
    Try you!
TELL. The lake may pity, but the
    Viceroy will not.
Come, venture, man!
SHEPHERD and HUNTSMEN. O save him!
    save him! save him!
RUODI. Though 'twere my brother, or
    my darling child,
I would not go. It is St. Simon's
    day,
The lake is up, and calling for its vic-
    tim.
TELL. Nought's to be done with idle
    talking here.
Time presses on—the man must be as-
    sisted.
Say, boatman, will you venture?
RUODI.   No; not I.
TELL. In God's name, then, give me
    the boat! I will,
With my poor strength, see what is to
    be done!
KUONI. Ha, noble Tell!
WERNI.   That's like a
    gallant huntsman!
BAUMGARTEN. You are my angel, my
    preserver, Tell.
TELL. I may preserve you from the
    Viceroy's power,
But from the tempest's rage another
    must.
Yet you had better fall into God's
    hands
Than into those of men. [To the HERDS-
    MAN.] Herdsman, do thou
Console my wife, should aught of ill be-
    fall me.
I do but what I may not leave undone.
            [He leaps into the boat.]
KUONI [to the FISHERMAN]. A pretty
    man to be a boatman, truly!

What Tell could risk, you dared not venture on.

RUODI. Far better men than I would not ape Tell.

There does not live his fellow 'mong the mountains.

WERNI [*who has ascended a rock*]. He pushes off. God help thee now, brave sailor!

Look how his bark is reeling on the waves!

KUONI [*on the shore*]. The surge has swept clean over it. And now

'Tis out of sight. Yet stay, there 'tis again!

Stoutly he stems the breakers, noble fellow!

SEPPI. Here come the troopers hard as they can ride!

KUONI. Heavens! so they do! Why, that was help, indeed.

[*Enter a troop of* HORSEMEN.]

1ST HORSEMAN. Give up the murderer! You have him here!

2ND HORSEMAN. This way he came! 'Tis useless to conceal him!

RUODI *and* KUONI. Whom do you mean?

1ST HORSEMAN [*discovering the boat*]. The devil! What do I see?

WERNI [*from above*]. Is't he in yonder boat ye seek? Ride on.

If you lay to, you may o'ertake him yet.

2ND HORSEMAN. Curse on you, he's escaped!

1ST HORSEMAN [*to the* SHEPHERD *and* FISHERMAN]. You help'd him off,

And you shall pay for it. Fall on their herds!

Down with the cottage! burn it! beat it down! [*They rush off.*]

SEPPI [*hurrying after them*]. Oh my poor lambs!

KUONI [*following him*]. Unhappy me, my herds!

WERNI. The tyrants!

RUODI [*wringing his hands*]. Righteous Heaven! Oh, when will come

Deliverance to this devoted land?

[*Exeunt severally.*]

SCENE II

A lime tree in front of STAUFFACHER'S *house at Steinen, in Schwyz, upon the public road, near a bridge.*

[WERNER STAUFFACHER *and* PFEIFFER, *of Lucerne, enter into conversation.*]

PFEIFFER. Ay, ay, friend Stauffacher, as I have said,

Swear not to Austria, if you can help it.

Hold by the Empire stoutly as of yore,

And God preserve you in your ancient freedom! [*Presses his hand warmly and is going.*]

STAUFFACHER. Wait till my mistress comes. Now do! You are

My guest in Schwyz—I in Lucerne am yours.

PFEIFFER. Thanks! thanks! But I must reach Gersau to-day.

Whatever grievances your rulers' pride

And grasping avarice may yet inflict,

Bear them in patience—soon a change may come.

Another emperor may mount the throne.

But Austria's once, and you are hers for ever. [*Exit.*]

[STAUFFACHER *sits down sorrowfully upon a bench under the lime tree.* GERTRUDE, *his wife, enters, and finds him in this posture. She places herself near him, and looks at him for some time in silence.*]

GERTRUDE. So sad, my love! I scarcely know thee now.

For many a day in silence I have mark'd

A moody sorrow furrowing thy brow.

Some silent grief is weighing on thy heart.

Trust it to me. I am thy faithful wife,

And I demand my half of all thy cares.

[STAUFFACHER *gives her his hand and is silent.*]

Tell me what can oppress thy spirits thus?

Thy toil is blest—the world goes well with thee—

Our barns are full—our cattle, many a score;

Our handsome team of sleek and well-
fed steeds
Brought from the mountain pastures
safely home,
To winter in their comfortable stalls.
There stands thy house—no nobleman's
more fair!
'Tis newly built with timber of the best,
All grooved and fitted with the nicest
skill;
Its many glistening windows tell of com-
fort!
'Tis quarter'd o'er with scutcheons of all
hues,
And proverbs sage, which passing trav-
ellers
Linger to read, and ponder o'er their
meaning.
STAUFFACHER. The house is strongly
built, and handsomely,
But, ah! the ground on which we built
it totters.
GERTRUDE. Tell me, dear Werner, what
you mean by that?
STAUFFACHER. No later since than yes-
terday I sat
Beneath this linden, thinking with de-
light
How fairly all was finished, when from
Küssnacht
The Viceroy and his men came riding by.
Before this house he halted in surprise:
At once I rose, and, as beseemed his rank,
Advanced respectfully to greet the lord,
To whom the Emperor delegates his power,
As judge supreme within our Canton here.
"Who is the owner of this house?" he
asked,
With mischief in his thoughts, for well
he knew.
With prompt decision, thus I answered
him:
"The Emperor, your grace—my lord and
yours,
And held by me in fief." On this he
answered,
"I am the Emperor's viceregent here,
And will not that each peasant churl
should build
At his own pleasure, bearing him as
freely

As though he were the master in the
land.
I shall make bold to put a stop to this!"
So saying, he, with menaces, rode off,
And left me musing with a heavy heart
On the fell purpose that his words be-
tray'd.
GERTRUDE. Mine own dear lord and
husband! Wilt thou take
A word of honest council from thy wife?
I boast to be the noble Iberg's child,
A man of wide experience. Many a
time,
As we sat spinning in the winter nights,
My sisters and myself, the people's chiefs
Were wont to gather round our father's
hearth,
To read the old imperial charters, and
To hold sage converse on the country's
weal.
Then heedfully I listened, marking well
What now the wise man thought, or good
man wished;
And garner'd up their wisdom in my
heart.
Hear then, and mark me well; for thou
wilt see,
I long have known the grief that weighs
thee down.
The Viceroy hates thee, fain would in-
jure thee,
For thou hast cross'd his wish to bend
the Swiss
In homage to this upstart house of
princes,
And kept them staunch, like their good
sires of old,
In true allegiance to the Empire. Say,
Is't not so, Werner? Tell me, am I
wrong?
STAUFFACHER. 'Tis even so. For this
doth Gessler hate me.
GERTRUDE. He burns with envy, too,
to see thee living
Happy and free on thine inheritance,
For he has none. From the Emperor
himself
Thou hold'st in fief the lands thy fathers
left thee.
There's not a prince i' the Empire that
can show

A better title to his heritage;
For thou hast over thee no lord but one,
And he the mightiest of all Christian kings.
Gessler we know, is but a younger son,
His only wealth the knightly cloak he wears;
He therefore views an honest man's good fortune
With a malignant and a jealous eye.
Long has he sworn to compass thy destruction.
As yet thou art uninjured. Wilt thou wait
Till he may safely give his malice scope?
A wise man would anticipate the blow.
STAUFFACHER. What's to be done?
GERTRUDE.   Now hear what I advise.
Thou knowest well, how here with us in Schwyz
All worthy men are groaning underneath
This Gessler's grasping, grinding tyranny.
Doubt not the men of Unterwald as well,
And Uri, too, are chafing like ourselves
At this oppressive and heart-wearying yoke.
For there, across the lake, the Landenberg
Wields the same iron rule as Gessler here—
No fishing-boat comes over to our side
But brings the tidings of some new encroachment,
Some outrage fresh, more grievous than the last.
Then it were well that some of you—true men—
Men sound at heart, should secretly devise
How best to shake this hateful thraldom off.
Well do I know that God would not desert you,
But lend his favor to the righteous cause.
Hast thou no friend in Uri, say, to whom
Thou frankly may'st unbosom all thy thoughts?
STAUFFACHER. I know full many a gallant fellow there,

And nobles, too,—great men, of high repute,
In whom I can repose unbounded trust.
                              [Rising.]
Wife! What a storm of wild and perilous thoughts
Hast thou stirr'd up within my tranquil breast?
The darkest musings of my bosom thou
Hast dragg'd to light, and placed them full before me;
And what I scarce dared harbor e'en in thought
Thou speakest plainly out, with fearless tongue.
But hast thou weigh'd well what thou urgest thus?
Discord will come, and the fierce clang of arms,
To scare this valley's long unbroken peace,
If we, a feeble shepherd race, shall dare
Him to the fight, that lords it o'er the world.
Ev'n now they only wait some fair pretext
For setting loose their savage warrior hordes,
To scourge and ravage this devoted land,
To lord it o'er us with the victor's rights,
And, 'neath the show of lawful chastisement,
Despoil us of our chartered liberties.
GERTRUDE. You, too, are men; can wield a battle-axe
As well as they. God ne'er deserts the brave.
STAUFFACHER. Oh wife! a horrid, ruthless fiend is war,
That strikes at once the shepherd and his flock.
GERTRUDE. Whate'er great Heaven inflicts, we must endure;
No heart of noble temper brooks injustice.
STAUFFACHER. This house—thy pride—war, unrelenting war,
Will burn it down.
GERTRUDE. And did I think this heart
Enslaved and fettered to the things of earth,
With *my* own hand I'd hurl the kindling torch.

STAUFFACHER. Thou hast faith in human kindness, wife; but war
Spares not the tender infant in its cradle.

GERTRUDE. There is a friend to innocence in heaven!
Look forward, Werner—not behind you, now!

STAUFFACHER. We men may perish bravely, sword in hand;
But oh, what fate, my Gertrude, may be thine?

GERTRUDE. None are so weak but one last choice is left.
A spring from yonder bridge, and I am free!

STAUFFACHER [embracing her]. Well may he fight for hearth and home, that clasps
A heart so rare as thine against his own!
What are the hosts of Emperors to him?
Gertrude, farewell! I will to Uri straight.
There lives my worthy comrade, Walter Fürst;
His thoughts and mine upon these times are one.
There, too, resides the noble Banneret
Of Attinghaus. High though of blood he be,
He loves the people, honors their old customs.
With both of these I will take counsel how
To rid us bravely of our country's foe.
Farewell! and while I am away, bear thou
A watchful eye in management at home;
The pilgrim, journeying to the house of God,
And pious monk, collecting for his cloister,
To these give liberally from purse and garner.
Stauffacher's house would not be hid. Right out
Upon the public way it stands, and offers
To all that pass an hospitable roof.
        [While they are retiring, TELL
          enters with BAUMGARTEN.]
TELL. Now, then, you have no further need of me.
Enter yon house. 'Tis Werner Stauffacher's,

A man that is a father to distress.
See, there he is, himself! Come, follow me.   [They retire. Scene changes.]

SCENE III

A common near Altdorf. On an eminence in the background a Castle in progress of erection, and so far advanced that the outline of the whole may be distinguished. The back part is finished; men are working at the front. Scaffolding, on which the workmen are going up and down. A slater is seen upon the highest part of the roof. All is bustle and activity.

[TASKMASTER, MASON, WORKMEN and
        LABORERS.]
TASKMASTER [with a stick, urging on the workmen]. Up, up! You've rested long enough! To work!
The stones here! Now the mortar, and the lime!
And let his lordship see the work advanced,
When next he comes. These fellows crawl like snails!
[To two laborers, with loads.] What! call ye that a load? Go, double it.
Is this the way ye earn your wages, laggards?

1ST WORKMAN. 'Tis very hard that we must bear the stones
To make a keep and dungeon for ourselves!

TASKMASTER. What's that you mutter? 'Tis a worthless race,
And fit for nothing but to milk their cows,
And saunter idly up and down the mountains.

OLD MAN [sinks down exhausted]. I can no more.

TASKMASTER [shaking him]. Up, up, old man, to work!

1ST WORKMAN. Have you no bowels of compassion, thus
To press so hard upon a poor old man
That scarce can drag his feeble limbs along?

MASTER MASON *and* WORKMEN. Shame, shame upon you—shame! It cries to heaven!

TASKMASTER. Mind your own business. I but do my duty.

1ST WORKMAN. Pray, master, what's to be the name of this Same castle, when 'tis built?

TASKMASTER. The Keep of Uri; For by it we shall keep you in subjection.

WORKMAN. The Keep of Uri?

TASKMASTER. Well, why laugh at that?

2ND WORKMAN. So you'll keep Uri with this paltry place!

1ST WORKMAN. How many mole-hills such as that must first Be piled above each other, ere you make A mountain equal to the least in Uri?

[TASKMASTER *retires.*]

MASTER MASON. I'll drown the mallet in the deepest lake, That served my hand on this accursed pile.

[*Enter* TELL *and* STAUFFACHER.]

STAUFFACHER. O, that I had not lived to see this sight!

TELL. Here 'tis not good to be. Let us proceed.

STAUFFACHER. Am I in Uri, in the land of freedom?

MASTER MASON. O, sir, if you could only see the vaults Beneath these towers. The man that tenants them Will never hear the cock crow more.

STAUFFACHER. O God!

MASON. Look at these ramparts and these buttresses, That seem as they were built to last for ever.

TELL. Hands can destroy whatever hands have rear'd. [*Pointing to the mountains.*] *That* house of freedom God hath built for us.

[*A drum is heard. People enter bearing a cap upon a pole, followed by a crier. Women and children thronging tumultuously after them.*]

1ST WORKMAN. What means the drum? Give heed!

MASON. Why, here's a mumming! And look, the cap—what can they mean by that?

CRIER. In the Emperor's name, give ear!

WORKMAN. Hush! silence! hush!

CRIER. Ye men of Uri, ye do see this cap! It will be set upon a lofty pole In Altdorf, in the market-place: and this Is the Lord Governor's good-will and pleasure, The cap shall have like honor as himself, And all shall reverence it with bended knee, And head uncovered; thus the king will know Who are his true and loyal subjects here; His life and goods are forfeit to the crown That shall refuse obedience to the order.

[*The people burst out into laughter. The drum beats, and the procession passes on.*]

1ST WORKMAN. A strange device to fall upon, indeed! Do reverence to a cap! A pretty farce! Heard ever mortal anything like this?

MASTER MASON. Down to a cap on bended knee, forsooth! Rare jesting this with men of sober sense!

1ST WORKMAN. Nay, were it but the imperial crown, indeed! But 'tis the cap of Austria! I've seen it Hanging above the throne in Gessler's hall.

MASON. The cap of Austria? Mark that! A snare To get us into Austria's power, by Heaven!

WORKMAN. No freeborn man will stoop to such disgrace.

MASTER MASON. Come—to our comrades, and advise with them!

[*They retire.*]

TELL [*to* STAUFFACHER]. You see how matters stand. Farewell, my friend!

STAUFFACHER. Whither away? Oh, leave us not so soon.

TELL. They look for me at home. So fare ye well.

STAUFFACHER. My heart's so full, and has so much to tell you.

TELL. Words will not make a heart that's heavy light.

STAUFFACHER. Yet words may possibly conduct to deeds.

TELL. All we can do is to endure in silence.

STAUFFACHER. But shall we bear what is not to be borne?

TELL. Impetuous rulers have the shortest reigns.

When the fierce Southwind rises from his chasms,
Men cover up their fires, the ships in haste
Make for the harbor, and the mighty spirit
Sweeps o'er the earth, and leaves no trace behind.
Let every man live quietly at home;
Peace to the peaceful rarely is denied.

STAUFFACHER. And is it thus you view our grievances?

TELL. The serpent stings not till it is provoked.
Let them alone; they'll weary of themselves
Whene'er they see we are not to be roused.

STAUFFACHER. Much might be done—did we stand fast together.

TELL. When the ship founders, he will best escape
Who seeks no other's safety but his own.

STAUFFACHER. And you desert the common cause so coldly?

TELL. A man can safely count but on himself!

STAUFFACHER. Nay, even the weak grow strong by union.

TELL. But the strong man is strongest when alone.

STAUFFACHER. Your country, then, cannot rely on you,
If in despair she rise against her foes.

TELL. Tell rescues the lost sheep from yawning gulfs:
Is he a man, then, to desert his friends?
Yet, whatsoe'er you do, spare me from council!
I was not born to ponder and select;
But when your course of action is resolved,

Then call on Tell: you shall not find him fail.

[*Exeunt severally. A sudden tumult is heard around the scaffolding.*]

MASON [*running in*]. What's wrong?

1ST WORKMAN [*running forward*]. The slater's fallen from the roof.

BERTHA [*rushing in*]. Is he dashed to pieces? Run—save him, help!
If help be possible, save him! Here is gold. [*Throws her trinkets among the people.*]

MASON. Hence with your gold,—your universal charm,
And remedy for ill! When you have torn
Fathers from children, husbands from their wives,
And scattered woe and wail throughout the land,
You think with gold to compensate for all.
Hence! Till we saw you, we were happy men;
With you came misery and dark despair.

BERTHA [*to the* TASKMASTER, *who has returned*]. Lives he?

[TASKMASTER *shakes his head.*] Ill-fated towers, with curses built,
And doomed with curses to be tenanted!
[*Exit.*]

SCENE IV

The House of WALTER FÜRST.

[WALTER FÜRST *and* ARNOLD VON MELCHTHAL *enter simultaneously at different sides.*]

MELCHTHAL. Good Walter Fürst.

FÜRST. If we should be surprised!
Stay where you are. We are beset with spies.

MELCHTHAL. Have you no news for me from Unterwald?
What of my father? 'Tis not to be borne,
Thus to be pent up like a felon here!
What have I done of such a heinous stamp,
To skulk and hide me like a murderer?
I only laid my staff across the fingers
Of the pert varlet, when before my eyes,

By order of the governor, he tried
To drive away my handsome team of oxen.
FÜRST. You are too rash by far. He
did no more
Than what the governor had ordered him.
You had transgress'd, and therefore
should have paid
The penalty, however hard, in silence.
MELCHTHAL. Was I to brook the fellow's saucy words?
"That if the peasant must have bread to
eat,
Why, let him go and draw the plough
himself!"
It cut me to the very soul to see
My oxen, noble creatures, when the knave
Unyoked them from the plough. As
though they felt
The wrong, they lowed and butted with
their horns.
On this I could contain myself no longer,
And, overcome by passion, struck him
down.
FÜRST. O, we old men can scarce command ourselves!
And can we wonder youth should break
its bounds?
MELCHTHAL. I'm only sorry for my
father's sake!
To be away from him, that needs so much
My fostering care! The governor detests
him,
Because he hath, whene'er occasion served,
Stood stoutly up for right and liberty.
Therefore they'll bear him hard—the poor
old man!
And there is none to shield him from their
gripe.
Come what come may, I must go home
again.
FÜRST. Compose yourself, and wait in
patience till
We get some tidings o'er from Unterwald.
Away! away! I hear a knock! Perhaps
A message from the Viceroy! Get thee in.
You are not safe from Landenberger's arm
In Uri, for these tyrants pull together.
MELCHTHAL. They teach us Switzers
what we ought to do.
FÜRST. Away! I'll call you when the
coast is clear. [MELCHTHAL retires.]

Unhappy youth! I dare not tell him all
The evil that my boding heart predicts!
Who's there? The door ne'er opens, but
I look
For tidings of mishap. Suspicion lurks
With darkling treachery in every nook.
Even to our inmost rooms they force their
way,
These myrmidons of power; and soon we'll
need
To fasten bolts and bars upon our doors.
[He opens the door, and steps
back in surprise as WERNER
STAUFFACHER enters.]
What do I see? You, Werner? Now, by
Heaven!
A valued guest, indeed. No man e'er set
His foot across this threshold, more esteem'd.
Welcome! thrice welcome, Werner, to my
roof!
What brings you here? What seek you
here in Uri?
STAUFFACHER [shakes FÜRST by the
hand]. The olden times and olden
Switzerland.
FÜRST. You bring them with you. See
how I'm rejoiced.
My heart leaps at the very sight of you.
Sit down—sit down, and tell me how you
left
Your charming wife, fair Gertrude
Iberg's child?
And clever as her father. Not a man
That wends from Germany, by Meinrad's
Cell,
To Italy, but praises far and wide
Your house's hospitality. But say,
Have you come here direct from Flüelen,
And have you noticed nothing on your way,
Before you halted at my door?
STAUFFACHER [sits down]. I saw
A work in progress, as I came along,
I little thought to see—that likes me ill.
FÜRST. O friend! you've lighted on my
thought at once.
STAUFFACHER. Such things in Uri ne'er
were known before.
Never was prison here in man's remembrance,
Nor ever any stronghold but the grave.

FÜRST. You name it well. It is the grave of freedom.

STAUFFACHER. Friend, Walter Fürst, I will be plain with you.
No idle curiosity it is
That brings me here, but heavy cares. I left
Thraldom at home, and thraldom meets me here.
Our wrongs, e'en now, are more than we can bear,
And who shall tell us where they are to end?
From eldest time the Switzer has been free,
Accustom'd only to the mildest rule.
Such things as now we suffer ne'er were known
Since herdsmen first drove cattle to the hills.

FÜRST. Yes, our oppressions are un-parallel'd!
Why even our own good lord of Atting-haus,
Who lived in olden times, himself declares
They are no longer to be tamely borne.

STAUFFACHER. In Unterwalden yonder, 'tis the same;
And bloody has the retribution been.
The imperial Seneschal, the Wolfshot, who
At Rossberg dwelt, long'd for forbidden fruit—
Baumgarten's wife, that lives at Alzellen,
He wished to overcome in shameful sort,
On which the husband slew him with his axe.

FÜRST. O, Heaven is just in all its judgments still!
Baumgarten, say you? A most worthy man.
Has he escaped, and is he safely hid?

STAUFFACHER. Your son-in-law conveyed him o'er the lake,
And he lies hidden in my house at Steinen.
He brought the tidings with him of a thing
That has been done at Sarnen, worse than all,
A thing to make the very heart run blood!

FÜRST [attentively]. Say on. What is it?

STAUFFACHER. There dwells in Melch-thal, then,
Just as you enter by the road from Kerns,
An upright man, named Henry of the Halden,
A man of weight and influence in the Diet.

FÜRST. Who knows him not? But what of him? Proceed.

STAUFFACHER. The Landenberg, to pun-ish some offence,
Committed by the old man's son, it seems,
Had given command to take the youth's best pair
Of oxen from his plough; on which the lad
Struck down the messenger and took to flight.

FÜRST. But the old father—tell me, what of him?

STAUFFACHER. The Landenberg sent for him, and required
He should produce his son upon the spot;
And when th' old man protested, and with truth,
That he knew nothing of the fugitive,
The tyrant call'd his torturers.

FÜRST [springs up and tries to lead him to the other side]. Hush, no more!

STAUFFACHER [with increasing warmth]. "And though thy son," he cried, "has 'scaped me now,
I have thee fast, and thou shalt feel my vengeance."
With that they flung the old man to the earth,
And plunged the pointed steel into his eyes.

FÜRST. Merciful Heaven!

MELCHTHAL [rushing out]. Into his eyes, his eyes?

STAUFFACHER [addresses himself in as-tonishment to WALTER FÜRST]. Who is this youth?

MELCHTHAL [grasping him convulsive-ly]. Into his eyes? Speak, speak!

FÜRST. Oh, miserable hour!

STAUFFACHER. Who is it, tell me?
[FÜRST makes a sign to him.] It is his son! All righteous heaven!

MELCHTHAL. And I
Must be from thence! What! into both
his eyes?
FÜRST. Be calm, be calm; and bear it
like a man!
MELCHTHAL. And all for me—for my
mad, wilful folly!
Blind, did you say? Quite blind—and
both his eyes?
STAUFFACHER. Ev'n so. The fountain
of his sight's dried up.
He ne'er will see the blessed sunshine
more.
FÜRST. Oh, spare his anguish!
MELCHTHAL. Never, never more!
[*Presses his hands upon his eyes
and is silent for some mo-
ments; then turning from one
to the other, speaks in a sub-
dued tone, broken by sobs.*]
O the eye's light, of all the gifts of
Heaven
The dearest, best! From light all beings
live—
Each fair created thing—the very plants
Turn with a joyful transport to the light,
And he—he must drag on through all his
days
In endless darkness! Never more for him
The sunny meads shall glow, the flow'rets
bloom;
Nor shall he more behold the roseate tints
Of the iced mountain top! To die is
nothing,
But to have life, and not have sight,—oh,
that
Is misery indeed! Why do you look
So piteously at me? I have two eyes,
Yet to my poor blind father can give
neither!
No, not one gleam of that great sea of
light,
That with its dazzling splendor floods my
gaze.
STAUFFACHER. Ah, I must swell the
measure of your grief,
Instead of soothing it. The worst, alas!
Remains to tell. They've stripp'd him of
his all;
Nought have they left him, save his staff,
on which,

Blind, and in rags, he moves from door to
door.
MELCHTHAL. Nought but his staff to
the old eyeless man!
Stripp'd of his all—even of the light of
day,
The common blessing of the meanest
wretch.
Tell me no more of patience, of conceal-
ment!
Oh, what a base and coward thing am I,
That on mine own security I thought,
And took no care of thine! Thy precious
head
Left as a pledge within the tyrant's grasp!
Hence, craven-hearted prudence, hence!
And all
My thoughts be vengeance and the des-
pot's blood!
I'll seek him straight—no power shall
stay me now—
And at his hands demand my father's
eyes.
I'll beard him 'mid a thousand myrmi-
dons!
What's life to me, if in his heart's best
blood
I cool the fever of this mighty anguish.
[*He is going.*]
FÜRST. Stay, this is madness, Melch-
thal! What avails
Your single arm against his power? He
sits
At Sarnen high within his lordly keep,
And, safe within its battlemented walls,
May laugh to scorn your unavailing rage.
MELCHTHAL. And though he sat within
the icy domes
Of yon far Schreckhorn—ay, or higher,
where,
Veil'd since eternity, the Jungfrau soars,
Still to the tyrant would I make my
way;
With twenty comrades minded like myself
I'd lay his fastness level with the earth!
And if none follow me, and if you all,
In terror for your homesteads and your
herds,
Bow in submission to the tyrant's yoke,
I'll call the herdsmen on the hills around
me,

And there beneath heaven's free and
boundless roof,
Where men still feel as men, and hearts
are true,
Proclaim aloud this foul enormity!
STAUFFACHER [*to* FÜRST]. 'Tis at its
height—and are we then to wait
Till some extremity——
MELCHTHAL.   What extremity
Remains for apprehension, when men's
eyes
Have ceased to be secure within their
sockets?
Are we defenceless?   Wherefore did we
learn
To bend the cross-bow,—wield the battle-
axe?
What living creature but, in its despair,
Finds for itself a weapon of defence?
The baited stag will turn, and with the
show
Of his dread antlers hold the hounds at
bay;
The chamois drags the huntsman down th'
abyss
The very ox, the partner of man's toil,
The sharer of his roof, that meekly bends
The strength of his huge neck beneath the
yoke,
Springs up, if he's provoked, whets his
strong horn,
And tosses his tormentor to the clouds.
FÜRST.   If the three Cantons thought
as we three do,
Something might, then, be done, with good
effect.
STAUFFACHER.   When Uri calls, when
Unterwald replies,
Schwyz will be mindful of her ancient
league.
MELCHTHAL.   I've many friends in Un-
terwald, and none
That would not gladly venture life and
limb,
If fairly backed and aided by the rest.
Oh, sage and reverend fathers of this
land,
Here do I stand before your riper years,
An unskill'd youth, whose voice must in
the Diet
Still be subdued into respectful silence.

Do not, because that I am young, and
want
Experience, slight my counsel and my
words.
'Tis not the wantonness of youthful blood
That fires my spirit, but a pang so deep
That e'en the flinty rocks must pity me.
You, too, are fathers, heads of families,
And you must wish to have a virtuous
son,
To reverence your grey hairs, and shield
your eyes
With pious and affectionate regard.
Do not, I pray, because in limb and for-
tune
You still are unassail'd, and still your
eyes
Revolve undimm'd and sparkling in their
spheres,
Oh, do not, therefore, disregard our
wrongs!
Above you, too, doth hang the tyrant's
sword.
You, too, have striven to alienate the
land
From Austria. This was all my father's
crime:
You share his guilt, and may his punish-
ment.
STAUFFACHER [*to* FÜRST]. Do thou re-
solve! I am prepared to follow.
FÜRST.   First let us learn what steps
the noble lords
Von Sillinen and Attinghaus propose.
Their names would rally thousands in the
cause.
MELCHTHAL.   Is there a name within
the Forest Mountains
That carries more respect than thine—
and thine?
To names like these the people cling for
help
With confidence—such names are house-
hold words.
Rich was your heritage of manly virtue
And richly have you added to its stores.
What need of nobles? Let us do the
work
Ourselves. Although we stood alone, me-
thinks,
We should be able to maintain our rights.

STAUFFACHER. The nobles' wrongs are
not so great as ours.
The torrent, that lays waste the lower
grounds,
Hath not ascended to the uplands yet.
But let them see the country once in
arms,
They'll not refuse to lend a helping hand.
FÜRST. Were there an umpire 'twixt
ourselves and Austria,
Justice and law might then decide our
quarrel.
But our oppressor is our emperor too,
And judge supreme. 'Tis God must help
us, then.
And our own arm! Be yours the task to
rouse
The men of Schwyz; I'll rally friends in
Uri.
But whom are we to send to Unterwald?
MELCHTHAL. Thither send me. Whom
should it more concern?
FÜRST. No, Melchthal, no; thou art
my guest, and I
Must answer for thy safety.
MELCHTHAL. Let me go.
I know each forest track and mountain
pass;
Friends too I'll find, be sure, on every
hand,
To give me willing shelter from the foe.
STAUFFACHER. Nay, let him go; no
traitors harbor there:
For tyranny is so abhorred in Unterwald,
No minions can be bound to work her
will.
In the low valleys, too, the Alzeller
Will gain confederates and rouse the
country.
MELCHTHAL. But how shall we com-
municate, and not
Awaken the suspicion of the tyrants?
STAUFFACHER. Might we not meet at
Brunnen or at Treib,
Hard by the spot where merchant vessels
land?
FÜRST. We must not go so openly to
work.
Hear my opinion. On the lake's left bank,
As we sail hence to Brunnen, right against
The Mytenstein, deep-hidden in the wood

A meadow lies, by shepherds called the
Rootli,
Because the wood has been uprooted there.
'Tis where our Canton bound'ries verge
on yours;—
[To MELCHTHAL] Your boat will carry
you across from Schwyz.
[To STAUFFACHER.] Thither by lonely
bypaths let us wend
At midnight, and deliberate o'er our plans.
Let each bring with him there ten trusty
men,
All one at heart with us; and then we
may
Consult together for the general weal,
And, with God's guidance, fix our onward
course.
STAUFFACHER. So let it be. And now
your true right hand!
Yours, too, young man! and as we now
three men
Among ourselves thus knit our hands to-
gether
In all sincerity and truth, e'en so
Shall we three Cantons, too, together
stand
In victory and defeat, in life and death.
FÜRST *and* MELCHTHAL. In life and
death.
          [*They hold their hands clasped
          together for some moments in
          silence.*]
MELCHTHAL. Alas, my old blind father!
Thou canst no more behold the day of
freedom;
But thou shalt hear it. When from Alp to
Alp
The beacon fires throw up their flaming
signs,
And the proud castles of the tyrants fall,
Into thy cottage shall the Switzer burst,
Bear the glad tidings to thine ear, and
o'er
Thy darken'd way shall Freedom's radi-
ance pour.

ACT II

SCENE I

The Mansion of the BARON OF ATTING-
HAUSEN. *A Gothic Hall, decorated with*

escutcheons and helmets. The BARON, *a grey-headed man, eighty-five years old, tall and of a commanding mien, clad in a furred pelisse, and leaning on a staff tipped with chamois horn.* KUONI *and six hinds standing round him with rakes and scythes.* ULRICH *of* RUDENZ *enters in the costume of a Knight.*

RUDENZ. Uncle, I'm here! Your will?

ATTINGHAUSEN. First let me share, After the ancient custom of our house, The morning cup with these my faithful servants! [*He drinks from a cup, which is then passed round.*] Time was, I stood myself in field and wood, With mine own eyes directing all their toil, Even as my banner led them in the fight; Now I am only fit to play the steward; And, if the genial sun come not to me, I can no longer seek it on the mountains. Thus slowly, in an ever narrowing sphere, I move on to the narrowest and the last, Where all life's pulses cease. I now am but The shadow of my former self, and that Is fading fast—'twill soon be but a name.

KUONI [*offering* RUDENZ *the cup*]. A pledge, young master! [RUDENZ *hesitates to take the cup.*] Nay, Sir, drink it off! One cup, one heart! You know our proverb, Sir?

ATTINGHAUSEN. Go, children, and at eve, when work is done, We'll meet and talk the country's business over. [*Exeunt* SERVANTS.] Belted and plumed, and all thy bravery on! Thou art for Altdorf—for the castle, boy?

RUDENZ. Yes, uncle. Longer may I not delay—

ATTINGHAUSEN [*sitting down*]. Why in such haste? Say, are thy youthful hours Doled in such niggard measure that thou must Be chary of them to thy aged uncle?

RUDENZ. I see my presence is not needed here, I am but as a stranger in this house.

ATTINGHAUSEN [*gazes fixedly at him for a considerable time*]. Alas, thou art indeed! Alas, that home To thee has grown so strange! Oh, Uly! Uly! I scarce do know thee now, thus deck'd in silks, The peacock's feather flaunting in thy cap, And purple mantle round thy shoulders flung; Thou look'st upon the peasant with disdain, And takest with a blush his honest greeting.

RUDENZ. All honor due to him I gladly pay, But must deny the right he would usurp.

ATTINGHAUSEN. The sore displeasure of the king is resting Upon the land, and every true man's heart Is full of sadness for the grievous wrongs We suffer from our tyrants. Thou alone Art all unmoved amid the general grief. Abandoning thy friends, thou tak'st thy stand Beside thy country's foes, and, as in scorn Of our distress, pursuest giddy joys, Courting the smiles of princes, all the while Thy country bleeds beneath their cruel scourge.

RUDENZ. The land is sore oppress'd, I know it, uncle. But why? Who plunged it into this distress? A word, one little easy word, might buy Instant deliverance from such dire oppression, And win the good-will of the Emperor. Woe unto those who seal the people's eyes, And make them adverse to their country's good— The men who, for their own vile, selfish ends, Are seeking to prevent the Forest States From swearing fealty to Austria's House,

As all the countries round about have done.
It fits their humor well to take their seats
Amid the nobles on the Herrenbank;
They'll have the Cæsar for their lord, forsooth,—
That is to say, they'll have no lord at all.
ATTINGHAUSEN. Must I hear this, and from thy lips, rash boy!
RUDENZ. You urged me to this answer. Hear me out.
What, uncle, is the character you've stoop'd
To fill contentedly through life? Have you
No higher pride than in these lonely wilds
To be the Landamman or Banneret,
The petty chieftain of a shepherd race?
How! Were it not a far more glorious choice
To bend in homage to our royal lord,
And swell the princely splendors of his court,
Than sit at home, the peer of your own vassals,
And share the judgment-seat with vulgar clowns?
ATTINGHAUSEN. Ah, Uly, Uly; all too well I see,
The tempter's voice has caught thy willing ear,
And pour'd its subtle poison in thy heart.
RUDENZ. Yes, I conceal it not. It doth offend
My inmost soul to hear the stranger's gibes,
That taunt us with the name of "Peasant Nobles!"
Think you the heart that's stirring here can brook,
While all the young nobility around
Are reaping honor under Habsburg's banner,
That I should loiter, in inglorious ease,
Here on the heritage my fathers left,
And in the dull routine of vulgar toil
Lose all life's glorious spring? In other lands
Deeds are achieved. A world of fair renown

Beyond these mountains stirs in martial pomp.
My helm and shield are rusting in the hall;
The martial trumpet's spirit-stirring blast,
The herald's call, inviting to the lists,
Rouse not the echoes of these vales, where nought
Save cowherd's horn and cattle bell is heard
In one unvarying dull monotony.
ATTINGHAUSEN. Deluded boy, seduced by empty show!
Despise the land that gave thee birth! Ashamed
Of the good ancient customs of thy sires!
The day will come when thou, with burning tears,
Wilt long for home, and for thy native hills,
And that dear melody of tuneful herds
Which now, in proud disgust, thou dost despise!
A day when thou wilt drink its tones in sadness,
Hearing their music in a foreign land.
Oh, potent is the spell that binds to home!
No, no, the cold, false world is not for thee.
At the proud court, with thy true heart, thou wilt
For ever feel a stranger among strangers.
The world asks virtues of far other stamp
Than thou hast learned within these simple vales.
But go—go thither,—barter thy free soul,
Take land in fief, become a prince's vassal,
Where thou might'st be lord paramount, and prince
Of all thine own unburden'd heritage!
O, Uly, Uly, stay among thy people!
Go not to Altdorf. Oh, abandon not
The sacred cause of thy wrong'd native land!
I am the last of all my race. My name
Ends with me. Yonder hang my helm and shield;

They will be buried with me in the grave.
And must I think, when yielding up my
  breath,
That thou but wait'st the closing of mine
  eyes
To stoop thy knee to this new feudal
  court,
And take in vassalage from Austria's
  hands
The noble lands which I from God received,
Free and unfetter'd as the mountain air!
  RUDENZ. 'Tis vain for us to strive
  against the king.
The world pertains to him:—shall we
  alone,
In mad, presumptuous obstinacy, strive
To break that mighty chain of lands
  which he
Hath drawn around us with his giant
  grasp?
His are the markets, his the courts,—
  his, too,
The highways; nay, the very carrier's
  horse,
That traffics on the Gotthardt, pays him
  toll.
By his dominions, as within a net,
We are enclosed, and girded round about.
—And will the Empire shield us? Say,
  can it
Protect itself 'gainst Austria's growing
  power?
To God, and not to emperors must we
  look!
What store can on their promises be
  placed,
When they, to meet their own necessities,
Can pawn, and even alienate the towns
That flee for shelter 'neath the Eagle's
  wings?
No, uncle! It is wise and wholesome
  prudence,
In times like these, when faction's all
  abroad,
To own attachment to some mighty chief.
The imperial crown's transferred from
  line to line,
It has no memory for faithful service:
But to secure the favor of these great
Hereditary masters were to sow
Seed for a future harvest.

  ATTINGHAUSEN.   Art so wise?
Wilt thou see clearer than thy noble sires,
Who battled for fair freedom's costly gem
With life, and fortune, and heroic arm?
Sail down the lake to Lucerne, there in-
  quire
How Austria's rule doth weigh the Can-
  tons down.
Soon she will come to count our sheep,
  our cattle,
To portion out the Alps, e'en to their
  summits,
And in our own free woods to hinder us
From striking down the eagle or the
  stag;
To set her tolls on every bridge and gate,
Impoverish us, to swell her lust of sway,
And drain our dearest blood to feed her
  wars.
No, if our blood must flow, let it be shed
In our own cause! We purchase liberty
More cheaply far than bondage.
  RUDENZ.   What can we,
A shepherd race, against great Albert's
  hosts?
  ATTINGHAUSEN. Learn, foolish boy, to
  know this shepherd race!
I know them, I have led them on in
  fight,—
I saw them in the battle at Favenz.
Austria will try, forsooth, to force on us
A yoke we are determined not to bear!
Oh, learn to feel from what a race thou'rt
  sprung!
Cast not, for tinsel trash and idle show,
The precious jewel of thy worth away.
To be the chieftain of a free born race,
Bound to thee only by their unbought
  love,
Ready to stand—to fight—to die with
  thee,
Be that thy pride, be that thy noblest
  boast!
Knit to thy heart the ties of kindred—
  home—
Cling to the land, the dear land of thy
  sires,
Grapple to that with thy whole heart and
  soul!
Thy power is rooted deep and strongly
  here,

But in yon stranger world thou'lt stand
    alone,
A trembling reed beat down by every
    blast.
Oh come! 'tis long since we have seen
    thee, Uly!
Tarry but this one day. Only to-day?
Go not to Altdorf. Wilt thou? Not to-
    day!
For this one day, bestow thee on thy
    friends.   [*Takes his hand.*]
    RUDENZ. I gave my word. Unhand me!
    I am bound.
    ATTINGHAUSEN [*drops his hand and
    says, sternly*]. Bound, didst thou
    say? Oh yes, unhappy boy,
Thou art indeed. But not by word or
    oath.
'Tis by the silken mesh of love thou'rt
    bound.   [RUDENZ *turns away.*]
Ay, hide thee, as thou wilt. 'Tis she, I
    know,
Bertha of Bruneck, draws thee to the
    court;
'Tis she that chains thee to the Em-
    peror's service;
Thou think'st to win the noble knightly
    maid
By thy apostasy. Be not deceived.
She is held out before thee as a lure,
But never meant for innocence like thine.
    RUDENZ. No more, I've heard enough.
    So fare you well.   [*Exit.*]
    ATTINGHAUSEN. Stay, Uly! Stay!
Rash boy, he's gone! I can
Nor hold him back, nor save him from
    destruction.
And so the Wolfshot has deserted us;—
Others will follow his example soon.
This foreign witchery, sweeping o'er our
    hills,
Tears with its potent spell our youth
    away!
O luckless hour, when men and manners
    strange
Into these calm and happy valleys came,
To warp our primitive and guileless
    ways.
The new is pressing on with might. The
    old,
The good, the simple, fleeteth fast away.

New times come on. A race is springing
    up
That think not as their fathers thought
    before!
What do I here? All, all are in the grave
With whom erewhile I moved and held
    converse,
My age has long been laid beneath the
    sod:
Happy the man who may not live to see
What shall be done by those that follow
    me!

SCENE II

*A meadow surrounded by high rocks and
wooded ground. On the rocks are tracks,
with rails and ladders, by which the peas-
ants are afterwards seen descending. In
the background the lake is observed, and
over it a moon rainbow in the early part
of the scene. The prospect is closed by
lofty mountains, with glaciers rising be-
hind them. The stage is dark; but the
lake and glaciers glisten in the moonlight.*

[MELCHTHAL, BAUMGARTEN, WINKELRIED,
MEYER VON SARNEN, BURKHART AM BÜHEL,
ARNOLD VON SEWA, KLAUS VON DER FLÜE,
    and four other peasants, all armed.]
    MELCHTHAL [*behind the scenes*]. The
    mountain pass is open. Follow me!
I see the rock, and little cross upon it:
This is the spot; here is the Rootli.
          [*They enter with torches.*]
    WINKELRIED.   Hark!
    SEWA. The coast is clear.
    MEYER. None of our comrades come?
We are the first, we Unterwaldeners.
    MELCHTHAL. How far is't i' the night?
    BAUMGARTEN.   The beacon watch
Upon the Selisberg has just called two.
          [*A bell is heard at a distance.*]
    MEYER. Hush! Hark!
    BÜHEL.   The forest chapel's
    matin bell
Chimes clearly o'er the lake from Switzer-
    land.
    VON FLÜE. The air is clear, and bears
    the sound so far.

MELCHTHAL. Go, you and you, and
light some broken boughs,
Let's bid them welcome with a cheerful
blaze.   [*Two peasants exeunt.*]
SEWA. The moon shines fair to-night.
Beneath its beams
The lake reposes, bright as burnish'd
steel.
BÜHEL. They'll have an easy passage.
WINKELRIED [*pointing to the lake*]. Ha!
look there!
See you nothing?
MEYER.   What is it? Ay, indeed!
A rainbow in the middle of the night.
MELCHTHAL. Formed by the bright re-
flection of the moon!
VON FLÜE. A sign most strange and
wonderful, indeed!
Many there be who ne'er have seen the
like.
SEWA. 'Tis doubled, see, a paler one
above!
BAUMGARTEN. A boat is gliding yonder
right beneath it.
MELCHTHAL. That must be Werner
Stauffacher! I knew
The worthy patriot would not tarry
long.
        [*Goes with* BAUMGARTEN *towards
        the shore.*]
MEYER. The Uri men are like to be the
last.
BÜHEL. They're forced to take a wind-
ing circuit through
The mountains, for the Viceroy's spies
are out.
        [*In the meanwhile the two peas-
        ants have kindled a fire on the
        centre of the stage.*]
MELCHTHAL [*on the shore*]. Who's
there? The word?
STAUFFACHER [*from below*]. Friends of
the country.
        [*All retire up the stage, towards
        the party landing from the
        boat. Enter* STAUFFACHER, ITEL
        REDING, HANS AUF DER MAUER,
        JÖRG IM HOFE, KONRAD HUNN,
        ULRICH DER SCHMIDT, JOST VON
        WEILER, *and three other peas-
        ants, armed.*]

ALL.   Welcome!
        [*While the rest remain behind,
        exchanging greetings,* MELCH-
        THAL *comes forward with*
        STAUFFACHER.*]
MELCHTHAL. Oh worthy Stauffacher,
I've look'd but now
On him, who could not look on me again,
I've laid my hands upon his rayless
eyes,
And on their vacant orbits sworn a vow
Of vengeance, only to be cool'd in blood.
STAUFFACHER. Speak not of vengeance.
We are here to meet
The threatened evil, not to avenge the
past.
Now tell me what you've done, and what
secured,
To aid the common cause in Unterwald,
How stand the peasantry disposed, and
how
Yourself escaped the wiles of treachery?
MELCHTHAL. Through the Surenen's
fearful mountain chain,
Where dreary ice-fields stretch on every
side,
And sound is none, save the hoarse vul-
ture's cry,
I reach'd the Alpine pasture, where the
herds
From Uri and from Engelberg resort,
And turn their cattle forth to graze in
common.
Still, as I went along, I slaked my thirst
With the coarse oozings of the lofty
glacier,
That thro' the crevices come foaming
down,
And turned to rest me in the herdsmen's
cots,
Where I was host and guest, until I
gain'd
The cheerful homes and social haunts of
men.
Already through these distant vales had
spread
The rumor of this last atrocity;
And whereso'er I went, at every door,
Kind words and gentle looks were there
to greet me.
I found these simple spirits all in arms

Against our rulers' tyrannous enroach-
ments.
For as their Alps through each succeed-
ing year
Yield the same roots,—their streams flow
ever on
In the same channels,—nay, the clouds
and winds
The selfsame course unalterably pursue,
So have old customs there, from sire to
son,
Been handed down, unchanging and un-
changed;
Nor will they brook to swerve or turn
aside
From the fixed even tenor of their life.
With grasp of their hard hands they wel-
comed me,—
Took from the walls their rusty falchions
down,—
And from their eyes the soul of valor
flash'd
With joyful lustre, as I spoke those
names,
Sacred to every peasant in the mountains,
Your own and Walter Fürst's. Whate'er
your voice
Should dictate as the right, they swore
to do;
And you they swore to follow e'en to
death.
—So sped I on from house to house, se-
cure
In the guest's sacred privilege;—and
when
I reached at last the valley of my home,
Where dwell my kinsmen, scatter'd far
and near—
And when I found my father, stript and
blind,
Upon the stranger's straw fed by the alms
Of charity——
STAUFFACHER. Great Heaven!
MELCHTHAL. Yet wept I not!
No—not in weak and unavailing tears
Spent I the force of my fierce burning
anguish;
Deep in my bosom, like some precious
treasure,
I lock'd it fast, and thought on deeds
alone.

Through every winding of the hills I
crept,—
No valley so remote but I explored it;
Nay, even at the glacier's ice-clad base
I sought and found the homes of living
men;
And still, where'er my wandering foot-
steps turn'd,
The selfsame hatred of these tyrants met
me;
For even there, at vegetation's verge,
Where the numb'd earth is barren of all
fruits,
Their grasping hands had been stretch'd
forth for plunder.
Into the hearts of all this honest race
The story of my wrongs struck deep, and
now
They, to a man, are ours; both heart and
hand.
STAUFFACHER. Great things, indeed,
you've wrought in little time.
MELCHTHAL. I did still more than this.
The fortresses,
Rossberg and Sarnen, are the country's
dread;
For from behind their rocky walls the foe
Swoops, as the eagle from his eyrie, down,
And, safe himself, spreads havoc o'er the
land.
With my eyes I wish'd to weigh its
strength,
So went to Sarnen, and explored the
castle.
STAUFFACHER. How! Risk thyself e'en
in the tiger's den?
MELCHTHAL. Disguised in pilgrim's
weeds I entered it;
I saw the Viceroy feasting at his board—
Judge if I'm master of myself or no!
I saw the tyrant and I slew him not!
STAUFFACHER. Fortune, indeed, has
smiled upon your boldness.
[*Meanwhile the others have arrived and
join* MELCHTHAL *and* STAUFFACHER.]
Yet tell me now, I pray, who are the
friends,
The worthy men, who came along with
you?
Make me acquainted with them, that we
may

Speak frankly, man to man, and heart to
heart.
MEYER. In the three Cantons, who, sir,
knows not you?
Meyer of Sarnen is my name; and this
Is Struth of Winkelried, my sister's son.
STAUFFACHER. No unknown name. A
Winkelried it was
Who slew the dragon in the fen at
Weiler,
And lost his life in the encounter, too.
WINKELRIED. That, Master Stauffacher,
was my grandfather.
MELCHTHAL [pointing to two peasants].
These two are men belonging to the
convent
Of Engelberg, and live behind the forest.
You'll not think ill of them because
they're serfs,
And sit not free upon the soil, like us.
They love the land, and bear a good
repute.
STAUFFACHER [to them]. Give me your
hands. He has good cause for thanks
That unto no man owes his body's
service.
But worth is worth, no matter where 'tis
found.
HUNN. That is Herr Reding, sir, our
old Landamman.
MEYER. I know him well. There is a
suit between us
About a piece of ancient heritage.
Herr Reding, we are enemies in court,
Here we are one.   [Shakes his hand.]
STAUFFACHER. That's well and bravely
said.
WINKELRIED. Listen! They come. Hark
to the horn of Uri!
    [On the right and left armed men
    are seen descending the rocks
    with torches.]
MAUER. Look, is not that God's pious
servant there?
A worthy priest! The terrors of the night
And the way's pains and perils scare not
him,
A faithful shepherd caring for his flock.
BAUMGARTEN. The Sacrist follows him,
and Walter Fürst.
But where is Tell? I do not see him there.

    [WALTER FÜRST, RÖSSELMÁNN
    the pastor, PETERMANN the
    sacrist, KUONI the shepherd,
    WERNI the huntsman, RUODI
    the fisherman, and five other
    countrymen, thirty-three in all,
    advance and take their places
    round the fire.]
FÜRST. Thus must we, on the soil our
fathers left us,
Creep forth by stealth to meet like mur-
derers,
And in the night, that should her mantle
lend
Only to crime and black conspiracy,
Assert our own good rights, which yet
are clear
As is the radiance of the noonday sun.
MELCHTHAL. So be it. What is woven
in gloom of night
Shall free and boldly meet the morning
light.
RÖSSELMANN. Confederates! Listen to
the words which God
Inspires my heart withal. Here we are
met
To represent the general weal. In us
Are all the people of the land convened.
Then let us hold the Diet, as of old,
And as we're wont in peaceful times to
do.
The time's necessity be our excuse,
If there be aught informal in this meet-
ing.
Still, whereso'er men strike for justice,
there
Is God, and now beneath his heav'n we
stand.
STAUFFACHER. 'Tis well advised.—Let
us, then, hold the Diet,
According to our ancient usages.—
Though it be night, there's sunshine in
our cause.
MELCHTHAL. Few though our numbers
be, the hearts are here
Of the whole people; here the best are
met.
HUNN. The ancient books may not be
near at hand,
Yet are they graven in our inmost
hearts.

Rösselmann. 'Tis well. And now,
then, let a ring be formed,
And plant the swords of power within
the ground.

Mauer. Let the Landamman step into
his place,
And by his side his secretaries stand.

Sacrist. There are three Cantons here.
Which hath the right
To give the head to the united Council?
Schwyz may contest that dignity with
Uri,
We Unterwald'ners enter not the field.

Melchthal. We stand aside. We are
but suppliants here,
Invoking aid from our more potent
friends.

Stauffacher. Let Uri have the sword.
Her banner takes,
In battle, the precedence of our own.

Fürst. Schwyz, then, must share the
honor of the sword;
For she's the honored ancestor of all.

Rösselmann. Let me arrange this
generous controversy.
Uri shall lead in battle—Schwyz in Council.

Fürst [gives Stauffacher his hand].
Then take your place.

Stauffacher. Not I. Some older
man.

Hofe. Ulrich, the Smith, is the most
aged here.

Mauer. A worthy man, but he is not
a freeman;
No bondman can be judge in Switzerland.

Stauffacher. Is not Herr Reding
here, our old Landamman?
Where can we find a worthier man than
he?

Fürst. Let him be Amman and the
Diet's chief!
You that agree with me, hold up your
hands!
[All hold up their right hands.]

Reding [stepping into the centre]. I
cannot lay my hands upon the books;
But by yon everlasting stars I swear
Never to swerve from justice and the
right.

[The two swords are placed before him, and a circle formed; Schwyz in the centre, Uri on his right, Unterwald on his left.]

Reding [resting on his battle-sword].
Why, at the hour when spirits walk the
earth,
Meet the three Cantons of the mountains here,
Upon the lake's inhospitable shore?
And what the purport of the new alliance
We here contract beneath the starry
heaven?

Stauffacher [entering the circle]. No
new alliance do we now contract,
But one our fathers framed, in ancient
times,
We purpose to renew! For know, confederates,
Though mountain ridge and lake divide
our bounds,
And every Canton's ruled by its own
laws,
Yet are we but one race, born of one
blood,
And all are children of one common
home.

Winkelried. Then is the burden of
our legends true,
That we came hither from a distant land?
Oh, tell us what you know, that our new
league
May reap fresh vigor from the leagues
of old.

Stauffacher. Hear, then, what aged
herdsmen tell. There dwelt
A mighty people in the land that lies
Back to the north. The scourge of
famine came;
And in this strait 'twas publicly resolved
That each tenth man, on whom the lot
might fall,
Should leave the country. They obey'd
—and forth,
With loud lamentings, men and women
went,
A mighty host; and to the south moved
on,
Cutting their way through Germany by
the sword,

Until they gained these pine-clad hills of
   ours;
Nor stopp'd they ever on their forward
   course
Till at the shaggy dell they halted, where
The Müta flows through its luxuriant
   meads.
No trace of human creature met their
   eye,
Save one poor hut upon the desert shore,
Where dwelt a lonely man, and kept the
   ferry.
A tempest raged—the lake rose moun-
   tains high,
And barr'd their further progress. There-
   upon
They view'd the country—found it rich
   in wood,
Discover'd goodly springs, and felt as
   they
Were in their own dear native land once
   more.
Then they resolved to settle on the
   spot;
Erected there the ancient town of Schwyz;
And many a day of toil had they to
   clear
The tangled brake and forest's spreading
   roots.
Meanwhile their numbers grew, the soil
   became
Unequal to sustain them, and they
   cross'd
To the black mountain, far as Weiss-
   land, where,
Conceal'd behind eternal walls of ice,
Another people speak another tongue.
They built the village Stanz, beside the
   Kernwald;
The village Altdorf, in the vale of Reuss;
Yet, ever mindful of their parent stem,
The men of Schwyz, from all the stranger
   race,
That since that time have settled in the
   land,
Each other recognize. Their hearts still
   know,
And beat fraternally to kindred blood.
      [*Extends his hand right and left.*]
   MAUER. Ay, we are all one heart, one
   blood, one race!

   ALL [*joining hands*]. We are one peo-
   ple, and will act as one.
   STAUFFACHER. The nations round us
   bear a foreign yoke,
For they have yielded to the conqueror.
Nay, e'en within our frontiers may be
   found
Some that owe villein service to a lord,
A race of bonded serfs from sire to son.
But we, the genuine race of ancient
   Swiss,
Have kept our freedom from the first till
   now.
Never to princes have we bow'd the knee;
Freely we sought protection of the Em-
   pire.
   RÖSSELMANN. Freely we sought it—
   freely it was given.
'Tis so set down in Emperor Frederick's
   charter.
   STAUFFACHER. For the most free have
   still some feudal lord.
There must be still a chief, a judge
   supreme,
To whom appeal may lie, in case of
   strife.
And therefore was it that our sires al-
   low'd,
For what they had recover'd from the
   waste,
This honor to the Emperor, the lord
Of all the German and Italian soil;
And, like the other free men of his realm,
Engaged to aid him with their swords in
   war;
And this alone should be the free man's
   duty,
To guard the Empire that keeps guard
   for him.
   MELCHTHAL. He's but a slave that
   would acknowledge more.
   STAUFFACHER. They followed, when
   the Heribann went forth,
The imperial standard, and they fought
   its battles!
To Italy they march'd in arms, to place
The Cæsars' crown upon the Emperor's
   head.
But still at home they ruled themselves
   in peace,
By their own laws and ancient usages.

The Emperor's only right was to ad-
judge
The penalty of death; he therefore named
Some mighty noble as his delegate,
That had no stake nor interest in the
land
He was call'd in, when doom was to be
pass'd,
And, in the face of day, pronounced de-
cree
Clear and distinctly, fearing no man's
hate.
What traces, here, that we are bonds-
men? Speak,
If there be any can gainsay my words!
    Hofe. No! You have spoken but the
simple truth;
We never stoop'd beneath a tyrant's yoke.
    Stauffacher. Even to the Emperor
we refused obedience,
When he gave judgment in the church's
favor;
For when the Abbey of Einsiedlen
claimed
The Alp our fathers and ourselves had
grazed,
And showed an ancient charter, which
bestowed
The land on them as being ownerless—
For our existence there had been con-
cealed—
What was our answer? This: "The
grant is void,
No Emperor can bestow what is our
own:
And if the Empire shall deny us justice,
We can, within our mountains, right
ourselves!"
Thus spake our fathers! And shall we
endure
The shame and infamy of this new yoke,
And from the vassal brook what never
king
Dared, in the fulness of his power, at-
tempt?
This soil we have created for ourselves,
By the hard labor of our hands; we've
changed
The giant forest, that was erst the haunt
Of savage bears, into a home for man;
Extirpated the dragon's brood, that wont

To rise, distent with venom, from the
swamps,
Rent the thick misty canopy that hung
Its blighting vapors on the dreary waste;
Blasted the solid rock; o'er the abyss
Thrown the firm bridge for the wayfar-
ing man:
By the possession of a thousand years
The soil is ours. And shall an alien
lord,
Himself a vassal, dare to venture here,
On our own hearths insult us,—and at-
tempt
To forge the chains of bondage for our
hands,
And do us shame on our own proper
soil?
Is there no help against such wrong as
this? [*Great sensation among the
people.*]
Yes! there's a limit to the despot's
power!
When the oppress'd looks round in vain
for justice,
When his sore burden may no more be
borne,
With fearless heart he makes appeal to
Heaven,
And thence brings down his everlasting
rights,
Which there abide, inalienably his,
And indestructible as are the stars.
Nature's primeval state returns again,
Where man stands hostile to his fellow
man;
And if all other means shall fail his
need,
One last resource remains—his own good
sword.
Our dearest treasures call to us for aid
Against the oppressor's violence; we stand
For country, home, for wives, for chil-
dren here!
    All [*clashing their swords*]. Here
stand we for our homes, our wives,
and children.
    Rösselmann [*stepping into the circle*].
Bethink ye well before ye draw the
sword.
Some peaceful compromise may yet be
made;

Speak but one word, and at your feet
you'll see
The men who now oppress you. Take
the terms
That have been often tendered you; re-
nounce
The Empire, and to Austria swear al-
legiance!

MAUER. What says the priest? To
Austria allegiance?

BÜHEL. Hearken not to him!

WINKELRIED. 'Tis a traitor's counsel,
His country's foe!

REDING. Peace, peace, confederates.

SEWA. Homage to Austria, after
wrongs like these!

VON FLÜE. Shall Austria extort from
us by force
What we denied to kindness and en-
treaty?

MEYER. Then should we all be slaves,
deservedly.

MAUER. Yes! Let him forfeit all a
Switzer's rights,
Who talks of yielding to the yoke of
Austria!
I stand on this, Landamman. Let this
be
The foremost of our laws!

MELCHTHAL. Even so! Whoe'er
Shall talk of tamely bearing Austria's
yoke,
Let him be stripp'd of all his rights and
honors;
And no man hence receive him at his
hearth!

ALL [raising their right hands].
Agreed! Be this the law!

REDING [after a pause]. The law it
is.

RÖSSELMANN. Now you are free—by
this law you are free.
Never shall Austria obtain by force
What she has fail'd to gain by friendly
suit.

WEILER. On with the order of the day!
Proceed!

REDING. Confederates! Have all gen-
tler means been tried?
Perchance the Emp'ror knows not of our
wrongs;

It may not be his will that thus we
suffer:
Were it not well to make one last at-
tempt,
And lay our grievances before the throne,
Ere we unsheath the sword? Force is at ·
best
A fearful thing e'en in a righteous cause;
God only helps when man can help no
more.

STAUFFACHER [to KONRAD HUNN].
Here, you can give us information.
Speak!

HUNN. I was at Rheinfeld, at the
Emperor's palace,
Deputed by the Cantons to complain
Of the oppressions of these governors,
And claim the charter of our ancient
freedom,
Which each new king till now has rati-
fied.
I found the envoys there of many a
town,
From Suabia and the valley of the
Rhine,
Who all received their parchments as they
wish'd
And straight went home again with merry
heart,
They sent for me, your envoy, to the
council,
Where I was soon dismiss'd with empty
comfort;
"The Emperor at present was engaged;
Some other time he would attend to
us!"
I turn'd away, and passing through the
hall,
With heavy heart, in a recess I saw
The Grand Duke John in tears, and by
his side
The noble lords of Wart and Tegerfeld,
Who beckon'd me, and said, "Redress
yourselves!
Expect not justice from the Emperor.
Does he not plunder his own brother's
child,
And keep from him his just inheritance?
The Duke claims his maternal property,
Urging he's now of age, and 'tis full
time

That he should rule his people and.domin-
ions;
What is the answer made to him? The
king
Places a chaplet on his head; 'Behold
The fitting ornament,' he cries, 'of
youth!'"
MAUER. You hear. Expect not from
the Emperor
Or right or justice! Then redress your-
selves!
REDING. No other course is left us.
Now, advise
What plan most likely to ensure suc-
cess.
FÜRST. To shake a thraldom off that
we abhor,
To keep our ancient rights inviolate,
As we received them from our fathers,—
this,
Not lawless innovation, is our aim.
Let Cæsar still retain what is his due;
And he that is a vassal, let him pay
The service he is sworn to faithfully.
MEYER. I hold my land of Austria in
fief.
FÜRST. Continue, then, to pay your
feudal service.
WEILER. I'm tenant of the lords of
Rappersweil.
FÜRST. Continue, then, to pay them
rent and tithe.
RÖSSELMANN. Of Zürich's Lady I'm
the humble vassal.
FÜRST. Give to the cloister what the
cloister claims.
STAUFFACHER. The Empire only is my
feudal lord.
FÜRST. What needs must be we'll do,
but nothing further.
We'll drive these tyrants and their min-
ions hence,
And raze their towering strongholds to
the ground,
Yet shed, if possible, no drop of blood.
Let the Emperor see that we were driven
to cast
The sacred duties of respect away;
And when he finds we keep within our
bounds,
His wrath, belike, may yield to policy;

For truly is that nation to be fear'd
That, when in arms, is temp'rate in its
wrath.
REDING. But prithee tell us how may
this be done?
The enemy is arm'd as well as we,
And, rest assured, he will not yield in
peace.
STAUFFACHER. He will, whene'er he
sees us up in arms;
We shall surprise him, ere he is pre-
pared.
MEYER. 'Tis easily said, but not so
easily done.
Two fortresses of strength command the
country—
They shield the foe, and should the King
invade us,
The task would then be dangerous in-
deed.
Rossberg and Sarnen both must be se-
cured,
Before a sword is drawn in either Can-
ton.
STAUFFACHER. Should we delay the
foe will soon be warned;
We are too numerous for secrecy.
MEYER. There is no traitor in the
Forest States.
RÖSSELMANN. But even zeal may heed-
lessly betray.
FÜRST. Delay it longer, and the keep
at Altdorf
Will be complete,—the governor secure.
MEYER. You think but of yourselves.
SACRIST. You are unjust!
MEYER. Unjust! said you? Dares Uri
taunt us so?
REDING. Peace, on your oath!
MEYER. If Schwyz be leagued
with Uri,
Why, then, indeed, we must perforce be
silent.
REDING. And let me tell you, in the
Diet's name,
Your hasty spirit much disturbs the
peace.
Stand we not all for the same common
cause?
WINKELRIED. What if we delay till
Christmas? 'Tis then

The custom for the serfs to throng the castle,
Bringing the governor their annual gifts.
Thus may some ten or twelve selected men
Assemble unobserved, within its walls,
Bearing about their persons pikes of steel,
Which may be quickly mounted upon staves,
For arms are not admitted to the fort.
The rest can fill the neighboring wood, prepared
To sally forth upon a trumpet's blast,
Whene'er their comrades have secured the gate;
And thus the castle will be ours with ease.

MELCHTHAL. The Rossberg I will undertake to scale.
I have a sweetheart in the garrison,
Whom with some tender words I could persuade
To lower me at night a hempen ladder.
Once up, my friends will not be long behind.

REDING. Are all resolved in favor of delay?

[*The majority raise their hands.*]

STAUFFACHER [*counting them*]. Twenty to twelve is the majority.

FÜRST. If on the appointed day the castles fall,
From mountain on to mountain we shall pass
The fiery signal: in the capital
Of every Canton quickly rouse the Landsturm.
Then, when these tyrants see our martial front,
Believe me, they will never make so bold
As risk the conflict, but will gladly take
Safe conduct forth beyond our boundaries.

STAUFFACHER. Not so with Gessler. He will make a stand.
Surrounded with his dread array of horse,
Blood will be shed before he quits the field,
And even expell'd he'd still be terrible.
'Tis hard, indeed 'tis dangerous, to spare him.

BAUMGARTEN. Place me where'er a life is to be lost;
I owe my life to Tell, and cheerfully
Will pledge it for my country. I have clear'd
My honor, and my heart is now at rest.

REDING. Counsel will come with circumstance. Be patient!
Something must still be trusted to the moment.
Yet, while by night we hold our Diet here,
The morning, see, has on the mountain tops
Kindled her glowing beacon. Let us part
Ere the broad sun surprise us.

FÜRST. Do not fear.
The night wanes slowly from these vales of ours.

[*All have involuntarily taken off their caps, and contemplate the breaking of day, absorbed in silence.*]

RÖSSELMANN. By this fair light which greeteth us, before
Those other nations, that beneath us far,
In noisome cities pent, draw painful breath,
Swear we the oath of our confederacy!
We swear to be a nation of true brothers,
Never to part in danger or in death!

[*They repeat his words with three fingers raised.*]

We swear we will be free, as were our sires,
And sooner die than live in slavery!

[*All repeat as before.*]

We swear to put our trust in God Most High,
And not to quail before the might of man!

[*All repeat as before, and embrace each other.*]

STAUFFACHER. Now every man pursue his several way
Back to his friends, his kindred, and his home.
Let the herd winter up his flock, and gain,
In silence, friends for our confederacy!

What for a time must be endured, endure,
And let the reckoning of the tyrants grow,
Till the great day arrive when they shall pay
The general and particular debt at once.
Let every man control his own just rage,
And nurse his vengeance for the public wrongs;
For he whom selfish interests now engage
Defrauds the general weal of what to it belongs.

[*As they are going off in profound silence, in three different directions, the orchestra plays a solemn air. The empty scene remains open for some time, showing the rays of the sun rising over the glaciers.*]

ACT III

Scene I

Court before Tell's *house.*

[Tell *with an axe.* Hedwig *engaged in her domestic duties.* Walter *and* Wilhelm *in the background, playing with a little crossbow.*]
Walter [*sings*]. With his cross-bow
  and his quiver,
The huntsman speeds his way,
Over mountain, dale, and river,
  At the dawning of the day.

As the eagle, on wild pinion,
  Is the king in realms of air,
So the hunter claims dominion
  Over crag and forest lair.

Far as ever bow can carry,
  Thro' the trackless airy space,
All he sees he makes his quarry,
  Soaring bird and beast of chase.

Wilhelm [*runs forward*]. My string
  has snapt! Wilt mend it for me,
  father?

Tell. Not I; a true born archer helps
  himself.   [*Boys retire.*]
Hedwig. The boys begin to use the
  bow betimes.
Tell. 'Tis early practice only makes
  the master.
Hedwig. Ah! Would to Heaven they
  never learnt the art!
Tell. But they shall learn it, wife, in
  all its points.
Whoe'er would carve an independent way
Through life, must learn to ward or plant
  a blow.
Hedwig. Alas, alas! and they will
  never rest
Contentedly at home.
Tell.   No more can I!
I was not framed by nature for a shepherd.
Restless I must pursue a changing
  course;
I only feel the flush and joy of life
In starting some fresh quarry every day.
  Hedwig. Heedless the while of all your
  wife's alarms,
As she sits watching through long hours
  at home
For my soul sinks with terror at the
  tales
The servants tell about your wild adventures.
Whene'er we part, my trembling heart
  forebodes
That you will ne'er come back to me
  again.
I see you on the frozen mountain steeps,
Missing, perchance, your leap from cliff
  to cliff.
I see the chamois, with a wild rebound,
Drag you down with him o'er the precipice.
I see the avalanche close o'er your head,—
The treacherous ice give way, and you
  sink down
Entombed alive within its hideous gulf.
Ah! in a hundred varying forms does
  death
Pursue the Alpine huntsman on his
  course.
That way of life can surely ne'er be
  blessed

Where life and limb are perill'd every
hour.
TELL. The man that bears a quick and
steady eye,
And trusts to God and his own lusty
sinews,
Passes, with scarce a scar, through every
danger.
The mountain cannot awe the mountain
child. [*Having finished his work, he
lays aside his tools.*]
And now, methinks, the door will hold
awhile.—
The axe at home oft saves the carpenter.
[*Takes his cap.*]
HEDWIG. Whither away?
TELL. To Altdorf, to
your father.
HEDWIG. You have some dangerous en-
terprise in view?
Confess!
TELL. Why think you so?
HEDWIG. Some scheme's on foot,
Against the governors. There was a Diet
Held on the Rootli—that I know—and
you
Are one of the confederacy, I'm sure.
TELL. I was not there. Yet will I not
hold back,
Whene'er my country calls me to her
aid.
HEDWIG. Wherever danger is, will you
be placed.
On you, as ever, will the burden fall.
TELL. Each man shall have the post
that fits his powers.
HEDWIG. You took—ay, 'mid the thick-
est of the storm—
The man of Unterwald across the lake.
'Tis a marvel you escaped. Had you no
thought
Of wife and children, then?
TELL. Dear wife, I had;
And therefore saved the father for his
children.
HEDWIG. To brave the lake in all its
wrath! 'Twas not
To put your trust in God! 'Twas tempt-
ing him.
TELL. The man that's overcautious
will do little.

HEDWIG. Yes, you've a kind and help-
ing hand for all;
But be in straits, and who will lend you
aid?
TELL. God grant I ne'er may stand in
need of it! [*Takes up his cross-bow
and arrows.*]
HEDWIG. Why take your cross-bow with
you? Leave it here.
TELL. I want my right hand, when I
want my bow.

[*The boys return.*]
WALTER. Where, father, are you going?
TELL. To granddad, boy—
To Altdorf. Will you go?
WALTER. Ay, that I will!
HEDWIG. The Viceroy's there just now.
Go not to Altdorf!
TELL. He leaves to-day.
HEDWIG. Then let him first be gone.
Cross not his path.—You know he bears
us grudge.
TELL. His ill-will cannot greatly in-
jure me.
I do what's right, and care for no man's
hate.
HEDWIG. 'Tis those who do what's right
whom most he hates.
TELL. Because he cannot reach them.
Me, I ween,
His knightship will be glad to leave in
peace.
HEDWIG. Ay!—Are you sure of that?
TELL. Not long ago,
As I was hunting through the wild
ravines
Of Schechenthal, untrod by mortal foot,—
There, as I took my solitary way
Along a shelving ledge of rocks, where
'twas
Impossible to step on either side;
For high above rose, like a giant wall,
The precipice's side, and far below
The Schechen thunder'd o'er its rifted
bed;—
[*The boys press towards him,
looking upon him with excited
curiosity.*]
There, face to face, I met the Viceroy.
He

Alone with me—and I myself alone—
Mere man to man, and near us the
    abyss.
And when his lordship had perused my
    face,
And knew the man he had severely fined
On some most trivial ground, not long
    before,
And saw me, with my sturdy bow in
    hand,
Come striding towards him, then his
    cheek grew pale,
His knees refused their office, and I
    thought
He would have sunk against the moun-
    tain side.
Then, touch'd with pity for him, I ad-
    vanced
Respectfully, and said, "'Tis I, my
    lord."
But ne'er a sound could he compel his
    lips
To frame in answer. Only with his hand
He beckoned me in silence to proceed.
So I pass'd on, and sent his train to seek
    him.
HEDWIG. He trembled then before you?
    Woe the while
You saw his weakness; that he'll ne'er
    forgive.
TELL. I shun him, therefore, and he'll
    not seek me.
HEDWIG. But stay away to-day. Go
    hunting rather!
TELL. What do you fear?
HEDWIG.   I am uneasy. Stay.
TELL. Why thus distress yourself with-
    out a cause?
HEDWIG. Because there is no cause.
    Tell, Tell! stay here!
TELL. Dear wife, I gave my promise I
    would go.
HEDWIG. Must you,—then go. But
    leave the boys with me.
WALTER. No, mother dear, I'm going
    with my father.
HEDWIG. How, Walter! will you leave
    your mother then?
WALTER. I'll bring you pretty things
    from grandpapa.   [Exit with his
                                father.]

WILHELM. Mother, I'll stay with you!
HEDWIG [embracing him]. Yes, Yes!
    thou art
My own dear child. Thou'rt all that's
    left to me. [She goes to the gate of
    the court, and looks anxiously after
    TELL and her son for a considerable
                                time.]

SCENE II

A retired part of the forest. Brooks dash-
    ing in spray over the rocks.

[Enter BERTHA in a hunting dress. Im-
    mediately afterwards RUDENZ.]
BERTHA. He follows me. Now to ex-
    plain myself!
RUDENZ [entering hastily]. At length,
    dear lady, we have met alone.
In this wild dell, with rocks on every
    side,
No jealous eye can watch our interview.
Now let my heart throw off this weary
    silence.
BERTHA. But are you sure they will
    not follow us?
RUDENZ. See, yonder goes the chase.
    Now, then, or never!
I must avail me of the precious mo-
    ment,—
Must hear my doom decided by thy
    lips,
Though it should part me from thy side
    for ever.
Oh, do not arm that gentle face of thine
With looks so stern and harsh! Who—
    who am I,
That dare aspire so high as unto thee?
Fame hath not stamp'd me yet; nor may
    I take
My place amid the courtly throng of
    knights
That, crown'd with glory's lustre, woo
    thy smiles.
Nothing have I to offer but a heart
That overflows with truth and love for
    thee.
BERTHA [sternly and with severity].
And dare you speak to me of love—of
    truth?

You, that art faithless to your nearest ties!

You, that are Austria's slave—bartered and sold

To her—an alien, and your country's tyrant!

RUDENZ. How! This reproach from thee! Whom do I seek,

On Austria's side, my own beloved, but thee?

BERTHA. Think you to find me in the traitor's ranks?

Now, as I live, I'd rather give my hand

To Gessler's self, all despot though he be,

Than to the Switzer who forgets his birth

And stoops to be the minion of a tyrant.

RUDENZ. Oh, Heaven, what must I hear!

BERTHA. Say! what can lie

Nearer the good man's heart, than friends and kindred?

What dearer duty to a noble soul

Than to protect weak, suffering innocence,

And vindicate the rights of the oppress'd?

My very soul bleeds for your countrymen.

I suffer with them, for I needs must love them;

They are so gentle, yet so full of power;

They draw my whole heart to them. Every day

I look upon them with increased esteem.

But you, whom nature and your knightly vow

Have given them as their natural protector,

Yet who desert them and abet their foes

In forging shackles for your native land,

You—you it is that deeply grieve and wound me.

I must constrain my heart, or I shall hate you.

RUDENZ. Is not my country's welfare all my wish?

What seek I for her but to purchase peace

'Neath Austria's potent sceptre?

BERTHA. Bondage, rather!

You would drive freedom from the last stronghold

That yet remains for her upon the earth.

The people know their own true int'rests better:

Their simple natures are not warp'd by show.

But round your head a tangling net is wound.

RUDENZ. Bertha, you hate me—you despise me!

BERTHA. Nay!

And if I did, 'twere better for my peace.

But to see him despised and despicable,—

The man whom one might love—

RUDENZ. Oh, Bertha! You

Show me the pinnacle of heavenly bliss,

Then, in a moment, hurl me to despair!

BERTHA. No, no! the noble is not all extinct

Within you. It but slumbers,—I will rouse it.

It must have cost you many a fiery struggle

To crush the virtues of your race within you.

But, Heaven be praised, 'tis mightier than yourself,

And you are noble in your own despite!

RUDENZ. You trust me, then? Oh, Bertha, with thy love

What might I not become!

BERTHA. Be only that

For which your own high nature destin'd you.

Fill the position you were born to fill;—

Stand by your people and your native land—

And battle for your sacred rights!

RUDENZ. Alas!

How can I hope to win you—to possess you,

If I take arms against the Emperor?

Will not your potent kinsmen interpose,

To dictate the disposal of your hand?

BERTHA. All my estates lie in the Forest Cantons,

And I am free when Switzerland is free.

RUDENZ. Oh! what a prospect, Bertha, hast thou shown me!

BERTHA. Hope not to win my hand by
Austria's favor;
Fain would they lay their grasp on my
estates,
To swell the vast domains which now
they hold.
The selfsame lust of conquest that would
rob
You of your liberty endangers mine.
Oh, friend, I'm mark'd for sacrifice,—
to be
The guerdon of some parasite, perchance!
They'll drag me hence to the Imperial
court,
That hateful haunt of falsehood and in-
trigue;
There do detested marriage bonds await
me.
Love, love alone,—your love can rescue
me.

RUDENZ. And thou couldst be con-
tent, love, to live here;
In my own native land to be my own?
Oh, Bertha, all the yearnings of my soul
For this great world and its tumultuous
strife,
What were they but a yearning after
thee?
In glory's path I sought for thee alone,
And all my thirst of fame was only love.
But if in this calm vale thou canst abide
With me, and bid earth's pomps and
pride adieu,
Then is the goal of my ambition won,
And the rough tide of the tempestuous
world
May dash and rave around these firm-
set hills!
No wandering wishes more have I to send
Forth to the busy scene that stirs be-
yond.
Then may these rocks, that girdle us,
extend
Their giant walls impenetrably round,
And this sequestered happy vale alone
Look up to heaven, and be my para-
dise!

BERTHA. Now art thou all my fancy
dream'd of thee.
My trust has not been given to thee in
vain.

RUDENZ. Away, ye idle phantoms of my
folly!
In mine own home I'll find my happi-
ness.
Here, where the gladsome boy to man-
hood grew,
Where ev'ry brook, and tree, and moun-
tain peak
Teems with remembrances of happy
hours,
In mine own native land thou wilt be
mine.
Ah, I have ever loved it well. I feel
How poor without it were all earthly
joys.

BERTHA. Where should we look for hap-
piness on earth,
If not in this dear land of innocence?
Here, where old truth hath its familiar
home,
Where fraud and guile are strangers,
envy ne'er
Shall dim the sparkling fountain of our
bliss,
And ever bright the hours shall o'er us
glide.
There do I see thee, in true manly worth,
The foremost of the free and of thy
peers,
Revered with homage pure and uncon-
strain'd,
Wielding a power that kings might envy
thee.

RUDENZ. And thee I see, thy sex's
crowning gem,
With thy sweet woman grace and wake-
ful love,
Building a heaven for me within my
home,
And, as the spring-time scatters forth
her flowers,
Adorning with thy charms my path of
life,
And spreading joy and sunshine all
around.

BERTHA. And this it was, dear friend,
that caused my grief,
To see thee blast this life's supremest
bliss
With thine own hand. Ah! what had
been my fate

Had I been forced to follow some proud
lord,
Some ruthless despot, to his gloomy
castle!
Here are no castles, here no bastion'd
walls
Divide me from a people I can bless.
RUDENZ. Yet, how to free myself; to
loose the coils
Which I have madly twined around my
head?
BERTHA. Tear them asunder with a
man's resolve.
Whatever the event, stand by thy peo-
ple.
It is thy post by birth.
[*Hunting-horns are heard in the
distance.*]
But hark! The chase!
Farewell,—'tis needful we should part—
away!
Fight for thy land; thou fightest for thy
love.
One foe fills all our souls with dread; the
blow
That makes one free emancipates us all.
[*Exeunt severally.*]

SCENE III

*A meadow near Altdorf. Trees in the
foreground. At the back of the stage a
cap upon a pole. The prospect is bounded
by the Bannberg, which is surmounted
by a snow-capped mountain.*

[FRIESSHARDT *and* LEUTHOLD *on guard.*]
FRIESSHARDT. We keep our watch in
vain. There's not a soul
Will pass, and do obeisance to the cap.
But yesterday the place swarm'd like a
fair;
Now the whole green looks like a very
desert,
Since yonder scarecrow hung upon the
pole.
LEUTHOLD. Only the vilest rabble show
themselves,
And wave their tattered caps in mockery
.at us.

All honest citizens would sooner make
A tedious circuit over half the town
Than bend their backs before our mas-
ter's cap.
FRIESSHARDT. They were obliged to
pass this way at noon,
As they were coming from the Council
House.
I counted then upon a famous catch,
For no one thought of bowing to the
cap.
But Rösselmann, the priest, was even
with me:
Coming just then from some sick peni-
tent,
He stands before the pole,—raises the
Host—
The Sacrist, too, must tinkle with his
bell,—
When down they dropp'd on knee—my-
self and all,
In reverence to the Host, but not the
cap.
LEUTHOLD. Hark ye, companion, I've a
shrewd suspicion
Our post's no better than the pillory.
It is a burning shame, a trooper should
Stand sentinel before an empty cap,
And every honest fellow must despise us
To do obeisance to a cap, too! Faith,
I never heard an order so absurd!
FRIESSHARDT. Why not, an't please
thee, to an empty cap?
Thou'st duck'd, I'm sure, to many an
empty sconce.

[HILDEGARD, MECHTHILD *and* ELSBETH
*enter with their children, and station
themselves around the pole.*]
LEUTHOLD. And thou art an officious
sneaking knave,
That's fond of bringing honest folks to
trouble.
For my part, he that likes, may pass the
cap:—
I'll shut my eyes and take no note of
him.
MECHTHILD. There hangs the Viceroy!
Your obeisance, children!
ELSBETH. I would to God he'd go, and
leave his cap!

The country would be none the worse
for it.

FRIESSHARDT [*driving them away*].
Out of the way! Confounded pack of
gossips!
Who sent for you? Go, send your hus-
bands here,
If they have courage to defy the order.

[TELL *enters with his cross-bow, leading
his son* WALTER *by the hand. They pass
the hat without noticing it and advance
to the front of the stage.*]

WALTER [*pointing to the Bannberg*].
Father, is't true that on the moun-
tain there
The trees, if wounded with a hatchet,
bleed?

TELL. Who says so, boy?

WALTER. The master herds-
man, father!
He tells us there's a charm upon the
trees,
And if a man shall injure them, the
hand
That struck the blow will grow from out
the grave.

TELL. There is a charm about them—
that's the truth.
Dost see those glaciers yonder—those
white horns—
That seem to melt away into the sky?

WALTER. They are the peaks that
thunder so at night,
And send the avalanches down upon us.

TELL. They are; and Altdorf long ago
had been
Submerged beneath these avalanches'
weight
Did not the forest there above the town
Stand like a bulwark to arrest their
fall.

WALTER [*after musing a little*]. And
are there countries with no moun-
tains, father?

TELL. Yes; if we travel downwards
from our heights,
And keep descending in the river's
courses,
We reach a wide and level country,
where

Our mountain torrents brawl and foam
no more,
And fair large rivers glide serenely on.
All quarters of the heaven may there be
scann'd
Without impediment. The corn grows
there
In broad and lovely fields, and all the land
Is fair as any garden to the view.

WALTER. But, father, tell me, where-
fore haste we not
Away to this delightful land, instead
Of toiling here, and struggling as we do?

TELL. The land is fair and bountiful
as heaven;
But they who till it never may enjoy
The fruits of what they sow.

WALTER. Live they not free,
As you do, on the land their fathers left
them?

TELL. The fields are all the bishop's
or the king's.

WALTER. But they may freely hunt
among the woods?

TELL. The game is all the monarch's—
bird and beast.

WALTER. But they, at least, may surely
fish the streams?

TELL. Stream, lake, and sea, all to the
king belong.

WALTER. Who is this king, of whom
they're so afraid?

TELL. He is the man who fosters and
protects them.

WALTER. Have they not courage to
protect themselves?

TELL. The neighbor there dare not his
neighbor trust.

WALTER. I should want breathing room
in such a land.
I'd rather dwell beneath the avalanches.

TELL. 'Tis better, child, to have these
glacier peaks
Behind one's back, than evil-minded men!
[*They are about to pass on.*]

WALTER. See, father, see the cap on
yonder pole!

TELL. What is the cap to us? Come,
let's begone.
[*As he is going,* FRIESSHARDT,
presenting his pike, stops him.]

FRIESSHARDT. Stand, I command you, in the Emperor's name!

TELL [*seizing the pike*]. What would ye? Wherefore do you stop my path?

FRIESSHARDT. You've broke the mandate, and must go with us.

LEUTHOLD. You have not done obeisance to the cap.

TELL. Friend, let me go.

FRIESSHARDT. Away, away to prison!

WALTER. Father to prison? Help! [*Calling to the side scene.*] This way, you men!

Good people, help! They're dragging him to prison!

[RÖSSELMANN *the Priest, and the* SACRISTAN, *with three other men, enter.*]

SACRISTAN. What's here amiss?

RÖSSELMANN. Why do you seize this man?

FRIESSHARDT. He is an enemy of the King—a traitor.

TELL [*seizing him with violence*]. A traitor, I!

RÖSSELMANN. Friend, thou art wrong. 'Tis Tell,

An honest man and worthy citizen.

WALTER [*descries* FÜRST *and runs up to him*]. Grandfather, help, they want to seize my father!

FRIESSHARDT. Away to prison!

FÜRST [*running in*]. Stay, I offer bail. For God's sake, Tell, what is the matter here?

[MELCHTHAL *and* STAUFFACHER *enter.*]

LEUTHOLD. He has contemn'd the Viceroy's sovereign power,

Refusing flatly to acknowledge it.

STAUFFACHER. Has Tell done this?

MELCHTHAL. Villain, thou knowest 'tis false!

LEUTHOLD. He has not made obeisance to the cap.

FÜRST. And shall for this to prison? Come, my friend,

Take my security and let him go.

FRIESSHARDT. Keep your security for yourself—you'll need it.

We only do our duty. Hence with him.

MELCHTHAL [*to the country people*]. This is too bad—shall we stand by and see them

Drag him away before our very eyes?

SACRISTAN. We are the strongest. Don't endure it, friends.

Our countrymen will back us to a man.

FRIESSHARDT. Who dares resist the governor's commands?

OTHER THREE PEASANTS [*running in*]. We'll help you. What's the matter? Down with them!

[HILDEGARD, MECHTHILD *and* ELSBETH *return.*]

TELL. Go, go, good people, I can help myself.

Think you, had I a mind to use my strength,

These pikes of theirs should daunt me?

MELCHTHAL [*to* FRIESSHARDT]. Only try—

Try, if you dare, to force him from amongst us.

FÜRST *and* STAUFFACHER. Peace, peace, friends!

FRIESSHARDT [*loudly*]. Riot! Insurrection, ho!

[*Hunting-horns without.*]

WOMEN. The Governor!

FRIESSHARDT [*raising his voice*]. Rebellion! Mutiny!

STAUFFACHER. Roar, till you burst, knave!

RÖSSELMANN *and* MELCHTHAL. Will you hold your tongue?

FRIESSHARDT [*calling still louder*]. Help, help, I say, the servants of the law!

FÜRST. The Viceroy here! Then we shall smart for this!

[*Enter* GESSLER *on horseback, with a falcon on his wrist;* RUDOLPH DER HARRAS, BERTHA *and* RUDENZ, *and a numerous train of armed attendants, who form a circle of lances round the whole stage.*]

HARRAS. Room for the Viceroy!

GESSLER. Drive the clowns apart. Why throng the people thus? Who calls for help?

[*General silence.*]

Who was it? I will know.
[FRIESSHARDT *steps forward.*]
And who art thou?
And why hast thou this man in custody?
[*Gives his falcon to an attendant.*]
FRIESSHARDT. Dread sir, I am a soldier of your guard,
And station'd sentinel beside the cap;
This man I apprehended in the act
Of passing it without obeisance due,
So I arrested him, as you gave order,
Whereon the people tried to rescue him.
GESSLER [*after a pause*]. And do you, Tell, so lightly hold your king,
And me, who acts as his viceregent here,
That you refuse the greeting to the cap
I hung aloft to test your loyalty?
I read in this a disaffected spirit.
TELL. Pardon me, good my lord! The action sprung
From inadvertence,—not from disrespect.
Were I discreet, I were not William Tell:
Forgive me now—I'll not offend again.
GESSLER [*after a pause*]. I hear, Tell, you're a master with the bow,—
And bear the palm away from every rival.
WALTER. That must be true, sir! At a hundred yards
He'll shoot an apple for you off the tree.
GESSLER. Is that boy thine, Tell?
TELL. Yes, my gracious lord.
GESSLER. Hast any more of them?
TELL. Two boys, my lord.
GESSLER. And, of the two, which dost thou love the most?
TELL. Sir, both the boys are dear to me alike.
GESSLER. Then, Tell, since at a hundred yards thou canst
Bring down the apple from the tree, thou shalt
Approve thy skill before me. Take thy bow—
Thou hast it there at hand—and make thee ready
To shoot an apple from the stripling's head!
But take this counsel,—look well to thine aim,
See that thou hitt'st the apple at the first,

For, shouldst thou miss, thy head shall pay the forfeit.
[*All give signs of horror.*]
TELL. What monstrous thing, my lord, is this you ask?
That I, from the head of mine own child!
—No, no!
It cannot be, kind sir, you meant not that—
God, in His grace, forbid! You could not ask
A father seriously to do that thing!
GESSLER. Thou art to shoot an apple from his head!
I do desire—command it so.
TELL. What! I
Level my cross-bow at the darling head
Of mine own child? No—rather let me die!
GESSLER. Or thou must shoot, or with thee dies the boy.
TELL. Shall I become the murd'rer of my child!
You have no children, sir—you do not know
The tender throbbings of a father's heart.
GESSLER. How now, Tell, so discreet upon a sudden?
I had been told thou wert a visionary,—
A wanderer from the paths of common men.
Thou lov'st the marvellous. So have I now
Cull'd out for thee a task of special daring.
Another man might pause and hesitate;—
Thou dashest at it, heart and soul, at once.
BERTHA. Oh, do not jest, my lord, with these poor souls!
See, how they tremble, and how pale they look,
So little used are they to hear thee jest.
GESSLER. Who tells thee that I jest?
[*Grasping a branch above his head.*]
Here is the apple.
Room there, I say! And let him take his distance—
Just eighty paces,—as the custom is,—

Not an inch more or less! It was his boast
That at a hundred he could hit his man.
Now, archer, to your task, and look you miss not!
HARRAS. Heavens! this grows serious—down, boy, on your knees,
And beg the governor to spare your life.
FÜRST [aside to MELCHTHAL, who can scarcely restrain his impatience].
Command yourself,—be calm, I beg of you!
BERTHA [to the governor]. Let this suffice you, sir! It is inhuman
To trifle with a father's anguish thus.
Although this wretched man had forfeited
Both life and limb for such a slight offence,
Already he has suffer'd tenfold death.
Send him away uninjured to his home;
He'll know thee well in future; and this hour
He and his children's children will remember.
GESSLER. Open a way there—quick! Why this delay?
Thy life is forfeited; I might despatch thee,
And see I graciously repose thy fate
Upon the skill of thine own practis'd hand.
No cause has he to say his doom is harsh
Who's made the master of his destiny.
Thou boastest of thy steady eye. 'Tis well!
Now is a fitting time to show thy skill.
The mark is worthy, and the prize is great.
To hit the bull's eye in the target—that
Can many another do as well as thou;
But he, methinks, is master of his craft
Who can at all times on his skill rely,
Nor lets his heart disturb or eye or hand.
FÜRST. My lord, we bow to your authority;
But oh, let justice yield to mercy here.
Take half my property, nay, take it all,
But spare a father this unnatural doom!
WALTER. Grandfather, do not kneel to that bad man!
Say, where am I to stand? I do not fear;

My father strikes the bird upon the wing,
And will not miss now when 'twould harm his boy!
STAUFFACHER. Does the child's innocence not touch your heart?
RÖSSELMANN. Bethink you, sir, there is a God in heaven,
To whom you must account for all your deeds.
GESSLER [pointing to the boy]. Bind him to yonder lime-tree straight!
WALTER. Bind me?
No, I will not be bound! I will be still,
Still as a lamb—nor even draw my breath!
But if you bind me, I can not be still.
Then I shall writhe and struggle with my bonds.
HARRAS. But let your eyes at least be bandaged, boy!
WALTER. And why my eyes? No! Do you think I fear
An arrow from my father's hand? Not I!
I'll wait it firmly, nor so much as wink!
Quick, father, show them that thou art an archer!
He doubts thy skill—he thinks to ruin us.
Shoot, then, and hit, though but to spite the tyrant! [He goes to the lime-tree, and an apple is placed on his head.]
MELCHTHAL [to the country people].
What! Is this outrage to be perpetrated
Before our very eyes? Where is our oath?
STAUFFACHER. 'Tis all in vain. We have no weapons here;
And see the wood of lances that surrounds us!
MELCHTHAL. Oh! would to Heaven that we had struck at once!
God pardon those who counsell'd the delay!
GESSLER [to TELL]. Now, to thy task!
Men bear not arms for nought.
'Tis dangerous to carry deadly weapons,
And on the archer oft his shaft recoils.
This right, these haughty peasant churls assume,
Trenches upon their master's privileges.
None should be armed but those who bear command.

It pleases you to wear the bow and bolt:—
Well,—be it so. I will provide the mark.
TELL [*bends the bow and fixes the arrow*]. A lane there! Room!
STAUFFACHER. What, Tell? You would
—no, no!
You shake—your hand's unsteady—your
knees tremble.
TELL [*letting the bow sink down*].
There's something swims before mine
eyes!
WOMEN. Great Heaven!
TELL. Release me from this shot! Here
is my heart! [*Tears open his breast.*]
Summon your troopers—let them strike
me down!
GESSLER. I do not want thy life, Tell,
but the shot.
Thy talent's universal! Nothing daunts
thee!
Thou canst direct the rudder like the bow!
Storms fright not thee, when there's a
life at stake.
Now, saviour, help thyself,—thou savest
all!
> [TELL *stands fearfully agitated
> by contending emotions, his
> hands moving convulsively, and
> his eyes turning alternately to
> the governor and heaven. Suddenly he takes a second arrow
> from his quiver and sticks it
> in his belt. The governor
> watches all these motions.*]
WALTER [*beneath the lime-tree*]. Come,
father, shoot! I'm not afraid!
TELL [*collects himself and levels the
bow*]. It must be!
RUDENZ [*who all the while has been
standing in a state of violent excitement, and has with difficulty restrained himself, advances*]. My lord,
you will not urge this matter further.
You will not. It was surely but a test.
You've gained your object. Rigor push'd
too far
Is sure to miss its aim, however good,
As snaps the bow that's all too straitly-
bent.
GESSLER. Peace, till your counsel's
ask'd for!

RUDENZ. I will speak!
Ay, and I dare. I reverence my king;
But acts like these must make his name
abhorr'd.
He sanctions not this cruelty. I dare
Avouch the fact. And you outstep your
powers
In handling thus an unoffending people.
GESSLER. Ha! thou grow'st bold, me-
thinks!
RUDENZ. I have been dumb
To all the oppressions I was doom'd to see.
I've closed mine eyes, that they might
not behold them,
Bade my rebellious, swelling heart be still,
And pent its struggles down within my
breast.
But to be silent longer were to be
A traitor to my king and country both.
BERTHA [*casting herself between him
and the governor*]. Oh, Heaven! you
but exasperate his rage!
RUDENZ. My people I forsook—re-
nounced my kindred—
Broke all the ties of nature, that I might
Attach myself to you. I madly thought
That I should best advance the general
weal
By adding sinews to the Emperor's
power.
The scales have fallen from mine eyes—
I see
The fearful precipice on which I stand.
You've led my youthful judgment far
astray,—
Deceived my honest heart. With best
intent,
I had well nigh achiev'd my country's
ruin.
GESSLER. Audacious boy, this language
to thy lord?
RUDENZ. The Emperor is my lord, not
you! I am free
As you by birth, and I can cope with you
In every virtue that beseems a knight.
And if you stood not here in that King's
name
Which I respect e'en where 'tis most
abused,
I'd throw my gauntlet down, and you
should give

An answer to my gage in knightly
fashion.
Ay, beckon to your troopers! Here I
stand;
But not like these [pointing to the people]
—unarmed. I have a sword,
And he that stirs one step——
STAUFFACHER [exclaims]. The apple's
down!
[While the attention of the crowd
has been directed to the spot
where BERTHA had cast herself
between RUDENZ and GESSLER,
TELL has shot.]
RÖSSELMANN. The boy's alive!
MANY VOICES.   The apple has
been struck!
[WALTER FÜRST staggers and is
about to fall. BERTHA supports
him.]
GESSLER [astonished]. How? Has he
shot? The madman!
BERTHA.   Worthy father,
Pray you, compose yourself. The boy's
alive.
WALTER [runs in with the apple].
Here is the apple, father! Well I
knew
You would not harm your boy.
[TELL stands with his body bent
forward, as though he would
follow the arrow. His bow
drops from his hand. When he
sees the boy advancing he
hastens to meet him with open
arms, and embracing him pas-
sionately sinks down with him
quite exhausted. All crowd
round them, deeply affected.]
BERTHA.   Oh, ye kind Heaven!
FÜRST [to father and son]. My chil-
dren, my dear children!
STAUFFACHER.   God be praised!
LEUTHOLD. Almighty powers! That was
a shot indeed!
It will be talked of to the end of time.
HARRAS. This feat of Tell, the archer,
will be told
While yonder mountains stand upon their
base. [Hands the apple to GESS-
LER.]

GESSLER. By Heaven! the apple's cleft
right through the core.
It was a master shot, I must allow.
RÖSSELMANN. The shot was good. But
woe to him who drove
The man to tempt his God by such a
feat!
STAUFFACHER. Cheer up, Tell, rise!
You've nobly freed yourself,
And now may go in quiet to your home.
RÖSSELMANN. Come, to the mother let
us bear her son!
[They are about to lead him off.]
GESSLER. A word, Tell.
TELL.   Sir, your pleasure?
GESSLER.   Thou didst place
A second arrow in thy belt—nay, nay!
I saw it well—what was thy purpose
with it?
TELL [confused]. It is the custom with
all archers, Sir.
GESSLER. No, Tell, I cannot let that
answer pass.
There was some other motive, well I
know.
Frankly and cheerfully confess the
truth;—
Whate'er it be, I promise thee thy life.
Wherefore the second arrow?
TELL.   Well, my lord,
Since you have promised not to take my
life,
I will, without reserve, declare the truth.
[He draws the arrow from his
belt and fixes his eyes sternly
upon the governor.]
If that my hand had struck my darling
child,
This second arrow I had aimed at you,
And, be assured, I should not then have
miss'd.
GESSLER. Well, Tell, I promised thou
shouldst have thy life;
I gave my knightly word, and I will keep
it.
Yet, as I know the malice of thy
thoughts,
I will remove thee hence to sure confine-
ment,
Where neither sun nor moon shall reach
thine eyes.

Thus from thy arrows I shall be secure.
Seize on him, guards, and bind him.

[*They bind him.*]

STAUFFACHER. How, my lord—
How can you treat in such a way a man
On whom God's hand has plainly been reveal'd?

GESSLER. Well, let us see if it will save him twice!
Remove him to my ship; I'll follow straight.
In person I will see him lodged at Küssnacht.

RÖSSELMANN. You dare not do't. Nor durst the Emperor's self
So violate our dearest chartered rights.

GESSLER. Where are they? Has the Emp'ror confirm'd them?
He never has. And only by obedience
Need you expect to win that favor from him.
You are all rebels 'gainst the Emp'ror's power,
And bear a desperate and rebellious spirit.
I know you all—I see you through and through.
Him do I single from amongst you now,
But in his guilt you all participate.
The wise will study silence and obedience.

[*Exit, followed by* BERTHA, RUDENZ, HARRAS, *and attendants.* FRIESSHARDT *and* LEUTHOLD *remain.*]

FÜRST [*in violent anguish*]. All's over now! He is resolved to bring
Destruction on myself and all my house.

STAUFFACHER [*to* TELL]. Oh, why did you provoke the tyrant's rage?

TELL. Let him be calm who feels the pangs I felt.

STAUFFACHER. Alas! alas! Our every hope is gone.
With you we all are fettered and enchain'd.

COUNTRY PEOPLE [*surrounding* TELL]. Our last remaining comfort goes with you!

LEUTHOLD [*approaching him*]. I'm sorry for you, Tell, but must obey.

TELL. Farewell!

WALTER [*clinging to him in great agony*]. Oh, father, father, my dear father!

TELL [*pointing to heaven*]. Thy father is on high—appeal to him!

STAUFFACHER. Hast thou no message, Tell, to send thy wife?

TELL [*clasping the boy passionately to his breast*]. The boy's uninjured; God will succor me!

[*Tears himself suddenly away and follows the soldiers of the guard.*]

ACT IV

SCENE I

Eastern shore of the Lake of Lucerne, rugged and singularly shaped rocks close the prospect to the west. The lake is agitated, violent roaring and rushing of wind with thunder and lightning at intervals.

[KUNZ OF GERSAU, FISHERMAN *and* BOY.]

KUNZ. I saw it with these eyes! Believe me, friend,
It happen'd all precisely as I've said.

FISHERMAN. Tell made a prisoner and borne off to Küssnacht?
The best man in the land, the bravest arm,
Had we resolved to strike for liberty!

KUNZ. The Viceroy takes him up the lake in person:
They were about to go on board as I
Left Flüelen; but still the gathering storm,
That drove me here to land so suddenly,
Perchance has hindered their abrupt departure.

FISHERMAN. Our Tell in chains, and in the Viceroy's power!
O, trust me, Gessler will entomb him, where
He nevermore shall see the light of day;
For, Tell once free, the tyrant well might dread
The just revenge of one so deep incensed.

KUNZ. The old Landamman, too—von
Attinghaus—
They say, is lying at the point of death.
FISHERMAN. Then the last anchor of
our hopes gives way!
He was the only man that dared to raise
His voice in favor of the people's rights.
KUNZ. The storm grows worse and
worse. So, fare ye well.
I'll go and seek out quarters in the
village.
There's not a chance of getting off to-
day. [*Exit.*]
FISHERMAN. Tell dragg'd to prison,
and the Baron dead!
Now, tyranny, exalt thy insolent front,—
Throw shame aside! The voice of truth
is silenced,
The eye that watch'd for us in darkness
closed,
The arm that should have struck thee
down, in chains!
BOY. 'Tis hailing hard—come, let us
to the cottage!
This is no weather to be out in, father!
FISHERMAN. Rage on, ye winds! Ye
lightnings, flash your fires!
Burst, ye swollen clouds! Ye cataracts
of heaven,
Descend, and drown the country! In the
germ,
Destroy the generations yet unborn!
Ye savage elements, be lords of all!
Return, ye bears; ye ancient wolves, re-
turn
To this wide, howling waste! The land is
yours.
Who would live here when liberty is
gone!
BOY. Hark! How the wind whistles,
and the whirlpool roars;
I never saw a storm so fierce as this!
FISHERMAN. To level at the head of his
own child!
Never had father such command before.
And shall not nature, rising in wild
wrath,
Revolt against the deed? I should not
marvel,
Though to the lake these rocks should bow
their heads

Though yonder pinnacles, yon towers of
ice,
That, since creation's dawn, have known
no thaw,
Should, from their lofty summits, melt
away,—
Though yonder mountains, yon primeval
cliffs,
Should topple down, and a new deluge
whelm
Beneath its waves all living men's abodes!
[*Bells heard.*]
BOY. Hark, they are ringing on the
mountain, yonder!
They surely see some vessel in distress,
And toll the bell that we may pray for
it. [*Ascends a rock.*]
FISHERMAN. Woe to the bark that now
pursues its course,
Rock'd in the cradle of these storm-toss'd
waves!
Nor helm nor steersman here can aught
avail;
The storm is master. Man is like a
ball,
Toss'd 'twixt the winds and billows. Far
or near,
No haven offers him its friendly shelter!
Without one ledge to grasp, the sheer
smooth rocks
Look down inhospitably on his despair,
And only tender him their flinty breasts.
BOY [*calling from above*]. Father, a
ship; and bearing down from Flüelen.
FISHERMAN. Heaven pity the poor
wretches! When the storm
Is once entangled in this strait of ours,
It rages like some savage beast of prey,
Struggling against its cage's iron bars!
Howling, it seeks an outlet—all in vain;
For the rocks hedge it round on every
side,
Walling the narrow pass as high as
heaven. [*He ascends a cliff.*]
BOY. It is the Governor of Uri's ship;
By its red poop I know it, and the flag.
FISHERMAN. Judgments of Heaven!
Yes, it is he himself.
It is the governor! Yonder he sails,
And with him bears the burden of his
crimes!

Soon has the arm of the avenger found
him!
Now over him he knows a mightier lord.
These waves yield no obedience to his
voice,
These rocks bow not their heads before
his cap.
Boy, do not pray; stay not the Judge's
arm!
BOY. I pray not for the governor—I
pray
For Tell, who is on board the ship with
him.
FISHERMAN. Alas, ye blind, unreason-
ing elements!
Must ye, in punishing one guilty head,
Destroy the vessel and the pilot too?
BOY. See, see, they've clear'd the
Buggisgrat; but now
The blast, rebounding from the Devil's
Minster,
Has driven them back on the Great Axen-
berg.
I cannot see them now.
FISHERMAN. The Hakmesser
Is there, that's founder'd many a gallant
ship.
If they should fail to double that with
skill,
Their bark will go to pieces on the rocks
That hide their jagged peaks below the
lake.
They have on board the very best of
pilots.
If any man can save them, Tell is he;
But he is manacled both hand and foot.

[*Enter* WILLIAM TELL, *with his cross-bow.
He enters precipitately, looks wildly
round, and testifies the most violent agita-
tion. When he reaches the centre of the
stage he throws himself upon his knees
and stretches out his hands, first towards
the earth, then towards heaven.*]
BOY [*observing him*]. See, father!
Who is that man, kneeling yonder?
FISHERMAN. He clutches at the earth
with both his hands,
And looks as though he were beside him-
self.
BOY [*advancing*]. What do I see?

Father, come here, and look!
FISHERMAN [*approaches*]. Who is it?
God in Heaven! What! William Tell!
How came you hither? Speak, Tell!
BOY. Were you
In yonder ship, a prisoner, and in chains?
FISHERMAN. Were they not bearing
you away to Küssnacht?
TELL [*rising*]. I am released.
FISHERMAN *and* BOY. Released? Oh,
miracle!
BOY. Whence came you here?
TELL. From yonder vessel!
FISHERMAN. What?
BOY. Where is the Viceroy?
TELL. Drifting on the waves.
FISHERMAN. Is't possible? But you!
How are you here?
How 'scaped you from your fetters and
the storm?
TELL. By God's most gracious provi-
dence. Attend.
FISHERMAN *and* BOY. Say on, say on!
TELL. You know what
passed at Altdorf?
FISHERMAN. I do—say on!
TELL. How I was seized
and bound,
And order'd by the governor to Küss-
nacht.
FISHERMAN. And how with you at
Flüelen he embarked.
All this we know. Say how have you
escaped?
TELL. I lay on deck, fast bound with
cords, disarm'd,
In utter hopelessness. I did not think
Again to see the gladsome light of day,
Nor the dear faces of my wife and chil-
dren,
And eyed disconsolate the waste of
waters.—
FISHERMAN. Oh, wretched man!
TELL. Then we put forth;
the Viceroy,
Rudolph de Harras, and their suite. My
bow
And quiver lay astern beside the helm;
And just as we had reached the corner,
near
The Little Axen, Heaven ordain'd it so,

That from the Gotthardt's gorge a hurricane
Swept down upon us with such headlong force
That ev'ry rower's heart within him sank,
And all on board look'd for a watery grave.
Then heard I one of the attendant train,
Turning to Gessler, in this strain accost him:
"You see our danger, and your own, my lord,
And that we hover on the verge of death.
The boatmen there are powerless from fear,
Nor are they confident what course to take;—
Now, here is Tell, a stout and fearless man,
And knows to steer with more than common skill.
How if we should avail ourselves of him
In this emergency?" The Viceroy then
Address'd me thus: "If thou wilt undertake
To bring us through this tempest safely, Tell,
I might consent to free thee from thy bonds."
I answer'd, "Yes, my lord, with God's assistance,
I'll see what can be done, and help us Heaven!"
On this they loosed me from my bonds, and I
Stood by the helm and fairly steered along,
Yet ever eyed my shooting-gear askance,
And kept a watchful eye upon the shore,
To find some point where I might leap to land;
And when I had descried a shelving crag,
That jutted, smooth atop, into the lake—
FISHERMAN. I know it. 'Tis at foot of the Great Axen;
But looks so steep, I never could have dreamt
'Twere possible to leap it from the boat.
TELL. I bade the men put forth their utmost might,

Until we came before the shelving crag.
For there, I said, the danger will be past!
Stoutly they pull'd, and soon we near'd the point.
One prayer to God for his assisting grace,
And straining every muscle, I brought round
The vessel's stern close to the rocky wall;
Then snatching up my weapons, with a bound
I swung myself upon the flattened shelf,
And with my feet thrust off, with all my might,
The puny bark into the hell of waters.
There let it drift about, as Heaven ordains!
Thus am I here, deliver'd from the might
Of the dread storm, and man, more dreadful still.
FISHERMAN. Tell, Tell, the Lord has manifestly wrought
A miracle in thy behalf! I scarce
Can credit my own eyes. But tell me, now,
Whither you purpose to betake yourself?
For you will be in peril, should the Viceroy
Chance to escape this tempest with his life.
TELL. I heard him say, as I lay bound on board,
His purpose was to disembark at Brunnen,
And, crossing Schwyz, convey me to his castle.
FISHERMAN. Means he to go by land?
TELL. So he intends.
FISHERMAN. Oh, then, conceal yourself without delay!
Not twice will heaven release you from his grasp.
TELL. Which is the nearest way to Arth and Küssnacht?
FISHERMAN. The public road leads by the way of Steinen,
But there's a nearer road, and more retired,
That goes by Lowerz, which my boy can show you.

TELL [*gives him his hand*]. May Heaven reward your kindness! Fare ye well.

[*As he is going, he comes back.*]

Did not you also take the oath at Rootli? I heard your name, methinks.

FISHERMAN. Yes, I was there, And took the oath of the confederacy.

TELL. Then do me this one favor: speed to Bürglen— My wife is anxious at my absence—tell her That I am free and in secure concealment.

FISHERMAN. But whither shall I tell her you have fled?

TELL. You'll find her father with her, and some more, Who took the oath with you upon the Rootli; Bid them be resolute, and strong of heart,— For Tell is free and master of his arm; They shall hear further news of me ere long.

FISHERMAN. What have you, then, in view? Come, tell me frankly!

TELL. When once 'tis *done*, 'twill be in every mouth. [*Exit.*]

FISHERMAN. Show him the way, boy. Heaven be his support! Whate'er he has resolved, he'll execute.

[*Exit.*]

SCENE II

Baronial mansion of Attinghausen. The BARON *upon a couch, dying.* WALTER FÜRST, STAUFFACHER, MELCHTHAL, *and* BAUMGARTEN *attending round him.* WALTER TELL *kneeling before the dying man.*

FÜRST. All now is over with him. He is gone.

STAUFFACHER. He lies not like one dead. The feather, see, Moves on his lips! His sleep is very calm, And on his features plays a placid smile.

[BAUMGARTEN *goes to the door and speaks with some one.*]

FÜRST. Who's there?

BAUMGARTEN [*returning*]. Tell's wife, your daughter; she insists That she must speak with you, and see her boy.

[WALTER TELL *rises.*]

FÜRST. I who need comfort—can I comfort her? Does every sorrow centre on my head?

HEDWIG [*forcing her way in*]. Where is my child? Unhand me! I must see him.

STAUFFACHER. Be calm! Reflect you're in the house of death!

HEDWIG [*falling upon her boy's neck*]. My Walter! Oh, he yet is mine!

WALTER. Dear mother!

HEDWIG. And is it surely so! Art thou unhurt?

[*Gazing at him with anxious tenderness.*]

And is it possible he aim'd at thee? How could he do it? Oh, he has no heart— And he could wing an arrow at his child!

FÜRST. His soul was rack'd with anguish when he did it. No choice was left him, but to shoot or die!

HEDWIG. Oh, if he had a father's heart, he would Have sooner perish'd by a thousand deaths!

STAUFFACHER. You should be grateful for God's gracious care, That ordered things so well.

HEDWIG. Can I forget What might have been the issue? God of Heaven! Were I to live for centuries, I still Should see my boy tied up,—his father's mark,— And still the shaft would quiver in my heart!

MELCHTHAL. You know not how the Viceroy taunted him!

HEDWIG. Oh ruthless heart of man! Offend his pride, And reason in his breast forsakes her seat; In his blind wrath he'll stake upon a cast A child's existence, and a mother's heart!

BAUMGARTEN. Is then your husband's fate not hard enough,
That you embitter it by such reproaches?
Have you no feeling for his sufferings?
HEDWIG [*turning to him and gazing full upon him*]. Hast thou tears only for thy friend's distress?
Say, where were you when he—my noble Tell,
Was bound in chains? Where was your friendship then?
The shameful wrong was done before your eyes;
Patient you stood, and let your friend be dragg'd,
Ay, from your very hands. Did ever Tell
Act thus to you? Did he stand whining by
When on your heels the Viceroy's horsemen press'd,
And full before you roared the storm-toss'd lake?
Oh, not with idle tears he show'd his pity;
Into the boat he sprung, forgot his home,
His wife, his children, and delivered thee!
FÜRST. It had been madness to attempt his rescue,
Unarm'd, and few in numbers as we were.
HEDWIG [*casting herself upon his bosom*]. Oh, father, and thou, too, hast lost my Tell!
The country—all have lost him! All lament
His loss; and, oh, how he must pine for us!
Heaven keep his soul from sinking to despair!
No friend's consoling voice can penetrate
His dreary dungeon walls. Should he fall sick!
Ah! In the vapors of the murky vault
He must fall sick. Even as the Alpine rose
Grows pale and withers in the swampy air,
There is no life for him but in the sun,
And in the balm of heaven's refreshing breeze.
Imprison'd! Liberty to him is breath;
He cannot live in the rank dungeon air!

STAUFFACHER. Pray you be calm! And hand in hand we'll all
Combine to burst his prison doors.
HEDWIG.   Without him,
What have you power to do? While Tell was free,
There still, indeed, was hope—weak innocence
Had still a friend, and the oppress'd a stay.
Tell saved you all! You cannot all combined
Release him from his cruel prison bonds.
                [*The* BARON *wakes.*]
BAUMGARTEN. Hush, hush! He starts!
ATTINGHAUSEN [*sitting up*]. Where is he?
STAUFFACHER.   Who?
ATTINGHAUSEN.   He leaves me,—
In my last moments he abandons me.
STAUFFACHER. He means his nephew. Have they sent for him?
FÜRST. He has been summoned. Cheerly, sir! Take comfort!
He has found his heart at last, and is our own.
ATTINGHAUSEN. Say, has he spoken for his native land?
STAUFFACHER. Ay, like a hero!
ATTINGHAUSEN. Wherefore comes he not,
That he may take my blessing ere I die?
I feel my life fast ebbing to a close.
STAUFFACHER. Nay, talk not thus, dear sir! This last short sleep
Has much refresh'd you, and your eye is bright.
ATTINGHAUSEN. Life is but pain, and even that has left me;
My sufferings, like my hopes, have passed away.   [*Observing the boy.*]
What boy is that?
FÜRST. Bless him. Oh, good, my lord!
He is my grandson, and is fatherless.
        [HEDWIG *kneels with the boy before the dying man.*]
ATTINGHAUSEN. And fatherless—I leave you all, ay all!
Oh, wretched fate, that these old eyes should see

My country's ruin as they close in death!
Must I attain the utmost verge of life
To feel my hopes go with me to the grave?

STAUFFACHER [to FÜRST]. Shall he depart 'mid grief and gloom like this?
Shall not his parting moments be illumed
By hope's delightful beams? My noble lord,
Raise up your drooping spirit! We are not
Forsaken quite—past all deliverance.

ATTINGHAUSEN. Who shall deliver you?

FÜRST. Ourselves. For know
The Cantons three are to each other pledged
To hunt the tyrants from the land. The league
Has been concluded, and a sacred oath
Confirms our union. Ere another year
Begins its circling course—the blow shall fall.
In a free land your ashes shall repose.

ATTINGHAUSEN. The league concluded! Is it really so?

MELCHTHAL. On one day shall the Cantons rise together.
All is prepared to strike—and to this hour
The secret closely kept, though hundreds share it.
The ground is hollow 'neath the tyrants' feet;
Their days of rule are numbered, and ere long
No trace of their dominion shall remain.

ATTINGHAUSEN. Ay, but their castles, how to master them?

MELCHTHAL. On the same day they, too, are doom'd to fall.

ATTINGHAUSEN. And are the nobles parties to this league?

STAUFFACHER. We trust to their assistance should we need it;
As yet the peasantry alone have sworn.

ATTINGHAUSEN [raising himself up, in great astonishment]. And have the peasantry dared such a deed
On their own charge, without the nobles' aid—
Relied so much on their own proper strength?
Nay then, indeed, they want our help no more;
We may go down to death cheer'd by the thought
That after us the majesty of man
Will live, and be maintain'd by other hands.
[He lays his hand upon the head of the child, who is kneeling before him.]
From this boy's head, whereon the apple lay,
Your new and better liberty shall spring;
The old is crumbling down—the times are changing—
And from the ruins blooms a fairer life.

STAUFFACHER [to FÜRST]. See, see, what splendor streams around his eye!
This is not nature's last expiring flame,
It is the beam of renovated life.

ATTINGHAUSEN. From their old towers the nobles are descending,
And swearing in the towns the civic oath.
In Uechtland and Thurgau the work's begun;
The noble Bern lifts her commanding head,
And Freyburg is a stronghold of the free;
The stirring Zürich calls her guilds to arms;—
And now, behold!—the ancient might of kings
Is shiver'd 'gainst her everlasting walls.
[He speaks what follows with a prophetic tone; his utterance rising into enthusiasm.]
I see the princes and their haughty peers,
Clad all in steel, come striding on to crush
A harmless shepherd race with mailèd hand.
Desp'rate the conflict: 'tis for life or death;
And many a pass will tell to after years
Of glorious victories sealed in foeman's blood.
The peasant throws himself with naked breast,

A willing victim on their serried lances.
They yield—the flower of chivalry's cut
down,
And freedom waves her conquering ban-
ner high!
[*Grasps the hands of* WALTER
FÜRST *and* STAUFFACHER.]
Hold fast together, then,—for ever fast!
Let freedom's haunts be one in heart and
mind!
Set watches on your mountain tops, that
league
May answer league, when comes the hour
to strike.
Be one—be one—be one——
[*He falls back upon the cushion.
His lifeless hands continue to
grasp those of* FÜRST *and*
STAUFFACHER, *who regard him
for some moments in silence,
and then retire, overcome with
sorrow. Meanwhile the serv-
ants have quietly pressed into
the chamber, testifying differ-
ent degrees of grief. Some
kneel down beside him and
weep on his body: while this
scene is passing, the castle bell
tolls.*]

[RUDENZ *enters hurriedly.*]
RUDENZ. Lives he? Oh say, can he
still hear my voice?
FÜRST [*averting his face*]. You are
our seignior and protector now;
Henceforth this castle bears another
name.
RUDENZ [*gazing at the body with deep
emotion*]. Oh, God! Is my repent-
ance, then, too late?
Could he not live some few brief moments
more,
To see the change that has come o'er my
heart?
Oh, I was deaf to his true counselling
voice
While yet he walked on earth. Now he
is gone,
Gone, and for ever,—leaving me the
debt—
The heavy debt I owe him—undischarged!

Oh, tell me! did he part in anger with
me?
STAUFFACHER. When dying, he was
told what you had done,
And bless'd the valor that inspired your
words!
RUDENZ [*kneeling down beside the dead
body*]. Yes, sacred relics of a man
beloved
Thou lifeless corpse! Here, on thy death-
cold hand,
Do I abjure all foreign ties for ever!
And to my country's cause devote myself.
I am a Switzer, and will act as one,
With my whole heart and soul. [*Rises.*]
Mourn for our friend,
Our common parent, yet be not dismay'd!
'Tis not alone his lands that I inherit,—
His heart—his spirit, have devolved on
me;
And my young arm shall execute the task,
For which his hoary age remain'd your
debtor.
Give me your hands, ye venerable fathers!
Thine, Melchthal, too! Nay, do not hesi-
tate,
Nor from me turn distrustfully away.
Accept my plighted vow—my knightly
oath!
FÜRST. Give him your hands, my
friends! A heart like his,
That sees and owns its error, claims our
trust.
MELCHTHAL. You ever held the peas-
antry in scorn.
What surety have we that you mean us
fair?
RUDENZ. Oh, think not of the error of
my youth!
STAUFFACHER [*to* MELCHTHAL]. Be
one! They were our father's latest
words.
See they be not forgotten!
MELCHTHAL. Take my hand—
A peasant's hand,—and with it, noble
sir,
The gage and the assurance of a man!
Without us, sir, what would the nobles
be?
Our order is more ancient, too, than
yours!

RUDENZ. I honor it, and with my
sword will shield it!
MELCHTHAL. The arm, my lord, that
tames the stubborn earth,
And makes its bosom blossom with in-
crease,
Can also shield a man's defenseless breast.
RUDENZ. Then you shall shield my
breast, and I will yours;
Thus each be strengthen'd by the other's
aid!
Yet wherefore talk we, while our native
land
Is still to alien tyranny a prey!
First let us sweep the foeman from the
soil,
Then reconcile our difference in peace!
            [After a moment's pause.]
How! You are silent! Not a word for
me?
And have I yet no title to your trust?—
Then must I force my way, despite your
will,
Into the League you secretly have form'd.
You've held a Diet on the Rootli,—I
Know this,—know all that was transacted
there!
And though I was not trusted with your
secret,
I still have kept it like a sacred pledge.
Trust me, I never was my country's
foe,
Nor would I e'er have ranged myself
against you!
Yet you did wrong—to put your rising
off.
Time presses! We must strike, and
swiftly too!
Already Tell has fallen a sacrifice
To your delay.
    STAUFFACHER. We swore to wait till
Christmas.
    RUDENZ. I was not there,—I did not
take the oath.
If you delay, I will not!
    MELCHTHAL. What! You would——
    RUDENZ. I count me now among the
country's fathers,
And to protect you is my foremost duty.
    FÜRST. Within the earth to lay these
dear remains,

That is your nearest and most sacred
duty.
    RUDENZ. When we have set the country
free, we'll place
Our fresh victorious wreaths upon his
bier.
Oh, my dear friends, 'tis not your cause
alone!—
I have a cause to battle with the tyrants
That more concerns myself. Know that
my Bertha
Has disappear'd,—been carried off by
stealth,—
Stolen from amongst us by their ruffian
hands!
    STAUFFACHER. And has the tyrant
dared so fell an outrage
Against a lady free and nobly born?
    RUDENZ. Alas! my friends, I promised
help to you,
And I must first implore it for myself!
She that I love is stolen—is forced away,
And who knows where the tyrant has
conceal'd her,
Or with what outrages his ruffian crew
May force her into nuptials she detests?
Forsake me not!—Oh, help me to her
rescue.
She loves you! Well, oh well, has she
deserved,
That all should rush to arms in her be-
half!
    STAUFFACHER. What course do you
propose?
    RUDENZ.   Alas! I know not.
In the dark mystery that shrouds her
fate,—
In the dread agony of this suspense,—
Where I can grasp at nought of cer-
tainty,—
One single ray of comfort beams upon me.
From out the ruins of the tyrant's power
Alone can she be rescued from the grave.
Their strongholds must be levell'd! every
one
Ere we can pierce into her gloomy prison.
    MELCHTHAL. Come, lead us on! We
follow! Why defer
Until to-morrow what to-day may do?
Tell's arm was free when we at Rootli
swore,

This foul enormity was yet undone.
And change of circumstance brings change
    of law;
Who such a coward as to waver still?
  RUDENZ [to WALTER FÜRST]. Mean-
    while to arms, and wait in readiness
The fiery signal on the mountain tops.
For swifter than a boat can scour the
    lake
Shall you have tidings of our victory;
And when you see the welcome flames
    ascend,
Then, like the lightning, swoop upon the
    foe,
And lay the despots and their creatures
    low.

SCENE III

The pass near Küssnacht, sloping down
from behind, with rocks on either side.
The travellers are visible upon the heights
before they appear on the stage. Rocks
all around the stage. Upon one of the
foremost a projecting cliff overgrown
with brushwood.

  TELL [enters with his cross-bow]. Here
    thro' this deep defile he needs must
    pass;
There leads no other road to Küssnacht:
  —here
I'll do it:—the opportunity is good.
Yon alder tree stands well for my con-
    cealment.
Thence my avenging shaft will surely
    reach him;
The straitness of the path forbids pursuit.
Now, Gessler, balance thine account with
    Heaven!
Thou must away from earth,—thy sand is
    run.

I led a peaceful, inoffensive life;—
My bow was bent on forest game alone,
And my pure soul was free from thoughts
    of murder—
But thou hast scared me from my dream
    of peace;
The milk of human kindness thou hast
    turn'd

To rankling poison in my breast; and
    made
Appalling deeds familiar to my soul.
He who could make his own child's head
    his mark
Can speed his arrow to his foeman's heart.

My children dear, my lov'd and faith-
    ful wife
Must be protected, tyrant, from thy
    fury!—
When last I drew my bow—with trem-
    bling hand—
And thou, with murderous joy, a father
    forced
To level at his child—when, all in vain,
Writhing before thee, I implored thy
    mercy—
Then in the agony of my soul I vow'd
A fearful oath, which met God's ear
    alone,
That when my bow next wing'd an arrow's
    flight
Its aim should be thy heart. The vow I
    made,
Amid the hellish torments of that mo-
    ment,
I hold a sacred debt, and I will pay it.

Thou art my lord, my Emperor's dele-
    gate;
Yet would the Emperor not have stretch'd
    his power
So far as thou. He sent thee to these
    Cantons
To deal forth law—stern law—for he is
    anger'd;
But not to wanton with unbridled will
In every cruelty, with ·fiend-like joy:—
There is a God to punish and avenge.

Come forth, thou bringer once of bitter
    pangs,
My precious jewel now,—my chiefest
    treasure—
A mark I'll set thee, which the cry of
    grief
Could never penetrate,—but thou shalt
    pierce it.—
And thou, my trusty bowstring, that so
    oft

Has served me faithfully in sportive scenes,
Desert me not in this most serious hour—
Only be true this once, my own good cord,
That hast so often wing'd the biting shaft:—
For shouldst thou fly successless from my hand,
I have no second to send after thee.

[*Travellers pass over the stage.*]

I'll sit me down upon this bench of stone,
Hewn for the wayworn traveller's brief repose—
For here there is no home.—Each hurries by
The other, with quick step and careless look,
Nor stays to question of his grief.—Here goes
The merchant, full of care,—the pilgrim, next,
With slender scrip,—and then the pious monk.
The scowling robber, the jovial player,
The carrier with his heavy-laden horse,
That comes to us from the far haunts of men;
For every road conducts to the world's end.
They all push onwards—every man intent
On his own several business—mine is murder. [*Sits down.*]

Time was, my dearest children, when with joy
You hail'd your father's safe return to home
From his long mountain toils; for, when he came,
He ever brought some little present with him.
A lovely Alpine flower—a curious bird—
Or elf-boat, found by wanderer on the hills.—
But now he goes in quest of other game:
In the wild pass he sits, and broods on murder,
And watches for the life-blood of his foe.—

But still his thoughts are fixed on you alone,
Dear children.—'Tis to guard your innocence,
To shield you from the tyrant's fell revenge,
He bends his bow to do a deed of blood!
[*Rises.*]

Well—I am watching for a noble prey—
Does not the huntsman, with severest toil,
Roam for whole days, amid the winter's cold,
Leap with a daring bound from rock to rock,
And climb the jagged, slippery steeps, to which
His limbs are glued by his own streaming blood—
And all this but to gain a wretched chamois.
A far more precious prize is now my aim—
The heart of that dire foe who would destroy me.
[*Sprightly music heard in the distance, which comes gradually nearer.*]
From my first years of boyhood I have used
The bow—been practised in the archer's feats;
The bull's eye many a time my shafts have hit,
And many a goodly prize have I brought home,
Won in the games of skill.—This day I'll make
My master-shot, and win the highest prize
Within the whole circumference of the mountains.
[*A marriage train passes over the stage and goes up the pass.* TELL *gazes at it, leaning on his bow. He is joined by* STÜSSI *the Ranger.*]

STUSSI. There goes the bridal party of the steward
Of Mörlischachen's cloister. He is rich!
And has some ten good pastures on the Alps.

He goes to fetch his bride from Imisee,
There will be revelry to-night at Küssnacht.
TELL. A gloomy guest fits not a wedding feast.
STÜSSI. If grief oppress you, dash it from your heart!
Bear with your lot. The times are heavy now,
And we must snatch at pleasure while we can.
Here 'tis a bridal, there a burial.
TELL. And oft the one treads close upon the other.
STÜSSI. So runs the world at present. Everywhere
We meet with woe and misery enough.
There's been a slide of earth in Glarus, and
A whole side of the Glärnisch has fallen in.
TELL. Strange! And do even the hills begin to totter?
There is stability for naught on earth.
STÜSSI. Strange tidings, too, we hear from other parts.
I spoke with one but now, that came from Baden,
Who said a knight was on his way to court,
And, as he rode along, a swarm of wasps
Surrounded him, and settling on his horse,
So fiercely stung the beast that it fell dead,
And he proceeded to the court on foot.
TELL. Even the weak are furnish'd with a sting.

[ARMGART enters with several children, and places herself at the entrance of the pass.]
STÜSSI. 'Tis thought to bode disaster to the country,—
Some horrid deed against the course of nature.
TELL. Why, every day brings forth such fearful deeds;
There needs no miracle to tell their coming.

STÜSSI. Too true! He's bless'd, who tills his field in peace,
And sits untroubled by his own fireside.
TELL. The very meekest cannot rest in quiet,
Unless it suits with his ill neighbor's humor.
[TELL looks frequently with restless expectation towards the top of the pass.]
STÜSSI. So fare you well! You're waiting some one here?
TELL. I am.
STÜSSI. A pleasant meeting with your friends!
You are from Uri, are you not? His grace
The governor's expected thence to-day.
TRAVELLER [entering]. Look not to see the governor to-day.
The streams are flooded by the heavy rains.
And all the bridges have been swept away. [TELL rises.]
ARMGART [coming forward]. The Viceroy not arriv'd?
STÜSSI. And do you seek him?
ARMGART. Alas, I do!
STÜSSI. But why thus place yourself
Where you obstruct his passage down the pass?
ARMGART. Here he cannot escape me.
He must hear me.
FRIESSHARDT [coming hastily down the pass and calls upon the stage]. Make way, make way! My lord the governor,
Is coming down on horseback close behind me. [Exit TELL.]
ARMGART [with animation]. The Viceroy comes!
[She goes towards the pass with her children. GESSLER and RUDOLPH DER HARRAS appear upon the heights on horseback.]
STÜSSI [to FRIESSHARDT]. How got ye through the stream,
When all the bridges have been carried down?
FRIESSHARDT. We've battled with the billows; and, my friend,
An Alpine torrent's nothing after that.

STÜSSI. How! Were you out, then, in that dreadful storm?

FRIESSHARDT. Ay, that we were! I shall not soon forget it.

STÜSSI. Stay, speak——

FRIESSHARDT. I cannot. I must to the castle,
And tell them that the governor's at hand. [Exit.]

STÜSSI. If honest men, now, had been in the ship,
It had gone down with every soul on board:—
Some folks are proof 'gainst fire and water both. [Looking round.]
Where has the huntsman gone, with whom I spoke? [Exit.]

[Enter GESSLER and RUDOLPH DER HARRAS on horseback.]

GESSLER. Say what you please; I am the Emperor's servant,
And my first care must be to do his pleasure.
He did not send me here to fawn and cringe
And coax these boors into good humor. No!
Obedience he must have. We soon shall see
If king or peasant is to lord it here.

ARMGART. Now is the moment! Now for my petition!

GESSLER. 'Twas not in sport that I set up the cap
In Altdorf—or to try the people's hearts—
All this I knew before. I set it up
That they might learn to bend those stubborn necks
They carry far too proudly—and I placed
What well I knew their eyes could never brook
Full in the road, which they perforce must pass,
That, when their eye fell on it, they might call
That lord to mind whom they too much forget.

HARRAS. But surely, sir, the people have some rights—

GESSLER. This is no time to settle what they are.
Great projects are at work, and hatching now.
The Imperial house seeks to extend its power.
Those vast designs of conquest, which the sire
Has gloriously begun, the son will end.
This petty nation is a stumbling-block—
One way or other, it must be subjected.

[They are about to pass on. ARMGART throws herself down before GESSLER.]

ARMGART. Mercy, lord governor! Oh, pardon, pardon!

GESSLER. Why do you cross me on the public road?
Stand back, I say.

ARMGART. My husband lies in prison;
My wretched orphans cry for bread. Have pity,
Pity, my lord, upon our sore distress!

HARRAS. Who are you, woman; and who is your husband?

ARMGART. A poor wild-hay-man of the Rigiberg,
Kind sir, who on the brow of the abyss
Mows down the grass from steep and craggy shelves
To which the very cattle dare not climb.

HARRAS [to GESSLER]. By Heaven! a sad and miserable life!
I prithee, give the wretched man his freedom.
How great soever his offence may be,
His horrid trade is punishment enough.
[To ARMGART.] You shall have justice.
To the castle bring
Your suit. This is no place to deal with it.

ARMGART. No, no, I will not stir from where I stand
Until your grace restore my husband to me.
Six months already has he been in prison,
And waits the sentence of a judge in vain.

GESSLER. How! would you force me, woman? Hence! Begone!

ARMGART. Justice, my lord! Ay, justice! Thou art judge:
The deputy of the Emperor—of Heaven.

Then do thy duty,—as thou hopest for justice
From Him who rules above, show it to us!

GESSLER. Hence, drive this daring rabble from my sight!

ARMGART [*seizing his horse's reins*]. No, no, by Heaven, I've nothing more to lose.—
Thou stirr'st not, Viceroy, from this spot, until
Thou dost me fullest justice. Knit thy brows,
And roll thy eyes—I fear not. Our distress
Is so extreme, so boundless, that we care
No longer for thine anger.

GESSLER. Woman, hence!
Give way, I say, or I will ride thee down.

ARMGART. Well, do so—there—
[*Throws her children and herself upon the ground before him.*]
Here on the ground I lie,
I and my children. Let the wretched orphans
Be trodden by thy horse into the dust!
It will not be the worst that thou hast done.

HARRAS. Are you mad, woman?

ARMGART [*continuing with vehemence*].
Many a day thou hast
Trampled the Emperor's lands beneath thy feet.
Oh, I am but a woman! Were I a man,
I'd find some better thing to do than here
Lie grovelling in the dust.
[*The music of the wedding party is again heard from the top of the pass, but more softly.*]

GESSLER. Where are my knaves?
Drag her away, lest I forget myself,
And do some deed I may repent hereafter.

HARRAS. My lord, the servants cannot force a passage;
The pass is block'd up by a marriage party.

GESSLER. Too mild a ruler am I to this people,
Their tongues are all too bold—nor have they yet
Been tamed to due submission, as they shall be.

I must take order for the remedy;
I will subdue this stubborn mood of theirs,
And crush the Soul of Liberty within them.
I'll publish a new law throughout the land;
I will—
[*An arrow pierces him,—he puts his hand on his heart, and is about to sink—with a feeble voice.*]
Oh God, have mercy on my soul!

HARRAS. My lord! my lord! Oh God!
What's this! Whence came it?

ARMGART [*starts up*]. Dead, dead! he reels, he falls! 'Tis in his heart!

HARRAS [*springs from his horse*]. This is most horrible! Oh, Heaven! sir knight,
Address yourself to God and pray for mercy,—
You are a dying man.

GESSLER. That shot was Tell's.
[*He slides from his horse into the arms of RUDOLPH DER HARRAS, who lays him down upon the bench. TELL appears above upon the rocks.*]

TELL. Thou know'st the archer, seek no other hand.
Our cottages are free, and innocence
Secure from thee: thou'lt be our curse no more.
[*TELL disappears. People rush in.*]

STÜSSI. What is the matter? Tell me what has happen'd?

ARMGART. The governor is shot—kill'd by an arow!

PEOPLE [*running in*]. Who has been shot?
[*While the foremost of the marriage party are coming on the stage the hindmost are still upon the heights. The music continues.*]

HARRAS. He's bleeding fast to death.
Away for help—pursue the murderer!
Unhappy man, is't thus that thou must die?
Thou wouldst not heed the warnings that I gave thee!

Stüssi. By Heaven, his cheek is pale!
His life ebbs fast.
Many Voices. Who did the deed?
Harras. What! Are the people mad,
That they make music to a murder?
Silence!
[*Music breaks off suddenly. People continue to flock in.*]
Speak, if thou canst, my lord. Hast thou no charge
To intrust me with?
[Gessler *makes signs with his hand, which he repeats with vehemence when he finds they are not understood.*]
What would you have me do?
Shall I to Küssnacht? I can't guess your meaning.
Do not give way to this impatience. Leave
All thoughts of earth, and make your peace with Heaven.
[*The whole marriage party gather round the dying man.*]
Stüssi. See there! how pale he grows!
Death's gathering now
About his heart;—his eyes grow dim and glazed.
Armgart [*holds up a child*]. Look, children, how a tyrant dies!
Harras. Mad hag!
Have you no touch of feeling, that you look
On horrors such as these without a shudder?
Help me—take hold. What! will not one assist
To pull the torturing arrow from his breast?
Women. We touch the man whom God's own hand has struck!
Harras. All curses light on you!
[*Draws his sword.*]
Stüssi [*seizes his arm*]. Gently, sir knight!
Your power is at an end. 'Twere best forbear;
Our country's foe is fallen. We will brook
No further violence. We are free men.
All. The country's free!

Harras. And is it come to this?
Fear and obedience at an end so soon?
[*To the soldiers of the guard, who are thronging in.*]
You see, my friends, the bloody piece of work
They've acted here. 'Tis now too late for help,
And to pursue the murderer were vain.
New duties claim our care. Set on to Küssnacht,
And let us save that fortress for the king!
For in an hour like this all ties of order,
Fealty and faith are scatter'd to the winds.
No man's fidelity is to be trusted.
[*As he is going out with the soldiers, six* Fratres Miseri-cordiæ *appear.*]
Armgart. Here come the brotherhood of mercy. Room!
Stüssi. The victim's slain, and now the ravens stoop.
Brothers of Mercy [*form a semicircle round the body, and sing in solemn tones*]. With hasty step death presses on,
Nor grants to man a moment's stay;
He falls ere half his race be run,
In manhood's pride is swept away:
Prepar'd, or unprepar'd, to die,
He stands before his Judge on high.
[*While they are repeating the last two lines, the curtain falls.*]

ACT V

Scene I

A common near Altdorf. In the background to the right the Keep of Uri, with the scaffold still standing, as in the Third Scene of the First Act. To the left, the view opens upon numerous mountains, on all of which signal fires are burning. Day is breaking, and bells are heard ringing from various distances.

[Ruodi, Kuoni, Werni, Master Mason *and many other country people, also women and children.*]

RUODI. Look at the fiery signals on the mountains!

MASON. Hark to the bells above the forest there!

RUODI. The enemy's expelled.

MASON. The forts are taken.

RUODI. And we of Uri, do we still endure
Upon our native soil the tyrant's keep?
Are we the last to strike for liberty?

MASON. Shall the yoke stand, that was to bow our necks?

Up! Tear it to the ground!

ALL. Down, down with it!

RUODI. Where is the Stier of Uri?

URI. Here. What would ye?

RUODI. Up to your tower, and wind us such a blast
As shall resound afar, from hill to hill,
Rousing the echoes of each peak and glen,
And call the mountain men in haste together! [*Exit* STIER *of* URI.]

[*Enter* WALTER FÜRST.]

FÜRST. Stay, stay, my friends! As yet we have not learn'd
What has been done in Unterwald and Schwyz.
Let's wait till we receive intelligence!

RUODI. Wait, wait for what? The accursed tyrant's dead,
And the bright day of liberty has dawn'd!

MASON. How! Do these flaming signals not suffice,
That blaze on every mountain top around?

RUODI. Come all, fall to—come, men and women, all!
Destroy the scaffold! Tear the arches down!
Down with the walls, let not a stone remain!

MASON. Come, comrades, come! We built it, and we know
How best to hurl it down.

ALL. Come! Down with it!
[*They fall upon the building at every side.*]

FÜRST. The floodgates burst. They're not to be restrained.

[*Enter* MELCHTHAL *and* BAUMGARTEN.]

MELCHTHAL. What! Stands the fortress still, when Sarnen lies
In ashes, and when Rossberg is a ruin?

FÜRST. You, Melchthal, here? D'ye bring us liberty?
Say, have you freed the country of the foe?

MELCHTHAL. We've swept them from the soil. Rejoice, my friend;
Now, at this very moment, while we speak,
There's not a tyrant left in Switzerland!

FÜRST. How did you get the forts into your power?

MELCHTHAL. Rudenz it was who, with a gallant arm
And manly daring, took the keep at Sarnen.
The Rossberg I had stormed the night before.
But hear what chanced. Scarce had we driven the foe
Forth from the keep, and given it to the flames,
That now rose crackling upwards to the skies,
When from the blaze rush'd Diethelm, Gessler's page,
Exclaiming, "Lady Bertha will be burnt!"

FÜRST. Good heavens!
[*The beams of the scaffold are heard falling.*]

MELCHTHAL. 'Twas she herself. Here had she been
Immured in secret by the Viceroy's orders.
Rudenz sprang up in frenzy. For we heard
The beams and massive pillars crashing down,
And through the volumed smoke the piteous shrieks
Of the unhappy lady.

FÜRST. Is she saved?

MELCHTHAL. Here was a time for promptness and decision!
Had he been nothing but our baron, then
We should have been most chary of our lives;
But he was our confederate, and Bertha

Honor'd the people. So, without a
thought,
We risk'd the worst, and rush'd into the
flames.
FÜRST. But is she saved?
MELCHTHAL. She is. Rudenz and I
Bore her between us from the blazing
pile,
With crashing timbers toppling all
around,
And when she had revived, the danger
past,
And raised her eyes to meet the light of
heaven,
The baron fell upon my breast; and then
A silent vow of friendship pass'd between
us—
A vow that, temper'd in yon furnace heat,
Will last through ev'ry shock of time and
fate.
FÜRST. Where is the Landenberg?
MELCHTHAL. Across the Brünig.
No fault of mine it was that he who
quench'd
My father's eyesight should go hence
unharm'd.
He fled—I followed—overtook and seized
him,
And dragg'd him to my father's feet.
The sword
Already quiver'd o'er the caitiff's head,
When at the entreaty of the blind old
man,
I spared the life for which he basely
pray'd.
He swore URPHEDE, never to return:
He'll keep his oath, for he has felt our
arm.
FÜRST. Thank God, our victory's un-
stain'd by blood!
CHILDREN [running across the stage
with fragments of wood]. Liberty!
Liberty! Hurrah, we're free!
FÜRST. Oh! what a joyous scene!
These children will,
E'en to their latest day, remember it.
[Girls bring in the cap upon a
pole. The whole stage is filled
with people.]
RUODI. Here is the cap, to which we
were to bow!

BAUMGARTEN. Commend us, how we
shall dispose of it.
FÜRST. Heavens! 'Twas beneath this
cap my grandson stood!
SEVERAL VOICES. Destroy the emblem
of the tyrant's power!
Let it be burnt!
FÜRST. No. Rather be preserved!
'Twas once the instrument of despots—
now
'Twill be a lasting symbol of our freedom.
[PEASANTS, men, women, and
children, some standing, others
sitting upon the beams of the
shattered scaffold, all pictur-
esquely grouped, in a large
semicircle.]
MELCHTHAL. Thus now, my friends,
with light and merry hearts,
We stand upon the wreck of tyranny;
And gallantly have we fulfill'd the oath
Which we at Rootli swore, Confederates!
FÜRST. The work is but begun. We
must be firm.
For, be assured, the king will make all
speed
To avenge his Viceroy's death, and re-
instate,
By force of arms, the tyrant we've ex-
pell'd.
MELCHTHAL. Why, let him come, with
all his armaments!
The foe within has fled before our arms;
We'll give him welcome warmly from
without!
RUODI. The passes to the country are
but few,
And these we'll boldly cover with our
bodies.
BAUMGARTEN. We are bound by an in-
dissoluble league,
And all his armies shall not make us
quail.

[Enter RÖSSELMANN and STAUFFACHER.]
RÖSSELMANN [speaking as he enters].
These are the awful judgments of the
Lord!
PEASANT. What is the matter?
RÖSSELMANN. In what times we
live!

FÜRST. Say on, what is't? Ha, Werner, is it you?
What tidings?
PEASANT. What's the matter?
RÖSSELMANN.   Hear and wonder!
STAUFFACHER. We are released from one great cause of dread.
RÖSSELMANN. The Emperor is murdered.
FÜRST.   Gracious Heaven!
[PEASANTS *rise up and throng round* STAUFFACHER.]
ALL. Murder'd, the Emp'ror? What! The Emp'ror! Hear!
MELCHTHAL. Impossible! How came you by the news?
STAUFFACHER. 'Tis true! Near Bruck, by the assassin's hand,
King Albert fell. A most trustworthy man,
John Müller, from Schaffhausen, brought the news.
FÜRST. Who dared commit so horrible a deed?
STAUFFACHER. The doer makes the deed more dreadful still;
It was his nephew, his own brother's child,
Duke John of Austria, who struck the blow.
MELCHTHAL. What drove him to so dire a parricide?
STAUFFACHER. The Emperor kept his patrimony back,
Despite his urgent importunities;
'Twas said, indeed, he never meant to give it,
But with a mitre to appease the duke.
However this may be, the duke gave ear
To the ill counsel of his friends in arms;
And with the noble lords, Von Eschenbach,
Von Tegerfeld, Von Wart and Palm, resolved,
Since his demands for justice were despised,
With his own hands to take revenge at least.
FÜRST. But say, how compass'd he the dreadful deed!

STAUFFACHER. The king was riding down from Stein to Baden,
Upon his way to join the court at Rheinfeld,—
With him a train of high-born gentlemen,
And the young Princes John and Leopold,
And when they'd reach'd the ferry of the Reuss,
The assassins forced their way into the boat,
To separate the Emperor from his suite.
His highness landed, and was riding on
Across a fresh plough'd field—where once, they say,
A mighty city stood in Pagan times—
With Habsburg's ancient turrets full in sight,
Where all the grandeur of his line had birth—
When Duke John plunged a dagger in his throat,
Palm ran him thro' the body with his lance,
Eschenbach cleft his skull at one fell blow,
And down he sank, all weltering in his blood,
On his own soil, by his own kinsmen slain.
Those on the opposite bank, who saw the deed,
Being parted by the stream, could only raise
An unavailing cry of loud lament.
But a poor woman, sitting by the way,
Raised him, and on her breast he bled to death.
MELCHTHAL. Thus has he dug his own untimely grave,
Who sought insatiably to grasp at all.
STAUFFACHER. The country round is fill'd with dire alarm.
The mountain passes are blockaded all,
And sentinels on ev'ry frontier set;
E'en ancient Zürich barricades her gates,
That for these thirty years have open stood,
Dreading the murd'rers, and th' avengers more.
For cruel Agnes comes, the Hungarian queen,
To all her sex's tenderness a stranger,

Arm'd with the thunders of the church,
to wreak
Dire vengeance for her parent's royal
blood
On the whole race of those that murder'd
him,—
Upon their servants, children, children's
children,—
Nay, on the stones that build their castle
walls.
Deep has she sworn a vow to immolate
Whole generations on her father's tomb,
And bathe in blood as in the dew of May.
MELCHTHAL. Know you which way the
murderers have fled?
STAUFFACHER. No sooner had they
done the deed than they
Took flight, each following a different
route,
And parted, ne'er to see each other more
Duke John must still be wand'ring in the
mountains.
FÜRST. And thus their crime has
yielded them no fruits.
Revenge is barren. Of itself it makes
The dreadful food it feeds on; its delight
Is murder—its satiety despair.
STAUFFACHER. The assassins reap no
profit by their crime;
But we shall pluck with unpolluted hands
The teeming fruits of their most bloody
deed,
For we are ransomed from our heaviest
fear;
The direst foe of liberty has fallen,
And, 'tis reported that the crown will
pass
From Habsburg's house into another line;
The empire is determined to assert
Its old prerogative of choice, I hear.
FÜRST and SEVERAL OTHERS. Has any
one been named to you?
STAUFFACHER. The Count
Of Luxembourg is widely named al-
ready.—
FÜRST. 'Tis well we stood so staunchly
by the Empire!
Now we may hope for justice, and with
cause.
STAUFFACHER. The Emperor will need
some valiant friends,

And he will shelter us from Austria's
vengeance.
[The peasantry embrace.]

[Enter SACRISTAN with Imperial
Messenger.]
SACRISTAN. Here are the worthy chiefs
of Switzerland!
RÖSSELMANN and SEVERAL OTHERS.
Sacrist, what news?
SACRISTAN. A courier brings this let-
ter.
ALL [to WALTER FÜRST]. Open and
read it.
FÜRST [reading]. "To the worthy men
Of Uri, Schwyz, and Unterwald, the
Queen
Elizabeth sends grace and all good
wishes!"
MANY VOICES. What wants the queen
with us? Her reign is done.
FÜRST [reads]. "In the great grief and
doleful widowhood
In which the bloody exit of her lord
Has plunged her majesty, she still re-
members
The ancient faith and love of Switzer-
land."
MELCHTHAL. She ne'er did that in her
prosperity.
RÖSSELMANN. Hush, let us hear!
FÜRST [reads]. "And she is well as-
sured
Her people will in due abhorrence hold
The perpetrators of this damned deed.
On the three Cantons, therefore, she relies,
That they in nowise lend the murderers
aid,
But rather that they loyally assist
To give them up to the avenger's hand,
Remembering the love and grace which
they
Of old received from Rudolph's princely
house."
[Symptoms of dissatisfaction
among the peasantry.]
MANY VOICES. The love and grace!
STAUFFACHER. Grace from the father
we, indeed, received;
But what have we to boast of from the
son?

Did he confirm the charter of our freedom,
As all preceding emperors had done?
Did he judge righteous judgment, or
afford
Shelter or stay to innocence oppress'd?
Nay, did he e'en give audience to the
envoys
We sent, to lay our grievances before
him?
Not one of all these things e'er did the
king,
And had we not ourselves achieved our
rights
By resolute valor, our necessities
Had never touch'd him. Gratitude to
him!
Within these vales he sowed not grati-
tude.
He stood upon an eminence—he might
Have been a very father to his people,
But all his aim and pleasure was to raise
Himself and his own house: and now may
those
Whom he has aggrandized lament for
him!
   FÜRST. We will not triumph in his
fall, nor now
Recall to mind the wrongs we have en-
dured.
Far be't from us! Yet, that we should
avenge
The sovereign's death, who never did us
good,
And hunt down those who ne'er molested
us,
Becomes us not, nor is our duty. Love
Must bring its offerings free and uncon-
strain'd;
From all enforced duties death absolves—
And unto him we are no longer bound.
   MELCHTHAL. And if the queen laments
within her bower,
Accusing Heaven in sorrow's wild despair;
Here see a people, from its anguish freed,
To that same Heav'n send up its thank-
ful praise.
For who would reap regrets, must sow
affection. [*Exit the Imperial Courier.*]
   STAUFFACHER [*to the people*]. But
where is Tell? Shall he, our free-
dom's founder,

Alone be absent from our festival?
He did the most—endured the worst of
all.
Come—to his dwelling let us all repair,
And bid the saviour of our country hail!
                [*Exeunt omnes.*]

SCENE II

Interior of TELL'S *Cottage. A fire burn-
ing on the hearth. The open door shows
the scene outside.*

   [HEDWIG, WALTER *and* WILHELM.]
   HEDWIG. Boys, dearest boys! your
father comes to-day.
He lives, is free, and we and all are free!
The country owes its liberty to him!
   WALTER. And I, too, mother, bore my
part in it;
I shall be named with him. My father's
shaft
Went closely by my life, but yet I shook
not!
   HEDWIG [*embracing him*]. Yes, yes,
thou art restored to me again!
Twice have I given thee birth,—twice
suffer'd all
A mother's agonies for thee, my child!
But this is past—I have you both, boys,
both!
And your dear father will be back to-day.

   [A MONK *appears at the door.*]
   WILHELM. See, mother, yonder stands
a holy friar;
He's asking alms, no doubt.
   HEDWIG.   Go lead him in,
That we may give him cheer, and make
him feel
That he had come into the house of joy.
      [*Exit, and returns immediately
               with a cup.*]
   WILHELM [*to the* MONK]. Come in,
good man. Mother will give you
food!
   WALTER. Come in and rest, then go
refresh'd away!
   MONK [*glancing round in terror, with
unquiet looks*]. Where am I? In
what country?

WALTER. Have you lost
Your way, that you are ignorant of this?
You are at Bürglen, in the land of Uri,
Just at the entrance of the Scheckenthal.

MONK [to HEDWIG]. Are you alone?
Your husband, is he here?

HEDWIG. I momently expect him. But
what ails you?
You look as one whose soul is ill at
ease.
Whoe'er you be, you are in want—take
that   [Offers him the cup.]

MONK. Howe'er my sinking heart may
yearn for food,
I will taste nothing till you've promised
me—

HEDWIG. Touch not my dress, nor yet
advance one step.
Stand off, I say, if you would have me
hear you.

MONK. Oh, by this hearth's bright,
hospitable blaze,
By your dear children's heads, which I
embrace—   [Grasps the boys.]

HEDWIG. Stand back, I say! What is
your purpose, man?
Back from my boys! You are no monk,
—no, no.
Beneath that robe content and peace
should dwell,
But neither lives within that face of
thine.

MONK. I am the veriest wretch that
breathes on earth.

HEDWIG. The heart is never deaf to
wretchedness;
But thy look freezes up my inmost soul.

WALTER [springs up]. Mother, my
father!

HEDWIG. Oh, my God!
[Is about to follow, trembles and
stops.]

WILHELM [running after his brother].
My father!

WALTER [without]. Thou'rt here once
more!

WILHELM [without]. My father, my
dear father!

TELL [without]. Yes, here I am once
more! Where is your mother?
[They enter.]

WALTER. There at the door she stands,
and can no further,
She trembles so with terror and with joy.

TELL. Oh, Hedwig, Hedwig, mother of
my children!
God has been kind and helpful in our
woes.
No tyrant's hand shall e'er divide us
more.

HEDWIG [falling on his neck]. Oh, Tell,
what have I suffer'd for thy sake!
[MONK becomes attentive.]

TELL. Forget it now, and live for joy
alone!
I'm here again with you! This is my
cot!
I stand again on mine own hearth!

WILHELM. But, father,
Where is your cross-bow left? I see it
not.

TELL. Nor shalt thou ever see it more,
my boy.
It is suspended in a holy place,
And in the chase shall ne'er be used again.

HEDWIG. Oh, Tell! Tell!
[Steps back, dropping his hand.]

TELL. What alarms thee, dearest wife?

HEDWIG. How—how dost thou return
to me? This hand—
Dare I take hold of it? This hand—Oh,
God!

TELL [with firmness and animation].
Has shielded you and set my country
free,
Freely I raise it in the face of Heaven.
[MONK gives a sudden start—
he looks at him.]
Who is this friar here?

HEDWIG. Ah, I forgot him.
Speak thou with him; I shudder at his
presence.

MONK [stepping nearer]. Are you that
Tell that slew the governor?

TELL. Yes, I am he. I hide the fact
from no man.

MONK. You are that Tell! Ah! it is
God's own hand
That hath conducted me beneath your
roof.

TELL [examining him closely]. You are
no monk. Who are you?

MONK. You have slain
The governor, who did you wrong. I, too,
Have slain a foe, who late denied me
    justice.
He was no less your enemy than mine.
I've rid the land of him.
    TELL [*drawing back*]. Thou art—oh,
    horror!
In—children, children—in without a word.
Go, my dear wife! Go! Go! Unhappy
    man,
Thou shouldst be——
    HEDWIG. Heav'ns, who is it?
    TELL. Do not ask.
Away! away! the children must not hear
    it.
Out of the house—away! Thou must not
    rest
'Neath the same roof with this unhappy
    man!
    HEDWIG. Alas! What is it? Come!
           [*Exit with the children.*]
    TELL [*to the* MONK]. Thou art the
    Duke
Of Austria—I know it. Thou hast slain
The Emperor, thy uncle and liege lord.
    JOHN. He robb'd me of my patrimony.
    TELL. How!
Slain him—thy king, thy uncle! And
    the earth
Still bears thee! And the sun still shines
    on thee!
    JOHN. Tell, hear me ere you——
    TELL. Reeking with the blood
Of him that was thy Emperor and kins-
    man,
Durst thou set foot within my spotless
    house?
Show thy fell visage to a virtuous man,
And claim the rites of hospitality?
    JOHN. I hoped to find· compassion at
    your hands.
You also took revenge upon your foe!
    TELL. Unhappy man! And dar'st thou
    thus confound
Ambition's bloody crime with the dread
    act
To which a father's direful need impell'd
    him?
Hadst thou to shield thy children's dar-
    ling heads?

To guard thy fireside's sanctuary—ward
    off
The last, worst doom from all that thou
    didst love?
To Heaven I raise my unpolluted hands
To curse thine act and thee! I have
    avenged
That holy nature which thou hast pro-
    faned.
I have no part with thee. Thou art a
    murderer.
I've shielded all that was most dear to
    me.
    JOHN. You cast me off to comfortless
    despair!
    TELL. My blood runs cold ev'n while
    I talk with thee.
Away! Pursue thine awful course! Nor
    longer
Pollute the cot where innocence abides!
           [JOHN *turns to depart.*]
    JOHN. I cannot live, and will no longer
    thus!
    TELL. And yet my soul bleeds for thee;
    —gracious Heaven!
So young, of such a noble line, the grand-
    son
Of Rudolph, once my lord and emperor,
An outcast—murderer—standing at my
    door,
The poor man's door—a suppliant, in de-
    spair! [*Covers his face.*]
    JOHN. If thou hast power to weep, oh
    let my fate
Move your compassion—it is horrible.
I am—say rather was—a prince. I might
Have been most happy, had I only curb'd
Th' impatience of my passionate desires.
But envy gnaw'd my heart—I saw the
    youth
Of mine own cousin Leopold endow'd
With honor, and enrich'd with broad do-
    mains,
The while myself, that was in years his
    equal,
Was kept in abject and disgraceful
    nonage.
    TELL. Unhappy man, thy uncle knew
    thee well
When he withheld both land and subjects
    from thee!

Thou, by thy mad and desperate act, hast set
A fearful seal upon his sage resolve.
Where are the bloody partners of thy crime?

JOHN. Where'er the demon of revenge has borne them;
I have not seen them since the luckless deed.

TELL. Know'st thou the Empire's ban is out,—that thou
Art interdicted to thy friends, and given
An outlaw'd victim to thine enemies!

JOHN. Therefore I shun all public thoroughfares,
And venture not to knock at any door—
I turn my footsteps to the wilds, and through
The mountains roam, a terror to myself.
For mine own self I shrink with horror back,
Should a chance brook reflect my ill-starr'd form.
If thou hast pity for a fellow mortal——
[Falls down before him.]

TELL. Stand up, stand up.

JOHN.   Not till thou shalt extend
Thy hand in promise of assistance to me.

TELL. Can I assist thee? Can a sinful man?
Yet get thee up—how black soe'er thy crime,—
Thou art a man. I, too, am one. From Tell
Shall no one part uncomforted. I will
Do all that lies within my power.

JOHN [springs up and grasps him ardently by the hand].   Oh, Tell,
You save me from the terrors of despair.

TELL. Let go my hand! Thou must away. Thou canst not
Remain here undiscover'd, and discover'd,
Thou canst not count on succor. Which way, then,
Wilt bend thy steps? Where dost thou hope to find
A place of rest?

JOHN.   Alas! alas! I know not.

TELL. Hear, then, what Heaven suggesteth to my heart.

Thou must to Italy—to Saint Peter's City—
There cast thyself at the Pope's feet,—confess
Thy guilt to him, and ease thy laden soul!

JOHN. But will he not surrender me to vengeance?

TELL. Whate'er he does, receive as God's decree.

JOHN. But how am I to reach that unknown land?
I have no knowledge of the way, and dare not
Attach myself to other travellers.

TELL. I will describe the road, and mark me well!
You must ascend, keeping along the Reuss,
Which from the mountains dashes wildly down.

JOHN [in alarm]. What! See the Reuss? The witness of my deed!

TELL. The road you take lies through the river's gorge,
And many a cross proclaims where travellers
Have perish'd 'neath the avalanche's fall.

JOHN. I have no fear for nature's terrors, so
I can appease the torments of my soul.

TELL. At every cross, kneel down and expiate
Your crime with burning penitential tears—
And if you 'scape the perils of the pass,
And are not whelm'd beneath the drifted snows
That from the frozen peaks come sweeping down,
You'll reach the bridge that hangs in drizzling spray;
Then if it yield not 'neath your heavy guilt,
When you have left it safely in your rear,
Before you frowns the gloomy Gate of Rocks,
Where never sun did shine. Proceed through this
And you will reach a bright and gladsome vale.

Yet must you hurry on with hasty steps,
For in the haunts of peace you must not linger.

JOHN. O Rudolph, Rudolph, royal grandsire! thus
Thy grandson first sets foot within thy realms!

TELL. Ascending still, you gain the Gotthardt's heights,
On which the everlasting lakes repose,
That from the streams of heaven itself are fed.
There to the German soil you bid farewell,
And thence, with rapid course, another stream
Leads you to Italy, your promised land.
[*Ranz des Vaches sounded on Alp-horns is heard without.*]
But I hear voices! Hence!

HEDWIG [*hurrying in*]. Where art thou, Tell?
Our father comes, and in exulting bands
All the confederates approach.

JOHN [*covering himself*]. Woe's me!
I dare not tarry 'mid this happiness!

TELL. Go, dearest wife, and give this man to eat.
Spare not your bounty. For his road is long,
And one where shelter will be hard to find.
Quick! they approach.

HEDWIG. Who is he?

TELL. Do not ask!
And when he quits thee, turn thine eyes away,
That they may not behold the road he takes.
[*DUKE JOHN advances hastily towards TELL, but he beckons him aside and exit. When both have left the stage, the scene changes.*]

SCENE III

The whole valley before TELL'S *house, the heights which enclose it occupied by peasants, grouped into tableaux. Some are seen crossing a lofty bridge, which crosses the Schechen.* WALTER FÜRST *with the two boys.* WERNER *and* STAUFFACHER *come forward. Others throng after them. When* TELL *appears, all receive him with loud cheers.*

ALL. Long live brave Tell, our shield, our liberator!
[*While those in front are crowding round* TELL, *and embracing him,* RUDENZ *and* BERTHA *appear. The former salutes the peasantry, the latter embraces* HEDWIG. *The music from the mountains continues to play. When it has stopped,* BERTHA *steps into the centre of the crowd.*]

BERTHA. Peasants! Confederates! Into your league
Receive me here, that happily am the first
To find protection in the land of freedom.
To your brave hands I now entrust my rights.
Will you protect me as your citizen?

PEASANT. Ay, that we will, with life and fortune both!

BERTHA. 'Tis well! And to this youth I give my hand,
A free Swiss maiden to a free Swiss man!

RUDENZ. And from this moment all my serfs are free!
[*Music, and the curtain falls.*]

JEPPE OF THE HILL

By LUDVIG HOLBERG

First produced 1722

TRANSLATED, ESPECIALLY FOR THIS WORK, BY M. JAGENDORF

CHARACTERS

JEPPE OF THE HILL
NILLE, *his wife*
JACOB SKOEMAGER
BARON NILUS
HIS SECRETARY
VALET
ERIC, *a lackey*
ANOTHER LACKEY
FIRST DOCTOR
SECOND DOCTOR
THE BAILIFF
THE BAILIFF'S WIFE
FIRST LAWYER
SECOND LAWYER
THE JUDGE
MAGNUS

Various attendants to the BARON *and to the* JUDGE

ACT I

SCENE—*A road in the village. At one extreme end is* JEPPE'S *house. At the other extreme end is* JACOB SKOEMAGER'S *inn. In the center stands a tree.*

NILLE. There isn't another lazy lummox in all the village like that husband of mine. If I didn't yank him by his hair from the bed he'd never come out of it. The blackguard knows full well to-day is market day, yet he's still in bed and I suppose he'll stay there until the cock crows again. Just the other day Master Paul said to me: "Nille, you are too hard on your man. After all he is and should be master in his house." I answered: "No, no, good Master Paul; if he'd run things his way, even for a single year, the squire would not get his rent nor the pastor his offering. In this short time he'd drink away any and everything in the house. You don't expect me to let a man run the house who'd sell out home, wife and children,—nay his very self for a cursed drink." At that Master Paul didn't say a word. He just stroked his beard. The bailiff agrees with me too. He says: "My dear little woman, pay no attention to the pastor. True, it says in the catechism you must honor and obey your husband. But it says in the lease, which isn't so old as the catechism, you must keep your farm in good order and pay your rent on time. And that you'll never do if you don't pull your husband's hair every day and drive him to his work." Just a minute ago I hauled him out of bed and then went to take a peep in the barn to see what work was to be done, and when I came back, what do you think? I found him sitting on a stool asleep, with his breeches—you must excuse me, on one leg. So off came the whip from the nail and my Jeppe got a trouncing until he was wide-awake. Master Eric I call that whip and it's the only thing of which Jeppe is afraid. Ho there, Jeppe . . . you cur, aren't you dressed yet? Do you want Master Eric to caress you again? Hey there, Jeppe, come out here.

[JEPPE *comes out and stands at the door.*]

JEPPE. For the Lord's sake! don't I need time to dress myself, Nille? I can't go to town like a pig without breeches or jacket.

NILLE. You jailbird, you could've put on ten pair of breeches since I dragged you out of bed.

JEPPE. Did you . . . did you put away Master Eric, Nille?

NILLE. I did, but I know the place where to find him if you don't get a move on. Come here! Look how he crawls! Come here! You'll go to town and get me two pounds of soft soap. Here is the money. But remember, if you aren't back on this very spot in four hours, Master Eric'll dance a polka on your back.

JEPPE. How can I walk four miles in four hours, Nille?

NILLE. Who said you are to walk? You are to run. Now I've told you what I want, you can act as your thick skull tells you. [*She goes back into the house.*]

JEPPE. Look at that sow going in to eat her breakfast while I, poor fool, must walk four miles without food or drink. I don't think there is another man cursed with such a witch. I honestly think she is first cousin to Satan. Everybody in the village says Jeppe drinks, but no one says why Jeppe drinks. In the ten years I was in the militia I didn't get the beatings I get in one day from my snake of a wife. She beats me; the bailiff drives me to work as if I were a beast, and the deacon makes a cuckold of me. Haven't I good reason to get drunk? Mustn't I use every means in nature to forget my troubles? If I were a fool I wouldn't take it so to heart; then I wouldn't have to drink. But everyone knows I am a very bright fellow, and I feel these things much more than others. That is why I must drink. My neighbor Moens Christoffersen, he is my friend, he often says to me: "Put the devil of courage in your big belly, Jeppe. You must learn to hit good and hard, then your wife'll soon have to behave." But I can't hit good and hard, and that for three reasons. First, I have no courage, second, because of that accursed Master Eric who is always hanging behind the bed. Just to think of him makes my back weep bitter tears. And third, if I say it myself, because I have a kind soul, and I am a good Christian. That's why I never try to take revenge. Even on the deacon. I pay my offerings regularly on all high holidays while he hasn't the decency to offer me a glass of beer on any ordinary week day of the year. But nothing ever hurt me so much as that insult last year when I told him a wild bull who wasn't afraid of any man suddenly got scared of me. Said he to me: "Don't you understand, Jeppe, why that happened? The bull saw that your horns were even bigger than his and he thought it best not to butt against one stronger than himself." I call you to witness, good people, if such words wouldn't cut a decent man to the very bone and marrow. I am so honorable I don't even wish my wife to die. On the contrary. When she lay sick last year of the yellow jaundice, I wanted her to go on living. For since hell is already full of ugly women, Lucifer would send her back and then she'd be worse than before. But if the deacon dies, I'd be happy—for my sake as well as for others. He brings me only aggravation and is of no use to the parish. He is an ignorant devil. He can't sing a decent note, and can't pour a straight candle. Ah, but his predecessor! Christoffer! There was a fellow of a different cut. He shouted his religion so you'd hear him over a dozen deacons put together. That's the kind of a voice he had. Yes, Moens Christoffersen, you and my other peasant neighbors, you can say lots of things but you have no Master Eric hanging behind your beds. If I had one wish in this whole world it'd be that my wife had no arm or I no back. Talk she can all she wants. . . . But while I am on my way I might as well drop in on Jacob Skoemager. Perhaps he'll give me a shilling's worth of brandy on credit. After all I must take something to strengthen my body. [*He stops before the inn.*] Ho there Jacob Skoemager! Are you up? Open, Jacob.

[JACOB SKOEMAGER *opens the door and comes out partly dressed.*]
JACOB SKOEMAGER. Good morning! Who the devil wants to come in so early?
JEPPE. Good morning, Jacob Skoemager.
JACOB SKOEMAGER. Many thanks, Jeppe. You are on the road pretty early to-day.
JEPPE. Let's have a shilling's worth of brandy, Jacob.
JACOB SKOEMAGER. With the greatest pleasure. Just give me the shilling.
JEPPE. You'll get it to-morrow, when I come back.

JACOB SKOEMAGER. There is no trust at Jacob Skoemager's. I know you must have a shilling or two around to pay for your drinks.
JEPPE. Curse me if I have more than the few shillings my wife gave me to buy something in the city.
JACOB SKOEMAGER. What are you going to buy?
JEPPE. I got to buy two pounds of soft soap.
JACOB SKOEMAGER. Oh, then you can easily say you paid one or two shillings more than it will cost.
JEPPE. I'm afraid my wife will find out. Then I'll be in a good mess.
JACOB SKOEMAGER. Poppycock! How will she find out? Can't you swear you spent all the money? You are dumb as an ox.
JEPPE. That's true, Jacob. I really could do that.
JACOB SKOEMAGER. All right. Come, out with the shilling.
[JEPPE *gives him a coin, and* JACOB *goes inside.*]
JEPPE. Ho there, don't forget to give me change.
JACOB SKOEMAGER [*returns with a pitcher and a glass. Pours it full*]. Your health, Jeppe. [*Drinks it.*]
JEPPE. That's drinking a potful, you guzzler.
JACOB SKOEMAGER. It's a fine old custom. The host always takes the first drink. [*He refills the glass and gives it to* JEPPE.]
JEPPE. I know, but devil take him who started it. Your health, Jacob.
[*Drains his glass.*]
JACOB SKOEMAGER. Thanks, Jeppe. And while you are about it you might as well drink for the other shilling as well. You surely wouldn't want to take it along; you'd only keep it until you drop in here on the way home for another drink of brandy. I swear to you I haven't a shilling change in the house.
JEPPE. Only a damned fool would wait that long. If it's to be drunk, it'll be drunk right now so that I know there is

something in my belly. But if you drink again I'll not pay for it.

JACOB SKOEMAGER [*pouring him a glass*]. To your health!

JEPPE. May God keep our friends and the devil take our enemies. Ah! That warms the belly! Ah! Ah!

JACOB SKOEMAGER. Good luck on the way, Jeppe!

JEPPE. Thanks, Jacob Skoemager.

[JACOB *goes back into the inn.* JEPPE *commences to sing.*]

A nice white hen and a gray speckled hen
They wanted to fight a big rooster. . . .
Oh if I only dared drink another shilling's worth! Oh, if I only dared! I think I'll do it. It wouldn't be such a terrible thing. I can't get away from this inn. But it's like somebody holding me with iron chains. I must go in. Hold on, Jeppe, what are you going to do? I can see Nille right now standing in the road, Master Eric in hand. No, I must turn back. If I only dared drink another shilling's worth! My belly says, drink; my back says, don't drink. Which shall I obey? Is my belly better than my back? I say yes. Shall I knock? Ho there, Jacob Skoemager! Come out. But look, there stands that cursed woman again before my eyes. If only her beatings wouldn't break the bones in my back . . . but she hits hard as a . . . Oh, may the Lord help poor me, what shall I do? Control your nature, Jeppe. Wouldn't it be a shame to get into trouble for a glass of brandy? No, this time it won't happen. I must go. . . . Oh, if I only dared drink just one more shilling's worth! It was my misfortune to taste it. That's it. Now I can't get away from it. Go ahead, legs! May the devil take you if you don't start moving! . . . No, the ruffians won't budge. They want to go to the inn. My legs are at war. My belly and legs want to go to the inn and my back wants to go to the city. Will you go ahead, you curs, you dirty beasts, you scoundrels! May the devil take the one that goes to the inn. I have more trouble getting my legs away from the inn than dragging my piebald nag from the stable. Oh, if only I could drink another shilling's worth! Perhaps Jacob Skoemager'll trust me for a shilling or two if I beg him for it. Ho there, Jacob, another glass of brandy—two shillings' worth.

[JACOB *comes from the inn with bottle and glass.*]

JACOB SKOEMAGER. Oh, is that you, Jeppe! Here again? I knew you had too little. What is a couple coppers' worth of brandy! That hardly wets the gullet.

JEPPE. That's true, Jacob, so now give me another good measure. [*Aside.*] Once it's down he'll have to trust me whether he wants to or not.

JACOB SKOEMAGER [*pours him a glass full of brandy*]. Here's your measure of brandy. [JEPPE *greedily reaches for it.*] First the money.

JEPPE. Come, you know the proverb: 'While I am drinking you surely can trust me.'

JACOB SKOEMAGER. You don't pay for drinks with proverbs in this place. If you don't pay in advance, you won't get a drop. We've sworn off trusting even the bailiff himself.

JEPPE [*weeping*]. Can't you trust me just once? You know I am an honest man.

JACOB SKOEMAGER. No credit.

JEPPE. Here is your money, you bullying beggar. Now it's done. [JACOB *pours him a glass.*] Now drink, Jeppe. [*Drinks.*] Ah that was good.

JACOB SKOEMAGER. Oh yes, that'll warm the cockles of your heart.

JEPPE. The best thing about brandy is that it gives a fellow such courage. Now I'm not thinking of my wife nor of Master Eric. It's that last glass that did it all. Do you know this song, Jacob?
Sweet Kitty and Master Peter sat at the
    table, Peteheia!
Speaking and saying many a silly thing,
    Polemeia!
About nightingales singing in summer
    time, Peteheia!
The vile fiends fly off with Nille the cate-
    meran, Polemeia!

I went out to the green forest one day,
Peteheia!
The deacon he's a dirty dog, Polemeia!
I sat on my gray old horse, Peteheia!
The deacon is a real jackass, Polemeia!
And if you'd like to know my wife's real
name, Peteheia!
She's known all over as lust and shame,
Polemeia!

It was I who made that song, Jacob.

JACOB SKOEMAGER. The devil you did!

JEPPE. Jeppe isn't the fool you think
he is. I also made a song about shoe-
makers. It goes like this.

The shoemaker with the bass and fiddle,
Philepom, philepom.

JACOB SKOEMAGER. O, you fool, that's
a song about a fiddler.

JEPPE. That's right. That's just what
it is. Listen, Jacob, give me another shill-
ing's worth of brandy. [*Gives him the
money.*]

JACOB SKOEMAGER. Fine. Now I know
you are a generous fellow, ready to give
my humble inn a chance to make a bit of
money.

[JEPPE *drains his glass.*]

JEPPE. Hey Jacob, give me four shill-
ings' worth more. [*Giving him the money.*]

JACOB SKOEMAGER. With pleasure.

[*Pours him glass after glass.*]

JEPPE [*drinking and singing*]. The
earth drinks water,
The sea drinks the sun,
The sun drinks the sea,
All the world is a-drinking,
Then why shouldn't be a-drinking
Poor fine me?

JACOB SKOEMAGER. Your health, Jeppe.

JEPPE. Nur zu.

JACOB SKOEMAGER. Prosit, only half a
glassful.

JEPPE. Ich tank ju, Jacob! Drink, man.
May the devil take you. That's all I ask
for.

JACOB SKOEMAGER. I see you can speak
German.

JEPPE. Sure. That's an old story. But

I don't like to speak it except when I'm
drunk.

JACOB SKOEMAGER. Then you speak it
at least once a day.

JEPPE. I was ten years in the militia;
don't you think I ought to understand
the language?

JACOB SKOEMAGER. Yes, I know, Jeppe.
We were two years in the same company.

JEPPE. That's right, now I remember.
They hanged you once when you ran away
at Viszmar.

JACOB SKOEMAGER. They were going to
hang me, but I was pardoned. A miss is
as good as a mile.

JEPPE. It's too bad they didn't hang
you. But weren't you along with me at
the auction in the meadow? You know
which one.

JACOB SKOEMAGER. Lord, where wasn't
I along!

JEPPE. I'll never forget the first greet-
ings the Swedes gave us. I think three
thousand or even four thousand men fell
there. Dasging fordyvled zu, Jacob. Du
kanst wol das remembering—I can't. I
must say I was a little afraid of the
battle.

JACOB SKOEMAGER. Yes, true. It's not
so easy to die. A fellow always becomes
religious when he goes against the enemy.

JEPPE. Yes, that's so. I also know that
feeling. The whole night before the auc-
tion I read David's Psalms.

JACOB SKOEMAGER. What I don't under-
stand is that you who have been a soldier
let yourself be so bullied by your wife.

JEPPE. I? Hm, if she were only here
now you'd see how I'd warm her hide.
Fill it up again, Jacob. I still have eight
shillings. When they are gone I'll drink
on trust. Give me a pitcher of beer.

In Leipzig lived a man,
In Leipzig lived a man,
In Leipzig lived a leather man,
In Leipzig lived a leather man,
In Leipzig lived a man.

The man he took a wife, etc.

JACOB SKOEMAGER. Your health, Jeppe.

JEPPE. Ho! H . . . o. Y . . . au.

Your health, and my health, and all good friends' health. Y . . . au.

JACOB SKOEMAGER. Don't you want to drink to the bailiff's health?

JEPPE. If you want me to. Give me another shilling's worth. The bailiff's a decent man. If you slip him a dollar he'll swear on his soul to his lordships that you can't pay the rent. Hang me if I have another copper. You'll trust me for a penny or two.

JACOB SKOEMAGER. No, Jeppe. You can't stand any more. I'm not the man to let my customers drink more than is good for them. I'd rather lose my trade than do that.

JEPPE. Just for one copper.

JACOB SKOEMAGER. No, Jeppe. You can't get another drop. Remember, you've got a long way to go.

JEPPE. You dirty cur, blackguard, beast, cut-throat. Y . . . au!

JACOB SKOEMAGER. Good-by, Jeppe! A happy journey. [He goes in.]

JEPPE. Jeppe, you are drunk as a beast. My legs don't want to carry me any more. Will you stand up, you knaves. [Fumbling around the door to the inn.] Where is that bell gone to? Ho there, Jacob! Dog of a shoemaker! Ho, for another copper's worth! Will you stand still, you dogs? No, may the devil take me if they'll stay still. Thanks much, Jacob Skoemager. Let's have another from the fresh barrel. Listen, friend, which is the road to the city? Stand still, I say. Look, the brute is drunk. You have drunk like a rogue. Jacob, is that a copper's worth of brandy? You measure like a Turk. . . . [He falls down mumbling incoherently, and remains on the ground, unable to get up. Falls asleep.]

[Enter BARON NILUS, his SECRETARY, VALET, ERIC and another lackey.]

BARON NILUS. It looks as though we'll have an excellent year. The harvest will be fine. Look how thick the barley is growing.

SECRETARY. Quite true, your lordship, but that means that the ton of barley won't bring more than five marks.

BARON NILUS. That does not matter. The peasants are always better off in a good season.

SECRETARY. I don't really understand how it is, your lordship, but no matter how good the year is, the peasants always complain and ask for seed-corn. The more they have the more they drink. Right here lives an innkeeper by the name of Jacob Skoemager who has a good deal to do with impoverishing the peasants. They say he puts salt in his beer so the more they drink of it the more thirsty they become.

BARON NILUS. We will have to put the fellow out. But what's this lying on the road? It must be a dead man. There is nothing but misfortune around here. Come here, quick, one of you, and see who it is. [They crowd around JEPPE.]

FIRST LACKEY. It is Jeppe of the Hill who has that devil of a wife. Ho there, Jeppe, get up! It's no use, you can beat him, or tear his hair from his head, he won't get up.

BARON NILUS. Let him sleep. . . . I'd like to have a little fun with him. You generally have clever ideas, can't you think of something diverting that will give us a bit of fun?

SECRETALY. I think it would be amusing to put a paper collar around his neck and cut off his hair.

VALET. I think it would be even funnier if you'd paint his face with ink and undress him completely. Then send him home and see what his wife will do to him.

BARON NILUS. A fine idea. But I'll wager Eric will think of something better still. Give us your suggestion, Eric.

ERIC (one of the lackeys). My idea is to take off all his clothes and put him in the master's best bed. Then to-morrow when he gets up we'll treat him as if he were his lordship, so that he won't know whether he is sane or insane. When we have finally convinced him that he is the baron, we'll get him drunk as he is right now and put him back into the very same dirt where he is now lying. If we do this cleverly he'll convince himself that either he was only dreaming or that he was actually in paradise.

BARON NILUS. Eric, you are a great fellow, that is why you always have great ideas. What if he wakes up in the middle of it?

ERIC. I'll vouch he won't, your lordship. If this is Jeppe of the Hill he is the biggest toper and heaviest sleeper in the whole community. Last year they tried setting off a rocket that was tied around his neck and it never woke him.

BARON NILUS. Then let us do it. Take him away quickly, put a fine shirt on him and put him in my best bed.

ACT II

A room, JEPPE *is seen lying in the baron's sumptuous bed. On the chair beside him lies a gold-embroidered dressing-gown. He wakes up, rubs his eyes, sits up, looks around, and falls back again in great fright. He rubs his eyes again, turns his nightcap in all directions, and examines it. Now he notices the fine shirt he has on, the dressing-gown and other beautiful things about him. He makes faces to scare children. Soft music has begun to play and when* JEPPE *hears it, he folds his hands and commences to weep. When the music stops he speaks.*

JEPPE. What's all this? What glory! How did I get here? Am I dreaming or am I awake? No,—wide-awake. Where are my wife and children? Where is my home, and where is Jeppe? Everything has changed; I too. What does it all mean? [*Calling in a faint and frightened voice.*] Nille! Nille! Nille! I believe I've come to heaven, Nille, by some accident. But is this really me? I think it is, and then again I think it isn't. If I feel my back that's still aching from the beatings I got, if I hear myself speaking, if I stick my tongue in the holes in my teeth, then I believe it's me; but if I look at my cap, at my shirt and all the other beautiful things I see, when I hear that sweet music, devil

take it if I can get it through my noodle that it is me. No, it's not me. I'll be cursed a thousand times if it's me. But perhaps I'm dreaming? No, I don't believe it. I'll pinch myself in the arm. If it doesn't hurt then I'm dreaming. If it does, then I'm not dreaming. [*Pinches himself.*] Yes, I felt it, so I'm awake. I'm honestly awake. None can argue me out of that. For if I wasn't I couldn't. . . . But when I think of it, how can I be awake? It's positive that I am Jeppe of the Hill. I know I am a poor peasant, a dolt, a knave, a cuckold, a hungry louse, a bit of vermin and a scoundrel—then how can I be emperor and lord of a castle? No, it's only a dream. The best thing is to be patient until I wake up. [*The music commences again to play and* JEPPE *weeps again.*] Can anything like that be heard in a dream? But it's impossible. If it's only a dream I wish I'd never wake again; and if I've gone crazy I don't want to ever be sane again. I'd drag any doctor who'd want to cure me before a judge. I'd curse anyone who'd wake me. But I'm neither dreaming nor crazy. I can remember that my father, God bless his soul, was Niels of the Hill; my grandfather, Jeppe of the Hill. My wife's name is Nille, and she has a whip called Master Eric. My sons' names are Hans, Christoffer and Niels. But wait a minute, I've got it. It's the eternal life. It's paradise. This is the heavenly kingdom. Probably I drank too much once again at Jacob Skoemager's, died and went straight to heaven. Dying isn't so hard as people make it out. I for one didn't feel a single thing. Perhaps at this very minute the pastor is standing in the pulpit and delivering a funeral sermon over me, saying: "That is the end of Jeppe of the Hill. He lived like a soldier and died like a soldier." They could argue whether I died on land or sea. I know I was quite wet when I left the world. Aha, Jeppe, that's very different from running four miles to town to buy soap. It's different from sleeping on straw, getting beatings from your wife and horns from the deacon. Oh, into what a happy life your hardships and misery have turned! I could cry from sheer joy, particularly when I think how I didn't deserve it. But one thing bothers me: I'm so thirsty my lips are glued together. If I desired to live again it'd be only to get a pitcher of beer. For what's the good of all the finery before my eyes and ears if I'm going to suffer of thirst. I remember the pastor used to say: "In heaven there is neither hunger nor thirst, and you'll meet there all your dead friends." But I am dying of thirst and I'm all alone—I don't see a soul. I thought I'd find at least my grandfather here; he was so fine a man that he died, and didn't owe a shilling to his lordship. I also know that other people lived as honest as I. Then why am I the only one in heaven? It can't be heaven. Then what is it? I'm not asleep; I'm not awake; I'm not dead; I'm not alive; I'm not crazy, I am not sane; I'm Jeppe of the Hill; I am not Jeppe of the Hill. I am poor; I am rich; I am a miserable peasant; I am an emperor. [Roaring.] O . . . o . . . ah. . . . Help! Help! Help!

[At his shouting ERIC, the VALET, and many others enter to watch the fun.]

VALET. I wish your lordship a happy morning. Here is your dressing-gown,— if your worship desires to rise. Eric, fetch quickly the towel and washbasin.

JEPPE. Oh, most worthy chamberlain, I'd very much like to get up, only I beg you please don't do me any harm.

VALET. God forbid that we should harm your lordship!

JEPPE. Oh, before you kill me, won't you please just tell me who I am.

VALET. Does not your lordship know who he is?

JEPPE. Yesterday I was Jeppe of the Hill, to-day . . . oh, I don't really know what to say.

VALET. We are happy indeed to see his lordship in such fine humor for jesting. But God save us! Why does your worship weep?

JEPPE. I am not your worship. I swear on my blessed soul that I am not. As far as I can remember, I am Jeppe Nielsen of the Hill. If you call my wife she'll tell you the same. But don't permit her to bring Master Eric along.

VALET. That is strange! What does that mean? Perhaps your lordship is not quite awake yet; he has never joked like this before.

JEPPE. Whether I am awake or not, I cannot tell; but this I do know, and I can say it too: I am one of our baron's peasants, called Jeppe of the Hill, and never in my life have I been baron or count.

VALET. Eric, I wonder what this means? I fear our master is falling sick.

ERIC. I think he has turned sleepwalker; it often happens that people get up, dress, read, eat and drink while they are asleep.

VALET. No, Eric, now I understand,— our master has hallucinations, brought about by illness. Quick, call a few doctors. . . . Oh, your worship, drive these thoughts from your mind. Your lordship is frightening the whole household. Doesn't my lord recognize me?

JEPPE. I don't know myself, so how can I know you?

VALET. Oh, is it possible that I hear such words from your gracious lordship, and see him in such a plight! Alas; the unfortunate house! to be visited by such misfortune! Doesn't my lord remember what he did yesterday when he went out hunting?

JEPPE. I was never a hunter—and no poacher; I know that means prison. No living soul can prove that I hunted even a hare in my lord's lands.

VALET. Why, it was only yesterday that I myself was out hunting with your gracious lordship.

JEPPE. Yesterday I was at Jacob Skoemager's and drank twelve shillings' worth of brandy. How could I have been hunting?

VALET. Oh, on bended knees I beg your worship to stop talking such nonsense.

Eric, have the doctors been summoned?
ERIC. They will soon be here.
VALET. Then let us put on his lordship's dressing-gown. Perhaps when he gets some fresh air he'll feel better. Will your worship kindly put on his dressing-gown?
JEPPE. Sure. Do with me what you like, so long as you don't kill me, for I am as innocent as an unborn babe.

[*Two doctors enter.*]
FIRST DOCTOR. We heard with the very deepest sorrow that your lordship is ill.
VALET. Yes, master doctor, he is in a very serious condition.
SECOND DOCTOR. How do you feel, gracious lord?
JEPPE. Fine, only I am still thirsty from the brandy I drank yesterday at Jacob Skoemager's. If I could get a pitcher of beer and they let me go, you and the other doctor can go hang so far as I'm concerned. I don't need any medicines.
FIRST DOCTOR. That is what I call delirious raving, my colleague!
SECOND DOCTOR. The more violent the fever the quicker it runs its course. Now we will feel his lordship's pulse. *Quid Tibi videtur, domine frater?*
FIRST DOCTOR [*feeling JEPPE'S pulse*]. I think he should be bled immediately.
SECOND DOCTOR. I do not agree with you; such diseases are cured in a different manner. His lordship had a strange, ugly, dream which so excited his blood and put his brain in such a turmoil that he imagines himself a peasant. We must now divert his attention with such amusements as usually give him the greatest pleasure. We must serve him the wines and foods he likes best and play for him the kind of music he most enjoys.
[*Lively music commences to play.*]
VALET. This is my lord's favorite piece.
JEPPE. Maybe.—Is there always such fun in a castle?
VALET. Whenever your lordship desires it, for he gives us our board and wages.

JEPPE. It's strange I can't remember the things that I used to.
SECOND DOCTOR. The disease from which my lordship suffers brings with it forgetfulness of what he used to do. I remember a few years ago one of my neighbors drank so much that he became deranged and thought he was minus his head.
JEPPE. I wish that would happen to Judge Christoffer; he has an illness that seems to work just the other way. He believes he has a great big head. From the way he judges he really hasn't any at all.
[*All laugh.*]
SECOND DOCTOR. It is a joy to see his lordship jest, but to get back to my story. The same man went through the whole town asking everyone if they had found the head he had lost. After a time he recovered it; he is now a sexton in Jutland.
JEPPE. He could have been that even if he had never found his head again.
[*Everyone laughs.*]
FIRST DOCTOR. Does my honored colleague recollect what happened ten years ago to a man who thought his head was full of flies? He couldn't get that delusion out of his mind until a very clever doctor cured him in this fashion: He covered his whole head with plaster which he covered in turn with dead flies. After a time he took the plaster off, showing the patient the flies he believed had come from his head. This cured him. I also heard of another man who after a long fever got the idea that if he made water, the whole country would be flooded. No one could get this out of his head. He said he was ready to die for the common welfare. This is how he was cured. They brought him a message, supposedly from a commander, that the town was threatened with siege, and since there was no water in the moat, he was to fill it and thus keep the enemy from entering. The sick man was delighted that he could serve his country and himself as well, and in this manner got rid of both his water and his sickness.

SECOND DOCTOR. I can cite another case that happened in Germany. A nobleman one day came to an inn. After dining, and getting ready to retire he hung a golden chain which he wore around his neck, on the wall in his sleeping chamber. The innkeeper noted this carefully as he accompanied the gentleman to the bedroom and wished him good-night. No sooner did he hear that the nobleman was asleep, than he stole into the chamber, took off sixty links from the chain and hung it back again. The guest rose in the morning, ordered his horse saddled, and dressed himself. When he came to putting on the chain he noticed that it was only half its former length. He began to shout that he had been robbed. The host who had been at the door listening ran in at once and putting on an air of great consternation exclaimed: "Lord! What an awful change in you." The traveller asked what he meant by that. "Oh my Lord," replied the innkeeper, "your head is twice as big as it was yesterday." And with that he held before him one of these mirrors that are so made that you appear twice the ordinary size. When the nobleman saw how big his head looked in the mirror, he burst into tears and said: "Now I understand how the chain has become too small." Then he mounted his horse and covered his head so that none could see him on the road. They say he kept a long time to his house, unable to get the silly idea out of his head, to wit, that it was not the chain that had become short but that his head had become large.

FIRST DOCTOR. There are endless examples of such obsessions. I remember hearing of a man who convinced himself that his nose was ten feet long and warned everyone not to come near him.

SECOND DOCTOR. Domine Frater has, I am sure, heard the story of the man who thought himself dead. A young man got the notion that he was dead, laid himself in a coffin and would neither eat nor drink. His friends did their utmost to show him how absurd this was. They tried every means to make him eat, but it was useless. In the end a very experienced doctor undertook to cure him by the most unusual method. He had a servant also pretend that he was dead and brought him with great ceremony to the place where the sick man was. At first the two looked at each other in silence. Finally the patient asked the other why he had come. The new arrival answered he was there because he was dead. Then they questioned each other as to how they had died and both explained in full. Later the same people who had been instructed what to do brought supper to the second man who sat up in his coffin and ate heartily. Said he to the sick man: "Don't you want a bite too?" The patient was surprised and asked if it was really proper for dead men to eat. "No one who doesn't eat," replied the other, "can remain dead for any length of time." In this way he allowed himself to be persuaded first to eat, then to rise and dress himself—in short he imitated the counterfeit sick man in every way until in the end he was all well and became normal like the one who set the example. I could tell endless tales of such delusions. That is just what has happened to his gracious lordship. He imagines himself a peasant, but if my lordship will get it out of his head, he will be immediately well again.

JEPPE. Is it really possible that I only imagine it?

FIRST DOCTOR. Certainly, My lord has heard from these stories what delusions can do.

JEPPE. Then I am not Jeppe of the Hill?

FIRST DOCTOR. Certainly not.

JEPPE. Then that cursed Nille is not my wife?

SECOND DOCTOR. Absolutely not, my lord is a widower.

JEPPE. And the whip called Master Eric is only something I imagine?

FIRST DOCTOR. Purely an illusion.

JEPPE. It isn't true either that I was to go to town yesterday to buy soap?

SECOND DOCTOR. No.

JEPPE. Nor that I drank up the money at Jacob Skoemager's?

VALET. Why, your lordship was yesterday with us on the hunt.

JEPPE. Nor that I am a cuckold?

VALET. Her ladyship has been dead for many years.

JEPPE. Oh now I am beginning to see my foolishness. I won't think about the peasant any more. Now I see that it was only a dream that put this silliness into my head. Funny what stupid notions a man can believe.

VALET. Will it please your lordship to take a little walk in the garden before breakfast is prepared.

JEPPE. Very good, you'd better hurry up, for I am hungry and thirsty.

[*They go out as the curtain drops.*]

ACT III

The scene is the same as in Act II. A screen hides the bed, a small table is set in front of it. JEPPE *enters from the garden followed by his attendants, the* VALET *and the* SECRETARY.

JEPPE. Ah ha! I see the table is all set.

VALET. Everything is ready, if it will please your worship to sit down.

[JEPPE *sits down. The others stand behind him, laughing constantly at his bad manners, as when he sticks all his fingers into his plate, when he belches, handles his knife clumsily, or cleans his nose with his fingers and lets the filth fly on his clothes.*]

VALET. Will my lord order the wine he desires?

JEPPE. You know yourself what I drink in the morning.

VALET. Your lordship always prefers Rhine wine, but if it is not to your worship's taste now, you can order a different kind immediately.

[*He hands him a glass of wine.*]

JEPPE [*tasting*]. No, that's a little too sour. You better put a bit of mead into it, then it'll be better. I've got a sweet tooth.

VALET. Here is some port if my lord would like to taste it.

JEPPE [*drinking*]. That's a good wine. To your health, all of you. [*Every time he drinks there is a sounding of trumpets.*] Ho there, watch out, fellow. Another glass of that pork wine. Do you understand me? Where did you get that ring on your finger?

SECRETARY. My lord gave it to me himself.

JEPPE. I don't remember. Give it back to me. I must have been drunk when I did it. Such rings you don't give away like that. Later on we'll see what else you fellows 've got. Servants shouldn't get more'n their board and wages. I swear I don't remember ever making presents. Why should I? Why, that ring is worth more'n ten rix-dollars. No, no, my good fellows, that won't do. You mustn't take advantage of your master's weakness when he's been drinking. When I am drunk I am apt to give away my breeches. When I've slept off my liquor I take my presents back. Otherwise I'd get into some mess with my wife Nille. . . . What am I talking about? I'm falling again into my old crazy ideas, and don't know who I am. Give me another glass of pork wine. Once again, to all your healths! Every one of you. [*Trumpet sounds.*] Pay attention to what I say, you lunkheads. It's a law from now on, if I give away anything in the evening when I am drunk, you must return it the next morning. When servants get more than they can eat, they become proud and despise their master. What wages do you get?

SECRETARY. My lord has always paid me two hundred rix-dollars a year.

JEPPE. The devil a two hundred you'll get from now on! What do you do to earn two hundred rix-dollars? I myself must work like a beast and stand on my feet in the hayloft from morn to night, and can't even . . . see, those peasant notions are coming back. Give me another glass of wine. [*He drinks and trumpets sound.*] Two hundred rix-dollars! That's what you call pulling wool over the very eyes of your master. Do you know what, my good fellows? After I am through with my meal, I have a good mind to hang every one of you in the courtyard. You'll soon learn that I don't stand for any fooling in money matters.

VALET. We will return whatever we have received from your lordship.

JEPPE. Oh yes, my lordship this and my lordship that. Compliment and flattery are very cheap these days. You are trying to feed me honey with your "lordships" until you've filched away all my money. Then you'll be your "lordship." With your mouths you say "lordship," with your heart it's "fool." You speak different from what you mean, you louts. You servants are like Abner who came to Roland, embraced him and said to him: "Hail, brother," and stuck a dagger in his heart at the same time. Jeppe is no fool. You may take my word for that. [*They all fall on their knees as though begging for mercy.*] Arise, all. Wait until I am through eating. Afterwards I'll see how things are and which ones are to be hung. Now I want to make merry. Where is the bailiff?

VALET. He is right outside.

JEPPE. Tell him to come in at once. [*One of the men goes out and returns with the* BAILIFF. *He has silver buttons on his coat and wears a sword.*]

BAILIFF. Has your lordship any orders?

JEPPE. Nothing except that you should be hanged.

BAILIFF. I haven't done any wrong, your worship, why should I be hanged?

JEPPE. Aren't you the bailiff?

BAILIFF. That I am, your worship.

JEPPE. And still you ask why you should be hanged?

BAILIFF. I have served your worship truly and honestly, and have been so diligent that your lordship has always praised me above all your other servants.

JEPPE. I know you've been diligent. I can well see that from your silver buttons. What are your wages?

BAILIFF. Fifty rix-dollars.

JEPPE [*getting up and walking up and down*]. Fifty rix-dollars. Then you must be hanged immediately.

BAILIFF. It couldn't be less for a whole year's hard work.

JEPPE. That's just why you'll be hanged. You have money for a coat with silver buttons, ruffles on your sleeves, a silk queue, for your hair and . . . you get only fifty rix-dollars a year. You must be stealing it from me, my poor man. Where else could you get it?

BAILIFF [*falling on his knees*]. O gracious lord, spare me for my wife's and children's sake.

JEPPE. Have you many children?

BAILIFF. Seven children living, your lordship.

JEPPE. Ho, ho, ho, seven children living. Away with him. Hang him at once, secretary.

SECRETARY. But your gracious lordship, I am not a hangman.

JEPPE. You'll soon learn to be. You already look the part. If you don't hang him, I'll have to have you hanged.

BAILIFF. O gracious lord, won't you pardon us!

JEPPE [*walks up and down, sits down, drinks and gets up again*]. Fifty rix-dollars, a wife and seven children. . . . If no one else will hang you, I'll do it myself. I know the kind of a fellow you are! You bailiffs! I know how you have treated me and the other peasants. There comes that accursed peasant idea again in my head! What I wanted to say is this: I know your kind and your carrying on so well, I could be a bailiff myself if I had to be. You get the milk and cream and the master gets dung, if you'll pardon my mentioning it. If this continues, I believe bailiffs'll become nobles and nobles bailiffs. If a peasant slips something into your or your wife's palm you tell your master: "The poor fellow is willing and hard-working. He has had no end of hard luck and that's why he can't pay. His land isn't worth anything, his cattle have the scab" . . . and more talk like that. That's the kind of words you feed your master. Take my word for it, my dear fellows, you can't blind me with that kind of talk. I am a peasant and my father was a peasant. . . . Look, there come those crazy notions again. I said I was a peasant's son because Abraham and Eve our first parents were peasants.

SECRETARY [*also falls on his knees*]. O, gracious lord, have pity on him for the sake of his unfortunate wife. How will they live when he is not there to provide for them?

JEPPE. Who said they were to live? You can hang them together with him!

SECRETARY. Oh my lord, she is such a pretty, neat, woman!

JEPPE. So, perhaps you are her lover? How you take her part! Let her come in here. [*One of the men run out and bring her in. She kisses his hand.*] Are you the bailiff's wife?

WOMAN. Yes, your gracious lordship, I am.

JEPPE [*puts his hand on her breasts*]. You are pretty. Would you like to stay with me to-night.

WOMAN. Your worship can command me to do anything, for I am in his service.

JEPPE [*to the* BAILIFF]. Do you allow your wife to stay with me here to-night?

BAILIFF. I thank your lordship for showing such honor to my humble house.

JEPPE. Look here, put a chair here so she'll eat with me. [*They sit down at the table and eat and drink. He notes the* SECRETARY *eyeing her all the time and becomes jealous.*] You'll get into trouble if you keep on looking at her.

[*Whenever he looks at the* SECRETARY *the latter looks on the ground.* JEPPE *sings an old-fashioned love song. Then he*

orders a polka to be played and tries to dance with her. But he is so drunk he falls down again and again. When he falls the fourth time he can't get up, and falls asleep.]

BARON [*who until now has played the* SECRETARY]. He is sound asleep. In playing this game we almost got into trouble. He was on the point of handling us very roughly. We would either have had to give up our little farce or submit to the maltreatment of this rude lout. From his conduct one can learn how tyrannical and overbearing low people become when they are suddenly raised from the mire to honor and high position. The rôle of secretary would have turned out ill for me. If he had ordered me whipped it would have spread an ill tale which would have made me look as foolish in the eyes of the people as the peasant. The best thing is to let him sleep awhile before we put him into his dirty work clothes again.

ERIC. Why, my lord, he sleeps the sleep of the dead. I can beat and pummel him and he won't feel it.

BARON. Take him out and let's put an end to our comedy.

ACT IV

The scene is the same as in Act I. JEPPE *is lying on a dirt heap near* JACOB SKOEMAGER'S, *in his old work clothes. He wakes and calls.*

JEPPE. Ho there! Secretary! Valet! Lackeys! Another glass of pork wine. [*He looks around, rubs his eyes and gets hold of his head and finds his old wide-brimmed hat. He rubs his eyes again, gets hold of his hat again and turns it in all directions. Then he looks at his clothes, recognizes himself again and begins to speak.*] How long was Abraham in paradise? Alas! now I recognize everything again: my bed, my jacket, my old hat, myself. This is different, Jeppe, from drinking pork wine out of gilded glasses and sitting at a table with lackeys and secretaries behind your chair. Good fortune, curses on it! never lasts long. Oh, that I, who just now was such a gracious lord, should find myself again in this miserable condition! My fine white bed is turned to a dirt heap, my gold embroidered hat into an old hat, my lackeys into pigs and I myself from a great gracious lord into a miserable peasant. I thought when I'd wake up, I'd find my fingers covered with golden rings, but they are covered with something very different, if you'll forgive me for mentioning it. I wanted to call my servants to account. And now I must prepare my own back for an accounting when I get home and tell what I did. I thought when I woke up I should reach out and find a glass of pork wine. Oh, oh, Jeppe, the stay in paradise was short and your joys ended too soon. But who knows if something won't happen to me again if I lay down and fall asleep again. Oh, if only it would! Oh, if I could get there again. [*He lies down and falls asleep again.* NILLE *enters, a whip in her hand.*]

NILLE. I wonder if he met with some misfortune on the way? What could it be? Either Lucifer carried him off or he is sitting in the inn drinking his money away. It was stupid of me to trust that drunkard with twelve whole shillings. But what's this? Isn't that him lying in the filthy dung heap snoring? Oh, miserable woman that I am, to have such a beast for a husband! Ah, but your back'll pay dearly for that. [*She steals up to him and gives him a blow on the back with Master Eric.*]

JEPPE [*waking*]. Ah! Oh! Help! Help! What's this? Where am I? Who is beating me? Why? Oh, oh!

NILLE. I'll teach you soon who it is. [*Beats him again and pulls his hair.*]

JEPPE. Oh, dearest Nille, don't beat me any more. You have no idea what has happened to me.

NILLE. Where have you been all this time, you drunken cur? Where is the soap I sent you to buy?

JEPPE. I couldn't get to town, Nille.

NILLE. Why couldn't you get to town?

JEPPE. I was taken up to paradise while I was on the way.

NILLE. To paradise? [*She commences to beat him again.*] To paradise! [*Beating him.*] To paradise! [*Continues beating him.*] Are you trying to make a fool of me besides?

JEPPE. Oh! Ow! Oh! As I am an honest man, I tell gospel truth.

NILLE. What truth?

JEPPE. That I was in paradise.

NILLE. In paradise! [*Beats him again.*]

JEPPE. Oh, darling Nille, don't beat me!

NILLE. Quick, confess where you were or I'll kill you.

JEPPE. I'll confess where I was if you stop beating me.

NILLE. Go on, tell me.

JEPPE. Swear you'll not beat me any more.

NILLE. No.

JEPPE. As true as I am an honest man and my name is Jeppe of the Hill, I was in paradise and I will tell you things that'll more than surprise you if you'll listen.

[NILLE *commences to beat him again and pulling him by the hair towards the house. Finally she throws him into the house.*]

NILLE. Now, you drunken sot, first sleep your liquor off and then we'll do some more talking. A swine like you doesn't go to paradise. Just think how that beast drank himself out of his mind. But this time he did it at my expense. He'll not get a bite of food or a drop of water for the next three days. By that time he'll be over his crazy idea of paradise.

[*Three armed men enter.*]

FIRST MAN. Doesn't a man by the name of Jeppe live here?

NILLE. Yes, he does.

SECOND MAN. Are you his wife?

NILLE. Yes, God help me in my misfortune.

THIRD MAN. We must see him and talk to him.

NILLE. He is dead drunk.

FIRST MAN. That doesn't matter. Get him out or your whole household will suffer.

[NILLE *goes into the house and soon* JEPPE *comes flying out with such force that he knocks one of the men over.*]

JEPPE. Oh! Oh! Good gentlemen, now you can see what kind of a wife I have to put up with.

FIRST MAN. You don't deserve any better, you are a criminal. [*They get hold of him and tie his hands behind him.*]

JEPPE. What crime have I committed?

SECOND MAN. You'll soon find out. You'll appear before the judge at once.

[*Enter two* LAWYERS, *a* JUDGE *and some clerks. The* JUDGE *sits down on a stool which one of the clerks has brought in.* JEPPE *is brought before him. One of the* LAWYERS *steps forward.*]

FIRST LAWYER. Here is a man, your honor, whom we can prove to have stolen into the baron's house, posed as his lordship, put on his clothes, and tried to maltreat the servants. This is an unheard-of insolence and we demand therefore, in the name of his lordship, that he be severely punished as an example and warning to other criminals.

JUDGE. Is the accusation against you true? Let us hear what you can reply to it, for we will not convict anyone who has not been heard.

JEPPE. Alas, poor me, what shall I say? I confess I deserve punishment but only for drinking away the money I was to have used for buying soap. It is true I was just now in the castle, but how I got there I don't know—and how I got out I don't know either.

FIRST LAWYER. Your honor knows now from his own admission, first, that he was drunk, and second, while in that stage of drunkenness he committed this unheard-of crime. It is now only a question of whether such a gross criminal act should be excused on the ground of intoxication. That I argue is impossible. For then offenders who have committed adultery or murder could also escape by pleading drunkenness. Even if he could prove that he really was drunk it would not help his case. For the law says that when a man commits a crime under the influence of drink he must answer for it when sober. You remember how a similar case was recently decided. Even though the criminal was led into impersonating a lord from sheer stupidity, such stupidity and ignorance could not save him from the death penalty. Punishment is meted out to act as a warning to others. I could go into details if I did not fear to retard the progress of this case.

SECOND LAWYER. Gracious judge, this case seems so strange to me that I cannot accept it even if there were witnesses to corroborate it. How could a simple peasant have stolen into the castle of my lord and impersonate him without assuming his manner and likeness as well? How could he get into my lord's bedchamber? How could he put on my lord's clothes without being seen by anyone? No, your honor, this accusation could only have been made up by this poor man's enemies. I hope therefore that he may be discharged.

JEPPE [*weeping*]. May God bless your mouth. I have a bit of tobacco in the pocket of my breeches and I hope you won't refuse it. It's as good as any honest man would want to chew.

SECOND LAWYER. Keep your tobacco, Jeppe. I am pleading for you not for gain, but out of pure, sheer Christian pity.

JEPPE. I beg your pardon, master attorney, I didn't think your kind of folks were so honorable.

FIRST LAWYER. The grounds for acquitting this criminal on which my colleague bases his plea rest entirely on conjectures. It is not a question here of whether or not such a thing happened. Witnesses and his confession have established his guilt beyond all doubt.

SECOND LAWYER. A confession made in fear has no value. It seems to me therefore that it would be only fair to give this poor man an opportunity to think over the matter and then to question him once again. Listen, Jeppe, and think well of what you say. Do you admit this charge against you?

JEPPE. No, I swear on my most sacred oath that what I swore before is all lies. I haven't been out of the house for three days.

FIRST LAWYER. Your honor, it is my humble opinion that no man can testify under oath whose guilt has been established by witnesses and who has confessed his crime.

SECOND LAWYER. I think he should.

FIRST LAWYER. I think he should not.

SECOND LAWYER. Particularly when the case is of so peculiar a nature.

FIRST LAWYER. There is no disputing witnesses and a confession.

JEPPE [to himself]. Oh, if they'd only go for each others' throats then I'd get at the judge and give him such a beating that he'd forget his law and order.

SECOND LAWYER. But listen, worthy colleague, even if the deed is confessed, the man deserves no punishment. For he committed neither murder nor robbery nor any kind of misdeed while on the premises.

FIRST LAWYER. That makes no difference: intentio furandi are one and the same thing as furtum.

JEPPE. Speak Danish, you black hound, then we'll be able to argue the business.

FIRST LAWYER. For when a man is apprehended, whether in the act of stealing, or after the stealing is done—in either case he is a thief.

JEPPE. Kind judge, I'll gladly let you hang me if only this lawyer will hang alongside of me.

SECOND LAWYER. Stop talking like that, Jeppe, you are only injuring your own case.

JEPPE. Then why don't you answer? [Low.] He stands there like a dumb beast.

SECOND LAWYER. But how is that furandi propositum proved?

FIRST LAWYER. Quicung; in aedes alienas noctu irrumpit, tanquam fur aut nocturnus grassator existimandus est; atqui reus hic ita, ergo—

SECOND LAWYER. Nego majorem, quod scilicet irruperit.

FIRST LAWYER. Res manifesta est, tot legitimis testibus exstantibus, ac confitente reo.

SECOND LAWYER. Quicung; vi vel metu coactus fuerit confiteri—

FIRST LAWYER. Bah! Where is the Vis, where is the Metus? That is just quibbling.

SECOND LAWYER. Ho, it's you who are quibbling.

FIRST LAWYER. Whoever accuses me of that is not an honorable man.

[They fly at each other. JEPPE leaps in between them and pulls off the first lawyer's wig.]

JUDGE. Respect for the court! Not another word. I've heard enough. [Reading his decision.] Inasmuch as Jeppe of the Hill, son of Niels of the Hill, grandson of Jeppe of the same has been proven both by witnesses and his own confession to have entered by stealth into the baron's castle, to have put on his clothes and to have maltreated his servants—he is condemned to die by poison, and after death to be hanged on the gallows.

JEPPE. Oh, oh! Gracious judge, have you no mercy!

JUDGE. No, absolutely not. The sentence shall be carried out forthwith in my very presence.

JEPPE. Oh! Can't I have at least a glass of brandy before I take the poison, so that I can die without fear.

JUDGE. Yes, that I permit.

[A glass of brandy is poured for him, which he drains. He holds out for another, drinks that; then for a third. After he has finished it he falls to his knees.]

JEPPE. Won't you have mercy?

JUDGE. No, Jeppe, it's too late now.

JEPPE. Oh, it is not too late. Your judgeship can change his judgment and say he judged the wrong way the first time. Such things have happened often. After all, we are all human.

JUDGE. No, you yourself will feel in a few minutes that it is too late, for the poison was mixed in the brandy you drank.

JEPPE. Oh, poor me! Have I already taken the poison! Oh, farewell, Nille. But no, you cur, you don't deserve that I should bid you good-by. Farewell, Jens, Niels, and Christoffer! Farewell, my daughter Martha; farewell, apple of my eye! I am sure that you are my daughter: you were born before the deacon came to our house. You have your father's face. We resemble each other like two drops of water. Farewell, my piebald horse and thanks for every time I rode you. Farewell, Feierfax, my true dog; farewell, Moens, my black cat; farewell, my oxen, my sheep and pigs. Thanks for your honest friendship, and for the happy days we spent together. Farewell . . . Oh, now I can't talk any more. I feel heavy and weak.

[He falls down in a faint.]

JUDGE. Everything is turning out well. The sleeping potion did its work and now he is sleeping like a log. Hang him up now, but take care that no harm comes to him. Just put the rope under his arms. Then we shall see how he acts when he awakes and finds himself on the gallows.

[They drag him over to the tree and the curtain drops.]

ACT V

The scene is the same as in Act IV. JEPPE is discovered hanging on the tree which is used as a gallows. NILLE is standing in front of him. The JUDGE stands to one side, unseen by NILLE.

NILLE [beating her breast and pulling her hair]. Oh, oh, is it possible that I see my good husband hanging on the gallows! Oh my dearest husband, forgive me if I did you any wrong! Oh, oh, now my conscience hounds me! Now I am sorry for the ugly way I treated you, but it is too late! Now I begin to miss you. Now I know for the first time what a fine man I've lost. Oh, now I'd save you with my own heart's blood if I could.

[She dries her eyes and continues weeping bitterly. In the meantime JEPPE'S sleeping potion has worn off and he awakes. He finds himself hanging and hears the lamenting of his wife.]

JEPPE. Don't weep, good wife, we must all go the same way. Go home, look after the house and take care of the children. You can have my red jacket made over for little Christoffer. Whatever is left you can use for Martha for a cap. And be sure to see that my piebald horse is well taken care of. I loved that animal as if it were my own blood brother. If I were not dead I'd tell you many more things. . . .

NILLE. Oh . . . oh . . . oh . . . What's that! What do I hear? Can the dead speak?

JEPPE. Don't be afraid, Nille, I won't hurt you.

NILLE. Dearest of husbands, how can you speak when you are dead?

JEPPE. How that is I don't know myself, but listen, my darling wife. Run as quick as your legs can carry you and bring me eight shillings' worth of brandy, for I am now more thirsty than when I was alive.

NILLE. For shame, you beast, you dirty sot, you poisonous sousepot! Didn't you drink enough brandy when you were alive? Do you still thirst, you mangy cur, even when you are dead? You're what I call a swine, through and through.

JEPPE. Shut up, you filthy mug, and bring me the brandy, quick! If you don't, devil take me if I don't haunt you every night. Remember, now I'm not afraid of Master Eric. I don't feel blows. [NILLE runs into the house and comes out with the whip and commences to beat him.] Ow, ow, ow! Stop, Nille, you are killing me over again. Ow! ow!

JUDGE [*coming forward*]. Listen, woman, you mustn't beat him any more. You needn't weep any more, for your sake we will pardon your husband his transgression and condemn him to life once again.

NILLE. Oh no, righteous judge, let him hang. It isn't worth giving him life again.

JUDGE. For shame, wicked woman! Away from here or I will hang you beside him.

[NILLE *runs away. The* JUDGE *goes up to* JEPPE *and frees him.*]

JEPPE. Oh, just judge, am I really alive again, or am I only a ghost?

JUDGE. You are alive. The court that takes life can also give it back. Do you understand that?

JEPPE. I can't get that through my head. I believe I am still a ghost.

JUDGE. You foolish fellow. It's simple to understand. Whoever takes something from you can also give it back.

JEPPE. Then I'd like to try and hang the judge just for a joke . . . and see if I can sentence him back to life.

JUDGE. No, that won't do. You are not a judge.

JEPPE. Then I'm really alive again?

JUDGE. That you are.

JEPPE. I'm not just a spook?

JUDGE. Certainly not.

JEPPE. I don't just wander around in spirit?

JUDGE. No.

JEPPE. I am the same Jeppe of the Hill that I was before?

JUDGE. Yes.

JEPPE. And not a spirit?

JUDGE. Certainly not.

JEPPE. Will you swear that's true?

JUDGE. Yes, I swear that you are alive.

JEPPE. Swear that the devil may carry you off if it is not so.

JUDGE. Oh, come, take our word for it and thank us that we were so kind as to sentence you back to life again.

JEPPE. I would thank you right well for taking me down if only you had not hanged me.

JUDGE. Be satisfied, Jeppe, and tell us when your wife beats you again. We'll find a remedy for it. Here are four rixdollars with which you can make merry for many a day. Don't forget to drink to our health.

[JEPPE *kisses the hand of the* JUDGE, *and the latter goes out.*]

JEPPE. I've lived half a hundred years and in all this time I haven't gone through so much as in these last two days. It's the devil of a story when I come to think of it. First a drunken peasant, then a baron, then peasant again. Now dead, now living on the gallows! That is the most marvelous of all. Perhaps when live people are hung, they die, if you hang them dead, they become alive again. Ah! but a glass of brandy right now would taste heavenly! Ho there, Jacob Skoemager.

[JACOB SKOEMAGER *comes from his inn.*]

JACOB SKOEMAGER. Welcome back from town. Well, did you get the soap for your wife?

JEPPE. You scamp, do you know to whom you are talking? Hat off! You are just common dirt next to me.

JACOB SKOEMAGER. I'd not stand this from any man but you, Jeppe. But since you bring me good money every day, I'll take no note of it.

JEPPE. I said hat off, you cobbler!

JACOB SKOEMAGER. What happened to you on the road that makes you so haughty?

JEPPE. I'd have you know I've been hung since I saw you last.

JACOB SKOEMAGER. Well, that's not so much to boast about. I don't grudge you your good fortune. But listen, Jeppe, where you drink your beer, there you should pour the dregs. You get drunk in other inns and come here to raise the devil.

JEPPE. Quick, hat off, varlet! Don't you hear what jingles in my pocket?

[*He jingles the money.*]

JACOB SKOEMAGER [*takes his hat off and*

puts it under his arm]. Heavens! Where did you get the money?

JEPPE. From my barony, Jacob. I'll tell you all that happened to me. But give me a glass of mead for I'm far too noble to drink Danish brandy.

JACOB SKOEMAGER [*runs in for a pitcher and glass, brings it out and pours* JEPPE *a glass*]. Your health, Jeppe!

JEPPE. Now I will tell you all that's happened to me. When I left you I fell asleep. When I awoke I was a baron and drank my gullet full of pork wine. After I was drunk on pork wine I awoke again on the dirt heap. I went asleep again hoping I'd sleep myself again into the baronship. Then I discovered it doesn't always work that way, for my wife woke me with the aid of Master Eric and pulled me home by the hair without showing the slightest respect to the man I had been. No sooner did I get in my room than I was kicked out again head first and found myself surrounded by a lot of constables who sentenced me to death and killed me with poison. When I was dead I was hung, and when I was hung I came to life again, and got four rix-dollars. That is the story. Now you figure out how all that could have happened.

JACOB SKOEMAGER. Ha, ha, ha, that's all a dream, Jeppe!

JEPPE. If I didn't have these four rix-dollars I'd also think it was a dream. Pour me another, I'll not think of this crazy story but get honestly drunk.

JACOB SKOEMAGER [*pouring him*]. Your health, master Baron. Ha, ha, ha!

JEPPE. I suppose you can't believe it, Jacob?

JACOB SKOEMAGER. No, not even if I stood on my head.

JEPPE. It can be true for all that, Jacob. You are dumb and often you don't understand things which are much simpler.

[*Enter* MAGNUS.]

MAGNUS. Ha, ha, ha. I'll tell you the craziest tale that happened to a man named Jeppe of the Hill. He was found dead drunk on the ground. His clothes were changed and he was put in the finest bed in the baron's castle and made believe he was the baron. After he woke up he got drunk again and they put on his old clothes and put him again on the dung heap. Then he awoke and talked himself into having been in paradise. I laughed myself sick when the bailiff's men told me the story. I'd give a rix-dollar to see the fool, ha, ha, ha.

JEPPE. What do I owe, Jacob?

JACOB SKOEMAGER. Twelve shillings.

[JEPPE *pays, wipes his mouth and starts walking off, deeply ashamed.*]

MAGNUS. Why is that man leaving so soon?

JACOB SKOEMAGER. It is the very man they played the joke on.

MAGNUS. Is that so? I must run after him. Listen, Jeppe, just a word. How are things in the other world?

JEPPE. Leave me alone.

MAGNUS. Why did you come back so quickly?

JEPPE. What's that to you?

MAGNUS. Oh, come, tell us something about the journey.

JEPPE. Leave me in peace, I say, or you'll get into trouble.

MAGNUS. Come, Jeppe, I am very anxious to learn a little more about it. [*He gets hold of his clothes and pulls him back.* JEPPE *tries to get away.*]

JEPPE. Help, Jacob Skoemager! Will you let that fellow harm me in front of your very inn?

MAGNUS. I am not doing you any harm, Jeppe. I am only asking you what the other world looks like. [*He holds on while* JEPPE *is trying to pull away.*]

JEPPE. Help! Help! Help!

MAGNUS. Did you see any of my ancestors there?

JEPPE. No, your forefathers must all be in another place, where I hope you and other blackguards go after their death.

[*He finally tears himself away and runs off.* JACOB *returns to his inn and* MAGNUS *goes off.*]

[*Enter the* BARON, *his* SECRETARY, *his* VALET, ERIC *and other lackeys.*]

BARON NILUS. Ha, ha, ha, the experience was worth its weight in gold. I never expected it would turn out so perfectly. If you could amuse me often like that, Eric, you'd stand very high in my good graces.

ERIC. My kind lord, I wouldn't dare play such comedies often for if he'd have beaten your lordship as he threatened, it would have turned into an ugly tragedy.

BARON NILUS. Upon my faith, quite true. I was afraid of the same thing, but I was so delighted with the adventure that I would rather have let myself be beaten; yes, I believe I'd even let you be hanged Eric, than give the story away. Didn't you feel the same way?

ERIC. No, your lordship. To be hanged for fun is a little too serious a sport. The joke would have cost too dear.

BARON NILUS. Why, Eric, that happens every day. How many take their life in sport one way or another! For example, take the man with a weak body. He knowingly drinks his life and health away. He'll constantly attack his constitution and risk life and health for an evening's pleasure. Then again, in Turkey great viziers are for the most part strangled or choked with a cord the very day they take office, or a few days later. Yet all are most eager for the office just to be hanged with a great title. Still another instance: officers sacrifice body and soul to achieve a reputation for bravery. They fight duels for no reason at all, even with those stronger than themselves who they know in advance will overcome them. I also believe there are hundreds of people in love who for a night's pleasure would let themselves be killed in the morning. You also see during sieges how soldiers desert in droves and run into beleaguered cities which they know must soon surrender. All for a day's pleasure—though they know full well they'll be hanged the very next. One acts no worse than the other. Even the philosophers in olden days threw themselves into every misfortune solely to be praised after their death. Therefore, Eric, I fully believe you would rather have allowed yourself to be hanged than spoil that perfectly beautiful story.

Of this adventure, we dear children this
    lesson shall learn,
That raising the low too quickly to places
    on high
    Is no worse than throwing the great
        from their pedestals proud
    Gained by great heroic deeds.
When peasant and artisan are put in
    leaders' command,
The scepter will quick to whip be trans-
    formed.
    For government, tyrants may easily
        gain,
    A Nero each hamlet might willful
        usurp.
Did Caius or Phalaris in day past act
With worse sovereignty than this lowborn
    lout?
    With rods and gallows, steel and
        wheels he threatened us
    When still but young in new-won
        fame.
Therefore never seek ruler from plow,
No peasant shall be lords as in days of
    yore.
    For old customs put in practice now
    Lead us only to tyranny and woe.

THE THUNDERSTORM

By ALEXANDER OSTROVSKY

Produced at St. Petersburg, 1860

TRANSLATED BY FLORENCE WHYTE AND GEORGE RAPALL NOYES *

CHARACTERS

SAVÉL PROKÓFYICH DIKÓY, † *a merchant, an important personage in the town*

BÓRIS GRIGÓRYICH, *his nephew, a young man, fairly well educated*

MÁRFA IGNÁTYEVNA KABÁNOV, § *a rich merchant's widow*

TÍKHON IVÁNYCH KABÁNOV, *her son*

KATERÍNA, *his wife*

VARVÁRA, *Tíkhon's sister*

KULÍGIN, ‡ *a tradesman, a self-taught watchmaker, in search of the secret of perpetual motion*

VÁNYA KUDRYÁSH, *a young man, clerk to Dikóy*

SHÁPKIN, *a tradesman*

FEKLÚSHA, *a pilgrim*

GLÁSHA, *a maid in the Kabánovs' house*

AN OLD LADY, *seventy, half crazy, with two servants*

Townspeople of both sexes

All the characters except BORÍS are dressed in Russian costume.

The action takes place in the town of Kalínov, on the bank of the Volga, in summer. Ten days elapse between the third and fourth acts.

---

* Reprinted from the edition published by Samuel French, copyright 1927, by permission of the translators.
† Savage.
§ Wild boar.
‡ Virgin soil.

ACT I

A public garden on the high bank of the Volga. Beyond the Volga a rural landscape. On the stage there are two benches and several bushes.

SCENE I

[KULIGIN, *seated on a bench and gazing at the river.* KUDRYASH *and* SHAPKIN *are walking about.*]

KULIGIN [*sings*]. " 'Mid the level valley, on the plateau's height———" [*He stops singing.*] It is wonderful; I would say it is really wonderful! Kudryash! See here, brother, for fifty years I have been gazing over the Volga and I cannot gaze enough.

KUDRYASH. What do you see?

KULIGIN. A wonderful view! Beautiful! My heart leaps at the sight.

KUDRYASH. Really!

KULIGIN. It's an inspiration! And you say, "Really!" You've seen it so often that you've grown indifferent, or else you don't appreciate how full of beauty nature is.

KUDRYASH. Well, it's no use talking to you! You are our town freak, a chemist.

KULIGIN. A mechanic, a self-taught mechanic.

KUDRYASH. It's all the same. [*A pause.*]

KULIGIN [*pointing to one side*]. Look, brother Kudryash, who's that waving his arms about down there?

KUDRYASH. Who is it? It's Dikoy scolding his nephew.

KULIGIN. A fine place he's found for it!

KUDRYASH. Any place'll do for him. He's not afraid of any one! Boris Grigoryich has fallen into his hands and so he rides on his back.

SHAPKIN. It'd be hard to find another such scold as Savel Prokofyich. He'll fall upon a man for nothing.

KUDRYASH. He's a blustering fool.

SHAPKIN. Madam Kabanov is a fine one too.

KUDRYASH. Well, at any rate, she does everything with the pretence of piety, but he acts as if he had just broken his chain.

SHAPKIN. There's no one to quiet him down, so he rages about.

KUDRYASH. There are too few lads of my kind around or we should have cured his impudence.

SHAPKIN. What should *you* have done?

KUDRYASH. We should have given him a good scare.

SHAPKIN. How?

KUDRYASH. Four or five of us in a bunch would have had a heart-to-heart talk with him in some alley, and he would have turned soft as silk. And he wouldn't have said a word to anyone about our little lesson; he'd only have minded his ways a bit.

SHAPKIN. He had a good reason for wanting to send you off to the army.

KUDRYASH. He wanted to, but he didn't do it, so it doesn't amount to anything. He won't enlist me; he knows mighty well that I won't sell my skin cheap. He scares you, but I know how to talk to him.

SHAPKIN. You don't say?

KUDRYASH. What's that *you don't say?* People know I'm a rough fellow—then what does he keep me for? Evidently he needs me. Well, consequently, I'm not afraid of him—let him fear me!

SHAPKIN. And doesn't he continually scold you?

KUDRYASH. How can he help scolding? He can't breathe without it. But I don't let him go on: he says a word and I say ten; he spits but clears out. No, I won't bow down to him any more.

KULIGIN. Is he a good example to copy! It's better to stand him.

KUDRYASH. Well, then, if you're so wise, teach him politeness first and then teach us! It's a pity that his daughters are small, not one of them grown up.

SHAPKIN. What'd happen then?

KUDRYASH. I'd do him a good turn! I'm a great fellow with the girls. [DIKOY *and* BORIS *pass by.* KULIGIN *takes off his hat.*]

SHAPKIN [to KUDRYASH]. Let's get out of the way; he'll keep it up. [*They go out.*]

SCENE II

[*The same.* DIKOY *and* BORIS.]
DIKOY. Did you come here to idle about? You lazy fellow, the devil take you!

BORIS. It's a holiday; what is there to do at home?

DIKOY. You can find something if you want to. If I've told you once I've told you twice: "Don't dare to come across my path." You're beyond words. Haven't you enough room? Wherever I go, there you are. Phew, you beast! Why do you stand there like a post? Am I talking to you or not?

BORIS. I'm listening. What more can I do?

DIKOY [*looking at* BORIS]. Get out! I don't want to talk to you, you Jesuit. [*Walking off.*] Always in the way!
[*He spits and goes out.*]

SCENE III

[KULIGIN, BORIS, KUDRYASH, *and* SHAPKIN.]
KULIGIN. What kind of business have you with him, sir? We don't understand it at all. You must like to live with him and stand his scolding.

BORIS. Why should I like it, Kuligin! I can't help it.

KULIGIN. Why so, sir, may I ask? If you can, sir, tell us about it.

BORIS. Why shouldn't I tell? Did you know my grandmother, Anfisa Mikhaylovna?

KULIGIN. Why, of course.

KUDRYASH. Of course.

BORIS. She took a dislike to my father because he married a noblewoman. On that account my father and mother lived in Moscow. Mother used to say that she couldn't live three days with father's people; they seemed so rough to her.

KULIGIN. Rough indeed! I should say so. One has to be used to it to stand it.

BORIS. Our parents educated us well in Moscow; they spared nothing for us. They sent me to the Academy of Commerce and my sister to a boarding school, but suddenly both died of the cholera and sister and I were left orphans. Then we heard that grandmother had died here and had provided in her will that uncle should give us our share when we were of age, on one condition.

KULIGIN. What condition, sir?

BORIS. That we should be respectful to him.

KULIGIN. That means, sir, that you will never see your inheritance.

BORIS. No, but that's not the whole story, Kuligin! First he'll begin to boss us; he'll abuse us in every way he pleases, and he'll end up just the same by giving us nothing or some trifle. And then he'll say he did it for charity, that even that was not *due* us.

KUDRYASH. That's the way the merchants here usually act. And then even if you were respectful to him, who's to prevent him from saying you weren't?

BORIS. Well, yes. Even now he says once in a while: "I've children of my own, why should I give money to other people's children? In that way I should impoverish my own family."

KULIGIN. That is to say, sir, your affairs are in bad shape.

BORIS. If it were only myself, it wouldn't matter! I should have thrown it up and left, but I'm sorry for my sister. He ordered her to come too, but my mother's folks wouldn't allow it; they wrote that she was ill. What kind of a life would she live here—it's dreadful to think of it.

KUDRYASH. Of course. Do they know anything at all about good breeding?

KULIGIN. What position do you hold in his establishment?

BORIS. None at all. "You may live in my house," he said, "and do what you are told. I'll arrange about your salary."

That means that within a year he will settle accounts with me as he sees fit.

KUDRYASH. That's his way. None of us ever dares to mention his salary, or he starts to storm at us with all his might. "How do you know what I am thinking about?" says he. "You can't read my mind. Perhaps I'll take a fancy to give you five thousand rubles." Just try to talk to him! Only in all his life never once has he taken such a fancy.

KULIGIN. What's to be done, sir! You must try to please him somehow.

BORIS. That's the trouble, Kuligin; it's entirely impossible to do it. Even his own people can't please him at all; how should I do so!

KUDRYASH. Who can please him when his whole life is nothing but one long quarrel? And it's mostly on money matters; not a single account can be settled without a row. Some are glad to give up their rights if he will only quiet down. It's a calamity when any one stirs him up in the morning! He picks on everybody the rest of the day.

BORIS. Every morning my aunt begs every one with tears in her eyes: "My friends, do not excite him! My dears, do not excite him!"

KUDRYASH. But you can't help yourself! He goes to the market and then all's over. He scolds at all the peasants. Even if they offer at a loss he won't leave without a row. And then he keeps it up all day.

SHAPKIN. In short he is a rowdy!

KUDRYASH. What a rowdy!

BORIS. And it's a calamity if some man whom he doesn't dare to berate offends him: then the people at the house have to look out for themselves!

KUDRYASH. O, how funny it was when a hussar scolded him on the ferry across the Volga. He did wonders.

BORIS. But how did the home folks fare? For two weeks after that everybody kept hiding in attics or closets.

KULIGIN. What's this? The people can't be leaving vespers? [*Several people pass by in the background.*]

KUDRYASH. Let's go and have a good time, Shapkin. What's the use of standing here? [*They bow and pass out.*]

BORIS. O, Kuligin, it's very hard for me here, for I'm not used to it. Everybody looks at me askance, as if I were in the way and disturbed them. I don't know the ways of the place. I know that these are all our native Russian ways, but nevertheless I can't grow used to them.

KULIGIN. And you never will grow accustomed to them, sir.

BORIS. Why?

KULIGIN. We have hard ways in our town, sir, hard ways! Among the townspeople, sir, you will see nothing but coarseness and stark poverty. And we can never break through the bark that binds us, sir; for by our honest labor we can never earn more than our daily bread. And the one who has money, sir, tries to enslave the poor in order to acquire still more money by their unrequited labor. Do you know how your uncle, Savel Prokofyich, answered the provost? The peasants came to the provost to complain that he would not pay a single one of them off. The provost began to talk to him. "Listen, Savel Prokofyich," he said, "pay the peasants in full! Every day they come to me with complaints!" Your uncle tapped the provost on the shoulder and said: "Is it worth our while, your Honor, to discuss such trifles? I employ numbers of those men every year: now you see, if I pay them off only a kopek short to each man, by that means I make thousands: so it's fine for me!" There it is, sir! And how they treat one another, sir! They seek to capture one another's trade, not so much from love of gain as from envy. They make war on each other; they entice into those tall mansions of theirs drunken clerks, such clerks, sir, as have not even the appearance of men—the human semblance is lost. And those fellows for a small consideration write malicious charges about their neighbors on stamped paper. And then begins a law suit between them, sir, and there's no end to the suffering. They sue and sue here, and then they carry the case to the provincial court; and there they are waiting for them and rubbing their hands with glee. "A tale is soon told but a case is not soon finished." They carry them on and on; they prolong them and prolong them; and they are even glad that it does drag on. That's just what they want. "I'll lose money," one says, "but it will cost him a kopek too!" I should have liked to put all that into verse——

BORIS. Do you know how to write verse?

KULIGIN. In the old style, sir. I have read Lomonosov and Derzhavin a great deal.—Lomonosov was clever, a student of natural science, but still he was of our class too, of the common people.

BORIS. You ought to have written it. It would have been interesting.

KULIGIN. How could I, sir? They would devour me, they would eat me alive. Even now, sir, I smart for my chatter; but I can't help it. I love to talk! I wanted to tell you about their family life, sir, but at some other time. It's worth hearing.

[FEKLUSHA *and another woman come in.*]

FEKLUSHA. Lovely, my dear, lovely! Wonderful beauty! How can one express it! You live in the promised land, and the merchants are all pious people, adorned with many virtues and generous and charitable! I am so well satisfied, my dear, completely satisfied! On account of their charity to us their goodness shall be increased to them, and especially to the house of the Kabanovs. [*Goes out.*]

BORIS. The Kabanovs?

KULIGIN. She is a hypocrite, sir! She gives freely to beggars, but has absolutely devoured her family. [*Pause.*] O, if I could only discover perpetual motion, sir!

BORIS. What should you do then?

KULIGIN. What, sir? Why, the English offer a million for it; I should use all the money for the good of society, for charity. The working classes need employment; there are hands to work, but there is nothing to do.

BORIS. And do you hope to discover perpetual motion?

KULIGIN. Certainly, sir! If I could only get a bit of money now for the models! Good-bye, sir! [*Goes out.*]

SCENE IV

[BORIS *alone.*]

BORIS. It would be a pity to disillusion him! What a fine man! He dreams and is happy, but I'm evidently doomed to waste my youth in this hole. I'm completely crushed already and still this nonsense creeps into my head! Well, what's the use? Am I in a condition for sentimentality? Exiled and down-trodden, yet I was fool enough to think of falling in love. And with whom? With a woman to whom I can never even manage to speak. [*A pause.*] And still the thought of her will not leave my head, no matter what I do. There she is. She is walking with her husband, and his mother is with them! What a fool I am! I'll have a peek at her from around a corner and then run along home. [*Goes out. From the opposite side* MADAM KABANOV, KABANOV, KATERINA, *and* VARVARA *come in.*]

SCENE V

[MADAM KABANOV, KABANOV, KATERINA, *and* VARVARA.]

MADAM KABANOV. If you wish to obey your mother, then when you arrive there do as I have bidden you.

KABANOV. But, mamma, how could I disobey you?

MADAM KABANOV. In these times old people are not much respected.

VARVARA [*aside*]. Much respect *you'll* get!

KABANOV. Why, mamma, I don't think that I ever act except as you wish.

MADAM KABANOV. I should believe you, my dear, if my own eyes had not seen and my own ears had not heard what sort of respect parents get from their children nowadays. You should remember how much mothers suffer from their children.

KABANOV. But, mamma, I——

MADAM KABANOV. If your mother has to speak harshly now and then on account of your uppishness I think you might be patient! What do you think about it?

KABANOV. But, mamma, when was I ever impatient with you?

MADAM KABANOV. Your mother is old and stupid, to be sure, but you young people must not expect too much from us old fools.

KABANOV [aside, with a sigh]. O heavens! [To his mother.] Why, mamma, do we ever dare to think of such a thing!

MADAM KABANOV. Parents are stern with you because of their love, they scold you because of their love, they are always hoping to teach you what is right. And that's not welcome in these days. And then the children go around saying to other people that their mother is a grumbler, that their mother won't allow them to take a step alone, that she makes their life wretched. And Heaven help us if some word or other doesn't happen to please the daughter-in-law! A rumor starts that the mother-in-law has eaten her up, flesh and bone.

KABANOV. Why, mamma, who ever talks about you?

MADAM KABANOV. I haven't heard them, my dear, I haven't heard them; I don't wish to lie. If I had heard them, my dear, I should not be talking like this. [She sighs.] O, what a sin! It is easy to go astray! A conversation touches the heart too closely, and you sin, you get angry. No, my dear, say what you please about me. No one can be kept from talking; if they don't dare to talk before your face they will behind your back.

KABANOV. May my tongue wither——

MADAM KABANOV. Stop, stop, don't swear; that's a sin. I have seen for a long while that your wife is dearer to you than your mother. Since you have been married I find that you have not your former love for me.

KABANOV. In what way do you see that, mamma?

MADAM KABANOV. In everything, my dear! What a mother cannot see with her eyes her heart tells her; she can feel things with her heart. Your wife may be leading you away from me—I am not sure yet.

KABANOV. No indeed, mamma, what are you saying?

KATERINA. As for me, mamma, I feel towards you just as if you were my own mother; and Tikhon loves you too.

MADAM KABANOV. You might keep still when you're not spoken to, I think. Don't interfere, woman. I won't hurt him— don't be afraid. You see, he's still my son; don't forget that! What struck you to flit before our eyes! To make people see how much you love your husband? We know it, we know it; you are always casting it in everybody's face.

VARVARA [to herself]. She's found a fine place to preach her sermon in.

KATERINA. You are wrong, mamma, in saying that about me. I am just the same alone as I am before other people, and I don't try to show off.

MADAM KABANOV. I didn't mean to talk about you; the words just slipped out.

KATERINA. Even if it was a slip—why do you wish to insult me?

MADAM KABANOV. What a fine lady! She's insulted right away.

KATERINA. Who likes to listen to false charges?

MADAM KABANOV. I know very well that my words do not please you, but what can I do about it? I am not an outsider and my heart aches on your account. I have seen for a long time that you want to have your own way. Well, wait a bit, you will have it; live in your own way when I am here no longer. Then you can do as you please, there will be no old people over you. But maybe you will remember me then.

KABANOV. But, mamma, we pray day and night for you, that God may give you health and happiness and prosperity.

MADAM KABANOV. Stop, please, that's enough. Perhaps you loved your mother when you were a bachelor: now you have no time for me; you have a young wife.

KABANOV. One thing does not hinder the other. My wife, of course, I care for, but I respect my mother just the same.

MADAM KABANOV. Then you would give up your wife for your mother? I can never believe that so long as I live.

KABANOV. But why do I have to give one up? I love them both.

MADAM KABANOV. Yes, yes, that's the way—spread it on thick! I know that I'm in the way.

KABANOV. Think what you please, have everything your own way; only I know that I am the most unhappy man ever born on earth, that I cannot possibly please you in any way.

MADAM KABANOV. Now you are pretending to be abused! What are you whining about? What kind of a husband are you? Take a look at yourself. Can your wife be afraid of you after that?

KABANOV. Why should she be afraid of me? It's enough for me that she loves me.

MADAM KABANOV. What—why should she be afraid of you! Have you lost your mind? If she's not afraid of you, she'll be still less afraid of me. What kind of order will there be in the house? It seems to me you are lawfully married to her—or doesn't the law mean anything to you? And if you have such silly ideas in your head, you had better not chatter about them before her at any rate, or before your sister, a young girl. She will marry some day, too, and if she listens to your nonsense her husband will have to thank you for the lesson later on. You see how much sense you have in your head, and yet you want to live independently.

KABANOV. No, mamma, I don't want to live independently. How could I do so?

MADAM KABANOV. Then you think you must be always tender to your wife? That you mustn't shout at her or threaten her?

KABANOV. But, mamma, I——

MADAM KABANOV [furiously]. Even if she has a lover! Well? And that would be of no consequence in your opinion, I suppose? Well, speak!

KABANOV. But, for God's sake, mamma.

MADAM KABANOV [quite calmly]. Fool! [She sighs.] What's the use of talking to a fool? It's only a sin. [A pause.] I'm going home.

KABANOV. We'll go right away too; we'll only take a turn or two on the boulevard.

MADAM KABANOV. Well, do as you please, only see that I don't have to wait for you! You know that I don't like that.

KABANOV. No, mamma! God forbid!

MADAM KABANOV. All right. [Goes out.]

SCENE VI

[The same, without MADAM KABANOV.]

KABANOV. There, you see, I'm always catching it from mamma, on your account. What a life!

KATERINA. How am I to blame?

KABANOV. I don't know who is to blame.

VARVARA. How could you know?

KABANOV. She kept always repeating: "Get married, get married; if I could only see you married!" And now she eats me up, she never lets me rest—all on your account.

VARVARA. How is she to blame! Mother pounces on her and on you too, and still you say you love your wife. I hate the sight of you. [She turns away.]

KABANOV. Well, tell me: what am I to do?

VARVARA. Play your part—keep still if you don't know any thing better to do. What are you standing shuffling like that for? I can see in your eye what you're thinking about.

KABANOV. Well, what is it?

VARVARA. It's very plain. You want to go to Savel Prokofyich's and have a drink with him. Isn't that so?

KABANOV. You've guessed right.

KATERINA. Hurry back, Tisha, or mother will begin to scold again.

VARVARA. Yes indeed, be quick or you know what you'll get.

KABANOV. How can I help knowing?

VARVARA. We're not very anxious to get a scolding on your account either.

KABANOV. I'll be back in a minute, wait for me. [Goes out.]

SCENE VII

[KATERINA and VARVARA.]

KATERINA. Are you sorry for me then, Varya?

VARVARA [looking to one side]. Of course I am.

KATERINA. Then you love me? [Kisses her eagerly.]

VARVARA. Why shouldn't I love you?

KATERINA. O, thank you! You're so good, I love you dearly. [A pause.] Do you know what came into my head?

VARVARA. What?

KATERINA. Why can't people fly?

VARVARA. I don't understand what you mean.

KATERINA. I tell you: I wonder why people can't fly like birds. You know, sometimes I imagine that I am a bird. When you stand on a hill, you just long to fly. You feel that you could take a run, raise your arms, and fly away. Do you want to try it now?

[She starts to run.]

VARVARA. What notions you get!

KATERINA [sighing]. I used to be so lively! I have shriveled up completely in your house.

VARVARA. Don't you think I can see that?

KATERINA. I was so different. I just lived and didn't worry about anything; I was like an uncaged bird. My mother was so fond of me; she dressed me up like a doll and never made me work; I used to do just as I pleased. Do you know how I used to live before I was married? I'll tell you all about it. I used to get up early. In summer I would go to the spring and bathe; I would carry back water and sprinkle all the flowers in the house. I had lots and lots of flowers. Then mamma and I would go to church, and the pilgrims too—our house used to be full of pilgrims and holy women When we came from church we would sit down to some work, usually gold thread on velvet, and the pilgrims would begin to tell about the places they had visited, what they had seen, and the lives of saints, or they would sing songs. So the time would pass till dinner. Then the older people would lie down to rest, and I would walk about the garden. Then I would go to vespers, and in the evening there would be more stories and songs. It was so nice!

VARVARA. But it is just the same at our house.

KATERINA. But everything here seems to be under restraint. I used to love dearly to go to church! It seemed as if I were in heaven. I could see no one, I didn't notice the time passing and I didn't hear all when the service ended. It seemed all to have happened in a second. Mamma said that every one used to look at me and wonder what was happening to me. And you know, on sunny days a shining column came down from the dome and in it smoke hovered like clouds and I seemed to see angels flying and singing in the column. Or else I would get up at night—we, too, used to have lamps burning everywhere at night—and I would go into some corner and pray till morning. Or early in the morning I would go into the garden when the sun was hardly up; I would fall on my knees and pray and weep, and I would not know myself why I prayed or why I wept—and so they would find me. And what I prayed about then, and what I asked for, I cannot imagine; I didn't need anything. I had enough of everything. And such dreams as I used to have, Varenka, wonderful dreams! of golden temples, or marvelous gardens where unseen voices would sing and cypress trees wafted forth their fragrance. And the mountains and trees were not the ordinary kind, but like those that are painted on the sacred images. Or I would fly and fly away through the air. And sometimes I dream now, but rarely, and then it is not the same.

VARVARA. Why?

KATERINA [*after a pause*]. I shall die soon.

VARVARA. Don't say that. What's the matter?

KATERINA. No, I'm sure that I am going to die. O, my dear, something evil is happening to me, something strange. I never was this way before. There is some strange feeling in my heart. It seems as if I were beginning to live again, or—I don't know.

VARVARA. What is the matter with you then?

KATERINA [*taking her by the hand*]. Varya, a misfortune will happen to some-one. I am so afraid, so afraid! I seem to stand on a precipice and some one is pushing me toward it, and I have nothing to hold to. [*She clutches her head with her hand.*]

VARVARA. What is the matter? Are you well?

KATERINA. Yes, I am well.—It would be better if I were ill—but something is wrong. Such a fancy keeps flitting through my head and I cannot escape from it. I begin to think and I cannot collect my thoughts; I try to pray and I cannot. I murmur words with my lips but my mind is on something else. The evil one seems to be whispering in my ear, whispering about something wicked. Then I imagine things that make me ashamed of myself. What is the matter with me? Some misfortune is going to happen! At night, Varya, I cannot sleep; I keep hear-ing that whisper in my dreams; some one speaks so caressingly to me, speaks en-dearingly like a cooing dove. I no longer dream those old dreams, Varya, about the trees of paradise and the mountains, but some one seems to embrace me, fiercely, fiercely, and he leads me somewhere and I follow him, follow——

VARVARA. And then?

KATERINA. But why am I talking like this to you? You are an unmarried girl.

VARVARA [*glancing around*]. Go on! I am worse than you are.

KATERINA. How can I tell you? I am ashamed.

VARVARA. Go on. You needn't be.

KATERINA. It becomes so oppressive at home, so oppressive that I could run away. And such ideas come to me that, if I were free, I would drift along the Volga now, in a boat, singing, or in a fine troika, embracing——

VARVARA. But not your husband.

KATERINA. How do you know?

VARVARA. How can I help knowing?

KATERINA. O, Varya, I have evil thoughts in my mind. How I have cried and struggled with myself, wretched girl that I am! But the temptation will not leave me. I cannot escape it. It is not right. It is a dreadful sin to love an-other than my husband, is it not, Varenka?

VARVARA. I cannot judge you! I have my own sins on my conscience.

KATERINA. What can I do? I am not strong enough. Where can I go? I shall kill myself from this suffering.

VARVARA. What are you saying? What is the matter? Wait, tomorrow brother will be going away and we will think of something; perhaps you can see each other.

KATERINA. No, no, we must not. What do you mean, what do you mean? God forbid!

VARVARA. What are you so afraid of?

KATERINA. If I see him even once I shall flee from the house and not return home for anything on earth.

VARVARA. Just wait, we'll see.

KATERINA. No, no, don't talk to me; I don't even want to listen.

VARVARA. Well, what is the pleasure in withering away here! Even if you die of despair, will any one pity you? Don't expect it. Why are you forced to torture yourself!

[*Enter an* OLD LADY *with a stick, followed by two lackeys in three-cornered hats.*]

Scene VIII

[*The same, and the* Old Lady.]

Lady. Well, my beauties! What are you doing here? Are you waiting for some young men, some gallants? Are you feeling happy? Are you? Does your beauty make you joyful? That is where beauty leads to. [*She points to the* Volga.] There, there into the deep flood. [Varvara *smiles.*] Why are you laughing? Don't feel joyful! [*She raps with her stick.*] All of you will burn in eternal fire. You will boil in the unquenchable pitch. [*Going out.*] That is where beauty leads to.   [*Goes out.*]

Scene IX

[Katerina *and* Varvara.]

Katerina. O, how she frightened me! I am trembling all over as if she had made me an evil prophecy.

Varvara. May it fall on your own head, you old hag!

Katerina. What was it she said? What did she say?

Varvara. It was all nonsense. There is no use listening to her chatter. She always raves like that. She has led a wicked life from her youth up. Ask any one what people say about her! And now she is afraid to die and she tries to frighten others with what she fears herself. Even the little boys in the town hide from her. She shakes her stick at them and shouts: [*Mocking the old woman.*] "You will all be burned in the fire!"

Katerina [*closing her eyes*]. O, be quiet! My heart has stopped beating.

Varvara. What is there to be afraid of? An old fool——

Katerina. But I am afraid. I am mortally afraid. She seems to be hovering before me all the time.   [*A pause.*]

Varvara [*looking around*]. I wonder why brother doesn't come. Here is a thunderstorm coming up.

Katerina [*terrified*]. A thunderstorm! Let's run home! Hurry!

Varvara. Have you gone crazy? How would you dare to show yourself at home without brother?

Katerina. No, no, let's run home, home! Never mind him!

Varvara. Why are you so afraid? That thunderstorm is still far away.

Katerina. If it's far off we can wait a little while, but really it would be better to go. We'd better go.

Varvara. Well, if anything is going to happen, you can't hide from it at home.

Katerina. Yes, but it's better, it's more comfortable; at home I can pray to God before the holy images.

Varvara. I didn't know that you were so afraid of a thunderstorm. I'm not afraid.

Katerina. How can you help being afraid, girl. Everyone must be afraid. It is not so dreadful that you may be killed, as that death may come suddenly and find you just as you are, with all your sins and with all your evil thoughts. I am not afraid to die, but when I think that I shall appear suddenly before God, just as I am here with you, after this conversation—that is what is so dreadful. What thoughts are in my mind! Such a sin! It is terrible to speak of it! [*A thunderclap.*] O! [Kabanov *comes in.*]

Varvara. There comes brother. [*To* Kabanov.] Hurry!   [*Thunder.*]

Katerina. O, hurry, hurry!

ACT II

A room in the Kabanovs' *house.*

Scene I

[Glasha *is gathering up the clothes into bundles;* Feklusha *comes in.*]

Feklusha. My dear girl, always at work! What are you doing, dear?

Glasha. I'm getting master ready to start.

Feklusha. Is he going away, our treasure?

Glasha. Yes, he's going away.

FEKLUSHA. For a long time, dearie?

GLASHA. No, not for very long.

FEKLUSHA. Well, a pleasant journey to him! And will his wife wail for him or not?

GLASHA. I don't know what to say about that.

FEKLUSHA. But she wails sometimes, doesn't she?

GLASHA. I've never heard her.

FEKLUSHA. I like awfully well to hear a woman who can wail finely! [A pause.] But you ought to look after that beggar woman, dearie, or she'll steal something.

GLASHA. Who can make you people out? You're always tattling on each other. Why can't you get along peacefully? You pilgrims don't fare badly at our house, but still you quarrel and wrangle. Are you not afraid of sinning?

FEKLUSHA. We can't live without sin since we live in this world. And I'll tell you what, dearie, you simple people have only one devil each to tempt you, but we pilgrims have, some of us, six; or some of us, twelve set over us, and we have to conquer them all. It's very hard, dearie.

GLASHA. Why have you so many?

FEKLUSHA. It's because the devil hates us for living such an upright life. But I'm not quarrelsome, dearie. I'm not guilty of that sin. I have one sin, to be sure, but I know myself what it is. I love dainty eating. Well, what of it? God sends me food according to my weakness.

GLASHA. And have you traveled far, Feklusha?

FEKLUSHA. No, dearie, I haven't gone far because of my weakness, but I have heard a lot. They say that there are countries, dearie, where the tsars are not orthodox, and sultans govern those lands. In one country the Turkish sultan, Mahmud, sits on a throne, and in another the Persian sultan, Mahmud; and they pass judgments, dearie, on all the people, and everything that they decree is unjust. And they cannot judge a single thing rightly, dearie—such limits has God set for them. We have just laws, but theirs, dearie, are unjust. What comes out one way under our laws comes out just the opposite way under theirs. And all the judges in those countries are corrupt too; so, dearie, when people send them petitions they write: "Judge me, thou corrupt judge." And then there is another land where all the people have dog's heads.

GLASHA. Why do they have dog's heads?

FEKLUSHA. Because they are infidels. I am going to visit the merchant folk, dearie, to see if they won't give me something to aid my poverty. Good-bye for now.

GLASHA. Good-bye. [FEKLUSHA goes out.] What countries there are! What wonderful, wonderful things there are in the world! And here we sit, knowing nothing about it. But still it is a fine thing that there are good people, so that you can hear what is happening out in the world: otherwise we should die fools.

[KATERINA and VARVARA come in.]

SCENE II

[KATERINA and VARVARA.]

VARVARA [to GLASHA]. Take the bundles to the cart; the horses have come. [To KATERINA.] They married you off too young; you never had a chance for a good time when you were a girl, so your heart hasn't calmed down yet. [GLASHA goes out.]

KATERINA. And it never will calm down.

VARVARA. Why not?

KATERINA. I was born so—with such a disposition! Do you know what I did when I was only six years old? Some one at home had hurt my feelings—it was in the evening and already dark. I ran out to the Volga, climbed into a boat and pushed it off from the shore. The next morning they found me seven miles away!

VARVARA. Did the young men ever notice you?

KATERINA. Of course they did.

VARVARA. But how about yourself? Didn't you care for any one?

KATERINA. No, I just laughed at them.

VARVARA. But, Katya, you don't love Tikhon.

KATERINA. Of course I do! I'm very sorry for him.

VARVARA. No, you don't love him. If you're sorry for him, then you don't love him. And there's no reason why you should, to tell the truth. And there's no use of your hiding it from me! I've noticed for a long while that you're in love with a certain man.

KATERINA. How did you notice that?

VARVARA. How funny you are! Am I a child? This is the first sign: when you see him, the expression of your face changes. [KATERINA *drops her eyes.*] And that's not all——

KATERINA [*with her eyes lowered*]. Well, who is he?

VARVARA. But you know yourself. Why should I say his name?

KATERINA. No, say it! What is his name?

VARVARA. Boris Grigoryich.

KATERINA. Yes, Varenka, yes, it is he. Only Varenka, for Heaven's sake——

VARVARA. O, don't worry! Only take care not to betray yourself.

KATERINA. I don't know how to deceive, or how to hide anything.

VARVARA. Well, but you can't get along without it; remember where you're living. In this house deceit is our rule of action. I didn't use to be a liar either, but I learned how when I had to. Last night I went out strolling, so I saw him and talked with him.

KATERINA [*after a long silence, her eyes lowered*]. Well, what then?

VARVARA. He told me to give you his regards. He says it's too bad you can't see each other anywhere.

KATERINA [*lowering her eyes still more*]. Where could we see each other? And what for?

VARVARA. He is so melancholy.

KATERINA. Don't talk about him to me, please don't. I don't want even to know him! I shall love my husband. Tisha, my darling, I will not change you for any one! I don't want to think about it, and you have upset me.

VARVARA. Well, don't think about it; who's forcing you?

KATERINA. You are not a bit sorry for me! You say, "Don't think about him," and then you remind me yourself. I don't want to think of him, but what can I do if the idea won't leave me. No matter what I think about, he stands before my eyes. I try to restrain myself but I can't do it at all. Do you know, last night the devil tempted me again? I almost left the house.

VARVARA. You are queer, on my word! For my part I believe in doing as you please, so long as no one finds it out.

KATERINA. I don't want to act that way. What's the use? I'd rather endure as long as I can.

VARVARA. But when you can't stand it what will you do?

KATERINA. What shall I do?

VARVARA. Yes, what will you do?

KATERINA. Whatever I take a fancy to.

VARVARA. Well, do it, just try it; and they will fairly eat you alive.

KATERINA. What do I care! I'll go away; that's the last they'll see of me.

VARVARA. Where will you go? You're a married woman.

KATERINA. Ah, Varya, you don't understand my character! Of course, Heaven forbid that it should happen! But when it becomes too wearisome for me here, then they won't be able to keep me here by any force. I'll jump out of the window and throw myself into the Volga. If I don't wish to live here, then I won't stay, though you cut my throat! [*Pause.*]

VARVARA. Do you know what we'll do, Katya? When Tikhon goes, we'll sleep in the garden, in the summer house.

KATERINA. What for, Varya?

VARVARA. Well, won't that be all right?

KATERINA. I'm afraid to sleep in a strange place.

VARVARA. What are you afraid of! Glasha will be with us.

KATERINA. All the same I'm scared! But maybe I will.

VARVARA. I wouldn't ask you, only mamma won't let me go alone, and I need to.

KATERINA [looking at her]. Why do you need to?

VARVARA [laughs]. We'll tell each other's fortunes there.

KATERINA. You must be joking.

VARVARA. Of course I am; did you think I meant it?   [A pause.]

KATERINA. Where is that Tikhon?

VARVARA. What do you want him for?

KATERINA. I just want to see him. He's going away soon.

VARVARA. He's closeted with mamma. She's wearing him down as the rust eats into iron.

KATERINA. What for?

VARVARA. For nothing at all: she's giving him a lesson. He'll be away two weeks on the road, out of her sight! Just think! Her heart is breaking because he is going off to do as he pleases! Now she's giving him her orders, one worse than the other; and she will lead him to the holy image and make him swear that he will do just as he has been told.

KATERINA. Even when he is free he is tied.

VARVARA. Much he's tied! As soon as he gets away he'll begin to drink. He's listening now and thinking to himself how he can break away as soon as possible.

[Enter KABANOV and MADAM KABANOV.]

SCENE III

[The same. KABANOV and MADAM KABANOV.]

MADAM KABANOV. Well, do you remember everything that I've told you?

Look out now, don't forget! Tie a string round your finger.

KABANOV. I remember it, mamma.

MADAM KABANOV. Well, now everything is ready. The horses have come. Say good-bye, and God be with you!

KABANOV. Yes, mamma, it's time to go.

MADAM KABANOV. Well!

KABANOV. What do you wish?

MADAM KABANOV. What are you standing there like that for? Don't you know how to act? Tell your wife how to behave when you are gone.

[KATERINA has dropped her eyes.]

KABANOV. O, I suppose she knows that herself.

MADAM KABANOV. Don't answer back! Give your orders so that I can hear what you say! Then when you come back you will ask whether she carried them all out.

KABANOV [standing in front of KATERINA]. Obey mamma, Katya.

MADAM KABANOV. Tell her not to be rude to her mother-in-law.

KABANOV. Don't be rude!

MADAM KABANOV. Tell her to respect her mother-in-law as her own mother.

KABANOV. Respect my mother, Katya, as your own mother.

MADAM KABANOV. Tell her not to sit with her arms folded, like a lady.

KABANOV. Keep busy while I'm gone.

MADAM KABANOV. Tell her not to gaze out of the windows.

KABANOV. But, mamma, when has she ever——

MADAM KABANOV. Come, come!

KABANOV. Don't gaze out of the windows.

MADAM KABANOV. Tell her not to look at the young men when you are gone.

KABANOV. But mamma, for Heaven's sake!

MADAM KABANOV [sternly]. It's no use making a fuss! You must do as your mother says. [With a smile.] It's always better to have your orders given.

KABANOV [confused]. Don't look at the young men.

[KATERINA looks at him sternly.]

MADAM KABANOV. Now you can talk together if you need to. Let's go, Varvara. [Both go out.]

SCENE IV

[KABANOV and KATERINA, who stands as if petrified.]

KABANOV. Katya! [A pause.] Katya, you're not angry with me, are you?

KATERINA [after a short pause, shaking her head]. No!

KABANOV. Why do you act like that? Come, forgive me!

KATERINA [still in the same condition, slightly shaking her head]. Bother you! [Covering her face with her hand.] She insulted me!

KABANOV. If you take everything to heart, you'll soon fall into consumption. What's the use of listening to her! She just has to say something! So let her talk; let it go in at one ear and out of the other. Well, good-bye, Katya!

KATERINA [throwing herself on her husband's neck]. Tisha, don't go away. For God's sake, don't go. Darling, I beg you.

KABANOV. That's impossible, Katya. If mamma sends me, how can I help going?

KATERINA. Well, then take me with you; take me!

KABANOV [freeing himself from her embrace]. That's impossible!

KATERINA. Why is it impossible, Tisha?

KABANOV. I should have a fine time going with you! You people have worn me out completely here. All I think of is how to get away, and you keep hanging on my neck.

KATERINA. Can you have ceased to love me?

KABANOV. No, I have not; but to escape such slavery a man would run away from the most beautiful of wives. Just think: no matter what sort of a fellow I am, still I am a man; and rather than spend his whole life in the way you see I do, anybody would run away, even from his wife. Now when I know that for two weeks I shall have no threats hanging over my head and no chains on my legs, what do I care for my wife?

KATERINA. How can I love you when you use such words?

KABANOV. Those words will do! How else should I talk? I can't understand what you're afraid of! You won't be alone, you know, you'll stay with mamma.

KATERINA. Don't mention her to me, don't torture my heart. O dear, O dear. [She cries.] Where can I go, unfortunate woman that I am? Who can I turn to? O God, I am lost!

KABANOV. Stop.

KATERINA [walks over to her husband and leans against him]. Tisha, dear, if you would stay or if you would take me with you, how I should love you, how I should pet you, my dear one. [Caressing him.]

KABANOV. I can't understand you, Katya. One time I can't get a word out of you, to say nothing of a caress, and another you come of your own accord.

KATERINA. Tisha, who are you leaving me to? There will be misfortune if you go; indeed there will.

KABANOV. Well, I can't take you, so there is nothing to be done.

KATERINA. Well, then, require a solemn oath from me.

KABANOV. What sort of oath?

KATERINA. Like this: that I should not dare, under any pretext, to speak to any stranger in your absence, nor to see any one, nor dare to think of any one but you.

KABANOV. But what for?

KATERINA. Calm my soul, do this favor for me!

KABANOV. How can you answer for yourself; any sort of fancy may come to you.

KATERINA [falling on her knees]. That should not see even my father or mother; that I may die without repentance if I——

KABANOV [*raising her up*]. What do you mean! What do you mean! That is a sin. I do not even want to hear such things! [*The voice of* MADAM KABANOV *is heard:* It is time, Tikhon! MADAM KABANOV, VARVARA *and* GLASHA *come in.*]

SCENE V

[*The same.* MADAM KABANOV, VARVARA *and* GLASHA.]
MADAM KABANOV. Well, Tikhon, it is time to go! God be with you! [*She sits down.*] Sit down, all of you. [*They all sit down. Pause.*] Well, good-bye. [*She rises, and they all rise.*]
KABANOV [*going to his mother*]. Good-bye, mamma!
MADAM KABANOV [*pointing to the floor*]. Bow down to my feet! [KABANOV *does so, then kisses his mother.*] Say good-bye to your wife.
KABANOV. Good-bye, Katya! [KATERINA *throws herself on his neck.*]
MADAM KABANOV. Why do you hang on his neck, you shameless woman! You are not saying good-bye to a lover. He is your husband, your master! Don't you know how to behave? Bow down to his feet. [KATERINA *does so.*]
KABANOV. Good-bye, sister! [*He kisses* VARVARA.] Good-bye, Glasha! [*He kisses* GLASHA.] Good-bye, mamma. [*He bows.*]
MADAM KABANOV. Good-bye! Long farewells make useless tears.
[KABANOV *goes out, after him* KATERINA, VARVARA *and* GLASHA.]

SCENE VI

[MADAM KABANOV *alone.*]
MADAM KABANOV. That's what it means to be young. It is funny just to watch them. If it were not your own family, you could laugh your fill. They don't know anything, they don't know how to act, not even how to say good-bye. It is a good thing when there are old people in the house; the home is upheld by them, while they are alive. But then the stupid things want their own way; and when they get it they go astray and bring good people into disgrace and ridicule. Of course, there are some who have compassion for them, but most people just laugh. Why, you can't help laughing. They invite guests and don't know how to seat them, and they even forget one of their own relatives. It is so ridiculous. And so the old customs are forgotten. You even hate to enter some houses; and if you do, you spit, and clear out as soon as possible. I don't know what will happen when the old people die, or how the world will go round. Well, it is a good thing that I shan't see it.

[KATERINA *and* VARVARA *come in.*]

SCENE VII

[MADAM KABANOV, KATERINA, *and* VARVARA.]
MADAM KABANOV. You used to boast that you loved your husband dearly; and I can see now how much you love him. Any other good wife who had just said farewell to her husband would wail for an hour and a half, lying on the porch. But you don't care at all, I see.
KATERINA. There's no use in it! And I don't know how. Why should I make people laugh!
MADAM KABANOV. It's not very difficult. You would have learned how if you loved him. If you don't know how to behave properly, you might have made a pretence of it; that would be more decent, anyhow: but it's quite plain that your love is only empty words. I'm going to say my prayers; don't disturb me.
VARVARA. I'm going out.
MADAM KABANOV [*affectionately*]. I don't care. Go on. Have a good time till your turn comes. You will have to sit at home enough then. [MADAM KABANOV *and* VARVARA *go out.*]

Scene VIII

[KATERINA *alone, meditating.*]
KATERINA. Well, now quiet will reign in our house. Ah, what weariness! If there were only some children! What a sorrow! I have no children; I would sit with them all the time and amuse them. I dearly love to talk with children; they are angels. [*Pause.*] If I had died when I was little it would have been better; then I should have looked down from heaven upon earth and rejoiced at everything. Or I should have flown around invisible wherever I chose; I should have flown over the fields from cornflower to cornflower on the breeze, like a butterfly. [*Meditating.*] I know what I will do; I will make a vow to do a piece of work; I will go to the shops and buy some linen; I will make it into clothes and then give it to the poor. They will pray for me. I will sit and sew with Varvara and we shall not notice how the time passes, and then Tisha will come back.

[VARVARA *comes in.*]

Scene IX

[KATERINA *and* VARVARA.]
VARVARA [*tying a kerchief on her head before the glass*]. I'm going out now, but Glasha will make our beds in the garden; mamma has agreed. In the garden, beyond the raspberry bushes, there is a gate that mamma locks and then hides the key. I've taken it and put another in its place so she won't notice it. Here it is; perhaps you may need it. [*She gives her the key.*] If I see him I'll tell him to come to the gate.
KATERINA [*frightened, thrusting away the key*]. What for? What for? I don't need it! I don't need it!
VARVARA. If you don't need it I shall; take it, it won't bite you.
KATERINA. What have you planned, you temptress! Is it possible? Did you think that I would— What do you mean? What do you mean?

VARVARA. Well, I don't like to discuss things forever, and I can't stop. It's time for me to go out walking. [*She leaves.*]

Scene X

[KATERINA, *alone, holding the key in her hands.*]
KATERINA. What is she doing? What is she plotting? O, she is insane, quite insane! This means ruin, it does! I ought to throw it away, to throw it far off, into the river, where it would never be found! It burns my hands like a live coal! [*After a moment's thought.*] This is how we women are lost. Who likes to live in bondage? All sorts of ideas come into one's head. An occasion presents itself, and one is glad and makes a headlong plunge. But how can one do so without thinking or considering! It's easy to fall into sin! But once done, you weep about it a whole lifetime in torment; and your bondage will seem still more bitter. [*Pause.*] Bondage is bitter, how bitter it is! Who would not weep over it! And most of all, we women. Take me for instance! I live and suffer and see no escape! And I shall not see any, I know that! The farther I go the worse it will be. And now, besides, this sin is upon me. [*Reflecting.*] If it were not for my mother-in-law! She ias ruined me—the house has grown loathsome to me on her account; even the walls are hateful to me. [*She looks thoughtfully at the key.*] Shall I throw it away? Of course, I must. Why did it fall into my hands? To tempt me, to ruin me? [*She listens.*] Someone is coming—my heart almost stopped beating. [*She hides the key in her pocket.*] No, there is no one! Why was I so frightened? And I hid the key. Well, that is where it belongs! Evidently fate so decrees. What sin will it be for me to look at him just once, from a distance? Even if I talk to him, there's really no harm in that! But what did I swear to my husband? But he didn't

want me to, himself. Perhaps a chance like this won't come again in my whole life. Then I shall reproach myself: "You had a chance but you weren't clever enough to take advantage of it." What am I saying? Why am I deceiving myself? Even if I die, I will see him. Who am I pretending to? Shall I throw away the key! No, not for anything on earth! It is mine now.—Come what may, I shall see Boris! O, if night would only come soon!

ACT III

TABLEAU I

A street. The gate of the KABANOVS' *house; a bench stands in front of the gate.*

SCENE I

[MADAM KABANOV *and* FEKLUSHA *are sitting on the bench.*]

FEKLUSHA. It's the end of the world, my dear Marfa Ignatyevna, the end of the world, according to all the signs. In your town there is still heavenly quiet, but in other towns it is simply like Sodom, my dear; such a noise, running about, and ceaseless coming and going. The people rush about so; one goes here and another there.

MADAM KABANOV. There is no need for us to rush about, dear; we live quietly.

FEKLUSHA. No, mother, you have quiet in town because many people, you for example, are adorned with virtues as if with flowers; because of this everything is done calmly and in good order. What does that rushing about signify, mother? Vanity, it is plain. In Moscow, for example, the people rush back and forth, no one knows why. That is nothing but vanity. They are a vain people, my dear Marfa Ignatyevna; that is why they run about. One of them imagines that he is going about his business; the poor man hurries on, he does not recognise people.

He fancies that someone is beckoning to him, but when he gets to the place it is empty; no one is there, and it is only a dream. So he goes away in sadness. Another fancies that he is overtaking an acquaintance. A sensible person could see with half an eye that no one is there; but the dreamer in his vanity thinks that he is overtaking someone. Vanity is really a sort of haze. Here people rarely even come outside their gates to sit a while on a beautiful evening like this, but in Moscow now there are promenades and amusements, the streets are noisy, groans are heard. What do you think, Mother Marfa Ignatyevna; they have begun to harness up the fiery dragon, all for the sake of haste!

MADAM KABANOV. I have heard of that, dearie.

FEKLUSHA. But I have seen it with my own eyes, mother. Of course some others do not see anything, on account of their vanity. They imagine it is an engine, and even call it an engine, but I have seen how it does like this with its feet. [*She spreads her fingers apart.*] Yes and it utters groans which people of holy lives can hear.

MADAM KABANOV. You can call it anything, an engine, if you like; people are stupid, they will believe anything. But if you showered me with gold I would not ride in one.

FEKLUSHA. What's to make you, mother! God preserve you from such a misfortune. And then, my dear Marfa Ignatyevna, I had a vision in Moscow. I was going along early in the morning —it was hardly light yet—when I saw someone with a black face standing on the roof of a tall, tall house. You know yourself who it was. He made a gesture with his hands as if he were sprinkling something, but nothing was sprinkled. Then I guessed that he was sowing tares, and the people during the day, in their vanity, would invisibly gather them. That is why they rush about so, that is why their women are so thin, their bodies do not fatten up at all. It seems as if they had lost something or were looking for something; their faces are so sad it is pitiful.

MADAM KABANOV. It's quite possible, my dear. In our times one can't be surprised at anything.

FEKLUSHA. These are hard times, my dear Marfa Ignatyevna, very hard, and the times are growing shorter.

MADAM KABANOV. What do you mean by shorter, my dear?

. FEKLUSHA. Of course we do not notice it in our bustle; how could we? But wise men notice that our times are growing shorter. Formerly summer and winter lasted a long, long time: you thought they would never end; but nowadays you do not notice it, they fly so. The days and hours seem to have stayed the same length, but on account of our sins the time is becoming shorter and shorter. That is what wise men say.

MADAM KABANOV. And it is going to be worse than this, dearie.

FEKLUSHA. If only we may not live to see it!

MADAM KABANOV. Perhaps we shall live to see it.

[*Enter* DIKOY.]

SCENE II

[*The same and* DIKOY.]

MADAM KABANOV. Why are you wandering about so late, my friend?

DIKOY. Who's going to stop me?

MADAM KABANOV. Who can stop you? Who needs to?

DIKOY. Well, then there's no use talking. Am I under anybody's orders? Why are you here? What the devil are you up to?

MADAM KABANOV. Well, don't yell so loud! Find someone easier than I am, I'm better than you. Find your way home. Come, Feklusha, let's go in. [*She rises.*]

DIKOY. Wait a minute, my friend! Don't get angry! You'll get home all

right yet; your house isn't beyond the mountains. There it is.

MADAM KABANOV. If you've come on business, don't yell, but talk sense.

DIKOY. I haven't come on business, but I'm drunk; that's all!

MADAM KABANOV. Well, now, do you want me to praise you for that?

DIKOY. I don't want praise or blame, but I'm just drunk; that's all there is to it. Until I sleep it off the thing can't be mended.

MADAM KABANOV. Then go along and sleep.

DIKOY. Where shall I go?

MADAM KABANOV. Go home; where else?

DIKOY. And what if I don't want to go home?

MADAM KABANOV. Why not, may I ask?

DIKOY. Because there is a fight on at my house.

MADAM KABANOV. Who is there to fight? You are the only fighter there.

DIKOY. Well, suppose I am; what of it?

MADAM KABANOV. What? Nothing. But it's no great honor that you've been fighting women all your life. That's what!

DIKOY. Well, then they ought to submit to me. Would you have me submit?

MADAM KABANOV. I'm mightily surprised at you; of all those people in your house not one can please you.

DIKOY. O rubbish!

MADAM KABANOV. Well, what do you want of me?

DIKOY. Just this: I want you to talk me down so that my anger may pass off. You are the only one in town who knows how to talk me down.

MADAM KABANOV. Feklusha, go and order something for us to eat. [FEKLUSHA *goes out.*] Let's go inside.

DIKOY. No, I won't go in; I'm worse inside.

MADAM KABANOV. What made you angry?

DIKOY. Ever since morning I've been so.

MADAM KABANOV. Some one must have asked you for money.

DIKOY. They seem to have planned it, the rascals; first one and then another has been pressing me the whole day long.

MADAM KABANOV. They must deserve it if they are pressing you.

DIKOY. I know that, but what do you want me to do with myself when I have such a disposition! I know that I must pay, but I can't do it with good grace. You are my friend, for instance, and I must pay you; but if you come and ask for money I'll abuse you. I'll pay all right, but I'll abuse you. Because if you only mention money to me my blood begins to boil; my blood fairly boils, that's all. Well, at such a time I'd abuse a man for nothing at all.

MADAM KABANOV. You have no older people over you, that's why you bluster.

DIKOY. No, my friend, keep still! Listen, this is what has often happened to me. In Lent I was fasting and the Devil brought a poor peasant across my path; he came for money for hauling wood; and he happened to come in an evil hour. I sinned; I berated him till you couldn't ask for anything better; I almost beat him. That's what kind of a disposition I have. Afterwards I begged his pardon. I got down on my knees; honest I did. I'm telling you the truth. I got down on my knees to a peasant. That's what my disposition leads me to: there in the courtyard, in the mud I got down on my knees to him before everybody.

MADAM KABANOV. And why do you work yourself up on purpose? That's not a good thing, my friend.

DIKOY. Why do you say "on purpose"?

MADAM KABANOV. I've seen it. I know why. When you see that they want to ask you for something, you purposely fall upon one of your people so that you may get angry, for you know that no one will go near you when you are angry. That's how it is, my friend.

DIKOY. Well, what of it? Every one hates to part with his property!

[GLASHA comes in.]

GLASHA. Marfa Ignatyevna, the lunch is ready, please.

MADAM KABANOV. Come in, friend! Have a bite of what God has given us!

DIKOY. Very well.

MADAM KABANOV. Please come in. [She shows DIKOY out and follows him. GLASHA folds her arms and stands by the gate.]

GLASHA. There comes Boris Grigoryich. I suppose he's after his uncle. Or is he just strolling? He must be taking a walk.

[BORIS comes in.]

SCENE III

[GLASHA, BORIS; later KULIGIN.]

BORIS. Is my uncle here?

GLASHA. Yes, he is here. Do you want him?

BORIS. They sent me from our house to find out where he was: but if he's here, let him stay; nobody wants him around. At home they're awfully glad he went out.

GLASHA. Our mistress should be his housewife; she'd soon finish him. Why am I standing here with you, like a fool! Good-bye! [Goes out.]

BORIS. O, Heavens, if I could only catch a single glimpse of her! I cannot go into the house: nobody calls here unless he's invited. Such a life! We live in the same town, almost side by side, but we see each other about once a week— and then in church or on the road; that's all! In this town a woman who is married might as well be buried. [Pause.] Not to see her any more at all—that would be easier to bear! As it is, I see her only now and then; and in company

at that, with a hundred eyes looking on.
My heart is just breaking; I can't reconcile myself. I start out for a walk and always find myself here by her gate. Why do I come here? It is impossible ever to see her, and then if talk should happen to be stirred up it would do her harm. Well, what a place I have struck! [*He walks away.* KULIGIN *comes towards him.*]
KULIGIN. What are you doing, sir? Taking a walk?
BORIS. Yes, I am taking a walk: the weather is very fine today.
KULIGIN. It is a very fine time to walk now, sir. It is so serene, the fresh air is scented with flowers from the meadows beyond the Volga:

Above us there extends the starry sky:
The stars uncounted, infinite the abyss.

Let us go on the boulevard, sir; there's not a soul there.
BORIS. All right, let's go.
KULIGIN. This is the kind of town we have, sir: they have built a boulevard and will not walk on it. They take walks only on holidays and then they are only pretending, for they just come to display their clothes. Now you will meet only a drunken clerk reeling home from the tavern. The poor people have no time to take walks, sir; they have to work day and night; they get only three hours sleep out of twenty-four. And what do the rich people do? Why shouldn't they walk about and breathe the fresh air? No, all their gates have been bolted long ago and their dogs let loose. Perhaps you think they are busy, or at their prayers? Not at all, sir— and their doors are not locked against thieves, but so that people may not see how they abuse their households and tyrannise over their families. How many tears are shed behind those bolts, unseen and unheard! But why should I tell you about it, sir? You can judge by your own case. And what depravity and drunkenness flourish behind those locks!

And everything on the sly, so that no one should see or know of it—God alone sees it. "You may look at me in company or on the street," they say, "but my family is no concern of yours. That's why I have locks and bolts and fierce dogs. The family," they say, "is a mysterious thing, a secret!" We know these secrets! These secrets, sir, are pleasant to him alone, but he makes the rest of his people howl like wolves. And what kind of a secret? Who does not know it? To cheat orphans, relatives, nephews, to bully the household so that they do not dare to mention the things he does there. That's the whole secret. Well, let them be. Do you know, sir, who take walks here? The young men and girls. They steal an hour or two from sleep and walk about in couples. There's a couple now.

[KUDRYASH *and* VARVARA *appear. They are kissing each other.*]
BORIS. They are kissing each other!
KULIGIN. That doesn't concern us.
[KUDRYASH *goes out.* VARVARA *goes to her gate and beckons to* BORIS. *He approaches her.*]

SCENE IV

[BORIS, KULIGIN, VARVARA.]
KULIGIN. I'm going to the boulevard, sir. Why should I disturb you? I'll wait there.
BORIS. All right. I'll come right away.
[KULIGIN *goes out.*]
VARVARA [*covering her face with her kerchief*]. Do you know the ravine behind the Kabanovs' garden?
BORIS. Yes.
VARVARA. Come there later on.
BORIS. Why?
VARVARA. You're stupid! Come and you'll find out. Well, now hurry, they're waiting for you. [BORIS *goes out.*] He didn't recognise me. Let him guess now. But I know that Katerina cannot contain herself; she'll slip out. [*She goes out through the gate.*]

TABLEAU II

Night. A ravine overgrown with bushes; above, the fence of the KABANOVS' *garden and the wicket gate: a foot-path leads down from above.*

SCENE I

[KUDRYASH *comes in with his guitar.*]
KUDRYASH. Nobody is here. What can she be doing over there! Well—I'll sit and wait. [*He seats himself on a stone.*] Well, I'll sing a song to pass the time away. [*He sings.*]

The Don Cossack led his horse to drink,
By the gate stood the youth and began to think,
By the gate he stood and his thoughts were rife,
For he pondered how he should kill his wife.
The wife her husband did entreat,
She kneeled down low at his swift feet,
"Thou, little father, my heart's delight!
Kill me not, not too soon, tonight!
Kill me, I pray thee, at midnight,
And let my little children sleep,
Our nearby neighbors their slumbers keep!"

[BORIS *comes in.*]

SCENE II

[KUDRYASH *and* BORIS.]
KUDRYASH [*stops singing*]. Aha! You're tame and peaceful, but you've come out to have a good time too.
BORIS. Is that you, Kudryash?
KUDRYASH. Yes, Boris Grigoryich.
BORIS. Why are you here?
KUDRYASH. I? I must need to be here, Boris Grigoryich, if I am here. I didn't come without any purpose. Where's God taking you?
BORIS [*looking the place over*]. I'll tell you, Kudryash: I have to stay here, but I think it will be all the same to you, if you go to another place.
KUDRYASH. No, Boris Grigoryich, you are here for the first time, I see, but I have a familiar seat here and my feet have worn the path to this spot. I am fond of you, sir, and am ready to do you any service; but don't meet me on this path at night, or, which Heaven forbid! —there will be trouble for you. It pays to have an understanding.
BORIS. What's the matter with you, Vanya?
KUDRYASH. What? Vanya! I know I'm Vanya. But you go your own way, that's all. Get a girl of your own and go walking with her, and no one will have anything to say. But don't meddle with another fellow's. That's not our style; if you do the young men will break your legs. On my girl's account I would do—I don't know what! I'll break your neck.
BORIS. You are getting angry for nothing at all; I'm not thinking of depriving you of anything. I shouldn't have come here if I hadn't been bidden.
KUDRYASH. Who bade you come?
BORIS. I couldn't make out; it was dark. Some girl stopped me on the street and told me to come right here, behind the Kabanovs' garden, where the path is.
KUDRYASH. What girl could it be?
BORIS. Listen, Kudryash. Can I speak frankly to you? You will not spread the news?
KUDRYASH. Speak out, don't be afraid! I'm as close-mouthed as a dead man.
BORIS. I don't know anything about things here, your customs or habits; but this is the affair——
KUDRYASH. You've fallen in love with some one?
BORIS. Yes, Kudryash.
KUDRYASH. Well, that's all right. We are quite free on that point. The girls go out as they please and their fathers and mothers don't care. Only the married women are shut in.
BORIS. That's just my trouble.

KUDRYASH. You surely haven't fallen in love with a married woman?

BORIS. Yes, with a married woman, Kudryash.

KUDRYASH. Ah, Boris Grigoryich, you must give her up.

BORIS. It's easy to say, give her up! Perhaps it would be the same to you; you would give up one and find another. But I can't do that! If I have fallen in love——

KUDRYASH. That means, then, that you just want to ruin her, Boris Grigoryich!

BORIS. God forbid. God preserve me! No, Kudryash, how could I? I don't want to ruin her! I only want to see her somewhere, nothing more than that.

KUDRYASH. How can you answer for yourself, sir? You know what kind of people there are here! You know yourself. They will eat her alive; they will nail her in a coffin.

BORIS. Do not say that, Kudryash! Do not frighten me, please!

KUDRYASH. Does she love you?

BORIS. I don't know.

KUDRYASH. Have you ever spoken with her?

BORIS. I have only been at her house once, along with uncle. But I see her in church, and we meet on the boulevard. Ah, Kudryash, if you could see how she prays. She has such an angelic smile, and her face seems to be radiant.

KUDRYASH. It is the young Mme. Kabanov, isn't it?

BORIS. Yes, Kudryash.

KUDRYASH. Ah, that is it! Well, I have the honor to congratulate you.

BORIS. Why?

KUDRYASH. Why, your affair must be going nicely if they told you to come here.

BORIS. It couldn't have been she who told me?

KUDRYASH. Then who was it?

BORIS. No, you're joking. That is impossible. [He clasps his forehead.]

KUDRYASH. What's the matter?

BORIS. I shall go mad for joy.

KUDRYASH. Oho, there is something to go mad about. Only look out not to make trouble for yourself and not to cause her misery. Even if her husband is a fool, her mother-in-law is a terrible woman.

[VARVARA comes in through the gate.]

SCENE III

[The same and VARVARA; later, KATERINA.]

VARVARA [sings by the gate]. Beyond the swift river my Vanya is strolling; There my dear Vanya is strolling . . .

KUDRYASH [continues]. "He buys his wares." [He whistles.]

VARVARA [comes down the path and, covering her face with a kerchief, walks up to BORIS]. Wait a while, my boy. You will see something. [To KUDRYASH.] Let's go to the Volga.

KUDRYASH. Why were you so long? I'm sick of waiting for you! You know that I don't like it. [VARVARA puts her arm around him and they go off.]

BORIS. I seem to be in a dream! This night, these songs and meetings! They are walking off, embracing each other. It is so new to me, so pleasant and agreeable! Here I am waiting for something, but what I am waiting for I don't know, and I cannot imagine; only my heart is beating and every nerve trembles. I cannot even think now what to say to her; my breath catches and my knees fail me! When my stupid heart suddenly begins to beat it won't calm down. There she comes. [KATERINA comes slowly down the path, her head covered with a large white kerchief and her eyes on the ground. Pause.] Is it you, Katerina Petrovna? [Pause.] I don't know how to thank you. [Pause.] If you only knew how I love you, Katerina Petrovna! [He tries to take her hand.]

KATERINA [frightened, but not lifting her eyes]. Don't touch me! Don't touch me! O, O!

BORIS. Don't be angry.

KATERINA. Leave me! Go at once, you accursed man! Do you know: I can never pray away this sin; never, all my life. It will lie on my soul like a stone.

BORIS. Do not drive me away.

KATERINA. Why did you come? Why have you come, my tempter? I am a married woman; I must live with my husband till the grave claims me.

BORIS. You bade me come yourself.

KATERINA. Understand me, my enemy: till the grave claims me!

BORIS. It would be better for me not to see you!

KATERINA [agitated]. What a fate I am preparing for myself! Do you know where fate is leading me?

BORIS. Calm yourself! [He takes her hand.] Sit down!

KATERINA. Why do you wish my ruin?

BORIS. How can I wish your ruin when I love you more than anything on earth, more than myself?

KATERINA. No, no! You have ruined me.

BORIS. Am I really a villain?

KATERINA [shaking her head]. You have ruined me, ruined me, ruined me!

BORIS. God preserve me! I would rather perish myself!

KATERINA. Well, have you not ruined me when I am leaving my home and come to you at night?

BORIS. It was your will.

KATERINA. I have no will. If I had any will of my own, I should not have come to you. [Raising her eyes, she looks at BORIS. A short pause.] Now your will controls me; don't you see! [She throws herself on his neck.]

BORIS [embracing KATERINA]. My life!

KATERINA. Do you know, now I should like to die suddenly!

BORIS. Why die, when it is so good for us to live?

KATERINA. No, I shall not live! I know, now, that I shall not live.

BORIS. Do not say such things, please: do not pain me.

KATERINA. It is all right for you, you are a free Cossack, but I——

BORIS. No one knows of our love. How can I help sparing you?

KATERINA. Ah, why should I be spared? No one is to blame; I brought it on myself. Do not spare me; ruin me! Let every one know and let every one see what I am doing! [She embraces BORIS.] If I was not afraid of sin for your sake, shall I fear the judgment of men? They say it is even easier for you when here on this earth you suffer for a sin you have committed.

BORIS. Well, why think of that, seeing that we are so happy now?

KATERINA. Yes. I shall have plenty of leisure to ponder and weep over it.

BORIS. I was afraid at first; I thought you would drive me away.

KATERINA [smiling]. Drive you away! How could I? I should not have the heart to! If you had not come, I think I should have gone to you myself.

BORIS. I didn't even know that you loved me.

KATERINA. I have loved you for a long time. You seem to have come here to tempt me. When I saw you I lost command of myself. From the very first time, I think if you had beckoned to me I should have followed you; if you had gone to the end of the earth I should have followed you and never looked back.

BORIS. Will your husband be gone long?

KATERINA. Two weeks.

BORIS. Then we will enjoy ourselves. There is plenty of time.

KATERINA. Yes, we will enjoy ourselves. And then—[She ponders.] they will lock me up—that is death! But if they don't lock me up I shall have a chance to see you!

[KUDRYASH and VARVARA come in.]

SCENE IV

[The same. KUDRYASH and VARVARA.]

VARVARA. Well, have you come to terms? [KATERINA hides her face on BORIS'S breast.]

BORIS. Yes.

VARVARA. Go and take a stroll; we'll wait here. When it is time Vanya will call. [BORIS and KATERINA *go out.* KUDRYASH *and* VARVARA *sit down on the stone.*]

KUDRYASH. That was a fine trick you thought of, to come through the garden gate. It's very convenient for us fellows.

VARVARA. I thought of it all myself.

KUDRYASH. You can be trusted for that. But won't your mother miss you?

VARVARA. No. The idea won't enter her head.

KUDRYASH. Well, if it should happen to?

VARVARA. Her first sleep is very sound; towards morning she is wakeful.

KUDRYASH. But how can you tell? Suppose the devil should get her up.

VARVARA. Well, suppose! The door to the courtyard is locked from the garden side. She will knock and knock and then go away; and in the morning we will say that we were so fast asleep that we didn't hear. And Glasha is on guard, too: if anything happens she will call immediately. You can't do it without some danger, anyhow; at any moment things may go wrong. [KUDRYASH *strikes some chords on the guitar.* VARVARA *leans on the shoulder of* KUDRYASH, *who, paying no attention to her, plays quietly.*]

VARVARA [*yawning*]. Do you know what time it is?

KUDRYASH. Past midnight.

VARVARA. How do you know?

KUDRYASH. The watchman struck the board just now.

VARVARA [*yawning*]. It's time. Call them! To-morrow we'll come out earlier and we'll have more time to stroll.

KUDRYASH [*whistles and sings in a loud voice*]. Time to go home, time to go home, But I do not want to.

BORIS [*from behind the scenes*]. I hear you.

VARVARA [*rising*]. Well, good-bye! [*She yawns, then kisses* KUDRYASH *coldly, like an old friend.*] To-morrow, remem-ber, come earlier. [*She looks in the direction where* BORIS *and* KATERINA *disappeared.*] Stop saying good-bye; you're not parting forever; you'll see each other again to-morrow.

[*She yawns and stretches.* KAT-ERINA *runs in and* BORIS *after her.*]

SCENE V

[KUDRYASH, VARVARA, BORIS *and* KATERINA.]

KATERINA [*to* VARVARA]. Well, let's go, let's go! [*They go up the path.* KATERINA *turns back.*] Good-bye!

BORIS. Till to-morrow.

KATERINA. Yes, till to-morrow. Tell me what you dream about! [*She goes to the wicket gate.*]

BORIS. I will, surely.

KUDRYASH [*sings with the guitar*]. Go strolling, maiden,
Al-le-li,
Till evening;
Till evening.

VARVARA [*by the gate*]. But I, the maiden,
Will strolling go;
Ah-le-li,
Till morning.

KUDRYASH. When dawn began to show,
Then homeward did I go.

ACT IV

In the foreground the narrow arched gallery of an old building beginning to fall into ruin; here and there grass and bushes; beyond the arches the bank and a view of the Volga.

SCENE I

[*Several persons of both sexes pass by under the arches, strolling about.*]

FIRST MAN. It's beginning to sprinkle, perhaps a storm is coming up?

SECOND MAN. It seems so.

FIRST MAN. It's a good thing there's a shelter.

[*All come under the arches.*]

A WOMAN. What a lot of people there are on the boulevard! It's a holiday and they've all come out. The merchants' wives are all dressed up.

FIRST MAN. They'll take shelter somewhere or other.

SECOND MAN. See what a lot of people will crowd in here now!

FIRST MAN [*looking at the walls*]. Look, my friend, it was painted here once. And now it still shows in spots.

SECOND MAN. O, yes. Of course it was painted. Now, you know, everything is deserted; it's tumbled down and overgrown. After the fire they didn't fix it up. You don't remember that fire; it was about forty years ago.

FIRST MAN. What can that be, my friend, that is painted here? It's rather hard to make it out.

SECOND MAN. That is hell fire.

FIRST MAN. O yes, my friend!

SECOND MAN. And all classes of people are going there.

FIRST MAN. Yes, yes, I understand now.

SECOND MAN. And people of all degrees.

FIRST MAN. Even negroes?

SECOND MAN. Yes, negroes too.

FIRST MAN. And what is this one, my friend?

SECOND MAN. That is the downfall of Lithuania. There is a battle, do you see? It shows how our men fought the Lithuanians.

FIRST MAN. What is Lithuania?

SECOND MAN. It is just Lithuania.

FIRST MAN. And they say, brother, that it fell upon us from heaven.

SECOND MAN. I can't tell you. If it fell from heaven, it fell from heaven.

A WOMAN. Do tell! Everyone knows that it fell from heaven; and wherever there was a battle with it, mounds have been heaped up as a memorial.

FIRST MAN. Really, my brother! Yes, that is quite true.

[DIKOY *comes in; behind him* KULIGIN, *without a hat. All bow and take respectful positions.*]

SCENE II

[*The same.* DIKOY *and* KULIGIN.]

DIKOY. O, I'm all wet. [*To* KULIGIN.] Leave me. Go away. [*Angrily.*] You stupid man!

KULIGIN. Savel Prokofyich, you see that it would be of general use to all the inhabitants, your Honor.

DIKOY. Clear out! Of what use? Who wants to use it?

KULIGIN. Why, you, perhaps, your Honor, Savel Prokofyich. It might be set up in an open place on the boulevard. And what expense would it be? Scarcely any: a stone pillar—[*He indicates the size of each thing with a gesture.*] a small copper dial, round like this, and a needle, an upright needle—[*He indicates it with a gesture.*] simplicity itself. I will fix it all myself, and I will draw all the figures myself. Then, your Honor, when you are taking a walk, or when anyone else is out walking, you can go over and see at once what time it is. And then it is such a beautiful spot, with a view and everything else, but it has an empty look. And then there are strangers, your Honor, who come here to see our views: it would be an ornament; it would make things pleasing to the eye.

DIKOY. Why do you come crawling around me with such nonsense. Suppose I don't want to talk to you? You ought to have found out first if I were in a mood to listen to you or not, you fool. Are you my equal? What a fine thing he has found out! So he butts straight in to talk about it.

KULIGIN. If it were intruding with an affair of my own, then you might blame me. But this is for public use, your Honor. Well, for the benefit of society, what do ten rubles signify? No more will be needed.

DIKOY. But perhaps you intend to steal them; who knows?

KULIGIN. But if I give my work for nothing, how can I be stealing anything, your Honor? Everybody here knows me; no one speaks ill of me.

DIKOY. Well, let them know you; I don't want to know you.

KULIGIN. Why do you insult an honest man, Savel Prokofyich?

DIKOY. Do I have to give an account to you? I do not give an account even to persons of more importance than you are. If I want to think something about you I'll think it. You are an honest man to other people, but I think you're a robber, that's all. Did you want to hear that from me? Then hear it! I say you are a robber, and that's the end of it. Are you going to start a lawsuit with me? Then understand that you are a worm. If I wish I will spare you, if I wish I will crush you.

KULIGIN. Don't talk like that, Savel Prokofyich! I am a humble man, sir; it's easy to insult me. But I will tell you this, your Honor: "Even in shirt sleeves honesty is to be respected."

DIKOY. Don't dare to be insolent to me! Do you hear?

KULIGIN. I am not saying anything insolent to you; but I am talking to you because perhaps you may think of doing something for the town some day. You have the means, your Honor, in abundance, if you only had the will for the good work. Now, take this, for example: we often have thunderstorms, but we have no lightning conductors.

DIKOY [proudly]. That's all nonsense!

KULIGIN. But how can it be nonsense, when they have made experiments?

DIKOY. What are your lightning conductors made of?

KULIGIN. Steel.

DIKOY [angrily]. Well, what next?

KULIGIN. Steel rods.

DIKOY [getting more and more angry]. I have heard that they are rods, you low creature, but what next? You keep saying they are rods—and what next?

KULIGIN. Nothing.

DIKOY. What are thunderstorms in your opinion, eh? Well, tell me.

KULIGIN. Electricity.

DIKOY [stamping his foot]. Electricity again! You certainly are a robber! Thunderstorms are sent to us as a punishment, so that we may repent; and you want to defend yourself with lightning-rods and such, Lord pardon us! What are you, a Tatar? Are you a Tatar? Tell me, are you a Tatar?

KULIGIN. Savel Prokofyich, your Honor, Derzhavin said:

My body moulders in the dust;
My mind directs the thunderbolt.

DIKOY. I ought to take you to the provost for those words; he will see to you! Ah, my respected friends, listen to what he says!

KULIGIN. There is no help for it; I must give up. But when I have a million, then I will talk. [Goes out, with an impatient wave of his hand.]

DIKOY. Are you going to steal from some one? Arrest him! What a cheating peasant! How should one behave with such people? I don't know. [Turning to the crowd.] You cursed people would lead anybody into sin! I didn't want to get angry today, but he seemed to want to make me angry. Plague take him! [Angrily.] Has the rain stopped?

FIRST MAN. It seems to have stopped.

DIKOY. Seems! Go out and look, you fool. Seems to!

FIRST MAN [coming out from under the arches]. It has stopped.

[DIKOY goes out, and all the others after him. The stage is empty for a time. VARVARA enters quickly under the arches and, concealing herself, looks about.]

SCENE III

[VARVARA, later BORIS.]

VARVARA. That looks like him! [BORIS walks across the back of the stage.] Ssst! [BORIS looks around.] Come here. [She

beckons with her hand. BORIS *comes in.*]
What are we going to do with Katerina?
Please tell me.

BORIS. What has happened?

VARVARA. A misfortune has happened,
that's all. Her husband has come back;
did you know that? We didn't expect
him, but he has come.

BORIS. No, I didn't know it.

VARVARA. She is completely beside her-
self.

BORIS. I had only ten short days of real
life, while he was away. Now I shall not
see her any more!

VARVARA. What a fellow you are! Lis-
ten! She trembles all over as if she had
the fever; she is very pale and roams
about the house as if she were searching
for something. Her eyes have a crazed
look! This morning she started to cry
and she fairly sobs aloud. Heavens, what
am I to do with her?

BORIS. But perhaps it will pass away!

VARVARA. I hardly think so. She
doesn't dare to raise her eyes to her hus-
band. Mamma has begun to notice it: she
goes around watching her out of the corner
of her eye; she looks like a snake, and
that makes Katerina still worse. It is
simply torture to look at her. And I am
afraid.

BORIS. What are you afraid of?

VARVARA. You don't know her. She
is a strange woman. She is capable of
anything. She does such things that——

BORIS. Ah, my God, what is to be done?
You should have had a good talk with
her. Isn't it possible to calm her?

VARVARA. I have tried to, but she won't
listen to anything. It's better to let her
alone.

BORIS. Well, what do you think she
might do?

VARVARA. Here's what: she might
throw herself at her husband's feet and
tell him everything. That's what I'm
afraid of.

BORIS [*frightened*]. Would she do that?

VARVARA. She might do anything.

BORIS. Where is she now?

VARVARA. She has just gone out on the
boulevard with her husband, and mamma
is with them. Go there yourself if you
like. But no, you had better not go or
she might lose control of herself com-
pletely. [*A clap of thunder in the dis-
tance.*] Isn't that thunder? [*She looks
out.*] And it's sprinkling. Here comes
the crowd. Hide there, somewhere, and
I'll stand out in plain sight so that they
won't suspect anything.

[*Several persons of both sexes
and various classes come in.*]

SCENE IV

[*Various persons, then* MADAM KABANOV,
KABANOV, KATERINA *and* KULIGIN.]

FIRST MAN. The young woman must be
very much frightened; she's hurrying to
shelter so fast.

A WOMAN. How can you hide from it?
If it's your fate, then you can't escape.

KATERINA [*running in*]. Ah, Varvara!
[*She takes her hand and holds it fast.*]

VARVARA. Why, what's the matter?

KATERINA. This means my death.

VARVARA. Control yourself! Collect
your thoughts!

KATERINA. No, I cannot! I cannot do
anything. My heart is aching.

MADAM KABANOV [*coming in*]. I say
that one ought to live so as to be always
ready for anything; then one would not
be so frightened.

KABANOV. But, mamma, what particu-
lar sins can she have committed? Just
the same as all the rest of us have; she
is just afraid because she was born so.

MADAM KABANOV. How do you know?
One person's soul is always a mystery to
another.

KABANOV [*jokingly*]. Maybe she did
something when I was gone. But I'm sure
nothing happened when I was here.

MADAM KABANOV. Maybe she did do
something while you were gone.

KABANOV [*jokingly*]. Katya, you had
better confess, my dear, if you are guilty

of anything. You cannot hide anything from me: no indeed! I know it all.

KATERINA [*gazing into* KABANOV'S *eyes*]. My dearest!

VARVARA. Why do you urge her? Don't you see that it is hard enough for her without your teasing? [BORIS *walks out from among the crowd and bows to the* KAHANOVS.]

KATERINA [*exclaims*]. Ah!

KABANOV. Why are you frightened? Did you think it was a stranger? He is an acquaintance!—Is your uncle well?

BORIS. Very well, thank God!

KATERINA [*to* VARVARA]. What more does he want of me? Isn't it enough for him that I suffer so? [*She clings to* VARVARA *and sobs*.]

VARVARA [*aloud, so that her mother can hear her*.] We have tried everything; we don't know what to do with her, and now strangers are coming around!

[*She makes a sign to* BORIS, *who retires to the side of the stage*.]

KULIGIN [*comes to the center and turns to the crowd*]. What are you afraid of, tell me if you please! Now every blade of grass and every flower is rejoicing, but we are hiding. We are afraid as if it were some disaster. Thunderstorms kill people, you say! This is not a thunderstorm, it is a blessing! Yes, a blessing! You say that everything is terrible! When the northern lights shine out we ought to admire them and marvel at the divine wisdom. "From northern lands the sunrise glows!" But you are terrified and think that it means a war or a plague. A comet appears, and one should not turn his eyes away; it is so beautiful! You have looked long enough at the stars—they are always the same—but this is something new; you ought to gaze at it and admire it! But you are afraid even to look at the sky; you tremble! You have made a bugbear of everything. O, what people! I am not afraid. Let us go, sir!

BORIS. Let us go! It is more frightful here. [*Goes out*.]

SCENE V

[*The same, without* BORIS *and* KULIGIN.]

MADAM KABANOV. What a sermon he did preach! That was worth listening to, I must say! What times these are, that such teachers have risen up. When an old man talks like that, what can you expect from the young ones?

A WOMAN. The whole sky is clouded over. It seems to be covered with a hat.

FIRST MAN. Ah, my friend, the storm rolls on like a ball; it seems as if something living were moving in it. It crawls and crawls upon us like a living creature!

SECOND MAN. Remember what I say, that this storm will not pass over without some misfortune. I tell you the truth, because I know. It will kill some one or burn down a house; you will see. Look, what a strange color!

KATERINA [*listening*]. What are they saying? They say it will kill some one.

KABANOV. Of course, they just say anything that comes into their heads.

MADAM KABANOV. Don't judge your elders! They know more than you do. Old people know the signs for everything. An old man does not say anything idly.

KATERINA [*to her husband*]. Tisha, I know who will be killed.

VARVARA [*aside, to* KATERINA]. You'd better stop talking now.

KABANOV. How do you know?

KATERINA. I shall be killed. Pray for me then!

[*The old lady with the two lackeys comes in.* KATERINA *hides herself with a cry*.]

SCENE VI

[*The same, and the* LADY.]

LADY. Why do you hide? There is no use hiding! I see you are afraid; you don't want to die! You want to live, of course you do; such a little beauty as you are! Ha, ha, ha! Beauty! You should pray God to take away your beauty!

Beauty is our ruin! You will destroy yourself, and you will tempt men; then you can exult in your beauty. You will lead many, many men into sin. Light-headed fellows fight duels; they kill each other with swords. Isn't that fine! Old men, honorable old men, forget about death, enticed by your beauty! And who will answer for it? You will have to answer for it all. Into the flood with your beauty! Yes, quick, quick! [KATERINA *hides.*] Where can you hide, you stupid thing! You cannot hide from God. [*A clap of thunder.*] You will all burn in everlasting fire. [*Goes out.*]

KATERINA. I am dying.

VARVARA. Why do you torment yourself? Go away a little and pray; it will comfort you.

KATERINA [*walks over to the wall and drops on her knees; then suddenly jumps up*]. O, O! The flames of hell! of hell! [KABANOV, MADAM KABANOV and VARVARA *surround her.*] My heart is broken! I cannot endure any more! Mother, Tikhon, I am guilty before God and before you! Did I not swear to you that I would not look on any one when you were gone! Do you remember? Do you remember? And do you know what I, wicked woman that I am, have done in your absence? The very first night I left the house——

KABANOV [*discounted, in tears, pulls her by the sleeve*]. Do not tell, do not tell! What are you thinking of! Mamma is here!

MADAM KABANOV [*sternly*]. Well, go on, since you have begun.

KATERINA. And all of the ten nights I sinned. [*She sobs.* KABANOV *tries to embrace her.*]

MADAM KABANOV. Let her alone! With whom?

VARVARA. She lies; she doesn't know herself what she is saying.

MADAM KABANOV. Keep still, I tell you! So that's it? With whom, I say?

KATERINA. With Boris Grigoryich. [*A clap of thunder.*] Ah! [*She falls senseless into her husband's arms.*]

MADAM KABANOV. Now, my son! That is where your freedom leads! I told you, but you wouldn't listen. Now you have found it out.

ACT V

Scene same as in Act I. Evening.

SCENE I

[KULIGIN *sitting on a bench,* KABANOV *walking along the boulevard.*]

KULIGIN [*sings*]. The darkness of night now covers the skies,
And all good people have shut their eyes. [*Seeing* KABANOV.] Good-day, sir. Are you going far?

KABANOV. I am going home. Have you heard about our trouble, my friend? Our whole family has been broken up.

KULIGIN. Yes, sir, so I have heard.

KABANOV. I went to Moscow, did you know? Before I left mamma lectured and lectured me, but as soon as I was away I went on a spree. I was so glad to be free. And I drank all along the road, and in Moscow I drank all the time: I just drank to beat the band! I tried to drink enough to make up for the whole year. I didn't think about home even once. And even if I had, it wouldn't have occurred to me what was happening there. Have you heard?

KULIGIN. Yes, sir.

KABANOV. I'm an unhappy man now, brother. I'm being ruined without any cause.

KULIGIN. Your mother is dreadfully severe.

KABANOV. Yes, yes. She is at the bottom of it all. But why am I made to suffer, please tell me? I went to Dikoy's and we had a drink; I thought it would be easier to bear; but no, it's worse, Kuligin. What my wife has done to me—nothing could be worse.

KULIGIN. It is a complicated affair, sir; it is hard to judge you.

KABANOV. No, wait a bit. There's something worse than that. It wouldn't be enough to kill her for that. Mamma says she ought to be buried alive for a punishment. But I love her; I should be sorry to lay a finger on her. I beat her a little, for mamma ordered me to. It makes me sad to look at her: understand that, Kuligin. Mamma keeps worrying at her, and she, like a ghost, walks about without saying anything. She only weeps; she is melting away like wax. It is killing me to watch her.

KULIGIN. You ought to settle it peacefully! You should forgive her and never remind her of it. You are not without sin yourself, I suppose!

KABANOV. I should say not!

KULIGIN. So just be careful not to reproach her when you're drunk. She would make you a good wife, sir, probably better than any other.

KABANOV. But you know, Kuligin, I shouldn't do anything myself, but mamma —you can't reason with her.

KULIGIN. It is time, sir, for you to live as you think best yourself.

KABANOV. How can I break myself in two? They say I have no mind of my own; so I must live by another's. I'll just drink away what little sense I have; then let mamma nurse me like a fool.

KULIGIN. Ah, sir, it's a sad business! And what about Boris Grigoryich?

KABANOV. They are sending the rogue to Tyakhta, among the Chinese. His uncle is sending him there as a clerk to some merchant he knows. He's sent there for three years.

KULIGIN. Well, how does he take it, sir?

KABANOV. He too is moping around and crying. His uncle and I set on him a while ago; we dressed him down finely, and he just kept silent. He has become like a wild man. "Do what you like with me," he says, "only don't torture her." Even he is sorry for her.

KULIGIN. He is a good man, sir.

KABANOV. He is all ready and the horses are harnessed! How he suffers; dreadfully! I can see that he wants to say good-bye to her. And a lot more, too! Enough of him! He is my enemy, Kuligin! He ought to be cut in pieces, so that he should know——

KULIGIN. We should forgive our enemies, sir!

KABANOV. Go and tell that to mamma, and see what she will say about it. All our family, friend Kuligin, is broken up now; we are not like relatives but enemies to each other. Mamma nagged and nagged Varvara, but she wouldn't stand it; she just skipped and ran away!

KULIGIN. Where did she go?

KABANOV. Nobody knows. They say she ran off with Vanya Kudryash; he can't be found anywhere either. And this, Kuligin, to be frank, is mamma's fault because she began to boss her and lock her up. "Don't lock me up," she said; "it will be worse!" And this is what happened. What shall I do now, tell me? Tell me how I am to live now! The house has become hateful to me; I'm ashamed to see people; I start to do something and my hands fall helpless. Now I am going home: am I going to find anything pleasant?

[GLASHA comes in.]

GLASHA. Tikhon Ivanyich, sir.

KABANOV. What now?

GLASHA. Things are wrong at home, sir.

KABANOV. Heavens! One thing after another! Tell me what has happened there.

GLASHA. Your wife——

KABANOV. What? Has she died?

GLASHA. No, she has gone out somewhere and we can't find her. We have worn ourselves out searching.

KABANOV. Kuligin, I must run and look for her, brother. Do you know what I am afraid of? She might lay hands on herself in her misery! She suffers so frightfully. If you look at her your heart breaks. Why didn't you keep your eyes open? Has she been gone long?

GLASHA. Not very long! It's our fault, we didn't watch her closely enough.

But then you can't be on the lookout every minute.

KABANOV. Well, why are you standing there? Run. [GLASHA goes out.] Let's go, Kuligin.

[*They go out. The stage is empty for a time. From the opposite side* KATERINA *comes in and walks slowly about the stage.*]

SCENE II

[KATERINA *alcne. This monologue and all the following scenes she speaks meditatively, as if half unconscious, drawling and repeating her words.*]

KATERINA. No, he is not to be found anywhere! What is he doing now, poor boy? If I could only say good-bye to him, and then—then die. Why did I lead him into misfortune? It's no easier for me! I ought to have perished alone! But now I have ruined myself, ruined him: I'm dishonored, he will always be under a cloud. Yes, I'm dishonored. He's under a cloud. [*Pause.*] Can I remember what he used to say? How he pitied me! What words did he say? [*She clasps her head.*] I don't remember; I've forgotten it all. The nights, the nights are so hard! They all go to bed, and I go too; they go to sleep and I go down to my tomb. It's so terrible in the dark! There's a noise and they sing as if they were burying some one, only so quietly I can hardly hear it, far, far from me. And how glad I am to see the light! But I don't want to get up—the same people again, the same talk, the same torture. Why do they look at me in such a way? Why don't they put people to death now? Why have they acted in this way? In former times, they say, they used to put people to death. They would have taken me and thrown me in the Volga, and I should have been glad. "If we put you to death," they say, "then your sin will be taken from you; live on and torture yourself with your sin." I've been tor-

tured enough for it. Must I be tortured much longer? . . . What shall I live for now? What for? I don't need anything now; nothing is dear to me, God's world itself is not dear to me! But death does not come. You call to it, but it does not come. Whatever I see or hear, I have the same pain here. [*She points to her heart.*] If I could still live with him, perhaps I should still find a little happiness. Well, well, now it's all the same; I've already destroyed my soul. How I long for him! How I long for him! If I cannot see you more, then at least hear my voice from afar. Wild winds, carry to him my sorrow and longing! Heavens, I am weary, weary! [*She walks to the bank and cries aloud.*] My joy, my life, my soul, I love you! Answer me! [*She weeps. Enter* BORIS.]

SCENE III

[KATERINA *and* BORIS.]

BORIS [*not seeing* KATERINA]. My God! That was her voice! Where is she? [*He looks about.*]

KATERINA [*running up to him and falling on his neck*]. At last I have seen you again. [*She weeps on his bosom. A pause.*]

BORIS. Well, now we have wept together; God brought you to me.

KATERINA. You have not forgotten me?

BORIS. How could I forget you? What do you mean?

KATERINA. Ah, no, I didn't mean that, not that. You are not angry?

BORIS. Why should I be angry?

KATERINA. Well, forgive me! I didn't mean to do you wrong; I couldn't control myself. No matter what I said or did; I was beside myself.

BORIS. Stop. What are you thinking of?

KATERINA. And you? What are you going to do now?

BORIS. I am going away.

KATERINA. Where are you going?

BORIS. Far away, Katya, to Siberia.

KATERINA. Take me away with you.

BORIS. I cannot, Katya. I'm not going of my own accord; uncle is sending me, and the horses are already harnessed. I only begged for a minute's leave from uncle. I wanted to say good-bye to the place where we used to see each other.

KATERINA. God be with you on your journey! Don't grieve for me. At first maybe it'll be hard for you; but then you will forget.

BORIS. Why talk about me? I'm a free lance. But how about you? How does your mother-in-law act?

KATERINA. She tortures me, she locks me up. She says to everybody and to my husband, "Do not believe her, she is sly." They all follow me about the whole day and laugh right in my face. They keep upbraiding me with you at every word.

BORIS. And your husband?

KATERINA. Now he is affectionate and again he is angry, and he drinks continually. I have grown sick of him, sick of him; his caresses are worse to me than his blows.

BORIS. Is it hard for you to bear, Katya?

KATERINA. So hard, so hard that it would be easier to die!

BORIS. Who would have known that you and I would have to suffer so on account of our love? I should have done better to run away then!

KATERINA. It was my undoing that I saw you. I have had little happiness, and so much sorrow, such bitter sorrow! And how much is to come! But why think of the future! I have seen you now and they cannot take that from me; I need nothing more, I only needed to see you. Now it has become far easier for me; it seems as if a mountain had fallen from my shoulders. And I kept thinking that you were angry at me, that you cursed me.

BORIS. How could you think so? How could you?

KATERINA. No; that was not what I meant, that was not what I wanted to say! I just longed to see you, that's it; and now I have seen you.

BORIS. I hope they will not find us here.

KATERINA. Wait, wait! What did I want to say to you? I've forgotten! I had to tell you something. My head is confused; I don't remember anything.

BORIS. It's time for me to go, Katya!

KATERINA. Wait, wait!

BORIS. What did you want to say?

KATERINA. I'll tell you in a moment. [After thinking.] O yes! As you travel along the road, don't pass by a single beggar; give something to every one, and tell him to pray for my poor sinful soul.

BORIS. Ah, if those people knew how hard it is for me to say good-bye to you! My God! God grant that it will be as pleasant for them some day as it is for me now. Good-bye, Katya! [He embraces her and starts to go.] You scoundrels! Scum of the earth! Ah, if I had the strength!

KATERINA. Wait, wait! Let me look at you for the last time. [She looks into his eyes.] Well, that's enough for me! Now go, and God be with you! Go, go quickly.

BORIS [walks away a few steps and then stops]. Katya, something is wrong! Are you planning to do something? I shall suffer on the road, thinking of you.

KATERINA. No, no! God be with you on your journey! [BORIS starts to go over to her.] You must not, you must not; it is enough.

BORIS [sobbing]. Well, God be with you. The only thing to pray for is that she should die as soon as possible, so that she may not suffer long. Good-bye. [He bows.]

KATERINA. Good-bye!

[BORIS goes out. KATERINA follows him with her eyes and stands meditating a few moments.]

SCENE IV

[KATERINA alone.]

KATERINA. Where shall I go now? Shall I go home? No, that is the same as going into a grave. Yes, home or the grave, the grave! It is better in the grave. A little grave under a tree! How pleasant! The sun warms it and the rain waters it; in spring the grass will grow on it, the tender grass—birds will fly to the tree, they will sing, they will raise their little ones. Flowers will bloom —yellow ones, red ones and blue—every kind—[*Thinking.*] every kind. How quiet it will be! How pleasant! It will be easier for me, I think! I don't want to think of life. To live again? No, no, I must not—it's no use! I loathe people, I loathe the house, I loathe its walls! I will not go there! No, no, I will not go. If I go to them they will walk about and talk, and what do I care? Ah, it has grown dark! And they are singing somewhere again. What are they singing? I cannot make it out. If I could only die now! What are they singing? It's all the same if death comes or if I myself—but I cannot go on living! It is a sin! Will they pray for me? Whoever loves me will pray anyway. They lay your hands crossed—in the coffin! Yes, like this—I remember. If they catch me they will take me home by force. Ah, I must hurry! hurry! [*She walks over to the bank. Aloud.*] My darling! My joy! Farewell! [*She goes out.*]

[MADAM KABANOV, KABANOV, KULIGIN *and a workman with a lantern come in.*]

SCENE V

[MADAM KABANOV, KABANOV *and* KULIGIN.]

KULIGIN. They say she was seen here.
KABANOV. Is it true?
KULIGIN. They are sure it was she.
KABANOV. Thank God that they saw her alive.
MADAM KABANOV. And you are frightened and crying! There is no need of it. Don't worry, you will still be burdened a long time with her.

KABANOV. Who would think of her coming here! It is such a busy place. Who would think of hiding here?
MADAM KABANOV. You see how she acts! She's a bad sort! She wants to live up to her character! [*From different directions people gather with lanterns.*]
ONE OF THE CROWD. Have you found her?
MADAM KABANOV. No. She seems to have been swallowed up.
SEVERAL VOICES. How can that be? This is a strange thing! Where can she have gone?
ONE OF THE CROWD. You will find her.
ANOTHER. Of course you will.
THIRD ONE. She will come back herself.
[*A voice behind the scenes:* Bring a boat.]
KULIGIN [*from the bank*]. Who is calling? Who is there?
A VOICE. A woman has thrown herself into the water!
[KULIGIN *and several other men run out.*]

SCENE VI

[*The same, without* KULIGAN.]
KABANOV. Heavens, that is she! [*He starts to run.* MADAM KABANOV *holds him back by the hand.*] Mamma, let me go; it is my death! I will pull her out or I myself will—— What is life worth to me without her!
MADAM KABANOV. I will not let you go, don't think it! Would you kill yourself for her! Is she worth it! Hadn't she shamed us enough before! See what she has done now!
KABANOV. Let me go!
MADAM KABANOV. There are enough without you. I'll curse you if you go.
KABANOV [*falling on his knees*]. If I could only look at her!
MADAM KABANOV. They'll pull her out. You'll see her.
KABANOV [*rises. To the crowd*]. Can you see anything, my friends?

FIRST OF THE CROWD. It's dark down there; we can't see anything.

[*A noise behind the scenes.*]

SECOND OF THE CROWD. They seem to be shouting something, but you can't make it out.

FIRST OF THE CROWD. That's Kuligin's voice.

SECOND OF THE CROWD. They're walking along the bank with a lantern.

FIRST OF THE CROWD. They're coming here. They're bringing her.

[*Several of the crowd return.*]

ONE OF THOSE WHO HAVE COME BACK. Kuligin is a brave fellow! Right near by, in the pool by the bank, we could see deep into the water with a light; he saw her gown and pulled her out.

KABANOV. Is she alive?

A SECOND. How could she be alive? She jumped from a high place: there is a precipice there; she must have fallen on an anchor. She wounded herself, poor thing! How could she be alive, fellows? She has only a small wound on her temple; there is only just one little drop of blood. [KABANOV *starts to run;* KULIGIN *meets him on the way with others, carrying* KATERINA.]

SCENE VII

[*The same and* KULIGIN.]

KULIGIN. Here is your Katerina. Do what you will with her! Her body is here, take it; but her soul is no longer yours: it is now before a Judge who is more merciful than you are! [*He lays the body on the ground and rushes out.*]

KABANOV [*throwing himself upon* KATERINA]. Katya, Katya!

MADAM KABANOV. Stop! It's a sin to weep for her!

KABANOV. Mamma, you have killed her! You, you, you——

MADAM KABANOV. What are you saying? Are you beside yourself? You have forgotten who you are talking to!

KABANOV. You have killed her! You, you!

MADAM KABANOV [*to her son*]. Well, I'll talk to you at home. [*She bows low to the people.*] I thank you, good people, for your services! [*All bow.*]

KABANOV. It is well with you, Katya! But why am I left to live on the earth and to suffer! [*He falls on his wife's body.*]

A DOLL'S HOUSE

By HENRIK IBSEN

Produced at Christiania, 1879

TRANSLATED BY WILLIAM ARCHER *

CHARACTERS

TORVALD HELMER
NORA HELMER
DR. RANK
NILS KROGSTAD
MRS. LINDEN

ANNA,
ELLEN } *Servants*

IVAR
EMMY } *The Helmers' Children*
BOB

SCENE: *Sitting-room in* HELMER'S *House* [*a flat*] *in Christiania.*

TIME: *The present day; Christmastide.*
The action takes place on three consecutive days.

ACT I

A room comfortably and tastefully, but not expensively, furnished. In the background, to the right, a door leads to the hall; to the left, another door leads to HELMER'S *study. Between the two doors a pianoforte. In the middle of the left wall, a door, and nearer the front a window. Near the window a round table with armchairs and a small sofa. In the right wall, somewhat to the back, a door; and against the same wall, farther forward, a porcelain stove; in front of it a couple of armchairs and a rocking-chair. Between the stove and the side door a small table. Engravings on the walls. A whatnot with china and bric-à-brac. A*

* Reprinted from the separate edition published by Walter H. Baker & Co., Boston, by permission of the publisher.

*small book-case of showily bound books.
Carpet. A fire in the stove. A winter
day.*
[*A bell rings in the hall outside. Pres-
ently the outer door is heard to open.
Then* NORA *enters, humming contentedly.
She is in out-door dress, and carries sev-
eral parcels, which she lays on the right-
hand table. She leaves the door into the
hall open behind her, and a* PORTER *is
seen outside, carrying a Christmas-tree
and a basket, which he gives to the maid-
servant who has opened the door.*]
NORA. Hide the Christmas-tree care-
fully, Ellen; the children mustn't see it
before this evening, when it's lighted up.
[*To the* PORTER, *taking out her purse.*]
How much?
PORTER. Fifty öre.
NORA. There's a crown. No, keep the
change. [*The* PORTER *thanks her and
goes.* NORA *shuts the door. She con-
tinues smiling in quiet glee as she takes
off her walking things. Then she takes
from her pocket a bag of macaroons, and
eats one or two. As she does so, she goes
on tip-toe to her husband's door and
listens.*]
NORA. Yes; he is at home. [*She be-
gins humming again, going to the table
on the right.*]
HELMER [*in his room*]. Is that my lark
twittering there?
NORA [*busy opening some of her par-
cels*]. Yes, it is.
HELMER. Is it the squirrel skipping
about?
NORA. Yes!
HELMER. When did the squirrel get
home?
NORA. Just this minute. [*Hides the
bag of macaroons in her pocket and wipes
her mouth.*] Come here, Torvald, and see
what I've bought.
HELMER. Don't disturb me. [*A little
later he opens the door and looks in, pen
in hand.*] "Bought," did you say? What!
all that? Has my little spendthrift been
making the money fly again?
NORA. Why, Torvald, surely we can
afford to launch out a little now! It's

the first Christmas we haven't had to
pinch.
HELMER. Come, come; we can't afford
to squander money.
NORA. Oh, yes, Torvald, do let us
squander a little—just the least little bit,
won't you? You know you'll soon be
earning heaps of money.
HELMER. Yes, from New Year's Day.
But there's a whole quarter before my
first salary is due.
NORA. Never mind; we can borrow in
the meantime.
HELMER. Nora! [*He goes up to her
and takes her playfully by the ear.*]
Thoughtless as ever! Supposing I bor-
rowed a thousand crowns to-day, and you
spent it during Christmas week, and that
on New Year's Eve a tile blew off the
roof and knocked my brains out——
NORA [*laying her hand on his mouth*].
Hush! How can you talk so horridly?
HELMER. But, supposing it were to
happen—what then?
NORA. If anything so dreadful hap-
pened, I shouldn't care whether I was in
debt or not.
HELMER. But what about the credi-
tors?
NORA. They! Who cares for them?
They're only strangers.
HELMER. Nora, Nora! What a woman
you are! But seriously, Nora, you know
my ideas on these points. No debts! No
credit! Home-life ceases to be free and
beautiful as soon as it is founded on bor-
rowing and debt. We two have held out
bravely till now, and we won't give in
at the last.
NORA [*going to the fireplace*]. Very
well—as you like, Torvald.
HELMER [*following her*]. Come, come;
my little lark mustn't let her wings
droop like that. What? Is the squirrel
pouting there? [*Takes out his purse.*]
Nora, what do you think I've got here?
NORA [*turning round quickly*]. Money!
HELMER. There! [*Gives her some
notes.*] Of course I know all sorts of
things are wanted at Christmas.
NORA [*counting*]. Ten, twenty, thirty,

forty. Oh! thank you, thank you, Torvald. This will go a long way.

HELMER. I should hope so.

NORA. Yes, indeed, a long way! But come here, and see all I've been buying. And so cheap! Look, here is a new suit for Ivar, and a little sword. Here are a horse and a trumpet for Bob. And here are a doll and a cradle for Emmy. They're only common; but she'll soon pull them all to pieces. And dresses and neckties for the servants; only I should have got something better for dear old Anna.

HELMER. And what's in that other parcel?

NORA [crying out]. No; Torvald, you're not to see that until this evening.

HELMER. Oh! ah! But now tell me, you little rogue, what have you got for yourself?

NORA. For myself? Oh, I don't want anything.

HELMER. Nonsense. Just tell me something sensible you would like to have.

NORA. No. Really I want nothing. . . . Well, listen, Torvald——

HELMER. Well?

NORA [playing with his coat buttons, without looking him in the face]. If you really want to give me something, you might, you know, you might——

HELMER. Well, well? Out with it!

NORA [quickly]. You might give me money, Torvald. Only just what you think you can spare; then I can buy myself something with it later.

HELMER. But, Nora——

NORA. Oh, please do, dear Torvald, please do! Then I would hang the money in lovely gilt paper on the Christmas-tree. Wouldn't that be fun?

HELMER. What do they call the birds that are always making the money fly?

NORA. Yes, I know—spendthrifts, of course. But please do as I say, Torvald. Then I shall have time to think what I want most. Isn't that very sensible, now?

HELMER [smiling]. Certainly; that is to say, if you really kept the money I gave you, and really bought yourself something with it. But it all goes in housekeeping, and f~~ sorts of useless things, and then I h find more.

NORA. But, Torva.

HELMER. Can you deny it, Nora dear? [He puts his arm round her.] It's a sweet little lark; but it gets through a lot of money. No one would believe how much it costs a man to keep such a little bird as you.

NORA. For shame! how can you say so? Why, I save as much as ever I can.

HELMER [laughing]. Very true—as much as you can—but you can't.

NORA [hums and smiles in quiet satisfaction]. H'm!—you should just know, Torvald, what expenses we larks and squirrels have.

HELMER. You're a strange little being! Just like your father—always eager to get hold of money; but the moment you have it, it seems to slip through your fingers; you never know what becomes of it. Well, one must take you as you are. It's in the blood. Yes, Nora, that sort of thing is inherited.

NORA. I wish I had inherited many of my father's qualities.

HELMER. And I don't wish you anything but just what you are—my own, sweet little song-bird. But, I say—it strikes me—you look so, so—what shall I call it?—so suspicious to-day——

NORA. Do I?

HELMER. You do, indeed. Look me full in the face.

NORA [looking at him]. Well?

HELMER [threatening with his finger]. Hasn't the little sweet-tooth been breaking the rules to-day?

NORA. No; how can you think of such a thing!

HELMER. Didn't she just look in at the confectioner's?

NORA. No, Torvald, really——

HELMER. Not to sip a little jelly?

NORA. No; certainly not.

HELMER. Hasn't she even nibbled a macaroon or two?

NORA. No, Torvald, indeed, indeed!

HELMER. Well, well, well; of course I'm only joking.

NORA [goes to the table on the right]. I shouldn't think of doing what you disapprove of.

HELMER. No, I'm sure of that; and, besides, you've given me your word. [Going toward her.] Well, keep your little Christmas secrets to yourself, Nora darling. The Christmas-tree will bring them all to light, I daresay.

NORA. Have you remembered to ask Doctor Rank?

HELMER. No. But it's not necessary; he'll come as a matter of course. Besides, I shall invite him when he looks in to-day. I've ordered some capital wine. Nora, you can't think how I look forward to this evening!

NORA. And I too. How the children will enjoy themselves, Torvald!

HELMER. Ah! it's glorious to feel that one has an assured position and ample means. Isn't it delightful to think of?

NORA. Oh, it's wonderful!

HELMER. Do you remember last Christmas? For three whole weeks beforehand you shut yourself up till long past midnight to make flowers for the Christmas-tree, and all sorts of other marvels that were to have astonished us. I was never so bored in my life.

NORA. I did not bore myself at all.

HELMER [smiling]. And it came to so little after all, Nora.

NORA. Oh! are you going to tease me about that again? How could I help the cat getting in and spoiling it all?

HELMER. To be sure you couldn't, my poor little Nora. You did your best to amuse us all, and that's the main thing. But, all the same, it's a good thing the hard times are over.

NORA. Oh, isn't it wonderful!

HELMER. Now, I needn't sit here boring myself all alone; and you needn't tire your dear eyes and your delicate little fingers——

NORA [clapping her hands]. No, I needn't, need I, Torvald? Oh! it's wonderful to think of! [Takes his arm.]

And now I'll tell you how I think we ought to manage, Torvald. As soon as Christmas is over—— [The hall-door bell rings.] Oh, there's a ring! [Arranging the room.] That's somebody come to call. How vexing!

HELMER. I am "not at home" to callers; remember that.

ELLEN [in the doorway]. A lady to see you, ma'am.

NORA. Show her in.

ELLEN [to HELMER]. And the Doctor is just come, sir.

HELMER. Has he gone into my study?

ELLEN. Yes, sir.

[HELMER goes into his study. ELLEN ushers in MRS. LINDEN in travelling costume, and shuts the door behind her.]

MRS. LINDEN [timidly and hesitatingly]. How do you do, Nora?

NORA [doubtfully]. How do you do?

MRS. LINDEN. I daresay you don't recognize me?

NORA. No, I don't think—oh, yes!—I believe—— [Effusively.] What! Christina! Is it really you?

MRS. LINDEN. Yes; really I!

NORA. Christina! and to think I didn't know you! But how could I—— [More softly.] How changed you are, Christina!

MRS. LINDEN. Yes, no doubt. In nine or ten years——

NORA. Is it really so long since we met? Yes, so it is. Oh! the last eight years have been a happy time, I can tell you. And now you have come to town? All that long journey in mid-winter! How brave of you.

MRS. LINDEN. I arrived by this morning's steamer.

NORA. To keep Christmas, of course. Oh, how delightful! What fun we shall have! Take your things off. Aren't you frozen? [Helping her.] There, now we'll sit down here cosily by the fire. No, you take the arm-chair; I'll sit in this rocking-chair. [Seizes her hand.] Yes, now I can see the dear old face again. It was only at the first glance—— But you're a little paler, Christina, and perhaps a little thinner.

MRS. LINDEN. And much, much older, Nora.

NORA. Yes, perhaps a little older—not much—ever so little. [*She suddenly stops; seriously.*] Oh! what a thoughtless wretch I am! Here I sit chattering on, and—— Dear, dear Christina, can you forgive me?

MRS. LINDEN. What do you mean, Nora?

NORA [*softly*]. Poor Christina! I forgot, you are a widow?

MRS. LINDEN. Yes; my husband died three years ago.

NORA. I know, I know, I saw it in the papers. Oh! believe me, Christina, I did mean to write to you; but I kept putting it off, and something always came in the way.

MRS. LINDEN. I can quite understand that, Nora dear.

NORA. No, Christina; it was horrid of me. Oh, you poor darling! how much you must have gone through!—and he left you nothing?

MRS. LINDEN. Nothing.

NORA. And no children?

MRS. LINDEN. None.

NORA. Nothing, nothing at all?

MRS. LINDEN. Not even a sorrow or a longing to dwell upon.

NORA [*looking at her incredulously*]. My dear Christina, how is that possible?

MRS. LINDEN [*smiling sadly and stroking her hair*]. Oh, it happens sometimes, Nora.

NORA. So utterly alone. How dreadful that must be! I have three of the loveliest children. I can't show them to you just now; they're out with their nurse. But now you must tell me everything.

MRS. LINDEN. No, no, I want you to tell me——

NORA. No, you must begin; I won't be egotistical to-day. To-day, I will think of you only. Oh! I must tell you one thing; but perhaps you've heard of our great stroke of fortune?

MRS. LINDEN. No. What is it?

NORA. Only think! my husband has been made Manager of the Joint Stock Bank.

MRS. LINDEN. Your husband! Oh, how fortunate!

NORA. Yes, isn't it? A lawyer's position is so uncertain, you see, especially when he won't touch any business that's the least bit . . . shady, as of course Torvald won't; and in that I quite agree with him. Oh! you can imagine how glad we are. He is to enter on his new position at the New Year, and then he will have a large salary, and percentages. In future we shall be able to live quite differently —just as we please, in fact. Oh, Christina, I feel so light and happy! It's splendid to have lots of money, and no need to worry about things, isn't it?

MRS. LINDEN. Yes; it must be delightful to have what you need.

NORA. No, not only what you need, but heaps of money—heaps!

MRS. LINDEN [*smiling*]. Nora, Nora, haven't you learnt reason yet? In our schooldays you were a shocking little spendthrift!

NORA [*quietly smiling*]. Yes; Torvald say I am still. [*Threatens with her finger.*] But "Nora, Nora," is not so silly as you all think. Oh! I haven't had the chance to be much of a spendthrift. We have both had to work.

MRS. LINDEN. You too?

NORA. Yes, light fancy work; crochet, and embroidery, and things of that sort, [*Significantly.*] and other work too. You know, of course, that Torvald left the Government service when we were married. He had little chance of promotion, and of course he required to make more money. But in the first year of our marriage he overworked himself terribly. He had to undertake all sorts of odd jobs, you know, and to work early and late. He couldn't stand it, and fell dangerously ill. Then the doctors declared he must go to the South.

MRS. LINDEN. Yes; you spent a whole year in Italy, didn't you?

NORA. We did. It wasn't easy to manage, I can tell you. It was just after Ivar's birth. But of course we had to go. Oh, it was a delicious journey! And it saved Torvald's life. But it cost a frightful lot of money, Christina.

MRS. LINDEN. So I should think.

NORA. Twelve hundred dollars! Four thousand eight hundred crowns! Isn't that a lot of money?

MRS. LINDEN. How lucky you had the money to spend!

NORA. I must tell you we got it from father.

MRS. LINDEN. Ah, I see. He died just about that time, didn't he?

NORA. Yes, Christina, just then. And only think! I couldn't go and nurse him! I was expecting little Ivar's birth daily. And then I had my Torvald to attend to. Dear, kind old father! I never saw him again, Christina. Oh! that's the hardest thing I've had to bear since my marriage.

MRS. LINDEN. I know how fond you were of him. And then you went to Italy?

NORA. Yes; we had the money, and the doctors insisted. We started a month later.

MRS. LINDEN. And your husband returned completely cured?

NORA. Sound as a bell.

MRS. LINDEN. But—the doctor?

NORA. What about him?

MRS. LINDEN. I thought as I came in your servant announced the Doctor——

NORA. Oh, yes; Doctor Rank. But he doesn't come as a doctor. He's our best friend, and never lets a day pass without looking in. No, Torvald hasn't had an hour's illness since that time. And the children are so healthy and well, and so am I. [*Jumps up and claps her hands.*] Oh, Christina, Christina, it's so lovely to live and to be happy!—Oh! but it's really too horrid of me!—Here am I talking about nothing but my own concerns. [*Sits down upon a footstool close to her and lays her arms on* CHRISTINA'S *lap.*] Oh! don't be angry with me!—Now just tell me, is it really true that you didn't

love your husband? What made you take him?

MRS. LINDEN. My mother was then alive, bedridden and helpless; and I had my two younger brothers to think of. I thought it my duty to accept him.

NORA. Perhaps it was. I suppose he was rich then?

MRS. LINDEN. Very well off, I believe. But his business was uncertain. It fell to pieces at his death, and there was nothing left.

NORA. And then——?

MRS. LINDEN. Then I had to fight my way by keeping a shop, a little school, anything I could turn my hand to. The last three years have been one long struggle for me. But now it's over, Nora. My poor mother no longer needs me; she is at rest. And the boys are in business, and can look after themselves.

NORA. How free your life must feel!

MRS. LINDEN. No, Nora; only inexpressibly empty. No one to live for. [*Stands up restlessly.*] That is why I couldn't bear to stay any longer in that out-of-the-way corner. Here it must be easier to find something really worth doing—something to occupy one's thoughts. If I could only get some settled employment—some office-work.

NORA. But, Christina, that's so tiring, and you look worn out already. You should rather go to some watering-place and rest.

MRS. LINDEN [*going to the window*]. I have no father to give me the money, Nora.

NORA [*rising*]. Oh! don't be vexed with me.

MRS. LINDEN [*going toward her*]. My dear Nora, don't you be vexed with me. The worst of a position like mine is that it makes one bitter. You have no one to work for, yet you have to be always on the strain. You must live; and so you become selfish. When I heard of the happy change in your circumstances—can you believe it?—I rejoiced more on my own account than on yours.

NORA. How do you mean? Ah! I see.

You mean Torvald could perhaps do something for you.

MRS. LINDEN. Yes; I thought so.

NORA. And so he shall, Christina. Just you leave it all to me. I shall lead up to it beautifully, and think of something pleasant to put him in a good humor! Oh! I should so love to do something for you.

MRS. LINDEN. How good of you, Nora! And doubly good in you, who know so little of the troubles of life.

NORA. I? I know so little of——?

MRS. LINDEN [smiling]. Ah, well! a little fancy-work, and so forth. You're a mere child, Nora.

NORA [tosses her head and paces the room]. Oh, come, you mustn't be so patronizing!

MRS. LINDEN. No?

NORA. You're like the rest. You all think I'm fit for nothing really serious——

MRS. LINDEN. Well——

NORA. You think I've had no troubles in this weary world.

MRS. LINDEN. My dear Nora, you've just told me all your troubles.

NORA. Pooh—these trifles. [Softly.] I haven't told you the great thing.

MRS. LINDEN. The great thing? What do you mean?

NORA. I know you look down upon me, Christina; but you've no right to. You're proud of having worked so hard and so long for your mother?

MRS. LINDEN. I'm sure I don't look down upon anyone; but it's true I'm both proud and glad when I remember that I was able to make my mother's last days free from care.

NORA. And you're proud to think of what you have done for your brothers?

MRS. LINDEN. Have I not the right to be?

NORA. Yes, surely. But now let me tell you, Christina—I, too, have something to be proud and glad of.

MRS. LINDEN. I don't doubt it. But what do you mean?

NORA. Hush! Not so loud. Only think, if Torvald were to hear! He mustn't—not for worlds! No one must know about it, Christina—no one but you.

MRS. LINDEN. What can it be?

NORA. Come over here. [Draws her beside her on the sofa.] Yes—I, too, have something to be proud and glad of. I saved Torvald's life.

MRS. LINDEN. Saved his life? How?

NORA. I told you about our going to Italy. Torvald would have died but for that.

MRS. LINDEN. Yes—and your father gave you the money.

NORA [smiling]. Yes, so Torvald and everyone believes; but——

MRS. LINDEN. But——?

NORA. Father didn't give us one penny. I found the money.

MRS. LINDEN. You? All that money?

NORA. Twelve hundred dollars. Four thousand eight hundred crowns. What do you say to that?

MRS. LINDEN. My dear Nora, how did you manage it? Did you win it in the lottery?

NORA [contemptuously]. In the lottery? Pooh! Any fool could have done that!

MRS. LINDEN. Then wherever did you get it from?

NORA [hums and smiles mysteriously]. H'm; tra-la-la-la!

MRS. LINDEN. Of course you couldn't borrow it.

NORA. No? Why not?

MRS. LINDEN. Why, a wife can't borrow without her husband's consent.

NORA [tossing her head]. Oh! when the wife knows a little of business, and how to set about things, then——

MRS. LINDEN. But, Nora, I don't understand——

NORA. Well you needn't. I never said I borrowed the money. Perhaps I got it another way. [Throws herself back on the sofa.] I may have got it from some admirer. When one is so—attractive as I am——

Mrs. Linden. You're too silly, Nora.

Nora. Now I'm sure you're dying of curiosity, Christina——

Mrs. Linden. Listen to me, Nora dear. Haven't you been a little rash?

Nora [sitting upright again]. Is it rash to save one's husband's life?

Mrs. Linden. I think it was rash of you, without his knowledge——

Nora. But it would have been fatal for him to know! Can't you understand that? He was never to suspect how ill he was. The doctors came to me privately and told me that his life was in danger —that nothing could save him but a trip to the South. Do you think I didn't try diplomacy first? I told him how I longed to have a trip abroad, like other young wives; I wept and prayed; I said he ought to think of my condition, and not thwart me; and then I hinted that he could borrow the money. But then, Christina, he got almost angry. He said I was frivolous, and that it was his duty as a husband not to yield to my whims and fancies—so he called them. Very well, thought I, but saved you must be; and then I found the way to do it.

Mrs. Linden. And did your husband never learn from your father that the money was not from him?

Nora. No; never. Father died at that very time. I meant to have told him all about it, and begged him to say nothing. But he was so ill—unhappily, it was not necessary.

Mrs. Linden. And you have never confessed to your husband?

Nora. Good Heavens! What can you be thinking of? Tell him, when he has such a loathing of debt? And besides— how painful and humiliating it would be for Torvald, with his manly self-reliance, to know that he owed anything to me! It would utterly upset the relation between us; our beautiful, happy home would never again be what it is.

Mrs. Linden. Will you never tell him?

Nora [thoughtfully, half-smiling]. Yes, some time perhaps—after many years, when I'm—not so pretty. You mustn't laugh at me. Of course I mean when Torvald is not so much in love with me as he is now; when it doesn't amuse him any longer to see me skipping about, and dressing up and acting. Then it might be well to have something in reserve. [Breaking off.] Nonsense! nonsense! That time will never come. Now, what do you say to my grand secret, Christina? Am I fit for nothing now? You may believe it has cost me a lot of anxiety. It has been no joke to meet my engagements punctually. You must know, Christina, that in business there are things called instalments and quarterly interest, that are terribly hard to meet. So I had to pinch a little here and there, wherever I could. I could not save anything out of the housekeeping, for of course Torvald had to live well. And I couldn't let the children go about badly dressed; all I got for them, I spent on them, the darlings.

Mrs. Linden. Poor Nora! So it had to come out of your own pocket-money.

Nora. Yes, of course. After all, the whole thing was my doing. When Torvald gave me money for clothes and so on, I never used more than half of it; I always bought the simplest things. It's a mercy everything suits me so well; Torvald never noticed anything. But it was often very hard, Christina dear. For it's nice to be beautifully dressed. Now, isn't it?

Mrs. Linden. Indeed it is.

Nora. Well, and besides that, I made money in other ways. Last winter I was so lucky—I got a heap of copying to do. I shut myself up every evening and wrote far on into the night. Oh, sometimes I was so tired, so tired. And yet it was splendid to work in that way and earn money. I almost felt as if I was a man.

Mrs. Linden. Then how much have you been able to pay off?

Nora. Well, I can't precisely say. It's difficult to keep that sort of business clear. I only know that I paid off everything I could scrape together. Sometimes I really didn't know where to turn. [*Smiles.*] Then I used to imagine that a rich old gentleman was in love with me——

MRS. LINDEN. What! What gentleman?

NORA. Oh! nobody—that he was now dead, and that when his will was opened, there stood in large letters: Pay over at once everything of which I die possessed to that charming person, Mrs. Nora Helmer.

MRS. LINDEN. But, dear Nora, what gentleman do you mean?

NORA. Dear, dear, can't you understand? There wasn't any old gentleman: it was only what I used to dream, and dream when I was at my wit's end for money. But it's all over now—the tiresome old creature may stay where he is for me; I care nothing for him or his will; for now my troubles are over. [*Springing up.*] Oh, Christina, how glorious it is to think of! Free from cares! Free, quite free. To be able to play and romp about with the children; to have things tasteful and pretty in the house, exactly as Torvald likes it! And then the spring is coming, with the great blue sky. Perhaps then we shall have a short holiday. Perhaps I shall see the sea again. Oh, what a wonderful thing it is to live and to be happy!

[*The hall door-bell rings.*]

MRS. LINDEN [*rising*]. There is a ring. Perhaps I had better go.

NORA. No; do stay. It's sure to be some one for Torvald.

ELLEN [*in the doorway*]. If you please, ma'am, there's a gentleman to speak to Mr. Helmer.

NORA. Who is the gentleman?

KROGSTAD [*in the doorway to the hall*]. It is I, Mrs. Helmer.

[*ELLEN goes. MRS. LINDEN starts and turns away to the window.*]

NORA [*goes a step toward him, anxiously, half aloud*]. You? What is it? What do you want with my husband?

KROGSTAD. Bank business—in a way.

I hold a small post in the Joint Stock Bank, and your husband is to be our new chief, I hear.

NORA. Then it is——?

KROGSTAD. Only tiresome business, Mrs. Helmer; nothing more.

NORA. Then will you please go to his study.

[*KROGSTAD goes. She bows indifferently while she closes the door into the hall. Then she goes to the fireplace and looks to the fire.*]

MRS. LINDEN. Nora—who was that man?

NORA. A Mr. Krogstad. Do you know him?

MRS. LINDEN. I used to know him—many years ago. He was in a lawyer's office in our town.

NORA. Yes, so he was.

MRS. LINDEN. How he has changed!

NORA. I believe his marriage was unhappy.

MRS. LINDEN. And he is now a widower?

NORA. With a lot of children. There! now it'll burn up. [*She closes the stove, and pushes the rocking-chair a little aside.*]

MRS. LINDEN. His business is not of the most creditable, they say.

NORA. Isn't it? I daresay not. I don't know—— But don't let us think of business—it's so tiresome.

[*DR. RANK comes out of HELMER'S room.*]

RANK [*still in the doorway*]. No, no; I won't keep you. I'll just go and have a chat with your wife. [*Shuts the door and sees MRS. LINDEN.*] Oh, I beg your pardon. I am *de trop* here too.

NORA. No, not in the least. [*Introduces them*]. Doctor Rank—Mrs. Linden.

RANK. Oh, indeed; I've often heard Mrs. Linden's name. I think I passed you on the stairs as we came up.

MRS. LINDEN. Yes; I go so very slowly. Stairs try me so much.

RANK. You're not very strong?

MRS. LINDEN. Only overworked.

RANK. Ah! Then you have come to town to find rest in a round of dissipation.

MRS. LINDEN. I have come to look for employment.

RANK. Is that an approved remedy for over-work?

MRS. LINDEN. One must live, Doctor Rank.

RANK. Yes, that seems to be the general opinion.

NORA. Come, Doctor Rank, you yourself want to live.

RANK. To be sure I do. However wretched I may be, I want to drag on as long as possible. And my patients have all the same mania. It's just the same with people whose complaint is moral. At this very moment Helmer is talking to such a wreck as I mean.

MRS. LINDEN [softly]. Ah!

NORA. Whom do you mean?

RANK. Oh, a fellow named Krogstad, a man you know nothing about—corrupt to the very core of his character. But even he began by announcing solemnly that he must live.

NORA. Indeed? Then what did he want with Torvald?

RANK. I really don't know; I only gathered that it was some Bank business.

NORA. I didn't know that Krog—that this Mr. Krogstad had anything to do with the Bank?

RANK. He has some sort of place there. [To MRS. LINDEN.] I don't know whether, in your part of the country, you have people who go wriggling and snuffing around in search of moral rottenness—whose policy it is to fill good places with men of tainted character whom they can keep under their eye and in their power? The honest men they leave out in the cold.

MRS. LINDEN. Well, I suppose the—delicate characters require most care.

RANK [shrugs his shoulders]. There we have it! It's that notion that makes society a hospital. [NORA, deep in her own thoughts, breaks into half-stifled laughter and claps her hands.] What are you laughing at? Have you any idea what society is?

NORA. What do I care for your tiresome society. I was laughing at something else—something awfully amusing. Tell me, Doctor Rank, are all the employees at the Bank dependent on Torvald now?

RANK. Is that what strikes you as awfully amusing?

NORA [smiles and hums]. Never mind, never mind! [Walks about the room.] Yes, it is amusing to think that we—that Torvald has such power over so many people. [Takes the box from her pocket.] Doctor Rank, will you have a macaroon?

RANK. Oh, dear, dear—macaroons! I thought they were contraband here.

NORA. Yes; but Christina brought me these.

MRS. LINDEN. What! I?

NORA. Oh, well! Don't be frightened. You couldn't possibly know that Torvald had forbidden them. The fact is, he is afraid of me spoiling my teeth. But, oh bother, just for once. That's for you, Doctor Rank! [Puts a macaroon into his mouth.] And you, too, Christina. And I will have one at the same time—only a tiny one, or at most two. [Walks about again.] Oh, dear, I am happy! There is only one thing in the world that I really want.

RANK. Well; what's that?

NORA. There's something I should so like to say—in Torvald's hearing.

RANK. Then why don't you say it?

NORA. Because I daren't, it's so ugly.

MRS. LINDEN. Ugly?

RANK. In that case you'd better not. But to us you might. What is it you would so like to say in Helmer's hearing?

NORA. I should so love to say—"Damn!"

RANK. Are you out of your mind?

MRS. LINDEN. Good gracious, Nora!

RANK. Say it. There he is!

NORA [hides the macaroons]. Hush-sh-sh.

[HELMER *comes out of his room, hat in hand, with his overcoat on his arm.*]

[*Going toward him.*] Well, Torvald, dear, have you got rid of him?

HELMER. Yes; he's just gone.

NORA. May I introduce you?—This is Christina, who has come to town——

HELMER. Christina? Pardon me, but I don't know——?

NORA. Mrs. Linden, Torvald dear—Christina Linden.

HELMER [*to* MRS. LINDEN]. A schoolfriend of my wife's, no doubt?

MRS. LINDEN. Yes; we knew each other as girls.

NORA. And only think! She has taken this long journey on purpose to speak to you.

HELMER. To speak to me!

MRS. LINDEN. Well, not quite——

NORA. You see Christina is tremendously clever at accounts, and she is so anxious to work under a first-rate man of business in order to learn still more——

HELMER. Very sensible indeed.

NORA. And when she heard you were appointed Manager—it was telegraphed, you know—she started off at once, and—Torvald dear, for my sake, you must do something for Christina. Now can't you?

HELMER. It's not impossible. I presume you are a widow?

MRS. LINDEN. Yes.

HELMER. And have already had some experience in office-work?

MRS. LINDEN. A good deal.

HELMER. Well then, it is very likely I may find a place for you.

NORA [*clapping her hands*]. There now! there now!

HELMER. You have come at a lucky moment, Mrs. Linden.

MRS. LINDEN. Oh! how can I thank you——?

HELMER [*smiling*]. There's no occasion. [*Puts his overcoat on.*] But for the present you must excuse me.

RANK. Wait; I'll go with you. [*Fetches his fur coat from the hall and warms it at the fire.*]

NORA. Don't be long, dear Torvald.

HELMER. Only an hour; not more.

NORA. Are you going too, Christina?

MRS. LINDEN [*putting on her walking things*]. Yes; I must set about looking for lodgings.

HELMER. Then perhaps we can go together?

NORA [*helping her*]. What a pity we haven't a spare room for you; but I'm afraid——

MRS. LINDEN. I shouldn't think of troubling you. Good-by, dear Nora, and thank you for all your kindness.

NORA. Good-by for a little while. Of course you'll come back this evening. And you too, Doctor Rank. What! if you're well enough? Of course you'll be well enough. Only wrap up warmly. [*They go out into the hall, talking. Outside on the stairs are heard children's voices.*] There they are! there they are! [*She runs to the door and opens it. The nurse* ANNA *enters with the children.*] Come in! come in! [*Bends down and kisses the children.*] Oh! my sweet darlings! Do you see them, Christina? Aren't they lovely?

RANK. Don't let's stand here chattering in the draught.

HELMER. Come, Mrs. Linden; only mothers can stand such a temperature. [DR. RANK, HELMER, *and* MRS. LINDEN *go down the stairs;* ANNA *enters the room with the children;* NORA *also, shutting the door.*]

NORA. How fresh and bright you look! And what red cheeks you have!—like apples and roses. [*The children talk low to her during the following.*] Have you had great fun? That's splendid. Oh, really! you've been giving Emmy and Bob a ride on your sledge!—Both at once, only think! Why you're quite a man, Ivar. Oh, give her to me a little, Anna. My sweet little dolly! [*Takes the smallest from the nurse and dances with her.*] Yes, yes; mother will dance with Bob too. What! did you have a game of snow-balls? Oh! I wish I'd been there. No; leave them, Anna; I'll take their things off.

Oh, yes, let me do it; it's such fun. Go to the nursery; you look frozen. You'll find some hot coffee on the stove. [*The nurse goes into the room on the left.* NORA *takes off the children's things, and throws them down anywhere, while the children talk to each other and to her.*] Really! A big dog ran after you all the way home? But he didn't bite you? No; dogs don't bite dear little dolly children. Don't peep into those parcels, Ivar. What is it? Wouldn't you like to know? Oh, take care—it'll bite! What! shall we have a game? What shall we play at? Hide-and-seek? Yes, let's play hide-and-seek. Bob shall hide first. Am I to? Yes, let me hide first.

[*She and the children play, with laughter and shouting, in the room and the adjacent one to the right. At last* NORA *hides under the table; the children come rushing in, look for her, but cannot find her, hear her half-choked laughter, rush to the table, lift up the cover, and see her. Loud shouts. She creeps out, as though to frighten them. Fresh shouts. Meanwhile there has been a knock at the door leading into the hall. No one has heard it. Now the door is half opened and* KROGSTAD *is seen. He waits a little; the game is renewed.*]

KROGSTAD. I beg your pardon, Mrs. Helmer——

NORA [*with a suppressed cry, turns round and half jumps up*]. Ah! What do you want?

KROGSTAD. Excuse me; the outer door was ajar—somebody must have forgotten to shut it——

NORA [*standing up*]. My husband is not at home, Mr. Krogstad.

KROGSTAD. I know it.

NORA. Then—what do you want here?

KROGSTAD. To say a few words to you.

NORA. To me? [*To the children, softly.*] Go in to Anna. What? No,

the strange man won't hurt mamma. When he's gone we'll go on playing. [*She leads the children into the left-hand room, and shuts the door behind them. Uneasy, with suspense.*] It's with me you wish to speak?

KROGSTAD. Yes.

NORA. To-day? But it's not the first yet——

KROGSTAD. No; to-day is Christmas Eve. It will depend upon yourself whether you have a merry Christmas.

NORA. What do you want? I certainly can't to-day——

KROGSTAD. Never mind that just now. It's about another matter. You have a minute to spare?

NORA. Oh, yes, I suppose so; although——

KROGSTAD. Good. I was sitting in the restaurant opposite, and I saw your husband go down the street.

NORA. Well!

KROGSTAD. With a lady.

NORA. What then?

KROGSTAD. May I ask if the lady was a Mrs. Linden?

NORA. Yes.

KROGSTAD. Who has just come to town?

NORA. Yes. To-day.

KROGSTAD. I believe she's an intimate friend of yours?

NORA. Certainly. But I don't understand——

KROGSTAD. I used to know her too.

NORA. I know you did.

KROGSTAD. Ah! you know all about it. I thought as much. Now, frankly, is Mrs. Linden to have a place in the bank?

NORA. How dare you catechise me in this way, Mr. Krogstad, you, a subordinate of my husband's? But since you ask you shall know. Yes, Mrs. Linden is to be employed. And it's I who recommended her, Mr. Krogstad. Now you know.

KROGSTAD. Then my guess was right.

NORA [*walking up and down*]. You see one has a little wee bit of influence. It doesn't follow because one's only a woman that—— When one is in a subordinate position, Mr. Krogstad, one ought really to take care not to offend anybody who —h'm——

KROGSTAD. Who has influence?

NORA. Exactly!

KROGSTAD [*taking another tone*]. Mrs. Helmer, will you have the kindness to employ your influence on my behalf?

NORA. What? How do you mean?

KROGSTAD. Will you be so good as to see that I retain my subordinate position in the bank?

NORA. What do you mean? Who wants to take it from you?

KROGSTAD. Oh, you needn't pretend ignorance. I can very well understand that it cannot be pleasant for your friend to meet me; and I can also understand now for whose sake I am to be hounded out.

NORA. But I assure you——

KROGSTAD. Come now, once for all: there is time yet, and I advise you to use your influence to prevent it.

NORA. But, Mr. Krogstad, I have absolutely no influence.

KROGSTAD. None? I thought you just said——

NORA. Of course not in that sense—I! How should I have such influence over my husband?

KROGSTAD. Oh! I know your husband from our college days. I don't think he's firmer than other husbands.

NORA. If you talk disrespectfully of my husband, I must request you to go.

KROGSTAD. You are bold, madam.

NORA. I am afraid of you no longer. When New Year's Day is over, I shall soon be out of the whole business.

KROGSTAD [*controlling himself*]. Listen to me, Mrs. Helmer. If need be, I shall fight as though for my life to keep my little place in the bank.

NORA. Yes, so it seems.

KROGSTAD. It's not only for the money: that matters least to me. It's something else. Well, I'd better make a clean breast of it. Of course you know, like every one else, that some years ago I—got into trouble.

NORA. I think I've heard something of the sort.

KROGSTAD. The matter never came into court; but from that moment all paths were barred to me. Then I took up the business you know about. I was obliged to grasp at something; and I don't think I've been one of the worst. But now I must clear out of it all. My sons are growing up; for their sake I must try to win back as much respectability as I can. This place in the bank was the first step, and now your husband wants to kick me off the ladder, back into the mire.

NORA. But I assure you, Mr. Krogstad, I haven't the power to help you.

KROGSTAD. You have not the will; but I can compel you.

NORA. You won't tell my husband that I owe you money?

KROGSTAD. H'm; suppose I were to?

NORA. It would be shameful of you! [*With tears in her voice.*] This secret which is my joy and my pride—that he should learn it in such an ugly, coarse way—and from you! It would involve me in all sorts of unpleasantness.

KROGSTAD. Only unpleasantness?

NORA [*hotly*]. But just do it. It will be worst for you, for then my husband will see what a bad man you are, and then you certainly won't keep your place.

KROGSTAD. I asked if it was only domestic unpleasantness you feared?

NORA. If my husband gets to know about it, he will of course pay you off at once, and then we'll have nothing more to do with you.

KROGSTAD [*stepping a pace nearer*]. Listen, Mrs. Helmer. Either you have a weak memory, or you don't know much about business. I must make your position clearer to you.

NORA. How so?

KROGSTAD. When your husband was ill, you came to me to borrow twelve hundred dollars.

NORA. I knew nobody else.

KROGSTAD. I promised to find you the money——

NORA. And you did find it.

KROGSTAD. I promised to find you the money under certain conditions. You were then so much taken up about your husband's illness, and so eager to have the money for your journey, that you probably did not give much thought to the details. Let me remind you of them. I promised to find you the amount in exchange for a note of hand which I drew up.

NORA. Yes, and I signed it.

KROGSTAD. Quite right. But then I added a few lines, making your father a security for the debt. Your father was to sign this.

NORA. Was to? He did sign it!

KROGSTAD. I had left the date blank. That is to say, your father was himself to date his signature. Do you recollect that?

NORA. Yes, I believe——

KROGSTAD. Then I gave you the paper to send to your father. Is not that so?

NORA. Yes.

KROGSTAD. And of course you did so at once? For within five or six days you brought me back the paper, signed by your father, and I gave you the money.

NORA. Well! Haven't I made my payments punctually?

KROGSTAD. Fairly—yes. But to return to the point. You were in great trouble at the time, Mrs. Helmer.

NORA. I was indeed!

KROGSTAD. Your father was very ill, I believe?

NORA. He was on his death-bed.

KROGSTAD. And died soon after?

NORA. Yes.

KROGSTAD. Tell me, Mrs. Helmer: do you happen to recollect the day of his death? The day of the month, I mean?

NORA. Father died on the 29th of September.

KROGSTAD. Quite correct. I have made inquiries, and here comes in the remarkable point—[Produces a paper.] which I cannot explain.

NORA. What remarkable point? I don't know——

KROGSTAD. The remarkable point, madam, that your father signed this paper three days after his death!

NORA. What! I don't understand——

KROGSTAD. Your father died on the 29th of September. But look here, he has dated his signature October 2d! Is not that remarkable, Mrs. Helmer? [NORA is silent.] Can you explain it? [NORA continues silent.] It is noteworthy too that the words "October 2d" and the year are not in your father's handwriting, but in one which I believe I know. Well, this may be explained: your father may have forgotten to date his signature, and somebody may have added the date at random before the fact of his death was known. There is nothing wrong in that. Everything depends on the signature. Of course it is genuine, Mrs. Helmer? It was really your father who with his own hand wrote his name here?

NORA [after a short silence throws her head back and looks defiantly at him]. No: I wrote father's name there.

KROGSTAD. Ah! Are you aware, madam, that that is a dangerous admission?

NORA. Why? You'll soon get your money.

KROGSTAD. May I ask you one more question? Why did you not send the paper to your father?

NORA. It was impossible. Father was ill. If I had asked him for his signature I should have had to tell him why I wanted the money; but he was so ill I really could not tell him that my husband's life was in danger. It was impossible.

KROGSTAD. Then it would have been better to have given up your tour.

NORA. No, I couldn't do that; my husband's life depended on that journey. I couldn't give it up.

KROGSTAD. And did you not consider that you were playing me false?

NORA. That was nothing to me. I didn't care in the least about you. I couldn't endure you for all the cruel difficulties you made, although you knew how ill my husband was.

KROGSTAD. Mrs. Helmer, you have evidently no clear idea what you have really done. But I can assure you it was nothing more and nothing worse that made me an outcast from society.

NORA. You! You want me to believe that you did a brave thing to save your wife's life?

KROGSTAD. The law takes no account of motives.

NORA. Then it must be a very bad law.

KROGSTAD. Bad or not, if I lay this document before a court of law you will be condemned according to law.

NORA. I don't believe that. Do you mean to tell me that a daughter has no right to spare her dying father anxiety? —that a wife has no right to save her husband's life? I don't know much about the law, but I'm sure that, somewhere or another, you will find that *that* is allowed. And you don't know that—you, a lawyer! You must be a bad one, Mr. Krogstad.

KROGSTAD. Possibly. But business— such business as ours—I do understand. You believe that? Very well; now do as you please. But this I may tell you, that if I'm flung into the gutter a second time, you shall keep me company.

[*Bows and goes out through hall.*]

NORA [*stands awhile thinking, then throws her head back*]. Never! He wants to frighten me. I'm not so foolish as that. [*Begins folding the children's clothes. Pauses.*] But——? No, it's impossible. I did it for love!

CHILDREN [*at the door, left*]. Mamma, the strange man is gone now.

NORA. Yes, yes, I know. But don't tell any one about the strange man. Do you hear? Not even papa!

CHILDREN. No, mamma; and now will you play with us again?

NORA. No, no, not now.

CHILDREN. Oh, do, mamma; you know you promised.

NORA. Yes, but I can't just now. Run to the nursery; I've so much to do. Run along, run along, and be good, my darlings! [*She pushes them gently into the inner room, and closes the door behind them. Sits on the sofa, embroiders a few stitches, but soon pauses.*] No! [*Throws down work, rises, goes to the hall-door and calls out.*] Ellen, bring in the Christmas-tree! [*Goes to table, left, and opens the drawer; again pauses.*] No, it's quite impossible!

ELLEN [*with the Christmas-tree*]. Where shall I stand it, ma'am?

NORA. There, in the middle of the room.

ELLEN. Shall I bring in anything else?

NORA. No, thank you, I have all I want.

[ELLEN, *having put down the tree, goes out.*]

NORA [*busy dressing the tree*]. There must be a candle here, and flowers there. —The horrid man! Nonsense, nonsense! there's nothing in it. The Christmas-tree shall be beautiful. I will do everything to please you, Torvald; I'll sing and dance, and——

[*Enter* HELMER *by the hall-door, with bundle of documents.*]

NORA. Oh! you're back already?

HELMER. Yes. Has anybody been here?

NORA. Here? No.

HELMER. Curious! I saw Krogstad come out of the house.

NORA. Did you? Oh, yes, by the bye, he was here for a minute.

HELMER. Nora, I can see by your manner that he has been asking you to put in a good word for him.

NORA. Yes.

HELMER. And you were to do it as if of your own accord? You were to say nothing to me of his having been here! Didn't he suggest that too?——

NORA. Yes, Torvald; but——

HELMER. Nora, Nora! and you could condescend to that! To speak to such a man, to make him a promise! And then to tell me an untruth about it!

NORA. An untruth!

HELMER. Didn't you say nobody had been here? [*Threatens with his finger.*]

My little bird must never do that again?
A song-bird must never sing false notes.
[*Puts his arm round her.*] That's so,
isn't it? Yes, I was sure of it. [*Lets her
go.*] And now we'll say no more about it.
[*Sits down before the fire.*] Oh, how cosy
and quiet it is here. [*Glances into his
documents.*]

NORA [*busy with the tree, after a short
silence*]. Torvald.

HELMER. Yes.

NORA. I'm looking forward so much to
the Stenborgs' fancy ball the day after
to-morrow.

HELMER. And I'm on tenterhooks to
see what surprise you have in store for me.

NORA. Oh, it's too tiresome!

HELMER. What is?

NORA. I can't think of anything good.
Everything seems so foolish and meaning-
less.

HELMER. Has little Nora made that
discovery?

NORA [*behind his chair, with her arms
on the back*]. Are you very busy, Torvald?

HELMER. Well——

NORA. What sort of papers are those?

HELMER. Bank business.

NORA. Already?

HELMER. I got the retiring manager to
let me make some changes in the staff,
and so forth. This will occupy Christmas
week. Everything will be straight by the
New Year.

NORA. Then that's why that poor
Krogstad——

HELMER. H'm.

NORA [*still leaning over the chair-back,
and slowly stroking his hair*]. If you
hadn't been so very busy I should have
asked you a great, great favor, Torvald.

HELMER. What can it be? Let's hear it.

NORA. Nobody has such exquisite taste
as you. Now, I should so love to look
well at the fancy ball. Torvald dear,
couldn't you take me in hand, and settle
what I'm to be, and arrange my costume
for me?

HELMER. Aha! so my wilful little
woman's at a loss, and making signals of
distress.

NORA. Yes, *please*, Torvald. I can't get
on without you.

HELMER. Well, well, I'll think it over,
and we'll soon hit upon something.

NORA. Oh, how good that is of you!
[*Goes to the tree again; pause.*] How
well the red flowers show. Tell me, was
it anything so very dreadful this Krog-
stad got into trouble about?

HELMER. Forgery, that's all. Don't
you know what that means?

NORA. Mayn't he have been driven to
it by need?

HELMER. Yes, or like so many others,
done it out of heedlessness. I'm not so
hard-hearted as to condemn a man abso-
lutely for a single fault.

NORA. No, surely not, Torvald.

HELMER. Many a man can retrieve his
character if he owns his crime and takes
the punishment.

NORA. Crime?

HELMER. But Krogstad didn't do that;
he resorted to tricks and dodges, and it's
that that has corrupted him.

NORA. Do you think that——?

HELMER. Just think how a man with
that on his conscience must be always
lying and canting and shamming. Think
of the mask he must wear even toward
his own wife and children. It's worst for
the children, Nora!

NORA. Why?

HELMER. Because such a dust-cloud of
lies poisons and contaminates the whole
air of home. Every breath the children
draw contains some germ of evil.

NORA [*closer behind him*]. Are you
sure of that!

HELMER. As a lawyer, my dear, I've
seen it often enough. Nearly all cases of
early corruption may be traced to lying
mothers.

NORA. Why—mothers?

HELMER. It generally comes from the
mother's side, but of course the father's
influence may act in the same way. And
this Krogstad has been poisoning his own
children for years past by a life of lies
and hypocrisy—that's why I call him
morally ruined. [*Stretches out his hands*

toward her.] So my sweet little Nora must promise not to plead his cause. Shake hands upon it. Come, come, what's this? Give me your hand. That's right. Then it's a bargain. I assure you it would have been impossible for me to work with him. It gives me a positive sense of physical discomfort to come in contact with such people.

[Nora *snatches her hand away, and moves to the other side of the Christmas-tree.*]

NORA. How warm it is here; and I have so much to do.

HELMER. Yes, and I must try to get some of these papers looked through before dinner; and I'll think over your costume, too. And perhaps I may even find something to hang in gilt paper on the Christmas-tree! [*Lays his hand on her head.*] My precious little song-bird.

[*He goes into his room and shuts the door behind him.*]

NORA [*softly, after a pause*]. It can't be—— It's impossible. It must be impossible!

ANNA [*at the door, left*]. The little ones are begging so prettily to come to mamma.

NORA. No, no, don't let them come to me! Keep them with you, Anna.

ANNA. Very well, ma'am.

[*Shuts the door.*]

NORA [*pale with terror*]. Corrupt my children!—— Poison my home! [*Short pause. She raises her head.*] It's not true. It can never, never be true.

ACT II

The same room. In the corner, beside the piano, stands the Christmas-tree, stripped, and the candles burnt out. NORA'S *walking things lie on the sofa.* NORA *discovered walking about restlessly. She stops by sofa, takes up cloak, then lays it down again.*

NORA. There's somebody coming. [*Goes to hall door; listens.*] Nobody; nobody is

likely to come to-day, Christmas Day; nor to-morrow either. But perhaps—— [*Opens the door and looks out.*] No, nothing in the letter box; quite empty. [*Comes forward.*] Stuff and nonsense! Of course he only meant to frighten me. There's no fear of any such thing. It's impossible! Why, I have three little children.

[*Enter* ANNA, *from the left, with a large cardboard box.*]

ANNA. At last I've found the box with the fancy dress.

NORA. Thanks; put it down on the table.

ANNA [*does so*]. But it is very much out of order.

NORA. Oh, I wish I could tear it into a hundred thousand pieces.

ANNA. Oh, no. It can easily be put to rights—just a little patience.

NORA. I'll go and get Mrs. Linden to help me.

ANNA. Going out again! In such weather as this! You'll catch cold, ma'am, and be ill.

NORA. Worse things might happen—— What are the children doing?

ANNA. They're playing with their Christmas presents, poor little dears; but——

NORA. Do they often ask for me?

ANNA. You see they've been so used to having their mamma with them.

NORA. Yes; but, Anna, in future I can't have them so much with me.

ANNA. Well, little children get used to anything.

NORA. Do you think they do? Do you believe they would forget their mother if she went quite away?

ANNA. Gracious me! Quite away?

NORA. Tell me, Anna—I've so often wondered about it—how could you bring yourself to give your child up to strangers?

ANNA. I had to when I came as nurse to my little Miss Nora.

NORA. But how could you make up your mind to it?

ANNA. When I had the chance of such

a good place? A poor girl who's been in trouble must take what comes. That wicked man did nothing for me.

NORA. But your daughter must have forgotten you.

ANNA. Oh, no, ma'am, that she hasn't. She wrote to me both when she was confirmed and when she was married.

NORA [embracing her]. Dear old Anna —you were a good mother to me when I was little.

ANNA. My poor little Nora had no mother but me.

NORA. And if my little ones had nobody else, I'm sure you would—nonsense, nonsense! [Opens the box.] Go in to the children. Now I must——. To-morrow you shall see how beautiful I'll be.

ANNA. I'm sure there will be no one at the ball so beautiful as my Miss Nora. [She goes into room on left.]

NORA [takes the costume out of the box, but soon throws it down again.] Oh, if I dared go out. If only nobody would come. If only nothing would happen here in the meantime. Rubbish; nobody will come. Only not to think. What a delicious muff! Beautiful gloves, beautiful gloves! Away with it all—away with it all! One, two, three, four, five, six—— [With a scream.] Ah, there they come—— [Goes toward the door, then stands undecidedly.]

[MRS. LINDEN enters from hall where she has taken off her things.]

NORA. Oh, it's you, Christina. Is nobody else there? How delightful of you to come.

MRS. LINDEN. I hear you called at my lodgings.

NORA. Yes, I was just passing. I do so want you to help me. Let us sit here on the sofa—so. To-morrow evening there's to be a fancy ball at Consul Stenborg's overhead, and Torvald wants me to appear as a Neapolitan fisher girl, and dance the tarantella; I learnt it at Capri.

MRS. LINDEN. I see—quite a performance!

NORA. Yes, Torvald wishes me to. Look, this is the costume. Torvald had it made for me in Italy; but now it is all so torn, I don't know——

MRS. LINDEN. Oh! we'll soon set that to rights. It's only the trimming that's got loose here and there. Have you a needle and thread? Ah! here's the very thing.

NORA. Oh, how kind of you.

MRS. LINDEN. So you're to be in costume, to-morrow, Nora? I'll tell you what—I shall come in for a moment to see you in all your glory. But I've quite forgotten to thank you for the pleasant evening yesterday.

NORA [rises and walks across room]. Oh! yesterday, it didn't seem so pleasant as usual. You should have come a little sooner, Christina. Torvald has certainly the art of making home bright and beautiful.

MRS. LINDEN. You, too, I should think, or you wouldn't be your father's daughter. But tell me—is Doctor Rank always so depressed as he was yesterday?

NORA. No; yesterday it was particularly striking. You see he has a terrible illness. He has spinal consumption, poor fellow. They say his father led a terrible life—kept mistresses and all sorts of things—so the son has been sickly from his childhood, you understand.

MRS. LINDEN [lets her sewing fall into her lap]. Why, my darling Nora, how do you learn such things?

NORA [walking]. Oh! when one has three children one has visits from women who know something of medicine—and they talk of this and that.

MRS. LINDEN [goes on sewing—a short pause]. Does Doctor Rank come here every day?

NORA. Every day. He's been Torvald's friend from boyhood, and he's a good friend of mine too. Doctor Rank is quite one of the family.

MRS. LINDEN. But tell me—is he quite sincere? I mean, doesn't he like to say flattering things to people?

NORA. On the contrary. Why should you think so?

MRS. LINDEN. When you introduced us yesterday he declared he had often heard my name; but I noticed your husband had no notion who I was. How could Doctor Rank——?

NORA. Yes, he was quite right, Christina. You see, Torvald loves me so indescribably he wants to have me all to himself, as he says. When we were first married he was almost jealous if I even mentioned one of the people at home; so I naturally let it alone. But I often talk to Doctor Rank about the old times, for he likes to hear about them.

MRS. LINDEN. Listen to me, Nora! You're still a child in many ways. I am older than you, and have more experience. I'll tell you something: you ought to get clear of the whole affair with Doctor Rank.

NORA. What affair?

MRS. LINDEN. You were talking yesterday of a rich admirer who was to find you money——

NORA. Yes, one who never existed, worse luck. What then?

MRS. LINDEN. Has Doctor Rank money?

NORA. Yes, he has.

MRS. LINDEN. And nobody to provide for?

NORA. Nobody. But——?

MRS. LINDEN. And he comes here every day?

NORA. Yes, every day.

MRS. LINDEN. I should have thought he'd have had better taste.

NORA. I don't understand you.

MRS. LINDEN. Don't pretend, Nora. Do you suppose I don't guess who lent you the twelve hundred dollars?

NORA. Are you out of your senses? You think *that!* A friend who comes here every day! How painful that would be!

MRS. LINDEN. Then it really is not he?

NORA. No, I assure you. It never for a moment occurred to me. Besides, at that time he had nothing to lend; he came into his property afterward.

MRS. LINDEN. Well, I believe that was lucky for you, Nora dear.

NORA. No, really, it would never have struck me to ask Doctor Rank. But I'm certain that if I did——

MRS. LINDEN. But of course you never would?

NORA. Of course not. It's inconceivable that it should ever be necessary. But I'm quite sure that if I spoke to Doctor Rank——

MRS. LINDEN. Behind your husband's back?

NORA. I must get out of the other thing; that's behind his back too. I must get out of that.

MRS. LINDEN. Yes, yes, I told you so yesterday; but——

NORA [*walking up and down*]. A man can manage these things much better than a woman.

MRS. LINDEN. One's own husband, yes.

NORA. Nonsense. [*Stands still.*] When everything is paid, one gets back the paper?

MRS. LINDEN. Of course.

NORA. And can tear it into a hundred thousand pieces, and burn it, the nasty, filthy thing!

MRS. LINDEN [*looks at her fixedly, lays down her work, and rises slowly*]. Nora, you're hiding something from me.

NORA. Can you see that in my face?

MRS. LINDEN. Something has happened since yesterday morning. Nora, what is it?

NORA [*going toward her*]. Christina [*Listens.*]—Hush! There's Torvald coming home. Here, go into the nursery. Torvald cannot bear to see dressmaking. Let Anna help you.

MRS. LINDEN [*gathers some of the things together*]. Very well, but I shan't go away until you've told me all about it.

[*She goes out to the left as HELMER enters from hall.*]

NORA [*runs to meet him*]. Oh! how I've been longing for you to come, Torvald dear.

HELMER. Was the dressmaker here?

NORA. No, Christina. She is helping

me with my costume. You'll see how well I shall look.

HELMER. Yes, wasn't that a lucky thought of mine?

NORA. Splendid. But isn't it good of me, too, to have given in to you?

HELMER [takes her under the chin]. Good of you! To give in to your own husband? Well, well, you little madcap, I know you don't mean it. But I won't disturb you. I dare say you want to be "trying on."

NORA. And you're going to work, I suppose?

HELMER. Yes. [Shows her bundle of papers.] Look here. [Goes toward his room.] I've just come from the Bank.

NORA. Torvald.

HELMER [stopping]. Yes?

NORA. If your little squirrel were to beg you for something so prettily——

HELMER. Well?

NORA. Would you do it?

HELMER. I must know first what it is.

NORA. The squirrel would jump about and play all sorts of tricks if you would only be nice and kind.

HELMER. Come, then, out with it.

NORA. Your lark would twitter from morning till night——

HELMER. Oh, that she does in any case.

NORA. I'll be an elf and dance in the moonlight for you, Torvald.

HELMER. Nora—you can't mean what you were hinting at this morning?

NORA [coming nearer]. Yes, Torvald, I beg and implore you.

HELMER. Have you really the courage to begin that again?

NORA. Yes, yes; for my sake, you must let Krogstad keep his place in the bank.

HELMER. My dear Nora, it's his place I intend for Mrs. Linden.

NORA. Yes, that's so good of you. But instead of Krogstad, you could dismiss some other clerk.

HELMER. Why, this is incredible obstinacy! Because you thoughtlessly promised to put in a word for him, I am to——

NORA. It's not that, Torvald. It's for your own sake. This man writes for the most scurrilous newspapers; you said so yourself. He can do you such a lot of harm. I'm terribly afraid of him.

HELMER. Oh, I understand; it's old recollections that are frightening you.

NORA. What do you mean?

HELMER. Of course you're thinking of your father.

NORA. Yes, of course. Only think of the shameful things wicked people used to write about father. I believe they'd have got him dismissed if you hadn't been sent to look into the thing and been kind to him and helped him.

HELMER. My dear Nora, between your father and me there is all the difference in the world. Your father was not altogether unimpeachable. I am; and I hope to remain so.

NORA. Oh, no one knows what wicked men can hit upon. We could live so happily now, in our cosy, quiet home, you and I and the children, Torvald! That's why I beg and implore you——

HELMER. And it's just by pleading his cause that you make it impossible for me to keep him. It's already known at the bank that I intend to dismiss Krogstad. If it were now reported that the new manager let himself be turned round his wife's little finger——

NORA. What then?

HELMER. Oh, nothing! So long as a wilful woman can have her way I am to make myself the laughing-stock of everyone, and set people saying 1 am under petticoat government? Take my word for it, I should soon feel the consequences. And besides, there's one thing that makes Krogstad impossible for me to work with.

NORA. What then?

HELMER. I could perhaps have overlooked his shady character at a pinch——

NORA. Yes, couldn't you, Torvald?

HELMER. And I hear he is good at his work. But the fact is, he was a college chum of mine—there was one of those rash friendships between us that one so often repents of later. I don't mind confessing it—he calls me by my Christian name; and he insists on doing it even when others are present. He delights in putting on airs of familiarity—Torvald here, Torvald there! I assure you it's most painful to me. He would make my position at the Bank perfectly unendurable.

NORA. Torvald, you're not serious?

HELMER. No? Why not?

NORA. That's such a petty reason.

HELMER. What! Petty! Do you consider me petty?

NORA. No, on the contrary, Torvald dear; and that's just why——

HELMER. Never mind, you call my motives petty; then I must be petty too. Petty! Very well. Now we'll put an end to this once for all. [*Goes to the door into the hall and calls.*] Ellen!

NORA. What do you want?

HELMER [*searching among his papers*]. To settle the thing. [ELLEN *enters.*] There, take this letter, give it to a messenger. See that he takes it at once. The address is on it. Here is the money.

ELLEN. Very well. [*Goes with the letter.*]

HELMER [*arranging papers*]. There, Madame Obstinacy!

NORA [*breathless*]. Torvald—what was in that letter?

HELMER. Krogstad's dismissal.

NORA. Call it back again, Torvald! There is still time. Oh, Torvald, get it back again! For my sake, for your own, for the children's sake! Do you hear, Torvald? Do it. You don't know what that letter may bring upon us all.

HELMER. Too late.

NORA. Yes, too late.

HELMER. My dear Nora, I forgive your anxiety, though it's anything but flattering to me. Why should I be afraid of a blackguard scribbler's spite? But I forgive you all the same, for it's a proof of your great love for me. [*Takes her in his arms.*] That's how it should be, my own dear Nora. Let what will happen—when the time comes, I shall have strength and courage enough. You shall see, my shoulders are broad enough to bear the whole burden.

NORA [*terror-struck*]. What do you mean by that?

HELMER. The whole burden, I say.

NORA [*firmly*]. That you shall never, never do.

HELMER. Very well; then we'll share it, Nora, as man and wife. [*Petting her.*] Are you satisfied now? Come, come, come, don't look like a scared dove. It is all nothing—fancy. Now you must play the tarantella through, and practice the tambourine. I shall sit in my inner room and shut both doors, so that I shall hear nothing. You can make as much noise as you please. [*Turns round in doorway.*] And when Rank comes, just tell him where I'm to be found. [*He nods to her and goes with his papers into his room, closing the door.*]

NORA [*bewildered with terror, stands as though rooted to the ground and whispers*]. He would do it. Yes, he would do it. He would do it, in spite of all the world. No, never that, never, never! Anything rather than that! Oh, for some way of escape! What to do! [*Hall bell rings.*] Anything rather than that—anything, anything!

[NORA *draws her hands over her face, pulls herself together, goes to the door and opens it.* RANK *stands outside, hanging up his greatcoat. During the following, it grows dark.*]

NORA. Good afternoon, Doctor Rank. I knew you by your ring. But you mustn't go to Torvald now. I believe he's busy.

RANK. And you?

NORA. Oh, you know very well I've always time for you.

RANK. Thank you. I shall avail myself of your kindness as long as I can!

NORA. What do you mean? As long as you can?

RANK. Yes. Does that frighten you?

NORA. I think it's an odd expression. Do you expect anything to happen?

RANK. Something I've long been prepared for; but I didn't think it would come so soon.

NORA [*seizing his arm*]. What is it, Doctor Rank? You must tell me.

RANK [*sitting down by the stove*]. I am running down hill. There's no help for it.

NORA [*draws a long breath of relief*]. It's *you?*

RANK. Who else should it be? Why lie to one's self? I'm the most wretched of all my patients, Mrs. Helmer. I have been auditing my life-account—bankrupt! Before a month is over I shall lie rotting in the churchyard.

NORA. Oh! What an ugly way to talk!

RANK. The thing itself is so confoundedly ugly, you see. But the worst of it is, so many other ugly things have to be gone through first. There is one last investigation to be made, and when that is over I shall know exactly when the break-up will begin. There's one thing I want to say to you. Helmer's delicate nature shrinks so from all that is horrible; I will not have him in my sick room.

NORA. But, Doctor Rank——

RANK. I won't have him, I say—not on any account! I shall lock my door against him. As soon as I have ascertained the worst, I shall send you my visiting card with a black cross on it; and then you will know that the horror has begun.

NORA. Why you're perfectly unreasonable to-day. And I did so want you to be in a really good humor.

RANK. With death staring me in the face? And to suffer thus for another's sin! Where's the justice of it? And in every family you can see some such inexorable retribution——

NORA [*stopping her ears*]. Nonsense, nonsense; now cheer up.

RANK. Well, after all, the whole thing's only worth laughing at. My poor innocent spine must do penance for my father's wild oats.

NORA [*at table, left*]. I suppose he was too fond of asparagus and Strasbourg paté, wasn't he?

RANK. Yes; and truffles.

NORA. Yes, truffles, to be sure. And oysters, I believe?

RANK. Yes, oysters; oysters of course.

NORA. And then all the port and champagne. It's sad all these good things should attack the spine.

RANK. Especially when the spine attacked never had the good of them.

NORA. Yes, that's the worst of it.

RANK [*looks at her searchingly*]. H'm——

NORA [*a moment later*]. Why did you smile?

RANK. No; it was you that laughed.

NORA. No; it was you that smiled, Doctor Rank.

RANK [*standing up*]. You're deeper than I thought.

NORA. I'm in such a crazy mood to-day.

RANK. So it seems.

NORA [*with her hands on his shoulders*]. Dear, dear Doctor Rank, death shall not take you away from Torvald and me.

RANK. Oh, you'll easily get over the loss. The absent are soon forgotten.

NORA [*looks at him anxiously*]. Do you think so?

RANK. People make fresh ties, and then——

NORA. Who make fresh ties?

RANK. You and Helmer will, when I'm gone. You yourself are taking time by the forelock, it seems to me. What was that Mrs. Linden doing here yesterday?

NORA. Oh! You're surely not jealous of Christina?

RANK. Yes, I am. She will be my successor in this house. When I'm gone, this woman will perhaps——

NORA. Hush! Not so loud; she is in there.

RANK. To-day as well? You see!

NORA. Only to put my costume in order—how unreasonable you are! [*Sits on sofa.*] Now do be good, Doctor Rank.

To-morrow you shall see how beautifully I dance; and then you may fancy that I am doing it all to please you—and of course Torvald as well. [*Takes various things out of box.*] Doctor Rank, sit here, and I'll show you something.

RANK [*sitting*]. What is it?

NORA. Look here. Look!

RANK. Silk stockings.

NORA. Flesh-colored. Aren't they lovely? Oh, it's so dark here now; but to-morrow— No, no, no, you must only look at the feet. Oh, well, I suppose you may look at the rest too.

RANK. H'm——

NORA. What are you looking so critical about? Do you think they won't fit me?

RANK. I can't possibly have any valid opinion on that point.

NORA [*looking at him a moment*]. For shame! [*Hits him lightly on the ear with the stockings.*] Take that. [*Rolls them up again.*]

RANK. And what other wonders am I to see?

NORA. You shan't see any more, for you don't behave nicely. [*She hums a little and searches among the things.*]

RANK [*after a short silence*]. When I sit here gossiping with you, I simply can't imagine what would have become of me if I had never entered this house.

NORA [*smiling*]. Yes, I think you do feel at home with us.

RANK [*more softly—looking straight before him*]. And now to have to leave it all——

NORA. Nonsense. You sha'n't leave us.

RANK [*in the same tone*]. And not to be able to leave behind the slightest token of gratitude; scarcely even a passing regret—nothing but an empty place, that can be filled by the first comer.

NORA. And if I were to ask for——? No——

RANK. For what?

NORA. For a great proof of your friendship.

RANK. Yes?— Yes?

NORA. No, I mean—for a very, very great service.

RANK. Would you really for once make me so happy?

NORA. Oh! you don't know what it is.

RANK. Then tell me.

NORA. No, I really can't; it's far, far too much—not only a service, but help and advice besides——

RANK. So much the better. I can't think what you can mean. But go on. Don't you trust me?

NORA. As I trust no one else. I know you are my best and truest friend. So I will tell you. Well, then, Doctor Rank, you must help me to prevent something. You know how deeply, how wonderfully Torvald loves me; he would not hesitate a moment to give his very life for my sake.

RANK [*bending toward her*]. Nora, do you think he is the only one who——

NORA [*with a slight start*]. Who——?

RANK. Who would gladly give his life for you?

NORA [*sadly*]. Oh!

RANK. I have sworn that you shall know it before I—go. I should never find a better opportunity—— Yes, Nora, now you know it, and now you know too that you can trust me as you can no one else.

NORA [*standing up, simply and calmly*]. Let me pass, please.

RANK [*makes way for her, but remains sitting*]. Nora——

NORA [*in the doorway*]. Ellen, bring the lamp. [*Crosses to the stove.*] Oh, dear, Doctor Rank, that was too bad of you.

RANK [*rising*]. That I have loved you as deeply as—anyone else? Was that too bad of me?

NORA. No, but that you should tell me so. It was so unnecessary——

RANK. What do you mean? Did you know——?

[ELLEN *enters with the lamp; sets it on table and goes out again.*]

RANK. Nora—Mrs. Helmer—I ask you, did you know?

NORA. Oh, how can I tell what I knew

or didn't know. I really can't say——
How could you be so clumsy, Doctor
Rank? It was all so nice!

RANK. Well, at any rate, you know
now that I am yours, soul and body.
And now, go on.

NORA [looking at him]. Go on—now?

RANK. I beg you to tell what you
want.

NORA. I can tell you nothing now.

RANK. Yes, yes! You mustn't punish
me in that way. Let me do for you what-
ever a man can.

NORA. You can really do nothing for
me now. Besides, I really want no help.
You'll see it was only my fancy. Yes, it
must be so. Of course! [Sits in the
rocking-chair smiling at him.] You're
a nice one, Doctor Rank. Aren't you
ashamed of yourself now the lamp's on
the table?

RANK. No, not exactly. But perhaps
I ought to go—for ever.

NORA. No, indeed you mustn't. Of
course you must come and go as you've
always done. You know very well that
Torvald can't do without you.

RANK. Yes, but you?

NORA. Oh, you know I always like to
have you here.

RANK. That's just what led me astray.
You're a riddle to me. It has often
seemed to me as if you liked being
with me almost as much as being with
Helmer.

NORA. Yes, don't you see?—there are
some people one loves, and others one
likes to talk to.

RANK. Yes—there's something in that.

NORA. When I was a girl I naturally
loved papa best. But it always delighted
me to steal into the servants' room. In
the first place they never lectured me, and
in the second it was such fun to hear them
talk.

RANK. Oh, I see; then it's their place
I have taken?

NORA [jumps up and hurries toward
him]. Oh, my dear Doctor Rank, I don't
mean that. But you understand, with
Torvald it's the same as with papa——

[ELLEN enters from the hall.]

ELLEN. Please, ma'am—— [Whispers
to NORA and gives her a card.]

NORA [glances at the card]. Ah! [Puts
it in her pocket.]

RANK. Anything wrong?

NORA. No, not in the least. It's only
—it's my new costume——

RANK. Why, it's there.

NORA. Oh, that one, yes. But it's an-
other that—I ordered it—Torvald mustn't
know——

RANK. Aha! so that's the great secret.

NORA. Yes, of course. Do just go to
him; he's in the inner room; do keep him
as long as you can.

RANK. Make yourself easy; he sha'n't
escape. [Goes into HELMER'S room.]

NORA [to ELLEN]. Is he waiting in the
kitchen?

ELLEN. Yes, he came up the back
stair——

NORA. Didn't you tell him I was en-
gaged?

ELLEN. Yes, but it was no use.

NORA. He won't go away?

ELLEN. No, ma'am, not until he has
spoken with you.

NORA. Then let him come in; but
quietly. And, Ellen——say nothing about
it; it's a surprise for my husband.

ELLEN. Oh, yes, ma'am, I under-
stand—— [She goes out.]

NORA. It's coming. It's coming after
all. No, no, no, it can never be; it shall
not!

[She goes to HELMER'S door and
slips the bolt. ELLEN opens
the hall-door for KROGSTAD,
and shuts it after him. He
wears a travelling coat, high
boots, and a fur cap.]

NORA. Speak quietly; my husband is
at home.

KROGSTAD. All right. I don't care.

NORA. What do you want?

KROGSTAD. A little information.

NORA. Be quick, then. What is it?

KROGSTAD. You know I've got my dis-
missal.

NORA. I could not prevent it, Mr.

Krogstad. I fought for you to the last, but it was no good.

Krogstad. Does your husband care for you so little? He knows what I can bring upon you, and yet he dares——

Nora. How can you think I should tell him?

Krogstad. I knew very well you hadn't. It wasn't like my friend Torvald Helmer to show so much courage——

Nora. Mr. Krogstad, be good enough to speak respectfully of my husband.

Krogstad. Certainly, with all due respect. But since you're so anxious to keep the matter secret, I suppose you're a little clearer than yesterday as to what you have done.

Nora. Clearer than you could ever make me.

Krogstad. Yes, such a bad lawyer as I——

Nora. What is it you want?

Krogstad. Only to see how you're getting on, Mrs. Helmer. I've been thinking about you all day. A mere money-lender, a penny-a-liner, a—in short, a creature like me—has a little bit of what people call "heart."

Nora. Then show it; think of my little children.

Krogstad. Did you and your husband think of mine? But enough of that. I only wanted to tell you that you needn't take this matter too seriously. I sha'n't lodge any information for the present.

Nora. No, surely not. I knew you would not.

Krogstad. The whole thing can be settled quite quietly. Nobody need know. It can remain among us three.

Nora. My husband must never know.

Krogstad. How can you prevent it? Can you pay off the debt?

Nora. No, not at once.

Krogstad. Or have you any means of raising the money in the next few days?

Nora. None that I will make use of.

Krogstad. And if you had it would be no good to you now. If you offered me ever so much ready money you should not get back your I O U.

Nora. Tell me what you want to do with it.

Krogstad. I only want to keep it, to have it in my possession. No outsider shall hear anything of it. So, if you've got any desperate scheme in your head——

Nora. What if I have?

Krogstad. If you should think of leaving your husband and children——

Nora. What if I do?

Krogstad. Or if you should think of —something—worse——

Nora. How do you know that?

Krogstad. Put all that out of your head.

Nora. How did you know what I had in my mind?

Krogstad. Most of us think of *that* at first. I thought of it, too; but I had not the courage——

Nora [*voicelessly*]. Nor I.

Krogstad [*relieved*]. No one hasn't. You haven't the courage either, have you?

Nora. I haven't, I haven't.

Krogstad. Besides, it would be very silly—when the first storm is over—— I have a letter in my pocket for your husband——

Nora. Telling him everything?

Krogstad. Sparing you as much as possible.

Nora [*quickly*]. He must never have that letter. Tear it up. I will get the money somehow.

Krogstad. Pardon me, Mrs. Helmer, but I believe I told you——

Nora. Oh, I'm not talking about the money I owe you. Tell me how much you demand from my husband——I'll get it.

Krogstad. I demand no money from your husband.

Nora. What *do* you demand then?

Krogstad. I'll tell you. I want to regain my footing in the world. I want to rise; and your husband shall help me to do it. For the last eighteen months my record has been spotless; I've been in bitter need all the time; but I was content to fight my way up, step by step. Now, I've been thrust down, and I won't be satisfied with merely being allowed to sneak back again. I want to rise, I tell you. I must get into the bank again, in a higher position than before. Your husband shall create a place on purpose for me——

NORA. He will never do that!

KROGSTAD. He will do it; I know him —he won't dare to refuse! And when I'm in, you'll soon see! I shall be the manager's right hand. It won't be Torvald Helmer, but Nils Krogstad, that manages the Joint Stock Bank.

NORA. That will never be.

KROGSTAD. Perhaps you'll——?

NORA. *Now* I have the courage for it.

KROGSTAD. Oh, you don't frighten me. A sensitive, petted creature like you——

NORA. You shall see, you shall see!

KROGSTAD. Under the ice, perhaps? Down in the cold, black water? And next spring to come up again, ugly, hairless, unrecognizable——

NORA. You can't terrify me.

KROGSTAD. Nor you me. People don't do that sort of thing, Mrs. Helmer. And, after all, what good would it be? I have your husband in my pocket all the same.

NORA. Afterward? When I am no longer——

KROGSTAD. You forget, your reputation remains in my hands! [NORA *stands speechless and looks at him.*] Well, now you are prepared. Do nothing foolish. So soon as Helmer has received my letter I shall expect to hear from him. And remember that it is your husband himself who has forced me back again into such paths. That I will never forgive him. Good-by, Mrs. Helmer. [*Goes through hall.* NORA *hurries to the door, opens it a little, and listens.*]

NORA. He's going. He is not putting the letter into the box. No, no, it would be impossible. [*Opens the door farther and farther.*] What's that? He's standing still; not going downstairs. Is he changing his mind? Is he——? [*A letter falls into the box.* KROGSTAD's footsteps are heard gradually receding down the stair.* NORA *utters suppressed shriek;*

pause.] In the letter-box. [*Slips shrinkingly up to the door.*] There it lies—— Torvald, Torvald—now we are lost!

[MRS. LINDEN *enters from the left with the costume.*]

MRS. LINDEN. There, I think it's all right now. Shall we just try it on?

NORA [*hoarsely and softly*]. Christina, come here.

MRS. LINDEN [*throws dress on sofa*]. What's the matter? You look quite aghast.

NORA. Come here. Do you see that letter? There, see—through the glass of the letter-box.

MRS. LINDEN. Yes, yes, I see it.

NORA. That letter is from Krogstad——

MRS. LINDEN. Nora—it was Krogstad who lent you the money!

NORA. Yes, and now Torvald will know everything.

MRS. LINDEN. Believe me, Nora, it's the best thing for you both.

NORA. You don't know all yet. I have forged a name——

MRS. LINDEN. Good heavens!

NORA. Now listen to me, Christina, you shall bear me witness.

MRS. LINDEN. How "witness"? What am I to——?

NORA. If I should go out of my mind— it might easily happen——

MRS. LINDEN. Nora!

NORA. Of if anything else should happen to me—so that I couldn't be here myself——

MRS. LINDEN. Now, Nora, you're quite beside yourself!

NORA. In case any one wanted to take it all upon himself—the whole blame, you understand——

MRS. LINDEN. Yes, but how can you think——

NORA. You shall bear witness that it's not true, Christina. I'm not out of my mind at all; I know quite well what I'm saying; and I tell you nobody else knew anything about it; I did the whole thing, I myself. Don't forget that.

Mrs. Linden. I won't forget. But I don't understand what you mean——

Nora. Oh, how should you? It's the miracle coming to pass.

Mrs. Linden. The miracle?

Nora. Yes, the miracle. But it's so terrible, Christina;—it mustn't happen for anything in the world.

Mrs. Linden. I will go straight to Krogstad and talk to him.

Nora. Don't; he will do you some harm.

Mrs. Linden. Once he would have done anything for me.

Nora. He?

Mrs. Linden. Where does he live?

Nora. Oh, how can I tell——? Yes; [Feels in her pocket.] here's his card. But the letter, the letter——!

Helmer [knocking outside]. Nora.

Nora [shrieks in terror]. What is it? What do you want?

Helmer. Don't be frightened, we're not coming in; you've bolted the door. Are you trying on your dress?

Nora. Yes, yes, I'm trying it on. It suits me so well, Torvald.

Mrs. Linden [who has read the card]. Then he lives close by here?

Nora. Yes, but it's no use now. The letter is actually in the box.

Mrs. Linden. And your husband has the key?

Nora. Always.

Mrs. Linden. Krogstad must demand his letter back, unread. He must make some excuse——

Nora. But this is the very time when Torvald generally——

Mrs. Linden. Prevent him. Keep him occupied. I'll come back as quickly as I can.

[She goes out quickly through the hall door.]

Nora [opens Helmer's door and peeps in]. Torvald!

Helmer. Well, now may one come back into one's own room? Come, Rank, we'll have a look— [In the doorway.] But how's this?

Nora. What, Torvald dear?

Helmer. Rank led me to expect a grand dressing-up.

Rank [in the doorway]. So I understood. I suppose I was mistaken.

Nora. No, no one shall see me in my glory till to-morrow evening.

Helmer. Why, Nora dear, you look so tired. Have you been practising too hard?

Nora. No, I haven't practised at all yet.

Helmer. But you'll have to——

Nora. Yes, it's absolutely necessary. But, Torvald, I can't get on without your help. I've forgotten everything.

Helmer. Oh, we'll soon freshen it up again.

Nora. Yes, do help me, Torvald. You must promise me.—Oh, I'm so nervous about it. Before so many people—this evening you must give yourself up entirely to me. You mustn't do a stroke of work! Now promise, Torvald dear!

Helmer. I promise. All this evening I will be your slave. Little helpless thing!—But, by the by, I must first—— [Going to hall door.]

Nora. What do you want there?

Helmer. Only to see if there are any letters.

Nora. No, no, don't do that, Torvald.

Helmer. Why not?

Nora. Torvald, I beg you not to. There are none there.

Helmer. Let me just see. [Is going. Nora, at the piano, plays the first bars of the tarantella.]

Helmer [at the door, stops]. Aha!

Nora. I can't dance to-morrow if I don't rehearse with you first.

Helmer [going to her]. Are you really so nervous, dear Nora?

Nora. Yes, dreadfully! Let me rehearse at once. We have time before dinner. Oh! do sit down and accompany me, Torvald dear; direct me as you used to do.

Helmer. With all the pleasure in life, if you wish it.

[*Sits at piano.* NORA *snatches the tambourine out of the box, and hurriedly drapes herself in a long parti-colored shawl; then, with a bound, stands in the middle of the floor.*]

NORA. Now play for me! Now I'll dance!

[HELMER *plays and* NORA *dances.* RANK *stands at the piano behind* HELMER *and looks on.*]

HELMER [*playing*]. Slower! Slower!

NORA. Can't do it slower.

HELMER. Not so violently, Nora.

NORA. I must! I must!

HELMER [*stops*]. Nora—that'll never do.

NORA [*laughs and swings her tambourine*]. Didn't I tell you so?

RANK. Let me accompany her.

HELMER [*rising*]. Yes, do—then I can direct her better.

[RANK *sits down to the piano and plays.* NORA *dances more and more wildly.* HELMER *stands by the stove and addresses frequent corrections to her. She seems not to hear. Her hair breaks loose and falls over her shoulders. She does not notice it, but goes on dancing.* MRS. LINDEN *enters and stands spellbound in the doorway.*]

MRS. LINDEN. Ah!

NORA [*dancing*]. We're having such fun here, Christina!

HELMER. Why, Nora dear, you're dancing as if it were a matter of life and death.

NORA. So it is.

HELMER. Rank, stop! this is the merest madness. Stop, I say! [RANK *stops playing, and* NORA *comes to a sudden standstill.* HELMER *going toward her.*] I couldn't have believed it. You've positively forgotten all I taught you.

NORA [*throws tambourine away*]. You see for yourself.

HELMER. You really do want teaching.

NORA. Yes, you see how much I need it. You must practise with me up to the last moment. Will you promise me, Torvald?

HELMER. Certainly, certainly.

NORA. Neither to-day nor to-morrow must you think of anything but me. You mustn't open a single letter—mustn't look at the letter-box!

HELMER. Ah, you're still afraid of that man——

NORA. Oh, yes, yes, I am.

HELMER. Nora, I can see it in your face—there's a letter from him in the box.

NORA. I don't know, I believe so. But you're not to read anything now; nothing must come between us until all is over.

RANK [*softly to* HELMER]. You mustn't contradict her.

HELMER [*putting his arm around her*]. The child shall have her own way. But to-morrow night, when the dance is over——

NORA. Then you will be free.

[ELLEN *appears in doorway, right.*]

ELLEN. Dinner is ready, ma'am.

NORA. We'll have some champagne, Ellen!

ELLEN. Yes, ma'am. [*Goes out.*]

HELMER. Dear me! Quite a feast.

NORA. Yes, and we'll keep it up till morning. [*Calling out.*] And macaroons, Ellen—plenty—just this once.

HELMER [*seizing her hands*]. Come, come, don't let's have this wild excitement! Be my own little lark again.

NORA. Oh, yes I will. But now go into the dining-room; and you too, Doctor Rank. Christina, you must help me to do up my hair.

RANK [*softly as they go*]. There is nothing in the wind? Nothing—I mean——

HELMER. Oh, no, nothing of the kind. It's merely this babyish anxiety I was telling you about. [*They go out right.*]

NORA. Well?

MRS. LINDEN. He's gone out of town.

NORA. I saw it in your face.

Mrs. Linden. He comes back to-morrow evening. I left a note for him.

Nora. You shouldn't have done that. Things must take their course. After all, there's something glorious in waiting for the miracle.

Mrs. Linden. What are you waiting for?

Nora. Oh, you can't understand. Go to them in the dining-room; I'll come in a moment. [Mrs. Linden *goes into dining-room;* Nora *stands for a moment as though collecting her thoughts; then looks at her watch.*] Five. Seven hours till midnight. Then twenty-four hours till the next midnight. Then the tarantella will be over. Twenty-four and seven? Still thirty-one hours to live.

[Helmer *appears at door, right.*]

Helmer. What's become of my little lark?

Nora [*runs to him with open arms*]. Here she is!

ACT III

The same room. The table with the chairs around it is in the middle. A lamp lit on the table. The door to the hall stands open. Dance music is heard from the floor above. Mrs. Linden *sits by the table, and turns the pages of a book absently. She tries to read, but seems unable to fix her attention; she frequently listens and looks anxiously toward the hall door.*

Mrs. Linden [*looks at her watch*]. Still not here; and the time's nearly up. If only he hasn't—— [*Listens again.*] Ah, there he is—— [*She goes into the hall and opens the outer door; soft footsteps are heard on the stairs; she whispers:*] Come in; there's no one here.

Krogstad [*in the doorway*]. I found a note from you at my house. What does it mean?

Mrs. Linden. I must speak with you.

Krogstad. Indeed? And in this house?

Mrs. Linden. I could not see you at my rooms. They have no separate entrance. Come in; we are quite alone. The servants are asleep and the Helmers are at the ball upstairs.

Krogstad [*coming into room*]. Ah! So the Helmers are dancing this evening. Really?

Mrs. Linden. Yes. Why not?

Krogstad. Quite right. Why not?

Mrs. Linden. And now let us talk a little.

Krogstad. Have we anything to say to each other?

Mrs. Linden. A great deal.

Krogstad. I should not have thought so.

Mrs. Linden. Because you have never really understood me.

Krogstad. What was there to understand? The most natural thing in the world—a heartless woman throws a man over when a better match offers.

Mrs. Linden. Do you really think me so heartless? Do you think I broke with you lightly?

Krogstad. Did you not?

Mrs. Linden. Do you really think so?

Krogstad. If not, why did you write me that letter?

Mrs. Linden. Was it not best? Since I had to break with you, was it not right that I should try to put an end to your love for me?

Krogstad [*pressing his hands together*]. So that was it? And all this —for the sake of money.

Mrs. Linden. You ought not to forget that I had a helpless mother and two little brothers. We could not wait for you, as your prospects then stood.

Krogstad. Did that give you the right to discard me for another?

Mrs. Linden. I don't know. I've often asked myself whether I did right.

Krogstad [*more softly*]. When I had lost you the very ground seemed to sink from under my feet. Look at me now. I am a shipwrecked man clinging to a spar.

Mrs. Linden. Rescue may be at hand.

Krogstad. It was at hand; but then you stood in the way.

MRS. LINDEN. Without my knowledge, Nils. I did not know till to-day that it was you I was to replace in the bank.

KROGSTAD. Well, I take your word for it. But now you do know, do you mean to give way?

MRS. LINDEN. No, for that would not help you.

KROGSTAD. Oh, help, help——! I should do it whether or no.

MRS. LINDEN. I have learnt prudence. Life and bitter necessity have schooled me.

KROGSTAD. And life has taught me not to trust fine speeches.

MRS. LINDEN. Then life has taught you a very sensible thing. But deeds you will trust?

KROGSTAD. What do you mean?

MRS. LINDEN. You said you were a shipwrecked man, clinging to a spar.

KROGSTAD. I have good reason to say so.

MRS. LINDEN. I am a shipwrecked woman clinging to a spar. I have no one to care for.

KROGSTAD. You made your own choice.

MRS. LINDEN. I had no choice.

KROGSTAD. Well, what then?

MRS. LINDEN. How if we two shipwrecked people could join hands?

KROGSTAD. What!

MRS. LINDEN. Suppose we lashed the spars together?

KROGSTAD. Christina!

MRS. LINDEN. What do you think brought me to town?

KROGSTAD. Had you any thought of me?

MRS. LINDEN. I must have work, or I can't live. All my life, as long as I can remember, I have worked; work has been my one great joy. Now I stand quite alone in the world, so terribly aimless and forsaken. There is no happiness in working for one's self. Nils, give me somebody and something to work for.

KROGSTAD. No, no, that can never be. It's simply a woman's romantic notion of self-sacrifice.

MRS. LINDEN. Have you ever found me romantic?

KROGSTAD. Would you really——? Tell me, do you know my past?

MRS. LINDEN. Yes.

KROGSTAD. And do you know what people say of me?

MRS. LINDEN. Did not you say just now that with me you would have been another man?

KROGSTAD. I am sure of it.

MRS. LINDEN. Is it too late?

KROGSTAD. Christina, do you know what you are doing? Yes, you do; I see it in your face. Have you the courage?

MRS. LINDEN. I need some one to tend, and your children need a mother. You need me, and I—I need you. Nils, I believe in your better self. With you I fear nothing.

KROGSTAD [seizing her hands]. Thank you—thank you, Christina. Now I shall make others see me as you do. Ah, I forgot——

MRS. LINDEN [listening]. Hush! The tarantella! Go, go!

KROGSTAD. Why? What is it?

MRS. LINDEN. Don't you hear the dancing overhead? As soon as that is over they will be here.

KROGSTAD. Oh, yes, I'll go. But it's too late now. Of course you don't know the step I have taken against the Helmers?

MRS. LINDEN. Yes, Nils, I do know.

KROGSTAD. And yet you have the courage to——

MRS. LINDEN. I know what lengths despair can drive a man to.

KROGSTAD. Oh, if I could only undo it!

MRS. LINDEN. You can——. Your letter is still in the box.

KROGSTAD. Are you sure?

MRS. LINDEN. Yes, but——

KROGSTAD [looking at her searchingly]. Ah, now I understand. You want to save your friend at any price. Say it out—is that your idea?

MRS. LINDEN. Nils, a woman who has once sold herself for the sake of others does not do so again.

KROGSTAD. I will demand my letter back again.

MRS. LINDEN. No, no.

KROGSTAD. Yes, of course; I'll wait till Helmer comes; I'll tell him to give it back to me—that it's only about my dismissal—that I don't want it read.

MRS. LINDEN. No, Nils, you must not recall the letter.

KROGSTAD. But tell me, wasn't that just why you got me to come here?

MRS. LINDEN. Yes, in my first terror. But a day has passed since then, and in that day I have seen incredible things in this house. Helmer must know everything; there must be an end to this unhappy secret. These two must come to a full understanding. They can't possibly go on with all these shifts and concealments.

KROGSTAD. Very well, if you like to risk it. But one thing I can do, and at once——.

MRS. LINDEN [listening]. Make haste. Go, go! The dance is over; we are not safe another moment.

KROGSTAD. I'll wait for you in the street.

MRS. LINDEN. Yes, do; you must take me home.

KROGSTAD. I never was so happy in all my life! [KROGSTAD goes, by the outer door. The door between the room and hall remains open.]

MRS. LINDEN [setting furniture straight and getting her out-door things together]. What a change! What a change! To have some one to work for; a home to make happy. I shall have to set to work in earnest. I wish they would come. [Listens.] Ah, here they are! I must get my things on.

[Takes bonnet and cloak. HELMER'S and NORA'S voices are heard outside; a key is turned in the lock, and HELMER drags NORA almost by force into the hall. She wears the Italian costume with a large black shawl over it. He is in evening dress and wears a black domino.]

NORA [still struggling with him in the doorway]. No, no, no; I won't go in! I want to go up-stairs again; I don't want to leave so early!

HELMER. But, my dearest girl——!

NORA. Oh, please, please, Torvald, only one hour more.

HELMER. Not one minute more, Nora dear; you know what we agreed! Come, come in; you are catching cold here! [He leads her gently into the room in spite of her resistance.]

MRS. LINDEN. Good evening.

NORA. Christina!

HELMER. What, Mrs. Linden, you here so late!

MRS. LINDEN. Yes, pardon me! I did so want to see Nora in her costume!

NORA. Have you been sitting here waiting for me?

MRS. LINDEN. Yes, unfortunately I came too late. You had already gone upstairs, and I couldn't go away without seeing you.

HELMER [taking NORA'S shawl off]. Well then, just look at her! I think she's worth looking at. Isn't she lovely, Mrs. Linden?

MRS. LINDEN. Yes, I must say——

HELMER. Isn't she exquisite? Every-one said so. But she is dreadfully obstinate, dear little creature. What's to be done with her? Just think, I had almost to force her away.

NORA. Oh, Torvald, you'll be sorry some day you didn't let me stop, if only for one half hour.

HELMER. There! You hear her, Mrs. Linden? She dances her tarantella with wild applause, and well she deserved it, I must say—though there was, perhaps, a little too much nature in her rendering of the idea—more than was, strictly speaking, artistic. But never mind—she made a great success, and that's the main thing. Ought I to let her stop after that —to weaken the impression? Not if I know it. I took my sweet little Capri girl—my capricious little Capri girl, I might say—under my arm; a rapid turn round the room, a courtesy to all sides, and—as they say in novels—the lovely apparition vanished! An exit should always be effective, Mrs. Linden; but I can't get Nora to see it. By Jove, it's warm here. [*Throws his domino on a chair, and opens the door to his room.*] What! No light here? Oh, of course! Excuse me——

[*Goes in and lights candles.*]

NORA [*whispers breathlessly*]. Well?

MRS. LINDEN [*softly*]. I have spoken to him.

NORA. And——?

MRS. LINDEN. Nora—you must tell your husband everything——

NORA [*almost voiceless*]. I knew it!

MRS. LINDEN. You have nothing to fear from Krogstad; but you must speak out.

NORA. I shall not speak!

MRS. LINDEN. Then the letter will.

NORA. Thank you, Christina. Now I know what I have to do. Hush!

HELMER [*coming back*]. Well, Mrs. Linden, have you admired her?

MRS. LINDEN. Yes; and now I'll say good-night.

HELMER. What, already? Does this knitting belong to you?

MRS. LINDEN [*takes it*]. Yes, thanks; I was nearly forgetting it.

HELMER. Then you do knit?

MRS. LINDEN. Yes.

HELMER. Do you know, you ought to embroider instead?

MRS. LINDEN. Indeed! Why?

HELMER. Because it's so much prettier. Look now! You hold the embroidery in the left hand so, and then work the needle with the right hand, in a long, easy curve, don't you?

MRS. LINDEN. Yes, I suppose so.

HELMER. But knitting is always ugly. Look now, your arms close to your sides, and the needles going up and down—there's something Chinese about it.— They really gave us splendid champagne to-night.

MRS. LINDEN. Well, good-night, Nora, and don't be obstinate any more.

HELMER. Well said, Mrs. Linden!

MRS. LINDEN. Good-night, Mr. Helmer.

HELMER [*going with her to the door*]. Good-night, good-night; I hope you'll get safely home. I should be glad to—but really you haven't far to go. Good-night, good-night! [*She goes*; HELMER *shuts the door after her and comes down again.*] At last we've got rid of her; she's an awful bore.

NORA. Aren't you very tired, Torvald?

HELMER. No, not in the least.

NORA. Nor sleepy?

HELMER. Not a bit. I feel particularly lively. But you? You do look tired and sleepy.

NORA. Yes, very tired. I shall soon sleep now.

HELMER. There, you see. I was right after all not to let you stop longer.

NORA. Oh, everything you do is right.

HELMER [*kissing her forehead*]. Now my lark is speaking like a reasonable being. Did you notice how jolly Rank was this evening?

NORA. Was he? I had no chance of speaking to him.

HELMER. Nor I, much; but I haven't seen him in such good spirits for a long time. [*Looks at* NORA *a little, then comes nearer her.*] It's splendid to be back in our own home, to be quite alone together! Oh, you enchanting creature!

NORA. Don't look at me in that way, Torvald.

HELMER. I am not to look at my dearest treasure?—at the loveliness that is mine, mine only, wholly and entirely mine?

NORA [*goes to the other side of the table*]. You mustn't say these things to me this evening.

HELMER [*following*]. I see you have the tarantella still in your blood—and that makes you all the more enticing. Listen! the other people are going now. [*More softly.*] Nora—soon the whole house will be still.

NORA. I hope so.

HELMER. Yes, don't you, Nora darling? When we're among strangers do you know why I speak so little to you, and keep so far away, and only steal a glance at you now and then—do you know why I do it? Because I am fancying that we love each other in secret, that I am secretly betrothed to you, and that no one guesses there is anything between us.

NORA. Yes, yes, yes. I know all your thoughts are with me.

HELMER. And then, when we have to go, and I put the shawl about your smooth, soft shoulders, and this glorious neck of yours, I imagine you are my bride, that our marriage is just over, that I am bringing you for the first time to my home, and that I am alone with you for the first time, quite alone with you, in your quivering loveliness. All this evening I was longing for you, and you only. When I watched you swaying and whirling in the tarantella—my blood boiled—I could endure it no longer; and that's why I made you come home with me so early.

NORA. Go now, Torvald. Go away from me. I won't have all this.

HELMER. What do you mean? Ah! I see you're teasing me! Won't! won't! Am I not your husband?

[A knock at the outer door.]

NORA [starts]. Did you hear?

HELMER [going toward the hall]. Who's there?

RANK [outside]. It's I; may I come in a moment?

HELMER [in a low tone, annoyed]. Oh! what can he want? [Aloud.] Wait a moment. [Opens door.] Come, it's nice of you to give us a look in.

RANK. I thought I heard your voice, and that put it into my head. [Looks round.] Ah! this dear old place! How cosy you two are here!

HELMER. You seemed to find it pleasant enough upstairs, too.

RANK. Exceedingly. Why not? Why shouldn't one get all one can out of the world? All one can for as long as one can. The wine was splendid——

HELMER. Especially the champagne.

RANK. Did you notice it? It's incredible the quantity I contrived to get down.

NORA. Torvald drank plenty of champagne too.

RANK. Did he?

NORA. Yes, and it always puts him in such spirits.

RANK. Well, why shouldn't one have a jolly evening after a well-spent day?

HELMER. Well spent! Well, I haven't much to boast of.

RANK [slapping him on the shoulder]. But I have, don't you see?

NORA. I suppose you've been engaged in a scientific investigation, Doctor Rank?

RANK. Quite right.

HELMER. Bless me! Little Nora talking about scientific investigations!

NORA. Am I to congratulate you on the result?

RANK. By all means.

NORA. It was good then?

RANK. The best possible, both for doctor and patient—certainty.

NORA [quickly and searchingly]. Certainty?

RANK. Absolute certainty. Wasn't I right to enjoy myself after it?

NORA. Yes, quite right, Doctor Rank.

HELMER. And so say I, provided you don't have to pay for it to-morrow.

RANK. Well, in this life nothing's to be had for nothing.

NORA. Doctor Rank, aren't you very fond of masquerades?

RANK. Yes, when there are plenty of comical disguises.

NORA. Tell me, what shall we two be at our next masquerade?

HELMER. Little insatiable! Thinking of your next already!

RANK. We two? I'll tell you. You must go as a good fairy.

HELMER. Oh, but what costume would indicate that?

RANK. She has simply to wear her every-day dress.

HELMER. Capital! But don't you know what you yourself will be?

RANK. Yes, my dear friend, I'm perfectly clear upon that point.

HELMER. Well?

RANK. At the next masquerade I shall be invisible.

HELMER. What a comical idea!

RANK. There's a big, black hat—haven't you heard of the invisible hat? It comes down all over you, and then no one can see you.

HELMER [with a suppressed smile]. No, you're right there.

RANK. But I'm quite forgetting what I came for. Helmer, give me a cigar, one of the dark Havanas.

HELMER. With the greatest pleasure. [Hands case.]

RANK [takes one and cuts the end off]. Thanks.

NORA [striking a wax match]. Let me give you a light.

RANK. A thousand thanks. [She holds match. He lights his cigar at it.] And now, good-by.

HELMER. Good-by, good-by, my dear fellow.

NORA. Sleep well, Doctor Rank.

RANK. Thanks for the wish.

NORA. Wish me the same.

RANK. You? Very well, since you ask me—sleep well. And thanks for the light.

[He nods to them both and goes out.]

HELMER [in an undertone]. He's been drinking a good deal.

NORA [absently]. I dare say. [HELMER takes his bunch of keys from his pocket and goes into the hall.] Torvald, what are you doing there?

HELMER. I must empty the letter-box, it's quite full; there will be no room for the newspapers to-morrow morning.

NORA. Are you going to work to-night?

HELMER. Not very likely! Why, what's this? Some one's been at the lock.

NORA. The lock——?

HELMER. I'm sure of it. What does it mean? I can't think that the servants——? Here's a broken hairpin. Nora, it's one of yours.

NORA [quickly]. It must have been the children.

HELMER. Then you must break them of

such tricks. H'm, h'm! There! at last I've got it open. [Takes contents out and calls into the kitchen.] Ellen, Ellen, just put the hall-door lamp out. [He returns with letters in his hand, and shuts the inner door.] Just see how they've accumulated. [Turning them over.] Why, what's this?

NORA [at the window]. The letter! Oh, no, no, Torvald!

HELMER. Two visiting cards—from Rank.

NORA. From Doctor Rank?

HELMER [looking at them]. Doctor Rank. They were on the top. He must just have put them in.

NORA. Is there anything on them?

HELMER. There's a black cross over the name. Look at it. What a horrid idea! It looks just as if he were announcing his own death.

NORA. So he is.

HELMER. What! Do you know anything? Has he told you anything?

NORA. Yes. These cards mean that he has taken his last leave of us. He intends to shut himself up and die.

HELMER. Poor fellow! Of course I knew we couldn't hope to keep him long. But so soon—and then to go and creep into his lair like a wounded animal——

NORA. What must be, must be, and the fewer words the better. Don't you think so, Torvald?

HELMER [walking up and down]. He had so grown into our lives. I can't realize that he's gone. He and his sufferings and his loneliness formed a sort of cloudy background to the sunshine of our happiness. Well, perhaps it's best so—at any rate for him. [Stands still.] And perhaps for us, too, Nora. Now we two are thrown entirely upon each other. [Puts his arm round her.] My darling wife! I feel as if I could never hold you close enough. Do you know, Nora, I often wish some danger might threaten you, that I might risk body and soul, and everything, everything, for your dear sake.

NORA [tears herself from him and says

firmly]. Now you shall read your letters, Torvald.

HELMER. No, no; not to-night. I want to be with you, sweet wife.

NORA. With the thought of your dying friend?

HELMER. You are right. This has shaken us both. Unloveliness has come between us—thoughts of death and decay. We must seek to cast them off. Till then we will remain apart.

NORA [*her arms round his neck*]. Torvald! good-night, good-night.

HELMER [*kissing her forehead*]. Goodnight, my little bird. Sleep well, Nora. Now I'll go and read my letters. [*He goes into his room and shuts the door.*]

NORA [*with wild eyes, gropes about her, seizes* HELMER'S *domino, throws it round her, and whispers quickly, hoarsely, and brokenly*]. Never to see him again. Never, never, never. [*Throws her shawl over her head.*] Never to see the children again. Never, never. Oh, that black icy water! Oh, that bottomless——If it were only over! Now he has it; he's reading it. Oh, no, no, no, not yet. Torvald, good-by. Good-by my little ones——!

[*She is rushing out by the hall; at the same moment* HELMER *tears his door open, and stands with an open letter in his hand.*]

HELMER. Nora!

NORA [*shrieking*]. Ah——!

HELMER. What is this? Do you know what is in this letter?

NORA. Yes, I know. Let me go! Let me pass!

HELMER [*holds her back*]. Where do you want to go?

NORA [*tries to get free*]. You sha'n't save me, Torvald.

HELMER [*falling back*]. True! Is it true what he writes? No, no, it cannot be true.

NORA. It is true. I have loved you beyond all else in the world.

HELMER. Pshaw—no silly evasions.

NORA [*a step nearer him*]. Torvald——!

HELMER. Wretched woman! what have you done?

NORA. Let me go—you shall not save me. You shall not take my guilt upon yourself.

HELMER. I don't want any melodramatic airs. [*Locks the door.*] Here you shall stay and give an account of yourself. Do you understand what you have done? Answer. Do you understand it?

NORA [*looks at him fixedly, and says with a stiffening expression*]. Yes; now I begin fully to understand it.

HELMER [*walking up and down*]. Oh, what an awful awakening! During all these eight years—she who was my pride and my joy—a hypocrite, a liar—worse, worse—a criminal. Oh! the hideousness of it! Ugh! Ugh! [NORA *is silent, and continues to look fixedly at him.*] I ought to have foreseen something of the kind. All your father's dishonesty——be silent! I say all your father's dishonesty you have inherited—no religion, no morality, no sense of duty. How I am punished for shielding him! I did it for your sake, and you reward me like this.

NORA. Yes—like this!

HELMER. You have destroyed my whole happiness. You have ruined my future. Oh! it's frightful to think of! I am in the power of a scoundrel; he can do whatever he pleases with me, demand whatever he chooses, and I must submit. And all this disaster is brought upon me by an unprincipled woman.

NORA. When I'm gone, you will be free.

HELMER. Oh, no fine phrases. Your father, too, was always ready with them. What good would it do to me if you were "gone," as you say? No good in the world! He can publish the story all the same; I might even be suspected of collusion. People will think I was at the bottom of it all and egged you on. And for all this I have you to thank—you whom I have done nothing but pet and spoil during our whole married life. Do you understand now what you have done to me?

NORA [*with cold calmness*]. Yes.

HELMER. It's incredible. I can't grasp it. But we must come to an understanding. Take that shawl off. Take it off I say. I must try to pacify him in one way or other—the secret must be kept, cost what it may. As for ourselves, we must live as we have always done; but of course only in the eyes of the world. Of course you will continue to live here. But the children cannot be left in your care. I dare not trust them to you—— Oh, to have to say this to one I have loved so tenderly—whom I still—but that must be a thing of the past. Henceforward there can be no question of happiness, but merely of saving the ruins, the shreds, the show of it! [*A ring; HELMER starts.*] What's that? So late! Can it be the worst? Can he——? Hide yourself, Nora; say you are ill.

[NORA *stands motionless. HELMER goes to the door and opens it.*]

ELLEN [*half dressed, in the hall*]. Here is a letter for you, ma'am.

HELMER. Give it to me. [*Seizes letter and shuts the door.*] Yes, from him. You shall not have it. I shall read it.

NORA. Read it!

HELMER [*by the lamp*]. I have hardly courage to. We may be lost, both you and I. Ah! I must know. [*Tears the letter hastily open; reads a few lines, looks at an enclosure; a cry of joy.*] Nora. [NORA *looks interrogatively at him.*] Nora! Oh! I must read it again. Yes, yes, it is so. I am saved! Nora, I am saved!

NORA. And I?

HELMER. You too, of course; we are both saved, both of us. Look here, he sends you back your promissory note. He writes that he regrets and apologizes—that a happy turn in his life—— Oh, what matter what he writes. We are saved, Nora! No one can harm you. Oh! Nora, Nora——; no, first to get rid of this hateful thing. I'll just see—— [*Glances at the I O U.*] No, I won't look at it; the whole thing shall be nothing but a dream to me. [*Tears the I O U and both letters in pieces, throws them into the fire and watches them burn.*] There, it's gone. He wrote that ever since Christmas Eve—— Oh, Nora, they must have been three awful days for you!

NORA. I have fought a hard fight for the last three days.

HELMER. And in your agony you saw no other outlet but—no; we won't think of that horror. We will only rejoice and repeat—it's over, all over. Don't you hear, Nora? You don't seem to be able to grasp it. Yes, it's over. What is this set look on your face? Oh, my poor Nora, I understand; you can't believe that I have forgiven you. But I have, Nora; I swear it. I have forgiven everything. I know that what you did was all for love of me.

NORA. That's true.

HELMER. You loved me as a wife should love her husband. It was only the means you misjudged. But do you think I love you the less for your helplessness? No, no, only lean on me. I will counsel and guide you. I should be no true man if this very womanly helplessness did not make you doubly dear in my eyes. You mustn't think of the hard things I said in my first moment of terror, when the world seemed to be tumbling about my ears. I have forgiven you, Nora—I swear I have forgiven you.

NORA. I thank you for your forgiveness. [*Goes out, right.*]

HELMER. No, stay. [*Looks in.*] What are you going to do?

NORA [*inside*]. To take off my doll's dress.

HELMER [*in doorway*]. Yes, do, dear. Try to calm down, and recover your balance, my scared little song-bird. You may rest secure, I have broad wings to shield you. [*Walking up and down near the door.*] Oh, how lovely—how cosey our home is, Nora. Here you are safe; here I can shelter you like a hunted dove, whom I have saved from the claws of the hawk. I shall soon bring your poor beating heart to rest, believe me, Nora, I will. To-morrow all this will seem quite different—everything will be as before; I shall not need to tell you again that I forgive you; you will feel for yourself that it is true. How could I find it in my heart to drive you away, or even so much as to reproach you? Oh, you don't know a true man's heart, Nora. There is something indescribably sweet and soothing to a man in having forgiven his wife —honestly forgiven her from the bottom of his heart. She becomes his property in a double sense. She is as though born again; she has become, so to speak, at once his wife and his child. That is what you shall henceforth be to me, my bewildered, helpless darling. Don't worry about anything, Nora; only open your heart to me, and I will be both will and conscience to you. [NORA enters, crossing to table in everyday dress.] Why, what's this? Not gone to bed? You have changed your dress.

NORA. Yes, Torvald; now I have changed my dress.

HELMER. But why now so late?

NORA. I shall not sleep to-night.

HELMER. But, Nora dear——

NORA [looking at her watch]. It's not so late yet. Sit down, Torvald, you and I have much to say to each other.

[She sits on one side of the table.]

HELMER. Nora, what does this mean; your cold, set face——

NORA. Sit down. It will take some time; I have much to talk over with you.

[HELMER sits at the other side of the table.]

HELMER. You alarm me; I don't understand you.

NORA. No, that's just it. You don't understand me; and I have never understood you—till to-night. No, don't interrupt. Only listen to what I say. We must come to a final settlement, Torvald!

HELMER. How do you mean?

NORA [after a short silence]. Does not one thing strike you as we sit here?

HELMER. What should strike me?

NORA. We have been married eight years. Does it not strike you that this is the first time we two, you and I, man and wife, have talked together seriously?

HELMER. Seriously! Well, what do you call seriously?

NORA. During eight whole years and more—ever since the day we first met— we have never exchanged one serious word about serious things.

HELMER. Was I always to trouble you with the cares you could not help me to bear?

NORA. I am not talking of cares. I say that we have never yet set ourselves seriously to get to the bottom of anything.

HELMER. Why, my dear Nora, what have you to do with serious things?

NORA. There we have it! You have never understood me. I have had great injustice done me, Torvald, first by my father and then by you.

HELMER. What! by your father and me?—by us who have loved you more than all the world?

NORA [shaking her head]. You have never loved me. You only thought it amusing to be in love with me.

HELMER. Why, Nora, what a thing to say!

NORA. Yes, it is so, Torvald. While I was at home with father he used to tell me all his opinions and I held the same opinions. If I had others I concealed them, because he would not have liked it. He used to call me his doll child, and play with me as I played with my dolls. Then I came to live in your house——

HELMER. What an expression to use about our marriage!

NORA [undisturbed]. I mean I passed from father's hands into yours. You settled everything according to your taste; and I got the same tastes as you; or I pretended to—I don't know which— both ways perhaps. When I look back on it now, I seem to have been living here like a beggar, from hand to mouth. I lived by performing tricks for you, Torvald. But you would have it so. You and father have done me a great wrong. It's your fault that my life has been wasted.

HELMER. Why, Nora, how unreasonable and ungrateful you are. Haven't you been happy here?

NORA. No, never; I thought I was, but I never was.

HELMER. Not—not happy?

NORA. No, only merry. And you have always been so kind to me. But our house has been nothing but play-room. Here I have been your doll-wife, just as at home I used to be papa's doll-child. And the children in their turn have been my dolls. I thought it fun when you played with me, just as the children did when I played with them. That has been our marriage, Torvald.

HELMER. There is some truth in what you say, exaggerated and overstrained though it be. But henceforth it shall be different. Playtime is over; now comes the time for education.

NORA. Whose education? Mine, or the children's?

HELMER. Both, my dear Nora.

NORA. Oh, Torvald, you can't teach me to be a fit wife for you.

HELMER. And you say that?

NORA. And I—am I fit to educate the children?

HELMER. Nora!

NORA. Did you not say yourself a few minutes ago you dared not trust them to me.

HELMER. In the excitement of the moment! Why should you dwell upon that?

NORA. No—you are perfectly right. That problem is beyond me. There's another to be solved first—I must try to educate myself. You are not the man to help me in that. I must set about it alone. And that is why I am now leaving you!

HELMER [jumping up]. What—do you mean to say——

NORA. I must stand quite alone to know myself and my surroundings; so I cannot stay with you.

HELMER. Nora! Nora!

NORA. I am going at once. Christina will take me in for to-night——

HELMER. You are mad. I shall not allow it. I forbid it.

NORA. It's no use your forbidding me anything now. I shall take with me what belongs to me. From you I will accept nothing, either now or afterward.

HELMER. What madness!

NORA. To-morrow I shall go home.

HELMER. Home!

NORA. I mean to what was my home. It will be easier for me to find some opening there.

HELMER. Oh, in your blind experience——

NORA. I must try to gain experience, Torvald.

HELMER. To forsake your home, your husband, and your children! You don't consider what the world will say.

NORA. I can pay no heed to that! I only know that I must do it.

HELMER. It's exasperating! Can you forsake your holiest duties in this way?

NORA. What do you call my holiest duties?

HELMER. Do you ask me that? Your duties to your husband and your children.

NORA. I have other duties equally sacred.

HELMER. Impossible! What duties do you mean?

NORA. My duties toward myself.

HELMER. Before all else you are a wife and a mother.

NORA. That I no longer believe. I think that before all else I am a human being, just as much as you are—or, at least, I will try to become one. I know that most people agree with you, Torvald, and that they say so in books. But henceforth I can't be satisfied with what most people say, and what is in books. I must think things out for myself and try to get clear about them.

HELMER. Are you not clear about your place in your home? Have you not an infallible guide in questions like these? Have you not religion?

NORA. Oh, Torvald, I don't know properly what religion is.

HELMER. What do you mean?

NORA. I know nothing but what our clergyman told me when I was confirmed. He explained that religion was this and that. When I get away from here and stand alone I will look into that matter too. I will see whether what he taught me is true, or, at any rate, whether it is true for me.

HELMER. Oh, this is unheard of! But if religion cannot keep you right, let me appeal to your conscience—I suppose you have some moral feeling? Or, answer me, perhaps you have none?

NORA. Well, Torvald, it's not easy to say. I really don't know—I am all at sea about these things. I only know that I think quite differently from you about them. I hear, too, that the laws are different from what I thought; but I can't believe that they are right. It appears that a woman has no right to spare her dying father, or to save her husband's life. I don't believe that.

HELMER. You talk like a child. You don't understand the society in which you live.

NORA. No, I don't. But I shall try to. I must make up my mind which is right —society or I.

HELMER. Nora, you are ill, you are feverish. I almost think you are out of your senses.

NORA. I never felt so much clearness and certainty as to-night.

HELMER. You are clear and certain enough to forsake husband and children?

NORA. Yes, I am.

HELMER. Then there is only one explanation possible.

NORA. What is that?

HELMER. You no longer love me.

NORA. No, that is just it.

HELMER. Nora! Can you say so?

NORA. Oh, I'm so sorry, Torvald; for you've always been so kind to me. But I can't help it. I do not love you any longer.

HELMER [keeping his composure with difficulty]. Are you clear and certain on this point too?

NORA. Yes, quite. That is why I won't stay here any longer.

HELMER. And can you also make clear to me, how I have forfeited your love?

NORA. Yes, I can. It was this evening, when the miracle did not happen. For then I saw you were not the man I had taken you for.

HELMER. Explain yourself more clearly; I don't understand.

NORA. I have waited so patiently all these eight years; for, of course, I saw clearly enough that miracles do not happen every day. When this crushing blow threatened me, I said to myself, confidently, "Now comes the miracle!" When Krogstad's letter lay in the box, it never occurred to me that you would think of submitting to that man's conditions. I was convinced that you would say to him, "Make it known to all the world," and that then——

HELMER. Well? When I had given my own wife's name up to disgrace and shame——?

NORA. Then I firmly believed that you would come forward, take everything upon yourself, and say, "I am the guilty one."

HELMER. Nora!

NORA. You mean I would never have accepted such a sacrifice? No, certainly not. But what would my assertions have been worth in opposition to yours? That was the miracle that I hoped for and dreaded. And it was to hinder that that I wanted to die.

HELMER. I would gladly work for you day and night, Nora—bear sorrow and want for your sake—but no man sacrifices his honor, even for one he loves.

NORA. Millions of women have done so.

HELMER. Oh, you think and talk like a silly child.

NORA. Very likely. But you neither think nor talk like the man I can share my life with. When your terror was over —not for me, but for yourself—when there was nothing more to fear,—then it was to you as though nothing had happened. I was your lark again, your doll

—whom you would take twice as much care of in the future, because she was so weak and fragile. [*Stands up.*] Torvald, in that moment it burst upon me, that I had been living here these eight years with a strange man, and had borne him three children—Oh! I can't bear to think of it—I could tear myself to pieces!

HELMER [*sadly*]. I see it, I see it; an abyss has opened between us—But, Nora, can it never be filled up?

NORA. As I now am, I am no wife for you.

HELMER. I have strength to become another man.

NORA. Perhaps—when your doll is taken away from you.

HELMER. To part—to part from you! No, Nora, no; I can't grasp the thought.

NORA [*going into room, right*]. The more reason for the thing to happen. [*She comes back with out-door things and a small travelling bag, which she puts on a chair.*]

HELMER. Nora, Nora, not now! Wait till to-morrow.

NORA [*putting on cloak*]. I can't spend the night in a strange man's house.

HELMER. But can't we live here as brother and sister?

NORA [*fastening her hat*]. You know very well that would not last long. Good-by, Torvald. No, I won't go to the children. I know they are in better hands than mine. As I now am, I can be nothing to them.

HELMER. But some time, Nora—some time——

NORA. How can I tell? I have no idea what will become of me.

HELMER. But you are my wife, now and always?

NORA. Listen, Torvald—when a wife leaves her husband's house, as I am doing, I have heard that in the eyes of the law he is free from all the duties toward her. At any rate I release you from all duties.

You must not feel yourself bound any more than I shall. There must be perfect freedom on both sides. There, there is your ring back. Give me mine.

HELMER. That too?

NORA. That too.

HELMER. Here it is.

NORA. Very well. Now it is all over. Here are the keys. The servants know about everything in the house, better than I do. To-morrow, when I have started, Christina will come to pack up my things. I will have them sent after me.

HELMER. All over! All over! Nora, will you never think of me again?

NORA. Oh, I shall often think of you, and the children—and this house.

HELMER. May I write to you, Nora?

NORA. No, never. You must not.

HELMER. But I must send you——

NORA. Nothing, nothing.

HELMER. I must help you if you need it.

NORA. No, I say. I take nothing from strangers.

HELMER. Nora, can I never be more than a stranger to you?

NORA [*taking her travelling bag*]. Oh, Torvald, then the miracle of miracles would have to happen.

HELMER. What is the miracle of miracles?

NORA. Both of us would have to change so that—— Oh, Torvald, I no longer believe in miracles.

HELMER. But I will believe. We must so change that——?

NORA. That communion between us shall be a marriage. Good-by.

[*She goes out.*]

HELMER [*sinks in a chair by the door with his face in his hands*]. Nora! Nora! [*He looks around and stands up.*] Empty. She's gone! [*A hope inspires him.*] Ah! The miracle of miracles——?!

[*From below is heard the reverberation of a heavy door closing.*

READING LIST

GENERAL

There is nothing in English on the whole subject of drama as full and authentic as the monumental works of Klein, Proelss, and Creizenach. However, the latest edition of the *Encyclopædia Britannica* is useful and dependable so far as it goes. See the article on *Drama*.

Readable outlines are:

Sheldon Cheney, *The Theater* (New York, 1929)
Ashley Dukes, *Drama* (New York, 1926)
Glenn Hughes, *The Story of the Theater* (New York, 1928)
Karl Mantzius, *A History of Theatrical Art* (6 vols., London, 1903ff.)
Brander Matthews, *The Development of the Drama* (New York, 1903)
Allardyce Nicoll, *The Development of the Theater* (New York, 1927)
Thomas Wood Stevens, *The Theater: From Athens to Broadway* (New York, 1932)
Donald Clive Stuart, *The Development of Dramatic Art* (New York, 1928)

The drama and theater, according to countries and peoples, are treated more or less fully in the following works:

ITALY

Joseph S. Kennard, *The Italian Theater* (2 vols., New York, 1932)
Maurice Sand, *History of the Harlequinade* (2 vols., New York, 1915)

SPAIN

James Fitzmaurice-Kelly, *A History of Spanish Literature* (New York, 1917)
Hugo Albert Rennert, *The Spanish Stage in the Time of Lope de Vega* (New York, 1909)

FRANCE

Eleanor Jourdain, *An Introduction to the French Classical Drama* (Oxford, 1912)

Frederick W. Hawkins, *The French Stage in the Eighteenth Century* (2 vols., London, 1888)
Brander Matthews, *French Dramatists of the Nineteenth Century* (New York, 1905)
John Palmer, *Molière* (New York, 1930)

GERMANY

Calvin Thomas, *A History of German Literature* (New York, 1917)
Georg Witkowski, *The German Drama of the Ninteenth Century* (New York, 1909)

SCANDINAVIAN COUNTRIES

R. B. Anderson, *Horn's History of the Literature of the Scandinavian North,* etc. (Chicago, 1895)
Edmund Gosse, *Northern Studies* (London, n. d.)

RUSSIA

K. Waliszewski, *A History of Russian Literature* (New York, 1911)
Leo Wiener, *The Contemporary Drama of Russia* (Boston, 1924)

READING LIST OF PLAYS

SUPPLEMENTING THE TEXTS PRINTED IN THE TWO VOLUMES OF *World Drama*

ITALY

Carlo Goldoni, *The Beneficent Bear* (Samuel French)
Niccolo Macchiavelli, *Mandragola* (Macaulay)

SPAIN

Pedro Calderon de la Barca, *The Physician of His Own Honor* (Macmillan)
Lope de Vega, *The Dog in the Manger* (*The Drama,* Victorian ed.)

FRANCE

Henry Becque, *The Vultures* (Little, Brown)
Pierre Corneille, *Cinna* (Modern Library)
A. Dumas fils, *Camille* (Samuel French)
J. B. P. Molière, *Tartuffe* (Modern Library)
Jean Racine, *Andromaque* (Modern Library)

GERMANY

J. W. von Goethe, *Faust* (Everyman's Library)
Friedrich Hebbel, *Maria Maddalena* (Everyman's Library)
G. E. Lessing, *Nathan the Wise* (Bohn Library)
F. Schiller, *Don Carlos* (Bohn Library)

SCANDINAVIAN COUNTRIES

Sweden
August Strindberg, *The Father* (Scribner's)
Norway
Henrik Ibsen, *Peer Gynt* (Scribner's)
Denmark
Ludvig Holberg, *The Political Tinker* (American-Scandinavian Foundation)

RUSSIA

Nikolay Gogol, *The Inspector-General* (Samuel French)
Leo Tolstoy, *The Power of Darkness* (Dramatic Publishing Co.)

(1)

A CATALOG OF SELECTED DOVER
BOOKS IN ALL FIELDS OF INTEREST

CONCERNING THE SPIRITUAL IN ART, Wassily Kandinsky. Pioneering work by father of abstract art. Thoughts on color theory, nature of art. Analysis of earlier masters. 12 illustrations. 80pp. of text. 5⅜ x 8½.   23411-8 Pa. $3.95

ANIMALS: 1,419 Copyright-Free Illustrations of Mammals, Birds, Fish, Insects, etc., Jim Harter (ed.). Clear wood engravings present, in extremely lifelike poses, over 1,000 species of animals. One of the most extensive pictorial sourcebooks of its kind. Captions. Index. 284pp. 9 x 12.   23766-4 Pa. $12.95

CELTIC ART: The Methods of Construction, George Bain. Simple geometric techniques for making Celtic interlacements, spirals, Kells-type initials, animals, humans, etc. Over 500 illustrations. 160pp. 9 x 12. (USO)   22923-8 Pa. $9.95

AN ATLAS OF ANATOMY FOR ARTISTS, Fritz Schider. Most thorough reference work on art anatomy in the world. Hundreds of illustrations, including selections from works by Vesalius, Leonardo, Goya, Ingres, Michelangelo, others. 593 illustrations. 192pp. 7⅛ x 10¼.   20241-0 Pa. $9.95

CELTIC HAND STROKE-BY-STROKE (Irish Half-Uncial from "The Book of Kells"): An Arthur Baker Calligraphy Manual, Arthur Baker. Complete guide to creating each letter of the alphabet in distinctive Celtic manner. Covers hand position, strokes, pens, inks, paper, more. Illustrated. 48pp. 8¼ x 11.   24336-2 Pa. $3.95

EASY ORIGAMI, John Montroll. Charming collection of 32 projects (hat, cup, pelican, piano, swan, many more) specially designed for the novice origami hobbyist. Clearly illustrated easy-to-follow instructions insure that even beginning papercrafters will achieve successful results. 48pp. 8¼ x 11.   27298-2 Pa. $3.50

THE COMPLETE BOOK OF BIRDHOUSE CONSTRUCTION FOR WOOD-WORKERS, Scott D. Campbell. Detailed instructions, illustrations, tables. Also data on bird habitat and instinct patterns. Bibliography. 3 tables. 63 illustrations in 15 figures. 48pp. 5¼ x 8½.   24407-5 Pa. $2.50

BLOOMINGDALE'S ILLUSTRATED 1886 CATALOG: Fashions, Dry Goods and Housewares, Bloomingdale Brothers. Famed merchants' extremely rare catalog depicting about 1,700 products: clothing, housewares, firearms, dry goods, jewelry, more. Invaluable for dating, identifying vintage items. Also, copyright-free graphics for artists, designers. Co-published with Henry Ford Museum & Greenfield Village. 160pp. 8¼ x 11.   25780-0 Pa. $10.95

HISTORIC COSTUME IN PICTURES, Braun & Schneider. Over 1,450 costumed figures in clearly detailed engravings—from dawn of civilization to end of 19th century. Captions. Many folk costumes. 256pp. 8⅜ x 11¾.   23150-X Pa. $12.95

STICKLEY CRAFTSMAN FURNITURE CATALOGS, Gustav Stickley and L. & J. G. Stickley. Beautiful, functional furniture in two authentic catalogs from 1910. 594 illustrations, including 277 photos, show settles, rockers, armchairs, reclining chairs, bookcases, desks, tables. 183pp. 6½ x 9¼. 23838-5 Pa. $9.95

AMERICAN LOCOMOTIVES IN HISTORIC PHOTOGRAPHS: 1858 to 1949, Ron Ziel (ed.). A rare collection of 126 meticulously detailed official photographs, called "builder portraits," of American locomotives that majestically chronicle the rise of steam locomotive power in America. Introduction. Detailed captions. xi + 129pp. 9 x 12. 27393-8 Pa. $12.95

AMERICA'S LIGHTHOUSES: An Illustrated History, Francis Ross Holland, Jr. Delightfully written, profusely illustrated fact-filled survey of over 200 American lighthouses since 1716. History, anecdotes, technological advances, more. 240pp. 8 x 10¾. 25576-X Pa. $12.95

TOWARDS A NEW ARCHITECTURE, Le Corbusier. Pioneering manifesto by founder of "International School." Technical and aesthetic theories, views of industry, economics, relation of form to function, "mass-production split" and much more. Profusely illustrated. 320pp. 6⅛ x 9¼. (USO) 25023-7 Pa. $9.95

HOW THE OTHER HALF LIVES, Jacob Riis. Famous journalistic record, exposing poverty and degradation of New York slums around 1900, by major social reformer. 100 striking and influential photographs. 233pp. 10 x 7⅞. 22012-5 Pa. $10.95

FRUIT KEY AND TWIG KEY TO TREES AND SHRUBS, William M. Harlow. One of the handiest and most widely used identification aids. Fruit key covers 120 deciduous and evergreen species; twig key 160 deciduous species. Easily used. Over 300 photographs. 126pp. 5⅜ x 8½. 20511-8 Pa. $3.95

COMMON BIRD SONGS, Dr. Donald J. Borror. Songs of 60 most common U.S. birds: robins, sparrows, cardinals, bluejays, finches, more—arranged in order of increasing complexity. Up to 9 variations of songs of each species. Cassette and manual 99911-4 $8.95

ORCHIDS AS HOUSE PLANTS, Rebecca Tyson Northen. Grow cattleyas and many other kinds of orchids—in a window, in a case, or under artificial light. 63 illustrations. 148pp. 5⅜ x 8½. 23261-1 Pa. $4.95

MONSTER MAZES, Dave Phillips. Masterful mazes at four levels of difficulty. Avoid deadly perils and evil creatures to find magical treasures. Solutions for all 32 exciting illustrated puzzles. 48pp. 8¼ x 11. 26005-4 Pa. $2.95

MOZART'S DON GIOVANNI (DOVER OPERA LIBRETTO SERIES), Wolfgang Amadeus Mozart. Introduced and translated by Ellen H. Bleiler. Standard Italian libretto, with complete English translation. Convenient and thoroughly portable—an ideal companion for reading along with a recording or the performance itself. Introduction. List of characters. Plot summary. 121pp. 5¼ x 8½. 24944-1 Pa. $2.95

TECHNICAL MANUAL AND DICTIONARY OF CLASSICAL BALLET, Gail Grant. Defines, explains, comments on steps, movements, poses and concepts. 15-page pictorial section. Basic book for student, viewer. 127pp. 5⅜ x 8½. 21843-0 Pa. $4.95

BRASS INSTRUMENTS: Their History and Development, Anthony Baines. Authoritative, updated survey of the evolution of trumpets, trombones, bugles, cornets, French horns, tubas and other brass wind instruments. Over 140 illustrations and 48 music examples. Corrected and updated by author. New preface. Bibliography. 320pp. 5⅜ x 8½. 27574-4 Pa. $9.95

HOLLYWOOD GLAMOR PORTRAITS, John Kobal (ed.). 145 photos from 1926-49. Harlow, Gable, Bogart, Bacall; 94 stars in all. Full background on photographers, technical aspects. 160pp. 8⅜ x 11¼. 23352-9 Pa. $12.95

MAX AND MORITZ, Wilhelm Busch. Great humor classic in both German and English. Also 10 other works: "Cat and Mouse," "Plisch and Plumm," etc. 216pp. 5⅜ x 8½. 20181-3 Pa. $6.95

THE RAVEN AND OTHER FAVORITE POEMS, Edgar Allan Poe. Over 40 of the author's most memorable poems: "The Bells," "Ulalume," "Israfel," "To Helen," "The Conqueror Worm," "Eldorado," "Annabel Lee," many more. Alphabetic lists of titles and first lines. 64pp. 5$\frac{3}{16}$ x 8¼. 26685-0 Pa. $1.00

PERSONAL MEMOIRS OF U. S. GRANT, Ulysses Simpson Grant. Intelligent, deeply moving firsthand account of Civil War campaigns, considered by many the finest military memoirs ever written. Includes letters, historic photographs, maps and more. 528pp. 6⅛ x 9¼. 28587-1 Pa. $11.95

AMULETS AND SUPERSTITIONS, E. A. Wallis Budge. Comprehensive discourse on origin, powers of amulets in many ancient cultures: Arab, Persian Babylonian, Assyrian, Egyptian, Gnostic, Hebrew, Phoenician, Syriac, etc. Covers cross, swastika, crucifix, seals, rings, stones, etc. 584pp. 5⅜ x 8½. 23573-4 Pa. $12.95

RUSSIAN STORIES/PYCCKNE PACCKA3bl: A Dual-Language Book, edited by Gleb Struve. Twelve tales by such masters as Chekhov, Tolstoy, Dostoevsky, Pushkin, others. Excellent word-for-word English translations on facing pages, plus teaching and study aids, Russian/English vocabulary, biographical/critical introductions, more. 416pp. 5⅜ x 8½. 26244-8 Pa. $8.95

PHILADELPHIA THEN AND NOW: 60 Sites Photographed in the Past and Present, Kenneth Finkel and Susan Oyama. Rare photographs of City Hall, Logan Square, Independence Hall, Betsy Ross House, other landmarks juxtaposed with contemporary views. Captures changing face of historic city. Introduction. Captions. 128pp. 8¼ x 11. 25790-8 Pa. $9.95

AIA ARCHITECTURAL GUIDE TO NASSAU AND SUFFOLK COUNTIES, LONG ISLAND, The American Institute of Architects, Long Island Chapter, and the Society for the Preservation of Long Island Antiquities. Comprehensive, well-researched and generously illustrated volume brings to life over three centuries of Long Island's great architectural heritage. More than 240 photographs with authoritative, extensively detailed captions. 176pp. 8¼ x 11. 26946-9 Pa. $14.95

NORTH AMERICAN INDIAN LIFE: Customs and Traditions of 23 Tribes, Elsie Clews Parsons (ed.). 27 fictionalized essays by noted anthropologists examine religion, customs, government, additional facets of life among the Winnebago, Crow, Zuni, Eskimo, other tribes. 480pp. 6⅛ x 9¼. 27377-6 Pa. $10.95

FRANK LLOYD WRIGHT'S HOLLYHOCK HOUSE, Donald Hoffmann. Lavishly illustrated, carefully documented study of one of Wright's most controversial residential designs. Over 120 photographs, floor plans, elevations, etc. Detailed perceptive text by noted Wright scholar. Index. 128pp. 9¼ x 10¾. 27133-1 Pa. $11.95

THE MALE AND FEMALE FIGURE IN MOTION: 60 Classic Photographic Sequences, Eadweard Muybridge. 60 true-action photographs of men and women walking, running, climbing, bending, turning, etc., reproduced from rare 19th-century masterpiece. vi + 121pp. 9 x 12. 24745-7 Pa. $10.95

1001 QUESTIONS ANSWERED ABOUT THE SEASHORE, N. J. Berrill and Jacquelyn Berrill. Queries answered about dolphins, sea snails, sponges, starfish, fishes, shore birds, many others. Covers appearance, breeding, growth, feeding, much more. 305pp. 5¼ x 8¼. 23366-9 Pa. $8.95

GUIDE TO OWL WATCHING IN NORTH AMERICA, Donald S. Heintzelman. Superb guide offers complete data and descriptions of 19 species: barn owl, screech owl, snowy owl, many more. Expert coverage of owl-watching equipment, conservation, migrations and invasions, etc. Guide to observing sites. 84 illustrations. xiii + 193pp. 5⅜ x 8½. 27344-X Pa. $8.95

MEDICINAL AND OTHER USES OF NORTH AMERICAN PLANTS: A Historical Survey with Special Reference to the Eastern Indian Tribes, Charlotte Erichsen-Brown. Chronological historical citations document 500 years of usage of plants, trees, shrubs native to eastern Canada, northeastern U.S. Also complete identifying information. 343 illustrations. 544pp. 6½ x 9¼. 25951-X Pa. $12.95

STORYBOOK MAZES, Dave Phillips. 23 stories and mazes on two-page spreads: Wizard of Oz, Treasure Island, Robin Hood, etc. Solutions. 64pp. 8¼ x 11. 23628-5 Pa. $2.95

NEGRO FOLK MUSIC, U.S.A., Harold Courlander. Noted folklorist's scholarly yet readable analysis of rich and varied musical tradition. Includes authentic versions of over 40 folk songs. Valuable bibliography and discography. xi + 324pp. 5⅜ x 8½. 27350-4 Pa. $9.95

MOVIE-STAR PORTRAITS OF THE FORTIES, John Kobal (ed.). 163 glamor, studio photos of 106 stars of the 1940s: Rita Hayworth, Ava Gardner, Marlon Brando, Clark Gable, many more. 176pp. 8⅜ x 11¼. 23546-7 Pa. $12.95

BENCHLEY LOST AND FOUND, Robert Benchley. Finest humor from early 30s, about pet peeves, child psychologists, post office and others. Mostly unavailable elsewhere. 73 illustrations by Peter Arno and others. 183pp. 5⅜ x 8½. 22410-4 Pa. $6.95

YEKL and THE IMPORTED BRIDEGROOM AND OTHER STORIES OF YIDDISH NEW YORK, Abraham Cahan. Film Hester Street based on Yekl (1896). Novel, other stories among first about Jewish immigrants on N.Y.'s East Side. 240pp. 5⅜ x 8½. 22427-9 Pa. $6.95

SELECTED POEMS, Walt Whitman. Generous sampling from *Leaves of Grass*. Twenty-four poems include "I Hear America Singing," "Song of the Open Road," "I Sing the Body Electric," "When Lilacs Last in the Dooryard Bloom'd," "O Captain! My Captain!"—all reprinted from an authoritative edition. Lists of titles and first lines. 128pp. 5³⁄₁₆ x 8¼. 26878-0 Pa. $1.00

THE BEST TALES OF HOFFMANN, E. T. A. Hoffmann. 10 of Hoffmann's most important stories: "Nutcracker and the King of Mice," "The Golden Flowerpot," etc. 458pp. 5⅜ x 8½. 21793-0 Pa. $9.95

FROM FETISH TO GOD IN ANCIENT EGYPT, E. A. Wallis Budge. Rich detailed survey of Egyptian conception of "God" and gods, magic, cult of animals, Osiris, more. Also, superb English translations of hymns and legends. 240 illustrations. 545pp. 5⅜ x 8½. 25803-3 Pa. $13.95

FRENCH STORIES/CONTES FRANÇAIS: A Dual-Language Book, Wallace Fowlie. Ten stories by French masters, Voltaire to Camus: "Micromegas" by Voltaire; "The Atheist's Mass" by Balzac; "Minuet" by de Maupassant; "The Guest" by Camus, six more. Excellent English translations on facing pages. Also French-English vocabulary list, exercises, more. 352pp. 5⅜ x 8½. 26443-2 Pa. $8.95

CHICAGO AT THE TURN OF THE CENTURY IN PHOTOGRAPHS: 122 Historic Views from the Collections of the Chicago Historical Society, Larry A. Viskochil. Rare large-format prints offer detailed views of City Hall, State Street, the Loop, Hull House, Union Station, many other landmarks, circa 1904-1913. Introduction. Captions. Maps. 144pp. 9⅜ x 12¼. 24656-6 Pa. $12.95

OLD BROOKLYN IN EARLY PHOTOGRAPHS, 1865-1929, William Lee Younger. Luna Park, Gravesend race track, construction of Grand Army Plaza, moving of Hotel Brighton, etc. 157 previously unpublished photographs. 165pp. 8⅞ x 11¾. 23587-4 Pa. $13.95

THE MYTHS OF THE NORTH AMERICAN INDIANS, Lewis Spence. Rich anthology of the myths and legends of the Algonquins, Iroquois, Pawnees and Sioux, prefaced by an extensive historical and ethnological commentary. 36 illustrations. 480pp. 5⅜ x 8½. 25967-6 Pa. $8.95

AN ENCYCLOPEDIA OF BATTLES: Accounts of Over 1,560 Battles from 1479 B.C. to the Present, David Eggenberger. Essential details of every major battle in recorded history from the first battle of Megiddo in 1479 B.C. to Grenada in 1984. List of Battle Maps. New Appendix covering the years 1967-1984. Index. 99 illustrations. 544pp. 6½ x 9¼. 24913-1 Pa. $14.95

SAILING ALONE AROUND THE WORLD, Captain Joshua Slocum. First man to sail around the world, alone, in small boat. One of great feats of seamanship told in delightful manner. 67 illustrations. 294pp. 5⅜ x 8½. 20326-3 Pa. $5.95

ANARCHISM AND OTHER ESSAYS, Emma Goldman. Powerful, penetrating, prophetic essays on direct action, role of minorities, prison reform, puritan hypocrisy, violence, etc. 271pp. 5⅜ x 8½. 22484-8 Pa. $6.95

MYTHS OF THE HINDUS AND BUDDHISTS, Ananda K. Coomaraswamy and Sister Nivedita. Great stories of the epics; deeds of Krishna, Shiva, taken from puranas, Vedas, folk tales; etc. 32 illustrations. 400pp. 5⅜ x 8½. 21759-0 Pa. $10.95

BEYOND PSYCHOLOGY, Otto Rank. Fear of death, desire of immortality, nature of sexuality, social organization, creativity, according to Rankian system. 291pp. 5⅜ x 8½. 20485-5 Pa. $8.95

A THEOLOGICO-POLITICAL TREATISE, Benedict Spinoza. Also contains unfinished Political Treatise. Great classic on religious liberty, theory of government on common consent. R. Elwes translation. Total of 421pp. 5⅜ x 8½. 20249-6 Pa. $9.95

PIANO TUNING, J. Cree Fischer. Clearest, best book for beginner, amateur. Simple repairs, raising dropped notes, tuning by easy method of flattened fifths. No previous skills needed. 4 illustrations. 201pp. 5⅜ x 8½. 23267-0 Pa. $6.95

A SOURCE BOOK IN THEATRICAL HISTORY, A. M. Nagler. Contemporary observers on acting, directing, make-up, costuming, stage props, machinery, scene design, from Ancient Greece to Chekhov. 611pp. 5⅜ x 8½. 20515-0 Pa. $12.95

THE COMPLETE NONSENSE OF EDWARD LEAR, Edward Lear. All nonsense limericks, zany alphabets, Owl and Pussycat, songs, nonsense botany, etc., illustrated by Lear. Total of 320pp. 5⅜ x 8½. (USO) 20167-8 Pa. $6.95

VICTORIAN PARLOUR POETRY: An Annotated Anthology, Michael R. Turner. 117 gems by Longfellow, Tennyson, Browning, many lesser-known poets. "The Village Blacksmith," "Curfew Must Not Ring Tonight," "Only a Baby Small," dozens more, often difficult to find elsewhere. Index of poets, titles, first lines. xxiii + 325pp. 5⅜ x 8¼. 27044-0 Pa. $8.95

DUBLINERS, James Joyce. Fifteen stories offer vivid, tightly focused observations of the lives of Dublin's poorer classes. At least one, "The Dead," is considered a masterpiece. Reprinted complete and unabridged from standard edition. 160pp. 5$\frac{3}{16}$ x 8¼. 26870-5 Pa. $1.00

THE HAUNTED MONASTERY and THE CHINESE MAZE MURDERS, Robert van Gulik. Two full novels by van Gulik, set in 7th-century China, continue adventures of Judge Dee and his companions. An evil Taoist monastery, seemingly supernatural events; overgrown topiary maze hides strange crimes. 27 illustrations. 328pp. 5⅜ x 8½. 23502-5 Pa. $8.95

THE BOOK OF THE SACRED MAGIC OF ABRAMELIN THE MAGE, translated by S. MacGregor Mathers. Medieval manuscript of ceremonial magic. Basic document in Aleister Crowley, Golden Dawn groups. 268pp. 5⅜ x 8½. 23211-5 Pa. $8.95

NEW RUSSIAN-ENGLISH AND ENGLISH-RUSSIAN DICTIONARY, M. A. O'Brien. This is a remarkably handy Russian dictionary, containing a surprising amount of information, including over 70,000 entries. 366pp. 4½ x 6⅛. 20208-9 Pa. $9.95

HISTORIC HOMES OF THE AMERICAN PRESIDENTS, Second, Revised Edition, Irvin Haas. A traveler's guide to American Presidential homes, most open to the public, depicting and describing homes occupied by every American President from George Washington to George Bush. With visiting hours, admission charges, travel routes. 175 photographs. Index. 160pp. 8¼ x 11. 26751-2 Pa. $11.95

NEW YORK IN THE FORTIES, Andreas Feininger. 162 brilliant photographs by the well-known photographer, formerly with *Life* magazine. Commuters, shoppers, Times Square at night, much else from city at its peak. Captions by John von Hartz. 181pp. 9¼ x 10¾. 23585-8 Pa. $12.95

INDIAN SIGN LANGUAGE, William Tomkins. Over 525 signs developed by Sioux and other tribes. Written instructions and diagrams. Also 290 pictographs. 111pp. 6⅛ x 9¼. 22029-X Pa. $3.95

PHOTOGRAPHIC SKETCHBOOK OF THE CIVIL WAR, Alexander Gardner. 100 photos taken on field during the Civil War. Famous shots of Manassas Harper's Ferry, Lincoln, Richmond, slave pens, etc. 244pp. 10⅝ x 8¼. 22731-6 Pa. $9.95

FIVE ACRES AND INDEPENDENCE, Maurice G. Kains. Great back-to-the-land classic explains basics of self-sufficient farming. The one book to get. 95 illustrations. 397pp. 5⅜ x 8½. 20974-1 Pa. $7.95

SONGS OF EASTERN BIRDS, Dr. Donald J. Borror. Songs and calls of 60 species most common to eastern U.S.: warblers, woodpeckers, flycatchers, thrushes, larks, many more in high-quality recording. Cassette and manual 99912-2 $9.95

A MODERN HERBAL, Margaret Grieve. Much the fullest, most exact, most useful compilation of herbal material. Gigantic alphabetical encyclopedia, from aconite to zedoary, gives botanical information, medical properties, folklore, economic uses, much else. Indispensable to serious reader. 161 illustrations. 888pp. 6½ x 9¼. 2-vol. set. (USO) Vol. I: 22798-7 Pa. $9.95
Vol. II: 22799-5 Pa. $9.95

HIDDEN TREASURE MAZE BOOK, Dave Phillips. Solve 34 challenging mazes accompanied by heroic tales of adventure. Evil dragons, people-eating plants, blood-thirsty giants, many more dangerous adversaries lurk at every twist and turn. 34 mazes, stories, solutions. 48pp. 8¼ x 11. 24566-7 Pa. $2.95

LETTERS OF W. A. MOZART, Wolfgang A. Mozart. Remarkable letters show bawdy wit, humor, imagination, musical insights, contemporary musical world; includes some letters from Leopold Mozart. 276pp. 5⅜ x 8½. 22859-2 Pa. $7.95

BASIC PRINCIPLES OF CLASSICAL BALLET, Agrippina Vaganova. Great Russian theoretician, teacher explains methods for teaching classical ballet. 118 illustrations. 175pp. 5⅜ x 8½. 22036-2 Pa. $5.95

THE JUMPING FROG, Mark Twain. Revenge edition. The original story of The Celebrated Jumping Frog of Calaveras County, a hapless French translation, and Twain's hilarious "retranslation" from the French. 12 illustrations. 66pp. 5⅜ x 8½. 22686-7 Pa. $3.95

BEST REMEMBERED POEMS, Martin Gardner (ed.). The 126 poems in this superb collection of 19th- and 20th-century British and American verse range from Shelley's "To a Skylark" to the impassioned "Renascence" of Edna St. Vincent Millay and to Edward Lear's whimsical "The Owl and the Pussycat." 224pp. 5⅜ x 8½. 27165-X Pa. $4.95

COMPLETE SONNETS, William Shakespeare. Over 150 exquisite poems deal with love, friendship, the tyranny of time, beauty's evanescence, death and other themes in language of remarkable power, precision and beauty. Glossary of archaic terms. 80pp. 5$\frac{3}{16}$ x 8¼. 26686-9 Pa. $1.00

BODIES IN A BOOKSHOP, R. T. Campbell. Challenging mystery of blackmail and murder with ingenious plot and superbly drawn characters. In the best tradition of British suspense fiction. 192pp. 5⅜ x 8½. 24720-1 Pa. $6.95

THE INFLUENCE OF SEA POWER UPON HISTORY, 1660–1783, A. T. Mahan. Influential classic of naval history and tactics still used as text in war colleges. First paperback edition. 4 maps. 24 battle plans. 640pp. 5⅜ x 8½.   25509-3 Pa. $12.95

THE STORY OF THE TITANIC AS TOLD BY ITS SURVIVORS, Jack Winocour (ed.). What it was really like. Panic, despair, shocking inefficiency, and a little heroism. More thrilling than any fictional account. 26 illustrations. 320pp. 5⅜ x 8½.
20610-6 Pa. $8.95

FAIRY AND FOLK TALES OF THE IRISH PEASANTRY, William Butler Yeats (ed.). Treasury of 64 tales from the twilight world of Celtic myth and legend: "The Soul Cages," "The Kildare Pooka," "King O'Toole and his Goose," many more. Introduction and Notes by W. B. Yeats. 352pp. 5⅜ x 8½.   26941-8 Pa. $8.95

BUDDHIST MAHAYANA TEXTS, E. B. Cowell and Others (eds.). Superb, accurate translations of basic documents in Mahayana Buddhism, highly important in history of religions. The Buddha-karita of Asvaghosha, Larger Sukhavativyuha, more. 448pp. 5⅜ x 8½.   25552-2 Pa. $12.95

ONE TWO THREE . . . INFINITY: Facts and Speculations of Science, George Gamow. Great physicist's fascinating, readable overview of contemporary science: number theory, relativity, fourth dimension, entropy, genes, atomic structure, much more. 128 illustrations. Index. 352pp. 5⅜ x 8½.   25664-2 Pa. $8.95

ENGINEERING IN HISTORY, Richard Shelton Kirby, et al. Broad, nontechnical survey of history's major technological advances: birth of Greek science, industrial revolution, electricity and applied science, 20th-century automation, much more. 181 illustrations. ". . . excellent . . ."–Isis. Bibliography. vii + 530pp. 5⅜ x 8¼.
26412-2 Pa. $14.95

DALÍ ON MODERN ART: The Cuckolds of Antiquated Modern Art, Salvador Dalí. Influential painter skewers modern art and its practitioners. Outrageous evaluations of Picasso, Cézanne, Turner, more. 15 renderings of paintings discussed. 44 calligraphic decorations by Dalí. 96pp. 5⅜ x 8½. (USO)   29220-7 Pa. $4.95

ANTIQUE PLAYING CARDS: A Pictorial History, Henry René D'Allemagne. Over 900 elaborate, decorative images from rare playing cards (14th–20th centuries): Bacchus, death, dancing dogs, hunting scenes, royal coats of arms, players cheating, much more. 96pp. 9¼ x 12¼.   29265-7 Pa. $11.95

MAKING FURNITURE MASTERPIECES: 30 Projects with Measured Drawings, Franklin H. Gottshall. Step-by-step instructions, illustrations for constructing handsome, useful pieces, among them a Sheraton desk, Chippendale chair, Spanish desk, Queen Anne table and a William and Mary dressing mirror. 224pp. 8⅛ x 11¼.
29338-6 Pa. $13.95

THE FOSSIL BOOK: A Record of Prehistoric Life, Patricia V. Rich et al. Profusely illustrated definitive guide covers everything from single-celled organisms and dinosaurs to birds and mammals and the interplay between climate and man. Over 1,500 illustrations. 760pp. 7½ x 10⅛.   29371-8 Pa. $29.95